To Dr. Duffield
with
Mr. Macleod's
best respects

HISTORY

OF

THE CHURCH OF SCOTLAND,

FROM THE INTRODUCTION OF CHRISTIANITY

TO THE

PERIOD OF THE DISRUPTION IN 1843.

BY THE

REV W. M. HETHERINGTON, A.M.,

TORPHICHEN.

AUTHOR OF THE "MINISTER'S FAMILY;" "HISTORY OF THE WESTMINSTER ASSEMBLY OF DIVINES," ETC., ETC., ETC.

NEC TAMEN CONSUMEBATUR.

NEW YORK:

ROBERT CARTER & BROTHERS,

No. 285 BROADWAY.

1856.

CONTENTS.

PREFACE.

The want of a History of the Church of Scotland, at once concise and entire, has long been felt. Separate periods have been very fully treated of by several authors, leaving for their successors little to do but to compress the voluminous records which they had collected; and ample materials exist to fill up the intermediate chasms, and to continue the narrative down to the present times. But as no attempt has hitherto been made to compress the histories of these detached periods, to fill up the intermediate chasms, and to continue the narrative, it is a matter of considerable difficulty for any person who has not much leisure to spend, nor ready access to public libraries, to obtain a connected view of the Church of Scotland throughout its entire history. Several very serious disadvantages have resulted from the want of such a work; a great degree of ignorance has been allowed to prevail respecting the true principles and character of the Church of Scotland; her enemies have availed themselves of this ignorance to misrepresent her past conduct, to calumniate the characters of her Reformers and Martyrs, and to assail her present proceedings, while many of her zealous friends are without the means of vindicating the past and defending the present; and numbers are remaining in a state of neutrality, liable to be misled, who require but accurate information to induce them at once to give their cordial support to the Church of their fathers. Nor can there be a doubt, that many are at present not merely neutral but hostile, who would become her strenuous defenders, if they possessed sufficient knowledge of her past and present history.

Impelled by these considerations, and by the strong persuasion, that by giving to the public a faithful record of the scriptural principles of the Church of Scotland, her sufferings in defence of the Redeemer's Headship and of Gospel truth and purity, and the mental, moral, and religious blessings which she has been instrumental in conferring on the kingdom, I should best aid in her vindication and defence, I have endeavoured to supply the long-felt want of a concise, continuous, and entire History of the Church of Scotland. I have not the presumption to imagine that my work will adequately supply the want. For reasons which seemed to me imperative, I have restricted myself within the limits which prevent the possibility of giving more than a tolerably full outline of a subject requiring several volumes to do it justice. Much peculiarly interesting and instructive matter,—both fitted to illustrate great principles, and characteristic of the interior life and private influence of the Presbyterian Church,—has been unavoidably, and very reluctantly, withheld, that the continuity of the main outline might not be broken, nor the general impression weakened by minute details.

References to authorities have been given in every matter of chief importance, except where these are already well known and universally admitted. It would have been easy to have adduced very many more; but while a superfluous array of references appears to me to savour of ostentation, and can be of little consequence to the general reader, for whom chiefly this work is intended, it is believed, that those who wish to prosecute their acquaintance with the subject, will find enough to authenticate every statement, and to direct them to sources where more minute details may be obtained. I have preferred to quote the testimony of opponents rather than that of friends, in many instances, as less liable to be disputed; and when several authorities support the same account, I have given the one most generally known, rather than the rarer, that the reader might the more easily verify my statement, if so disposed. The edition of Knox's History of the Reformation to which reference is made, is that which Dr. M'Crie regarded as the most authentic. No pains have been spared in the investigation of every point respecting which conflicting opinions have been entertained; and in forming my own judgment I have been guided chiefly by the testimony of those who were amply acquainted with the events which they related, and whose characters give the highest value to their evidence.

With regard to the sentiments contained in the work, I cannot but be aware, that while stating my own feelings and opinions, what I have written will not be equally agreeable to all. I have no wish to give unnecessary offence to any; but in my opinion, no person ought to attempt to write history, who has not both an honest desire to ascertain the truth, and sufficient courage to state it freely and impartially when ascertained. And it is perfectly impossible to write the History of the Church of Scotland, without relating events which cannot fail to excite strong moral indignation against the two systems by which that Church has, at different periods, been persecuted and oppressed. It has been my desire to abstain from unnecessary asperity of language, even when detailing acts of perfidy and cruelty, rarely equalled in the annals of persecution; not because I think that Scottish Prelacy has any peculiar claim to be leniently treated, but because the plain and simple statement of the truth will best display the spirit and character of that intolerant system.

Painful, indeed, has been the task of tracing the course of worldly policy and ecclesiastical corruption and despotism, which prevailed throughout the last century and the beginning of the present; and most reluctantly have I felt myself constrained to record the deeds which were done in Scotland during the long reign of Moderatism. But it was felt to be an imperative duty to do so, both as required by historical fidelity, and as rendered peculiarly necessary by the present circumstances of the Church. It would be a very instructive chapter in the history of the errors which the spirit of the world has superinduced upon Christianity, to give a full view of the rise, progress, and complete developement of the system which has been called Moderatism. I have not, however, sought to do so, further than appeared absolutely necessary for the purpose of displaying so much of its real essence and character as might sufficiently prove, that the true Presbyterian Church of Scotland is not justly chargeable with the actions of a secular system, which had its origin in hostile elements, which gradually usurped, and long exercised over her the most cruel and oppressive tyranny, and whose whole procedure was one continuous endeavour to destroy her principles and subvert her constitution.

To those Gentlemen who have kindly favoured me with the perusal of valuable books, to which I could not otherwise have easily obtained access, I take this opportunity of returning my grateful thanks. And I now lay my work before the public, in the hope, that what was undertaken solely from a strong conviction of duty to the Divine Head of the Church, to the Church of Scotland, and to my countrymen in general, may, through the blessing of God, be of some avail in removing ignorance and prejudice, correcting erroneous misrepresentations, and enabling the community to form an accurate conception of the real principles and character of the Church of Scotland.

In preparing this edition of the History of the Church of Scotland, it has been thought expedient to continue the narrative of events till the Disruption which took place in May last, and resulted in the formation of what is now termed THE FREE CHURCH OF SCOTLAND,—in which are still preserved entire the constitutional principles, the unfettered freedom, the vital energy, the doctrinal purity, and the spiritual fervency, that have, in its best periods, always distinguished the testimony-bearing Church of our fathers.

W. M. H.

FREE MANSE, TORPHICHEN,
October 1843.

HISTORY

OF THE

CHURCH OF SCOTLAND.

CHAPTER I.

FROM THE INTRODUCTION OF CHRISTIANITY INTO SCOTLAND, TO THE COMMENCEMENT OF THE REFORMATION.

Introductory Remarks—Statement of General Principles involved in all Church History—Divine Truth infused into the Social System—Opposition from Man's Fallen Nature—Characteristic Principles of different Churches—Of the Church of Scotland—Introduction of Christianity into Scotland—The Culdees—Peculiarities of their System—Introduced into England—Augustine the Monk—He and his followers oppose the Culdees—They retire to Scotland—The Prelatic System of Rome introduced—the Culdees at length overborne and suppressed—The leading Tenets of the Culdees—Progress of Popery—Its Wealth and Power—State of Scotland at the Commencement of the Reformation.

THERE are certain general principles involved in all Church History, greatly more profound in their character and important in their consequences than those which appear in, or can be deduced from, the records of Civil History. The civil historian has to deal with man merely as the mortal inhabitant of this world; and, however deeply his philosophical knowledge of the human mind may enable him to penetrate into those undeclared motives by which sovereigns and statesmen are often influenced, and the affairs of nations controlled, there is still one department, and that the mightiest of all, into which it is not his province to enter. He may unravel the twisted intrigues of mere worldly policy; he may detect and confute the sophistries of worldly wisdom; but, except he be something more than a philosophical historian, he will remain utterly unable to understand the meaning and the power of conscience, influenced by religion, and impelling men frequently to act directly contrary to every thing which he would deem politic and expedient. Not only this class of motives, but the course of events also, will often be found to lie equally beyond his reach adequately to comprehend and explain. He will often find means and arrangements apparently the wisest and most sufficient, utterly fail of accomplishing the proposed end; while others, which seem ill advised and feeble, will be crowned with the most remarkable success. Frequently, therefore, must he content himself with recording the course of events, of which the impelling causes and controlling agencies are to him altogether unknown. Man as he is, in short, impelled by the passions and allured by the interests of his known and common nature,—circumscribed, as he at present appears, within the limits of space and time, of his earthly pursuits and mortal life,—forms the object of the civil historian's important yet incomplete researches.

But Church History has to deal with the deeds and characters of men in that very department into which the civil historian cannot enter. It views man as a moral and spiritual being, fallen from his original condition of purity and happiness, the slave of guilty passions, degraded by low and grovelling pursuits, and blinded by inveterate prejudices, yet capable of recovery from his depraved and miserable condition, and at present under a dispensation divinely fitted to restore him to more than the purity and elevation from which he fell. He is seen, therefore, as constantly impelled by the one or the other of two contending influences, directly hostile to each other;—the one, the influence of his fallen and corrupt nature, striving to perpetuate all its own evil tendencies, and to impede and pervert all the efforts of its opponent; the other, the influence of revealed religion, of Christianity, striving to expel corruption, remove prejudices, and heal the moral maladies of the soul, by the infusion of the new and sacred principles of eternal truth. Church History has, therefore, for its peculiar province, the infusion into the soul of fallen man of the sacred principles of divine revealed truth,—their influence in the social system, as they strive to pervade and mould it anew,—the opposition which they meet with from the inherent depravity of the heart,—the struggles of these contending influences of good and evil, of the world and religion,—the convulsions occasionally thereby produced,—and the changes which take place in the aspect and structure of society, as the one or the other from time to time obtains ascendency, puts forth its power, and exhibits its native character. It is thus evident that the history of the Church of any land is the history of the moral and spiritual life of that land; and that it claims, as its own peculiar domain, that very region of moral and spiritual principles and motives into which the secular historian, as such, cannot even enter, and yet without some knowledge of which, much of what is most important in the history of every nation can never be understood and explained.

In tracing the Church History of any country, we must expect to meet with much that we must both deplore and condemn. For although the principles which Christianity introduces into the soul of man, and thereby into the social system, are in themselves absolutely perfect, yet they are rarely perfectly received, and never have been perfectly developed. Divine truth does not, indeed, contract any portion of human error by entering into the mind of man; but the depraved and prejudiced human mind obtains in general only a partial reception and distorted view of its great principles. The inevitable consequence is, that its genuine effects are very greatly impaired by the disturbing influence of human depravity and prejudice. Some of the most important religious principles are frequently obscured, because they have been either imperfectly understood, or are so opposed to the natural predilections of fallen man as to be disliked, and therefore perverted. They do indeed reappear from time to time, as peculiar junctures, under the guiding of Divine Providence, call them forth; until their true character and value being thus forced upon the perception of the general mind, they are at length received, and opportunity thereby given for the similar process of developement to others, which had been equally neglected or opposed. This is the case, whether such principles have direct reference to the government, the doctrine, or the discipline of the Christian Church, as might easily be shown from the general records of Church History.

There is also a necessary continuity of character, as of being, in the life and history of any Church; and that character can never be rightly understood, however familiar we may be with the details of its general history, unless we have a clear and true conception of those leading principles which have always formed the master element of its essential existence. By keeping them steadily in view, we shall be able to trace distinctly all the various changes and alternations of its course, marking and understanding not merely those external events which are manifest to the world, but those unseen influences which move, and mould, and animate the whole. Even in periods of comparative stagnation, when there seems to be a cessation of all active and vital impulses, the knowledge of what forms the essential characteristics of a national Church may enable us to detect the otherwise imperceptible progress of a deep and calm under-current, preparing for some new and mighty developement of silently-ripened energies, by which the whole structure of society may be convulsed, and constrained to assume a new aspect, more in conformity with the character of its inward moral and religious life.

Every person who has paid much attention to Church History must be aware that, of the great leading principles of Christianity, some have been held in peculiar reverence, and defended with peculiar determination, by one national Church, and some by another; and from this has arisen in each that distinctive characteristic by which the various portions of the Church general maintain their individuality, notwithstanding their common resemblance. It would require too wide a survey, and perhaps involve a discussion too vague, to point out the distinctive characteristics of the chief national Churches throughout the Christian world; but there can be little difficulty in making specific mention of that great Christian principle which the Church of Scotland has always striven to realize and defend,—namely, THAT THE LORD JESUS CHRIST IS THE ONLY HEAD AND KING OF THE CHURCH; whence it follows, by necessary consequence, THAT ITS GOVERNMENT IS DERIVED FROM HIM ALONE, AND IS DISTINCT FROM, AND NOT SUBORDINATE IN ITS OWN PROVINCE TO, THE CIVIL MAGISTRATE. The very remoteness of Scotland from Rome, the seat first of imperial, and subsequently of ecclesiastical power, tended to allow for a time a more free developement of that great principle, and of its legitimate consequences, than would have been possible had it been more accessible to the influence of Roman supremacy. It might, perhaps, be thought by some, that the Presbyterian form of church government, rather than the great principle of the sole Sovereignty of Christ, has been, and is, the characteristic tenet of the Church of Scotland. But it requires only a little deeper investigation, or profounder thought, to enable any impartial and unprejudiced person to see, that the great principle of Christ's sole Sovereignty must prohibit the Church which holds it from the adoption of any merely human inventions or arrangements in that form of government which He has given to the Church, his free spiritual kingdom, of which the Holy Scriptures contain the only authoritative enactment and declaration.

It is not our purpose to enter here into the controversy respecting forms of church government, farther than merely to state our full conviction, that it can be proved, and often has been proved, that the Episcopalian, or rather let us term it now, and throughout this work, the Prelatic form of church government, is one of merely human invention; whilst the Presbyterian is of divine origin and authority, and consequently is that which would of necessity be adopted and retained by any Church which held as its leading principle the sole headship and kingly dominion of the Lord Jesus Christ. But it is enough at present merely to have stated these general principles, and suggested their application. If the candid reader will bear them in mind during his perusal of the following pages, he will soon be able to decide for himself respecting their truth and their importance.

The first introduction of Christianity into Scotland cannot, it appears, be now exactly ascertained. It would be in vain to refer to the legendary records of ancient Scottish kings, given by some of our historians, as furnishing authoritative information respecting the events of a period so far beyond the boundaries of our nation's authentic annals. Perhaps the earliest indication that the light of Christianity had begun to dawn upon the remote regions of Caledonia, that can at all be depended upon, may be found in the words of Tertullian, who asserts, that "those parts of Britain which were inaccessible to the Romans had become subject to Christ." And although we are not to attach to the fervid language of a rhetorician the same degree of credit which we yield to the direct statements of a historian, yet, remembering the extreme rapidity with which Christianity was propagated throughout the Roman empire in the apostolic age, it is by no means improbable that it should have reached Britain, and even penetrated to the mountains of Caledonia, before the close of the second century. The violence of the persecutions which raged in every part of Rome's dominion's during the third century, may readily be supposed to have driven many of the Christians beyond the boundaries of the empire, and thus to have aided indirectly in the diffusion of the gospel, and especially to have promoted its introduction into the territories of unsubdued nations. Many of those persecuted Christians may then have found a refuge among the unconquered districts of Scotland and Ireland, where they would, of course, endeavour to instruct the rude but not inhospitable natives in the knowledge of the truth as it is in Jesus.

In what manner these early Christian refugees commenced what may be termed their missionary labours among the Scots and Picts,—and whether, as some authors assert, the greater number of them resorted to Ireland, and there assembling themselves together, resumed the form of primitive ecclesiastical government to which they had been accustomed,—are questions into which it would be fruitless to inquire, it being now almost impossible to arrive at any certainty on these points. The records of those remote times are so obscure and contradictory, that they rather furnish material for conjecture, than data from which any satisfactory inferences may be drawn. There are, however, a few points on which all ancient records seem to agree. These, therefore, we may assume as generally admitted facts, although party-writers have endeavoured to deduce from them the most opposite conclusions; and while we do not venture to claim for ourselves absolute impartiality and freedom from all biassing predilections, we shall do our utmost to guard against the influence of prejudices,—to state nothing but what we believe, after very careful investigation, to be the truth,—and to frame no inferences but what seem to us to be natural, direct, and inevitable.

There is reason to believe, as has been already stated, that the knowledge of Christianity was to some extent communicated to the people of Scotland and Ireland as early as towards the close of the second, and more especially during the third, century of the Christian era, in the times of those fierce persecutions which, while they were meant to exterminate, were actually overruled to promote the progress of the Christian religion. There is no reason, however, to think that those persecuted and banished Christians attempted at that early period to construct any distinct frame of ecclesiastical government. They seem rather to have dwelt in comparatively isolated solitude, each in his own retreat, and each communicating to his own immediate neighbours as much instruction as he could impart, or they could be persuaded to receive. If any dependence may be placed upon the fabulous records of those ages, there were too many convulsions and semi-revolutions in both Scotland and Ireland, caused by the contensions of rival races and petty monarchies, to have permitted the construction of any regular form of church government; so that for a considerable period, while Christianity was gradually pervading both countries, it was doing so almost imperceptibly, through the exertions of individuals, without system and without combination, farther than that invisible but strong harmony which is caused by identity of principle and aim. In this manner Christianity might have been, and indeed appears to have been propagated extensively throughout the British Isles, before it began to assume the external aspect of a Church, with a regular system and form of government. But when persecution ceased, in consequence of the fall of Paganism before the progress of Christianity, and Rome began to be regarded as the central seat of ecclesiastical government, the Bishop of Rome very early assumed a sort of supremacy over the whole Christian Church, and took it upon him to interfere with the arrangements of the whole Christian world. To this, in all probability, we owe the visit of Palladius, about the object and consequences of which so much fruitless controversy has arisen.

According to the Archbishop Ussher, Palladius was sent from Rome to "the Scots believing on Christ," in the year 431, by Celestine, at that time Bishop of Rome, as their "first bishop," (*primus episcopus*).* Some writers assert, that by the word "*Scots*" we are to understand the Irish to be meant; and are further to learn, that Palladius was sent to be ***Primate*** of Ireland! It is not necessary to waste space in the discussion of assertions which contain their own refutation in their absurdity. Whatever else may have been among the secret objects of the Roman Bishop Celestine in the mission of Palladius, it appears sufficiently evident from the above-quoted ex-

* Ussher, Primord., p. 801. See also Jamieson's History of the Culdees, pp. 7, 8.

pression, that the chief one was to introduce Episcopal government among the Scottish and Irish Christians; whence it clearly follows, that previously no such form of ecclesiastical government was known, if indeed there did exist previously either organization or government at all, beyond the mental harmony which subsisted among those who held one faith, were animated by one Spirit, trusted in one Saviour, and worshipped one God.

Whether the mission of Palladius were chiefly to Ireland or not, it may not now be possible to determine with certainty; but there is reason to believe that he not only visited Scotland, but that he died there, at Fordoun, in the Mearns.* The very common opinion that Palladius was sent expressly to refute the errors of Pelagius, which are said to have become prevalent among the British Christians, we are disposed to regard as without sufficient foundation. The Pelagian heresy was scarcely known till the year 412, and that chiefly among the African Churches; and it is not at all likely that it had even reached, much less made extensive progress among, the simple-minded Christians of Scotland and Ireland, before the year in which the mission of Palladius is recorded to have taken place.

Nothing certain is known respecting the direct effects produced by the mission of Palladius. It is indeed stated by Marianus Scotus, that after him St. Patrick was consecrated by Celestine, and sent as archbishop to Ireland, where, in the course of forty years, he converted the whole island to the faith;† but this account cannot be relied on, in consequence of its opposition to other and more authentic records. There is no proof whatever that St. Patrick had any connection with Rome; while there is strong reason to believe that he was a native of Scotland, and that the Christianity which he communicated to Ireland was, both in forms and doctrines, what he had himself been taught by his Scottish instructors. What the form of church government was which St. Patrick instituted in Ireland, appears very plainly, even from the statement of Archbishop Ussher. "We read," says that learned and candid prelate,—"we read in Nennius, that at the beginning St. Patrick founded 365 churches, and ordained 365 bishops, besides 3000 presbyters" (or elders).* What kind of *bishops* these were, is sufficiently apparent from the fact that there was one for each church, and also from the number of the elders,—about eight to each bishop. It was, in short, manifestly the same institution which ultimately became the Presbyterian Church of Scotland,—a parish minister, with his session of elders, in each church and parish that had received the gospel. But it is time to quit the regions of dark and half-fabulous antiquity, and to direct our attention to what, though still obscure, has been brought into somewhat of a more definite form, by those writers who have preserved to us an outline of the aspect of primitive Christianity in Scotland, in the remarks they have made on the Culdees.

* Jamieson's Hist. Culd., p. 9.

† Ibid., p. 8.

It is not our intention to investigate at any length the questions which have been so long agitated respecting the origin, the doctrines, and the form of church government of the Culdees, but rather to state briefly and consecutively all that is clearly known concerning them.

The name Culdees appears to have been given to those Christians who fled from persecution, and sought refuge in those districts of Scotland which were beyond the limits of the Roman empire. Different explanations have been suggested of the name itself; some deriving it from Latin, and assuming it to have been an abbreviation of *Cultores Dei*, worshippers of God; others from the Gaelic expression, *Gille De*, servants of God; and others from the Gaelic *Cuil* or *Ceal*, a sheltered place, a retreat. We would combine the two latter opinions, and suppose that the Culdees derived their name from the union of these two facts in their early history, namely, that they were refugees, and dwelt generally in comparatively secret retreats and hiding-places; and that they were known to be in a peculiar manner servants of God. Their early possession of the island of Iona, and concentration there as their chief seat, we would regard also as the result of a combination of circumstances:

* Discourse on the Religion of the Irish and British p. 77.

The same necessity which drove them to Scotland would impel them to seek some tolerably secure place of safety, to which they could at all times retreat from danger. The marked and important intercourse between the Dalriad Scots and the Irish, which subsisted at that period, would point out some interjacent island as affording easy access to either country and people. For these reasons Iona would readily recommend itself to them, as at once a safe retreat, even from its insignificance in point of size, and at the same time allowing free and convenient intercourse with Picts, Scots, and Irish. It thus became their chief residence; and in it first appeared that form of ecclesiastical government, the rudimental principles of which they had either brought with them, or into which Christianity itself naturally tended to mould a society of single-hearted believers.

The first definite accounts which have reached us respecting the Culdees are those which relate to Columba, who is said to have been a native of Ireland, and of royal extraction. He is reported to have founded the monastery, or rather abbey, of Iona, in the year 563, and to have been himself the first abbot. He took with him, we are told, from Ireland to Iona, twelve companions, over whom he possessed no other kind of superiority than that of being president for life. Neither the office nor the designation of bishop, in its prelatical sense, appears to have been known among them. The institution of Iona formed, in truth, a regular presbytery, as it has long existed in Scotland, with this slight difference, that the presidency, or what we term the moderatorship, was permanently enjoyed by the abbot, whom even Bede terms the "Presbyter-Abbott." Upon the death of this permanent president, or presbyter-abbot, the remaining presbyter-monks met and chose a successor from among themselves, to whom was accordingly given the permanent presidency, but without any such rite as that of consecration, or any thing which could indicate elevation to an office essentially superior in itself. He was, in fact, nothing more than "the first among equals," placed so by the choice of his brethren, for the purpose of maintaing order in their meetings together for deliberation and consultation. This peculiarity was well known to the venerable Bede, who terms it "an unusual constitution" (*ordo insusitatus*), as indeed it must have appeared to one who had been himself accustomed to the constitution of a diocesan and prelatic Episcopacy.

It deserves to be remarked, that the number of the council or college of presbyter-monks of Iona was fixed at twelve; and that, when the Culdees formed new settlements, they adhered to the same number. This was, in all probability, caused by their veneration for the primitive apostolic council of twelve; and indicates, either that the Culdees must have reached Scotland in a very early age, while apostolic forms were still uncorrupted and prelacy unknown; or that they followed the sacred Scriptures as closely as possible, regarding them as the only and the sufficient standard of both faith and ecclesiastical government. We find them also appealing to the authority of the Apostle John, in their controversy with the Romanized English clergy respecting Easter, which indicates both the earliness of their origin and the quarter whence they derived their tenets and their institutions. An additional proof of their early origin and unperverted belief and practice appears in the fact, that though generally termed monks by ecclesiastical writers of that age, to whom the term had become familiar, they did not hold the tenet of monastic celibacy, but were married men, and were even frequently succeeded in their official station and duties by their own sons. From this we can scarcely avoid drawing the conclusion, that those who held a form of Christianity so primitive, so simple, and so pure, must have branched off from the central regions and stem of the Christian Church at a very early period indeed,—almost before any corruption had begun to disfigure the institutions, and pollute the doctrines and customs, of the apostles. For these and other reasons the second century seems not too early a date to assign to the origin of Christianity in Scotland.

Little is known respecting the progress made by the Culdees in propagating Christianity among the Scots and Picts, impeded as their efforts must have been by the almost incessant hostilities in which these tribes were engaged, That they did make some progress, however, is certain, from the various semi-monastic settlements which they formed in the districts inhabited by each people, as at Dunkeld, Abernethy, Arbroath, Brechin, Monimusk, &c. It deserves to be noted also, that in each of these settlements the Culdees retained the institutions of Iona already specified, namely, a council of twelve presbyter-monks, with a life-president or presbyter-abbot, chosen from among their own number by themselves, and continuing of the same order, than which they acknowledged no higher.

Although the intestine feuds of the Scots and Picts must have greatly retarded the progress of Christianity among them, yet their neighbours of the southern part of the island were in a much worse condition. It is well known that, on the final departure of the Romans from Britain, the enfeebled Britons applied to the Saxons for aid against the invasions of the Scots and Picts; and were themselves, after a protracted and bloody struggle, completely subdued by their faithless auxiliaries. The effect of these devasting wars was the complete ascendency of the Saxons in England, and the entire extinction of Christianity in the territories upon which they had seized; the remainder of the British race, with what of Christianity survived among them, being driven into the mountain fastnesses of Wales, where, accordingly, the relics of the primitive Culdee system continued for a considerable time to exist.*

At length there came a period of comparative tranquillity; and the Christianity which had been preserved in the northern regions began to find its way southward. Bede informs us, that Oswald, king of the Northumbrian Saxons, had been himself educated at Iona; and immediately upon his obtaining the sovereignty, he sent to the Scottish elders (*majores natu*), requesting them to send him what would now be termed an ordained minister (*antistes*), by whose doctrine and ministry his subjects might be instructed in the Christian faith.† From this period and downwards, the Culdees prosecuted their missionary labours among the Saxons with great activity. At first their success was but indifferent. Corman, their first missionary, was a man of austere manners, and failed to render himself and his ministry acceptable to the rude and warlike Saxons. They next sent Aidan, one of the presbyter-monks of Iona, having first ordained him as a preaching presbyter. He formed a settlement at Lindisfarne, constructing it upon the model of that of Iona; and it became a new salient point from which Christianity might make its aggressive movements into England. Such, nevertheless, was the veneration entertained for Iona, and such also, in all probability, its superiority in the means of instructing aspirants for the Christian ministry, that several of the immediate successors of Aidan, in the presbyter-abbotship of Lindisfarne, were sent thither from the primitive seat of the Culdees.

But while the simple primitive Christianity of the Culdees was making rapid progress among the Pagan Saxons, a more formidable opposition was preparing to meet it. The attention of Pope Gregory the Great was accidentally directed to Britain; and he sent Augustine the Monk, with forty missionary attendants, to attempt the conversion of the Saxons. The imposing pomp, and keen subtilty and artifice, of the Italian monk and his associates, speedily acquired an ascendency which the simple Culdee presbyters could not gainstand. The controversy respecting the proper time for observing Easter, and other points of form and ceremony in which the Culdees differed from the Roman Church, was formally begun by Augustine, in a synod held by him in the year 603. This was the commencement of the corruption and tyranny of the Romish Church in Britain. The Romish party continued to advance, employing all the craft and despotism with which they were so familiar, and bearing down their opponents; and in a synod held at Whitby in the year 662, for the purpose of deciding the controversy, Colman, at that time presbyter-abbot (termed also, in conformity with the names then become prevalent, bishop) of Lindisfarne, was overborne by the arrogant manner and confident assertions which his opponent Wilfrid had learned

* Keith, Preface, pp. viii. and xv.; Jamieson's Hist. Culd., pp. 35 and 259.

† Bede, Hist., lib. iii. c. 17; Jamieson's Hist. Culd., pp. 36, 37.

at Rome; but rather than abandon the tenets which he had been taught by his elders, as he termed them, he relinquished his position at Lindisfarne, and returned to Iona.

From this time forward the Romish influence made rapid aggressive progress. The adaptation of the Romish system to the natural pride and ambition of man, lent it a mighty impulse: and the Culdees were either allured to exchange their presbyter-abbot for a prelatic and diocesan bishop, or compelled to abandon their settlements and return to Scotland. Indeed the name bishop was often applied to the presbyter-abbot of the Culdees by the writers of that period; and so far as it was applied in its primitive sense, it was his due, there being no distinction between an *ordained presbyter* and a *scriptural bishop.* Still, their difference from the Romish diocesan bishop, or prelate, was marked even by those writers, in the peculiar appellation, "bishops of the Scots," by which they were designated.

It is not our intention to trace minutely the encroachments of the prelatic Romish party, as they not only expelled the Culdees from England, but also, following up the ever-intolerant policy of Rome, assailed them in Scotland itself, and ceased not their hostile efforts till they procured their final suppression. It deserves, however, to be peculiarly observed, that what chiefly excited the hostility of the Romish party was the want of Prelacy among the Culdees, even more than their differing in other points from the superstitious rites and ceremonies of Popery; and that the introduction of Prelacy was the direct means by which the pure scriptural system of worship and government held by the early Scottish Church was at last overthrown. Nor let it pass unmarked, that England's influence and example were the direct causes of the corruption and subversion of Scotland's more ancient and purer faith. This might be rendered evident, beyond the possibility of contradiction, did our limits permit us to trace minutely the successive events which led to this disastrous result; such as the residence for a time in England of some of our most powerful kings, especially Malcolm Canmore, and David I., who, returning to Scotland with their minds filled with prejudices in behalf of the pomp and splendour of the English Prelacy, made it their most strenuous endeavour to erect buildings, and organize and endow a hierarchy, which might vie in dignity and grandeur with those of their more wealthy neighbours. The ruinous effects were soon apparent. In vain did the best of the Scottish clergy oppose these innovations; their more ambitious brethren were but too ready to grasp at the proffered wealth and honour; and at length, to save themselves from the usurpations of the archbishop of Canterbury, who strove to assert supremacy over the Scottish Church, they yielded up their spiritual liberty to the Roman pontiff, in the year 1176.

It can scarcely fail to strike every thoughtful reader, that the history of the Culdees presents, in its main outline, a very close resemblance to the general aspect and characteristic incidents subsequently exhibited in the history of the Church of Scotland, at and since the time of the Reformation. When left to itself, and free from external influence, the Scottish Church has always been remarkable for its simplicity of forms and purity of doctrine, taking the word of God as its sole rule and guide in both; the wealthier and more worldly Church of England has always hated and sought to overthrow a Church which contrasted so strongly with its own external pomp and internal corruption and inefficacy: and the monarchs and nobility of Scotland, being Anglicised, have striven to introduce forms of worship, and a system of despotic ecclesiastical government and corrupt doctrine, equally opposed to the simplicity and purity of the Scriptures, and to the grave, manly, and free spirit of the Scottish people.

It is at all times a melancholy task to trace the progress of a persecuted, oppressed, and falling cause, whether that cause be of religious or of civil liberty, which, indeed, suffer together and alike. We shall, therefore, very briefly state the most marked incidents in the suppression and extinction of the Culdees. After the Synod of Whitby, in the year 662, the Culdees generally either retired from England, or submitted to the institutions and doctrines of Rome, which from that time forward held supreme ascendency among the English. Soon after that period arose the furious contests between the Scots and Picts, which ended in the complete overthrow of the latter, and their entire national extinction, the conquered and the conquerors becoming so thoroughly blended together, that the Picts ceased to be known as a separate people.

It appears that during these wars the Culdees suffered severely. The annals of Ulster state that, in the year 716, "the family of Iona was expelled beyond Drum-Albin, by Nectan, king of the Picts." This seems to have been connected with an attempt by Nectan to introduce the form of the Anglican Church into his dominions; as we find that a Saxon priest, Ecgberht, was at the same time placed in Iona; while the Pictish king applied to Ceolfrid, abbot of Girvey, for architects to erect a church after the Roman manner. It was probably his intention to transfer the chief seat of ecclesiastical government from Iona to Abernethy, his own capital, whereby he might expect that his personal influence would enable him to accomplish his intended religious innovations.

The premature death of Nectan put an end to these attempts; and Iona recovered its shaken supremacy, and enjoyed about sixty years of comparative tranquillity. But a more terrible enemy appeared. The Danes and Norwegians began their piratical invasions of the Western Isles; and in 801, Iona itself was burned, and a great number of the Culdees slain, by these fierce invaders. About the year 877, the Culdees of Iona fled from another Danish invasion to Ireland, carrying with them the relics of Columba. Still a considerable number of the Culdees continued to cleave to the long-hallowed abode of their ancestors, though now sadly shorn of its ancient splendour. But their perils and sufferings continued; and in 905, the Danes again pillaged the monastery, and killed the abbot, with fifteen of his presbyters. In 1059, the monastery was destroyed by fire; but still the devoted Culdees lingered among the scathed ruins of their venerated Iona. A large body of them, indeed, appear to have sought refuge in Dunkeld, where they endeavoured to perpetuate their simple scriptural institutions; but Iona continued to be inhabited by Culdees till the year 1203, when "Ceallach built a monastery, in opposition to the learned of the place."* Thus the Romish usurping power seized upon the very citadel; and this seems effectually to have driven the remains of the persecuted Culdees from Iona, which they never again recovered. The only further accounts of them which can be gleaned from the incidental notices, represent them as scattered throughout the districts of the western counties of Scotland, especially in Kyle and Cunningham; where, though their name soon became extinct, their tenets were preserved in a great measure pure from papal corruption, till about the time that the Lollards, the followers of Jerome and Huss, and of Wickliffe, appeared like the faint day-break of the Reformation.

Although we have traced chiefly the fortunes of the original settlement of the Culdees at Iona, it must not be forgotten that there were many other similar settlements of them in Scotland; and that in latter times some of these were even more prominently the scenes of contest with the encroaching Anglo-Roman Church than was Iona, and maintained the conflict for a longer period. In the year 1176, the abbot of Dunkeld permitted himself to be made a diocesan bishop. It was not till the year 1230, or about that time, that the Culdees of Monimusk were deprived of their peculiar privileges; and in the year 1297, the Culdees of St. Andrews made the last attempt at resisting the usurpations of the bishop of that see, by an effectual appeal to Rome. This, therefore, may be taken as the date of the final suppression, by prelatic and papal fraud and tyranny, of the primitive, scriptural and presbyterian Church of Scotland.

Before concluding this brief sketch of the Culdees, it may be expedient to state the main points of doctrine and ritual, as of ecclesiastical government, in which they differed from the corrupt Church of Rome. For although Bede and other writers make most mention of the disputes and controversies respecting the celebration of Easter, and the peculiar form of the clerical tonsure, and such like idle fooleries, from which some

* Jamieson's Hist. Culd., p. 301.

have hastily concluded that there was, after all, nothing but the most trifling and unessential distinctions between the Culdees and their Anglo-Roman opponents; yet a closer examination may enable us to discover, what a little more reflection would have led us to conjecture, that they differed in some points of vital importance, although the popish and prelatic party, with their usual cunning, contrived to make the public aspect of the controversy one of mere rites and ceremonies. It may, indeed, be here stated, as an axiomatic principle, which we shall have frequent occasion of applying and verifying, that the opposers of pure religion never venture to assail what is manifestly sacred, if they can obtain the slightest hold of what is merely ritual or civil. From incidental notices, however, it may be gathered that the Culdees were opposed to the Church of Rome in such essential doctrines as the following:—

They rejected that dark and tyrannical tenet of Popery, *auricular confession*, and also its natural sequents, *penance*, and *authoritative absolution;* confessing their sins to God alone, as believing that He alone could forgive sins.

They opposed the idolatrous doctrine of *the real presence*, or *transubstantiation;* holding the sacrament of the Lord's Supper to be indeed a healing ordinance and an appointed means of grace to all faithful receivers, but at the same time in its own nature essentially commemorative.

They rejected and opposed the *idolatrous worship* of *angels*, and *saints*, and *relics*, and all these peculiar superstitious practices by means of which the Roman Church so grossly imposed upon credulous ignorance, and promoted its own wealth and influence; and so sensible do they appear to have been in their apprehension of the danger lest idolatry should creep into their pure system, that they would not permit any of their churches to be dedicated to, or designated by the name of, any saint or angel.

They neither admitted *praying to saints for their intercession*, nor *prayers for the dead.* For they were persuaded, that while we are in the present world, we may help each other either by our prayers or by our counsels; but when we come before the tribunal of Christ, "neither Job, nor Daniel, nor Noah, can intercede for any one, but every one must bear his own burden;"—so scriptural were their views on these points.

They strenuously denied the popish doctrine of *works of supererogation;* utterly disclaiming all merit of their own, and hoping for salvation solely from the mercy of God, through faith in Jesus Christ; stating as their view of that essential point of Christian doctrine, "That the faithful man does not live by righteousness, but the righteous man by faith."

It has been already shown that the ecclesiastical constitution and government of the Culdees was diametrically opposed to prelatic Episcopacy; and it ought to be stated, both as a consequence and as an additional proof, that they were unacquainted with the episcopalian rite of *confirmation.*

And, as an additional proof of their freedom from superstitious usages of merely human invention, they, in the sacrament of baptism, made use of any water that was conveniently at hand, as did the apostles, rejecting the "consecrated chrism" introduced by the Romanists, and still retained wherever popish and prelatic institutions prevail.*

When to the preceding doctrinal tenets of the Culdees we add their freedom from the pernicious system of an unmarried priesthood, their repugnance to the lordly rule of a disocesan Prelacy, and the scriptural simplicity of their presbyterial form of church government, we cannot fail to be struck with the close resemblance which they bear to the authoritative doctrines and institutions of the Word of God; to the opinions and desires of the great men of the Reformation,—of Luther and Melancthon, Calvin and Beza, Cranmer and Ridley, Knox and Melville; and to the constitutional confession and government of the Presbyterian Church of Scotland. And we have been at some pains to extricate, as far as may now be done, the tenets of our old ancestral faith from the confused and faded records of bygone ages, because we regarded that as the best method of ascertaining what were the actual life-germs and essential principles of that

* For authorities in proof of the preceding statement of the differences between the Culdees and the Romish Churches, see Jamieson's Hist. Culd. chap. x.

primitive, apostolic, and scriptural form of Christianity which was so early enjoyed by our fathers; and because we are persuaded that, however much externally overborne by the corrupt prelatic Church of Rome, its influence never perished, but, after having for a season lain concealed, yet not unfelt, within the strong and independent heart of Scotland, while the fierce storms of English invasion and civil broils were sweeping over and devastating the land, it sprang again into energetic action, when the voice of reformation went forth, awakening Europe, and became the moving and moulding life-power of our reformed, or rather resuscitated, national Church.

We have given the outline of all that is with any degree of certainty known respecting the Culdees, in one continued narrative, for the purpose of presenting it to the reader in the most intelligible form, unbroken by reference to contemporaneous events. But some of these demand a portion of our attention, before proceeding with the main course of our narrative. The chief of these we shall now proceed to state with all practical brevity.

It has been already stated, that the Christianizing labours of the Culdees were met and borne back from England by the efforts of the Romish Church, which even then was greatly corrupted; and also, that the system established in England speedily began to be imitated by our own somewhat Anglicised sovereigns and clergy. But it must be observed, that neither king nor clergy had the slightest intention of subjecting the Church of Scotland to that of England. Indeed, there occur some noble instances of the determined manner in which the Scottish kings repelled the aggressions of the archbishops of Canterbury and York, when endeavouring to extend their supremacy over the Church of Scotland; in particular, the conduct of Alexander I., in the contest which arose in 1109, is deserving of the highest approbation. Yet this monarch was, in these attempts at usurpation by the English archbishops, only reaping the fruits of his own innovations, as it was by him chiefly that bishoprics were first erected in Scotland.

During the reign of his successor, David I., Popery obtained complete footing in Scotland, by the erection of an immense number of monasteries and abbeys, and the vast wealth which these scenes of corruption speedily acquired. Still, however, the Church of Scotland maintained its independence, refusing to submit to the dictation of that of England Even after that unfortunate defeat which threw William the Lion into the power of the English monarch, and after he had consented to surrender the independence of the kingdom, that he might regain his personal liberty, the Scottish clergy refused to submit to equal degradation. The archbishop of York was now the claimant for this supremacy; and in the year 1176, an assembly of the English and Scottish clergy was held at Northampton, on a citation for that purpose by the Pope's legate. It would appear that Prelacy had already begun to do its work, in producing a mean spirit of subserviency; for not one of the Scottish prelates ventured to oppose the arrogant claim of the archbishop of York. But a young canon, named Gilbert Murray, rose and addressed the assembled dignitaries, in a tone of bold and manly independence worthy of his country and his cause, repelling the arrogant pretensions of the arch-prelate, and asserting the freedom of the Church of Scotland.* The result was an appeal to Rome, and the declaration, by a papal bull, of the independence of Scotland, in all matters ecclesiastical, of any other power than the Pope or his legate. Although this incident proves that the national spirit of a Scot was still stronger in some than the unnationalising spirit of Popery, yet the result was productive to the country of an evil scarcely, if at all, less than that which it was intended to repel. It unquestionably tended to increase the intercourse between the Scottish ecclesiastics and Rome, and thereby to introduce more rapidly, and to diffuse more widely, the pernicious errors of Popery.

That the Romish system, thus unhappily introduced, made rapid progress, and speedily became prevalent throughout the kingdom, cannot be doubted; but the records of these things are so meagre, that no specific details can be given. During the fierce wars by which Scot-

* Jamieson's Hist. Culd., pp. 240-244; Spotswood, p. 38.

and was devastated, in consequence of the attempts of Edward I. of England to annex it to his own dominions, it may be well supposed that little opportunity existed for either the improvement of religious institutions, or their temporal aggrandizement. But soon after Scotland had secured its national independence, we find fresh indications of the growing power, wealth, and profligacy of the clergy. So early, indeed, as the reign of Malcolm II., which began in 1004, the ecclesiastical courts had obtained the sole right of judging in all matters pertaining to dowries and testaments; and also, the passing of a law, that all men might bequeath property to the Church.* This soon became a fertile source of gain, ignorant people being persuaded by the wily priests, that by such bequests they might secure the salvation of their souls, whatever might have been the criminality of their course of life. Besides, while the priesthood were by these means acquiring great wealth, they possessed the only education which existed in the country, and were by no means desirous of communicating it to either the nobility or the common people. They thus became indispensable in the management of all public matters, and soon engrossed the chief official stations in the kingdom. That some of them discharged the duties of these stations with decided ability, need not be denied; but that they at the same time neglected their sacred duties, and allowed the country to remain in a state of great ignorance and barbarism, is equally certain.

In the meantime the social structure of Scotland had gradually reached the last stage of developement of which such a system was capable. The feudal system had been superinduced upon the patriarchal or clan system. Those of the great barons who were of Norman extraction, comprising nearly all the Lowland nobility, maintained the feudal system in all its stern inflexible despotism. The sovereign they regarded as but the highest of their own order, to whom they owed a merely nominal or formal allegiance; each other they viewed as rivals, against whom they might wage open war or frame machinations, as seemed the safest policy; and the people they considered as mere serfs, born to obey, and toil, and bleed, as each haughty tyrant might be pleased to command. In the Highlands the system of clanship prevailed; in which, though the system itself was perfectly despotic, yet it was somewhat mitigated by the idea essential to it, that there subsisted a family relationship between the chief and every clansman; so that, in theory at least, the tie was one of nature's formation, the authority that of a father, and the obedience that of children. In both the feudal and the clan systems the tendency was to divide the nation, or to keep it divided, into a number of jealous and conflicting sections, and to render it a constant scene of strife, anarchy, and blood, such as neither the power of the king, which was little more than nominal, nor the supremacy of the laws, which was scarcely recognised except in theory, was able to restrain. The condition of the body of the people, exposed to the wild violence of factious and implacable nobles, may be more easily imagined than described. Nor is it our purpose to do more than merely suggest the public aspect of affairs in Scotland previous to the Reformation, leaving its minuter delineation to the professedly civil historian, to whom that province belongs.

Reference has already been made to the excessive grants of land and other wealth bestowed upon the Romanized clergy by several of the Scottish kings, especially by David I., and the encouragement thereby given to that avaricious class of men. We have also seen that the ruin of the more ancient and purer faith and discipline of the Culdees was effected by the same instrumentality,—prelates, abbots, and church dignitaries of every name and order, alike detesting a system, the simplicity and purity of which formed a strong and manifest condemnation of their own. At the same time, we are not unaware, that although the encouragement given to the popish system may have at first arisen in a great measure from religious motives operating on minds comparatively ignorant, there may have been not a little of an influence very different in character, by which the Scottish kings were induced to promote the wealth and power of the clergy. They may have regarded the ecclesiasti-

* Regiam Majestatem, pp. 11 and 66.

cal body as the most likely counterbalance to the exorbitant power of the feudal nobility, which could be organized. And it must be admitted, that in many instances the prelates of the Church did lend important assistance to the sovereign, and also exercised some influence in imparting civilization to the community. Let it be observed also, that to whatever extent the prelates did counteract the nobility, to that extent they provoked the jealousy of these proud and overbearing men, who were not unlikely to remember past hostilities in a day of retribution, even though that retribution had begun on far other and holier grounds. The enormous wealth which the all-grasping Romish Church had acquired, while it confirmed the influence of that Church, tended equally to increase the bitter hatred of the nobility, who both envied and scorned the wealth and the luxurious indulgence of the pampered priesthood. The existence of this feeling, and its baneful consequences, we shall have ample occasion hereafter to display.

But instead of continuing our own observations, we cannot better conclude this introductory chapter than by copying, from Dr M'Crie's Life of Knox, the following account of the state of religion in Scotland before the Reformation.

"The corruptions by which the Christian religion was universally disfigured before the Reformation, had grown to a greater height in Scotland than in any other nation within the pale of the Western Church. Superstition and religious imposture, in their grossest forms, gained an easy admission among the rude and ignorant people. By means of these, the clergy attained to an exorbitant degree of opulence and power, which were accompanied, as they always have been, with the corruption of their order, and of the whole system of religion.

"The full half of the wealth of the nation belonged to the clergy; and the greater part of this was in the hands of a few individuals, who had the command of the whole body. Avarice, ambition, and the love of seculiar pomp, reigned among the superior orders. Bishops and abbots rivalled the first nobility in magnificence, and preceded them in honours; they were privy-councillors, and lords of session as well as of parliament, and had long engrossed the principal offices of state. A vacant bishopric or abbacy called forth powerful competitors, who contended for it as for a principality or petty kingdom: it was obtained by similar arts, and not unfrequently taken possession of by the same weapons. Inferior benefices were openly put to sale, or bestowed on the illiterate and unworthy minions of courtiers, on dice-players, strolling bards, and the bastards of bishops. Pluralities were multiplied without bounds; and benefices, given *in commendam*, were kept vacant during the life of the commendator, nay, sometimes during several lives; so that extensive parishes were frequently deprived, for a long course of years, of all religious service,—if a deprivation it could be called, at a time when the cure of souls was no longer regarded as attached to livings originally endowed for that pupose. The bishops never on any occasion condescended to preach; indeed, I scarcely recollect an instance of it mentioned in history, from the erection of the regular Scottish Episcopacy, down to the Era of the Reformation. The practice had even gone into desuetude among all the secular clergy, and was devolved wholly on the mendicant monks, who employed it for the most mercenary purposes.

"The lives of the clergy, exempted from secular jurisdiction, and corrupted by wealth and idleness, were become a scandal to religion, and an outrage on decency. While they professed chastity, and prohibited, under the severest penalties, any of the ecclesiastical order from contracting lawful wedlock, the bishops set an example of the most shameless profligacy before the inferior clergy,—avowedly kept their harlots, provided their natural sons with benefices, and gave their daughters in marriage to the sons of the nobility and principal gentry, many of whom were so mean as to contaminate the blood of their families by such base alliances, for the sake of the rich dowries which they brought.

"Through the blind devotion and munificence of princes and nobles, monasteries, those nurseries of superstition and idleness, had greatly multiplied in the nation; and though they had universally degenerated, and were notoriously become the haunts of lewdness and debauchery, it was deemed impious and sacrilegious to reduce their number, abridge their privileges, or alienate their funds. The kingdom was swarmed with ignorant, idle, luxurious monks, who, like locusts, devoured the fruits of the earth, and filled the air with pestilential infection; with friars, white, black, and gray; canons regular and of St Anthony, Carmelites, Carthusians, Cordeliers, Domicians, Franciscan Conventuals and Observantines, Jacobins, Premonstratensians, Monks of Tyrone and of Vallis Caulium, and Hospitallers or Holy Knights of St. John of Jerusalem; nuns of St. Austin, St. Clair, St. Scholastica, and St. Catharine of Sienna; with canonesses of various classes.

"The ignorance of the clergy respecting religion was as gross as the dissoluteness of their morals. Even bishops were not ashamed to confess that they were unacquainted with the canon of their faith, and had never read any part of the sacred Scriptures, except what they met with in their missals. Under such masters the people perished for lack of knowledge. That book which was able to make them wise unto salvation, and intended to be equally accessible to 'Jew and Greek, Barbarian and Scythian, bond and free,' was locked up from them, and the use of it in their own tongue prohibited under the heaviest penalties. The religious service was mumbled over in a dead language, which many of the priests did not understand, and some of them could scarcely read; and the greatest care was taken to prevent even catechisms, composed and approved by the clergy, from coming into the hands of the laity.

"Scotland, from her local situation, had been less exposed to disturbance from the encroaching ambition, the vexatious exactions, and fulminating anathemas of the Vatican court, than the countries in the immediate vicinity of Rome. But from the same cause, it was more easy for the domestic clergy to keep up on the minds of the people that excessive veneration for the holy see, which could not be long felt by those who had the opportunity of witnessing its vices and worldly politics. The burdens which attended a state of dependance upon a remote foreign jurisdiction was severely felt. Though the popes did not enjoy the power of presenting to the Scottish prelacies, they wanted not numerous pretexts for interfering with them. The most important causes of a civil nature which the ecclesiastical courts had contrived to bring within their jurisdiction, were frequently carried to Rome. Large sums of money were annually exported out of the kingdom, for the confirmation of benefices, the conducting of appeals, and many other purposes; in exchange for which were received leaden bulls, woollen palls, wooden images, old bones, and similar articles of precious consecrated mummery.

"Of the doctrine of Christianity almost nothing remained but the name. Instead of being directed to offer up their adorations to one God, the people were taught to divide them among an innumerable company of inferior divinities. A plurality of mediators shared the honour of procuring the Divine favour with the 'one Mediator between God and man;' and more petitions were presented to the Virgin Mary, and other saints, than to 'Him whom the Father heareth always.' The sacrifice of the mass was represented as procuring forgiveness of sins to the living and the dead, to the infinite disparagement of the sacrifice by which Jesus Christ expiated sin and procured everlasting redemption; and the consciences of men were withdrawn from faith in the merits of their Saviour, to a delusive reliance upon priestly absolutions, papal pardons, and voluntary penances. Instead of being instructed to demonstrate the sincerity of their faith and repentance by forsaking their sins, and to testify their love to God and man by practising the duties of morality, and observing the ordinances of worship authorised by Scripture, they were taught that if they regularly said their *aves* and *credos*, confessed themselves to a priest, punctually paid their tithes and church-offerings, purchased a mass, went in pilgrimage to the shrine of some celebrated saint, refrained from flesh on Fridays, or performed some other prescribed act of bodily mortification, their salvation was infallibly secured in due time; while those who were so rich and pious as to build a chapel or an altar, and to endow it for the support of a priest, to perform masses, obits, and dirges, procured a relaxation of the pains of purgatory for themselves or their relations, in proportion to the extent of their liberality. It is difficult for us to conceive how empty, ridiculous, and wretched those harangues were which the monks delivered for sermons. Legendary tales concerning the founder of some religious order, his wonderful sanctity, the miracles which he performed, his combats with the devil, his watchings, fastings, flagellations; the virtues of holy water, chrism, crossing, and exorcism; the horrors of purgatory, and the numbers released from it by the intercession of some powerful saint,—these, with low jests, table-talk, and fireside scandal, formed the favourite topics of the preachers, and were served up to the people instead of the pure, salutary, and sublime doctrines of the Bible.

"The beds of the dying were besieged, and their last moments disturbed, by avaricious priests, who laboured to extort bequests to themselves or to the Church. Not satisfied with exacting tithes from the living, a demand was made upon the dead: no sooner had the poor husbandman breathed his last, than the rapacious vicar came and carried off his corpse-present, which he repeated as often as death visited the family. Ecclesiastical censures were fulminated against those who were reluctant in making these payments, or who showed themselves disobedient to the clergy; and for a little money they were prostituted on the most trifling occasions. Divine service was neglected; and, except on festival days, the churches, in many parts of the country were no longer employed for sacred purposes, but served as sanctuaries for malefactors, places of traffic, or resorts for pastime.

"Persecution, and the suppression of free inquiry, were the only weapons by which its interested supporters were able to defend this system of corruption and imposture. Every avenue by which truth might enter was carefully guarded. Learning was branded as the parent of heresy. The most frightful pictures were drawn of those who had separated from the Romish Church, and held up before the eyes of the people, to deter them from imitating their example. If any person, who had attained a degree of illumination amidst the general darkness, began to hint dissatisfaction with the conduct of churchmen, and to propose the correction of abuses, he was immediately stigmatized as a heretic, and if he did not secure his safety by flight, was immured in a dungeon, or committed to the flames. And when at last, in spite of all their persecutions, the light which was shining around did break in and spread through the nation, the clergy prepared to adopt the most desperate and bloody measures for its extinction.

"From this imperfect sketch of the state of religion in this country, we may see how false the representation is which some persons would impose on us; as if Popery were a system, erroneous, indeed, but purely speculative,—superstitious, but harmless, provided it had not been accidentally accompanied with intolerance and cruelty. The very reverse is the truth. It may be safely said, that there is not one of its erroneous tenets, or of its superstitious practices, which was not either originally contrived, or afterwards accommodated, to advance and support some practical abuse, to aggrandize the ecclesiastical order, secure to them immunity from civil jurisdiction, sanctify their encroachments upon secular authorities, vindicate their usurpations upon the consciences of men, cherish implicit obedience to the decisions of the Church, and extinguish free inquiry and liberal science."*

To this very masterly summary of the state of religion in Scotland before the Reformation nothing need be added; and it must convince every reflecting reader, that such a state of matters could not be much longer endured by a people like the Scottish, who, though held in deep ignorance, were naturally shrewd and sagacious, despisers of idleness and luxury, and filled with an indestructable love of liberty, which even their civil feuds and public wars served in no inconsiderable degree to stimulate and confirm. And the more protracted and severe that the burden of spiritual despotism had been, it was to be expected that it would be followed by a correspondingly mighty and extensive revulsion and recoil. Nor should it be forgotten,

* M'Crie's Life of Knox, pp. 9-15, 6th edit.

that widely as Popery had shed its baleful influence, it had not been able wholly to exterminate the purer faith and simpler system of the ancient Culdees, especially in Ayrshire, and perhaps also in Fife,—the districts adjacent to St. Andrews and Iona,—the earliest abodes and the latest retreats of primitive Christianity in Scotland.

CHAPTER II.

FROM THE BEGINNING OF THE REFORMATION TO THE MEETING OF THE FIRST GENERAL ASSEMBLY.

From the Beginning of the Reformation to the Meeting of the first General Assembly in 1560—State of Affairs in Rome—Introduction of Wickliffe's Opinions—Patronages—Lollards of Kyle—Patrick Hamilton the first Scottish Martyr—Persecutions in St. Andrews, Edinburgh, and Glasgow—Cardinal Beaton—Barbarous Persecution at Perth—George Wishart—His Preaching,—and Martyrdom—Death of Cardinal Beaton—John Knox in the Castle of St. Andrews—His Confinement in the Galleys—Returns to Scotland—Proceedings of the Queen-Regent and the Reformers—The First Covenant—The Lords of the Congregation—Martyrdom of Walter Mill—Political Intrigues—Final Return of Knox—Destruction of the Monasteries at Perth—Knox at St. Andrews—Growing Strength of the Reformers—Conventions of Estates—Siege of Leith—Death of the Queen-Regent—Meeting of Parliament and Treaty of Peace—First Confession of Faith—First General Assembly of the Church of Scotland.

In the preceding chapter a brief sketch has been presented to the reader of the usurpations of the prelatic and corrupt Church of Rome, and the final suppression of the Culdees, which we may regard as having been accomplished in the year 1297, that being the date of the last documents signed by them as a public body. But though from that time the Culdee form of church government and discipline may be regarded as extinct, there is no reason to believe that their religious tenets were consigned to oblivion at the same instant. Indeed, such a result may be regarded as absolutely impossible. All forcible attempts to suppress religion but compel it to burn with increased intensity, and to be retained with increased pertinacity, within the secret heart; unless, indeed, such attempts be carried to the extreme of utterly exterminating the adherents of the persecuted faith,—a dire result which has been several times produced in different nations. There is, besides, evidence, although but slight, to prove that the doctrine of the Culdees continued to survive long after the suppression of their forms of church government. Sir James Dalrymple refers us to a clause in the bull of Pope John XXII. in 1324, conceding to Robert Bruce the title of King of Scotland, and removing the excommunication; in which clause that pontiff makes mention of many heretics, whom he enjoins the king to suppress.* There is every reason to believe that these were the adherents of the Culdees, against whom some of the Scottish Romanized clergy had complained to the pope.

The great schism which happened in the Church of Rome, through the contentions of rival popes, gave occasion, as is well known, to those who had secretly disapproved of papal corruption, of assailing Popery more openly than before, and more boldly demanding some measure of reformation. Wickliffe, the morning star of the Reformation, began then openly both to censure the abuses of the Church of Rome, and to proclaim those great doctrines of Christianity which it had been the policy of that corrupt Church to conceal. It might have been expected that his doctrines would find a ready reception among the adherents of the Culdees of Scotland, if any were still remaining; and accordingly we find, that John Resby, an Englishman, and a scholar of Wickliffe's, was condemned for maintaining that the pope was not the vicar of Christ, and that no man of a wicked life ought to be acknowledged pope.† For holding and teaching these opinions, with certain others deemed also heretical, he was burned to death in the year 1407. It would appear that this cruel deed had for a time prevented at least the open avowal of similar doctrines in Scotland; as the next victim of popish tyranny was found at the distance of twenty-five years. This victim was Paul Craw, a Bohemian, and a follower of John Huss. It does not appear on what account he had come to Scotland; but having begun to disseminate the opinions of the Bohemian reformer, he was laid hold of by the instigation of Henry Wardlaw, bishop of St. Andrews, convicted of denying the

* Sir J. Dalrymple's Historical Collections, p. 52.
† Spotswood, p. 56,

doctrines of transubstantiation, auricular confession, and praying to saints, then handed over to the secular powers, and by them committed to the flames, at St. Andrews, in the year 1432. That he might not at the stake promulgate his opinions among the spectators by his last dying declaration, his destroyers adopted the barbarous policy of forcing a ball of brass into his mouth, then gazing, as they thought, in safety, on the agonies of the voiceless sufferer.

The popish clergy seem to have thought their triumph complete, and themselves at liberty to prosecute with even increased energy their schemes of aggrandisement. One method in which this was prosecuted deserves to be particularly noticed, as intimately connected with a subject to which we shall have repeated occasion to refer in the course of this work, viz., the subject of patronage. It has not been exactly ascertained at what time the system of lay patronage was introduced in Scotland.

The Late Dr. Mc'Crie, whose opinions on all matters of church history are of the very highest authority, held that it could not have been introduced before the tenth century. The first mention of Scottish patronages and presentations with which we are acquainted occurs in the Book of Laws of Malcolm II., who ascended the throne in the year 1004;* and although the critical acumen of Lord Hailes has succeeded in casting considerable doubt upon the genuine antiquity of these laws, this much may at least be said, that no claim more ancient can be pretended for the asumed right of patronage in Scotland, at the same time that by these laws the right of deciding respecting "the advocation of kirks and the right of patronage," pertains to the jurisdiction of the Church. For a time, it would appear, the Scottish clergy followed the usual policy of the papal Church, holding out every inducement to men to bequeath large sums for the erection and endowment of churches, monasteries, &c., as the best mode of securing their salvation; and allowing to such donors and subsequently to their heirs, the right of presenting to the benefices thus bequeathed. But when they had obtained a very large proportion of the wealth of the kingdom into their own possession, these crafty churchmen became anxious to resume the patronages into their own hands; and putting the same machinery of superstition again to work, they prevailed on the lay patrons to resign the right of presentation to the Church, by annexing it, as it was called, to bishoprics, abbacies, priories, and other religious houses. The benefices thus annexed or appropriated were termed patrimonial, and were not longer subject to the patronage of laymen. The civil power became at length alarmed at the prospect of the lands and wealth of the kingdom being thus placed in the hands of a body of men who were not only beyond the control of the civil law, but were in fact the subjects of a foreign power. An attempt was therefore made to check this practice of annexation, by a statute in the reign of James III., in the year 1471; but so effectual had the schemes of the clergy been, that at the period of the Reformation there were in Scotland only two hundred and sixty-two non-appropriated benefices out of the whole number, consisting of about nine hundred and forty. Even of these two hundred and sixty-two a considerable number, though not annexed, were in the hands of bishops, abbots, and the heads of other religious houses; so that the crafty and avaricious popish clergy might deem themselves secure, being possessed of more than half the wealth of the kingdom, and that, too, placed beyond the power of any control, except that of an appeal to Rome,—a danger which they might well regard as not very formidable.

[1494.] But while the priesthood were thus strenuously endeavouring to consolidate their power, and to increase their splendour, obtaining the erection of an archbishopric, first at St. Andrews, and then at Glasgow, they did not seem to be aware that the spirit of religious reformation was diffusing itself silently but rapidly throughout the kingdom, especially in the western districts of Kyle, Carrick, and Cunningham. At length they began to take alarm, and shaking off their golden dreams, they prepared to crush their hated antagonists. Robert Blacater, the first archbishop of Glasgow, prevailed on James IV. to summon be-

* Regiam Majestatem, pp. 2, 11.

fore the great council about thirty persons, male and female, natives mostly of the above-named western districts; the chief of whom was George Campbell of Cessnock, Adam Reid of Barskimming, John Campbell of New-mills, Andrew Schaw of Polkemmet, and the Ladies of Stair and Polkellie.* This memorable trial of the Lollards of Kyle, as they were opprobiously termed, took place in the year 1594. The articles which they were accused of holding have been recorded both by Knox and Spotswood with little variation, except that Knox's account is rather more full than the other. Their main tenor is chiefly in condemnation of the worship of the Virgin Mary, of saints, reliques, images, and the mass; and also of the various arrogant pretensions and licentious abuses of the prelates and the priesthood, without any very clear statement of the leading doctrines of pure Christianity. It appears, indeed, exceedingly probable, that the Lollards of Kyle did little more than revive the old contest between the Culdees and the prelates; and that the designation given to them by their popish enemies was not in consequence of their having actually imbibed the tenets of Lollard the Waldensian, but that it was applied to them partly as a term of reproach, and partly with a view to prejudge their cause. For it has always been the policy of those who were engaged in persecuting religion, to slander, misrepresent, and affix to it a calumnious name, and then to assail it under this maliciously-imposed disguise. Few men have ever persecuted religion avowedly as such; but how often have they called religion fanaticism, and then persecuted its adherents under the calumnious designation of fanatics!

Providentially for the Lollards of Kyle, James IV. himself presided at the trial,—a monarch who, with all his faults, had yet too much of manliness and candour to permit his judgment to be greatly swayed by the malignity of the prelates. Adam Reid appears to have taken the chief part in the defence, and to have answered with such spirit, point, and humour, as to amuse James, and baffle the bishop completely. The result was, that they were dismissed, with an admonition to beware of new doctrines, and to content themselves with the faith of the Church.

* Knox's History of the Reformation, p. 2; Spotswood, p. 60.

No new persecutions for heresy occurred during the reign of James IV., and after his death on the fatal field of Flodden, the attention of the nobility and the clerical dignitaries was too much occupied with the prosecution of their own selfish and factious designs, to bestow much regard upon the progress of religious opinions. James Beaton had been translated from Glasgow to the archbishopric of St. Andrews, and, in conjunction with the Douglas faction, ruled the kingdom with considerable ability during the minority of the young king, James V. According to Spotswood, Beaton "was neither violently set, nor much solicitous, as it was thought, how matters went in the Church." Still, notwithstanding their political cares, the clergy were aware that the writings of the Continental Protestant divines were beginning to be introduced, as appears from an act of parliament passed in 1525, strictly prohibiting the importation of all such writings, and also forbidding all public "disputations about the heresies of Luther, except it be to the confusion thereof, and that by clerks in the schools alenarlie" [alone.]* Nor was their anxiety unfounded. There is great reason to think that some of these Protestant writings had about this time fallen into the hands of a youth whose rank and talents shed lustre on the cause which he espoused.

Patrick Hamilton, a youth of royal lineage, and not less distinguished by the possession of high mental endowments, was the chosen instrument by means of whom "the Father of lights" rekindled in Scotland the smouldering beacon of eternal truth.

Being designed by his relations for the Church, there had been conferred on him, even in infancy, the abbacy of Ferne,—a foretaste of the wealth and honours to which he might aspire, and a stimulus to quicken his ambition. But while his friends were anticipating for him a splendid career of worldly pomp and power, a very different path was preparing for him. The ambitious and worldly, yet ignorant

* M'Crie's Life of Knox, p. 23, 6th edit.

priesthood, by whom he was surrounded, began to mark with jealous eye his altered manner, to note suspiciously the praise he gave to the study of ancient literature in preference to the dry logic of the schools, and the severe terms in which he condemned the abounding corruptions of the Church. Partly, perhaps, to avoid the danger to which he was thus exposing himself, but chiefly to obtain a more complete knowledge of the doctrines of the Reformation, he resolved to visit the Continent in 1526. With this view he naturally directed his course to Wittemberg, where he was speedily honoured with the friendship and esteem of Luther and Melancthon. After enjoying the benefit of their society for a short time, he proceeded to the University of Marbourg, where he obtained the instructions of the celebrated Francis Lambert. But the more that his own mind acquired of the knowledge of divine truth, the more earnestly did he long to return and communicate that knowledge to his beloved countrymen.

The return to Scotland of this noble youth at once attracted all eyes, as if a new star had appeared in the heavens. His instructions were listened to with the deepest attention, and the doctrines which he taught began to spread rapidly throughout the kingdom. His high birth, reputation for learning, the attractive elegance of his youthful aspect, and the persuasive graces of his courteous demeanour, rendered his influence almost irresistible; and the popish clergy saw no safety to their cause but in his destruction. They framed their murderous plans with fiend-like ingenuity. Being apprehensive that the young king might not readily be persuaded to sanction the death of one who stood to him in the near relationship of cousin, they contrived to send him on a pilgrimage to the shrine of St. Dothess, or Duthack, in Ross-shire. They next decoyed Patrick Hamilton to St. Andrews, on the pretence of wishing to have a free conference with him on religious subjects. Pursuing their perfidious plot, they caused Alexander Campbell, prior of the Blackfriars, to hold several interviews with him, and even to seem to concede to his opinions so far as to draw from him a full avowal of them. Their measures being now ripe for execution, they caused him to be apprehended under night, and committed to the Castle.

The very next day he was brought before the archbishop, and a large convention of bishops, abbots, priors, and other dignitaries and doctors of the Church, and there charged with maintaining and propagating certain heretical opinions. John Knox declares, that the articles for which he was condemned were merely those of "*pilgrimage, purgatory, prayers to saints, and prayers for the dead*," although matters of greater importance had been in question. Spotswood, on the other hand, specifies thirteen distinct articles, of much graver character, which were condemned as heretical, and he condemned for holding them. The probability is, that both statements are true; that the articles specified by Spotswood are those "matters of greater importance" to which Knox alludes; but that in declaring the sentence publicly, no mention was made of any but the four topics stated by Knox, because for his accusers to have done otherwise would have been to have published tenets themselves, which they wished to consign to oblivion. Such, indeed, has been the policy of persecutors in all ages,—to fix the attention of the public, as far as possible, on the external aspect and the nonessentials of the subject in dispute, thereby to conceal the truth, while they are destroying its defenders. So acted the Romanized English prelates towards the Culdees, as we have already seen; and so, as we shall afterwards see, acted the persecutors of the Church of Scotland in different periods of her history.

[1528.] The sentence of condemnation was pronounced; and, to give it all the weight of authority, every person of name and rank, civil and ecclesiastical, was induced to sign it; amongst whom was the Earl of Cassilis, a boy of thirteen years of age. Arrangements were then made to carry it into effect, that very day. The pile was erected in front of the College of St. Salvador, and the youthful martyr hurried to the stake. Before being bound to the stake, he divested himself of his outer garments, and gave them to his servant, who had attended him faithfully and affectionately for a number of years, accompanying the gift with these tender and pathetic words:—

"This stuff will not help me in the fire, and will profit thee. After this you can receive from me no more good, but the example of my death, which, I pray thee, keep in mind; for, albeit it be bitter to the flesh, and fearful in man's judgment, yet it is the entrance into eternal life, which none shall possess that denies Christ Jesus before this wicked generation." A train of gunpowder, laid for the purpose of setting fire to the pile, exploded ineffectually, scorching his left side and face, but leaving the mass unkindled. While they were procuring materials of a more combustible nature, the calm spirit of the scorched sufferer poured itself forth in earnest exhortations and instructions to the pitying spectators. The treacherous Friar Campbell attempted to disturb him by calling on him to recant, and pray to the Virgin Mary, which drew from the dying martyr a severely solemn reproof, ending with an appeal and citation to the judgment-seat of the Lord Jesus. The pile was then effectually kindled; and as the flames blazed up around him, his voice rose calm and clear,—"How long, O Lord, shall darkness cover this realm? How long wilt thou suffer this tyranny of man? Lord Jesus, receive my spirit!"—and with these words his spirit returned to God who gave it.*

Thus died Patrick Hamilton, the first Scottish martyr, on the last day of February 1528, and in the twenty-fourth year of his age. He died a victim to the malice and the treachery of the popish priesthood; but his death did more to recommend the cause for which he suffered to the heart of Scotland, than could have been accomplished by a lengthened life, —as a sudden flash of lightning at once rends the gnarled oak of a thousand years, and yields a glimpse of the strong glories of heaven.

[1529.] The report of the martyrdom of this noble youth spread rapidly throughout the kingdom, and men began to inquire why Patrick Hamilton was burned, and what were the opinions he had held and maintained to the death. When these opinions were related, the public mind was not only excited, but enlightened also; and many began to call in question much which they had never before doubted, and to admit sacred truths with which they had till then been utterly unacquainted. Several even of the friars began to preach and defend doctrines savouring strongly of the Reformation, and, at the same time, to declaim loudly against the licentious and ungodly lives of the bishops and the chief men of the ecclesiastical body.

* Knox, p. 6; Spotswood, p. 65.

The archbishop and his familiars, alarmed and irritated, spoke of burning some, in order to terrify and silence others; but a bystander, with a mixture of shrewdness and mockery, warned the archbishop to act warily, and if he burned any more, to burn them in cellars; "for the smoke," said he, "of Mr. Patrick Hamilton hath infected as many as it blew upon." So rapidly, indeed, did these reforming doctrines spread, that in a short time Alexander Seaton, a Dominican friar, and confessor to the king, publicly preached in a strain directly subversive of the very essence of Popery. The following were his leading propositions:—That Christ Jesus is the end and perfection of the law,—that there is no sin where God's law is not violated,—and that to satisfy for sins lies not in man's power, but the remission thereof cometh by unfeigned repentance, and by faith apprehending God the Father, merciful in Jesus Christ his Son.* Such doctrines, publicly preached by a bold and eloquent man, occupying an influential position, gave dire offence to the corrupt priesthood, who accordingly called him to account for certain heretical opinions which he was accused of holding. His able defence, and the favourable regard of the king, which he then enjoyed, saved him for that time; but the archbishop secretly influenced the young and licentious monarch against a man who was too faithful and severe a monitor; and Seaton, becoming aware of the secret machinations against him, fled to Berwick, and wrote to the king a remarkable letter, defending himself, retorting the charge against his enemies, and demanding the protection of just and impartial laws. This letter is given at length in Knox's History of the Reformation, and is well deserving of an attentive perusal, as containing the first attempt, by a Scottish reformer, to point out the duty of the

* Knox, Historie, p. 16.

civil magistrate respecting religious matters; asserting it to be the duty of the king, to which he is "bound by the law of God, to cause every man, in any case accused of his life, to have just defence, and his accusers produced conform to their own law." It will be observed, that while this asserts the power and the duty of the sovereign in what regards the life, and by consequence the property, of the subject, it leaves the accused person to be tried by the laws of that court which he is assumed to have offended, and by consequence to suffer, if convicted, the punishments which such court may be competent to inflict. To this letter, and the principle very ably stated in it, we direct the reader's attention the more, in consequence of the misrepresentations of party writers, who refer to it as admitting the right of the king to judge directly in matters of doctrine.

[1534.] The fierce persecuting zeal of the Archbishop Beaton, and his counsel of prelates, abbots, priors, &c., was ineffectual. Many learned men, especially Gawin Logie, principal of St. Leonard's, and John Winram, the sub-prior, either directly taught or secretly connived at the teaching of the reformed doctrines; while considerable numbers of the inferior orders of the clergy abandoned the errors of Popery, cast aside the impure and extravagant legends of saints, and became earnest preachers of the gospel. Fear and rage inflamed the hearts of the persecutors, and increased their cruelty. Norman Gourlay and David Straiton were condemned at Edinburgh; and, after being half-strangled, were cast into the flames, at Greenside, on the 17th August, 1534. Henry Forrest was burned at St. Andrews about the same time.

In February 1538, Robert Forrester, gentleman, Duncan Simpson, priest, Friar Kyllor, Friar Beveridge, and Dean Thomas Forrest, were condemned to death, and burned in one huge pile on the Castle Hill of Edinburgh. There is an incident connected with the last-named person, which deserves attention, as exhibiting the ignorance of the bishops. We give it in the words of Archbishop Spotswood:—"This poor man, not long before, had been called before the bishop of Dunkeld, his ordinary, for preaching every Sunday to his parishioners upon the epistles and gospels of the day, and desired to forbear, seeing his diligence that way brought him in suspicion of heresie. If he could find a *good gospel* or a *good epistle*, that made for the liberty of the holy Church, the bishop willed him to preach that to his people, and let the rest be. The honest man replying, *that he had read both the New Testament and the Old, and that he had never found an ill epistle or an ill gospel in any of them.* The bishop said, *I thank God I have lived well these many years, and never knew either the Old or the New: I content me with my portuise and pontificall; and if you, Dean Thomas, leave not these fantasies, you will repent when you cannot mend it.* Dean Thomas answered, that he believed it was his duty to do what he did, and that he had laid his account with any danger that might follow."*

In the course of the same year, (1538) Jerom Russell, a friar, and a young man named Kennedy, of Ayr, were both burned at the same stake in Glasgow. At first, the heart of Kennedy, glowing with all the fresh feelings of youth, shrunk from the prospect of such an early and fearful death; but spiritual strength being graciously imparted to him in his hour of weakness, he fell on his knees, breathed forth his fervent thanks to God for the heavenly comfort he had received, and then exclaimed, "Now I defy death! Do what you please; I praise God, I am ready!" This scene made such an impression upon the archbishop of Glasgow, that he would have spared the lives of the heroic martyrs, had he not been urged on to the dreadful deed by the bloody brotherhood around him. The two young sufferers perished together at the stake, exhorting each other to endure patiently their short agonies, for the sake of Him who died to destroy death, and to purchase for his followers eternal life; and their calm Christian fortitude awoke the deep sympathies of the pitying and admiring spectators.

Hitherto the persecution of the reformers had been carried on nominally under the authority of James Beaton, archbishop of St. Andrews, who, however, was in his latter years greatly under the influ-

* Spotswood, pp. 66, 67.

ence of his nephew, David Beaton, a man of great talents, still greater ambition, and immitigable cruelty of disposition. He had been educated in France; and after his return to Scotland, he was sent by the king to negotiate respecting the marriage of his own sovereign with a French princess. This was an object on which the hearts of the Scottish clergy were most earnestly bent, being apprehensive lest James should comply with the proposal of Henry VIII. of England to give to the Scottish monarch his own daughter in marriage. The deep designs of the clergy were successful. The minds of Henry and James were estranged from each other; and first a daughter of the French king, and, upon her early death, Mary of Guise, became successively united in marriage to the Scottish king. For these services the King of France prevailed upon the pope to raise David Beaton to the rank of a cardinal, by which title he is hereafter to be designated.

Upon the death of James Beaton, in the year 1539, the cardinal succeeded him in the archbishopric of St. Andrews, and very speedily gave proof of his determination to employ still sharper measures for the extermination of the reformers and their tenets. He called together all his adherents of the clerical body, together with a considerable number of the nobility, to St. Andrews; and there, presiding in state, proceeded to declare the dangers to which the Church was exposed from the prevalence of heresy, which, he said, found too much countenance even at court, and the necessity of instituting still more rigorous measures for the suppression of heresy. He then named Sir John Borthwick as infected with heretical opinions, and cited him to appear and answer to the charge. But Borthwick, having been aware of his danger, had fled to England; and not appearing when summoned, was condemned in absence, and burnt in effigy, in May 1540, both at St. Andrews and Edinburgh. The king was at that time thought to be favourably disposed towards the reformers, influenced, probably, by his friendship for Sir David Lindsay, whose poetical genius attracted the admiration of the youthful monarch, himself possessing a taste and somewhat of a talent for poetry. But matters of grave political importance and civil dissensions intervened, turning aside the king's favour, and directing the active energies of the cardinal into another channel.

Allusion has been already made to the wish of Henry VIII. to form an alliance with James V., by offering to him his daughter in marriage. Against this the cardinal and whole clergy of the kingdom remonstrated in the strongest terms. They were afraid that the influence and example of Henry might induce James to favour the Reformation, in which case their power and their wealth must inevitably perish. They pointed out to James the danger of his being imprisoned, as his ancestor James I. had been should he venture into England; and they offered to provide him funds for the support of an army, should war arise in consequence of his refusing to hold an interview with Henry. The reader of Scottish history must be well aware that the reign of James V. was one continued contest between the king and the nobility. His first great conflict was with the house of Douglas, which he succeeded in overthrowing, after a protracted and dubious struggle. Pursuing what had been the policy of the race of Stuart, especially since the time of James I., the king strove to reduce the power of the great feudal barons; and this induced him to yield more readily to the persuasions of the clergy than he might otherwise have done, and also to promote unworthy favourites to those stations of dignity and power which the nobility were accustomed to regard as their birthright. But though the intrigues of the clergy might sway the councils of the king, they could do him little service in the field. The wars with England produced but a series of disgraceful defeats, the nobles allowing themselves to be routed and taken prisoners by mere handfuls of their antagonists. These disastrous events broke the heart of the unhappy monarch, who died at Falkland on the 14th day of December 1542, leaving the shattered sovereignty to his infant daughter, the ill-fated Mary, who was born seven days before his death.

Both Knox and Spotswood assert that Cardinal Beaton suborned a priest, called

Henry Balfour, to forge a document purporting to be the will of the king, in which the cardinal, and the Earls of Huntly, Argyle, and Murray, were appointed governors of the kingdom during the minority of the infant queen. But this daring attempt was defeated in a meeting of the chief nobility at Edinburgh; and James Hamilton, earl of Arran, next heir to the crown, was appointed regent and governor of the kingdom.

The defeat of the cardinal, and the appointment of Arran to the regency, were productive of great advantage to the cause of the Reformation. After the king's death, there was found a list which had been furnished to him by the cardinal, containing the names of some hundreds of persons of various ranks, and possessed of property and wealth, whom they denounced as heretics, and by whose forfeited riches the coffers of the king might, according to their suggestions, be easily replenished. The knowledge of this nefarious scheme tended not a little to bring odium on the cardinal and his party, and to strengthen the cause of their opponents. The regent Arran had also been for some time favourable to the Reformation, to which the lamented death of his relative, the martyr Patrick Hamilton, may easily be thought to have greatly contributed. In a parliament held the same year, 1542, an act was passed, declaring it lawful for all to read the Scriptures in their native language. Against the passing of this act the cardinal and the bishops strove with all the energy of fury and despair, but strove in vain. The effect was instantaneous and great. Copies of the sacred volume, which had been most carefully concealed, and perused with secrecy and fear, were now to be seen, as Knox says, lying on every gentleman's table, and the New Testament, especially, borne about in almost every person's hands.* For a time the regent gave direct encouragement to the Reformation, and employed as his own chaplains Thomas Guillaume or Williams, and John Rough, both zealous and faithful preachers of the reformed doctrines. And, as if for the purpose of settling the Reformation upon a firm and extensive basis, a treaty was concluded with Henry VIII. for a contract of marriage between his son Edward and the infant queen of Scotland.

So far all seemed prosperous; but a great reverse was at hand. The regent, though a plausible, was a weak and fickle man, liable at all times to be wrought upon and biassed by those of greater decision and energy of character. With this, his constitutional failing, the wily cardinal was well acquainted; and, to avail himself of it, invited from France, John Hamilton, abbot of Paisley, the regent's own illegitimate brother, and David Panter, afterwards bishop of Ross, two able and designing men, by whose influence he hoped to accomplish his design. Too well did they succeed in their subtile enterprise. In a short time the regent's mind became so much alienated from the reformers, that his chaplains were under the necessity of withdrawing from court to save their lives; Williams retiring to England, and Rough to Kyle. Sir David Lindsay, Kirkaldy of Grange, and other gentlemen who favoured the reforming party, were also obliged to retire; and the regent became completely the tool of the cardinal and the popish faction. He accordingly broke off the agreement with England, abjured the reformed religion, and entered heartily into the great master-scheme of the cardinal, to give the young queen in marriage to the Dauphin of France.

[1543.] Cardinal Beaton having thus recovered his ascendency in the government of the kingdom, renewed his efforts to suppress the Reformation, by means of the most merciless and exterminating persecution. He began his barbarous career at Perth, where five men and one woman were brought before him, accused of heresy. They were tried, condemned, and sentence of death passed upon them,—the men to be hanged, the woman to be drowned. The case of the poor woman, named Helen Stark, deserves to be more particularly recorded. She was the wife of one of the above-mentioned men, and had recently given birth to a child. During the anguish of her travail, she had been urged by her female assistant to pray to the Virgin Mary, and had answered that she would only pray to God, in the name of Jesus Christ. For this she was accused of heresy, and condemned to die. On the day of execution

* Knox, p. 34.

she earnestly requested that she might die along with her husband. Her pathetic appeal was harshly refused; but she accompanied him to the fatal spot, bearing her infant in her arms, and exhorting her husband to patience and constancy in the cause of Christ. He was murdered before her eyes; and as soon as life had left his quivering frame, she was dragged to a pool of water close at hand, with her babe still clinging to her bosom. When she had withdrawn her precious infant from its last enjoyment of nature's resting place and nature's nourishment, and consigned it to the charge of a pitying neighbour, and to the care of Him who is the orphan's stay, she felt that for her the bitterness of death was past, and being cast into the whelming waters, died without a struggle, full of the steady fortitude and the heavenly comfort of a Christian martyr.*

Not satisfied with these victims, the cardinal pursued his bloody circuit through Angus and Mearns, inflicting upon some fines, upon others imprisonment, and persecuting others to the death, taking with him the feeble regent, that he might have the appearance of his sanction to the perpetration of these cruel deeds.

[1544.] He was soon to stain his soul with the blood of a more distinguished victim. This was the celebrated George Wishart, brother of the Laird of Pittarrow, in Mearns. He had been banished by the instigation of the bishop of Brechin, for teaching the Greek language in Montrose, and had resided for some years at the University of Cambridge. In the year 1544, he returned to his native country in the company of the commissioners who had been sent to negotiate a treaty with Henry VIII. of England. Immediately upon his arrival in Scotland, he began to preach the doctrines of evangelical truth, with such warm and persuasive eloquence as at once to attract, and soften, and convince the crowding audiences, who wept, and glowed, and trembled as he preached. In the accounts transmitted by cotemporary writers of this eminent Christian martyr, we seem to trace the features of a character of surpassing loveliness, bearing a close resemblance in its chief lineaments to that of the beloved Apostle John,—so mild, gentle, patient, and unresisting,—his lips touched with a live coal from off the altar, and his heart overflowing with holy love to God, and compassionate affection to mankind. The citizens of Montrose, and especially of Dundee, felt and owned the power of his heavenly eloquence; and much of his time and labours were spent in the latter city.

[1545.] The cardinal was soon informed of Wishart's preaching, and of the deep impression it was producing in Dundee. Instigated by him, Robert Mill, a man of great authority in the town, openly commanded him to leave the place, and trouble them no more with his sermons. Expressing his pity and regret that they were thus refusing to listen to the message of salvation, he took his departure, along with some of his friends, to Ayrshire. There his preaching was attended with equal success, and, of course, excited equal hostility in the breasts of the bishops and clergy. The archbishop of Glasgow hastened to the town of Ayr, to prevent Wishart from preaching in the church; and the sheriff of the county prevented him from preaching in the church of Mauchline. But this was a small hindrance to the zealous martyr. He could preach in the market-place, in the fields, or on the hill-side, with equal readiness, and with equal success in convincing his hearers.

Hearing that the plague had visited Dundee, he hastened to return thither, that he might bring the hopes and consolations of the gospel to perishing men in their hour of extreme need. There he braved the horrors of the plague, ministering comfort to the miserable sufferers, both speaking to their souls, and supplying their temporal necessities. Even when engaged in this work of mercy, an attempt was made upon his life by a priest; and he escaped narrowly from a plot laid to get him into the power of the cardinal. Soon afterwards he proceeded to Edinburgh, and from thence to Haddington, beset by enemies, yet for a time delivered from their snares. During his abode in that neighbourhood he was very constantly attended by John Knox, who was at that time residing as tutor in the family of Douglas of Langniddrie, and

* Spotswood, p. 75.

who scrupled not to wear a sword for the defence of his beloved friend, the gentle and unresisting Wishart.

[1546.] But the time of his martyrdom was at hand. After preaching at Haddington, he went to Ormiston, accompanied by the proprietor, and by Crichton of Brunston and Sandilands of Calder. John Knox wished to have accompanied him also, but Wishart refused to permit him, saying, "Go back to your pupils: one is sufficient for one sacrifice." During the night, the house was beset by armed horsemen, headed by the Earl of Bothwell; while the regent and the cardinal were but a short way distant with a larger force, so that resistance was in vain. Ormiston, however, refused to yield up Wishart, till Bothwell pledged his honour to protect his life from the cardinal's hatred; or, if he should find that to be impracticable, to restore him again to the protection of his friends. But the cardinal and the queen-dowager persuaded Bothwell to violate his pledge; and Wishart was carried to St. Andrews, and left there a prisoner, in the power of his deadly foe.

While the cardinal was summoning together his prelatic council, that he might with the utmost pomp and ostentation proceed to the destruction of his victim, David Hamilton of Preston endeavoured to persuade the regent not to consent to the death of so distinguished a servant of God. The regent yielded so far as to write to the cardinal not to precipitate the trial of Wishart till he should himself come to St. Andrews. The cardinal haughtily returned this answer: "That he wrote not to the governor as though he depended in any measure upon his authority, but out of a desire he had that the heretic's condemnation might proceed with a show of public consent, which, since he could not obtain, he would himself do that which he held most fitting."*

He proceeded accordingly to the execution of his bloody purpose; gave orders that Wishart should be summoned to trial; and marched in state to the Abbey Church, accompanied by the archbishop of Glasgow, and a great number of bishops, abbots, and other clerical dignitaries, and attended by a large body of retainers in military array. The sub-prior, John Winram, by the cardinal's command, preached a sermon on the nature of heresy, but expressed in such guarded terms, that it gave no countenance to the ruthless deed about to be perpetrated. Then rose up John Lauder, a priest, and entering fully into the spirit of the cardinal, began, in a strain of the coarsest and most ferocious invective, to enumerate eighteen articles of accusation against Wishart. He answered them all calmly and mildly, but with great strength of reasoning, and full proof of all his opinions from the Scriptures. He was nevertheless condemned by the unanimous voice of the assembled popish prelates and clergy, and sentence passed adjudging him to be burned to death, as a heretic, on the following day.

Wishart passed the intervening night in the chamber of the captain of the castle, occupying the greater part of it in prayer. Early next morning, the 2d day of March, 1546, after refusing to hold intercourse with two friars who had been sent to hear his confession, he requested to converse with Winram, the sub-prior. Winram came immediately, and after some private conversation, returned to the cardinal, to request that the sacrament might be given to the prisoner. This was refused; but being invited by the captain to breakfast with him, Wishart prayed, exhorted, and distributed bread and wine to those who were present,—thus commemorating, as fully as circumstances would permit, the dying love of Him for whose sake he was himself so soon to die. He then retired to his private apartment, and remained in prayer till those came who were appointed to take him to the place of execution. They divested him of his usual attire, clad him with a loose garment of black linen, and fastened bags of gunpowder to various parts of his body; and when thus arrayed, he was conducted to an outer room near the gate of the castle, to wait there till the rest of the hideous preparations should be completed.

The cardinal, in the meantime, had commanded a stake to be fixed in the ground, and combustible materials to be piled around it, in front of one of the castle-gates, near the priory; and, lest the friends of Wishart should attempt a

* Spotswood, p. 79.

rescue, he had also given directions that all the cannons and other ordnance of the castle should be pointed to the place of execution. The battlements and windows of the fore-tower of the castle were hung with tapestry and spread with rich cushions, that the cardinal and the prelates might, in state, and at their ease, feast their eyes upon the torments of the martyred servant of the Lord.

All things being now prepared, Wishart was led to the stake, with his hands bound behind his back, a rope round his neck, and an iron chain about his waist. When he reached the spot, he kneeled down and prayed aloud saying thrice, "O, thou Saviour of the world, have mercy on me! Father of heaven, I commend my spirit into thy holy hands!" He then rose and addressed the people, exhorting them not to be offended with the Word of God, notwithstanding the torments which they saw prepared for him; entreated them to accept, believe and obey the Word of God; and expressed entire forgiveness of his enemies and persecutors. Then the executioner, casting himself upon his knees, before the martyr, begged to be forgiven for the deed he was about unwillingly to do. Wishart desiring him to draw near him, kissed his cheek, saying, "Lo, here is a token that I forgive thee; my heart, do thine office!" The sounding of a trumpet gave the signal; the martyr was tied to the stake, and the fire was kindled around him, exploding the gunpowder, but not putting an end to his sufferings. The captain perceiving him still alive, drew near the pile, and bade him be of good courage. Wishart replied with unfaltering voice, "This fire torments my body, but no way abates my spirit." Then looking towards the cardinal, he said, "He who in such state from that high place feedeth his eyes with my torments, within few days shall be hanged out at the same window, to be seen with as much ignominy as he now leaneth there in pride." As he ended these words, the executioner tightened the rope that was about his neck; and the fire now blazing fiercely, he was speedily consumed to ashes.*

Thus died George Wishart, one of the most amiable, eloquent, and truly pious men that ever endured the tortures and obtained the crown of Christian martyrdom. But his death, while it seemed the triumph of the cardinal's power, proved to be the consummation of his guilt, and the knell summoning him to judgment. While the fierce popish faction extolled the zeal and the courage of the cardinal, in thus, by his own authority exterminating heretics, and avenging the cause of holy mother Church, a great body of the people were stirred with indignation against the shedders of innocent blood, and several men of birth and influence began to talk openly of the necessity of putting an end to the bloodthirsty career of the cardinal, unless they were willing tamely to yield themselves up to be butchered at his pleasure. Of those who thus talked, the chief were John Lesly, brother to the Earl of Rothes; Norman Lesly, son to the same Earl; William Kircaldy of Grange, who afterwards acted a distinguished part in the Reformation; Peter Carmichael; and James Melville, of the family of Carnbee. To these were joined several other men of less note, but equally determined; and they began to plot how they might best succeed in their determination to put the cardinal to death.

The cardinal was not unaware of the indignation which his cruelties had excited; but his haughty spirit determined him to brave the hostility which he had provoked. For this purpose he gave his illegitimate daughter in marriage to the Earl of Crawford, thereby to confirm his personal influence; and began to fortify more strongly his archiepiscopal palace, or castle, at St. Andrews. This latter scheme, from which he hoped security, prepared the way of his death. The conspirators came privately, and separate from each other, so as to avoid causing suspicion, to St. Andrews, on the evening of the 28th of May. Next morning, as the workmen employed in fortifying the castle were assembling, they entered separately, till the whole number, sixteen in all, had obtained admission. They then seized the porter, took possession of the keys, and secured the gates; and going from room to room, either put out the domestics, or locked them up. Having thus mastered the

* For a more full account, see Spotswood, pp. 75-82; Knox, Historie, pp. 43-63; Foxe, Martyrology.

castle, they proceeded to the apartment occupied by the cardinal, who was still asleep,—so quietly had the whole affair been conducted. Starting at length out of his slumbers, the cardinal demanded the cause of the noise; and learning that the castle was in the hands of his enemies, he at first attempted to escape, and finding that to be impracticable, he barricaded his chamber door, and then held parley with those by whom it was assailed. The assailants refused to promise him his life; and, as the door resisted their efforts to force it, they called for a fire to burn it open. Upon this the door was opened, and the cardinal throwing himself despairingly into a chair, cried out, "I am a priest, I am a priest; ye will not slay me!" John Lesly and Peter Carmichael struck him hastily with their daggers, but James Melville interposed, and putting them aside, said, "This work and judgment of God, although it be secret, yet ought to be done with greater gravity." Then turning to the cardinal, and presenting the point of his sword to his breast, he continued, "Repent thee of thy former wicked life, but especially of the shedding of the blood of that notable instrument of God, Mr. George Wishart; which, albeit, the flame of fire consumed before men, yet cries it for vengeance upon thee, and we from God are sent to avenge it. For here, before my God, I protest, that neither the hatred of thy person, the love of thy riches, nor the fear of any trouble thou couldest have done to me in particular, moved or moveth me to strike thee, but only because thou hast been, and remainest, an obstinate enemy against Christ Jesus and his holy evangel." With these words he struck the wretched and trembling man twice or thrice through the body; whose expiring breath was spent in crying, "I am a priest, I am a priest! fy, fy! all is gone!" Thus died David Beaton, cardinal, and archbishop of St. Andrews, without uttering one word of repentance or of prayer, on the 29th day of May, 1546, leaving behind him a name unrivalled in Scottish annals for the fearful combination of evil qualities of which his character was composed,—unscrupulous ambition, far-reaching treachery, deliberate malice, gross licentiousness, and relentless cruelty.*

Scarcely was the Cardinal dead when a tumult arose in the town, caused by those who had been expelled from the castle; and a large body of the populace collected and began loudly to demand to see the cardinal, or to know what was become of him. To allay the tumult, the conspirators exposed the dead body from the same window, or over the same part of the battlements, where the cardinal had, a short time before, reclined in haughty state, gazing on the martyrdom of Wishart. Thus were the prophetic dying words of the martyr fulfilled; and many of the people, when they beheld the strange spectacle, remembering at the same time the previous prediction, began to regard the event as a signal instance of the just judgment of God, and, abandoning all thought of tumultuary revenge, returned quietly to their homes.

That the death of Cardinal Beaton was an act of deliberate murder, and therefore in itself highly criminal, no right-thinking man will deny. At the same time it ought to be kept in mind, that such actions bear in our eyes a much blacker aspect than they did in the estimation of men of that period. Some of the conspirators may also have been excited by resentment for private injuries, others by motives of state policy and the influence of English gold; but a desire to deliver their country from his oppression, and especially to avenge the death of Wishart, seems to have been unquestionably the predominating feeling by which they were impelled to the deed. The attempt which has been recently made, by a modern historian, to blacken the characters of all parties concerned, and even to implicate the martyr Wishart himself, deserves no other answer than to be at once indignantly repelled, or, if an answer, not more than may be contained in a brief appended note.† To every reader accustomed to investigate moral evidence, the true nature of the transaction will at once be manifest; and by all such, a fair estimate of the moral delinquency of men who thought themselves called upon to avenge the wrongs of their country and the murder of their friend, by committing a deed

* Knox, Historie, pp. 64, 65.

† See Note in Appendix.

of lawless justice on the person of a criminal too high for the reach of law, will, without difficulty, be formed; and with these remarks we quit the subject.

Soon after the death of Cardinal Beaton, a number of gentlemen of Fife, who favoured the reforming party, entered into the castle of St. Andrews, thus both giving countenance to the deed of the conspirators, and securing a place of strength in which they could defend themselves while they were endeavouring to make their peace with the regent. This, however, it was not so easy to accomplish, instigated as he was by the clergy to avenge in the most exemplary manner the death of their leader. The regent laid siege to the castle in August; but it was by this time so well garrisoned and supplied with both provisions and ammunitions from England, that the besiegers could make no impression upon it, and at length entered into terms of agreement and a suspension of hostilities with the defenders. John Rough, formerly chaplain to the regent before his relapse into Popery, had entered into the castle of St. Andrews, along with the Fifeshire gentlemen, previous to the commencement of the siege; but upon the suspension of hostilities he extended his preaching to the town, to which he then gained ready access. He was there encountered by John Annan, a popish priest and dean, and being inferior to his antagonist in learning, made application for aid to one who was destined to become the MAN of the age.

[1547.] This was JOHN KNOX, the great SCOTTISH REFORMER. He had been educated for the Romish Church; but his bold and penetrating mind could not be held in the trammels of mere priestly and scholastic authority, and at a very early period of his public life he showed his disposition to disregard antiquated dogmatism, and to walk freely on the paths of light and liberty pointed out by the Word of God. His mind had received some benefit in its early researches by the teaching of the regent's two chaplains, Guillaume and Rough; but the clear doctrines, the heart-warm love, and the heavenly piety of the martyr Wishart, completed his conversion to the reformed faith. About the beginning of April 1547, he entered the castle of St. Andrews, partly drawn by respect to those by whom it was held, and partly induced to seek an asylum within it from the hostility of the popish clergy, who seemed already to have marked him out as a dangerous opponent, and therefore to be cut off as soon as possible; but chiefly to aid Rough in the controversy with Annan. Soon after his arrival, the people of the place, together with Rough, resolved to give John Knox a solemn and public call to be their minister. He was at first overwhelmed with anxiety when he thought of the awful responsibility of the ministerial office, but durst not refuse the call; and from that hour manifestly regarded himself as devoted, with all his energies of mind and body, to the preaching of the everlasting gospel.*

Knox being thus publicly called to his great work, proceeded immediately to place the controversy between the Reformers and the Papists on its proper basis. Instead of waging a skirmishing warfare of outposts, he directed his efforts against the very heart of the enemy's position. Instead of contending about rites and ceremonies, the licentious lives of the priesthood, and minor errors and perversions of doctrine, he boldly stated, and offered to maintain, the proposition, that the papal Church of Rome is Antichrist. From the hour when that proposition was boldly announced, are we disposed to date the real beginning of the Reformation in Scotland; because from that hour it was manifest that there could be no compromise,—no retaining of anything in form, government, or doctrine, which had no other authority than what was derived from the practice or the teaching of an apostate and antichristian body,—no appeal to any other standard than the Word of God.

A public disputation was held in the presence of the sub-prior, between Knox and the priests; the effect of which was prodigious upon the numerous audience, who now clearly perceived that the popish party were unable to maintain their cause in argument. Nor were the prelates unaware of their danger; and therefore they prepared to overwhelm by force what they could not oppose successfully from reason and Scripture. Having procured assistance from France, they again besieged the castle, not only

* Life of Knox, by Dr M'Crie, pp. 32, 33.

by land, but also by sea, by means of the French galleys, which blockaded the harbour, thereby cutting off their supplies from England. After a gallant resistance, the defenders were obliged to capitulate, on the 31st day of July 1547, making their terms with the French commander, and stipulating that their lives and liberties should be preserved. These terms, however, were not kept; for immediately upon the return of the French fleet to France, the prisoners, instead of being set at liberty, were confined to the galleys as slaves.*

The triumph of the popish party was great; but it was of brief duration. The Duke of Somerset, protector of England in the minority of Edward VI., resenting the perfidy of the regent and his counsellors, invaded Scotland at the head of a powerful army, and inflicted on the Scottish forces a severe defeat at the battle of Pinkie. This had little other affect than that of throwing the ruling party in Scotland more completely into the arms of France, and thereby hastening the decisive struggle. In a parliament held at Stirling in 1548, it was resolved to send the young Queen of Scotland to France, first to be educated there, and then married to the dauphin.

After hostilities had continued for some time between Scotland and England, of a harassing rather than of a destructive character, a peace was concluded, in which France also was embraced; and, in consequence of the application of the English ambassadors, John Knox was released from the galleys, and allowed to return to England. He resided for some time in that country; and while there, refused the offer of the bishopric of Rochester, which he could not accept because he regarded prelacy as without the sanction of scriptural authority. From England Knox proceeded to the Continent; and, after being for some time pastor of a Protestant church at Frankfort, whence he withdrew on account of the usurpation and intolerance of an English prelatic party, went to Geneva, where he remained till his return to Scotland in the year 1555.

But during this interval some things occurred which deserve to be mentioned, that the series of events may not be left unconnected. After the taking of the castle of St. Andrews, and the banishment of its defenders, the popish party continued their efforts for the suppression of the incipient Reformation; in which they promised themselves the more complete success that Knox was now no longer present to defend it. Adam Wallace, who was tutor to the family of Ormiston, was accused of heresy, and burned on the Castle Hill of Edinburgh. Several gentlemen of property, accused of favouring the reforming party, were banished, and their estates forfeited. Councils of the clergy were held at Linlithgow, and at Edinburgh, for devising measures, not only to extirpate heresy, but also to reform such glaring abuses as excited public odium, hoping thereby to allay the general desire of further reformation. Some of the regulations passed by these councils were good in themselves, but as they were left to be carried into execution by the very persons who were interested in the perpetuation of abuses, they remained themselves generally inoperative. In the meantime, the reforming party were left without a leader. several of the nobility, and the inferior barons of considerable influence, continued to favor the views of the reformers, but contented themselves with retaining their opinions, and waiting for a more propitious juncture. The zeal of the persecutors seemed also to abate. They flattered themselves that they had succeeded in suppressing heresy in Scotland; and they returned to their old employment of engaging in political intrigues.

There was at this time a double course of intriguing carried on; and, on the one side, by a person who proved herself an adept in the art,—namely, the queen-mother. It was her desire to obtain the regency, and yet not to give direct offence to the Earl of Arran. She contrived therefore, to form a party against him among the nobility and gentry who were attached to the principles of the Reformation, to whom, secretly, she promised protection. At length Arran, feeling his influence departing, resigned the regency, which was given to the queen-mother, Mary of Guise, on the 10th of April 1554. She thus reached the summit of her ambition; and had

* Knox, Historie, p. 77; Spotswood, p. 88.

the state of torpor into which the Reformation had been cast continued, she might, in all probability, have enjoyed her power for a considerable time, and with no little reputation; for she was possessed of superior abilities, untroubled by conscientious scruples, and able to gild over her designs by plausible artifice and deep dissimulation.

But the mind of Scotland was not allowed to remain long in this state of torpidity. The accession of Mary to the English throne on the lamented death of Edward VI. produced an immediate change in religious matters throughout the island. The fierce persecution which arose in England drove several of the English Protestants to Scotland, where they renewed the public preaching, which had been for some time in a great measure suppressed. Of these the most distinguished were William Harlow and John Willock, the latter of whom was afterwards colleague to John Knox.

At length, in the end of harvest, in the year 1555, John Knox himself returned to Scotland, and resumed his reforming labours, with double energy, zeal, and success. From Edinburgh, where he first recommenced his toils, he proceeded, along with the justly celebrated John Erskine of Dun, to Angus and Mearns, where he preached in public for a month, rekindling in that district the embers of the Reformation. His next position was at Calder House, where he resided for some time as the friend and guest of Sir James Sandilands, preceptor, or provincial grand-master of the Knights of St. John, who had been for some time attached to the reformed faith, and was a person of distinguished talents, blameless life, and great weight and dignity of character. In his mansion Knox held intercourse with Lord Erskine, subsequently Earl of Mar, and Regent; the Lord of Lorn, afterwards Earl of Argyle; and Lord James Stewart, an illegitimate son of James V., afterwards Earl of Murray, "the Good Regent." By his intercourse with these noblemen, Knox was at that time framing the nucleus of what subsequently grew into a power capable not only of assuming an attitude of self-defence, but of wielding the kingdom.

From Calder House Knox went to Ayrshire, accompanied by Campbell of Kinyeangh, and traversed that district, preaching wherever he had an opportunity, to increasing, attentive, and deeply impressed audiences. The Earl of Glencairn, who alone had opposed the martyrdom of Adam Wallace, gave the full weight of his countenance and support to the teaching of Knox. Continuing his reforming progress Knox again visited Calder, the district of Angus and Mearns, and finally returned to Edinburgh.

[1556.] By this time the priesthood were thoroughly roused out of their vain security; and, determining to stem the tide ere it should reach its flood, they summoned Knox to appear in the Blackfriars Church at Edinburgh, on the 15th of May 1556. Knox at once determined to comply with this summons, and confront his opponents; and with that intention came to Edinburgh a little before the day appointed, accompanied by Erskine of Dun, and several other gentlemen. But the clergy were not prepared to deal summarily with this dauntless antagonist. They were not sure how far the queen-regent would support them, and they deserted the diet, and allowed Knox to keep the field unchallenged. He, on his part, did not let slip the opportunity: he preached openly in Edinburgh, deepening the impression formerly made, and increasing the alarm and confusion of his enemies. Some of the nobility, who were equally impressed and astonished with the convincing power of his fervid eloquence, persuaded him to write to the queen-regent, hoping that, if she could be prevailed on to hear him, she too might be converted to the reformed faith. But after glancing carelessly over his letter, she handed it to the archbishop of Glasgow, saying, in a tone of mockery, "Please you, my Lord, to read a pasquil." So vanished the hope of her reformation.

While John Knox was thus strenuously engaged in promoting the Reformation, in his native country, letters came from his former flock in Geneva, earnestly pressing him to return to his charge among them. After revisiting those parts of Scotland where he had previously preached, and spending a few days at

Castle Campbell with the aged Earl of Argyle, he departed for Geneva in July 1556. He was no sooner gone than the clergy renewed their summons; and upon his failing to appear, he was condemned of heresy, and burned in effigy at the market-cross of Edinburgh,—an achievement sufficiently showing the fangless malice of his enemies.

Although John Knox had left Scotland, the reformed doctrines continued to be preached in different parts of the country. John Douglas, a Carmelite friar, renouncing the errors of Popery, became chaplain to the aged Earl of Argyle; and when the archbishop of St. Andrews endeavoured to persuade the earl to dismiss his suspected chaplain, he positively refused, and continued to protect him till his own decease. Willock, about the same time, arrived from the Continent; and Paul Methven began to preach the Protestant doctrines in Dundee, as did others in Angus and Mearns.

The clergy perceiving that their own power was now insufficient for the suppression of what they termed heresy, prevailed on the queen-regent to summon the preachers before the council of state, and there to have them accused of stirring up sedition among the people,—a device to which persecutors have very often since resorted, for the purpose of at once accomplishing the object, and escaping the odium of persecution. But this device was, in this instance, completely frustrated. When the preachers came to Edinburgh, such numbers of their friends came along with them, that it was judged dangerous to proceed to extremities. A proclamation was, however, issued, ordering all who had come to the town without having been commanded, to repair immediately to the borders, and there remain fifteen days under the banner of the lieutenant-general. The Protestant gentlemen, penetrating easily into the object of this proclamation, assembled together, and, instead of obeying it, proceeded to court, and forced themselves with little ceremony into the presence of the queen, then sitting in council with the bishops. Chalmers of Gadgirth, a bold and zealous man, spoke in the name of all:—"Madam, we know that this proclamation is a device of the bishops, and of that bastard, (the primate of St. Andrews) that stands beside you. We avow to God, that ere we yield, we will make a day of it. These idle drones oppress us and our tenants; they trouble our preachers, and would murder them and us. Shall we suffer this any longer? No, madam, it shall not be." And therewith every man put on his steel bonnet. The queen-regent had recourse to fair words, disavowed the proclamation, and discharged the citation of the preachers. Thus that storm blew past.*

A few days after this there was a ludicrous tumult of the people, at a procession in honour of St. Giles, when the image was thrown scornfully to the ground, drawn through the mire of the streets, its head beaten off, the body thrown into the North Loch, and then dragged out and burned. These events so discouraged the queen and the clergy, that they thought it expedient to abandon their persecuting schemes, and to endeavour to procure an accession of strength before they should again provoke the courage of the Protestant gentry and the tumults of the people. This accession of strength they expected to obtain by procuring an act of the Scottish parliament to confer the crown-matrimonial of Scotland on Francis the Dauphin, and husband of Mary; by which scheme there would be so close a union between France and Scotland, the king of the one country being also the king of the other, that French power would give the popish clergy paramount influence in Scotland, and enable them to extirpate the Reformation by force.

[1557.] But while the queen-regent and the prelates were concocting this deep scheme, the Scottish protestants became anxious for the return of Knox from Geneva. A letter was accordingly sent to him in March 1557, signed by the Earl of Glencairn, and Lords Erskine, Lorn, and James Stewart, inviting him in their own name, and in that of their brethren, to return to Scotland, where he would find them all ready to receive him, and to jeopard their lives and fortunes in the cause of true religion. Having consulted Calvin and his other friends at Geneva, and been by them advised to comply with the request, Knox prepared to take

* Knox, Historie, p. 94.

what he expected to be a final farewell of Geneva, and then proceeded on his journey through France to Dieppe. When he arrived at Dieppe, he received letters from Scotland of a tenor so discouraging as to cause him to delay his farther journey till he should receive additional information as to the real state of matters in his native country. While at Dieppe he wrote a letter to the nobility by whom he had been invited, upbraiding them sharply for their timidity and fickleness of purpose. Being unwilling to abandon the enterprise, he continued to reside at Dieppe for several months, expecting a more favourable answer from Scotland; and employing his time in writing some very long and able letters of a public character, in particular, one against the erroneous tenets of the Anabaptists, and another to the Scottish nobility on their duties in general, and on the question of resistance to supreme rulers. Not receiving such answers, and so directly as he wished, he returned again to Geneva in the beginning of the year 1558.

In the meantime matters were rapidly maturing in Scotland. Notwithstanding the discouraging letters which Knox had received at Dieppe, the chief of the nobility who invited him were still prepared to stand by their invitation; and, in fact, renewed it, in a letter sent to Geneva by a special messenger. And although the return of Knox was delayed, yet his letters from Dieppe seemed to have little less influence than his presence might have had. The lords and chief gentry, devoted to the reforming interests, resolved to meet at Edinburgh, and, by a general consultation, to determine what was now best for them to do. They came to the noble resolution that they would persevere in their defence of the reformed religion; and, that they might have the confidence and strength of confirmed union, they resolved to frame a common bond or covenant, engaging them to mutual support in defence of each other and of the gospel.* This very remarkable document, which has been commonly called The First Covenant, was subscribed at Edinburgh, on the 3d of December 1557; and on account of its great importance, both in its own time, and as setting the example of similar covenants, we shall present it to the reader entire, merely modernizing the spelling.

"We, perceiving how Satan, in his members the antichrists of our time, cruelly doth rage, seeking to downthrow and destroy the evangel of Christ and his congregation, ought, according to our bounden duty, to strive in our master's cause, even unto the death, being certain of the victory in him: the which, our duty being well considered, we do promise before the Majesty of God and his congregation, That we, by his grace, shall with all diligence continually apply our whole power, substance, and our very lives, to maintain, set forward, and establish the most blessed Word of God, and his congregation; and shall labour at our possibility to have faithful ministers, purely and truly to minister Christ's evangel and sacraments to his people. We shall maintain them, nourish them, and defend them, the whole congregation of Christ, and every member thereof, at our whole powers, and wairing [expending] of our lives against Satan and all wicked power that does intend tyranny and trouble against the foresaid congregation. Unto the which holy word and congregation we do join us; and also do renounce and forsake the congregation of Satan, with all the superstitions, abominations and idolatry thereof. And moreover shall declare ourselves manifestly enemies thereto, by this our faithful promise before God, testified to his congregation, by our subscription at these presents. At Edinburgh the 3d day of December 1557 years. God called to witness."*

This bond, or covenant, was subscribed by the Earls of Argyle, Glencairn, and Morton, Archibald, lord of Lorn, John Erskine of Dun, and a great number of other distinguished men among the lesser barons and influential country gentlemen. From the repeated recurrence of the word *congregation* in this document, the chief subscribers were after this called Lords of the Congregation; and the people who adhered to them were called the Congregation.

Though they had thus both ascertained and confirmed their strength, the Lords of the Congregation were desirous to act in the most temperate manner, and

* The First Covenant, 3d December 1557.

* Knox, Historie, p. 101.

not to provoke an actual conflict, unless it could not possibly be avoided. They resolved, therefore, to rest satisfied with requesting the queen-regent to cause all country curates and pastors to perform the services of religion in the English language; consenting that the reformed preachers should teach in private houses only, till permission should be obtained for them to preach in public. This petition was presented to the queen-regent by Sir James Sandilands. To this she returned a plausible answer, promising to grant the prayer of the petition as far as might be practicable, and, in the meantime, granting protection to the Protestant preachers till some uniform arrangement might be established by parliament, provided there should be no public meetings held in Edinburgh and Leith. In consequence of this interim arrangement, the chief Protestant preachers were received into the houses of the Lords of the Congregation, and restricted their teaching in a great measure to the households where they resided.

[1558.] The popish clergy being now unable to wreak their vengeance on the chief Protestant preachers, determined to show no mercy to any whom they could get within their power. There was an aged priest, named Walter Mill, who had been accused of heresy in the days of Cardinal Beaton, but had contrived to escape at that time from his murderous hands. Mill had continued to live in comparative concealment, for several years, occasionally preaching in public, but more commonly in private, in different quarters of the kingdom. Being lately discovered by one of the archbishop's spies, he was seized and brought to trial at St. Andrews. The venerable man, bowed down with the weight of years, for he was upwards of four-score, defended himself on the day of his trial with great spirit and ability. He was, nevertheless, condemned to be burned at the stake; but so great was the compassion felt for him, and such the horror awakened by this barbarous outrage of all that man holds sacred in the hoary head of drooping human nature, that no person could be got to aid in the execution of the sentence, till the archbishop commanded one of his own domestics to perpetrate the crime. On the 28th of April 1558, Mill expired amidst the flames, uttering these words, "As for me, I am fourscore and two years old, and cannot live long by course of nature; but a hundred better shall rise out of the ashes of my bones. I trust in God, I shall be the last that shall suffer death in Scotland for this cause."*

This barbarous deed stirred the heart of the reforming party in Scotland, like the sound of a trumpet. The people of St. Andrews raised a great pile of stones on the spot where he was burned, to commemorate his martyrdom. The Lords of the Congregation complained to the queen-regent against the unparalleled barbarity of the bishops. And the Protestant preachers availing themselves of the ferment throughout the kingdom, broke through the restraints to which they had submitted for the sake of peace, and began to preach with increased fervour and publicity. But the measures of the queen-regent were not yet matured, and therefore she renewed her deep dissimulation.

She declared to the Protestant lords that she was not guilty of the death of Walter Mill, who, being a priest, belonged properly to the jurisdiction of the Church. She engaged to do every thing in her power to procure redress in a legal form from parliament; and succeeded in deceiving the Lords of the Congregation, whom she could not venture openly to offend till she had procured their aid in accomplishing her own deep scheme.

In the parliament which met in October 1558, she contrived to balance the bishops, the party headed by Arran, and the Lords of the Congregation, against each other, in such a manner as to procure the consent of all that the crown matrimonial should be given to Francis, who would thereby be king of both France and Scotland. In the same parliament, previous to the completion of this arrangement, the Lords of the Congregation were prepared to present a petition seeking the redress of the grievances in religious matters of which they had previously complained; but the wily regent contrived to induce them to withhold it for the present, and to content themselves with publicly reading such a pro-

* Knox, p. 122; Spotswood, pp. 95-97.

test as should completely reserve their right to have the subject re-introduced when another opportunity should occur. To the protest the queen-regent answered verbally, that she would remember what was protested, and put order afterwards to all that was in controversy. With this promise the Protestant lords were satisfied, and their suspicions lulled asleep. But having now gained her object in securing the crown-matrimonial to the Dauphin of France, she gave private assurance of support to the archbishop of St. Andrews, and consulted with him how most thoroughly and speedily to suppress the Reformation.

Dr. Robertson* has stated very clearly and convincingly the deep and daring scheme of the princes of the house of Lorraine, brothers of the queen-regent of Scotland, with which that able and unscrupulous princess was fully acquainted, and which formed in truth the leading principle of all her own political machinations. It was to the following effect: The formation of a league between France and Spain for the utter destruction of the Reformation throughout Europe; and as England was the most powerful Protestant kingdom, and Elizabeth was now its sovereign, it was necessary that she should be dethroned, and the crown bestowed on a popish monarch. As Mary, the young queen of Scotland, was the nearest heir to the English crown, it was thought that the best method of accomplishing their design would be, by suppressing the Reformation in Scotland, establishing the French and popish influence in that country, and through it assailing Elizabeth. It was essential to the complete arrangement of this gigantic scheme that the crown-matrimonial of Scotland should be secured to the Dauphin of France, Mary's husband; and for this reason did the queen-regent employ all her artifice to blind and cajole the Lords of the Congregation, and to induce them to consent to recognise Francis and Mary as king and queen of Scotland, distinctly promising that she would then, supported by the authority of the kingly name, make such arrangements as should protect their preachers and themselves from the malice and hatred of the bishops, and promote the reformation of religion.*

* Robertson's History of Scotland.

Having now accomplished her purpose, the queen-regent prepared to throw aside the mask which she had so long worn. Accordingly, in the end of December 1558, with her concurrence, the preachers of the reformed doctrines were summoned to appear at St. Andrews, before the archbishop, on the 2d day of February following, to answer for their conduct in usurping the sacred office, and disseminating heretical doctrines. Upon this, a deputation of the Protestants waited on the queen-regent, and endeavoured to dissuade her from permitting the adoption of such violent measures; declaring, that after what had recently taken place in the instance of the martyr Mill, they were determined to attend and see justice done to their preachers, and that, if the prosecution went on, there would be such a number present to witness it as had been rarely seen in Scotland. This declaration so far alarmed the regent, that she caused the trial to be postponed; at the same time summoning a convention of the nobility, to be held at Edinburgh on the 7th of March, 1559, to advise upon the most proper measures for settling the religious differences by which the nation had been so long agitated; and, that these matters might be fully discussed, the primate, at her request called a provincial council of the clergy, to meet in the same place on the 1st of March.

[1559.] The convention of nobility and council of clergy met at the time appointed, and the Protestants having also assembled at Edinburgh, appointed commissioners to lay their representations before each of these bodies. To the council of clergy they gave in certain preliminary articles of reformation, in which they craved that the religious service should be performed in the native tongue; that such as were unfit for the pastoral office should be removed from their benefices; that, in future, bishops should be admitted with the assent of the barons of the diocese, and parish priests with the assent of the parishioners; and that measures should be adopted for pre-

* Knox, Historie, p. 110; Spotswood, p. 120; M'Crie's Life of Knox.

venting immoral and ignorant persons from being employed in ecclesiastical functions. It deserves to be noticed, that there was another paper laid before the council, drawn up by persons attached to the Romish Church, also "craving redress for several grievances complained of in the ecclesiastical administration of Scotland." This latter paper, indicating the existence of a reforming party within the Romish Church itself, gave serious alarm to the council, and increased their determination to adopt strong and decisive measures at once. They accordingly ratified, in the strongest terms, all the controverted doctrines; ordered strict inquiry to be made after all such as absented themselves from the celebration of mass; and threatened with excommunication all who should disseminate or adhere to the doctrine of the Reformation. A secret treaty, it appears, had been framed between the clergy and the queen-regent, in which they engaged to raise a large sum of money to enable her to levy and maintain forces wherewith to overthrow and suppress the reformers.

The Protestant party becoming aware of this secret treaty, and perceiving the turn that matters were now taking, broke off the negociations in which they had been engaged, and left Edinburgh. They were no sooner gone than a proclamation was made at the market-cross by order of the queen-regent, "prohibiting any person from preaching or administering the sacraments without authority from the bishops; and commanding all the subjects to prepare to celebrate the ensuing feast of Easter, according to the rules of the Catholic Church." This proclamation the Protestants regarded as equivalent to a declaration of direct hostility against them and their religious belief; and perceived that they must either now take their stand, or prepare to abandon all that they held most sacred. They did not hesitate, but disregarded the proclamation, neglecting the superstitious and idolatrous rites of Popery, and worshipping God according to the directions contained in His own Word, and the light of conscience. The queen-regent had now advanced too far to retract; and accordingly, Paul Methven, John Christison, William Harlaw, and John Willock were summoned to stand trial before the Justiciary Court at Stirling, on the 10th of May 1550, for disregarding the proclamation, teaching heresy, and exciting seditions and tumults among the people.

Being reluctant to proceed to extremities, the Protestants sent the Earl of Glencairn and Sir Hugh Campbell of London to wait on the queen, and remonstrate against these violent proceedings; but she haughtily replied, that "maugre [in spite of] their hearts, and all that would take part with them, these ministers should be banished Scotland, though they preached as soundly as ever St. Paul did." The deputation reminded her of the promises she had repeatedly made to protect them, to which she unblushingly replied, that "it became not subjects to burden their princes with promises, farther than they pleased to keep them." Roused, rather than intimidated, by this language, they answered, that if she violated the engagements she had come under to her subjects, they would regard themselves as absolved from their allegiance to her. This bold and resolute answer caused her to pause and resume her tone of simulated mildness, and at length she promised to suspend the trial of the preachers, and take the whole affair into serious consideration.

That very night, according to Spotswood, after the departure of the deputation, the queen received information that the town of Perth had embraced the reformed doctrines. Enraged to find all matters going so contrary to her wishes, she sent for Lord Ruthven, provost of that town, and commanded him to go immediately to suppress these innovations. To this he answered, that "he could make their persons and their goods subject to her, but had no power over their minds and consciences." She furiously exclaimed, that "he was too malapert to give her such an answer, and she would make both him and them repent it." In the same spirit of revenge, she broke the promise she had given to Glencairn and Loudon, ordered the processes against the preachers to go on, and summoned them peremptorily to stand their trial at Stirling on the appointed day.

Affairs now swept rapidly forward to the crisis that had been long inevitable.

The Protestant nobility and gentlemen determined to accompany their preachers to Stirling on the day appointed. The townsmen of Dundee, and those of Montrose, together with the chief inhabitants of Angus and Mearns, assembled at Perth; but before proceeding to Stirling, it was judged expedient to send Erskine of Dun before them, to assure the queen of their peaceful dispositions, and that their only object was to join with their preachers in making a public confession of their faith, and to aid them in their just defence. The wily queen again resorted to dissimulation; and succeeded in persuading Erskine to remain at Stirling, and to write to the assembled Protestants at Perth, requesting them to return to their houses, and promising that the trial should not proceed against the ministers. Some, confiding in the queen-regent's promise, did return to their homes; but a considerable number, remembering her previous acts of treachery, remained at Perth, till they should see the issue. At this very important juncture the Protestant party received an accession of strength in the opportune arrival of John Knox in Scotland.

It has been already stated that he had returned to Geneva, after the discouraging letters which he received at Dieppe. But when he received a fresh invitation from the Lords of the Congregation, and farther learned in what extremities his Scottish reforming brethren were placed, he at once determined to hasten to his native country, and devote his life to the great and sacred cause of the Scottish Reformation. He was refused permission to journey through England; but taking shipping at Dieppe, he sailed to Leith, where he landed the 2d of May 1559.

Nothing can more strikingly prove the importance of this timely arrival of the great Scottish reformer, than the consternation it excited in the hearts of his antagonists. The day for the trial of the preachers was close at hand, and their enemies were busily engaged in completing their treacherous plots against the lives of those devoted men. For several days the provincial council of the clergy had been sitting in the monastery of the Grayfriars; and on the morning of the 3d of May, they had again met and resumed their deliberations. While they were thus engaged, on a sudden one of the fraternity entered the monastery, and rushed into the presence of the council, breathless with haste, and pale with terror, exclaiming in broken words—"John Knox! John Knox is come! he is come! he slept last night in Edinburgh!" The council was panic-struck. In dumb dismay they contemplated the ruin of all the plans which they had given their gold and stained their souls with guilt to fabricate. At once stunned and terrified, they ceased to deliberate, broke up the council, and dispersed in great haste and confusion.

A messenger was instantly sent to the queen-regent with the unwelcome information; and within a few days Knox was proclaimed an outlaw and a rebel, in virtue of the sentence formerly pronounced against him by the clergy. He staid but one day in Edinburgh; and being resolved to cast himself at once into the heart of the conflict, and to share the dangers of his brethren, he hurried to Dundee, and joined those who were preparing to proceed to the trial at Stirling. With them he hastened to Perth, where the main adherents of the Reformation were by this time assembled, waiting the result of the negotiations between the queen-regent and Erskine of Dun, of which mention has been already made.

The queen, as already stated, had promised, to Erskine that the trial of the preachers should be postponed; but when the day of trial came, they were summoned, and, not appearing, they were outlawed, and all persons were prohibited, "under pain of rebellion, to assist, comfort, receive, or maintain them in any sort." At the same time, the gentlemen who had given security for their appearance were fined. Indignant at this act of gross deceit and injury, and apprehensive of personal danger, Erskine contrived to escape from Stirling unobserved, and hastened to Perth with the intelligence of what had taken place. An event immediately followed the return of Erskine to Perth, which has often been grievously misrepresented, to the prejudice of the reformers, very unjustly, by the favourers of Prelacy; and as Dr.

M'Crie has given a very full account of it in his Life of Knox, we extract the passage.

"It happened that, on the same day on which the news came of the queen's treacherous conduct at Stirling, Knox, who remained at Perth, preached a sermon, in which he exposed the idolatry of the mass and of image-worship. The audience had quietly dismissed, and a few idle persons only loitered in the church, when an imprudent priest, wishing to try the disposition of the people, or to show his contempt of the doctrine which had just been delivered, uncovered a rich altar-piece, decorated with images, and prepared to celebrate mass. A boy, having uttered some expressions of disapprobation, was struck by the priest. He retaliated by throwing a stone at the aggressor, which, falling on the altar-piece, broke one of the images. This operated as a signal upon the people present, who had sympathised with the boy; and in course of a few minutes, the altar, images, and all the ornaments of the church, were torn down and trampled under foot. The noise soon collected a mob, which, finding no employment in the church, flew, by a sudden and irresistible impulse, upon the monasteries; and although the magistrates of the town and the preachers assembled as soon as they heard of the riot, yet neither the persuasions of the one, nor the authority of the other, could restrain the fury of the people, until the houses of the gray and black friars, with the costly edifice of the Carthusian monks, were laid in ruins. None of the gentlemen or sober part of the congregation were concerned in this unpremeditated tumult; it was wholly confined to the lowest of the inhabitants, or, as Knox designs them, 'the rascal multitude.' If this disorderly conduct must be traced to a remote cause, we can impute it only to the wanton and dishonourable perfidy of the queen-regent.

"In fact, nothing could be more favourable to the designs of the regent than this riot. By her recent conduct she had forfeited the confidence of the Protestants, and even exposed herself in the eyes of the sober and moderate of her own party. This occurrence afforded her an opportunity of turning the public indignation from herself, and directing it against the Protestants. She did not fail to improve it with her usual address. She magnified the accidental tumult into a dangerous and designed rebellion. Having called the nobility to Stirling, she, in her interviews with them, insisted upon such topics as were best calculated to persuade the parties into which they were divided. In conversing with the Catholics, she dwelt upon the sacrilegious overthrow of those venerable structures which their ancestors had dedicated to the service of God. To the Protestants who had not joined their brethren at Perth, she complained of the destruction of the charter-house, which was a royal foundation; and, protesting that she had no intention of offering violence to their consciences, promised to protect them, provided they would assist her in punishing those who had been guilty of this violation of public order. Having inflamed the minds of both parties, she collected an army from the adjacent countries, and advanced to Perth, threatening to lay waste the town with fire and sword, and to inflict the most exemplary vengeance on all who had been instrumental in producing the riot."*

A considerable body of French troops strengthened the queen's army, and increased the danger of the Protestants, who were also weakened by the retreat of many of their own party, confiding in the previous pacific declarations of the queen. But messengers had been sent by the reformers from Perth, requesting their friends to come to their defence with all possible expedition; and so readily were these entreaties responded to, that before the queen's army had reached Perth, the reformers were enabled to assume an attitude of self-defence sufficiently imposing to cause the queen to propose overtures of accommodation. The promptitude of the Earl of Glencairn, on this emergency, deserves particular mention. In an almost incredible short space of time, he assembled about two thousand five hundred men, and marched from Ayrshire to Perth, bringing this large reinforcement to his brethren there, while they were treating with the queen-regent.

The queen employed the Earl of Argyle and Lord James Stewart to treat

* M'Crie's Life of Knox, pp, 159, 160.

with the Lords of the Congregation at Perth; and an agreement was entered into, in which it was stipulated, that the town should be left open to the queen; that none of the inhabitants should be called in question for what had taken place; that the French should not enter the town; and that, when the queen retired, there should be no garrison left in it. To these terms the reformers agreed; at the same time stating, that they did not expect the queen to keep faith with them any longer than till she obtained the power to break it with safety to herself; and Argyle and Stewart, declaring that if she should violate the treaty, they would leave her, and openly take part with their brethren, to whom they considered themselves bound by the most sacred ties. Before quitting Perth, the Lords of the Congregation framed and subscribed another bond pledging them to mutual support and defence in the cause of religion, or any cause dependent thereupon, by whatsoever pretext it might be coloured and concealed. This has been generally called THE SECOND COVENANT. It was subscribed in the name of the whole Congregation, by the Earls of Argyle and Glencairn, Lord James Stewart, the Lords Boyd and Ochiltree, and Matthew Campbell of Terringland, on the 31st of May 1559.*

A very short time was sufficient to prove how much reason the Protestants had to distrust the most solemn promises of the queen-regent. No sooner had she obtained complete possession of the town of Perth than she began to violate her engagement, treating the inhabitants with the greatest violence, changing their magistrates forcibly, and substituting creatures of her own, exacting oppressive fines from some, and conniving at the murder of others who had been friendly to the reformers, and, upon her departure, leaving a garrison in the town, contrary to the express stipulations of the treaty. Argyle and Lord James Stewart remonstrated strongly against such conduct, and were answered, that "she was not bound to keep promises made to heretics; and that she would make little conscience to take from all that sect their lives and inheritance, if she might do it with so honest an excuse."† These noblemen feeling their own honour implicated, forsook her, and went to the Congregation, resolving never again to place any confidence in her promises.

The Lords of the Congregation now resolved to temporize and negotiate no longer, but to take immediate steps for abolishing the idolatrous and superstitious rites of Popery, and setting up the reformed worship in all places to which their authority or influence extended. And as Lord James Stewart was prior of St. Andrews, and had now cordially and entirely joined with the reformers, he gave an authoritative invitation to John Knox, to meet him in that city on a certain day, and to preach publicly in the Abbey Church. Knox, who had been preaching in several places along the east coast of Fife, hastened to comply with this invitation, and on the 9th of June arrived at St. Andrews. The archbishop, hearing of this design to storm Popery in its stronghold, hastily collected an armed force, and having at their head hurried to St. Andrews, sent information to Knox, that if he appeared in the pulpit, he would give orders to fire upon him.

The juncture was one of an extremely critical nature. The Lords of the Congregation were but slenderly accompanied; the disposition of the townsmen was in a great measure uncertain; and the queen-regent had advanced to Falkland, about twelve miles distant, at the head of a considerable army, consisting chiefly of the French troops, who were thoroughly devoted to her interests, and as thoroughly hostile to the Reformation. Argyle and Lord James Stewart were alarmed at the dangerous aspect of affairs, and yet reluctant to abandon their intention. They felt that to be baffled at the very outset of their great enterprise would be a severe if not a fatal discouragement; and yet they were unwilling to put the life of Knox, as well as their own lives, in such imminent peril. In this perplexity they sent for Knox himself, to have his own judgment in this emergency. That judgment was one becoming him "who never feared the face of man." Reminding them that he had been first called to preach the gospel in that very town,—reft from it by the tyranny of France, at the procurement of the

* Knox, p. 138. † Knox, p. 130; Spotswood, p. 133.

bishops,—that now the opportunity was presented to him, for which he had longed, and prayed, and hoped,—he entreated them not to hinder him from once more preaching in St. Andrews. "As for the fear of danger that may come to me, let no man be solicitous; for my life is in the custody of Him whose glory I seek. I desire the hand and weapon of no man to defend me. I only crave audience; which, if it be denied here unto me at this time, I must seek farther where I may have it."

The dauntless courage of the great reformer communicated itself to the lords. Like him, they ceased to think of danger, when the call was that of sacred duty; and next day, the 16th of June, Knox appeared in the pulpit, and preached to a numerous audience, including the archbishop, many of the inferior clergy, and the scowling bands of armed retainers prepared for the assassination of the fearless preacher. But the hand of God was with him, restraining the fury of the adversary, and moulding anew the melted hearts of the people. The subject of his discourse was, our Saviour's ejecting the profane traffickers from the temple of Jerusalem; which he applied to the duty incumbent on all Christians, according to their different stations, to remove the corruptions of the Papacy, and purify the Church. On the three following days he preached in the same place, and on similar subjects; and such was the effect of his doctrine, that the magistracy and the inhabitants agreed to set up the reformed worship in the town; and immediately stripped the church of images and pictures, and demolished the monasteries.

The archbishop of St. Andrews hastened to the queen-regent with this dire information. Being apprised, at the same time, that the lords at St. Andrews were accompanied by a small retinue, she resolved to surprise them before their friends could come to their support, and gave orders to prepare to march on Cupar. But the Protestants in the adjacent counties, being aware of the danger of their friends, hastened to their aid with such celerity, and in such numbers, that they were able to anticipate the queen's movements, and take up a position confronting her army on Cupar-moor. The resolute aspect of the Protestant army again appalled the queen; and dreading a disastrous defeat, should she risk a battle, she proposed a suspension of hostilities. The Protestant lords had now received too many proofs of her duplicity to be again circumvented by mere promises. They, therefore, stipulated that the French troops should be removed out of Fifeshire; and that commissioners should, within ten days, be sent to St. Andrews, for the purpose of settling all differences between her and the Congregation. The troops were removed; but no commissioners were sent. The Lords of the Congregation determined, therefore, to adopt more decisive measures, and to redress by their own efforts those grievances which they could not get otherwise remedied.

Mustering once more their strength, they advanced to Perth, and expelled the garrison left there by the queen. Thence by a rapid movement they proceeded to Stirling, seized upon it, and continuing their march, took possession of Edinburgh itself; the queen-regent, as they approached, retiring with her forces to Dunbar. In the meantime the dread of the direct and immediate vengeance of the popish clergy being removed, the rest of the kingdom quickly followed the example of Perth and St. Andrews, in abolishing the popish worship; and in the course of a few weeks, "at Crail, at Cupar, at Lindors, at Stirling, at Linlithgow, at Edinburgh, and at Glasgow, the houses of the monks were overthrown, and all the instruments of idolatry destroyed."*

On their arrival at Edinburgh the Lords of the Congregation sent deputies to Dunbar, to assure the queen that they had no intention of throwing off their allegiance, and to induce her to accede to reasonable terms of accommodation. One preliminary point was agreed upon, —that the sentence of outlawry against the ministers should be rescinded, and that they should be allowed to preach publicly to those who chose to hear them. Knox was chosen by the people of Edinburgh to be their minister, on the 7th of July, and immediately began his labours among them. But the wiles of the queen were not yet exhausted. She prolonged the negotiations till she learned

* M'Crie's Life of Knox, p. 165

that the greater part of the Protestant forces had returned to their homes, and then advanced suddenly with her army to Edinburgh. Leith having declared for the regent, and the castle of Edinburgh being under the command of Lord Erskine, who was unfavourable to the Protestants, they felt that they could not defend the town, and agreed to evacuate it, on condition that the inhabitants should be left at liberty to use that form of worship which they should prefer. The lords then retired to Stirling, taking with them John Knox, and leaving Willock in his place, who continued to preach in St. Giles' Church after the arrival of the regent.

The King of France dying about this time was succeeded by Mary's husband, and thus the crowns of France and Scotland seemed to be united, and the deep scheme of the princes of Lorraine on the point of being realized. Letters were sent by the new king and queen to Lord James Stewart, for the purpose of detaching him, if possible, from the Protestant party; but he remained firm to his faith and covenant engagement. At the same time, an additional supply of money and troops were sent from France to the queen-regent to enable her to crush and exterminate the Reformation in Scotland. The hopes of the regent began to revive; and she commenced fortifying Leith, both as commanding strength in an important position, and a port through which she might readily at all times receive supplies from France into the very heart of the country. But though these matters were favourable to the queen-regent, there were others of a counterbalancing character. The Earl of Arran, son to the former regent, the Duke of Chatelherault, returned at this time from France, having narrowly escaped imprisonment on account of having expressed himself favourable to the Protestant doctrines. After having held an interview with the Protestant lords at Stirling, this young nobleman went to Hamilton to his father, and succeeded in prevailing on him to quit the party of the queen-regent, and join the Lords of the Congregation.

The accession of the Hamiltons to the Protestant party gave a new turn to affairs. The queen-regent immediately put in practice all her diplomatic arts to detach the Hamiltons from the Congregation, if possible, or to sow jealousy and cause dissension among them. Failing in these endeavours, she issued declarations to the public, in which she strove to fix the charge of rebellion upon the Congregation generally, and, in particular, accused Lord James Stewart and the Duke of Chatelherault of aiming severally at the crown. These insidious declarations were met by counter-declarations, in which the accused parties vindicated themselves from these charges, and exposed the course of treachery and cruelty by which her conduct had been all along characterised. This war of diplomacy, however, was not likely to lead to any satisfactory result; and the Protestant lords began to prepare for more decisive measures. They assembled in Edinburgh on the 21st of October 1559, in such numbers as to form a convention of the estates of the kingdom, and entered upon a formal deliberation what ought to be done to rescue the country from such a state of civil dissension, and especially from the lawless outrages committed by the French troops in the queen-regent's army.

In this convention of estates both Knox and Willock were requested to state their sentiments respecting the duty of subjects to their rulers in cases of oppression. Willock held that the power of rulers was limited both by reason and by Scripture, and that they might be deprived of it upon valid grounds; implying that he thought the conduct of the queen-regent had passed these limits, and given to her subjects these valid grounds. Knox assented to Willock's opinions, and added, that the assembly might, with safe consciences, act upon it, provided they attended to the three following points:—"First, that they did not suffer the misconduct of the queen-regent to alienate their affections from their due allegiance to their sovereigns, Francis and Mary; second, that they were not actuated in the measure by private hatred or envy of the queen-dowager, but by regard for the safety of the commonwealth; and, third, that any sentence which they might at this time pronounce should not preclude her readmission to office, if she afterwards discovered sorrow for her conduct, and a disposition to submit to the advice of the estates of the realm. After this, the whole assembly, having severally delivered their opinions, did, by a solemn deed, suspend the queen-dowager from her authority as regent of the kingdom, until the meeting of a free parliament; and, at the same time, elected a council for the management of public affairs during this interval.

The conduct of Knox and Willock, in giving their opinions on this very important matter, has been very often and very severely censured. But those who have done so have in general displayed either an anxious desire to avail themselves of any opportunity of blackening the character and aspersing the motives of the Scottish reformer, or so little acquaintance with the great principles of civil and religious liberty, as to render their opinion of very slight value. Genuine Christianity, instead of impairing the worth of man's natural and civil rights and privileges, gives to them an infinitely increased importance, as the rights and privileges of the freemen of the Lord; rendering it absolutely impossible for a true Christian either to enslave others or to submit to be himself enslaved. And let it be ever most gratefully remembered, that to the Reformation we owe that true civilization which not only strikes off the fetters from the body, but cultivates also the mind,—which not only liberates men from civil, mental, and moral thraldom, but also, at the same time, elevating them in the scale of existence, renders them worthy to be free. The mind of Knox was too deeply imbued with these great principles, and his heart too fearless, for him to hesitate in giving a frank avowal of his sentiments, be the danger and the obloquy thereby to be encountered what they might; and yet, let it be observed, that while he vindicated the right of subjects to protect themselves against unlawful despotism, both in this and in other instances, he carefully guarded against the opposite extreme, of encouraging subjects wantonly to violate the allegiance due to their sovereigns. But instead of farther attempting to vindicate Knox from the aspersions cast upon him by writers of a servile character, let us direct the attention of the reader to a noble passage in M'Crie's Life of Knox, where the principles of civil and religious liberty are explained and defended with great eloquence of language and power of reasoning.*

This act, suspending the commission of the queen-regent, was proclaimed in all the chief towns throughout the kingdom, and intimated formally to the regent herself, summoning her at the same time to dismiss the French troops from Leith, and yield the town. To this declaration and summons, an answer, charging the Protestants with rebellion, and uttering a bold defiance of their power, was returned; and hostilities immediately began. But the success of the Protestant lords and their army was not equal to their hopes and the goodness of their cause. There arose, in fact, a division among them, of a kind to which such enterprises as they were engaged in must always be exposed. The very essence of the contest was of a strictly religious character, and had been begun by men whose sole object it was to rescue the pure and undefiled Christianity of the Bible from the gross corruptions of Popery. But many had now joined the early reformers from a variety of motives, apart from those of religion; and even those in whom religious motives predominated still retained so great an admixture of selfish and worldly policy, as to embarrass extremely the conduct of those with whom they professed to act. A double policy must always be an unsafe one. And, perhaps, there is nothing which has ever done more evil to man than the debasing intermixture of worldly motives in matters of a purely religious and sacred character. But on this subject we shall not further dwell at present, as it will repeatedly meet us hereafter, and in circumstances fitted to display its nature and bearing more clearly.

The accession of the Hamiltons and their adherents appeared to strengthen the Protestants very much; yet the divisions which almost immediately sprung up proved more detrimental to their cause than their increase of numbers was beneficial. And as the Duke of Chatelherault, being the man of greatest rank among them, was placed nominally at their head, his timid and vacillating

* M'Crie's Life of Knox, pp. 183-192.

character diffused its contagion among them, and rendered their councils undecided and their conduct irresolute. They failed in some encounters with the French; and fresh supplies arriving at Leith, they became so discouraged as to abandon the siege, and retreat to Stirling, in a state of great dejection. They were also deficient in money to pay and support their forces, many of whom were of a mercenary character, regarding little on which side they fought, provided they obtained pay, and were occasionally gratified with pillage. Upon the retreat of the Lords of the Congregation, the French issued from Leith, took possession of Edinburgh, with the exception of the castle, which Lord Erskine continued to hold in a kind of armed neutrality, advanced to Stirling, pillaging the country as they went, and crossed into Fifeshire, skirting the coast, and continuing their ravages as they proceeded towards St. Andrews.*

In this extremity the Protestants found it necessary to apply more pressingly to Queen Elizabeth for aid from England. This had indeed been done some months before, when they became convinced that hostilities must ensue; and the intercourse with England had been conducted chiefly by Knox and Henry Balnaves of Hallhill, on the Scottish side, and Cecil on the English. Knox apprized Cecil of the great popish league, devised by the princes of Lorraine, for the suppression of the Reformation throughout Europe, to which the dethronement of Elizabeth was essential; and suggested a great counter-league of Protestant powers, of which Elizabeth should be the head. Cecil could appreciate the scheme; but it was not so easy to induce Elizabeth to engage in it, requiring, as it necessarily did, great and immediate sacrifices and exertions for a remote, and what might appear a contingent, good. Assistance in money was sent, but with a sparing hand; and part of it was intercepted, and fell into the possession of the queen-regent. But now, when the Protestant cause appeared to be sinking in Scotland, in consequence of the direct aid received by the queen-regent from France, the English court perceived the necessity of sending an army to the assistance of the Congregation. A short time before the Protestants retired from Edinburgh, they were joined by William Maitland of Lethington, one of the ablest statesmen of his time, who had previously been secretary to the queen-regent. Upon his arrival, Knox, who had no relish for the intrigues of mere politicians, immediately relinquished the direct management of all diplomatic matters to Lethington, expressing great satisfaction at being relieved from duties so uncongenial to his mind. Lethington was sent to England to endeavour to procure assistance; and it was finally resolved that an English force should be sent to Scotland to co-operate with the Protestant lords in expelling the French troops out of the kingdom. A contract to that effect was concluded at Berwick, between the Duke of Norfolk and the Scottish commissioners, on the 27th of February 1560.*

[1560.] The war now assumed a more determined aspect. The French troops, being aware of the approach of the English, returned to Leith, and prepared to defend it to the last extremities. Before the arrival of the English forces, the queen-regent was allowed by Lord Erskine to enter into Edinburgh castle; thus withdrawing herself from being personally exposed to the dangers and horrors of a war which she herself had caused. Several sharp encounters took place between the besiegers and the besieged; but as the English fleet had the command of the sea, no supplies could be transmitted from France to the garrison of Leith, which was daily becoming weaker. The French court employed every art of policy to induce Elizabeth to abandon the support of the Protestant lords, and almost succeeded. But being at length convinced that England's own security and best interests were involved in the support of Scotland, she gave orders to prosecute the siege with the utmost vigour. The resolution of Elizabeth convinced the Court of France that it was in vain to prolong the contest. A treaty was therefore proposed between France and England, the basis of which was, that the troops of both countries should be withdrawn from Scotland, and ambassadors were appointed to meet

* Knox, Spotswood, Buchanan.

* Knox, Spotswood.

in Edinburgh, to complete its arrangement and ratification.

While the ambassadors were on their way to Scotland, the queen-regent, who had been for some time declining in health, became seriously ill; and, sending for some of the chief Lords of the Congregation, expressed her regret at the sufferings which the kingdom had endured. She also sent for John Willock, and conferred with him for some time on religious matters; but, after his departure, received extreme unction, according to the rites of the Romish Church, and expired, on the 9th Knox says, Spotswood says the 10th, of June 1560.*

On the 16th of June the ambassadors arrived in Edinburgh, and began their negotiations. The death of the late queen-dowager had removed one of the main obstacles to peace; and the troubled state of political matters in France tended to make the ambassadors of that country more disposed to pacification than they might otherwise have been. It proceeded, however, with the usual tardiness of state diplomacy, and was signed on the 7th of July 1560. By this treaty it was provided, that the French troops should be immediately removed from Scotland; that an amnesty should be granted to all who had been engaged in the late resistance to the queen-regent; that the principal grievances of which they complained in the civil administration should be redressed; that a free parliament should be held in the month of August next, to settle the other affairs of the kingdom; and that, during the absence of their sovereigns, the government should be administered by a council of twelve, all natives of the kingdom, to be partly chosen by Francis and Mary, and partly by the estates of the nation. On the 16th July the French army embarked at Leith, and the English troops began their march to their own country; and on the 19th the Congregation assembled in St. Giles's Church, to return public thanks to God for the restoration of peace, and for the success which had crowned their exertions.

The parliament, which had met formally during the presence of the ambassadors on the 10th of July, adjourned until the 1st day of August, according to the treaty, both dates being specified in the records of its acts. When the circumstances in which they were assembled, and the affairs on which they were called to deliberate, are taken into consideration, this must be regarded as the most important meeting of the estates of the kingdom that had ever been held in Scotland. It engrossed the attention of the nation, and the eyes of Europe were fixed on its proceedings. Although a great concourse of people resorted to Edinburgh on that occasion, yet no tumult or disturbance of the public peace occurred. Many of the lords spiritual and temporal who were attached to Popery absented themselves; but the chief patrons of the old religion, as the archbishop of St. Andrews, and the bishops of Dumblane and Dunkeld, countenanced the Assembly by their presence, and were allowed to act with freedom as lords of parliament.

"The all-important business of religion was introduced by a petition presented by a number of Protestants of different ranks; in which, after rehearsing their former endeavours to procure the removal of the corruptions which had infected the Church, they requested parliament to use the power which Providence had now put into their hands for effecting this great and urgent work. They craved three things in general; that the antichristian doctrine maintained in the Popish Church should be discarded; that means should be used to restore purity of worship and primitive discipline; and that the ecclesiastical revenues, which had been engrossed by a corrupt and indolent hierarchy, should be applied to the support of a pious and active ministry, to the promotion of learning, and to the relief of the poor. They declared, that they were ready to substantiate the justice of all their demands, and, in particular, to prove that those who arrogated to themselves the name of clergy were destitute of all right to be accounted ministers of religion; and that, from the tyranny which they had exercised, and their vassalage to the court of Rome, they could not be safely tolerated, and far less intrusted with power, in a reformed commonwealth."*

The attentive reader will mark, in the

* Knox, Spotswood.

* M'Crie's Life of Knox, pp. 200, 201; Knox, pp. 237, 238.

preceding outline of this petition, the statement of certain great principles which he will have occasion subsequently to trace in active operation. He will mark the request, not only for purity of worship, but also for *primitive discipline*,—a point of vital importance in any Church, but one which worldly-minded men will always hate and oppose. He will mark, also, that while our Scottish reformers still wished ecclesiastical revenues to be devoted to *ecclesiastical*, and not *civil* purposes, they did so, not for the sake of their own aggrandizement, but purely for the public good, purposing a threefold division and application of them,—one-third for the support of colleges and schools, one-third for the support of the poor, and the remaining third for the support of the ministers of religion. No other national Church ever exhibited a spirit at once so generous and self-denying, and so wisely and nobly zealous in devising large and liberal schemes for promoting the welfare of the kingdom. But such schemes were far too generous to find favour in the sight of the avaricious nobility and gentry, and far too enlightened to be adequately understood, either by the men of that age, or even yet, of our own. Unfortunately for the public welfare, in all ages and countries, men of the world, judging others by themselves, cannot understand, and will not believe, the self-denying and generous spirit of true religion, and therefore always regard with jealousy every proposal made by the servants of Christ; and even the more manifestly self-denying and generous it is, the more suspicious are they that it must contain some peculiarly deep design. The applicability of these remarks will soon be made evident.

When this petition was laid before parliament, it soon became apparent that it went much farther than many of the politicians were disposed to permit. Maitland of Lethington had previously said, in reference to the discourses which Knox had preached from the book of Haggai, "We may now forget ourselves, and bear the barrow to build the house of God." This scoffing comment showed plainly enough what were his sentiments; and there were but too many ready to concur with and support him. In answer to the first topics of the petition, the parliament required the reformed ministers to lay before them a summary of doctrine which they could prove to be consonant with the Scriptures, and which they desired to have established. The following ministers were appointed to perform the task:—John Winram, John Spotswood, John Willock, John Douglas, John Row, and John Knox; and in the course of four days, they presented a Confession of Faith as the product of their joint labours, and an expression of their unanimous judgment. It agreed with the Confessions which had been published by other reformed Churches. In the statement of doctrinal tenets it is very clear and distinct, and eminently evangelical; but though a very valuable and excellent summary of Christian faith, it is perhaps more coloured with the circumstances of the times than is necessary, and in some respects less specific and decided than is desirable. For an admirable outline of it the reader may consult M'Crie's Life of Knox; from which work we extract the following condensed account of its ratification.

"The Confession was first read before the Lords of Articles, and afterwards before the whole parliament. The Protestant ministers attended in the house to defend it, if attacked, and to give satisfaction to the members respecting any point which might appear dubious. Those who had objections to it were formally required to state them. And the farther consideration of it was adjourned to a subsequent day, that none might pretend that an undue advantage had been taken of him, or that a matter of such importance had been concluded precipitately. On the 17th of August the parliament resumed the subject, and previous to the vote, the Confession was again read, article by article. The Earl of Athole, and Lords Somerville and Borthwick, were the only persons of the temporal estate who voted in the negative, assigning this as their reason, 'We will believe as our forefathers believed.' 'The bishops spake nothing.' After the vote establishing the Confession of Faith, the Earl Marischal rose, and declared, that the silence of the clergy had confirmed him in his belief of the protestant doctrine; and he protested that if any of the ecclesiastical estate should afterwards oppose the doctrine which had just been received, they should be entitled to no credit, seeing, after full knowledge of it, and ample time for deliberation, they had allowed it to pass without the smallest opposition or contradiction. On the 24th of August, the parliament abolished the papal jurisdiction, prohibited, under certain penalties the celebration of mass, and rescinded all the laws formerly made in support of the Roman Catholic Church, and against the Reformed faith."*

With these acts Sir James Sandilands of Torphichen was sent to France, in order to obtain, if possible, their ratification by the king and queen. This, however, they refused to give, trusting to the possibility of yet restoring the Romish Church in Scotland; but as their hostility was known, their refusal gave little disturbance to the reformers, by whom indeed it seems to have been expected. As in the treaty of Edinburgh it had been expressly agreed that, in the parliament which was to be held in August, the religious matters in dispute should be considered and grievances redressed, the reformers held themselves entitled to regard all the decisions of that parliament as in reality ratified by anticipation; and accordingly their next care was to devise what steps should now be taken for the complete diffusion and establishment of the Reformation throughout the kingdom.

Previous to the meeting of parliament, and during the calm which intervened between the treaty of Edinburgh and the later period, a temporary arrangement had been made, by which the chief of the reformed ministers were appointed to reside in the most populous and important towns. John Knox was appointed to Edinburgh; Christopher Goodman (who had been Knox's colleague at Geneva, and had of late come to Scotland) was appointed to St. Andrews; Adam Heriot to Aberdeen; John Row to Perth; Paul Methven to Jedburgh; William Christison to Dundee; David Ferguson to Dumferline; and David Lindsay to Leith. But as the country parts of the kingdom were at least equally in need of ministers and instruction, and there were not yet any thing like a sufficient number of reformed ministers to supply the urgent necessities of the case, another expedient was devised. It was resolved to divide the counties into departments, and appoint one of the Protestant party to take the general charge of religious matters throughout each of these departments, and to bear the name of Superintendents, as indicative of the general charge which they were to take of the interests of religion in their respective districts. These superintendents were, John Spotswod for the Lothians; John Winram for Fife; John Willock for Glasgow; John Erskine of Dun for Angus and Mearns; and John Carsewell for Argyle.* It was intended by the reformers to have divided Scotland into ten districts, and to have appointed a superintendent for each; but the difficulty of obtaining suitable persons prevented the appointment of any more than the above-named five.

From the fact of the appointment of these superintendents, Episcopalian writers have striven to represent the Scottish reformers as favourable to diocesan Prelacy. The utter absurdity of this notion has been demonstrated so conclusively by many authors, that we need not expend our time in its refutation; it is enough to refer to Calderwood, Stevenson, and M'Crie, or to the First Book of Discipline, in which it manifestly appears that the superintendents had no one thing in common with prelates, except the charge of religious matters in an extensive district,—a charge by the one class of men laboriously executed, and by the other made a source of honour and emolument; thus, even in this apparent similarity, proving their inherent and essential difference. It may be added, that not only was there no essential difference between the ordination of the superintendent and the minister, but Erskine of Dun filled the office of a superintendent before he was ordained at all; and farther, that when it was proposed to make the bishop of Galloway superintendent over Galloway, the proposal was rejected, lest the appointment of one who had been a bishop should give some colour to the idea that the office was Prelacy under a different name.†

Soon after the parliament had finished

* M'Crie's Life of Knox, p. 203; see also Knox p. 253; Spotswood, p. 150. Calderwood, p. 14.

* Knox, p. 236; Spotswood, p. 149.
† Knox, Historie, p. 263; Calderwood, p. 32.

its labours and been dissolved, the reformed ministers and the leading Protestants determined to meet and deliberate respecting the measures to be next adopted. On the 20th day of December 1560, they met accordingly, in Edinburgh, "To consult upon those things which are to forward God's glory, and the weil of his Kirk, in this realme." And this was the first meeting of the FIRST GENERAL ASSEMBLY OF THE CHURCH OF SCOTLAND."*

We have thus briefly traced the progress of the Reformation in Scotland, from its first scarcely perceptible beginning, struggling against the opposition of powerful, treacherous, and merciless antagonists, until, "strong only in the Lord and in the power of His might," it surmounted all obstacles, and the ministers and elders of the Church of Scotland convened and held their General Assembly, in the name and by the sole authority of Him by whom they had been so mightily upheld, and whom alone they recognized as Head and King of the Church of Scotland. We have seen how long the early Church of Scotland, the Culdees, resisted the encroachments and the corruptions of Prelacy and Popery; with what difficulty these adherents of primitive Christianity were overborne; how pertinaciously the people of Scotland clung to their early belief; and how readily the tenets of Wickliffe and other early reformers were received in those districts where the Culdee system had most prevailed. The dying declarations of the Scottish martyrs have called forth our admiration, and touched our sympathies; and we have traced the steady unswerving course of the undaunted Knox, as he bore right onward to the accomplishment of his one great aim,—the establishment of the blessed gospel of Christ in his native land. And we must have traced the course of these great events with unperceiving eye indeed, if we have not marked the hand of Providence guiding them all in a most peculiar manner. Even circumstances the most seemingly adverse were so overruled as to contribute to the purity and completeness of the Scottish Reformation. The alternating direct hostility and alien intrigues of the court and the civil rulers, preventing the vitiating influence of worldly policy from interfering with and warping the views of our re formers, who were thus not only left, but even constrained, to follow the guidance of the sacred Word of God alone; while in almost every other country, England for example, the Reformation was either biassed in its course, or arrested at that stage of its progress in which worldly statesmen conceived it could be rendered more subservient to their own designs. But this, which is the glory and excellency of the Church of Scotland, we shall find to have been the cause of nearly all the perils wherewith she has been encompassed, and the sufferings through which she has passed, from the Reformation to the present day.

* Booke of the Universall Kirk of Scotland.

CHAPTER III.

FROM THE FIRST GENERAL ASSEMLLY, IN 1560, TO THE YEAR 1592, AND THE GREAT CHARTER OF THE CHURCH.

First Book of Discipline—Opposition of the Nobility to its Regulations—Queen Mary's Return to Scotland—Contests respecting the Mass, and respecting the Liberty of the Assembly, and the Patrimony of the Church—Proceedings against the Popish Bishops—Trial of Knox for convening the Ministers—Defence by Knox of the Freedom of the Pulpit—Marriage of the Queen to Darnley—Patronage—Death of Rizzio—First National Fast—Murder of Darnley—Marriage of the Queen to Bothwell—Flight of Bothwell, and Mary's Imprisonment—Act of Parliament 1567, recognising the Church—Powers and Jurisdiction of the Church, and its Condition at this time—The Regent Murray—his Assassination—The Regent Morton—Attempts for the Restoration of Prelacy—Convention of Leith, 1572—Tulchan Bishops—Death of John Knox—Continued Struggles of the Church against the Tulchan Bishops—Andrew Melville comes to Scotland—Commission to draw up a System of Ecclesiastical Polity and Jurisdiction—Patrick Adamson—Opposition of Melville—Morton resigns the Regency, and King James assumes the Government—The Second Book of Discipline—Conference respecting it—Its Ratification evaded—Condemnation of Episcopacy by the Assembly—Erection of Presbyteries, and Engrossment of the Second Book of Discipline in the Records of the Assembly—First National Covenant subscribed by the King—Robert Montgomery—Proceedings of the Church in his case—The Raid of Ruthven—Proceedings of the King against Melville—The Black Acts of 1584—Sufferings of the Church—Change of Measures for the better—Act of Annexation—Alarm on account of the Spanish Armada—The King sails to Norway—Peaceful State of the Church and Kingdom—The King returns and eulogizes the Church—Collision between the Court of Session and the Church—Act of Parliament of 1592, called the Great Charter of the Church of Scotland.

THE act of the Scottish parliament, passed on the 24th August 1560, in accordance with the petition of the Scottish reformers, abrogated and annulled the pa pal jurisdiction, and all authority flowing therefrom; but it enacted no ecclesiastical jurisdiction whatever in its stead. This it left the reformed Church to determine upon and effect by its own intrinsic powers. And this is a fact of the utmost importance, which cannot be too well known and kept in remembrance. It is, indeed, one of the distinctive characteristics of the Church of Scotland, that it owes its origin, its form, its jurisdiction, and its discipline, to no earthly power. And when the ministers and elders of the Church of Scotland resolved to meet in a General Assembly, to deliberate on matters which might tend to the promotion of God's glory and the welfare of the Church, they did so in virtue of the authority which they believed the Lord Jesus Christ had given to His Church. The parliament which abolished the papal jurisdiction made not the slightest mention of a General Assembly. In that time of comparatively simple and honest faith, even statesmen seem instinctively to have perceived, that to interfere in matters of ecclesiastical jurisdiction, so as to appoint ecclesiastical tribunals, specify their nature, and assign their limits, was not within their province. It had been well for the kingdom if statesmen of succeeding times, certainly not their superiors in talent and in judgment, had been wise enough to follow their example.

The first meeting of the General Assembly of the Church of Scotland was held, as has been already stated, on the 20th of December 1560. The number that convened was but small,—it consisted of forty members, only six of whom were ministers; but they were men of great abilities, of deep piety, and of eminent personal worth, fitted and qualified by their Creator for the work which he had given them to do. The very next step which was taken proved both their qualifications and their zeal. It was very clearly seen by the reformers, that the power of discipline was essential to the well-being of a Church, since without it purity could not be maintained, either among the people or the ministers themselves. They determined, therefore, to draw up a book in which there should be a complete system of ecclesiastical government; and the same eminent men by whom the Confession of Faith had been composed were appointed to undertake the new and scarcely less important task. This, indeed, they had been previously desired to do by the privy council, as appears from the preamble of their production. They applied themselves to their task in the same spirit as before, having respect, indeed, to the circumstances and the exigencies of the time, but looking to Divine direction and authority alone. "They took not their example," says Row, "from any Kirk in the world; no, not from Geneva;" but their plan from the sacred Scriptures. Having arranged the subject under different heads, they divided these among them; and, after they had finished their several parts, they met together and examined them with great attention, spending much time in reading and meditation on the subject, and in earnest prayers for Divine direction. When they had drawn up the whole in form, they laid it before the General Assembly, by whom it was approved, after they had caused some of its articles to be abridged. At the close of the brief records of the first General Assembly, there is an intimation that the next meeting was to be held on the 15th day of January following;* but no record appears to have been kept of that meeting; yet, as we find the Book of Discipline referred to in the next meeting of May the same year, we may conclude that it was in January that it was approved and ratified by the Assembly. It was also submitted to the privy council; but although many of the members highly approved of the plan, it was keenly opposed by others. "Every thing," says Knox, "that repugned to their corrupt affections was termed, in their mockery, 'devout imaginations.' The cause we have before declared: some were licentious, some had greedily gripped the possessions of the Church, and others thought that they would not lack their part of Christ's coat."† This points out clearly enough the cause of the opposition made to the Book of Discipline,—partly aversion to the strict discipline which it appointed to be exercised against vice, and partly from reluctance to comply with its requisition for the appropriation of the

* Booke of the Universall Kirk, p. 5.
† Knox, p. 256.

revenues of the Popish Church to the support of the new religious and literary establishments. But though not formally ratified by the privy council, it was subscribed by the greater part of the nobility and barons, members of the council, and thereby virtually ratified. The document deserves to be recorded:—

"At Edinburgh, 17th January 1561.

"We, who have subscribed these presents, having advised with the articles herein specified, as is above mentioned, from the beginning of this book, think the same good, and conform to God's Word in all points,—conform to the notes and additions hereto eiked; and promise to set the same forward to the uttermost of our powers. Providing that the bishops, abbots, priors, and other prelates and beneficed men which else have adjoined themselves to us, bruik [enjoy] the revenues of their benefices during their lifetimes; they sustaining and upholding the ministry and ministers, as herein is specified, for the preaching of the Word, and ministering of the sacraments."

To this,—termed by several writers "An act of the secret council," which indeed it was, being subscribed by a large majority,—there were affixed the names of the Duke of Chatelherault, the Earls of Arran, Argyle, Glencairn, Rothes, Marischal, Monteith, and Morton, Lords James Stewart, Boyd, Yester, Ochiltree, Lindsay, Sanquhar, St. John of Torphichen, the Master of Maxwell, the Master of Lindsay, Drumlanrig, Lochinvar, Garlies, Balgarnie, Cunninghamhead, Alexander Gordon, bishop of Galloway, Alexander Campbell, dean of Murray, and others of less note.

As the Book of Discipline contains the deliberate opinions of the Scottish reformers respecting what they regarded as the fundamental principles of the Church which they were labouring to establish in Scotland, it seems necessary to give a brief abstract of those principles, that the reader may the better know what the Church of Scotland, from its beginning, has either been or striven to be.

The ordinary and permanent office-bearers of the Church were of four kinds: the minister or pastor, to whom the preaching of the gospel and administration of the sacraments belonged; the doctor or teacher, whose province it was to interpret Scripture and confute errors, including those who taught theology in schools and universities; the ruling elder, who assisted the minister in exercising ecclesiastical discipline and government; and the deacon, who had the special charge of the revenues of the Church and the poor. To these permanent office-bearers there were added two others, of a temporary character. It has been already stated, that, in the arrangement entered into previous to the first General Assembly, there were only twelve reformed ministers to preach the gospel throughout the whole kingdom; and that, to accomplish the utmost possible amount of duty by so small a number, seven were placed in the chief towns, and large country districts were assigned to each of the remaining five. These five were called superintendents; and their duty was, to travel from place to place throughout their districts, for the purpose of preaching, planting churches, and inspecting the conduct of the country ministers, where there were any, and of another temporary class of men termed Exhorters and Readers. This latter class consisted of the most pious persons that could be found, who, having received a common education, were able to read to their more ignorant neighbours, though not qualified for the ministry. When the readers were found to have discharged their duty well, and to have increased in their own knowledge, they were encouraged to add a few plain exhortations to the reading of the Scriptures; and then they were termed Exhorters. If they still continued to improve, they might finally be admitted to the ministry. To search out, employ, and watch over the conduct of such men, giving them instruction from time to time, was the chief duty of the superintendent, from which, indeed, he derived his name, so naturally expressive of his duty,—a duty the very nature of which shows it to have been temporary, and intended to expire whenever the necessities which called it into being should have been removed by a sufficiency of qualified ministers.

No person was allowed to preach, or to administer the sacraments, till he was regularly called to his employment.

"Ordinary vocation [calling] consisteth in election, examination, and admission." "It appertaineth to the people, and to every several congregation, to elect their minister." "For altogether this is to be avoided, that any man be violently intruded or thrust in upon any congregation; but this liberty, with all care, must be reserved to every several church, to have their votes and suffrages in election of their ministers." The examination was appointed to take place "in open assembly, and before the congregation," to satisfy the church as to his soundness in the faith; his "gifts, utterance, and knowledge;" his willingness to undertake the charge; the purity of his motives; and his resolution to discharge the duties of his office with diligence and fidelity. Admission then took place by the person being solemnly set apart by prayer, at first without imposition of hands, which, however, was afterwards appointed to be done. Superintendents were admitted in the same way as other ministers, were tried by the same church courts, liable to the same censures, and might be deposed for the same crimes.

The affairs of each congregation were managed by the minister, elders, and deacons, who constituted the kirk-session, which met regularly once a week, and oftener if business required. There was also a meeting, called the weekly exercise, or prophesying, held in every considerable town, consisting of the ministers, exhorters, and educated men in the vicinity, for expounding the Scriptures. This was afterwards converted into the presbytery, or classical assembly. The superintendent met with the ministers and delegated elders of his district twice a-year, in the provincial Synod, which took cognizance of ecclesiastical affairs within its bounds. And the General Assembly, which was composed of ministers and elders commissioned from the different parts of the kingdom, met twice, sometimes thrice, in a year, and attended to the interests of the National Church.

Public worship was attended to in such a manner, as to show the estimation in which it was held by our reformers. On Sabbath days the people assembled twice for public worship; and, the better to instruct the ignorant, catechising was substituted for preaching in the afternoon. In towns a sermon was regularly preached on one day of the week besides the Sabbath: and on almost every day the people had an opportunity of hearing public prayers and the reading of the Scriptures. Baptism was never dispensed unless it was accompanied with preaching or catechising. The Lord's Supper was administered four times a-year in towns; the sign of the cross in baptizing, and kneeling at the Lord's table, were forbidden; and anniversary holidays were abolished.

Education was very justly regarded as of the utmost importance, and deserving every possible encouragement. It was stated as imperatively necessary, that there should be a school in every parish, for the instruction of youth in the principles of religion, grammar, and the Latin tongue; and it was farther proposed, that a college should be erected in every "notable town," in which logic and rhetoric should be taught, along with the learned languages. It was even suggested that parents should not be permitted to neglect the education of their children; but that the nobility and gentry should be obliged to do so at their own expense; and that a fund should be provided for the education of the children of the poor, who discovered talents and aptitude for learning.

To carry these important measures into effect, permanent funds were requisite; and for these they naturally looked to the patrimony of the Church. The hierarchy had been abolished, and the popish clergy excluded from all religious services, by the alterations which the parliament had introduced; and whatever provision it was proper to allot for the dismissed incumbents during life, it was unreasonable that they should continue to enjoy those emoluments which were attached to offices for which they had been found totally unfit. No successors could be appointed to them; and there was not any individual or class of men in the nation, who could justly claim a title to the rents of their benefices. The compilers of the Book of Discipline, therefore, proposed that the patrimony of the Church should be appropriated, in the first instance, to the support of the new ecclesiastical establishment. Under this designation they included the *ministry*, the *schools*, and the *poor*. For the ministers they required, that such "honest provision" should be made as would give "neither occasion of solicitude, neither yet of insolencie and wantonnesse." The stipends of ministers were to be collected by the deacons from the tithes; but all illegal exactions were to be previously abolished, and measures taken to relieve the cultivators of the ground from the oppressive manner in which the tithes had been gathered by the clergy, or by those to whom they had farmed them. The revenues of bishoprics, and of cathedral and collegiate churches, with the rents arising from the endowments of monasteries and other religious foundations, were to be divided, and appropriated to the support of the universities, or of the churches within their bounds.

The reformers were well aware of the necessity of establishing and maintaining a systematic course of discipline. "As no commonwealth can flourish or long endure without good laws, and sharp execution of the same, so neither can the Kirk of God be brought to purity, neither yet be retained in the same, without the order of ecclesiastical discipline, which stands in reproving and correcting of the faults which the civil sword either doth neglect or may not punish."* "To discipline must all the estates within the realm be subject, as well as the rulers as they that are ruled; yea, and the preachers themselves, as well as the poorest within the Kirk." These quotations may alone serve to show, that there was nothing in which the Scottish reformers approached nearer to the primitive Church, than in the rigorous and impartial exercise of ecclesiastical discipline, the relaxation of which, under the papacy, they justly regarded as one great cause of the universal corruption of religion. "In some instances they might carry their rigour against offenders to an extreme, but it was a virtuous extreme, compared with the dangerous laxity, or rather total disuse, of discipline which has gradually crept into almost all the churches that retain the name of reformed; even as the scrupulous delicacy with which our forefathers shunned the society of those who had transgressed the rules of morality, is to be preferred to modern manners, by which the vicious obtain easy admission into the company of the virtuous."*

There is one almost casual expression in that part of the Book of discipline which treats of Church censures, of too much importance to be passed by without notice, tending, as it does, to throw a flood of light on the character of the age, and to vindicate the reformers from one of the heaviest of the accusations brought against them,—"correcting of the faults which either the civil sword *doth neglect* or may not punish." Every person at all acquainted with the history of those times will see the deep meaning of these very pregnant words. Rent as the kingdom had long been into feudal factions there was scarcely anything in it deserving the name of public justice. Every ambitious nobleman was ready to defend the most notorious criminals, for the purpose of strengthening his "following," by the accession of fierce, lawless, and unscrupulous adherents. Impartiality in the administration of justice, and the suppression of crime, neither did exist, nor was possible in such a state of matters; and the popish clergy, being themselves as licentious and unjust as either people or nobles, were not disposed to attempt enacting or enforcing laws by which they might themselves be condemned and punished. There was, therefore, an absolute necessity that the reformed Church of Scotland should take decided measures, not only for the teaching of truth, but also for the suppression of vice and immorality, as far as its authority could possibly reach, and much farther than in a better state of society would have been either necessary or desirable. Yet, even when impelled by these urgent considerations, the Church of Scotland never attempted to dictate in civil matters, nor even called upon the secular authorities to inflict civil penalties for the purpose of enforcing discipline purely ecclesiastical. That the Church called upon the parliament to suppress *idolalry*, and to abolish the *papal jurisdiction* in the kingdom, is admitted; but this cannot justly be regarded as any thing more than the public voice of the Church calling upon the civil magistrate to do his own duty in his own province, as *idolatry* is a viola-

* First Book of Discipline, chap. ix.

* M'Crie's Life of Knox, p. 251.

tion of natural religion, and even of reason itself, and the *papal jurisdiction* involves the national crime of allegiance to a foreign secular power, which no well-governed country can safely tolerate. A slight apparent confusion between the secular and the ecclesiastical jurisdictions arose from the fact that the parliament, or the magistracy of particular burghs, had enacted punishments of a corporal kind, against certain crimes which were ordinarily tried in the church courts; but the infliction, as well as the enacting of them, pertained to the civil magistrate.*

Such were the fundamental principles, and the chief points of the government and discipline of the Church of Scotland as stated in the Book of Discipline, drawn up by John Knox and the most eminent of the Scottish reformers; approved by the General Assembly; and subscribed by the majority of the nobles, and inferior barons, and gentry, composing the privy council of the kingdom. Had it obtained the complete sanction of the civil government, and its principles and arrangements thereby been brought into full operation, many, if not all of the calamities which speedily fell upon the kingdom, might have been averted. But statesmen had not then learned, neither indeed have they yet, the important difference between principles, which have in them the energy of imperishable vital powers, and external arrangements, which are either the results of the operation of principles, or are the mere mounds by which short-sighted men attempt to modify and restrain the aspect and growth of the internal agency, which they understand not, but wish to coerce Arrangements may be altered almost at will; but principles, when once fully stated, can never be destroyed. They may be repressed, fettered, turned awry in their operations; but they continue to operate powerfully even when unseen, causing convulsion after convulsion as they rend asunder and throw off the uncomforting external moulds into which they have been forced; and must inevitably continue thus to act, till they obtain a free and unconstrained developement, congenial to their own nature. The principles stated in the First Confession of Faith, and the First Book of Discipline, of the Church of Scotland, were disliked, opposed, repressed, and turned aside by the worldly-wise statesmen of that day, as they have often been in subsequent times; but they took up their abiding residence in the mind and heart of Scotland,—in the deliberate judgment and conviction of its intellect, and the fervent regard of its affection; and the struggle then begun will continue, till, sooner or later, they be completely realized.

It has been already stated, that the Protestant nobility readily enough consented to the suppression of the papal jurisdiction, and the public sanctioning of the reformed doctrines, especially as these measures were understood to imply a prospective confiscation of the exorbitant wealth of the Romish clergy. But they were by no means equally satisfied with the remaining main propositions of the reformers,—the regulations of discipline, and especially the appropriation of the patrimony of the suppressed Church to the purposes, ministerial, educational, and charitable, of the new ecclesiastical establishment. They had for some time cast a covetous eye on the rich revenues of the popish clergy. Some of them had seized upon church lands, or retained the tithes in their own hands. Others had taken long leases of them from the clergy for small sums of money, and were anxious to have these private bargains legalized. From this arose one great cause of their aversion to have the Book of Discipline ratified, lest they should be obliged to surrender the spoil they had unjustly obtained. The plan of the Church was, they said, a "devout imagination," a mere visionary scheme, which showed indeed the goodness of their intentions, but which it was impossible to carry into practical effect. In short, they determined to retain by force the greater part of the Church revenues, thus fraudfully seized upon, for their own advantage.

Several public events of great importance occurred about this time, by which the affairs of the Church were not a little influenced, and which, therefore, must be briefly stated. Francis, the young king of France, and in virtue of the matrimonial crown as husband of Mary, king of

* Baillie's Vindication, p. 17.

Scotland also, died in December 1560. Mary immediately lost all power at the French court, and indicated her willingness to return to Scotland. Her natural brother, Lord James Stewart, was sent by the Scottish parliament to France, in the expectation that he might induce her to be favourable to the reformed Church; and Lesly, afterwards bishop of Ross, was deputed by the Romish party to promote their interests. Mary manifested no disposition to favour the Reformation; but seemed disposed to place much confidence in the political sagacity of her brother, endeavouring, at the same time, to draw him aside from his adherence to the reformed Church, in which she was partially successful.

Previous to the return of Mary, the second General Assembly was held at Edinburgh, on the 27th of May 1561. Its proceedings were chiefly directed to the object of obtaining a specific ratification of certain topics contained in the Book of Discipline, respecting the suppression of idolatry, and the providing of maintenance for the reformed preachers, which the privy council thought proper to grant.

On the 19th of August, in the same year, Queen Mary landed at Leith, and was conducted to Holyrood-house, in the midst of great demonstrations of joy at her safe arrival, by a people predisposed to the most devoted loyalty, provided their allegiance to an earthly sovereign was not strained to the violation of the infinitely higher allegiance which they owed to the King of kings. There was but too much certainty, that they would soon be put to choose whether they would violate their conscience or offend their queen. Mary had unfortunately been trained up from her infancy in a blind attachment to the tenets and observances of Popery; and, before she left France, her uncles of the house of Guise or Lorraine had used every means to strengthen this prejudice, and to inspire her with hatred to the religion which had been embraced by her people. She was taught that it would be the glory of her reign to bring back her kingdom to its former obedience to the papal sway, and to co-operate with the popish princes on the Continent in extirpating heresy. To this was added as a strong inducement, that they would not only support her in chastising her rebellious subjects, but would assist her also to prosecute her claims to the English crown Mary brought with her to Scotland these prepossessions and schemes; and she adhered to them throughout her life with the most determined pertinacity. She did, indeed, temporise for a time, as the Protestants were in the possession of all power in the kingdom; but she resolved to withhold her ratification of the late proceedings, and to embrace the first favourable opportunity to overturn them, and re-establish the ancient system.*

The Protestants, on the other hand, remembering well the deep dissimulation of her mother, and aware of the fierce bigotry of the Guisan family, were jealous of their young queen, and had strictly prohibited the deputies sent to France from promising her more than the private exercise of her religion,—if, indeed, even that could be tolerated. Between such conflicting principles and aims, it was impossible but that a collision should speedily ensue. Nor was occasion long wanting for the exhibition of that hostility which was so deeply entertained by both parties. As if to seize the earliest opportunity of proving her attachment to her own faith, Mary gave orders for the celebration of a solemn mass in the chapel of Holyrood-house, on the first Sabbath after her arrival. This service, it will be remembered, had been prohibited by an act of the late parliament, and had not been publicly performed since the conclusion of the civil war. This most unwise step of the queen gave such offence to the people, that it was with the utmost difficulty they were prevented from breaking into an open tumult, and inflicting punishment on the perpetrators of what they regarded as a direct violation at once of the laws of God and of the nation. An act of the privy council was framed, prohibiting all innovations in the religion found by the queen on her arrival; but, at the same time, prohibiting all tumultuary interference with the French attendants "for any cause whatsoever," by which they were protected in their religious usages, despite the known hostility of her Protestant

* See M'Crie's Life of Knox, note UU.

subjects. Against this act of council the Earl of Arran alone of the nobility protested briefly; but a more full and formal protest was made by the Protestant ministers. John Knox took occasion to deliver his mind fully and openly on the subject in a sermon preached by him on the following Sabbath; in which he declared, "That one mass was more fearful unto him than if ten thousand armed enemies were landed in any part of the realm, of purpose to suppress the whole religion: for, said he, in our God there is strength to resist and confound multitudes, if we unfeignedly depend upon Him, of which we have had experience; but when we join hands with idolatry, it is no doubt but both God's presence and defence will leave us; and what shall then become of us?*

Let the Christian reader note well the reasoning on which Knox founds his dread of the mass; and let him put to himself this question, and ponder well what answer must be returned to it:—"Can religion be reformed really and successfully without the direct aid of God, and can it be defended in any other manner?" The man of the world may imagine that it can; but he will not produce one instance that it ever was. Neither will it be possible to produce one instance of a great and real reformation of religion taking place, without the chief human agents being themselves fully persuaded that they are enjoying the direct aid of God, and, in the strength of that belief, proceeding confidently forward with measures the success of which, according to every merely human calculation, is absolutely hopeless. For the same reason they will be found rejecting those schemes which human prudence and political sagacity would most recommend; and expressing their dread of nothing so much as of the unhallowed intermixture of worldly wisdom in their sacred welfare, especially when that intermixture involves the crime of conniving at what they believe to be direct or implicit violation of the laws of Him who alone can give the victory. For they well know, that as their enterprise can be brought to a successful issue through the aid of God alone, so, whatever has the tendency to cause Him to withdraw that aid,—whether by direct violation of His commandments, or by such temporizing conduct as implies distrust of His all-sufficient support,—must lead infallibly to their own punishment, in the overthrow of their undertaking, or the indefinite postponement of its success. So thought and believed John Knox; and hence his dread of one permitted mass, as tending to cause God to withdraw his support, and to leave them to the punishment which their faithless and temporizing devices had deserved. Such opinions and rules of action, we well know, are termed fanatical by sages and the learned, by the philosophers and statesmen of the world; but the Christian knows their truth, and the reflecting historian may learn and mark their reality and their value. We shall have repeated occasion to trace them, and to note their importance, in our subsequent pages.

The report of Knox's animadversions upon her conduct was speedily conveyed to the queen. She seems to have resolved to try the possible amount of that personal influence with him which she had found so effectual with a great number of the Protestant lords; of whom it was customary to say, that they came to court very zealous defenders of the true religion, but, after a few days' residence there, the fire-edge wore off them, and they became as temperate as the rest. If such were her expectations, she was completely disappointed; and finding that she had now to deal with a man who could neither be flattered nor overawed, she seems to have ever afterwards regarded him with mingled feelings of respect, terror, and hatred. Knox had, on his part, made it his study to avail himself of such an opportunity to discover the real character of the queen; and when some of his friends asked his opinion of her, he answered, "If there be not in her a proud mind, a crafty wit, and an indurate heart against God and his truth, my judgment faileth me."* Few will now deny that his judgment proved to be but too accurate. The estimate which he formed of the queen's character, and the coldness which he perceived spreading among the Protestant lords, had no other effect upon him than to make him the more watchful

* Knox, p. 287.

* Knox, p. 292.

over public procedure, and the more determined in the defence of the Church.

A meeting of the General Assembly was held in December, the same year, 1561, of which the Booke of the Universall Kirk gives no account, probably because its time was spent in disputations, without producing any direct result. These disputations, however, have been recorded by Knox himself; and a brief account of them is necessary, as showing the altered sentiments of some of the Protestant lords. A considerable number of them at first absented themselves from the meeting of the Assembly; and when reproved, they retorted by disputing the propriety of such conventions without her majesty's pleasure. Maitland of Lethington, now made secretary of state, took upon him to encounter the reasoning of Knox. "Take from us the liberty of assemblies, and take from us the gospel," said the reformer. "If the liberty of the Church must depend upon her allowance or disallowance, we shall want not only assemblies, but the preaching of the gospel." It was then proposed that the Book of Discipline should be ratified by the queen; but this was pointedly opposed by the secretary. "How many of those that subscribed that book will be subject to it?" said he scoffingly. It was answered, "All the godly." "Will the Duke?" said Lethington. "If he will not," replied Lord Ochiltree, "I wish that his name were scraped, not only out of that book, but also out of our number and company; for to what end shall men subscribe, and never mind to keep word of that which they promise?" Lethington answered, that many subscribed it, *in fide parentum*, as children are baptized. Knox replied, that "the scoff was as untrue as it was unbecoming; for the book was publicly read, and its different heads discussed, for a number of days, and no man was required to subscribe what he did not understand." "Stand content," said one of the courtiers: "that book will not be obtained." "Let God," replied Knox, "require the injury which the commonwealth shall sustain, at the hands of those who hinder it."

Another subject which caused keen and protracted altercation between Knox and the court party, was their management in settling the provision for the ministers of the Church. Hitherto they had lived chiefly on the benevolence of their hearers, and many of them had scarcely the means of subsistence, but repeated complaints having obliged the privy council to take up the affair, they came at last to a determination, that the ecclesiastical revenues should be divided into three parts; that two of these should be given to the ejected popish clergy, and that the third part should be divided between the court and the protestant ministry! Well might Knox exclaim, when he heard of this disgraceful arrangement, "If the end of this order, pretended to be taken for the sustentation of the ministers, be happy, my judgment fails me! I see two parts freely given to the devil, and the third part must be divided betwixt God and the devil." Even the lords of the privy council seem to have felt that their own nefarious deed was little better than a mockery; for when the scheme was proposed among them, the Earl of Huntly, himself a popish nobleman, addressed the others jestingly, by "Good morrow, my lords of the two parts."* The privy council appointed certain persons to fix the sums which were to be appropriated to the court and to the ministry, and also the particular salaries which were to be allotted to individual ministers, according to the circumstances in which they were placed. The officers for this purpose composed a board under the privy council, which was called the "Court of Modification." The persons thus appointed to "modify the stipends," were disposed to gratify the queen, and her demands were readily answered; while the sums allotted to the ministers were as ill paid as they were inadequate. Lethington again displayed his sneering and bitter nature, asserting that "if the ministers were sustained, the queen would not get, at the year's end, to buy her a pair of new shoes." "To these dumb dogs the bishops," answered Knox, "ten thousand was not enough; but to the servants of Christ, that painfully preach the Gospel, an hundred merks† must suffice! How can that be sustained?"

The preceding particulars have been

* Knox, pp. 296-300. † 100 merks Scots=£5, 11s. 1 3-4d.

the more exactly related, because, slight as they may seem, they indicate very correctly the main grounds of the hostility which began to arise between the Protestant nobility and the ministers, and also serve to point out the course which that hostility was likely soon to take, and, in fact, did take. The more that the nobility became accustomed to the loose manners prevalent in a court formed, as far as possible, on the model of the licentious court of France, the less were they inclined to conform themselves to the strict and pure morality of the Book of Discipline. And having given two-thirds of the patrimony of the Church to the popish clergy during the remainder of their lives, they had rendered it impossible to comply with the scheme for supporting the poor and endowing schools and colleges. The dilapidated state of the crown revenues had long rendered the Scottish monarchs in a great measure dependent on the gifts which they received at times from the wealthiest of the nobility, but more generally from the dignitaries of the Church. Had a portion of these two-thirds of the Church revenues been devoted to the maintenance of the crown, it might have been a wise and a just method of employing them, and lightening the public burdens of the country; but nothing could be more unjust than to leave them in the possession of such unworthy persons, and then to rob the laborious preachers of the gospel, and give the pillage of their stinted allowance to the queen. There is reason to believe, that when the queen consented to this arrangement, she anticipated the overthrow of the reformed Church, and the re-establishment of the popish; and, in that case, she expected to retain the entire third in her own hands, in addition to what benefactions she might receive from the popish clergy. Although this expectation was never realized, the arrangement gave rise to another evil, which might have been, and perhaps was foreseen. The two-thirds were secured to the ejected clergy during their lives; but upon their deaths, how was this large revenue to be bestowed? It might revert to the Church, and then the scheme of the Book of Discipline might be accomplished. This ought to have been the case; but some of the more fore-casting nobles had a very different scheme in view. If they could construct a kind of pseudo-prelacy, they might induce some creatures of their own to accept the title, while they should themselves, in the ame of those mercenary sycophants, draw and enjoy the revenues. This device seems to have been concocted between Lord. Erskine, afterwards Earl of Mar, and the Earl of Morton.

[1562.] The next General Assembly met in June 1562. In it several matters of importance were transacted, tending to the completion of the judicatorial arrangements of the Church; such as the appointment of the method of trying, and, if necessary, censuring, superintendents, ministers, and elders; authority to excommunicate the "inobedient;" and it was added, that "the magistrate, subject to the rule of Christ, be not exeemed from the same punishment, being found guilty and inobedient."* It is observable also, that in this Assembly the formal style of supreme authority was used— "The haill Kirk appoints and decerns."

The only matters of public importance which occurred during the early part of that year were, the elevation of Lord James Stewart to the earldom of Murray; by which title he is henceforth to be known; and the rebellious enterprise of the Marquis of Huntly, in which he fell in battle. The death of Huntly weakened the popish party, and seemed to confirm the influence of the Earl of Murray; but the infamous Earl of Bothwell, about the same time began that course of daring intrigues which ended in the ruin of the queen, and his own miserable death in a Danish prison.

During the course of the summer of that year, in consequence of the paucity of ministers and superintendents, John Knox was sent as a visitor, to preach and plant churches in Galloway, and George Hay in Ayrshire. Returning through the latter district, Knox held a public disputation with the Abbot of Crassaguel. who had been induced to attempt the defence of Popery in that manner. About the same time John Craig was appointed colleague to John Knox in Edinburgh, who was now beginning to sink beneath the intensity of his labours, which he had so long endured.

* Booke of the Universall Kirk, p. 10.

Another meeting of the General Assembly took place in December, the same year, in which it continued steadily to advance in the course of reformation, and of what might be not inaptly termed self-construction. As many of the former parish priests continued to reside in their parishes, and, without any formal abjuration of Popery, pretended to act as parish ministers, the Assembly, to remedy this evil, prohibited from serving in the ministry all who had not satisfied the Church of their soundness in the faith, and had not been examined and approved by the superintendent; and it was added, "This act to have strength as well against them that are *called bishops*, as others." The same Assembly erected provincial synods, to meet regularly twice a-year, with power to translate as well as to appoint ministers. A commission was also nominated to treat with the lords of the privy council, for the purpose of coming to an understanding as to the jurisdiction of the Church, manifestly with the view of averting the danger of any collision arising between two coordinate jurisdictions, the separate provinces of which had not been defined and settled by mutual agreement.* So early did the Church of Scotland anticipate that danger, all the while proceeding in the exercise of that jurisdiction which belonged to its sacred character and inherent powers.

[1563.] In the spring of the year 1563, an event occurred which had nearly hastened a direct conflict between the popish and the reformed parties earlier than the temporizing policy of the queen would have wished. The knowledge of her favour, and the perceived disagreement between the Protestant lords and the ministers, gave such encouragement to the popish party, that many of them openly celebrated mass at Easter. It will be recollected that this had been prohibited by the parliament of 1560, on pain of very severe penalties, amounting even to death for the third offence. The Protestants, highly incensed at this open violation of the law, resolved to enforce it themselves, without farther application to the queen, and even in disregard of her threatened displeasure. The queen at first endeavoured to induce Knox himself to mitigate the zeal of the western gentlemen; but, foiled in this attempt by his firmness, she promised to cause summon the offenders, and see justice done. Knox seems almost to have believed her for once serious. He gave a favourable report of her intentions, and this tended to allay the jealousy and indignation of the public mind.

Mary seemed now on the point of realizing the fruits of her deep and crafty policy. And, in order the more completely to lull the Protestants into security, she, on the 19th of May, caused the archbishop of St. Andrews, and a number of the principal Papists, to be arraigned before the Lord Justice-General, for transgressing the laws; and they, aware probably of her politic design, having come in her majesty's will, were committed to ward. The Protestants in general were highly delighted with this instance of justice and impartial-seeming administration of the laws of the queen; and began to entertain sanguine expectations that she would now ratify the reformed religion, and perhaps conform to it herself. Following up her scheme, she convoked a parliament, which met on the 21st of May. When Knox urged the Protestant lords to procure from the queen in this Parliament the complete ratification of the reformed Church, they declined, referring to the present more favourable conduct of the queen, and the inexpediency of urging such matters so rapidly forward as to incur the hazard of giving her offence, and thereby renewing her former hostility. The altercation between Knox and the Earl of Murray on this subject became so hot, that it caused a total suspension of all friendly intercourse between them, which lasted for nearly two years, greatly to the injury of the Protestant cause. So far had the crafty policy of the queen prevailed with the nobility, that instead of demanding the ratification of the treaty of Edinburgh, and the establishment of the Protestant Church, they consented to receive an act of oblivion, securing indemnity to those who had been engaged in the late civil war. The very mode of its enactment virtually implied the invalidity of the treaty in which it had been embodied; for the Protestant lords, on their bended knees, supplicated as a boon from

* Booke of the Universall Kirk, pp. 12, 13.

their sovereign, what they had formerly won with their swords, and repeatedly demanded as their right.

John Knox publicly and severely reprehended the conduct of the Protestant lords; and, adverting to the report of the queen's marriage, which was then prevalent, predicted the consequences which would ensue, if ever the nobility consented that their sovereign should marry a Papist. For this boldness, he was summoned to appear before the queen in council, and a very sharp altercation ensued between them, in which Knox defended himself with unshaken firmness, alike unmoved by her threatenings or her tears. She was persuaded, however, by the lords of the council, to abandon the idea of a prosecution. "And so," says Knox, "that storm quieted in appearance, but never in the heart."

The storm in the heart had soon another opportunity of bursting forth. During the residence of the queen at Stirling, in the month of August, the domestics whom she had left behind her in Holyrood-house celebrated the popish worship with greater publicity than had been usual, even when she was present. This gave great offence to the inhabitants of Edinburgh; and a slight popular tumult, not attended with injury, or even danger to any one, ensued. Reports, extremely exaggerated, were carried to the queen, who declared her determination not to return to Edinburgh until this riot was punished; and commanded two of the Protestants to be indicted to stand trial for the offence said to be committed. Dreading an intention to proceed to extremities against these men, and that their condemnation would be a preparative to some hostile attempt against their religion, the Protestants in Edinburgh resolved that Knox, agreeably to a commission which he had received from the Church, should write a circular letter to the principal gentlemen of the reformed faith, informing them of the circumstances, and requesting their presence on the day of trial. It will be recollected, that a similar course of procedure had been repeatedly adopted by the reformers in their previous contests with the queen-regent, so that it was completely accordant with the usage of the Church and nation. He wrote the letter according to their request; but a copy of it falling into the hands of Sinclair, bishop of Ross, and president of the Court of Session, was by him transmitted to the queen at Stirling. She communicated it to her privy council, who, to her great satisfaction, pronounced it treasonable. This was what the queen had long wished; and she accordingly gave orders that an extraordinary meeting of councillors, assisted by other noblemen, should be held at Edinburgh, to try the cause; and the reformer was summoned to appear before this convention.

Previous to the day of trial, great influence was used in private to persuade him to acknowledge that he had committed a fault, and to throw himself on the queen's mercy. This neither the entreaties of friends nor the threats of enemies could prevail upon him to do. On the day of trial, the public mind was excited to an intense degree of anxiety. The cause of the Reformation appeared to depend on the issue; and both parties regarded it with the most tremulous and eager interest. Secretary Lethington took the disreputable office of accuser; but was repeatedly and unbecomingly interrupted by the queen herself, when she thought he was not prosecuting the matter with sufficient point and force. Knox defended himself with such skill and ability as to refute every accusation brought against him. The main charge was that of illegally convoking the queen's lieges, and charging herself with cruelty. This charge he met and answered, so as completely to baffle both thc sophistry of Lethington, and the angry vehemence of the queen. At length he was ordered to retire for that night; and the judgment of the council was taken respecting his conduct.

All of them, with the exception of the immediate dependents of the court, gave it as their opinion that he had not been guility of any breach of the laws. The secretary, who had assured the queen of his condemnation, was enraged at this decision. He brought her majesty, who had previously retired, again into the room, and proceeded to call the votes a second time. This attempt to overawe them incensed the nobility. "What!" said they, "shall the laird of Lethington have power to control us? or shall the presence of a woman cause us to offend God, and to condemn an innocent man, against our consciences?" They then repeated the vote which they had already given, absolving Knox from all offence, and, at the same time, praising his modest appearance, and the judicious manner in which he had conducted his defence.*

The effects of this trial were various and extensive. The Protestant part of the community were justly indignant at the attempt made upon Knox, and alarmed with the proof thereby given of the queen's determined hostility. On the other hand, the queen could not control her indignation at the reformer's escape; and the effects of her resentment fell upon those who had voted for his exculpation, or failed to procure his conviction. The Earl of Murray lost her confidence; and even Lethington sunk in her favour. They attempted to induce Knox to soothe her by a voluntary submission; but to this he would not consent. They next attempted to weaken his influence among his brethren of the ministry, representing to them that Knox exercised a despotic and popish authority in the Church, inconsistent with their freedom and equality.

These secret machinations were met by Knox with his usual open and manly intrepidity of character. At the meeting of the General Assembly in December of the same year, he refused to take part in the public deliberations of the Church, till an inquiry should be made into his conduct in writing the late circular letter, and it should be declared whether he had gone beyond the commission with which he had been intrusted. The court party endeavoured to prevent the discussion of this question; but it was taken up, and the Assembly decided, by a great majority, that he had been charged with such a commission, and that in the advertisement which he had lately given he had not exceeded his powers.

In the preceding Assembly, held in June, one of the most important principles of our existing system of church government was established. It was "statute and ordained," that any person thinking himself aggrieved by the sentence of the kirk-session should have liberty to appeal to the Synod, and, if necessary, from the Synod to the General Assembly, "from which it shall not be lawful to the said party to appeal." There were also various other regulations framed for the perfecting of the judicatorial powers and arrangements of the Church.

It has been already stated, that in the December meeting of Assembly, John Knox was vindicated from the accusation of having convoked the Protestant ministers and elders on his own authority alone. By the same Assembly John Willock was appointed moderator, or president, "to prevent confusion in reasoning." He was the first moderator of the Church of Scotland. This Assembly also passed an act, expressing their consent, "that for their own parts, tenants, and occupiers of the ground should have their own teinds or tithes upon composition;"—a most important arrangement for setting free agricultural industry, preventing harsh and vexatious exactions, and removing one great cause of strife between the Church and the people. This act is another clear proof of the wise and enlightened views of the Scottish reformers, who were in almost every respect very far in advance of their age. It may be mentioned also, that non-residence was prohibited, and one minister suspended, by this Assembly.

[1564.] The year 1564 was not signalized by any events of peculiar importance; but the hostility between the Protestant ministers and the courtiers continued unabated. In the month of June a conference was held between the principal statesmen and the ministers of the Church, respecting the liberty demanded and exercised by the latter of animadverting freely in the pulpit on every topic which concerned the purity of public morals and the welfare of religion. In an elaborate debate with Lethington, Knox defended the leading points of his conduct and doctrine on this subject, which had given offence to the court. "This debate," says Principal Robertson, "admirably displays the talents and character of both the disputants; the acuteness of the former, embellished with learning, but prone to subtlety; the vigorous understanding of the latter, delighting in bold sentiments, and superior to

* Knox, pp. 338-343; M'Crie's Life of Knox, pp. 264-269.

all fear."* The reader who wishes to peruse a full statement of this debate may turn to Knox's History of the Reformation in Scotland, or to the account of it given in Dr. M'Crie's Life of the reformer.†

An Assembly was held in June, in which a committee was appointed to "reason and confer anent the causes of the whole Kirk and jurisdiction thereof," and to report to next Assembly. Permission to go to foreign parts was refused to a minister applying for it, and he was "ordained" not to leave his congregation. The sentence of suspension was taken off from another, and he was restored to his ministry. Another minister was deposed for contumacy. Thus did the Church proceed, completing its arrangements, asserting its authority, and carrying its decrees into actual execution, irrespective of the frowns or smiles of parliaments and courts.

The Assembly met again in December the same year, and directed seven articles respecting the prohibition of the mass, the provision of the ministry, the reparation of kirks, &c., to be presented to the privy council and the queen, requiring an answer to each of the particulars. The rest of its time was occupied with matters of discipline.

[1565.] The year 1565 began with events at first apparently of little moment, yet containing the germs of what proved to be the cause of great individual and national calamity. Towards the close of the preceding year, Matthew Stewart, earl of Lennox, after an exile of twenty years, obtained permission to return to Scotland, and was soon afterwards followed by his son, Henry Stewart, Lord Darnley. It will be remembered by those who are acquainted with Scottish history, that Lennox, besides being himself of royal extraction, had received from Henry VIII. in marriage, his own niece, the Lady Margaret Douglas, uterine sister of James V. of Scotland.

Darnley was thus the nearest heir to both the English and the Scottish crowns, failing any direct heirs from the two reigning queens, Elizabeth and Mary. There was, therefore, at least a political convenience in a union between him and Mary, as likely to preclude any competition for the crown of either country.

It does not appear, however, that Mary was swayed by such considerations, but by the sudden and strong passion which she conceived for the young nobleman himself, almost at the first interview between them. Some of the deeper politicians had, it appears, anticipated as much; and, in particular, Lethington had exerted himself to procure permission from Elizabeth for the return of Lennox and Darnley to Scotland; aware, as he himself declared, that he was thereby likely to incur the direct hostility of the powerful house of Hamilton, whose hopes of succession to the Scottish throne would be thwarted. The Protestant lords, those of them at least whom court influence had not succeeded in corrupting, were from the first dissatisfied with the queen's regard to Darnley, and opposed to her marriage. Darnley, had not, indeed, exhibited any peculiar regard for any religion; but so far as he had indicated his predilections, he appeared to be inclined to Popery. Every endeavour was made by the queen to procure the consent of the nobility to her marriage with Darnley. She even promised to grant the royal sanction to the legal establishment of the Protestant religion, which had been hitherto evaded, as soon as a parliament could be conveniently assembled. On this condition she procured the consent of the greater part of the nobles; but the Earl of Murray continued to refuse, nor could either the entreaties or the threatenings of the queen move him to consent to a measure which his better judgment strongly condemned.

The queen, finding herself thus opposed, resolved upon the ruin of Murray. For this purpose she recalled his personal enemy, the notorious Bothwell, to court, and restored the Huntly family to their forfeited estates and titles. Having thus strengthened her party, Mary hastened her marriage with such precipitation as to anticipate any opposition; and on the 19th of July 1565, the nuptials were solemnized, and Darnley proclaimed king, without the consent of the estates of the kingdom. As Murray had refused his consent to the marriage, Darnley was determined to revenge this oppo-

* Robertson's Hist. of Scotland, vol. ii. p. 109.
† Knox's Hist. pp. 348-366; M'Crie, pp. 273-283.

sition, and during his brief period of influence over the queen, prevailed on her to summon the earl to court. Aware of his danger, Murray refused to come, and was immediately proclaimed an outlaw. He prepared to defend himself: and was joined by the Hamiltons, the Earls of Argyle, Glencairn, and Rothes, Lords Boyd and Ochiltree, and several inferior barons. The queen allowed them no time to consolidate their strength; but hastily levying an army, advanced against them, herself leading on her troops with masculine spirit and energy, and pursuing them from place to place till they took refuge in England.

While these events were in progress, the General Assembly met in Edinburgh on the 25th of June. This was before the queen's marriage, and while she was busied in those artifices by which she hoped to accomplish her purpose. Desirous to secure support from any quarter so long as difficulties were apprehended, she had for a time endeavoured to conciliate the Protestant ministers, and had appointed a conference at Perth, in addition to her promises to call a parliament and ratify the establishment of the reformed Church. Trusting a little to these favourable appearances, the Assembly drew up six articles for her majesty's consideration, desiring her to ratify and approve them in the parliament about to be held. These articles were of the same general tenor as those which had been repeatedly presented before; though they were perhaps somewhat more fully stated, in expectation, probably, of a ratification, which would require minute and specific detail in legal form. The queen, who had no intention of calling a parliament, evaded an immediate answer, and continued to encourage their expectations till after her marriage to Darnley. This took place, it will be remembered, on the 19th of July. At length, on the 21st of August, an answer was returned, sufficiently unfavourable. To put an end to all their hopes of her own conversion, she plainly declared that "her majesty neither will nor may leave the religion wherein she has been nourished and brought up." Her answer to the second article must be stated more fully, as it has frequently been strangely misrepresented and misconstrued in subsequent times, and especially of late.

The article itself was to the following effect:—"That provision be made for the sustentation of the ministers, as well for the time present as for the time to come; that such persons as are presented to the ministry may have their livings assigned to them; that vacant benefices may be dispensed to qualified and learned persons, able to preach God's Word; that no bishopric, abbacy, &c., having many kirks annexed thereto, may be disponed to any one man."

To this the queen answered as follows:—"That her majesty thinks it noway reasonable that she should defraud herself of so great a part of the patrimony of her crown, as to put the patronages of benefices forth of her own hands; for her own necessities in bearing of her great and common charges will require the retention of a good part in her own hands."

When the Assembly met in December the same year, the queen's answers were taken into consideration, and the replies of the Assembly ordered to be again transmitted to her majesty. The reply to the second article was as follows:—"It is not our meaning that her majesty, or any other patron within this realm, should be defrauded of their just patronages. But we mean, whensoever her majesty, or any other patron, does present any person to a benefice, that the person presented should be tried and examined by the judgment of learned men of the Kirk, such as are presently the superintendents appointed thereto: and as the presentation of benefices pertains to the patron, so ought the collation thereof, by law and reason, appertain to the Kirk: of the which collation the Kirk should not be defrauded, more than the patrons of their presentation; for otherwise it shall be lesum [lawful] to the patrons absolutely to present whomsoever they please, without trial or examination: What then shall abide in the Kirk of God but ignorance without all order? As to the second point, concerning the retention of a good part of the benefice in her majesty's own hands, this point abhors so far from good conscience, as well of God's law as from the public order of our common laws. Howsoever the retention of patronages of benefices may appertain to herself, the retention thereof in her own hands undisponed to qualified persons, is both ungodly, and also contrary to all public order, and brings no small confusion to the poor souls of the common people, who by these means should be instructed of their salvation."*

It must, we think, be evident to every unprejudiced and intelligent person, that the queen's answer contained a sophism of that kind which consists in evasively substituting one thing for another, confounding the distinction between them, and reasoning from the substituted topic, as if it were the real one. The article of the petition requested that provision be made for the sustentation of the ministers. The queen makes the topic of patronage the chief point of her answer, yet so as to exhibit her intention to avail herself of the patronage for the purpose of retaining the benefice. It will be remembered that there were only about two hundred strictly lay patronages at the time of the Reformation. With these, viewing them as dependent upon and guarded by civil enactments, the Church did not take it upon herself, of her own authority, to interfere, however much disposed to condemn them, as contrary to the principles and rules of Scripture. This was well known to the person by whom the queen's answer was framed, probably Lethington; and for this reason they were put prominently forward in the answer. But in the reply of the Church the two topics are separated,—the lay patronages left as they were, and the unprincipled and injurious retention of the fruits of the benefice pointed out and condemned. The iniquitous nature of the claim might be placed in a still stronger light, when it is remembered, that two-thirds of the patrimony of the Church had already been either allowed to the rejected clergy, or seized upon by the rapacious nobility; and now the queen, under pretence of her right to certain patronages, unblushingly proposed to retain the fruits of the benefices in her own hands. Those who think to defend patronage by referring to such a transaction, must be either unacquainted with its true nature themselves, or must calculate largely on the ignorance of the public.

* Booke of the Universall Kirk, pp, 34-37.

In the same Assembly the following question was proposed: "What order ought to be used against such as oppress children!" The Assembly's answer was,—"As concerning punishment, the civil magistrate ought therein to discern. As touching the slander, the offenders ought to be secluded from participation in the sacraments till they have satisfied the Kirk, as they shall be commanded." In this clear answer the respective provinces of the civil and the ecclesiastical judicatories are distinctly specified.

[1566.] The year 1566 was pregnant with events of a dark and disastrous character. A decree had been passed by the Council of Trent for the extirpation of the Protestant name; and the popish princes had combined for carrying it into execution. In the beginning of February, a messenger arrived from the cardinal of Lorraine, Mary's uncle, with a copy of that infamous combination known in history as the League of Bayonne, and Mary did not hesitate to set her name to the bloody bond. She seems to have considered herself now possessed of sufficient power to proceed to those extremities which, there is too much reason to believe, she had always contemplated. Darnley had professed himself a convert to Popery, and several of the noblemen had followed his example. Murray and the chief of the Protestant lords were in exile; and to render their return impossible, Mary summoned them to appear before a parliament which was appointed to meet on the 12th of March. The Lords of the Articles were chosen according to the queen's pleasure; the popish ecclesiastics were restored to their place in parliament; and the altars to be erected in St. Giles's Church, for the celebration of the Romish worship, were already prepared.

But the hand of Providence arrested these guilty machinations. Many of the Protestant lords, who had hitherto supported the queen's measures against their former confederates, began to take alarm, some from disappointed ambition, and some from better feelings and worthier motives. The League of Bayonne, and the queen's accession to it, was not unknown to them: and they could not hope long to escape the fate to which all adherents of the Protestant religion were thereby destined, if they did not anticipate the danger. They knew also, that Rizzio, the queen's private secretary, an Italian by birth, was in the confidence of the Continental princes, and the secret manager of their dark intrigues. This person had been for some time treated with an undue degree of confidential regard by the queen, and the jealousy of the king had been excited against him. The nobility formed a secret combination to seize upon Rizzio, and put him to an open and ignominious death; and availing themselves of Darnley's jealousy, they obtained the accession of both him and his father to the plot. It is unnecessary to state the details, which are familiar to all. Rizzio was assassinated; the popish councillors fled from the palace; the exiled lords returned out of England; and the queen's prospects of accomplishing her designs being entirely frustrated, the parliament was prorogued, without accomplishing any of the objects for which it had been assembled. It may be mentioned, in passing, that Mr. Tytler takes the credit, as he probably regards it, of having discovered that John Knox was one of those who were engaged in the conspiracy for the assassination of Rizzio.* Certainly so grave a charge, and so improbable, was never brought forward and maintained on evidence so slender, nay, so absolutely incredible. Its utter groundlessness has been demonstrated by the Rev. Thomas M'Crie, son of the historian of Knox; and the calumnious accusation deserves no farther notice.†

The wrath of the queen against the murderers of Rizzio was so extreme, that it burned out, for a time, all other wrath. The exiled lords, Murray, Glencairn, Ochiltree, and others, were forgiven, or passed over, though not restored to favour as before. But although the Queen managed to detach her weak husband from the confederacy, and thus broke it asunder, she never forgave him, nor showed him the least regard. She had dried her tears that she might "study revenge," as she herself declared; and in the daring and unprincipled Earl of Bothwell she found a fitting instrument.

* Tytler's Hist. of Scotland, vol. vii. p. 25 and 427.

† See Mr. M'Crie's Historical Sketches, Appendix, and note in Appendix.

Her condition retarded for a time the prosecution of her designs; and on the 19th of June she gave birth to a prince, afterwards James VI. of Scotland and I. of England.

Little of importance was transacted in the Assembly which met in June, with the exception of an act appointing a national fast, which was the first instance of the kind since the Reformation. The act was as follows:—"The haill Assembly, in respect of the perils and dangers wherewith the Kirk of God is assaulted, and that by mighty enemies, considered a general fast to be published throughout this realm in all kirks reformed."

In the December meeting of Assembly, permission was granted to John Knox to visit England; and a letter was addressed by the Assembly to the English Church, for the purpose of endeavouring to allay the contentions then raging respecting the forms, ceremonies, and dresses, which the high prelatic party wished to impose upon their more simple-minded brethren. In this apparently trivial cause of contention, it may be remarked, lay the germs of the division of the Church of England into two great parties, the High Churchmen and the Puritans, and, more remotely, of the great civil war of next century. This Assembly also "Ordained a humble supplication to be made to the Lords of the Secret Council, anent the commission of jurisdiction supposed granted to the bishop of St. Andrews, to the effect that their Honours stay the same, in respect that these causes, for the most part judged by his usurped authority, pertain to the true Kirk." Thus did the General Assembly not only define and assert, but vigilantly defend its proper jurisdiction.

[1567.] The public affairs of the year 1567 seemed the bursting of the black thunder-cloud which had hung its baleful gloom over the greater part of the preceding year. The weak, rash, and vindictive Darnley had become an object of utter abhorrence to the ill-fated, haughty, and revengeful queen. Her own too manifest predilection for Bothwell encouraged that licentious and aspiring man to proceed to the perpetration of a crime of the blackest dye, by which he trusted to reach the summit of his ambition. Darnley, despised, dispirited, and suffering under disease, was decoyed to Edinburgh, lodged in a solitary dwelling at the Kirk of Field, and murdered on the morning of the 10th of February, the house in which he lay being blown up with gunpowder. Bothwell was accused of the crime; but his own ill-got power, and the favour of the queen, screened the murderer from justice.

The marriage of Mary to the infamous Bothwell completed at once her crimes and her ruin. After an abortive attempt by Bothwell to obtain possession of the infant prince, the nobility formed a confederacy to avenge the king's death, and protect their infant sovereign. The perpetration of some deed of great enormity seems frequently to paralyze the criminal. Mary's energy of character appeared to have forsaken her immediately after the murder of Darnley. No longer could she, by either force or guile, conquer or circumvent her antagonists. Her troops would not fight for her and her blood-stained paramour; Bothwell fled, and Mary was committed to Lochleven Castle. Her subsequent escape from Lochleven,—the rallying of the Hamiltons and their adherents round her standard,—her defeat, flight to England, protracted imprisonment, and melancholy death,—are all well known to the readers of Scottish history, and need not farther occupy our pages.

During these troubled and guilty times the Assembly met in June, as usual, and soon after adjourned to July. At the latter meeting, the confederate lords specified a number of articles highly favourable to the Church, which they expressed their intention to have granted at the next lawful parliament that should be held.

Before the next meeting of Assembly, in December, the regency had been conferred on the Earl of Murray, who had returned from France, and was thus raised to the head of the government. On the 15th of December parliament met. John Knox preached at the opening of parliament, and exhorted them to begin with the affairs of religion, in which case they would find better success in their other business. The parliament ratified all the acts which had been passed in 1560, in favour of the Protestant religion and against Popery. Several new statutes of a similar kind were added. It was provided, that no prince should afterwards be admitted to the exercise of authority in the kingdom, without taking an oath to maintain the Protestant religion; and that none but Protestants should be admitted to any office, with the exception of those that were hereditary, or held for life. It was ordained, that the examination and admission of ministers be only in the power of the Church, reserving the presentation of lay patronages to the ancient patrons. The ecclesiastical jurisdiction exercised by the Assemblies of the Church was formally ratified, and commissioners appointed to define more exactly the causes which came within the sphere of their judgment. The thirds of benefices were appointed to be paid at first-hand to collectors nominated by the Church, who, after paying the stipends of the ministers, were to account to the Exchequer for the surplus. And the funds of provostries, prebendaries, and chaplainries, were appropriated to maintain bursars in colleges.*

No difference of tone or manner appears in the proceedings of the General Assembly, which met on December the 25th, a few days subsequent to the meeting of that parliament by which its existence and jurisdiction were legally recognised and ratified. It went calmly and steadily forward in the prosecution of those sacred duties which owed neither their existence, their validity, nor their continuation, to any earthly power. Commissioners were appointed to cooperate with "six persons of parliament, or secret council," nominated by the regent, "for such affairs as pertain to the Kirk, and jurisdiction thereof." "Adam, called bishop of Orkney," was deprived of all "function of the ministry," for marrying the queen to Bothwell. John Craig was commanded to give in a written statement of his conduct in proclaiming the banns of marriage between the queen and Bothwell; from which statement it appeared that he had acted in a manner to deserve not only acquittal, but approbation. The Countess of Argyle submitted to the discipline and censure of the Church, "for having given her assistance and presence to the baptizing of the king in a papistical manner."

The reformed Church was now le-

* Act Parl. Scot. III., pp. 14-25. See also Appendix.

gally recognised as the only National Church,—not, it will be observed, created by statute; not deriving its existence from acts of parliament, as has been strangely and perversely, if not ignorantly asserted; but distinctly and specifically recognised as pre-existent, and the powers and jurisdiction which it had already been exercising, in virtue of the sacred character and authority derived from its Divine Head and King, merely ratified and confirmed, so as to place it in a state of safety from the open assaults and persecutions of any human power. It has been thought necessary to be somewhat minute in tracing the rise of the Church of Scotland, and the manner in which it exercised its ecclesiastical powers previous to its recognition by parliament, for the purpose of showing that those powers are wholly and purely self-originated, and not one of them created and conferred by statute law. While still struggling against direct persecution, or the secret stratagems of insidious foes, the General Assembly of the Church of Scotland rose into personal and active being,—put forth supreme legislative powers in regard to the constitution and government of the Church,—sanctioned the office of elder on the authority of the sacred Scriptures,—gave existence and powers to kirk-sessions,—appointed the important though temporary office of superintendents and visitors,—erected provincial synods,—and inflicted on offenders of all ranks, according to their offence and its distinctive judgments, the disciplinary and executive sentences of suspension, deposition, and excommunication. And is it now to be asserted that the Church of Scotland is the "creature of the state!"—the creature of a hostile power, which would have crushed it in its infancy, had that been possible!—or that the Church of Scotland lost her inherent powers by means of the very enactments which gratefully recognised and sanctioned them! Such assertions mere lawyers may utter and pretend to believe; but the common sense and right feelings of mankind in general will ever reject them with indignant scorn; and the true Christian will do as did his venerated ancestors,—reject and resist them with uncompromising firmness and unyielding fortitude, while he pities and prays for his blind and self-willed antagonists.

The limits to which we purpose restricting ourselves in this work will not permit us to enter into details of a very minute character; but one or two statements may be made, calculated to interest the reader. It has been stated that the first General Assembly, in 1560, contained but *forty* members, only *six* of whom were ministers; and that there were no more than *twelve* Protestant ministers at that time in Scotland. When the Assembly met on the 20th of December 1567, exactly seven years afterwards, the Church of Scotland could number two hundred and fifty-two ministers, four hundred and sixty-seven readers, and one hundred and fifty-four exhorters. How mighty the increase in so short a period! And yet these seven years had been spent in an incessant struggle against a hostile government, bent on the destruction of the Church by every artifice that craft and malice could suggest. And while the Church was thus waxing stronger and stronger in spite of all opposition, its internal progress in improvement of doctrine and discipline was not less rapid, steady, and decided, than its manifest external increase. Offenders of every kind and degree were compelled to yield obedience to its sacred authority: noblemen and ladies of the highest rank submitted to its disciplinary censures; lordly prelates were constrained to bow their unmitred heads before its rebuke; over the refractory members of its own body,—over one even of its early champions, Paul Methven,—its power was extended in the impartial administration of even-handed spiritual justice; and even the stormy tumults of a fierce and turbulent populace were often quelled and hushed into peace and silence at the utterance of its calm and grave command. Whence comes that invincible and all-controlling energy? How were these wondrous deeds achieved? May we not answer in the solemn words of the inspired prophet,—"Not by might, nor by power, but by my Spirit, saith the Lord of Hosts." That there must have been a marvellous amount of the divine influence accompanying all the exertions of the Church of Scotland, when the walls of her temple were thus built in troublous times, we cannot, and we do not doubt: for nothing else could have given to means so inadequate a triumph so complete. And let it be well marked and understood, that there is perhaps no clearer proof of the presence of the Spirit of God in the movements of a Church, than when that Church pursues unswervingly the course marked out by the principles of the Word of God, refusing to be turned aside by all the motives which human prudence, apparent expediency, and worldly policy can suggest; and no surer evidence that she has begun to forsake God, and to be by Him forsaken, than when she begins to mould her measures into conformity with the crooked and selfish schemes so natural to the guileful heart and darkened mind of fallen and sinful man.

[1568.] Although the mind of the community was intensely occupied with the contentions which arose between the partizans of Mary and the adherents of the regent, the affairs of religion were not neglected. The Assembly held its usual meetings, and continued to watch over the religious welfare of the kingdom with undiminished vigilance. Proceeding with the completion of their ecclesiastical arrangements, they passed an act in July, regulating the constitution of Assemblies, and prescribing who the members were to be, and how they were to be elected. An act was passed also for the suppression of a book entitled the *Fall of the Roman Kirk*, in which the king was named as the "Supreme Head of the primitive Kirk." By this it was emphatically proved that the Church of Scotland would own no earthly Head. The Assembly renewed its applications to the civil powers for a better distribution of the patrimony of the Church, and a more adequate support to the minister; but although Murray was personally disposed to grant the request, his political power was not sufficiently confirmed to enable him to act according to his own inclination. He returned answers couched in the most favourable terms; but there were too many of his own supporters among those who had seized upon the property of the Church, for him to venture to dispossess the spoliators of their ill-got gains. The utmost that he could accomplish was, to cause a more regular and faithful payment of the third part of the ancient Church revenues, and to prevent any new encroachments from being made upon them.

[1569.] It is neither our province nor our inclination to trace civil affairs, or to intermingle more of them in this work than may be necessary for the right understanding of the affairs of the Church. The civil matters of chief importance which occurred during this period were those which arose out of the struggle between Murray and the partizans of Mary, headed by the Hamilton family. Lethington joined the queen's party, and became the very soul of all their measures. Not only did he plan and conduct the intrigues with the Duke of Norfolk, but he even contrived to seduce Kirkaldy of Grange from his long friendship with Murray. The firm, prudent, and vigorous conduct of the regent enabled him for a time to make head against all open adversaries; and he steadily refused to protect himself from the danger of assassination, by cutting off such persons as were strongly suspected of plotting against his life. The noble magnanimity of his nature would not permit him to resort to such a method for preserving a life more valuable to his country than it seemed to be to himself. In vain was he repeatedly warned to be on his guard. It seemed to be his maxim, that it was better to die than to live haunted by suspicious fears. And notwithstanding the almost incessant conflicts with the opposite faction in which he was engaged, he reformed abuses, maintained public order, and administered justice with steady and impartial hand, so as to earn from his grateful country the honourable appellation of THE GOOD REGENT.

No transactions of any peculiar importance took place in the Assembly in this year. It may, however, be stated, that the Assembly renewed, in urgent terms, the expression of their earnest desire, "that the jurisdiction of the Kirk may be separated from that which is civil." To this the Church was impelled by the conviction, that the drawing of a clear and definite line of distinction between the jurisdiction of the Church and the civil magistrate was essentially necessary for securing the purity of the Church and the peace of the community; and while the ecclesiastical courts were anxious to prevent encroachments upon their own sacred province, they were equally desirous to avoid the accusation, or even the suspicion, of being disposed to interfere with matters purely secular. The often-repeated and earnest request of the Church to have the boundaries between the civil and the ecclesiastical jurisdictions distinctly marked out, ought to vindicate her from the charge of grasping at powers not naturally within her sphere.

[1570.] The year 1570 was ushered in by an event pregnant with disaster to the kingdom and the Church of Scotland. The Regent Murray had hitherto baffled every attempt to overthrow his power by direct hostility; and, as invariably happens, the failure of every successive attempt to shake his influence served but to give it additional firmness and solidity. Despairing of success by open force, his enemies became the more resolved to employ the hand of the private assassin. A fitting instrument was soon found for the perpetration of the bloody crime. Hamilton of Bothwellhaugh, a nephew of the archbishop of St. Andrews, whose life Murray had spared after the battle of Langside, undertook the murder of the man who had restored him to life and liberty. With cool, deliberate determination, he followed the regent from place to place, till he found an opportunity as Murray was passing slowly through a narrow and crowded street in Linlithgow; and, taking his stand at the window of a room carefully prepared for concealment, shot his victim through the body with a musket-ball, on the 23d day of January 1570. The murderer fled to Hamilton, where he was received with great applause by the base instigator of his crime.* The wound proved mortal in the course of a few hours; but it deserves to be recorded, that while the friends of the dying regent, standing around his bed, were lamenting that he had spared the life of his murderer, he replied, that nothing should ever make him regret having done a deed of mercy.

So died the Good Regent Murray, a man of great natural ability, thoroughly tried in many an adverse scene, of unimpeachable integrity, a skilful warrior, a wise statesman, an upright judge, and an impartial ruler. The chief aspect of his private character was that frank and open manliness which suspects no evil because it entertains none; and a deep and earnest personal piety imparted a sacred grace to all the virtues which adorned him as a man and a Christian. During the short period of his regency he gave to the world one of the brightest examples ever yet recorded in its annals, of that rare and truly glorious character, a CHRISTIAN STATESMAN.*

The death of the Regent Murray was not only lamented by the Church to which he had been a protector, if not a benefactor, but was soon regretted by all parties as a national calamity. Several months elapsed before a successor in the regency could be appointed, in consequence of the nearly-balanced power of the contending parties. At length the choice fell upon the Earl of Lennox, not so much on account of his personal fitness for the arduous duties of that high station, as because of his relationship to the young king, whose grandfather he was. It soon appeared that Lennox was deficient in the abilities necessary for swaying the government of a nation so rent by faction as Scotland at that time was; one party supporting the young king and the regency, the other contending for the restoration of the queen. The whole kingdom was devastated by fierce and relentless civil wars; the two contending parties being so equally matched, that neither could acquire a decided superiority over its antagonist. The Church lent its influence to the support of the king's party and the regency, but was unable to mitigate to any extent the fury of the civil broils by which the kingdom was distracted.

Little of importance was transacted in the meetings of Assembly in this year, the distressed state of the country engrossing the attention of all classes. It may, however, be noticed, that the hostility of the queen's faction was so great

* Spotswood, p. 233; Calderwood MSS.; Bannatyne's Journal, p. 4; Buchanan.

* For a strikingly accurate and able view of the character of Murray, see M'Crie's Life of Knox, pp. 307-309.

against Knox, that his own congregation prevailed on him to leave Edinburgh, the castle being in the possession of his enemies, and to retire to St. Andrews. While residing in the latter town, he was engaged in some controversy with Robert and Archibald Hamilton, partly in vindicating his own character from calumnious aspersions, partly in defending the liberty of the pulpit from the attempt of one of the professors to subject it to the judgment of the university.

[1571.] In the Assembly which met in March 1571, there were six articles stated respecting the jurisdiction of the Church, to be proposed to the regent and the privy council, for their approbation. The chief of these were,—that the Church have the judgment of true and false doctrine,—of election, examination, and admission to the ministry,—and of all matters concerning the discipline of the Church,—with the power to enforce its own decisions by admonition, deposition, and excommunication. It ought to be observed, that the Church did not ask the civil power to grant her jurisdiction in these matters, for she had exercised it in them all previous to her recognition in 1567; but merely that she should meet no obstruction in the exercise of her own inherent and essential powers.

But a storm was at hand, by which the Church of Scotland was to be severely tried. Reference has been repeatedly made to the avaricious conduct of the nobility, in seizing upon the revenues of the Church, and keeping the ministers in poverty. It will be remembered also, that the popish prelates had been allowed to retain two-thirds of the revenues of the larger benefices during their lifetime, although they were no longer recognised as any part of the National Church. Several of these larger benefices had begun to become vacant by the death or the forfeiture of the incumbents, and it was necessary to determine in what manner they were to be disposed of. Had the uniform request of the Church been attended to, this would not have been a matter of any difficulty: she had always required that they should be divided, and applied to the support of the religious and literary establishments. Willingly would the nobility have seized these large benefices as they became vacant, and appropriated them to themselves without scruple, could they have done so without a violation of all law and reason too glaring for even these unscrupulous men. To have secularized them at once was a measure for which they were not prepared; and, indeed, they must have been well aware, that to do so would only be to throw another element of strife into the seething whirlpool of contention with which the country was agitated. The Earl of Morton found means to solve this difficulty. Upon the death of Hamilton, archbishop of St. Andrews, Morton obtained a grant empowering him to dispose of the archbishopric and its revenues. As it was unseemly for him to hold a benefice which the law declared to be ecclesiastical, while his avarice stimulated him not to let the golden prize elude his grasp, he devised the scheme of appointing to the archbishopric a minister with whom he had entered into a previous arrangement, that while his nominee held the title, he should enjoy the principal part of the revenues. In pursuance of this scheme, Morton nominated John Douglas, rector of the University of St. Andrews, to the archbishopric. This nefarious transaction set the example to the nobility, who perceiving how it might be imitated for their own private and selfish ends, supported Morton, and prepared to render it systematic and universal.

The danger to the interests of religion certain to arise out of this selfish and corrupt scheme, did not escape the penetrating eye of Knox, by whom, indeed, it had been previously suspected. He was at that time at St. Andrews, too weak in bodily health to be able to attend a meeting of Assembly, which was to be held at Stirling in August 1571, in consequence of the dangerous state of Edinburgh, the castle being still in possession of the queen's party. In a letter to this Assembly, he warned them of the nature of the struggle in which they were about to engage, the certainty that it would be severe and protracted, and the necessity of courage, perseverance, and the most strenuous exertions in so good a cause.* The Assembly gave in their remonstrances to a parliament which met in Stirling

* Booke of the Universall Kirk, p. 128.

in the end of August, especially protesting against Douglas taking a seat in parliament and voting, on pain of excommunication. Morton, on the other hand, whose influence was paramount in parliament, commanded him to vote, as archbishop of St. Andrews, on pain of treason.* The commissioners of the Church presented also the articles respecting the jurisdiction of the Church, which had been previously agreed upon by the Assembly.

While the parliament was sitting at Stirling, a bold attempt was made by the queen's party to end the war by one blow. A considerable body of men marched under night with great speed and secrecy to Stirling, entered the town before any alarm was given, assailed the houses in which the nobility were lodged, seized on them, and on the regent himself, and endeavoured to carry them off prisoners to Edinburgh. But their progress had been retarded by the vigorous defence made by the Earl of Morton, who beat back the assailants till the house was set on fire, and thereby gave time to the Earl of Mar to hasten from the castle to the rescue of the regent and the nobility. Finding themselves baffled in their attempt, the assailants fled; but the regent was killed by command of Lord Claude Hamilton, in revenge for the death of the archbishop of St. Andrews. This disastrous event took place on the 3d of September; and on the 5th, the Earl of Mar was appointed regent. This change in the regency was productive of no advantage to the Church; for though Mar was not disposed to tyrannize himself, he had several years before laid hold of a large portion of church property, which he was not inclined to relinquish, and he was, besides, very much under the influence of the Earl of Morton, whose feelings were decidedly hostile to the Church, as he had sufficiently indicated only a few days before, when he told the commissioners of the Church, that "he would lay their pride, and put order to them."†

The Earl of Mar, however, was not disposed to press forward these innovations with so high a hand as Morton would have done. Morton procured from him letters prohibiting the collectors of tithes in St. Andrews from raising the money, because they had refused to bestow the sums raised on his creature Douglas; but Erskine of Dun having written a very strong remonstrance to the regent against such proceedings, this direct aggression was recalled. In this letter Erskine manifests a very clear perception of the essential distinction between the civil and ecclesiastical jurisdictions. "There is," says he, "a spiritual jurisdiction and power, which God has given unto his Kirk, and to them that bear office therein; and there is a temporal jurisdiction and power given of God to kings and civil magistrates. Both the powers are of God, and most agree to the fortifying one of the other, if they be right used. But when the corruption of man enters in, confounding the offices, usurping to himself what he pleases, nothing regarding the good order appointed of God, then confusion follows in all estates. The Kirk of God should fortify all lawful power and authority that pertains to the civil magistrate, because it is the ordinance of God. But if he pass the bounds of his office, and enter within the sanctuary of the Lord, meddling with such things as appertain to the ministers of God's Kirk, then the servants of God should withstand his unjust enterprise, for so are they commanded of God."*

This clear and strong assertion of the distinction between the respective jurisdiction of the courts civil and spiritual, is of double importance, both as showing the sentiments of such a man as John Erskine of Dun, whose chief failing was a tendency to yield disputed matters for the sake of peace; and also as proving beyond all question what were the views on that vital point of the Church of Scotland in the days of the first reformers. It may be added, that in the same letter Erskine "lamented from his very heart the great disorder used in Stirling at the last parliament, in creating bishops, placing them, and giving them vote in parliament as bishops, in despite of the Kirk, and high contempt of God, the Kirk opposing herself against that disorder:" so little favour did the idea of Protestant bishops find in the opinion of our re-

* Calderwood, p. 48; Bannatyne's Memorials, p. 183.
† Calderwood, p. 48.

* Bannatyne's Mem., pp. 197-204; Calderwood, p. 48.

forming ancestors. Even Dr. Cook terms this measure "plainly subversive of ecclesiastical right;"* although that reverend and learned historian appears to regard the subversion of ecclesiastical right as consisting in this measure being "adopted without the concurrence of the Church, and even in express opposition to it;" whereas, he seems to insinuate, to have first corrupted the Church, and then changed its constitution, would have been no such subversion. The regent appears to have been of the same opinion; for he changed his measures so far as to recall the letters which had drawn forth Erskine's remonstrance; and wrote an explanatory letter, in which he complains that his intentions were misunderstood, and that "the fault of the whole stands in this, that the policy of the Kirk of Scotland is not perfect, nor any solid conference among godly men, that are well willed and of judgment, how the same may be helped."†

It would appear that the regent's influence had prevailed upon Erskine to yield farther than his own principles would have sanctioned. A convention of ministers had been appointed to confer with the privy council, on the 6th of December. This was postponed, in consequence of Erskine's letter to the regent; but another was soon afterwards appointed to meet in Leith, for the same purpose.

[1572.] On the 12th of January 1572, the regent convened the superintendents and certain ministers at Leith, to consult on the best method of allaying the dissension which had arisen between the court and the Church. This convention imprudently and wrongfully assumed to itself the powers of a General Assembly; and, advancing in its erroneous course, devolved the whole business on a few of its members, authorising them to meet with such persons as should be appointed by the privy council, and agreeing to ratify whatever they might determine, agreeably to their instructions. A joint committee was accordingly formed of six of the privy council and six ministers, who proceeded with strange and reckless haste in the arrangement of matters of such great national importance.‡

The convention of Leith agreed that, "in consideration of the present time," the titles of archbishops and bishops, and the bounds of dioceses, should remain as formerly, at least until the king's majority, or until the parliament should make a different arrangement; that such as were admitted to bishoprics should be of due age and scriptural qualifications; that they should be chosen by a chapter, or assembly of learned ministers; and that they should have no greater jurisdiction than was already possessed by superintendents, but should, like them, be subject to the General Assemblies of the Church in Spiritual, as they were to the King in temporal matters. The reader is requested to mark well this latter article, subjecting these prelates to the authority of the General Assembly. It was inserted, doubtless, for the purpose of inducing the Church to agree the more readily to this great innovation; but remaining unrepealed, it proved in after years the means by which the Church was enabled to overthrow Prelacy, and restore the original constitution of the Presbyterian Church of Scotland. Arrangements of a similar nature were made with regard to abbacies, priories, &c.; so that, while the holder of these large benefices were to be admitted to sit in parliament, and to be members of the College of Justice, as such dignitaries had done before the Reformation, they were to be admitted after due trial by the Church, and still to be amenable to her supreme court. This agreement was immediately confirmed by the regent and council, who engaged to persuade the lay patrons of churches to conform to such of its regulations as concerned them.

By this strange heterogeneous compound of Popery, Prelacy, and Presbytery, the avaricious nobility imagined they had secured their long-cherished design of obtaining for themselves the real possession of the wealth of the Church, while it was nominally held by these mean sycophants: and although the true nature of the transaction was

* Cook's History of the Church of Scotland, vol. i. p. 169. † Bannatyne's Mem., p. 206.

‡ The names of the persons forming this convention deserve to be recorded, not to their honour: the Earl of Morton, Lord Ruthven, Robert, abbot of Dunfermline, Sir John Bellenden, Mr. James M'Gill, and Colin Campbell of Glenorchy, of privy council; John Erskine, John Winram, Andrew Hay, David Lindsay, Robert Pont, and John Craig, ministers. See Spotswood, p. 260; Calderwood, MSS., vol. ii. p. 310, &c printed Calderwood, pp. 50-54.

not suffered to appear in their records, the object was well enough understood by the country in general, as appears from the designation given to the new order of bishops. In allusion to a custom at that time prevalent in the Highlands, of placing a calf's skin stuffed with straw, called a *tulchan*, before cows to induce them to give their milk, those who were placed in this new prelatic order were called *tulchan bishops.* "The bishop," says Calderwood, "had the title, but my lord got the milk or commoditie."

Having thus obtained the apparent sanction of the Church to these guileful proceedings, the nobility, led by Morton, hastened to put them in execution. The archbishopric of St. Andrews was conferred on John Douglas, as had been previously attempted; and he was publicly installed in his office, his ordination being performed by men who were not themselves bishops. The Earl of Morton had the effrontery to request John Knox to inaugurate Douglas; but he positively refused, and pronounced an anathema against both the giver and the receiver of the bishopric; and when the Assembly met in St. Andrews a few weeks afterwards, and the matters agreed upon by the convention of Leith came to be discussed, Knox opposed himself directly and zealously to the making of bishops.* Even Patrick Adamson at that time was a strenuous opponent of Prelacy; though, as James Melville shrewdly conjectures, his zeal may have been caused at his disappointment at not obtaining one of the new bishopricks. "There were," said Adamson, "three sorts of bishops: my lord bishop, my lord's bishop, and the Lord's bishop. My lord bishop was in the papistrie; my lord's bishop is now, when my lord gets the benefice, and the bishop serves for nothing but to make his title sure; and the Lord's bishop is the true minister of the Gospel."† It had been well for Adamson if he had always continued to maintain and act upon such sound and scriptural opinions.

At the Assembly which met in Perth, in August the same year, the convention of Leith came again under consideration, and a committee was appointed to examine the subject. The report of the committee disclaimed the intention of giving any countenance to popish superstitions, by the titles recognised in the convention; and protested that the heads and articles thereat agreed on be received only as an *interim*, till farther order may be obtained at the hands of the king's majesty, regent, and nobility, for which they will press as occasion shall serve.* To that Assembly John Knox sent a letter, in which he took a solemn farewell of them, and of all public affairs, commending the Church earnestly to the protection of God, and imploring the divine grace to strengthen them for the contest they had still to wage. In a message accompanying that letter he proposed several topics for their consideration, to be turned into acts of Assembly if approved of; and in these topics may be traced the deep and far-seeing prudence of the great Reformer. He did not advise a direct opposition to the articles of the convention of Leith, being probably but too well aware, that those to whom the management of the affairs of the Church would now fall, did not possess the courage and decision of mind requisite for such a struggle; but he recommended a measure which, if it had been adopted and enforced, would have defeated the mercenary views of both the nobility and their tulchan bishops. But though his advice was approved of, the courage and energy to carry it into execution were not found; and the articles of the ill-omened convention were allowed for a time to produce their baneful consequences, in the corruption of the Church, and the enjoyment of their pillage by the rapacious nobility.

The public national affairs of this year may be very briefly stated. The earl of Mar, who had been elevated to the regency upon the death of Lennox, was, though not a little of an avaricious man, well-disposed and unwilling to excite strife, or to see it prolonged. But he was overruled by the earl of Morton, and thereby brought into collision with the Church; and he was not able either to compel the queen's party to submit, or to procure a satisfactory termination of those dire hostilities by which the king

* Melville's Diary, p. 24.
† Ibid., p. 25; Calderwood, p, 55.

* Booke of the Universall Kirk, p. 133.

dom was devastated. Anxiety of mind is said to have contributed greatly to the bringing on of the disease of which he died on the 29th of October 1572. Soon after his death the earl of Morton succeeded to the regency, of which he had for some time wanted little but the name. On the very day in which Morton was appointed regent, the 24th of November, John Knox, the Scottish reformer, rested from his long and arduous labours; and on the 26th, the newly-elected regent, accompanied by all the nobility at that time in Edinburgh, and a great concourse of people, attended his funeral. When the body was lowered into the grave, the regent, himself one of the daring race of Douglas, gazing thoughtfully into the open sepulchre, gave utterance to what, from his lips, was a most emphatic eulogium, "THERE LIES HE WHO NEVER FEARED THE FACE OF MAN."

The death of Knox at such a juncture was a serious calamity to the Church of Scotland. Morton knew well that he had now men of a different character to deal with,—men who might be cajoled, and could be daunted. He proceeded, therefore, with the execution of his schemes more openly and forcibly, and also made more use of those intrigues in which he was such an adept, than he would have attempted to do, bold and designing as he was, if he had still had to encounter the piercing sagacity and dauntless courage of John Knox. In like manner, the Assembly felt the want of his clear judgment and intrepid spirit in its councils. It reeled and staggered like a storm-tossed vessel, when the pilot's hand has ceased to guide the rudder. There still remained, indeed, a number of excellent men, sincerely attached to the principles upon which the Reformation had been established in Scotland, and not incapable, in more peaceful times, to have defended them. But they were comparatively paralyzed by their recent loss, by the new difficulties with which they had to contend, and by the combined subtlety and sternness of that bold bad man, the regent Morton.

[1573.] Morton accordingly, advanced almost unchecked in his career. To this he was incited by an additional reason, which now began to influence his mind. He had entered into a close correspondence with queen Elizabeth, and guided all his policy according to her maxims and example. And perceiving how skillfully she contrived to make her influence, as head of the Church of England, bend all the bishops into complete subserviency to her will, and through them, to mould the mind of the nation, he was the more confirmed in his determination to change the entire constitution of the Church of Scotland, till it should become as prelatic and as accommodating as that of England. This, he had sagacity enough to perceive, could be done only by rendering it as corrupt and worldly as possible; which, again, could be best accomplished by placing sycophants and unprincipled men in these nominally influential positions which he had created and forced upon the Church. But, not content with his tulchan bishops, he endeavoured further to impoverish the Church, that he might thereby both enrich himself,—a matter which he never neglected,—and at the same time induce its poverty, if not its will, to consent to his pernicious measures. He contrived to draw into his own hands the thirds of benefices, offering more sure and ready payment to the ministers than had been made previously by their own collectors, and promising to make the stipend of each minister local, and payable in the parish where he laboured. But no sooner had he obtained the thirds into his own hands, than he joined two, three, or even four parishes together, appointing to them, by means of his obedient creatures, the tulchan bishops, but one minister, who was obliged to preach in them by turns. Morton paying him as if he had but one charge, and retaining the remaining stipends for his own purposes.

Against this nefarious conduct the Church continued to remonstrate, but in vain. The utmost that the Assembly could do was to attempt to control the proceedings of the bishops as much as was practicable, in virtue of the authority over such persons which, even by the convention of Leith, they continued to possess.

[1574.] The struggle continued, with somewhat of increasing energy on the part of the Church, and with at least undiminished determination on that of the regent. The Assembly not only asserted its supremacy over bishops, but even exercised it with unexpected firmness, both by a strong remonstrance presented to the regent, and by directly censuring the bishop of Dunkeld for his improper conduct,—evincing clearly the determination of the Church of Scotland to maintain and exercise its jurisdiction. It may be stated in passing, that the assembly had proceeded to take both these steps before the influence of Andrew Melville could have even begun to be felt, as he did not arrive in Scotland till the beginning of July, and the assembly by which the bishop of Dunkeld was censured met on the 7th of August, only a few weeks after Melville's arrival, and while he was still residing in privacy with his relations. The noticing of such a matter will not seem too minute to those who are aware how much Episcopalians are in the habit of ascribing the decided Presbyterian form of church government in Scotland to the personal inflence of Andrew Melville, who had brought, say they, from Geneva the opinions of Calvin and Beza, and succeeded in infusing them into the Scottish ministers, who had previously been favourable to a modified prelacy. This modified prelacy they pretend to find, partly in the superintendents appointed by John Knox, and partly in the tulchan bishops of the convention of Leith, whom they affect to regard as merely the natural, but somewhat more properly appointed and ordained, successors of the superintendents. Our readers are, we trust, in the possession of information sufficient to enable them to detect at once the fallacy of all such statements, and to come to the conclusion unhesitatingly, that the reformed Church of Scotland was from the beginning, and always has been, so far as she has been enabled to exhibit and act upon her own principles, decidedly opposed to Prelacy, taking neither her creed, her form of government, nor her discipline, from any other church, but from the word of God alone, and in principle, aim, and endeavour, always essentially and determinedly Presbyterian.

Andrew Melville, as has been already stated, arrived in Scotland in the beginning of July 1574, after an absence of ten years from his native country. Though personally a stranger, his eminent character as a man of learning and talents was well known to his countrymen. The regent Morton, aware that such a man must soon acquire extensive influence over the public mind, attempted to secure him for an agent in the prosecution of his own designs. For this purpose he caused some of his own confidential friends to wait on Melville, and propose that he should act as domestic instructor to the regent, with a promise of advancement to a situation more suited to his merits, on the first vacancy that might occur. Had Melville acceded to this proposal, and fallen into the regent's schemes, he might have enabled that crafty statesman to rivet securely the fetters with which he was striving to bind the Church, instead of being mightily instrumental in wrenching them asunder. But though it does not appear that Melville was at that time at all aware of Morton's designs, his predilections led him to prefer an academical life to that of a courtier, and he therefore declined the proposal.

[1575.] The Assembly which met in March 1575, went boldly forward in the reforming process begun by its predecessor of the year before, and passed an act requiring the knowledge of Latin in every person appointed to a benefice; which act was intended to oppose the corrupt practice of many of the nobility, who were in the habit of appointing ignorant persons, servants, and even children, to benefices; such appointments being readily ratified by the corrupt and servile bishops, regarding it probably as the regular discharge of an essential part of their *tulchan* function. A small committee was also appointed to confer with the regent's commissioners respecting the policy and jurisdiction of the Church. As this subject had been very frequently made the topic of application, the convention of estates had come to the conclusion that some measure must be framed to put an end to the uncertainty which prevailed on such matters. Spotswood says that the regent sent to the General Assembly to require of them whether they would stand to the policy agreed to at Leith; and if not, to desire them to settle upon some form of government at which they would abide.* The Assembly was not unwilling to follow up this suggestion. They not only appointed a committee to confer with the parliamentary commissioners, but also selected such of their own body as were known to have most thoroughly studied the subject, directing them to prepare a complete outline of ecclesiastical policy and discipline, to be submitted to the Assembly for consideration, and, if approved of, for ratification. It deserves to be remarked, that the regent did not presume to appoint commissioners to draw up a book of discipline which the Church must receive; but requested them to frame, according to their own principles, some form of government by which they would abide. In this very instance there is the most distinct recognition of the inherent right of the Church to act freely upon its own principles, in the formation of its rules of government and discipline.

In the Assembly which met in August the same year, John Dury, one of the ministers of Edinburgh, protested that the examination of the conduct of the bishops should not prejudge what he and other brethren had to object against the lawfulness of their name and office. This protest led to a discussion, in which Andrew Melville took a distinguished part, and the discussion brought on a formal reasoning on the question, "Have bishops, as they are now in Scotland, their function from the Word of God, or not? and ought the chapters appointed for electing them to be tolerated in a reformed Church?" To these searching questions, answers of a somewhat indefinite character were returned by those whom the Assembly had appointed to confer and report; but the very moving of such questions was a sufficiently significant indication of the opinions held by the Church of Scotland.

In the meantime, Morton, who was well aware of the prevalent feelings of the Church, and knew also that it was in vain to attempt direct compulsion, endeavoured to corrupt the most influential ministers, that he might by their means mould the Assembly to his mind. To gain Andrew Melville was his great object; and this he tried to do by offering to him the living of Govan, Melville being at that time principal of Glasgow college. Not succeeding in this attempt, he tried a higher bribe, and offered Melville the archbishopric of St. Andrews, upon the death of Douglas. But all bribes were equally ineffectual, and the crafty regent thought proper to conceal his displeasure.

[1576.] The question respecting bishops, which had been raised in the preceding Assembly, received a tolerably distinct answer in that which met in April 1576. This answer was, "That the name of bishop is common to all who are appointed to take charge of a particular flock, in preaching the Word, administering sacraments, and exercising discipline with the consent of their elders; and that this is their chief function according to the Word of God." And still proceeding with their important work, a large commission was appointed to prosecute the formation of a complete and systematic work on the policy and jurisdiction of the Church. Spotswood complains piteously, that in these Assemblies, in which the office of a bishop, as then exercised by the tulchan prelates in Scotland, was called in question, not one of six bishops who were present spoke a single word in defence of their office. They may be forgiven; some abuses are so glaringly indefensible, that even those who could tolerate their existence cannot muster effrontery enough to defend them.

Although the regent had failed to bribe Melville to aid in his nefarious attempts, he found others more accessible to his golden persuasives. Patrick Adamson, who, on the installation of Douglas, had expressed his condemnation of "my lord's bishop" so pointedly, had been gained over by Morton, and was by him presented to the archbishopric of St. Andrews. This was stated to the Assembly which met in October, and he was required to submit himself to trial before admission, agreeably to the act which had been passed to that effect. Adamson, declined on the ground that the regent had forbidden him to comply, "in respect the said act and ordinance of the Kirk is not accorded on." The Assembly prohibited the chapter from proceeding in the matter; but Morton commanded them to proceed, in disregard of the Assem-

* Spotswood, p. 276.

bly's prohibition, and gave him admission to the archbishopric.

[1577.] The contest between Morton and the Church continued, the regent being unwilling to relinquish his favourite tulchan system, and the Church being equally determined to put an end to an abuse so manifest and pernicious. At the meeting of the Assembly in April 1577, Adamson was interdicted from the exercise of his prelatic authority, until he should be regularly admitted by the Church; and a commission was appointed to summon him before them, investigate his case, and judicially determine it. A committee was appointed to confer with the regent respecting the discipline and jurisdiction of the Church; and those who were engaged in preparing the systematic work on those points, were required to proceed with their labours.

It was probably on this occasion that the regent, irritated at the steady opposition of the Church, and also at his failure to influence Melville by mercenary considerations, attempted to intimidate and overbear him. Morton complained that the Church and the kingdom were kept in a perpetual state of confusion and strife by certain persons, who sought to introduce their own private conceits and foreign laws on points of ecclesiastical government. Melville replied, that he and his brethren took the Scriptures, and not their own fancies, or the mode of any foreign Church, for the rule and standard of the discipline which they defended. Morton said, as Queen Mary had formerly done, that the General Assembly was a convocation of the kings's subjects, and that it was treasonable for them to meet without his permission. To this Melville answered, that if it were so, then Christ and his apostles must have been guilty of treason, for they called together great multitudes, and taught and governed them, without asking the permission of magistrates. The regent, unable to refute the reasoning of Melville, and almost losing command of his temper, biting the head of his staff, growled, in that deep under-tone which marked his occasional fits of cold, black, ruthless anger,—"There will never be quietness in this country till half-a-dozen of you be hanged or banished." "Tush, Sir," replied Melville, "threaten your courtiers after that manner. It is the same to me whether I rot in the air or in the ground. The earth is the Lord's. My country is wherever goodness is. *Patria est ubicunque est bene.* I have been ready to give my life where it would not have been half so well expended, at the pleasure of my God. I have lived out of your country two years, as well as in it. Let God be glorified; it will not be in your power to hang or exile his truth."*

Morton felt himself for once outdared; but, however indignant, he did not venture to put his threats into execution. He seems to have been aware that to proceed to use force would be to ensure the defeat of his intentions; and therefore he gave a comparatively favourable answer to the Assembly respecting their labours in preparing a Book of Policy. But as his intentions were by no means altered, he endeavoured to turn the Assembly aside from its endeavours to perfect its own policy, by employing Adamson to frame a number of frivolous and captious questions, to which he wished answers to be given. He was also not a little embarrassed in political matters. His administration had been so severe, accompanied with so much of a base avaricious spirit, that it had become intolerable to a large portion of the kingdom, including many of the most influential of the nobility. He felt his power on the wane, and would have been disposed to court the support of the Church, of which he gave some intelligible indications, had the crisis of his fate not come on too rapidly to give time for a sufficient modification of his measures.

[1578.] On the 6th of March 1578, Morton resigned his regency, and King James formally assumed the reins of government, although, being still only in his twelfth year, it was in reality little more than a nominal assumption, the real power passing from Morton, not into the hands of the king, but of a new court favourite. When the Assembly met in April 1578, they proceeded to consider the system of ecclesiastical polity which their committee had been employed for some time in framing; and its articles having been read over one by one, the whole received, after mature deliberation, the

* Melville's Diary, pp. 52, 53.

sanction of the General Assembly. The system of ecclesiastical government and discipline thus deliberately prepared and formally sanctioned, is known by the name of the Second Book of Discipline; and from that time forward was, and continues still to be, the authorised standard of the Church of Scotland, in respect of government and discipline.

The same Assembly agreed, that the bishops should, for the future, be addressed in the same style as other ministers; and in case of a vacancy occurring in any bishopric, they prohibited the chapters from proceeding to a new election before next meeting of Assembly. Commissioners were also appointed to lay the Book of Discipline before the king and council; and in case a conference was desired respecting it, commissioners were named for such conference. Thus did the Church advance in the maturing of her own principles and forms of government and discipline; and having completed what she thought requisite for regulating her own conduct in matters of a spiritual character, she sought that ratification of the system by the civil court which should protect her from the undue interference of any hostile power, and at the same time give civil effect to all such ecclesiastical decisions as naturally involved civil consequences.

The Assembly which met in the following June extended to all future time the act regarding the election of bishops, ordaining that no new bishops should be made thenceforward. It was also ordained, that the existing bishops should "submit themselves to the General Assembly concerning the reformation of the corruption of that estate of bishops in their own persons," under pain of being excommunicated, in the event of their obstinate refusal. The bishop of Dunblane, who was present, immediately submitted, according to the act.

Soon after this Assembly closed its sittings, a conference took place between the commissioners of the Church and a commission appointed by the parliament, at that time met in Stirling, where the king was then residing. Spotswood has preserved the results of this conference in the marginal remarks made upon a copy of the Book of Discipline which was laid before the commission of Parliament.* In these marginal comments the most important of the articles are marked as "agreed;" some, chiefly relating to church government, are "referred to further reasoning," and others are agreed to with some slight verbal explanations. Upon the whole, so far as this conference was concerned, the Church had reason to regard her essential principles and regulations as adopted and ratified by the state virtually, and waiting but a more full discussion to be formally confirmed. By the same parliament an act was passed closely resembling the acts of 1567, and ratifying and approving all acts and statutes previously made, agreeable to God's Word, for the maintenance of the liberty of the "true Kirk of God."

Another Assembly was held in October the same year, partly to consider the result of the conference at Stirling, and partly to proceed in the exercise of their own inherent authority, stripping the prelates of their usurped and misused powers, and removing their corruptions.

[1579.] Before the Assembly again met, and before the Parliament had completely ratified the Book of Discipline, which it had seemed on the point of doing, the Earl of Morton regained his ascendency, and once more swayed the councils of the nation, although no longer in his own name. The favourable sentiments of the king were soon changed; and as the Church continued to exercise its authority over the tulchan bishops manufactured by Morton, the king was prevailed upon to interfere with its jurisdiction, and to arrest, by means of orders in council, the execution of the acts of the Assembly, and its sentences of excommunication. The Assembly which met in July 1579, received a letter from the king, in which he objected to the proceedings against the bishops. The letter did not, however, deter the Assembly from both persevering in its course, and remonstrating against this interference with its inherent right of spiritual jurisdiction.

A parliament was held in October the same year, in which the attempted encroachments of the king were not countenanced; but, on the contrary, two of the acts of 1567 were expressly re-enacted,

* Spotswood, pp. 289-302.

and inserted anew in the record. Little however, was done in this parliament either for or against the Church. The elements of political strife and intrigue were too numerous and active to allow mere politicians to direct their attention to what they have always regarded as matters of comparatively slight importance. The Earl of Morton was no longer regent; but the influence of the veteran statesman was still so great, that the young aspirants to political power felt that their own ascendency could be securely founded only on his ruin. The king had already shown his disposition to favoritism,—that prevalent vice of weak and irresolute minds; and, as might have been expected, his favourites were those who could rule by flattering, not guide by instructing him. These favourites were Esme Stewart, his own cousin, whom he speedily raised to the dukedom of Lennox; and Captain James Stewart, second son of Lord Ochiltree, afterwards created Earl of Arran. The former had been brought up in France, and was, on his arrival in Scotland, an adherent of the Church of Rome, though not long afterwards he declared himself a convert to the Protestant faith. The latter was a bold, unprincipled, licentious man, capable of any crime, and possessing considerable craft in devising, as well as daringness in executing, his ambitious designs. To such men, it may be easily supposed, the Church of Scotland was an object of dislike; and, so far as their influence extended, they, especially Arran, were its natural foes.

[1580.] The Assembly, perceiving that their desire to have the corrupt form of pseudo-prelacy abolished, and the Book of Discipline ratified, was continually evaded by the civil magistrate, whether regent or king, resolved to put forth their own inherent powers, both in removing abuses, and in completing their own judicial and disciplinary arrangements. Accordingly, the Assembly which met in Dundee in July 1580 passed an act declaring, that the office of a bishop, as it was then used and commonly understood, was destitute of warrant and authority from the Word of God, was of mere human invention, introduced by folly and corruption, and tended to the great injury of the Church; ordaining farther, that all such persons as were in possession of the said pretended office should be charged *simpliciter* to demit it, as an office whereunto they were not called by God; appointing the places and times at which they should appear before the provincial synods, and signify their submission to this act. This remarkable act was agreed to by "the whole Assembly with one voice, after liberty given to all men to reason in the matter, none opposing himself in defending the said pretended office."* So great was the influence of the Assembly, that notwithstanding the reluctance of the "pretended bishops" to relinquish their usurped power and wealth, and the opposition of the nobility to the loss of their *tulchans*, and of the *milk* thereby extracted, the whole assumed order submitted, with the exception of five, in the course of the year in which the act abolishing Episcopacy was passed.†

[1581.] The year 1581 was an important one in the history of the Church of Scotland. The labours of the ablest men in the Church had been expended for several years in the preparation of a regular system of ecclesiastical polity. This had been at length matured, made the subject of conference with the privy council, their remarks considered by the Church, and the book again laid before the king and council, with the earnest request that it might obtain the full ratification of an act of parliament. But finding their endeavours still thwarted and evaded, the Assembly resolved to temporize no longer; but as they had already guided their conduct generally in accordance with its principles, they determined now to erect it, by an act of Assembly, into the condition of their avowed and accredited standard of government and discipline. Several of its provisions had been already in operation. Even in 1579 the Assembly had proceeded so far towards the erection of presbyteries, that they had decreed that "the exercise [or weekly meeting of the ministers and elders of contiguous, parishes] might be judged a presbytery."‡ The king, following, as usual the course of the Church, sent to the As-

* Booke of the Universall Kirk, p. 194.
† Calderwood MSS., vol. ii. p. 636.
‡ Booke of the Universall Kirk, p, 192.

sembly, which met at Glasgow in April 1581, by his commissioner, Cunningham of Caprington, a request that the Assembly would proceed with the erection of presbyteries, for the purpose of "bringing the ecclesiastical discipline to be far better exercised and executed over all the realm than it had previously been." This request was readily complied with; and an act was passed erecting at once thirteen presbyteries, and recommending the speedy extension of the system throughout the kingdom.

By another act of the same Assembly, the Second Book of Discipline was ordained to be registered in the acts of the Church, and to remain therein, *ad perpetuam rei memoriam*, and copies thereof to be taken by every presbytery.* By the same Assembly another act was passed, ratifying what has often been termed Craig's Confession of Faith, because it was drawn up by John Craig. It is also known by the designation of THE FIRST NATIONAL COVENANT OF SCOTLAND, and forms the first part of every subsequent national covenant entered into by the Church and people of Scotland. The occasion of its being framed and subscribed at this time was the jealousy entertained by the nation of the Duke of Lennox and other nobles, who either openly avowed their adherence to the Church of Rome, or were suspected of attachment to the creed of that dreaded and detested perversion of Christianity. This covenant was subscribed by the king himself, his household, and the greater part of the nobility and gentry throughout the kingdom, and ratified by the Assembly, as has been stated above, and the signing of it zealously promoted by the ministers in every part of the country. The interim office of "readers" was suppressed by this Assembly, because there was now a sufficient number of ministers to supply the churches throughout the kingdom. In this it will be observed that the Church acted with regard to readers exactly as it had done with regard to the other interim offices of superintendents and visitors. They had been called into existence, as an extraordinary office, to meet the necessities of the time; and when these necessities ceased, the extraordinary offices naturally expired, leaving the ordinary and permanent to carry on the healthful functions of the matured Church.

* Booke of the Universall Kirk, p. 218.

As the Second Book of Discipline, being thus engrossed in the acts of Assembly, must be regarded as the standard of the Church of Scotland in respect of government and discipline, it seems expedient to give a brief summary of its leading propositions, referring those who wish more minute information to the work itself.

It begins by stating the essential line of distinction between civil and ecclesiastical power. This it does by declaring, that Jesus Christ has appointed a government in his Church, distinct from civil government, which is to be exercised by such office-bearers as He has authorised, and not by civil magistrates, or under their direction. Civil authority has for its direct and proper object the promoting of external peace and quietness among the subjects; ecclesiastical authority, the direction of men in matters of religion, and which pertain to conscience. The former enforces obedience by external means, the latter by spiritual means; yet, "as they be both of God, and tend to one end, if they be rightly used, to wit, to advance the glory of God, and to have good and godly subjects," they ought to co-operate within their respective spheres, and fortify each other. "As ministers are subject to the judgment and punishment of the magistrates in external matters, if they offend, so ought the magistrates to submit themselves to the discipline of the Church, if they transgress in matters of conscience and religion." The government of the Church consists in three things,—doctrine, discipline, and distribution. Corresponding to this division, there are three kinds of church-officers,—ministers, who are preachers as well as rulers; elders, who are merely rulers; and deacons, who act as distributors of alms and managers of the funds of the Church. The name *bishop* is of the same meaning as that of pastor or minister: it is not expressive of superiority or lordship; and the Scriptures do not allow of a pastor of pastors, or a pastor of many flocks. There should be *elders*, who do not labour in word and doctrine. The eldership is a spiritual function, as is the ministry. These functionaries ought to assist the pastor in examining those who come to the Lord's table, and in visiting the sick; but their principal office is to hold assemblies with the pastors and doctors, who are also of their number, for establishing good order and execution of discipline. The office-bearers of the Church are to be admitted by election and ordination. None are to be intruded into any ecclesiastical office "contrary to the will of the congregation to which they are appointed." Ecclesiastical assemblies are either particular (consisting of the office-bearers of one congregation, or of a number of neighbouring congregations), provincial, national or ecumenical, and general. The presbytery, or eldership as it is called, has the inspection of a number of adjoining congregations in every thing relating to religion and manners, and has the power of ordaining, suspending, and deposing ministers, and of exercising discipline within its bounds. The provincial synod possesses the power of all the presbyteries within a province. The General Assembly is composed of commissioners, ministers and elders, from the whole churches in the realm, and takes cognizance of every thing connected with the welfare of the National Church. Appeals for redress of grievances may be taken from every subordinate court to its next superior one, till they reach the General Assembly, whose decision in all matters ecclesiastical is final. All the ecclesiastical assemblies have lawful power to convene for transacting business, and to appoint the times and places of their meeting. The patrimony of the Church includes whatever has been appropriated to her use, whether by donations from individuals, or by law and custom. To take any part of this by unlawful means, and apply it to the particular and profane use of individuals, is simony. It belongs to the *deacons* to receive the ecclesiastical goods, and to distribute them according to the appointment of presbyteries. The purposes to hich they are to be applied are the four following:—The support of ministers; the support of elders where that is necessary, and of a national system of education; the maintenance of the poor and of hospitals; and the reparation of places of worship, and other extraordinary charges of the Church or commonwealth. Among the remaining abuses which ought to be removed, the following are particularly specified:—The titles of abbots, and others connected with monastic institutions, with the places which they held, as churchmen, in the legislative and judicial courts; the usurped superiority of bishops, and their acting in parliament and council in the name of the Church, without her commission; the exercise of criminal jurisdiction and the pastoral office by the same individuals; the mixed jurisdiction of commissaries; the holding of pluralities; and patronages and presentations to benefices, whether by the prince or any inferior person, which lead to intrusion, and are incompatible with "lawful election and the assent of the people over whom the person is placed, as the practice of the apostolical and primitive Kirk, and good order, crave."

"Such is the outline of the Presbyterian plan of church government, as delineated in the Second Book of Discipline. Its leading principles rest upon the express authority of the Word of God. Its subordinate arrangements are supported by the general rules of Scripture; they are simple, calculated to preserve order and promote edification, and adapted to the circumstances of the Church for which they were intended. It is equally opposed to arbitrary and lordly domination on the part of the clergy, and to popular confusion and misrule. It secures the liberty of the people in one of their most important privileges,—the choosing of those who shall watch for their souls,—without making them the final judges of the qualifications of those who shall be invested with this office. While it establishes an efficient discipline in every congregation, it also preserves that unity which ought to subsist among the different branches of the Church of Christ,—secures attention to those numerous cases which are of common concern and general utility,—and provides a remedy against particular acts of injustice and mal-administration arising from local partialities and partial information, by the institution of larger assemblies acting as courts of appeal and review, in which the interests of all are equally represented, and each enjoys the benefit resulting from the collective wisdom of the whole body. It encourages a friendly co-operation between the civil and ecclesiastical authorities; but it, at the same time, avoids the confounding of their limits,—prohibits church courts from 'meddling with any thing pertaining to the civil jurisdiction,'—establishes their independence in all matters which belong to their own cognizance,—and guards against what is the great bane of religion and curse of the Church—a priesthood which is merely the organized puppet of the state, and moves and acts only as it is directed by a political administration. It is a form of ecclesiastical polity whose practical utility has been proportioned to the purity in which its principles have been maintained. Accordingly, it has secured the cordial and lasting attachment of the people of Scotland: whenever it has been wrested from them by arbitrary violence, they have uniformly embraced the first favourable opportunity of demanding its restoration; and the principal secessions which have been made from the national Church in this part of the kingdom have been stated, not in the way of dissent from its constitution, as in England, but in opposition to departures, real or alleged, from its original and genuine principles."*

To the above quoted just estimate of the merits of the Second Book of Discipline, it would be presumptuous and unnecessary to add a single sentence. And it would be well if those who declaim against the Church of Scotland, would have the candour to make themselves acquainted with its standard of government and discipline, before they proceed to misrepresent, villify, and condemn, what they neither know nor understand. It is a melancholy thought, but, we fear, too near the truth, that the opposition, and even bitter hatred, which the Church of Scotland has had to encounter in every age, has arisen from the fact, that her standards of faith and government are too pure and spiritual to be readily apprehended by the darkened mind, or relished by the corrupt heart, of fallen and sinful man. This at least is certain, that her bitterest enemies have always been among the most worldly-minded or the most depraved, and her warmest friends among the wisest, best, and holiest of their age and nation. That a weak, vain, and tyrannical king, and a licentious court, should hate and endeavour to subvert so pure a Church, was only what might have been expected; that some of her own ambitious or backsliding office-bearers should have been ready to become tools in the hands of her enemies, for the sake of their own self-interested views or base indulgencies, was also but too natural; but that men can still be found eager to blacken the character of our heavenly-minded reformers, and attempt to overthrow the Church which these great men expended their noble lives in establishing, is a matter that must awaken in every well-informed and spiritually enlightened mind the deepest grief and the most painful reflections. Is it indeed so, that an institution avowedly divine in its origin and principles, cannot be tolerated by kings, and governments, and men of rank and power, unless it will consent to abandon all claim to that sacred origin and authority in virtue of which alone it exists, to sacrifice all its God-given principles, intrinsic powers, and divinely appointed jurisdiction, and submit to become the slave, bedecked and pampered, but fettered and enthralled, of licentious and worldly despotism? Such might have been the sad and depressing thoughts of Knox and Melville, in the early days of the Church of Scotland; and her subsequent history will often force on the thoughtful reader musings of a similarly melancholy character.

But to proceed with the narrative of events. The king and his dissolute and avaricious favourites viewed these proceedings of the Church with equal hatred and alarm. They were well aware, that unless they could preserve the prelatic element in the Church, they would lose both their power of corrupting and biassing its courts, and of laying hold of the revenues of the larger benefices through the instrumentality of their cringing sycophants the tulchan bishops. An opportunity soon presented itself of putting their schemes in execution. Boyd, archbishop of Glasgow, died in June 1581; and a grant of the revenues of the archbishopric was made by the privy council to the duke of Lennox. But as these

* M'Crie's Life of Melville, pp. 124, 125.

revenues could not be drawn in his own name, it was necessary to revive the tulchan system, and procure some hireling to hold the title, and hand over to Lennox the greater portion of the revenues. The transaction was so base, and so directly opposed to the whole acts of the Assembly, especially the more recent ones condemning and wholly abolishing the episcopal name and office, that Lennox had some difficulty in finding a person at once sufficiently knavish and reckless to enter into what even Spotswood terms this "vile bargain." At length, Robert Montgomery, minister of Stirling, "a man," says Robertson, "vain, feeble, presumptuous, and more apt, by the blemishes of his character, to have alienated the people from an order already beloved, than to reconcile them to one which was the object of their hatred,"—this worthless man consented to make himself the base instrument of a licentious courtier's sacrilegious avarice.

The Assembly which met in October entered promptly into the consideration of this simoniacal transaction, and called Montgomery to the bar. After proceeding a certain length, the matter was remitted to the presbytery of Stirling, to deal farther in it as necessity might require; and Montgomery was prohibited from accepting the condemned prelatic office, and from leaving his charge at Stirling. The members of the synod of Lothian were summoned to appear before the privy council, on account of having interfered with Montgomery in obedience to the orders of the Assembly. They appeared; and Robert Pont, who was at that time one of the Lords of Justiciary, in their name, after protesting their readiness to yield all lawful obedience, declined the judgment of the council, as incompetent, according to the laws of the land, to take cognizance of a cause which was purely ecclesiastical.

[1582.] The Assembly met in April 1582 at St. Andrews, and immediately proceeded to take up the case of Montgomery, which had been referred to them by the presbytery of Stirling. The king sent a letter to the Assembly, requesting them not to proceed against Montgomery for any thing connected with the archbishopric. The answer was, that they would touch nothing so far as belonged to the civil power, but in other respects would discharge their duty. Soon after, a messenger-at-arms entered the house, and charged the moderator and members of Assembly, on the pain of rebellion, to desist entirely from the prosecution. After serious deliberation, they agreed to address a respectful letter to his Majesty; resolved that it was their duty to proceed with the trial; ratified the sentence of the presbytery of Stirling, suspending him from the exercise of the ministry; and having found eight articles of the charge against him proved, declared that he had incurred the censures of deposition and excommunication. Overawed by this calm and resolute conduct, Montgomery hastened to the house, and like a self-convicted culprit, humbly crouching before them, acknowledged that he had heavily offended God and His Church, craved that the sentence might not be pronounced, and solemnly promised to interfere no farther with the bishopric. The Assembly accepted his submission, and delayed pronouncing the sentence; but, aware of his character, gave instructions to the presbytery of Glasgow to watch his conduct, and in case he violated his engagement, to inform the presbytery of Edinburgh, who were authorized to appoint one of their number to pronounce the sentence of excommunication against him.

The event showed the wisdom of these precautions. Instigated by Lennox, who longed to realize the fruits of his "vile bargain," Montgomery revived his claim to the prelacy; and when the presbytery of Glasgow met to do as they had been directed by the Assembly, he procured an order from the king to stay their procedure, and, at the head of an armed force, entered the house where they were sitting, and presented the order. They refused compliance; and the moderator was dragged from the chair, insulted, beaten, and cast into prison. The presbytery, nevertheless, discharged their duty, found him guilty, and transmitted the result to the presbytery of Edinburgh, who appointed one of their own number to pronounce the sentence. In spite of the rage and the threatenings of the court, the sentence was pronounced, and intimated publicly in all the surrounding churches. A proclamation was immediately issued by the privy council, declaring the excommunication of Montgomery null and void. The ministers of Edinburgh were repeatedly called before the council and insulted; and John Dury was banished from the capital, and prohibited from preaching.

But if the king and the courtiers were furious, the Church was roused and resolute, and its councils were guided by men equal to the emergency. An extraordinary meeting of Assembly was convened, and a spirited remonstrance was drawn up, to be presented to the king and council, complaining of the late proceedings, and craving a redress of grievances. In this very remarkable document they commence the statement of grievances by thus addressing the king:—"That your majesty, by device of some councillors, is caused to take upon you a spiritual power and authority, which properly belongeth unto Christ, as only King and Head of the Church, the ministry and execution whereof is only given unto such as bear office in the ecclesiastical government in the same. So that in your highness's person some men press to erect a new popedom, as though your majesty could not be full king and head of this commonwealth, unless as well the spiritual as temporal sword be put into your highness's hands,—unless Christ be bereft of his authority, and the two jurisdictions confounded which God hath divided, which directly tendeth to the wreck of all true religion."*

A deputation, at the head of which was Andrew Melville, was appointed to go to Perth, where the king was then residing, and to present this remonstrance. When information of these proceedings reached the court, the favourites expressed the highest indignation; and an apprehension generally prevailed, that if the ministers ventured to approach the court, their lives would be sacrificed on the spot. Their more timid and wary friends entreated them not to appear; but Melville answered, "I am not afraid, thank God, nor feeble-spirited in the cause and message of Christ; come what God pleases to send, our commission shall be executed." Having next day obtained access to the king in council, he presented the remonstrance. When it had been read, Arran, looking around the assembly with a threatening countenance, exclaimed, "Who dares subscribe these treasonable articles?" "WE DARE," replied Melville; and advancing to the table, he took the pen from the clerk, and subscribed. The other commissioners immediately followed his example. Even the unprincipled and daring Arran was overawed by the native supremacy of religious principle and true moral courage, and sunk from his look of domineering sternness into the sullen scowl of impotent and baffled malice. Lennox addressed the commissioners in a conciliatory tone; and they were peaceably dismissed. Certain Englishmen who happened to be present expressed their astonishment at the bold carriage of the ministers, and could scarcely be persuaded that they had not an armed force at hand to support them.*

But though the deputation escaped personal violence, the king and his favourites were not disposed thus to relinquish the contest. A warrant was given to the Duke of Lennox to hold what was called a chamberlain's court, to inquire into the late sedition, and have its authors and abetters duly punished. This court was to be held in Edinburgh on the 27th of August; but before the arrival of that day, an event took place which completely changed the aspect of public affairs. The haughty and tyrannical conduct of Lennox and Arran had excited the hostility of the greater part of the nobility; and, roused from their lethargy by witnessing the free and energetic behaviour of the Church, they resolved to rescue the country from the disgraceful servitude under which it groaned. A combination for effecting this purpose was formed; the person of the king was seized, and restrained for a time to Ruthven castle, whence this enterprise obtained the name of the Raid of Ruthven. The Duke of Lennox was compelled to retire to France, where he soon after died; Arran was removed from all intercourse with the king; and a proclamation was issued, recalling all the

* Booke of the Universall Kirk, p. 256; Calderwood, p. 127.

* Calderwood, p. 128; Melville's Diary, p. 95; M'Crie's Life of Melville, pp. 182, 183.

late despotic measures, and putting an end to all hostile procedure against the Church.

When the Assembly met in the month of October, the lords connected with the Raid of Ruthven sent a deputation to explain the grounds of the late proceedings. They declared, that the causes which moved them were, the dangers to which they perceived the Church and religion, the king and his estate, were exposed, and the confusion and disorder of the commonwealth; requesting the Assembly to give the sanction of their public approval to the enterprise. The Assembly acted with becoming caution in the matter. Ministers were required to state whether it was consistent with their own knowledge that such grievances were prevalent in the kingdom; and a deputation was sent to the king, to receive his own account of the transaction, and his own feelings regarding it. The king's answer agreeing with the declaration of the lords, and the statements of the ministers from all parts of the country, the Assembly then expressed their approbation of the reformation of the commonwealth intended and begun.

The same Assembly proceeded to the trial and deposition of the corrupt prelates; and commission was given to frame articles to be presented to the king, council, and estates, for the farther removal of abuses, and maintenance of the liberty and purity of the Church. The notorious Montgomery, seeing little prospect of accomplishing his base designs, offered to submit to the discipline of the Church, and begged to be again received into her communion.

[1583.] While the king remained under the care of the new administration, peace and contentment prevailed throughout the kingdom. He publicly declared his satisfaction with what had taken place; and, lest any suspicion might remain, emitted an act of indemnity to all in any way connected with the Raid of Ruthven. The Church was not only permitted, but even encouraged, to advance in her course of reformation: and a confidential intercourse was commenced between the court and the Assembly, which seemed to indicate the opening of a more propitious era. Yet the Assembly was not lulled into security; for when certain articles were proposed for their consideration by the king and council, with a request that a commission might be appointed with powers to deliberate and conclude, the Assembly, remembering well the convention of Leith, answered significantly, "that they had found by experience, commission given to brethren with power to conclude, to have done great hurt to the Church."

But the period of peace and prosperity was near its close, and a storm was ready to burst forth with increased violence. The king, whose mind and morals had been deeply corrupted by his former licentious favourites, became utterly impatient of the restraint in which he was kept by the new administration. Contriving to elude the vigilance of the lords, he hastened to St. Andrews, summoned his former courtly flatterers, and cast himself once more into the arms of the unprincipled Earl of Arran. Immediately the hostile proceedings against the Church were resumed, although for a time the royal and courtly displeasure was directed chiefly against individuals. John Dury was banished from Edinburgh, and restricted to the neighbourhood of Montrose; and severe threatenings were uttered against all who had expressed approbation of the Raid of Kuthven.

[1584.] The year 1584, black in the annals of the Church of Scotland, was ushered in by the commencement of that storm which was soon to shake and devastate the kingdom. On the 15th of February, Andrew Melville was summoned to appear before the privy council, to answer for seditious and treasonable speeches, alleged to have been uttered by him in his sermon and prayers on a fast which had been kept during the preceding month. He appeared, gave an account of what he had really said, and proved his innocence; but the council resolved to proceed with his trial. He then stated objections, which he subsequently put into the form of a protest, the chief point of which was, that his trial should be remitted, *in the first instance*, to the ecclesiastical courts, as the ordinary and proper judges of his ministerial conduct, according to Scripture, the law of the kingdom, and an agreement lately made between certain commissioners of the privy council and of the Church. This modified declinature of the direct and primary jurisdiction of the privy council over the conduct of ministers in the discharge of the pastoral functions, gave dire offence to the king, who was jealous to excess of every limitation of his absolute prerogative; and roused the despotic heart of Arran to a degree of ungovernable fury. Nothing could appal the dauntless spirit of Melville. Unclasping his Hebrew Bible from his girdle, and throwing it on the table, he said, "*These* are my instructions: see if any of you can judge of them, or show that I have passed my injunctions." Entreaties and menaces were in vain employed to induce him to withdraw his protest; he steadily refused, unless his cause were remitted to the proper judges. He was then formally accused, and the deposition of a number of witnesses taken. But although most of them were his enemies, nothing could be extracted from their evidence that tended in the slightest degree to criminate him. Notwithstanding this, he was found guilty of declining the judgment of the council, and behaving, as they said, irreverently before them; and was condemned to be imprisoned in the castle of Edinburgh, and to be farther punished in his person and goods at his majesty's pleasure. Having learned that his place of confinement was changed to Blackness Castle, kept by a creature of Arran's, and that if once there, he would either never leave his dungeon alive, or only to ascend the scaffold, he fled to Berwick, which he reached in safety, while Arran was preparing a troop of cavalry to convey him to Blackness.*

This harsh and unjustifiable conduct at once roused and alarmed the kingdom. The ministers of Edinburgh prayed publicly for Melville; and the universal lament was, that the king, under the influence of evil council, had driven into exile the most learned man in the kingdom, and the ablest defender of religion and the liberties of the Church. The privy council issued a proclamation, declaring that his exile was voluntary; but at the same time an act of council was passed, ordaining that such preachers as were accused should henceforth be apprehended without the formality of a legal charge. This contradictory procedure tended still more to increase the public dissatisfaction, and to deepen the general alarm.

This contest between the court and Andrew Melville it has been thought necessary to state with some minuteness, because it brings before the reader plainly one of the chief subjects on account of which the Church of Scotland has been often exposed to peril, and almost always to misrepresentation and calumny. The claim that a minister should be tried, *in the first instance*, by an ecclesiastical court, for every accusation brought against him in regard to doctrine and the discharge of his pastoral functions, has been attempted to be identified with the claim maintained by the popish clergy, of entire immunity from the civil jurisdiction, even in matters civil, and in crimes of every kind. That the two claims are essentially different, must be obvious to every clear and unprejudiced mind. Even the bare statement of them as above, makes it evident that they are totally dissimilar. But it has ever been the policy of the enemies of the Church of Scotland, first to misrepresent her principles, and then to condemn their own misrepresentation and to punish their slandered victims, as if they were indeed convicted criminals. It is easy to brand a good cause with a bad name, and then to assume the plausible aspect of preventers of evil, or avengers of wrong, when, in reality, those who so act, are themselves the calumniators of good and the assailants of right. The Church of Scotland has never denied the right of the civil magistrate to take cognizance of every crime by which the public morality and peace were or might be injured; but as the liberty of the pulpit is essential to the free and fearless delivery of the gospel message, and as that liberty would be but a name, were the minister to be dragged before a civil tribunal upon the accusation of every ignorant, spiteful, or malicious informer, she has always asserted the right of the minister to be tried, *in the first instance*, by an ecclesiastical court Should the partiality of such a court shelter a delinquent from condign punishment, it is still competent for the civil magistrate to pro-

* Calderwood, pp. 144-147; M'Crie's Life of Melville, pp. 197-204.

ceed against him in the exercise of that authority which the antecedent judgment of the Church could neither supersede nor invalidate. And, if accurately examined, this liberty will be found to be the very palladium of civil liberty itself. The freedom of opinion has never existed in any country where religious freedom was unknown; indeed, free public opinion had no existence till the Reformation broke the fetters of religious despotism and made men free indeed. And in the time of the Scottish Reformation, the press, with its mighty influences, had not sprung into being,—parliamentary proceedings were the records of tyranny or faction,—the courts of justice obeyed too generally the arbitrary will of the sovereign, or exhibited the one-sided results of partizanship,—and it was from the teachers of religion that the people first learned to know that they were something more than the slaves of their feudal lords or regal despots,—that being rational, responsible, and immortal creatures, they were entitled to think, and reason, and act, as conscious of their mysterious nature, and worthy of their high destinies. "Despotism," says M'Crie, "has rarely been established in any nation without the subserviency of the ministers of religion. And it nearly concerns the cause of public liberty, that those who ought to be the common instructors and the faithful monitors of all classes, should not be converted into the trained sycophants of a corrupt, or the trembling slave of a tyrannical, administration."

Soon after the flight of Melville, a proclamation was issued against all who had been concerned in the Raid of Ruthven, who were commanded to leave the kingdom within a given time. An abortive attempt was made by the threatened party to defend themselves; but the Earl of Gowrie having been seized, the others fled to England, and Arran obtained the uncontrolled management of the king and the government. Gowrie was executed notwithstanding the act of indemnity, and the express forgiveness of the king to him personally. Arran urged impetuously forward his schemes at once of tyranny and revenge. When the Assembly met at St. Andrews in April, few in number, and dispirited in consequence of the conduct of the court, they were peremptorily commanded by the king's commissioner to rescind the former act expressing approval of the Raid of Ruthven, and to pass another condemning that transaction as treasonable. This the Assembly declined to do; but instead of taking a determined stand against such an encroachment on their liberties, they broke up their meeting, and withdrew from the scene of immediate danger.

A parliament was held in May, in which the proceedings were of a most extraordinary character. The Lords of the Articles were sworn to secrecy while they were preparing the business of the parliament; and the meetings of the parliament were held with closed doors. In spite of these precautions, it became known that measures subversive of the Presbyterian form of church government were intended. One minister was seized, when entering the palace-gate to supplicate the king in behalf of the Church, and sent to Blackness. And when, on the 25th of May, the acts of parliament were proclaimed, Pont and Balcanquhall protested formally at the market-cross of Edinburgh, and immediately fled to Berwick. Adamson and Montgomery sat in this infamous parliament as bishops, directing the despotic measures against the church and the kingdom.

The acts passed by this parliament, known as "*the Black Acts of* 1584," were to the following effect:—That to decline the judgment of his majesty or of the privy council in any matter was treason: That those were guilty of the same crime who should impugn or seek the diminution of the power and authority of the three estates of parliament: [By this, all that the Church had done in the abolition of Prelacy was declared treasonable]. That all subjects were prohibited from convening any assembly, except the ordinary courts, to consult or determine on any matter of state, civil or ecclesiastical, without the special commandment and license of his majesty: [This was intended for the suppression of Presbyteries, Synods, and General Assemblies.] That commissions should be given to the bishops, along with such others as the king might appoint to pu order in all ecclesiastical matters in their dioceses; and, That none should presume, in private or public, in sermons, or familiar conferences, to censure the conduct of the king, his council, and proceedings, under the penalties of treasonable offences, to be executed with all rigour. These BLACK ACTS, containing the very essence of despotism, were passed on the 22d of May, publicly proclaimed on the 25th, and basely submitted to by the nobility, barons, and gentry, being opposed alone by the ministers, the dauntless guardians of civil and religious liberty. "There was a spirit awakened in Scotland, mightier far than acts of parliament or the influence of the court. The spirit of her ministers was not crushed: they fought on steadily to the end."*

Great was the sufferings and protracted the struggle of the Church. Upwards of twenty ministers were compelled to save their lives by a flight to England. A bond was drawn up by Adamson, to be subscribed by all ministers within forty days, obliging themselves to submit to the king's power over all estates, spiritual and temporal, and to the bishops, under the pain of losing their stipends; with certification, that they who did not submit within the given time shoud not be received afterwards, but underlie the penalty without relief. The most of them refused to subscribe; but an ambigious and deceptive clause was introduced by Adamson, by which several were beguiled into subscription.

[1585.] But as the arrogance and tyranny of Arran were boundless, and as the kingdom in general sympathized with the suffering ministers, and as even James himself began to grow weary of his domineering favourite, it became evident that a change of administration must speedily ensue. The banished lords returned from England in October 1585; crowds of supporters flocked to them from all quarters; they advanced towards Stirling, where the king and Arran then were; and entering the town, Arran fled, and the king received them into favour, and deprived his unworthy minion of all his previous ill-got power and honours.

By this new change of administration the Church was at once rescued from direct persecution; but the lords were more intent on securing their own interests with the capricious and yet obstinate monarch, than on restoring the rights and privileges of which the Church had been deprived by Arran's infamous parliament. They excused themselves by the common plea of temporising insincerity, that it was not expedient yet to annoy the king by pressing the abolition of Prelacy, to which he was so much attached. And, at the same time, the Church was somewhat divided, in consequence of some ministers having been induced to subscribe the servile bond of the Black Acts. Animadversions, supplications, and declarations, passed between the king and the Assembly, which met in December; but nothing of a definite nature was concluded.

[1586.] In April, 1586, the synod of Fife excommunicated Adamson, pretended archbishop of St. Andrews; and Adamson retaliated by excommunicating Andrew Melville, his nephew James, and some other ministers. This matter was brought before the Assembly in May, and after long and sharp controversy, the king used every method to gain his purpose, by intimidation, by flattery of individuals, and by deceptive promises, the sentence was held to be regarded as not pronounced, many protesting against this deliverance. The king was peculiarly urgent with the Assembly to have the pre-eminence of bishops over their brethren recognized, if not on the ground of *jurisdiction*, yet on that of *order;* but the utmost he could obtain was the answer, "That it could not stand with the word of God; only they must tolerate it, if it be forced upon them by the civil authority.*

[1587.] Scarcely anything of marked importance occurred during the year 1587. Some slight contests there were, indeed, between the king and the ministers, respecting praying for Queen Mary, who was still alive, but her life placed in the most imminent peril, in consequence of the jealousy of Elizabeth and the plots of the Papists. By a parliament held in July, such lands of the Church as had not been already bestowed inalienably upon the nobles or landed gentry, were

* Dean of Faculty Hope—Speech, Auchterarder Case, p. 205.

* Calderwood, p. 512.

annexed to the crown. This act, detaching the Church lands from all connection with ecclesiastical persons, was a fatal blow to the order of bishops, rendering the subsequent endeavours of James and his successors to restore them to their pristine dignity and authority utterly hopeless. It might have proved a fertile source of revenue to the crown, had not the facile disposition of James led him to bestow the titles to these lands lavishly on almost any one who requested them; as, being generally held at that time by annuitants, he could not himself immediately obtain possession, and little valued property in prospect. But he accompanied his own prodigal act with one of injustice, in conferring, along with these Church lands, the patronages which had formerly belonged to their ecclesiastical proprietors, and which he thus arbitrarily converted into lay patronages. Of this arbitrary conduct even Sir George Mackenzie says, "There could be nothing so unjust as these patronages." Against them the Church promptly and strongly protested, in the Assembly which met in August the following year.*

[1588.] The year 1588 was one of great importance for Scotland and for Europe. We have had occasion to refer to the leagues of the popish sovereigns for the utter destruction of Protestantism, in which both the queen-regent and Queen Mary were deeply implicated, and on account of which they were continually the objects of jealousy and distrust to their Protestant subjects. Nor did King James escape similar suspicion and distrust. In the early part of his reign, when guided by his favourites Lennox and Arran, it was currently believed that the former was in correspondence with the popish sovereigns on the Continent, and that the proceedings of James against the Church were chiefly intended either to overthrow the Church of Scotland, and reintroduce Popery, or at least to secure the support of the great Continental powers in his pretensions to the throne of England on the death of Elizabeth. And although there is no reason to suppose that James did really intend the overthrow of the reformed religion in this country, yet a certain suspicion respecting his own stability on the Scottish throne, in case of his mother's liberation, induced him to desire to keep on favourable terms with the popish sovereigns, and that party in his own realm. While the death of Mary relieved him from one cause of his embarrassment, it tended to throw him into another line of policy scarcely more favourable to the Presbyterian Church of Scotland. Keeping in view his succession to the English throne, he thought it necessary to conciliate the English Church as far as possible, by making known his decided preference to a prelatical form of church government. To this, indeed, his own despotic principles naturally inclined him, having found by experience how much more easily a bench of bishops, seated among the temporal lords, might be brow-beaten or cajolled, than a free Assembly of high principled and fearless Presbyterian ministers.

The same considerations led him to concur readily in the political schemes of Elizabeth. And as Philip of Spain, after long preparation, was now putting in motion the whole power of his vast empire for the dethronement of the English queen, the Scottish monarch consented to make common cause with her against the common enemy of the Protestant faith. Nobly did the Scottish Church exert herself in this dark and threatening period. An extraordinary meeting of the Assembly was called, to deliberate what steps ought to be taken in this ominous aspect of public affairs. A deputation was sent to the king, to rouse him to due activity; and though he at first seemed inclined to resent this, as an interference with his administration, yet the formidable nature of the impending danger induced him to name a committee of the privy council, to co-operate with the commissioners of the Church in providing for the public safety. A solemn bond of allegiance and mutual defence was framed, approved by his majesty, zealously promoted by the ministers of the Church, and sworn by all ranks, knitting the kingdom together by a sacred and patriotic tie. The Spanish armada, fondly termed invincible, was soon after checked and baffled by the determined courage and persevering energy of the English fleet, then smitten and

* Calderwood, p 227; Booke of the Universall Kirk, p 335.

scattered over the stormy ocean by the avenging hand of Omnipotence.

[1589.] This signal deliverance, and the zeal and energy displayed by the Church in the hour of danger, produced a beneficial influence upon both the king and the nation. An insurrection attempted by the popish party, of whom the Earls of Huntly, Errol, and Crawford were the leaders, was speedily put down; and the king was earnestly urged to suppress Popery, and especially to expel from the kingdom the jesuit emissaries of the king of Spain. And the Church, putting forth its own powers, excommunicated Patrick Adamson, for performing the ceremony of marriage, uniting the popish Earl of Huntly to a lady of the Lennox family.

On the 22d of October, the same year, the king set sail for Norway, to meet the princess of Denmark, to whom he had been previously contracted; and their marriage was solemnized at Upsal, on the 24th of November. Before he departed he had appointed a provisional government to conduct public affairs during his absence; nominating Robert Bruce, one of the ministers of Edinburgh, an extraordinary member of the privy council; and declaring that he reposed more confidence in him and his brethren, for preserving the country in peace, than he did in all his nobility. Nor was he disappointed. During the six months that the king was absent, the kingdom exhibited a scene of unwonted tranquillity; and the king was so sensible of the valuable services of the Church, that in his letters to Bruce, he declared that he was "worth the quarter of his kingdom."

[1590.] When the king returned in May 1590, he took the earliest opportunity of acknowledging his grateful sense of the valuable services rendered to him by the Church, and gave promise of removing all remaining grievances, and providing better measures for the future. In the Assembly which met in August, he pronounced his celebrated panegyric on the purity of the Church of Scotland. "He praised God that he was born in such a time as in the time of the light of the Gospel, and in such a place as to be king in such a Kirk, the sincerest Kirk in the world." "The Kirk of Geneva," continued he, "keepeth Pash and Yule. What have they for them? they have no institution. As for our neighbour Kirk in England, their service is an evil-said mass in English; they want nothing of the mass but the liftings. I charge you, my good people, ministers, doctors, elders, nobles, gentlemen, and barons, to stand to your purity; and I, forsooth, so long as I brook my life and crown, shall maintain the same against all deadly." This speech was received by the Assembly with a transport of joy, "there was nothing heard for a quarter of an hour, but praising God, and praying for the king."*

[1591.] Nothing of public importance occurred in the year 1591, except the recantation of Patrick Adamson, whose dissolute life had at length so disgusted the king, that he ceased to protect and support him; and the miserable victim of ambition was reduced to such extremities, as to be supported by the charity of Andrew Melville, the man whom he had so often maligned and persecuted; and who, in his time of distress, pitied, relieved, and forgave him. The unhappy man, tortured by remorse, and wasted by immorality, sunk into dotage, and died early in the following year.†

An incident took place the same year, which we should not have deemed of sufficient importance to mention, had it not been for the reflex value given to it by the occurrence of modern times. It was a collision between the judicatories of the Church and the Court of Session. The transaction was of a somewhat complicated nature. Graham of Hallyards, it appears, had corrupted a notary public to authenticate by his signature a forged instrument, by means of which Graham intended to defraud the feuars of some property belonging to his wife. The matter becoming suspected, the notary was imprisoned, and during his confinement confessed to Patrick Simpson of Stirling, the minister by whom he was visited, that he had been guilty of the crime. Graham accused Simpson of having suborned the poor notary; and the Assembly took up the case, as implicating the character of the minister. The Lord President, and two other Lords of Session, appeared before the Assembly, requiring them not to proceed with a cause which was within the jurisdiction

* Calderwood, p. 286.

† Ibid., pp. 259-264.

of the Court of Session, and already before that court. The Assembly declared that they had no intention to interfere with any civil matter; but that, as the case in question related to the character of a minister, and to his discharge of his pastoral functions, it was ecclesiastical, and belonged *primario* to the jurisdiction of the Church. Another attempt was made by the Court of Session to set aside this determination; but the Lord Justice Clerk being "demanded if he acknowledged the judgment and jurisdiction of the Kirk or not?" he answered, "that he acknowledged with reverence the judgment of the Assembly in all causes appertaining to them; objecting, however, that this was a civil cause, and that therefore the Lords were *primario judices*." The Assembly repelled the objection, found themselves judges in the first instance, and, notwithstanding the protest of the Lord Justice Clerk, proceeded to try and determine the case. The civil court thought proper to relinquish any farther direct interference, but tried the cause in their own way, and left the Church to do the same; which seems, indeed, to be the proper mode of avoiding collisions between co-ordinate jurisdictions.*

[1592.] On the 22d of May 1592, the General Assembly met at Edinburgh, Robert Bruce, moderator. As the king had appeared more favourable to the Church ever since he had experienced its power to promote the peace of the country during his absence in Norway, this was thought a fitting time to procure an amicable settlement of the protracted conflicts between the Church and the court. Articles, embodying the chief requests of the Church, were accordingly drawn up and presented to the king. When the parliament met in June, the same year, these articles were taken into consideration, and an act was passed, greatly through the influence of the Chancellor Maitland, not, indeed, granting all that the Church desired, but of a much more complete and satisfactory nature than any previous legislative enactment.

The act 1592 ratified the General Assemblies, Synods, Presbyteries, and particular Sessions of the Church; declaring them, with the jurisdiction and discipline belonging to them, to be in all time coming most just, good, and godly, notwithstanding whatsoever statutes, acts, and laws, canon, civil, or municipal, made to the contrary. It ratified and embodied also some of the leading propositions in the Second Book of Discipline, relating to the power of these judicatories. It appointed General Assemblies to be held once every year, or oftener, *pro re nata*, as occasion should require; the time and place of next meeting to be appointed by his majesty or his commissoner, or, provded neither of them should be present, by the Assembly itself. It declared that the act of the parliament 1584, respecting the royal supremacy, should be in nowise prejudicial to the privileges of the office-bearers of the Church concerning heads of religion, matters of heresy, excommunication, the appointment or deprivation of ministers, or any such essential censures, warranted by the Word of God. And it declared the act of the same parliament, granting commission to bishops and other judges appointed by his majesty in ecclesiastical causes, to be null, and of no avail, force, or effect in time coming; and ordained presentations to be directed to presbyteries, who should have full power to give collation to benefices, and to manage all ecclesiastical causes within their bounds, provided they admitted such qualified ministers as were presented by his majesty or other lay patrons. In another part of the same act it was provided, that in case a presbytery should refuse to admit a qualified minister presented by the patron, it should be lawful to the patron to retain the whole fruits of that benefice in his own hands. Such were the main provisions of the celebrated act 1592; and, notwithstanding several imperfections, both in what it enacts and in what it omits, it was then, and has ever since been regarded, as THE GREAT CHARTER OF THE CHURCHOF SCOTLAND.*

* Spotswood, p. 384; Booke of the Universall Kirk, pp. 354, 355; Baillie, Vindication, pp. 62, 63.

* It deserves to be peculiarly remarked, that some of the peculiarities of the act 1592, c, 116, are directly favourable to the Church in that very respect in which they have been thought unfavourable. No express mention is made of the Second Book of Discipline, but certain of its main topics are ratified, while others are apparently passed over. Hence it has been argued, that nothing has been ratified to the Church but what is specifically mentioned in the act itself, and that every other proposition in the Book of Discipline must be held to have been rejected. The true reason of this peculiarity in the act appears to be the following:—

By this act of parliament the Church of Scotland was placed in a much better position for promoting the public welfare, which is the great end of any Church, than she had previously occupied. Not that she regarded any parliamentary enactment as the basis of her religious constitution, but as merely a legal recognition of those sacred and intrinsic powers, which she had always claimed as belonging to her by scriptural institution, and the gift of her Divine Head and King; and which she had already, in her Books of Discipline, stated, proved, and put into execution on the sole authority of the Word of God. The attentive reader must have perceived how steadily the Church pursued her course, amidst the ever-shifting phases of the political world; at one time countenanced and supported; at another, opposed, calumniated, and persecuted, according to the varying character and aims of successive civil administrations. But while politicians intrigued, rose into power, plunged into criminal excesses, fell, and perished, the Church displayed the calm grandeur of an institution resting upon the fixed principles of eternal truth, and, whether suffering or triumphant, maintaining her integrity, and following with firm, though bleeding steps, the path of right, of mercy, and of love to God and man. From this statesmen might have learned —will they yet learn?—that the Church may be cast down, but cannot be destroyed; that their own devices against her will but issue, sooner or later, in their own ruin; that even sound political sagacity might warn them not to incur the hazard of shattering into fragments their own frail schemes of human expediency against the adamantine strength of sacred principles; and that their wisest measure would be, to secure to a spiritual Church the freest and fullest possible developement of its own sacred laws and discipline, assured that they would thereby best promote that which ought to be their chief object,—the true welfare of the nation.

When the Second Book of Discipline was laid before the privy council, certain articles, chiefly those relating to government and jurisdiction by Assemblies, Synods, and Presbyteries, were referred to farther consideration, whilst others were at once ratified. Now, on comparing the copy of the Book of Discipline in Spotswood, where the marginal comments of the privy council are given, with the act 1592, it is remarkable that none of those marked "*agreed*" are contained in the act, while the chief of those marked "*referred*" are. From this the conclusion seems inevitable, that having already agreed to these in the privy council, it was not held necessary to specify any but those which had been left for future consideration, and, consequently, that partly by the concurrence of the privy council in 1578, and partly by the act 1592, thus combined, the whole of the Second Book of Discipline was ratified, and became the law of the land, as well as the law of the Church.

CHAPTER IV.

FROM THE GREAT CHARTER OF THE CHURCH, IN 1592, TO THE RATIFICATION OF THE FIVE ARTICLES OF PERTH, IN THE YEAR 1621.

Remarks on the Act 1592—Detection of the Conspiracy of the Popish Lords—Duplicity of the King—Excommunication of the Popish Lords by the Synod of Fife—Act of Abolition—Secret Motives of the King—Ratification of the Synod's Sentence by the Assembly—Support given to the King by the Church—Proposal of a regular arrangement for fixed and local Stipends—Reforming Assembly of 1596—Renewal of the National Covenant—Fresh Alarms from the Popish Lords—Deceitful conduct of the King—Interview between the King and Andrew Melville—Jealousy between the Court and the Church—Proceedings against David Black—He declines the Jurisdiction of the Civil Court, *in the first instance*—The Church addresses the King—A Tumult in Edinburgh—Proceedings of the Court—The Ministers of Edinburgh expelled—First Corrupt General Assembly held at Perth—Commissioners of the Church appointed to deliberate with the King—Proposal to admit Representatives from the Church into Parliament, 1697—Partially carried in 1598—Completed in 1600—Three Ministers secretly appointed to Bishoprics—The Basilicon Doron—The Gowrie Conspiracy—Injurious Consequences to the Church—Robert Bruce banished by the King—The Covenant virtually renewed by the King—Assembly of 1602, the last free Assembly—Case of Semple—The Accession of James to the Throne of England—Hampton Court Conference—Proposals for a Union of Scotland and England—Alarm of the Church—Arbitrary Prorogation of the Assembly—Held at Aberdeen in 1605, notwithstanding the Royal Prorogation—Banishment of the Ministers—Parliament restores the Temporalities of Bishops in 1606—Andrew Melville summoned to London, imprisoned, and banished—Constant Moderators appointed—Parliament restores the Civil Jurisdiction to Bishops in 1609—Court of High Commission in 1610—The Assembly restores the Ecclesiastical Jurisdiction of Bishops in 1610—This Act ratified by Parliament in 1612—New Confession of Faith in 1616—Calderwood banished—Five Articles of Perth in 1618—Ratified by Parliament in 1621—Reflections.

ALTHOUGH the act of parliament passed in the year 1592, and commonly known as the Great Charter of the Church of Scotland, was then, and must always be, regarded as a very important measure, giving legislative sanction to most of the chief principles of the government and discipline of the Church, yet it was not without several decidedly serious defects. It was evasive in its recognition of the Book of Discipline, as if leaving it open to dispute whether the engrossing of some of the provisions of that book, formerly "referred," was to be regarded as an implicit sanction of the whole, seeing that the privy council had already "agreed" to the rest; or whether it might not be held that every part was excluded except what was expressly mentioned. The former view must have been that which was entertained by the Church, and which not merely every man of candour will entertain, but which also every clear reasoner will see to be necessary, otherwise the act is self-contradictory and absurd. But still, the ambiguity of the act in that respect has given occasion to the legal sophist, in several periods, to bring forward specious objections against the discipline of the Church of Scotland, on the plea of its wanting full statutory authority. Another decided evil was the clause which half prohibited the Assembly from meeting except when the time and place of its next meeting had been appointed by his majesty or his commissioner; its own authority being enough only when neither the king nor his representative was present. This afterwards enabled the king repeatedly to suspend its meetings altogether; and, when it did meet without his previous appointment, gave some colour to his hostile proceedings against its leading members. But the most injurious part of the act 1592 was that which imposed upon both the Church and the people the intolerable yoke and enslaving fetters of lay patronage. How fatal the "binding and astricting" clause has been to the Church, her whole subsequent history testifies, and perhaps no period more so than the present.

The reader will perceive that these defects in this enactment left the Church still exposed to danger on the very points on which she had been always most fiercely and perseveringly assailed. The freedom of the Assembly, and its right to meet for the discharge of its important duties whenever necessity required, had been gainsaid by Secretary Lethington in Queen Mary's days; had been questioned by the Regent Morton, and had been for a time neutralized or overborne by King James, during the period of the tulchan bishops. This was again placed in peril, and that too, by a regular legislative enactment, on the strength of which the king might proceed to greater severities and more plausibly than had been formerly done. The evasive nature of the recognition of the Book of Discipline showed the unchanged hostility entertained by the king and the nobility against a system of moral and religious discipline too pure and uncompromising to find favour in the estimation of dissolute, haughty, and worldly-minded men. That the enforcement of ecclesiastical discipline would still be resisted, was therefore abundantly apparent, notwithstanding the evasive sanction of the act of parliament. And it was equally evident that, by the rigid retention of lay patronages, the king and the nobility were determined to keep possession of the means whereby they might either corrupt the Church, or contrive to hold fast her patrimony within their sacrilegious grasp.

But although there thus remained these strong elements of antagonism between the king and the Church, there was no urgent reason why they might not have continued in a state of dormancy for an indefinite length of time. That the Church did not wish to urge matters to an immediate contest, was evident from the very fact of her receiving the act 1592, defective as it was, without opposition, and even with gratitude. And had the king been sincere in his expressions of friendship and estimation, he needed not to have provoked hostility by an early and harsh enforcement of the harmful powers which that act enabled him to retain. Their mere existence in the statute-book ought to have been enough to satisfy him that the Church could not, even were she disposed, make any dangerous encroachments upon his cherished prerogatives. And had they been allowed to remain solely as latent but complete preventive checks against any sudden democratic movement of the Church, the whole of what even his jealousy of his arbitrary prerogative deemed necessary might have been peacefully secured; and when that jealousy had subsided, he might have removed these defects from the enactment, and thereby perfected the constitution of the country, by the harmonious agreement and mutually supporting connection of Church and State; exerting themselves in their respective spheres, undisturbed by mutual jarrings and suspicions, for the advancement of the great end of both

—the promotion and the security of the civil and sacred welfare of the nation. Such was not, however, to be the case. A short time was sufficient to show that James had caused the elements of strife to be retained in the act 1592, expressly for the purpose of putting them into execution on the earliest opportunity, for the overthrow of a Church whose principles, spirit, and discipline were too sacred, independent, and pure, to suit the taste and comport with the habits of a monarch at once crafty and despotic, and of courtiers both avaricious and dissolute. It may seem strange that James, who had experienced so much treachery on the part of his nobility, and been exposed to personal danger from their factious and daring attempts; and, on the other hand, had found such constant fidelity to his cause, and zeal in his behalf, in every time of peril, from the Church, notwithstanding his injurious treatment of it,—that with such strong and repeated proofs which was the more trustworthy party, he could still favour the schemes of the treacherous and selfish aristocracy, and distrust and persecute the faithful and disinterested Church. But it has always been the fault and the misfortune of kings and statesmen to give their countenance to sycophants and mercenary tools, whom they can manage and employ for any purpose, however guilty and base, rather than to men whose principles are too lofty for them to comprehend, and whose integrity is beyond their power to move. And James knew well that he could mould and bias his courtiers by the artifices of that "kingcraft" in which he thought himself a most accomplished adept; but that in the high-souled ministers of the Presbyterian Church, when met together in their own free General Assembly, he encountered men whom neither his arts could blind nor his threatenings overawe. Hence his determination to retain, even in the act recognising and ratifying the liberty of the Church, a seeming innocuous clause, by which he might be able to prohibit the meetings of the Assembly, whenever he apprehended from it a decided opposition to his schemes; or to call it together when he should have succeeded in corrupting its members by means of the patronage-enforcing clause.

The preceding remarks we have deemed it expedient to make, for the purpose of placing before our readers clearly the position of the Church after the passing of the great charter of 1592, and the dangers still to be apprehended from the defects of that enactment, and the pernicious elements which it contained. But we must now resume the narrative, and trace the progress of events.

The act 1592 almost took the Church by surprise. The ministers had striven so long for a legislative ratification of the liberty of the Church, of General Assemblies, Synods, and Presbyteries, and of discipline, and had met so many disappointments, evasions, and direct violations of the most solemn promises from the ruling powers, that though they continued to strive, they seem almost to have ceased to expect success. They appear to have acted on the great general principle, that for the discharge of known duty man is responsible,—for success he is not; and that therefore their duty was to continue their exertions, and leave the result to God, in whose hands are the issues of all events. Yet they have been censured for accepting a measure which fell so far short of what they sought to obtain, and which contained elements capable of being roused into the most pernicious activity. But it should be considered that men who are very far above taking expediency as their rule in matters of duty, may, with a safe conscience, accept of a measure comparatively defective, for which they could not have striven; regarding it as, though not a satisfactory, and consequently not a final settlement, yet, upon the whole, a great advancement towards a better state of matters than had previously existed, and containing a ratification of the most essential of their own leading principles. Such appear to have been the sentiments of the most active and influential of the ministers when this very important act was passed; and while they disapproved of those points in it which have been specified, still, as it went beyond their general expectation, they received it with joy and gratitude. It may be mentioned also that, between the passing of the act and its being publicly proclaimed, the enemies of the Church attempted to deny that any such measure either had been or would be enacted by the parliament; and their very hostility and opposition would tend to secure for it the more ready and cordial acceptation by all who were friendly to the Church.*

A very short time elapsed, after the passing of this act, when the Church had again occasion to show that her intrinsic powers had not been fettered by an act which professed to ratify her freedom; and that to enter into a solemn compact with the State was not to lay aside her native spiritual independence, and to assume a gilded yoke. Towards the end of the year 1592, the jealousy of all sound-hearted Protestants, and especially of the ministers,—those vigilant guardians both of the purity of religion and of the public welfare,—was strongly excited, partly by the known presence and activity of priests and Jesuits within the kingdom, and partly by indefinite intimations of danger from abroad. The sense of impending peril, the more alarming on account of its unascertained character and extent, alarmed the country in general, but seemed to give no uneasiness to the king. An extraordinary meeting of the ministers was convoked in Edinburgh on the 15th of November, and measures were framed calculated to provide for the safety of the Church and kingdom, by exerting the utmost vigilance for the detection of the popish machinations; and to these measures the king gave his approbation.

The necessity and the wisdom of these precautions became very soon evident. Andrew Knox, minister of Paisley, having received secret intelligence respecting one of the popish emissaries, hastened to the island of Cumray, accompanied by a number of Glasgow students and some neighbouring gentlemen, and seized George Ker, brother of Lord Newbattle, as he was on the point of embarking for Spain. A number of letters were found in his possession from priests in Scotland; and several blanks subscribed by the popish Earls of Huntly, Errol, and Angus, with a commission to William Crighton, a Jesuit, to fill up the blanks, and address them to the persons for whom they were intended. Graham of Fintry was soon afterwards apprehended; and being both examined before the privy

* Melville's Diary pp. 198, and 201.

council, they testified to the genuineness of the signatures, and confessed the nature and extent of the conspiracy. It was, indeed, one of a most perilous and flagrant character. The king of Spain was to have landed thirty thousand men on the west coast of Scotland, part of whom were to invade England, and the remainder, in concert with the forces which the three earls promised to have in readiness, were to suppress the Protestants, and to procure the re-establishment of the Romish religion in Scotland.*

[1593.] The privy council and the ministers of Edinburgh having thus received proof positive of the dangerous conspiracy existing in the kingdom, issued letters calling upon the well-affected to hasten to the capital, for the purpose of consulting what steps were to be taken in a matter of such a formidable character. At the same time they earnestly besought the king, who was at the time absent, to hasten to Edinburgh, and aid his faithful subjects in the defence of the commonwealth. The Earl of Angus, unaware that the conspiracy had been detected, happening to come to the capital at the same time, was seized and committed to the castle. Upon his majesty's arrival, instead of thanking his people for the zeal and vigilance which they had displayed in behalf of the religion and liberties of the country, he broke out into peevish and ill-timed complaints of their conduct in seizing the Earl of Angus, and in convoking the lieges without his previous command, which he resented as a grievous encroachment upon his prerogative. They answered, as such men might have been expected to answer, "That it was no time to attend on warnings when their religion, prince, country, lives, lands, and all were brought into jeopardy by such treasonable dealings." But when their whole proceedings were detailed, and the full nature and extent of the conspiracy made known to him, his petulant fume passed off, he called Angus "a traitor of traitors," and declared that the crime of the conspirators was too great for his prerogative to pardon, promising to proceed to trial of the accused "with all diligence and severity."

* Melville's Diary, p 205; Calderwood, pp. 275-280.

James now thought it necessary to act with at least the appearance of sincerity. A proclamation was issued, specifying the general nature of the detected conspiracy, and commanding all who hated subjection to foreign tyranny to abstain from intercourse with popish priests, on pain of treason; and to hold themselves in readiness to defend the country, "as they should be certified by his majesty, or otherwise find the occasion urgent." And as some suspicion of the king's sincerity had been excited by his first expression of displeasure with the prompt zeal of his people, he thought proper to pass an act of council, prohibiting all from attempting to procure the pardon of the conspirators. The nation immediately testified its delight with the king's conduct, by framing and extensively subscribing a bond in defence of religion and the government, and preparing zealously to protect and support the king and the public peace. The king marched northwards against the conspirators; but they merely concealed themselves from immediate apprehension; and the king, notwithstanding his own act of privy council, received favourably those who were sent to intercede in behalf of the detected traitors.

The General Assembly met at Dundee on the 24th of April, according to their own previous arrangement, and without waiting to be called together by his majesty. The proceedings of that Assembly, although of no great moment, furnished sufficient indication of the growing jealousy between the king and the Church. The Assembly appointed commissioners to present to the king an address and petition, containing several articles in regard to which they craved redress. One was, that he would adopt strong measures for the suppression of the popish party, and in the meantime that they should be excluded from all public official situations, and denied access to his majesty's presence. Another was, that his majesty would consider the great prejudice done to the Church by the erection of the tithes of different prelacies into titular lordships. The king, on the other hand, by his commissioner, directed the attention of the Assembly to that part of the act 1592 which required its meetings to be held by the appointment of his majesty, intimating that he could not with honour see that provision infringed; and further, requested them to make an act prohibiting any minister, on pain of deposition, from uttering in public any animadversions on the conduct of his majesty or the privy council. The Assembly agreed to the provision of the act 1592, it being reserved to them to meet on their own authority, provided his majesty or his commissioner were not present, and ordained that no minister "utter any rash or irreverent speeches against his majesty or council, but that all their public admonitions proceed upon just and necessary causes, in all fear, love, and reverence, under pain of deposition."* These proceedings could give little satisfaction to either party, and indicated but too plainly a mutual distrust, likely ere long to come to an open rupture. Some steps were taken by that Assembly to prevent further dilapidation of Church property, and for the enforcement of discipline and the maintenance of public morality and peace.

The parliament met in July, and proceeded with the trial of the popish lords; but Ker had been permitted to escape a short while previously; and the parliament listened to the offers of submission made by the conspirators, and rejected the bill of attainder against them, on the pretext of want of evidence. Great and general was the dissatisfaction caused by this injudicious lenity to men guilty of repeated acts of treason; and strong suspicions arose in the minds of many that his majesty's own attachment to the Protestant faith was but hollow and insincere. The synod of Fife, at its meeting in September, determined to take such steps as were competent to it, as a church court, towards counteracting the injurious lenity of the king and parliament. On the ground that the Earls of Angus and Errol had, when students at St. Andrews, within the bounds of that synod, subscribed the Confession of Faith, and thereby rendered themselves amenable to its jurisdiction, and that Huntly had murdered the Earl of Murray within its bounds, the synod of Fife proceeded to pass the sentence of excommunication against these apostate conspirators, and

* Booke of the Universall Kirk, pp. 385, 386.

sent intimation of what had been done throughout the country. Intimation was also given, that a general meeting of commissioners from the different counties of the kingdom, consisting of noblemen, gentlemen, burgesses and ministers, was to be held at Edinburgh on the 17th of October. The king was extremely annoyed with these measures. They were so completely in unison with his former declarations against the popish conspirators, and so naturally resulting from the bond of defence previously subscribed with his concurrence, that he could not justly find direct fault with them, and yet so contrary to his recent treatment of the traitors that he could not approve of them. With his usual craft, he attempted to tamper with several of the noblemen and the ministers, to prevent the intimation of the sentence of excommunication, and also to impair the effect of the coming convention. Not succeeding in his schemes, he again dissembled; and being about to proceed to the borders to suppress some seditious and turbulent affairs, he promised that he would show no favour to the conspirators.

On the very same day on which this promise was given, the king admitted the conspirators to his presence at Fala, and made arrangements with them respecting their trial. The convention appointed commissioners to follow James to Jedburgh, and lay their complaints before him. The reception given by his majesty to his faithful and zealous subjects was very different from that which he had granted to the traitors a few days before. He termed the convention an unlawful meeting, complained of the sentence of excommunication, and even threatened to call a parliament for the purpose of overthrowing Presbyterian and restoring Prelacy. When he had expended his wrath in idle threats, he grew calmer, and returned to the petition of the commissioners a written answer, containing promises sufficiently fair, but as idle.* It is unnecessary to dwell upon the wretched tergiversation of the king in this very important matter. A convention of estates was held at Linlithgow in October, and arrangements were made for the final trial of the rebel lords at Holyrood-house in the following month.

* Melville's Dairy, p. 208.

The conclusion of the trial was the passing of what was termed an "act of abolition," by which the popish lords were ordained to give satisfaction to the Church, and to embrace the Protestant faith, or else to leave the kingdom within a limited time; the process against them was dropped and consigned to oblivion; and they were declared "free and unaccusable in all time coming" of the crimes laid to their charge, provided they did not for the future enter into any treasonable correspondence with foreigners.

This arrangement was equally unsatisfactory to the Church and to the greater part of the nation. It was well understood at that time, and might be still, that the determined adherents of Popery could easily obtain absolution from Rome for any oaths or concessions made to Protestants, provided they continued to plot the destruction of the Protestant religion; and therefore, that to think of binding such men with oaths and protestations, however solemn, was about as wise as to think of fettering a beast of prey with a skein of rotten silk. Nor was it without reason that James was himself distrusted. He had repeatedly broken his most solemn pledges, and brought his word into such suspicion, that the more earnestly he protested, the less he was believed. Besides, the ruling motives of his whole policy were well known to such men as Andrew Melville and Robert Bruce. They were aware of his secret intercourse with England, for the purpose of promoting his succession to the throne of that kingdom; and they knew that he would hesitate at nothing, however base and deceptive, which seemed likely to forward his views. He knew that there was a strong popish party still in England, and he was desirous of conciliating them and procuring their support, which he sought to do by his lenient treatment of his own popish rebels. To this it may be added, that the political principles of papists were more agreeable to a monarch so devoted to despotic power and uncontrolled prerogative as James, than could possibly be the free spirit which lived and breathed in the Presbyterian Church of Scotland. For the same reason Episcopacy obtained his peculiar favour; as his cunning enabled him to perceive, that he might more easily exercise an influence upon prelates who derived from him their wealth and titles, and who, as seekers of such selfish preeminence, were likely to be worldly-minded and sycophantish men, than he could ever hope to do upon ministers who, deriving nothing from him, owed him nothing but natural allegiance. And he had another reason for wishing to restore Prelacy; he thought that his doing so would recommend him to the favour and support of the English prelates, who both hated and feared the Presbyterian Church government of Scotland, as a standing rebuke to their own unscriptural system. All these reasons combined to induce this crafty yet weak-minded monarch to favour the treacherous abettors of despotism, civil and religious, and to discountenance the friends of genuine freedom,—a line of policy which he pursued throughout his life, and left as a dire heritage to his successors, and which they followed with infatuated pertinacity, till the ill-omened race reaped the baneful fruits of generations of falsehood and oppression, and became extinct after years of exiled, discrowned, unhonoured, and unpitied wretchedness.

[1594.] It is for the civil historian to relate the minor turmoils of the nation; such as those caused by the turbulent and ambitious earl of Bothwell, the successor in title and in character of him by whom Darnley was murdered and Mary disgraced and ruined, but an illegitimate scion of the royal race, being a grandson of James V. The only reason why such events are mentioned here is, that their effects were not unfrequently felt in ecclesiastical matters; as, for example, where Bothwell, anxious to gain strength, pretended to befriend the Church, and thought thereby to procure the support of individual ministers at least, if not of the Assembly, so completely did the Church stand aloof from him and his measures, that he was able to deceive and ensnare but one minister; and upon the complaint of the king, that minister was deposed, till he should satisfy his majesty and the Church.*

The same Assembly which so readily testified its abhorrence of treason, by punishing one of its own members who had been accused of favouring that crime, dealt in the same manner with those higher delinquents whose greater offence the king seemed more willing to forgive. The sentence of excommunication pronounced against the conspirators by the synod of Fife, was approved and ratified by the Assembly; but Lord Home, who had also been excommunicated, appearing and confessing his offence, abjured popery, and was released from the sentence. It deserves to be remarked, that the moderator of the Assembly, Andrew Melville, not being satisfied with Lord Home's professions of repentance, but doubting their sincerity, felt conscientious scruples respecting pronouncing the act of the absolution; and the Assembly, with a due regard to his feelings, appointed another person to discharge that duty. In more modern times, men who made no pretension to tenderness of conscience themselves, showed no such toleration of the conscientious convictions and difficulties of others. Yet this is not strange, though deplorable; for men naturally estimate others by their own standard; and he who knows that for him to plead tenderness of conscience would be hypocrisy, regards that plea in others as entitled to no better name.

Another instance of the loyalty, public spirit, and energy of the Church may be stated. The popish lords, who had previously entered into a treasonable correspondence with the King of Spain, and who had been so leniently treated by James, were again detected continuing their treacherous plots. The king, irritated into sincerity, gave commission to the Earl of Argyle to march against the traitors, and subdue them by force, while he himself proposed to proceed by Aberdeen, to see the command fully executed. Argyle encountered the rebel lords, but sustained a partial defeat. On the day after this conflict the king left Edinburgh, and marched towards Aberdeen, taking with him Andrew and James Melville, and some other ministers, to witness his zealous discharge of his determination to suppress wholly the popish conspirators. But before any decisive measures had been taken, the money raised by the king for the support of the army was so far expended, that the troops were on the point of being disbanded for want of pay. In this emergency, James Melville was

* Booke of the Universall Kirk, p. 408.

sent back to Edinburgh for the purpose of inducing the ministers to raise, by the contributions of their congregations, a sum of money to assist the king. This mission he accomplished with extraordinary speed and success, and thereby enabled the king to keep his forces together till the object of the expedition was effected, by the demolition of the strong holds of the conspirators. Even this was nearly defeated by the vacillation of the unstable monarch. Scarcely had James Melville left the camp, when James was on the point of frustrating the whole scheme, by yielding to the advice of those who wished him to spare the rebels. The energy and high principle of Andrew Melville prevailed even in the councils of the camp, and saved his sovereign from this disgrace. A little, a very little real wisdom might have enabled James to perceive who were his best friends and wisest councillors, and upon whom he might with the greatest confidence depend in any time of emergency; but unfortunately for himself and the kingdom, he loved flattery better than advice, and preferred courtly sycophants to bold and honest patriots.

[1595.] An Assembly was held at Montrose in June 1595, in which no matters of great importance were transacted; but some suggestions were brought forward, containing the germs of much possible good, although afterwards employed for evil. It was proposed that the acts of Assembly should be examined, and those which had special reference to the practice of the Church extracted, and joined with the Book of Discipline, for the information and guidance of all ministers throughout the kingdom. The proposal was not carried into execution; but it served to show how completely the Book of Discipline was regarded by the Church as her standard of government. A commission was also given to certain brethren to inquire into the state of the revenues of the Church in every presbytery, to prevent dilapidations, and to secure that they should be expended in the support of the ministry, according to their original destination. But the suggestion of greatest moment arose from a desire to provide a remedy for an abuse which had been productive of great injury to the cause of religion. From the time of the regent Morton's administration it had been customary for men in power to endeavour to throw two or three parishes into one, appointing but one minister for all, and retaining the fruits of the remaining benefices in their own hands; and also to change the amount of the teind (or tithe) from year to year, so as not unfrequently to compel the minister to leave his charge from positive want of the necessaries of life. The act of annexation, and the erection of titular lordships, had greatly increased the process of spoliation. To remedy these grievances the Assembly proposed that some of the most intelligent of the ministers from every province should make themselves well acquainted with the affairs of their own districts, and then convene in Edinburgh, and draw up a statement respecting the number of parish churches which ought to be in each presbytery, the amount of available tithes, by whom held, and on what tenure; that, acting upon the certain knowledge thus acquired, a continuing form, or durable arrangement, might be made, by which such injurious proceedings might for the future be prevented. This "constant plat," as it was termed, might have been productive of much good had it been carried into effect; but the king, seeing the anxiety of the Church to have the arrangement made, availed himself of it as a measure, by promising to ratify which he might induce the ministers to comply with some ensnaring scheme of his own.

[1596.] The year 1596 is peculiarly memorable in the history of the Church of Scotland. "It had," says James Melville, "a strange mixture and variety; the beginning thereof with a show of profit, in planting the churches with perpetual local stipends; the midst of it very comfortable for the exercise of reformation and renewing the covenant; but the end of it tragical, in wasting the Zion of our Jerusalem, the church of Edinburgh, and threatening no less to many of the rest.* The first thing which occupied the attention of the Assembly was an overture from John Davidson, minister of Prestonpans, concerning the necessity of reforming the many prevalent corruptions of the Church and the country.

* Melville's Dairy, p. 222.

The overture met with unanimous approbation, the conscience of every man present convincing him of his own need of humiliation and repentance. Order was given that a written form of confession should be drawn up, containing an enumeration of the evils to be reformed, under the four following heads: corruptions in the persons and lives of the ministers of the gospel; offences in his majesty's house; the common corruptions of all estates; and offences in the courts of justice. On the motion of Melville, the means to be employed for reforming ministers, and the censures to be inflicted on them for particular acts of delinquency, were specified. As confession is the primary step of reformation, the members of Assembly agreed to meet by themselves, for the purpose of jointly confessing their sins, and "making promise before the Majesty of God" to amend their conduct. They met accordingly in the Little Church, on Tuesday the 30th of March. John Davidson, the author of the overture, was chosen to preside and lead their devotional exercises. So deeply searching were his words, that they wrought conviction in every heart; and his earnest and humble confession of sin drew tears of sincere penitence from every eye. While they were in this frame of mind, he called upon them to pause, and in the privacy of their own souls to acknowledge, each man for himself, his personal guilt before God. For a quarter of an hour a solemn stillness reigned, broken only by deep-drawn sighs and heavy, half-stifled sobs, as each man searched apart the dark chambers of his own bosom. After another fervent prayer and impressive address, they rose from their seats at his desire, and lifting up their right hands, they renewed their covenant with God, "protesting to walk more warily in their ways, and to be more diligent in their charges." "There have been many days," says Calderwood, "of humiliation for present judgments, or imminent dangers; but the like for sin and defection was never seen since the reformation."*

As this solemn confession of sin regarded the nation, that it might be done nationally, the Assembly ordained that it should be repeated in the several synods and presbyteries, and that it should also be extended to congregations. This ordinance was obeyed with such a degree of readiness and fervour, and with such manifestations of sincere contrition, as proved that it both sprang from and was accompanied by the all-pervading power of the Spirit of God. At Dunfermline the synod of Fife met, and conducted the duties of the solemn transaction in a peculiarly impressive manner. The synod was addressed by David Ferguson, one of the first six ministers engaged in the Reformation, and now the sole survivor; who, after giving a brief account of the perils that had been encountered, and difficulties surmounted in that great work, urged his younger brethren to fidelity and zeal in their less hazardous toils and duties. Many a dark and stormy day had the reforming patriarch seen and struggled through; and his grave words must have sounded to his younger brethren like the voice of warning, admonition, and encouragement, breathed forth to his sons by a departing father.

Men of the world may smile at the thought; but we do not hesitate to say, that we regard this solemn confession of sin and renewal of the covenant as an express means employed by Divine Providence to prepare the Church for the wasting conflict in which she was soon to be engaged,—the fiery trial through which she was soon to pass. It was the communication of spiritual strength enabling her to live through a period of dreary oppression and prostrate suffering, without which she must have perished; like the food given to Elijah by the angel, to sustain him in his journey through the wilderness, which would otherwise have been "too great for him."

The attempt to establish the mode of supporting the ministry on a firm and satisfactory basis, called by the writers of that period the "constant plat," occupied a portion of the attention of the Assembly. The scheme proposed for consideration was drawn up by Secretary Lindsay, and may be seen at length in Melville's Diary.* It deserves the attention of public men yet, containing many suggestions which, if carried into effect,

* Calderwood, pp. 317, 318; Melville's Dairy, pp. 232, 233; Booke of the Universall Kirk, pp. 426-429.

* Melville's Dairy, pp. 223-229.

would greatly promote the welfare of the community. But its principles were too sound, and its arrangements too liberal, to gain the favour of the king and his avaricious courtiers; who, having seized upon what even this scheme terms "the patrimony of the Church," could not be prevailed upon to make restitution of the pillage. The main principles of Lindsay's scheme were the same as those which had been proposed by Knox and the early reformers:—That the whole tithes should be regarded as the patrimony of the Church; and that they should be expended in the support of the ministers of the gospel, a national system of education, and the poor of the land. Could this scheme have been carried into effect, it must have prevented many evils, and produced benefits altogether incalculable. It would have placed the ministers in that happy medium, congenial to the spirit of Presbytery, alike remote from the evils and temptations of wealth and of poverty,—rendering the return of Prelacy impracticable, and delivering the Church from those insidious arts by which James sought to gain the aid of the poor and the ambitious. It might also have produced such a harmonious adjustment of all the great interests of the community,—at once cultivating the national mind and mitigating the bitter evils of poverty and want,—as would have secured the peace and happiness of the commonwealth to a degree that never yet has been experienced in any age or country. But, like every scheme of Christian benevolence devised by the Church of Scotland, and from time to time re-produced by her friends, it was frustrated by the narrow and selfish views of kings and statesmen, who seem never yet to have learned that to secure the nation's good, and not their own aggrandisement, is the very end of their public being, and that, indeed, their own true welfare and that of the community are one.

To proceed with our narrative: Rumours of a near impending Spanish invasion began to pervade the kingdom. While men's minds were in a state of great anxiety on account of these tidings, and after the king had himself given orders for military musters, and urged the ministers to exhort their people to take arms, provide supplies, and prepare to meet the meditated attacks,—while the public mind was in this state of tremulous excitement, an additional element of alarm was given by the tidings that the popish lords had secretly entered the kingdom. The affairs of the court tended to increase the public distrust and anxiety. Since the death of Chancellor Maitland the administration of affairs had been entrusted to eight persons, commonly called *Octavians*, the greater part of whom were either known or suspected Papists. It was at once believed that they were privy to the return of the conspirators, and would exert themselves to procure for those traitors both indemnity and admission to his majesty's councils; in which case the nation might speedily be exposed to all the horrors of a popish persecution, of which it had not yet lost the remembrance.

It soon appeared that these suspicions were too well founded. A meeting of the privy council was summoned at Falkland, to take into consideration an offer of submission by Huntly, for himself and his associates. Certain ministers, whom the court judged more complying than the rest, were invited to attend this meeting, to give their advice. Plausible arguments were employed by the friends of the exiled noblemen, to induce the council to sanction their return, lest, like Coriolanus and Themistocles, they should join the enemies of their country; but Andrew Melville, who had of his own accord joined the other ministers, uttered a bold and strong remonstrance against receiving into favour convicted traitors and popish apostates, enemies at once of their native country and of the gospel. Melville was commanded to withdraw, his presence not having been required, which he did, having thus first exonerated his conscience. The council came to the resolution that Huntly might be restored upon his acceding to such conditions as the king and council should prescribe. This resolution gave so much offence, that the king thought proper twice to declare publicly that he did not mean to act upon it; yet a short time afterwards a convention of estates was held at Dunfermline, and the Falkland resolution there approved of and ratified.

His majesty's manifest breach of faith

increased the public alarm so greatly, that the commissioners of the Assembly and some country gentlemen met at Cupar in Fife, and appointed a deputation to wait on the king, and petition him to prevent the evil consequences which must result from such proceedings. It had been agreed that James Melville should be the person to address his majesty, because of his courteous manner, and the favourable regard which the king had shown him. Scarcely had he begun to speak when the king interrupted him, challenged the meeting at Cupar as seditious, and accused them of exciting causeless fears in the minds of the people. As James Melville was beginning a reply, couched in his mildest terms, his uncle, Andrew, finding that the occasion demanded a full and uncompromising statement of first principles, quitted the subordinate position which he had been willing for the time to occupy, and confronting the king, began to address him. James endeavoured authoritatively to command Melville to silence; but his high spirit was roused, and could not be overborne. Seizing the king's robe by the sleeve, in the earnestness of his mind and action, and terming him "*God's silly vassal*," he addressed him in a strain such as few kings have ever had the happiness to hear, "uttering their commission as from the mighty God."

"Sir," said he, "we will always humbly reverence your majesty in public; but since we have this occasion to be with your majesty in private, and since you are brought in extreme danger of your life and crown, and along with you the country and the Church of God are like to go to wreck, for not telling you the truth and giving you faithful counsel, we must discharge our duty, or else be traitors both to Christ and you. Therefore, Sir, as divers times before I have told you, so now again I must tell you, there are two kings and two kingdoms in Scotland: there is King James, the head of the commonwealth, and there is Christ Jesus, the King of the Church, whose subject James the Sixth is, and of whose kingdom he is not a king, nor a lord, nor a head, but a member. Sir, those whom Christ has called and commanded to watch over his Church, have power and authority from Him to govern his spiritual kingdom, both jointly and severally; the which no Christian king or prince should control and discharge, but fortify and assist; otherwise they are not faithful subjects of Christ and members of his Church. We will yield to you your place, and give you all due obedience; but again, I say, you are not the head of the Church; you cannot give us that eternal life which we seek for even in this world, and you cannot deprive us of it. Permit us then freely to meet in the name of Christ, and to attend to the interests of that Church of which you are the chief member. Sir, when you were in your swaddling clothes, Christ Jesus reigned freely in this land, in spite of all his enemies. His officers and ministers convened and assembled for the ruling and welfare of his Church, which was ever for your welfare, defence and preservation, when these same enemies were seeking your destruction. Their assemblies since that time continually have been terrible to these enemies, and most stedfast to you. And now, when there is more than extreme necessity for the continuance and discharge of that duty, will you (drawn to your own destruction by a most pernicious counsel) begin to hinder and dishearten Christ's servants and your most faithful subjects, quarrelling them for their convening, and the care they have of their duty to Christ and you, when you should rather commend and countenance them, as the godly kings and emperors did? The wisdom of your counsel, which I call devilish, is this, that you must be served by all sorts of men, to come to your purpose and grandeur, Jew and Gentile, Papist and Protestant; and because the Protestants and ministers of Scotland are over strong, and control the king, they must be weakened and brought low by stirring up a party against them, and, the king being equal and indifferent, both should be fain to flee to him. But, Sir, if God's wisdom be the only true wisdom, this will prove mere and mad folly; His curse cannot but light upon it; in seeking both ye shall lose both; whereas in cleaving uprightly to God, His true servants would be your sure friends, and He would compel the rest counterfeitly and lyingly to give over themselves and serve you."*

* Melville's Dairy, pp. 245, 246.

The dignity and power of these high sentiments overbore the petulant anger of the king; his heart was awed, and his soul felt for a space the hallowed energy of sacred truth. He uttered no wrathful reply; he attempted not to dispute the principles to which he had been compelled to listen; but declaring that the popish lords had returned without his previous knowledge, he pledged his word that the proposals which they had made to the privy council should not be received till they left the kingdom, and that even then he would show them no favour before they satisfied the Church. So ended that remarkable interview between the king and Melville, in which the latter gave free expression to the sentiments and principles which the Church of Scotland has always held as essential to the constitutional freedom and purity of the Christian Church. That such pinciples would not find favour in the eyes of an arbitrary monarch, was not surprising; but that men who at least affect to be strenuous advocates of religious and civil liberty, should reprehend them as lawless and rebellious, might well excite feelings of indignant astonishment, were it not for the painful truth, that men of the world will not perceive and acknowledge the inseparable connection between religious freedom and civil liberty, the former as the sacred cause, the latter as the effect. Religious freedom cannot long exist without producing civil liberty; and civil liberty can neither come into being without religious liberty, nor survive it, even for a day. The Church was then, and evermore must be, the parent and the guardian of liberty, sacred and civil, and therefore doubly dear to every free-born and free-hearted Christian man.

The solemn pledge of the king was soon found to be, as formerly, a frail security. Steps for restoring the popish conspirators were taken, of which public intimation sufficiently intelligible was given, by the invitation of the Countess of Huntly to the baptism of the Princess Elizabeth, and the appointment of Lady Livingston, an adherent to the Romish Church, to have charge of the person of the royal infant. These ominous proceedings were not unmarked by the nation's vigilant guardians. The commissioners of the Assembly met at Edinburgh in October, and wrote circular letters to all the presbyteries, pointing out the imminent dangers of the present crisis, and specifying the measures necessary to be taken, to meet, and, if possible, to avert the peril. These remedial measures were, the appointment of a day of humiliation and prayer,—the renewal of the excommunication of the popish conspirators,—the summoning of a certain number of ministers from different parts of the kingdom, to form, along with the presbytery of Edinburgh, an extraordinary council of the church, to receive information, deliberate, and convoke, if necessary, a meeting of the General Assembly.

This energetic procedure of the Church convinced the court that something more than mere deceit would be necessary for the subversion of religious and civil liberty. It was therefore determined to make a direct assault upon the privileges of the Church, hoping thereby forcibly to subdue, since they could not guilefully delude her. This intention came first to the knowledge of the commissioners at an interview which they had requested with the king, for the purpose of endeavouring to remove the jealousies which existed between them. On that occasion, the king told them plainly, that there could be no agreement between him and them, "till the marches of their jurisdiction were rid," and unless the following points were yielded to him:—That the preachers should not introduce matters of state into their sermons; that the General Assembly should not be convened without his authority and special command; that nothing done in it should be held valid until ratified by him in the same manner as acts of parliament; and that none of the church courts should take cognizance of any offence which was punishable by the criminal law of the land. Some, even in the present day, will think that the Church ought at once to have assented to these conditions. But those who are adequately acquainted with the history of that period will be well aware, that to have done so, would have been putting it into the king's power to establish at once a pure despotism; while those who have studied the nature of ecclesiastical jurisdiction, as contradistinguished from that of civil courts, must also know, that to have complied with the king's demands would have been yielding up the very essence of every thing which constitutes a Church, and placing all matters of doctrine, government, and discipline, entirely under his control. Such an institution as that would have been might have been termed the king's Church, but could have been no longer the Church of Christ.

The slighest shadow of doubt respecting the ultimate designs of the court, if any had still remained, was soon removed by the information that David Black, minister of St. Andrews, had been summoned to answer before the privy council for certain expressions said to have been used by him in his sermons. It was now evident that the entire overthrow of the liberties of the Church was intended; and the commissioners resolved to make a firm and united resistance to this premeditated attack. They wrote to the presbyteries to warn them against any attempt to disunite them, directing their attention particularly to those subjects likely to be controverted, and to the acts of privy council and parliament by which the liberties of the Church had received the sanction of the civil powers. To avoid, if possible, a direct collision, they endeavoured to persuade the king to abandon the prosecution of Black; but finding all their efforts ineffectual, and being well aware that if they did not resist this attempt, it would speedily become a precedent for subjecting the whole jurisdiction of the Church to the arbitrary will of the king, they came to the resolution of advising Black to decline the judgment of the privy council, as incompetent to decide, *in the first instance*, on the accusation brought against him. A declinature having been drawn up to that effect, it was sent through the presbyteries, and in a very short time subscribed by upwards of three hundred ministers.

There was now an open and avowed contest between the civil and ecclesiastical authorities; and not merely the peace of the kingdom, but the interests of religion for generations were involved in the issue. The Church displayed an extraordinary degree of unanimity in this dangerous crisis: even those who were not peculiarly distinguished for zeal in ordinary cases cast aside their lethargy, and joined warmly in the defence of the threatened right of the Church. Spotswood himself was, or seemed to be, peculiarly forward to defend the men and the cause, whom he was afterwards more than suspected of at that very time secretly betraying, and whom he afterwards basely and falsely calumniated. Previous to giving in his general declinature, Black was summoned before the council, *super inquirendis*, about unspecified matters into which inquiry was to be made; and when he objected to this mode of procedure as inquisitorial and illegal, he was then told that the accusation was restricted to matters complained of by the English ambassador, as assailing the character of Elizabeth. So trivial was the first form of accusation, that even the king said he "did not think much of the matter; only he should take some course for pacifying the English ambassador; but take heed that you do not decline the judicatory; for if you do, it will be worse than any thing that has fallen out." The English ambassador was easily pacified; but that did not serve the king's purpose; and accordingly a new charge was brought against him, ranging over the alleged improper language of the three preceding years. In vain did Black produce testimonials from the provost and the professors of St. Andrews; the council was determined to proceed. On the day fixed for hearing the cause, he was assisted by Pont and Bruce; but the council rejected the declinature, disregarded the testimonials, found the charges against him proved, and sentenced him to be confined beyond the Tay, until his majesty resolved what farther punishment should be inflicted.

This unjust and oppressive sentence was not pronounced without a very solemn warning having been previously given by the Church. On the morning of Black's trial, the commissioners presented to the king and council an address, containing their deliberate sentiments respecting the nature of the contest in which they were engaged, and the momentous consequences which it involved. A portion of this document must be given, for the vindication of the

Church of Scotland from the calumnies of her enemies, and for the exposition of the truly Christian and patriotic sentiments by which the ministers were animated.

"We are compelled, for clearing of our ministry from all suspicion of such unnatural affection and offices towards your majesty and the state of your majesty's country, to call that great Judge who searcheth the hearts, and shall give recompence to every one conform to the secret thought thereof, to be judge betwixt us and the authors of all these malicious calumnies. Before His tribunal we protest, that we always bore, now bear, and shall bear, God willing, to our life's end, as loyal affection to your majesty as any of your majesty's best subjects within your majesty's realm, of whatsoever degree; and, according to our power and calling shall be, by the grace of God, as ready to procure and maintain your majesty's welfare, peace and advancement, as any of the best affectioned whosoever. We call your majesty's own heart to record, whether you have not found it so in effect to your majesty's straits, and if your majesty be not persuaded to find the like of us all, if it shall fall out that your majesty have occasion in these difficulties to have the trial of the affection of your subjects again. Whatsoever we have uttered, either in our doctrine or in other actions toward your majesty, it hath proceeded of a zealous affection toward your majesty's welfare, above all things next to the honour of God, as we protest; choosing rather by the liberty of our admonitions to hazard ourselves, than by our silence to suffer your majesty to draw on the guiltiness of any sin that might involve your majesty in the wrath and judgment of God. In respect whereof we most humbly beseech your majesty so to esteem of us and our proceedings, as tending always, in great sincerity of our hearts, to the establishing of religion, the surety of your majesty's estate and crown (which we acknowledge to be inseparably joined therewith), and to the common peace and welfare of the whole country. We persuade ourselves, that howsoever the first motion of this action might have proceeded upon a pu·pose of your majesty to have the limits of the spiritual jurisdiction distinguished from the civil, yet the same is entertained and blown up by the favourers of those that are, and shall prove in the end, the greatest enemies that either your majesty or the cause of God can have in this country; thinking thereby to engender such a misliking betwixt your majesty and the ministry as shall by time take away all farther trust, and in end work a division irreconcilable, wherethrough your majesty might be brought to think your greatest friends to be your enemies, and your greatest enemies to be your friends. There is no necessity at this time, nor occasion offered on our part, to insist on the decision of intricate and unprofitable questions and processes; albeit, by the subtle craft of adversaries of your majesty's quietness, some absurd and almost incredible suppositions (which the Lord forbid should enter in the part of Christians, let be in the hearts of the Lord's messengers) be drawn in and urged importunately at this time, as if the surety and privilege of your majesty's crown and authority royal depended on the present decision thereof. We must humbly beseech your majesty to remit the decision thereof to our lawful Assembly, that might determine thereupon according to the Word of God. For, this we protest in the sight of God, according to the light that he hath given us in his truth, that the special cause of the blessing that remaineth and hath remained upon your majesty and your majesty's country, since your coronation, hath been, and is, the liberty which the Gospel hath had within your realm; and if your majesty, under whatsoever colour, abridge the same directly or indirectly, the wrath of the Lord shall be kindled against your majesty and the kingdom, which we, in the name of the Lord Jesus, forewarn you of, that your majesty's and your council's blood lie not upon us."*

These solemn and evidently heart-wrung remonstrances had no effect upon James and his council: they were so intent upon their great design of humbling the Church, that the earnest pathos and fervent piety of the ministers made no impression upon their callous and haughty hearts. Still, with astonishing forbear-

* Calderwood, pp. 344, 345.

ance and patience, the commissioners of the Church continued to strive for peace, if it could be obtained without the abandonment of sacred principles. Again they sought an interview with his majesty, for the purpose of attempting an agreement; but nothing would satisfy the king, except the complete submission of Black to every point of his accusation. The ministers answered with sad and solemn earnestness, "that if the matter concerned only the life of Mr. Black, or that of a dozen others, they would have thought it of comparatively trifling importance; but as it was the liberty of the Gospel, and the spiritual sovereignty of the Lord Jesus, that was assailed, they could not submit, but must oppose all such proceeding, to the extreme hazard of their lives." This declaration, uttered by Bruce in his grave and serious manner, moved the heart of the king for a moment, till he even shed tears; and that night he pondered anxiously and rested little, perceiving that his attempt was likely to be followed by consequences which he had not anticipated.* But his courtly parasites soon regained their ascendency: the Lord President Seaton persuaded him that he could not, without loss of honour, abandon the prosecution; his remorse passed away; and again he prosecuted his designs, with even increased asperity and violence.

The king, by a proclamation, ordered the commissioners of the Asssembly to leave Edinburgh, declaring their powers unwarranted and illegal; and an act of council was passed, ordaining the ministers, before receiving payment of their stipends, to subscribe a bond, in which they promised to submit to the judgment of the king and the privy council as often as they were accused of seditious or treasonable doctrine; and commanding all magistrates in burghs, and noblemen and gentlemen in country parishes, to interrupt and imprison any preachers whom they should hear uttering such language from pulpits. At the same time a circular missive was prepared, for calling a convention of Estates, and a General Assembly, to be held at Edinburgh, on the 15th of the following February, to take into consideration "the whole order and policy of the Kirk." From this it was perfectly evident that the entire overthrow of the Presbyterian Church was intended.

On the 17th of December, a rumour being spread that the Earl of Huntly had arrived in the capital, and been admitted to the presence of the king, the ministers and the citizens became greatly alarmed; which was increased by the fact, that a charge had just been given to twenty-four of the most zealous of the townsmen to remove from Edinburgh. In this state of excitement an evil-disposed person (supposed to be an emissary of that courtier party called the *Cubiculars*) gave an alarm that the Papists were coming to massacre the Protestants. Absurd as this outcry would have appeared in a cooler moment, it was enough to raise a temporary tumult, through the combined influence of fear and imagination. No injury, however, was done to any one, either in person or property; and by the exertions of the ministers and the magistrates the tumult was speedily quieted This tumult, although utterly insignificant in itself, gave the king and the courtiers the opportunity for which they had so long wished, of a colour to their own violent proceedings. Next morning early the king quitted Holyrood-house and hastened to Linlithgow. Immediately upon his departure, a proclamation was issued, requiring all in public office to repair to him at Linlithgow, and commanding all strangers instantly to leave the capital. Fiercer proclamations immediately followed. The ministers of Edinburgh were ordered to enter into confinement in the castle; the magistrates were commanded to apprehend them; and the tumult was declared to be "a cruel and barbarous attempt against his majesty's royal person, his nobility, and council, at the instigation of certain seditious ministers and barons;" and all who had been accessory to it, or should assist them, were declared to be liable to the penalties of treason. A short time afterwards the king entered Edinburgh at the head of a hostile array, as if he had been taking possession of a captured town, breathing forth denunciations of vengeance, and threatening to raze the city to the ground, and to erect a monument where it stood, to perpetuate the

* Calderwood, p. 349; Life of Bruce; Livingstone's Memorable Characters, p. 74.

memory of such an execrable treason! The terrified citizens crouched before the storm of royal wrath, surrendered all their rights civil and sacred, subscribed such a bond as the king pleased to impose, and being sufficiently humbled and enslaved, were, by what Spotswood terms his majesty's unparalleled "grace and clemency," restored to favour.

1597. During this royal and courtly paroxysm the ministers of Edinburgh were advised by their friends to withdraw from the capital; which they reluctantly did, after Bruce had written a very able and eloquent apology for himself and his colleagues. This apology was copied by Spotswood himself, to aid in its dissemination, and in the copying he contrived to "give it a sharper edge."* A letter written by the Edinburgh ministers to Lord Hamilton, requesting him to intercede with the king in behalf of the Church, was also falsified, as there is strong reason to believe, by the same treacherous hand, while Spotswood was all the time pretending the utmost zeal in defending the liberties of the Church. It were well that every reader of Spotswood were aware of the deceitful and perfidious part acted by that designing and ambitious man, that they might know how little trust is to be reposed in any of his statements, and that writers on the prelatic side might, for very shame, cease to repeat his gross and malicious fabrications.

Affairs being in this condition,—the ministers of Edinburgh in exile or concealment, the citizens humbled and prostrate, and a false imputation cast upon the whole conduct of the Church,—the king proceeded to the execution of his long-cherished scheme. Fifty-five questions respecting the government and discipline of the Church, drawn up by Secretary Lindsay, were published in the name of the king, and a convention of estates and a meeting of the General Assembly were called by royal authority, to meet at Perth in the end of February, to consider these questions. But the spirit of the Church was not yet broken. Answers to his majesty's propositions were prepared by the synods, of Lothian and Fife; and while the king was requested to prorogue the extraordinary meeting which he had called, the Presbyteries, in case he should not comply, were instructed in the line of conduct which they should pursue; and not a minister of any note could be prevailed upon to subscribe the bond of submission framed and promulgated by the king.*

This prompt and energetic conduct convinced the king that sheer power would never enable him to triumph over men who could suffer and die, but not violate their duty to God. But there was yet one resource; the General Assembly might be vitiated by the introduction of false, ambitious, and unprincipled brethren, and thereby the Church made to fall by a suicidal blow. Sir Patrick Murray, one of the gentlemen of the bed-chamber, was sent to the northern parts of the kingdom, to visit the presbyteries of Angus, and Aberdeenshire, and to induce the ministers of those remote districts to subscribe his majesty's bond, and to come to Perth to the ensuing Assembly. Partly by flatteries and misrepresentations, and partly by striving to raise a spirit of jealousy in the northern ministers against the ascendancy of their south-country brethren, the royal emissary sped so well, that, when the Assembly met, it was found that the royal assentators formed a majority.

The first struggle was on the question, whether this was a lawful Assembly? and after a debate of three days, the affirmative was carried by a majority of votes, some even of the south-country ministers being corrupted by the royal intrigues. His majesty's questions were next taken into consideration; and such answers were given to the leading propositions, which alone were laid before them, as enabled the king to introduce his measures in a more plausible manner than formerly, with the seeming sanction of the Church.† Thus did the king succeed in partially accomplishing by stratagem and "kingcraft," to use his own term, what force and persecution could not effect.

The next meeting of the Assembly was held at Dundee, by the kings appointment, in May; and notwithstanding all his majesty's artifice, and the aid of his northern battalions, it was with the utmost

* Calderwood, p. 369.

* Melville's Dairy, pp. 256, 257.

† Booke of the Universall Kirk, pp. 443, 444.

difficulty that he was able to carry his measures. The Assembly of Perth was declared lawful, with an explanation; its acts were approved, but with certain qualifications; and the additional answers now given to the king's questions were very guardedly expressed. To advance his schemes with an Assembly so much on its guard, required all the peculiar cunning of the crafty monarch; but craft was his element, and false pretences were his weapons; and thus he prevailed over men who were too honest themselves thoroughly to understand his guile. He requested them to appoint a committee of their number, with whom he might advise on certain important affairs which they could not at present find leisure to determine, such as the arrangements to be made respecting the ministers of Edinburgh and St. Andrews, the planting of vacant churches in general, and the providing of local and fixed stipends for the ministers throughout the kingdom. To this the Assembly agreed, and nominated fourteen ministers, to whom, or any seven of them, they granted power to convene with his majesty, for the above purposes, and to give him advice "in all affairs concerning the weal of the Church, and entertainment of peace and obedience to his majesty within his realm."* This was indeed, as Calderwood says, "a wedge taken out of the Church, to rend her with her own forces." It enabled the king to frame and mature his devices, and to introduce them into the Church through what might be termed his ecclesiastical council. By their means also, he called before him presbyteries, reversed their decisions, and restored one suspended minister to his office,—a species of direct interference with ecclesiastical government to which at least one parallel might be pointed out, with this important difference—that what the king prevailed on his ecclesiastical council to do, a modern civil court has done of itself.

Availing himself of the advantage he had gained, James induced his ecclesiastical council to present a petition to the parliament which met in December, requesting that the Church might be represented, and have a voice in the supreme council of the nation. This petition the king induced the parliament to grant; and it was declared that Prelacy was the third estate of the kingdom; that such ministers as his majesty should please to raise to the dignity of prelates should have full right to sit and vote in parliament; and that bishoprics, as they became vacant, should be conferred on none but such as were qualified and disposed to act as ministers or preachers. This spiritual power to be exercised by bishops in the government of the Church, was left by parliament to be arranged by his majesty and the General Assembly. Thus the introduction of episcopacy was attempted to be concealed under the pretext of giving to the Church a vote in the national councils, for the security of her rights and the advancement of her welfare.

It will be observed by the attentive and intelligent reader, that even in this innovation there was an intermixture of constitutional propriety. It was so contrived that the proposal for representatives in parliament came first from the commissioners of the Church; and when the parliament agreed to the request, its enactment provided only that all ministers appointed to prelacies should have vote in parliament; that is, it restored the political rank of prelates, but left to the Church its own province untouched, to restore or not the prelatic office. And had the Church not been so much corrupted by the king, but refused to allow ministers to accept of prelacies, the act of parliament must have remained a dead letter, and the scheme proved abortive. It may be added, that the king had a double object in view in the matter,—both to obtain the means of silencing the bold and free admonitions and censures of the Church, by subjecting the ecclesiastical to the civil judicatories, and to acquire a body of creatures of his own within the parliament, by whose assistance he might control all its proceedings. The measure in short, was a deadly blow aimed at the very heart of liberty, civil and religious, as subsequent events ere long very clearly proved.

[1598.] Measures being thus far prepared, the next step was to prevail upon the Church to accede to the arrangement proposed by the act of parliament; and for this purpose the commissioners,

* Booke of the Universall Kirk, p. 461.

who were wholly gained over by the king, wrote a circular letter to their brethren, putting the most plausible construction on the scheme, and in particular representing it as essential to the procuring of legislative sanction to the "constant plat,"—the provision for a permanent ministry and fixed local stipends. This letter gave rise to long and keen debates in the several synods, particularly in that of Fife, where it was strongly opposed by both the Melvilles, by the venerable reforming patriarch Ferguson, and by Davidson, who, pointing out clearly that the proposed parliamentary voter was a bishop in disguise, exclaimed, "Busk, busk, busk him as bonnilie as ye can, and fetch him in as fairlie as ye will, we see him weill eneuch; we see the horns of his mitre."*

A meeting of the General Assembly was convoked by the king, at Dundee, in the Month of March 1598, expressly for the purpose of taking the late act of parliament into consideration. The most strenuous exertions were made by his majesty to get the Assembly packed and constructed according to his mind. The Aberdeenshire legion was again importunately summoned to the scene; his own ecclesiastical council was thoroughly trained for its appointed task; every means had been used to bring, as elders from the presbyteries, those noblemen and gentlemen who had already voted for the measure in parliament; and even after the Assembly met, several days were spent, before entering into business by his majesty, in holding private personal intercourse with the members, endeavouring to corrupt, intimidate, or cajole them into compliance. Not even then did he venture to proceed with his pernicious scheme, till he had banished Andrew Melville, not only from the Assembly, but even out of the town. The business was then introduced by a speech from his majesty himself; in which, after descanting complacently on the great services he had rendered the Church, and his anxiety still farther to promote her welfare, which, he alledged, could only be done by the proposed measure, he solemnly disclaimed any intention of bringing in popish or Anglican bishops, averring that his sole object was,

* Melville's Dairy, p. 289.

that some of the best and wisest of the ministry chosen by the General Assembly, should have a place in the privy council and parliament, to sit in judgment on their own affairs, and not to stand, as they had too long stood, at the door, like poor suppliants, disregarded and despised.*

The question was put in this form,—"Whether it was necessary and expedient, for the welfare of the Church, that the ministry, as the third estate of this realm, should, in the name of the Church, have a vote in parliament." A warm and protracted debate ensued, all the best and ablest ministers rejecting earnestly that elevation to wealth, rank, and power, which weak, worldly-minded, and ambitious men so greatly covet. It was at length carried in the affirmative, by the slender majority of ten, after all the artifices which the king had employed, and carried chiefly by the votes of the elders, a number of whom, it was asserted, had no commission. A protest was then given in by Davidson against the proceedings of this and the two foregoing Assemblies, on the ground of their not being free, but overawed by the king, and restricted in their due and wonted privileges; to which protest upwards of forty ministers adhered. It was then agreed by the Assembly, that fifty-one ministers should be chosen to represent the Church, according to the ancient number of the bishops, abbots, and priors; and that their election should belong partly to the king and partly to the Church. But when resolutions respecting the manner of electing the parliamentary representatives, the duration of their commission, their names and revenues, were proposed, many of the king's party began to waver, alarmed at the consequences of their own act; and it was deemed expedient to leave these matters for further consideration by the presbyteries, synods, and the next Assembly, which was appointed to meet at Aberdeen in July 1599.

Numerous meetings and conferences were held throughout the kingdom; and the more that the measure was investigated, the less was it approved of by the ministers. In a conference held at Falkland, the whole measure met such a de-

* Calderwood, p. 413.

cided opposition, that the king thought proper to prorogue the appointed meeting of Assembly, and had recourse again to that private influence to which he owed his previous success.

[1599.] In November 1599, another conference was held at Holyrood-house, called by the king, and attended by ministers from all parts of the country. The whole subject was then fully discussed, chiefly, it appears, for the purpose of ascertaining the arguments likely to be used against the measure in the next Assembly, that the court party might be prepared with their answers. The substance of this remarkable conference is given by James Melville in his Diary, and will well repay a careful perusal, by those who wish to ascertain the real sentiments of the Church of Scotland at this memorable period of her history. The conclusion of this conference was, that James, finding the discussion going decidedly against him, broke it off in anger, threatening that he would leave the refractory ministers to sink deeper and deeper into poverty; and would, besides, of his own authority, put into the vacant bishoprics persons who would accept of them, and who would do their duty to him and to his kingdom.*

[1600.] On the 28th day of March 1600, the General Assembly met at Montrose. The most intense interest was felt by the whole kingdom in the meeting and the proceedings of this Assembly; as it was manifest that upon its decision would depend the continuation or the overthrow of the Presbyterian form of church government in Scotland. The previous conferences had made both parties aware of each other's arguments, and, in a great measure, of each other's strength; and each appears to have entertained strong expectations of success. On the one hand, the staunch Presbyterians, holding firm by the great principles of the Reformation, by the acts of parliament formerly passed in their favour, and, above all, by the clear and plain language of Scripture, confided in the goodness of their cause, and trusted in the support of their divine Head and King. On the other, the court party, aware of the dislike entertained by the sovereign, the nobility, and all the looser-living part of the community, against the strictness and impartiality of Presbyterian discipline, and knowing the influence which the temptations of wealth, rank, and power must always exercise upon the selfish minds of poor and ambitious men, trusted that, by these considerations, and by the personal exertions of the crafty monarch himself, the triumph of their measure would be secured.

Andrew Melville had been chosen by the presbytery of St. Andrews as one of their representatives, and went accordingly to Montrose; but the king, dreading his influence and his power of argument, strictly prohibited him from taking his seat in the Assembly. He remained, nevertheless, in the town, and gave his brethren the benefit of his advice, during the course of the proceedings. After some preliminary business had been arranged, the Assembly proceeded to the consideration of that which was the great object of its meeting,—the propriety of ministers voting in parliament. The opponents of the measure brought forward a formidable train of arguments against it, such as its supporters felt it impossible to answer; who thereupon had recourse to evasions, and deceptive endeavours to draw their antagonists from their impregnable position. The king, perceiving his party evidently losing ground, and the whole scheme exposed to imminent peril, interposed his arbitrary authority, declaring that the preceding Assembly had already decided the general question in the affirmative, that its decision must be held final on that point, and that they had only to determine respecting minor arrangements. This interference on the part of his majesty saved his measure from defeat; for there is reason to think, that if the general question had been then put to the vote, the whole scheme would have been negatived. For, on the subordinate but kindred question, whether the parliamentary voters should retain their place for life, or be annually elected, it was carried, in spite of all the influence of the court, by a majority of three, in favour of annual election. Yet James, in the exercise of his favourite "king-craft," prevailed upon the clerk to draw up the minute stating that vote in such a manner as essentially to change its meaning,

* Melville's Dairy, pp. 296-308.

and virtually to grant the very thing which it was intended to reject; and in this vitiated form he contrived to procure for it the sanction of the Assembly, towards the close of its sittings, when its vigilance was diminished.*

To render the introduction of this measure somewhat less intolerable than it would otherwise have been, the court party agreed to all the "caveats" or cautions which had been proposed in the conference at Falkland, for protecting the liberties of the Church, and guarding against the introduction of Prelacy. The voters were to have the name, not of bishops, but of commissioners of the Church, in parliament. The General Assembly, with the advice of synods and presbyteries, were to nominate six in each province, of whom his majesty should choose one, as the ecclesiastical representative of that province. The commissioner was to be allowed the rents of the benefice to which he should be presented, after provision had been made out of them for the churches, colleges, and schools. And, that he might not abuse his power, it was provided,—That he should not propose any thing to parliament, convention, or council, in the name of the Church, without her express warrant and direction, nor consent to the passing of any act prejudicial to the Church, under the penalty of deposition from his office: That at each General Assembly he should give an account of the manner in which he had discharged his commission, and submit, without appeal, to the censure of the Assembly, under the pain of infamy and excommunication: That he should rest satisfied with the part of the benefice allotted to him, without encroaching upon what was assigned to other ministers within his province: That he should not dilapidate his benefice, nor dispose of any part of its rents, without the consent of the General Assembly: That he should perform all the duties of the pastoral office within his own particular congregation, subject to the censures of the presbytery and synod to which he belonged: That in all parts of ecclesiastical government and discipline, he should claim no more power or jurisdiction than what belonged to other ministers, under the pain of deprivation: That in meetings of presbytery and other church courts he should behave himself in all things, and be subject to censure, in the same manner as his brethren: That he should have no right to sit in the General Assembly without a commission from the presbytery: That, if deposed from the office of the ministry, he should lose his vote in parliament, and his benefice should become vacant: And that the very fact of ambitiously soliciting the office should itself, on conviction, be a sufficient cause of deposition and all its consequences. It was ordained, that these "caveats" should be inserted, "as most necessary and substantial points," in the body of an act of parliament to be made for confirming the vote of the Church; and that every commissioner should subscribe and swear to observe them, when he was admitted to that peculiar appointment.*

It will be admitted that these regulations were well adapted to render the king's measures as harmless as possible, if strictly observed. But, to use the words of Spotswood, "it was neither the king's intention, nor the minds of the *wiser sort*, to have these cautions stand in force; but, to have matters peaceably ended, and the reformation of the policy made without any noise, the king gave way to these conceits."† And yet these "conceits" were publicly ratified by act of Parliament, and Spotswood himself, as well as others of "the wiser sort," solemnly swore to observe them. But to such an accomplished master of "king-craft" as James, and to such worldly-wise churchmen as Spotswood and his coadjutors, the violation of national faith, and the direct perjury of men styling themselves ministers of the gospel, seemed but a slight sacrifice to make for the introduction of their beloved Prelacy into a church and a kingdom, both of which cordially abhorred and dreaded its very name and nature, as equally a corruption of the Christian ministry and an instrument of political despotism.

The perfidious designs of the king and the "wiser sort" were very soon displayed. A meeting of the commissioners of the General Assembly was called

* Calderwood, pp. 438, 439; M'Crie's Life of Melville ii. pp. 58-62.

* Booke of the Universall Kirk, pp. 482-487.
† Spotswood, p. 435.

by the king in the month of October following, to have their advice respecting the settlement of ministers in Edinburgh, and to consult on other matters to be proposed to parliament for the good of the Church and kingdom. Pursuing his usual policy, the king got James Melville and two other ministers appointed on a committee to transact some other business; and during their absence, he, with the consent of those present, summarily nominated David Lindsay, Peter Blackburn, and George Gladstanes, to the vacant bishoprics of Ross, Aberdeen, and Caithness. This transaction was carefully concealed from the absent members until the meeting was dissolved; and the bishops appointed in this clandestine manner sat and voted in the ensuing parliament, in direct violation of the cautions to which they had so lately given their consent. But these cautions, though thus early violated, and though their protective power was thus proved to be ineffectual to prevent the lawless deeds of a treacherous king and perfidious churchmen, were not therefore of no avail. Their enactment served to show the mind and the principles of the purer part of the Church of Scotland; and, remaining on the statute-book unrepealed, like the clause of the convention of Leith subjecting bishops to the General Assembly, they, together with that clause, being revived and called into operation in better times, gave to the Church of Scotland the means and the power of deposing and excommunicating her perjured betrayers.

If the Church of Scotland had been in any doubt respecting the arbitrary intentions of the king, that doubt must have been completely dispelled by two different works published by the royal author about this time. These were, his *Free Law of Free Monarchies*, and his *Basilicon Doron*, or instructions of the king to his son, Prince Henry. In the former of these productions his majesty expresses with abundant clearness his notions of a free monarchy, which according to him, is the government of "a free and absolute monarch,"—a king free to do what he pleases,—in short, a perfect despotism, in which the arbitrary will of the sovereign is above all law with a parliament to register and execute his commands, and a people his passively-obedient and unresisting slaves. In the latter, the Basilicon Doron, the extent and nature of the king's hatred of the Presbyterian Church was revealed, as may be seen from the propositions extracted from that treatise, and condemned by the synod of Fife. These propositions were the following:—That the office of a king is of a mixed kind, partly civil and partly ecclesiastical: That a principal part of his function consists in ruling the Church: That it belongs to him to judge when preachers wander from their text; and that such as refuse to submit to his judgment in such cases ought to be capitally punished: That no ecclesiastical assemblies ought to be held without his consent: That no man is more to be hated of a king than a proud puritan: That parity among ministers is irreconcilable with monarchy, inimical to order, and the mother of confusion: That puritans had been a pest to the commonwealth and Church of Scotland, wished to engross the civil government as tribunes of the people, sought the introduction of democracy into the State, and quarrelled with the king because he was a king: That the chief persons among them should not be allowed to remain in the land: And that parity in the Church should be banished, Episcopacy set up, and all who preached against bishops rigorously punished.*

Surely no man of common intelligence and candour will deny that the Church of Scotland had good reason to be jealous of a monarch who could pen such gross slanders and outrageous opinions; and yet, at the very same time, the royal dissembler was publicly and loudly declaring that nothing was farther from his mind than the introduction of the prelatic system into Scotland! But oaths and laws were in his view fetters of iron to Presbyterian ministers and the community, and threads of gossamer to kings and prelates. The policy of principle he knew not, because he was himself unprincipled; but the policy of falsehood, cunning, and sycophancy, he well understood and practised, and crowded its whole essence into his favourite ecclesi

* Melville's Diary, p. 295.

astico-political aphorism, "*No bishop, no king*," which his own comment explains to mean, No bishop, no despot.

An event occurred in the same year, 1600, the consequences of which proved exceedingly detrimental to the Church of Scotland. This was that mysterious event known in history by the name of the Gowrie conspiracy, the true nature of which has never been fully unveiled. Leaving the discussion of such topics to the civil historian, to whose province they belong, we proceed to state the baneful consequences to the Church arising out of this strange conspiracy. An order was issued by the privy council, commanding all ministers to give thanks for his majesty's deliverance, according to a prescribed form; and for not using the very words of that form, the ministers of Edinburgh were called before the council, and candidly acknowledged that they were not thoroughly convinced of Gowrie's treason, although they respected the king's account of the matter, and were willing to express thankfulness that he had been delivered from danger, provided they were not at the same time obliged to express any opinion respecting its nature and extent. Five of them were immediately banished from the capital, and prohibited from preaching in Scotland. Of these, four soon submitted; but the remaining one, Robert Bruce, not being convinced, would not violate his conscience by saying what he did not believe, and was banished from the kingdom. He was afterwards allowed to return to his native country, but not to Edinburgh; and his offence was never forgiven,—an offence in which nearly all the kingdom, and almost every historian, shared. After his return he was banished for a time to Inverness; then allowed to reside in his own house at Kinnaird, near Stirling; then removed to the vicinity of Glasgow, watched and persecuted by the bishops, and beloved and revered by every good and pious man throughout the kingdom, many of whom, and among others the celebrated Alexander Henderson, owed their conversion to his instrumentality. But James could never forgive him for two dire offences; he had rendered great services to his country, and he had been injured by the king; for the one the sovereign hated him, because it could neither be denied nor compensated; and for the other, because it is natural for malignant men to hate those whom they injure. To this may be added, that the king bore towards Bruce that instinctive antipathy which men of little minds cherish against those in the presence of whom their dwarfish intellect shrinks into its native insignificance, rebuked and crouching.*

A considerable number of the ministers throughout the country were brought into much trouble on account of their expressing sympathy with the ministers of Edinburgh, and with Bruce in particular. And it deserves to be mentioned, that the king availed himself of the confusion and distress into which this affair had cast the Church, for completing his eversive schemes; for it was while James Melville and two of his like-minded brethren were conversing with the persecuted ministers of Edinburgh, that James nominated three of his creatures to the vacant bishoprics, as above related.†

[1601.] A meeting of the General Assembly was held at Burntisland in May 1601, by the appointment of James, who called it two months earlier than had been previously arranged. He was induced, probably, to take this step, partly in consequence of the failure of an embassy which he had sent to Rome to propitiate the papal influence, and partly because of the odium which he had incurred by the slaughter of the Earl of Gowrie, the accusation of treason against whom the mass of the nation could not be induced to believe. To this Assembly James Melville sent a letter, pointing out very faithfully the corruptions still remaining in the Church and nation, and urging his brethren to fidelity in the discharge of their public duty; but this letter the king thought proper to suppress. A letter to the same effect, but expressed in stronger terms, written by the venerable John Davidson, was read in the Assembly, contrary to his majesty's inclination. Davidson's letter was instrumental in leading the Assembly back to the sacred ground so frequently occupied by its predecessors. They entered into a serious deliberation on the "causes of the general defections from the purity, zeal, and practice of the true religion in all

* Calderwood pp. 444-446. † Ibd., pp. 445, 446.

estates of the country, and how the same may be most effectually remedied." The king himself either yielded to, or for a short while participated in, the general feeling. He rose up and addressed the Assembly with great appearance of sincerity, tears moistening his eyes as he spoke. He confessed his offences and mismanagement in the government of the kingdom; and lifting up his hand, he vowed in the presence of God and of the Assembly, that he would, by the grace of God, live and die in the religion presently professed in the realm of Scotland, defend it against all its adversaries, minister justice faithfully to his subjects, reform whatever was amiss in his person or family, and perform all the duties of a good and a Christian king better than he had hitherto performed them. At the request of his majesty, the members of Assembly in a similar manner renewed their vows; and it was ordained that this mutual vow should be intimated from the pulpits on the following Sabbath, to convince the people of the good dispositions of his majesty, and the cordiality subsisting between him and the Church.*

Various other matters were transacted in this Assembly, of little public importance, with one exception,—a proposal to review and improve the common translation of the Bible, and the metrical version of the Psalms. Into this proposal the king entered with great cordiality, availed himself of the opportunity of displaying his acquaintance with the Scriptures, and his knowledge of their original languages, and subsequently set himself to the task of attempting a new poetical version of the Psalms.

Although the king had, in the Assembly held at Burntisland, made the most solemn declaration of love to the Church of Scotland, yet as soon as his fit of devotion, and perhaps of remorse, wore off, he returned to his course, and continued to prosecute his measures for the subversion of that Church which he so often swore to maintain. Upon the representation of his parasite Gladstanes, he confined Andrew Melville within the precincts of the College of St. Andrews; and he continued to demand from Bruce concessions which he well knew that upright man could never make, that he might have some pretext for continuing to prosecute and oppress him. And when the synod of Fife met, and proceeded, with accustomed sincerity and boldness, to express complaints and animadversions respecting public matters, the king endeavoured first to circumvent, and then to intimidate James Melville, in neither of which attempts did he succeed.

[1602.] The Assembly had been appointed to meet in July 1602, at St. Andrews; but the king, on his own authority, postponed it till November, changing the place of meeting to the chapel at Holyrood-house. This arbitrary mode of dealing with the meetings of the Assembly excited considerable apprehension, numbers of the most faithful ministers regarding it as, what in all probability it was intended for,—a mode of familiarizing the minds of the ministers generally with the idea that the meeting of the Assembly was wholly dependent on the pleasure of his majesty, and might be postponed indefinitely, or altogether disallowed, whenever he should think proper. A protestation against this arbitrary procedure was given in by James Melville. Yet when the Assembly fairly entered upon its duties, it was soon apparent that a great number of the ministers were still true Presbyterians. Several important acts were passed concerning the visitation, examination, and censure of synods, presbyteries, pastors, and congregations; and regulations were framed of a very searching nature, well calculated to test the conduct and character of the Church, both office-bearers and ordinary members, and to prevent that laxity of discipline and morals which the prelatic party were but too certain to introduce, should their machinations be successful.

In this Assembly's records we find mention of a case of some importance, as indicative of the views of the Church, respecting the appointment of ministers at that period. The synod of Glasgow brought a complaint against Mr. George Semple, who had been presented to the parish of Killelane, and whom the synod had forbidden to intermeddle with the ministry in that parish, for various reasons, but especially on account of a great dislike which several of the parishioners

* Melville's Dairy, pp. 329-331; Caldorwood, pp. 447-456; Booke of the Universall Kirk, pp, 491-499.

entertained against him. The Assembly inquired into the case, acquitted Mr. Semple of the charges brought against his character in general; but, in respect of the great dislike between him and the parishioners, "think it not good that he be planted minister at the said kirk, and therefore ordained him to desist therefrom, and demit the presentation made to him of the benefice thereof."*

This Assembly was the last which was recognised by the Church of Scotland as a free and lawful Assembly, from that time till the year 1638. And indeed even the Assembly of 1602 can scarcely be called a free Assembly. It was held in the very precincts of the palace; some of the most influential men in the Church were violently prevented from attending it; and on several occasions the king and his minions interrupted the proceedings when these began to take a course of which the despotic monarch and his flatterers did not approve; as, for instance, when an accusation was brought against Spotswood, that he had been present at the superstitious and idolatrous popish service of the mass, when he was recently in France, the court party interfered, and contrived to prevent the process against him from going forward.

[1603.] On the last day of March 1603, intelligence of the death of Queen Elizabeth having reached Scotland, James was proclaimed king of Scotland, England, France, and Ireland: and in the High Church of Edinburgh on the following Sabbath, he addressed the assembled people, and once more declared his approbation of the Church of Scotland, disclaiming all intention of making any farther alteration in its government. But even in the moment of his exultation on account of his easy accession to such an increase of wealth and power, he relented not in his determination to perpetrate the punishments which he had inflicted on Bruce and Davidson, unless they would confess themselves guilty of an offence in a matter in which they saw nothing guilty or offensive. If they could have flattered and falsified, they might easily have regained his favour; that is, they might have regained, by ceasing to deserve it; but because they could not be other than honest and conscientious men, they could not recover the favour of their vain, weak-minded, and obstinate sovereign.

The Presbyterian Church of Scotland had little reason to expect that its government and discipline would obtain additional favour from a sovereign who had long plotted their overthrow, now that he had obtained a vast accession of wealth and power, and was surrounded by the dignitaries of the prelatic Church of England. Still, it was not from the English bishops, so much as from their own treacherous countrymen, that the Scottish ministers were most apprehensive of danger; according to the well-known fact, that the renegade becomes the greatest zealot. The Hampton Court conference between the High Church party and the puritan Non-conformists, which took place soon after James's arrival in London, indicated with sufficient distinctness what might be expected; especially when his majesty, in his first speech in parliament, expressed his tender indulgence of papal errors, and his utter detestation of the puritans, with "their confused form of policy and parity," whom he termed "a sect insufferable in any well-governed commonwealth." The proposal for a union of the two kingdoms gave additional alarm to the Church of Scotland, who saw in such a measure, especially after the utterance of such sentiments, the greatest danger to the Presbyterian establishment.

In this dangerous juncture the synod of Fife again put itself boldly in the front of the conflict. When the Scottish parliament met to deliberate upon the proposal for a union, the synod of Fife applied for liberty to hold a General Assembly; and when this was declined, the synod addressed the commissioners of the Assembly, reminded them of their duty and their responsibility to the Church at all times, and particularly in this hour of danger. They adjured the commissioners to defend the government of the Church of Scotland, as not resting upon conventional grounds, capable of being changed or altered, but upon Divine authority, equally as the other articles of religion did; declaring that they would rather suffer death itself than see the overthrow of the Presbyterian Church. This spirited remonstrance had a most beneficial effect. The parliament passed

* Booke of the Universall Kirk, p. 529.

an act in conformity with its views, declaring, that the commissioners for the union should have no power to treat of any thing that concerned the religion and ecclesiastical discipline of Scotland.* This, it may be remarked, was of the very same nature as the celebrated Act of Security, passed about a century afterwards, as the basis of the union then really formed; and we shall have occasion to show how little such an act was able to accomplish directly the purpose for which it was intended, but yet, as in the other instances, of how much service it may finally be productive. A great constitutional principle, law or declaration, may remain for any indefinite length of time not dead but dormant; and may at length be aroused into potential activity, so as to realize the full developement of that precious germ which it so long preserved.

[1604.] Events very soon proved that the dangers dreaded by the Church were not imaginary. When the time approached that the General Assembly should meet, which had been appointed to be on the last Tuesday of July 1604, at Aberdeen, his majesty prorogued it till the conferences respecting the union should be over, and postponed its meeting till the same month of the following year. But the presbytery of St. Andrews being resolved to exonerate themselves from the blame of allowing their sacred rights to be violated without remonstrance, enjoined their representatives to keep the appointed meeting, notwithstanding the royal prorogation, which they accordingly did; and finding none present to assist them in holding an Assembly, they took a formal protest that they had done their duty, and that the danger to the privileges and rights of the Church, arising from the cowardly neglect of others, should not be imputed to them.

This bold and faithful conduct acted like the kindling of a beacon in the time of a threatened invasion. The next meeting of the Synod of Fife bore the aspect of a General Assembly, so many delegates from all parts of the kingdom assembled, to consult what course should now be taken in defence of their religious liberties. This synodical meeting, and an extraordinary one subsequently held at Perth, went as direct to the cause of these evils as they constitutionally could, charging not the king, but the parliamentary bishops, with hindering the meeting of the Assembly, for the purpose of prolonging their own powers, and of evading the censures which their conduct had deserved. It was resolved that petitions should be sent from all the synods, requesting his majesty to allow the Assembly to meet for the transaction of important business. The terror and wrath of the parliamentary bishops and expectant commissioners were great; and Gladstanes procured an order from the king to throw the two Melvilles into prison, in revenge for their activity,—an order which the privy council did not deem it expedient at the time to execute.

[1605.] But the king had resolved upon his course; and when the time for the meeting of the General Assembly again drew near, it was again prorogued, notwithstanding the numerous petitions sent to court, requesting its meeting to be allowed. And, as if to remove all doubt respecting his design, his majesty, in proroguing the Assembly, mentioned no time for its next meeting. This rendered it evident that nothing less than its entire suppression was intended, and, by inevitable consequence, the overthrow of the Presbyterian Church of Scotland, and the erection of Prelacy. This was directly contrary to the act of parliament 1592, in which it was expressly stipulated that the Assembly should meet at least once every year; it was contrary even to the acts of parliament and Assembly passed for the introducing of commissioners of the church into parliament, who were annually to render to the Assembly an account of their conduct, subject to censure and deposition if they had acted improperly. The suppression of the meeting of Assembly was a virtual bestowal of permanence in their function on these parliamentary bishops and commissioners, and to that extent was directly eversive of the constitution and government of the Presbyterian Church. It was therefore imperatively necessary for the Church now to oppose these perfidious

* Calderwood, pp. 479-482; M'Crie's Life of Melvile, vol. i. pp. 108, 109

and arbitrary encroachments, and to defend her sacred liberties, or to be for ever enslaved.

When the Assembly was thus prorogued, the time of its meeting was so near at hand that several presbyteries had already chosen their representatives. The interval was too short to admit of such deliberations and transmission of opinions as would have enabled the whole Church to act in a body, and according to one systematic plan; but nine presbyteries resolved to send their representatives to Aberdeen, with instructions to constitute the Assembly, and adjourn it to a particular day, without proceeding to transact any business. For it was still hoped that his majesty might be prevailed upon to alter his course; and the Church was extremely reluctant to take any exasperating steps, but merely to secure formally its sacred and statutory rights.

On the 2d of July 1605, nineteen ministers met, after sermon in the session-house of Aberdeen; and the king's commissioner, Straiton of Lauriston, presented to them a letter from the lords of the privy council, addressed "To the brethren of the ministry convened at their Assembly in Aberdeen." The very address of this letter not only authorized the Assembly, but rendered it necessary, that it should be formally constituted before the letter could with propriety be read. This was done accordingly; and while they were engaged in reading the letter, a messenger-at-arms entered, and, in the king's name, charged them to dismiss, on the pain of rebellion. The Assembly declaring their readiness to comply with this order, requested the commissioner to name a day and place for their next meeting; and upon his refusal, the moderator appointed the Assembly to meet again in the same place on the last Tuesday of September ensuing, and then dissolved the meeting with prayer. It was afterwards pretended by the commissioner, that he had prohibited the Assembly by open proclamation at the market-cross of Aberdeen on the day before it met; but when Andrew Melville charged him, in presence of the king, with having falsified the date, he had nothing to answer, and could not produce a single person who had heard the proclamation on that day.*

Is there one man who understands the principles and values the rights of religious and civil liberty, that will condemn the proceedings of this much calumniated Assembly? The right of the ministers of the Church of Scotland to meet at least once a-year in a General Assembly, had been always asserted, had been secured by acts of parliament, and had received repeatedly the express sanction of his majesty. And when these sacred rights and legislative enactments were attempted to be destroyed by the arbitrary will of the sovereign, on the bare authority of a royal proclamation, the ministers of the Church of Scotland would have been unworthy of the names they bore, the station they occupied, and the great cause in defence of which they stood forth, had they acted in any other manner than they did,—had they not confronted every danger, rather than submit to measures which aimed at the establishment of a perfect despotism. It does not seem too much to say, that these high principled christian ministers were the chosen instruments, in the hand of the Divine Head and King of the Church, for the preservation of that sacred principle,—the right of the office-bearers and members of the Christian Church to meet and deliberate respecting religious matters, and to exercise a spiritual jurisdiction therein, free from all civil control. And though for a time the strong arm of power might crush the devoted defenders of that sacred principle, the principle itself, when once fully made known and resolutely asserted, was indestructible, because it was true, and because God was its defender.

The wrath of the king, when informed of the meeting of the Assembly at Aberdeen, knew no bounds. He instantly sent orders to Scotland to proceed with the utmost rigour against the ministers who had presumed to contravene his command. Fourteen of the most eminent were sent to prison to wait their trial, John Forbes, moderator of the late Assembly, and John Welsh, son-in-law of Knox, being confined in separate dungeons in the castle of Blackness. Acting

* Calderwood, pp. 492-494.

according to the principles of the Church of Scotland, they declined the jurisdiction of the privy council in a matter purely ecclesiastical; and this being, as formerly, regarded as an aggravation of their offence, they were indicted to stand trial for high treason before the Court of the Justiciary at Linlithgow. The able defence of Forbes and Welsh, supported by the legal reasonings of Thomas Hope, and countenanced by Andrew Melville, could not avail to rescue the victims from the gripe of the tyrant. Every species of corruption was employed by James's unworthy minions to secure a verdict against them, which was at length obtained by a majority of no more than three.*

Six eminently pious and able ministers were thus condemned and cast into prison, to wait his majesty's pleasure what sentence should be pronounced. Eight more remained for trial; and the relentless despot sent orders to proceed without delay to a repetition of the same perversion of law and justice. But the heart of Scotland began to swell with sympathy for the sufferers; and the privy council sent intimation to the king, that it would not be safe to proceed with the trial in the present temper and feeling of the nation. James yielded to the remonstrance so far as to release the eight ministers from prison, but banished them to the remotest parts of the kingdom. The six who had been convicted, after suffering fourteen months' imprisonment in the Castle of Blackness, were banished into France.

Such were the first-fruits of the introduction of Prelacy into Scotland,—the violation of acts of parliament, the corruption of courts of justice, and the banishment of ministers eminently distinguished by personal piety, and by success in the discharge of their sacred duties; and so early was the foundation laid in Scottish experience for what has become a national proverb,—"that prelatic Episcopacy never appeared in Scotland but as a persecutor."

[1606.] In the month of February 1606, an evasive attempt was made by the king, at the instigation of the bishops, to procure the consent of the synods to five articles, intended to secure the bishops and commissioners from the consequences of their violation of all the cautions they had sworn to observe, and also to admit the power which the king claimed over the meetings of the General Assembly. But although the synods were cunningly summoned to meet on the same day all over the kingdom, so that there could be no interchange of opinion among them, the result was, that only one synod, that of Angus, assented to the proposed articles.

* Calderwood, pp. 499-516.

A parliament was held at Perth in August the same year, for the purpose chiefly of proceeding with the restoration of Prelacy. In order to effect this, it was necessary to repeal the statute annexing the temporalities of bishoprics to the crown, and to restore them to those who should be nominated to the episcopal office. This intention becoming known, the ministers from all quarters repaired to Perth, remonstrated against this design, and finally gave in a protest to each of the three estates. This protest was signed by forty-two ministers, three of whom not long afterwards accepted bishoprics, to their perpetual disgrace. The protest itself may be seen in Calderwood, and also in the introduction to Stevenson; and deserves an attentive perusal, as an able embodiment of the opinions entertained by the leading men in the Church at that period,—opinions which all ages would do well to cherish. An arrangement was made between the nobility and the prelatic party to the following effect: That the wealth and lands formerly possessed by abbots, priors, &c., in virtue of which those persons had voted in parliament, and as representing which so many commissioners of the Church had recently been admitted to sit and vote, should be alienated from the Church, and erected into temporal lordships; and that, on the other hand, there should be seventeen prelacies erected, and the bishops restored to all their ancient honours, dignities, privileges, and prerogatives. In the preamble to the strange and arbitrary act by which this base arrangement was ratified, and which was for a considerable time kept as secret as possible, his majesty is recognized as "absolute prince, judge, and governor over all estates, persons, and causes, both spiritual and temporal.*

A short while previous to the meeting

* Act Parl. Scot. iv. pp. 281-283; Calderwood, p. 532.

of parliament, letters were sent by the king to six of the most distinguished of the ministers who had not been already seized on account of the Aberdeen Assembly. These six were, Andrew and James Melville, William Scott, John Carmichael, William Watson, James Balfour, Adam Colt, and Robert Wallace. They were commanded to repair to London, that his majesty might treat with them concerning such things as would settle the peace of the Church, and would justify to the world the measures which his majesty, after such extraordinary condescension, might find it necessary to adopt for repressing the obstinate and turbulent. The ministers had little doubt what would be the issue. The course of the king's conduct in times past pointed out with sufficient plainness what was his probable design. Like the tyrant of antiquity, James knew that the safest method of reducing a nation to slavery was to begin by cutting off its leading and free-spirited men. Bruce and Welsh were already in exile; and if the Melvilles could also be removed, he might secure the comparatively easy accomplishment of his favourite scheme,—the overthrow of the Church of Scotland, and the establishment of Prelacy.

The heart sickens at the very recital of such a continued course of royal knavery and prelatic treachery; and we feel compelled to trace with more rapid and summary course the remaining stages of this disgraceful period of our national history. When the six ministers arrived at London, they were admitted to an interview with the king, and questioned respecting their opinion of the Assembly which met at Aberdeen, notwithstanding the royal prorogation. Every endeavour was used to draw them into the use of language which might furnish a plausible pretext for instituting proceedings against them; and at length, on the despicable charge against Andrew Melville, of having written an epigram censuring pointedly the superstitious ceremonies which he had been compelled to witness in the Chapel Royal, he was brought to trial as guilty of a treasonable act. Notwithstanding the singularly able and eloquent defence of Melville, he was committed to the Tower, subjected to a tedious imprisonment of four years, and at length allowed to go to Sedan, where he remained till his death. His nephew was also prohibited from returning to Scotland, and the remaining four from returning to their parishes, although not implicated in the offence charged against him; but thus the crafty tyrant contrived to cut down the tallest.

The king and his bishops thinking themselves now tolerably secure of carrying their measures, hastened with keen speed to the work. Missives were addressed by the king to the several presbyteries, informing them that an Assembly was to be held at Linlithgow on the 10th of December, and naming the persons whom they were to send as representatives. Thus even the choice of their own representatives was to be taken away before the king could expect to threaten or cajole the Presbyterian ministers into the reception of his beloved Prelacy. Some of the presbyteries refused to grant any commission to the king's nominees; and others strictly prohibited them from taking part in the decision of any ecclesiastical question. When this packed Assembly met, a letter from his majesty was read, recommending the appointment of constant moderators of presbyteries, and that the bishops should be the moderators of the presbyteries within whose bounds they resided. Even in this carefully-selected Assembly it required all the art of the king's commissioner, and a repetition of the deceitful protestations and cautions of the perjured prelates, to carry a measure so repugnant to every Presbyterian principle. It was carried, however; and when sent to his majesty to be ratified, it returned with an interpolation, appointing the bishops to be moderators of provincial synods, as well as of presbyteries. Legal charges were sent to all the synods and presbyteries to admit the constant moderators; and the synod of Angus confirmed its bad pre-eminence by being the only one that did not refuse.* Fierce, violent, and outrageous were the attempts made by the king's agents to force the bishops as constant moderators upon the synods and presbyteries, and in almost every instance unsuccessfully.

* Calderwood, pp. 550-554.

though many ministers were thrown into prison, and disgraceful tumults raised by the prelatic party.

[1607.] The whole of the year 1607 was employed by the prelates and their supporters in their endeavour to force the constant moderators upon synods and presbyteries, by every method which craft could devise or tyranny execute.

[1608.] But the bishops perceiving that these forcible measures were rousing the spirit of the country, had recourse to a stratagem which wrought more effectually. A conference was held at Falkland, between the Prelatists and the faithful presbyterians, with the pretext of attempting to come to an amicable arrangement, and put an end to the strifes and divisions by which the country was distracted. Following up this policy, an Assembly was held at Linlithgow about the end of July, in which the Prelatists repeated their wish for a peaceful and amicable discussion on the points in dispute, some of them pretending that they began to be of opinion that Prelacy was more agreeable to Scripture than the Presbyterian form of church government. This fallacious pretext produced the desired effect. It lulled many of the vigilant Presbyterians into security, or directed their attention to speculative discussions, while their wily antagonists were pressing forward their machinations practically.

[1609.] A parliament was held at Edinburgh in 1609, in which the bishops were present, but none of the ministers received intimation of its meeting, that they might, as usual, present their requests to the national legislature. Considerable progress was accordingly made by the prelates in the prosecution of their measures. Spotswood, now archbishop of Glasgow, was made a Lord of Session; and the bishops were empowered to modify and fix the stipends of ministers,—a power which they did not scruple to employ for the pupose of bribing adherents, and of starving antagonists. Thus were the bishops restored by Parliament to the civil jurisdiction formerly held by the popish prelates.

[1610.] On the 16th of February 1610 a commission was given under the great seal of the two archbishops of St. Andrews and Glasgow, to hold two courts of high Commission. These courts, it may be mentioned here, were united in 1615, when Spotswood was translated to St. Andrews, and thereby became possessed of what in popish times had been the primacy. Never was a more tyrannical court instituted than that of High Commission. It was regulated by no fixed laws or forms of justice, and was armed with the united terrors of civil and ecclesiastical despotism. It had the power of receiving appeals from any ecclesiastical judicatory; of calling before it all persons accused of immorality, heresy, sedition, or an imaginary offence; or finding them guilty upon evidence which no court of justice would have sustained; and of inflicting any punishment either civil or ecclesiastical, or both, which it thought proper. "As it exalted the bishops far above any prelate that ever was in Scotland, so it put the king in possession of what he had long desired, namely, the royal prerogative and absolute power to use the bodies and goods of his subjects at his pleasure, without form or process of law: so that our bishops were fit instruments of the overthrow of the freedom and liberty both of the Church and realm of Scotland."*

An Assembly was held at Glasgow on the 8th of June, the same year. Previous to its meeting, the king, by the direction of the bishops, sent circular letters to the presbyteries, nominating as on a former occasion, their representatives; and the Earl of Dunbar was sent from London as king's commissioner, well provided with golden persuasives to use in lack of better arguments. His majesty's dictatorial letter was read; threats and promises were plentifully employed; and at length the whole of the prelatic measures were carried, only five votes being given against them. The Aberdeen Assembly of 1605 was condemned; the right of calling and dismissing Assemblies was declared to belong to the royal prerogative; the bishops were declared moderators of diocesan synods, and all presentations to benefices were appointed to be directed to them; and the power of excommunicating and absolving offenders, and of visiting the churches within their respective dioceses,

* Melville's Hist. of Decl. Age. pp. 270-276; Calderwood, pp. 616-619.

was conferred on them. Thus did this packed, and intimidated, and bribed convention (often called the *Angelical Assembly*, in allusion to the *angels*, a gold coin used in bribing the mercenary prelatists), consent to the introduction of the corrupt and corrupting prelatic system of church government. Not more strongly contrasted are Prelacy and Presbytery in their forms and ceremonies, than in the methods by which they were established in Scotland. The faithful preaching of the gospel, open and manly argument, and the pure lives of its teachers, were the means employed by Presbytery to fix itself in the heart of Scotland: arbitrary power, dissimulation, perfidy, treachery, corruption, and persecution, were the methods by which Prelacy was introduced, nourished, and confirmed. Till these facts have perished from the records of history, little else will be required by any right-hearted and unprejudiced man, to enable him to answer the question, Which of the two systems is of human invention, and which of divine institution?

The perfidious acts of the Glasgow Assembly were kept for a time concealed till the prelates were ready to have them enforced. Yet great opposition was made in many parts of the country, and the persecution of faithful ministers was resumed. Spotswood, Lambe, and Hamilton, went to London to obtain consecration of their episcopal functions, and that they might afterwards legitimately consecrate their prelatic brethren.

[1612.] Nearly two years elapsed between the Glasgow Assembly and the ratification of its acts by the parliament, in October 1612; but in the ratification the acts were so far changed as to render them more according to the wish of the prelates, especially of Spotswood, who directly asserts that this act rescinded and annulled that of 1592.* By the influence of the same ambitious man, also, the Courts of High Commission were subsequently united in 1615, and he was placed at the head of this prelatic inquisition.

[1616.] No Assembly was held till August 1616, when it was summoned to meet at Aberdeen. It is chiefly remarkable on account of a new Confession of Faith, drawn up by the prelatic party, sufficiently orthodox in its doctrines, but meagre and evasive in respect of church government and discipline, for a very evident reason.* By this accommodating Assembly the popish lords were received into favour, and subscribed the new Confession. The prelatic party had indeed outgrown the patriarchs of the Reformation.

[1617.] In 1617 the king paid a visit to his ancient kingdoms; expecting, probably, to find matters more to his liking under the prelatic sway than formerly. He soon found, however, that the ancient spirit was not wholly fled. A considerable number of the ministers gave in a protestation against a proposal that the king, with the advice of the prelates and some of the ministry, should have power to enact ecclesiastical laws; and when David Calderwood was summoned before the Court of High Commission on account of this protestation, he declined its jurisdiction. Some sharp altercation passed between him and the king, which Calderwood has himself recorded in a very graphic manner.† The result was, that he was banished out of the kingdom, and compelled to depart during the stormy winter weather, the king coarsely saying, that should he be drowned it would save him from a worse fate. A sort of Assembly was held at St. Andrews in the end of October, for the purpose of completing the prelatic innovations; but it proved rather premature, and that completion was reserved for the following year.

[1618.] On the 25th of August 1618, the General Assembly met at Perth, in obedience to the royal mandate. During the preceding summer months, every possible device which craft or despotism could suggest, had been used to prepare such an Assembly as would be sufficiently subservient; and when the Assembly met, nothing was left undone to ensure a prelatic triumph. They met in what was called the Little Kirk, in which a long table was placed in the centre, benches arranged on each side of it, and at the head a cross table, with chairs for his majesty's commissioners and the moderator. The nobility, gentry, and prelates placed themselves on the benches, leaving

* Spotswood, p. 518.

* Calderwood, pp. 666-673. † Calderwood, pp. 681-683.

the ministers to stand behind them, unaccommodated with seats, as if indicating the subordinate part which they were to perform; and Spotswood took the moderator's chair, without being elected to that office. When it was proposed that the moderator should be elected according to the usual order of procedure, Spotswood would not permit it, on the ground that as the Assembly was held within the bounds of his diocese, he was entitled to preside. The ministers were then required to give in their commissions; but these commissions were not examined publicly, so that it could not be known whether they were all genuine or not, till the conclusion of the proceedings, when it was ascertained that many of them were not legal. The question was asked by some of the ministers, whether all the noblemen, barons, and burgesses present were to vote, since many of them had no commissions as elders. Spotswood answered, that all who had come in compliance with his Majesty's missives should vote, although this was directly contrary to the constitution of the Assembly. The dean of Winchester was then introduced, who read a long letter from the king, strongly recommending the measures which he proposed, and warmly expostulating with the Church on account of its reluctance to comply with his suggestions. The dean followed up this letter with a speech, strenuously urging compliance with all the king's desires and suggestions, in a strain of sycophantic adulation.

The struggle immediately began between the faithful ministers and the innovating prelatic party. A private conference was held for the purpose of putting the proposed articles into regular form for the consideration of the Assembly. In the conference Spotswood endeavored to procure the sanction of these articles by a vote, which would have precluded the liberty of reasoning in the Assembly, and in this he was partially successful. When the articles were laid before the Assembly on the 27th, a scene of tyrannical violence ensued, such as has been seldom equalled. Spotswood addressed the Assembly in the most haughty and domineering style, urging submission to his majesty's desires, commanding implicit and immediate obedience, deriding the idea that any ministers would submit to be expelled from their parishes and stipends rather than yield, and assuring them that the people would not support them, or, if such a thing should happen, "wishing that the king would make him a captain, and never one of these braggers would come to the field." Others of the prelates followed in a similar strain and spirit; and every attempt made by the faithful Presbyterians to reason and argue was overborne by the rude clamours and taunting jeers of the haughty barons and more haughty prelates. A protestation against such a course of procedure was given in by some of the ministers; but after a few sentences had been read it was cast aside and neglected. The vote was then loudly demanded by the self-chosen moderator, and the king's letter was again read, to overawe the opposing ministers. In putting the vote the question was often crouched in these terms:—"*Will you consent to these articles, or disobey the king?*" and Spotswood even declared, that whosoever voted against these articles, his name should be marked and transmitted to his majesty. Thus surrounded by the half-armed retainers of the nobility, and threatened with the vengeance of the king, the ministers were compelled to proceed to the vote in the midst of confusion and alarm. Even then many stood true and unshaken; but the *Five Articles of Perth*, as they are usually called, were carried by a majority,—one nobleman, Lord Ochiltree, one doctor, and forty-five ministers, voting in the negative. These *Five Articles* were,—*kneeling at the communion,—the observance of holidays,—episcopal confirmation,—private baptism,—and the private dispensation of the Lord's Supper.* Thus by a formidable combination of fraud and violence, the king and his minions succeeded in perpetrating another glaring innovation upon the government, discipline, and ritual of the Presbyterian Church; yet so narrowly, that if none had voted except those who had commissions, the attempt would have been defeated.* These articles being thus forcibly carried in the Assembly, the Court of High Commission set about enforcing their observance, by means of civil penalties;

* Calderwood, pp. 697-713.

thus yielding another practical proof, that civil and religious liberties perish or exist together.

[1621.] Trusting that the spirit of the nation was now subdued, after three years of High Commission tyranny, the parliament was summoned to meet in Edinburgh on the 25th of July 1621, chiefly for the ratification of the Five Articles of Perth. The faithful ministers who still survived to watch over the welfare of the Church, endeavoured to move the parliament by earnest remonstrances, but in vain; the course was predetermined, and the result prepared. At length all preliminary arrangements being completed, the parliament proceeded to vote for the ratification or rejection of the Five Articles, without deliberation, and as if they had formed but one topic. Even then the opposition was very strong. Fifteen lords and fifty-four commissioners of shires and burghs voted against the measure, and it was carried by a small majority. On Saturday the 4th of August 1621, this vote, subversive of the Presbyterian Church of Scotland, was thus carried, chiefly by means of men who had solemnly sworn to maintain what they had thus conspired to overthrow. This day, sadly memorable in the annals of the Church of Scotland, was marked also by a singular coincident event, recorded by the historians of that time. The morning had been lowering and gloomy, and as the day advanced the gloom waxed deeper and deeper, as the gathering clouds seemed to concentrate their huge voluminous masses around over the city. At the very moment when the Marquis of Hamilton and the Lord High Commissioner rose to give the formal ratification to the acts, by touching them with the sceptre, a keen blue flash of forked lightning blazed through the murky gloom, followed instantaneously by another and another, so dazzingly bright as to blind the startled and terrified parliament, in the act of consummating its guilty deed. Three terrific peals of thunder followed in quick succession, appalling the trembling conclave, as if the thunder-voice of heaven were uttering denouncements of vengeance against the insulters of the dread majesty on high. Then descended hailstones of prodigious magnitude, and sheeted rains so heavy and continuous, as to imprison for an hour and a-half the parliament which had perpetrated this act of treason against the King of kings, by subjecting His Church to an earthly monarch. This dark and disastrous day was long known in Scotland by the designation of "BLACK SATURDAY,"—"black with man's guilt and with the frowns of heaven."*

We have now reached the close of another period of the Church of Scotland's eventful history,—a period full of instruction for the thoughtful Christian reader. It is painful to peruse the records of a crafty monarch's fraud and tyranny,—of aristocratic selfishness and avarice,—of the perjury and deceit of ambitious and sycophantic churchmen, longing for prelatic pre-eminence in wealth and power,—and of the sufferings to which the true-hearted and noble-minded defenders of the Church of Scotland were exposed, as they strove faithfully, though ineffectually, to maintain her principles and defend her rights. Yet it affords a signal illustration of the great truth, that the Church of Christ and the world are each other's natural antagonists, and that the more closely a Church cleaves to its Divine Head and King, obeying His precepts and following His example, the more certain is it to incur the hostility of crafty, irreligious, and wordly-minded men of every rank and station. It shows also, that the greatest danger a Church has to encounter is that arising from internal corruption. King James could not overthrow the Church of Scotland till he had gained over some of its ministers, and thereby succeeded in corrupting its courts, so as to obtain its own apparent sanction to his successive invasions of its rights and privileges. And it deserves also to be remarked, that even when zealously working the ruin of the Church, there was in all the crafty despot's measures a strange tacit recognition of one of the leading principles which he sought to overthrow,—the independent right of the Church to regulate its own procedure on its own authority. Every one of the destructive acts by which Presbytery was overthrown and Prelacy introduced, was so contrived as to have its origin in some court or commission of the Church,—never first in a civil court; thereby prac-

* Calderwood, p. 783; Spotswood, p. 542.

tically admitting, not only that the Church courts were possessed of complete co-ordinate jurisdiction, but even that they were supreme in ecclesiastical matters. When the parliament even seemed to take the primary step, it was only in affairs manifestly civil, such as the restoration of the civil emoluments and civil jurisdiction to prelates; but the existence of the prelatic function itself, and the elevation of ministers to the prelacy, were matters with which the parliament did not interfere, till the Church had been induced to pass the acts which were competent alone to her jurisdiction. The hatred shown by the king to declinatures of civil jurisdiction in matters ecclesiastical, may be regarded as a proof that he was aware how constitutionally sound and religiously just was the claim of the Presbyterian Church; and that he, as a tyrant, detested it the more, because of its constitutional and sacred character.

CHAPTER V.

FROM THE RATIFICATION OF THE FIVE ARTICLES OF PERTH, IN THE YEAR 1621, TO THE NATIONAL COVENANT IN 1638.

Despotic Letter from the King.—Conduct of his Majesty and the Prelates.—John Welch.—Robert Bruce.—Proceedings of the Court of High Commission against the Ministers, Universities, Probationers, and People.—David Dickson.—Robert Boyd.—Robert Blair.—The People and Magistrates of Edinburgh.—Death of King James.—Charles I.—Despotic Temper and proceedings of Charles.—Changes in the Courts of Session and Justiciary.—Commission of Teinds.—Proposed Act of Revocation.—Intention to assimilate the Church of Scotland to that of England.—Ambition and Rashness of the younger Prelates.—Revivals of Religion at Irvine, Stewton, and Shotts.—Growth of Arminianism among the Prelatic Party.—Visit of the King to Scotland.—"Act anent the Royal Prerogative and the Apparel of Churchmen."—Fraudulent manner in which it was carried.—Edinburgh made a Bishopric.—Trial of Balmerino.—Diocesan Courts of High Commission.—Book of Canons.—Pride and Ambition of the Prelates.—The Liturgy.—Riot in Edinburgh at its Introduction.—Arbitrary Conduct of the Prelates.—The Feelings of the Kingdom roused.—Alexander Henderson.—The Presbyterians crowd to Edinburgh.—The Privy Council.—Commotions.—Violent Proclamations.—Increased Agitation.—The Presbyterians accuse the Prelates of being the direct Cause of all the National Troubles.—The Formation of the Four Tables.—Deceitful Proceedings of the Privy Council.—Evasive Proclamations.—Pernicious Advice given to the King by Spotswood and Laud.—Conduct of the Earl of Traquair.—Skilful Management of the Presbyterians.—Duplicity of the Privy Council.—Injudicious Proclamation.—THE NATIONAL COVENANT.

DURING the interval which elapsed between the passing of the Five Articles of Perth in the Assembly 1618, and their ratification by the parliament of 1621, there had been a continual struggle between the prelates and the Presbyterian ministers; the former endeavouring to enforce obedience to these articles by the authority of the Court of High Commission; the latter protesting, refusing obedience, and resisting, notwithstanding the sufferings to which they were exposed. But still something was wanting to complete the power of the prelates, and to give a more legal aspect to their aggressions; for the minds of men in general revolted against the glaring tyranny of the High Commission,—a court depending solely upon the arbitrary will and command of the sovereign, but not recognised by constitutional law. The act of parliament ratifying the Five Articles of Perth supplied what had been wanting, and gave a constitutional sanction to the despotism and the treachery of these subversive measures. It was not the intention of either the king or the prelates to allow this power to remain unemployed. A short time after the passing of the act, Spotswood, archbishop of St. Andrews, received a letter from the king, not merely giving full warrant to proceed to extremity in the enforcement of the Five Articles, but even urging forward men who were already abundantly disposed to tyrannize over and persecute their brethren. "The greatest matter," said the king, in this remarkable letter, "the puritans had to object against the church government was, that your proceedings were warranted by no law, which now, by this last parliament, is cutted short; so that hereafter that rebellious, disobedient, and seditious crew must either obey or resist God, their natural king, and the law of the country. It resteth therefore to you to be encouraged and comforted by this happy occasion, and to lose no more time to procure a settled obedience to God, and to Us, by the good endeavours of our commissioner, and our other true-hearted subjects and servants. The sword is now put into your hands: go on therefore to use it, and let it rust no longer, till ye have perfected the service entrusted to you."* Such were the instructions of the infatuated king to his not less infatuated prelatic minions, for the destruction of a Church which he had termed "the

* Calderwood, p. 784.

sincerest Church in the world," and had repeatedly sworn to defend. And the enormity of these instructions is certainly not diminished, if, as Calderwood suggests, and other authors more distinctly assert, this letter was actually a mere transcript of one sent to the king by Spotswood, to be copied and returned to Scotland, stamped with the royal authority,—a procedure which it appears, was often adopted by the treacherous and tyrannical Scottish prelates.* A letter of a similar import was also sent to the privy council, commanding all the officers of state to conform, under pain of dismission; and enjoining them to see that all persons filling any subordinate official station, members of the Courts of Session and Justiciary, advocates, sheriffs, magistrates of burghs, and even clerks and sheriff-officers, should render implicit obedience, or be declared incapable of holding office.

The Court of High Commission was not composed of men likely to let the sword of double despotism which had been put into their hands rust for want of being used. Its freshly whetted edge was directed keenly against the faithful ministers, and against all who refused to mould their faith according to acts of parliament. And, as if for the very purpose of proving that the cruelty of the king and of the prelates was equally fierce and implacable, its effects were exhibited almost simultaneously by his majesty and by them. The celebrated John Welch, who had suffered a banishment of fourteen years duration on account of the part he took in the prorogued Assembly of Aberdeen in 1605, had fallen into such a state of ill health, that a return to his native country was recommended, as the only means of saving his life. By great solicitations he obtained permission to return to London; but when his wife, a daughter of John Knox, obtained an interview with the king, and requested that her dying husband might be allowed to breathe once more his native air, his majesty, with coarse oaths, refused, unless she would persuade her husband to submit to the bishops. "Please your majesty," replied the heroic matron, lifting up her apron, and holding it forth as if in the act of receiving her husband's decolated and falling head, "I would rather kep [receive] his head there!"—James would not even permit the dying man to preach, till, hearing that he was at the point of death, he in mockery sent permission then, when he believed it could not be accepted. But Welch joyfully hastened to embrace the opportunity of once more proclaiming the glad tidings of salvation; and having preached long and fervently, returned to his chamber, and within two hours rested from his labours, and escaped from the cruel and insulting tyranny of his oppressors.

About the same time Robert Bruce, who had been residing for some years in his own house at Kinnaird, having been permitted to return from Inverness, was accused of seditious conduct, and of transgressing the bounds of his confinement. He was imprisoned for a time in the Castle of Edinburgh, and then sentence passed that he should again be sent to Inverness, and restricted to that town and four miles around it during the king's pleasure; this sentence being accompanied by the sneering expression, "We will have no more popish pilgrimages to Kinnaird,"—in allusion to the frequent intercourse between Bruce and the most pious people of the surrounding country, who resorted to Kinnaird to enjoy the benefit of his instructive conversation. The prelatic party exulted in the opportunity of inflicting their mean malicious vengeance upon a man whom the king, in an unwonted fit of truth and gratitude, had pronounced worth the quarter of his kingdom. But what was meant as a punishment to him, became a precious blessing to the people of Inverness and its vicinity, who acquired then a relish for the pure gospel, which there is reason to believe, has never since been lost.

[1622.]—Not contented with these severe proceedings against the venerable fathers of the Church, the prelates directed their attention to every minister of eminence throughout the kingdom, requiring from each submission to the Perth Articles. They had a twofold purpose in demanding urgently the compliance of such men: by far the majority of the people regarded these articles with extreme dislike; and the prelates were well aware, that if they could prevail upon the

* Wodrow's Collection of Lives, particularly the lives of Gladstanes and Spotswood.

best ministers to subscribe, those ministers would either bring with them the people who were strongly attached to them, or they would lose that popular influence which they possessed. There was another alternative which they seem not to have taken into their calculation; they do not appear to have thought it probable that those ministers would continue to resist, braving the terrors of the Court of High Commission, and by their sufferings increasing the popular detestation of the prelatic system, much more than all their arguments could have done. They were aware that they would themselves have yielded to any measure, when, by so yielding, they would both escape personal suffering and obtain the prospect of personal wealth, rank and power; and they could not conceive nor credit the higher principles of their antagonists. But it has often been the lot of cunning men to overreach themselves; and such was the lot of the Scottish prelates. The prelates held a Court of High Commission early in January 1622, and commenced their despotic course by summoning before them the Rev. Messrs. Dickson of Irvine, Dunbar of Ayr, Row of Carnock, Murray of Dunfermline, and Johnstone of Ancrum. All these were men of great piety, much beloved by their people, and highly respected in the districts of the country where they respectively resided. Their submission was therefore earnestly desired by the prelates; or, at least, their forcible removal to distant parts of the country, where, being unknown, they would possess little influence, and their oppressors would the more easily carry forward their pernicious designs.

Of all these ministers, the case of Mr. David Dickson of Irvine seems to have excited the most attention. This eminent man was assailed by the prelates at one time in the language of entreaty, at another in that of fierce vituperative threats, to induce him to submit. His own congregation employed every effort for his protection; and the earl of Eglinton personally entreated the prelates not to remove him from his charge. But all entreaties were ineffectual; he had declined the jurisdiction of that despotic court, the High Commission, and this was an offence which could not be forgiven. He was banished to Turriff, in the synod of Aberdeen, where, however, he continued to exercise his ministry, greatly to the advantage of the inhabitants of that district, till he was afterwards permitted to return to Irvine. The other ministers, whose names were mentioned above, were also subjected to similar penalties, some being banished to one part of the country, others to another, and only one, so far as appears, permitted to remain in his own parish, but strictly prohibited from passing beyond its boundaries.*

The tyranny of the prelatic party fell not less heavily on the people than on the ministers; for the people were every where as much opposed to compliance with the Perth Articles as their pastors could be, and in some places much more so; for in every parish where the minister was prelatic the opposition was of course made by the people alone. In such instances the prelatic ministers strove to persuade, or to force, the people to comply with the Five Articles of Perth; and as the article which commanded kneeling at the communion was that which was most exposed to public observation, it gave rise to the greatest part of the contentions by which the peace of the country was destroyed. Many most disgraceful scenes of strife and confusion took place, even at the communion-table, in consequence of the prelatic party attempting forcibly to compel the people to submit to what they justly regarded as an attitude not warranted by Scripture, and bearing a close resemblance to the idolatrous service of the Church of Rome. Notwithstanding all their exertions, they could not prevail upon the people to comply. A few, and those in general the least respectable in character, did gratify the prelates by adopting their superstitious ceremonies; but by far the greater number either ceased to communicate at all, or resorted to the churches of those ministers who continued to follow the simple and scriptural customs of their fathers.

The universities did not escape the vigilance of the prelates, who were aware of the influence which the opinions of eminent professors naturally exercise upon the minds of their students. The celebrated Robert Boyd of Trochrigg was first obliged to leave Glasgow College,

* Calderwood, pp. 792-794.

in consequence of the hostility of Archbishop Law; and having been appointed principal of Edinburgh College, the prelatic party complained to the king, and obtained from his majesty a positive command to the magistrates to urge Mr. Boyd to conform to the Perth Articles, on pain of being expelled from his office. He accordingly removed, to the joy of the prelatists, and to the great grief both of the students and of the religious part of the inhabitants. About the same time Mr. Robert Blair was deprived of his professorship in Glasgow, and obliged to retire to Ireland, where he became minister of Bangour, and was honoured in being made the instrument of much spiritual good in that country. In addition to the removal of true Presbyterians from the professorships, the prelatic party did all in their power to corrupt the young aspirants to the ministry; proceeding even to the extent of exacting an oath from these young students, before investing them with the office of preaching, that they would conform to the Perth Articles, and submit to the prelatic form of Church government. This ensnaring oath they rigidly enforced; and if any conscientious young man expressed unwillingness to bind himself by such an obligation, he was at once rejected. By this process it was hoped, that all the growth of the Church would be directed into the prelatic channel, so that within the course of another generation it would become universal, and Episcopacy would be as firmly settled in Scotland as in England.

The prelates do not seem to have been aware of some symptoms which even then were beginning to appear, and speedily assumed a formidable aspect. Of these, the two most important were, the alienation of the nobility, and the increasing direct hostility of the people. Even so early as the Perth Assembly of 1618, the prelates had given offence to the nobility by their haughty and overbearing manners; and as prosperity did not tend to abate their insolence, it soon became intolerable to the proud Scottish barons. An ill-suppressed jealousy from that time prevailed, which waited but an opportunity to rise into open strife,—so soon, at least, as the selfish interests of the rival parties should manifestly bear in opposite directions. That the people were opposed to all their proceedings, the prelatic party were well aware; but considering themselves "lords over God's heritage," they disregarded equally the entreaties and the expressions of dissatisfaction addressed to them by the poor suffering congregations of the oppressed Presbyterian Church. Spotswood and his coadjutors thought that these popular discontents would soon subside, when they had succeeded in removing from their parishes the most eminent of the ministers who refused to conform to the Articles of Perth. And when they were not startled by sudden outbursts of popular indignation, they flattered themselves that the kingdom was acquiescing in their measures, or at least passively submitting to what could not any longer be successfully opposed. They might have heard, from time to time, of private meetings for prayer, among the more pious ministers and their adherents; but they seem in general to have despised those private meetings, being themselves ignorant of the sacred might of prayer. They do not seem to have marked the difference between a ripple on the surface, and a deep, calm under-current: the ripple dies away with the breeze that produced it; but the under-current moves steadily on, imperceptible to the eye, but irresistible in its silent and viewless power.

[1623.] The tyranny of the prelates continued throughout the year 1623, displacing non-conforming ministers, insulting congregations, enforcing the oppressive enactments of previous years, and relaxing those only which had been made against papists. The intercourse at that time existing between his majesty and the court of Spain, during the negotiations for the marriage of the prince to the Spanish infanta, may have been the cause of this toleration to the adherents of the Papal Church; but certainly it had no tendency to gratify the people of Scotland, who saw more favour shown to the corrupt Church of Rome than to their own, although the one was prohibited, and the other established, by the most solemn national enactments.

[1624.] A contest arose in Edinburgh in 1624, which excited considerable attention, and had no slight effect in deepening and confirming the popular feeling against the prelatic party. It had been customary for many years, that, previous to the communion Sabbath, a day was appointed on which all who were at enmity with each other were summoned to appear before the kirk-session, that they might be exhorted to lay aside their strife, give and accept forgiveness, and thereby prepare to make the communion indeed a feast of mutual love. It was usual at the same time to institute some general inquiries into the conduct of the members of the session, both minister and elders, with regard to the manner in which they had discharged their duties, each member withdrawing during the inquiry into his course of life and behaviour. While engaged in the discharge of this customary investigation, one of the citizens complained that Mr. William Forbes, recently appointed minister of one of the city churches, had taught that there might easily be a reconciliation effected between the Church of Rome and the Protestant Churches. This complaint was repeated by other respectable citizens, who requested that Mr. Forbes might be questioned by the presbytery, whether he really meant to teach doctrines subversive of the Reformation.

Forbes, who had been brought from Aberdeen to Edinburgh expressly on account of his high prelatic opinions, was excessively indignant that the people should presume to express disapprobation of his doctrine. And his brethren making it a common cause, applied to Spotswood, and through him obtained from the king an order empowering a select number of the privy council to try those citizens for their conduct in expressing disapprobation of the doctrine of the ministers; and, in particular, for having requested that the communion might be observed in the former manner, and not according to the Articles of Perth. The result was, that William Rigg, one of the magistrates of Edinburgh, was deprived of his office, and imprisoned in the Castle of Blackness till he should pay a ruinous fine; and five other highly respectable citizens were punished, some by imprisonment, others by banishment to remote parts of the country.

The prelatic party being somewhat alarmed by the spirit manifested in this trial, complained to the king that several of the non-conforming ministers who had been deprived of their parishes, were in the habit of resorting to Edinburgh, and holding "private conventicles," whereby the people were stirred up, and the public peace disturbed. In answer to this complaint, the king sent a proclamation, prepared, says Calderwood, as was constantly reported, by the archbishop of St. Andrews; in which, after reprehending, in very severe terms, the conduct of the citizens in listening to the "turbulent persuasions of restless ministers, either deprived from their functions, or confined for just causes," he strictly prohibited all such privats conventicles. A short while afterwards his majesty sent a letter of censure to the magistrates of Edinburgh, reprehending them severely for not giving obedience to the Perth Articles, and for remissness in the enforcement of these articles upon others; threatening to remove from the town the Courts of Session and Justiciary, if these orders were not more punctually obeyed.

Every attentive reader of history must often be struck with the close similarity in language and sentiment of men who lived in periods very remote from each other. It seems that oppressors are always the men who most loudly complain of resistance: the despot most vehemently exclaims against rebellion; and the subverters of pure religion cry out against the turbulence of restless ministers. But it appears to be very natural, and certainly it is very easy, for men to disguise a bad cause under a good name, and to try to blacken a good cause by fixing upon it an offensive designation.

[1625.] King James had determined to have Christmas celebrated with extreme pomp and ceremony, as a public triumph; and had given orders to that effect; but the plague breaking out in Edinburgh, suspended his scheme. As Easter approached he renewed his commands, to prepare for celebrating the communion on that day, in conformity with the Articles of Perth, threatening very severe punishment to all who should refuse implicit obedience. But the close of his despotic career was at hand. On the 27th of March 1625, he departed this life, leaving behind him a kingdom sunk from glory to disgrace through his mean misgovernment; filled with the elements of private strife and social discord, fermenting and heaving onward to a revolution;—a son, the inheritor of his despotic principles, and of all the evils which they had engendered;—and a name, lauded by a few prelatic flatterers, who could term their "earthly creator" the "Solomon of the age," but scorned by the haughty, mocked by the witty, despised by men of learning and genius, and not hated, only because pitied and deplored, by the persecuted yet loyal and forgiving Church of Scotland.

The death of King James paralyzed the power of the prelatic party for a time, and allowed many of the persecuted Presbyterians to escape from actual, and also from threatened sufferings. The proceedings against the Edinburgh citizens were suspended, Robert Bruce returned from Inverness, David Dickson was allowed to resume without interruption the discharge of his ministry at Irvine, and many other sufferers for the sake of truth and conscience obtained a temporary respite. The direct reason of this cessation of the prelates from their tyrannical procedure was, that the Court of High Commission expired with the monarch, from whose arbitrary will it derived its existence. The people of Scotland could not fail to perceive, that the prelates were the instigators, and even the perpetrators, of all the judicial despotism under which they had so long groaned; so that this very cessation of their sufferings would increase their detestation of the system under which they had suffered, and of the men by whom these sufferings had been inflicted.

Although the death of one sovereign and the accession of another caused a suspension of the active progress of prelatic domination, till the intentions of the new monarch should be known, and allowed a brief breathing time to the ministers and people, yet the relief was but slight, and the favourable hopes entertained by the Presbyterians were soon clouded with doubts. Soon after his accession to the throne, Charles I. wrote to Archbishop Spotswood, directing him to proceed with the affairs of the Church as formerly, and assuring him that it was his majesty's special will to have all the laws enforced which had been enacted in the former reign concerning ecclesiastical affairs; and, as if to remove all remaining doubt respecting his intentions, the king issued a proclamation on the 1st of August, commanding conformity to the Perth Articles, and ordering severe and rigorous punishment to be inflicted on all who dared to disobey. Next month, September, a royal letter was sent to the town-council of Edinburgh, commanding them to choose for magistrates those only who observed the Articles of Perth. By this arbitrary command a sufficiently plain indication was given of the principles held by the young king, and a proof that he meant to carry into effect that despotism which his father held in theory, but wanted firmness and tenacity of purpose to enforce.

The greater firmness of purpose by which Charles was characterized impelled him to the adoption of more decisive, but also more dangerous measures, than those which his father had employed. One of these, essential to his future schemes, was at the same time both ungracious in itself, and calculated to excite the jealousy of the nobles with regard to a matter in which they felt peculiarly sensitive. Charles was well aware, that if he expected Prelacy to take ere long the same high ground in Scotland which it occupied in England, he must not merely secure to the prelates their titles, but also reinstate them in the possession of their wealth and power. The first step towards the execution of that design was taken in November 1625, when by proclamation his majesty revoked all the deeds of his father in prejudice of the Crown. This, it was tolerably evident, was preparatory to a resumption of those crown lands, many of them previously church lands, which his father had erected into temporal lordships, and bestowed upon his unworthy favourites, and upon others whose support he wished to secure. But as no direct consequences immediately followed the proclamation, the jealousy of the nobles partially subsided, though it did not entirely pass away.

[1626.] Although the king's attention was very much occupied with the Spanish war in which he was engaged with little success, and also with those beginnings of resistance to his arbitrary conduct in England which ought to have warned him to desist from his dangerous course, he nevertheless found leisure to interfere in Scottish affairs enough to increase the dissatisfaction already prevalent. The Scottish nobles were not sufficiently servile for a monach so arbitrary. He resolved, therefore, to make extensive changes throughout the whole public administration of the kingdom, removing men of independent mind, and introducing those who would be subservient to his will. He remodelled the Courts of Session and the Justiciary, the privy council, and the Lords of the Exchequer, placing several of the prelates in the two latter departments; and he erected a Commission of Grievances, which occupied the position of the Star Chamber in England, reviving also the Court of High Commission, created in the former reign. By these changes the king hoped to cut off all opposition, and to obtain the means of carrying all his measures into execution.

These alterations having been made, and a little time allowed for the new officials to become acquainted with their duties, a convention of estates was held in July the same year, for the purpose of proceeding with the recovery of the tithes and the church lands. But the opposition of the nobility was still too strong; and all that the convention did was naming four of each estate as a commission, to examine the state of the teinds, to ascertain who were the proprietors, and by what tenure they were held. The titulars and possessors of teinds not relishing this intended inquiry, sent the Earls of Rothes, Linlithgow, and Loudon, as a deputation to endeavour to prevail upon the king to abandon that measure; but their efforts proved ineffectual.

About the same time Charles did one of the few even seemingly prudent acts of his strangely imprudent life. He ordained that such of the ministers as had been admitted before the Assembly of 1618, should not be compelled to conform to the Perth Articles, provided they did not publicly assail the king's authority and the form of church government; and that all who had been banished, confined, or suspended, should be restored to their charges on the same condition; but that conformity should be strictly enforced on all who had been admitted since 1618, and on every new entrant into the ministry. This measure was one of deep and dangerous policy; and its steady operation would have been far more deadly to the Presbyterian Church than the most direct and fierce persecution. But the intolerant zeal of the prelates could not endure this wary policy, even on account of what made it dangerous,—its lenient aspect. It is probable that this scheme was devised by Spotswood; but the younger prelates, and those who expected to reach the prelacy, were beginning to obtain a greater influence with the king than his more aged and sagacious counsellors.

[1627.] Early in the year 1627, commissioners from the Church were sent to the king, to supplicate his majesty for certain important alterations and improvements in ecclesiastical matters. An attempt was made to give to this deputation the aspect of being a full representation of the whole Church, both the Prelatic and the Presbyterian parties; but the overbearing conduct of the prelatists caused the Presbyterian commissioner to withdraw, so that the purpose remained unaccomplished.

The commissioners for the teinds also prosecuted their labours, but with little success. Yet a tolerably complete return of the state of teinds throughout the country having been obtained, it was resolved that every man should have liberty to purchase back his own teind at a reasonable price, and all were required to come to the commissioners for that purpose. Although this measure was introduced at first with a view to prepare for the restoration of Prelacy to all its golden honours, it has proved, on the whole, very beneficial to the Church and the people of Scotland, by being instrumental in removing the obstacles which the method of levying tithes in kind opposes to national prosperity and peace.

[1628.] In the spring of 1628, a meeting of synod was held in Edinburgh, in which, after long and earnest reasoning, it was resolved to send a deputation to his majesty, to entreat release from the compulsive obligation to comply with the Perth Articles, especially that of kneeling at the communion, to which the people could not be brought to submit. But the king expressed himself highly displeased that the people durst presume to petition against a measure which had his approbation; and commanded that condign punishment should be inflicted on the petitioners, to deter others from the like presumption. The result was, there was no communion at Edinburgh that year.

The king seems to have thought that the public mind was now sufficiently prepared for the act of revocation which he meditated. In order, however, to introduce it as plausibly as might be, he privately purchased the abbey of Arbroath from the Marquis of Hamilton, and the lordship of Glasgow from the Duke of Lennox, and gave them to the two archbishops of St. Andrews and Glasgow, giving to the transaction such an aspect as if these two noblemen had voluntarily surrendered that property. By this and several similar private purchases of estates, Charles hoped to induce the nobility and gentry to comply with the act of revocation. But when he sent the Earl of Nithsdale to propose the measure to a convention of estates, with this inducement, that those who would willingly submit should experience his majesty's favour, while the most rigorous proceedings should be instituted against those who refused, the nobility instantly determined to resist, and to employ force if arguments should not prevail. It was resolved at a private meeting of the irritated barons, that if Nithsdale should continue to press the measure, he and his adherents should be assailed and put to death in the open court. So determinedly was this purpose entertained, that Lord Belhaven, a man blind by very age, requested to be placed beside one of Nithsdale's party, and he would make sure of that one. Being set beside the Earl of Dumfries, and holding him fast with one hand, apologizing for doing so, as necessary for support in his blindness, he clutched fast with the other the hilt of a dagger, which he kept concealed in his bosom, ready to plunge it into the heart of his victim, should the signal for violence be given. But the Earl of Nithsdale read enough in the stern and frowning looks of the Scottish barons around him, to induce him to suppress the main part of his instructions, and to give up the attempt as hopeless.*

* Burnet's History of his own Times, folio edition of 1724, pp. 20, 21.

[1629.] Nothing of peculiar public importance occurred during the year 1629,—nothing, indeed, except the continuation of the insolence displayed and the persecutions inflicted on the Presbyterian ministers and people by the prelates. Some attempts were made to induce the king himself to interpose in behalf of his suffering people; but he paid no attention to the statement of grievances which they laid before him. Previous to this time there had been some symptoms of division in the prelatic party, although Spotswood continued to be regarded as its head; but now the younger prelates began to undermine his influence with the king. The most active of these intriguers was John Maxwell, at that time one of the ministers of Edinburgh, and soon afterwards bishop of Ross. This able and unscrupulous man contrived to work himself into the confidence of the notorious Laud, by whose pernicious counsels the king was almost entirely guided. In this manner there arose a decided and growing dissention among the prelates; and the violence of the younger and more impetuous party had the effect of stimulating the rash despotism of the king, and increasing the hostility of the nobles, who could not brook the insolence and pride of these haughty churchmen.

[1630.] In the year 1630, Maxwell, who had been at London on some private commission, brought down from the king a letter to Spotswood, directing him to convene the other prelates, and the most prelatic of the ministers, and to inform them, that it was his majesty's pleasure that the whole order of the Church of England should be received in Scotland. "This," Wodrow says in his life of Spotswood, "was the first motion for the English liturgy in Scotland, in King Charles's reign." The most prudent of the prelates, apprehensive of the consequences, opposed this measure as too dangerous, considering the already excited state of the country, and it was postponed. In July the same year, at a convention of estates, the non-conforming ministers gave in a paper of grievances, of which they craved redress; but though it was supported by several of the nobility, it was not permitted to be read.

[1631.] The year 1631 is chiefly remarkable for the progress made by the commissioners of teinds, in the discharge of their duty. The landed proprietors began to perceive the advantage of obtaining possession of their own teinds at a moderate price, and many accordingly applied to the commissioners, and made the purchase. Some attempts were made this year by the prelatic party to introduce organs, choristers, surplices, and the other mummeries of the cathedral service, with little success.

[1632.] Some changes took place among the prelates this year, by which, instead of being strengthened, they were hurried forward to their suicidal doom. Law, archbishop of Glasgow, died, and Lindsay, bishop of Ross, was appointed to succeed him, and Maxwell was raised to the bishopric of Ross. But this promotion only opened the way to others, to which his elevation to the prelacy rendered him eligible; and in a short time Maxwell became a lord of session, a lord of exchequer, and a member of the privy council; by which accumulation of offices, belike, he thought that he was most convincingly proving the scriptural character of Prelacy, and his own indubitable claims to the sacredness of pure apostolical succession!

All further innovations were suspended for a time, in consequence of his majesty having intimated that it was his intention to visit his ancient kingdom next year, to be formally crowned king of Scotland, and to make all the arrangements which might be desirable for promoting the peace and happiness of that portion of his dominions. The preparations fc that visit, which were made on the most magnificent scale, so thoroughly occupied the public mind, that almost every thing else was disregarded, all men vieing with each other how they might best do honour to the long-expected visit of their native king.

The preceding brief outline of the progress of public events, from the accession of Charles to the year in which he purposed to visit Scotland, has been given, that the reader might obtain a continuous view of the external aspect of what was done or attempted. And for the same reason it is now intended to retrace the same period of years, that a continuous view may be obtained of matters immeasurably more important than the despotism of kings, the plots of courtiers, and the perfidious ambition of prelates.

Reference has already been made to the remarkable effects which frequently attended the preaching of Robert Bruce, both before he was banished from Edinburgh, and in his various places of confinement. Had the prelates understood the influence of a man thus highly honoured by success in his divine Master's work, they would have either left him untouched, or put him to utter silence. But while they sent him, in the wantonness of their malicious power, from district to district of the kingdom, they even compelled him to kindle in many quarters that sacred fire by which they were destined to be consumed. Many able and fervent young ministers were deeply impressed by what they heard uttered by the venerable man; and thus his principles were infused into the minds of men in the rising prime of life, able and willing to expend their unbroken energies in the sacred cause. There were few of the eminent men of that day who did not cheerfully acknowledge how much, under God, they owed to Bruce.

But there were many other ministers of decided piety, whose labours the Head of the Church also owned and blessed to a very great extent. Of these, David Dickson of Irvine deserves particular mention. It has been already stated, that he was so greatly beloved by his congregation, that when brought before the court of the tyrannical prelates, every effort was made by the devoted flock to secure the enjoyment of their pastor's precious labours. They did not at first succeed; but in the year 1624, he was allowed to return to Irvine, and remain there during their majesty's pleasure. Suffering in Christ's cause gives a very deeply spiritual character to a Christain minister's labours. Soon after Mr. Dickson's return to his charge, striking effects began to appear among his people, and in the adjoining parish of Stewarton, where he frequently preached. This remarkable revival of vital religion began, it appears, in 1625, and lasted for about five years. "This," says Fleming, "by the profane rabble of that time was called *the Stewarton sickness;* for in that parish first, but afterwards through much of that country, particularly at Irvine under the ministry of Mr. Dickson, it was remarkable; where it can be said (which diverse ministers and Christians yet alive can witness), that for a considerable time few Sabbaths did pass without some evidently converted, or some convincing proof of the power of God accompanying his Word. And truly this great spring-tide, as I may call it, of the gospel, was not of a short time, but of some years' continuance; yea thus, like a spreading moor-burn, the power of godliness did advance from one place to another, which put a marvellous lustre on those parts of the country, the savour whereof brought many from other parts of the land to see its truth."*

Another token for good to the suffering Church of Scotland occurred in the year 1628. At a meeting of the synod in Edinburgh in the spring of that year, it had been agreed upon to apply to his majesty that a general fast might be held all over the kingdom. The ostensible causes adduced for this proposal by the prelates, were the dangerous state of Protestant Churches abroad, the prevalence of vice and immorality at home, and to implore the divine blessing upon his majesty's arms being at that time involved in hostilities both with France and with the House of Austria. To these causes, the Presbyterians naturally added the consideration of their own suffering state, and of the oppressive innovations forced upon the people. Much of the searching power of the Holy Spirit seems to have been granted to both ministers and people during their solemn fast; and many felt, that in humbling themselves before God, and making an earnest confession of sin, both national and individual, they obtained a strength not their own,—a spiritual strength,—preparing them for greater sufferings, and giving earnest of final deliverance. And let any truly pious person imagine the contrast between the cold, formal, and insincere services of the prelatists, and the deep, earnest, heart-wrung supplications of the Presbyterian sufferers, breathing the very essence of spiritual contrition, and he cannot fail to perceive one mighty cause of the disrespect with which he former were regarded, and the powerful hold which the latter possessed of the nation's heart.

* Fleming's Fulfilling of the Scriptures, vol. i. p. 355.

In no individual instance probably, was the converting power of the Spirit more signally displayed than at the Kirk of Shotts, on Monday the 21st of June 1630. It appears that John Livingstone, a young man of about twenty-seven years of age, who was at that time domestic chaplain to the Countess of Wigton, had gone to attend the dispensation of the Lord's Supper at the Kirk of Shotts. There had been a great confluence of both ministers and people from all the adjoining country; and the sacred services of the communion Sabbath had been marked with much solemnity of manner and great apparent depth and sincerity of devotional feeling. When the Monday came, the large assembly of pious Christians felt reluctant to part without another day of thanksgiving to that God whose redeeming love they had been commemorating. Livingstone was prevailed upon to preach, though reluctantly, and with heavy misgivings of mind, at the thought of his own unworthiness to address so many experienced Christians. He even endeavoured to withdraw himself secretly from the multitude; but a strong constraining impulse within his mind caused him to return, and proceed with the duty to which he had been appointed. Towards the close of the sermon, the audience, and even the preacher himself was affected with a deep unusual awe, melting their hearts and subduing their minds, stripping off inveterate prejudices, awaking the indifferent, producing conviction in the hardened, bowing down the stubborn, and imparting to many an enlightened Christian, a large increase of grace and spirituality. "It was known," says Fleming, "as I can speak on sure ground, that nearly five hundred had at that time a discernible change wrought on them, of whom most proved lively Christians afterwards. It was the sowing of a seed through Clydesdale, so that many of the most eminent Christians of that country could date either their conversion, or some remarkable confirmation of their case, from that day."*

* For a more full account, see Gillies's Collections, vol. i. p. 310, *et seq.*; and Fleming's Fulfilling of the Scriptures, vol. i. pp. 355, 356.

Mr. Livingstone, the honoured instrument by which this great work was wrought, was one of those against whom the tyranny of the suspicious prelates had been directed. He had been called to be their pastor by the people of Torphichen; but because he would not take the oath of conformity to the Perth Articles, Spotswood would not allow him to be continued in the charge. This, indeed, was the current policy of the prelates,—a policy which may generally be expected to be pursued by every party when contests run high and victory is doubtful. But in the case of the prelates, and indeed in every case of a contest between right and wrong, the most politic measure will prove injurious to those who employ it. When such men as Livingstone were excluded from a parish by the prelates, they were actually compelled to extend their influence over a wider sphere than would otherwise have been either possible or right. And not unfrequently, as in his case, they were received into the families of some of the nobility, where their unassuming manners and deep personal piety produced the most beneficial results, both to their protectors, and to the cause for which they suffered. In this manner both the ejected ministers and the rejected probationers tended, by their fervent and widely diffused labours, to prepare the great body of the nation for that struggle and revulsion which was ere long to take place. And when the reader who is at all acquainted with Scottish ecclesiastical history marks among these home missionaries the names of Livingstone, and Blair, and Rutherford, and Douglas, and Gillespie, and Dunbar, and Hogg, and Dickson, and many others of almost equal eminence, he may easily imagine how mighty must have been the influence which their sufferings and their toils produced in the very heart of Scotland.

There is yet another general reflection which must not be omitted, in order to complete our survey of all the elements then fermenting in the kingdom. Soon after the introduction of Prelacy into Scotland by the machinations of King James, the tenets of Arminius began to be entertained by those worldly-minded men, as much more congenial to their low notions of Christianity, and their own characters and habits. But Arminianism made little progress till after the ratification of the Five Articles of Perth, when the prelatic party felt themselves secure, and ventured to follow more openly the bent of their inclination. In the meantime, a large proportion of the Church of England had greedily imbibed these erroneous tenets, thereby widening the division between them and the party called Puritans. As soon as the Arminian party were headed by the cunning, narrow-minded, bigoted and malevolent Laud, they advanced with rapid strides to the possession of uncontrolled power in the kingdom, and especially in the favour of the Sovereign. The younger Scottish prelates, headed by Maxwell, set themselves to emulate Laud, and almost surpassed him in their ardent advocacy of Arminianism. But however this might recommend them to the king and the English prelates, it had a very different effect among their own countrymen in general. For the erroneous tenets of Arminius, however plausible in the eyes of men of superficial minds, will never stand the scrutiny of a searching intellect, if directed to the investigation with warm and real interest. Least of all will such tenets give satisfaction to a heart on which the light of God's Word has shone, revealing its desperate wickedness,—to a soul which has been quickened from its deadness in sin by the life-giving power of the Holy Spirit. In so far, therefore, as Arminianism prevailed among the prelatic party, to that extent were they regarded as weaklings and aliens, by the manly and searching intellect of Scotland; and in so far as vital religion revived and was diffused throughout the kingdom, to that extent did the right-hearted Scottish nobles and peasantry detest a system which introduced such men, and men who vitiated the oracles of the living God, and strove to reduce the Gospel of the Lord Jesus Christ to a code of human morality.

It is scarcely necessary to add to these mighty elements, this further consideration, although it had its influence, that the men who were the keenest sticklers for empty forms and ceremonies,—who did not hesitate to violate their oaths, and strive to compel others to the perpetration of the same crime, throwing a whole na tion into suffering and confusion for the attainment of what they themselves admitted to be not a matter of conscience, but merely of convenient and seemly order,—that these men were generally notorious for vice, profligacy, Sabbath-breaking, and every species of immorality. Had even the cause been good, the perfidious and tyrannical manner of its introduction, and the characters of the men by whom it was introduced, would have ruined it in the estimation of every man who had an eye to discern and a heart to feel.

Some of the defenders of Prelacy have said, that Scotland never saw it in its true aspect,—that if we had, we would have received it, and made it cordially our own. Certainly Prelacy never appeared in Scotland but as a tyrannical and persecuting system; therefore we have little cause to love it. But we can see it in England, with all its blushing honours and unblushing abuses thick upon it,—with its clergy secularized, and its people uninstructed; and what we see of it there has no tendency to recommend it to our favourable regard, or to make us languish for its reintroduction to Scotland.

[1633.] Such was the state of Scotland, and of the contending parties by which it was agitated when Charles I. prepared to pay a visit to his ancient kingdom. Had he been disposed to inquire into the state of the country, with a sincere desire to remedy all proved evils, and redress all manifest grievances,—and had he been able to lay aside his own prejudices, or even to prevail upon himself to investigate matters for himself, and not to trust entirely to the statements of persons who were interested in deceiving him,—the result might have been most propitious. As it was, it proved highly disastrous. Unfortunately his whole conduct was pre-determined before he left London. He wished to enjoy the pageantry of a Scottish coronation; he intended to hold a parliament for procuring money; and he was resolved to take measures for reducing the Church of Scotland into perfect conformity with that of England. For the management of the latter point he brought with him Laud, who may not inaptly be designated his evil genius, by whose malign influence he was perpetually turned aside from the path of safety, and hurried along that of ruin.

It is not our intention to describe the pride, pomp and circumstance of his majesty's triumphal procession, his entrance into the capital of his ancient kingdom, and the more than semi-popish pageantry of his coronation. Suffice it to state, that the most enthusiastic reception was given to their monarch by a people who were almost instinctively loyal, and who were prone to gratify him in every thing which their higher allegiance to God could permit. Still even in the height of their enthusiastic loyalty, they were compelled to feel, that in the most important matters there existed no harmony of sentiment and feeling between their sovereign and them. The manifest preference shown by the king to all the rites, ceremonies, and gaudy exhibitions of Prelacy, strengthened the distrust already entertained, that no good was intended to the Presbyterian Church. Ample proof was soon given that these apprehensions were but too well founded.

Previous to the meeting of parliament the king arranged matters in the most likely way to secure the accomplishment of his designs. He introduced ten Englishmen into the privy council of Scotland, one of whom was the notorious Laud. The Lords of the Articles were so chosen as to be composed almost entirely of those who were known to be subservient to the king, and ready to comply with any thing which he might require. All matters being thus arranged, the parliament met for the despatch of business on the 25th of June. Their first act was one granting to Charles a larger subsidy than had ever before been given to a Scottish king. So far all was harmony and good-will; but the next measure aroused a different spirit. It was intituled, "An act anent his Majesty's Royal Prerogative, and Apparel of Churchmen." This was a combination of two acts, one passed in 1606, acknowledging the king's supremacy over all persons, and in all causes; and another passed in 1609, by which King James was empowered to prescribe apparel and vestments to all judges, magistrates, and churchmen. The act 1606 had been but too often enforced, to the sad experience of many banished ministers and destitute congregations; but the act 1609, concerning vestments, had been allowed to lie dormant. They were now joined together and made one, in the expectation that the strength of the prerogative clause would carry with it the weakness of the other. To this combined act great opposition was made, the Earl of Rothes heading the opposition. Rothes desired that the acts might be divided, expressing his willingness to vote for the prerogative clause, if it stood alone. The king declared that it was now one act, and that he must either vote for it or against it, as such. Rothes began to argue, that the second clause was contrary to the liberties of the Church, and ought not to be further considered until at least the mind of the Church should be ascertained; but the king rudely interrupted him, commanded the vote to be taken without further reasoning, and, calling for a list of the members, which had been previously prepared, he sternly said, "I have all your names here, and I will now know who are good subjects and who are bad."* The question was then put; Rothes promptly voted, "Not content." His example was followed by fifteen earls and lords, several barons, and forty-four commissioners of counties and burghs.† Even Burnet affirms that the act was rejected by the majority; but the clerk of register, knowing well the king's wish, declared that it was carried in the affirmative. Rothes asserted that the contrary was the case; but the king, whose attempt to overawe the parliament must have made him aware of the truth, dishonourably supported the clerk's false assertion, saying that it must be held good unless the Earl of Rothes would go to the bar, and accuse him of falsifying the record of parliament—an offence which was capital; and in that case, if he should fail in the proof, he was liable to the same punishment.‡ This perilous step Rothes declined to take; consequently the act was declared to have passed, though its power was greatly paralyzed by the despotic and nefarious nature of the transaction, which speedily became known to the whole kingdom.

So dissatisfied were the lords, both with this act itself, and the forcible and fraudulent manner in which it had been carried, that they resolved to present to the king a supplication, explaining and excusing their conduct, and remonstrating against the manner in which their freedom to deliberate had been overborne. This supplication was drawn up by Hague, the king's solicitor, himself, as Burnet says, a sincere and zealous Presbyterian. It was read over to Lord Balmerino and the Earls of Rothes and Cassilis. Balmerino disapproved of some expressions in it, and procured a copy, that he might deliberately peruse and alter it, according to his own judgment. Rothes carried a copy of it to the king, that he might, if possible, obtain his majesty's permission to present it, without further exciting his displeasure; but the king would not so much as look upon it, and commanded him to proceed no further in that matter. Accordingly it was not presented, and was regarded by its authors as consigned to oblivion. But it ere long appeared that the king and the prelates could neither forget nor forgive whatsoever thwarted them.

In the meantime the oppressed Presbyterian Church of Scotland did not neglect the opportunity of his majesty's presence in the kingdom, and the meeting of parliament, to endeavour to obtain some redress of their grievances. A number of the most eminent of the ministers repaired to Edinburgh, met together, and deliberated in what manner they ought to proceed. It was resolved to present to his majesty and the parliament a petition containing a full statement of the grievances of the Church, expressed in the most respectful terms, and humbly supplicating redress. This petition was suppressed by the clerk register, who was a fierce prelatist; upon which a new pet tion was prepared, mentioning the one given into the hands of the clerk register, and requesting his majesty to cause it to be read and considered. That the latter petition might not also be suppressed, Mr. Thomas Hogg, who had been deposed from his ministry at Dysart, by the High Commission, delivered it per sonally to the king. His majesty perused it with unmoved countenance, but re turned no answer. Too well the neg lected sufferers saw that no redress was

* Kirkton. p. 30.

† Rutherford's Letters, part iii. letter 40.

‡ Burnet's History of his own Times, pp. 21, 22

to be expected from the king: but they did not despair; but they presented their supplications to the King of kings, in the full confidence that He would not reject their prayers.

The remainder of the time spent by Charles in Scotland tended but to increase the alienation between him and his best subjects. He studiously neglected, and even insulted, those who had opposed his designs; and heaped honours upon those who had showed themselves willing to prostrate the liberties of the Church and the kingdom at his feet. At length he took his departure, little gratified with the result of a visit from which he had promised himself a vast accession of strength. He was already deeply involved in contentions with his English parliament; and he seems to have anticipated, that by his visit to Scotland he would secure the support of that kingdom, and be thereby enabled to coerce the people of England into submission to his arbitrary sway. Little did he understand the character of either country, or the nature of the principles by which at that time both were so deeply moved. There seemed, indeed, to rest upon Charles I. and all his advisers,—those at least in whom he most confided,—a cloud of infatuation, concealing or distorting every truth, and giving a delusive aspect to error.

Some may perhaps be disposed to say, that the act respecting the vestments of churchmen was not a matter of such importance as to justify the opposition made to it. But it must be observed, that the passing of such an act, without consulting the Church on the matter, involved the whole question respecting the liberty of the Church; and especially, joined as it was to the clause respecting the royal prerogative, it implied no less than that the power of dictating to the Church in every matter, whether of vital importance or comparatively trivial, was a part of the royal prerogative. In fact, it virtually admitted, and very soon would have rendered operative, the principle, that the king was the Head of the Church,—a principle directly subversive of the Church of Scotland, which has never admitted any Head but the Lord Jesus Christ alone.

[1634.] Previous to the departure of the king, he declared that he had found a man whose high merits deserved that a bishopric should be made for him. This man of rare eminence was Mr. William Forbes, one of the ministers of Edinburgh,—the same person who had been brought from Aberdeen to the capital, in consequence of his known attachment to Prelacy and Arminianism, and whose scornful disregard of his respectable parishioners had been the cause to them of heavy fines and protracted imprisonment. In recompense of these meritorious deeds, Edinburgh was constituted a bishopric, and Forbes appointed its first prelate,—an appointment not calculated to soothe the oppressed and insulted citizens. The new bishop determined to justify the choice of his majesty, by proceeding immediately, in the most rigorous manner, to enforce obedience to the Perth Articles; and issued a circular order to all the presbyteries within his diocese, commanding them to conform, on pain of his ecclesiastical censure. The majority of the Edinburgh presbyteries yielded; but several others not only refused to comply, but even boldly warned the haughty prelate of the sinful and dangerous nature of his own conduct, in thus wantonly aggrieving the conscience of both ministers and people in matters for which he could find no warrant in the Word of God. Before, however, his fiery zeal had time to proceed to the extremities which he had threatened, he was, happily for his own memory, removed from the scene by death, and succeeded by Lindsay, bishop of Brechin, to which latter see Sydserf was appointed.

An event occurred about the same time, the consequences of which proved exceedingly detrimental to the character and schemes of the king. It has been already mentioned, that a supplication had been prepared to be presented to his majesty, by those lords who disapproved of the act of parliament respecting the prerogative and the attire of churchmen; and that, though it was not presented, Lord Balmerino retained a copy of it in his own possession. It would appear that Balmerino still entertained hopes of this petition being useful, as explaining to the king the feelings and sentiments actuating a number of his most faithful subjects, and had showed it in confidence to one Dunmoor, a legal friend whom he trusted, for the purpose of obtaining his aid in modifying its phraseology, so as to be as little offensive to the king as it could possibly be rendered. Dunmoor was allowed to take it home with him, on the promise of keeping it concealed from every one; but he so far violated his pledge as to show it to Hay of Naughton, on promise of secrecy. Hay surreptitiously obtained a copy, and carried it to Archbishop Spotswood, who immediately posted off with it to London, commencing his journey, according to his custom, on a Sabbath-day. The king, whose own conscience must have secretly condemned him for the tyrannical and fraudulent manner in which he had compassed the passing of that act, and instigated by Spotswood and Laud, resolved to wreak his vengeance on Balmerino. It required some ingenuity to frame a plausible ground of accusation against that nobleman. This the malignity of Spotswood supplied, by the distorted application of one of James's despotic acts respecting what is termed *leasing-making*, or the crime of sowing dissention between the king and his subjects. By this act, writing or saying any thing which might tend to bring discredit on the king and the government was declared capital; and even to know who was the author of any such seditious matter, and not to reveal it, was held to involve equal guilt, and to expose to the same punishment. But this latter clause had never been put in execution; and yet on the strength of it alone was Balmerino to be tried for his life.

The management of the trial was intrusted to the Earl of Traquair, who was at that time rising rapidly into court favour. Traquair was not a man to be deterred by any scruples of conscience from the invidious and dangerous task. He selected such a jury as he thought he could trust, and got some of Balmerino's personal enemies appointed to be assessors to the justice-general, that he might secure both the declaration of the law and the verdict of the jury. Balmerino defended himself with great ability. When the verdict of the jury was about to be required, Gordon of Buckie,—then a very aged man, but who had in his youth been distinguished for daring and reckless ferocity of character, shown especially in the murder of "the bonnie Earl of Murray," the good regent's son, —this aged homicide arose, and with a tremulous voice, desired them to consider what they were about. "It was," he said, "a matter of blood, and they would feel the weight of that as long as they lived. He had in his youth been drawn into shed blood, for which he had the king's pardon; but it cost him more to obtain God's pardon: it had given him many sorrowful hours, both day and night." The tears, as he spoke, ran down his furrowed cheeks; and for a time the chill sensation of sympathetic horror held the guilty conclave silent.* But Traquair, to break the force of this pathetic appeal, reminded them that the question which they had to determine, was simply whether or not Balmerino had concealed his knowledge of the author of a production said to be seditious. The result was, that seven of the jury voted for acquittal, and seven voted guilty; the casting vote of Traquair secured the condemnation of Balmerino, and sentence of death was immediately pronounced,—the execution to be delayed till the pleasure of the king should be known. Intense had been the interest excited by this trial; and no sooner was the result divulged than public indignation swelled to a storm. Secret meetings were held, at which plans of the most daring character were proposed. It was resolved that the prison should be forced, and Balmerino set at liberty; or, if that attempt failed, to revenge his death by the slaughter of that portion of the jury by whose verdict he had been condemned. Traquair perceiving the danger, hastened to the king, informed him of the state of public feeling, and solicited a pardon for the condemned nobleman, which his majesty reluctantly granted.

Scarcely any thing could have been more injurious to the character and the schemes of the king than this trial. It not only proved beyond all doubt the arbitrary disposition of Charles himself, who could brook no opposition to his despotic will, not even in the constitutional form of an humble supplication and remonstrance; but it also showed clearly,

* Burnet's History of his own times, pp. 24, 25.

that the main object at which he aimed, in his zeal for the establishment of Prelacy in Scotland, was, that he might obtain in the prelates a set of nominal lords, creatures of his own, who would be wholly subservient to his commands, and enable him to reduce the kingdom to a state of utter slavery. If any thing had been wanting either to excite or to confirm the jealousy of the Scottish nobility, who were already irritated at the arrogance of the prelates, it was supplied by the trial of Balmerino. In it they saw revealed the very heart of his majesty's design,—that a change in church government was the means, but absolute despotism the end, at which he aimed; and much as many of them disliked the severe impartiality of Presbyterian discipline, they felt that they had more in common with men who were the friends of freedom, sacred and national, however strongly opposed to that licentiousness which is the bondage of the soul, than they could have with those who could indeed tolerate all immoralities, but were the banded foes of all true liberty, civil and religious. Thus were the nobles, the ministers, and the people, gradually drawn together into one common cause, by the infatuated conduct of their common oppressors; and the remembrance of the manner in which they had in former times asserted and defended their liberties, began again to suggest the idea of a bond of union, whence all parties might derive mutual protection and support. But the crisis was not yet come; and the prelatic party were allowed to fill up the measure of their guilt.

Nor were they slack in their guilty career. They marked not the tempest blackening around the national horizon; they felt not the ground-swell beginning to heave beneath their feet, indicative of the coming earthquake. Exulting in their fallacious prosperity, they continued to urge forward with reckless haste the measures which were to issue in their own destruction. Although they had not been yet able to enforce obedience to the Perth Articles, they urged the propriety of having a Book of Canons framed for the government of the Church, and a Liturgy prepared for its form of worship. This Spotswood and the older prelates opposed, regarding the attempt as yet too dangerous; but the younger and more reckless party, encouraged by Laud, expressed their confidence that the attempt might be made with perfect safety. Some difference of opinion also existed whether the English Book of Canons and Liturgy should be adopted, or one framed expressly for Scotland; but upon the representation of the more cautious party, that the very fact of these new arrangements coming from England would give them the appearance of conveying a studied insult to the national feeling of independence, and thereby greatly increase the hostility against them, it was finally agreed that a Book of Canons and a Liturgy should be framed in Scotland, and communicated to Laud, Juxon, and Wren, for their revision and approval. This matter was finally determined upon in September. About the same time the Court of Exchequer was remodelled, a number of the barons removed, and four of the vacancies filled by the aspiring prelates.

[1635.] Early in the year 1635, prelatic ambition obtained another triumph. The Earl of Kinnoul, lord chancellor of Scotland, a nobleman of the antique mould, who had repeatedly checked the arrogance of the prelates, and on one occasion had refused precedency to Spotswood, even when solicited by Charles himself, died in December of the preceding year. The high office thus left vacant was conferred on Spotswood, who was thus raised to the highest pinnacle of rank on which a Scottish subject could be placed. Some of the older prelates dying about the same time, several changes took place, in all of which not wisdom, worth, and learning were advanced, but men of ambitious and intriguing minds obtained the stations of greatest honour and emolument. Elated with this success, they now proceeded to enforce an enlargement of their Court of High Commission, for which his majesty's letters patent had been a short while previously obtained. Before this time only archbishops could hold Courts of High Commission: now they were empowered to hold such courts in every diocese, each prelate in his own, where, assuming to himself any six ministers, he could call before him and sit in judgment upon any person, of whatsoever quality.

'These courts," says Burnet, "were thought little different from the Courts of Inquisition."* Sydserf, now made bishop of Galloway, immediately raised one of these courts in his diocese, banished Gordon of Earlston to a remote part of the kingdom, suspended Robert Glendinning, minister of Kirkcudbright, who had reached the venerable age of seventy-nine, and began that persecuting process against Samuel Rutherford, which ended in his banishment to Aberdeen.

In April the same year a meeting of the prelates was held in Edinburgh, to see what progress had been made in the framing of the Book of Canons. After the Scottish prelates had brought it as near to perfection as they could, it was sent to Laud, under the care of Maxwell, bishop of Ross, the leader of the younger prelates. Having obtained the high benefit of Laud's supervision and amendments, the Book of Canons was confirmed under the great seal, by letters patent bearing date 23d May 1635. The Book of Canons, thus revised and sanctioned by the regal fiat, was sent, not to Edinburgh, but to Aberdeen, that arsenal of Scotland's woes, to be printed, and then circulated by the prelates throughout their respective dioceses. The canons contained in this book were subversive of the whole constitution of the Church of Scotland. The first decrees excommunication against all who should deny the king's supremacy in ecclesiastical affairs: the next pronounces the same penalty against all who should dare to say that the worship contained in the Book of Common Prayer (a book not yet published, nor even written) was superstitious or contrary to the Scriptures. The same penalty was decreed against all who should assert that the prelatic form of church government was unscriptural. Every minister was enjoined to adhere to the forms prescribed in the Liturgy, on pain of deposition; which Liturgy, as before stated, was not yet in existence. It was decreed also, that no General Assembly should be called, but by the king; that no ecclesiastical business should even be discussed, except in the prelatic courts; that no private meetings, which were termed conventicles, and included presbyteries and kirk sessions, should be held by the ministers for expounding the Scriptures; and that on no occasion in public should a minister pour out the fulness of his heart to God in extemporary prayer. Many minute arrangements were also decreed respecting the ceremonial parts of worship, as fonts for baptism, communion-altars, ornaments in church, modes of dispensing the communion elements, the vestments of the clerical order, and all such other idle mummeries as the busy brain of Laud could devise, or the fantastic fooleries of Rome suggest. Such are some of the chief regulations in the Book of Canons; and yet, although every Presbyterian must have perceived at once that they were totally subversive of the constitution of the Presbyterian Church, his majesty's declaration was made, with consummate effrontery, to assume them to have been taken from the acts of the General Assemblies held in former years.*

Great was the indignation felt all over Scotland when the character of the Book of Canons came to be known; and innumerable were the discussions respecting its papistical regulations which immediately ensued. The prelatic party endeavoured feebly to defend it; but their antagonists condemned it unsparingly and in the strongest terms. The nobility were secretly gratified to find it so glaringly offensive, believing that its regulations never could be enforced, and perceiving that its failure must shake the credit and diminish the power of the prelates, whose ambitious usurpation of the highest offices in the State they could not brook. The people almost universally detested the Book of Canons, regarding it as directly popish, and intended to prepare for the introduction of Popery itself. All the hostility, however, thus increased and extended against the prelatic innovations, did not break out into any positive tumults; but it gave an immense additional power to the deep under-current of the popular mind, and pointed its course directly against those regal and prelatic measures which were now universally felt to be equally injurious to civil liberty, freedom of conscience, and the purity of sacred worship.

[1636.] During the year 1636, the

* Burnet's History of his own Times, p. 26.

* Stevenson's History of the Church of Scotland, edition 1840, pp. 159-164; Cruickshank, vol. i. p. 41; Neale's History of the Puritans, vol. ii p. 277, &c.

contending parties seemed to be silently mustering their strength, preparatory to a conflict which should prove fatal to the one or the other. But there was this very significant difference between the modes of preparation, that the prelatic party strained every nerve to obtain an accession to that political and civil power which was already exorbitant, and upon which alone they seemed to rely for support in the hour of peril; while the Presbyterians were doubly earnest in their prayers to God, in whose wisdom to guide, and strength to uphold them, they placed all their confidence. The only other method adopted by the ministers was, that of informing their people of the nature and course of the proceedings which the prelatic party were urging forward with such high-handed tyranny. Attempts have often been made to convict these pious men of the grave crime of neglecting the most important duty of their office, the preaching of salvation through the Redeemer, and converting the pulpit into a place for uttering seditious and inflammatory harangues. This is an accusation easily made, but fortunately as easily refuted. The writings of these culumniated men still exist, and never have been surpassed for the heart-searching earnestness of practical piety, purity, and depth of devotional feeling, loftiness of spirituality, and even peace-loving gentleness of temper, which they contain and display. To prove this statement, nothing more is necessary than to direct the reader to the letters of Samuel Rutherford, the greater part of which were written in those very stormy times, and many of them while he was himself suffering persecution because of his refusal to yield to prelatic despotism. And would these watchmen of our Zion have been guiltless, if they had neglected to warn those over whom they had been appointed overseers, that days of sharp and fiery trial were at hand? Would they have been true shepherds, if they had seen the wolf about to break in upon the fold, and given no alarm? True, their silence would have been more favourable to the wolfish invaders; and, no doubt, by a wolfish conclave their loud and earnest warnings would be vehemently censured and condemned. But let those who still re-echo and renew these accusations beware, lest they bring upon themselves the suspicion, or confirm the belief, that they, too, belong to the same ravening and blood-thirsty herd.

The prelates, as has been already stated, had procured admission to the privy council, the exchequer, and the courts of session and justiciary, so that at least the half of the civil offices in the kingdom were filled by these aspiring churchmen. The office of lord high treasurer becoming vacant, Maxwell, bishop of Ross, grasped eagerly at that high office, in addition to three other civil offices which he already enjoyed. But the nobility, disgusted with his insatiable ambition, concurred in requesting the king to confer it on Traquair, who was already in high favour with the sovereign. Baffled ambition is the very spirit of implacable revenge. From that time forward Ross and Traquair cherished a deadly mutual hatred, and strove to thwart each other's designs. The two rivals strove to counterplot each other about the continuation or the breaking up of the commission for the teinds; but in this also Traquair proved an overmatch for his antagonist. The prelates had begun to find, that when the teinds were valued and purchased, they lost the power of drawing the revenues of the diocese into their own possession, nothing remaining but what was alloted for the local stipends of the ministers. They therefore now wished the commission terminated, for their own avaricious ends. But Traquair persuaded the king to continue that court, and even contrived to persuade several of the prelates to support his views.

These contests for wealth and power had engrossed the prelates so much for a time, that the Book of Canons had been allowed allowed to sink into comparative oblivion. This apparent calm in the public mind the prelates seemed to regard as a positive acquiescence by the nation in the progressive changes of church government and discipline which they were labouring to introduce; and accordingly came to the conclusion that the Liturgy also might now with perfect safety be published and enforced. Some authors assert that Traquair encouraged them to urge forward the Liturgy, with the very intention of precipitating their ruin; but this seems scarcely credible, as he was himself certain to share in both the obloquy and the danger. However that might be, the prelates themselves were sufficiently desirous of having their long-contemplated purpose accomplished. A Liturgy, or Book of Public Worship, was framed by the bishops of Ross and Dunblane, on the model of the English Prayer-Book, and sent to London for the revision of Laud. It was returned with innumerable corrections and additions, all tending to give it a more popish character. "I have seen," says Kirkton, "the principal book, corrected with Bishop Laud's own hand, where in every place which he corrected, he brings the word as near the missal as English can be to Latin."* A proclamation was brought from Court by the bishop of Ross, and published by an act of privy-council in December 1636, announcing the completion of the work, and commanding all faithful subjects to receive with reverence, and conform themselves to, the public form of religious service therein contained. To conform to that Liturgy, so popish in its character, and imposed in such an arbitary manner, was impossible without being prepared to yield up every vestige of liberty, civil and religious, and to violate all that conscience held most sacred.

[1637.] Even after this last element of strife had been thrown into the surcharged and boiling heart of the community, the long-collected storm of popular indignation did not at once burst forth. The proclamation itself was so far premature, that the Liturgy was not yet printed off and ready for distribution; and although it had been determined that the period of its universal adoption should be at Easter, that period was allowed to elapse, except that some of the bishops, who had obtained early copies, began to use the Liturgy in their own churches about that time. Some of the more wary of the prelates were apprehensive of the coming tempest, even by the deep preternatural stillness by which it was preceded; while others regarded the stillness as a proof that the spirit of the people was broken and humbled, and that no resistance would be made. In May and June a few copies of the Liturgy began to appear, and to be circulated about the country; which gave to men the opportunity of ascertaining the real character of the production, and of forming a deliberate resolution how to act when the crisis should take place. In the beginning of July the prelates procured an order from the privy council, empowering them to raise letters of horning (the technical phrase in Scottish law for a kind of outlawry) against the ministers who should manifest reluctance to receive the Liturgy, ordering them to provide for the use of their parishes two copies of the Service Book each, within fifteen days after they received the order, on pain of being declared and treated as rebels against the king and the law.*

But even in the moment of the closing struggle the spell of infatuation seemed to rest upon the prelates. In every stage of their proceedings something occurred which caused them to throw away the mask, and reveal their true motives, proving that self-interest, and not zeal for religion, was their ruling principle. The two archbishops of St. Andrews and Glasgow, Spotswood and Lindsay, were both at that time busily engaged in making such arrangements as would have largely increased their revenues, but would to the same extent have diminished those of the Duke of Lennox and the Earl of Traquair. To prevent this, Traquair exerted all his court influence; and, about the middle of July, procured from the king an order to dissolve the commission for teinds till further advisement. By this order all the schemes of the arch-prelates were at once suspended, and their golden harvest subjected to a fatal blight. Both resolved to journey to London for the purpose of endeavouring to procure redress, but thought that their prospect of succeeding with his majesty would be greatly promoted if they could carry with them the gratifying intelligence that the Liturgy had been actually introduced into the Church of Scotland. Up till this time they had been favourable to delay till the angry feelings of the people might subside; but now, when their pecuniary interests were affected, they became the most urgent to proceed immediately. They accordingly procured his majesty's letter, requiring the Liturgy to be used in all the churches of Edinburgh,

* Kirkton, p. 30.

* Baillie's Letters, vol. i. p. 3.

and an act of the privy council to enforce obedience to the royal mandate. Spotswood, goaded on by his love of money, summoned the ministers together, announced to them his majesty's pleasure, and commanded them to give intimation from their pulpits, that on the following Sabbath, the public use of the Liturgy was to be commenced. One only of the ministers, Mr. Andrew Ramsay, refused; the rest promised obedience.

This announcement sounded to Scotland like a trumpet-call to arms. During the intermediate week all was anxious, but no longer silent, expectation. Several brief but vigorous pamphlets appeared, condemning the Liturgy, and the prelates for urging forward that daring innovation without the sanction of either Parliament or Assembly; numerous meetings for prayer and consultation were held simultaneously, though not by concert; and the low murmur of indignant Scotland's voice began to be heard like the awakening thunders on far distant hills, or the deep sound of the advancing ocean-tide.

The 23d day of July 1637 was the day on which the perilous experiment was to be made, whether the people of Scotland would tamely submit to see the religious institutions of their fathers wantonly violated and overthrown, for the gratification of a despotic monarch and a lordly hierarchy. Several of the prelates were in the capital, to grace the innovation with their presence. The attention of the public was directed chiefly to the cathedral church of St. Giles. There the dean of Edinburgh prepared to commence the intended outrage on the national Church and the most sacred feelings of the people. A deep melancholy calm brooded over the congregation, all apparently anticipating some display of mingled wrath and sorrow, but none aware what form it might assume, or what might be its extent. At length, when their feelings, wound up to the highest pitch, were become too tremulously painful much longer to be endured, the dean, attired in his surplice, began to read the service of the day. At that moment an old woman, named Jenny Geddes, unable longer to restrain her indignation, exclaimed, "Villain, dost thou say mass at my lug!" and seizing the stool on which she had been sitting, hurled it at the dean's head. Instantly all was tumultuous uproar and confusion. Missiles of every kind were flying from all directions, aimed at the luckless leader of the forlorn hope of Prelacy; and several of the most vehement rushed towards the desk, to seize upon the object of their indignation. The dean, terrified by this sudden outburst of popular fury, tore himself out of their hands and fled, glad to escape, though with the loss of his sacerdotal vestments. The bishop of Edinburgh himself then entered the pulpit, and endeavoured to allay the wild tumult, but in vain. He was instantly assailed with equal fury, and was with difficulty rescued by the interference of the magistrates. When the most outrageous of the rioters had been thrust out of the church, the dean attempted to resume the service; but the tumultuary din of the mob on the outside, shouting aloud their hostile cries, breaking the windows, and fiercely battering the doors, compelled him to terminate the mangled service abruptly. Great exertions were required to protect the prelates from the fury of the excited rioters, whose long-pent feelings had now burst forth in a torrent of ungovernable violence.

This riot, as the reader will perceive, bears every mark of having been entirely an unpremeditated burst of popular indignation. Yet writers on the prelatic side have attempted to represent it as a preconcerted scheme of the leading Presbyterian nobility and ministers. It does not seem necessary to enter into the controversy further than to state, that their assertions are directly contradicted by well authenticated facts; and that although the most searching investigations were instituted by the magistrates of Edinburgh, immediately after the riot, not the slightest trace was found of any pre-arrangements having been made, and none but the lowest of the people, whose passions are generally least under control, were found to have been concerned in it. Indeed it was almost wholly confined to females; and the utmost search of the magistrates enabled them to detect, apprehend, and commit to prison, only some six or seven servant girls. It was, in fact, merely the result of a new outrage given to feelings long suppressed, and thereby collected into a degree of concentrated strength, making their final outburst the more impetuous, but also the more natural,—like a spark of fire thrown into a high-piled mass of combustible materials, and causing a sudden and tremenduous explosion. In the church of the Greyfriars, where the bishop of Argyle officiated, no other interruption was that day experienced but groans of deep sorrow, and the shriller wailings of lamentation; but had one single word or act of violence been used, the sorrow might have been in an instant converted into the wild uproar of fury; for in such a state of excited feelings the passions of the heart can change with the suddenness of lightning.

Great was the consternation and astonishment of the prelatic party when this unexpected storm of popular wrath dashed the Liturgy from their trembling hands. They had calculated on nothing worse than a few weak and sullen murmurs from the people, and perhaps the obstinate resistance of a portion of the ministers in different parts of the country, whom they could easily banish and replace by creatures of their own. But when matters began to assume a more serious aspect than they had expected, they stood amazed and stupified. No preparation had been made to overawe and suppress popular tumult; and although the rioters were mostly women of the lowest ranks, they began to suspect a more formidable body of antagonists; and their fears exaggerated the nature and extent of their dangers. Spotswood, whose cupidity had induced him to urge forward the introduction of the Liturgy, and who had hoped to carry the tidings of its reception in triumph to London, now thought it expedient to extenuate his failure by transmitting to the king an inflated account of the riot, casting all the blame of its occurrence upon Traquair, who had been detained from the capital on the eventful day by the marriage of a relation. At the same time he put forth his high commission powers in the most vehement manner, laying the town under an episcopal interdict, suspending all public worship, even on the hallowed day of God, because the Liturgy had been rejected. This he did without communicating with the privy council, who, on their part, were sufficiently annoyed at what had taken place, and not in a temper to tolerate either the folly or the arrogance of the mortified and angry primate. They accordingly sent to his majesty their own account of what had taken place, extenuating the affair, and accusing the bishops of having caused it by all by their own vanity and rashness.

These mutual recriminations between the privy council and the prelates tended to paralyze the executive at the very moment when decision and energy were most required. Meanwhile, the intelligence of what had taken place in Edinburgh spread throughout the kingdom like the kindling of a beacon-fire, and gave the signal of open resistance to this invasion of their sacred rights,—a signal most willingly received by a high-minded people, thus wantonly injured in what they held most precious. They seemed to perceive, in the paltry riot of Edinburgh, the cloud like a man's hand rising out of the sea, soon to cover the whole skies, and descend in showers of new life and energy. The thrilling fervour of the people told their long oppressed ministers that the day of their deliverance was drawing near, and that they had now but to guide that strong national feeling which was rising in its might, and would soon, if rightly directed, burst through and sweep away those feeble barriers within which regal and hierarchical despotism had striven to confine it. Nor were they wanting in their duty to the people, to themselves, and to the Church of their fathers, in this momentous crisis.

Still it was prelatic infatuation that forced on the contest. Foiled in Edinburgh, the prelates resolved to try whether they might not be more successful in the country. Accordingly the two archbishops determined to compel all the ministers within their bounds to procure and use the Liturgy. Renewing the former imperious mandate, Spotswood charged Alexander Henderson, George Hamilton, and James Bruce, the three most eminent ministers within his diocese, to purchase two copies of the Service Book each, for the use of their parishes, within fifteen days after the date of the charge, under the pain of rebellion. The archbishop of Glasgow gave a similar charge to all the ministers within his bounds. This called into the field of action the man who was destined to become the leader of his party. Alexander Henderson declared himself willing to purchase the book, that he might make himself acquainted with its contents; but refused to promise that he would use it in public, boldly affirming, that in matters which referred to the worship of God, no man could be bound to a blind and servile obedience. But as the danger to which they were exposed by this charge was both formidable and near at hand, the ministers resolved to apply to the privy council for a suspension of the charge itself. Accordingly Henderson hastened to the metropolis, to present a petition in his own name, and in that of his two brethren. He there met with William Castelaw from Stewarton, Robert Wilkie from Glasgow, and James Bonar from Maybole, who had been sent by their respective presbyteries for the same purpose, chiefly by the advice of David Dickson and the Earl of Loudon. This meeting, unanticipated, so far as appears, encouraged the ministers to go forward with their petitions, by making them fully aware of the rapidly-extending harmony of sentiment and feeling throughout the kingdom. On the 23d of August they presented their petitions to the council; and, at the same time, many letters were addressed to the councillors by noblemen and gentlemen from all parts of the country, requesting that the reading of the Liturgy might not be forcibly imposed on the ministers. The council, by an act dated the 25th, declared, that the letters and charges respecting the Service Book, extended only to the buying thereof, and no further. At the same time the council wrote to the king, giving him a tolerably full and fair account of the state of the country, of the universal dissatisfaction which the attempted forcible introduction of the Liturgy had caused, and of the dangerous consequences which might be dreaded were the attempt to enforce its reception immediately renewed, or punishment inflicted on those by whom it was opposed. It was left to his majesty, after taking these statements into consideration, to determine by what means these perilous commotions might be best allayed, and their cause removed or mitigated. To the petitioners the council gave the additional satisfaction of a promise, that their supplication should receive a full answer on the 20th of September ensuing.

The prelates were exceedingly disappointed and enraged by these proceedings of the council. They now saw themselves deserted by the nobility, and they never had possessed the support of the people. But they relied upon the influence of Laud over the king, and upon his majesty's despotic principles, which but too thoroughly coincided with their own; and in the blind wrath of mortified pride they determined to persevere in their course. Partly by transmitting false accounts to the king, and partly by Laud's suppressing all the true accounts sent by others, the prelates deceived his majesty, and induced him to send a very sharp reply to the letter of the privy council. In that letter he severely reproved the magistrates of Edinburgh for permitting the riot, and the privy council itself for its feeble management of public affairs; commanding further, that a sufficient number of the council should remain in the capital till the reading of the Liturgy should be established; that no magistrate should be chosen for any of the burghs who was not ready to conform, and that the bishops should use the Liturgy in their own churches.*

The king's severe and despotic letter again acted like a spark thrown upon a train of gunpowder, or like the kindling of a beacon. Roused, rather than intimidated, the Presbyterians crowded to Edinburgh from all parts of the kingdom, as to the spot on which the country's welfare should be lost or gained. In the course of three days, twenty-four noblemen, many barons, about a hundred ministers, commissioners from sixty-six parishes, and also from a number of the principal burghs, with many of the gentry from the counties of Fife, Stirling, Lothian, Ayr, and Lanark, arrived in the metropolis, all animated by the same spirit, and resolved to defend the purity and freedom of their national religion.† Less than a month had elapsed since the petitioners against the prelatic innovation

* To this last command the bishop of Brechin yielded a singular compliance. He armed himself with pistols, and taking his own family, all likewise armed, to church before the people were assembled, fastened the doors, and so read the Liturgy in triumph. (Baillie, vol. i. p. 24.)

† Baillie, p. 15.

were only four ministers; and now the whole kingdom, as by a simultaneous impulse, had started from its apparent lethargy and poured its confluent streams of living energy into the capital. In such a mighty and universal movement a thoughtful statesman would have seen, as Sir Philip Sidney did in Holland, the manifested will of God, and would have bowed before the sacred majesty of what he thus perceived to be a spiritual element, which none but the Divine Spirit could have caused so to pervade the general heart of the community. But sacred principles are incomprehensible to men of secular minds.

Instead of all these numerous petitions, it was thought expedient that one should be presented, in which all the petitioners should express their concurrence. This was done accordingly, and presented to the privy council by the Earl of Sutherland; and although the council declined to give an answer till they should have received his majesty's instructions, the petitions were given to the Duke of Lennox, to be by him presented to the king. Lennox had expressed himself much impressed by the extent of the national feeling, declaring that he was sure his majesty was greatly misinformed, else he never could persevere in urging a measure which was thus alienating the whole of his most faithful subjects; and hopes were entertained that his mediation with the king would procure a favourable answer. But not trusting too much to the fallacious visions of hope and court favour, the Presbyterians wisely improved the opportunity, when so many of them were together, and drew up several important papers, detailing their principles and opinions, by which their unexpected spontaneous harmony of sentiment was confirmed into a thorough union of heart and mind.

Soon after the departure of the numerous supplicants from Edinburgh, some popular commotions agitated the city, in consequence of the conduct of the provost, who was a determined prelatist, and therefore strove to thwart the people, repressing their petitions, and still urging the use of the Liturgy, even while it was suspended in other parts of the kingdom. These commotions were not, however, now caused only by the sudden impulses of the lowest ranks, but were joined and guided by many of all classes, and were sufficiently formidable to overawe the council, and constrain them to comply with the wishes of the citizens. Their petitions were received, and a promise was given that they should receive his majesty's answer against the 17th of October.

The intimation of this expected communication from the king having been sent throughout the country by Archibald Johnston of Warriston, advocate, caused the immediate reappearance of the Presbyterians in Edinburgh, and in still greater numbers than formerly. Commissioners from above two hundred parishes presented petitions to the privy council, before the tenor of the king's despatches had been divulged. The numerous petitioners then held meetings to deliberate what further steps were necessary to be taken. But as their numbers were now so great that they could not conveniently meet all in one place, they separated themselves into four divisions, and met in as many different places, each order—noblemen, gentry, burgesses, and ministers—meeting apart from the others. Each of these meetings was opened with prayer; after which all were asked individually, whether they disapproved of the Service Book. When all had answered that they did, both on account of its matter, and the manner in which it had been attempted to be imposed on the country, the ablest and most intelligent proceeded to point out more specifically the erroneous character of the book, and the aggravated nature of the grievances already sustained, and still further threatened. This judicious procedure tended still more completely to concentrate and unite the opinions of the petitioners.*

While engaged in these deliberations they were suddenly informed, that an act of council, proceeding upon his majesty's letters, had been that instant proclaimed, dissolving the standing committee of privy council in so far as concerned the affairs of the Church, and commanding the supplicants to leave town within twenty-four hours, under pain of rebellion. Another proclamation almost immediately followed, intended as a punish-

* In these discussions Baillie seems to have acquitted himself greatly to the satisfaction of his auditors, (Baillie, p. 17.)

ment to the city, commanding the privy council and the Court of Session to be removed from Edinburgh to Linlithgow till November, and thereafter to Dundee. And still descending with their vindictive measures, another proclamation commanded a book written by Gillespie, entitled, "A Dispute against the English Popish Ceremonies," to be called in and burned. It was not difficult to perceive by what hands these proclamations had been fabricated. Indeed, some hints respecting the probable character of the expected communications from his majesty had previously been uttered by the prelates, who were offended with the former leniency of the privy council, and had represented to the king, that the riots in Edinburgh had been caused by ill-affected persons resorting thither from the country.

These proclamations had the effect of constraining the Presbyterian petitioners to proceed to a bolder and more decisive step than any they had previously taken, and, instead of continuing to act merely on the defensive, to become themselves assailants. They resolved to lay before the privy council a formal complaint against the prelates, accusing them directly of being the cause of all the troubles that disturbed the nation, by their lawless and tyrannical attempts to force the Book of Canons and the Liturgy upon an unwilling Church and people. Two forms of the proposed complaint were drawn up, the one by Lord Balmerino and Alexander Henderson, the other by the Earl of Loudon and David Dickson, the latter of which was unanimously adopted. Baillie acknowledges that he was himself the only person who felt any difficulty in agreeing to it, being apprehensive that it went too far; but after weighing it maturely in his mind, he subscribed it, and never repented of having done so.* It complained of the arbitrary nature of the proclamation commanding them to leave the town, while they were peaceably waiting for an answer to their supplication. It then proceeded to point out some of the pernicious characteristics of the Books of Common Prayer and of Canons, as containing the seeds of divers superstitions, idolatry, and false doctrine, and as being subversive of the discipline established in the Church, and confirmed by many acts of parliament; and it concluded by declaring the belief of the complainers, that all these wrongs had been committed by the bishops, contrary to his majesty's intention, craving that these matters might be brought to trial, and decided according to justice, and that this complaint might be fully represented to his majesty, that their grievances and wrongs might be redressed, and religion permitted to remain as it had been placed by the principles and arrangements of the Reformation.*

This important document was, in the course of a few hours, subscribed by twenty-four of the nobility, several hundreds of gentlemen, all the ministers in town, amounting to about three hundred, and all the commissioners of burghs present. Soon afterwards, having been sent to the country, it was subscribed by fourteen nobles more, gentlemen without number, nearly all the ministers in the kingdom, and by every town except Aberdeen, which still continued to retain its most unenviable distinction.

The vindictive proclamation removing the courts from Edinburgh caused another temporary riot, and was the means of procuring to the citizens the restoration of those ministers who had been deposed on account of their opposition to the Liturgy, and also so much control over the town council as to secure some of that body to act as commissioners along with the other supplicants, thereby restoring the link uniting the metropolis to the rest of the kingdom. The favourable results of this riot, if riot it ought to be termed, may be partly attributed to the open defence of the conduct of the citizens made by some of the most influential of the nobility, as well as to the fact that people of the highest respectability took part in the commotion, and did so avowedly on the most sacred grounds, in the defence of religious purity and freedom. "Let any one," said the Earl of Rothes, "who hath found the comfort, and knoweth the binding power, of true religion, judge if this people deserve that censure and imputation which the bishops would cast upon them for opposing their project. Who pressed that

* Baillie, p. 19.

† Stevenson, pp. 181, 182.

form of service contrary to the laws of God and this kingdom? Who dared, in their conventicles, contrive a form of God's public worship contrary to that established by the general consent of this Church and state?" "If any fault or violence have been committed by any of the subjects in resisting or seeking the abolition of that book, they might retort, that the bishops framing, and the council authorizing it, were the first and principal causes, necessitating either disobedience to God, and breach of our laws, or else resisting those evils which would bring the judgment of God on the land."*

The next meeting of privy council was held on the 15th of November. Again did the Presbyterians assemble in the capital, and in still increased numbers. The council, apprehensive of a renewal of tumultuary commotions in the town, requested the nobles to use their influence with their friends to induce them to return quietly to their homes. The petitioners signified their willingness to make such an arrangement as would allow the greater part to withdraw, no more remaining than were requisite to conduct all necessary matters, and were empowered by the whole to act in their behalf. Following up this suggestion, which had indeed been so far practically employed before as a matter of convenience, it was arranged, that as many of the nobility as pleased, two gentlemen from every county, one minister from every presbytery, and one burgess from every burgh, should form a general commission, representing the whole body of the Presbyterians. Still more to concentrate their efforts, it was resolved that the general body of commissioners should meet only on extraordinary occasions, and a smaller number should be selected, who might reside permanently at Edinburgh, watching the progress of events, and ready to communicate with the whole body on any emergency. This smaller committee was composed of sixteen persons—four noblemen, four gentlemen, four ministers, and four burgesses; and from the circumstance of their sitting in four separate rooms in the parliament-house, they were designated THE FOUR TABLES. A member from each of these constituted a chief Table of last resort, making a supreme council of four members. In this manner was constructed one of the most active and efficient councils that ever guided the affairs of any community, vigilant, prompt, and energetic, placed in the very centre of the body politic, conveying life and intelligence through its entire frame, and able to rouse it into instantaneous action at one thrilling call.

When these exceedingly judicious arrangements had been completed, the great body of the petitioners were solemnly exhorted to return to their homes, to reform their personal habits, to act according to their religious profession, and to be earnest and constant in faith and prayer to Him in whose hands are the hearts of kings, and from whom alone they could hope for safety to the crown, peace to the country, and deliverance to the Church. These exhortations produced a deep impression upon the assembled thousands, and were at once obeyed. The people quietly withdrew from the scene of agitating anxiety, committing the cause of the distressed Church to the protection of its divine Head and King fearing God, and having no other fear.

About the beginning of December a meeting of privy council was appointed to be held at Linlithgow, to receive the communications transmitted from his majesty by the Earl of Roxburgh. The Tables were instantly on the alert, and summoned the whole of the commissioners of the Church to the capital, to be prepared for any emergency, but at the solicitation of Traquair and Roxburgh, consented to abstain from going to Linlithgow. There is reason to believe that Roxburgh had it in charge to employ every method by which the Presbyterians might be weakened; such as, to detach some of their supporters by bribes and promises of preferment, and to seize and imprison the leading men whom he could not otherwise influence; but the first method being indignantly rejected, the second was abandoned as too perilous. Three proclamations were, however, issued by the council; in one of which his majesty declared his abhorrence of Popery, and his determination to allow nothing but what should tend to the advancement of religion, "as it is presently professed within this his majesty's ancient

* Rothes's Relation, p. 15.

kingdom of Scotland; and that nothing is, or will be, intended to be done therein against the laudable laws of that his majesty's native kingdom." With this proclamation the Presbyterians saw no reason to be satisfied. It was but too evident that its language was equivocal, and might be interpreted to mean, that his majesty would allow nothing but what should tend to the advancement of Prelacy, and that he regarded the laws establishing that system as "laudable laws," which nothing should be done against. They resolved, therefore, to abide by their own plain and unequivocal complaints, and not to allow themselves to be circumvented and deceived, either by the arts of courtiers or the kingcraft of the sovereign.

In vain did Traquair and Roxburgh endeavour to persuade the petitioners to rest satisfied with the proclamation. Finding them on their guard in this matter, the next attempt was to induce the petitioners to divide their petitions, and make application separately, on the plea that by doing so their conduct would bear less the appearance of combination, and be proportionally less offensive to the king. But the Tables were aware of the maxim, "divide and conquer," and therefore refused to expose themselves and their cause to the danger of division and defeat. Yet once more did the council attempt to draw the Presbyterians into a snare, requesting them to abandon their accusation of the prelates, and to limit their petition to the subject of the Book of Canons and the Liturgy. This stratagem also failed, in consequence of the unalterable resolution of the Tables to adhere to the principles stated in their complaint, and to regard the prelates as parties accused of high offences against the National Church, which they had striven to subvert by the introduction of a hierarchy not recognised in its constitution. The privy council then attempted to evade receiving the general petition of the Tables; but such was the indefatigable perseverance of the Presbyterian leaders, that the council was in a manner besieged, and compelled to receive the deputation, and listen to their complaint. Baillie has preserved the speeches of the deputation, which are indeed a noble specimen of high religious principle, loyalty, and eloquence, honourable alike to the men and to the cause. They are said to have produced such an impression upon Lord Lorn, afterwards Earl of Argyle, as to detach him from the prelatic party, and to incline him to that of the Presbyterians, of which he subsequently proved a steady and able supporter.

Information of the state of affairs was sent by the privy council to the king, through the Earl of Traquair, accompanied by Hamilton of Orbiston, who was appointed to take charge of the petition and complaint of the Presbyterians. Some faint hopes were entertained, that when his majesty should receive full and accurate accounts of the real state of affairs in Scotland, he might be induced to abandon the pernicious attempt to violate the conscience of an entire kingdom, by forcing upon the people religious ceremonies to which they were determinedly opposed; and a hierarchy which they both detested and feared. But unhappily for both the king and the kingdom, an evil agency was strenuously at work, prompting the misguided and obstinate monarch to provoke his destiny. Sir Robert Spotswood, president of the Court of Session, hastened to London, and, aided by Laud, prejudiced the mind of the king against all sound and wise council; and the archbishop, seconding his son's misrepresentations, suggested that the Presbyterians would submit, were his majesty to resort to measures more decisive than any he had yet adopted,—that it required but a proclamation condemning the proceeding of the Tables, and prohibiting them, under pain of treason, to put an end to the whole opposition. This advice was but too congenial to the despotic temper of Charles. It prevailed against the opinions of those who counselled a milder course; and Traquair was commanded to be in readiness to return to Scotland early in the following year, to bear down all opposition, and see his majesty's orders carried into effect.

[1638.] In the beginning of February 1638, the Earl of Traquair returned from England, bearing with him those arbitrary commands with which his majesty hoped to dishearten and disunite the Presbyterians. He was immediately requested by some of the leading nobles to inform them respecting the nature of the measures which he was empowered to propose; but he declined to give any answer till the meeting of the privy council, which was appointed to be held at Sterling on the 20th of February. The Presbyterians, however, had already received secret information respecting the real character of Traquair's commission; and the intelligence having been speedily sent throughout the country, great numbers began to flock to Sterling, to act as occasion might require. Traquair endeavoured to dissuade them from thus assembling in dangerous numbers; and they consented so far as to promise to send Rord Rothes and Lindsay only, as a deputation. Learning soon after that the intended proclamation would not only prohibit any supplicants from appearing before the council, but also would command them to be incarcerated as traitors if they should attempt it, they changed their plan, and determined to repair to Sterling in such numbers as should prove a sufficient mutual protection. And as they were resolved that they at least would act honourably, whatever might be the conduct of their antagonists, they sent information of this change of purpose to Lord Traquair. Somewhat irritated at the failure of his stratagem, Traquair told them that by asking too much they were defeating their own object; that if they had contented themselves with supplicating release from the Book of Canons and the Liturgy, they might have been successful; but his majesty would not suffer one of his estates to be brought under subjection to them. This hasty answer confirmed all their apprehensions. It showed the king's determination to retain Prelacy under the designation of one of the estates of the kingdom,—an estate essentially subservient to him, by the dexterous use of which he might vitiate every court, undermine all the bulwarks of liberty, and succeed in establishing a perfect and absolute despotism, civil and religious. This, indeed, there is every reason to believe, was his majesty's unavowed but real design,—a design happily frustrated by the promptitude, firmness, and energy which God bestowed upon our Presbyterian ancestors.

Traquair had now but one resource left, and that an abundantly mean one,—to attempt the accomplishment by stealth of what dissimulation and threats had failed to effect. He resolved to hasten under night to Sterling, and there issue the proclamation, before the Presbyterians could arrive, on the morning of the 20th, which happened to be a Monday. Even this proved abortive. His design was detected; the zealous Presbyterians sent two of their number to anticipate this new movement; and when the members of privy council appeared in Sterling to publish the proclamation, they were met by the Lords Home and Lindsay, who read a protest, and affixed a copy of it on the market-cross, beside that of the proclamation, leaving them there, bane and antidote together.

Nothing could have been more injudicious than his majesty's proclamation. The Presbyterians were all along extremely unwilling to believe, and still more so to affirm, that they regarded the king as in any degree the direct cause of their troubles, accusing the ambitious and corrupt prelates of being both the instigators and the agents in all the innovations which had been made, and the oppressions under which the country had groaned, ever since the institution of their inquisitorial and despotic Courts of High Commission. But in this proclamation the king declared "that the bishops were unjustly accused as being authors of the service book and canons, seeing whatever was done by them in that matter was by his majesty's authority and orders." The proclamation further expressed entire approbation of these innocent books; condemned all meetings and subscriptions against them, prohibiting all such proceedings, under pain of rebellion; and ordaining that no supplicant should appear in any town where the council were sitting, under pain of treason.* In this manner did the king openly take upon himself all the blame of those measures against which the great body of the nation had petitioned and complained, as if to tell the kingdom that no redress should be granted to any of their grievances.

It might have been thought that the depths of meanness and duplicity had now been explored. But the council found a still lower deep. Great numbers of the Presbyterians had arrived in Sterling before the day was far advanced,

* Baillie, pp. 32, 33.

and the council entreated their leaders to persuade them to withdraw, lest any tumult should arise; promising that no act of ratification should be passed, and that their protest and declinature against the prelates sitting as members of council should be received. Yet no sooner had the mass of the supplicants withdrawn, than the council admitted two of the prelates, ratified the proclamation, and refused to receive the protest and declinature; thus violating their own pledged honour, and degrading the faith of courts beneath the level of common falsehood. Several high-minded nobles, who had hitherto supported the prelatic measures, recoiled from the contamination of this act, and soon afterwards joined the Presbyterians. The publication of this proclamation in other towns was met with equal promptitude by a protest; and thus, according to the received opinions on such matters in Scotland, the binding force of the proclamation was neutralized, till the subjects of which it treated should be freely and fully discussed in Parliament and Assembly.

These proceedings hastened on the crisis. The Presbyterians now saw clearly that the king himself was determined to support the prelates, and ruin them, if in his power. Unless, therefore, they were prepared to bow their necks beneath prelatic despotism in the Church, and arbitrary power in the State, they must maintain their position; and to do so without a more decided and permanent bond of union than that which the Tables afforded was impossible. So reasoned the nobility. On the other hand, Henderson, Dickson, and some more of the leading men among the ministers, looking more deeply into the matter, became convinced that the Church and the nation were suffering the natural and penal consequences of their own defections. And calling to mind how greatly God had blessed the previous Covenants, in which the nation had bound itself by the most solemn obligations to put away all idolatry, superstition, and immorality, and to worship God in simplicity and faithfulness according to his own Word, they arrived at the important conclusion, that their duty and their safety were the same, and would consist in returning to God, and renewing their covenant engagements to Him and His holy law.

This great idea re-assured their minds; yet they were aware that it would require to be cautiously introduced to the notice of the weaker and less decided of the brethren. A public fast was intimated, in which the confession of the defections of the Church and nation formed naturally a leading subject of the addresses which the most eminent of the ministers were selected to deliver to crowded audiences of earnest and deep thinking men. In this manner the idea of renewing the Covenant was infused into their minds, while the sacred duties in which they were engaged had for a time entirely banished all narrow, selfish, and worldly considerations. On the immediately following day, Monday the 26th of February, the subject was openly mentioned; and it was found that already there was a strong and very prevalent inclination to renew the Covenant. Alexander Henderson and Johnston of Warriston were appointed to draw it up, and Rothes, Loudon, and Balmerino to revise it. The utmost care was taken that it should contain nothing which could justly give offence to even the most tender and scrupulous conscience. Objections of every kind were heard and considered, and forms of expression altered, so as to remove whatsoever might seem liable to objection. Baillie and the brethren of the west country appear to have been the most scrupulous, but all their difficulties were removed or answered.

The Covenant consisted of three parts; the first, the Old Covenant of 1581, exactly as at first prepared; the second, the acts of Parliament condemning Popery, and confirming and ratifying the acts of the General Assembly,—this was written by Johnston; and the third, the special application of the whole to present circumstances,—this was the production of Henderson, displaying singular clearness of thought and soundness of judgment.

At length the important day, the 28th of February, dawned, in which Scotland was to resume her solemn covenant union with her God. All were fully aware, that on the great transaction of the day, and on the blessing of God upon it, would depend the welfare or the woe of the

Church and kingdom for generations to come. By day-break all the commissioners were met; and the Covenant being now written out, it was read over, and its leading propositions deliberately examined, all being invited to express their opinions freely, and every objection patiently heard and answered. From time to time there appeared some slightly doubtful symptoms, indicative of possible disunion; but these gradually gave way before the rising tide of sacred emotion with which almost every heart was heaving. Finally, it was agreed that all the commissioners who were in town, with as many of their friends as could attend, should meet at the Grayfriars church in the afternoon, to sign the bond of union with each other, and of covenant with God.

As the hour drew near, people from all quarters flocked to the spot; and before the commissioners appeared, the church and churchyard were densely filled with the gravest, the wisest, and the best of Scotland's pious sons and daughters. With the hour approached the men; Rothes, Loudon, Henderson, Dickson, and Johnston appeared, bearing a copy of the Covenant ready for signature. The meeting was then constituted by Henderson, in a prayer of very remarkable power, earnestness, and spirituality of tone and feeling. The dense multitude listened with breathless reverence and awe, as if each man felt himself alone in he presence of the Hearer of prayer. When he concluded, the Earl of Loudon stood forth, addressed the meeting, and stated, explained, and vindicated the object for which they were assembled. He very judiciously directed their attention to the covenants of other days, when their venerated fathers had publicly joined themselves to the Lord, and had obtained support under their trials, and deliverance from every danger; pointed out the similarity of their position; and the consequent propriety and duty of fleeing to the same high tower of Almighty strength; and concluded by an appeal to the Searcher of hearts, that nothing disloyal or treasonable was meant. Johnston then unrolled the vast sheet of parchment, and in a clear and steady voice read the Covenant aloud. He finished, and stood silent. A solemn stillness followed, deep, unbroken, sacred. Men felt the near presence of that dread Majesty to whom they were about to vow allegiance; and bowed their souls before Him, in the breathless awe of silent spiritual adoration.

Rothes at length, with subdued tone, broke the silence, stating that if any had still objections to offer, they should repair if from the south or west parts of the kingdom, to the west door of the church, where their doubts would be heard and resolved by Loudon and Dickson; if from the north and east, to the east door where the same would be done by Henderson and himself, "Few came, proposed but few doubts, and these few were soon resolved." Again a deep and solemn pause ensued; not the pause of irresolution, but of modest diffidence, each thinking every other more worthy than himself to place the first name upon this sacred bond. An aged nobleman, the venerable Earl of Sutherland, at last stepped slowly and reverentially forward, and with throbbing heart and trembling hand subscribed Scotland's Covenant with God. All hesitation in a moment disappeared. Name followed name in swift succession, till all within the church had given their signatures. It was then removed into the churchyard, and spread out on a level grave-stone, to obtain the subscription of the assembled multitude. Here the scene became, if possible, still more impressive. The intense emotions of many became irrepressible. Some wept aloud; some burst into a shout of exultation; some, after their names, added the words, *till death;* and some opening a vein, subscribed with their own warm blood. As the space became filled, they wrote their names in a contracted form, limiting them at last to the initial letters, till not a spot remained on which another letter could be inscribed. There was another pause. The nation had framed a Covenant in former days, and had violated its engagements: hence the calamities in which it had been and was involved. If they, too, should break this sacred bond, how deep would be their guilt! Such seem to have been their thoughts during this period of silent communing with their own hearts; for, as if moved by one spirit,—and doubtless they were moved by the One Eternal Spirit, —with low heart-wrung groans, and faces bathed in tears, they lifted up their right hands to heaven, avowing, by this sublime appeal, that they had now "joined themselves to the Lord in an everlasting COVENANT, that shall not be forgotten."*

CHAPTER VI.

FROM THE SUBSCRIBING OF THE COVENANT IN 1638, TO THE RESTORATION OF CHARLES II. IN 1660.

The Covenant Subscribed throughout the Kingdom with great zeal—Plans of the Prelatists—Applications of both Parties to the King—The Covenant Subscribed in the Highlands—The King resolves to enter into temporizing Negotiations with the Covenanters—The Marquis of Hamilton appointed Lord High Commissioner—Deceitful and fruitless Negotiations of Hamilton—Preparations for a Meeting of Assembly—The General Assembly of 1638 held at Glasgow—Struggles of Hamilton—Triumph of the Assembly—Summary of its most important Acts—Reflections—Supplication to the King—His Resentment, Schemes of Revenge, and Preparations for War—Deliberations and Preparations of the Covenanters—Montrose at Aberdeen—The King resolves to invade Scotland—The Covenanters arm—Their appearance at Dunse Law—The King enters into a Treaty—Defection of Montrose—The King displeased with the Proceedings of the Assembly and Parliament—Prepares again for War—The Covenanters prepare also—Contentions in the Assembly respecting Private Meetings of a Religious Character—Reflections—The Army of the Covenanters enter England—The Scottish Commissioners in London—The Idea of Religious Uniformity in the Two Kingdoms suggested—Repeated in the Assembly—First Commission of Assembly—The Covenanters resolve to enter into Treaty with the English Parliament—THE SOLEMN LEAGUE AND COVENANT—Reflections—The Westminster Assembly of Divines—Contemporaneous Events in England and Scotland—Montrose—Charles in the Army of the Covenanters—The Confession of Faith—The Engagement—Divisions in Scotland—Death of Charles I.—Loyalty of the Covenanters—Charles II. proclaimed King—Signs the Covenant—Cromwell in Scotland—Suppression of the General Assembly—Internal State of the Church—Divisions—Resolutioners and Protesters—Restoration of Charles II.

NEVER, except among God's peculiar people the Jews, did any national transaction equal in moral and religious sublimity that which was displayed by Scotland on the great day of her sacred National Covenant. Although it was computed that there could not be less than sixty thousand people from all parts of the kingdom assembled at that time in Edinburgh, there was not the slightest appearance of confusion or tumult; and on the evening of that solemn day, after hours of the deepest and most intense emotion, when every chord of the heart and every faculty of the mind had been excited to the utmost pitch of possible endurance, the mighty multitude melted quietly and peacefully away, each to his own abode, their souls filled with holy awe and spiritual elevation, by the power of the sacred pledge which they had mutually given to be faithful to their country and their God. What but the Spirit of God could have thus moved an entire people to the formation of such a bond, in which every worldly consideration was thrown aside, every personal interest trampled under foot, every kind of peril calmly confronted, solely for the maintenance of religious truth, purity, and freedom? Worldly politicians might well stand amazed; selfish and ambitious prelates might be confounded and appalled; and a despotic sovereign and his flatterers might cherish fierce resentment, when they heard of the wonderful transaction: and men of similar views, characters, and feelings, may still pour forth their virulent invectives against Scotland's Covenant, and the men who framed and signed it, obeying the divine impulse by which they were guided and upheld; but we do not hesitate to state our opinion, that the sublime deed of that great day will ever, by all who can understand and value it, be regarded as the deed and the day of Scotland's greatest national and religious glory.

On the next day, the 1st of March, the Covenant was again publicly read in a large meeting of those who had come too recently to the capital to have had leisure to take its main propositions into sufficiently deliberate consideration. Freely were its principles stated, that no man might bind himself to a measure the full nature of which he did not comprehend; and yet so remarkable was the unanimity of the meeting, that about three hundred ministers at once added their names to the large number already subscribed. The Covenant was then carried to the most public parts of the city, to afford an opportunity to people dwelling in the different districts of adding to it their signatures; and whereever it appeared, it was hailed with joyful welcome, as a bond of unity and a pledge of sacred peace. Great numbers are said to have followed it from place to place, imploring the blessing of God upon it, with gushing tears and fervent

* For a more full account see Baillie's Letters, Rothe's Relation, Row's History, Alton's Life of Henderson, &c.

supplications, that this return of their country to its ancient covenant union with God might be the means of averting the Divine indignation, and procuring deliverance from their calamities. Copies of it were soon afterwards written, and sent to every part of the kingdom, that by being universally signed, it might become indeed a National Covenant. It was almost everywhere received with feelings of reverence and gratitude. No compulsion was required to induce men to subscribe a bond, the placing their names on which they held to be at once a high honour and a solemn duty; nor would compulsion have been permitted, had it been required. "The matter was so holy," says the Earl of Rothes, "that they held it to be irreligious to use violent means for advancing so good a work." And in his answer to the Aberdeen Doctors, Henderson says, that "some men of no small note offered their subscription, and were refused, till time should prove that they joined from love to the cause and not from the fear of man."* Before the end of April there were few parishes in Scotland in which the Covenant had not been signed by nearly all of competent age and character. It deserves to be stated, in confirmation of the thoroughly religious character both of the Covenant itself, and of the feelings regarding it or those by whom it was subscribed, that Baillie, Livingstone, and every writer of the period of any respectability, agree in declaring that the subscribing of the Covenant was everywhere regarded as a most sacred act, and was accompanied in many instances with remarkable manifestations of spiritual influence, and in all with decided amendment in life and manners. It awed and hallowed the soul, imparted purity to the heart, and gave an earnest and foretaste of peace,—that peace which the world can neither give nor take away,—peace of conscience and peace with God.

We do not affect to conceal that some slight instances of popular violence took place in some parts of the country, where either the people had previously suffered injurious treatment from the prelates and their partizans, or where attempts were made by that party forcibly to prevent the signing of the Covenant. But these scenes of intemperate zeal or petty retaliation were almost entirely the sudden ebullitions of passion among a few women and boys, unattended by serious consequences. Not an instance is recorded of personal injury having been sustained by a prelatist, but one, and that to a very trifling extent.* And when it is remembered how long the country had groaned beneath the prelatic yoke,—how many of the most faithful ministers had been banished from their attached congregations,—and how much injurious and oppressive treatment both ministers and people had suffered from the Court of High Commission,—the chief cause of wonder is, that so little of a vindictive spirit was displayed by the nation, when arising in its might, to shake off the galling domination of its proud oppressors. But this truly glorious blending of strength and forbearance, of judgment and mercy, was merely a new manifestation of the Presbyterian spirit and principles, first shown at the Reformation, when Popery was overthrown, but the popish priesthood spared,—repeated in this, the Second Reformation, when Prelacy was condemned, but the prelatic faction rarely exposed to the slightest degree of that retaliation which they had so wantonly provoked,—again to be re-exhibited in still more trying circumstances by the truly Christian-minded Presbyterians, but never imitated by their antagonists in their periods of triumph. The Presbyterian Church of Scotland has often suffered persecution, but has never been guilty of committing that great crime.

The prelates had always declared, when urging forward their innovations, that the greater part of the nation would readily receive the Canons and Liturgy, and that the opposition was that merely of a very few, who might be safely despised; but now, when the Covenant was received with such cordiality and gratitude throughout the kingdom, they were overwhelmed with shame, consternation, and despair, mingled with bursts of fury and passionate longings for revenge. Spotswood, who better under-

* Answers to the Aberdeen Doctors, &c., p. 9.

* Even the prelates, in their artiches of information, mention only four instances of popular violence. (Burnet's Memoirs of the Duke of Hamilton, p. 41.) Other authors mention about as many more, but not so well authenticated.

stood the character of his countrymen than the younger prelates, exclaimed, "Now all that we have been doing these thirty years past is thrown down at once;" and, yielding to despair, he fled to London, and remaining chiefly there in a state of gloomy dejection, survived the ruin of his pride and power little more than a year.

The privy council felt almost equally paralyzed. After a deliberation of four days at Stirling, during which they were receiving hourly intelligence of the rapidly-extending influence of the Covenant, they resolved to send to the king information of the state of affairs, suggesting the necessity of listening to the remonstrances of the aggrieved nation, and giving promise of redress, to the extent at least of refraining from the enforcement of the Book of Canons and Liturgy, and mitigating the despotic conduct of the High Commission. About the same time, the Covenanters, as they began to be designated, and as we may henceforth term them, sent a deputation to London, to give his majesty a faithful representation of the real state of public matters, and of the views and wishes of his oppressed subjects. The prelates were already in London; so that the representatives of all parties in Scotland were at one time within the precincts of the court, affording an opportunity to his majesty of obtaining full and accurate information of the condition of the kingdom, had he been disposed to seek it. But he had already listened to the partial statements of the prelates, and formed his determination. They, anxious to extenuate their own failure, had still represented the Covenanters as weak in station, influence, and numbers, and, however violent in their procedure, forming but a small faction in the kingdom. They had suggested that the north was steady to his majesty's interest; and that the south was so divided, that if the powerful families of Hamilton, Douglas, Nithsdale, and some others, should raise their forces, and form a junction with Huntly and the Highland chiefs, the Covenanters might be easily overpowered, and the whole kingdom brought into complete subjection to his commands.* Such were the counsels of the prelates, who seem to have regarded a civil war as a slight matter, provided they could recover that wealth and power which they had so grievously abused. Unfortunately their pernicious advice sunk deep into the mind of Charles, impelling him to those measures which involved the kingdom in the miseries of revolutionary strife, and issued in the death of the beguiled and infatuated monarch. Well indeed may Prelacy canonize as a martyr the sovereign who perished, the victim of its dark, bloody, and fatal policy.

The Earl of Haddington, to whom the Covenanters had sent their deputation, and with whom they maintained a secret but very constant correspondence, was aware of the advice which had been given to the king, and of the measures which were in contemplation. Orders had been given to seize Livingstone the moment he arrived, and to throw him into prison; but Haddington concealed him, presented the supplication of the Covenanters, which was, however, returned unopened; and sent the messenger back to Scotland, with private information of the secret designs of the court. The Covenanters lost no time in counteracting the dangerous policy recommended by the prelates. Deputations were sent to those districts of the country where the Covenant had been but partially signed, and on the support of which the prelates mainly relied for the ultimate triumph of their cause. These deputations met with success beyond their most sanguine hopes. In some of the seats of learning, as at St. Andrews and Glasgow, the ministers and professors subscribed but partially; but even in these towns, the magistrates, burgesses, and citizens joined their countrymen almost universally. Even in the Highlands the Covenant was welcomed with perfectly amazing cordiality. Clans that rarely met but in hostile strife, and, if they did so meet, never parted without exchanging blows, met like brothers, subscribed the bond of national union, and parted in peace and love. Nowhere was this unwonted but most lovely sight more signally displayed than at Inverness. There the fierce feuds of ages melted and disappeared beneath the warming and renewing power of that Divine influence which so strongly and brightly shone around

* Baillie, vol. i. pp. 70, 71.

he Covenant, as the snows melt from their native mountains, when the summer sun is high in the smiling heavens.

Thus did her sacred Covenant first make Scotland truly a nation, melting and fusing into one united mass the heterogeneous and jarring elements which had previously lain partially compacted together in space, but uncombined, and mutually repelling and repelled. Then, too, was seen a portion of the good which God brings out of what man intends for evil; for then was seen some of the fruits of the zealous and faithful labours, among these warm-hearted Highlanders, of the pious ministers who had been from time to time torn away from their own congregations, and banished to the remote regions of the north, there in tears to sow a seed which was now springing up in gladness. James and the prelates had sent Bruce, and Dickson, and Rutherford, and others, to Inverness, Aberdeen, and other Highland districts, as if to show the inhabitants what true religion was, and thus to prepare them for the Covenant, although they did not mean it so. But such has often been the mysterious course of all-wise Providence, to pour contempt upon the wicked desires of ungodly men, overruling their machination, and causing them to promote the very cause which they are seeking to destroy.

Meanwhile the king was busily engaged in concerting his schemes; and for a time it seemed as if he were truly desirous to learn the real state of matters before he should come to a final determination. He sent orders to the Earl of Traquair, Roxburgh, and Lorn, to repair to London without delay; and he required from the most eminent Scottish lawyers a legal opinion whether the conduct of the Covenanters were not treasonable. Sir Thomas Hope, then Lord Advocate, and two other distinguished lawyers, gave their opinion, that there was nothing decidedly illegal in the proceedings of the Covenanters. Lord Lorn also spoke very strongly in defence of these injured and calumniated men; and laid before his majesty a full account of the actual state of the country. About the same time the king received the unwelcome intelligence, that the Covenant had been received with enthusiastic delight, even in those parts of the country where the prelates had assured him it would be indignantly rejected. This rendered the prelatic cry for war a more doubtful question; especially as the English nobility concurred in recommending peace, being better aware of the wide-spread discontent existing in that kingdom also, than was its blindly-obstinate sovereign.

Perceiving that he must for the present abandon his warlike designs, the next care of the king was to engage the Covenanters in negociations, partly in the hope of dividing them, and partly to gain time till he might muster power enough forcibly to overwhelm them. He resolved, therefore, to appoint a commissioner to treat with his Scottish subjects, to hear their grievances, and, if he could not flatter and delude them into submission, at least to lull them into security, or wear them out by procrastination. The choice of a person to undertake this difficult task was a matter of vital importance, as its success would greatly depend upon his skilful management. At last the Marquis of Hamilton was appointed lord high commissioner, and intrusted with the hazardous and disreputable enterprise of attempting to deceive or overawe a nation famed for courage and sagacity, and now doubly vigilant and thoroughly united. Aware of the perilous nature of the task, Hamilton would willingly have declined it; but the king would take no denial, and he was obliged to prepare to meet it as he might. For this reason he strove to secure himself against the possible consequences of the dark intrigues in which he must be involved; and knowing well the character of those who were urging the king to the adoption of hostile measures, one of Hamilton's first steps was to secure the absence from the court of all the Scottish courtiers, and especially of the prelates. After he had seen them all sent off, he left London himself; but not thinking his protection yet sufficiently secure, he delayed his journey at Berwick, and remained there till he had procured from the king private instructions, ample powers, and a secret pardon for whatever he might say or do in the matter, which might be represented by his enemies as contrary to the king's intentions.

In that strange specimen of state diplomacy, the real intentions of the king are revealed, and are enough to cause any man of common honesty to blush for shame. It states, that Hamilton was expected, and even required, to enter into the most intimate intercourse with the Covenanters,—to pretend friendship and compassion,—and to throw them off their guard and detect their schemes, that he might the more easily circumvent and overpower them. "For which end," says his majesty, "you will be necessitated to speak that language which, if you were called to account for by us, you might suffer for it. These are therefore to assure you, and, if need be, hereafter to testify to others, that whatsoever ye shall say to them to discover their intentions, ye shall neither be called in question for the same, nor yet it prove in any way prejudicial to you."* It may be hoped that a high-minded nobleman, such as Hamilton, would feel it indeed a degrading and irksome employment, when thus required to act the part of a spy and a deceiver; and when courtly and prelatic historians assail the Covenanters in the language of vituperation and reproach, they may be reminded that the whole conduct of Charles was a tissue of despotism and treachery, fatal to his character and ruinous to his cause.

The Covenanters received warning of the secret intentions of the king, and of the real object of Hamilton's commission; but though thus aware of the treacherous devices to be put in motion against them, they resolved to act as became their sacred cause, and, whilst guarding against deceit and guile, to make their own course one of truth and rectitude. For this reason they drew up and promulgated two papers, of a public nature. The one was sent to the nobles at court, stating plainly the articles required for the peace of the Church and kingdom of Scotland, that they might be aware what was demanded, and be prepared to advise his majesty accordingly. The other contained a general statement of the plan of procedure which would require to be followed in the approaching negociations with the high commissioner; and was sent through the kingdom, to prevent division of sentiment, and to secure that unity of heart, mind, and effort, which was essential to their safety.

On the 10th of May the king sent to the Scottish privy council intimation of his commission to the Marquis of Hamilton, requiring them all to meet his Grace at Dalkeith on the 6th of June, to render him all due honour, and to support him in the discharge of his high trust. The Covenanters, on their part, sent information of the approaching negociations to all their supporters, requiring them to come to Edinburgh in such numbers as should protect them from any meditated hostile attempt. And still placing their trust in the Divine guidance and support, a general fast was appointed to be held on the 3d of June, to humble themselves before God, and to supplicate his protection. The fast was kept in the most solemn and impressive manner, and had a powerful effect in preparing the kingdom for the approaching struggle, enabling them to keep their position on ground avowedly sacred. At the same time, the Covenanters, whose councils were still guided by the Tables, resolved that they would not attend the commissioner at Dalkeith, but would remain in a united body at Edinburgh, and by that means avoid the danger of being divided by the subtle insinuations of their crafty opponents. Having received information that the king meant to subdue them by force, they judged it expedient to prevent that force from being concentrated in the heart of the country; and therefore placed a guard on the Castle of Edinburgh, that it might not receive any large supplies of provisions and military stores.

Hamilton at first refused to come to Edinburgh, which was completely in the possession of the Covenanters; but after some concessions had been made, he consented to make the Palace of Holyrood his residence. Accordingly it was concerted that on the 19th of June the Marquis of Hamilton should make his public entry into Edinburgh in state, as lord high commissioner from the king. The Covenanters prepared to give him a stately reception. Both parties agreed that he should approach by Musselburgh along the level sea-line,—a circuitous route, but one peculiarly adapted for display. All the nobles who had signed

* Hardwicke's State Papers, vol. ii. p. 141.

the Covenant, gentry from all parts of the kingdom, the magistrates of Edinburgh, all the ministers who had assembled in the capital, and an immense multitude, loosely calculated at about sixty thousand, went out to meet the commissioner, and arranged themselves along the beach, covering the undulating outline with a more numerous assemblage of people than had been seen in Scotland for centuries. As Hamilton rode slowly along the line of this vast mass of his collected countrymen, hearing on every side not the fierce battle-cry of armed men, nor the giddy shouts of mere holiday rejoicers, but earnest and fervent prayers for the preservation of the liberties and religion of the country, he was deeply moved, and could not suppress tears of sympathy, declaring his strong desire that King Charles himself had been present to witness a scene so affecting, and even sublime. On a little eminence near the end of this extended multitude, stood upwards of five hundred ministers, wearing their cloaks and bands, and prepared to address the commissioner; but when he came to the place where they stood, he declined receiving their addresses in public, bowed to them, and uttering a single complimentary sentence, continued his progress.

From what he had seen on that single day, the commissioner must have learned that the state of Scotland had been grievously misrepresented to his majesty; that there were not, in truth, two parties in the country, but on the one side a Presbyterian nation, and on the other a prelatic faction, contemptible in numbers, despicable in character, and detested on account of their long career of treachery and despotism. But he knew that the king had placed himself at the head of that base and weak faction, and was prepared, for their sakes, and to gratify his own arbitrary temper, to trample upon the dearest rights and most sacred privileges of an entire kingdom; and he was constrained to suppress his generous sympathy, and to resume the course of heartless and tortuous policy with which he was commissioned.

And now began the unequal contest between diplomatic craft and the straightforward honesty of honourable and religious men,—unequal, inasmuch as the wily dissimulation of designing craft is perpetually over-reaching or betraying itself, while unbending integrity of purpose goes right onward to its aim, and, having nothing to conceal, is in no dread of detection. We cannot afford space to follow the contending parties through the shifts and changes of their varying negotiations, but must confine ourselves to a brief statement of the most important points of the complicated proceedings of that eventful time.

In an early interview which they obtained, the Covenanters informed the commissioner that all negotiations would prove fruitless, unless he were empowered to grant a free General Assembly, in which their complaints respecting the innovations introduced by the prelates, and the conduct generally of those men, might be investigated, judged of, and, if proved culpable, censured and condemned according to their demerits,—and a parliament, by which acts proved to be unconstitutional might be rescinded, and redresses authoritatively and conclusively granted. Hamilton replied, that he would answer their statements and requests by a proclamation. They promptly gave him to know, that they would be in readiness to meet every proclamation with a distinct protest, to whatsoever extent it should fall short of the necessities of the case and the just demands of the nation. The commissioner seemed disposed to try the resolution of the Covenanters. He commanded preparations to be made for issuing the proclamation; and the Covenanters made similar arrangements to meet it with their protest, the nobility and gentlemen mustering in considerable numbers around their official representatives, each man with his sword loosened in its sheath, in readiness to repel any sudden attack by the military attendants of the commissioner. Seeing the determined front displayed by the Covenanters, Hamilton changed his procedure, abandoning the proclamation, and resuming the path of crooked and wily dissimulation.*

It is always more difficult for a cunning man to understand honesty, than for an honest man to detect craft. Hamilton could not comprehend the designs of the Covenanters; but they could easily see through his thin evasions. He now

*Baillie, Burnet, and Stevenson.

thought it expedient to offer them both an Assembly and a Parliament, provided they would abandon the Covenant. They answered, that they would as soon renounce their baptism. And at the request of the Tables, Henderson wrote an able paper, containing a clear and strong statement of the reasons why they could neither rescind nor alter in the slightest degree their sacred Covenant. Still more completely to convince the commissioner of the futility of any such expectation, they prepared a supplication, in which the request of a free General Assembly and a Parliament was publicly and avowedly stated as that without which they could not be satisfied; and at the same time they caused another paper to be extensively circulated, containing suggestions of the measures which it might be necessary to adopt, should the commissioner resort to force, or protract the negotiations to an intolerable length. In these suggestions a significant hint was given, that both a General Assembly and a Parliament might possibly be called, without the royal authority, if that were much longer withheld; and also, that if violence were used for enforcing obedience, a committee might be chosen, to consider what was fit and lawful to be done for the defence of their religion, laws, and liberties.

These bold and energetic measures startled the commissioner, and convinced him that any longer continuation of his temporizing policy would be in vain, and that his majesty must either yield to every one of the main points demanded by the Covenanters, or must prepare to subdue them by open force. And as his instructions did not enable him to proceed to either of these alternatives, he determined to return to London, give the king a full account of Scottish affairs, ascertain the state of the royal preparations for the commencement of hostilities, and return fully empowered to act as necessities might require. This was indeed the only course which he could now pursue; but even this was to be marred by double dealing. On one day he left town, and proceeded a few miles on his journey: on the next, supposing the Covenanters now off their guard, he hastily returned, and proceeded to publish a declaration of his majesty's intentions, plausible, but characteristically evasive. It promised that the Liturgy should not be pressed but in a *fair and legal way;* that the High Commission should be rectified by the aid of the privy council, so that it should not impugn the laws, nor be a just grievance to loyal subjects; and that whatsoever concerned the peace and welfare of the Church should be taken into consideration in a free Assembly and Parliament, which should be called with his majesty's first convenience. The Covenanters had experienced his majesty's duplicity too often to be deluded by so flimsy a pretext. They met it therefore by a protestation, which had been previously prepared for any sudden emergency, and which this weak stratagem gave them a fair opportunity to publish. Hamilton seems, nevertheless, to have imagined he had gained his point, and pressed the privy council to ratify this declaration. Many consented; but the Covenanters having given to each member of council a paper containing reasons against its ratification, they were induced by its perusal to rescind the act of ratification. Rothes, Montrose, and Loudon obtained an interview with the commissioner himself, presented to him these reasons, and urged upon him the necessity of a more frank and conciliatory course. Hamilton, irritated by his failure, replied to them in a haughty and dictatorial tone. This drew from Loudon the bold declaration, that they knew no other bands between a king and his subjects but those of religion and laws: if these were violated, men's lives were not dear to them. Overborne by threatenings they would not be, for such fears were past with them.* After this abortive attempt, the Marquis of Hamilton left Scotland on the 8th of July, and went to London for fresh instructions.

During the course of these fruitless negotiations the king maintained a constant intercourse by letters with the commissioner; and it is painful to peruse these glaring proofs of the infatuated monarch's disgraceful and perfidious dissimulation. A few instances must be given, in proof of this assertion, and in vindication of the Covenanters. "I give you leave to flatter them with what hopes you please; your chief end being now to win time, until I be ready to suppress them."—"I

* Baillie, vol. i. p. 92.

have written this to no other end than to show you that I will rather die than yield to those impertinent and damnable demands."—"I do not expect that you should declare the adherers to the Covenant traitors, until you have heard from me that my fleet hath set sail for Scotland. In a word, gain time by all the honest means you can, without forsaking your grounds."—"There be two things in your letter that require answer, to wit, the answer to their petition, and concerning the explanation of their damnable Covenant." In another letter, after stating how far his military preparations were in readiness, and what was their amount, his majesty adds,—"Thus you may see that I intend not to yield to the demands of those traitors the Covenanters."* All these and many similar instructions to the commissioner to prevaricate, to deceive, and to gain time, while the king was busy levying forces, collecting military stores, preparing a fleet, and hiring foreign troops to suppress his faithful subjects by this combination of treachery and power, were sent to the Marquis of Hamilton privately, while that nobleman was engaged in pacific negotiations with the Covenanters. History can scarcely furnish an equal instance of a monarch's faithlessness, dissimulation, and forethought despotism. Bolder tyranny the world has often seen, but rarely any so deliberately dishonourable. And as these private instructions to the commissioner were all to a considerable extent known to the Covenanters, it cannot appear strange that they received every proposal with suspicion, and expressed distrust of every declaration, how strong soever might be its asseveration, and to whatsoever extent it might wear the aspect of sincerity.

While the king and the marquis were using every "honest means" to gain time, the covenanters took care to lose none. Aware that the king intended to send some forces to the north, to co-operate with those which Huntly was expected to raise, they resolved to paralyze effectually that right arm of prelatic and regal tyranny, during the breathing space allowed by the absence of the commissioner. And as Aberdeen, by the influence of Huntly and of its cloistered sages, had yet stood out against the Covenant, Henderson, Dickson, and some others, were sent to try whether the dreary darkness which brooded over that town and neighbourhood, might not be partially dispelled. The deputation was at first but coldly welcomed; permission to preach in the city churches was refused; and the doctors strove to engage them in a fruitless scholastic disputation. But the deputation was composed of men of energy and decision. They returned brief answers to the sophistic subtleties of their learned opponents; and since the churches were refused, they preached in the open air, explained the Covenant, and produced arguments for its subscription. At the close of their addresses the Covenant was produced for signature; and that evening about five hundred respectable citizens adhibited their names. They then traversed the adjacent country; and within little more than a week, forty-four ministers, many gentlemen, and a large proportion of the people, signed the Covenant. Returning to Aberdeen, they again preached where they had done before, and obtained a considerable number of additional adherents to the sacred cause. Having thus, by the powerful demonstration of the Divine Spirit accompanying their exertions, succeeded in pouring a stream of light and life into those regions of previous gloomy stagnation, they returned to Edinburgh, leaving in the town and vicinity of Aberdeen a power sufficient to prevent the possibility of any great hostile combination there.

The Marquis of Hamilton returned to Holyrood-house on the 10th of August, furnished, indeed, with ampler powers to treat than before, but still enjoined to use every diplomatic stratagem. One new artifice by which it was hoped the Covenanters might be divided, was the re-promulgation of the Confession or Covenant of 1581. If this could be got numerously signed, it might either neutralize the Covenant recently produced, or so divide the nation as to enable his majesty to balance one part of the kingdom against another, and so to reduce both under his power. But that which was first put in operation was a set of demands which Hamilton gave to the Tables, requiring written answers to them before

* Burnet's Memoirs of the Hamiltons, pp. 46-68.

he would consent to call an Assembly. These demands were at first eleven in number, but subsequently were reduced to two; first, that no layman should have voice in choosing the ministers to be sent from the presbyteries to the General Assembly, nor any but the ministers of the same presbytery; the second, that the Assembly should not go about to determine things established by act of parliament, otherwise than by remonstrance or petition to parliament. If Hamilton could have obtained the assent of the Covenanters to these propositions, his victory over them would have been secure. By the first, the ministers would have been divided from the laity, and left powerless in the hands of their enemies; by the second, all the innovations of James's reign would have been confirmed, as they had all been ratified by parliament. But although the leading Covenanters easily perceived the fatal character of these propositions, it was not so easy to unite the whole body in returning proper answers. The first had nearly accomplished the commissioner's insidious design. Many of the ministers looked with some degree of jealousy upon the power of the laymen, and would not have been displeased to see that power diminished. For that reason they were disposed to assent to the first proposition; while the other three Tables would by no means comply with any such measure. At length, chiefly by the skilful management of Henderson and Dickson, this dangerous discussion terminated in the rejection of the commissioner's demands, and in the restoration of that unanimity of sentiment and purpose among the Covenanters which constituted their strength.

The danger thus encountered, and the re-union thus produced, both tended to point out to the Covenanters the path at once of duty and of safety. They now resolved to bring matters to a crisis, and to compel the commissioner to abandon his deceitful policy, by avowing their determination, that if the royal mandate were further delayed, they would call a General Assembly, on the sole authority which every Christian Church must be held intrinsically to possess, for the purpose of regulating all matters of worship and discipline, according to the institutions of the gospel, and the example of the apostles. The reasons on which this decisive resolution was based were published in their own defence, and for the instruction of all their adherents, and are still deserving of a thoughtful perusal by every true Presbyterian.*

Hamilton now felt that temporizing policy would no longer be endured, and also that his anticipations of creating a disunion among the Covenanters were at an end. But their demand went beyond his powers to grant, and was perilous to refuse, lest a refusal should impel them to put their purpose into immediate execution. He requested, therefore, a delay of twenty days, that he might return to the king, and obtain a final answer, promising to be again in Scotland with his majesty's ultimate decision before the 20th of September. The Covenanters consented to this delay, and employed the intermediate time in sending instructions to every presbytery how to proceed in the election of members for the approaching Assembly. This was necessary, in consequence of the lengthened period which had elapsed since an Assembly had been held at all, there having been none since 1618; and as all the Assemblies since 1597 had been more or less corrupted by regal interference. the proper course of procedure, in the calling of a free Assembly according to pure Presbyterian principles, had almost sunk into oblivion. These instructions were of the utmost importance, both in guiding the proceedings of the Covenanters throughout the kingdom, and in furnishing them with information on topics certain to come under discussion in the ensuing Assembly, with which many were at that time very little acquainted. Having taken these preliminary steps, the Covenanters waited calmly the return of the commissioner, and the ultimate answer of the king.

When the commissioner returned from London, a deputation from the tables waited on him at Dalkeith, and were told in general terms that his majesty had granted all their requests, but that the particulars could not with propriety be divulged till they had been communicated to the privy council. The council met the same day, when his majesty's letter

* These reasons are to be seen in Stevenson, edit. 1840. pp. 243, 246.

was produced, requiring them to subscribe the Covenant or Confession of 1581, which, as it contained chiefly an abjuration of Popery, was often termed the Negative Confession. The utmost efforts of Hamilton could not prevail upon more than about thirty of the council to subscribe, and that not till a clause was added, declaring that the subscribers understood it according to its original meaning, when, as the reader will recollect, even tulchan Episcopacy had been condemned and abolished, presbyteries erected, and the Second Book of Discipline entered on the records of the Assembly. Even thus explained, the commissioner entertained some hope that it might either cause division among the Covenanters, or at least produce a similar compact union of the royal and prelatic party; and with this view he published an act of council, calling upon all loyal subjects to subscribe the king's Covenant, with a general bond, resembling that of 1589. Commissioners were appointed to convey this rival Covenant throughout the kingdom, and every artifice was employed to procure the utmost possible number of signatures. But the Presbyterian Covenanters, perceiving clearly the intention of the commissioner, met the proclamation of the king's Covenant by a protestation and a warning against the ensnaring tendency of this new device;* and sent a deputation to every presbytery, with a copy of the protestation, and instructions how to act. So successful were these precautionary measures, that the king's Covenant obtained no more than about twenty-eight thousand signatures, of which number twelve thousand were procured in Aberdeen and its vicinity by the strenuous exertions of Huntly. This new stratagem had consequently no other effect than that of proving, even by an arithmetical demonstration, the weakness of the prelatic faction.

The next step of the privy council was the publication of two important acts,—the one calling a General Assembly to be held at Glasgow on the 21st of November, and warning the bishops and other commissioners of kirks to attend; he other summoning a parliament to meet at Edinburgh on the 15th day of May 1639, for settling and confirming peace in Church and State. The king's declaration was then publicly proclaimed, in which his majesty prohibited the enforcement of the Book of Canons, the Liturgy, and the Five Articles of Perth; abolished the Court of High Commission; declared all persons subject to the trial and censure of the competent judicatory; allowing free entrance into the ministry without the taking of any other oath than that contained in the act of parliament; granted a general pardon of all offences which had arisen out of the recent contentions; appointed a fast to avert the Divine displeasure, and procure a peaceable end to the distractions of the Church and kingdom; and recommended the subscription of the Confession and Covenant of 1581.

Had these terms been granted at the beginning of the negotiations between the king and the Covenanters, they would have given universal satisfaction, and been received with equal joy and gratitude. But after the many repeated instances of tergiversation and insincerity which had been detected, the Covenanters were compelled to regard every declaration of the king's with suspicion, and to look narrowly into every one of his promises, lest it should contain some evasive expression, by which it might be nullified, or even reversed. And unhappily even this plausible declaration of his majesty's sentiments did contain such neutralizing and evasive elements. It was understood to subject the prelates to the trial and censure of the Assembly; but it cited them to appear as constituent members of that very court by which they were to be tried; and the urgency with which the king pressed the subscription of the Covenant of 1581, showed clearly that he expected, by its instrumentality, to divide and conquer the Presbyterian Covenanters; besides that the bond contained an insidious clause for the maintenance of religion "as at present professed,"—a clause manifestly susceptible of such a construction as would convert it into one for the defence of Prelacy. The Presbyterians, therefore, resolved that they would no longer submit to such paltering in a double sense; that they would take care to have the Assembly

* This a' le document is prese ved by Stevenson, pp. 256, 264.

framed and constituted according to the fundamental and imperishable principles of the Presbyterian Church; and that the prelates should be tried and censured according to their demerits, and Prelacy itself entirely abolished, so that their National Church might be delivered from bondage and oppression, and established once more on a basis which no law can give, and ought not to attempt removing,—the warm affections of an intelligent, truly loyal, and earnestly religious people.

Great anxiety was felt by all parties, in the interval between the calling and the meeting of this most important General Assembly. Notwithstanding the artifices of the commissioner, and the exertions of the prelatic party, the Covenanters were eminently successful in securing the return of the most able and faithful of the ministers as commissioners, and the most zealous and influential of the nobility and gentry as ruling elders; so that before the Assembly met they were assured of its freedom and integrity, so far as depended upon the majority of its members. The mode in which they were to proceed against the prelates was a matter which required much and careful deliberation. The Earl of Rothes, and some other leading men of the Tables, petitioned the commissioner for a warrant to command the prelates to appear before the Assembly to stand trial for the offences charged against them; but this he refused to grant. The Covenanters were not, however, to be thus defeated in a point of such vital moment. It was arranged that a complaint should be prepared in form of a libel or regular accusation, to be laid before the Assembly by a considerable body of the nobility, gentry, burgesses, and ministers, who were not members of that court. The accusation embraced both their official and personal delinquencies. The first part of the charge referred to the "caveats" or cautions passed in the Assembly 1600, and ratified by King James, the ostensible object of which was to guard against the abuse of their powers by the prelates and commissioners of the Church, at that time introduced to parliament; but the real intention having been to delude the Church by the semblance of a security which could be easily broken through or set aside. These caveats, however, had been allowed to remain unrepealed, and now formed a leading element in the accusation against the prelatic party, by whom every one of them had been repeatedly violated. The prelates were accordingly charged collectively with having transgressed these caveats, usurped a lordly supremacy over the Church, taught heretical and false doctrines, and, personally, with having been guilty of irreligious conduct, and the perpetration of the grossest immoralities, which were distinctly specified according to each individual case. The accusations were sent to each of the prelates, and also to all the presbyteries, where they were directed to be read publicly in every church.

The prelates prepared an elaborate defence, bearing the general form of a declinature of the Assembly's jurisdiction, with their reasons for that line of procedure; which were said to have been sent to court, and revised by the sovereign's own hand. All being now nearly prepared, and the time at hand, the commissioner made his last attempt to interfere with the construction of the Assembly, by endeavouring to bring as many of the members as possible under such legal processes as might incapacitate them from taking their seat. This was instantly met by a remonstrance so strong, pointed, and resolute, that Hamilton felt the inexpediency, and even danger, of carrying this last scheme into effect.

The only remaining part of the preparations made by both parties is one which scarcely falls within our province to relate, as being more of a civil, or rather military, than of an ecclesiastical character. Allusion has already been made to the large naval and military armaments in preparation by the king. These were vigorously prosecuted by his majesty, in the midst of all his pacific declarations; and as this was well known to the Covenanters, they began to consider themselves entitled to prepare for the defence of their civil and religious liberties, so manifestly endangered. With this view, arms, ammunition, and provisions were quietly collected by the nobility and many of the towns; and General Leslie, a veteran officer of great skill and courage, who had served long under Gustavus, king of Sweden, was called home to take command of the army, if they should finally be compelled to rise in self-defence.

The Marquis of Hamilton was well aware that the crisis could no longer be retarded; but how best to meet it cost him many an anxious thought. Gladly would he have prorogued the meeting of Assembly, but that he was aware that the Covenanters had determined to hold it, even though he should attempt its prorogation. He resolved, therefore, at last to allow it to be held according to the proclamation already issued, and to do his utmost to bias, control, or overawe it, so as to prevent, if possible, the condemnation of the prelates; and should all his efforts prove ineffectual, he would dissolve it, with this advantage, that time had been gained, and his majesty's preparations for actual war would be in a state of greater forwardness.

On the Friday before the meeting of Assembly, the Covenanters, both those who were members of Assembly and those who were their friends and supporters, came in great crowds to Glasgow; and on the next day the commissioner and his friends entered town from Hamilton, and were met with much appearance of respectful and stately courtesy by the Presbyterian chiefs. The marquis had then another opportunity of seeing how completely the cause which he was commissioned to circumvent or oppress was the cause of the Scottish nation. Little more than a year had elapsed from the time when four humble petitioners met at the door of the privy council, to supplicate for protection against the oppressive conduct of the prelates; and now his majesty's lord high commissioner beheld arrayed against these men, or rather against that abjured system, the irresistible might of all the physical, mental, moral, and religious strength of a united people. We may imagine how his heart must have sunk within him when he contemplated the task imposed upon him by his infatuated sovereign,—the task of deluding or coercing his sagacious and high-minded countrymen, and of trampling in the dust those civil and religious liberties which were to them dearer than life itself,—a task which no foreign power had been ever able by its utmost efforts to achieve, and which he must have seen to be equally ungracious and desperate.

The Assembly had been indicted to meet on the Wednesday; and the three intervening days were spent in making preliminary arrangements, and especially, on the part of the Covenanters, in humbling themselves before God, and imploring his direction and support through the arduous duties in which they were about to engage, and for the right discharge of which they felt their own wisdom to be indeed utterly insufficient. And it ought to be carefully remarked, for the instruction of all succeeding ages, that during the whole course of their negotiations and deliberations, humble acknowledgments of their own folly and weakness, earnest prayer to God, and strong faith in his heavenly guidance, were always the master elements by which their actions were guided and their hopes upheld.

On Wednesday the 21st of November 1638, the General Assembly met, and commenced the discharge of its all-important duties. We cannot afford space to give more than the briefest outline of its proceedings; which, however, is the less to be regretted, since the very fact of their extreme importance has caused them to be very fully recorded by many authors whose works are in general circulation.* Both parties, the commissioner and the Covenanters, acted warily, yet firmly, from the very first hour on which the Assembly met. They were equally well aware, that a false movement on either side would give to the antagonist an advantage which it might not be possible to counteract; and, like two contending armies led by skilful generals, they watched each other's operations with deep, calm, forecasting prudence, cool resolution, and deliberate energy. The choice of a moderator was to the Assembly, in such a juncture, a matter of great moment, but not of doubt, except on one account. Alexander Henderson was universally admitted to be beyond all competition the fittest man, for knowledge, gravity, self-command, and soundness of judgment; but they dreaded to lose his ability in debate by placing him in the

* See Baillie, Stevenson, Burnet, Peterkin's Records of the Kirk of Scotland, &c., &c.

moderator's chair. Yet the necessity of having at their head a man who could both direct their own deliberations and defend them to the commissioner with courtesy and firmness, overruled all other considerations, and he was unanimously chosen to occupy that post of honour, toil, and danger.

The commissioner wished to have had the commissions of the members scrutinized before the choice of a moderator; but this the Assembly very properly resisted, as without a moderator their proceeding would have been informal and invalid. Again, the regular course of proceedings was interrupted by a proposal from his grace to have the declinature of the prelates read, before the Assembly had been duly constituted; but this, too, was rejected on the same general principle. Yet once more did Hamilton attempt to vitiate the court, by demanding six assessors with him, to take part in the deliberations, and to vote on all questions; and still the Assembly kept its position, and would enter on no public business till a moderator of their own choice had been formally placed in the chair. The marquis at length gave way, protesting, meanwhile, against the decision of the Assembly on each of these points, and being met by counter protestations; and, as above related, the Assembly chose for its moderator, Alexander Henderson. The choice of a clerk caused a new struggle; but again the Covenanters prevailed, and Archibald Johnston was placed in that office.

The contest still continued, and on what appeared mere matters of arrangement. The declinature of the prelates was now brought forward by the commissioner, and requested to be read before proceeding with the trial of the commissions of members; but as this paper contained a protestation against the whole members, and would have borne the aspect of a disqualification of them all, the Assembly refused to hear the declinature till the commissions had been all tried, that the court might be placed in a state of valid integrity before hearing a paper on the contents of which it must pass judgment.

These preliminary points having been thus arranged, the decisive movement could no longer be delayed. The declinature of the prelates was presented to the Assembly by Dr. Hamilton of Glassford, who appeared as their procurator. An instantaneous effect took place, which they appeared not to have foreseen. The Covenanters took instruments, that by this very declinature the prelates had acknowledged their citation, had appeared by their procurator, and that therefore, their personal absence was wilful. Dr. Hamilton was accordingly cited *apud acta*, and they were recognised as at the bar of the Assembly. A committee was then appointed to answer the declinature; and when the marquis protested against this procedure, a counter protest was immediately produced. The next was the seventh day of the Assembly's meeting; and both parties were conscious, that upon the events of this day would depend the issue of their long and arduous struggle. A slight preliminary skirmish engaged their attention on the early part of the day. This was caused by the Assembly's committee pronouncing their opinion that the five books which had been produced, purporting to be the records of the Church from the time of the Reformation, were genuine and authentic. This the lord high commissioner opposed, well knowing that if these records were sustained as authentic and authoratative, they would furnish principles, regulations, and precedents amply sufficient to justify the condemnation of the prelates. But the Assembly, deeply grateful to that divine Providence which had signally preserved these records, aud caused their restoration to the Church in such a momentous crisis of its history, received these precious volumes gladly, and gave to them the stamp of unanimous approbation. The answers to the declinature of the prelates were then read, and approved of by the Assembly, although Dr. Balcanquhal, the commissoner's clerical adviser, attempted to lead the discussion away from the matter in hand, and to involve them in scholastic subtleties. The moderator now put the question to the Assembly whether they found themselves competent to sit in judgment on the case of the prelates, notwithstanding their declinature. The commissioner immediately declared, that he could not permit the Assembly to persevere in this course of procedure, so contrary to the express intentions of his majesty. He complained that the Assembly was vitiated by the introduction of what he termed lay elders, and by undue influence used in the election of members; and he required the Assembly to dissolve, promising to procure from the king authority for the meeting of another, in which all such evils might be avoided. Against this Henderson, Rothes, and Loudon reasoned and protested, expressing at the same time their deep regret if his grace should forsake the Assembly, but their determination to continue its sittings till it should have accomplished those important duties for the discharge of which it had been called. The commissioner put an end to the discussion by saying, "I stand to the king's prerogative, as supreme judge over all causes civil and ecclesiastical: to him the Lords of the clergy have appealed, and therefore I will not suffer their cause to be further reasoned here." This he uttered with great apparent emotion, even with tears, in which he was joined by many, who thought they saw in his departure the final dispelling of all their hopes of a pacific settlement to those troubles by which the Church and the kingdom had been so long afflicted and oppressed.

The Marquis of Argyle (the same nobleman hitherto designated Lord Lorn, but who had succeeded to the higher title by the recent death of his father) attempted to avert or delay the crisis, by introducing a discussion respecting the two apparently conflicting Covenants; but Hamilton waived the subject, and called on the moderator to dissolve the meeting by prayer. This Henderson refused to do; upon which the commissioner protested in his majesty's name against whatever might be done by the Assembly, declared it dissolved by the same authority, and prohibited all further proceedings. The Earl of Rothes immediately produced a protestation against the departure of the commissioner, and his attempt to dissolve the meeting in this summary manner, while its most important duties were still unfulfilled. Argyle remained after the commissioner retired, and thus gave his countenance to the Assembly in this hour of peril. Nothing daunted or confused by what had taken place, Henderson addressed the Assembly in a very noble speech, full of the calm magnanimity of the Christian character, and instinct with the sacred principles of spiritual and eternal truth. Several other eminent members of this great Assembly spoke, and all in a similar spirit of Christian faith and Christian fearlessness. At this moment of deep and wide-spread emotion, an incident occurred, simple in itself, yet rising into the region of true moral sublimity. Lord Erskine, son of the Earl of Mar, a young nobleman of high character and distinguished talents, rose from the gallery where he was seated among the youthful nobility, and requested permission to address the Assembly. He then declared, while the starting tears attested the sincerity of his declaration, that he had hitherto abstained from subscribing the Covenant, against the light and the conviction of his own conscience; begged that he might now be allowed to affix his name to that sacred bond; and implored the Assembly to pray that his sin in resisting the call of duty might be forgiven him. Several others followed the example of this noble youth; so that, at the very moment when the frowns of royal wrath were darkening over the Assembly, the light of God's favour shone upon it, and the impelling power of the Spirit of truth, in answer to their earnest prayers, sent to the rescue the glowing energies of ingenuous youth, like a fresh stream of new life pouring its warm might into the sacred bosom of Scotland's reviving Church.

The moderator, availing himself of this encouraging event, put the question, Whether the Assembly would adhere to the protestation against the commissioner's departure, and continue together till they should have concluded the important business on account of which they had met? This was carried almost unanimously; there being only three or four opposing votes. The next question was, Whether the Assembly found themselves competent judges of the prelates and their adherents, notwithstanding their declinatures and protestation; and this also was unanimously carried in the affirmative, or, if not unanimously, with only three or four dissentient voices.

The struggle was now at an end; and the Assembly proceeded regularly and calmly forward to the completion of its remaining business. Next day the Marquis of Hamilton issued a proclamation, commanding the Assembly to dissolve; which was, as usual, met by a protestation, and no further notice was taken of the matter. The remaining deeds of the Assembly may be stated in a few sentences. An act was passed, annulling all the corrupt Assemblies by which Prelacy had been introduced,—those, namely, of the years 1606, 1608, 1610, 1616, 1617, and 1618. As a necessary consequence, all the innovations and changes made by these Assemblies were declared illegal, and all the obligations imposed on ministers by their authority pronounced no longer binding. An act was passed, condemning the Five Articles of Perth, the Book of Canons, the Liturgy, and the Book of Ordination, as introduced without warrant of either civil or ecclesiastical authority; and the Court of High Commission also, as having neither act of Assembly nor of Parliament in its support, and regulated by no law, human or divine. Then directing their attention to the deceptive use which had been attempted to be made of the Confession or Covenant of 1581, it was clearly proved from the language of acts of Assembly before and at that time, that diocesan Episcopacy had been and was then abjured and condemned by the Church; and upon this demonstration the Assembly passed an act, declaring, "that all Episcopacy different from that of a pastor over a particular flock was abjured in this Kirk, and is to be removed out of it." Baillie informs us, that he was himself the only person who hesitated to vote for this motion; and that his hesitation went no further than to give a brief explanation of his views.* This trial of the prelates had been prosecuted for many days with great care and deliberation; and all the accusations having been fully proved, the moderator was appointed to pronounce the sentence of Assembly. This he did, after having preached a sermon suitable to the occasion, in what Ballie terms, "a very grave and dreadful manner." Eight were deposed and excommunicated; four merely deposed; and two deposed from the prelatic station, but allowed to officiate as pastors of single congregations. Diocesan Episcopacy, or rather Prelacy (as we have all along preferred to term it, as its proper designation), having been thus condemned and abolished, the next step naturally was the passing of an act restoring to kirk-sessions, presbyteries, synods, and General Assemblies, the full enjoyment of those constitutional privileges, liberties, powers, and jurisdictions, according to the Book of Discipline, of which they had been deprived by prelatic usurpation. In completing the restoration of the Presbyterian Church, the Assembly did not forget certain points which at such a time might have seemed of comparatively minor importance. The principle that no person be intruded into any parish contrary to the will of the congregation, was re-enacted; and presbyteries were directed to see that schools were provided in every landward parish, and such support secured to schoolmasters as should render education easily accessible to the whole population of the kingdom. Many other beneficial enactments were made, which our limits will not permit us to enumerate.

* Baillie, vol. i. p. 158.

At length, on Thursday the 20th of December, this great and truly noble General Assembly having brought all these important matters to a satisfactory conclusion, prepared to close its labours. The next Assembly was appointed to meet at Edinburgh on the third Wednesday of July, 1639, in virtue of its own intrinsic powers, whether it should be called by his majesty or not; with this reservation, that if the king should of his own accord call a meeting of the Assembly on a different day, they should with all diligence and respect attend the time and place of his majesty's appointment. Several grave addresses and admonitions were then delivered by the moderator and other venerable members; and after prayer, praise and the apostolical benediction, Henderson pronounced the Assembly concluded, adding these remarkable words, "*We have now cast down the walls of Jericho. Let him that rebuildeth them beware of the curse of Hiel the Bethelite.*"

We have traced with some minuteness, and with feelings of deep veneration and gratitude, the proceedings of this ever-memorable General Assembly. And when our readers mark with what calmness, prudence, solemnity, and earnestness of devotional feeling its whole proceedings were conducted,—how much patience, in the midst of innumerable attempts to retard, violate or disturb its progress,—how little of vindictive spirit against the prelates from whom many of the members had sustained great personal injury,—how steadily they maintained the principles of loyalty to a monarch by whom, at the same time, they had too much reason to believe they were both hatred and betrayed, willing to regard him as deceived, and not intentionally tyrannical,—how generously, in the midst of all their harassing anxieties, they directed their attention to the wants and the welfare of the whole population of their beloved native land, securing, to the utmost of their power, to the poor man those inestimable blessings, the free and pure preaching of the Gospel, and the education of his children,—and, above all, how nobly, fearlessly, and piously, Scotland's National Church vindicated the sole sovereignty of the Lord Jesus Christ, her only and Divine Head and King,—it must, we think, be humbly and gratefully owned, that much of the presence and the power of the Spirit of wisdom, peace and truth, was there; and that a glory, sacred and imperishable, must ever rest on the memory of that venerable General Assembly whom God honoured to accomplish Scotland's SECOND REFORMATION.

It would be inexpedient to interrupt the progress of the narrative by any protracted disquisitions; but we trust we may be forgiven for directing the attention of the reader to one or two important lines of thought. The whole proceedings of the Assembly of 1638 present the most signal illustration that could be conceived of one of our introductory remarks, namely, the re-appearance at peculiar junctures, of those great principles which constitute the moral and religious life of a nation, although they may have been for a time so much obscured and overborne, that a superficial observer might have thought them sunk into entire and perpetual oblivion.

The great principles of the Reformation had pierced into the very core of Scotland's heart, and had there deposited their vital energies; but their growing development had been at first obstructed by the selfishness and rapacity of the nobles, and subsequently fettered and cast into dark imprisoned torpor by the king himself, who wished to substitute a frame of church government and discipline of an entirely different and uncongenial nature. But though thus repressed, and apparently dormant, these principles were not extinct. They formed the hidden life of Scotland still; awaiting but the time when the Divine Spirit, by whom they had been breathed into the nation, should again revive, awaken and call them forth, and the hand of Providence should rend asunder the fettering cerements within which they had been starkly swathed, and bid them live and act anew. In the second Reformation there was not one principle called into action which had not been either in active operation, or at least distinctly stated, in the first. Nor was there a single step taken for which there could not be shown both a precedent in the previous history of the Presbyterian Church of Scotland, and a direct authority from Scripture. And even in those parts of their proceedings which to some have appeared most questionable, such as continuing to sit notwithstanding the departure of the commissioner, and the deposition and excommunication of the prelatic party, their conduct will be found, when fairly examined, to have been altogether beyond the reach of censure,—nay, deserving of the highest approbation. To the king, in all civil matters, they rendered the most implicit obedience; while they calmly but resolutely refused to yield him that obedience in religious matters, which could not have been granted without violating their allegiance to Christ, as the only Head and King of the Church. At the same time they most pointedly not only admitted the right, but asserted the duty, of a Christian sovereign to defend the liberties and maintain the purity of a Christian Church. They clearly distinguished between his power *in the Church*, as a member of it and nothing more, and his power to regulate external arrangements, and enact and enforce national laws, *concerning the Church*, as a Christian king, bound by his own solemn oaths to be a nursing father to the Church, to protect and cherish it, and by that means, and through its unfettered instrumentality, best to promote the moral and religious welfare of the kingdom. And in the deposition and excommunication of the prelatic party, nothing was done but what was in direct accordance with many acts both of Assembly and of Parliament; and, what is of infinitely greater importance, all was founded on the explicit authority of the Word of God. Before a single prelate was deposed or excommunicated, he was proved, by incontrovertible evidence, to have been guilty of false doctrine, of introducing popish ceremonies, of attempts to subvert the church government and discipline which he had sworn to maintain, of tyrannical violations of national laws, and of such gross personal crimes and immoralities as rendered him utterly unworthy to hold any office in a Christian Church. Even then, so tenderly were those abandoned men treated, that a regular form of procedure was appointed for their expression of penitence and restoration to the Church, as members and ministers, should they be moved to repentance, and seek to be restored. Pride is not a sentiment which any human being ought ever to cherish, and therefore we dare not say that Scotland has reason to be proud of the great men who composed that Assembly and conducted its proceedings; but we will say, that every true Presbyterian must ever hold them in the highest esteem and veneration, while with humble gratitude we adore the gracious and merciful Redeemer, who shed down on them so abundantly the promise of the Father, the Holy Spirit, enlightening, guiding, and supporting them in their truly glorious defence of the unalienable prerogatives of his spiritual kingdom.

[1639.] The Covenanters had now completely taken their ground, from which they well knew that they could not retreat; but they were anxious to avoid hostilities if possible. For this reason, several of their leading men waited on the Marquis of Hamilton, before his departure from Edinburgh, to entreat his friendly mediation with the king. Hamilton was too well acquainted with his majesty's sentiments and intentions to anticipate any favourable result; and therefore not only refused to undertake the task of attempting to mitigate the king's resentment, but replied to the Covenanters in terms of reproach and threatening. But they were too earnestly desirous of peace to be deterred from prosecuting their loyal and pacific course by one ungracious refusal; and they accordingly determined to send their supplication to his majesty himself, by one of their own body, however perilous the enterprise. The supplication was couched in the most dutiful and submissive language, putting it in the king's power to come to an amicable arrangement with his faithful subjects, not only without submitting to any humiliating conditions, but with ample security to his honour and dignity. A little, a very little, more judgment and less passion on the part of his majesty might even then have put an end to all existing contentions, and prevented the subsequent miseries and sufferings both of the nation and of the ill-starred monarch. Mr. George Winram of Liberton undertook the hazardous duty of carrying the supplication to London, and of attempting to have it presented to the king, although aware that his life would be endangered by the unwelcome mission. His majesty thought proper to permit it to be read to him by the Marquis of Hamilton; but the only answer he returned was by uttering, in a tone between indignation and mockery, the Scottish proverb, "When they have broken my head, they will put on my coul." The supplication was presented on the 15th of January; and although Winram waited till the middle of March, he could obtain no other answer; but his presence in London so long enabled him to transmit to Scotland valuable information respecting the king's designs and preparations.

As the displeasure of the king was so great, so his preparations for war were on a scale so extensive as to indicate clearly that he intended nothing less than the complete subjugation of the kingdom. His majesty's plan was, to levy an army of thirty thousand infantry and six thousand cavalry; to put strong garrisons in Berwick and Carlisle; to send a division of five thousand men to Aberdeenshire to form a junction with the Marquis of Huntly, who might either divide the Covenanters, or operate on their rear; to send a strong fleet under the Marquis of Hamilton to the Frith of Forth, for the purpose of blockading the harbours, intercepting supplies of arms and ammunition, and spreading alarm along the coasts of Fife and Lothian; and having completed these arrangements, to place himself at the head of his main army, and advance into Scotland in such force as to bear down all opposition. To complete the scheme, the Earl of Antrim was to raise at least ten thousand men, and invade Argyleshire; and the Earl of Strafford was to take the command of a naval armament, and with it to sail up the Frith of Clyde, to rouse and encourage the Marquis of Hamilton's adherents, and to sweep the seas and devastate the shores of the west of Scotland.* To meet the heavy expenditure of such extensive preparations, the king resorted to the natural but unconstitutional process of procuring supplies of money from the private resources of those who approved of the object for which war was to be waged; and, as was to be expected, the English bishops contributed liberally for the support of this hierarchical war.

Nor were the Covenanters blind to their perilous condition. However reluctant to resort to even a defensive war, they felt it to be their duty to put themselves into the best state for either defending their civil and religious liberties, like men who knew their value, or at least exhibiting such a resolute and imposing front as should induce his majesty to grant favourable terms rather than hazard an encounter where victory was uncertain and defeat would be ruinous. But as it was in their estimation a matter of the utmost importance to clear their proceedings from the imputation of rebellion so pertinaciously charged upon them by their enemies, they published an "Information to all good Christians within the kingdom of England," vindicating their past conduct and their present intentions from the calumnious aspersions of the prelatic party. This paper was extensively circulated in England, and was successful in removing many prejudices, and awaking a considerable feeling of approbation. To counteract this, the king employed Dr. Balcanquhal, who had been Hamilton's clerical adviser at the Glasgow Assembly, to write an account of the whole of the proceedings in Scotland which had led to the present state of affairs. This paper, after being revised by Charles himself, was published as a royal manifesto, and is known by the title of "The Large Declaration." A proclamation was about the same time published by the king, of the same purport, which was also speedily answered by the Covenanters; and the answer was perused with great attention and considerable sympathy in England.

Having thus done every thing in their power to prove the goodness of their cause and their own earnest desire of peace, the Covenanters proceeded to deliberate concerning the propriety of even a defensive war. Considerable numbers of them entertained the opinion, that resistance to the civil magistrate was unlawful for Christians, how despotic and oppressive soever might be his couduct. And so far as suffering the penalties of even an unjust and tyrannical law was involved in the question, the majority would have submitted, with no other kinds of opposition than those of remonstrances and supplications, though there were others who held bolder opinions on that subject. But all were compelled to perceive that the king had much more in view than to allow them even the hard alternative of obedience or punishment, which in matters distinctly religious must always subject men to penalties, till the civil magistrate can be prevailed on to relax his requirements. The intention of his majesty, it was easily seen, was positively, to compel them to adopt all those changes in religious worship which he might think proper to introduce, and to prohibit absolutely and unconditionally those modes of worship which they believed to be most accordant with the Word and will of God. The alternative was not obedience, or the forfeiture of certain civil advantages and the infliction of certain temporal penalties; but obedience, or imprisonment, exile and death; or rather it was, obey the king though you should thereby be disobedient to God. With deep and anxious solicitude they set themselves to the investigation of this momentous question; and, after the most profound and studious perusal of eminent divines and jurists, and especially of the Bible, they arrived at the conclusion, that a Christian people were entitled to take up arms in defence

* Burnet's Memoirs, p. 113.

of their religious liberties against any assailant.*

We do not attempt to give even an outline of the elaborate writings of the Covenanters on this highly important question; chiefly because the most of their leading propositions have long been received into the national mind, and even form essential elements in the British constitution, so far at least as civil liberty is concerned. They were, however, at the time, far beyond the general sentiments of the age,—loftier, nobler, and more true than those, the defence of which rendered illustrious the boasted Hambdens and Sidneys of England. But we deem it right to direct the attention of the reader to this almost startling truth, that while the empire at large has imbibed and ratified their sentiments with regard to civil liberty, which was with them in reality a subordinate consideration, those sacred principles of religious freedom, of sole allegiance to Christ in matters of faith, in defence of which alone they resolved to confront their earthly sovereign, have not yet been thoroughly received into the national mind, and have never been regarded with equal favour by the historian, the philosopher, or the statesman. Why has this been the case? Because, while all men can so far understand their natural rights, and value their civil liberties, no man can understand sacred rights and value spiritual liberties till he has been made a freeman of the Lord. Therefore is the main principle of the Covenanters still assailed, and must be still defended, though we trust no longer with the weapons of earthly warfare. A man may lose his civil liberties, or submit to civil wrongs, and be a Christian still; but a Christian cannot yield up his religious liberty without committing grievous sin, sinking into the condition of a slave, and forfeiting his hopes of heaven.

Having thus arrived at the important conclusion that it was their clear and imperative duty to defend their religious liberties, the Covenanters commenced their preparations for defence with great promptitude and energy. A committee, on the plan of the Tables, was appointed to sit at Edinburgh, and to exercise full executive powers, holding correspondence with subordinate committees in every county, and giving simultaneous directions to the kingdom. And as the ministers had now become almost universally convinced of the lawfulness of a defensive war, they no longer felt any hesitation in recommending that measure to the people, rousing their courage, and stimulating their religious zeal. Arms and ammunition were procured in considerable quantities; the most experienced officers were distributed throughout the kingdom, to instruct others, and to begin, if not the actual levies of troops, at least the occasional training of such men as expressed willingness to serve when required. It was debated whether assistance should be sought from foreign powers; but this was overruled, as of a more questionable character than merely standing on their own defence; and the utmost that was permitted was, that letters might be written to certain continental kings and states, requesting them to intercede with Charles on behalf of his Scottish subjects. Even this was very partially done. The letter to the king of France was written and subscribed by a few of the nobles, but never forwarded to its destination, though the bare fact of its having been written and signed exposed the Earl of Loudon to the extreme peril of his life a short while afterwards.

But while the country was thus rapidly arming in self-defence, it was resolved that theirs should not be the first overt act of hostility. They even submitted to several minor outrages of a warlike nature, willing to postpone the actual collision to the latest possible period, in the faint hope that some pacific arrangement might yet be made. Many Scottish merchants and travellers were seized in England and Ireland, and treated as rebels; the Marquis of Huntly seized upon the city of Aberdeen, and put it in a state of fortified defence; and the Popish lords began to arm in different quarters of the kingdom; while English troops were not only assembling rapidly at York, but also hovering in threatening bands along the borders, and the Irish were preparing to invade the western coasts. At this time the castles of Edinburgh and Dumbarton were both in the hands of the royalists; but as the Covenanters perceived

* Baillie, vol. i. p. 189.

the danger of leaving these strong fortresses in the possession of their enemies when they should be compelled to march southward to repel the invaders, it was determined to anticipate and remove that peril. They were accordingly both seized on the same day; and so well had the Covenanters laid their schemes, that these important strengths were secured without the loss of a single life. Dalkeith was also taken without a blow, and a large quantity of military stores fell into the hands of the captors. The Earl of Montrose was sent to the north, to counteract the influence of Huntly; and as Montrose was not so scrupulous as the other leaders of the Presbyterians, he speedily reduced Aberdeen, forcibly compelled the citizens to subscribe the Covenant,* and having obtained possession of Huntly himself, not by the most honourable means, carried that dangerous nobleman with him to Edinburgh.

To complete their defensive arrangements, they resolved to fortify Leith, and by that means to protect the capital from assault by sea. As this was an object of great importance, it was undertaken and carried forward with corresponding energy. The nobles of the Covenant began the works with their own hands, which were prosecuted night and day without intermission, all classes and ranks vieing with each other in carrying forward the labour, and even ladies of distinction stimulating the enthusiastic ardour of the men by personally sharing in their toils. In an almost incredibly short period Leith was completely fortified; and the towns along the Fifeshire coast were put in a state of defence by the erection of batteries on the most commanding positions.

These prompt and decisive measures put an end to the king's hopes of paralyzing the Covenanters by internal disunion, and there remained but two alternatives, —either to subdue Scotland by the force of English and Irish arms, or to treat with it on fair and equal terms. Unhappily Charles chose the former alternative, even though there were not wanting symptoms which ought to have caused him to pause in his perilous enterprise. Indications sufficiently intelligible were given to him, that the high heart of England was disinclined to the invasion of Scotland in such a cause. Many saw clearly that the king's success in subjugating the Scottish Covenanters would enable him to forge for themselves the fetters of absolute despotism; and not few entered more deeply into the question, and perceived in his attempt the real spirit of Popery, regarding it as a distinction of little moment whether a foreign prelate or a native monarch should assume and exercise that lordship over the conscience which belongs to God alone. Some of the nobility declared that they would not aid in the invasion of Scotland till the consent of parliament had been sought and obtained; and, in general, the supplies of both men and money fell far short of the king's expectations. Still, as Charles could not believe that the Covenanters would dare to meet him on the field, he adhered to his warlike resolutions; and, having mustered his forces at York in the beginning of April, he sent the Marquis of Hamilton with a fleet to the Frith of Forth, and began his own march at the head of his army, to invade his ancient kingdom.

After a series of ominous delays, the Marquis of Hamilton arrived with his fleet in the Frith; but no sooner was he descried, than the beacons were lighted, and brave men rushed from all quarters to the points of danger, like descending mountain torrents. Instead of being able to effect an "awful diversion," as the king had commanded him, by landing and laying waste the country "with fire and sword,"* he found himself actually surrounded by forces immensely superior to his own. All his efforts were therefore reduced to a paper warfare, in which, as formerly, he found himself overmatched by his able antagonists. At length he was summoned to meet the king near Berwick, to strengthen the operations by land, since his attempts by sea were so ineffectual. When the parliament met in Edinburgh, it was immediately prorogued by the king; and to this prorogation they yielded without the slightest opposition, contrary to the expectation and the wish of their enemies. But in this they merely acted in accordance with their own high and well-defined principles; they yielded

* It deserves to be noted, that this was the first instance in which any were compelled to subscribe the Covenant, and that this was done by Montrose on his own sole authority.

* Burnet's Memoir, pp. 121-123.

to the king all due and constitutional obedience in matters purely civil, refusing only that obedience in spiritual matters to which he was not entitled, and which they could not render without sin.

Another slight alarm was raised in the north by the reising of Huntly's adherents, who seized Aberdeen, and threatened a descent upon the southern provinces. This was again speedily suppressed by Montrose, who now treated the inhabitants of Aberdeen and the adjacent country with considerable severity, levying a heavy contribution, and committing some acts of pillage upon the defenceless inhabitants, inconsistent with his present religious profession, though sufficiently natural to his real character, as afterwards developed.

War was now begun; but still the Covenanters were anxious for peace, if it could be obtained without the sacrifice of religious purity and truth. Repeatedly did they send deputations to his majesty, while on his march; but the haughty monarch refused to listen to their supplications, and would hear of nothing but the renunciation of the Covenant and the Glasgow Assembly, and an unconditional submission to his royal will. It was now time to move forward in their united might; but, animated by the same religious spirit which had guided all their past conduct, they would not go till they had done their utmost to secure the hope that God had gone before them. A solemn fast was held, and many earnest prayers were offered up to the Lord of Hosts, imploring Him to guide all their movements, and to crown them with victory in that sacred cause which they regarded as most truly His own. The committee next issued directions to the kingdom to regulate the conduct of their adherents in the muster and the march to head-quarters. They then marched forward in two divisions; the main body, under General Leslie, halted at Dunglas; and a strong detachment, under Monro, took up a position at Kelso. The latter body came first into contest with a division of the king's forces, which had been sent forward to publish a proclamation, and at sight of the Scottish troops, turned and fled with great precipitation;—proving thereby, no' their want of courage, but their want of inclination to fight in such a quarrel.

The result of this rencounter, and the nature of the royal proclamation commanding them to lay down their arms within eight days, on pain of being declared rebels, their lands forfeited, and a price set on their heads, convinced the Scottish leaders that their reluctance to proceed to hostilities was regarded by the king as caused by fear, and not the effect of conscientious loyalty. They determined to relieve his majesty from this mistake, and accordingly advanced to Dunse Law, where they encamped within sight of the royal army, at a distance of little more than six miles. When they first pitched their tents on Dunse Law, on the 1st of June, the army was about twelve thousand strong, but in a few days it was increased to nearly twice that number, full of courage, and confident in the goodness of their cause.

The army of the Covenanters presented such a spectacle as has been rarely witnessed. The hill on which they had taken up their position is of a conic form, about a Scottish mile in circumference, rising gradually to the height of a bowshot, where it terminates in a plain of nearly thirty acres in extent. This level summit was bristled round with forty field-pieces, commanding the two roads that led to the capital. Around the sides of the hill were pitched the tents of the army, each regiment in its own respective cluster. A banner-staff was planted firmly at each captain's tent-door, from which floated the Scottish colours, displaying not only the national arms, but also this inscription in golden letters, "FOR CHRIST'S CROWN AND COVENANT," explanatory of the sacred cause for which this dauntless banner was again spread on the winds. A minister of the highest character and abilities was attached to each regiment; and regularly as morning dawned and evening fell, the troops were summoned, by beat of drum, or sound of trumpet, to their devotional duties, which were conducted generally by the same reverend pastors to whose prayers and exhortations they had listened on days of Sabbath stillness, among their own rural and peaceful homes. The army was chiefly composed of Scotland's thoughtful and high-souled peasantry,—men strong of frame and bold of heart, to whom religious liberty was dear because they had felt and known its priceless value, and therefore were prepared to peril life itself in its defence. Led on by their time-honoured nobility, encouraged by their beloved pastors, and convinced by the goodness of their cause that Heaven was on their side, these dreadless men looked forward to the hour of battle as to that of certain victory. Theirs was not the fiery courage of untamed blood and reckless hardihood, but the calm, deliberate fortitude of men who feared God, and knew no other fear. It was not strange that Charles recoiled from encountering such a foe.*

Perceiving the formidable strength and dauntless resolution of the Scottish army, Charles became anxious to treat with men on whom he now saw that he could not trample. Yet pride withheld him from making the first proposals otherwise than by stealth. No sooner did the Covenanters learn that the king might now listen to overtures for the peaceful termination of the struggle, than they sent an embassy to supplicate his majesty to bestow on their requests and statement of grievances a favourable audience. Both parties being now willing to come to pacific terms, the adjustment of preliminaries was not a matter of extreme difficulty, although the king was careful to maintain such punctilious forms as should, in his opinion, save his honour, and not too greatly mortify his pride. As it was not pride, but religious principle, by which the Covenanters were actuated, they were content to make every reasonable concession, and to soothe the monarch's wounded feelings to the utmost. Yet the negotiations were at one time nearly interrupted at the instigation of the Scottish prelates, who were willing to peril their sovereign's life, and the peace of their native land, in the prosecution of their own avaricious and revengeful desires. But a significant hint from Leslie of his intention to advance his army within cannon-shot of the royal camp, caused an immediate change in the lowering aspect of affairs, and the negotiations were not only resumed, but brought to a speedy conclusion. Although the king would not grant directly the requests of the Covenanters, he thought it prudent to accede to articles of pacification in which they were virtually involved. He consented to the ratification of all that had been deceptively promised by the Marquis of Hamilton to the Glasgow Assembly, though he would not allow that Assembly to be specifically named. To this was added, that an Assembly should be held at Edinburgh on the 6th of August, to which all ecclesiastical matters were to be referred for decision; and a Parliament was to sit on the 20th of the same month, to determine civil affairs, and to ratify the acts of Assembly. On these terms it was further agreed that the forces on both sides should be disbanded, the fleet leave the shores, and the castles be rendered back to the king. To express his royal gratification, his majesty expressed his intention to honour both the Assembly and the Parliament with his presence,—an intention which he did not carry into effect. This treaty was signed on the 18th of June, and publicly proclaimed in both camps the same day.

It is painful to be obliged to state, that not only during these negotiations did the king too manifestly degrade himself by double-dealing and treachery, but that even in concluding the treaty of pacification, he entertained the fixed determination to violate all its most important stipulations as soon as his power should ever be equal to his will. This perfidious conduct was not unknown to the Covenanters; and although they did not publicly avow distrust of the king, nor declare their jealousy of his dissimulation, it would argue a degree of imbecility of which they cannot be suspected, if they had allowed themselves to be circumvented by such manifest deceit. Their part of the treaty they performed by instantly breaking up their encampment, disbanding their troops, and placing the fortresses in the hands of the royalists; but they retained their veteran officers in pay, and broke not up that internal organization by means of which they were able almost instantaneously to raise and re-concentrate the power of the kingdom. Charles lingered some time before he disbanded his army; and after that had been partially done, sent for the leading Cove-

* For a more full account, see Baillie, pp. 210-214; Stevenson, pp. 373, 374.

nanters to wait on him at Berwick. Burnet admits that he did so with the intention of trying what fair treatment might do with them. Six only of them went, or rather were allowed to go, as the probable object of the king was suspected. Of these Montrose was one; and so effectual were the king's arguments or promises with him, that before he left the royal presence, that ambitious nobleman had pledged himself to promote his sovereign's designs, and to remain among the Covenanters that he might the more effectually betray them It is difficult to say whether the conduct of the king or of Montrose was most dishonourable,—the one in persuading to treachery the, other in consenting to become a traitor; or most criminal, the king in violating the faith of the recent treaty, Montrose in committing perjury by breaking his solemn Covenant engagement.

Defeated in all his intentions, and disappointed in all his hopes, the king declined to go to Edinburgh according to his promise; but before his return to England, appointed a lord high commissioner to represent him in the Assembly and in parliament. Hamilton declined holding this high office, though requested by the king; and the Earl of Traquair was appointed. A list of instructions were given by the king to Traquair, for the direction of his conduct in the Assembly, in which a spirit of even mean and bitter spite against the last Assembly is betrayed, and its whole character is that of shifting and deceitful evasiveness. The last article of it requires Traquair to protest, that in case any thing has escaped his notice, prejudicial to his majesty's service, "his majesty may be heard for redress thereof, in his own time and place." By this it is manifest that the king intended to revoke every concession which the commissioner had made, whenever it should be in his power. With regard to the parliament, he felt even more at liberty, as Traquair had suggested that none of its acts could be valid without the presence of the prelates, as the third estate, and, therefore, they might be passed and afterwards thrown aside whenever his majesty thought proper.*

The General Assembly met on the 12th of August. In such an outline as the present work, we cannot record more than the most important acts passed by this Assembly. As the king had expressed his determination not to ratify the acts of the Glasgow Assembly, which, on the other hand, the Covenanters would not disavow, the expedient was adopted of re-enumerating its acts in the preambles of those now to be passed. In this manner the corruptions which had so long troubled the Church, were re-stated, and formally condemned, by which means all the prelatic innovations were once more abolished, and a clause was added, securing the annual meeting of Assemblies, and the regular meeting of synods, presbyteries, and kirk-sessions. Considerable difficulty was experienced in dealing with the recusant prelatists, but this, too, was surmounted by hearing the accusations against them afresh, framing a condemnation of the errors of which they were accused, and dealing leniently with those who expressed contrition for their faults, and submitted to the Assembly. The Large Declaration, written by Balcanquhal, but published as the king's manifesto, was condemned, and a supplication was prepared, requesting his majesty to cause the offensive book to be suppressed. The National Covenant was next renewed; and the Assembly petitioned the privy council to give it the sanction of an act of council, requiring it to be subscribed by all his majesty's subjects. This was accordingly done, the whole council subscribing, and Traquair himself subscribing as commissioner, that it might have as full sanction as the representative of royalty could give it, with this explanatory declaration, that it was one in substance with the Confession or Covenant of 1581. The minor acts of this Assembly were a proposal by Henderson for a committee to frame a full Confession of Faith—another for a Catechism,—and an act resembling that since called the Barrier Act, prohibiting any change in the laws of the Church till the motion to that effect had been communicated to all synods and presbyteries, and returned to the next Assembly ripely considered. The next Assembly was appointed to meet at Aberdeen; and after warm and earnest expressions of gratitude to the king and his commissioner, and of fervent thanksgiving and

* Burnet's Memoir, pp. 149, 150.

praise to God for his countenance and support, was formally dissolved in the usual manner.

Information of the proceedings of the Assembly had been sent to the king from time to time during its sittings, and his majesty's comments were returned to his commissioner. Whether from inadvertence, or thinking that since the king's whole concessions were deceptive, it could not much matter about the strictness of the language, the commissioner had permitted himself to subscribe and ratify the act condemning the prelatic innovations, although it contained the following strong statement: "That Episcopal government, and the civil places and power of kirkmen, be holden still as unlawful in this Kirk." The word *unlawful* the king could not tolerate, though he would not have objected to the condemnation of Prelacy as "contrary to the constitution of the Church of Scotland;" and, therefore, he "absolutely commanded" Traquair not to ratify that act in parliament, unless the language were changed according to his suggestion.* One might be disposed to regard his majesty's distinction as merely a petty quibble, since what is *unconstitutional* ought to be held as *more than unlawful* by every man of sound judgment; but it is too well known that many men pay more respect to the letter of the law than to the spirit of the constitution; and besides, Charles held that he possessed, in virtue of his high prerogative, the power of altering the constitution of both Church and State, according to his own arbitrary will; consequently, the word *unconstitutional* was a much less formidable obstacle in his estimation than the word *unlawful*. Like superficial thinkers in general, he did not perceive that constitutional principles are the life-powers of a community, while laws are but the variable forms through which they manifest their essential energies. Under the strong coercion of his majesty's "absolute command," Traquair endeavoured to prevail upon the parliament to amend the errors which he had permitted to pass the Assembly; but after much intriguing and successive adjournments, he was obliged to prorogue its further sitting till the 2d of June 1640, and to hasten to court for the purpose of endeavouring to appease the royal indignation.

[1640.] The Scottish parliament sent the Earls of Loudon and Dunfermline to London for a similar purpose; but the king was so highly incensed with their pertinacious adherence to their own views, that after having reluctantly granted them audience, and listened to the statement which they were commissioned to make, he commanded the Earl of Loudon to be committed to the Tower, on a charge of treason, founded on the letter to the King of France, of which mention was made above. So vehement was the wrath of the king, that he issued the tyrannical order, that Loudon should be beheaded within the Tower before nine o'clock of the following morning, and without the formalities of a trial. This bloody warrant the lieutenant of the Tower carried to the Marquis of Hamilton, who, aware of the fearful consequences which would inevitably ensue, hastened to the king, and earnestly besought him to recall the warrant. At first he sternly, and with violent language, refused to comply; but at length the marquis prevailed, chiefly by pointing out the dire effects to himself and his cause which such a deed would certainly produce, and with suppressed and sullen revengefulness he permitted the victim to be rescued from his deadly gripe.

The king was now resolved once more to take the field, and reduce the Covenanters to subjection by force of arms. But the main obstacle to the accomplishment of this sanguinary resolution consisted in the difficulty of meeting the expenditures in which he would be necessarily involved. All his resources were drained by his previous ineffectual attempt; and he saw no method of obtaining a sufficient sum of money but that of calling an English parliament, and endeavouring to procure a grant of adequate supplies. Above eleven years had elapsed since a parliament had been held; during which period the arbitrary conduct of the king, and the hideous cruelties perpetrated by the Star-Chamber, had so alienated the kingdom, that Charles dreaded to call a parliament, lest, instead of granting a subsidy, it should proceed first to the consideration of grievances. What could not be avoided must

* Burnet's Memoir, p. 158.

be met; but what was dreaded took place. When the parliament met, they would not listen to the demand of a subsidy till they had inquired into their own wrongs, and sought redress. The king indignantly dissolved the parliament, and set himself to raise the necessary funds by every means in his power. By the most strenuous exertions he so far replenished his treasury as to be able to take the field in the month of July, at the head of 19,000 foot and 2,000 cavalry.*

Although perfectly aware of all the king's proceedings, the Covenanters manifested no rash eagerness to resort to defensive warfare, till every pacific method had been tried. They held the parliament on the day to which it had been prorogued; and, notwithstanding the absence of the Earl of Traquair, they calmly and regularly proceeded with the transactions for which the parliament had met, and ratified all the acts of the preceding Assembly, besides reforming their own constitution. At the same time they made repeated applications to the Marquis of Hamilton, and to several of the English nobility, that they would intercede with the king, and, if possible, persuade him to consent to a peaceful settlement of the nation's troubles. Some private intercourse appears to have taken place between the Covenanters and the disaffected party in England, by which the movements of the former were not a little influenced.† Being convinced that hostilities were inevitable, the Covenanters again sounded the alarm, and were answered immediately by the mustering thousands of the bold and religious peasantry, and the gallant nobles of Scotland, accompanied, as before, by many faithful and zealous ministers.

In the meantime the General Assembly met at Aberdeen on the 28th of July, and began their duties, while all around them was ringing with the din of war. Unhappily, all was not peace within the Assembly. The absence of many of the leading men left the business to be conducted by others of inferior talents, and less tact in the management of a popular assembly. The cause of the contention was not new; it had come before the preceding Assembly, but had been partly soothed down by the sagacious management of Henderson, and partly repressed into a subordinate position by the presence of matter of more urgent character. During the domination of the prelatic party, many religious people had withdrawn from the ministry of men from whom they derived no spiritual instruction; but to supply the want to the utmost of their power, they had adopted the measure of meeting together in private, and engaging in reading of the Scriptures, exhortation, and prayer, for their mutual edification. Several of those who had been in Ireland and other countries for a considerable time, had become so confirmed in this custom, that even after the Glasgow Assembly, the abolition of Prelacy, and the restoration of the purer and simpler modes of Presbyterian worship, they still continued their practice of holding these private religious meetings. The most pious ministers saw nothing offensive or improper in such private meetings of Christian worshippers; but there were others who looked on them with less favourable regard. Some of the ministers had, while on the Continent, witnessed scenes of gross profanity among the Aanabaptists, and other ignorant and enthusiastic sects, and dreaded that similar abuses would spring up in the prayer-meetings of their grave and sober countrymen. Others were still so deeply tainted with the prelatic leaven, that they viewed these meetings as so many conclaves of conspiracy against their own ecclesiastical dignity and privileges. There were others also, among the ministers, men of more comprehensive and far-seeing minds, who dreaded from such meetings the rise of a species of Independency in Scotland, which, they were aware, was beginning to raise its head very powerfully in England. Undoubtedly the wisest measure would have been either to have taken no public notice of such meetings, or to have done so in terms of approbation; and for the ministers themselves to have attended them, joined in them, given to the humble and pious worshippers all the instruction in their power, and thus not only to have prevented schism and alienation, but to

* Burnet's Memoirs, p. 173. † Burnet's Own Times, p. 17.

have re-directed all those streams of private devotion into the channels of the National Church.

It may be remarked in passing, that the number of sects which spring up in any country, the erroneous nature of the tenets held by these sects, and the wild extravagance into which they rush, supply, when fairly and judiciously investigated, so many almost infallible tests of the real character of the Church of that country. For if that Church has done its duty in communicating religious instruction to the people, they will carry with them, even should they leave its pale, the sacred knowledge which they had acquired, and will retain such an amount of sacred principles, and present such an aspect of regulated propriety, that no large-hearted Christian will feel himself at liberty to speak of them in terms of scorn. While, on the other hand, if they have been neglected and left in ignorance, they will infallibly display that ignorance in their insanely delusive, or darkly fanatical notions, and in the glaring absurdity or profane impiety of their conduct. This test we may have occasion hereafter to apply with regard to the Churches both of England and of Scotland; at present it is enough to suggest it, partly as connected with the contentions in the Assembly at Aberdeen, and partly for a subject of reflection to the reader.

The person by whom this subject was brought before the Assembly was Henry Guthry, at that time one of the ministers of Stirling.* His character is well known by all who are acquainted with Scottish ecclesiastical history, by whom his eagerness to repress private religious worship will be sufficiently understood. To those who may not have access to other sources of knowledge, it will probably be enough to state, that his subsequent conduct caused him to be deposed from the ministry in 1648; that after the restoration of Charles II. he was made bishop of Dunkeld; and that he wrote memoirs of Scottish affairs in his own times, which abound in misrepresentations and calumnies. Such was the man who took it upon him to act the part of a discourager of private religious meetings for worship, and a maker of strife in church courts.

* Baillie, vol. i. pp. 249-255.

Owing to the various causes already specified, his attempts were but too successful; and after some days of bitter contention, the Assembly passed an act respecting family worship, limiting it to the members of each family, and prohibiting the expounding of the Scriptures, except by ministers or those in training for the ministry, of whose qualifications the Presbytery had expressed approbation. This unseemly and ill-omened contention may be regarded as the first insertion of that wedge by which the Church of Scotland was afterwards rent asunder; and it deserves to be remarked that it was pointed and urged on by a prelatist.

The army of the Covenanters had again mustered at their former station on Dunse Law; but after remaining there about three weeks, and feeling that their resources would soon be exhausted should they continue inactive, they deliberated seriously on advancing into England to meet their assailants. This was a more questionable measure than their former defensive position, and they felt all the responsibility in which it might involve them.* But they felt also, that there were but two alternatives, the one or the other of which they must adopt,—either to advance in a peaceful manner towards the royal army, or to disband their forces, and submit to the mercy of an enraged monarch, and his cruel instigators, the relentless prelates. Many reasons might be adduced why the Covenanters ought not to have entered England; but their best vindication will be found in the dire necessity which compelled them either to advance and secure their religious and civil liberties, or to remain and bow their degraded necks beneath the yoke of double despotism. They chose the nobler alternative; prepared and published manifestoes explaining the reasons of their expedition, and most solemnly disclaiming all hostile intentions against the English nation; then, humbly committing their cause to God, they crossed the Tweed, and marched towards Newcastle, as peacefully as if they had been passing through the heaths and valleys of their beloved native land.

We shall not further trace the movements of the Scottish army. Its success at the crossing of the Tyne—its march

* Rushworth, vol. iii. p. 1223, *et seq.*

towards York,—the reluctance of the English to support the king's despotic designs,—the pacification of Ripon,—the transfer of the place of treaty to London,—and the first meeting of the long parliament,—must all be left to the civil historian, as not legitimately within our province, further than that, in tracing the reflex influence which these events exercised on ecclesiastical matters, so much must be stated as to render the subject intelligible.

[1641.] The residence in Scotland of the Scottish Commissioners for the Treaty, from the latter part of the year 1640 till August 1641, when the treaty was finally concluded, was productive of the most important consequences to both countries. Henderson, Baillie, Blair, and Gillespie, some of the most eminent of the Scottish ministers, were appointed to accompany the commissioners to London, and to remain with them in the capacity of chaplains.* The great abilities of these distinguished men attracted the attention of the English of all ranks in a very remarkable manner, and recommended the Presbyterian system of Church government much more effectually than arguments alone could have done. Nor was this strange. Henderson was a man of uncommon prudence and sagacity, profound judgment, decided eloquence, and the most attracting amenity of manners. Baillie, though greatly inferior to Henderson in mental powers, and somewhat fickle in disposition, arising from a facile temper and constitutional timidity, was one of the most learned men of his time. Blair was also a very learned man, had passed through many sharp trials, and, having been brought much into contact with the Independents, had thoroughly studied the questions in controversy with that religious body, on which account he was made one of the deputation. And Gillespie, though still a very young man, had already proved himself to be endowed with powers and possessed of acquirements of the very highest order; his learning was both extensive and singularly minute; his intellect clear, acute, and powerful, qualifying him for eminence in debate; and his high and fervid eloquence was pervaded by that electric energy which is an essential attribute of true genius. The presence of such men in London for so many months, and the free intercourse which they enjoyed with all classes of society, gave an impulse to the heart of England which proved irresistible.

During this residence of the Scottish commissioners in the English capital, the views of all parties expanded; and an idea which had been previously but dimly entertained by many, began to assume a definite form in the minds of the leading men. That idea was, the possibility which such a juncture seemed to present of establishing uniformity in the religious worship of the three kingdoms. In one respect this was no new idea. It had been entertained by both King James and the present sovereign; but they both sought to realize it by the strong compulsion of civil power, forgetting that men may be reasoned into the reception of opinions, but cannot be compelled; and proceeding upon the utterly false notion that the civil magistrate has a right to dictate in matters of religion. Viewing this great question in a very different light, and perceiving that the English nation was now wellnigh as weary of the despotic rule of Laud as they had been of their own prelatic tyrants, the Scottish commissioners began to hope that England might be persuaded to change her Church government, and bring it into closer uniformity with that of Scotland's National Church. They did not entertain the presumptuous wish to dictate to England in so grave a matter; the whole amount of the influence which they ever dreamt of exercising was, to suggest the measure to the English mind; and, if it should be favourably received and undertaken, to aid their English brethren by those advices and that information which their own experience might enable them to give. That these were in reality the sentiments of the Scottish Covenanters, however much they have been misrepresented by party writers, the following extract from a paper entitled "Arguments given in by the Commissioners of Scotland unto the Lords of the Treaty, persuading Conformity of Church government as one principal means of a con-

* Baillie, vol. i p. 269.

tinued Peace between the two Nations," will, we trust, clearly prove.

"As we account it no less than usurpation and presumption for one kingdom or church, were it never so mighty and glorious, to give laws and rules of reformation to another free and independent church and kingdom, were it never so mean, civil liberty and conscience being so tender and delicate that they cannot endure to be touched but by such as they are wedded unto, and who have lawful authority over them; so have we not been so forgetful of ourselves, who are the lesser, and of England, which is the greater kingdom, as to suffer any such arrogant and presumptuous thoughts to enter into our minds; our ways also are witnesses of the contrary, against the malicious, who do not express what we are or have been, but do still devise what may be fuel for a common combustion. Yet charity is no presumption, and the common duty of charity bindeth all Christians at all times, both to pray and profess their desire, that all others were not only almost but altogether such as themselves, except their afflictions and distresses; and, besides common charity, we are bound as commissioners in a special duty to propound the best and readiest means for settling of a firm peace. As we love not to be curious in another commonwealth, nor to play the bishop in another diocese, so may we not be careless and negligent in that which concerneth both nations. We do all know and profess, that religion is not the only mean to serve God and to save our own souls, but that it is also the basis and foundation of kingdoms and states, and the strongest band to the subjects under their prince in true loyalty, and to knit their hearts one to another in true unity. Nothing is so powerful to divide the hearts of people as division in religion; nothing so strong to unite them as unity in religion; and the greater zeal in different religions, the greater division; but the more zeal in one religion, the more firm union. In the paradise of nature the diversity of flowers and herbs is pleasant and useful; but in the paradise of the Church, different and contrary religions are unpleasant and hurtful. It is therefore to be wished, that there were one Confession of Faith, one form of Catechism, one Directory, for all the parts of the public worship of God, and prayer, preaching, administration of sacraments, &c., and one form of Church government in all the churches of his Majesty's dominions."*

Even before these views were communicated to the Lords of the Treaty by the Scottish commissioners, great numbers of petitions had been presented to parliament from different parts of England, some praying for the total extirpation of Prelacy, and others for a reformation in the liturgy, discipline, and government of the Chruch; but all agreeing in representing some decided change as necessary for the peace of the kingdom. The parliament indicated no unwillingness to have the question of Church government fully investigated, and no peculiar desire to maintain the prelatic hierarchy; but gave no intimation of their own ultimate intentions on the subject, if, indeed, they had already framed any definite design, which they probably had not. So far the subject was in a proper train; for while a civil government may with perfect propriety either repeal the laws which have respect to the civil status of a national Church, or frame new enactments for the purpose of giving civil effect to ecclesiastical arrangements, it would be an unconstitutional overstepping of its own province to dictate to a Church in what manner to construct its government, to frame its creed, and to determine its discipline.

While the treaty was proceeding slowly at London, interrupted by the trial of Strafford, the General Assembly met at St. Andrews, 20th July 1641; but as the Scottish parliament was to meet at Edinburgh about the same time, the Assembly adjourned till the 27th July, on which day it was to resume its sittings at Edinburgh. Before that day several of the Scottish commissioners had returned; and Henderson was appointed moderator, on account of several difficult matters, which, it was felt, would require the guiding hand of such a man to conduct with safety. The contest of the preceding year respecting private meetings was renewed, Henry Guthry being still bent on their entire suppression, to which others would not consent. By the wise

* Extracted from a very interesting volume of public documents printed at the time.

and temperate management of Henderson a peaceful settlement of this irritating topic was affected; the Aberdeen act was consigned to oblivion, and a new act passed, giving sanction to all that pious private Christians could wish, and guarding against the dangers of abuses in their religious meetings. A communication was received from several ministers in England, requesting the opinion of the Assembly respecting Church government, especially with reference to the system of Independents, or, as it may be termed, the Congregational system. The Assembly, as might be expected, gave its approbation strongly in favour of the Presbyterian system. Following out the idea which had been suggested by the commissioners in London, Henderson proposed to the Assembly the propriety of framing a full and systematic scheme of all things required in a regularly-constituted Church, namely a Confession of Faith, a Catechism, and a Directory for all parts of the public worship of God. The Assembly not only admitted the desirableness of such a measure, but assigned the task of executing it to Henderson himself, permitting him to retire from his pastoral duties, that he might devote his whole time and strength to the discharge of so important a duty, and empowering him to call to his assistance such of his brethren as he knew to be most highly qualified.*

One constitutional element was introduced by this Assembly, which has been productive of much good to the Church, and also of some harm. This was the appointment of a Commission of Assembly, empowered to finish the business which the Assembly had not been able to accomplish during its regular sitting, to attend during the meeting of parliament, to visit the universities, and generally to attend to the welfare of the Church. This Commission was at first to consist of about forty ministers and sixteen elders; but subsequently it was so enlarged as to include all the members of Assembly, to have four regular meetings, with power to adjourn, and its quorum to amount to thirty-one, of whom twenty-one were to be ministers.

King Charles had been no inattentive spectator of the respect shown to the Scottish commissioners in London; and he was perfectly aware that his discontented subjects in England hoped for support from the Scottish army, should their disagreement with their sovereign proceed to an open rupture, as it threatened to do. He formed, therefore, the resolution to visit Scotland once more in person, and attempt either to disunite the Covenanters, or to prevent them from entering into a closer union with the English parliament. He had, on a former occasion, gained over Montrose, and he probably anticipated equal success with a considerable number more of the ambitious Scottish nobility, if he were once among them. He had determined to act a part; but to such vigilant eyes as were around him it was too apparent that he was only acting. He was courteous to the Covenanters, almost to flattery. He lavished honours on those who had been in arms against him; but he remained sternly unforgiving to Balmerino, whose life he had formerly sought. He was so eager to sign and ratify every act of parliament and Assembly, that he could scarcely be prevailed upon to give them a first cursory perusal. The Covenant was subscribed by the parliament openly, and with his majesty's consent; and during the whole time of his residence in Scotland, the king conformed to the Presbyterian mode of worship, expressing no longing for the Liturgy. There was in all this too much compliance to argue full sincerity; and the Covenanters had experienced too much of the unhappy king's dissimulation on former occasions, to be able at once to throw aside all suspicion. Even if they had, they must have been startled from credulous security, first by some slight indications of danger, and finally by one terrific and portentous event, enough to rouse and appal the most lethargic.

The Earl of Montrose was at that time a prisoner in Edinburgh, accused of a treacherous correspondence with the king. An alarm, known in history by the name of the "Incident," startled the capital with terror, and caused the sudden flight of Hamilton and Argyle from the apprehended danger of assassination.* And their souls were horrified by the intelligence from Ireland, that the Papists

* Baillie, vol. i. p. 365

* Burnet's Memoirs, p. 186.

had arisen in a body, and massacred countless thousands of the unsuspecting and defenceless Protestant inhabitants.* While their hearts were throbbing at the recital of the atrocious barbarities perpetrated by Irish Papists, they could not forget, that on several previous attempts of insurrection by these deluded and blood-thirsty men, Charles had refused to proclaim their conduct rebellious; and yet that, when they in the most peaceful manner asserted their own religious freedom, they were instantly proclaimed rebels, and orders issued for their destruction by fire and sword. They cannot, therefore, be blamed,—they ought rather to be praised,—that while they accepted gladly their monarch's ratification of their religious liberties, they were not deluded by his "king-craft."

When the king returned to London, he was assailed by the unwise complaints of the prelates, that his concessions to the Scottish Church had rendered the overthrow of Episcopacy almost inevitable in England also. At the same time the English parliament laid before him a statement of national grievances, which still more increased his dissatisfaction with their conduct and with his own. The jealousy between the king and the parliament had now reached that extreme point which the slightest increase would convert into avowed hostility. By that fatality which attended the whole of the royal and prelatic measures, the provocation was given by the very parties who should have been most anxious to avoid it. The bishops left the House of Lords, on the pretext that they could not attend it with personal safety; protesting, at the same time, that whatever legislative enactments should take place in their absence should be null and void. This was instantly resented by the Commons as a treasonable attempt to paralyze the government of the country, and throw the kingdom into anarchy. The king's almost simultaneous attempt to seize forcibly the persons of some of the leading members of parliament, completed the breach between him and them, and drove their quarrel to the dread arbitrament of war. In vain did the Scottish commissioners offer their mediation, and strive to procure an amicable adjustment of all disputed points. Their mediation was rejected indignantly by the king, who regarded them as in a great degree the prime movers of all these contests, by having set the example of successful resistance to his arbitrary will.

The Covenanters had now a very difficult part to act. Their loyalty to the king had never been shaken, even when in arms against his despotic attempts; and they were unwilling to contribute towards overwhelming him in that struggle which he had himself provoked. At the same time, the contest in which the English parliament was engaged bore so close a resemblance to their own, that their sympathies naturally flowed towards men contending for civil and religious liberty. An uneasy neutrality was all they could for a time determine to maintain, watching anxiously the progress of events, and feeling deeply interested in both of the contending powers.

[1642.] When the assembly met at St. Andrews, on the 28th of July 1642, it began to be apparent that the political movements in England were about to involve Scotland also in the wild and maddening whirl of civil war. Both the king and the parliament addressed letters to the Assembly, each blaming the other for the fierce collision which had taken place, and both endeavouring to obtain the support of the Covenanters. The more wary of the leading men were averse from taking any precipitate step; and the answers to these letters were written by Henderson in the most guarded terms. But there were others who were eager to encourage the English parliament, regarding it but an act of gratitude to lend assistance to that body from whom they had obtained aid in their own hour of need. The General Assembly at this time, and for several subsequent years, manifested its sympathy for the distressed state of the Presbyterian Church in Ireland, by sending ministers to that country to administer the ordinances of religion among the destitute congregations; and from this time forward a warm reciprocal attachment subsisted between the Presbyterians of Scotland and Ireland, and a deep interest in each other's welfare, which recent circumstances have greatly strengthened. Little else of public moment was transacted at this Assembly,

* Burnet's Memoirs, p.187; Baillie, vol. i. p. 396.

with the exception of some discussion respecting patronage, which the Church wished to modify, so far, at least, that the patron might not present whomsoever he pleased, but select one out of a list of six to be furnished to him by the presbytery.

At a subsequent meeting of Commission a communication was received from the English parliament, intimating their intention to call an assembly of divines, to deliberate respecting the formation of such a Confession of Faith, Catechism, and Directory, as might lead to the desired uniformity between the Churches of the two kingdoms, and requesting commissioners from the Scottish Church to assist in their deliberations. Commissioners were nominated to be in readiness, but their departure was delayed till the English Assembly should actually meet, which, however, did not take place till the following year.

Before the king left Scotland in 1641, he had empowered a semi-parliament, or convention of estates, to meet from time to time in Edinburgh, for the conservation of the public peace; and this convention naturally assumed the whole conduct of public affairs. There had always been a considerable number of the nobility strongly opposed to the Covenanters and devoted to the king, and several more had been gained to that side during his majesty's late visit. The consequence was, that party spirit divided all their deliberations, and tended to drive them both to extremes. They ceased to consider whether they ought to remain in a state of neutrality during the war between the king and the parliament or not, and were only anxious to determine which party they should assist. In the meantime, the king had been generally successful in his military operations, and the parliament was reduced to a state of great danger. Had the Scottish army then joined the king, there can be little doubt that by their assistance he would speedily have reduced the insurgents to subjection. But the Covenanters knew well that he would be no sooner placed firmly on his seat of power than he would trample them beneath his feet and overthrow all the work of religious reformation which they had been toiling to erect.

[1643.] Such was the perilous state of public affairs, and such the views and feelings of the Covenanters, when various proofs of additional dangers came to light. A plot was discovered, in which the royalists were to have raised an army in Scotland, to be headed by Hamilton and Montrose, and led to the assistance of the king. Another of a still more formidable nature was also detected, from which it appeared that the king had entered into a combination with the perpetrators of the recent fearful massacre in Ireland, for the purpose of inducing them to invade Scotland, effect a junction with the royalists there, suppress the Covenanters, and then advance into England, and assist him against the parliament.* These discoveries alarmed the convention to such a degree, that they resolved to abandon their neutral ground, and enter into a treaty with the English parliament as soon as commissioners from it should arrive.

The General Assembly met at Edinburgh on the 2d of August; and feeling that they were on the brink of another eventful crisis, they began by setting apart a day for solemn fasting and supplication for Divine guidance through the perils of such dark and troublous times. Henderson was again chosen moderator. After a few days spent in routine business, the English commissioners arrived, consisting partly of civilians to transact business with the Scottish convention, and partly of ministers to confer with the Assembly. The result of these conferences was, the framing of that well-known bond of union between the two countries, THE SOLEMN LEAGUE AND COVENANT,—a document which we may be pardoned for terming the noblest, in its essential nature and principles, of all that are recorded among the international transactions of the world. It was written by Alexander Henderson, read by him to the Assembly on the 17th August, received and approved of with emotions of the deepest solemnity and awe, with whispered prayers and thanksgivings and outgushing tears, then carried to the convention of estates, and by them unanimously ratified.† It was subsequently sent to London, where on the 25th of September, it

* Baillie, vol. ii. pp. 73, 74.

† Records of Church of Scotland, p. 253; Baillie vol. ii pp. 90, 95.

was accepted and subscribed by the English parliament and the Westminster Assembly of Divines. The Solemn League and Covenant bound the united kingdoms to endeavour the preservation of the reformed religion in the Church of Scotland, in doctrine, worship, discipline, and government, and the reformation of religion in the kingdoms of England and Ireland, according to the Word of God, and the example of the best-reformed Churches,—the extirpation of Popery and Prelacy,—the defence of the king's person, authority, and honour,—and the preservation and defence of the true religion and liberties of the kingdom in peace and unity.

Perhaps no great international transaction has ever been so much misrepresented and maligned as the Solemn League and Covenant. Even its defenders have often exposed it and its authors to severe censures by their unwise modes of defence. There can be no doubt in the mind of any intelligent and thoughtful man, that on it mainly rests, under Providence, the noble structure of the British constitution. But for it, so far as man may judge, these kingdoms would have been placed beneath the deadening bondage of absolute despotism; and in the fate of Britain, the liberty and civilization of the world would have sustained a fatal paralyzing shock. This consideration alone might bid the statesman pause before he ventures to condemn the Solemn League and Covenant. But to the Christian we may suggest still loftier thoughts. The great principles of that sacred bond are those of the Bible itself. It may be that Britain was not then, and is not yet, in a fit state to receive them, and to make them her principles and rules of national government and law; but they are not on that account untrue, nor even impracticable; and the glorious predictions of inspired Scripture foretell a time when they will be more than realized, and when all the kingdoms of this earth shall become the kingdoms of Jehovah and of his Anointed, and all shall be united in one solemn league and covenant under the King of kings and Lord of lords. And though that time may be yet far distant, who may presume to say that the seemingly premature and ineffectual attempt to realize it by the heavenly-minded patriarchs of Scotland's Second Reformation was not the first faint struggling day-beam piercing the world's thick darkness, and revealing to the eye of faith an earnest of the rising of the Sun of righteousness? True, the clouds soon darkened down and hid that herald day-beam; but not less certainly does the day approach, although its dawning hour be shaded in the deepest gloom. A sacred principle was then infused into the heart of nations, which cannot perish; a light then shone into the world's darkness, which cannot be extinguished; and generations not remote may see that principle quickening and evolving in all its irresistible might, and that light bursting forth in its all-brightening glory.

But we must not further pursue this line of thought, however attractive. Another and a less delightful course of reflection demands our notice. It has often been said, that the Covenanters were circumvented by the English parliament, and were drawn into a league with men who meant only to employ them for their own purposes, and then either cast them off, or subdue them beneath a sterner sway than that of Charles. Were it even so, it might prove the treachery of the English, but would expose the Covenanters to no heavier accusation than that of unsuspecting simplicity of mind. They ought to have first ascertained, men say, what form of Church government England intended to adopt, before they had consented to the league. And yet the same accusers fiercely condemn the Scottish Covenanters for attemping to force their own Presbyterian forms upon the people of England. The former accusation manifestly destroys the latter. That the Covenanters did not attempt to force Presbyterians upon England, is proved by the fact, that they entered into the league without any such specific stipulation; and they sought no such stipulation, because it was contrary to their principles either to submit to force in matters of religion, or to attempt using force against other free Christian men. It argues, therefore, ignorance both of their principles and of their conduct, to bring against them an accusation so groundless and sc base. They consented to lend their aid to England in her day of peril, in which peril they were themselves involved: bu they left to England's assembled divines the grave and responsible task of reforming their own Church; lending merely, as they were requested, the assistance of some of their own most learned, pious, and experienced ministers, to promote the great and holy enterprise. For that they have been and they will be blamed by witlings, sciolists, and infidel philosophers; but what England's best and greatest men sought with earnest desire, and received with respect and gratitude, Scotland need never be ashamed that her venerable covenanted fathers did not decline to grant.

Yet in one respect they did, in our opinion, err. They allowed their Solemn League to involve them too deeply in matters of a strictly civil character. This was, indeed, what England chiefly sought; but the very fact that in their preliminary conferences the English commissioners argued for a civil league alone, ought to have made the Scottish doubly wary of the dangers into which they might be drawn. Their best apology, however, consists in the fact, that they were compelled by stern necessity to save the civil liberties of England, or to incur the eminent hazard of losing speedily their own religious freedom. They had gained, by a long and arduous, but bloodless struggle, all for which they strove; and they might naturally cherish the hope that the same result would crown the efforts of their English brethren. Thus were they, by necessity and hope, drawn into a new and more desperate contest, destined to have a very different termination, which their utmost efforts were not able to avert. Being once engaged in this new conflict, they were inevitably borne along in the mighty movements of the more powerful nation, and made to share, with equal unwillingness, in its crimes and in its self-inflicted punishment. And let it be carefully observed, that the difference between the conduct of the English parliament in the great civil war, and of the Covenanters, in their time of struggle, consisted in, and was caused by this,—that in England it was essentially a contest in defence, or for the assertion of civil liberty,—in Scotland for religious purity and freedom. In England, therefore, it was guided by a secular principle, and permitted the free developement of all the stormy passions that rage within the heart of striving and revengeful human nature; in Scotland, it was governed, chastened, and even hallowed, by the controlling presence of a sacred principle, by which man's wrath was checked, subdued, or turned aside, till truth prevailed, and victory was crowned with peace. England's fierce wars for civil liberty laid her and her unfortunate assistant prostrate beneath the feet of an iron-hearted usurper and despot. Scotland's calm and bloodless defence of religious purity and freedom secured to her those all-inestimable blessings, broke the chains of her powerful neighbour, revealed to mankind a principle of universal truth and might, and poured into her own crushed heart a stream of life, sacred, immortal. and divine.

As the very object for which the Solemn League and Covenant was framed was to secure the utmost practicable degree of uniformity in the religious worship of both countries, and as the English divines had already met at Westminster to take the whole subject into the most deliberate consideration, and had requested the assistance of commissioners from the Church of Scotland, the General Assembly named some of the most eminent of their ministers and elders as commissioners to the Westminster Assembly. These were, Alexander Henderson, Robert Douglas, Robert Baillie, George Gillespie, and Samuel Rutherford, ministers: and the Earl of Cassilis, Lord Maitland (afterwards Lauderdale), and Sir Archibald Johnston of Warriston, elders. It does not appear that either the Earl of Cassilis or Robert Douglas attended the Westminster Assembly during its protracted labours; but so efficient were the other commissioners, that their absence produced no injury to the cause of Presbytery. We have already briefly characterised Henderson, Baillie, and Gillespie; and few need to be informed respecting the character of Rutherford, his well known "Letters" being in almost universal circulation, and held in the highest esteem by all who are able to appreciate their merits. But even these "Letters" convey an inadequate view of that extraordinary man. His writings on the great controversial subjects of the period show him to have been not only very learned, but also and especially to have been one of the deepest thinkers of that or any age. Many have asserted that his work called "Lex Rex" is of anti-monarchical, and even democratic character; and on the strength of such an accusation it was condemned and burnt by the sycophantic minions of Charles II. That it is opposed to despotism is very certain; but it is as certain that it contains no principle contrary to those embodied in the British constitution. Such principles, indeed, had not been then recognised and assented to by either kings or parliaments; but if their statement by Rutherford was premature, let it always be remembered that some person must sow the seed of which others may reap the fruit; and it ill becomes those who are practically enjoying what he theoretically maintained, to repeat even yet the slanderous accusations uttered by the enemies of liberty against a work which they have not done themselves the justice to peruse.

It would lead us into what might seem a digression beyond our province, and certainly beyond our limits, to attempt any adequate account of the Westminster Assembly. As, however, it is intimately connected with the history of the Church of Scotland, we must very briefly give an outline of its character and proceedings. Before the arrival of the Scottish commissioners, both the English parliament and the Westminster Assembly had determined on the abolition of Prelacy in the Church of England. It was also fully resolved, that a great reformation should take place in all religious matters; but what form of Church government, and what rules of discipline should be adopted, were subjects on which the greatest differences of opinion prevailed. There were three great parties in the Westminster Assembly:—First, the Erastians, who held that it belonged only to the civil magistrate to inflict church censures, as well as civil punishments; and, generally, that the civil magistrate is the proper head, the source and ruler of all power, ecclesiastical as well as civil. That party was active and vehement, but not numerous, consisting chiefly of lawyers, and only one or two ministers. Secondly, the Independents, who held that every individual congregation of Christians has an entire and complete power of jurisdiction over its members in all religious matters, to be exercised by its elders within itself, and by its own sole authority. These amounted to ten or twelve, and were men of considerable ability, and exceedingly pertinacious in maintaining their opinions. Thirdly, the Presbyterians, who formed the majority of the Assembly, and generally coincided with the opinions of the Scottish commissioners. But as this latter party, though most numerous, was but indifferently acquainted with the Presbyterian polity, having little knowledge of any other than the Prelatic form of Church government, the task of explaining and vindicating Presbytery devolved chiefly upon the Scottish divines, who were admirably qualified for the important duty.*

The first struggle in the Westminster Assembly was with the Erastians, and took place at the very commencement of their labours. In preparing for their great task, they had stated that, "in inquiring after the officers belonging to the Church of the New Testament, we find that Christ, who is Priest, Prophet, King, and Head of the Church, hath fulness of power, and containeth all other offices by way of eminency in himself. He being ascended far above all heavens, and filling all things, hath given all officers necessary for the edification of his Church."† From this preface necessarily followed the proposition, that the government of the Church was distinct from that of the civil magistrate,—neither derived from it, nor subordinate to it. This the Erastians opposed; but though they were easily defeated in the Assembly, they triumphed in the parliament, which, after many evasions, finally refused to sanction that important proposition. The struggle with the Independents was of much longer duration. Many weeks were often expended in debating a single topic, for that party within the Assembly were in a state of intimate connection with the political Independents in the army, who dreaded nothing so much as the conclusion of the Assembly's labours, their possible ratification by the parliament, and the consequent termination of

* Baillie, *passim.*
† Lightfoot, Pitman's edit., vol. xiii., p. 23

hostilities before their own schemes were ready for execution. We cannot prosecute the task of tracing the intrigues of the Independents in the Assembly, in parliament, and in the army, but we may briefly state the result. They contrived to embarrass, retard, and overreach the Assembly, till they were able to subvert all its labours, so far as England was concerned; they kept the parliament in a state of confusion and indecision with their intrigues, till they had the power to suppress it altogether; and they contrived so to balance the king's obstinacy against both Assembly and parliament, as to paralyze both him and them, till having obtained the opportunity which they sought, they put the unhappy monarch to death, and placed the sceptre in the iron grasp of military despotism.

There is one point on which an almost universal misunderstanding, to give it the most gentle designation, prevails. The Presbyterians are perpetually accused not only of wishing to force their peculiar ecclesiastical polity upon England, but also of such extreme *intolerance*, that they would not permit that liberty of conscience to others which they so strenuously demanded for themselves. Into a full discussion of this subject our limits will not permit us to enter; but truth and duty compel us to offer a few remarks. It will be remembered that the Independents formed only a small minority in the Westminster Assembly, and consequently it was impossible that their form of Church government could obtain the sanction of that body. Finding their endeavours unsuccessful in the Assembly, they had recourse to political intrigues, and to give the most plausible aspect to their proceedings, they put forth a claim for general toleration of all forms and kinds of religious worship. Be it observed, that they became advocates of toleration only after they had failed in obtaining the ascendency of their own opinions. And to what did this toleration amount? To the unrestrained license of every man, or knot of men, to utter sentiments in public, however blasphemous and revolting to reason and common sense; and to practise, in the name of worship, immoralities and indecencies of a nature too gross to be mentioned! That we do not characterise too strongly the tenets and conduct of the almost innumerable sects whom this plea of general toleration would have included, must be obvious to every person tolerably acquainted with the history of the period.* Against a *toleration* of this kind not only the Presbyterians, but also the most respectable and religious of the Independents themselves, strenuously protested. But the political party prevailed; the cry of toleration was a specious war-cry; and even to the present day is often raised by people in whose mouths it means mere licentiousness.

Allusion has already been made to a principle which accounts for the number of strange fanatical sects which appeared in England at this period. The prelatic Church of England had allowed the body of the community to remain in deep ignorance; and when that Church was overthrown so suddenly, and nothing ready to supply its place, the people were left to follow all the wild and enthusiastic fancies which such a time of intense excitement was certain to produce in strong but uncultivated minds. In Scotland, on the other hand, the overthrow of Prelacy had no other effect than that of permitting the Presbyterian Church to put forth its native powers among a people by whom its principles were understood and cherished, and its discipline beloved and revered. And notwithstanding all the calumnies which have been heaped upon our Presbyterian ancestors, it may be safely and most truly averred, that intolerance, in the right sense of the word, never was the characteristic of the Presbyterian Church. Expressions of a severe aspect against that toleration which included all kinds of blasphemous and immoral licentiousness, may be found in the writings of our fathers, and may be warped and misinterpreted by party writers; and we may even admit that they were not at all times sufficiently guarded in their language; but if any thing like a fair allowance be made for the spirit of the times, and the peculiar circumstances amidst which they acted and wrote, they will stand completely vindicated from the charge of intolerance and spiritual despotism.

* For a sufficient account of this subject, let the reader consult Edward's Gangrena.

[1644.] But we must leave the Westminster Assembly, and return to what more particularly concerns the Church of Scotland. The subscribing of the Solemn League and Covenant bound the two kingdoms of England and Scotland by a mutual defensive bond, in all that regarded religion, which both thus vowed to maintain. In consequence of this mutual league, the Scottish army again entered England, for the purpose of co-operating with that of the parliament. This took place on the 19th of January 1644, under the command of General Leslie, now Earl of Leven, Lieutenant General Baillie, and Major-General David Leslie. A great change speedily took place in the state of affairs in England, the king being unable to make head against the combined armies. The course of the military operations which took place we do not intend to trace. It may, however, be stated, that the English parliament was warm or cold in its professions of regard to the Solemn League and Covenant, and to the uniformity of religion in the two kingdoms exactly in proportion to its need of Scotland's military aid;*—proving completely what has been suggested, that the contest in England was chiefly waged for the sake of civil liberty, but in Scotland for the purity and freedom of religion.

Nothing of peculiar importance was transacted in the General Assembly which met at Edinburgh on the 31st of May 1644. Its time was occupied chiefly with letters from the Scottish commissioners at Westminster, and from the English divines, and with returning answers to these letters. A new presbytery was erected at Biggar; the declaration of the Scottish royalist nobles at Oxford was censured; and some additional salutary acts were passed for the encouragement of learning, similar to those of former Assemblies.

[1645.] The Assembly met on the 22d of January 1645, earlier than had been intended, on account of urgent business which demanded its attention. Baillie, Gillespie, and Warriston, had come to give an account of the progress made by the Westminster Assembly; and Montrose was spreading terror and devastation through the kingdom, which was comparatively defenceless, in consequence of its most experienced generals and best troops being in England. The report of the commissioners was received with great approbation, and the directory for public worship which they brought with them received the sanction of the Assembly. A very important act was passed for the advancement of learning, the principles and regulations of which reflect great credit on the enlightened men by whom it was framed. Another very remarkable act was that entitled "A Solemn and Seasonable Warning," &c., in which a clear and strong view is taken of the causes of the national disasters by which they were at that time agitated and alarmed. A remonstrance was also written, addressed to the king, in which the Assembly expressed the most earnest desire for peace on religious terms; and letters were sent to the Westminster Assembly.

All historians admit that the meteor-like career of Montrose was one of the causes of his sovereign's ruin. It gave the unfortunate king so much confidence in what he esteemed a propitious change in the aspect of his affairs, that he broke off negociations with his antagonists; and it furnished another proof of the deceitful character of his whole dealings, endeavouring to keep them in terms of treaty till he might be able to overpower them. The career of Montrose, if what his admirers call brilliant, was but brief. He was surprised and defeated by David Leslie, at Philiphaugh, near Selkirk, on the 13th of September, and with his defeat vanished the last hopes of Charles to re-establish his power by force of arms. With regard to the military achievements of Montrose, the barbarities which he perpetrated, and the retaliations alleged to have been committed by the army of the Covenanters, we do not think it necessary to occupy space, further than to state, that while we have no sympathy with those who luxuriate over tales of wholesale butchery on the battle-field, and cities sacked amid all the nameless atrocities of civil war, we have as little with those who either wail piteously over the death of the chief murderer, or exult in that melancholy fate which generally overtakes the bloody and deceitful man.

[1646.] The defeat of his own army

* Baillie, passim.

and of that of Montrose also, reduced the unhappy king to a state of desperation; and after a few miserable months of irresolution, he at last fled in disguise to the Scottish army, early in May 1646. Rumours had previously been spread that he might possibly take that very step, and the Covenanters were particularly anxious that he should not, foreseeing clearly the dangerous position into which it would throw them.* Soon after the king's arrival in the Scottish army they marched northwards to Newcastle, where they remained during the tedious negotiations which followed. The Scottish nobility, army, and nation in general, would most willingly have encountered every danger in his defence, if he could have been prevailed upon to ratify the Covenant. But the infatuated monarch remained obstinate; and as they regarded the sanctity of an oath as more binding than the mere feelings of natural loyalty and affection to the person of their sovereign, they felt themselves constrained to leave him to his fate. Yet they perceived both his danger and their own; and in order to save him, if possible, Alexander Henderson left London and hastened to Newcastle, for the purpose of endeavoring to persuade the obstinate king to abandon his inveterate prejudices, subscribe the Covenant, and rally round him the brave hearts and strong arms of his faithful and unconquered Scottish subjects. Charles would not be persuaded. He was possessed by the idea, that neither of the contending parties could do without him, and consequently that, even though he had been beaten in the field, they must yield to him when they found that he would not yield to them.

The English parliament sent propositions to his majesty, by acceding to which he might obtain peace, and the restoration to a large measure of regal power; but he would not accede to their propositions, any more than to the Scottish Covenant. Henderson, worn out with his many and arduous toils, and overwhelmed with affliction on account of the miseries which the infatuated king was so manifestly bringing upon himself and the kingdom, relinquished his hopeless task, returned to Edinburgh in a state of great weakness, and on the 19th of August yielded up his spirit to Him who gave it. Thus passed away from earth one of those gifted men whom the Ruler of all events sends forth in time of great emergency, to mould the minds of his fellow-men, and aid in working out the will of the Most High. He was one of the most distinguished of an age fertile in great men; and with all due veneration for the names of Knox and Melville, we do them no discredit when we place that of Henderson by their side,—the "first three" of the Church of Scotland's worthies.

The General Assembly met at Edinburgh on the 3d of June 1646. Its acts were neither numerous nor important, having reference chiefly to the troubled state of the kingdon, and to such acts of fasting, humiliation, and prayer, as might tend to avert the judgments of God from a guilty and suffering land. A short but respectful letter was sent to the king, expressing the earnest wish that God would incline his majesty's heart to the speedy following of the counsels of truth and peace.

For a short time there was calmness and silence in the kingdom,—not the silence of peace, but that of breathless expectation. All men perceived that upon the determination of the king would depend the cessation of the struggle, or its fresh outburst into tenfold violence. The revolutionary party in England dreaded that his majesty might yield, and gradually recover his power, limited undoubtedly, but rendered thereby the more secure. The Presbyterians hoped and prayed that he might submit so far as that with a safe conscience they might indulge their loyal feelings. The prelatists alone identified his cause and their own, seeing no prospect of restoration to wealth and power unless he should regain unlimited ascendency. And the king knew well, that no other party but the prelatic would submit to that arbitrary prerogative which he was determined to forego only with his life. In vain did the Scottish noblemen and ministers implore him with tears to subscribe the Covenant. He peremptorily refused; and as they could not defend him without incurring the fearful guilt of perjury, they were compelled to leave him to perish in his blind wilfulness.

Into the controversy respecting the question whether the Scottish army was

* Baillie, vol. ii. p. 341.

induced to yield Charles to the English parliament by the payment of the arrears due to them, we do not enter, further than to say, that there is not, in our opinion, the slightest ground in genuine historical documents to prove that there was any connection whatever between the receiving of the arrears and the yielding up of the king; while there is ample evidence, that Charles, having lost all hope of beguiling the Scots into an act at once of perfidy and perjury, was himself desirous of attempting to negotiate separately with his English subjects, believing them to be more tractable. If there was infamy in the transaction, that infamy ought to rest solely and exclusively upon the English parliament and army, who strained every nerve and employed every artifice to compel or delude their Scottish brethren into compliance with their pernicious schemes, and rested not till they had added to the guilt of a broken Covenant the murder of a dethroned king.

[1647.] The General Assembly which met at Edinburgh on the 4th of August 1647, is chiefly memorable for its ratification of the Confession of Faith of the Westminister Assembly of Divines, and for the adoption of that translation and metrical version of the Psalms which is still used in the Church of Scotland. This, therefore, may be regarded as the Assembly by which was completed the Second Reformation of the Scottish Church, and the full arrangement of its Confession, form of Worship and Discipline, as they exist at the present day, and as we trust they will ever exist, till the second coming of Him who is the only Head and King of the Church. Several important acts were passed by this Assembly; in particular, some very excellent directions for private worship, and an elaborate "Brotherly Exhortation" to their brethren of England. It may be added, that Gillepsie's able work, entitled "Aaron's Rod Blossoming," received the approbation of this Assembly; and eight of its leading propositions were engrossed in one of the acts.*

In the meantime, the unanimity which had given strength to Scotland in the earlier stages of this great contest began to be rent asunder by political intrigues. Although the Covenanters had been compelled to abandon the king on account of his impregnable obstinacy, they still cherished sentiments of devoted loyalty to him as their sovereign, and a sincere attachment to monarchy, as, when duly limited, the best form of civil government. They deplored the king's willfulness; they mourned the ruin which it was bringing on the whole country; they remonstrated with the English parliament, and did every thing to procure the safety of the king and the peace of the kingdom which it was in their power to do, short of violating their National Covenant. But the intrigues of the Hamiltonian party began to prevail in the Scottish parliament. Lauderdale joined them, regardless of his Covenant vow; and even Loudon was for a time carried away in the tide of defection. The Duke of Hamilton was still the ostensible head of the royalist party in Scotland; but his brother the Earl of Lanark, surpassed him both in zeal and activity, and was the prime mover in all the intrigues of the party. At length, in a private interview with King Charles at Garisbrook Castle, in the Isle of Wight, on the 27th of December, a secret treaty was concluded, in which Lanark and Lauderdale, in the name of their party, engaged to raise an army in Scotland for the purpose of assisting his majesty in his attempts to regain possession of the English throne,—his majesty engaging, on his part, to confirm Presbyterian church government for three years, till an assembly of divines, aided by twenty commissioners of his nomination, should frame such a form of church government and discipline as they should find to be most agreeable to the Word of God. He engaged also, that all schism and heresy should be effectually suppressed. This private treaty, known by the name of the Engagement, caused the overthrow of the Church and kingdom of Scotland.*

[1648.] Early in 1648 the rumour of the Engagement began to transpire in Scotland; and when the parliament met in March, and the terms of this private treaty were divulged, a vehement disunit-

* In that peculiarly acute and profound work will be found the very essence of the Westminster Assembly's most important discussions on the subject of church government, with the arguments employed against both the Erastians and the Independents, and answers to the most elaborate productions of their chief writers.

* Burnet's Memoirs, p. 334.

ing struggle began. The faithful Covenanters perceived at once, that the Engagement involved the violation of their most solemn vows. The Commission of the Church immediately met, and deliberated what steps ought to be taken in this new crisis. They did not deliberate long. They felt the deep power of the Covenant upon their souls too mighty for any earthly consideration to shake; and, accordingly they framed a declaration, pointing out the sinfulness of an Engagement which involved direct perjury, and must draw down the Divine displeasure on both Church and State. But the purely political or royalist party had obtained the ascendency in the parliament; and the earnest remonstrances of the sincere Covenanters were disregarded. The arguments of the ministers confirmed those of the nobility who regarded religion as of more importance than any earthly consideration, and brought back some whom political and personal motives had led astray, among whom was the Earl of Loudon; but the majority held on their course, and determined to fulfill the Engagement to the utmost of their power.

The Assembly met at Edinburgh on the 12th of July, and made choice of George Gillespie to be moderator. They not only approved of the declaration and other similar writings of the Commission, but passed an act condemnatory of that act and declaration of the parliament which enjoined all subjects to subcribe a bond, equivalent to an oath, in support of the Engagement. They further published a declaration and exhortation to all members of the Church of Scotland, pointing out the unlawfulness of the Engagement, and warning against the dangers in which it would certainly involve the Church and nation. An able answer was also written to the committee of estates, proving by scriptural arguments that the Engagement was inconsistent with the safety and security of religion. And, as the Hamiltonian faction was well aware of the power which the Church had recently put forth, when it raised the kingdom like one man for the defence of religious liberty, they employed every artifice to bring as many ministers as possible to their side, by that means either to procure support or to neutralize opposition. To meet this dangerous divisive policy, the Assembly passed an act censuring those ministers who either favoured the Engagement openly, or abstained from pointing out its sinfulness, and warning their people against entering its bond. A respectful but firm supplication was also written to his majesty showing the insufficiency of the concessions promised by him in the Engagement, and its positive sinfulness, as tending to involve the kingdom in perjury; and imploring him to comply with the Covenant, and thereby to enable them, with a safe conscience, to give him that support which their sincere loyalty and affection prompted them to bestow so far as their duty to God would permit.*

From this time forward Scotland presented a melancholy contrast to the ten preceding years, in which strict adherence to the Covenant had given it union and strength irresistible. It was now divided into three contending parties. First, the sincere Covenanters, led in the parliament by Argyle and Loudon, and in the Church by Rutherford and Gillespie; second, the framers of the Engagement, led by Hamilton, Lanark, and Lauderdale, who wished to take an intermediate position, and who were joined by a considerable number of the ministers, of whom Baillie was the most respectable. The third party was headed by Traquair and Callender, and was composed chiefly of those who were determined royalists of the cavalier caste, and paid little respect to either oaths or treaties, provided they could get their purposes accomplished. The two latter parties were easily induced to coalesce, and their junction gave them a decided preponderance in the political councils of the nation. That the genuine Covenanters could not unite with such men, will excite neither wonder nor surprise in the minds of those who are able to appreciate their principles; and that the chiefs of the Engagement should attempt to overwhelm them by invectives, and try to represent them as seditious and fanatical, is only what was to be expected. But that men can yet be found to repeat such slanderous calumnies, might appear incredible, were it not matter of daily occurrence.

* Records of the Church of Scotland, pp. 497-508, 518

They were, and are, accused of an unwarranted and intolerable interference with civil matters, with which the churchmen of them at least had nothing to do. But was not the whole struggle of that memorable period expressly on account of religion? Had it not been from the first a religious contest on both sides? And was not their bond of union strictly a religious covenant? Nay, the Hamiltonian party sought to inveigle the ministers into approbation of the Engagement, finding no fault with their intermeddling with such matters, provided they would support that measure; and when the ministers could neither be deceived nor overawed, but continued steadfastly to adhere to their solemn vows, warning others of the guilt and danger of perjury, then only were they accused of overstepping their province, and interfering with what was beyond their jurisdiction. Politicians have in all ages and countries shown themselves willing enough to employ and praise the ministers of religion, provided they would act as sycophants and tools; but when they act as the vigilant watchmen of sacred rights, warning the nation of coming danger, then they are exposed to the most virulent and vituperative censure; then are they charged with arrogant presumption in offering their opinions on those public measures which essentially affect the interests of religion; then they are branded as men who wish to subvert the order of society, and bring the State into subserviency to the Church. So was it in the days of our ancestors,—so is it now—and so will it ever be, as long as there is need for the Christian precept, "Be not conformed to the world."

One of the direct results of this division between the Covenanters and the mere politicians, was the necessity of appointing new commanders to the hastily-levied and ill-equipped army of the Engagers; for neither the Earl of Leven nor David Leslie would abandon the Covenant. The Duke of Hamilton, therefore, was made general,—led his army into England,—was defeated by Cromwell,—and died on the scaffold,—the unhappy victim of ill-judging devotion to his sovereign's person rather than his cause.* Even before the army of the Engagers had left Scotland, there were symptoms of insurrection among the people, who, refusing to join the Engagement, were severely harassed by those employed to levy troops. A small band of insurgents assembled at Mauchline, but were easily suppressed by Middleton. As soon as the tidings of Hamilton's defeat reached Scotland, the opponents of the Engagement assembled, assumed arms, and, led by the Marquis of Argyle and the Earls of Cassilis, Eglinton, and Loudon, advanced towards Edinburgh in such strength as the remaining Engagers could not hope successfully to resist. By this, termed the Whigamore's Raid, a complete change of administration was effected, and the Covenanters acquired the ascendancy in the Scottish parliament. The new administration easily convinced Cromwell that they were in no respect accessory to the Engagement which had caused the invasion of England by the Scottish army; and thus hostilities between them and that remarkable man were for the time averted.

[1649.] The Scottish parliament met on the 4th of January 1649, and proceeded to take steps for the peace and security of the kingdom. One of these was of a very stringent nature, and has been much censured. It was obvious to all, that the late Engagement could not have been framed if all men in power had been Covenanters, and had remained true to their vows. While therefore, the new parliament repealed all the acts that had been made for its enforcement, and ratified the protestation against it, this was naturally followed by the idea, that unless men of such principles were excluded from places of public trust and influence, the very same evil might at no distant date return. An act was accordingly passed, called the Act of Classes, on account of its dividing into four separate classes, according to their respective degrees of delinquency, the characters of persons not to be intrusted with power. Men will term this act one of bigotry and intolerance: it evidently aimed at the construction of what the world has never yet seen,—a Christian government, composed of men whose ruling principle should be to "fear God and honour the king."

* Burnet's Memoirs, p. 400; Ibid., pp. 367, 375.

While this parliament was sitting, they received intelligence that the English parliament, now moulded according to the mind of the army, was about to proceed with the trial of King Charles. The most strenuous exertions were made by the truly loyal Covenanters to prevent the fearful event in which a trial by such men would too surely issue. But all their endeavours were in vain; and the English parliament, having first broken the Solemn League and Covenant, consummated their guilt by the decapitation of their king. It is impossible not to deplore the fate of that unfortunate, ill-advised, and obstinate monarch; but it is as impossible to deny that his insincerity and double-dealing caused his overthrow and death. For when, by the discovery of private correspondence, it was clearly proved, that in the very act of framing treaties he was devising schemes for setting them aside, it became plain to his antagonists that they must ultimately become the victims of a monarch whom no treaties could bind, unless they secured their own lives by the death of their implacable foe.

The leaders of the English parliament and army were, besides, men of republican principles, and desired the abolition of the monarchy itself. Not so the Scottish Covenanters. They, even by the terms of their Covenant, were the vowed supporters of a monarchy based upon and pervaded throughout by Scripture principles. No sooner, theretore, did they receive the melancholy intelligence of their sovereign's death, than they hastened to proclaim his son king, by the designation of Charles II.; not omitting, however, in their proclamation, the significant intimation that their support of his pretensions to the throne would involve the necessity of his subscribing the Covenant. This proclamation was made on the 5th of February. At the same time, the Confession of Faith was formally ratified by parliament.

On the 9th of March 1649, the Scottish parliament passed an act abolishing patronage in the Church of Scotland, "as being unlawful and unwarrantable by the Word of God, and contrary to the doctrines and liberties of this Church;" recommending to the General Assembly to determine upon a settled rule for the appointment of ministers for all time coming.* It will be observed, that in this instance the parliament acted according to the dictates of sound reason and constitutional principle. So far as patronage was considered as a civil right, it was for the civil power to restrict or abolish it; but as the appointment of ministers was clearly an ecclesiastical matter, it was not for parliament to interfere with it, but merely to call on the Assembly to state its own method, and then give to that such civil ratification as should carry with it the civil consequences which it involved. And it was a parliament composed almost wholly of Covenanters, by which this truly liberal and enlightened act was passed.

The General Assembly met at Edinburgh on the 7th of July 1649. This Assembly emitted several able declarations respecting the religious affairs of the kingdom, the prevailing errors and abuses, and the best methods of promoting and maintaining peace, righteousness, and purity, which are the essential elements of national welfare. A letter was also addressed to the young king, who was still on the Continent, warning him earnestly against listening to the evil council of those who had already plunged the kingdom into the horrors of war, and beseeching him to sanction those great National Covenants, which would open the door for him to enter upon his royal government with the favour of God and the cordial love of his faithful and loyal subjects. Another act was passed regarding the reception, on proof of repentance, of those who had been suspended from church privileges on account of their connection with the Engagement, and generally of all those who, from prelatic and despotic predilections, had opposed the Covenant, and were known by the designation of "malignants," by which was meant, persons ill-affected towards the progress of religious reformation. Then taking up the subject of the appointment of ministers, according to the request of the parliament, the Assembly passed an act, entitled "Directory for the Election of Ministers.' The chief points of that directory are, that the session, which at that time was elected by the congregation,

* Acts of Parliament, see Appendix.

should elect a minister, and intimate their election to the congregation for their approbation. If they consented, the presbytery were to proceed to the trial of his qualifications; if a majority dissented, the presbytery were to judge of the same, and, unless they found the dissent to be founded on causeless prejudices, another election was to take place; but if a minority dissented, without being able to verify their ground of objection, the trials and ordination should proceed, all possible diligence and tenderness being used to bring all parties to a harmonious agreement. In the case of a disaffected or malignant congregation, the presbytery was to provide them with a minister.* It will be seen at a glance, that this well-known act was in perfect harmony with the constitutional principles of the Church of Scotland, as contained in the writings and declarations of the early fathers of the First Reformation, and in the First and Second Books of Discipline; and as by its means they were now finally brought into full developement and free operation, it formed the concluding act of the completed Second Reformation.

The Church of Scotland may now be said to have reached mature organization, but it was a period when the whole kingdom was so completely filled with elements of strife, threatening an immediate and tremendous convulsion, that it could not obtain one peaceful day in which to exhibit the free movements of its graceful and majestic form. Yet it was well—it was providential—that it had obtained this full developement before it was assailed by that terrific storm which smote it to the earth, and by which, at an earlier stage of its existence, it might have been utterly destroyed. All its vital powers were now called into native operation; all its arrangements were completed; and it might have been expected that it was about to enter on a glorious career of pure, faithful, and energetic zeal, in establishing the reign of religion in the hearts of the entire community. But the kingdom of Christ has ever been a suffering kingdom; and it may be, that when a church has most nearly realized the character and aspect of the true gospel Church, then is its hour at hand, not of triumph, but of sharpest and most fiery trial. It may be further remarked, that by this time several of the great men who had been chiefly instrumental in effecting the Second Reformation, had been called to their final rest. After the death of Henderson, Gillespie was the man of greatest influence; but he, too, died in December 1648. Baillie was not only timid and wavering, but naturally inclined to follow the guidance of men of worldly rank and power, and to sacrifice principle at the call of what he deemed expediency. Rutherford did not possess that cast of mind requisite for the management of great affairs in times of difficulty. Robert Douglas appears to have been the fittest man to have led the councils of the Church; but he was deficient in penetration, confided too easily in other men, and did not sufficiently follow the dictates of his usual sound judgment. James Guthrie and Patrick Gillespie were both men of great abilities and decided piety; but both were somewhat too impetuous in temper, and liable to speak and act with injudicious rashness, more likely to lead the Church into additional dangers than to extricate her from those with which she was already surrounded. In these adverse circumstances, the Church was left to encounter her long and fiery trial, that both her endurance and her preservation might be manifestly the result, not of man's wisdom, but of the imperishable life infused into her by her Divine Head.

[1650.] Commissioners had been sent to Holland in the preceding year, to treat with Charles II., but had returned without coming to any satisfactory conclusion. Early in the year 1650, the parliament again sent commissioners to Breda, where the young king at that time was, once more to enter into negotiations with him on the foundation of the Covenant. The commissioners found Charles surrounded with dissolute and unprincipled men, likely enough to lead him into evil, had he not been inclined, or to strengthen those evil inclinations which were already but too apparent in his whole conduct and character. He was at that very time listening to the sanguinary councils of Montrose, by whose means he hoped to gain Scotland, without any treaty, the terms of which might hamper his future

* Acts of Assembly, see Appendix

proceedings. The intelligence of Montrose's defeat and capture reached him in time to induce him to comply with the requirements of the Scottish parliament, though not till he had convinced the more faithful of them that there was nothing to be expected from him but duplicity and gross licentiousness. Livingstone, who was one of the commissioners from the Church, gives us ample proof that Charles had broken the treaty, both in its spirit and its letter, even before he left Breda.* Indeed, the treaty might justly have been declared null by the cottish parliament. In the capture of Montrose a commission was found from the king, giving him authority to levy troops, and subdue the kingdom by force of arms; and so highly did the parliament resent this treachery, that they sent to recall their commissioners; but the one into whose hands this document fell concealed it from the rest, and by showing it privately to the king, convinced him that he could no longer safely temporize. He accordingly hurried on board, and set sail for Scotland in company with the commissioners, bringing with him also a number of the very men whom the Act of Classes had declared incapable of public trust. Before he landed, Charles subscribed the Solemn League and Covenant; although Livingstone, who doubted his sincerity, was anxious that it should be postponed till his majesty should reach Scotland, and give some satisfactory proofs of his sincerity. The young king landed on the 16th of June 1650, near the mouth of the river Spey, and advanced to Stirling, where he was met by the chief nobility of the kingdom.

But instead of producing peace and unanimity in Scotland, the arrival of Charles was a signal for the instantaneous outburst of strife and confusion. His loose, licentious habits, and depraved heart, were not likely to conciliate the affections and respect of the Covenanters; while he could not brook what he regarded as the unnecessary strictness of their opinions and manners. And although he complied with all the stipulations of the parliament, and affected regard for the ministers, it was but too apparent to all men of penetration that he both hated and despised all the best men of the kingdom. In the meanwhile the Assembly met at Edinburgh in July; bu its records have not been published. We learn, however, from other sources, tha great dissatisfaction was expressed by the more zealous of the ministers with the whole behaviour of Charles, both in his deceitful conduct towards the commissioners at Breda, and since his arrival in Scotland. A commission was appointed to deal with those who had taken part with Montrose, and several ministers were deposed for that and similar offences. The proceedings of this Assembly were interrupted by the approach of Cromwell, who was advancing at the head of a veteran army, to expel the young king.

Charles now thought it was necessary to give greater satisfaction to the Church, in order to procure a more cordial and universal support. But the mode of doing so led to a complete and deplorable failure. He was advised to make a new declaration, such as should satisfy the desires of the most scrupulous. This advice was given both by his secular friends, and by the wary and semi-political party in the Church. In this declaration, subscribed by the king in August at Dunfermline, Charles avowed that he renounced Popery and Prelacy, and "would have no enemies but the enemies of the Covenant,—no friends but the friends of the Covenant." Patrick Gillespie requested the king "not to subscribe that declaration, no, not for the three kingdoms, if he were not satisfied in his soul and conscience, beyond all hesitation, of its righteousness." "Mr. Gillespie, Mr. Gillespie," answered the king, "I am satisfied, I am satisfied, and therefore will subscribe."* This ample declaration produced an effect directly the reverse of that anticipated by its worldly-wise advisers. Instead of completely satisfying the scrupulous, it confirmed their suspicions of the king's sincerity. This men of the world stigmatize as intolerant and narrow-minded distrust, but in worldly transactions they act upon the same principle. Is there anything which more certainly awakens suspicion of a man's sincerity than his strong and vehement professions of zealous friendship to a person or cause to

* Life of Livingstone, pp. 31-36.

* Cruickshank, p. 58; Hind let Loose, p. 98.

which his whole previous conduct and his known sentiments have been decidedly hostile? So thought and felt the more scrupulous ministers; and, as reason perceives, and subsequent events testified, they thought and felt rightly.

The explanation of the whole matter may be briefly stated. There were then, as there always have been, two great parties of public men; the one composed of those who judge and act according to principle; the other, of those who are guided by expediency. The first, led by P. Gillespie, J. Guthrie, S. Rutherford, and Warriston, were anxious not to press the king to the subscription of the Covenant till they should have some evidence that he was in such a state of mind as might render it in him indeed a religious act, correspondent to the nature of the solemn obligation which it involved. Till that time they were perfectly willing that he should be their king; but should remain as much as possible aloof from all intercourse with profane and irreligious men. The other party thought it inexpedient to be so strict. They considered it enough if the king should subscribe the Covenant literally, however little his mind might be accordant with its spirit; not, apparently, perceiving, that this would be an act of profane impiety, to which they could not hope the blessing of God to be given. Their worldly prudence suggested to them the absolute necessity of a complete national union, to resist the formidable invasion of the dreaded Cromwell; but they failed to perceive, that a union not of principle, but of compromise, can never be firm and permanent. They were willing to tamper with the sacredness of an oath, in order to frame a political bond; and by this unhallowed expedient they forfeited the protection of Him whose Covenant they thus profaned. They ought to have remembered that the Covenant of 1638, which had proved an ark of safety in a not less stormy sea of troubles, was sacredly guarded, as far as possible, from being subscribed by any of whose purity of character and devotion to the cause suspicions were entertained. The one party, in short, viewed all political and national transactions through the clear medium of religion, and therefore saw them in their true character and aspect: the other viewed religion itself through the turbid and warping medium of political expediency, and therefore saw neither religion nor politics in their true nature, bearing, value, and reciprocal influences. It may be that the strictly religious party were too rigidly severe; but unquestionably their error was immeasurably less than that of those who, following the suggestions of short-sighted human policy, urged upon the king an oath, which for him to take was perjury in the very act, and the inevitable consequences of which were an impious mockery of Heaven, and the putting of power into the hands of men by whom it was certain to be abused.

When Cromwell approached Edinburgh he was confronted by the Scottish army under the command of David Leslie; and so skilful were the movements of Leslie, that Cromwell found it impossible either to draw him to a battle, or to produce any impression on his lines. The English general was constrained to retire, and was placed in the utmost peril by the masterly position taken up by the Scottish army near Dunbar. But urged by the importunities of the committee of estates, Leslie descended from his commanding position; and before his army had recovered from the confusion of this ill-timed movement, it was assailed by Cromwell, thrown into disorder and completely routed. This disastrous battle was fought on the 3d of September 1650.

The shattered Scottish army rallied at Stirling, while Cromwell advanced deliberately, securing his conquest as he moved. Soon after this disastrous conflict a measure was proposed in the Scottish parliament, which had the effect of completely rending asunder the strength of the kingdom. This was the proposal to modify or rescind the Act of Classes, so as to admit to the army those who had been by that act declared incapable of public service, and by that means to repair the loss incurred by the battle of Dunbar. The difficulty was to procure the consent of the Church to this repeal; for since many of the malignants, as they were termed, had been excommunicated, and since, by the law of the land, no excommunicated person could be employed in public service, it was necessary to have the excommunication taken off before the parliament could grant them re-admission. But the Church was by no means satisfied that such men would form any real accession of strength, though they would swell the numerical forces of the kingdom. About the same time a considerable body of troops was raised in the western counties, composed chiefly of men whose opinions coincided with those of the strictly religious Covenanters. A long and pointed remonstrance, written by P. Gillespie, was addressed by them to the committee of estates, censuring their rashness in admitting the king to desecrate the Covenant by swearing contrary to his known intentions—"teaching his majesty dissimulation and outward compliance, rather than any cordial conjunction with the cause and covenants;" and charging this and similar violations of their vows as the cause of the nation's heavy calamities. This western remonstrance gave great offence to the prudent politicians of both Church and State. A meeting of the committee of estates soon afterwards, at Stirling, was induced to censure this remonstrance; and in December, at Perth, an ensnaring question was put to a very thin meeting of the Commission of Assembly, respecting what persons should be permitted to rise in arms and join the forces of the kingdom against the invaders. In answer to this, the Commission passed two resolutions favourable to the admission of all fencible persons in a time of such great and evident necessity, with the exception of excommunicated and profane persons, and of such as were professed enemies and opponents of the Covenant. Instantly the parliament, without regarding the exceptions, passed an act rescinding the Act of Classes, and throwing open all places of public trust and power to the malignants, upon their making such professions of regret for past misconduct as such persons made no scruple of doing, without entertaining the remotest intention of any change for the future.*

These resolutions were openly condemned by J. Guthrie and his colleague David Bennet, both from the pulpit and in a letter to the Commission, in which they protested against the recent resolutions, which were, in their view, a sinful junction with the malignants. From this time forward the two parties in the Church were known by the names of Resolutioners and Protesters; the former being those who were carried away by secular and prudential views of expediency; the latter, the uncompromising adherents of the Covenant. Many of the Resolutioners were men of great piety and worth, but somewhat deficient in firmness and decision of character; lovers of peace to such an extent, as to be willing to sacrifice some of their own principles for its attainment. Of these David Dickson was one; but some years afterwards, when the perfidy of Charles and the malignants had become evident, he, on his death-bed, acknowledged his error, and admitted that the Protesters had seen these matters in a truer light than the Resolutioners had done. On the other hand, there is reason to believe that the Protesters injured their own good cause by the somewhat intemperate vehemence of this proceedings.

[1651.] The repeal of the Act of Classes had greatly increased the number of the adherents of Charles; and it was determined to delay his coronation no longer. Accordingly he was publicly crowned at Scoon on the 1st of January 1651. A sermon was preached before the ceremony by Robert Douglas; and the crown was placed upon his head by the Marquis of Argyle. The National Covenant and the Solemn League and Covenant were then read, and the king solemnly swore to observe and keep them both. The oath to defend and support the Church of Scotland was then administered to him; and kneeling and holding up his right hand, he uttered the following awful vow: "By the Eternal and Almighty God, who liveth and reigneth for ever, I shall observe and keep all that is contained in this oath!"

Following up their policy, they endeavoured to suppress all opposition; and ordered Guthrie and Bennet to repair to Perth, and answer to the king and the committee of estates for their having dared to preach against the resolutions, and for their letter to the Commission. They appeared; but it was to give in a declinature of his majesty and the council as proper judges of doctrine and of the discharge of duties strictly ministerial. They were restricted to Perth and Dun-

* Balfour's Annales.

dee for a short time; but however willing to wound, their antagonists were as yet afraid to strike, and the prosecution was allowed to drop.*

An Assembly was appointed to meet at St. Andrews in July, whence it was transferred to Dundee; but intimation was at the same time given, that all who were not satisfied with the resolutions should be cited to the General Assembly, as liable to censure. This rendered the Protesters incapable of being members, was a virtual prejudging of the question between them and their brethren, and completely vitiated the character of the Assembly as a deliberate body. Against this course of procedure the Protesters again protested, denying the freedom and lawfulness of the Assembly itself. For this, James Guthrie, Patrick Gillespie, and James Simpson were deposed; but, protesting against this sentence, they continued to discharge their ministerial functions.†

The small western army was suppressed by Cromwell without difficulty; and Strachan, one of its leaders, a man of unstable mind, joined the usurper. While in Glasgow, Cromwell attended the churches of some of the Presbyterian ministers, who did not hesitate to pray for the king, and to term the protector a usurper to his face. Some of his Independent preachers held a disputation in his presence with the Presbyterian ministers, on the principles of church government, to which that singular man listened with great apparent interest. It is probably that the Protector's intention in thus entering into personal and familiar contact with the people, and especially with the ministers of Scotland, was for the purpose of obtaining the means of forming his opinion respecting their character and principles on the sure ground of his own penetrating discernment. He knew that the king and his party could not be trusted; and he was anxious to ascertain whether the other party, though opposed to him in many points, might not be so far conciliated as to submit peacefully to his government when they should perceive resistance to be hopeless. That this was the real design of Cromwell, it would be hazardous to affirm; but the conjecture has this to recommend it, that completely accounts for the conduct of that deep-thinking and far-seeing man, during his stay in Scotland, and after his return to England, in his public treatment of the former country. Having made his observations, and formed his plans, Cromwell proceeded to put them in execution.

Charles had taken up a strong position in the vicinity of Stirling, which the protector perceived it would be dangerous to assail. He therefore turned the position of the king's army by crossing the Firth at Queensferry; and marching northwards, seized upon Perth, and cut the king off from his supplies. Charles resolved upon a daring and desperate attempt to gain or lose the whole kingdom. He broke up from his camp at Stirling, and marched with all the expedition in his power into England, hoping that the royalists there would rise and join him before Cromwell could approach. But they were too much dispirited to make the attempt; and Charles was overtaken and defeated at Worcester, on the 3d of September 1651, exactly a year after the battle of Dunbar. The king fled, and, after a number of perilous adventures, escaped to France, to mourn his blighted hopes, or rather to waste his unhonoured youth in dissipation and licentiousness. Cromwell did not think it necessary to return to complete the subjugation of Scotland, but left that task, no longer a difficult one, to General Monk.

[1652.] The unhappy contest between the Resolutioners and the Protesters continued to divide the Church so completely, that it no longer presented a rallying point for either of the political parties. The Resolutioners were the more numerous; but the Protesters were favoured by the English, so that their power remained nearly balanced. An Assembly was attempted to be held at Edinburgh in July 1652, the Resolutioners assuming the right of calling, constituting, and conducting it, which was opposed by the Protesters, with a new protestation, subscribed by sixty-five ministers and about eighty elders. After spending about a fortnight in useless altercations, it dissolved, and its acts were not recorded.*

[1653.] Another attempt was made to hold an Assembly at Edinburgh in July

* Cruickshank, vol. i. p. 63. † Lamont's Diary, p. 40.

* Lamont's Diary, p. 55.

1653, but Lieutenant-Colonel Cottrel, at the head of a body of troops, entered the house where the ministers were assembled, demanded on whose authority they met,—whether that of Charles or the protector? and, after the interchange of a few sentences with the moderator, Mr. D. Dickson, ordered them to leave the house, led them through the streets surrounded by a band of soldiers, till he had conducted them a mile out of town; and then commanded them to depart to their respective homes within the course of a day, otherwise they should be held guilty of a breach of the peace, and liable to punishment. In this manner was the General Assembly also laid prostrate beneath the power of the iron-handed ruler of the English Commonwealth.*

No further violence was used by Cromwell against the Church of Scotland. Some of the Resolutioners were exposed to danger, because they would not cease to pray for the king; but no force was used to prevent them, and no punishments were inflicted. Synods and presbyteries continued to hold their meetings as formerly, subject to an occasional visit from some of those strange enthusiasts who abounded in the English army, and were equally disposed for polemical as for military contests. The contentions, meanwhile, between the Resolutioners and the Protesters continued to rage with unabated bitterness, although with much less pernicious results than would have taken place had the Assembly been regularly meeting from year to year. In that case, this schism, the first which had taken place in the church of Scotland since the Reformation, must have led to the positive expulsion of the weaker party, and thereby to an incurable division in the Presbyterian Church. As it was, amid all their contests, they were perpetually holding meetings to treat of a termination to their unseemly strife, and the formation of a brotherly union. Yet there was a constant endeavour by each party to increase its own strength by every practicable method, and to weaken its antagonist In this the Protesters were more successful than their opponents. Patrick Gillespie was appointed to the principalship of Glasgow College, where his influence had a strong effect in drawing the students and the young preachers to espouse his party. Rutherford was professor of theology at St. Andrews, where his influence was still more direct and extensive. Even at Aberdeen, a large proportion of the young aspirants to the ministry attached themselves to the party of the Protesters. In this manner the youth and growth of the Church was directed in a very decided manner to that party which was unquestionably the most distinguished for piety and zeal; which was another preparative for the great approaching trial.

* Lamont's Diary, pp. 69-71.

[1655.] Another circumstance which contributed not a little to strengthen the Protestors, was the direct and authoritative support given to them by Cromwell. In 1655 Cromwell gave a commission to Gillespie and some of his brethren, empowering them to settle the affairs of the Church. This curious document proves, that with all his previous attachment to the Congregational system, the protector was in favour of an Established Church; and while it was obviously intended to exclude all but Protesters, it expressly provided that, in the induction of ministers, respect should be had to the choice of the most religious part of the people, though that should not be the majority.* Baillie complains much of the severe proceedings of the Protesters, in deposing some ministers, rejecting aspirants, and settling young men of their own party in preference to Resolutioners; but even with all his querulous complaints, it is plain that they acted a much more lenient and impartial part than they had it in their power to have done, and than their opponents did, at the commencement of the struggle, when they set the example of deposition. Many unseemly contests undoubtedly took place; and at times the Protesters, supported by the English troops, appear to have dealt harshly towards some of their keen opponents; but, nevertheless, from all that has been recorded respecting that period, it appears that it was one of remarkable religious prosperity. The very contention of the two great parties rendered indifference in religious matters impossible on the part of either pastors or people. And although the General Assembly was suspended, no other part of church government and dis-

* Nicoll's Diary, pp. 163-166.

cipline experienced the slightest interruption; or, rather, every other part was thrown into more intense and vigorous action. The whole vitality of the kingdom seemed to be poured into the heart of the Church, and all the strong energies of the Scottish mind were directed to religious topics in a more exclusive manner than they had ever previously been. The very fact of the kingdom's complete civil prostration beneath the power of Cromwell closed every other avenue of thought and action, and even compelled men to give their entire being to the pursuit of earnest, fervent, personal religion. "I verily believe," says Kirkton, "there were more souls converted to Christ in that short period of time, than in any season since the Reformation, though of triple its duration;"* and keeping the above considerations in mind, we may admit that the account which he gives of the state of religion at that time in Scotland, though highly coloured, is nevertheless, in all its main lineaments, a faithful representation of the truth.

Throughout the whole of Scotland during the period of Cromwell's domination, there prevailed a degree of civil peace beyond what had almost ever before been experienced. This, too, should be taken into account, when we peruse the memoirs and annals of the period; for there being no great public events to record, these gossiping chroniclers filled their pages with minute details respecting the contests between the two parties in the Church, for lack of other materials to employ their talent for journalizing. It ought to be remembered also, that although the Protesters enjoyed the favour and support o the protector to a considerable extent, and might have done so much more if they had wished it, they never compromised their principles, nor stooped to flatter the usurper. Very few of them were prevailed upon to take the "*tender*," or acknowledgment of his authority and that of the English Commonwealth, without a king or House of Lords, because they regarded it as implying a violation of the Covenant.† Patrick Gillespie appears to have been the only minister in Scotland that ever prayed publicly for the protector. It is further to be remarked, that when we read the writings of that period, we perceive at once a striking difference between those of the Resolutioners and those of the Protesters. The writings of the Protesters are thoroughly pervaded by a spirit of fervent piety, and contain principles of the loftiest order, stated in language of great force, and even dignity, of which we find but few similar instances in the productions of the Resolutioners. To prove this assertion, it is enough to name the works of Rutherford, Blair, Binning, Guthrie of Fenwick, Durham, Traill, Gray, Guthry of Stirling, and many others, scarcely their inferiors. Among the Resolutioners, we find none deserving to be matched with these, but Leighton, who afterwards became a prelate; David Dickson, who acknowledged that his party had erred; and Robert Douglas, who also lived long enough to see that he had been mistaken and deceived.

Before quitting the subject of the Resolutioners and Protesters, there is one point to which it is desirable that the reader's attention should be directed. It will be remembered that the direct topic which caused the contest between the two parties was the question respecting the propriety of repealing the Act of Classes, and admitting men of all professions in religion, and all varieties of character, into the army, and to other places of power and influence in a time of such danger. This the political-expediency party resolved to do, and against this the strict Covenanters protested. It is evident that the difference of opinion between them arose from the different positions from which they viewed the same subject. Both were fully aware of the perilous state of the nation, and of the necessity of adopting some strong measure to meet the emergency. But the one party trusted chiefly in a combination of human strength, though obtained by a sacrifice of religious principle; the other, in the confession and abandonment of past errors, the restoration and more strict enforcement of religious purity, and that calm trust in the protection and the strength of God, under which, by such procedure, they hoped to place their cause. The one party regarded national division as the main cause of the nation's weakness; the other ascribed their calamities

* For a more ample account see Kirkton, pp. 48-65.

† Rutherford opposed the tender very keenly. Lamont's Diary, p. 51.

to the prevalence of national sins, especially to that violation of the National Covenant which consisted in entrusting its enemies with the power to do it injury. It is needless for shallow thinkers to imagine they can decide the question summarily, by terming the one party men of enlightened and liberal sentiments, and the other narrow-minded and intolerant bigots. The Covenanters had seen the storm of war borne back innocuous from their mountain bulwarks but a few years before, when not a man was allowed to take up arms in the sacred cause of religion who was not believed to be personally under its influence. They had, besides, the analogy of all scriptural history in their favour; so that the views they held appeared to have the sanction of recent facts and of the Word of God. And had their opponents been as truly patriotic as they pretended, instead of seeking political influence before they would lend their aid, might they not have formed themselves into a separate army, hung on the enemy's flanks and rear, distracted his attention, cut off his supplies, and thereby promoted in the most liberal and unselfish manner, and to the utmost of their power, the rescue of their country from the strong invader? This would have entitled them to the honourable appellation of men of truly enlightened minds and genuine patriotism; but their whole conduct, then and subsequently, proved them to have been influenced chiefly by ambitious, selfish, and despotic principles.

Let the reader take up the question, and muse upon it deeply, in the form of the following hypothetic proposition:—Are there not principles and rules applicable to wars strictly religious, by which all operations should be governed and directed, essentially different from those involved in ordinary warfare? What we mean to suggest is this: that in wars strictly religious, which are of course solely defensive (for religion may not be propagated by the sword, although it may, in extraordinary cases, be so defended), no principle of merely secular policy can be admitted without vitiating the cause; no principle can be held and acted upon which has not the clear warrant of the Word of God, either in stated precept or recorded example. On the other hand, in ordinary warfare, means may be employed, and results anticipated, more according to the calculations and arrangements of human wisdom, skill, and genius. Not that, in the latter case, the overruling influence of Providence is more in abeyance than in the former, but that its direct power is less conspicuously displayed. Now, the Covenanters regarded the war as as of a strictly religious character, otherwise they would not have engaged in it at all; and therefore they could not, they dared not, employ means on which they could not implore and expect the blessing of the Lord of Hosts. Men of no religion may deem this view fanatical; but it will require more than the usual amount of reason and philosophy—we speak not to such men of religion—which they bring to bear upon the subject, before they prove it to be either irrational and absurd, or inconsistent with the providential government of the "Most High, who doeth according to his will in the armies of heaven, and among the inhabitants of the earth."

It is unnecessary to dwell on the minor details which took place during the remainder of the Protectorate. After the death of Oliver Cromwell a series of intrigues commenced, which ended in the restoration of Charles II. In Scotland these intrigues were chiefly guided by Robert Douglas, the leader of the Resolutioners, through the instrumentality of James Sharp, who at that time affected, perhaps entertained, as thoroughly as such a man could, a warm zeal for the interests of the Presbyterian Church of Scotland. Monk, who had remained in Scotland since its subjugation by Cromwell, appeared for a time to favour the Presbyterian cause, and continued to hold intercourse with Douglas through the medium of Sharp. The epistolary correspondence between Douglas and Sharp, preserved in Wodrow, clearly proves the duplicity, selfishnes, and treachery of Sharp, and prepares us for the dark and cruel tyranny which that hollow-hearted and ruthless man subsequently exercised towards the Church which he had first betrayed, and then set himself to persecute.*

* For a very full, accurate, and impartial view of the period that elapsed between the death of Charles I. and the restoration of Charles II., the reader is referred

Charles II. entered London in triumph on the 29th of May 1660; and with his restoration to the sovereignty begins a new era of the Church of Scotland's history, the record of which is one of sufferings, and lamentations, and woe.

CHAPTER VII.

FROM THE RESTORATION OF CHARLES II. TO THE REVOLUTION OF 1688.

State of Affairs at the Restoration—James Sharp—Council of State—Apprehension of Argyle and of James Guthrie—Middleton's Parliament—Oath of Allegiance—Act Recissory—Proceedings of the Church—Trial and Execution of Argyle and Guthrie—Deposition and Banishment of several Ministers—Proclamation of the King's determination to restore Prelacy—Consecration of four Scottish Bishops in London—Prohibition of all Presbyterian Church Courts—Proceedings of the Prelatic Parliament—Oaths and Declaration against the Covenant—Reformation—Diocesan Meetings—Act of Glasgow—Ejection of nearly Four Hundred Ministers—Consequences—Trial and Death of Warriston—Re-erection of the Court of High Commission—Persecutions—Proclamation against Conventicles—Causes of the Rising of Pentland—The Rising itself, Discomfiture, and Fatal Consequences—Martyrdom of Hugh M'Kail and others—Severities of the Army—The Bond—Mitchell's Attempt—Increased Severities—The First Indulgence—Dissentions caused by it—Field-preaching—The Accommodation proposed by Leighton—Continued Persecution—Second Indulgence—Proceedings against Conventicles and Field-preaching—The Highland Host—Barbarities committed by them—Continued Persecution, Instances—Death of Archbishop Sharp—Declaration of Rutherglen—Battle of Drumclog—The West-country Army—Dissensions—Battle of Bothwell Bridge—Trials, Executions, and Increased Oppression—General Persecution, Instances—The Society People—Queens-ferry Paper and Declaration of Sanquhar—Skirmish at Ayramoss—Death of Cameron and others—The Torwood Excommunication—Trial and Death of Cargil—Persecutions and Martyrdoms, Instances—The Test—Proceedings against Argyle—His Escape—Circuit Courts—Murders in the Fields—Proceedings against the Society People—Their bold and resolute Conduct—Death of Charles II.—James VII.—Unsuccessful Attempt of Argyle—His Capture, Trial, and Execution—Dunottar Castle—Transportation to the Colonies as Slaves—The King's Letter to Parliament—Schemes for restoring Popery—Acts of Indulgence—Toleration—Liberty of Conseience—Trial and Execution of Renwick—The Society People—Letter of the Scottish Prelates to the King—Letter of the Presbyterian Ministers to the Prince of Orange—The Revolution.

[1660.] The Restoration of Charles II. to the throne of his ancestors, without the guard of precautionary conditions of any kind, and the strange frenzy of extravagant loyalty which seized upon the whole kingdom like some uncontrollable epidemic, so strongly contrasted with the conduct and temper exhibited by the nation but a few years before, would require for the explanation of a change so sudden and so grea., an investigation more minute, searching, and profound, than it has ever yet received. Into that subject, however, we cannot enter, further than merely to remark, that for the fundamental error of restoring the king to full power, without any prelimiting conditions for regulating the exercise of that power, the Church of Scotland, as a body, was not to blame. So early as the 6th of February 1660, six of the leading ministers met in Edinburgh, and agreed to send Mr. James Sharp to London, to hold intercourse with Monk, according to that wily politician's desire; and gave to him instructions by which he was to regulate all his stipulations in behalf of the Church of Scotland.* At that time the design of restoring the king had not been divulged; but these instructions were equally applicable whatever form of civil government should be established,—a matter with which the Presbyterian Church did not wish directly to interfere, though decidedly favourable to monarchy. Sharp seems to have been chosen as the agent of the Church at this juncture, because of his success in some previous negotiations during the time of Cromwell, when he had been sent by the Resolutioners to counteract the influence of the Protesters. His conduct on that occasion gave great satisfaction to his party, and is praised in the most extravagant terms by Baillie, who calls him "that very worthy, pious, wise, and diligent young man, Mr. James Sharp." His character was better understood by Bishop Burnet; and as it is difficult for a Presbyterian to mention his name and character in such terms as he deserves, without being thought to be influenced by violent and vindictive feelings, it may be expedient to quote the language of the prelatic historian.

"Among these, Sharp, who was employed by the Resolutioners of Scotland, was one. He carried with him a letter from the Earl of Glencairn to Hyde, made soon after Earl of Clarendon, recommending him as the only person capable to manage the design of setting up Episcopacy in Scotland; upon which he was received into great confidence. Yet, as he had observed very carefully the success of Monk's solemn protestations

o the "History of the Church of Scotland during the Commonwealth," by the Rev. James Beattie, recently published.

* Wodrow, Dr. Burn's edit. p, 5.

against the king and for the commonwealth, it seems he was so pleased with the original, that he resolved to copy after it, without letting himself be diverted from it by scruples. For he stuck neither at solemn protestations, both by word of mouth and by letters (of which I have seen many proofs), nor at appeals to God of his sincerity in acting for the Presbytery, both in prayers and on other occasions, joining with these many dreadful imprecations on himself, if he did prevaricate. He was all the while maintained by Presbyterians as their agent, and continued to give them a constant account of the progress of his negotiation in their service, while he was indeed undermining it. This piece of craft was so visible, he having repeated his protestations to as many persons as then grew jealous of him, that when he threw off the mask, about a year after this, it laid a foundation of such a character of him, that nothing could ever bring people to any tolerable thoughts of a man whose dissimulation and treachery was so well known, and of which so many proofs were to be seen under his own hand."*

To this nothing need be added regarding the man; but what must be thought of the system which needed such a man and such arts for its introduction? Yet, let this be said,—few, very few, Episcopalians have ever expressed their approbation of either Sharp or his treachery to the Church of Scotland; and no system is justly chargeable for all the faults of its adherents. In truth, men are always either better or worse than their system or their party. A good man may be attached to a bad system or party; but he will avoid as far as possible what is evil in it, and cleave chiefly to what is good, and will accordingly be better than his system or his party. A bad man may be attached to a good system or party; but he will acquire and exhibit little of what is good in it, and will draw forth, embody, and display peculiarly what is evil, and will therefore be worse than his system or party. Thus Sharp, and the greater part of the Scottish prelates, were worse than their system, unscriptural as we believe that system of Church government to be, and as we think its unreluctant employment of such men sufficiently proves it.

The correspondence which took place between Douglas and Sharp, during the residence of the latter in London, is highly instructive, both in showing the views entertained by the large party in the Church of Scotland, whose counsels were directed by Douglas, and in detecting the duplicity of Sharp. A very able paper was transmitted by Douglas to Sharp, on the 26th of March, containing the matured opinions of that sagacious man concerning the settlement of the government in the three kingdoms. In that document, Douglas proceeds strongly to advocate the restoration of Charles, and the establishment of the Presbyterian form of church government in Scotland, England, and Ireland; admitting, at the same time, the perfect right of England and Ireland to determine for themselves, and disclaiming all intention of using force. Yet in the same paper, he does not hesitate to lay it down as an incontrovertible proposition, that "Episcopacy and other forms are men's devices, but Presbyterian government is a divine ordinance."* Such, indeed, was the general opinion of the period. It was at a considerably subsequent time that the idea of defending Prelacy, on the ground of its being a divine institution, began to grow prevalent, though it had been previously held by a few; and it was, of course, solely on the ground of its political capabilities that kings and statesmen were so anxious to have it established. Sharp easily perceived in what direction the politicians were endeavouring to steer; but he did every thing in his power to conceal it from Douglas, lest some strong resolution should be adopted by the Church of Scotland, and his design frustrated. Douglas proposed that a commission should proceed to London to make the mind of the Church clearly known; but Sharp urged the inexpediency of such a step with so much plausibility, that it was abandoned. He knew well, that if Douglas himself had been on the spot, his own machinations would have been discovered, and all his golden hopes at once destroyed.

In the meantime, Douglas had enough

* Burnet's History of his Own Times, vol. i. p. 92.

* Wodrow, vol. i. p. 15.

to do to manage matters at home. The majority of the Resolutioners placed full confidence in him, and allowed themselves to be directed according to his judgment; but the Protesters could not be moved from their position. They distrusted the king, the courtiers, and their brethren of the opposite party in the Church, and would not unite with them in the measures they were proposing. This continued antagonism was productive of the most pernicious results. It kept the Church of Scotland in a state of equipoise, or rather paralysis. Neither party could give utterance to what might justly be regarded as the national mind; for their opinions mutually counterbalanced each other, so that the nation seemed to have no decided will or wish on the subject. This was exactly the condition in which the most deadly enemy of the Presbyterian Church could have wished it to be placed. Had either party possessed a decided preponderance, the politicians would not have dared to assail it; or, had they been able to unite, as in the early days of the Covenant, they might have bid defiance to every assailant. In numbers the Protesters were the weaker party, but in unwavering integrity of principle and character the stronger. They could not form a coalition with the Resolutioners without a sacrifice of principle and conscience; while the other party might have joined them without sacrificing any thing but expediency and pride. They were destined to be more united ere long; but not till both had been thrown into the furnace.

It deserves to be particularly remarked, that the Protesters made repeated advances to their brethren, and that Douglas was prevented from complying with their proposals for a union, chiefly through the insidious policy of Sharp, who continued to assure him that the safety of the Church would consist in its majority keeping aloof from the Protesters, against whom the king cherished an irreconcilable enmity. He intimated also his majesty's willingness to ratify the proceedings of the Assembly of 165', in which the Protesters had been condemned, regarding this as a clear proof of the royal feelings.

With one other remark we shall conclude these comparatively preliminary notices of the state of affairs at the Restoration. The whole nature of the great convulsion through which the nation had passed had tended to draw forth into the most marked contrast two very opposite states of mind, or aspects of character. The essential subject of the contest was religion; the one party seeking to govern and restrain it; the other striving to procure for it not only freedom, but supremacy in its own department. Of necessity, the defenders of religion were men of graver manners and more thoughtful minds than its opponents. But in the heat and anger of the struggle many joined each party who valued little the intrinsic nature of the subject in dispute, and deemed it enough to assume the external characteristics of the party which they joined. The consequence was, that such adherents presented the most ridiculously exaggerated caricature of their respective parties; so that a stern and gloomy fanaticism came to be regarded as the characteristic of a Presbyterian, while drinking, swearing, and licentiousness of every kind were the tokens by which a royalist was known. Accordingly, the restoration of the king was a signal for the universal display of these characteristics of loyalty. "A spirit of extravagant joy," says Burnet, "spread over the nation, that brought on with it the throwing off the very professions of virtue and piety. All ended in entertainment and drunkenness, which overrun the three kingdoms to such a degree, that it very much corrupted all their morals."* "Men did not think," says Kirkton, "they could handsomely express their joy, except they turned brutes for debauch; yea, many a sober man was tempted to exceed, lest he should be condemned as unnatural, disloyal, and insensible."† The effect may be easily imagined, both in degrading the royalist party, and in disgusting their opponents, driving them to the opposite extreme, and rendering the chasm between them more wide, deep, and impassable. It will account also for much of the exaggerated language used by party writers on both sides, while describing not the essential characteristics, but the distorted caricatures, of the two contending parties.

* Burnet's History of his Own Times, p. 92.
† Kirkton, p. 65.

Little more than a month was sufficient to ripen the schemes of those who wished to establish an arbitrary government, and to give them courage to commence the putting of these schemes into execution. A council of state was formed for the administration of affairs in Scotland, composed of men decidedly hostile to the Presbyterian cause. The Earl of Middleton, a fierce, rude, and unprincipled soldier of fortune, was made commissioner for holding the parliament, and general of the forces, and thus head of both the legislative and executive departments. The Earl of Glencairn was chancellor; the Earl of Lauderdale, who had been one of the commissioners to the Westminster Assembly, was appointed secretary of state; the Earl of Rothes, son of the celebrated Rothes, who gave such important aid in the time of the Covenant, was president of the council; the Earl of Crawford, lord treasurer; and Sir Archibald Primrose, clerk register. Private instructions were given to Middleton to try the inclination of the country for Prelacy, and to devise the best method of introducing it. For this purpose it was necessary to remove those whose opposition might have been formidable. The Marquis of Argyle was justly regarded as the most powerful supporter of the Covenant; and he had many enemies among the Scottish nobility, in addition to which the king himself regarded him with decided hostility. Argyle, nevertheless, unconscious of evil, repaired to London, and requested an audience of the king; but no sooner was Charles informed of his arrival than he commanded him to be committed to the Tower. This took place on the 8th of July. On the 14th of the same month, orders were sent to Edinburgh to imprison Sir James Stewart, Sir John Chiesly, and Sir Archibald Johnston of Warriston. The two former were seized, but Warriston made his escape, although a proclamation was immediately issued, offering a reward for his apprehension, and subjecting every person who should conceal him to the penalties of treason.

On the 23d of August, the committee of estates met in Edinburgh, to commence the administration of national affairs. The first act gave but too clear an indication what the course of their procedure was likely to be. Ten ministers and two elders had met that day in the house of a friend in Edinburgh, for the purpose of framing a humble address and supplication to the king, congratulating his return, expressing their loyalty, reminding him of his own and of the nation's Covenant, and praying that his reign might be prosperous. They were all Protesters, and had determined upon taking this step in consequence of the opposite party, beguiled by Sharp, refusing to join with them in a general address from the whole Church. Their intention was, to transmit the supplication to their brethren throughout the country, that it might obtain as many signatures as possible, and then to call a larger meeting, from which it might be sent to his majesty. No sooner did the committee receive intelligence of this private meeting, than they sent a party of soldiers, seized their papers, and committed themselves to prison, from whence one of them, James Guthrie, came not out but to trial and execution.* It was remarked, that this violent and illegal apprehension of these ministers took place on the very day of the month on which, exactly an hundred years before, the Scottish parliament had passed an act abolishing Popery, and permitting the free progress of the Reformation. They were now attempting to abolish Presbytery at the command of a king who was secretly a papist, and who would have been glad to have brought the nation once more into the dark and enslaving bondage of the Roman apostacy.

In the beginning of September Sharp came from London, and brought a letter from the king, addressed to Robert Douglas, but to be communicated to the Presbytery of Edinburgh. It was prepared, as Wodrow states, by Sharp himself, and was cunningly adapted to gratify the Resolutioners, and to throw all blame upon the Protesters. It produced the effect intended. All suspicion was lulled asleep, the most extravagant expressions of delighted gratitude were poured forth, and copies of it were sent to every presbytery, to prove to the kingdom the truthful fidelity of his majesty, and to show how groundless and unjust were the jealous suspicions of the Protesters. Yet

* Wodrow, vol. i. pp. 66-72.

the letter contained expressions of a character so manifestly evasive that it might well have excited suspicion, even had there been no previous cause of distrust. It startled the unscrupulous Middleton, who declared that he thought it beneath the dignity of a king thus to equivocate with his people and deceive them.*

Some proclamations were, about the same time, issued by the committee of estates against all unlawful meetings and seditious papers, all seditious slanderers of his majesty's government, and all remonstrators and their adherents. It was evident against whom these were fulminated, and for what purpose; but the committee could stoop to still meaner employment. About the middle of September a proclamation was issued against Rutherford's "Lex Rex," and J. Guthrie's "Causes of God's Wrath," and all were ordered to bring in their copies of those books, that they might be burned. They would have shown more wisdom by either leaving these works unnoticed, or by appointing their ablest reasoner to try his strength in answering them. The principles and arguments of the "Lex Rex" have not yet received, and will not soon receive, a refutation; and it had been well if the committee had so regulated their conduct as to avert that Divine wrath, the causes of which had been so forcibly stated by Guthrie.

In October a proclamation was issued calling a parliament to meet in December, which was subsequently prorogued till January, to allow more time for the maturing of the measures then to be proposed. In that proclamation there were some ominous intimations of the spirit by which it was likely to be pervaded. The royal prerogative was mentioned as that "by which alone the liberties of the people can be preserved;" the people were significantly told, that petitions or addresses were to be made only to the parliament or committee of estates; and an act of indemnity was promised after the honour of the king and the prerogative of the crown should have been asserted. In the time which elapsed before the meeting of parliament, every kind of exertion was made, by bribery, intimidation, and party influence, to procure the election of persons entirely at the devotion of the court; and as no act of indemnity had yet been passed, many of the staunch adherents of the Covenant were deterred from seeking to be elected, and some of them were cited before the parliament, to prevent them being returned as members. The result was the election of a parliament, the decided majority of which was composed of royalists and malignants, as those were termed who had been either the direct opponents of the Covenant, or who had deserted it, and were the more bent on its entire destruction; together with a considerable number of persons whose estates had been ruined during the preceding troublous times, and who were prepared to support any measures by which they could hope to repair their broken fortunes.

[1661.]—The new parliament was opened by the Earl of Middleton, as representative of his majesty, on the 1st of January 1661, and proceed to the despatch of public business on the 4th of that month. Some of the proceedings of this parliament require to be attentively considered, in consequence of the subversive use made of them at a subsequent period. The very constitution of the parliament was vitiated from the first. An act had been passed in 1651, when the king himself was present, requiring every member of all succeeding parliaments to sign and subscribe the Covenant before entering upon business, without which its constitution, and all its acts, were declared void and null. This was not done; but instead of it another oath was proposed, termed in its title "an oath of parliament," and in the body of the act "an oath of allegiance." In it there occur the following expressions:—"I acknowledge my said sovereign only supreme governor of this kingdom over all persons and in all causes," "and shall at my utmost power defend, assist, and maintain his majesty's jurisdiction aforesaid, against all deadly, and never decline his majesty's power and jurisdiction. There can be no doubt that these clauses admitted of a double interpretation. So far as their meaning applied to civil matters alone, they would not have been opposed by any of the Covenanters; but there was no such limitation specified, and therefore it was evident, that the first

* Burnet's Own Times, vol. i. p. 109.

might be construed to admit his majesty's supremacy in ecclesiastical causes as well as in civil matters; and that the second was intended to prevent the declining of the king's jurisdiction in religious affairs, as the Church of Scotland had always done. Subsequent events proved that such was the express intention of the oath; but it was thought proper to conceal this for a time; and when the Earls of Cassilis and Melville, and the Laird of Kilbirnie, refused to take the oath without its being understood as not extending the royal supremacy beyond civil matters, they were allowed to take it in that limited sense, but not permitted to have their explanation recorded. Middleton and the Chancellor Glencairn publicly declared that the oath was not intended to give his majesty any ecclesiastical, but only a civil supremacy; yet a short time afterwards, when the Presbyterian ministers expressed their willingness to take it in this sense, they were not allowed.*

Having thus established the king's supremacy, they proceeded to evolve its consequences by a series of acts as consistent with the strong premise as the most rigid logic of despotism could require. They declared it to be his majesty's prerogative to choose all officers of state, councillors, lords of session; to call hold, and prorogue, and dissolve all parliaments, conventions, and meetings; and that all meetings held without the royal warrant are void and null; that no convocations, leagues, or bonds, can be made without the Sovereign; and that to the king belongs the sole power of making peace and war. A tolerable broad foundation was thus laid for the erection of absolute despotism; but some obstructions needed to be taken away. The chief of these was the Solemn League and Covenant; and an act was accordingly passed, absolving the lieges from its obligation, and prohibiting its renewal without his majesty's special warrant and approbation. Another act was passed, approving of the Engagement in 1648, and condemning the conduct of those who opposed it, terming them "a few seditious persons." And to concentrate and confirm all the arbitrary acts already passed, another was framed, requiring not only all persons in civil official stations, but "all other persons who shall be required by his majesty's privy-council, or any having authority from them, to be obliged to take and swear the oath of allegiance, and the acknowledgment of the king's prerogative." The next act of this reckless parliament was the act recissory, not merely repealing certain acts of parliament for reasons stated, but at one broad sweep annulling all the parliaments held since 1633, with all their proceedings, and thus totally abolishing all the laws made in favour of the Presbyterian Church, as well as those in favour of civil liberty, which had been enacted during the late reign, and many of them with the full sanction of the king himself.

"This," says Burnet, "was a most extravagant act, and only fit to be concluded after a drunken bout. It shook all possible security for the future, and laid down a most pernicious precedent."† Nothing could more clearly prove the intimate connection between civil and religious liberty than this very act. The whole design of this parliament was to destroy the Church of Scotland; but in the attempt to accomplish this deed they were under the necessity of destroying not only all the existent laws of the land, but all the security which law itself can give, by not only repealing laws, but even annihilating the legislature of the kingdom. Such conduct amounted to a virtual dissolution of the social compact, by putting an end to all trust in public deeds, and leaving to men no alternative but submission to absolute despotism, or the wild recoil of utter anarchy. Yet even this glaring violation of all legislative principles was carried, after some oppsition, in this "drinking parliament," as it was commonly termed, in allusion to the intemperance of Middleton and the royalists.

Since by the act recissory the whole government of the Church of Scotland was virtually overthrown, another act was passed, "concerning religion and church government," in which his majesty declares his intention to secure the government of the Church "in such a frame as shall be most agreeable to the Word of God, most suitable to monarchical government, and most complying with the public peace and the quiet of the kingdom;" "in the meantime allowing the

* Wodrow, vol. i. pp. 92, 93.

† Burnet's Own Times, p. 119.

present administration by sessions, presbyteries, and synods." There could be little doubt as to the meaning of this act, in which the settlement of church government was left to the king, and the Presbyterian form "allowed" to remain evidently no longer than till his majesty's plans should be fully matured. And a sufficient indication was given what was the nature of these plans, by an act appointing the 29th of May to be kept as a solemn anniversary thanksgiving for his majesty's restoration; and another restoring patronages and presentations, "as what they knew had been still a dead weight upon, and really inconsistent with, the Presbyterian Establishment.'"*

Such is a brief outline of the public acts of Middleton's parliament, especially with regard to the Church. It might seem strange that such acts could have been passed by any parliament composed of men not actually born in slavery, and so habituated to bondage as to have become enamoured of their chains, and eager to impose the same ornaments upon all others. Where were Scotland's bold and free barons, who had never been accustomed to bend their haughty necks beneath the arbitrary yoke of any sovereign? Some of the best were dead, or in disgrace and danger; others were plunged in debt, and eager to repair their shattered fortunes by court favour; and a large majority of them were addicted to those glaring vices which had become the badges of the royalists,—drunkenness and immorality,—which they knew the Presbyterian Church would censure; and therefore they were eager to destroy a Church whose purity they both feared and hated. "Vices of all sorts," says Burnet, "were the open practices of those about the Earl of Middleton. Drinking was the most notorious of all, which was often continued through the whole night till the next morning." They came to the parliament reeling from the over-night debauches, and passed acts subversive of the whole civil and religious constitution of the country with less care than they bestowed upon their preparations for the next scene of revelry and wickedness. It was not strange that such besotted slaves of sin were the enemies of religious freedom; and that, in their hatred of religion, they were ready to sacrifice civil liberty in their fierce desire to subject the preaching of the gospel and the discipline of the Church to equal thraldom. This, while it explains their conduct, stamps the brand of infamy more deeply both on the men, and on the system which such men and such measures were employed to introduce.

* Wodrow, vol. i. p. 106.

But where was the Church of Scotland, that it did not raise aloud its voice in bold and indignant condemnation of such proceedings? It was paralyzed by its own unhallowed internal divisions. The Protesters were awed into comparative silence by the seizure and imprisonment of James Guthrie, their ablest and boldest leader; and the Resolutioners were still partly possessed by the blind spirit of party contention, and partly beguiled by the wily subtleties of the traitor Sharp. Yet some attempts were made by the ministers to prevent the utter subversion of the Church. The ministers of Edinburgh presented petitions, supplications, and remonstrances, against the act recissory and other acts of similar character, but without effect. When the synods began to hold their meetings in April and May, endeavours were made to frame addresses to the parliament respecting the danger to which the Church was exposed by the recent enactments; but as those addresses were generally proposed by the Protesters, the Resolutioners opposed them, urging the feeble but pernicions plea, so commonly used by men of time-serving and undecided character, that it was unseasonable and unexpedient to apply to parliament in the present circumstances.* Such was the case in the synod of Glasgow; and though the Protesters could have carried their measure by a majority, yet, to prevent the appearance of division, they agreed to delay, and meantime to utter an equivocal declaration, such as men of all views might support. This declaration was of course futile, and they were prevented from holding another meeting; which ought to be a warning to the Church to be equally prompt and decided in her Divine Master's cause, and never to defer till to-morrow the sacred duty of to-day.

The synod of Fife, which had in for

* Wodrow, vol. i. p. 117.

mer days often borne the brunt of the conflict in times of danger to the Church, were engaged in preparing a petition for a new act, ratifying the privileges of the Church, when they were interrupted by the Earl of Rothes, ordered to depart, and obeyed the order without a protestation against this infringement of the shadow of liberty left by the late parliament. The synod of Dumfries was interrupted and dissolved in the same forcible manner, and yielded with equal submissiveness. The synod of Galloway better maintained the character of the Church of Scotland. Mr. Park, the moderator, protested against this procedure, as an injurious encroachment upon the spiritual liberties of a court of Christ, incompetent to the civil magistrate; and refused to withdraw till he had regularly dissolved the meeting with prayer. The synod of Lothian was so far overawed by the presence and the interference of the court, as to suspend six or seven faithful and pious ministers of the Protesters, on the absurd and groundless charge of rebellion. And the synod of Ross deposed the celebrated Thomas Hog, minister of Kiltearn, although he had not signed the protestation, but merely because he was known to be opposed to Prelacy, for the honours and emoluments of which some of these northern brethren were longing. Yet so strong is conscience in hearts not utterly seared, that the moderator, a keen prelatist, in pronouncing the sentence of deposition, did it with an air of veneration, and in tones of deep respect, reminded the venerable man, that Christ himself had suffered great wrong from the scribes and pharisees.† The synod of Aberdeen, as Burnet tells us, was the only body that made an address looking towards Episcopacy,—so consistently did it preserve its bad pre-eminence, as the least enlightened part of Scotland, and the first to return to its scarcely half-broken darkness.

Having by these unconstitutional enactments prepared the way for the entire overthrow of the Church of Scotland, the parliament proceeded to ratify their destructive acts with the blood of some distinguished victims. The first of these in time, as well as in rank, was the Marquis of Argyle. That distinguished nobleman had been too firm and steady an adherent to the Presbyterian cause to find favour with the king and the prelatic party: he was too powerful to be permitted to remain in the enjoyment of liberty and life; and the Earl of Middleton hoped to obtain a grant of his forfeited estates. In addition to these public causes of hostility against Argyle, the king cherished a personal hatred of him, partly because Argyle had checked some of his licentious conduct when formerly in Scotland, and partly because he had himself broken his promise to marry Argyle's daughter, and consequently hated the man whom he had injured.* His indictment, however, carefully avoided allusion to the real causes for which his life was sought, and bore reference to his public acts,—first, during the late civil contentions,—secondly, with regard to his treatment of the royalists, and particularly of Montrose,—and thirdly, his concurrence with Cromwell during the period of the protectorate. Argyle defended himself with great eloquence and force of reason, so as nearly to baffle the malice of his enemies, although his death had been determined even before his trial commenced. To secure his condemnation, Monk sent to the Scottish administration some private letters in which Argyle had expressed concurrence with his government. By this base act Monk secured the condemnation of a man whose guilt, if guilt it could be called, was immeasurably less than his own, Argyle having only submitted to a power which he could not successfully oppose, wielded by Monk himself. The sentence was passed, adjudging him to be guilty of high treason, and condemning him to be beheaded, and his head to be affixed in the same place where that of the Marquis of Montrose had been. He received the sentence kneeling; and then rising, said, "I had the honour to set the crown upon the king's head, and now he hastens me to a better crown than his own."†

Between the time of his condemnation and his execution, Argyle enjoyed not merely tranquillity of mind, but such a perception of the love of God as filled his soul with heavenly gladness, and with the very peace of God. When his lady and

† Wodrow, vol. i. p. 129.

* Kirkton, p. 50. † Wodrow, vol. i. p. 150.

some of his friends exclaimed against the cruelty of his enemies, he replied, "Forbear, forbear! truly I pity them; they know not what they are doing; they may shut me in where they please, but they cannot shut out God from me." To some ministers who were with him in the prison he said, that shortly they would envy him who was got before them, adding emphatically, "Mind that I tell you; my skill fails me if you who are ministers will not either suffer much or sin much; for though you go along with these men in part, if you do not do it in all things, you are but where you were, and must suffer; and if you go not at all with them, you shall but suffer;"—words worthy to be held in lasting remembrance, for the deep wisdom which they contain. On the day of his execution, the 27th of May, his soul was filled with all a martyr's holy and inexpressible joy. "What cheer, my Lord!" said the Rev. Mr. Hutchison. "Good cheer, Sir; the Lord hath again confirmed and said to me from heaven, "Son be of good cheer, thy sins are forgiven thee.'" And when taking leave of his friends, after having freely stated that he was naturally of a timid disposition, but that God had taken away all fear from him, he said, "I could die like a Roman, but choose rather to die as a Christian." He ascended the scaffold with steady step, calm pulse, and unmoved countenance, spoke a grave and earnest address to the assembled multitude, breathed forth a fervent prayer, kneeled down beneath the sharp axe of the decapitating instrument, prayed, gave the signal, the weapon fell, and his spirit returned to God who gave it.

So fell the first and noblest Scottish victim of royal tyranny and prelatic ambition, leaving behind him a name and character which enemies have in vain striven to blacken and depreciate; which needs no other vindication than a simple statement of the truth; and which Scotland still holds, and long will hold, in deep and affectionate remembrance.

The next victim was James Guthrie, minister of Stirling, of whose seizure and imprisonment mention has already been made. The chief accusation against him was his declinature of the king and council's competency to judge, *in the first instance*, respecting matters purely ecclesiastical, such as presbyterial acts and letters, preaching, and the discharge of what belonged peculiarly to the ministerial function. This declinature had been presented to the king and council at Perth in February 1651; and though the king had managed to procure a sentence of deposition against him in the packed Assembly of St. Andrews and Dundee, yet as that assembly was not recognised as free and lawful by the Church, the sentence fell into abeyance, and Guthrie continued to discharge his ministerial duties, till he was seized by the Committee of of Estates, as above related. When brought to trial, he defended himself with such eloquence, knowledge of law and strength of argument, as utterly amazed his friends and confounded his enemies. He proved clearly that his declinature was agreeable to the Word of God, to the Confession of Faith, accordant with the doctrine and practice of the Church of Scotland from the period of the Reformation, and confirmed and sanctioned by many acts of parliament, and therefore had the support of both divine and human laws. His enemies could not answer his arguments, nor prove the relevancy of their own accusations; but he had been the leader of the Protesters; his death might strike terror into that truly Presbyterian party, and induce them to yield; and he had pronounced sentence of excommunication on the Earl of Middleton many years before, for which that vindictive man sought to be revenged. He was therefore pronounced guilty of high treason, and condemned to die as a traitor, on the first of June.

"My lord," said this eminent man to his partial judge, "my conscience I cannot submit; but this old crazy body and mortal flesh I do submit, to do with it whatsoever you will, whether by death, or banishment, or imprisonment, or any thing else; only I beseech you to ponder well what profit there is in my blood. It is not the extinguishing me or many others that will extinguish the Covenant and the work of reformation since the year 1638. My blood, bondage, or banishment will contribute more for the propagation of those things than my life or liberty could do, though I should live many years." But his persecutors would have their malice gratified, and their thirst for blood satiated. The Christian martyr is beyond the reach of fear. So was it with Guthrie. On the day of his execution he was not merely serene,—he was unusually cheerful. "He spoke," says Burnet, "an hour upon the ladder, with the composedness of a man that was delivering a sermon rather than his last words. He justified all he had done, and exhorted all people to adhere to the Covenant, which he magnified highly." When on the scaffold, adds another relation, he lifted the napkin off his face, just before he was turned over, and cried, "The Covenants, the Covenants, shall yet be Scotland's reviving."

Thus died the Rev. James Guthrie, who may, with strict propriety, be termed the first Scottish martyr for Christ's Crown and Covenant, inasmuch as the very essence of the accusation brought against him consisted in his declining to subject Christ's kingly and sole dominion over his Church to the arrogated supremacy of any earthly court or monach. In this, indeed, he but followed the example of Knox, and Melville, and Bruce, and Black, and Welch, and Calderwood, —in short, of all the great and pious men of both the First and Second Reformations of the Church of Scotland; but he was the first who died for that great and sacred truth, for which others had suffered bonds, affliction, and banishment. He died; but the cause for which he suffered martyrdom cannot die. It is living now, and once more putting forth those sacred energies before which all human opposition must ultimately be consumed like stubble in the flames. It is, indeed, the chief of those great principles which form the essential characteristics of the Church of Scotland, inclosed imperishably within its very heart, disappearing in times of defection or of lethargy, but reviving and putting forth its undiminished might ever when the reawakening call of God quickens its vital and eternal powers.

Another victim was sacrificed along with Guthrie, named William Govan, who was accused of being implicated in the death of Charles I. But though this was not proved against him, he had been engaged in the Western Remonstrance, and generally had favored the Protesters, which, in the estimation of Middleton's parliament, were crimes of unpardonable enormity.

The parliament seemed to think that blood enough had been shed for the present; but their tender mercies were still cruel. Several ministers of distinguished talents and character were apprehended, cast into prison, and finally banished. Of these, the most remarkable were M'Ward of Glasgow and Simpson of Airth, who were both banished to Holland. Moncrieff of Sconie and Trail of Edinburgh were deposed from the ministry, and exposed to many sufferings and dangers, in addition to the protracted imprisonment which they had endured. But Patrick Gillespie was more leniently treated, partly in consequence of his having many friends in the parliament, and partly because he made submissive acknowledgments of having given offence to his majesty by the Remonstrance, which none of the other sufferers could be induced to make. He was deposed from the ministry, and confined to Ormiston and six miles round it, but exempted from severer punishment. Yet he was, of all the ministers, the most disliked by the king, chiefly because of the direct intercourse which he had held with Cromwell. When his majesty heard that Guthrie had been put to death, he asked, "And what have you done with Mr. Patrick Gillespie?"—adding, "Well, if I had known you would have spared Mr. Gillespie, I would have spared Mr. Guthrie." The true explanation of Patrick Gillespie's conduct appears to be this: he was at least as much a man of the world as he was a Christian minister, and allowed his conduct to be swayed as much by political motives as by Christian principles. A man of such a mixed character will rarely act with thorough consistency, and generally his worldly and self-interested motives will, in the hour of danger, obtain the ascendency over those higher principles which they had been too often permitted to intermingle with and vitiate.

The deadly gripe of the parliament was attempted to be laid on a man of a very different mould,—the heavenly-minded Rutherford. Not content with burning his work entitled "Lex Rex," they summoned him to appear before them at Edinburgh, to answer to a charge of high treason. He was at that time lying on his death-bed. "Tell them," replied he, "that I have received a summons already to appear before a superior Judge and judicatory, and I behove to answer my first summons; and ere your day arrive, I will be where few kings and great folks come."

It was now thought that the Presbyterian spirit of Scotland was sufficiently humbled, and that Prelacy might be introduced without further delay. Some of the leading men pressed the king to proceed forthwith with the intended change of church government in Scotland, and Sharp prepared for another journey to London, to complete his treachery. Before his departure he had the dissimulation, or the effrontery, to visit Robert Douglas, and pretend that the king wished to make that distinguished man Archbishop of St. Andrews. Douglas answered that he would have nothing to do with it; and when Sharp rose to withdraw, Douglas called him back and thus addressed him, "James, I see you will engage,—I perceive you are clear,—you will be Bishop of St. Andrews; take it, and the curse of God with it;"—and laying his hand heavily on the apostate's shoulder as he spoke, moved him to the door.*

The subversive process now went on rapidly. A new privy council was formed for the permanent management of public affairs in Scotland. Soon after the meeting of the council, a letter, bearing date the 14th of August, was sent by his majesty to them, declaring his "firm resolution to interpose his royal authority for restoring the Church of Scotland to its rightful government by bishops." This letter was published by proclamation with the addition of penalties, to which all should be liable who might fail in rendering obedience. Such was the result of his majesty's often-repeated oaths and declarations to maintain and defend the Presbyterian Church of Scotland. And it deserves to be remarked, that this proclamation was of the most arbitrary character, resting the whole change upon the royal prerogative alone, without reference to the advice of council, parliament, or Assembly. This, indeed, was the natural result of the absolute prerogative which had been made the ruling principle of the whole preceding parliamentary enactments. The arbitrary will of the sovereign had been distinctly declared to be the source of all authority; and the repealing of acts and annulling of parliaments having left no other source of authority, the language of despotism was the fitting medium for declaring the restoration of Prelacy.

* Kirkton, p. 135.

All preliminary steps were now completed; and Sharp again hastened to London, to receive episcopal consecration, taking with him some of his brethren, who, like himself, were ready to purchase Prelacy at the cost of perjury. These were, Andrew Fairfoul, James Hamilton, and Robert Leighton. Of the character of Sharp it is unnecessary to write a single word. Fairfoul appears to have been vain, facetious, somewhat learned, and loose in his moral conduct. Hamilton was a weak, trimming, unprincipled man, equally readly to pretend extreme zeal for the Covenant, and to adjure and betray it. But what had Leighton to do in such company, and on such an errand? That pious, amiable, modest, and gentle-hearted man seems to have been selected expressly to present to Scotland the abstract possibility that a prelate might be a man deserving of esteem and love. It might be, too, that some of more sagacious mind might anticipate from Leighton's moderation and kindliness of heart, a greater influence in recommending Prelacy, than could be expected from the arbitrary and oppressive conduct and disreputable character of his brethren.

When they arrived at London, it was ascertained that Sharp and Leighton had not received episcopal ordination, having been both ordained since the abolition of Prelacy in Scotland. The English bishops refused to consecrate them to the prelatic office till they should be re-ordained as deacons and priests. This Sharp at first opposed, as contrary to the precedent in 1610, when Spotswood had not been required to receive prelatic ordination before his elevation to a bishopric. But the English prelates had begun to insist on the Divine institution of Prelacy,—a notion introduced into the English Church by Bancroft, and carried to its extreme height by Laud, but which the great and good men of England's

Reformation never entertained. Leighton regarded the whole matter as an indifferent ceremony, which might be omitted or performed, according to the custom of different churches; and Sharp was too intent on reaching the summit of his ambition to offer any protracted resistance. On the 12th of December 1661, these four men were formally consecrated to the episcopal office, and concluded the service of the day with feasting and revelry, to a degree which shocked the heart of Leighton. He said to Burnet, "that in the whole progress of that affair there appeared such cross character of an angry Providence, that how fully soever he was satisfied in his own mind as to Episcopacy itself, yet it seemed that God was against them, and they were not like to be the men that would build up his Church; so that the struggling about it seemed to him like a fighting against God.* It was not strange that he should come to that conclusion; but it was strange that he persevered so many years in what he regarded as little better than fighting against God, till at last he was constrained to abandon the fearful attempt, wounded in conscience, and almost broken-hearted.

[1662.] On the 2d of January 1662, the council received a letter from his majesty, announcing the consecration of the prelates, and prohibiting the meeting of Synods, Presbyteries, and Kirk-Sessions, till they should be authorised by the archbishops and bishops; calling upon the nobility, gentry, and burgh magistracy, to give all countenance and encouragement to the bishops, and threatening that severe and exemplary notice would be taken of every one who should presume to reflect or express any disrespect to their persons, or the authority with which they were intrusted. This was speedily followed by a proclamation from the council of the same tenor, and a letter to sheriffs and magistrates throughout the kingdom, intimating the prohibition of all meetings of Synods, Presbyteries, and Sessions, till they should be ordered by the bishops. By this proclamation the Presbyterian Church was more completely overthrown than it had been during the reign of James VI.; for then Synods, Presbyteries, and Kirk-Sessions continued to meet by virtue of their own intrinsic powers, cramped merely with constant moderators, possessing a negative upon the proceedings of these church judicatories. But now they were not to be held at all, till called by the prelates, and to possess no power except what these despots should be pleased to grant.

One good effect resulted from this arbitrary proclamation; it put an end to much of the rivalry which had existed between the Resolutioners and the Protesters, though too late to be of much avail. Robert Douglas exclaimed, "Our brethren the Protesters have had their eyes open, and we have been blind;" and David Dickson said, "The Protesters have been much truer prophets than we." Wood of St. Andrews, also, who had maintained a long and painful contest with Rutherford, acknowledged that he and his party had been mistaken in the views they took of matters. But their disunion had been of too long continuation to admit of a ready and cordial coalition, even in such a time of general danger and distress. Sorrow and dejection filled the minds of the great majority, instead of that prompt and decisive energy which might even yet have prevented the subversion of the Church, had it been put forth as in the early days of the Covenant. In a state of silent stupor they generally submitted to the blow; a very few Presbyteries only having the courage to meet and protest against this invasion of their spiritual liberties. Why had the Church of Scotland so soon lost its primitive spirit, and sunk into such cowardly despair? Because it had sinned in passing these baneful "Resolutions," expressive of acquiescence in the schemes of deceptive expediency devised by worldly politicians; and therefore were its councils distracted, and its strength was become weakness. The fiercest storm of royal wrath and prelatic revenge was indeed directed against the high-principled and clear-sighted Protesters; but who will say that it was not better to die the noble death of a Christian martyr, like Guthrie, than to sink, like Baillie, to the grave, beneath the piercing anguish of a disappointed and a broken heart? "Pray," said the Earl of Loudon to his

* Burnet's Own Times, vol. ii. pp. 140, 141.

pious countess, "that I may die before the meeting of parliament, when I must either sin or meet the fate of Argyle."

On the 8th of April, Sharp and his three brother prelates reached Berwick, having travelled from London all in one coach; but there Leighton left them, being thoroughly weary of their company, and hastened privately to Edinburgh, to escape the infamy of that pompous processional entrance which the others courted and obtained. Soon after their arrival, six others were consecrated to the prelatic function, but without that re-ordination to which Sharp and Leighton had submitted, as if to prove the incompatibility of Prelacy to the Scottish character, and the impossibility of manufacturing bishops in Scotland according to the high episcopalian rules. When the parliament met, a deputation was sent to invite the prelates to take their seats, as the third estate of the realm. The very first act passed by this parliament, which met on the 8th of May, was one "for the restitution and re-establishment of the ancient government of the Church by archbishops and bishops." After a false preamble respecting the evils sustained by the community during the late rebellion, as the late Reformation is termed, in consequence of casting off the "sacred order of bishops," that order is restored to all its accustomed dignities, privileges, and jurisdictions, and to all power of ordination, censure, and discipline, "which they are to perform with advice and assistance of such of the clergy as they shall find to be of known loyalty and prudence." The act further annuls every kind and degree of church power and jurisdiction "other than that which acknowledgeth a dependence upon and subordination to the sovereign power of the king as supreme."* This, certainly, was enough to gratify the utmost desire of the most thorough Erastian, ancient or modern, and might be studied with advantage by those who regard the Church as purely the "creature of the State." No wonder that the men who had sworn to maintain Christ's kingly government of his Church regarded Prelacy, thus introduced, and avowing no allegiance but that due to an earthly monarch, as involving a virtual transfer of the Divine Redeemer's eternal crown to the brows of a sinful and mortal man.

An act was also passed "for the preservation of his majesty's person, authority, and government;" probably one of the most pure pieces of despotism that ever emanated from any legislative body. It involves in the guilt of treason "all covenants and leagues for reformation;" brands the covenants as unlawful oaths against the fundamental laws and liberties of the kingdom, though the king himself has sworn them; stigmatizes all protestations and petitions as unlawful and seditious: rescinds the acts of the Assembly of 1638, and all ratifications of them; prohibits, on the severest penalties, all writing, speaking, painting, preaching, praying, &c., tending to stir up a dislike of his majesty's royal prerogative and supremacy in cases ecclesiastical, or the government of the Church by archbishops and bishops. Such are the leading clauses of this arbitrary act, unquestionably a fine specimen of prelatic legislation, and a sufficient proof that in Scotland at least, tyranny and Prelacy are inseparably connected. But their schemes were not yet fully developed. Another act prohibited any person to teach in universities, or to preach, keep schools, or to be tutors to persons of quality, who did not own prelatic government, and obtain a license from the prelates. By another act, all persons in public trust were ordained to sign a declaration condemning as unlawful all leagues and covenants among subjects, upon any pretext whatever; and particularly the National Covenant and the Solemn League and Covenant, which were declared by the subscriber to be of no obligation upon himself or any of the subjects. It did not seem to the prelates enough for a man to say that he ceased to regard the Covenants as binding upon himself he must also affirm the same of others, though he could know nothing of their conscientious opinions. One cannot help conjecturing, that the prelates, somewhat uneasy under their own perjury, were anxious that the whole kingdom should be plunged into similar guilt, or that men should become as accustomed to oaths, as to regard their violation as a matter of no real moment, inferring neither guilt nor infamy. One or other of

* See the act in Wodrow, vol. i, pp. 257, 258.

two consequences such a multiplicity of ensnaring and often self-contradictory oaths were sure to have: they would either involve the nation in wide-spread irreligion and immorality, or would bring into trouble, poverty, and suffering, all who venerated the sanctity of an oath. For it has always been observed, that where these solemn bonds are made too common, they cease to bind: they are iron fetters to the good, but threads of gossamer to the bad. A government which multiplies oaths of office, proves itself to have little consciousness of their awful sanction, manifests distrust of its subjects, and holds forth a snare to tempt ambitious and self-interested men to the commission of perjury. So was it with the Scottish prelatic parliament. The numerous oaths which they imposed shut out from places of public trust nearly all men of the highest worth, opposed no obstacle to the admission of the wicked, and became directly instrumental in the infliction of the most extensive and relentless persecution.

The act of indemnity, so long expected, came at last, but came in a character which sufficiently proved its paternity. In addition to a list of persons excepted from the benefit of this act, it had, in the form of an appended exception, what was in reality another act, empowering a committee to impose fines upon as many as they thought proper, and to whatsoever amount they pleased. A list of persons to be fined was accordingly made, including all who were known or suspected to be favourable to the Presbyterian Church. The avowed object of this list was, by means of these fines, to depress the Presbyterians and enrich the royalists and the favourers of Prelacy. The parliament terminated its sittings by passing an act, the effect of which was the immediate ejection of the ministers of Edinburgh, and of several other ministers in different parts of the country soon after, who held the laws of God in higher estimation than acts of parliament.

When the parliament rose, the privy council assumed the management of public affairs, and proceeded to enforce those arbitrary enactments in a congenial spirit. They published an act respecting diocesan meetings, commanding all ministers to repair to the meetings which the prelates were about to hold, to give their concurrence to them, and to refrain from holding any other ecclesiastical meetings on pain of the censures provided in such cases. These diocesan meetings were generally termed the Bishop's Courts; and notwithstanding the threatenings of the privy council and the prelates, very few of the ministers attended them. Indeed, they could not, without abandoning all their Presbyterian principles, and, in particular, that principle essentially Presbyterian, that all ecclesiastical jurisdiction is derived from Christ alone, whereas the jurisdiction of the prelates was avowedly derived from the king alone, so that to attend the diocesan meeting would have been to violate their allegiance to Christ.* The case was different during the semi-prelacy established by King James; for then the Presbyterian church courts had not been suppressed, but merely invaded, and the ministers held it even their duty to retain as much of their privileges as they could, to keep possession of their sacred judicatories, and to resist the invading prelates to the utmost. But now these judicatories had been wholly abolished, were attempted to be reconstructed on prelatic principles alone, and could not be so much as entered by a true Presbyterian, without abandoning all his own most sacred principles, and doing violence to his conscientious convictions.

But the wild career of Middleton was now near its close, although, like an eastern tornado, its last fierce burst of fury was the most destructive. There had, from the time of the king's restoration, been a constant rivalry between Middleton and Lauderdale, and each had been continually plotting to ruin the power of his rival. Lauderdale's situation near the person of the monarch gave him an advantage which Middleton attempted to counterbalance by his zeal in the destruction of the Presbyterian Church; and this had stimulated him to press forward his pernicious schemes with a degree of precipitation too impetuous to admit of taking a deliberate estimation of their possible consequences in case of failure or recoil. Having finished his tyrannical labours in the parliament and council, he began a tour through the west of Scotland, for the double purpose of enjoying the festive en-

* See Apologetical Relation, section viii. pp. 91-100.

tertainments given to him by the obsequious nobility, and of urging upon the Presbyterians the declaration recently passed by parliament. When he came to Glasgow, the archbishop, Fairfoul, laid before him the most grievous complaints, that none of the younger ministers within his diocese, entered since 1649, had attended his courts, or acknowledged his prelatic superiority; that he was exposed to the odium which attends that office in Scotland, but possessed nothing of its power; and that, unless some more effectual steps were taken, the prelatic office itself would sink into general contempt. Middleton requested him to state his plan, and he would immediately put it in execution. Fairfoul proposed that an act of council might be passed and proclaimed, peremptorily banishing all the ministers who had entered since the year 1649, from their houses, parishes, and respective presbyteries if they did not before the 1st day of November ensuing, procure presentations from the patrons, and present themselves to the prelates to receive collation and admission to their charges; assuring the commissioner, that there would not be ten in his diocese that would not rather sacrifice their principles than lose their stipends.* The result proved the folly of a prelate judging Presbyterian ministers by his own standard.

The council met at Glasgow on the 1st of October, and passed an act, known by the designation of "the Act of Glasgow," in exact conformity with the archbishop's suggestions. Burnet informs us, that the Duke of Hamilton, who was one of the council, told him, that "they were all so drunk that day that they were not capable of considering any thing that was laid before them, and would hear of nothing but the executing the law without any relenting or delay."† The Presbyterian ministers obeyed the law. They submitted to the very letter of its penalty. On the last Sabbath of October they preached and bade farewell to their deeply-attached congregations; and on that day, as Burnet states, above two hundred churches were at once shut up, and abandoned equally by pastors and by people. "I believe," says Kirkton, "there was never such a sad Sabbath in Scotland, as

* Wodrow, vol. i. p. 282. † Burnet's Own Times, vol. i. p. 154.

when the poor persecuted ministers took leave of their people."* In many instances the congregations could not repress their feelings, but wept aloud, till their lamentations resembled the wild wailings of a city taking by storm. This desolating blast fell first on the western counties, but it soon extended over the southern and midland parts of the kingdom, till it caused the ejection of nearly four hundred ministers in the course of a few months, involving a large portion of Scotland in sudden spiritual destitution.†

Great was the astonishment, and even consternation, felt by the prelatic party at the wide devastation caused by the Act of Glasgow. They had committed the grievous error which unprincipled men are so apt to do, of concluding what the Presbyterian ministers would do by what they would themselves have done in similar circumstances, and they saw their error when it was too late easily to repair it. They could not but perceive that the unpopularity of their proceedings would be very greatly increased by the firm and high-principled conduct of the ministers, submitting readily to the loss of all that human nature holds dear, rather than they would violate their sacred principles. The more wary of the prelates, and in particular Sharp himself, had intended to follow a very different method for the securing of their triumph over the Presbyterian Church. Their plan was gradually to depose the leading men of the Presbyterian ministers, not more rapidly, nor in greater numbers, than they would be able to supply with successors of tolerable education and character, so that in the course of a generation, an entire change might be effected by almost imperceptible degrees, and Prelacy quietly but firmly be established. This dangerous policy was at once rendered impossible by the Act of Glasgow; and that there is little reason to doubt, that while the most sagacious of the prelatists deplored the sudden precipitation of the struggle, the Presbyterians, amidst all their sufferings, rejoiced at the false movement of their enemies. Need we hesitate to say, that God confounded the councils of

* Kirkton, p. 150.

† Wodrow gives a list of ejected ministers, amounting to 412, but several of them had been deposed before the Act of Glasgow, so that the number cast out by that Act fell somewhat short of 400. See Wodrow vol. i. pp. 324-329.

Ahithophel, and caused the crafty to be taken in their own snares?

An attempt was made by the council to retrieve this false step, by an act passed at Edinburgh on the 23d of December, extending the term within which ministers might receive presentation and collation, to the 1st day of February 1663; but the penalties for non-compliance were not relaxed, and a fine of twenty shillings Scots was ordered to be exacted from all the people who did not attend their parish churches. As the testimony of an adversary is always held peculiarly valuable, we may here conclude our account of the proceedings of this year by extracting Bishop Burnet's statement of the consequences resulting from the Act of Glasgow.

"There was a sort of an invitation sent over the kingdom, like a hue-and-cry, to all persons to accept of benefices in the west. The livings were generally well endowed, and the parsonage-houses were well built, and in good repair. And this drew many very worthless persons thither, who had little learning, less piety, and no sort of discretion. The new incumbents who were put in the place of the ejected preachers, were generally very mean and despicable in all respects. They were the worst preachers I ever heard; they were ignorant to a reproach; and many of them were openly vicious. They were a disgrace to their orders and the sacred functions, and indeed were the dregs and refuse of the northern parts. Those of them who rose above contempt or scandal were men of such violent tempers, that they were as much hated as the others were despised.

"The former incumbents, who were for the most part Protesters, were a grave, solemn sort of people. Their spirits were eager, and their tempers sour; but they had an appearance that created respect. They were related to the chief families in the country either by blood or marriage, and had lived in so decent a manner that the gentry paid great respect to them. They used to visit their parishes much, and were so full of the Scriptures, and so ready at extempore prayer, that from that they grew to practise extempore sermons. They had brought the people to such a degree of knowledge, that cottagers and servants would have prayed extempore. By these means they had a comprehension of matters of religion greater than I have seen among people of that sort any where. As they (the ministers) lived in great familiarity with their people, and used to pray and to talk oft with them in private, so it can hardly be imagined to what a degree they were loved and reverenced by them."*

Let the candid reader look on these two pictures, drawn by the hand of a prelate from personal observation and knowledge, and say whether it was possible that the people of Scotland could regard with favour a system, the unconstitutional and tyrannical introduction of which drove to the wilds their own faithful, pious, and beloved ministers, and forced upon them the desecrating services of such an irreligious and immoral crew of the very lowest spawn of Prelacy. But these curates, as they were designated somewhat incorrectly, had obtained "presentations from patrons and collation from the bishops;" and these qualifications would, in the estimation of some people, cover any multitude of sins. Others, however, will be disposed to think, as the bereaved and oppressed people of Scotland did, that the very fact of patrons and prelates so readily concurring to thrust such men into churches, which their presence could only desecrate, furnished a very strong proof of the unchristian origin of both patronage and Prelacy. Will any sane man say, that that system is of divine origin which directly expels from the Church such men as Douglas, Traill, and Hutcheson of Edinburgh, Livingston of Ancrum, Blair of St. Andrews, Wylie of Kirkcudbright, Welch of Irongray, and Brown of Wamphray, and forces into it such men as even Burnet cannot write of without contempt? But we must proceed, though the heart sickens at the consciousness of the dreadful character of the narrative on which we are now more distinctly to enter. So strong, indeed, is our reluctance to dwell on scenes of almost unmingled horror,—so great is the repugnance which we feel to relate the bloody and inhuman brutalities perpetrated by Prelacy in Scotland,—that we purpose to sketch the outline of prelatic persecution as briefly, and with as little reference to its darker ter-

* Burnet's Own Times, vol. i. pp. 156-158.

rors, as may be possible, consistently with the historian's duty.

[1663.] The year 1663 began with great hardships to both the ejected ministers and the deprived people of Scotland. The ministers were compelled to leave their houses, the scenes of their ministry, the people whom they had been accustomed to instruct with such anxious and successful care in the knowledge of the way of salvation,—all that they held dear on earth, and much that had been to them both earnest and foretaste of heaven,—and to hasten away to other districts, chiefly to those north of the Tay, in the depth of a stern, inclement Scottish winter, because they would not bring upon their souls the guilt of perjury. The people were at once deprived of the highly-valued labours of their beloved pastors, at the very time when the course of religious instruction to which they had been accustomed was producing its most beneficial effects, and when they were become most able to appreciate truly the worth of an evangelical ministry. It soon became a question of deep moment, whether they could conscientiously attend the churches where the prelatic curates preached, but not long a question of difficult solution. Great numbers of the people were beyond all comparison better acquainted with their Bibles than the curates were; and it would be insulting to the memory of the Scottish Covenanters to compare them, in point of moral character, with the dissolute and licentious creatures of the prelates. To attend the ministry of such persons was absolutely impossible for men who had any feeling of what was due to the hallowed day of God, and to the sacred nature of religious ordinances; nay, even their regard to the welfare of their own souls forbade them to listen to men whose whole conduct was such as to render their interference with holy things a hideous profanation. The people therefore refused to attend the ministry of the curates, whom they could not look upon without equal disgust and indignation.

It will be remembered, that the Glasgow Act included directly only those ministers who had entered into their charges since 1649. But there were considerable numbers of more aged ministers, who had entered previous to that year, and who were accordingly left for a time in the possession of their parishes. To the churches of these men the people flocked from great distances when their own ministers were cast out, and thus continued for a time to obtain instruction to which they could listen without violation to their consciences. Some of the ejected ministers also were allowed to reside in their parishes, though not in the manses or parsonages; and the people collected together in great numbers at those hours in which they were accustomed to have family worship, that they might enjoy the private expositions and prayers of their beloved pastors. To such an extent did this proceed, that often no room could be obtained large enough to contain the assembled worshippers, who were constrained, both minister and people, to betake themselves to the open air, there to adore the God who made heaven and earth. This was the origin of what were termed conventicles and field-meetings in Scotland, against which, a few years afterwards, the rage of the persecutors burned so fiercely. Even at the very beginning of this method of seeking the benefit of a gospel ministry, the people were exposed to abusive treatment. The act of 23d December had imposed a fine upon those who did not attend their own parish churches; and the rude soldiery, instigated by the curates, began the practice of intercepting people on their way to the churches of the old and unexpelled ministers, and exacting the fine specified in the proclamation. Other occasions of persecution also began to be common. In several instances, the people, especially the females, opposed the entrance of curates forcibly, till their resistance was overcome by military power. This the wiser part of the Covenanters deplored, as calculated to give some colour of justice to the harsh retaliation inflicted by the armed supporters of the prelatic intruders; but the prelatists were not slow in availing themselves of every opportunity of inflicting vengeance upon their opponents.

Allusion has already been made to the political rivalry between Middleton and Lauderdale, and to the effect which it had in stimulating the former to press forward the establishment of Prelacy upon the ruins of the Presbyterian Church, as the best method, in his opinion, of securing the favour of the king. His majesty, however, saw clearly that the Glasgow Act was an impolitic measure, more likely to injure the cause of Prelacy than to promote it; and, though well enough satisfied with Middleton's zeal, was by no means disposed to hazard the failure of his schemes for any regard to the fortunes of his most zealous adherent. Lauderdale availed himself of this opportunity to assail his rival, and prepared for a final effort to overthrow him. The avarice of Middleton supplied what was wanting for his ruin. The king thought proper to send to the Scottish council a letter suspending the payment of the fines imposed on non-conformists; but Middleton, eager to get hold of the money, prevented the proclamation of his majesty's letter postponing the term of payment. This Lauderdale represented as a daring violation of the royal prerogative; and the king, offended more with this tampering with his authority, than with all the despotic proceedings of Middleton against the liberties of the people, deprived him of that power which he had so greatly abused, and sent him in a kind of honourable banishment to Tangier, where he soon afterwards died in consequence of a fall.*

Lauderdale became now the chief manager of Scottish affairs; but this brought no mitigation to the sufferings of the Presbyterians. He had, indeed, been himself at one time not only a Covenanter, but even one of the commissioners from the General Assembly to the Westminster Assembly of Divines; and at the Restoration he at first advocated the establishment of the Presbyterian Church as that of the three kingdoms.† Perceiving the king's rooted aversion to the Presbyterian Church, Lauderdale, with the supple pliancy of a courtier, abandoned his cause, and, with the spirit of a renegade, became the deadly persecutor of the religion from which he had apostatized. And now, when elevated to the chief power in Scotland, he deemed it expedient to remove any lingering suspicion which might still attach to him on account of his former conduct, by taking prompt and effectual measures for the suppression of the Church which he had most solemnly vowed to defend.

A parliament was held in Edinburgh, on the 18th of June, at which Lauderdale was present, to commence his career of power, assisted by the Earl of Rothes, with whom he was in close political connection. The first act of the new administration was one which paralyzed the parliament, by restoring the old method of electing the Lords of the Articles. The second was intituled, an "Act against Separation and Disobedience to Ecclesiastical Authority." Its object was, to prevent people from leaving the curates and following the ejected ministers; and to effect that purpose, it declares of the latter, "that their daring to preach, in contempt of the law," is sedition, and they are subjected to punishment as seditious persons; while all men are enjoined to attend "such ministers as by public authority are or shall be admitted to their parishes," those who absent themselves being liable to be fined, each nobleman, gentleman, and heritor, the fourth part of a year's rental, and each tenant the same proportion of his moveable property, deducting the payment of the rent due to his landlord: and each burgess to lose the liberty of trading within burgh towns, and the fourth part of his moveable property. This act was commonly termed "The Bishop's drag-net," and formed the foundation of a great part of the oppressive exactions afterwards levied throughout the kingdom. The privy council were directed to be careful to see this act put in due execution, by inflicting not only the specified censures and penalties, but also such other corporeal punishments as they should think fit,—a clause of dark import, destined ere long to be interpreted and enforced with terrific cruelty.

Another act was passed, enforcing the signing of the declaration condemnatory of the Covenants, without which no person was eligible to places of public trust; to which was now added, that those who should refuse to sign it should "forfeit all the privileges of merchandising and trading." From this it seems to have been the dire policy of Lauderdale and the prelates, to render it impossible for any man even to live in the kingdom without

* Burnet's Own Times, vol. i. pp. 200-222.

† It was at that time that the King uttered the well-known expression, "Presbytery is not a religion for a gentleman."

submitting to Prelacy. The last act of any importance passed by this servile parliament was one for establishing a national synod, modelled after the plan of the English convocation, but still more abortive, inasmuch as it was never once held, the prelates finding that their work could be more expeditiously and effectually done by the privy council itself, and by the Court of High Commission, which was soon afterwards revived. Lauderdale finished this parliament by the vain parade of an act, offering to his majesty an army of twenty-two thousand infantry and two thousand cavalry, if necessary, to aid in the preservation of Christendom against the Turks; unless, indeed, the act had a private interpretation, and was designed to show the king that an army could be raised for him in Scotland, in case his English subjects should grow refractory.

During the sitting of parliament, the privy council thought proper to meet and pass some acts manifestly beyond their powers, especially while the superior legislative body was assembled. The two archbishops had been by this time made members of the privy council, and to this may be fairly ascribed both its encroachment upon parliamentary privileges, and the despotism of its acts. The first, which was proclaimed on the 13th of August, is known as "The Mile Act." It commands all the ministers included within the Act of Glasgow "to remove themselves and their families, within twenty days, out of the parishes where they were incumbents, and not to reside within twenty miles of the same, nor within six miles of Edinburgh or any cathedral church, nor within three miles of any burgh royal within the kingdom," under the penalties of the laws against movers of sedition. Every person must see that it was physically impossible to comply with the terms of this act, coupled with a former one which prohibited any two of the ejected ministers from residing within the boundaries of the same parish. Four hundred spots such as the act describes could not have been found within the kingdom, though all its lonely wilds had been selected with geographical exactness. But it requires no comment to point out the blundering cruelty of these absurd tyrants. Another act of council was passed on the 7th of October, which rendered the despotic series nearly complete. Its first part was directed against the Presbyterian ministers who had fled from Ireland to escape the prelatic persecution there, rendering them liable to the penalties of sedition if they dared to reside or preach in Scotland: its second part directed the curates to read out from the pulpit lists of such people in their parishes as absented themselves from public worship in these parishes, which intimation should be sufficient ground for proceeding against such persons if they did not instantly submit; and not only magistrates, but "officers of the standing forces," are required to give their assistance to ministers in the discharge of their office, to put the law in execution, and to enforce the penalties expressed in the acts of parliament and council.* The effect of this was, to authorise the curates to act as spies and informers against their parishioners, and the army to act as executioners of the law almost on their own responsibility,—functions which both these classes of persons soon proved themselves equally ready to perform with the most ruthless cruelty.

The only public instance of actual martyrdom which occurred this year was that of Warriston. He had escaped from the hands of his enemies about two years before, and had fled to the continent for safety. While he was at Hamburg, he had an attack of sickness, and was attended by Dr. Bates, who had been one of the king's physicians, and was by him subjected to such improper medical treatment as to deprive him almost entirely of the use of his faculties.† His memory departed to such a degree that he could not remember what he had said or done a quarter of an hour before. In this deplorable condition, the wreck of his former self, he was basely given up by the French monarch to an emissary of Charles, brought to Edinburgh, tried, and condemned to death. The pitiable spectacle of the helpless old man, reduced to premature imbecility by the treacherous conduct of the royal physician, failed to excite the compassion of his persecutors; nay, Sharp and the other prelates triumphed in the weak and

* Wodrow, vol. i. pp. 341 343.

† Apologetical Relation, pref.

wavering accents of him whose bold and fervid eloquence had often formerly held Assemblies and parliaments mute in silent admiration. But God did not forsake his aged servant when compassed round with his exulting and merciless enemies. The night before his execution he was visited with that deep, calm, refreshing sleep, which the Father of mercies "gives to his beloved," and awoke in the morning marvellously restored. His memory returned, and all his faculties were remarkably revived, while his soul was filled with that "peace of God which passeth all understanding." He prepared a speech, which he read with clear and audible voice on the scaffold, where also he prayed aloud with such fervour, liberty, and power, as astonished every auditor. His last accents were those of prayer and praise; and almost without a struggle he expired, with his clasped hands held up to heaven in the attitude of adoration.*

The more general sufferings of the Church this year consisted in the expulsion of a great number of the best ministers from their parishes, the intrusion of the curates, and the grief which overwhelmed the bereaved people. At Kirkcudbright and Irongray the women opposed the entrance of the curates in a very determined manner, which drew down, not only upon themselves, but upon the whole parishes, and even districts of country which they inhabited, the severe displeasure of the council and the prelates, and gave occasion to the exaction of very heavy fines from persons suspected of being attached to the Presbyterian Church. The two deadly elements recently introduced by the prelates began to do their work. The curates began to prosecute their congenial labour of acting as spies and informers, conveying private information to the ruling powers against every man whom they knew or suspected to be opposed to their base ministry and baser characters, keeping a list of all such persons, and delating them from time to time, as their malicious dispositions prompted them. The army also began to be extensively employed in the levying of fines, in which they were cheered on by the curates with inhuman eagerness. Orders had been given by the privy council to Sir James Turner to lead a body of troops to the west and south of Scotland, to levy fines and compel submission to the prelates. Sir James was a fit instrument for their purposes. He was a military adventurer, selfish, cruel, and unprincipled, ready to sell his sword to whatever party would pay the highest price for it, and regarding no law, human or divine, except the orders of his superior in command, as he has himself distinctly stated. This mercenary soldier received orders to follow the directions of the curates, and to pillage the defenceless country people to the heart's content of their oppressors. In this Turner and his "lambs" rejoiced as a bloodless campaign, where they might without danger indulge all their vicious propensities, as if in an enemy's country, and receive the thanks of the council for their service. When sent to any refractory Presbyterian to levy the imposed fine, if it was not instantly paid, they took free quarters in his house, revelled in riot and drunkenness, destroyed much more than the amount demanded, and inflicted the most wanton insults and barbarous outrages on the unoffending people, without distinction of age or sex, or, rather, with such distinctions as age and sex rendered possible. One of the most common of the practices of these plunderers was, to go to some public-house in the vicinity of a church where a Presbyterian minister not yet ejected preached, and after drinking till nearly the time when public worship terminated, then to hasten to the church, place themselves at the church-door, and demand of every person upon oath, as they came out, whether they belonged to that parish. If they could not say they did, the fine was immediately exacted, and when money could not be obtained, they seized upon their Bibles, hats, bonnets, plaids, and any part of their clothing which could easily be carried away and sold; returning from the violated house of prayer laden with booty, as from a sacked and plundered city.

[1664.] The beginning of the year 1664 was signalized by the re-erection of the Court of High Commission. Sharp, it appears, was not satisfied with the privy council, which, in his opinion, did not display sufficient zeal and activity in the suppression of the Presbyterians. In

* Naphtali, pp. 177-182.

particular, he entertained suspicions of the Earl of Glencairn, the chancellor, regarding his influence as tending to retard and mitigate the course of persecution. He therefore hastened to London, and prevailed upon the king to grant a commission for the re-erection of that dreadful court, to which should be intrusted the execution of all laws concerning ecclesiastical matters. This commission was obtained on the 16th of January 1664, and was, if possible, more arbitrary in its character than its predecessor had been. Its basis was the essence of despotism. "His majesty, by virtue of his royal prerogative in all causes, and over all persons, as well ecclesiastical as civil, has given and granted," &c. In this commission there are nine prelates and thirty-five laymen; the quorum is five, of which one must be a prelate. They were empowered to summon before them and punish all the deposed ministers who presumed to preach, all attenders of conventicles, all who kept meetings at fasts and the sacrament of the Lord's Supper, and all who write, speak, preach, or print against Prelacy. They were empowered to inflict censures of suspension and deposition; to levy fines and imprison; to employ magistrates and military force for the apprehension of their victims; and finally, "to do and execute what they shall find necessary and convenient for his majesty's service in the premises."* Surely the heart of Sharp must have leapt for joy when placed at the head of this court of absolute despotism. This was certainly prelacy restored to its full glory, under the dignified auspices of a perjured apostate.

The proceedings of the Court of High Commission were such as were to be expected from its spirit and construction. It at once assumed the power of both the swords, and acted equally as an ecclesiastical and as a civil court. Holding the most intimate intercourse with the curates, who formed an organized espionage co-extensive with the nation, the Court of High Commission obtained information respecting every sincere Presbyterian throughout the kingdom, summoned every one whom it was their pleasure to oppress, and, without the formalities of citing witnesses and hearing evidence, either passed sentence upon the bare accusation, or required the oath of supremacy to be taken, and, upon its being refused, inflicted whatever sentence they thought proper, short of death. Some were reduced to utter poverty by fines; some were imprisoned till they contracted fatal diseases; some were banished to the remotest and most unhealthy and inhospitable parts of the kingdom; and some were actually sold for slaves.* Of the great numbers summoned to appear before this terrible court of inquisition, not one is recorded to have escaped without suffering punishment, and often to an extreme degree of severity.

One addition was made to the persecuting acts already in force against the ejected ministers, to the effect that no person should give charitable relief to them in their absolute starvation, on the pain of being regarded as disaffected, and movers of sedition. This appears to have been done at the instigation of Alexander Burnet, archbishop of Glasgow, who said that the only method to be taken with the fanatics, as he was pleased to call them, was to starve them out.† About the same time a party of soldiers were sent to the parish of Dreghorn, to quarter upon the people, and compel them, by direct force, to attend the preaching of the curate, who had been thrust into the parish after the expulsion of its former minister. This seems the climax of intrusion; first, to force an unworthy creature into a parish contrary to the strongly-expressed dissent of the congregation, and then, when they abstained from attending his profanation of the ministry, to send a band of armed men to drive them like a flock of sheep to the place, not of worship, but of desecration.

[1665.] The persecution of the Presbyterians continued during the year 1665 with unabated rigour; but the persecuting system was now so completely matured, that little addition could be made to it. The prelates continued to let loose the soldiery upon the country, and to encourage them to those excesses in outrage and plunder to which they were, of their own accord, sufficiently prone. The death of the Earl of Glencairn, in the preceding year, gave Sharp hopes of obtaining the chancellorship; but this was

* Wodrow, vol i. pp. 384-386.

* Wodrow, vol. i. p. 390. † Kirkton, p. 218.

frustrated, as the Scottish nobility began to be disgusted with the arrogance of that aspiring arch-prelate. The Earl of Rothes was intrusted with the general management of Scottish affairs, under the control of Lauderdale; and so far as Rothes was personally concerned, the persecution was somewhat relaxed; but in the Court of High Commission, and in the privy council, the prelates continued to exercise the chief sway. Some dim apprehensions appear to have been entertained, that the continued course of prelatic tyranny might at last provoke the country to rise into resistance; for, during the summer of this year, Sir James Turner was empowered to search the houses of the people for arms, and carry them forcibly away. The act of fines was also renewed, that this method of wearing out the Presbyterians might still be an available weapon in the hands of the prelates. On the 7th of December, a proclamation was issued by the council "against conventicles." This proclamation was of the same general import as those which have already been specified, prohibiting the preaching, or even private meetings for worship, of the ejected ministers; only that it went considerably beyond them in the power which it gave of inflicting punishment, not only to the privy council, but to all such as had or should have his majesty's commission to that effect. This was speedily interpreted to imply, that even a private soldier, because he acted under the royal authority, might, at his own discretion, seize, fine, drag to prison, or punish, "as he should think fit," any person who either held a conventicle, that is, worshipped God, others being present and joining in worship, attended one, or allowed one to be held in his house. The fearful use soon made of this proclamation we shall have occasion to relate.

[1666.] The year 1666 is sadly memorable in the annals of the Church of Scotland. During the space of the six preceding years, Prelacy had been speeding on in its career of oppressive cruelty, trampling under foot the dearest rights and privileges, civil and sacred, of the Presbyterian people. It seemed as if there was a positive determination to drive the country beyond all possible endurance, that they might have the opportunity of exterminating the population, if they could not otherwise extirpate Presbytery. Early in the spring, Sir James Turner was again sent to devastate the south and west of Scotland. Nithsdale and Galloway were the chief scenes of his wasting visitations on this occasion; and his oppressive conduct far outwent any of his previous campaigns. The soldiers availed themselves of the extension of their powers which the late act against conventicles seemed intended to give, and exacted fines at their pleasure from each and all. Gentlemen were made answerable for their wives, children, servants, and tenantry; and tenants were fined if their landlords were held to be disaffected. Like a swarm of eastern locusts, the soldiery literally devoured the country, wasting what provisions they could not use, and reducing the miserable inhabitants to utter starvation. If any person dared to complain, the only answers were neglect or increased abuse. In the course of a few weeks the sum of fifty thousand pounds Scots was raised in the west; and the exactions in Galloway were still more oppressive, and the presence of the plunderers of longer continuation.*

Seven months had this excessive barbarity continued, not only with unabated vigour, but even increasing in its severity in proportion as the exhausted state of the country rendered it more difficult to levy fines from a people already reduced nearly to starvation; when one act of shocking brutality put an end to the patient endurance of intolerable wrongs, and compelled the country to rise in the attitude of self-defence. On the 13th of November, while four countrymen, who had been wandering in concealment from the devastators, were taking some refreshment in the village of Dalry, in Upper Galloway, information was brought to them that three or four soldiers were inflicting the most barbarous abuse upon a poor old man, whom they had seized in order to compel him to pay the ruinous fines which they demanded. They hastened to the spot, and found the aged victim lying on the ground bound hand and foot, and the soldiers proceeding to strip him naked, in order to execute their hideous threat of stretching him upon a red-

* Wodrow, vol. ii. p. 8, Naphtali, pp. 125 126, 235

hot gridiron. The voice of outraged humanity was louder than the cold whisper of cowardly prudence, and they interposed to rescue the venerable sufferer. The soldiers turned upon them with drawn swords, so that they were compelled to fight in their own defence. A brief struggle ensued, in which one of the soldiers was wounded; upon which his comrades yielded and were disarmed.*

The reflection of a few moments showed the countrymen in what imminent peril they had placed their lives by this unpremeditated act of humanity. They knew well that their deed would be designated rebellion, and that they need not hope for mercy, should they be seized. The people of the village and neighbourhood were equally well aware that they would be counted participators in the crime because they had not supported the soldiers. Tamely to yield, would, they knew, be death; to rise generally in self-defence might secure more favourable terms, and, if unsuccessful, could but be death. They resolved, therefore, to adopt the more manly and rational alternative of self-defence; and early next morning surprised a party of about a dozen soldiers, who were quartered in the vicinity, before they were aware of the seizure of their comrades. One soldier, who would not yield, was killed in the struggle; the rest submitted, and were disarmed and made prisoners. Several of the neighbouring gentlemen now joined the insurgents, and they marched hastily to Dumfries, where Sir James Turner was, made him prisoner, and disarmed all the troops who where with him. They then proceeded in a body to the market-place, and publicly avowing that their object was self-defence alone, they drank his majesty's health, and prosperity to his government, to manifest their unshaken loyalty. And in proof of their humanity, it must be recorded, that notwithstanding the intense and protracted oppression to which they had been subjected, no violence was offered even to Turner, who had been the chief agent of the persecution. One Gray, an Edinburgh merchant who happened to be in Dumfries, and joined them there, proposed the putting Sir James to death; but this was withstood by Neilson of Corsack, whose property had been almost utterly ruined by the soldiery.

* Kirkton, p. 230; Wodrow, vol. ii. p. 17.

Having received a small addition to their numbers at Dumfries, they resolved to march towards Ayrshire, in order to form a junction with the grieviously oppressed inhabitants of that district, on whose sympathy and support they confidently calculated. They accordingly marched forward in that direction, and meeting with Colonel Wallace, put themselves under his command. But they were miserably disappointed in their expectations. The spirit of the west country seemed to be completely broken; and instead of rallying round the standard of religious liberty, they remained quietly in their homes, waiting the issue, willing to avail themselves of freedom, should it be gained, but unwilling to expose themselves to danger in the attempt to snap asunder the chains of slavery. The small band of insurgents moved from place to place, according to their expectations of being joined by their countrymen, but everywhere experienced the same discouragement. It was at length seriously debated, whether they ought not to separate, and seek comparative safety in a private return to their own abodes; for the rising had been so sudden and unexpected, that there existed no preconcerted understanding among the sufferers in the different parts of the country; and very many considered the enterprise as far too important to be undertaken without the previous arrangements which would secure a wide-spread simultaneous movement. To this it may be added, that a number of leading gentlemen in the west had a short time before been seized on suspicion, by an order of the council.

In the meantime the alarm of the prelates was great. The Earl of Rothes had gone to London a day or two before the commencement of the insurrection; and Sharp himself had, in consequence, become the head of the privy council. Immediately upon the intelligence reaching Edinburgh, the council met, despatched the tidings to the king, and gave orders to raise an army for the suppression of this dreadful rebellion and "horrid conspiracy," as they termed it in their terror. Dalziel of Binns was appointed to the command of the army; and all noblemen, gentlemen, and magistrates were urgently ordered to put the country in a state of defence. Edinburgh assumed the appearance of a beseiged city; Glasgow the same; the ferries of the Forth were secured; and Stirling bridge barricaded so as to resist the approach of an army. A guilty conscience sounds a loud alarm, and the prelates appear to have believed that the whole kingdom was about to rise in arms, and inflict that vengeance which their own hearts told them that they so fully deserved. So prompt and extensive were their defensive measures, that long before the insurgents had obtained any considerable accession to their strength, Dalziel's army had mustered at Glasgow in far more than sufficient force both to crush them and to overawe the western counties.

The small and unsupported band of Presbyterian sufferers, learning that the army was approaching, and receiving little assistance from their friends, drew towards the hilly part of the country, marching from Cumnock by Muirkirk to Douglas, where they halted, and consulted whether they should there disperse or continue in arms. The result of their deliberations was a firm determination to persevere, and either to secure their religious liberties, or to fall in their defence. They could not, they said, expect a clearer warrant to rise in self-defence than they at present had, when every thing dear to them as men and Christians was at stake. They were persuaded that the hand of Providence was in the matter; that there was a distinct call of sacred duty for them to go forward; and whether it might be God's pleasure to assert His own cause by their means at that time, by granting them victory and deliverance, though but an handful, or to employ them merely as suffering witnesses for the truth, still it seemed to be their duty to persevere, till they should have as clear a warning to desist as they already had to begin the enterprise. "We will follow on," said these heroic Christian soldiers, "till God shall do his service by us; and though we should all die at the end of it, we think the giving of a testimony enough for all."*

They then marched to Lanark, where they halted till they renewed the Covenant, and prepared and published a declaration setting forth the cause of their appearing in arms, and vindicating themselves against the charge of rebellion. By this time Dalziel was close at hand, and they had no choice but to give him battle, or make a rapid march on Edinburgh. In the hope of being joined by friends as they advanced, they resolved still to shun an engagement, and continue their forward movement. After a dreadfully fatiguing march through the pathless moors between Lanark and Bathgate, they arrived at the latter place, late at night, and when they arrived, finding no shelter, were compelled to continue their exhausting march. When morning dawned, it was found that the half of their little army had melted away, worn out by excessive fatigue, and their spirits exhausted by this destructive march of a day and night, drenched with heavy rains, and without food, shelter, or repose. Next day they continued their march to Collington, about three miles from Edinburgh; but there they learned that no assistance was to be expected from that town, nor from their friends in the east country. A messenger came to them there, sent by the Duke of Hamilton, to persuade them to lay down their arms, in the hope of an indemnity which the duke promised to endeavour to procure. But as no mention was made of redressing their grievances, they refused to submit to such terms. Again the former messenger, the laird of Blackwood, returned, and offered Dalziel's word of honor for a cessation of arms for a day, till a letter might be sent to the privy council, to ascertain what answer could be given to their demands. There is reason to believe, that this cessation of arms was offered by Dalziel as a stratagem, to keep them in suspense, till he should be ready to assail them; and no answer was returned by the council to their demands, the object being to keep them in suspense.

Colonel Wallace seems to have suspected the design of his antagonists, and therefore began to retreat, taking the direction most likely to enable him to retire in safety. He moved towards higher grounds, less accessible to cavalry round-

* Wallace's Narrative, in M'Crie's Lives of Veitch and Brysson, p. 402.

ing the shoulder of the Pentland Hills, intending to retreat by Biggar, along the skirts of the mountain range. Towards evening, on the 28th of November, he halted on the side of a ridge called Rullion Green, to call in the stragglers and to refresh the men. Scarcely had he taken up this position when the van of Dalziel's army appeared, which had advanced through a pass farther westward, with the evident design of cutting off the retreat of the Covenanters. Wallace's army did not exceed nine hundred, while Dalziel's was at least thrice as numerous. But as Wallace had taken up a strong position, his antagonist hesitated some time before proceeding to the attack. At length a party of the royal cavalry advanced to charge the Covenanters, who detached an equal number to meet them. A sharp encounter took place on the level ground between the armies till the royalists recoiled and fled. Again did they assail the Covenanters, and again were beaten back to their main army. A third charge proved equally unsuccessful. But by these successive encounters the Covenanters had been drawn from their position, nearer to the plain; and Dalziel now put his whole force in motion to assail them. Wallace hesitated a moment whether to resume his position and act on the defensive, till night should terminate the conflict; but, aware that the next morning would find his own force diminished, and that of his enemy increased, while, even if defeated, the nature of the ground, and the fading light, would enable him to retreat with little loss, he resolved to meet the shock. While Dalziel was advancing, the Covenanters spent the grim battle-pause in prayer, and then stood ready for the final struggle. Once more did they beat back their first assailants; but while their left wing and main body were pressing victoriously forward, their right was defeated, and Dalziel, charging with an overwhelming force on their unprotected flank, threw them into inextricable confusion, and pursuing his advantage, scattered their broken ranks, and drove them precipitately from this well-fought field.*

The pursuit was not continued long, for night speedily closed in, casting its favouring shades over the wearied and broken Covenanters. A considerable part of Dalziel's cavalry was composed of gentlemen, who were not eager to shed unnecessarily the blood of their persecuted and unfortunate but brave countrymen. About fifty were killed in the battle, and as many taken in the pursuit. The soldiers, after the conflict, stripped the dead and dying, and left their naked bodies exposed to the chill severity of a November night, freezing their blood before life was quite extinct. Next day the prisoners were dragged to Edinburgh, the army entering the town in triumph, as if they had achieved a glorious victory over fierce invaders, the citizens gazing on the hapless victims through tears of unavailing pity. They were cast into prison till the privy council should determine what punishment should be inflicted. Thus was suppressed that unpremeditated and ill-supported insurrection, commonly termed the Rising of Pentland, taking its designation from the place where the battle was fought.

And now began a scene of horrors, which may not be altogether passed over, and yet which sickens the heart too much to permit us to dwell on its dreadful details. The cowardly terror of the prelates had been extreme, and now their thirst of vengeance could not be satisfied. Rothes was still in London; consequently, till his return, Sharp retained the presidency of the council, and all its acts were issued in his name. First, the lord treasurer was ordered to secure the property of all who had been at Pentland, which was equivalent to an act of general confiscation of the greater part of Galloway and Ayrshire. Next, General Dalziel was commanded to "search for and apprehend all persons who had been in arms with the rebels, or were suspected, or who had given shelter or assistance to them:" and was empowered to quarter upon their lands with his forces. Soon afterwards a proclamation was issued, forbidding all subjects to correspond with or conceal the persons of a great number of gentlemen, ministers, and elders, mentioned by name, or, "any others concerned in the late rebellion;" and commanding them to pursue, seize, and deliver them up to justice, on pain of being regarded as equally criminal; and the prelatic cu-

* Wallace's Narrative, pp. 415-419.

rates were particularly enjoined to furnish lists of all suspended persons,—an employment worthy of such men, and in which they engaged with great alacrity and zeal.

The trial of the prisoners was then begun,—a trial in which condemnation had been predetermined before evidence was sought. Eleven of them were brought before the Court of Justiciary; and, after a brief form of trial, were condemned to be hanged, and their heads and right hands cut off and disposed of as the council might see fit. One of them died of his wounds before the day of execution: the other ten were hanged on one gibbet on the 7th of December. Their heads were fixed up at Kirkcudbright, Kilmarnock, and Hamilton, and their right hands at Lanark, because they had sworn the Covenant there. The joint testimony and dying speches of these martyrs for Christ's crown and covenant are recorded in Naphtali, and prove convincingly that it was indeed for the cause of religion that their blood was shed.* Other five were tried without the aid of counsel, and put to the same death on the 14th of December.

The death of John Neilson of Corsack demands more particular mention. He was a gentleman of considerable property in Galloway, of superior talents, and of unblemished character. But in this last particular consisted his unpardonable crime. He was too much of a Christian for the curates, and consequently he was included in their list, and exposed to the ruinous exactions of Sir James Turner and his brutal soldiery. When the people of Galloway rose in self-defence, he joined them; and, notwithstanding the cruel treatment whieh he and his family had received from Turner, Mr. Neilson argued strenuously and successfully against the proposal of some to put the oppressor to death. As the prelates could not conceive that the persecuted Presbyterians would have dared to rise in self-defence unless there had been a widely extended conspiracy, they determined to extort a confession of the nature and extent of this plot from such of the prisoners as were certain to be acquainted with it if it existed. For this reason they resolved to put Neilson to the torture of the *boot.* In vain did they crush his leg in this fearful engine of torture; shrieking nature attested his agony, but his soul was clear of the guilt wherewith he was charged, and he would not blacken it by making a false acknowledgment of a crime of which he was innocent. When the persecutors found that they could extort nothing from him but groans and anguish, they condemned him to suffer, along with his guiltless friends, the shorter pangs of death.*

Hugh M'Kail was the next victim of torture. He was a young preacher, learned, eloquent, and eminently pious. He had been but a short while with the insurgents, and had left them before the day of the battle, unable to endure the fatigue to which they were exposed; but he had, on one occasion, when preaching, and having cause to speak of the sufferings of the Church in all ages, said, that it had been persecuted by a Pharaoh on the throne, a Haman in the State, and a Judas in the Church; and though he made no application of this statement, it had reached the ears of Sharp, was thought himself alluded to under the character of Judas. For this he would have been laid hold of at the time, had he not gone abroad, and escaped for a little the prelate's rage. But he was now in the hands of his enemy, and was to suffer the dire effects of implacable revenge.

When he was brought before the council, he was interrogated respecting the leaders of the insurrection, and what correspondence they had, either at home or abroad. He declared himself utterly unacquainted with any such correspondence; and frankly stated how far he had taken part in their proceedings. The instrument of torture was then laid before him, and he was informed that, if he did not confess, it should be applied next day. On the following day, he was again brought before the council, and again ordered to confess, on the pain of immediate torture. He declared solemnly that he had no more to confess. The executioner then placed his leg in the horrid instrument, applied the wedge, and proceeded to his hideous task. When one heavy blow had driven in the wedge, and crushed the limb severely, he was again urged to confess, but in vain. Blow after blow succedeed, at consider

* Naphtali, pp. 182-192.

* Wodrow, vol. ii., p. 53.

able intervals, protracting the terrible agony; but still, with true Christian fortitude, the heroic martyr possessed his soul in patience. Seven or eight successive blows had crushed the flesh and sinews to the very bone, when he protested solemnly in the sight of God, that he could say no more, though all the joints of his body were in as great torture as that poor leg. Yet thrice more the wedge was driven in, till the bone itself was shattered by its iron compression, and a heavy swoon relieved him from longer consciousness of the mortal agony. He was carried back to prison; and soon afterwards condemned to death.

Between the day of his condemnation and that of his death, his mind was in a continual state of holy joy and heavenly peace. When brought to the place of execution, he was more than serene; he was filled with unutterable transport. His last speech breathed the very spirit of the Christian martyr's triumph: its conclusion is inexpressibly sublime. "And now I leave off to speak any more to creatures, and turn my speech to thee, O Lord. And now I begin my intercourse with God, which shall never be broken off. Farewell, father and mother, friends and relations; farewell, the world and all delights; farewell, meat and drink; farewell, sun, moon, and stars. Welcome, God and Father; welcome, sweet Jesus, the Mediator of the New Covenant; welcome, blessed Spirit of grace, and God of all consolation; welcome, glory; welcome, eternal life; welcome, death. O Lord, into thy hands I commit my spirit; for thou hast redeemed my soul, Lord God of truth."*

Thus passed from earth, on the 22d of December 1666, one of the brightest, purest, and most sanctified spirits that ever animated a mere human form; a victim to prelatic tyranny, and a rejoicing martyr for Christ's sole kingly dominion over his Church, and for that sacred Covenant in which the Church of Scotland had vowed allegiance to her Divine and only Head and King. Till the records of time shall have melted into those of eternity, the name of that young Christian martyr will be held in most affectionate remembrance and fervent admiration by every true Scottish Presbyterian, and will be regarded by the Church of Scotland as one of the fairest jewels that ever she was honoured to add to the conquering Redeemer's crown of glory.

It is almost too disgraceful to human nature to record, that before the death of M'Kail, and after several executions had taken place, a letter came from the king, prohibiting any more lives from being taken; but Sharp and Burnet suppressed this letter till after the death of M'Kail, so that they may justly be charged with the cold, deliberate murder of that guiltless youth, and of violating the most sacred prerogative of the crown, that they might perpetrate the monstrous deed.* This barbarous conduct of Sharp, which was generally known at the time, tended greatly to increase the detestation in which he and his coadjutors were held by the people. Indeed, the sufferings of the unfortunate victims who were put to death after the Pentland insurrection, and especially their dying speeches, produced a deep impression throughout the whole of Scotland. It was easy to brand the insurrection with the name of rebellion, and to assert that the victims suffered on account of their having been guilty of treason; but the conduct of the men themselves on the scaffold, the speeches they uttered there, and the written testimonies they left behind them, wrought conviction in the hearts of their sympathizing countrymen, and awoke a response which acts of privy council could no more check than they could stem the rising tide. Men began to ask, whether that could be a bad cause for which such martyrs suffered so heroically; and whether that could be a good cause which resorted to such methods to secure its triumph? And many who had disliked and opposed the west country Whigs, as they were sometimes termed, began to entertain a still stronger dislike to the prelates, who had displayed such a relentless and persecuting spirit, and such utter disregard of all liberty, civil and religious. It is not, we trust, necessary to vindicate the Pentland insurrection now; for the very same principles which urged these martyrs of civil and religious liberty to take up arms in their own defence,

* Naphtali, pp. 218-234.

* Wodrow, vol. ii, p. 38; Kirkton, p. 255; Memoirs of Veitch, p 37; Burnet's Own Times, vol. i. p. 237.

were afterwards espoused by the whole empire at the Revolution, and cannot now be gainsaid by any man who is not in his heart a tyrant or a slave.

[1667.] Soon after the privy council had glutted their vengeance with the public execution of a considerable number of persons both at Edinburgh and in different parts of the country, the army was sent to the disaffected districts, under the command of General Dalziel, with full powers to him to gratify his savage disposition by inflicting whatsoever barbarities he pleased upon the unoffending people. It was not necessary for him to go through the tardy process of a trial; the previous acts of council had given to persons bearing his majesty's commission, powers which a little straining would make amply sufficient for all tyrannical purposes; and Dalziel felt no difficulty in straining them to the utmost, and putting the whole country under military law. At Kilmarnock, where he took up his head-quarters, he not only let loose the soldiery,—he hounded them on with the most relentless ferocity. Suspicion of having been with the insurgents, or given them food, or of entertaining favourable sentiments with regard to them and their cause, was by him considered proof enough, on the strength of which he might inflict any punishment which caprice or cruelty might dictate. Money was extorted from those who had any; upon others the troops were quartered till they had "eaten up" every kind of sustenance, and reduced their victims to starvation; numbers were crowded into a dungeon in the prison so densely, that they could only stand upright day and night, though sick and dying from its noisome and pestilential vapours; some were, without trial, and upon the bare orders of the general, shot dead, stripped naked, and left weltering in their blood upon the spot were they had thus been murdered; and one woman, merely because a man had fled through her house and escaped the pursuit of the soldiers, was cast into a pit swarming with noxious reptiles.

In Galloway, the military command was intrusted to Sir William Bannatyne instead of Sir James Turner; but the change was even for the worse to the persecuted Presbyterians. To all the cruelties of Dalziel or Turner, Bannatyne added the most atrocious indulgence in lascivious licentiousness, both in his own conduct and that of the soldiery. Female chastity was exposed to every nameless outrage, the presence of parents or husbands being no protection to young maidens or married women, but exposing to insult, wounds and death, those men who presumed to defend their daughters, their sisters, or their wives, from the infamous attempts of Bannatyne and his brutal crew.* That in acts of mere cruelty Bannatyne was not inferior to Dalziel himself, appears from his treatment of a woman in the parish of Dalry, whom he tortured by tying matches betwixt her fingers and setting them on fire, because she was supposed to have assisted her husband in escaping from the hands of his pursuers. To such an extent did they proceed in their barbarity, that one of her hands was entirely destroyed, and she died of the effects of the torture within a few days.

But the prelates and the council had another object in view than merely the gratification of their cruelty. They wished to secure to themselves and their friends the property of those who either had been, or were suspected of having been, concerned in the Pentland rising. They therefore contrived to procure an opinion from the Court of Session, that persons accused of treason might be condemned in absence, a sentence of death passed upon them, and their estates forfeited. In consequence of this unprecedented opinion, the property of the most considerable gentlemen in several districts of Clydesdale and Galloway fell into the hands of these rapacious persecutors, and in a short time Dalziel and his lieutenant, Drummond, received the estates of Caldwell and Kersland, as a reward for their services.

But symptoms of a change of measures began to appear. Several of the nobility had become weary of this incessant course of persecution in which they were kept by the prelates, as well as disgusted with the pride of these domineering churchmen. The majority of the council was composed of prelates and officers in the army; and the Scottish barons felt themselves insulted and degraded by the con-

* Wodrow, vol. ii. p. 15.

duct and the company of such men. Lauderdale was quite aware of this state of matters, and contrived to countermine the prelatic party, and to procure a letter from the king to the council, giving permission to imprison and try all suspected persons, but not sanctioning the arbitrary forfeitures; and at the same time an intimation was given to Sharp to confine himself to his own diocese, and not intermeddle with public affairs. This disappointment checked their zeal considerably; and when, some time afterwards, a positive order came from his majesty, commanding the army to be disbanded, with the exception of the guards, they were in despair, Burnet, archbishop of Glasgow, exclaiming, "Now that the army is disbanded, the gospel will go out of my diocese."* What idea that arch-prelate entertained of the gospel, may be easily conjectured. Now that the army was to be disbanded, it came to be a serious question with the privy council how the country was to kept in peace without a military power. It formed no part of their scheme to promote peace by abstaining from committing outrages upon the country. But they were divided between the enforcement of the declaration and the framing of a new document to be termed the Bond of Peace. Chiefly through the influence of Sir Robert Murray, the council determined upon the bond of peace, which was accordingly passed. About the same time an act of indemnity to those who had been concerned in the late insurrection was transmitted from the king, and also passed by the council, but clogged with so many exceptions that it proved an indemnity in name rather than reality. "In the beginning," says Wodrow, "it pardoned all; in the middle very few; and in the end none at all." Both the act of indemnity and the bond of peace were published on the 9th of October.

The bond of peace varied somewhat in its forms, but its chief provision was, that the person taking it bound and obliged himself to keep the public peace, and not to rise in arms against or without his majesty's authority; and in the act of council enforcing it, noblemen, gentlemen, and heritors were compelled to become bound for themselves, their tenants, and servants, under the penalty of a full year's rent. The enforcement of this bond was likely enough to fill the coffers of the treasury; but there was another effect which it might have had, and was probably intended to have,—it caused not a little discussion among religious and conscientious people whether it might be taken with propriety. It was so comprehensive in its terms, that it might be explained as consenting to the existing forms of government in the Church, as well as in the State; and if so, none who were opposed to Prelacy could with sincerity subscribe any such bond. The differences of opinion entertained by the Presbyterians concerning the bond of peace, did not produce any dissensions among them; and it was not long till very different measures put an end to the danger of disunion on that account. The council, during some of their sittings towards the close of the year, gave proof of their critical acumen by emitting a proclamation against Brown of Wamphray's "Apologetical Relation," and the well-known book called "Naphtali, or the Wrestlings of the Church of Scotland." These works, however, survive, notwithstanding the impotent wrath of men who hate the truth because it condemns them, and will survive so long as truth is valued, martyrs held in honour, and tyranny abhorred.

[1668.] In the beginning of the year 1668, the council, in which the prelatic party had for a time lost their ascendency, thought proper to inquire into the conduct of Sir James Turner, whose cruelty and oppression had caused the insurrection, and of Sir William Bannatyne, whose still greater enormities were not unlikely to provoke another similar attempt. Turner proved that he had not exceeded his commission; but yet he was deprived of his military rank, as some atonement to the feelings of the country. Bannatyne was convicted of having perpetrated such barbarities as humanity could not endure, and he was sentenced to banishment. He retired to the continent, and was soon afterwards killed by a cannon-ball at the seige of Grave. But while the council thought proper to remove these bloody men from places of trust, there was little abatement in the severities employed against those who

* Wodrow, vol. ii. p. 89.

had been concerned in the late insurrection, or those who refused to subscribe the bond of peace. In a letter to the king, mention is made of the numbers who had yielded, and of those who still held out; and in a private letter from Tweeddale to Lauderdale, it was more minutely stated, that two hundred and eighteen had submitted, three hundred and nine refused, eighty had been killed in the the field, forty executed, thirty-one had died in the counties of Galloway and Dumfries, thirty had fled, and twenty forfeited; amounting to about seven hundred sufferers out of a small army not exceeding nine hundred when broken at Pentland.*

The acts against conventicles were this year enforced with greater rigour than they had previously been, in consequence of the repeated complaints of the curates, that some of the ejected ministers continued to preach, and that where such was the case, the people almost universally deserted their own ministry. Warrants were accordingly issued to apprehend all ejected ministers, or others, who should keep conventicles; and the magistrates of burghs were obliged to sign a bond to pay a certain sum if a conventicle should be held within their jurisdiction. Several eminent ministers were seized in consequence of this increased severity, of whom the most distinguished were, Michael Bruce, who had been a minister in Ireland, Thomas Hogg, minister at Kiltearn, and John Wilkie, a very aged man, whose infirmities rendered him physically incapable of committing the alleged crime for which he was oppressed, not having been out of his own house above twice during the course of a whole year.

Notwithstanding these severities, the oppression of the Presbyterians was considerably relaxed upon the whole, and there appeared some probability that even more favourable terms would be granted. But an incident occurred which had a most injurious effect in every point of view, both in leading to a renewal of the persecution, and in giving a degree of plausibility to the accusations urged against the Presbyterians. This was an attempt made by a preacher of the name of James Mitchell to assassinate Archbishop Sharp. Mitchell had been to some extent implicated in the insurrection which was suppressed at Pentland, and was excepted from the indemnity. After having wandered about for some time in daily peril of his life, and having seen many of his friends perish on the scaffold, others driven into banishment, their property confiscated, and their families reduced to starvation, the sense of intolerable wrong, national and individual, so far influenced his mind, that he determined to avenge his suffering country upon the perjured and relentless author of her sufferings. This determination he disclosed to no person, but provided himself privately with a pair of pistols, and watched for an opportunity of meeting with Archbishop Sharp. On the 11th of July he perceived the primate's carriage ready for its owner's reception, and immediately took up such a position as might place the person of his enemy within his reach. The archbishop entered the coach and took his seat; Mitchell stepped forward, aimed, and fired the pistol; but at that moment Honeyman, bishop of Orkney, in entering the carriage, stretched forth his arm, and received the ball in his wrist. Thus it was turned aside from Sharp, and the excited sufferer saved from the commission of a great crime. The cry immediately rose that a man was killed, and people began to rush to the spot where the deed had taken place; but when this cry was met by the response "that it was only a bishop," the crowd quietly dispersed. Mitchell escaped from observation and pursuit, and remained undetected for several years.*

This criminal attempt by a man whom persecution had driven nearly mad, was productive of very injurious consequences to the cause of Presbyterians. For although, as a party, they were not in the slightest degree implicated in Mitchell's guilty attempt, it was charged against them; and on the pretence of searching for the assassin, or for persons concerned, as was alleged, in a murderous conspiracy of which he was merely the agent, great numbers of people were brought into trouble, and subjected to grievous hardships. Several persons were apprehended on suspicion; and, among others,

* Wodrow vol. ii. p. 107; Sir J. Turner's Memoirs.

* Wodrow, vol. ii. pp. 115, 116; Naphtali, pp. 250-260.

three women, two of whom were widows. One of them, a minister's widow, was threatened with the torture of the boot, which would have been inflicted had not Rothes jestingly said, "It was not proper for gentlewomen to wear boots." She was, however sentenced to be imprisoned, and then banished to the colonies.*

[1669.]—The proceedings against conventicles, as they were called, continued during the early part of the year 1669; and in order to enforce the suppression of these meetings as effectually as the want of a sufficient military force would admit, there were appointed collectors of fines, who were sent to the several disaffected districts. But these collectors fell far short of the soldiery in their exactions; so that the Presbyterians obtained some mitigation of their sufferings. The archbishop of Glasgow exerted himself to the utmost to oppress the non-conforming ministers; but when they were called before the council, their defence was so calmly urged, and with such strength of reason, that the proceedings against them were allowed to drop, greatly to the mortification of the disappointed archbishop.

But the chief event of this year was the passing of the first indulgence. It has been already mentioned, that the nobility had become weary of the continued course of persecution in which the intolerance and cruelty of the prelates kept them engaged; and that Sharp's duplicity and tyranny had at length impelled the king to prohibit his further interference in the affairs of the nation. In England, also, a more temperate line of policy had been pursued since the fall of Clarendon; and Charles himself had become impatient of the continual complaints addressed to him from all quarters against prelatic cruelty, and had expressed his intention to be no longer the king of a party, but the king of the whole people."† Lauderdale had no peculiar regard for the prelates, and had repeatedly interfered to check the persecuting zeal of Sharp. Tweeddale was still more favourable, and had held interviews with some of the ejected ministers, with a view to ascertain whether some terms of mutual accommodation might not be framed, or some measure adopted, calculated to restore comparative peace to the country. At length, on the 15th of July, a letter from the king was laid before the council by Tweeddale, containing the indulgence. Its chief provisions were, that the privy council should "appoint so many of the ejected ministers as had lived peaceably and orderly," either to return to the parishes whence they had been expelled, if still vacant, or to such others as the council should approve of; that they should be allowed to receive the stipend of such parishes, upon condition of their receiving the consent of the patron, and collation from the bishop, to which, if they would not submit, they should only possess the manse and glebe; that they should be strictly enjoined to keep presbyteries and synods, that is, to attend diocesan meetings held by the prelates, for there were no truly Presbyterian meeting; that they should not allow the people from the other parishes to attend their churches and receive ordinances; and that all these favours should be withdrawn if they should publicly speak or preach against the ecclesiastical supremacy of the king. In conclusion, it is declared, that seeing all pretences for conventicles are thus taken away, if any should thereafter presume to hold or frequent them, "our express pleasure is, that you proceed with all severity against the preachers and hearers as seditious persons, and contemners of our authority.

This indulgence appeared to the prelates to be greatly too favourable to the persecuted Presbyterians; and meetings were held to devise by what methods it might be rendered as little beneficial to the ejected ministers as possible. It could not be set aside, since it was the king's declared will; but Sharp consoled his afflicted brethren, by promising to do his utmost to "make it a bone of contention to the Presbyterians."* His device, it appears, was, to revive the old contest between the resolutioners and the protesters, by proposing that the indulgence should be granted to the resolutioners alone.† But this contest had sunk into comparative insignificance, in consequence of the fiercer fires of the persecution into which the whole Church had been thrown, and by which they had

* Wodrow, vol. ii. p. 118. † Ibid, p. 115.

* Wodrow, vol. ii. p. 131. † Burnet's Own Times, vol. i. p. 278.

been, as it were, fused into union. Yet Sharp's wily scheme was so far followed, that when the council selected those to whom the indulgence was to be offered, they endeavoured to induce those who had been of the resolutioners to accept the ensnaring boon, and in many instances they were but too successful.

At first ten were selected to whom the indulgence was offered; and of those the most distinguished was George Hutchison, who had been one of the ministers of Edinburgh before the Glasgow Act. Hutchison, in his own name and that of his brethren, returned thanks to his majesty and the council for this act of clemency; guarding their acceptance, however, by saying, "We having received our ministry from Jesus Christ, with prescriptions from him for regulating us therein, must, in the discharge thereof, be accountable to him." This cautious statement gave satisfaction to no party. Those of the council who most strenuously asserted the royal supremacy, were displeased with it, as containing a denial of that high prerogative; while on the other hand, the greater part of the Presbyterian ministers regarded it as a weak and sinful betrayal of the great doctrine of Christ's sole supremacy. And certainly, if the reader has entered fully into the principles which have been repeatedly brought before his notice in the preceding pages of this history, he must be aware that the indulgence proceeded upon a principle clearly subversive of the Presbyterian Church. Its very existence depended upon the king's supremacy in matters ecclesiastical; without which he could have neither the right nor the power, on his own sole authority, and by his absolute command, to depose, suspend, restore and limit ministers in the discharge of their strictly ministerial functions. Viewing it, therefore, solely as a matter of principle, we have no hesitation in saying, that not one of the ejected ministers ought to have accepted the indulgence, because it was impossible to do so without sacrificing the fundamental and essential principle of the Presbyterian Church—that which constitutes its glory and its life—the sole sovereignty of Christ.

The whole number of ministers who were included in the first indulgence amounted to forty-two. All of them made some form of protestation against the royal supremacy, or at least some declaration of the opposite principle; and very few accepted of either the direct presentation of a patron, or collation from a bishop. Their wish appears to have been to obtain liberty to resume the discharge of their ministerial duties without molestation, though at the same time without receiving any stipend, and so far their conduct was disinterested and unselfish; but it proved extremely detrimental to the cause of the Church of Scotland. It divided the ejected ministers into two parties, the Indulged and the Non-indulged, and thereby put an end to that unanimity which their common sufferings had reproduced, and which, since the Pentland insurrection had been increasing so steadily, as to promise ere long to be beyond the power of kings and councils to subdue. Much has been written respecting the indulgence, and the propriety of complying with it, for the sake of peace and liberty to preach the gospel. But the whole discussion may be resolved into the question, which of three things ought to have been chosen by the Church; whether unanimously to accept the indulgence, in which case she would at once have become prelatic; or unanimously to reject it, in which case it would fall harmlessly to the ground; or some to receive and some to reject, in which case the Church would be divided, weakened, and trampled in the dust. The first could not be chosen without injury; the second would have been the choice of high principle and sound prudence; the third was the course followed, recommended by the usual weak and shortsighted arguments of expediency, and proved to be the course of ruin. The fatal effects resulting from this division, caused by partial compliance with the indulgence, might teach, if men could be taught by the experience of others, how dangerous it is to quit the path which clear principle points out, however beset with perils, and to turn aside into the crooked by-ways of human expediency, allured by the fallacious hopes of peace and safety.

It appears that a little reflection showed the privy council that they had proceeded rashly in giving immediate effect to the

* Brown's History of the Indulgence, *passion.*

indulgence, merely upon the authority of his majesty's letter, as it was contrary to several existing laws, which could not be repealed or superseded without a meeting of parliament. At the same time there was a proposal to unite the Scottish and English parliaments into one, which also would require to be discussed in the parliaments of the respective countries. For these reasons a parliament was called, after an interval of eight years. Its first act, passed on the 16th of November, was intended to legalize the indulgence. It certainly accomplished that purpose, and not a little more. It commenced by stating the necessity of clearly asserting his majesty's power and authority in relation to matters and persons ecclesiastical; and then proceeded to declare, "That his majesty hath the supreme authority and supremacy over all persons and in all causes ecclesiastical within this his kingdom; and that, by virtue thereof, the ordering and disposal of the external government and policy of the Church doth properly belong to his majesty and his successors, as an inherent right of the crown; and that his majesty and his successors may settle, enact, and emit such constitutions, acts, and orders, concerning the administration of the external government of the Church, and the persons employed in the same, and concerning all ecclesiastical meetings, and matters to be proposed and determined therein, as they in their royal wisdom shall think fit." It is wholly unnecessary to offer any comment on an act which utterly abolished all church power whatever, and elevated the king at once to the state and power of a royal pope. Indeed, it put it completely into the power of the king or his successor to restore Popery whenever he might think proper; and Burnet is of opinion that Lauderdale, who knew the sentiments of the Duke of York, procured the passing of this act for that very purpose.*

This act proved to be of too potent a character for even the prelates. Alexander Burnet, archbishop of Glasgow, had been exceedingly opposed to the indulgence; and now when this act was passed, he saw that it placed his own order as much in the power of the sovereign as it did the Presbyterian ministers.

* Burnet's Own Times, vol. i. p. 284.

"So now the Episcopal party, that were wont to put all authority in the king as long as he was for them, began to talk of law."* A meeting of the clergy of that diocese was held, and a strong remonstrance was drawn up against the indulgence. When it was transmitted to the king, he termed it another Western Remonstrance, said it was as bad as Guthrie's, and ordered the archbishop to be deposed. Leighton, bishop of Dunblane, was translated to the archbishopric of Glasgow, where he soon afterwards took a leading part in attempting to arrange the terms of an accommodation with the Presbyterian ministers.

[1670.] The year 1670 began with severe measures against the indulged ministers, at the instigation of the prelates because they did not conform in all particulars to the very terms of the indulgence. They were prohibited from lecturing, because the curates did not or could not lecture. They were watched narrowly as to their conduct in granting ordinances to people who came from other parishes. And they were called before a committee appointed by the privy council, and compelled to answer generally as to the manner in which they discharged their ministry. This must have shown them that, in complying with the indulgence, they had really subjected themselves to the arrogated supremacy of the king and the council in ecclesiastical matters.

And as the indulgence had, according to its own statement, taken away all pretence for conventicles, the acts against these meetings were enforced with increased severity. This was the more practicable, in consequence of an act passed by the parliament respecting the militia, in which the power of arming the subjects, and keeping them as a standing force for any purpose in which his majesty might think proper to employ them, was declared to be an inherent right of the crown. By this act, the loss of the army, which had been disbanded, was amply supplied, and a sufficient military force again put into the hands of the council. Several ministers were seized and punished for keeping conventicles; and a considerable number of country gentlemen were subjected to

* Burnet's Own Times, p. 283.

heavy fines for giving countenance to these meetings. But, instead of being discouraged and ceasing to meet together, both ministers and people seemed to become the more resolute as they were the more severely treated. What were termed field-conventicles, or field meetings, began to be frequently held, and numerously attended. The first of these field-meetings, at which people appeared in arms for their own defence, was held at Beath-hill, in the parish of Dunfermline, about the middle of June. Worship was conducted chiefly by the Rev. John Blackadder, who had been ejected several years before, and had resolutely refused to conform. Great numbers attended from the whole country round; and when some officers of militia came, as if to disturb and break up the meeting, they were met by men of determined courage, armed for self-defence, and compelled either to remain and listen quietly, or to promise to depart peaceably, and leave the people to worship God beneath the open canopy of heaven. There is related to have been a very remarkable manifestation of spiritual influence in the sacred services of that day, great solemnity, and deep devotional feeling, impressions which were never obliterated from the hearts and minds of many of the worshippers.*

Two other large meetings of the same kind were held the same year—one at the Torwood, and another at Carnwath; but neither of them quite equalled that of Beath-hill. They were, however, sufficient to alarm the prelatic party, and to excite the bitter indignation of the council. When the parliament met in the end of July, they proceeded to pass the most sanguinary enactments against conventicles, with the manifest determination of utterly suppressing them, though it should be by the entire exterminaton of the persons by whom they were held. On the 3d of August an act was passed "anent deponing," or giving evidence on oath, against those who either held or frequented conventicles. In this, "all and every subject, of what degree, sex, or quality soever," were commanded to "depone upon oath" their knowledge of any person holding or frequenting these meetings, under the penalty of "fining, imprisonment, or banishment to the plantations." By this it was intended to compel people to give evidence against their nearest relatives and dearest friends. Another act "anent field-conventicles" was of a still more crimson hue. It prohibits all "outed ministers," and "other persons not authorised by the bishop of the diocese," from preaching, expounding Scripture, or praying except in their own houses, and to their own family alone; appointing heavy and ruinous fines to be exacted from all who should violate these restrictions, and rendering the heads of every household answerable for each other and for the members of their families. It further ordains that those who "convocate" or conduct such conventicles in the fields, "shall be punished with death and confiscation of their goods;" and a reward is offered to any person who should seize and secure the persons of those who preached at these field-meetings, with an indemnity for any slaughter that might be committed in the seizure. This most atrocious act was to endure for three years, "unless his majesty should think fit that it continues longer." Two other acts—one against persons procuring baptism for their children from any other than the ministers licensed by government—the other against people separating themselves from the congregations where these government ministers preached—completed the persecuting enactments of this parliament.

The object of the indulgence might have been now sufficiently apparent. For these most iniquitous acts plainly proved, that mercy was not its intention, but merely such a division among the Presbyterians as might draw off all the timid and wavering, and leave the more determined to swift and utter destruction. There is a fearful meaning in the limitation of the act at first to three years; as if the persecutors contemplated the annihilation within that time, of the entire body of Presbyterians in Scotland. But when the malice of man wages war against the cause of God, the result is not doubtful. The very means employed with such relentless cruelty against the Presbyterians were overruled to the increasing of their numbers, their courage, and their progress in vital religion.

* Blackadder's Memoirs, pp. 144-148.

These barbarous enactments, so far from putting an end to field-meetings, roused the people to the determination to frequent them more than they had previously done, and to come in such numbers, and prepared with such defensive weapons, as might protect them against any sudden assault of their persecuting enemies. And the very danger which men had thus to encounter in the worship of God, had a powerful tendency to elevate their minds above that listlessness and torpidity which too often prevail in congregations met in their usual place of worship, and as a matter of ordinary occurrence. They must have loved the gospel, who thus braved every peril that they might hear it freely and fully proclaimed by men whose very act of proclaiming it exposed them to the loss of life; or they whose native courage loved the wild thrill of heart which rises at the encounter of danger, would soon love the gospel for the very danger's sake. And we may dimly imagine, though we cannot fully realize, the intense earnestness with which they would listen to the bold and fervent eloquence of a minister who indeed preached as a dying man to dying men, not knowing but that his sermon might be abruptly closed with his expiring groans, and his blood and theirs be mingled together on the trodden heath, before the day was done. Nor need we doubt that all these strong emotions would be raised to the highest pitch of which they were capable, by the scarcely perceived yet mighty influence of the scenery amidst which these field-meeting were generally held,—that sensations and feelings of the solemn, the sublime, and the glorious, would be wrought into their minds from the grave austerity of vast upland moors, the stern majesty of frowning crags and lofty mountains, and the overclouded or serene illimitable skies, from which the sun, like the broad eye of heaven looked down upon their worship. To all these incalculably powerful natural influences, the records of these times give us good reason to add, what was infinitely more mighty than them all, the felt presence of the Spirit of God accompanying the administration of word and ordinance, and sealing divine truth upon the souls of the quickened, melting, and adoring multitudes.

The latter part of this year was chiefly occupied by the discussions to which Leighton's attempt at an accommodation between the Prelatists and the Presbyterians gave rise. When Alexander Burnet was removed from the archbishopric of Glasgow by the king's orders, Leighton, at that time bishop of Dumblane, was appointed commendator or administrator of the vacant archiepiscopal see. This eminent man had kept as much as possible aloof from direct participation in the atrocities perpetrated by his brethren; and when appointed to the more influential position of Glasgow, he set himself to attempt some accommodation between his party and that of the persecuted Presbyterians. His first step was a very necessary one. It was an inquiry into the conduct of the prelatic clergy within his own diocese, with the view of correcting the abuses that were prevalent among them. From this attempt he was soon obliged to desist, in consequence of finding it utterly impossible to correct abuses so universal and so enormous; besides, that his attempts to be impartial in his inquiries were greatly checked by a lay committee which the council had ordered to assist, but which really impeded him. He next attempted to try the force of argument upon the nonconforming ministers and people, and selected six of the most learned and pious of the prelatic clergy to travel over the western counties, and endeavour to proselytise the people. Gilbert Burnet, at that time professor of theology in Glasgow, was one of these six, and has recorded their endeavours, and their unsuccessfulness, in his History of his Own Times. "We were indeed amazed," says he, "to see a poor commonalty so capable to argue upon points of government, and on the bounds to be set to the power of princes in matters of religion. Upon all these topics they had texts at hand, and were ready with their answers to any thing that was said to them. This measure of knowledge was spread even among the meanest of them, their cottagers and their servants."* From this alone men might deduce one of the reasons why the Presbyterian ought to be preferred to the Prelatic form of church government by a wise and patriotic legislature. By the

* Burnet's Own Times, vol. i. p. 293.

Presbyterian Church the whole body of the people are educated and thought to think and reason; by the Episcopalian this never yet has taken place, nor even been attempted, in its actings as a national church.

In further prosecution of his scheme of accommodation, Leighton procured a meeting of some of the most distinguished of the indulged ministers to be held in Edinburgh in August, and subsequently another at Paisley in December. Much reasoning passed between Leighton and them, on the point of the difference between Prelacy and Presbytery, and the possibility of some intermediate form, partaking of some of the essential features of both, by the adoption of which harmony might be restored. It was not difficult to see that any real and permanent accommodation was absolutely impossible, unless the Presbyterian ministers were prepared to abandon every essential point of their own form of church government and discipline, one by one, as the prelatic power chose to make its insidious but irresistible advances. They could not but know that Prelacy had been thrust upon the Church of Scotland in King James's days, in a great measure by the device of the constant moderators; and Leighton's proposal not only retained these, but did not abolish the negative vote of the presiding prelate, so that presbyteries and synods, so constituted would have been but a name. The attempted accommodation, was, therefore, finally abandoned, greatly to the regret of Leighton, who was, we are persuaded, sincerely desirous of peace, and pitied the sufferings of his oppressed country, having on one occasion declared that he could not approve of the severities employed against the nonconformists, even for the purpose of planting Christianity in a heathen land, much less for the mere substitution of one form of church government for another.* Yet he cannot be exonerated from the blame of having been accessory to these severities, through his compliance with the scheme of overthrowing the Presbyterian Church, and establishing Prelacy on its ruins. And however much we must deplore that such a stain should rest on the memory of such a man, historical truth condemns his public conduct as that of a persecutor although his gentle spirit shrunk from the contemplation of the bloody scenes in which his unnatural connection with Scottish Prelacy involved him.

[1671.] No great events signalized the year 1671. The indulged ministers, indeed, experienced some of the tender mercies of the council, by being confined within their parishes, and threatened to be deprived of their stipends, because they had not strictly obeyed all the directions contained in the indulgence. Several heavy fines were exacted, and people imprisoned in irons, for frequenting conventicles. Popery began to raise its head openly in various parts of the country, and experienced no such molestation as was directed unsparingly against the Presbyterians. The island, or rather rock, of the Bass, was purchased by the crown, and converted into a state prison, of which Lauderdale was made captain, —the place, the purpose, the office, and the man, all in dreadful harmony.

[1672.] The aspect of affairs grows darker as we enter upon the year 1672. Lauderdale was created a duke, as if to testify the king's satisfaction with his previous administration and to encourage him to proceed in his atrocious career His marriage to Lady Dysart, "a woman," says Sir Walter Scott, "of considerable talent, but of inordinate ambition, boundless expense, and the most unscrupulous rapacity," had a very pernicious effect in rendering him still more overbearing and incapable than he had previously been. The fines, which had been hitherto sufficiently oppressive, were increased and exacted with double rigour. The acts against conventicles and field-preachings were enforced with immitigable cruelty. The ejected ministers were hunted from place to place, as if they had been wolves, who were to be exterminated as a matter of public duty. An act was passed against what parliament was pleased to term "unlawful ordinations," by which was meant all except prelatic ordination. The intention of this act was manifestly to secure the final extinction of the Presbyterian Church, by preventing the ordination to the ministry of young men who might supply the vacancies caused by the death of the old. It caused great hardship to the whole

* Pearson's Life of Leighton, pp. 62, 63; Burnet.

Presbyterian community, and, could it have been fully enforced, must have proved fatal in the course of a single generation. As it was, it rendered it necessary for young men to be sent to Holland, where a presbytery was constituted of banished Scottish ministers, by whom these young men were ordained. It had another effect, which, of course, the prelates did not contemplate. The Scottish ministers in Holland were some of the most eminent men, in learning and abilities, of their age. Not only had they studied the subjects deeply for the maintenance of which they had been banished, before they suffered that punishment, but their exile furnished them with leisure to prosecute these studies, with the advantage of being aloof from the scene of conflict, their personal interests not involved in it, and themselves thereby enabled to take calmly both more comprehensive and profounder views of the whole matters in dispute, than would have been possible had they been in Scotland. These views they communicated to the men who came for ordination, and who returned to Scotland thoroughly imbued with the knowledge, and confirmed in the love, of the great and essential doctrine of the Presbyterian Church. In this manner the vital principles of Presbytery were not only kept alive; they were strengthened into more intense activity and uncompromising endurance.

Several other oppressive enactments were passed by this parliament, respecting baptism, the keeping of the 29th of May, and a prolongation of the act against conventicles. But as these differed from the acts already specified only in their increased severity, it is not necessary to state their provisions.

But the most important matter of this year was the second indulgence, which was promulgated by the council on the 3d of September. The main peculiarity of this indulgence consisted in its sending a number of the previously non-indulged ministers either to the parishes of those who had accepted the first indulgence, where they were to reside and perform, along with them, the functions of the ministry, or to other parishes not previously indulged; but in either case the arrangement coupled them together two by two, and confined each couple within the limits of the respective parishes to which they were appointed. This scheme, it appears, was founded upon a suggestion of Burnet's, supported by Leighton, who said that when burning coals were scattered all over the house, in danger of setting it on fire, it might be prevented by gathering them all into the hearth, where they might burn out in safety?* It had for its object, undoubtedly, the collecting together into the narrowest possible bounds, the nonconforming Presbyterian ministers; and as its concluding clause strictly prohibited these ministers from preaching in any other churches than those of the parishes in which they were confined, or out of doors even in the churchyards, and all others from preaching at all, it seemed calculated to suppress field-preaching, and prevent the diffusion of Presbyterian sentiments through the country. It had also another effect. Like the first indulgence, it divided the sentiments of the ministers whether it ought to be complied with or rejected; and, unable to come to any unanimity of opinion, some accepted, others rejected, great divisions were caused, and corresponding weakness ensued.

When recording events which take their aspect from mental, moral, and religious opinions, we are often struck with the strange contrast presented between men's principles and their course of conduct. Had the Presbyterian ministers looked only to the inevitable conclusion to which their principles must lead, they would not have hesitated one moment about rejecting the indulgence. The true nature of the question was brought into more distinct developement by the second indulgence than it had been by the first. It was manifestly this, "Whether the civil magistrate may of himself, and immediately, without the voice of the church and the previous election of the people, assign and send ministers to particular congregations, to take the fixed and pastoral oversight of them, prescribe rules and directions to them for the exercise of the ministry, and confine them rigidly to those special congregations." When the question is thus stated in its simple and essential form, no true Presbyterian can hesitate to say that it

* Burnet's Own Times, vol. i. p. 341.

must at once be met by a prompt and decided negative. It was indeed so met by some; for when the indulgence with its directions were offered to Mr. Blair, minister of Galston, he took the paper into his hand, saying, "My Lord Chancellor, I cannot be so uncivil as to refuse a paper offered to me by your lordship:" then letting it fall to the ground, he added, "but I can receive no instructions from you for regulating the exercise of my ministry; for if I should receive instructions from you, I should be your ambassador, not Christ's."* For this he was immediately committed to prison; and the dissensions among the ministers increased, some approving the decided conduct of Mr. Blair, others condemning his want of prudence, as they were pleased to term his bold and candid statement of his principles. Death, in the course of a few months, relieved Mr. Blair from his imprisonment, but did not diminish the indignation and alarm which his seizure had excited.

[1673.] The only peculiarities in the course of the year 1673, of sufficient importance to be mentioned, were the proceedings which arose out of the indulgence, and the rise and growth of an opposition to Lauderdale's administration. The number of ministers directly opposed to prelatic tyranny having been considerably reduced by the second indulgence, the council went forward with less hesitation in the persecution of those who still refused; and thus the indulgence actually proved the means of increasing the sufferings of the true Presbyterians. In a new act against conventicles, the council had the confidence to assert, that the suppression of these meetings was "of great concernment to religion;" so that, under the hypocritical guise of a regard for the interests of religion, they persecuted the faithful followers of the Lord Jesus. And in order that information might be readily given against the field-meetings, a third part of the fines appointed to be levied was now to be given to the informer, a third part to the exactors of the fines, and the remaining third to his majesty. Several of the ejected and non-indulged ministers were seized and committed to the Bass, among whom were Robert Gillespie and Alexander Peden, and positive orders were issued for the apprehension of others, who were specifically mentioned by name, particularly Gabriel Semple and John Welsh. It may give some idea of the ruinous amount of the fines levied upon the gentlemen who countenanced the field-meetings, to state, that in the small county of Renfew upwards of £30,000 sterling was exacted from eleven gentlemen, not of the greatest wealth.*

A considerable number of the nobility began to complain of the intolerable severity of Lauderdale's administration, the chief of whom was the Duke of Hamilton; but Lauderdale's proceedings were too much in accordance with the inclinations of the king himself for his power to be easily shaken. Yet the opposition in the council caused a little relaxation of the severities enforced against the Presbyterians.

[1674.] The struggle in the council against Lauderdale was terminated early in the year 1674, by its dissolution, and the appointment of a new one, in which the supporters of that ruthless tyrant formed a decided majority. This victory was signalized, as was to be expected, by the immediate resumption of the persecuting career of the prelatic party. A committee of council was appointed, including Sharp, with full council-powers to meet when and where they pleased, and to take what steps they might think necessary for the complete suppression of field-conventicles. Orders were issued to apprehend twenty ministers, mentioned by name; and a reward of £400 sterling offered for the seizure of Welsh or Semple, and about £55 for each of the others, a full indemnity being at the same time secured for any slaughter committed in their apprehension. Yet, notwithstanding those sanguinary measures, field-preachings increased greatly, both in the frequency with which they were held, and in the numbers by whom they were attended. The very atrocity of the acts of council roused the minds of both ministers and people; and they seemed now more resolved than ever to brave every danger, not counting their lives dear to them in defence of the liberty of the gospel, and fully determined that, come what

* Wodrow, vol. ii. 216; Brown's History of the Indulgence.

* Wodrow, vol. ii. pp. 226-227.

might, they would obey God rather than man.

Early in this year James Mitchell, who made the attempt upon the life of Sharp, narrated above, was apprehended; and, upon being assured that his life would be spared, made a confession of his crime. Finding, however, that proceedings were about to be instituted against him, he retracted his confession; and there being no other evidence, he was re-committed to prison.

A paper of "grievances" was laid before the council by the prelatic clergy of the diocese of Glasgow, filled with the most bitter calumnies against the Presbyterians, and urging the adoption of more effectual measures for the suppression of field-preachings. Having mentioned the calumnies of the prelatic clergy, it may be expedient to explain briefly a subject on which so many erroneous statements have so long prevailed. It seems to be taken for granted, that the Covenanters of this persecuting time were the mere dregs of society in Scotland, and that all the noble, the gentle, the learned, and the respectable belonged to the other side. The reverse would be much nearer the truth. A very considerable portion of the nobility were much more Presbyterian than Prelatic in their feelings, though they thought it expedient to temporize, through dread of the persecution to which their prominent position in society would expose them. And, in many instances, while the noblemen attended the privy council and the parliament, without taking a very active part in the persecuting enactments there passed, their ladies gave direct countenance and encouragement to the Presbyterian Church. The greater proportion of the landed proprietors in Fifeshire, the western counties, Dumfries-shire, and Galloway, were staunch Presbyterians, as the very lists of persons fined for giving countenance to conventicles, and refuge to the ejected ministers, incontestibly prove. Nearly all the tenantry throughout the counties where the persecution raged were covenanted Presbyterians; and it is well known that in every civilized country, and especially in Scotland, that class of people forms the very heart and soul of the nation. Every intelligent observer will at once admit, that in the middle classes of society exists the greatest amount of piety, morality, unbending integrity, and manly independence of character; and nearly the entire middle classes were true Presbyterians. Learning forms but a very unsafe criterion; for there are too many proofs that a man may be very learned, and yet be irreligious, and immoral, and profane. Nevertheless, we should be doing great injustice to the persecuted ministers were we to compare them for a moment to the prelatic clergy of that period in any possible respect. Of the truth of this there needs no more than the testimony of Bishop Burnet, though much more might very easily be given. The real truth of the matter, however, much as it has been generally misrepresented by prejudiced and party writers, is, that the prelatic party in Scotland consisted chiefly, nay, almost exclusively, of men of neither religion nor morality,—of ambitious and dissipated courtiers, military adventurers, a few perjured and apostate ministers, eager for the wealth and honours of the prelacy, a swarm of uneducated, irreligious, and immoral men, thrust hastily into the ministry to fill the room of the ejected ministers, and the very lowest dregs of society. When, therefore, men write about the prevalence of ignorance and crime at that period, their statements, so far as they are true, are applicable almost exclusively to the prelatic nobles, the prelates themselves, their curates, and the very lowest grade of the common people, who formed at once the bulk of the prelatic congregations, where any existed, and the ready and brutal instruments of prelatic persecution, along with the rude and licentious soldiery, whose bloody steps they traced as regularly as did the wild dog and the carrion crow, and for the same hideous purposes.* It must be added, that wherever the field preachings prevailed, there immediately followed a very perceptible diminution of crime of every kind, even in those districts which had previously been notorious for irreligion and vice. Of this some very remarkable proofs might be cited, as, for instance, the great change which took place in some of the border counties, whose pillaging

* Should this view be disputed, it shall be proved; but we are not disposed to dwell on such subjects, unless compelled for the sake of truth, and for the vindication of our maligned and martyred ancestors.

moss-troopers speedily became peaceful and honest.*

When the council met in Edinburgh, a petition was presented to them by a considerable number of females, some of them ladies of rank, others minister's widows, imploring the council to mitigate their severe proceedings against the faithful ministers, and to grant them permission to exercise their sacred functions. For this "unwarrantable crime," as it was termed, several of these ladies were imprisoned, and three of them banished from the town of Edinburgh! so determined were the oppressors to prosecute their tyranny to the utmost, that they punished as crimes even the respectful petitions and complaints of widowed women.†

In the meantime the indulged Presbyterian ministers felt grievously the bondage under which they had brought themselves, by their sinful compliance with an arrangement which their own conscience could not approve. They saw, besides, that the entire extinction of Presbytery was the object of their tyrannical antagonists; and they attempted to maintain some shadow of Presbyterian church government, by the formation of meetings resembling presbyteries and synods, to which delegates were sent, and where they deliberated respecting their common duties, mourned over their common sufferings, and adopted measures for the training of young men for the ministry, when their own cloudy and troubled day should have set in the darkness of the tomb.

[1675.] The chief topics of the year 1675, so far as it is distinguished from preceding years, were the establishing of garrisons in several parts of the country, the act of intercommuning, and the dissensions among the prelates. The first of these measures arose from the rapid progress of field-preachings, which it was found impossible to suppress by the means hitherto employed. For this reason an act of council was passed, appointing garrisons to be placed in the houses of two noblemen and ten gentlemen, in those parts of the country where conventicles and field-preachings, were most prevalent. In each instance the garrison was placed in the residence of a friend to the suffering Presbyterians, that he might be oppressed and reduced to poverty by the free quarters of the soldiery, while they were watching their opportunity to seize upon the ministers by whom these forbidden meetings were held.

The issuing of "letters of intercommuning," as they were called, was one of the most oppressive and inhuman deeds ever perpetrated by despotism. After mentioning by name above an hundred persons, of whom sixteen or eighteen were ministers, and who were all declared to be in a state of rebellion on account of their holding and frequenting conventicles, this document proceeds in the following terms:—"We charge and command all and sundry our lieges and subjects, that they, nor none of them, presume, nor take upon hand, to reset, supply, or intercommune with any of the foresaid persons, our rebels, nor furnish them with meat, drink, house, harbour, victual, nor no other thing useful or comfortable to them, nor have intelligence with them by word, writ, or message, or any other manner of way, under the pain to be reputed and esteemed art and part with them in the crimes foresaid, and pursued therefor with all rigour, to the terror of others." By this fiend-like measure the nearest relatives were prohibited from assisting each other; the wife might not assist the husband, nor the husband the wife; the brother might not comfort the brother, nor the parent give food and shelter to the son, if the sufferers had been intercommuned. Every feeling of humanity,—every tie of nature,—every bond of affection, was outraged; and for what? That Prelacy might be established in Scotland? Yes, for that, and something more; that the supremacy of the king equally in spiritual as in civil matters might be confirmed, a pure despotism erected, religion trampled under foot, the sovereignty of the Lord Jesus Christ over his Church abolished, and Christianity reduced to a political engine for swaying the community. And Scottish Prelacy assisted willingly in the prosecution of this truly diabolical scheme, by measures such as, Sir Walter Scott says, might have been suggested by Satan.*

* Wodrow, vol. ii. p. 451; Kirkton, p. 392. † Wodrow, vol. ii. pp. 268, 269.

* Tales of a Grandfather, vol. ii. p. 22.

It is not necessary to relate the contests which arose among the prelates, in consequence of the overbearing conduct of Sharp. They issued in the king's employing his ecclesiastical supremacy for the deposition of one bishop and four of the ordinary clergy, without the intervention of any church court.† This might have somewhat stunned the prelatists, when they were made to feel their own tyrannical devices turned against themselves. But they had still the comfort of knowing that their own pliant consciences would not urge them into any protracted opposition to the king; and that his majesty, having found them such serviceable instruments in his attempts against the liberties of the nation, would not visit them with any chastisement more severe than was necessary for reducing them to their former state of ready subserviency.

[1676.] The appointment of garrisons caused the year 1776 to be one of the most oppressive which Scotland had yet undergone. Each of these became a den of robbers, out of which issued at pleasure an armed band, wasting the country, pillaging from every quarter round them, and inflicting every kind of personal outrage upon men, women, and children, under the pretence of suppressing conventicles. A new proclamation was issued against these meetings, pressing the full execution of all the former persecuting decrees, and laying additional restrictions upon the indulged ministers; and inflicting fines on the proprietors of those lands where conventicles were held, although they neither knew of them, nor were able to prevent them. Yet these meetings increased, both in frequency of being held, and in the numbers by whom they were attended. Frequently the most remote, lonely, and inaccessible places were chosen, on the brink of some vast morass, or in the heart of some deep-cleft ravine, and men were stationed on commanding positions within sight, to give warning of the enemy's approach; and in such circumstances the persecuted wanderers worshipped God, and partook of the symbols of redemption. A commission of council was now appointed, containing the two archbishops, Sharp and Burnet, the latter of whom had been restored to Glasgow when Leighton relinquished the hopeless task of mitigating Prelacy and deceiving Presbyterian ministers, and, shocked with the bloody barbarities which he could not prevent, withdrew to England, after expressing his wish that he and the other prelates had been cast into the Forth with millstones fastened to their necks.

† Wodrow, vol. ii. p. 304.

One of the persecuting incidents of this year merits attention, on account of the light which it casts on the spirit and temper of the persecuting party. An attempt was made by one Captain Carstairs to seize the Rev. James Kirkton, one of the ejected ministers, for which Carstairs had no warrant. Kirkton was rescued by Baillie of Jerviswood. For this Baillie was called before the council, and having related the matter, would have been set at liberty, had not Sharp insisted that Carstairs must be supported, "otherwise it could not be expected that any one would prosecute the fanatics." But it was difficult to find a reasonable pretext for punishing Baillie for rescuing a friend when illegally seized. To obviate this difficulty, Sharp procured a warrant for the apprehension of Kirkton, and antedated it, so that it might give the appearance of legality to the attempt of Carstairs; and on the strength of this fabricated document Baillie was imprisoned four months, and compelled to pay a heavy fine, which was given to Carstairs to encourage him in the seizure of fanatics.* Some of the council could not consent to this base deed, and on that account the Duke of Hamilton and the Earl of Kinkardine were removed, to make way for less scrupulous supporters of Prelacy, who would readily second the perfidy of Sharp.

[1677.] The year 1677 is chiefly remarkable for the passing of those acts of council, and application to his majesty founded on them, which led to raising an armed force among the Highlands, and bringing it, like an invading army, upon the western counties. The assaults upon the large field meetings had been so frequent, that it had become customary for the persecuted Presbyterians to carry arms in self-defence; and on several occasions they had overawed the soldiers, and compelled them to consult their own

* Wodrow, vol. ii. pp. 327, 328; Kirkton, pp. 367-372 Burnet, pp. 399, 400.

safety by a prudent and peaceful retreat. In Fife, Captain Carstairs had attacked a few resolute men who were met together in a dwelling-house, and had been beaten off, one of the soldiers being wounded in the encounter. Availing themselves of these events, the prelatic party represented the whole south of Scotland as in a state of incipient insurrection, requiring a force for its suppression beyond what the small body of regular troops, together with the militia, could afford. A proclamation was issued about the same time, both calling on the gentlemen of the western counties to put down all conventicles, and to subscribe a bond, making themselves answerable for the conduct of their wives, children, servants, tenantry, and cottagers. The county gentlemen declined the bond, and answered, "that they found it not within the compass of their power to suppress conventicles,' at the same time recommending more tolerant measures. Upon this the council applied to the king for assistance by troops from the north of England and from Ireland, and suggested the raising of the Highland clans for the same purpose. The king willingly acceded to their request and suggestion; and on the 26th of December a commission was issued for raising the Highlanders, and employing them "against the places infested with rebellious practices;" empowering them to take free quarters; and "indemnifying them against all pursuits, civil and criminal, for killing, wounding, apprehending, or imprisoning, all such as should make opposition."*

[1678.] the year 1678 was ushered in by the invasion, as it may be well termed, of the Highland Host. Orders were given to the Marquis of Athole, and the Earls of Mar, Murray, Caithness, Perth, Strathmore and Airly, to raise their men, and advance to Stirling. There they were joined by the milita under the command of the Earl of Linlithgow, forming, when united, an army of about 10,000 men, 8,000 of whom were Highlanders. A committee of council was appointed to accompany them, and give encouragement and sanction to their proceedings. Alarmed by these formidable preparations, several of the noblemen and gentlemen of the western counties resolved to go to court, and by a fair and true statement of Scottish affairs, endeavor to obtain from the king himself orders to countermand this invasion; but the privy council immediately issued a proclamation, "prohibiting noblemen and others to go out of the kingdom without license." Thus prevented from access to the king, the western gentlemen applied to the council, where they were met by the furious tyranny of Lauderdale, who, with frantic vehemence, making bare his arm to the shoulder, as if about to plunge it into blood, swore a dreadful oath, that he would compel them to take the bond.*

On the 25th of January the Highland host and the militia marched from Stirling, directing their course by Glasgow to the western counties. They had with them a small train of artillery, and pioneering implements, as if to assail fortified places; and, in addition to their usual weapons, they carried with them large quantities of iron fetters, with which to manacle their captives, and thumb-screws and other instruments of torture. At Glasgow the bond against conventicles, field-meetings, and intercommuned persons, was repromulgated; and the savage horde moved onward, disarming the people, devastating the country, and perpetrating every imaginable kind of outrage. In vain did the people protest against being obliged to subscribe a bond which was in its own nature illegal, inhuman, and impossible: they must subscribe it, or be ruined in their fortunes, and suffer every kind of personal abuse short of death. The wild host held on its course. No army appeared to be fought, no tumultuary meetings to be dispersed, no resistance to be overborne. But there were towns which could be sacked, houses which could be pillaged, property which could be destroyed, and men and women who could be insulted and abused; and in the perpetration of all these barbarities the ferocious invaders were not only permitted but encouraged to revel unrestrained. Several aged men, and several women, including two ladies of rank, died in consequence of the abuse inflicted on them by these northern barbarians. A more minute specification of the enormities committed by the Highland host may not be given, as too hideously revolting to

* Wodrow, vol. ii. p. 370.

* Burnet's Own Times, vol. i. p. 418.

human nature to be expressed in language, or more than dimly suggested to the shuddering heart and recoiling mind. Even the face of the country bore witness to their ravages, which far surpassed those generally committed by an invading army in a hostile territory. Descending upon the fairest and most fertile scenes of Scotland, like a swarm of locusts in the regions of the east, they spread terror and ruin around them, leaving the country where they had appeared a waste and desolate wilderness.

Another device was employed by the council for the purpose of giving fuller scope to their persecuting zeal. On the 14th of February an act was passed "for securing the public peace,"* in which they contrived to include what is termed in Scottish law, *a writ of lawburrows*, by which a man who is afraid of violence from his neighbour, upon making oath to the circumstances affording ground for such apprehension, may have the party bound over to keep the peace, under security. By this act the king was made to apply for a writ of lawburrows against all in the western countries who had refused to sign the bond, on the pretence that his majesty had just grounds of apprehending injury from them. This seemed an attempt to involve the loyal Presbyterians in a personal quarrel with the king; and in the meantime it furnished a pretext for maintaining a standing army. When the western gentlemen complained that the whole district would be laid utterly waste by the interruption of all agricultural labour in consequence of these most oppressive proceedings, Lauderdale answered, that "it were better that the west bore nothing but windlestraws and sandy laverocks, than that it should bear rebels to the king."† Being thus driven to despair, they determined to brave the terrors of the proclamation which prohibited them from leaving the kingdom, and fourteen peers and fifteen gentlemen, headed by the Duke of Hamilton, went to London to lay their complaint before the king himself. But the interest of Lauderdale prevailed so far, that the supplicants received no favour from his majesty, nor any promise of redress.

* Wodrow, vol. ii. p. 400. † Tales of a Grandfather, vol. ii. p. 30.

Lauderdale appears, however, to have been somewhat alarmed at so strong a manifestation of hostility to his measures; and accordingly an act of council was passed about the end of February, ordering the Highland host to return to their own homes. They retired laden with booty of every description, from the plate and jewels taken from people of rank and wealth, to the most common furniture, household implements, and clothing of the cottager, and even to wearing apparel torn from the persons of all, both men and women, on whom they could lay their hands. No exact account can be given of the loss sustained by the western counties from this devastating inroad of the Highlanders; but, at a moderate computation, the county of Ayr alone is said to have suffered, from fines and plunder, to the value of about £137,499.* This is a very limited estimate of the direct loss of property sustained in that one county: the extent of personal injury inflicted can neither be estimated nor expressed.

Burnet suggests another reason for the recall of the Highland host. The intention of Lauderdale in bringing them down upon the western counties, he says, was to provoke the people into actual rebellion, partly to give some appearance of reason for the maintenance of a standing army, and partly that he and his adherents might divide among them the confiscated estates of such noblemen and gentlemen as they might succeed in driving to the desperate necessity of arming in self-defence. But the persecuted Presbyterians were aware of this malignant scheme, and therefore determined to suffer unresistingly, rather than fall into the snare laid for them by their cunning and relentless foe.† Foiled by their wonderful endurance, and perceiving that some even of his own party were recoiling with horror from the atrocities of his unparalled despotism, Lauderdale so far gave way as to recall the Highlanders, and to withdraw the bond and the writ of lawburrows. But at the same time he contrived to procure from his majesty a letter to the council expressing approbation of all their recent proceedings.

* Wodrow, vol. ii. p. 426.
† Burnet's Own Times, vol. i. pp. 418, 419; Kirkton, p. 390.

When the Highland host withdrew, the king's guards and the militia were again placed in garrison in different parts of the country, to suppress the field-preachings to the utmost of their power. But what ten thousand had not been able fully to accomplish, two thousand could not effect; and field-preachings were again held in several parts of the country, and attended by great numbers. At one, in particular, held at Whitekirk, nearly opposite the Bass, the soldiers were beaten off by the country people, and compelled to retire, one man being wounded in the brief conflict. For this, one man, James Learmont, was executed, chiefly in consequence of the relentless fury of Sharp. At another field-meeting the soldiery were more successful, dispersing the meeting, and seizing upon a number of the people, who, after suffering imprisonment, were sentenced to be banished to the plantations.

These numerous field-meetings roused the fury of Lauderdale and the prelates, who procured from the king an order calling a convention of estates to meet in July, to deliberate in what manner "field-conventicles, these rendezvouses of rebellion," as his majesty's letter was pleased to term them, might be most effectually suppressed. On the 10th of July, the convention passed an act imposing a cess or assessment of eighteen hundred thousand pounds Scots, or about £150,000 sterling, to be raised in five years by yearly payments of about £30, 000 sterling, for the maintenance of an army sufficiently strong to suppress those dreaded and detested field-meetings.* Not only was this measure in itself oppressive, but it also proved a new cause of contention among the Presbyterians. It immediately became a question among them whether they could in conscience pay an assessment which was imposed for the avowed purpose of maintaining an army to prevent the public preaching of the gospel. Some argued that it was of the nature of general taxation, which, as subjects, they were bound to pay, whatever use might be made of the money by the ruling powers of the State; others reasoned from the necessity of the case, since their refusal would only expose them to greater suffering, and to the utter spoliation of their entire property, by which their enemies would obtain much more than the specified amount; and the more resolute maintained that it was sinful to pay it, knowing precisely for what purpose it was levied, and how it was to be expended. It seems clear that the latter opinion was the correct one. For the fact, that this cess was imposed avowedly for the purpose of supporting an army to suppress the public preaching of the gospel in what were termed field-conventicles, deprived it of the character of common taxation, by which a general fund is raised to defray all the expenditure of the government, and where it is impossible to specify the particular use of any portion of the public money so raised. Yet the conduct of the Covenanters in declining to pay this cess has been appealed to in modern times, as a justification of the conduct of men who refused to pay an ancient and legal tax, levied for the purpose of supporting the preaching of the gospel, by men of whose doctrines they approved, and whom they acknowledged to be faithful and able servants of the Lord Jesus. This unhappy disagreement between the different parties of the Presbyterians tended greatly to increase the divisions among them, which had been already caused by the indulgence and other similar schemes of their crafty and merciless oppressors. On the strength of this assessment, it was resolved to raise and maintain a standing army of five thousand foot and five hundred cavalry, in addition to the life-guards, which had been continued in force after the previous disbanding of the army. It may be mentioned, that about this time James Graham of Claverhouse began to distinguish himself by his fierce and cruel treatment of the Covenanters, earning for himself that name of infamy and terror by which he will be known and held in detestation, notwithstanding the laudations of writers of romance, till the moors and mountains which witnessed his bloody deeds shall have perished amid the ruins of dissolving nature.

One event occurred in the beginning of this year, which demands notice, but which was omitted in order to avoid interrupting the narrative respecting the Highland host and other public transactions. This was the trial and execution

* Wodrow, vol. ii. p. 490.

of James Mitchell, who, in the year 1668, attempted to assassinate Archbishop Sharp. He had been apprehended, as above related, in the year 1674, and had confessed his guilt, on the promise of safety to his life; but was imprisoned for two years, first in Edinburgh, and afterwards in the Bass. In 1676 he was again brought to trial; when, finding that the promise of life was about to be broken, he refused to acknowledge his confession, and there being no other evidence against him, he was put to the torture of the boot. He behaved with great courage and firmness under this inhuman treatment, refusing to gratify the malice of his tormentors by uttering one word tending to criminate himself or others, till, after nine successive blows had crushed his leg almost to a jelly, he fainted under the excessive agony, and was again cast into prison. It was proposed to crush the other leg in the same manner; but this was prevented in consequence of a letter received by Sharp intimating that, if he persisted in his cruel intention, he should have a shot from a steadier hand.* After languishing two additional years in prison, he was again brought from the Bass to Edinburgh in the beginning of January 1678. The accusation was conducted by the Lord Advocate, well known as "the bloody Mackenzie," and the defence by Sir George Lockhart. As there was still no evidence except the prisoner's confession upon the promise that his life should be spared, the only way in which they could reach his life was by denying that any such promise had been given. Four members of the privy council—the Duke of Lauderdale, the Earl of Rothes, Lord Hatton, brother of Lauderdale, and Archbishop Sharp—positively swore that no assurance of life had been given to Mitchell to induce him to confess. Mitchell produced a copy of the act of council in which that assurance had been given, and craved that the register itself might be examined. This was refused, and sentence passed, condemning him to death. When the trial was over, the lords examined the register of the council, and found the act containing the assurance of life on which Mitchell had founded his defence. Lauderdale would have spared him, but Sharp strenuously insisted upon his death, as the only way of securing his own person against similar attempts. Lauderdale yielded, with a profane jest; and Sharp's cowardly and revengeful heart was gratified by this act of judicial murder. Such was the conduct of Archbishop Sharp, the great apostle of Scottish Prelacy,—conduct which even Burnet says "was probably that which, in the just judgment of God, and the inflamed fury of wicked men, brought him afterwards to such a dismal end."* "Doubtless," says Laing, "the fanaticism of Mitchell was of the most daring and atrocious nature; but his guilt is lost in the complicated perfidy, cruelty, perjury, and revenge, which accomplished his death.†"

[1679.] The year 1679 is one, the records of which would be most appropriately written in blood. Lauderdale had succeeded in repelling the accusations brought against him by the best of the Scottish nobility; and he had now an army at his command sufficiently strong, as he thought, to suppress the Presbyterians entirely. But it was necessary for that purpose to adopt measures more summary and destructive than had yet been attempted. Early in the month of January the council transmitted to his majesty, for his approbation, a series of overtures, or propositions, "for the suppression of the present schisms and disorders of the Church;" to which the king returned an early answer, expressing himself well pleased with them, and empowering the council to put them into effectual execution. Some of these propositions were peculiarly atrocious; such as,—authorising the soldiers to disperse all conventicles by force of arms, with an indemnity for whatever slaughter they might commit;—enjoining them to seize on the preachers and as many of the hearers as possible,—to strip those whom they could not take with them of their upper garments, as a means of future apprehension and conviction;—and offering rewards of £500 sterling for the apprehension of Mr. John Welsh, 3000 merks for any intercommuned minister, and 900 merks for any other preacher. Detachments of the newly levied army were stationed in dif-

* Law's Memorial's, p. 85.

* Burnet's Own Times, vol. i. p. 416. † Laing's History, vol. ii. p. 80.

ferent parts of the country, encouraged to their bloody work by the commands of the council, and assisted by the prelates and their underlings the curates. One effect of these oppressive measures was very soon apparent. It became certain death for the Presbyterians to meet for the worship of God, except in such large numbers as might enable them to defend themselves against their assailants. The field-meetings became therefore more rare in their occurrence, but correspondingly more formidable, both in the numbers who attended, and the army-like aspect which they began to wear. The preachers were generally accompanied by a band of armed men, who were resolved to protect their ministers at the hazard of their lives; and when they met for public worship, they chose strong positions, and posted armed sentinels all around them, to watch the movements of the enemy, and to warn their friends for a timely flight or a resolute resistance. At one of these meetings in the parish of Lesmahago, near Lanark, on the 30th of March, the soldiers, not daring to attack the main body, attempted to gratify their malice by plundering some women on the outskirts of the meeting. Upon this a party of men left the meeting, and compelled the plunderers to give back their pillage, and retire. About the same time two soldiers were murdered at Loudon Hill, not by the Presbyterians, but, as Wodrow has proved, by some of the mean villains employed as Government spies.*

These occurrences, as might be expected, roused the wrath of the persecutors to tenfold fury, and more violent and oppressive orders were immediately issued by the council; and a committee was appointed to be ready to act at all times and to issue such orders as circumstances might seem to require, the two archbishops being members of committee. On the 1st of May a new order of council was issued, commanding the Earl of Linlithgow to send a strong military force against the Rev. Messrs. Welsh, Cameron, Kid, and Douglas, and the party which accompained them, to seize them wherever they might be found, "and, in case of resistance, to pursue them to the death, declaring that the said officers and soldiers shall not be called in question therefor, civilly or criminally." This was equivalent to a proclamation of war against these ministers and every person who should endeavour to protect their lives; and it appears to have been so regarded by the more rash and daring of the persecuted Presbyterians. It was unquestionably the direct cause of the insurrection which soon afterwards took place.

In the meantime another event occured which had no little influence in precipitating the conflict. Archbishop Sharp had been in Edinburgh attending the meeting of privy council which issued the preceding order. Other measures were proposed, which would require the direct sanction of his majesty; and Sharp resolved to go to London himself, to aid in the arrangement of one great, and what he hoped might prove a conclusive, effort for the utter destruction of the Presbyterian Church of Scotland. The shire of Fife he regarded as under his peculiar care; and being much provoked that conventicles were frequently held in his domain, he had resolved to suppress them with the utmost rigour, and for that purpose had appointed a person named Carmichael, to employ all the methods commanded by the council without mercy or mitigation. Carmichael was an instrument suitable for such a purpose. His barbarities drove the people to despair, and in their misery they determined either to put him to death, or to terrify him so far as to compel him to leave that part of the country. For this purpose nine persons, some of them gentlemen of considerable property and rank, met on the morning of the 3d of May, prepared to carry their intention in effect. Carmichael, however, had received information that some gentlemen had been inquiring for him, and kept himself concealed. Being thus disappointed, they were on the point of separating, when they were informed that Sharp was approaching. Startled and excited by this unexpected intelligence at such a moment, one of them exclaimed, "Our arch-enemy is delivered into our hands;" and proposed that they should put him to death. Hackston of Rathillet opposed his design, but could not prevail upon his companions to abandon it; and though he would take no part in the matter, he consented to remain with them.

* Wodrow, vol. iii. pp. 37, 38.

The party then rode forward to Magus Moor, about three miles from St. Andrews, where they descried the prelate's coach, and immediately galloped on to intercept him. Perceiving himself pursued, Sharp cried out to his coachman, "Drive, drive," in that extreme terror of his life which his many cruelties to the Presbyterians may well have suggested to his dark and troubled mind. At length one of the pursuers overtook the coach, dismounted the postilion, cut the traces, and put an end to the unhappy prelate's flight, calling out to him, "Judas, be taken!" When the whole party had come up, they commanded Sharp to come out of the coach, and prepare himself for death, judgment, and eternity. The miserable man shrieked aloud for mercy, and clung to his daughter, who was with him in the carriage. Upon his refusing to come out, they fired into the carriage, but being unwilling to injure the person of the lady, their unsteady aim did not take effect, and they again commanded him to come forth, otherwise they would drag him out. At length he came out, repeating his vehement cries for mercy, offering to save their lives,—to give them money,—to abandon his prelatic station,—if they would but spare his life. His cries for mercy were in vain. They reminded him of his apostasy,—of the eighteen years of bloodshed of which he had been the chief cause,—of his repeated acts of perjury,—of his withholding the king's letter till nine sufferers, whom it would have saved, were put to a cruel and ignominious death; and having thus set his crimes in terrible array before his face, they again exhorted him to pray to God for that mercy which he himself had never shown to man. Still the wretched man could raise no cry to heaven,—a circumstance which appalled the assassins, and caused them to stand aghast at such a spectacle of utter despair. He availed himself so far of their half-recoiling horror as to creep grovelling towards Hackston, who remained on horseback a little apart, imploring him to interpose and save his life; but Hackston answering, "I shall never lay a hand on you," turned aside, and left him to his fearful fate.* They then fired upon him, and he fell to the ground; but when they were about to depart, perceiving him still alive, they returned and despatched him with their swords. So perished that deeply guilty and most miserable man, whose life had been one tissue of unbounded perfidy and remorseless cruelty, having been the cause to his suffering country of a greater amount of woe and ruin than ever was inflicted on it by any other human being. Yet, though his death may be justly viewed as an instance of the retributive judgment of God, the deed of those by whom his blood was shed cannot be regarded in any other light than as an act of murder. True, it was such a deed as Greece celebrated with loudest praises in the case of Harmodius and Aristogeiton, and Rome extolled when done by Cassius and Brutus; but the weapons of a Christian's warfare are not carnal, nor do the precepts of the gospel allow private individuals to stain their hands in blood, though for the purpose of avenging a public wrong, and rescuing their suffering country from the criminal oppression inflicted by a lawless and cruel tyrant. And therefore, though few will doubt that Sharp deserved to die, none will approve the conduct of those men, outraged grievously though they had been, who, in the exercise of what Bacon terms "wild justice," took upon themselves the office of his executioners.

When the intelligence of Sharp's death reached the council, they immediately despatched information to the king, and issued proclamations offering a large reward for the seizure of the murderers. In this their efforts were ineffectual; for these men, after remaining together till night, separated, and betook themselves to different parts of the country for better concealment. Several of them joined their friends in the west, but carefully abstained from stating their participation in the fatal deed—so well were they aware that the principles or impulses which had excited them to the slaughter of the arch-persecutor, were disavowed and condemned by almost the entire of the persecuted Presbyterians. Yet prelatic writers have generally accused the whole body of entertaining similar opinions, and approving of the unhappy prelate's assassination; and the ensnaring question, "Whether they approved of the killing

* Wodrow, vol. iii. pp. 40-46; Kirkton, pp. 411-421; Burnet's Own Times, vol. i. p. 471.

of the archbishop?" was frequently put by the soldiers to their prisoners, immediate death being the frequent consequence of an unsatisfactory answer. Many of those to whom this question was put would have readily interposed to save the life of the wretched victim, but would not express condemnation either of the deed itself, or of those by whom it was committed, not considering themselves entitled to judge the motives of other men, or to determine respecting such matters.

On the 13th day of May, a new proclamation was issued against conventicles, sufficiently expressive of the council's determination to wage henceforth a war of extermination. After rehearsing the previous acts against appearing in arms, especially at field-meetings, those "rendezvouses of rebellion," his majesty is made to express a degree of self-censure for his past *clemency!* and a determination that his subjects should no longer be led astray by such improper *lenity!* Authority is then given to judges and officers of the forces "to proceed against all such, who go with any arms to these field-meetings, as traitors;" and, lest this should seem to express lenity to those who went unarmed, the concluding clause expressly involves them in the same danger. The act of council on which this proclamation was formed was the last act to which Sharp set his persecuting hand, it having been proposed by him, and passed with some difficulty, on the 1st of May, before he left Edinburgh to meet his fate. From this circumstance this tyrannical act was termed "the bishop's legacy."*

The extreme of patient endurance was now almost overpast. The persecuted Presbyterians saw no alternative between sinking into a state of absolute slavery of both soul and body, and assuming arms in defence of their liberties, civil and religious. They would not submit to the prelatic yoke,—they would listen to the preaching of the pure gospel by their own ministers; and when their own lives and those of their pastors were assailed by the lawless soldiery, they conceived themselves entitled, by every law of God, nature, and reason, to defend themselves. To this extent who will say they were wrong? But intolerable oppression began, after long endurance, to drive them beyond what cooler reason in happier times can sanction. Some of the more impetuous, especially among the laymen, began to enquire whether it was not their duty to do something more than stand on the defensive. They thought the time was come when they were called upon to make a bold and public declaration of their sentiments, condemning the various steps by which the country had been reduced to such a state of misery, and censuring the conduct of those who continued to give any colour to the proceedings of the persecutors by subscribing their ensnaring bonds, or tamely submitting to their oppressive tyranny. Sentiments of this kind were strongly advocated by a gentleman named Robert Hamilton, son of Sir Thomas Hamilton of Preston, a man of personal piety, but of narrow and contracted views, ill-directed zeal, and overbearing temper. His opinions were adopted by a considerable number of the more youthful and ardent of the people, and by Cameron, Cargill, and Douglas, among the intercommuned ministers. It was at length resolved to make a public declaration of these sentiments; and accordingly, on the 29th of May, Robert Hamilton, Douglas, and about eighty armed men went to Rutherglen, extinguished the bonfires which had been kindled to celebrate the Restoration, burned the persecuting acts of parliament and council, read their own declaration and testimony, and then peaceably retired, leaving a copy of their declaration affixed to the market-cross.*

The Rutherglen declaration was magnified by the prelatic party into a daring act of open rebellion; and on Saturday the 31st of May, Graham of Claverhouse set out from Glasgow in quest of the party who had made this public manifestation. When he arrived at Hamilton, he surprised Mr. King, one of the intercommuned ministers, and about fourteen unarmed countrymen. Learning that a field-meeting was to be held next day near Loudonhill, he determined to assail and disperse it; and set out in the morning, taking with him his prisoners, bound together two by two. Before he came in sight of the Presbyterian party, they had received information of his approach, and had come to the determination to

* Wodrow, vol. iii. 58-60.

* Wodrow, vol. iii. p. 66.

prevent the meeting from being dispersed, by placing themselves in his line of march, a considerable space in advance of their friends, intending also to rescue the prisoners should they find it in their power. Mustering about forty horse, and one hundred and fifty foot, indifferently armed, but full of courage, they took up their position at a place called Drumclog, where they were somewhat protected by the swampy nature of the ground, and by a broad ditch which ran along their front. Hamilton took the chief command, supported by Hackston of Rathillet, Balfour of Kinloch or Burleigh, John Paton, William Cleland, Henry Hall, and some others of less note. When Claverhouse approached, and marked the strength of their position, and the resolute front which they presented, he perceived that they were not likely to be routed without a struggle, and therefore left a small party to guard the prisoners, commanding them to be shot should he be defeated.* Hamilton gave an order of a similar import that no prisoners should be taken. The battle was begun by Claverhouse, who commanded his men to fire upon the Covenanters. They returned his fire with effect; and, after the interchange of several volleys, Balfour and Cleland burst through their own line of defence, rushed upon their assailants, and, after a sharp conflict, put them to flight. Thirty or forty of the soldiers fell in the battle and the pursuit, and five were taken prisoners, one of whom was shot by Hamilton; the rest were saved by the interposition of the other officers.

After this encounter, the victorious Presbyterians deliberated what course to follow,—whether to disperse, or to remain together for their mutual protection. The latter opinion was speedily adopted, as they were well aware that their baffled and enraged enemies would exact a cruel revenge the moment it was in their power. They determined, therefore, to remain together in arms, both for their own defence, and to see whether the country would rally round them in sufficient strength to enable them to procure relief from the tyranny under which they had so long groaned. Next day they advanced to Hamilton, and, being joined by considerable numbers, they resolved to march on Glasgow, and dislodge the army from that town. But before they arrived, the troops under the command of Lord Ross and Claverhouse had prepared such means of defence as the countrymen could not force; and, after sustaining a slight loss, they retired, and encamped on Hamilton Moor, on the left bank of the Clyde.

Scarcely had the insurgents withdrawn, when the royal troops also left Glasgow, and retreated in hasty confusion towards Stirling to the main army. Proclamations and acts of council were issued, of which it is difficult to say whether they abound most in the language of terrified exaggeration or ferocious cruelty. Considerable exertions were made to increase the army, and the Duke of Monmouth, the king's illegitimate son, was sent down to take the chief command.

In the meantime, the army of the insurgents had received a considerable accession in point of numbers, but was paralyzed by dissension and disagreement. As the insurrectection, like that which terminated at Pentland, had arisen out of an unforeseen event, there was no previous concert of opinions and plans for their guidance; and when numbers began to flock to their army, it was considered necessary to frame and publish a declaration, stating the causes of their rising in arms, and the ruling principles by which they were actuated. Hamilton and his party were for taking the Rutherglen declaration as the basis of their new manifesto, and even purposed to emit a testimony against the indulgence and the payment of the cess; but as many who had joined them had submitted to both these measures, such persons would not consent to a declaration by which their own conduct would be directly condemned. These, on the other hand required that the manifesto should contain a declaration of their unshaken loyalty to the king, notwithstanding the oppressive tyranny which had been practised in his name; while Hamilton and his friends would not consent to acknowledge the king and his government regarding his right to the crown, as forfeited by his violation of the Covenant, which he had sworn, and by his long-continued and severe despotism. Neither

* Wilson's Relation, p. 7.

party would submit to the other, and all their councils became scenes of tumult and angry contention, discouraging the army, keeping back many who would have joined them, inducing others to abandon a divided and falling cause, and holding them spell-bound while their enemies were preparing to crush them. They seized on Glasgow, and advanced about a dozen miles towards Edinburgh, then hesitated, returned to their former position on Hamilton Moor, near Bothwell Bridge, and resumed their unhappy and most pernicious contests. There were eighteen ministers in their army, none of whom had taken the indulgence; and only two, Cargill and Douglas, espoused the opinions of Hamilton and his party. Not one of the sixteen approved of the indulgence, but they disapproved of condemning it in their manifesto, as certain to prevent a great number of true Presbyterians from joining the common cause. For this they were sharply censured by their opponents, and accused of downright Erastianism, as much as if they had themselves taken the indulgence. Yet how far they were from entertaining Erastian opinions must be evident from the fact, that their leader was Mr. Welsh, who had been intercommuned for field-preaching, and for whose seizure a reward of five hundred pounds sterling had been offered. That he could have been tainted with Erastian principles may well be deemed incredible; but while he was willing to peril his own life in preaching the gospel to any who had a desire to hear it, he was reluctant to hazard the success of the Presbyterian army and cause, by publishing a declaration which must alienate many, and which, in his opinion, the circumstances and necessities of the case did not require. Counter declarations were framed and proposed; ministers contended against ministers, and officers against officers; the body of the army caught the spirit of contention, and they lay in their camp tossing and confused till the army of their enemies was upon them.

"It is scarcely within the province of a historian to attempt deciding a question of such a nature as that which divided the Covenanters; yet, as it is so closely connected with the principles of the Church of Scotland, a few remarks may be offered. In one point of view it would seem that the opinions of Hamilton and the stricter party, were sounder and more consistent than those of their opponents. The indulgence was unquestionably based upon the act of supremacy, and, therefore, inconsistent with the fundamental principles of the Presbyterian Church. But it was not so clear a matter that a condemnation of it was imperatively required till an Assembly of the whole Church could be held, and the matter fairly and deliberately adjudged. The direct contest was with Prelacy and the act of supremacy in matters ecclesiastical; and could these have been removed, the indulgence would have perished of itself. It was for those who had complied with it to confess and lament their own defection, publicly, if they thought proper; but it does not seem a matter of positive duty in the non-indulged to have issued a condemnation of any thing more than the direct causes of their wrongs and sufferings. And especially, the significant suppression of any recognition of the king's authority as the lawful sovereign of the kingdom, indicated the existence of views, the open promulgation of which would expose the Presbyterians to the accusation of rebellion, with more appearance of justice than any thing which had yet taken place, and might be ruinous to their prospects of success. Besides, it actually involved that very mingling of things civil and spiritual, which leads inevitably to either Erastianism or Popery. It was true that Charles was a tyrant; and it may be the opinion of jurists, that subjects are bound by no law, human or divine, from rising up in vindication of their civil liberties, and hurling a lawless tyrant from his throne. But that is not an argument which Christians and Christian ministers, simply as such, can use. A Christian may be the loyal subject of a heathen monarch; and, even when persecuted, is not entitled, on that account, to rebel and wage war against his persecutor. Yet, when Christian subjects are exposed equally to the loss of their civil and religious liberties, it is not surprising that they should forget the nice distinctions which are required to guide them in determining what declarations they should issue, and what mode of self-defence they should employ. It seems probable, also, that Hamilton and his party were led to adopt and hold their opinions by misunderstanding the conduct of the Covenanters of the preceding generation, and especially with regard to the Act of Classes, excluding malignant and disaffected persons from places of trust, whose whole previous conduct proved that they would immediately use their power for the overthrow of religious reformation. And as this could not possibly be held with regard to those who had merely submitted to the indulgence, the cases were not parallel, and the rule of the one could not justly apply to the other. After all, however, this may be said in favour of the very strictest of the Presbyterians, that the principles which they held were the very same which nine years afterwards pervaded the whole nation, drove the race of Stuarts from the throne, and secured the liberty of Britain, by what all men with one consent rejoice to term the Glorious Revolution; and it would not be easy for any man who defends the principles which led to that great national deliverance, to show his consistency in condemning those of the persecuted Covenanters.*

At length, on the morning of the Sabbath day, June 22d, the royal army, commanded by the Duke of Monmouth, arrived at Bothwell, within a quarter of a mile of the bridge, which was in possession of the Presbyterian forces. Even then their baneful contentions did not cease. A deputation went to the duke, and presented a supplication for a redress of grievances. He refused to treat with them while they remained in arms; but expressing that he would be able to obtain from his majesty both mercy and redress if they would immediately lay down their arms and submit themselves to his clemency, he offered them half an hour to consider and answer these terms. That half hour was spent in hot altercation; and when it was past, the duke sent a detachment to attempt the passage of the bridge. It was bravely defended for an hour by a body of the Presbyterians under the command of Hackston, and Ure of Shargarton. At length their ammunition failed; and when they sent for a supply, they received orders to fall back upon the main army. Nothing could have been more insane than such a command; but being now defenceless and unsupported, they were constrained reluctantly to comply. Even then their native courage signalized itself by one gallant deed. Looking back, and seeing that a party of the royalists had already followed them to the southern bank of the river, they wheeled about, charged them hand to hand, and driving them headlong across the bridge, regained possession of that important post. Having thus almost instinctively pointed out the path which might have led to safety, if not to victory, they were again obliged to the inert mass, whom neither danger could excite nor courage rouse. Slowly the enemy's forces crossed the steep and narrow bridge, while the western army looked on in a state of helpless and unmoving stupor. One charge sufficed to cast the weltering mass into complete confusion; and, bereft of even the courage of despair, they fled, not in bands, but in scattered and defenceless rout, hewn down on every side by the remorseless hands of their fierce pursuing foes. Claverhouse, burning with the desire of revenge for his defeat at Drumclog, urged on the pursuit and the slaughter with inexorable fury, till night compelled him to quit his murderous work, wearied, but not satiated, with bloody butchery. Few fell in the battle, about four hundred perished in the flight, and about twelve hundred remaining together in a body, surrendered at discretion on the field.*

Such was the fate of that unconcerted and ill-conducted insurrection of the persecuted Presbyterians which terminated in the disastrous battle of Bothwell Bridge. But disastrous as the battle was, it was but the prelude to horrors of an unutterably more dreadful aspect. The unfortunate prisoners were stripped almost naked, and compelled to lie down upon the ground, while a strong guard kept watch over them, and fired upon

* Both parties into which the persecuted sufferers were henceforth divided were Presbyterians and Covenanters, and equally deserve both appellations; but the minority, consisting chiefly of the followers of Hamilton, Cameron, Cargill, &c., may be termed the strict Covenanters, to distinguish them from the larger body, who continued to adhere to the Covenant but not with such unbending firmness.

* Wodrow, vol. iii. pp. 88-100; Russell's Account appended to Kirkton; Wilson's Relation; Ure of Shargarton, in M'Crie's Lives of Veitch and Brysson; Blackadder's Memoirs.

them if but a single man raised his head or turned his body where he lay. Next day they were bound together two and two, and driven to Edinburgh by the brutal soldiery, like cattle to a slaughter-house. There they were enclosed within the Greyfriar's churchyard for a period of five months, half-naked, half-starved, and exposed to all the vicissitudes of the season, unsheltered save by the tomb-stones, and a few rude sheds erected towards the close of the autumnal months. In the mean time, Claverhouse and some others proposed to burn Glasgow and Hamilton, and lay the surrounding country waste; but to these savage proposals the Duke of Monmouth would not give his consent; and even exerted himself to check the severities of the council, and mitigate the sufferings of the persecuted insurgents. A proclamation was, however, speedily issued, containing a list of the gentlemen and ministers supposed to be implicated in what was termed "the late rebellion," declaring them traitors, adding, "or any others who concurred or joined in it." An indemnity was soon after published for all who would submit, but it was so ample in its exceptions as to be a nullity, so far as regarded the insurgents. A bond was also formed to be offered to the prisoners, the terms of which were such that few of them felt at liberty to subscribe it, even to save themselves from death or banishment. They could not conscientiously term the insurrection "rebellion;" and they would not bind themselves to take up arms in self-defence. Yet this they must do, or prepare to suffer the extreme of tyrannical cruelty. Some of the prisoners were prevailed upon to take this bond; others refused, and were condemned to slavery in the plantations. About two hundred and fifty of them were crowded into one vessel, to be transported to Barbadoes and sold for slaves; but a storm wrecked the ship, and, being confined within the hold, from which the captain refused to release them even when the vessel was foundering, not more than fifty escaped alive. Two ministers, the Rev. Messrs. Kid and King, had been taken after the battle; and on the 14th of August they were both executed in Edinburgh. Five other prisoners were carried to Magus Moor, and there hanged, as if to appease the manes of the perjured Sharp.*

But even these atrocities were slight, compared with those committed by the army. "The bloody Claverhouse," at the head of a strong detachment, was let loose upon the western and southern counties, and swept across them, like a demon of destruction guiding an exterminating whirlwind. Torture, rapine, and murder, marked his path. Those who fled were hunted down and shot in the fields; and these whose age or sex rendered them incapable of flight, were tortured, abused, and butchered by their own hearthside. The hoary head of threescore years and ten was dashed to the earth in blood; the shrinking form of woman was exposed to violence and fiery agonies, and the tender limbs of youth were mangled, or their heads cut to the skull, with twisted cords, in the barbarous attempt to wring from their anguish a discovery where their dearest relatives were concealed. But humanity recoils from the hideous recital of such horrors, perpetrated by the command, beneath the eye, and often by the hand, of that relentless ruffian, the favourite hero whom the admirers of Scottish Prelacy delight to honour.

To aid the sword in completing the ruin of the Presbyterians, circuit courts were appointed to be held in the different counties which remained most steady to their religious principles, empowered to "prosecute with the utmost rigour all suppliers, intercommuners, or correspondents with the rebels who had been at Bothwell," and to forfeit and burn in effigy those who did not appear upon citation.† Lists were speedily made up of all who had been at Bothwell, or were suspected to have been there, or were *suspected of being suspected* to have been favourably inclined towards the insurgents. The curates were, as formerly, the chief informers; and in innumerable instances gratified their personal malice and revenge, by naming persons against whom they bore a private grudge, or who had shown dislike to Prelacy. By these means all Presbyterians possessed of any property were either dragged to

* Wodrow, vol. iii. 112-140.

† Wodrow vol. iii. p. 141.

prison, or subjected to the most ruinous exactions, extermination being the object of their persecutors. Yet, as if to hide their fierce intentions, and to cast the odium upon their victims, an act was passed rescinding the acts against house-conventicles, and offering a new shadow of indulgence to Presbyterian ministers.

About the same time the final struggle between Lauderdale and his opponents took place; a full discussion of the demerits of his administration being held in the presence of the king and two English noblemen, the Earls of Essex and Halifax. It ended, as was to be expected, in the king's giving a complete acquittal to his despotic minion, and even expressing approbation of his most sanguinary proceedings. This approbation he expressed in private, in terms worthy of the most unprincipled tyrant. "I perceive," said the heartless despot, "that Lauderdale has been guilty of many criminal actions against the people of Scotland; but I cannot find that he has done any thing contrary to my interest;"*—as if the interest of a just sovereign could ever be different from that of his people. But though Charles protected Lauderdale in this last struggle, and in letters to the council approved of all his proceedings, he nevertheless allowed him to sink out of public employment, the chief power in Scotland being held for a short period by Monmouth, and then by the Duke of York.

[1680.] The year 1680 was remarkable for what appears a new aspect assumed by a section of the persecuted Presbyterians, but what in reality, if impartially considered, may rather be regarded as a more full developement of Presbyterian principles, somewhat biassed and exaggerated through the force of circumstances. The defeat of the western army at Bothwell Bridge was greatly caused, as has been already stated, by the contentions between the stricter party and those of more accommodating views. After that fatal day, the division between the two parties not only continued, but became wider, till it ended in a complete separation, Richard Cameron and Donald Cargill being the only ministers whom those zealous opponents of all practical tyranny and lax submissiveness of principle would acknowledge. This division proved highly injurious for a time to the Presbyterian cause, not only by the weakness which such disunion always must produce, but also by the tendency which it had to leave the disunited parties to fall into opposite extremes. The strict Presbyterians, termed sometimes "Cameronians," and sometimes "Society People," by keeping aloof from all others, and conversing only with those of their own sentiments, acquired a character of stern, inflexible determination, and poured their whole mental strength into a channel not too direct, but much too narrow, and became too prone to condemn the weaknesses as well as the errors of many whom gentler treatment might have made their friends. On the other hand, those of greater natural timidity and less strength of principle, who startled not only at the prospect of danger, but also at the practical conclusions to which certain abstract principles seemed to lead, being left to themselves, tempted by indulgence after indulgence, tried by bond after bond, yielding to one compliance after another, fell gradually away from several of the great principles to which they ought to have adhered, and in their own defence, as they imagined, were led to censure or condemn views and doctrines which, in more propitious circumstances, they would have been prompt to defend. In this manner both parties were left insensibly to diverge somewhat from the straight line along which a more comprehensive view of their own leading principles would have conducted them; and, while almost equally exposed to the machinations and the violence of their relentless enemies, they began to regard each other with mutual dislike, and at times to commit the folly and the crime of assailing each other in terms of bitter mutual recrimination.

The first public manifestation of the principles held by the stricter party of the Presbyterians took place incidentally, and before their views had been thoroughly matured. The direction of their deepest thoughts had been indicated during the dissensions at Bothwell Bridge, by their refusal to make any public avowal of allegiance to the king in their declaration. Subsequent reflection, in the midst of the most cruel and unmerited persecu-

* Burnet's Own Times, vol. i. p. 470.

tion, had only served to confirm their opinions; and they had arrived at the conclusion, that when sovereigns violate their solemn engagements with their subjects, and become tyrants, the people are released from theirs, and are no longer bound to support and defend those by whom they are oppressed. Few will now deny the abstract truth of this proposition; but in those days it was regarded as the very essence of treason and rebellion. They had, it appears, begun to draw up a general statement of their principles, at first in the form of a mere outline, to guide their deliberations while endeavouring to mature it into what might form a bond of union. While in this indigested condition, the paper was in the possession of Henry Hall of Haughhead, who in company with Mr. Cargill, was lurking in the neighbourhood of Queensferry. Their concealment had become known to the curates of Borrowstounness and Carriden, who gave information to the governor of Blackness Castle, by whom they were surprised at Queensferry on the 3d of June. The brave resistance of Henry Hall secured the escape of Cargill, but he was himself mortally wounded in the conflict, and died as they were conveying him to Edinburgh. The paper containing the rude outline of the intended declaration above alluded to, was found on his person. It is known by the name of the Queensferry Paper, from the place where it was seized; and, though an unfinished, is nevertheless a very remarkable production.*

This paper contains a statement materially the same with those on which both the First and Second Reformations were based,—an avowal of the Scriptures as the only rule of faith and conversation,—a pledge to promote the kingdom of God by every possible and lawful method, and to attempt the rescue of religious truth from all oppression,—a declaration of adherence to the covenanted Reformation of the Presbyterian Church,—a bold disowning of all authority which opposes the Word of God and persecutes on account of religion,—and a bond of mutual protection and defence. But the most objectionable part of this paper was the following rash declaration: "We do declare, that we shall set up over ourselves, and over what God shall give us power of, government and governors according to the Word of God;—that we shall no more commit the government of ourselves, and the making of laws for us, to any one single person, this kind of government being most liable to inconveniences, and aptest to degenerate into tyranny." This rash declaration of an intention of attempting to change the form of government, was eagerly laid hold of by all the enemies of the Presbyterian Church, and urged against the whole body, as if it had been the unquestionable purpose of them all, instead of being the unsigned and unauthenticated opinion of some unknown individuals among them, driven into a state of desperation by long-continued and intolerable outrage. But it was no part of the characteristic conduct of the prelatic tyrants to exercise candour with regard to the opinions of their Presbyterian opponents, or rather victims; and they had been too long in the habit of vending the most malicious calumnies against them, to let slip so good an opportunity of blackening their character and their cause. Therefore was the Queensferry Paper keenly seized upon and universally referred to, as containing the real sentiments of the entire Presbyterian community. In order so far to counteract the injurious consequences resulting from the unpropitious promulgation of this rash paper, Cameron, Cargill, and their adherents, framed another more deliberately, containing a more matured view of their principles and opinions, and excluding the objectionable clause respecting a change in the form of government; but at the same time renouncing allegiance to the reigning monarch, on account of his perjury, usurpation of ecclesiastical supremacy, and tyranny in matters civil; and declaring war against him and his supporters, as a tyrant and usurper, and an enemy of the Lord Jesus Christ and his cause and Covenant. This document, after having been publicly read, was affixed to the market-cross of Sanquhar on the 22d of June, whence it came to be termed the Sanquhar Declaration.*

* Wodrow, vol. iii. pp. 205-211.

* Wodrow, vol. iii. p. 218; Hind let Loose; Informatory Vindication.

The publication of the Sanquhar Declaration had no effect in mitigating the wrath of the persecutors, nor even in repelling their calumnies. In their proclamations they contrived so to blend the Queensferry Paper with the Sanquhar Declaration, as to lead to the conclusion that they were identical; at the same time holding them forth as the real sentiments of the entire body of the suffering Presbyterians. Nor did they fail to avail themselves of the opportunity which these papers seemed to afford, of issuing new and more cruel and exterminating commands to the army to pursue, seize, imprison, or kill all who were suspected of being concerned in these bold declarations. Cameron, Cargill, and ten other persons, were declared traitors, and a high price set on their heads; and the magistrates throughout sixteen different parishes were ordered to summon before them all the inhabitants, male and female, above sixteen years of age, and take their oaths "whether any of the foresaid traitors were in that parish, and where, and when." General Dalziel and the other officers of the army were also ordered to apprehend every disaffected person, and send all such under a sufficient guard to Edinburgh. These violent proceedings were, as usual, productive of two different effects. They deterred some from joining the resolute band led by Cameron and Cargill; but they served to knit that band into closer union, and to confirm their determination to maintain the ground they had taken, and to bear aloft the banner of civil and religious liberty, as long as as there should be a living hand to grasp it, and a living breast to form for it a defensive rampart.

It deserves to be especially remarked, that the persecuting party, in their desire to cast obloquy upon their victims, caused great numbers of the Queensferry Paper and the Sanquhar Declaration to be printed and circulated throughout both England and Scotland, and by that means disseminated the free and daring sentiments contained in these documents to an immeasurably greater extent than could have been in the power of their authors to have accomplished, however desirous they might have been. And when we read these papers, and compare them with the great national declarations which form the basis of the Revolution, we can not resist the conviction, that in the former we perceive the small germ out of which arose British liberty, that plant of renown, under the world-wide branches of which all tribes and kindreds of mankind rejoice. Almost the only real difference between the Declaration of the Cameronians, or rather the true Presbyterians, and that of the Convention of Estates at the Revolution, consisted in the former being the act of a small band of enlightened and determined patriots, the latter that of the nation. While, therefore, none who approve the latter can consistently condemn the former, every generous heart will bestow the meed of warmest approbation upon those who, in the midst of reproach, danger, and death, laid the foundation-stone and began the structure, cemented with their blood, of civil and religious liberty, which men of less heroic mould were permitted in calmer and brighter days to rear.

The consequence of these daring declarations on the one hand, and revengeful measures on the other, soon appeared. Strong bands of soldiery overran the country in all directions, and the country people were either compelled to give information by threats and tortures, or gave it to avoid being suspected and treated accordingly. At the same time the followers of Cameron and Cargill kept together in larger numbers than before, consequently were the more exposed to information and discovery. On the 22d of July, information was given to Bruce of Earlshall, who commanded a large body of military, that Cameron, and a party of armed men with him, were at a place called Ayrsmoss, or Airdsmoss, in the parish of Auchinleck. Seeing the enemy approaching, and perceiving that escape was impossible, the persecuted party resolved to stand on their defence, and either to hew out for themselves a path of retreat, or to sell their lives dearly. Hackston of Rathillet, who was among them, took the command of the small band, amounting to twenty-three horse and forty foot, indifferently armed. Being drawn up in battle-array, they waited the attack; and during the brief interval, Cameron, in a short but fervent prayer, committed their cause to God, using repeatedly this pathetic expression, "Lord, spare the green and take the ripe." The encounter was sharp, but of short duration. At the first shock, the Covenanters, led by Hackston and Cameron, broke the front line of the enemy, and, had they been vigorously seconded, might have cut their way through the reeling ranks of their antagonists; but the foot keeping their position on the skirt of the moss, the soldiers closed round the gallant band, who, with instinctive Scottish bravery, forming back to back, their faces to their foes, continued the unequal conflict till nine were killed on the spot, and the rest were wounded, struck down, and made prisoners. Rathillet, severely wounded and overpowered with numbers, was made prisoner; but after the conflict, the bodies of Cameron and his brother were found lying side by side among the slain. Twenty-eight of the soldiers were killed in this fierce skirmish; and several of the Covenanters died of their wounds within a few days.*

Cameron's head and hands were cut off and carried to Edinburgh, to be fixed up in some elevated position; even the person who did the deed saying, "These are the head and hands of a man who lived preaching and praying, and died fighting and praying." But previous to this they were taken to his father, at that time in prison, who was cruelly asked if he knew them. The venerable man taking them in his hands and kissing them, while the tears fell fast upon the faded relics, exclaimed, "I know them, I know them; they are my son's, my own dear son's: it is the Lord; good is the will of the Lord!" Hackston, wounded, bleeding, and exhausted as he was, was carried to Edinburgh; and as he was known to have been present at the murder of Sharp, though he laid not a hand upon that cruel apostate, the council determined to glut their fiend-like thirst of revenge in his torments. When taken to the place of execution, his right hand was cut off, and, after a considerable interval, his left. He was then hung up by the neck; and while struggling in the agonies of death, his breast was cut open, and his heart torn out and exposed on the point of the executioner's knife, while its palpitations and the convulsed quivering of his frame showed that life and consciousness were not yet gone. Several other victims perished on the scaffold; but their death was not attended by such unparalleled atrocity, the recital of which makes the heart to shudder with horror and indignation.*

Such monstrous cruelty was not found to be a very effectual way of making proselytes to Scottish Prelacy, nor even of terrifying men into crouching submission to the dictates of despotism. The blood-stained banner which fell from Cameron's dying hand, was caught up, and borne aloft by Cargill with unshrinking resolution. And, as if to testify in the most signal manner his abhorrence of the tyrannical persecutors, Cargill publicly excommunicated the king, the Duke of York, the Duke of Monmouth, the Duke of Lauderdale, the Duke of Rothes, General Dalziel, and Sir George Mackenzie. This solemn sentence of excommunication he pronounced at a field-preaching held at Torwood in Stirlingshire, in the month of September, after enumerating the series of grave offences against the laws of God and man of which they had been guilty. This act was much censured by many at the time; but this at least may be said in its defence, that whether Mr. Cargill was entitled on his own authority to pronounce such a sentence or not, it was one which these perjured and blood-stained men deserved. Nor was it regarded by the culprits themselves as an empty fulmination, deserving nothing but contempt. It roused their wrath in the first instance, and afterwards haunted several of them like a voice of doom, from whose indefinite terrors they could not escape. During the course of the following year, the Duke of Rothes fell dangerously ill; and perceiving the hand of death upon him, he sent for some of the persecuted Presbyterian ministers, to seek for instruction from them, not his cherished prelates, in his parting hour. To one of them he said,—"We all thought little of what that man did in excommunicating us; but I find that sentence binding upon me now, and will, I fear, bind to eternity." The faithful minister having spoken to the despairing sinner of that infinite atonement which can expiate every degree of guilt, prayed fervently for re-

* Wodrow, vol. iii. p. 219; Life of Cameron, pp. 203, 204.

* Wodrow, vol. iii. pp. 222, 223; Cloud of Witnesses.

pentance and mercy to the unhappy man. Some of the noblemen in an adjacent room hearing his voice, said, "That is a Presbyterian minister that is praying;" and turning to the bishops, added, "not one of you can pray as they do, though the welfare of a man's soul should depend upon it. The Duke of Hamilton remarked,—"We banish these men from us, and yet, when dying, we call for them; this is melancholy work!"* How mighty is the voice of conscience even in a hardened heart, when that heart is stirred to its inmost depths!

Before the close of this year, the Duke of York came to Edinburgh, and assumed the main direction of public affairs in Scotland, Lauderdale having sunk into a degree of dotage through excessive indulgence in his animal appetites. There was also another reason. The course of English politics was at that time setting strongly against the Duke of York's succession to the crown, in consequence of his bigoted attachment to Popery; and it was thought expedient to remove him from court for a season, till, by a series of intrigues, some change might be effected in the public mind. During the duke's previous visit to Scotland he had striven to acquire some popularity, and had succeeded to a considerable extent among the selfish and ambitious, who were likely to be his most fitting instruments when his designs should be matured. His present coming to Scotland proved a signal for increased severity against the persecuted Presbyterians, and especially against the followers of Cameron and Cargill. Of this he gave a fearful indication in presiding at the council when one Spreul, an apothecary, was subjected to the torture of the boot; for while the greater part of the noblemen hurried away from the court, that they might not witness the dreadful spectacle, the Duke of York remained, and gazed on with grim delight, feasting his cruel eyes with the victim's agonies.†

[1681.] The first trial which took place in the year 1681 was that of two young women, Isabel Alison and Marion Harvey. The accusation against these females was, that they had heard Mr. Cargill preach, would not renounce the Sanquhar Declaration, and had expressed sympathy for the sufferings of some of the victims of prelatic tyranny. The most ensnaring questions were put to them by Sir George Mackenzie, with the view of drawing from them answers which might by his fiendish ingenuity be distorted into treasonable language. To its indelible disgrace the court pronounced the sentence of guilty; and the innocent and helpless martyrs were brutally hanged on the 26th of January, for the heinous crime of hearing the gospel preached in the fields.*

About this time there appeared a small sect, who assumed the name of "Sweet Singers," but were generally termed Gibbites, from their leader, John Gib, a sailor in Borrowstounness. Their number never exceeded thirty persons, of whom four were men, and the rest chiefly young and ignorant females. Their tenets may be most briefly and accurately characterised by stating, that they were an absurd compound of some of the most extravagant notions of the Quakers, with some of the extreme speculative views of the strict Covenanters. While, with the former, they claimed inspiration, disregarded learning, and rejected the names of the months and the days of the week, with the latter they disowned the king,—adding, and "all authority throughout the world." Cargill attempted to reason them out of their absurdities, both in an interview held with them for that purpose, and by letter, but in vain. They despised admonitions and remonstrances, and spurned at reproof, condemning alike all denominations of Christians in the world who would not countenance their extravagancies. They were, in a short time, seized in a body; and, when examined by the council, displayed such ignorance and folly, that they were judged fitter for hard labour in the house of correction than any other punishment. This proved to them a sanatory process; and when liberated, they generally returned to their homes, resumed their occupations, and ceased to exist as a sect.† But the persecuting party did not allow their name to perish. It afforded too good an opportunity of casting obloquy upon the

* Cruickshank, vol. ii. p. 116; Life of Cargill, p. 46.
† Wodrow, vol. iii. p. 253; Burnet's Own Times, vol. . p. 583.

* Wodrow, vol. iii. pp. 275, 276; Cloud of Witnesses.
† Wodrow, vol. iii. pp. 348-356.

true Presbyterians, who were falsely represented as holding the same opinions. This the prelatists could not but know to be false, since one of the avowed tenets of the Gibbites was the renouncing of the Covenant, the Confession of Faith, and the Sanquhar Declaration, for the defence of which the Presbyterians were suffering the extreme of persecution. Let the judicious reader compare this single instance of what may truly be termed fanaticism in Scotland, after above twenty years of persecution, with the almost innumerable multitude of sects which have sprung up in every other country in times of similar excitement and suffering,—in Germany, for example, at the Reformation, or in England during the time of Cromwell,—and he can scarcely fail to be astonished at the contrast. We have already suggested what seems the only explanation. The multiplicity and extravagance of sects is the consequence of the ignorance of the people, which has left them incapable of distinguishing between what is true and what is false, what is rational and what is absurd. Hence the wild follies of the sectarians in Germany, when emerging out of Popish ignorance; and hence, also, the extravagance of English sectarians, when striving to escape out of Prelatic twilight. And, on the contrary, the fact that only four men, and twenty-five or twenty-six women, fell into enthusiastic delusions during the persecution in Scotland, and in a parish where there had been a prelatic incumbent for twenty years, may be regarded as a conclusive proof of the superior efficiency of the Presbyterian Church, in communicating sound and lasting instruction, such as the utmost malice of its deadly enemies could neither destroy nor pervert. The conduct of the council, too, proves sufficiently, that while they unjustly termed the whole of the Presbyterians "fanatics," they knew the difference between those who were truly so, and whom, therefore, they could despise and dismiss without the infliction of punishment, and those whom they knew to be animated by principles of indestructible might, because of eternal truth, before which they themselves bowed with guilty terror, and to which they paid the strange homage of the most deadly hatred. Had the Presbyterians been indeed the wild and gloomy fanatics which their persecutors represented them to be, they might have been safely left to pursue their own foolish and self-destructive course; they would soon have died out when they had reached the extreme of their absurdities; but the guilty souls of the perjured prelatists and the tyrannical council told them, that there was in the Presbyterian Church an amount of truth, which they must either destroy by violence, or be by it themselves destroyed. They called them *fanatics*, *traitors*, and *rebels;* and under these abusive names they strove to conceal their hatred against true and vital religion; but all the while they knew that these names were unjustly applied, and that they were themselves the fanatical devotees of sin, and actual traitors and rebels against the dread Majesty of the King Eternal.

Cargill still continued to brave the terrors of persecution, and to bear aloft with firm and fearless hand the banner of the Covenant. Against him the hottest rage of the tyrannical party was directed, and troops of soldiers scoured the country in all directions in pursuit of him. Hunted from place to place, he still continued to preach in the fields, in the most solitary moors and mountain fastnesses, to the undaunted few that dared to hear him. But his noble warfare was nearly accomplished. His last sermon was preached upon Dunsyre common, between Clydesdale and Lothian, on the 10th day of July. That night, accompanied by two of his adherents, Walter Smith and James Boig, he slept at Covington Mill. But information respecting his movements had been given to Irvine of Bonshaw, who had obtained a military commission; and he, at the head of a strong party of dragoons, beset the house by daybreak, and seized Mr. Cargill and his two companions. Bonshaw, whose border predatory habits had qualified him for such adventures, laid hold of his prisoner, exclaiming with savage delight, "O blessed Bonshaw, and blessed day that ever I was born, that have found such a prize this morning!" the reward of 5000 merks, which had been set upon Cargill's head, being the only thing for which his heart could rejoice. The cruel moss-trooper then placed Cargill upon an unsaddled horse, tying with his own hands the feet of his prisoner beneath the animal's belly, so hard as to cause severe pain to the sufferer.*

The prisoners were all taken to Edinburgh and brought to trial. Little proof was sought, and indeed little was required, as they all readily admitted that they had done what the council had called treason. Yet some compunction seems to have seized the council, for they hesitated whether to confine Cargill to the Bass for life, or to pass the sentence of death upon him. They were equally divided when it came to the vote of the Earl of Argyle, who gave his voice for death, by which the question was decided, and he was condemned to die.† This fatal vote was afterwards remembered by the Covenanters, when Argyle wished them to join his insurrection, and it prevented them from uniting with him and being involved in his overthrow. It was also remembered with deep remorse by the unhappy nobleman himself, when his own hour came to meet a similar doom. Cargill, the two that were taken with him, and two others taken about the same time, were executed on the 27th of July, and their heads fixed on spikes above two of the gates of Edinburgh. They all died in full possession of the peace and joy of martyrs, Cargill declaring that he went up the ladder with less fear or perturbation of mind than ever he entered a pulpit to preach.

Instead of continuing to relate the bloody deeds of the persecutors, it seems expedient to mention some of their legislative enactments. It was now nine years since a parliament had been held in Scotland, and the king determined that one should be called, appointing the Duke of York to be the royal commissioner. The chief objects which the king had in view in calling this parliament were to procure some new enactments against the Covenanters, and a legislative sanction to the Duke of York's succession to the crown, as appeared plainly, both from his majesty's letter to the parliament, and from their obsequious answer, in which these were made the leading topics. The subject of the Duke of York's succession had already been discussed in the English parliament, and a bill for securing it had been rejected in the House of Lords, on account of the duke's avowed adherence to Popery. It seems to have been the opinion of the Romish politicians, that there would be less opposition made in Scotland; and that, if the duke's succession were ratified in the latter kingdom, England would rather submit than incur the hazard of a civil war. It was, besides, a part of the great scheme for the re-establishment of Popery in both countries,—a scheme which was the ruling principle of the whole policy of both the royal brothers.

The parliament began its labors by passing a short yet unbiguous act, ratifying all former acts respecting religion. In the second act there was no such ambiguity. It was respecting the succession to the crown, and asserted in the most stringent terms, "That the kings of this realm, deriving their royal power from God Almighty alone, do succeed lineally thereto, according to the known degrees of proximinity in blood, which cannot be interrupted, suspended, or diverted by any act or statute whatsoever; and that no difference in religion, nor no law or act of parliament made, or to be made, can alter or divert the right of succession." All attempts or designs to alter the succession were declared to be treason. Such was what Wodrow calls the "everlasting act" of this subservient parliament, —an act the futility of which the duke was afterwards to experience, though its enactment must have delighted his despotic heart. Another act, for securing the peace of the country, bore directly against the Presbyterians, and exposed them to still greater severities and more arbitrary treatment than they had previously endured, dreadful as their oppression had already been. On the 31st of August was passed the crowning act of this slavish parliament,—the infamous Test Act. The assumed object of this act was for the security of the Protestant religion "against Popery and fanaticism;" and for that purpose it contained an oath which was to be taken by all persons occupying places of trust and public employment, with the exception of papists. The two main propositions of the oath were, an avowal of belief in, and adherence to, the First Confession of Faith drawn up by the early

* Wodrow, vol. iii. pp. 279-284; Cruickshank, vol. ii. p. 107; Life of Cargill, p. 44.

† Life of Cargill, pp. 50, 51

reformers; and an acknowledgment that the king "is the only supreme governor of this realm, over all persons, and in all cases, as well ecclesiastical as civil." It contained also a distinct renunciation of the covenants, and a bond not to attempt any change in the government of either Church or State, as by law established, which of necessity implied the entire and final abandonment of every Presbyterian principle.*

It was manifestly impossible for any man of candid, upright, and honorable mind to take an oath, containing propositions directly opposed to each other, and inferring duties, the performance of which, according to the literal meaning of the terms, was absolutely impracticable. But the making of oaths had been so long a customary expedient of the Scottish administration, that but few public men retained any regard for the sacred obligation which they implied; and it was more consistent with the dark and treacherous policy of the Duke of York to employ men totally devoid of conscientious scruples, and prepared for any extreme which tyranny could devise, than to retain such as had some regard for truth, integrity, and religious principles. An immediate contest accordingly arose between the unscrupulous minions of despotism, and those who had still some attachment to religious and civil liberty. Some refused the Test at once, and were immediately cast into prison. The Duke of Hamilton hesitated, but subsequently took the oath. The Earl of Queensberry took it with an explanation, but such a one as was not calculated to give offence; declaring that he did not hold himself bound to oppose alterations in Church or State, in case it should seem good to his majesty to make them. A considerable number of the prelatic clergy refused to take the test, and some of them carried their opposition so far as to leave their situations rather than be guilty of what amounted to perjury. Not one prelate, however, carried his opposition so far, although one, the bishop of Aberdeen, exhibited considerable reluctance to take an oath so full of absurdity, and so capable of evil. Paterson, bishop of Edinburgh, framed an evasive explanation of the test, which had the effect of reconciling the greater part of the prelatic clergy who had at first refused; and the adherents of Popery had no difficulty in taking an oath which some of them might know to be intended to strengthen their party, and from which they all knew that they could very easily procure absolution.

But the might of the storm fell first upon the Earl of Argyle. The well-known hereditary attachment of this nobleman's family to Presbyterian principles had made him an object of suspicion to the Duke of York, who on his coming to Scotland, had resolved either to gain Argyle wholly to his own designs, or to compass his destruction. Even before that time, Argyle had been distrusted by the Scottish council; but as he had concurred generally in their persecuting measures, and in some instances strongly, as in the case of Cargill, there had been hitherto no grounds for instituting proceedings formally against him. The desired opportunity was furnished by the test. He declined taking this absurd and impious bond, and offered to relinquish all his hereditary jurisdiction, and exhibit his loyalty merely as a private subject: but having been informed that he would be allowed to take the test with an explanation, he consented to do so. The explanation he gave was, "that he took it in as far as it was consistent with itself, and with the Protestant religion." The Duke of York at first expressed himself satisfied; but learning from Sir George Mackenzie, that the explanation might be so strained as to appear of treasonable import, he issued a command to Argyle to enter the Castle of Edinburgh as a prisoner. Argyle complied, and was brought to trial before the Court of Justiciary, headed by Queensberry as justice-general. The indictment, drawn by Mackenzie, was such a wretched piece of sophistry, that it seems surprising that the judges did not frown it out of court at once, as contradictory alike to law and reason. But unhappily the opinions and decisions of lawyers and judges are not always such as can be defended by rules of logic and approved of by right reason.

Argyle was ably defended by Lockhart and Dalrymple; and when the judges came to express their decision, there were but four present, besides the

* Wodrow, vol. iii

justice-general; and these four were equally divided in opinion. As Queensberry had himself qualified the test, he regarded it as unseemly in him to give a casting vote against Argyle; and therefore Lord Nairn, who had been absent, from the pleadings in consequence of his age and infirmity, was sent for to decide a cause which he had not heard. The pleadings were, however, read over to him, during which he fell asleep; and being awakened at the close, he gave his vote against Argyle. After this mockery of justice, by which the relevancy of the indictment was sustained, Argyle was tried before a jury of his peers, and pronounced guilty of treason, and a letter sent to the king for liberty to the justiciary to pronounce sentence upon the verdict. His majesty might have so modified the sentence as to preserve Argyle's life; but as it was now apparent that the death of this nobleman was intended, his friends contrived to procure information respecting the tenor of the king's answer before that answer had reached the Scottish council. Having ascertained that the sentence of death was to be passed, but its execution to be delayed during the king's pleasure, he resolved to escape from prison, if possible, before his enemies were fully aware of the tenor of his majesty's answer. That very night, the 20th of December, he effected his escape, disguised as a page, and bearing the train of Lady Sophia Lindsay. A proclamation was almost immediately issued, declaring the sentence of death against him, and the forfeiture of his lands and titles, and offering a reward for his apprehension; but notwithstanding the keenness of the pursuit in all directions, he reached London undiscovered, guided by Mr. Veitch, one of the ejected and intercommuned Presbyterian ministers, and soon afterwards took refuge in Holland. When these tyrannical proceedings became generally known in England, they excited universal surprise and indignation. Lord Halifax told the king that he did not understand the law of Scotland, but that English law would not have hanged a dog for such a crime. And the Earl of Clarendon, when he heard the sentence, "blessed God that he lived not in a country where there were such laws" Throughout Scotland the alarm and resentful detestation of all true Presbyterians were unbounded; and some intelligible indications were given that the heart of the country was almost roused to a sterner resistance than had yet been manifested. Even children indulged their feelings in mock trials of dogs, for the crime of taking the test with a qualification.* From such things, slight and trifling as they might appear, the despotic rulers ought to have learned that a time of retribution was at hand. For when the youth of a nation become the assertors of any great principle, its triumph cannot be remote; it grows with their growth and strengthens with their strength, so that their manhood and its supremacy are realized together.

[1682.] When Cargill perished on the scaffold, that determined band of Covenanters who had adhered to him were left without a minister, no man for a time daring to take up a position so imminently perilous. In this emergency these fearless and high-principled men resolved to form themselves into a united body, consisting of societies for worship and religious intercourse in those districts where they most abounded; and for the more effectual preservation of their opinions, and security against errors, in the absence of a stated ministry, these smaller societies appointed deputies to attend a general meeting, which was empowered to deliberate upon all suggestions, and adopt such measures as the exigency of the times required. The first meeting of these united societies was held on the 15th of December 1681, at Logan House, in the parish of Lesmahagow, Lanarkshire, where it was resolved to draw up a public testimony against the defections and dangers of the times. But this testimony was not promulgated till the beginning of the year 1682, into the annals of which we have accordingly placed it. On the 12th of January, about forty men, armed for self-defence, if necessary, entered the town of Lanark, where, having publicly burnt the Test Act, they solemnly read their declaration and testimony, and affixed a copy of it to the market-cross.†

From the fact that these people, in the absence of a stated ministry, formed them-

* Wodrow, vol. iii. pp. 296-344.

† Wodrow. vol. iii. p. 357.

selves into societies for mutual religious intercourse and edification, they came to be designated the Society People, a term frequently applied to them by Wodrow, as that of Cameronians has been generally given to them by other historians. Superficial readers are liable to be misled by names, of the origin and application of which they have no accurate conception. But the affixing of a new name to a party is no sure proof that it has taken new grounds. That "persecuted remnant," as they called themselves, had indeed taken up no new principles; the utmost they can be justly charged with is, merely that they had followed up the leading principles of the Presbyterian and Covenanted Church of Scotland to an extreme point, from which the greater part of Presbyterians recoiled; and that in doing so, they had used language capable of being interpreted to mean more than they themselves intended. Their honesty of heart, integrity of purpose, and firmness of principle, cannot be denied; and these are noble qualities; and if they did express their sentiments in strong and unguarded language, it ought to be remembered, that they did so in the midst of fierce and remorseless persecution, ill adapted to make men nicely cautious in the selection of balanced terms wherein to express their indignant detestation of that unchristian tyranny which was so fiercely striving to destroy every vestige of both civil and religious liberty.

The declaration of Lanark re-asserted and confirmed those of Rutherglen and Sanquhar, renewed the disavowal of allegiance to the king on account of his long and continued tyranny, condemned the recent acts of parliament, and boldly asserted the right of freemen to extricate themselves from under a tyrannous yoke, "Shall the end of government be lost," said that spirited paper, "through the weakness, wickedness, and tyranny of governors? Must the people, by an implicit submission and deplorable stupidity, destroy themselves, and betray their posterity, and become objects of reproach to the present generation, and pity and contempt to the future? Have they not, in such an extremity, good ground to make use of that natural power they have to shake off that yoke which neither we nor our forefathers were able to bear?"* Such were the sentiments of that greatly oppressed and much slandered people; and instead of condemning severely the strong language which they use, we may rather admire the free and manly sentiments which they so well express, at a time when nearly the whole aristocracy of the land were bowing their necks beneath the most degraded bondage, and uttering the language of fawning and sycophantic slavery.

When the intelligence of this Lanark declaration reached Edinburgh, the council made an exhibition of empty fury, by ordering the magistrates to burn that paper, together with the Solemn League and Covenant, by the hands of the common hangman; which was accordingly done, with much unmeaning ceremony, at the market-cross. The town of Lanark was then fined in six thousand merks, for not preventing the publication of this declaration in their jurisdiction, although the strength of the Covenanters was such that the magistrates dared not attempt to interrupt them.

The absence of the Duke of York, who had gone to London soon after the rising of the Scottish parliament, caused some relaxation of the severities directed against the Presbyterians, so that fewer perished on the scaffold this year than had done for several years before. Yet this comparative leniency was not so great as to prevent the death of several, the imprisonment of many more, and the utter destruction of estate and property to a still greater number. A commission was given to Claverhouse to proceed to Galloway with a troop of horse, to compel all to take the test, and to punish at discretion all who refused, or whom he suspected of being disaffected persons. So well did he execute his orders, that the council conferred on him a vote of thanks for his zeal against the Presbyterians. Similar commissions were given to Major White, and Urquhart of Meldrum, to promote ecclesiastical conformity in the same manner in which they showed themselves no less willing instruments of oppression. About the same time the Scottish prelates wrote a formal letter to the Archbishop of Canterbury, applauding in the most fulsome language of adulation, the measures pursued by

* Informatory Vindication, p. 251.

the Duke of York in Scotland, ascribing the increased prosperity of their order to his "gracious owning and vigilant protection" of them, and to his "eminent zeal against the most unreasonable schism;"—so naturally did Scottish Prelacy take refuge and find protection beneath the wing of an avowed and bigoted Papist.

The Duke of York paid his last visit to Scotland in May. Having found the storm of hostility against him considerably abated in England, he thought it desirable for him to reside there; but deemed it expedient, before quitting Scotland finally, to place the administration of affairs in that Kingdom in the hands of his devoted friends. The Earl of Queensberry was accordingly appointed treasurer; Gordon of Haddo was created Earl of Aberdeen, and made chancellor; and the Earl of Perth was constituted justice-general. Queensberry was peculiarly characterised by avarice, Aberbeen by cunning, and Perth by cruelty: and with three such men at the head of affairs in Scotland, the Duke might well regard his interests as tolerably secure. Yet before departing, which he did on the 15th of May, the duke strenuously recommended to the council the suppression of the Presbyterians, advising them to send additional troops to the most suspected counties. They thanked him for the excellent pattern of government which he had placed before them, begged the continuance of his kindness, and promised constant devotion to his service in every respect.*

After the departure of the duke, the council showed the utmost alacrity in complying with his directions. Full powers were given to the Earl of Dumfries, General Dalziel, and Claverhouse, to search for and punish all who were suspected to be rebels, or disaffected to the government either in Church or State,—their commission giving them liberty to plunder, fine, and imprison at discretion. Nor did they hesitate to stain their own hands in blood, several victims perishing on the scaffold by the sentence of the council.

On the 15th of June, a general meeting of delegates from the united societies was held at Talla-linn, Tweedsmuir, chiefly for the purpose of checking some erroneous opinions resembling those of the Gibbites, which two or three of their members were accused of holding. No declaration was either issued or proposed, nor any thing of a public nature done, except that, by mutual exhortation and prayer, the sufferers were encouraged to persevere in the maintenance of their great and sacred principles. Yet, the curate of the parish having sent information to the council after the meeting had quietly dispersed, misrepresenting it as a large armed assembly, a violent proclamation was immediately issued, censuring the people of the district for not having given instant information, and giving orders how that was in future to be done. All were strictly commanded, that wheresoever any number of men convocated in arms, or where any one or two of such as had been declared traitors or fugitives were seen, intimation was immediately to be given to the next authorities, who were to raise the inhabitants and pursue the fugitives "with hue and cry," till they should be apprehended and sent to Edinburgh; with certification that all who neglected to give information, or refused to join in the pursuit, should be held equally guilty with the proscribed offenders.* Even this furious proclamation was found ineffectual, through the natural reluctance which every man of common humility felt to allow himself to be transmuted into a bloodhound, for the purpose of hunting down his fellow-creatures, whose only guilt consisted in their resolute determination to obey God rather than man, in spite of persecution. To render it more effectual, commissions were given to military officers, to confer with the sheriffs and other authorities; to call before them every suspected person; and to pronounce sentence, and order immediate execution, with or without the concurrence of the magistrates.† It is scarcely necessary to direct the attention of any reader to this act of council, which contains the very essence of despotism, by placing in the same hands both judicial and executive power. Yet it was only the completion of what had been previously begun, though in a less formal manner, when the soldiery were empowered to question those whom they seized on

* Wodrow, vol, iii. pp. 365, 366.

* Wodrow, vol. iii. p. 376. † Ibid., vol. iii. p. 379.

matters involving life and death; and it may be added, it was the natural consequence of the doctrine of the king's absolute supremacy, by which both the legislative and the executive functions of government were merged in the royal prerogative, than which there cannot be a more entire and perfect despotism.

The military judges received most efficient aid from the curates, who furnished them with lists of suspected persons, and procured informers of the lowest and vilest of the populace to bear witness against them. The mode in which the curates prepared these lists sufficiently proves the character of these men. If any person did not attend upon their ministry,—if he spoke in terms of respect and pity of the sufferers,—if he was overheard reading the Bible in private, or conducting family worship in his own house,—any person guilty of any of these practices was immediately suspected of being a staunch Presbyterian, and information lodged against him by the curate. Such was the manner in which these wolves devoured their flocks.* Several instances of human barbarity occurred, with the recital of which we will not shock our readers.

One trial of a more public nature, which occurred towards the end of the year, must be mentioned. This was the trial of Hume of Hume, a gentleman who was known to be friendly to the cause of the persecuted wanderers, and whom, therefore, it was determined to destroy. All the main charges brought against him failed through utter want of proof; but this did not lead to his release. It was ascertained that he had been near the house of M'Dowal of Mackerston when some disturbance arose, which had been termed rebellion; and though he offered proof that he was altogether unacquainted with the occurrence of that disturbance, and had gone to the vicinity merely to purchase a horse, he was not allowed to bring forward evidence in his own defence, was condemned to death, and executed on the strength of that unsubstantial rumour. His friends, aware of his danger, had made application at court, and had actually procured a pardon, which reached Edinburgh two days before the day of execution; but the Earl of Perth kept it back, and allowed the judicial murder to be committed. His estate was forfeited, and his widow and five children exposed to the extremes of poverty.†

[1683.] The beginning of the year 1863 was signalized by an extension of the system of instituting commissions for the prosecution of the Presbyterians. Numerous fines were levied by these commissions, in many cases upon persons who had been previously reduced to great distress by these exorbitant exactions. Circuit courts were also renewed this year, for the purpose of extending the oppressive measures of the prelatic party over the whole of the western and southern counties. Great numbers were thrown into prison, several were banished or sent to the Bass, and a considerable number perished on the scaffold. Among these was Andrew Guillan, who had been present at the murder of Sharp, though he merely held the horses of the chief assassins while they were committing the bloody deed. Him the persecutors put to a cruel death, similar to that inflicted on Hackston of Rathillet. Lawrie of Blackwood was brought to trial for holding converse with rebels, and allowing some who had been at Pentland and Bothwell to retain their farms on his estate. It was not proved that any of the tenantry were in the lists of intercommuned persons; and it could not be known to him, as he resided generally in Edinburgh, whether any of them had been in arms at Bothwell or not. At the Pentland insurrection he had been employed by General Dalziel to hold intercourse with the insurgents, for the purpose of endeavouring to persuade them to submit; and it was not proved that he had subsequently maintained any correspondence with them. Yet he was condemned, and, though his life was spared, his estate was forfeited. This caused great alarm, as there were very few landed proprietors in the south and west of Scotland against whom similar charges might not have been brought; and his sentence was equivalent to the placing of the whole property of the kingdom at the arbitrary disposal of the council, upon false charges of constructive treason.‡

* Wodrow, vol. iii. p. 383, *et seq.*

† Wodrow, vol. iii. pp 416-419.

‡ Burnet's Own Times, vol. i. p. 526.

Many began to entertain serious intentions of abandoning their country, and seeking in foreign lands that liberty which was denied them in their own,—feeling that there was more than an empty threat in the saying of the Duke of York, "that Scotland would never be at peace till the whole country south of the Forth was turned into a hunting-field."

Since the death of Cargill there had been no ministers bold enough to preach in the open field; and those whom Wodrow calls "the Society People" had been left without the blessings of a stated ministry and the dispensation of religious ordinances. But Mr. James Renwick, who had for some time kept company with the persecuted wanderers in previous years, had been to Holland, and having completed his education at Groningen, and obtained ordination from the Presbytery there, he returned to Scotland, and accepted an invitation from the Covenanters to be their minister. He commenced his ministerial career in September, preaching in the fields at a place called Darmead, where a general meeting of the persecuted party had been assembled. In this, his first public sermon, Renwick thought proper to give a full statement of his views and opinions respecting the path of duty and peril on which he was about to enter. In this, it appears, he expressed himself somewhat rashly, particularly in stating with what ministers he could not hold intercourse, mentioning some by name, and assigning the reasons why he must continue to testify against their defections, by standing aloof from their communion. This open avowal of his sentiments, exposed Renwick at once to great obloquy. He was accused of having excommunicated a great number of the best ministers in Scotland, this construction being put upon his specific censure of their defections; and the effect was a more complete separation between the Society People and their less resolute Presbyterian brethren than had previously existed. He deplored this hurtful disagreement, and expressed great regret that his unguarded language should have given occasion to it; but he could not violate his principles for the sake of peace.* His was, nevertheless, a heart that loved peace, and was full of natural gentleness; but he seemed to feel himself devoted to a task too mighty and important to allow any personal feelings to impede his course. He had once more raised aloft the banner of the Covenant, and spread its folds abroad on the free mountain winds, and he was determined to keep it floating there while life was his, and to shed his last drop of blood in its defence. And if, in declaring this high enterprise, his tongue did utter strong and burning words, surely there was more concession to be made to such a man, at such a time, and in such a cause, than to those who had stooped to accept an indulgence from prelatic tyrants, and who, being thereby half enslaved, shrunk from the bold accents of liberty, and basely censured what they wanted courage to imitate.

The return of Renwick, and the recommencement of field-preaching, roused anew the wrath of the persecutors, as was manifested in an act of council published on the 8th of October, imposing heavy fines upon the districts where Renwick had been known to preach.* This, however, was but a faint beginning of a course of remorseless persecution, which raged for several successive years, with more intense and wide-spread fury than had previously been known. For not only is it a well-known fact, that a course of persecution becomes the more bloody the longer it continues, from the hardening and unhumanizing reflex influence of their own conduct upon the persecutors; but also, there was, in the case of the Scottish sufferers, after Renwick's arrival, something which excited at once the malice and the fear of their baffled foes. The prelatic party had begun to exult in the apparent discomfiture and submission of their victims, and thought they had now little more to do than to divide the spoil, when suddenly the lonely solitudes again resounded with the voice of prayer and praise, breathed forth by the free and fearless adherents of Scotland's covenanted Presbyterian Church, and they began to feel that the battle was yet to be fought, and with men who knew not to yield. They might have begun to learn that there is an imperishable life in the great principles of truth,

* Life of Renwick, pp. 40-44.

* Wodrow, vol. iii. p. 446.

against which the utmost power of men may rage and dash as vainly as do the wind-swept waves, when they cast their foam against the everlasting rocks.

That event known in English history by the name of the "Rye-house Plot" occurred this year, and was wrested into a cause of additional suffering to the Scottish Presbyterians. Being so much a matter of English history, we shall not enter into details, further than is necessary for explaining in what manner it was made to bear upon the affairs of Scotland. It has already been mentioned, that the excessive oppression under which they groaned had caused a number of Scottish gentlemen to deliberate upon the propriety of entering upon a voluntary exile to the colonies. Several of them went to London to prepare for emigration; but while there, they learned that some English patriots were endeavouring to concert a scheme by which they might rescue their country from tyranny, and prevent the Duke of York's succession to the crown in the event of his brother's demise. At the head of this conspiracy were Monmouth, Shaftesbury, Russell, and Sidney. The Scottish deputation entered into correspondence with these patriotic men; and a considerable number of free-hearted nobility and gentry began to enter warmly into the enterprise, among whom were, Lord Melville, the Earl of Tarras, Sir Patrick Hume of Polwarth (afterwards Lord Marchmont), Baillie of Jerviswood, Sir John Cochrane, Campbell of Cesnock, and others. They entered into a correspondence with the Earl of Argyle in Holland, which was conducted chiefly through the Rev. William Carstares, one of the Presbyterian ministers. A short intercourse with the English plotters was enough to show the Scottish gentlemen that the enterprise could not succeed; and they abandoned it before it was discovered. In the meantime there was an underplot, conducted by men of different character and views, which had for its object the death of the king, and the change of the monarchy into a republic. With this, neither the English nobility nor the Scottish Presbyterians were at all acquainted; but upon its discovery the government endeavoured to identify the two, and especially to charge the whole upon the Presbyterians, or "the fanatics," as irreligious men delighted to call them. The results of this malicious accusation did not fully manifest themselves till the following year.

[1684.] The year 1684 begins the last and bloodiest period of the persecution, termed by the sufferers themselves, "killing time." All the terrible enginery of persecution was now brought into full operation; and the practised hands and callous hearts of the oppressors wielded their murderous weapons without remorse. When disappointed in one instance, their savage spirits thirsted the more intensely for a deeper draught of blood from some less protected source. Public judicial murders gave sanction and encouragement to that indiscriminate slaughter perpetrated by the soldiery throughout the country, till the entire west and south of Scotland was one field of blood.

The Justiciary Court began its fearful career on the 28th of February; and before it had continued its sittings longer than four days, three Presbyterians obtained the crown of martyrdom. In a few days another guiltless victim met a similar fate. But these were opportunities of gratifying only their love of cruelty; and other victims must be sought, possessing property, the confiscation of which would gratify their avarice. Their grasp was first laid on Sir Hugh Campbell of Cesnock, who was accused of being accessory to the Rye-house plot. Finding that there was no evidence whatever to corroborate that charge, and being still determined to secure their victim, a new accusation was framed, charging him with participation in the insurrection of Bothwell Bridge. Two witnesses were produced; but when confronted with Cesnock, and solemnly abjured by him to speak the truth, they retracted their previous statements. The spectators shouted with delight, Sir George Mackenzie stormed furiously, terming this shout a "Protestant roar," declaring that he "had always had a kindness for the Presbyterian persuasion till now, and that he was convinced it hugs the most damnable trinket in nature."* In vain he strove to browbeat the jury; they returned a verdict of not guilty, and

* Wodrow, vol. iv. p. 91.

Cesnock was—acquitted?—no!—he was remanded to prison, his estate forfeited, and shortly afterwards he was sent to the Bass. The jury were compelled to make an apology, and the witnesses were laid in irons. Such was the justice shown to Presbyterians by their lawless persecutors.

To compensate for this disappointment, the Military Commission Court condemned and executed five Presbyterians at Glasgow, after a mock trial, upon evidence not only slight, but contradictory, and utterly incompetent to substantiate the charge, which was merely that they had either been at Bothwell, or had at least held intercourse with the "rebels." But the joy of the persecutors was great when they seized Captain John Paton of Meadowhead, who had held a command both at Pentland and Bothwell. This gallant gentleman boldly acknowledged and defended what he had done, answering every charge with such courage and dignity that the council, struck with admiration, entertained some intentions of sparing his life, to which, however, the prelates would not consent. He met his death on the scaffold with as much fortitude as he had exhibited in the battle-field, but with the superadded dignity of Christian forgiveness to his murderers.*

The absolute injustice as well as cruelty of the courts, were shown peculiarly in the trials of Spence, Carstares, and Jerviswood. Mr. William Spence had been Secretary to the Earl of Argyle, and it was thought that he must be capable of giving important information respecting the supposed connection of the Scottish Presbyterians with the Rye-house Plot. He had been kept for some time in prison heavily loaded with iron fetters, which were struck off that he might be examined by torture. The torture of the boot failed to wring from him any such disclosure as the council wished. He was then sent back to prison; and an order of almost unparaleled atrocity was issued by the council, that a party of soldiers should keep watch beside the exhausted sufferer, and not permit him to sleep day nor night till he should confess. Several days together, Burnet says eight or nine, was this fearfully barbarous order enforced; and when even this could not shake his constancy, he was subjected to the torture of the thumbkin or thumb screw. The utmost which they succeeded finally in extorting from the worn-out sufferer, was his assistance in decyphering a letter written in secret characters by Argyle, in which the purpose of preventing the Duke of York's succession was mentioned, but nothing tending to corroborate the charge of intended assassination. The names of Carstares and Baillie of Jerviswood were contained in Argyle's letter, and this exposed them to the wrath of the council.

Carstares had been apprehended in England, at first by mistake for a different person, and retained in custody on account of being suspected to have some knowledge of the meditated insurrection for which Russell and Sidney died; and also because he was believed to be in the confidence of the Scottish exiles in Holland. He was sent down to Scotland to be tried, contrary to the provisions of English law; and the mention of his name in the papers decyphered by Spence exposed him to the severity of the Scottish council. He endured the torture of the thumbkin for an hour and a half with unwavering fortitude, refusing to answer any questions by which he might be led to criminate other parties. When released from torture and remanded to prison, he learned that the information derived from Spence contained nearly all that the questions to be proposed to him could involve, and accordingly he consented to answer without further torture, stipulating that his answers should not be used as evidence against the persons accused, nor himself confronted with them as a witness. These stipulations were, as usual, immediately violated, and an unfair account of his confession published, and attempted to be used against Jerviswood, on whose death the council was bent. It deserves to be recorded, to the credit of Carstares, that he was in the possession of state secrets greatly more important than those which the council were attempting to wring from him, the offer to discover which would have secured him from torture, and the discovery of which might have frustrated the success of the subsequent enterprise of the Prince of Orange. But when Carstares had answered to the

* Wodrow, vol. iv. p. 65; Scottish Worthies, p. 366.

questions directly put by the council, they seem to have concluded that he was acquainted with nothing more; and, after a short additional imprisonment, he was permitted to leave the kingdom and retire to Holland, where he remained till the time of the Revolution.*

The trial of Baillie of Jerviswood came next, and demands attention, as peculiarly atrocious. Baillie was a man of great natural abilities, soundness of judgment, and high integrity and blamelessness of character. He was now considerably advanced in years, and his constitution greatly broken and enfeebled by sufferings and imprisonment; yet his life, evidently drawing near its close, was sought by his enemies, because they were aware of the high estimation in which he was held by the Presbyterians, whose proceedings and plans might be comparatively paralyzed by the loss of such a man. The main accusation against Jerviswood had reference to the conspiracy of the English patriots, Russell and Sidney, but there was a miserable deficiency of evidence to substantiate the charge. Every attempt was made by the "bloody Mackenzie" to supplement this deficiency; even the confession of Carstares was brought forward as corroborative evidence, contrary to the express stipulations into which the council entered with Carstares himself. Baillie was manifestly dying, but this only stimulated the council to hasten forward his trial, that they might enjoy the gratification of shaking rudely the ebbing sands of his life. When brought before the court, the venerable man was wrapped in his dressing-gown, as he had arisen from his sick-bed, and attended by his sister-in-law, daughter of the celebrated Warriston, who supported him from time to time with cordials during the course of the trial. Mackenzie pressed the charges against him with the most malignant bitterness of language. At last the venerable man slowly rose, defended himself against the articles of the accusation, solemnly declared his detestation of all plots against the lives of his majesty and his royal brother; then fixing his eyes on Mackenzie, asked how he could in public so violently accuse him of what in private he had declared he did not believe him guilty? The advocate quailed beneath the searching power of that calm clear eye, and confusedly stammered out, "Jerviswood, I own what you say; my thoughts there were as a private man; but what I say here is by special direction of the privy council," and pointing to the clerk, added, "he knows my orders." "Well," replied Jerviswood, "if you have one conscience for yourself and another for the council, I pray God forgive you, I do;"—then turning to the justice-general, he said, "my lord, I trouble your lordship no farther." But neither the dignity of truth nor the pathetic language of innocence could move the cruel conclave. He was pronounced guilty, and condemned to die the same day, his head to be cut off, his body quartered, and the mutilated parts to be affixed upon conspicuous places in the chief towns in the kingdom. When this barbarous sentence was intimated to him, he answered, "My lords, the time is short—the sentence is sharp; but I thank my God, who hath made me as fit to die as you are to live." The brief interval between the sentence and its execution was to him one of joy unspeakable and full of glory. His bodily weakness and sufferings were unfelt, in the anticipation of the glory, honour, and immortality of that heavenly inheritance into which he was about to enter. The hour came. His devoted sister-in-law, Warriston's heroic daughter, supported his sinking frame to the scaffold; stood with him there, while, leaning on her shoulder, he attempted to address the deeply agitated and sympathizing spectators; and left him not till, after the drums of the military had drowned his voice, and the rude hand of the executioner had hurried on the final deed, she beheld his earthly sufferings closed, withdrawing then from a place where she had undergone what may well be termed a martyrdom of the heart.*

When such was the treatment of men of considerable rank, it may well be supposed that those in humble life would be subjected to injustice still more glaring, and cruelties still more intense. Such was indeed the case. The circuit courts which had been appointed to be held in the districts most noted for the at

* Dr M'Cormack's Life of Carstares, pp. 17-22.

* Wodrow, vol. iv. pp. 104-112.

tachment of the people to Presbyterian principles, executed their dreadful commission with unprecedented barbarity. To be accused was almost always the sure forerunner of to be condemned. To hesitate or refuse to take the test was ground enough for the exaction of ruinous fines from those who possessed any property, or for death to those who had none. The curates were not only encouraged, but further enjoined, to ply their dreadful and degrading trade of spies and informers. Other spies of a still viler cast were employed to pretend to be Covenanters, to frequent the company of the persecuted wanderers, to discover their retreats, and then to give such information as might lead to their surprise and seizure. Renwick continued to preach in the fields in spite of the rage of the persecutors; and, notwithstanding the keenness with which he and his followers were hunted from place to place, he still escaped from their toils, and held aloft, as he had vowed to do, the banner of the Covenant.

About this time an incident occurred which tended greatly to increase the fury of the persecutors. There had been a meeting of the Covenanters in the neighbourhood of Drumlanrig, where the soldiers found these resolute men too numerous to be safely attacked. But when they dispersed, the soldiers scoured the country in the neighbourhood of the place of meeting, and intercepted eight or nine of the stragglers, among whom was the minister. When the Covenanters learned that the minister had been seized, they hastily mustered in small parties, each speeding to some advantageous spot to attempt a rescue. The soldiers took the most direct route to Edinburgh, and marched up Enterkin pass with their prisoners. This was immediately observed by the countrymen, who swiftly scaled the mountain side, and placed themselves in a commanding position before the approach of the dragoons. A more suitable position for such an enterprise could not be desired. The road is cut out of the steep side of a sheer precipitous mountain, not broader than to admit of two horses abreast, exceedingly steep on the upper side, unguarded by wall or bank on the under, from which the mountain descends almost perpendicularly to the bottom of a narrow glen, along which a mountain-stream toils, foaming through the shattered rocks that block its rugged channel. Nothing of vegetation is to be seen but a few loose tufts of wiry grass whistling in the wind, striving ineffectually to bind together the sharp slaty splinters which cover the vast bulk of the barren mountain, so that it is impossible to recover the footing once lost on that pass of fear. As the soldiers were slowly winding up that tremendous path, they were suddenly hailed by a voice from the misty hill-side above them, calling on them to stop and deliver up their minister and the other prisoners. The officer in command refused with a loud oath. He was immediately shot through the head, and fell from his horse, which, startling back, staggered over the precipice, rolling and bounding with increased velocity till it descended in a mangled indistinguishable mass into the rocky bed of the raving torrent. The rest of the soldiers stood petrified with horror at this appalling catastrophe, feeling that their own lives were completely at the mercy of the men posted above them on the hill. But these men were not revengeful. They wished not to spill the blood of their enemies, if they could otherwise rescue their friends. Again they demanded the minister and the other prisoners; and the officer second in command, aware that resistance was in vain, consented to yield them up, saying to the minister, "Go, sir; you owe your life to this damned mountain." "Rather, Sir," said the minister, "to that God who made this mountain."*

When the intelligence of this rescue reached Edinburgh, the rage of the council was unbounded. Furious proclamations were issued, and strong detachments of troops sent to traverse the adjacent country, and apprehend all who were suspected of having been in any respect implicated in the deed. Nor were they long without finding victims on which to inflict their vengeance. Three men were found asleep in the fields, fired upon, and

* Memoirs of the Church of Scotland, by De Foe, pp. 188-193; Wodrow, vol. iv. p. 173. Wodrow's account differ somewhat from that given by De Foe, but the latter is here mainly followed, as, from having personally explored the pass, and gleaned the traditionary accounts still current in the district, the author is satisfied of its accuracy.

wounded by the soldiers where they lay, then seized, hurried to Edinburgh, and put to death the very day on which they reached the capital, without the shadow of a proof that they were concerned in the rescue at Enterkin path. But this did not satiate their thirst of revenge. The whole district was laid under military law, and unparalleled atrocities were perpetrated by the licentious and infuriated soldiery. The people were hunted from their homes *and shot to death in the fields without* mercy; their houses were pillaged, and then reduced frequently to ashes, the women and children being abused, and then left to houseless misery and starvation. Three women were seized, and with difficulty escaped banishment, for lending assistance in her hour of travail to the wife of one who was suspected to have been at the rescue. Desolation covered the country wheresoever the fierce exterminators directed their ruthless ravages.

But while peculiar districts were thus exposed to excessive devastation, in consequence of peculiar events, the concentrated malice of the persecutors was directed incessantly against the unyielding remnant of true Covenanters. They were hunted like beasts of prey from moss to mountain, from cliff to cavern. In vain did they make their beds in the dark heaths, beneath the canopy of heaven, or in natural caves in the rocky glens, or in artificial lurking-places among the shaggy thickets. No retreat was sufficiently wild and secret to secure them from the keen eye of the prowling informer, and the relentless pursuit of their vindictive enemies. Thus driven from the haunts of men, outlawed, given up to pitiless butchery it would have been strange indeed if they had not, like a stag at bay, turned on their pursuers, and compelled them to know that there were extremities of persecution which human nature would not endure. At length, after their patience and Christian resignation had been tried to the extremest pitch, they did come to the determination of warning their enemies not to press further upon that perilous boundary, the crossing of which might make the great law of self-preservation the sole rule of duty, and when stern retaliation might become the only method by which that great law could act. This formidable warning they gave to their relentless persecutors, by publishing what they termed "the apologetic declaration and admonitory vindication of the true Presbyterians of the Church of Scotland, especially against intelligencers and informers." This very remarkable paper bears to have been drawn up on the 28th of October, and was to be affixed on the market-crosses of the chief towns in Scotland, on the 8th of November, which was accordingly done. It is of such importance, that an extract must be given.

This "apologetical declaration" begins by narrating the course of persecution which had impelled the sufferers to disown the authority of the tyrannical sovereign and government under whose cruel sway they were so mercilessly wasted; it then declares that they "utterly detest and abhor that hellish principle of killing all who differ in judgment and persuasion from us, it having no bottom upon the Word of God, or right reason; and after stating the incessant danger in which they lived, the hardships to which they were exposed, and the cruel deaths inflicted on their friends, through the instrumentality of spies, informers, and the remorseless soldiery, this document proceeds in the following strain:—

"We do hereby delare unto all, that whosoever stretch forth their hands against us while we are maintaining the cause and interest of Christ against his enemies, in defence of the Covenanted Reformation, all and every one of such shall be reputed by us enemies to God and the covenanted work of reformation, and punished as such, according to our power and the degree of their offence, chiefly if they shall continue, after the publication of this our declaration, obstinately and habitually with malice to proceed against us, any of the aforesaid ways. Now, let not any think that (our God assisting us) we will be so slack-handed in time coming to put matters in execution, as heretofore we have been, seeing we are bound faithfully and valiantly to maintain our Covenants and the cause of Christ. Therefore, let all these aforesaid persons be admonished of their hazard; and particularly all ye intelligencers, who by your voluntary informations endeavour to render us up into the enemies' hands, that our blood may be shed; for by such courses ye both endanger your immortal souls, if repentance prevent not, seeing God will make inquisition for shedding the precious blood of his saints, and also your bodies, seeing you render yourselves actually and maliciously guilty of our blood, whose innocency the Lord knoweth. However, we are sorry at our very hearts that any of you should choose such courses, either with bloody Doeg to shed our blood, or with the flattering Ziphites, to inform persecutors where we are to be found. So we say again, we desire you to take warning of the hazard that ye incur, by following such courses; for the sinless necessity of self-preservation, accompanied with holy zeal for Christ's reigning in our land, and suppressing of profanity, will move us not to let you pass unpunished. Call to your remembrance, all that is in peril is not lost, and all that is delayed is not forgiven. Therefore, expect to be dealt with as ye deal with us, so far as our power can reach, not because we are actuated by a sinful spirit of revenge, for private and personal injuries, but mainly because by our fall reformation suffers damage."*

It is, we think, impossible to peruse this remarkable document without strong emotions of mingled sorrow, regret, and admiration;—sorrow, to contemplate the sufferings which such men had been compelled so long to endure; regret, that these sufferings had driven them to the use of language, if not the adoption of sentiments, which might be perverted into something like a sanction of summary retaliation and lawless bloodshed, notwithstanding the earnestness with which they disclaimed such principles; and admiration of the invincible courage and perseverance which they displayed in the defence of civil and religious liberty, and in the maintenance of the fundamental principle of the Presbyterian Church of Scotland,—the sole sovereignty of the Lord Jesus Christ over his spiritual kingdom, the Church.

The effects resulting from this declaration were varied. To a certain extent it accomplished the intended object. The informers, both curates and their base emissaries, were appalled, and shrunk from the possible encounter with men rendered desperate by the deep sense of intolerable oppression, who knew no falsehood and who felt no fear, and for whom to act was easier than to threaten. They dared not, therefore, follow the persecuted remnant to their desolate retreats, as formerly; and, consequently, some diminution took place in the deadly accuracy with which the military executioners had previously been guided to the haunts of their victims. But the rage of the council was stimulated beyond all former precedent: and failing somewhat in their comparatively private methods of destruction, they resolved to wield all their public weapons with more terrific energy than they had ever yet put forth. An act of the privy council was passed on the 22d of November, well designated "the bloody act," ordaining "every person who owns, or does not disown, the late traitorous declaration, upon oath, whether he have arms or not, to be immediately put to death, before two witnesses, and the person or persons having commission from the council to that effect." And that this "bloody act" might not remain inoperative for want of commissions, these were given to several noblemen, gentlemen, and military officers, empowering and requiring them "to convocate all the inhabitants (in certain parishes named), men and women, above fourteen years of age; and if any own the late declaration, you shall execute them by military execution upon the place; and if any be absent, ye shall burn their houses and seize their goods, &c. And as to the families of such as you condemn or execute, you shall make prisoners of all persons in their families above the age of twelve years, in order to transportation." An oath, termed the "abjuration oath," was also framed, according to which every person was called upon "to abjure and renounce, by solemn oath, the late traitorous apologetical declaration;" and a proclamation was at the same time issued, "prohibiting all past the age of sixteen years to presume to travel without certificates of their loyalty and good principles, by taking the oath of abjuration; with certification, that all who shall adventure to travel without such certificate, which is to serve for a free pass, shall be holden and used as connivers with the

* Wodrow, vol. iv. pp. 148, 149; Informatory Vindication, pp. 255-256.

said rebels."* The indulgence was also recalled, and all the indulged ministers were obliged to give bond not to exercise any part of their ministry in Scotland.

The dread machinery of extermination seemed now complete. The preaching of the gospel by any Presbyterian minister was entirely prohibited, on the penalties of imprisonment, exile, or death. The power of enforcing contradictory oaths, such as the test, and judicial oaths, such as that of abjuration, was given to lawless military commissions, extended even to common troopers and private sentinels, with authority to inflict instant death on all who should refuse or hesitate thus to violate their conscience. No man might journey from one part of the country to another, however urgent the call of duty or of business, without a pass from these armed legislators; and many were shot dead by the soldiers, without taking the trouble to inquire whether they had obtained the pass, that paper being found in their possession by the murderers when they were pillaging the dead bodies. And as the speeches, testimonies, and declarations of the persecuted party had made their principles familiar to their enemies, the latter contrived to frame a few leading questions to be put by the military inquisitors, the refusal to answer which was to be held as a sufficient proof of guilt, entitling the banditti to inflict torture or death upon their victims at their pleasure. These questions were generally the following:—"Will you renounce the Covenant?"—"Will you pray for the king?"—"Was the killing of the Archbishop of St. Andrews murder?"—"Was the rising at Bothwell Bridge rebellion?"—"Will you take the test?"—"Will you abjure the late treasonable declaration?" The effect of such questions may very easily be imagined. Many thousands would have cheerfully lost their lives rather than have renounced the Covenants. To pray for the king, as a sinful human being, they were quite willing, but not as thereby acknowledging his right to exercise a sinful supremacy in matters spiritual, and an arbitrary despotism in civil affairs. They regarded the question respecting the death of Sharp as an illegal attempt to extort from them a sentence of condemnation upon the assassins, which they were not entitled to pronounce, nor their enemies to require. Neither did they feel at liberty to call the rising at Bothwell Bridge rebellion, as they considered it essentially an act of self-defence, and therefore justifiable. The test and the abjuration they regarded as not only illegal and ensnaring oaths, but as positively sinful, containing false principles, and involving the subjugation of Christianity to the arbitrary will of a perjured, licentious, and Popish tyrant. It was not strange, therefore, that when the rude soldiers put these questions to the people, they generally received such answers as put it in their power to inflict instant death upon the faithful Presbyterians, or such hideous tortures as might be prompted by the wild caprice of their savage natures.

[1684.] As the year 1684 closed with the framing of the "bloody acts" already specified, so 1685 began by their being put into relentless execution. Several prisoners had been seized about the close of the preceding year, and instantly sacrificed, even before the passing of the new persecuting enactments. The new year was begun in the same spirit, and with fuller powers of vengeance. About the middle of January, two men were hanged at Edinburgh for not disowning the late declaration; on the same day six men were shot in Galloway, because they were detected by the military in the act of prayer. Another man, sick of a fever, not giving satisfactory answers to the interrogations put to him, was dragged from his bed, and murdered at his own door. Other two seemed willing to take the abjuration oath, but being told by the military judge that they must take the test also, refused, and were put to death on the spot, the monster exultingly exclaiming, "they thought to have cheated the judges, but I have cheated them." In some places the whole inhabitants of a village or a parish were called together, and commanded to take the test and the abjuration oath, without distinction of age or sex, surrounded by the troops, with loaded muskets and drawn swords, prepared to revel in their blood if they should hesitate.*

A slight pause in these dreadful butch-

* Wodrow, vol. iv. pp. 155, 156, 161, 164; Life of Renwick, p. 78

* Wodrow, vol. iv.

eries took place upon the death of Charles II., which happened on the 6th day of February. The cause of his death is generally stated to have been apoplexy; but there are very strong reasons to suspect that he was poisoned.* It is not necessary to offer any remarks upon the character of a monarch whose whole life was a tissue of private crime and public perfidy and dishonour. "His ambition," says Fox, "was directed against his subjects; unprincipled, ungrateful, mean, and treacherous, to which may be added, vindictive and remorseless. I doubt whether a single instance can be produced of his having spared the life of any one whom motives of policy or revenge prompted him to destroy."

Intelligence of the death of Charles was speedily forwarded to Scotland, and the Duke of York was immediately proclaimed king in such terms as must have satisfied the most absolute despot, he being declared "our only righteous king and sovereign, over all persons, and in all causes, as holding his imperial crown from God alone." The Scottish council, with perfect consistency, held it unnecessary for James to take the coronation oath, for they had already recognised the will of the sovereign as the source of all law, civil and sacred; and to have required from their monarch an oath that he would govern according to his own will, would have been a mockery indeed. Yet this omission left room for the statement of an important principle within the course of a few years, furnishing another instance of the truth, that lawless deeds ultimately destroy their perpetrator. All public functionaries were continued in their offices; and the military commission courts, which had been instituted for the destruction of the Presbyterians, were renewed, and even extended.

A meeting of parliament had been called by the late king, to have commenced its sittings in March; but it was summoned anew by James, and met on the 28th of April. Queensberry was appointed commissioner; and as the test was in full operation, every person conscientiously attached to the Presbyterian Church was necessarily excluded. It would be instructive to dwell somewhat minutely on the proceedings of this purely Prelatic parliament, did space permit, as its slavish spirit, and the gross flatteries in which its leading members indulged, present a startling contrast to the conduct and language of the purely Presbyterian parliament of 1649. A few of the leading acts of this parliament must be mentioned. By one of them it was declared, "That the giving or taking the National Covenant or the Solemn League and Covenant, or writing in defence thereof, or owning them as lawful or obligatory upon themselves or others, shall infer the crime and pains of treason." Another converted all the illegal and oppressive acts of council into statute law. A third declared the giving of supplies, or the concealing of supplies given to or demanded for traitors, to be treason, and to be judged accordingly. By other acts it was ordained, that the punishment of death should be extended to hearers as well as preachers at conventicles; that the worshipping of God, in a private house, if five individuals more than the members of the family were present, was treason; and that the test should be imposed upon all heritors, life-renters, and tacksmen, *Papists alone excepted.* And, to complete their proofs of superlative loyalty, this prelate parliament passed acts of attainder against several Presbyterian noblemen and gentlemen, annexing their forfeited estates to the crown.*

This obsequious parliament had not yet quite finished its labours, when intelligence arrived, that a double invasion of the kingdom was on the point of taking place, conducted in England by the Duke of Monmouth, and in Scotland by the Earl of Argyle, "for the purpose of recovering the religion, rights, and liberties of the kingdom from the usurpation of James Duke of York, and a popish faction." It belongs to the province of the civil historian to narrate events of a character so much more civil than ecclesiastical as must needs be an attempt like that of Monmouth and Argyle. For it is

* Burnet's Own Times, vol. i. pp. 606-610.

* Wodrow, vol. iv. pp. 266-282. It may be stated, as a proof that this parliament had some perception of the dangerous tendency of their proceedings, that they passed an act by which lands might be entailed to perpetuity. They were bent on the utter ruin of all Presbyterian families; but thought, by this measure, to secure their own ill-got gains from similar ruin, should a change of administration take place. For the law of entail, with all the obstacles which it presents to the progress of society, Scotland has that Prelatic parliament to blame.

perfectly plain, even from the language of Argyle's declaration, that the main object of his enterprise was to redress the civil wrongs and grievances of the nation. He did not, certainly, and he could not, omit the statement of those persecutions on account of religion under which the nation had so long groaned and bled; but still it was manifest, that both he and the greater part of those who joined with him were more intent upon the restoration of the civil than of the religious liberties of the kingdom. The fate of the enterprise may be very briefly told.

Before leaving Holland, symptoms of dissension had appeared among the leaders of the expedition. Argyle was its natural leader, as the man of the highest rank and greatest personal influence in Scotland; but he appears to have been deficient in military talents, and in that high energy and decision of character so necessary in the leader of a dangerous enterprise. All their councils partook of the same indecision, no one man of the party possessing that degree of genius which would have given him unquestioned ascendency over the rest. The first attempt was made in the Highlands, but with little success. They then moved to the Lowlands,—met forces greatly superior in numbers,—avoided a general engagement,—began to be dispirited, and to melt away,—divided, a very few continuing with Argyle till he was taken, a large party following Sir John Cochrane,—till, after having crossed the Clyde, and been engaged in a sharp skirmish at Muirdykes, near Lochwinnoch, where they beat back their assailants, they separated, every man seeking his personal safety by flight.*

So ended this unfortunate attempt. The persecuted Covenanters, or Cameronians as they are often called, declined uniting with Argyle, on the ground chiefly that the declaration of that nobleman did not sufficiently assert the essential principles in behalf of which they were willing to suffer and to die; that it made no direct mention of the Covenants, nor of Presbyterian Church government; and that some of the leaders had been implicated in the persecuting measures of the prelatists, and such as Sir John Cochrane, who directed Earlshall to Airdsmoss where Cameron was killed: nor had they forgot that Argyle himself had given his vote for the putting of Cargill to death: and on these grounds they held it right to avoid the hazard, and, it might be, the sin of entering into a close alliance with men whom they still regarded with distrust, both on account of their principles and their previous conduct. Even had they been willing to join with Argyle, they had not the opportunity of doing so. The country between him and where they chiefly resorted was completely in the possession of the enemy; and they were not sufficiently numerous to have forced their way openly through the opposing troops. Their standing aloof, which was chiefly caused by their adherence to their own high principles, had the effect of preserving them from a portion of the ruin produced by Argyle's failure; and their junction with him, had it been practicable, could not have given such an accession of strength as to have ensured his success. Their conduct, therefore, need not be either censured or deplored; and were we disposed to enter into a more minute investigation of the subject, it might be shown to have been not undeserving of the meed of approbation, both for soundness of principle and for consistency.

Argyle, after his capture, was conducted to Edinburgh, and imprisoned in the castle. His trial was short, yet strange. Instead of being condemned for his invasion of the kingdom, and attempt to dethrone the sovereign, he was sentenced to death on the ground of his former refusal to take the test without a qualification. There was a pertinacious consistency of despotism in this determination to abide by a previous unjust and tyrannical sentence; but it shocked the public mind much more than condemnation on the ground of his recent attempt could have done, and in that view his death was in all probability much more serviceable to the cause of liberty than his life could have been. The interval between the passing of the sentence and its execution was brief; but it was spent by Argyle in such a manner as to raise his character in the estimation of all men to a degree immeasurably beyond what it had previously reached. He acknowledged his

* Wodrow, vol. iv. pp. 282-320; Memoirs of Veitch and Brysson, pp. 305-340.

former sinful compliances with the guilty deeds of the council, in language of deep contrition, admitting his own unworthiness to be the instrument of deliverance to his suffering country; his personal piety was displayed signally in that calm and profound peace of mind which the prospect of an ignominious death could not for a moment ruffle, and which breathed no word of reproach against his revengeful enemies; and, though his own enterprise had failed, he expressed the utmost confidence in the near and complete deliverance of his beloved native land from tyranny and oppression. On the scaffold he was attended by two ministers—one appointed by the council, Annand, dean of Edinburgh, and the other one of his own choice, Chartris, who had been laid aside for refusing to take the test; but no Presbyterian minister was allowed to be with him. When, after his speech, he declared that he forgave all men their wrongs against him, as he desired to be forgiven of God, Annand repeated these words, adding, "this nobleman dies a Protestant;" upon which Argyle, stepping forward, added emphatically, "I die not only a Protestant, but with a heart-hatred of Popery, Prelacy, and all superstition whatsoever." Then, kneeling down, he embraced the instrument of execution, prayed earnestly, gave the signal, and joined his martyred father.* Thus died the Earl of Argyle, on the 30th day of June 1685, another noble martyr in the great and sacred cause of Scottish civil and religious liberty.

Several other victims of less note, but not less excellence of character, speedily followed Argyle. Rumbold, an English officer, who had served under Cromwell, was executed in the same barbarous manner as Rathillet had been. The Rev. Thomas Archer, a young minister of great promise, who had been severely wounded in the skirmish at Muirdykes, was hanged. Gavin Russel and David Law died by a similar sentence; and upwards of twenty of Argyle's own clan were hanged at Inverness, while great numbers were banished to the plantations.

The preceding public events have been related in a consecutive order, for the sake of perspicuity; and for the same reason we must now give a brief continuous narrative of the sufferings of the persecuted Presbyterians. The pause occasioned by the death of one sovereign and the accession of another was of brief duration; and the military judges resumed their murderous career with increased eagerness, making the whole south and west of Scotland one scene of indiscriminate carnage. Claverhouse had been elevated to the dignity of a privy councillor, and Dumfriesshire and Galloway were assigned to him as his peculiar domain. To Grierson of Lagg, and Windram, were given districts of the latter county, over which they might spread devastation at will; while Claverhouse himself, like a superior fiend, traversed the whole province, cheering on the red exterminators, a bloodier and fiercer glare of destruction marking the spot where he was present, or the path along which he had swept. The employment of spies, who could assume the appearance and imitate the language and manners of the wandering Covenanters, was one of the favourite methods pursued by Claverhouse, that by their information he might trace the persecuted men to their most sacred lurking-places. At times, marking out a district, and mustering a sufficient force, he would drive all the inhabitants into one spot, gird them round with the armed soldiery, and compel them to swear allegiance to James, and to take the test and the oath of abjuration, instant death being the penalty of refusal or hesitation. At other times he would collect all the children from six to ten years of age, draw up a line of soldiers before them, and order them to pray, for the hour of death was come; then, while in the agony of mortal terror, would offer them their lives if they would discover where their friends, their fathers, or their elder brothers were concealed, causing occasionally the troops to fire over their heads, to increase their fear and stimulate their discoveries. Nor did he hesitate to stain his own hands with the blood of guiltless victims, rather than they should escape, when the troops showed signs of reluctance. Of this the death of John Brown of Priesthill is a fearful instance.

John Brown lived at a place called Priesthill, in the parish of Muirkirk, and earned his subsistence by the humble

* Wodrow, vol. iv. pp. 300-307.

employment of a carrier. He was a man of deep personal piety, but had not joined in any acts of open resistance to the government. He was, however, hated by the curate, because of his sincere attachment to Presbyterian principles, his refusal to attend upon that worthless man's degraded ministry, and the shelter which his solitary abode occasionally furnished to the persecuted wanderers and their ministers. Of this information had been given to Claverhouse, who immediately determined on his death. On the morning of the 1st of May, day having scarcely dawned, Brown, while at work in the fields, was surprised by a troop of dragoons, led by Claverhouse himself. He was brought back to his own house, and there the usual ensnaring questions were put to him, the brief examination closing by Claverhouse saying to him, "Go to your prayers, for you shall immediately die." Calmly the martyr kneeled down upon the heath, and poured forth the emotions of his heart in a strain of such fervent and lofty devotion as to move the rude and hardened soldiery, if not to tears of repentance, at least to strong, though transient remorse. Thrice was he interrupted by the relentless Claverhouse, who exclaimed that "he had given him time to pray, but not to preach." Turning to the merciless man, he answered, "Sir, you know neither the nature of preaching nor of praying, if you call this preaching," and continued his devotions, untroubled, unconfused. When he stopped, Claverhouse bade him take farewell of his wtfe and children. Turning to the afflicted woman, who was standing beside him, with one infant in her arms and another clinging to her knee, he said, "Now, Isabel, the day is come that I told you would come, when I first spoke to you of marriage." "Indeed, John," replied she, "I can willingly part with you." "Then," said he, "that is all I desire; I have no more to do but die; I have been in case to meet death for many years." After he had kissed his wife and children, Claverhouse ordered six soldiers to fire. They hesitated; the prayers of the martyr were still sounding in their souls; they positively refused. Enraged at their delay and refusal, Claverhouse with his own hand shot him through the head; then turning to the new-made widow, in a voice of fiend-like mockery, said, "What thinkest thou of thy husband now, woman?" "I ever thought much good of him," she answered, "and as much now as ever." "It were but justice to lay thee beside him," exclaimed the murderer. "If you were permitted," replied she, "I doubt not but your cruelty would go that length; but how will you answer for this morning's work?" "To man I can be answerable," said the ruthless persecutor; "and as for God I will take him in my own hand!" and wheeling about, rode off at the head of his horror-stricken troop. The poor woman laid down her fatherless infant on the ground, gathered together the scattered brains of her beloved husband, then taking the kerchief from her neck and bosom, wound it about his mangled head, straighted his stiffening body, covered it with her plaid, and sat down and wept over him, with one infant on her knee, and the other again clasped closely to her desolate heart. Not a friend or a neighbour was near in the dismal solitude of that dark hour, to aid her in performing the last sad duties of humanity, "it being a very desert place, where never victual grew;" but she was not alone, for her soul felt the strong support of her very present God.*

From the murder of John Brown, Claverhouse proceeded to the county of Dumfries, where another victim fell into his hands, and was dragged to the house of Johnstone of Westerraw or Westerhall. This man, Andrew Hislop, Claverhouse would have spared—his mind, as he himself afterwards acknowledged, not being able to shake off the deep impression which John Brown's prayer had made; but Johnstone insisted on his death, and orders were given to a Highland officer who was with the party to shoot the man. He refused, and drew off his troop, declaring that he would fight Claverhouse and his dragoons rather than do so barbarous a deed. Claverhouse then commanded three of his own men to execute the sentence, and this time they did not refuse. Placing the innocent man before them, they desired him to draw his bonnet over his eyes. Raising it higher on his dauntless brow, and stretching out his

* Wodrow, vol. iv. pp. 244, 245; Life of Peden, pp. 72-74.

hand, in which he held his Bible, he replied, that he could look his death-bringers in the face without fear, charging them to answer for what they had done, and were about to do, at the great day, when they should be judged by that book—and so fell a dreadless martyr for the truth.*

On the same day in which Hislop was thus murdered, the 11th of May, a still more hideous crime was committed near Wigton, in Upper Galloway. Gilbert Wilson occupied a farm belonging to the laird of Castlestewart, in the parish of Penningham. He and his wife had both yielded to the acts enforcing conformity to Prelacy; but his children had imbibed higher principles, and refused to conform. At length they were compelled to quit their father's house and join the persecuted wanderers, that they might avoid falling into the hands of the soldiers. Margaret Wilson, aged about eighteen, her brother Thomas, aged sixteen, and their sister Agnes, aged only thirteen, were all thus compelled to seek refuge in the wild moors of Upper Galloway; and by the dreadful intercommuning act, their parents were forbid to give them food or shelter, under the penalty attached to treason. In the slight pause of persecution which took place at the death of Charles, the two sisters ventured to quit the desert solitudes, and to come to Wigton, where they resided a short time in the house of an aged and pious widow, named Margaret M'Lauchlan. A base wretch, named Stuart, gave information against them, and they were all three dragged to prison. After they had lain there for some weeks, and had suffered much inhuman treatment, they were brought to trial before Lagg and Major Windram, who commanded the military force in that district. As if to stretch this mockery of justice to the utmost extreme at once of cruelty and of intense absurdity, these three helpless women were accused of rebellion at Bothwell Bridge and Airdsmoss, and also of having been present at twenty conventicles. This accusation it was impossible to urge; but they were required o take the abjuration oath, which all three refused, and were accordingly condemned to die. The specific terms of the sentence were, that they should be tied to stakes fixed within the flood-mark in the water of Blednock, where it meets the sea, and there be drowned by the tide. From this dreadful doom the entreaties of the distracted father prevailed so far as to rescue the innocent girl of thirteen, yet only by the payment of one hundred pounds sterling to the merciless and mercenary murderers. But nothing could avail to save the lives of the young woman and her widowed friend.

The day of execution came, the 11th of May, bright, it may be, with the fresh smiles of the reviving year, but dark and terrible to many a sympathizing heart. Windram and his troop guarded the victims to the place of doom, accompanied by a crowd of people, filled with fear and wonder, and still doubting whether yet the horrid deed would be done. The stakes were driven deep into the oozy sand. That to which the aged widow was tied was placed farthest in, that she might perish first. The tide began to flow,—the water rose around them,—the hoarse rough billows came advancing on, swelling and mounting inch by inch, over limb, and breast, and neck, and lip, of the pious and venerable matron, while her young companions in martyrdom, still in shallower water, gazed on the awful scene, and knew that in a few minutes more her sufferings would be the same. At this dreadful moment some heartless ruffian asked Margaret Wilson what she thonght now of her fellow-martyr in her dying agonies? Calmly she answered, "What do I see but Christ, in one of his members, wrestling there? Think you that we are the sufferers? No, it is Christ in us; for he sends none a warfare on their own charges." But the water now began to swell cold and deadly round and over her own bosom; and, that her last breath might be expended in the worship of God, she sung the 25th psalm, repeated a portion of the 8th chapter of the Epistle to the Romans, and prayed till her voice was lost amid the rising waves. Before life was quite extinct the torturers cut the cords that bound her to the stake, dragged her out, waited till she was restored to consciousness, and then asked her if she would pray for the king. She answered, "I wish the salvation of all men, and the damnation

* Wodrow, vol. iv. p. 250.

of none." "Dear Margaret," exclaimed one of the spectators, in accents of love and sorrow, "Say God save the king! say God save the king!" With the steady composure of one for whom life had few attractions and death no terrors, she replied, "God save him, if he will, for it is his salvation I desire." Her relatives and friends immediately cried aloud to Windram, "Oh, Sir, she has said it, she has said it!" The ruthless monster, reluctant thus to lose his victim, required her to answer the abjuration oath. In the same firm tone she answered, "I will not; I am one of Christ's children; let me go!" By his command she was again plunged into the heaving waters, and, after a brief struggle, the spirit of this virgin martyr entered into the rest and peace of everlasting happiness.*

This and similar instances of heroic Christian fortitude were termed by the persecutors, and will still be termed by their apologists, instances of obstinate fanaticism. And men who wish to be regarded as peculiarly persons of enlightened minds and liberal sentiments, will affect to pity the narrow and gloomy bigotry, as they will term it, which impelled these Christian martyrs to encounter death in every form the most terrific, rather than abandon the principles of eternal truth. But the true Christian alone can comprehend by what sacred might it was that not only the strength of manhood, but the weakness of age, womanhood, and infancy, was upheld and enabled to triumph gloriously in the midst of persecutions so fierce and barbarous that the heart turns with sick and shuddering horror from the bare recital. Their hearts were filled with "the peace of God which passeth all understanding," beyond the power of human rage to disturb; their souls had obtained both an earnest and foretaste of heaven, in that love of God and communion with him which had been imparted to them by "the spirit of adoption;" and feeling that "the Son had made them free," they recognised it as their bounden duty and their great privilege to defend the rights, and liberties of Christ's spiritual kingdom, willing to die rather than violate their allegiance to their Divine Redeemer, by yielding to a sinful mortal that sole supremacy and lordship over the conscience which belongs to Him alone, and that high and undivided sovereignty over His Church, which is the inalienable prerogative of the Mediator's crown. These principles they held, and by these principles they triumphed over every foe; for thus were they enabled to do all things, and bear all things, "through Christ strengthening them," and to go forward along their perilous and blood-dyed path undismayed and invincible, strong in the Lord and in the power of His might."

With the brief recital of one instance more of the horrors of the "killing time," we shall quit that dreadful period. When the tidings of the Earl of Argyle's enterprise reached the council, orders were immediately given to remove the prisoners confined in Edinburgh, probably that there might be room for the incarceration of the new victims, on whom they expected speedily to lay their grasp. On the 18th of May, these prisoners, both men and women, about two hundred and forty in number, were collected together, hurried to Leith, embarked in open boats, and conveyed in this manner to Burntisland. There they were crammed into two small rooms in the prison, incapable of affording tolerable space for half the number, and kept in that condition for two days, without being permitted to taste so much as bread and water. The oath of supremacy was then tendered to them. About forty accepted, and were sent back to Edinburgh; the rest, refusing to acknowledge an avowed Papist to be the head of the Church, were prepared for their northward journey. Their hands were tied together behind their backs, and in this helpless condition they were driven forward by the rude unfeeling soldiers, who heaped upon them mockery and abuse of every kind. The sufferings which they endured in their journey were so great that several died by the way, and many contracted diseases from which they never recovered. They reached Dunnottar, the place of their destination, on the 24th of May, and were immediately thrust into a dark vault in the castle, which had but one small window on the side next the sea, was full of mire, ankle deep, and was of such narrow dimensions as to allow scarcely more than room to

* Wodrow, vol. iv. pp. 247-249.

stand upright. In this dreadful dungeon they remained almost the whole summer, crowded together, men and women, in one dense mass, without the slightest means of preserving what decency requires; compelled to purchase the worst provisions at the most extravagant prices, so long as they had any money, even water being refused without a heavy price. Not even the horrors of the Black Hole of Calcutta surpassed those of Dunnottar Castle; for, in the former, the sufferings of the victims, if more intense, were of shorter duration, while the persecuted Scottish Presbyterians died many deaths in the lingering agonies of these slow dreadful months. At length disease began to release them more quickly from their miseries; and the governor's lady, having been induced to look into the hideous dungeon, was so shocked and appalled with the scene which met her brief gaze, that she prevailed upon her husband to remove the women to an apartment by themselves, and to put the men into other places, where they might at least breathe a less noisome and pestilential air. But many died of the diseases which they had already contracted, and about the end of the year the wasted survivors were banished to the plantations for slaves,—the men after having their ears cut off, and the women branded with hot irons on the face. Many died on the passage; the remainder met with humane treatment and Christian pity from the American settlers, which their own countrymen had denied them.*

Although the Society People declined joining in Argyle's enterprise, yet they were no inattentive or careless spectators of its progress, and especially of the events which had directly led to it. The succession of the Duke of York, an avowed Papist, to the throne, they regarded with the utmost abhorrence; and immediately published a full and able declaration against it, and also against the legality and validity of that servile parliament, which had been called by him whom they did not hesitate to term a usurper. But this declaration, though even more pointed and argumentative than its predecessors, did not so strongly attract the notice of the council, probably because their attention was for the time engrossed by the more dangerous movements of Argyle and his adherents. The Covenanters, though they did not join Argyle, manifested their sympathy with his enterprise by assisting in the escape of his scattered followers, notwithstanding the certainty that they were thereby increasing their own dangers, and provoking the rage of the victorious enemy. John Nisbet of Hardhill, who had been engaged in the insurrections both of Pentland and of Bothwell Bridge, fell into the hands of the persecutors in November, and accordingly sealed his testimony in the cause of true religion with his blood.

[1686.] The fires of persecution began to grow fainter, and the sword was less incessantly bathed in blood, during the year 1686; not, however, because the rage of the persecutors had abated, but partly because the exterminating process had so far reduced the number of accessible victims, that they could not now so easily lay hold on objects on whom to exercise their barbarities. Their progress had been like that of Roman conquest, characterised in such briefly and terribly emphatic terms by the historian; they had made a solitude,—they called it peace.

There was also another cause which tended to abate the violence of the persecution. The king appears to have thought the state of the country now nearly ripe for that great change, to produce which had been the main though unavowed cause of the greater part of the previous persecuting enactments. Both Charles and James knew well that the Presbyterian Church formed the strongest obstacle to the restoration of Popery, and neither of them expected Prelacy to offer any very determined or protracted opposition to it. They therefore directed all their efforts against Presbytery, confidently anticipating, that if it were destroyed, they would easily induce Prelacy to accept what would be a comparatively slight change, from a hierarchy acknowledging the headship of the king, to a hierarchy acknowledging the headship of the pope. In this they erred; for the Episcopalian Church, though prelatic, was still truly Protestant. Yet there was much probability in the error; for they had experienced so much subserviency from the prelates, that they were

* Wodrow, vol. iv. pp. 322-328, 333.

led to conclude that they could command nothing with which the prelates would not comply. Still it was thought expedient to cover the ulterior designs of the Popish monarch a little longer under some plausible pretexts, and to remove a few more obstacles before the final attempt should be made.

The first step towards restoring the Papists to power had been already made by their exemption from taking the test, which was still urged upon Presbyterians. The next was to repeal the penal statutes against them, and the disabilities under which they were placed. For this purpose a parliament was summoned to meet at Edinburgh on the 29th of April. When parliament met, the Earl of Murray, his majesty's commissioner, produced a letter from the king, the most prominent topic of which was, a glowing encomium on the loyalty and peacefulness of his Roman Catholic subjects; concluding with recommending them to the care of the parliament, that they "might not lie under obligations which their religion could not admit of;" "by doing whereof you will do us most acceptable service." In vain did the commissioner employ all his eloquence to enforce compliance with the suggestion of his majesty's letter. In vain did several of the prelates argue strenuously for the complete toleration of Popery. A considerable proportion of the parliament saw, in such a toleration, the first step towards the complete ascendency of a religion from which they could expect nothing else but a persecution as severe as that which they had employed against the Presbyterians; and, however willing to inflict injuries upon others, and to violate to the utmost of their power every conscientious principle or scruple entertained by the Church of Scotland, they were sufficiently reluctant to be exposed themselves to similar injuries. The recent events which had occurred in France tended greatly to confirm this dread of Popery, where the unjust revocation of the edict of Nantz exposed innumerable French Protestants to every kind of suffering. The public mind caught the alarm, both in England and Scotland, and this had no small influence in preventing the Scottish parliament's compliance with the king's desire. In more guarded terms than any Scottish parliament since the Restoration had been accustomed to use, they promised to take the subject into their serious consideration, and to go as great lengths therein as their consciences would allow, not doubting that his majesty would be careful to secure the Protestant religion. Baffled and disappointed, the commissioner prorogued the parliament, which met no more during the reign of James.

The weight of the king's indignation fell upon some of the prelates who had presumed to oppose his wish. The archbishop of Glasgow and the bishop of Dunkeld were deprived of their benefices. Paterson, who had been exceedingly active in striving to promote the king's views, was made archbishop of Glasgow; and one Hamilton, "noted for profaneness and impiety, which sometimes broke into blasphemy,"* was made bishop of Dunkeld. But the greater part of these servile and unprincipled men signed an address to his majesty, offering to concur with him in all he desired, provided the laws might still continue in force and be executed against the Presbyterians.†

But the previous servility of the Scottish parliaments had put into his majesty's hand a weapon which he was resolved to wield against them. They had admitted his absolute supremacy in the strongest possible terms, and he now employed this absolute supremacy to accomplish what the parliament had shrunk from doing. On the 21st of August, a letter was addressed to the council, from which he had previously expelled the best men, replacing them by sycophants, in which his majesty gives them to know, that "it was not any doubt he had of his power that made him bring his designs before the parliament, but merely to give them an opportunity of showing their duty to him; that he now, according to his undoubted right and prerogative, takes the Roman Catholics under his royal protection, allowing to them the free exercise of their religion, and giving to them the chapel of Holyrood-house for a place of public worship, appointing chaplains and others, whom he recommended to special protection." Thus had the Prelatic party prepared the way for the restoration of Popery, by their yielding up all power

* Burnet's Own Times, vol. i. p. 681. † Burnet's Own Times, vol. i. p. 680.

and law to the absolute supremacy of the monarch, upon whose will, according to their own principles, must depend the religion of his subjects. And they could not, without the most glaring inconsistency, offer any resistance to the despotic conduct of a sovereign whose will they had declared to be the fountain of law, which no man was entitled to question or resist. But the Presbyterians were still the bold guardians of the nation's liberties, civil and sacred, and under their protection that inestimable charge was safe.

In the meantime, there were some movements taking place among the Presbyterians of considerable importance. Several conferences were held between the persecuted followers of Renwick, and that larger body who had partially submitted to the indulgences of former years, or remained silent and passive, while their more daring brethren maintained an open conflict. The object of these conferences was to attempt a union among all Presbyterians, both for mutual protection and to be ready for any propitious moment in which to secure their common rights and liberties. But the desired union was found impracticable. The larger body had unquestionably yielded a sinful compliance with much that was directly subversive of Presbyterian principles; but their pride would not allow them to acknowledge their errors. On the other hand, the society people or Cameronians, or, more properly, the strict Covenanters, would not consent to any union without a previous acknowledgment from their brethren that they had indeed fallen into greivous and sinful defections. There were, besides, some points of minor importance on which their disputes were equally warm, and with much less reason. The result was, that it was found impracticable to form a union of all Presbyterians, although it was earnestly desired by the wisest and the best of both parties. When the subject is contemplated at this distance of time, we may form a more dispassionate opinion on the conduct of both parties than either of them could have done; and our opinion is, that decidedly the greatest amount of blame rests not on the Covenanters, but on their brethren, who had meanly and unfaithfully yielded far more to fear than now they were required to yield to principle. Had they posssessed magnanimity enough to have admitted that they had failed in the hour of conflict, through human weakness, there is no reason to doubt that the high-hearted and dauntless Covenanters would have ceased to stickle pertinaciously for less important matters, and almost the entire body of the Scottish Presbyterians might have been prepared to assume a more commanding attitude at the Revolution, such as would have secured a more complete re-establishment of all their great principles than they actually obtained.

The celebrated Alexander Peden died early in this year, after a reconciliation had been effected between him and Renwick, from whom he had been for a time estranged. Renwick was joined by Mr. David Houston and Mr. Alexander Shields, and field-preaching was continued, although the king, in the midst of his zeal for toleration to the Papists, issued a furious proclamation against them, offering a large reward to any person who should seize Renwick, alive or dead.

[1687.] Although the king had failed in obtaining from parliament that ready submission to his wishes, which he had expected with regard to the legislative repeal of the penal statutes against Papists, he was by no means disposed to mention his intention, but thought it expedient to adopt another mode of procedure. His plan was now to quit the crimson robe of the fierce persecutor, and to assume the garb of universal toleration. Accordingly, on the 12th of February 1687, a letter was sent to the council, accompanied by a proclamation, in which his majesty, "by his sovereign authority, prerogative royal, and absolute power, which all his subjects are to obey without reserve, did give and grant his royal toleration to the several professors of Christian religion." "In the first place," continues his majesty, "we allow and tolerate the *moderate** Presbyterians to meet in their private houses, and there to hear all such ministers as either have, or are willing to accept of our indulgence, and none other." But all those who held or attended field-preachings were still subjected to the utmost rigour of law. Then comes the main object of the pro

* Is this the origin of that ill-omened designation.

clamation, in which, by his prerogative and absolute power, his majesty at once abrogates and annuls all acts of parliament and laws against Roman Catholics, gives them the free and public exercise of their worship, and renders them eligible to all places of public trust, abolishing the test, and enacting a new oath, which affirmed chiefly the entire supremacy and absolute power and authority of the sovereign.*

This, which was called King James's First Indulgence, gave satisfaction to no party but the Papists. The Prelatists were irritated and alarmed to see their own weapons wrested out of their hands, dreading that the power which they had so long and relentlessly employed against the Presbyterians might soon be put into the hands of Papists, and directed against themselves. The Presbyterians generally regarded it with suspicion and distrust, viewing it as not intended for their relief, but as a deceptive mode of restoring Popery; and the Covenanters not merely rejected it, but set its threats at defiance, and continued their field-preachings as usual.

On the 31st of March a second indulgence was published, by which the council were empowered to dispense with the oath, and to suffer Presbyterian ministers to preach in private houses during his majesty's pleasure. This was equally disregarded by the Presbyterians, with this exception, that some of the ministers preached in private houses, having been requested to do so, irrespective of the indulgence; and this was represented by the council, in their letter to the king, as the compliance of the whole body. The king, imagining that his schemes were producing the desired effect, issued a still more extensive toleration to the Dissenters in England; but neither did this hollow and crafty stratagem delude that conscientious body of Christians, who, greatly to their honour, declined to avail themselves of the power of retaliation against the Established Church, which was so far placed within their reach.

At length a third indulgence was granted to the Scottish Presbyterians, dated from London on the 28th of June, and from Edinburgh on the 5th of July,

* Wodrow, vol. iv. pp. 417-419.

In this third indulgence, his majesty, in his usual strain, "by his sovereign authority, prerogative royal, and absolute power," suspends all penal and sanguinary laws made against any for non-conformity to the religion established by law; granting to the Presbyterians "leave to meet and serve God after their own way and manner, be it in private houses, chapels, or places purposely hired or built for that use, so that they take care that nothing be preached or taught among them which may any ways tend to alienate the hearts of our people from us or our government." It was, however, expressly provided that they were not to meet in the open fields; and all the laws against field-preaching were left "in full force and vigour," on the ground that, after this act of royal grace and favour, there was not a shadow of excuse left for them.

His majesty had now declared himself an advocate for liberty of conscience and universal toleration. But few were deceived by these hypocritical pretences. All true Protestants, whether Episcopalians, Presbyterians, or Dissenters, perceived clearly enough, that direct favour to the Papists was intended; and it was not unfairly surmised that, by the universal toleration, the king hoped to throw the various denominations of Protestants into such a state of rivalry and collision, that they would weaken each other, and prepare for the establishment of Popery upon their ruins. There is little reason to doubt that such was his majesty's aim and expectation; but both the immediate and the ultimate consequences were very different from what he intended and hoped. In England a sharp controversy was carried on against the distinctive tenets of the apostate Church of Rome, in which, as might be expected, both from the goodness of their cause and the high talents of the learned and eminent men who engaged in it, the English divines were signally victorious. The universities also joined in the opposition to Popish ascendency; even royalist Oxford, notwithstanding its previous declaration of passive obedience, resisted when oppression was directed against itself. The nation began to awaken, alarmed by the rapid strides which his majesty was making towards Popery, and by the utter disregard for all liberty, civil and religious, which he displayed in his impetuous haste to accomplish what he regarded as the great object of his life.

In Scotland the third indulgence led to a result different in aspect, but not more favourable to the designs of the king. Almost all the Presbyterian ministers in the kingdom availed themselves of the opportunity which it gave them of resuming public worship, and collecting again their scattered congregations. Many, both ministers and people, were released from prison, returned to their long-lost homes, and engaged with renewed fervour in the reconstruction of the Presbyterian Church by the revival of its unforgotten forms of government and discipline, the reunion of its scattered but still living members, and the resuscitation of its imperishable principles. Several of the ejected or intercommuned ministers who had fled to Holland, returned and resumed the discharge of their sacred duties among their countrymen in their own beloved native land. Thus did the Presbyterian Church begin to "shake herself from the dust, and to put on her beautiful garments;" yet the yoke was not wholly loosened from her neck, nor was her robe unstained. A meeting of ministers from different parts of the country was held in Edinburgh, to deliberate respecting the course which ought to be followed in this change of circumstances. It was generally agreed, that the benefit of this indulgence should be accepted; but a strong difference of opinion arose, whether an address of thanks should be transmitted to the king. Fortunately for the character of the Presbyterian Church, so large a number of the ministers disapproved of any address of thanks to a Popish tyrant for giving what he had no right either to give or withhold, that the meeting separated without consenting to transmit such an address as from the body, leaving it to individual ministers to act as they might think proper in the matter. This, however, while it prevented a total loss of character, was an ominous manifestation of weakness, and want of resolute adherence to Presbyterian principles. Not merely no address of thanks should have been sent from them as a body, but there should have been a prohibition issued, forbidding any to do what in reality amounted to at least a partial admission of the royal supremacy in matters spiritual. Yet a considerable number of the ministers concurred in writing and transmitting an address of thanks, but ill accordant with the free and independent principles of the Presbyterian Church.*

The firm, unyielding Covenanters adopted a more consistent course. The conferences in which they had been engaged with their more compliant brethern during the preceding year had caused them to institute a thorough inquiry into the nature and value of their own leading principles, the result of which was the publication, early in this year, of a work entitled "An Informatory Vindication," &c. In this work they republished their former declarations, giving a mitigated explanation of some objectionable sentiments and expressions, but reasserting the great principles in defence of which they had suffered, and were willing still to suffer, every extreme of persecution. The writing of this work had tended both to give clearness to their conception of what these principles were, and to confirm them in their resolute determination to resist every infringement of what they firmly believed to be principles of infinite value and eternal truth. They therefore rejected at once any and every indulgence or toleration of man's inalienable right to worship God according to the direction of His own revealed word and will, and the dictates of an enlightened conscience; especially when such indulgence was founded upon and proceeded from that pernicious principle, the unlimited prerogative and absolute power of the monarch,—a principle equally inconsistent with the laws of God and the liberties of mankind. Alike defying the tyrant's threats and spurning his favours, they resolved to hold on their unswerving course, to continue their field-preachings, and to oppose the exercise of arbitrary power on the one hand, and a course of weak and sinful submission on the other.† Men may censure their conduct as too rigidly unaccommodating but none who understand the subject will deny that at least "their failings leaned to virtue's side," and that

* Wodrow, vol. iv. p. 428.

† Faithful Contendings, p. 310; Hind Let Loose, p. 182.

their principles and proceedings bore a closer resemblance to those of the First and Second Reformations, than did the measures adopted by the greater number of the more compliant and larger party. Still, notwithstanding these dissensions, *the Presbyterian cause grew and prospered generally.* Some important regulations were framed by the meeting of ministers, for the guidance of the body in the great work, on which they were about to enter, of reviving the worship, government, and discipline of the Presbyterian Church.

[1688.] The year 1688, destined to be so memorable in the annals of civil and religious liberty, wore at its beginning in Scotland the aspect of returning persecution. The bold language and unyielding behaviour of Renwick and the Covenanters provoked the council, and led to redoubled efforts for the seizure of that fearless asserter of religious purity and freedom, and for the enforcement of all the acts against field-preaching. A proclamation was issued also, condemning all books which defended the conduct of the Presbyterians, censured that of the persecutors, and assailed Popery; from which the Bible was scarcely exempted, although its suppression was deemed yet premature.* Several instances of cruelty and oppression inflicted upon the persecuted wanderers might be mentioned; but omitting these, we proceed to relate the sufferings and death of the last and one of the most distinguished victims of prelatic tyranny.

It has been already stated, that the small band of determined Covenanters refused to accept the indulgence offered by King James, which was accepted by so many Presbyterian ministers. In this refusal Renwick not only heartily concurred, but was anxious that those who might accept it should at least guard against giving utterance to any such sentiments as might disgrace the Presbyterian cause, and widen the breach between them and him, which he so much deplored. For this purpose he wrote a paper containing his views, and went privately to Edinburgh to lay it before the meeting of ministers held there. When this was done, he went to Fife, where he continued preaching some time, and then returned to Edinburgh, where he lodged for the night. On the very next day, the 1st of February, early in the morning, he was seized, dragged before the council, committed to prison, and heavily fettered like a condemned felon. His accusation was based chiefly on his disowning the king, refusing to pay the cess, condemning the toleration, maintaining the right of self-defence, and continuing to hold field-preachings. All these points he openly and unhesitatingly admitted and defended, never once shrinking from a full and clear avowal of the principles which he had taught. The pleasing simplicity of his manners, the manly and candid frankness of his answers, the unflinching integrity of his sentiments, and the youthful elegance of his handsome person, all combined to command the respect and awaken the compassion of his council, who manifested an unusual desire to save his life. After he was condemned to die, he was asked if he wished longer time to be granted to him; his answer was, "It is all one to me: if it be prolonged, it is welcome; if it be shortened, it is welcome: my Master's time is the best." The day of execution was however, postponed, and considerable efforts were made to induce him to yield, or to make such a concession as would have justified the council in sparing his life. He was visited by one of the bishops, by some of the curates, and by the lord advocate; but he remained unshaken in his principles, and calmly resolute to lay down his life rather than consent to their violation in the slightest degree. He had been exposed to much calumny and reproach for his unbending maintenance of them, in his conferences with other Presbyterian ministers; and he judged rightly, to abandon them through the fear of death, if unconvinced that they were erroneous, would cast great discredit upon these principles, discourage those who had been his faithful followers and fellow-martyrs, and be utterly ruinous not only to his own character, but also and especially to his peace of mind. For him to die was infinitely less terrible than to disown the Covenants, cast a stumbling-block in the way of God's people, and violate his own allegiance to Christ.

Finding that there was no prospect of

* Wodrow, vol. iv. p. 444.

his submission, orders were given for his execution. On the day appointed, the 17th of February, he obtained permission for his mother and sisters to spend a little time with him in the prison. To them he spoke even in terms of joyful anticipation of his near approaching death-hour, addressing to them the kind and gentle language of warm and pure affection, which, while it smoothes the stream of sorrow, increases its depth and perpetuity. When the hour approached, the council, apprehensive of the effect which might be produced, sent to request him neither to pray nor address the people from the scaffold; intimating that, if he would not comply the drums should be beat so that not a word should be heard. He refused to comply; and accordingly, whenever he attempted to speak, his voice was drowned, or nearly so, in the harsh discordant sound of the beaten drums. Yet a few broken sentences were caught by the keen ears of his admiring followers and friends, and treasured up as the precious fragments of a distinguished martyr's dying testimony.* So died James Renwick, three days after he had completed his 26th year; a youth in years, but an experienced Christian, and a most faithful, zealous, and indefatigable minister; in temper mild, gentle, and patient,—in manners courteous and amiable,—in controversial discussion clear, vigorous, and eloquent, as his writings amply prove,—in principle a Presbyterian of the ancient and heroic mould, inflexible as Knox and vehement as Melville, though unequal to either in genius and power. This singularly pious and highly-gifted youth was the last who publicly sealed with his blood his testimony in behalf of Scotland's Covenant, and the Divine Mediator's sole sovereignty over his Church.

The dreadless banner of the Covenant, which Renwick had so long upheld, was not allowed to fall prostrate to the earth when his hand was cold in death. It was seized and borne aloft by the Rev. Alexander Shields, who had previously been a sufferer in the same cause, and who, having been called by the society people to be their minister, boldly stept into that honourable but most perilous path of duty. They held a large general meeting in the parish of Galston, where Mr. Shields preached in defiance of the sanguinary laws still in force against them. The soldiery were sent immediately to pursue the delinquents; but though they pillaged the country severely, only one youth fell into their hands, who was killed on the spot without so much as the form of a trial. Several of the indulged ministers were interrupted in their ministry and brought to trial on account of alleged violations of the terms of the late indulgence. By these proceedings the country was made fully aware that the king's boasted universal toleration was not intended to be a measure of mercy, but merely a deceptive pretext for the restoration of Popery to universal power in the kingdom.

It is not our province to trace the civil events of this period, by which the revolution was effected, especially as it may be assumed that these are familiar to almost every reader. A few sentences will contain an outline sufficient for our purpose, which is merely to preserve the continuity of the narrative, that what belongs peculiarly to the church of Scotland may chiefly engage our attention, and at the same time be seen in proper sequence and natural connection.

The attention of all lovers of freedom had for some time been directed to the Prince of Orange, husband of James's eldest daughter, and heir-presumptive to the crown. But on the 10th of June the queen gave birth to an infant prince, by which the joy of the Papists was raised to the highest pitch, and the nation generally alarmed by the dread of a succession of Popish sovereigns. At the same time, the acquittal of the seven bishops, who had been committed to the Tower by James because of their petitioning against being compelled to read one of his arbitrary indulgences from the pulpit gave occasion to the display of the nation's joy at the defeat of absolute power. The vigilant eye of William marked well the importance of the juncture. He saw the Scottish Presbyterians availing themselves of the king's deceptive truce, to muster their strength, and to recover that position which belonged to them as forming the great majority of the population in the kingdom. He perceived that James had succeeded in alienating the af-

* Wodrow, vol. iv. pp. 445-454; Life of Renwick; Cloud of Witnesses.

fections of the English Church and people, while yet his popish support was inconsiderable. The nation, he perceived, was ripe for a change, and the favourable moment was come, which, if not promptly seized, might never return. The birth of the infant prince put an end to all indecision, as it put an end to his hope of ascending the throne by natural succession. Having made the necessary preparations for an enterprise so momentous, he committed the cause solemnly to God, set sail, and landed at Torbay, without having encountered any opposition, on the 5th of November.

In the meantime, James had been acting like a man under the spell of infatuation. In England he ceased not to irritate the feelings of that high-spirited people, already provoked beyond endurance by his despotism. He attempted the perilous measure of remodelling the army, from which he was compelled to desist. He drew the greater part of the forces from Scotland, with the view of employing them to keep his refractory English subjects in obedience, but leaving his Scottish minions destitute of power to maintain his interests in that country against the rising and rapidly increasing strength of the Presbyterians. A proclamation was issued for raising the militia in Scotland; but that was little else than putting arms into the hands of his opponents. Yet the Scottish council showed their willingness, if not their power, by transmitting an address making offer of their lives and fortunes to the king, and requesting directions how to act in such a dangerous juncture. When the Prince of Orange issued his declaration and manifesto, that document was prohibited to be circulated or read; but the zealous Covenanters assisted greatly in spreading it throughout the length and breadth of the land, in spite of all prohibitions, and it was received with general satisfaction. On the 3d of November, all the Scottish prelates, except two, concurred in sending a letter to the king, containing the most extravagant eulogiums on that tyrant and his course of government, avowing their steadfast allegiance to him, "as an essential part of their religion," and wishing him "the hearts of his subjects and the necks of his enemies."* Any thing more servile, and at the same time despotic and persecuting in its spirit, it is impossible to imagine; and as this was the last public act of Scottish Prelacy, at the close of its bloody reign, it deserves to be recorded, as a proof that it was still the same slavish, intolerant, irreligious, and persecuting system which it had ever been, and as a warning also, that Prelacy and civil and religious freedom cannot exist together in Scotland.

On the 10th of December there occurred a riot in Edinburgh, caused chiefly by the students of the college and the city apprentices, which ended in their driving a body of troops out of Holyrood House, which had been fortified and garrisoned, rifling the Abbey, and burning the images and other idolatrous symbols employed in the popish worship. This riot the council had not power to quell; and the Duke of Perth, the chancellor, fled from the capital in terror of his life. On the 14th the council published an act for disarming Papists, and at the same time protecting their persons and property against tumults, which was intended to prevent the recurrence of similar riotous scenes. On the 24th they issued a proclamation, founded upon a rumour that the Irish Papists had been called on by the king to invade Scotland. In this proclamation they require all Protestant subjects to put themselves in a state of defence, for securing their religion, lives, liberties, and properties, against the attempts of Papists; and all heritors are summoned to meet, well armed and provided, at the head burghs of their respective counties, and to place themselves under the command of the persons named in the proclamation. This was a virtual repeal of the whole proceedings of the government during the preceding twenty-eight years, in which to appear armed in defence of life and religion was condemned and punished as treason. After this act the Scottish privy council voluntarily dissolved and disappeared, leaving the people in a great measure to their own government, and to the defence of that form of religion to which they were most attached. This, therefore, we may regard as the end of the long and bloody persecution

* Wodrow, vol. iv. p. 463. The address of the Presbyterian ministers to the Prince of Orange furnishes a noble contrast to this servile letter, as will be shown in its proper place.

which the Church of Scotland endured from perjured and remorseless Prelacy, and the absolute despotism of the Brother Tyrants.

It would not have been strange if the Presbyterians had inflicted a terrible retribution on their merciless oppressors. But they acted in general like men conscious of a glorious cause, which they might not permit their own passions to sully and disfigure. When the rumour that an Irish invasion was intended reached the Covenanters, they immediately mustered in a considerable body, and prepared to defend their country and their friends from the invaders; but finding the rumour groundless, they resolved to take that opportunity of expelling the prelatic curates from the parishes which they had so long polluted with their presence and devastated with their cruelty. They accordingly seized upon these wretched men, turned them out of their usurped abodes, marched them to the boundaries of their respective parishes, and sent them away, without offering them further violence.* No plunder, no bloodshed, stained the hands of the Covenanters. As their constancy through the long period of fiery trial had been almost unparalleled, so their high-principled self-government was conspicuous in their hour of bloodless triumph. How gloriously different the conduct of the Scottish Presbyterians from that of their prelatic persecutors, rendering it manifest to the world, as if written with a sunbeam, which of these two forms of Church government possessed most of the principles, and displayed most of the character of the gospel of peace and good-will.

When the landing of the Prince of Orange, and the revolution which followed, put an end to the persecution which had continued for twenty-eight years, a computation was made, from which it appeared, that above eighteen thousand had suffered by death, slavery, exile or imprisonment, inflicted in the vain endeavor to destroy the Presbyterian Church of Scotland, and establish Prelacy on its ruins.† This is exclusive of the desolation spread over the country by oppressive fines, assessments, and the lawless pillage of the licentious soldiery, by which whole districts were almost turned into a wilderness. Surely those who talk of the possibility of Prelacy ever becoming the religion of Scotland, must expect it to be preceded by such a revolution both in the constitution of the human mind and in the frame of nature, as shall completely sweep away all records of the past; for so long as our mountains, heaths, and glens, are studded with the gray memorials of our martyred fathers, and so long as the free blood courses more warmly and the heart beats higher in one true Scottish bosom, at the narrative of their glorious sufferings and the savage cruelty of their merciless persecutors, so long must it be absolutely impossible for Prelacy to be regarded in Scotland with any other feelings than those of indignant reprobation, as alike hostile to the principles of civil liberty, and contrary to the mild and gracious spirit of Christianity.

In taking a retrospective glance over that dark and stormy period of the Church of Scotland's history between the Restoration and the Revolution, there are some topics which force themselves upon the mind so strongly as to demand a brief investigation before proceeding further. What was the ruling motive which induced Charles and James to persecute the Presbyterian Church with such relentless cruelty? In the case of Charles, it could not have been his preference of Prelacy on religious grounds, as he was evidently a man of no religion at all. In the case of James, it was as manifest, that if he preferred that form of church government, it was only because he regarded it as less directly opposed to Popery, on the re-establishment of which his heart was bent. The steady and unswerving perseverance with which the whole course of public affairs was guided in Scotland, towards the effecting of one object, during so many years, proves clearly that some one ruling principle was in continual operation all the while. That principle, we think, Burnet's "History of His Own Times" furnishes the means of detecting. From that work, as well as from many other sources, we learn that Charles had joined the Church of Rome before he left France. Burnet tells us further, that soon after the restoration, Charles in con-

* Cruickshank, vol. ii. p. 474; Burnet's Own Times, vol. i. p. 805.

† Memoirs of the Church of Scotland, pp. 290-294.

versation with him, reprobated the liberty that, under the reformation, all men took of inquiring in matters of religion, from which they proceeded to inquire into matters of state; adding, that he thought government was a much safer and easier thing when the authority was believed infallible, and the faith and submission of the people were implicit. The king's predilection for Popery was evidently not on the ground of conscience, but because by its means alone he could hope to acquire absolute power, and to reduce the people to the implicit obedience of slaves. To effect this tyrannical intention was the constant endeavor of both Charles and his brother; and there are many significant indications, that even in the case of James, the love of Popery was subordinate to the love of despotism. This view completely explains both the direct endeavors and the evasive changes and fluctuations of these two reigns. Lauderdale appears to have early penetrated into the king's designs, and to have made the attempt to realize them the ruling aim and effort of his whole administration. Remembering also, that it was the presence of the Scottish army in England which turned the wavering balance in favor of the parliament during the civil wars, he made it his steady endeavour to bring Scotland into a state of such complete subserviency to the king, that a powerful army might be raised in support of his majesty, should any contest arise between him and his English subjects. In this view, the act which Lauderdale procured from the Scottish parliament in 1663, offering to the king an army of twenty thousand foot and two thousand cavalry to be at his own disposal, was no empty bravado, as it has generally been regarded, but a significant hint from that despotic statesman, that the time for the monarch's assumption of absolute power was near at hand. The oath of supremacy, and the acts enforcing it became, when viewed in this light, not only perfectly intelligible, but pregnant with meaning of fearful import. They were all so many steps towards that absolute despotism which the king desired to establish, and that state of utter slavery to which he wished to reduce the kingdom. It is not necessary to suppose that the prelatic party were fully aware of this intention, and were willing to become the base instruments by which it should be accomplished; yet their conduct and their written sentiments not only supported, but too often seemed to lead the way to the full establishment of the most arbitrary and cruel tyranny, And it must never be forgotten, that the execrable design of reducing Britain to a state of abject slavery was, under Providence, frustrated solely by the unconquerable fortitude with which the Presbyterian Church of Scotland endured every extremity of suffering which a long, relentless, and desolating persecution could inflict.

At the same time it must be observed, that the resistance of the Presbyterian Church proceeded from a far higher principle than merely the determination to defend the civil liberties of the country,—a principle without which civil liberty can never be fully realized, and which, in free and active operation, would render the dire counterparts—absolute power and abject slavery—for ever impossible. This great principle, as abstractly stated and most tenaciously maintained by the Church of Scotland, is, "That the Lord Jesus Christ is the sole Head and King of the Church, and hath therein appointed a government distinct from that of the civil magistrate." In the form in which it practically appears, this great principle realizes such a disjunction of the civil and the ecclesiastical powers from each other as to assign and secure to each a separate, co-ordinate, and independent supreme court for the exercise of their respective functions. The direct consequence of this great and sacred principle, thus realized, is, that it preserves the whole region of the conscience entirely free from the control of external power; and where the conscience is free, men cannot be enslaved. The attempt to establish an absolute despotism, involved, of necessity, the destruction of this principle: and the oath of supremacy was the weapon by which it was directly and fiercely assailed. The cruel policy of the assailants needs little explanation. It was an easy matter for them to enact an unjust and irreligious law, such as that which virtually declared that the sovereignty of the Church should be taken from Christ, and given to the king, and then to shout, "Obey the law, obey the law!" proclaiming men rebels and traitors, and persecuting them to the death, because they could not yield obedience to a law which required the violation of their allegiance to the Divine Redeemer, but chose to obey God rather than man in matters of religion. It requires but little Christian principle, metaphysical acumen, or knowledge of the general principles of jurisprudence, to perceive that no law can possibly be binding upon man which is manifestly contrary to the law of God. So reasoned and so felt our covenanted fathers; and in defence of that sacred and eternal principle they "endured a great fight of afflictions," through which they were triumphantly borne by the mighty power of God, unfolding and realizing in the fearful struggle, what, though of subordinate importance, was still of inestimable value, that noblest charter of civil liberty which man has ever framed, the British Constitution.

The only accusation which can, with any degree of propriety, be urged against the Covenanters is, that they did to a certain extent misunderstand and overpass some of the essential distinctions between things civil and things sacred. But this cannot justly either excite our surprise or call forth our censure. Few seem yet to have any accurate perception of these distinctions; and many seem disposed to deny that they either do or can exist, or, at least, that they can be so specifically marked out as to prevent the incessant mutual encroachments of the civil and the ecclesiastical jurisdictions upon the respective provinces which rightfully belong to each. It was not strange, therefore, that the Covenanters partially erred, especially when engaged in such a deadly struggle. The contest was, on their part, at first waged solely in defence of the central principle of religious liberty. But as civil and religious liberty exist or perish together, they were soon compelled to contend equally for both, and thus the scene of conflict was both enlarged and altered, involving a complication of interests which tended to produce confusion. It was this which led them to the idea of disowning the king, and declaring what they explained to be a "defensive war" against him, as against a lawless tyrant, whose own acts involved the invalidation of his right to reign. The Revolution was indeed a substantial confirmation of the justness of their bold opinions. But still, for any section of a community to proclaim and act upon such opinions, must unavoidably expose them, as citizens, to the charge of rebellion, and as ministers and members of the Christian Church, to the charge of interfering with matters beyond their legitimate province. There seem to be but two conditions by which such a course of procedure can be fully justified, either of which can rarely occur, and the one of which cannot be known beforehand, and, therefore, ought not to be assumed as a primary cause. These are, *the direct command of God*, of which the Bible relates various instances; and *ultimate success*, which, correctly speaking does not justify the attempt, but merely ratifies the deed, from which it may be inferred, that the enterprise was accordant with the will of Divine Providence. This *second* condition, we are aware, may be both misunderstood and misrepresented, as if it were identical with the false principle, that the end justifies the means. What we mean is this, that when an attempt is made by any considerable party in a nation, for an object which appears to be in accordance with Scripture, reason, and civil liberty, its failure may prove it to have been premature, but will not prove it to have been wrong; whereas its success will go far to prove it to have been essentially right. The *first*, many of the Scottish Covenanters conceived themselves to have, both by reasoning from Scripture analogies, and from the directly unchristian character of the principles attempted to be enforced by their opponents: the *second* they obtained when the Revolution completed what they had begun and carried forward with determined resolution, heroic fortitude, and Christian patience; and it must be remarked, that they never doubted of the ultimate triumph of their sacred cause, even in the most disastrous periods, and amidst the darkest horrors of the fierce exterminating persecution directed against them by their despotic and merciless oppressors. Any censure, therefore, which could justly be pronounced against them, must be exceedingly slight, and, when compared with the vast debt of gratitude due to them by the entire empire, must become almost invisible, like a speck in the sun. Still, while such must be the sentiments of every enlightened lover of freedom, it is the true spiritually-minded Christian alone who can enter fully into the feelings of these much-enduring and devoted men, comprehend the true nature of the great and sacred principles in defence of which they encountered the perils and suffered the extremities of poverty, imprisonment, exile, torture, and death, and appreciate the real value of the service rendered by them to the cause of vital piety, and to the interests of the Divine Redeemer's spiritual kingdom.

CHAPTER VIII

FROM THE REVOLUTION, IN THE YEAR 1688, TO THE TREATY OF UNION IN 1707.

Meeting of the Convention of Estates—Declaration and Claim of Right—Petition of the Covenanters—Their Loyalty and Patriotism—Condition of the Church and Country—King William and Carstares—The Prelatists—Meeting of Parliament—Acts abolishing Prelacy, ratifying the Confession of Faith, establishing the Presbyterian Church, and abolishing Patronage—Meeting of the General Assembly—Acts of Assembly—Remarks on the Revolution Settlement—State of the Conflicting Parties—The restored Ministers, the Conformists, the Covenanters—Views of the King, of the Church, and of the Jacobites, and Prelatic Party—Origin of the Moderate Party—The Commission—The Assembly forcibly adjourned—Its Firmness—Act of Parliament for settling the Quiet and Peace of the Church—Its Character and Consequences—A Mutual Compromise—A New Collision threatened—The King and Carstares—Meetings of the Assembly—Proceedings of the Church—Conduct of the Jacobites and Prelatists—Act against intruding into Churches—Competing Calls and Transportations—The Rabbling Act—Misrepresentations of the Prelatic Party—Death of King William—Queen Anne—Political Intrigues against the Church—Proposals for a Union—Act of Security—The Union—General View of the State of the Church

The dissolution of the Scottish privy council relieved the country instantly and completely from a tyranny and persecution under which it had groaned and bled for a period of twenty-eight terrible years; but it left the kingdom in a state of anarchy dangerous to the peace and welfare of the community. Had the Presbyterians been influenced at all by the spirit of revenge, there was nothing to have prevented them from inflicting a dreadful retribution upon their paralyzed and defenceless oppressors in their hour of utter weakness. Nothing, therefore, could have given a more perfect proof of the injustice and falsehood of the accusations formerly urged so vehemently against them on account of the pernicious, treacherous, and murderous principles which they were said to hold, than the fact, that when their principles had free scope, the most remarkable characteristic which they displayed was the forgiveness of their fallen enemies. The expelling of the curates, which has been already noticed, was in truth nothing else but the ejection of lawless intruders from positions and property on which they had wrongfully seized, with the view of having them restored to their rightful owners. Still, the condition of the country was full of peril, which was held in check by the power of religious principle alone; and it was the manifest interest of all classes to reconstruct the disorganized frame of society as speedily as possible. On this account men of all political parties hastened to London, to hold intercourse with each other and with the Prince of Orange, to ascertain their respective strength, and to deliberate on the course to be pursued.

[1689.] The legislature of England met in the form of a convention, avoiding the term *parliament*, as not being called by the king, and, after considerable discussion, voted, "That James the Second, having endeavored to subvert the constitution of the kingdom, by breaking the original contract between the king and the people, and, by the advice of Jesuits and other wicked persons, having violated the fundamental laws, and withdrawn himself out of this kingdom, has abdicated the government, and the throne is become vacant." After some further discussion, the vacant throne was given to the Prince and Princess of Orange, as joint sovereigns, the title constantly running William and Mary, King and Queen of England,—the sole administration resting in the king. On the 8th of January, 1689, William assembled the leading Scottish noblemen and gentlemen who were in London, and after referring to his Declaration, told them that he had called them together to ask their advice respecting the best method of securing the civil and religious liberties of their country. Their advice was, that he would assume the administration of affairs till a convention of estates could be held in Edinburgh, and a proper settlement be effected, which convention they requested to be empowered to meet on the 14th of March; and to this he gave his assent.

The Scottish convention met on the day appointed, the short interval having been employed by the two contending parties,—the adherents of James, who were generally Prelatists, and the supporters of the Revolution, who were Presbyterians,—in the most strenuous endeavours to muster their whole strength for the struggle. It had been stipulated by the meeting in London, that in the election of representatives to the convention, none who were protestants should be excluded from legally voting, or from being returned as members. This at once removed the disabilities under which the oppressive acts of the preceding reigns had laid the greater part of the Presbyterians, and enabled them to send to the convention a majority of right-minded men. Still the peril was great. Claverhouse, who had been created Viscount Dundee by James, was fully determined to maintain the right of that despot by war; and had brought with him to Edinburgh a considerable body of armed and desperate men to overawe the convention. There were no military forces in the kingdom to prevent Dundee from any extreme to which his daring and ferocious spirit might impel him; and the castle was held by the Duke of Gordon, who also favoured the interests of the fallen monarch. In this dangerous juncture recourse was had to the Cameronian Covenanters, as the only body which both possessed the power and the inclination to protect their country's liberties, and might be trusted in this hour of peril. They were requested to come to Edinburgh, armed and prepared to resist any outrage which might be offered to the convention or the town by Dundee, their former relentless persecutor. This was a noble tribute to the character of these much injured and greatly calumniated men. They had formerly been hunted down as disturbers of peace and the very enemies of society; they were now sought and hailed as conservators of peace, and protectors of the public welfare.

T e first trial of strength in the convention took place on the subject of choosing a president. The Duke of Hamilton was named by the Presbyterians; the Prelatists gave their support to the Marquis of Athol. The Duke of Hamilton was chosen by a majority of fifteen; and as this proved the superiority of the Presbyterian party, a considerable number of that wavering class of politicians who act from selfish motives, joined the side which they saw to be the strongest, increasing its majorities, though adding nothing to its moral influence. The struggle was no longer doubtful, so far as regarded the transfer of the crown from James to William; but the adjustment of the many great interests therein involved, was still a matter of an extremely difficult nature. Viscount Dundee, having in vain attempted to disturb or overawe the convention, abandoned the wily arts of the politician, and determined to have recourse to the sword. His abrupt and threatening departure ruined the plans of the adherents of James, by precipitating them into a conflict for which they were not prepared, and by relieving the convention in a great measure from the impediments which the supporters of despotism, had they remained, might have thrown in the way of the Revolution Settlement. The convention then ratified the London Address, in all its tenor and conditions. A committee was next appointed, similar to the Lords of the Articles, for preparing the overtures for settling the government; and in this committee the prelates were omitted, —by which a sufficiently intelligible intimation was given what was likely to be the fate of Prelacy. Two letters were presented to the convention, the one from King James, the other from the Prince of Orange; the first was disregarded, the other treated with great respect. An answer to the Prince's letter was prepared, and then the convention proceeded to declare their opinion respecting the state of the nation, and the necessary remedial measures. This declaration was publicly read and agreed to, on the 4th of April, the day on which the Prince's letter in reply was received; and having been embodied in the "Claim of Right," in the conclusion of which was contained an offer of the Scottish crown to William and Mary, together with a brief and simple oath of allegiance, the whole document was read, and the king and queen publicly proclaimed in Edinburgh, on the 11th day of April, 1689.

A few sentences of this most important document must be engrossed in the body of this work, in vindication of the principles and conduct of the oppressed and persecuted Church of Scotland. It begins as follows:—

"Whereas King James VII. being a professed Papist, did assume the regal power, and acted as king, without ever taking the oath required by law, whereby the king, at his accession to the government, is obliged to swear to maintain the Protestant religion, and to rule the people according to the laudable laws, and did, by the advice of wicked and evil counsellors, invade the fundamental constitution of this kingdom, and alter it from a legal limited monarchy to an arbitrary despotic power; and in a public proclamation asserted an absolute power to cass, annul, and disable all the laws, particularly the laws establishing the Protestant religion, and did exercise that power to the subversion of the Protestant religion, and to the violation of the laws and liberties of the kingdom." (Then follows an enumeration of the arbitrary acts, complained against, forming, in fact, a brief outline of the history of the persecuting period.) "Therefore, the estates of the kingdom of Scotland find and declare that King James VII. being a professed Papist, did assume, &c. (in the same terms as above,) WHEREBY HE HATH FORFEITED THE RIGHT TO THE CROWN, AND THE THRONE IS BECOME VACANT."

The reader will observe, that this declaration of the Scottish convention of estates is the same in spirit, and almost the same in words, as the declarations emitted by the covenanted Presbyterians, on account of which they were calumniated and persecuted as rebels and traitors. The only essential difference between their declarations and that of the convention is, that the Covenanters took for their central and leading principle that which forms the essence of religious liberty, and at the same time renders absolute civil despotism impossible, namely, the sole sovereignty of Christ, as the only Head and King of his free spiritual kingdom, the Church. This the convention did not declare,—in all probability they neither understood nor held it; but so far as their declaration went, it stated the very same reasons for the tyrant's forfeiture of the crown which had been repeatedly stated by the followers of Cameron, Cargill and Renwick, and in defence of which these high-principled men had cheerfully laid down their lives.

A short time previous to the issuing of the convention's Declaration and Claim of Right, a petition was laid before them, embodying the sentiments and requests of the maligned Cameronian Covenanters, in a strain at once of sublimity and pathos, such as rarely has been surpassed.

"We prostrate ourselves, yet under the sorrowing smart of our still bleeding wounds, at your honours' feet, who have a call, a capacity, and, we hope, a heart to heal us; and we offer this our petition, conjuring your honours to hearken to us. By all the formerly felt, presently seen, and, for the future, feared effects and efforts of Popery and tyranny,—by the cry of the blood of our murdered brethren,—by the sufferings of the banished freeborn subjects of this realm, now groaning in servitude, having been sold into slavery in the English plantations of America, by the miseries that many thousands forfeited, disinherited, harassed, and wasted houses have been reduced to,—by all the sufferings of a faithful people, for adhering to the ancient covenanted establishment of religion and liberty, and by all the arguments of justice, necessity, and mercy, that ever could join together, to begin communication among men of wisdom, piety, and virtue,—humbly, beseeching, requesting, and craving of your honours, now when God hath given you this opportunity to act for His glory, the good of the Church, of the nation, your own honour, and the happiness of posterity,—now when this kingdom, the neighbouring, and all the nations of Europe, have their eyes upon you, expecting you will acquit yourselves like the representatives of a free nation, in redeeming it from slavery otherwise inevitable,—that you will proceed without any delay to declare the wicked government dissolved, the crown and throne vacant, and James VII., whom we never owned, and resolved in conjunction with many thousands of our countrymen never to own, to have really forfeited, and rightly to be deprived of, all right and title he ever had, or ever could pretend to have hitherto, and to provide that it may never be in the power of any succeeding ruler to aspire unto or arise to such a capacity of tyrannizing." (They then petition that the crown may be bestowed on William, with such necessary provisions as may secure liberty civil and religious, specify the king's duty to profess and preserve the pure religion and the work of reformation, and conclude thus:)—"Upon such terms as these we render our allegiance to King William, and hope to give more pregnant proofs of our loyalty to his majesty, in adverse as well as prosperous providences, than they have done, or can do, who profess implicit subjection to absolute authority so long only as Providence preserves its grandeur."*

Such were the earnest, free, and dignified, loyal, and pious sentiments of men who had been slandered, reviled, and persecuted for the space of twenty-eight years; and whose characters, principles, and memory, the greatest author of modern times has vainly striven to blacken and disgrace, his own reputation alone suffering from the malignant and abortive attempt, through the fatal recoil which ignorant and calumnious falsehood sustains, when it dares to encounter unsullied and majestic truth.† Their loyalty and patriotism were not confined to words. In the distressed state of the country, a civil war commencing, led on by the fierce and infuriated Dundee (Claverhouse), with few troops in the kingdom, and some of these disaffected to the new sovereign, and others almost undisciplined, the generous Covenanters stood forward in defence of their native land, and offered to raise a regiment for public service, stipulating only that the officers should be men of conscience, honour, and fidelity, and unstained by the persecuting proceedings of the late reigns, and that their service should be for the defence of the nation and the preservation of religion, in opposition to Popery, Prelacy, and tyranny. These terms were gladly accepted; and in one day, without beat of drum, or the expenditure of levy-money, they raised a regiment of eight hundred men, commonly termed the Cameronian regiment, commanded by the Earl of Angus, and Lieutenant-Colonel Cleland; the latter of whom had led a party of the insurgents both at Drumclog and Bothwell Bridge, and was afterwards killed in the gallant and successful defence of Dunkeld by that regiment against a far superior force of Highlanders. Such, indeed, was their loyalty and zeal, that they even offered to raise two more regiments, if their services should be required, for the protection of the nation's liberties; a sufficient proof that they were neither the narrow-minded fanatics, nor the miserable handful, which their enemies and persecutors pretended, but in reality a powerful body of high-hearted and patriotic men.

It deserves to be remarked, that in the Claim of Right, which forms the basis of the Revolution Settlement, the convention did not rest satisfied with the rather ambiguous mention of the Protestant religion, but inserted a clause in the following terms: "That Prelacy, and the superiority of any office in the Church above Presbyters, is, and hath been, a great and insupportable grievance and trouble to this nation, and contrary to the inclinations of the generality of the people, ever since the Reformation, they having been reformed from Popery by Presbyters, and, therefore, ought to be abolished." The insertion of such a clause was imperatively necessary in order to satisfy the Presbyterians, who had at least as much reason to dread Prelacy as they had to dread Popery itself, having suffered from Prelacy a persecution unspeakably more intense than ever Popery had been in a condition to inflict.

The Revolution Settlement was now as complete as the temporary expedient of a convention of estates could legally render it; and in order to confirm it in the amplest manner, without incurring the danger of intrigues and divisions, the king empowered them to pass an act converting the convention into a parliament, to meet formally on the 5th of June, and for despatch of business on the 17th of the same month, in which the Earl of Crawford was to preside, the

* Cruickshank, vol. ii. pp. 279, 280; Memoirs of the Church of Scotland, pp. 303-308.

† See Sir Walter Scott's Old Mortality; and Dr. M'Crie's Vindication of the Covenanters, in his Miscellaneous Works.

Duke of Hamilton representing his majesty as commissioner. The general confusion prevailing in the kingdom at this time rendered the sitting of the parliament short, and comparatively unsatisfactory. Yet some important measures were carried and others proposed. On the 22d of July an act was passed "abolishing Prelacy, and all superiority of any office in the Church in this kingdom above Presbyters," and rescinding those acts of parliament passed in the reign of Charles II., by which Prelacy had been established. An "overture for settling church government in Scotland" was then laid before the parliament by the Duke of Hamilton, but was so ill received, that it was withdrawn. An act was prepared, and with some difficulty passed, excluding from places of public trust those persons who had either been ready instruments of tyranny and persecution in the former reigns, or had exerted themselves against the recent propitious changes which had rescued the nation from civil and religious despotism. But this the commissioner refused to ratify, and it was not again revived in any subsequent parliament. The dissensions in the parliament continued to run high, increased on the one hand by rumours of conspiracies among the adherents of James, who began to be termed Jacobites, and who were composed of Papists, Prelatists, and supporters of absolute power, whether of any religious creed, or of none; and on the other, by the disappointment of the Presbyterians, who had as yet experienced little return of gratitude from the king for having so greatly contributed to that Revolution which transferred to his brow the crown of three kingdoms. It was accordingly adjourned, and appointed to meet again early in the beginning of the following year.

Having thus traced a brief outline of the main civil events which took place during the first year of the new reign, and while the nation was still tossing in all the fitful uncertainties which characterize a state of transition, it is necessary to direct our attention a little more closely to the actual condition of the Presbyterian Church, which was now struggling from amidst the ruins in which it had been so long overwhelmed and kept prostrate. When King James's last indulgence was issued, several of the exiled and intercommuned ministers returned from abroad, and availed themselves of its provisions so far as to recommence preaching, some in the parishes from which they had been formerly ejected, in barns or in meeting-houses erected expressly for their accommodation; others in such places as their friends could procure in the most favourable situations. Some of these were again interrupted, driven from their places of worship, and imprisoned, or otherwise silenced, before the abdication of James, and the dissolution of the persecuting privy council. And when, by the act of forfeiture passed by the convention, the despotic power was abolished and religious liberty secured, all the surviving Presbyterian ministers were at once allowed to come forward, ready for the reconstruction of their national temple. It then appeared, that of upwards of four hundred ministers, who had been ejected to make way for Prelacy, only about sixty survived to see the restoration of Presbytery. Well might the worn and wasted band gaze sadly on each other, as they contemplated the great work which was to be done, and their own inadequacy to accomplish the arduous task.

The difficulties to be encountered were both numerous and formidable. They had to meet the determined and deadly hostility of the defeated Prelatists throughout the kingdom; under which designation must be classed not only the few who favoured Prelacy on purely religious grounds, if any such there were, but also, and especially, all secular politicians, all ambitious or licentious men of the world, all Papists, and all who hated religion because they loved immorality. They had also to attempt the very difficult task of uniting all Presbyterians into one compact harmonious body, able both to confront their enemies, and to insure the respect and support of their friends. But the greater part of the Presbyterian ministers in Scotland, at that juncture, were those who had either partially conformed to Prelacy, or had accepted of the indulgences which had from time to time been offered, and had repeatedly excited such unhappy and pernicious divisions among them. These men conscious of their feeble-minded and faithless defections, were on that very account the more ready to take offence at the slightest allusion to their former conduct by their more consistent brethren. There was, therefore, the utmost reason to dread the instantaneous rising of such internal dissensions as would prevent the possibility of reuniting the Presbyterian body into such a harmonious form as might enable it to become again the Established Church of the nation. The danger of such a disastrous result was greatly increased by two entirely opposite causes. On the one hand, those who were merely, or chiefly, political Presbyterians, strongly urged upon the ministers, that all mention of past defections, errors, and weaknesses among their brethren should be most carefully avoided, so that offence might neither be given nor received; on the other, the unyielding Covenanters, who had not shrunk from the hottest of the conflict, whose firm and steady strength had contributed greatly to the protection of the convention, and by that means had lent effectual aid to the assertors of freedom, and who were doubtless somewhat elated to see so many of their boldest principles in the course of being realized,—these high-minded and inflexible men urged upon the whole Presbyterian body the absolute necessity of making a full acknowledgement of all past errors and defections, and of resting satisfied with nothing short of the revival of the National Covenants, and the restoration of the Church to the position she had occupied in the year 1649. It was absolutely impossible that views so diametrically opposed to each other could both be adopted; and it was almost inevitable that the wish and the endeavour to frame some compromise, or to take up some intermediate position, would plunge the Church into inextricable difficulties, and perhaps also into serious errors.

The peculiar character and views of King William, and the advice given to him by those in whom he reposed the greatest confidence, did not tend to diminish the difficulties of the Scottish Presbyterians. There is no reason to doubt that William was well aware of the value of true religion, and was himself considerably under its influence. But he was a statesman in the strictest sense of the term; and his mind was so engrossed with the great idea of maintaining the balance of power in Europe against the gigantic strength of France, that every other thing occupied but a subordinate place and value in his thoughts. A complete union between Scotland and England he regarded as of essential importance, to enable him to meet the compact might of the French monarchy; and though personally favourable to the Presbyterian form, yet seeing the improbability that he could persuade England to accept of it, he was desirous to induce Scotland to consent to a modified Episcopacy. He did not regard any form of church government as of divine authority; and therefore thought it practicable to induce both kingdoms to abate somewhat of their distinctive peculiarities, and to meet and unite in some intermediate arrangement. For that reason he abstained from a full recognition of Presbytery in Scotland at first, waiting to try the effect of returning peace to produce unanimity; and when he did consent to the establishment of the Presbyterian Church in Scotland, he did so in terms which have been thought to admit of a somewhat lax interpretation, declaring it to be "agreeable to the Word of God," instead of "grounded upon the infallible truth of God's Word," which was the form of expression used by Knox, at the first establishment of the Presbyterian Church. The same course of policy led him to desire in Scotland itself a union of the prelatic clergy of the two preceeding reigns and the restored Presbyterians; though, how he could expect any degree of cordiality to subsist between humbled and fangless persecutors and their rescued, yet wounded and still bleeding victims, it is not easy to imagine. By prosecuting this specious yet most baneful policy, dictated do doubt by that great deceiver of the world's sages and statesmen, expediency, William both alienated and so far paralyzed his Presbyterian friends, to whom chiefly he owed the British crown, left power in the hands of enemies and traitors, and excited those feelings of discontent in the minds of the one party, and turbulent anticipations of change and counter-revolution in the other, by which his whole reign was rendered a scene of distraction and turmoil.

Nor was it fortunate for either William or the Church of Scotland, that Carstares, whom he had made his private chaplain, and on whose advice he so much relied in the management of Scottish affairs, held opinions so congenial to those of his royal master. Carstares was unquestionably a man of great ability, and his resolution and fidelity had borne a severe trial on a former occasion. But, though a sincere Presbyterian, he seems to have been so more from political than from religious considerations, and to have viewed a religious establishment more as an engine of state than as a Church of Christ. The great Presbyterian principle, that the Lord Jesus is the only Head and King in his Church, he does not seem to have understood or felt, at least neither his conduct nor any of his writings give any indication that it formed the ruling principle in his views of ecclesiastical polity. That he was a sincere friend to the Church of Scotland, is certain; but the defective nature of his own perception of its great principles not only prevented him from making any effort to obtain their free developement, but even led him to obstruct and thwart what it ought to have been the business of his life to promote. It was, therefore, morally impossible that Carstares should give to the king the wisest and the best advice with regard to the establishment of the Presbyterian Church, since he did not himself understand the very essence of the Presbyterian system of Church government. Some will think this a strange assertion, when employed respecting a man of such eminence as Carstares, and one to whom the Church of Scotland is in reality under deep obligations. Let them studiously compare the principles and conduct of Carstares with those of the great men who conducted the First and Second Reformations in Scotland, and they will be compelled to feel, whether they fully understand the cause or not, that in him they perceive but a cold reflected lunar light,—in them the life-giving power and fervour of direct sunshine. He was a Presbyterian greatly, if not chiefly, through the force of education and habit, and by the convictions of human prudence and political sagacity; and therefore, he strove for the re-establishment of the Presbyterian Church as most likely to confirm his sovereign's throne, and most agreeable to the inclinations of the people;—they were Presbyterians by the grace of God and the indwelling power of divine truth within their souls; and, therefore, they strove for the establishment of a Presbyterian Church, as directly founded upon the Word of God, and therefore of divine institution and authority. Yet the errors of Carstares were those chiefly of omission: to the extent to which his own defective views enabled him to reach, he had an accurate conception of the Presbyterian polity and discipline, and did his utmost to obtain its establishment, and to protect it in times of danger.

Another point demands our observation. On the 13th of April a proclamation was issued by the convention of estates, against the owning of King James, and appointing public prayers for William and Mary, as king and queen of Scotland; with certification, that those who refused should be deprived of their benefices. This proclamation was disregarded by a great number of the prelatic clergy, who neither read it as required, prayed for William and Mary, nor kept a day of thanksgiving, subsequently appointed. They were, besides, discovered to be in close correspondence with the exiled king, and with Dundee, both giving him information and doing their utmost to furnish him with supplies of men and money. This was very different from any thing which the Presbyterians had done during any period of the persecution; and to have allowed it to pass unpunished would have been giving direct encouragement to a counter-revolution. The matter was therefore taken up by the privy council, during the interval between the convention and the parliament, and after the adjournment of the latter, and prosecutions were instituted against the delinquents. From the records of council it appears that, in all, two hundred and two were publicly tried for disobeying the proclamation and maintaining direct intercourse with the armed supporters of James, twenty-three were acquitted, and one hundred and seventy-nine were deprived of their benefices.* Such was the sentence pronounced against them; but in a very great number of instances this sentence was not enforced, and these men continued to enjoy their official situations and emoluments, notwithstanding their direct and pertinacious hostility to the existing government of the country. This has been termed persecution; and loud and vehement have been the vituperative outcries of prelatic writers against the Presbyterian Church, accusing it of excessive cruelty and intolerance the moment it obtained power. But the whole procedure was the work of the convention and the council; the Presbyterian ministers were not consulted in the matter; and the process had been begun nearly three months before the passing of the act abolishing Prelacy. One inevitable consequence, however, was the increased hatred with which the Prelatists regarded the Presbyterians, rendering William's scheme for a compromise, and a union founded upon it between those rival parties, the more hopelessly impracticable.

It has been already stated, that William's general views of state policy led him to be anxious for a thorough union of all interests and parties in the empire. He well knew that this was impossible so long as men were not only divided, but keenly opposed to each other in religious matters. Having failed to induce the prelatic Church of England to abate its haughty pretensions, and having ascertained that the Scottish Presbyterians were not disposed to submit to the replacing upon their necks of that bloody yoke from which they had yet but scarcely escaped, he proposed a general toleration, intended to give immediate religious liberty to all Protestants, and to prepare the way gradually for that complete union which he so much desired. But the true principles of toleration were at that time little, if at all, understood; and instead of giving satisfaction to the contending parties, the greatest hazard was incurred, of giving offence to all, and completely frustrating his own favourite object. It is, indeed, scarcely possible to use the very word *toleration* even now without being misunderstood by some party, and offence being taken on the ground of that misunderstanding. When the mere politician uses the word, he too generally means nothing more than that he regards all religious creeds and forms with equal indifference; and that, in his opinion, it is a matter of convenience or expediency, whether a certain amount of encouragement should be shown to all alike, or to none at all. The mode of viewing the matter every man of principle must unhesitatingly condemn; and it may safely be presumed, that few of any Christian denomination would support religious toleration on the plea that religious truth could not be known, and, since it might possibly be in the possession of some party, it was best to tolerate all. Even if statesmen and mere politicians should take that ground, it is not likely that sincere Christians will. Yet almost all will admit, that error cannot be suppressed, nor truth taught, by means of civil pains and penalties, which, therefore, ought never to be employed in matters of religion; but surely it might be easily perceived, that abstaining from conferring power on those who hold certain opinions is a very different thing from inflicting pains, penalties, persecution, and death. The utmost that the Church of Scotland ever required was the former,—the mere abstaining from conferring power on men by whom it was certain to be abused; while Prelacy, not content with excluding Presbyterians from places of public trust, followed them into private life, assailed them in person and property, drove them from their houses, hunted them to the wildest dens and lurking-places, and inflicted upon them every kind and degree of suffering which the most intolerant and savage persecution could suggest and execute. The true Presbyterian cannot adopt the politician's plea, which is scepticism and indifference, for he believes that truth may be known, and that he has been taught to know it; but while he tolerates no error, he persecutes no erring man, but pities, forgives, loves, and endeavours to instruct him, that he may be relieved from the darkness and the bondage of ignorance and be rendered capable of enjoying that full and glorious liberty experienced by those alone whom truth has made free indeed.

The only direct steps taken by the

* Records of the Privy Council; Life of Carstares, pp. 41 42.

Presbyterian ministers in the course of the year 1689, were the resumption of their churches, where that was rendered practicable by the departure of the curates; the holding of several meetings with each other, preparatory to the re-establishment of their general forms of government and discipline; and the drawing up of an address to the Prince of Orange, early in the year, before the meeting of the convention. The free, generous, and noble sentiments contained in that address, contrast strongly with the spirit, equally servile and tyrannical, of the address transmitted by the Scottish prelates to James, on the very eve of his abdication.* The very comparison of those two documents alone, might have been enough to have convinced William to which of these Churches his entire and strenuous support was due, if he were indeed sincere in his assumed character of a defender of religious and civil liberty.

[1690.] When parliament met in April 1690, it was felt by the conflicting parties that their proceedings would be of vital importance in determining the completed form which the Revolution Settlement must now assume. The Earl of Melville was appointed commissioner, instead of the Duke of Hamilton, and the Earl of Crawford president,—changes which augured well of the king's favourable intentions, both of those noblemen being sound Presbyterians, particularly the latter, who was distinguished by an upright integrity of character, and an earnest sincerity of religious principle, but rarely seen in men of rank. The Jacobites were considerably weakened by the defeat and death of Dundee, and the suppression of the insurrection raised by him, and also by the detection of subsequent plots in which they had been engaged. Their attempts had satisfied William of the truth of what Carstares had told him, that the stability of his government would depend upon the Presbyterians; and had correspondingly disposed him to grant their requests. The private instructions to that effect which he gave to the commissioner were sufficiently ample, proving that he was prepared to grant larger concessions than he did, had they been seriously and urgently required, while he was desirous to retain as much direct influence in ecclesiastical affairs as might be practicable. On the 25th of April an act was passed, rescinding the act of supremacy, which had been the cause of so much suffering to the Church of Scotland. On the same day another important act was passed, restoring to their churches all that were still alive of the Presbyterian ministers who had been ejected since the 1st of January 1661, and ordering the removal of the prelatic incumbents from these usurped parishes. Some difficulty arose about the passing of an act restoring the Presbyterian form of church government partly from the attempts of those who favoured Prelacy, and partly from the king's reluctance to make any decided recognition of the divine right of Presbytery, which might preclude the possibility of some future modification of both that and the prelatic form, such as might enable them to be moulded into one. When the draught of the proposed act was sent to him for his approbation, he made several remarks on its language, altering some expressions so far as to allow at least a possible construction of the meaning according to his views, yet leaving to the commissioner "some latitude," in case he might find it necessary to adhere more closely to the original form than his majesty's alterations seemed to allow.* At length, on the 7th of June, that important act was passed, "ratifying the Confession of Faith, and settling Presbyterian church government."

In this act Prelacy is again termed a "great and insupportable grievance, and contrary to the inclination of the generality of the people, ever since the Reformation, they having been reformed from Popery by Presbyters:" the Presbyterian government is characterized as "the government of Christ's Church within this nation, agreeable to the Word of God, and most conducive to the advancement of true piety and godliness, and the establishing of peace and tranquillity within this realm." The act then "ratifies and establishes the Confession of Faith, now read in their presence, and voted and approven by them, as the public and avowed confession of this Church;" "as also, they do establish, ratify, and confirm the Presbyterian church government and discipline, ratified and established by the

* Wodrow, vol. iv. pp. 481, 482.

* Life of Carstares, pp. 44-46.

act of 1592, reviving, renewing, and confirming the foresaid act in the whole heads thereof, except that part of it relating to patronages, which is hereafter to be taken into consideration;" "and allowing and declaring that the church government be established in the hands of, and exercised by these Presbyterian ministers who were outed since the 1st of January 1661, and such ministers and elders only as they have admitted and received, or shall hereafter admit and receive." The General Assembly was allowed also "to try, and purge out, all insufficient, negligent, scandalous, and erroneous ministers, by due course of ecclesiastical proofs and censures."

On the 19th of July the subject of patronage was taken into consideration, and an act passed, "discharging, cassing, annulling, and making void the power of presenting ministers to vacant churches;" and declaring, "that in the case of the vacancy of any parish, the heritors of the said parish, being Protestants, and the elders, are to name and propose the person to the whole congregation, to be either approven or disapproven by them," their reasons to be stated if they disapproved, to be judged of by the Presbytery. And in lieu of the right of patronage, the patrons were empowered to raise from the heritors and life-renters of the several parishes the sum of 600 merks (£33. 6s. 8d.), on the payment of which the patron was bound to execute a renunciation of his right in favour of the parish. By the same act the teinds or tithes, to which no person could show an heritable title, and which had been considered always as the proper patrimony of the Church, were also made over to the patron, who, however, was bound to sell to each heritor the teinds of his own lands, at the rate of six years' purchase, subject to the deduction of the ministers' stipends. In this manner a very valuable compensation was given to patrons for relinquishing the right of patronage, as it was termed,—a right which in by far the majority of cases was a most flagrant wrong, a direct and illegal usurpation. But the friends of the Presbyterian Church were so desirous to be released from the grievous yoke of patronage, that they were content to submit to the loss of their rightful property, if, by the same means, they could obtain deliverance from that galling and pernicious bondage. The act was drawn up by a true Presbyterian, Sir James Stewart of Goodtrees, assisted by three ministers, Gabriel Cunningham, Hugh Kennedy, and Gilbert Rule. Goodtrees told the historian Wodrow, that the design of those who framed the act was to bring the matter of settling ministers as near the ancient primitive χειροτονια as the circumstances of the time would permit; that they were carefully cautious not to bring the heritors and elders into the patron's room in the matter of presentation, when the patronage was abolished; which in their judgment would have been as great slavery, if not worse, and a mere substitution of many patrons in the room of one. "And therefore they were very careful to abstract the word *present*, which might have imported something like this, and of design put in the word *propose* in its room." Goodtrees further expressed his astonishment that people still confounded these two, and supposed that the heritors and elders were in the patron's place, when they were only to *propose*, and the people to *approve*, or, if they disapprove, to give their reasons to the presbytery. The express intention of the act was to abolish patronage entirely, to put an end to presentations, and to cause the voice of the people to be heard as much as possible in the choice of ministers, and the assigning of the six hundred merks as an equivalent was intended to prevent the possibility of a subsequent parliament rescinding the act and restoring patronage.* Such were the legislative enactments for the re-establishment of the Presbyterian Church; and, that they might take full effect, a meeting of the General Assembly was appointed to be held in Edinburgh on the 16th of October.

On the appointed day, the 16th of October 1690, after a violent and illegal interruption of nearly forty years, the General Assembly again met for the discharge of its sacred duties. The first day was appointed as a day of fasting and humiliation, previous to entering upon the discharge of any official duties, when Mr. Gabriel Semple, who had assisted in

* Wodrow, MS. as given in the evidences of Dr. M'Crie, in the Patronage Report, pp. 361, 362.

renewing the Covenants at Lanark before the battle of Pentland Hills, preached,—Mr. Gabriel Cunningham acting as interim moderator till the Assembly was properly constituted, when Mr. Hugh Kennedy, one of the ministers of Edinburgh, was elected.* Lord Carmichael was the commissioner appointed by his majesty; and produced a letter from the king, strongly recommending calm and peaceable procedure. The reply of the Assembly was expressed in the most temperate language; and was followed by a declaration, "that it was not the mind of the Assembly to depose any incumbent simply for his judgment anent the government of the Church, or to urge reordination, nor to ratify any sentences against any ministers but such as were either ignorant, insufficient, scandalous, or erroneous." Proceeding in the same spirit, the Assembly received into the national Church the three Cameronian ministers, Messrs. Shields, Linning, and Boyd. But in the very act of receiving these ministers offence was given to their inflexible adherents, by the refusal of the Assembly to enter so fully into the subject of grievances and defections as that strict section of zealous Presbyterians required. The consequence was, that though the ministers were admitted, the people recoiled, continued to remain aloof, and ultimately succeeded in obtaining a sufficient number of ministers holding similar opinions to form themselves into a separate body, since known by the designation of the Reformed Presbytery.

An act of Assembly appointing a national fast, and stating the causes of it, gave rise to a long and somewhat perilous discussion. The more zealous party insisted that there should be a full enumeration of all the sinful deeds of the nation, whether committed by the rulers, the Church, or the people generally; but the same dread of uttering any thing which might tend to rekindle strife, or to widen divisions, induced the Assembly to avoid any very specific mention of several topics, and to restrict their confession as much as possible to general acknowledgments of public guilt displayed in the conduct of all ranks and classes in the kingdom. The Assembly then rescinded all the sentences passed by Resolutioners and Protesters against each other, during their time of angry contention; appointed a commission to visit the northern districts of the kingdom, and to inquire into the conduct of the ministers in those parts of the country, giving them full instructions for their course of procedure, and enjoining them to act with temperate caution towards the accused, and giving urgent directions respecting the dissemination of the Scriptures among the Highlanders in their own language, and the settling of no ministers among them who were ignorant of Gaelic. A letter was sent to the king, informing him respecting what had been done, and was intended; and Messrs. Gilbert Rule and David Blair were appointed to confer with his majesty concerning the affairs of the Church. Such is a brief outline of the proceedings of the first General Assembly after the Revolution.

So much has been written regarding the Revolution Settlement, both in terms of approbation and censure, that it seems necessary to offer a few remarks on it, less in the character of a logician or a churchman, than in that of a historian, for the purpose of directing the reader's attention to those points, the consideration of which may enable him to form his own judgment respecting its merits and demerits. The situation of the General Assembly, when it met, was one of peculiar difficulty. It was not merely surrounded by numerous and conflicting hostile forces, but it contained also within itself many jarring and discordant elements, threatening to produce instantaneous disruption. The king's desire for the admission of the prelatic party was well known, and the danger of offending him was great; Carstares was incessantly and strongly urging the necessity of compliance with his majesty's desires; the prelatists were loud in their complaints and vehement in their demands for such a measure of power as would have enabled them speedily to have resumed their persecuting and exterminating career; and the Jacobites were secretly instigating the enemies of William to employ every method for embroiling the Church in internal strife, till their schemes for a counter-revolution should be ripe. Within the Church there were three parties: the aged minis-

* Acts of Assembly, and MS. Minutes.

ters who had been ejected at the commencement of the persecution, and, having escaped its deadly perils, were now the proper representatives of the Church of the Second Reformation; the ministers who had, to a greater or lesser degree, conformed to Prelacy, accepted the indulgences, and become tainted somewhat with a tendency to laxity and indifference in doctrine, discipline, and government; and the unconquered Covenanters, who had followed Cameron, Cargill, and Renwick, spurning every weak compliance, braving every danger, and sealing cheerfully their testimony in defence of Christ's Crown and Covenant with their blood. The ministers of the first party were not more than sixty, those of the last only three, while those of the middle party amounted to more than double the number of both the others combined. It was perfectly manifest, therefore, that no measure which the more faithful and zealous party should propose could be carried, if the middle party should resolve to oppose it; and there was no reason to hope that men who had tamely submitted to the tyranny of Charles and James, and even bowed beneath the prelatic yoke, would readily assume an attitude of bold resistance to the Erastian policy of William. Accordingly, from the very hour when it met, the Assembly was laid under an almost fatal necessity of entering into a compromise, and keeping in comparative abeyance what its wisest and best members knew to be the great and essential principles of the true Presbyterian Church.

Such being the estate of affairs, it was not strange that the Revolution Settlement was defective in several very important respects. The chief of these arose out of the Erastian policy of William, and his unwise desire to include the prelatic clergy within the established Church of Scotland, in both of which views he was supported by the temporizing management of Carstares. This is manifest from the two leading maxims recommended to his majesty by that politic divine; which were, to avoid giving the slightest ground to either of the contending parties, for supposing that he entertained more regard for the one than the other; and, to be extremely cautious in giving up any one branch of the royal prerogative.* By adhering to these maxims, William discouraged and offended the Presbyterians, not only without conciliating the prelatists, but even giving occasion to them to entertain the hope that he would cast off the Presbyterians and restore Prelacy. There is no reason to think that such was ever his intention, though it has often been asserted by prelatic writers. His scheme was to retain as much of an Erastian power within the Presbyterian Church as might be possible, and for that reason he was extremely reluctant to consent to the abolition of patronage. For the same reason, the act re-establishing the Church revived the act of the year 1592, instead of the more perfect acts which were passed at the close of the Second Reformation, carefully avoiding all mention of the National Covenant and the Solemn League and Covenant. To have mentioned these and acknowledged their obligation, would unquestionably have put an end to all possibility of including the prelatists within the National Church; and it might have given, at the same time, ground of serious alarm to the Church of England, which his majesty was not in a condition to hazard. But even with these conflicting interests and designs operating to the detriment of the Revolution Settlement, it approaches very near to what it ought to have been,—much more so than many will allow. The various acts restoring Presbyterian church government never assume the tone of conferring power, but merely remove obstructions by rescinding the tyrannical and unconstitutional enactments of Charles and James, and thereby permitting the Church to put forth anew its own intrinsic powers. These acts gave nothing to the Church which she did not previously possess; they did not even pretend to restore what had been taken away; but they broke the fetters which had been forcibly imposed, and allowed the Church to resume the exercise of her own indestructible energies and inalienable rights, derived from her own Divine and only Head and King. This was at least a tacit recognition of the great truth, that the State can neither give nor take away any of the truly

* Life of Carstares, pp. 40, 42.

essential powers of a Church. These are derived from Christ alone. The State may obstruct their public and national exercise, or give them freedom and encouragement; but it can neither create them nor destroy them, though it may destroy itself in the wicked and vain attempt.

The conduct of the Church is, perhaps, more censurable than that of William. It was the duty of the Church to take care that none of her inherent principles should be overborne and fall into abeyance at such a juncture. She could not of herself repeal any act of parliament; and her appropriate attitude was that of calmly and respectfully, but firmly, stating her own principles and powers, and leaving it to the State to rescind those despotic and unchristian enactments which impeded their free exercise. Where that was not obtained, it was her duty to remonstrate and petition; and if still unsuccessful, then to enter such declarations and protests as should reserve her rights till a more propitious period might arrive, when they could be re-asserted and obtained. Instead of this, yielding to the force of external circumstances and internal dissensions, she abstained from the bold and free statement of those great principles which at the same time she continued to hold, seeking a temporary peace by a weak suppression or concealment of what she thought it inexpedient to avow, yet could not abandon. Though the acts of parliament made no mention of the Second Reformation and the National Covenants, it was the direct duty of the Church to have declared her adherence to both; and though the State had still refused to recognise them, the Church would, by this avowal, have at least escaped from being justly exposed to the charge of having submitted to a violation of her own sacred Covenants. In the same spirit of compromise, the Church showed herself but too ready to comply with the king's pernicious policy, of including as many as possible of the prelatic clergy within the National Church. This was begun by the first General Assembly, and continued for several succeeding years, though not to the full extent wished by William, till a very considerable number of those men whose hands had been deeply dyed in the guilt of the persecution were received into the bosom of that Church which they had so long striven utterly to destroy. It was absolutely impossible that such men could become true Presbyterians; and the very alacrity with which many of them subscribed the Confession of Faith, only proved the more clearly that they were void of either faith or honour. Their admission into the Presbyterian Church of Scotland was the most fatal event which ever occurred in the strange eventful history of that Church. It infused a baneful poison into her very heart, whence, ere long, flowed forth a lethal stream, corrupting and paralyzing her whole frame. It sowed the noxious seed which gradually sprang up, and expanded into the deadly upas-tree of Moderatism, shedding a mortal blight over the whole of her once fair and fruitful vineyard, till it withered into a lifeless wilderness.

It was, in short, the weak policy of all parties at that time, to temporise and watch the progress of events; to keep concealed, or at least undeveloped, their own ruling principles, without any intention of abandoning them; and thus, by a process of general and deceptive compromise, to give time to the still seething elements of the great revolutionary movement to subside and gradually crystallize into their most congenial forms. The king so far relinquished his Erastianism as to abolish Prelacy and patronage, and to pass general enactments giving the sanction of law to the liberated Presbyterian Church; but he carefully avoided all mention of the Second Reformation and the National Covenants, although the very act abolishing patronage was in itself a virtual ratification of all that tthe Church had done in that period of her greatest purity and faithfulness. The Church abstained from the direct mention of her Covenants, partly in compliance with the known wishes of his majesty, and partly in consequence of the reluctance of many of her own members to refer to those sacred bonds, the very mention of which would have been a severe condemnation of their own previous conduct; but there are such allusions to the Covenants in several of the acts of that Assembly, as to show distinctly that the best and ablest of the ministers still acknowledged their obligation, and wished to act in their spirit. The Jacobites and the Prelatic party were sufficiently lavish of their professions of loyalty to King William, and of their earnest desire of such moderate measures of church policy as might comprehend all forms and persuasions within one National Church; but they were at the same time maintaining a private intercourse with James, and cherishing the hopes of speedily obtaining such an ascendency in both Church and State as might enable them to repeal all that had been done, and resume their reign of terror.* The Cameronian Covenanters alone disdained to stoop to compromise or concealment, boldly avowed their principles, and loudly censured the Church for want of faithfulness and zeal, especially, because in the Revolution Settlement no direct recognition had been made of the National Covenants, and of the Reformation which these solemn bonds had been so instrumental in effecting; but while they deserve the praise due to courage and consistency, it may be doubted whether their own conduct did not tend to injure the very cause which they wished to promote. Had they joined the Church in a body, without any compromise, recording their protests against those omissions of which they complained, they might have contributed powerfully to counteract the pernicious influence of those men of lax principles and prelatic tendencies who were but too willing to enter; whereas by standing aloof, and indulging too much in the utterance of sharp and bitter censures of their brethren, they gave a repulsive aspect to their cause, alienated the minds of many whom a different course would have gained, and furnished somewhat of plausibility to the statements of those who loved to declaim against the intolerance of Presbyterians, and who were ready enough to refer to the language and conduct of the Cameronians as the inevitable result to which Presbyterian principles led, instead of being, as it really was, the intemperate outbreak of honest but imprudent zeal, in high-minded and fearless men, who had been roused by persecution and irritated by disappointment.

Every candid reader will perceive, that the Revolution Settlement, though not so full and perfect as it might have been made, did, nevertheless, contain and display, either directly or virtually, all the great principles of the Presbyterian Church for which she had so long contended, removing several restrictions which had been left in force by the act of 1592, in particular the clause relating to patronage; and realized to both the Church and the kingdom an amount of civil and religious liberty greatly beyond what had ever previously been enjoyed. By the ratification of the Confession of Faith, the great and sacred principle of Christ's sole Headship and Sovereignty over the Church, and its direct consequence, her spiritual independence, were affirmed; and by the abolition of patronage, the religious rights and privileges of the Christian people were secured, as far as security could be given by human legislation. Its defects were of a negative rather than of a positive character; and though some vitiating elements were allowed to remain, and some others introduced, of which it could not have been very safely predicted whether the progress of events would cause their development or their extinction, still it merits its lofty designation, the Glorious Revolution; and for it, and the precious blessings which it secured to the empire at large, our grateful thanks are due, under Providence, to the persecuted but unconquerable Presbyterian Church of Scotland.

Soon after the Assembly rose, the Commission which had been appointed to visit and purify the Church, by making inquiry into the state of religion and the conduct of ministers throughout the kingdom, began its labours. The instructions given by the Assembly were exceedingly cautious, for the purpose of preventing any thing which might even bear the semblance of severity and oppression. The Commission were not empowered to depose any minister summarily, nor to receive every kind of accusation: the only charges which they were allowed investigate were, "Doctrine inconsistent with the Confession of Faith," and "Conversation unbecoming the grace of the Gospel," and these were to be substantiated by sufficient evidence. A considerable number of worthless men were deposed from the ministry, on account of

* Burnet's Own Times, vol. ii. p. 74.

their grossly vicious and immoral conduct; few for unsoundness of doctrine; and very few for a conscientious adherence to the forms of Episcopacy. The greatest error committed by the Church of Scotland consisted in a degree of leniency, and readiness to admit "on the easiest terms" into the bosom of the Church its most deadly enemies, which almost amounted to either a suicidal infatuation, or a treacherous dereliction of principle.

[1691.] The year 1691 was chiefly employed by the Church of Scotland in repairing its broken walls, and rebuilding its ruined temple, impeded by the most violent assaults which its inveterate enemies, the Jacobites and the Prelatists, now thoroughly united, could make. Loud were the outcries of oppression raised by the disarmed tyrants, whose own deeds in their day of power had made Scotland a field of blood. Their complaints were carried to the ears of William, and repeated incessantly in the most exaggerated terms, till they made some impression on his mind, and induced him to write twice to the Commission, urging the admission of the prelatic clergy. Irritated by the failure of his scheme, based on a compromise, the king adjourned the meeting of the Assembly from November 1691 till January 1692, in the hope that this mark of his displeasure might render the Church more compliant.

[1692.] The General Assembly met on the 15th of January 1692, and received a letter from his majesty, conveying sufficiently plain indications of his dissatisfaction with the proceedings of the Commission. He censured them for not having complied with his desire, that those who were willing to conform should be admitted to the full possession of all the rights and privileges enjoyed by themselves; and, that there might be no doubt respecting the full amount of what he wished, he signified his pleasure that those of the Episcopalian persuasion who were willing to sign the Confession of Faith should not only retain their churches, but also be admitted to sit and act in church judicatories; and that the Commission of Assembly should be composed of one-half Presbyterians, and the other half of these admitted Prelatists.* This was an extent of compromise to which the Church was not prepared to submit. The General Assembly had frankly consented that the curates should not be disturbed in the possession of their churches and stipends on account of their views of church government,—a degree of toleration and forbearance totally unknown to Prelacy in any age or country; but to admit their persecutors to the enjoyment of equal power of government in the Church which they had striven to destroy, was what the king ought never to have asked, and what the Assembly could not grant. At the same time, the conduct of the Prelatists was violent and insulting in the extreme. They seemed to regard themselves as on the point of being not only restored to equal power, but of obtaining a decided ascendency; and they gave no obscure indications of the temper and spirit in which they were prepared to exercise it. But the Assembly remained firm; and when the commissioner, the Earl of Lothian, found that they could neither be intimidated nor deluded, he, in his majesty's name, declared the Assembly dissolved. The moderator asked whether it were to be dissolved without a day being named for the meeting of another. His grace replied, that his majesty would appoint another in due season, of which they should receive timely notice. The moderator then declared the intrinsic power of the Church to meet in the name of the Lord Jesus Christ, the only Head and King thereof, for the discharge of its necessary spiritual affairs; and that its dissolution now should be without prejudice to its right to meet annually, according to the laws of the kingdom. He then named the third Wednesday of August 1693 for the next meeting, and concluded in the usual form, dissolving the Assembly after prayer, and praise, and blessing.†

Great was the excitement caused by this most injudicious procedure on the part of the king; but the calmness of the ministers, waiting with deliberate intrepidity the issue of their adherence to their principles, and to the constitution of the

* MS. Minutes of the Assembly; Volume of Tracts.

† Burnet's Own Times, vol. ii. pp. 87, 88; MS. Minutes; Tracts; Willison's Fair and Impartial Testimony pp. 25, 26; Hog's Memoirs, pp. 64, 65.

country, contributed greatly to prevent the ferment from producing any convulsion. They had done their duty, and they were ready patiently to meet the result. The fearful massacre of Glencoe, which took place about the same time, tended also both to divide the attention of the public mind, and to direct its indignation so strongly against the Scottish administration, that they did not dare to provoke additional hostility by further interference with the Church. A season of half-suppressed dissatisfaction, intrigue, and jealousy prevailed, tending greatly to alienate the mind of Scotland from William, and fostering the hopes of the Jacobites, that they might ere long succeed in overturning the government, and bringing back the exiled king.

[1693.] In the spring of the year 1693, the Scottish parliament again met, in circumstances certainly very far from propitious, though somewhat less fraught with the elements of strife than had been the case during the preceding year. The chief management of affairs was intrusted to Secretary Johnston, son of the celebrated Warriston, chiefly because of the respect entertained for that family by the Presbyterians. The great difficulty to be surmounted was with regard to the General Assembly. The king had no intention of calling an Assembly, and the Church was determined to hold one on the day specified by the last moderator, in virtue of its own inherent powers. But great apprehensions were entertained that, if this was done, the king might be so highly offended as to proceed to enforce coercive measures, and probably to throw the kingdom into a convulsion. The great endeavour of Johnston was, to persuade the Church to desist from meeting on the appointed day; and to induce the ministers to submit so far, he promised to prevail upon the parliament to address the king, requesting that an Assembly might be held. By great exertions he succeeded in the accomplishment of his scheme, and by this new compromise partially saved the honour of both the king and the Church, neither directly yielding to the other, and both abandoning the antagonist attitudes which they had assumed.*

But there were other and scarcely less perilous matters to manage. The Jacobite party, and especially the prelatic clergy, had still continued to evade as far as possible the direct recognition of William as king. A new oath was framed for the purpose of putting an end to these evasions, termed the Oath of Assurance, because it declared William and Mary king and queen, both *de jure* and *de facto*—both rightfully and in reality. This oath caused nearly equal dissatisfaction to both the Prelatic clergy and the Presbyterian ministers. The former were disposed to refuse it, because it was contrary to their secret, yet determined, allegiance to James; the latter, because they regarded the imposition of any civil oaths as a qualification to sit in church courts, as an Erastian encroachment upon the freedom of a Christian Church, although they had no positive objection to the oath itself. The enactment of this oath was, neverthless, carried in the parliament, there being a tacit understanding that it would not be rigorously enforced.

Another act was passed on the 12th of June, "for settling the quiet and peace of the Church," the object of which was to promote the admission of the prelatic clergy to the full enjoyment of all the privileges of the Presbyterian Church. After ordaining that no person be admitted as a minister or preacher within this Church, till he take the oaths of allegiance and assurance,—subscribe the Confession of Faith, acknowledge Presbyterian church government, and conform to its worship and discipline,—the act, after addressing his majesty with an humble request to call a General Assembly for the ordering of the affairs of the Church, and the admission to the exercise of church government of those ministers prossessing churches who had not yet conformed, provides, "that if any of the said ministers who have not been hitherto received into the government of the Church, shall offer to qualify themselves, and to apply in manner foresaid, they shall have their majesties' full protection, aye and until they shall be admitted and received in manner foresaid." The meaning of the latter clause is, that if the Assembly should refuse to admit to a participation in church government those of the Prelatists who might apply for it, his majesty would not attempt to compel the Assembly to admit them, but

* Carstares' State Papers. p. 160.

would secure to them the possession of their churches, manses, and stipends. Even in that act there is a distinct recognition of the independence of the Church in spiritual matters. Anxious as the king was to secure the admission of the prelatic incumbents into the National Church of Scotland, he did not attempt to employ any directly compulsive measures for attaining the object on which he was so much bent. Admission to an equal share in church government was for the Church alone to give or to withhold; but the enjoyment of the fruits of the benefice was a civil matter, and that he could bestow according to his pleasure,—with the strong conviction, that those who possessed the wealth would ere long obtain possession also of the power.

The baneful effects of this act did not immediately appear in their full extent; for the heavings of the Revolution had not yet completely subsided. The Prelatists still entertained the hope that the exiled monarch might be yet restored; and therefore they were not eager in pressing for admission into the Presbyterian Church, which they could not enter without swearing allegiance to William, and obedience to Presbyterian church government, which their whole heart longed to subvert; and the Presbyterians, aware of the king's strong desire for a "comprehension" of both parties within the National Church, of which they could not approve, and of the jealousy with which he regarded themselves,—influenced also by a temperate and forgiving Christian spirit towards their enemies,—did not eagerly institute proceedings against those of the Prelatists who still refused to conform and make application to be admitted, but allowed them to retain possession of their manses, stipends, and even churches, sending merely from time to time Presbyterian ministers to preach and instruct the people in those parishes where the curates still continued to reside. But in the course of a series of years the pernicious consequences of the act became but too apparent, in the numbers of unfaithful, irreligious, and worldly-minded men, who were admitted into the Church, and who, joining naturally with the lax moderate party already within it, gave to that party the ascendency which it so long enjoyed and so grievously abused.

These acts it seemed expedient to state and explain at considerable length, because of the erroneous notions which prevail so widely regarding them. It is not strange that the leaders and adherents of that party which owed its being to the defects of the Revolution Settlement, should endeavour to represent these defects as positive merits.* And there are many so enamoured of that which professes to secure "quiet and peace," that they yield at once the homage of their weak applause to whatsoever employs these terms, however fallaciously,—unable apparently to distinguish between that peace which is but the appalling stillness of a deadly lethargy, and that peace which is the harmonious movement of warm and energetic life. But it is desirable for the true friends and members of the Church of Scotland to know, that almost all the defects which have at any time marred her beauty and impaired her usefulness, have been caused by the unwise and unhallowed influence of kings, and statesmen, and politicians of a lower order, within her pale and without, obstructing the free developement of her pure scriptural principles, and endeavouring to infuse into her system the elements of a worldly policy, more congenial to themselves, but fatally pernicious to any true Christian Church.

It has been already stated that a species of mutual compromise took place between the State and the Church, for the purpose of avoiding a destructive collision. The General Assembly, in consequence of this arrangement, was not held on the day named by the moderator; but a proclamation was issued appointing it to meet at a later period of the same year. The absence of the king on the continent, and the entire engrossment of his mind by wars and continental politics, led to another adjournment, so that no meeting of Assembly was held that year at all, and additional time was thereby allowed for the animosity of the antagonists either to ripen or subside. It soon appeared that the former had been the case, to a remarkable degree.

[1694.] A short time previous to the

* Cook's History of he Reformation, vol. iii. p. 453

meeting of the Assembly, which had been appointed to take place in March 1694, the ministers applied to the privy council to be released from the necessity of taking the oaths of allegiance and assurance, especially since these oaths had not been enforced with regard to the Prelatists. The council refused to comply with this request; and instructions were issued in the name of his Majesty, not to permit any member to take his seat till he had taken the oaths. The ministers were equally resolute not to take the oaths, and yet to hold an Assembly. They had consented to refrain from holding the previous meeting appointed by their own intrinsic authority and rights, in order to avoid an immediate collision, and to allow time to his Majesty to reconsider the line of conduct on which he was entering; but they had reached the extreme limits of prudent forbearance, and they would not submit to the sacrifice of a sacred principle and inherent right, to whatsoever perils the assertion of principles indestructible and rights inalienable might expose them. Such was the state of matters when Lord Carmichael, who had been appointed commissioner, arrived in Edinburgh. Perceiving clearly the extreme peril in which the peace and safety of both Church and nation was placed, the commissioner immediately despatched a messenger to the king, who had recently returned to London, with an account of the state of affairs, and a request for further instructions. At the same time the ministers sent a memorial to Carstares, earnestly requesting his interference with his Majesty in behalf of the Church at this critical juncture. When the express reached the King, Carstares happened not to be at hand, and before he returned to court, William, by the advice of Stair and Tarbet, who represented the conduct of the Church as obstinate and rebellious, renewed his orders in more peremptory terms, and commanded them to be returned by the same messenger. Carstares returned the same evening, received and perused the memorial which had been sent to himself, immediately inquired into the nature of the despatches which had been ordered to be sent off to Scotland; having ascertained this point, and availing himself of his known free intercourse with the king, he went to the messenger, and in his majesty's name demanded from him the papers with which he had been intrusted. It was now late, but the welfare of the Church and kingdom was wavering on the point of the passing moment, and Carstares hastened to the king The lord in waiting informed him that his majesty had retired to repose; but Carstares insisted on being admitted to his presence even at that unseasonable hour. Entering the chamber, he found the king fast asleep; but turning the curtain aside, and falling on his knees, he gently awoke him. The king, surprised to see him at so late an hour, and in such a posture, inquired what was the matter. "I come," he answered, "to beg my life." "Is it possible," said the king, "that you can have been guilty of a crime that deserves death?" He acknowledged that he had, and then produced the despatches which he had brought back from the messenger. "Have you indeed presumed," exclaimed William, frowning severely, "to countermand my orders?" Carstares begged leave to be heard only a few words, and then he would submit to any punishment which his majesty might think proper to inflict. The king gave him permission to explain his conduct, and listened attentively to his statement respecting the peculiar principles, views, and position of the Church of Scotland, and the malicious intrigues and misrepresentations of her enemies, and to the clear proof which he adduced, that the Presbyterians were the only party in that country who were truly attached to his majesty's person and government. The king remained for a moment in deep and thoughtful silence, then commanded him to throw the despatches into the fire, and drew up new instructions to the commissioner in whatsoever terms he thought best, and he would sign them. Carstares immediately wrote to his grace, signifying that it was his majesty's pleasure to dispense with putting the oaths to the ministers. This was signed by the king, and sent off by the messenger, who was commanded to use the utmost expedition in his power, that he might reach Edinburgh before any collision should take place.

The short delay caused by these transactions had retarded the messenger so much that he did not reach the Scottish capital till the morning of the day on which the Assembly was to meet. The most intense anxiety prevailed universally respecting the possible events of that day. The commissioner was bound by his instructions to dissolve the Assembly, or rather to prevent its being held, unless the oaths were previously taken; and the ministers were resolved to assert and maintain the intrinsic rights and liberties of the Church, as independent of the civil magistrate; but both looked forward to the struggle with dark anticipations of disaster to the Church, and ruin to the peace and welfare of the community. The messenger arrived,—the instructions were read,—and it was felt, that He in whose hands are the hearts of kings had interposed and given deliverance to his own free spiritual kingdom in the hour of extremest danger.* This timely concession, made by the king to the just claims and sacred inherent rights of the Church of Scotland, may be regarded as one of the most important and instructive events recorded in her history; proving that the path of duty is the path of safety,—that when adherence to sacred principle, like a divine command, says, "Go forward!" a divine power will point out and guide along the opening way,—and that the cloud which seemed surcharged with danger will descend pregnant with blessings. It was deeply felt by all parties, that the Presbyterian Church was now indeed the Established Church of Scotland.

The General Assembly met, in the full enjoyment of its spiritual independence, on the 29th of March. Grateful, but not unduly elated with the victory which God had granted to their firm adherence to their principles, they proceeded to the discharge of their important duties; and instead of exhibiting pride and severity in the hour of triumph, they passed an act respecting the instructions to be given to the Commission for receiving the ministers who had conformed to Prelacy into ministerial communion, granting very nearly all that the king had required for giving facility to the admission of these ministers.† This certainly approached more nearly to what may be termed undue concession than to persecution; and indeed heavy complaints were made by many, and severe reproaches uttered by some, against the conduct of the Assembly, as indicating great laxity of principle, and tending to unfaithfulness in the important duty of preserving the purity and efficiency of the Church,—a charge which it would not be easy to meet with a complete and satisfactory vindication.

Other acts of that Assembly deserve attention, as indicating the state both of the Church and of the country, such as an "Act appointing some ministers for the supply of the north,"—"Act for the better regulating transportations of ministers,"—"Act anent intrusion upon kirks,"—and "Act against fixing in the Lowlands of preachers who have the Irish (Gaelic) language." It will be remembered that throughout the whole history of the Church of Scotland, the northern districts had been the least thoroughly Presbyterian, and the readiest to comply with whatever Erastian and Prelatic measures were proposed by the king and the government. The Highland counties had not indeed been ever fully reformed from Popery, and therefore were the more disposed to rest in, or return to, the intermediate state of Prelacy; nearly all the Highland ministers accordingly conformed cheerfully and at once to Prelacy at the restoration of Charles II. At the Revolution a large proportion of them refused to conform again to the Presbyterian Church, and did their utmost to keep the people in the same state of hostility against the Revolution Settlement, both in Church and State. Some of them were ejected by the privy council; but by far the greater number were allowed to remain in the possession of their ecclesiastical position and temporal emoluments. It was evidently a matter of great importance for the General Assembly to provide such a remedy for this injurious state of affairs as it was competent for them to do. They did not seek to have these ministers silenced and ejected by the civil power, as the Prelatists had done to them; but they sent supplies of able and zealous ministers to those districts where either there were vacant churches, or where prelatic darkness prevailed. This they accomplished

* Life of Carstares, pp. 57-61. * Assembly of 1694, act xi.

by appointing the southern synods to send such proportions of their members as should furnish sixteen among them, who were to remain in the north three months, to be replaced by a similar number for an equal time, throughout the course of the year.* This process was continued from year to year for a considerable time, the number sent gradually diminishing as the churches became supplied with Presbyterian ministers permanently settled.

This mode of sending merely temporary supplies was rendered inevitable by the paucity of ministers in the whole kingdom. For during the time of the persecution there were few that could obtain means and opportunities of being educated for the ministry, and it was held treason for the ejected Presbyterian ministers to ordain young men even when properly qualified. It was consequently impossible at once to supply all the parishes in the kingdom with regular ministers, though there had been no obstruction. And, besides, many of the Highland congregations understood no language but Gaelic, on which account it was that preachers who could speak that tongue were not permitted to settle in the Lowlands. Great encouragement was at the same time offered to the Highland youth, by giving them bursaries, to induce them to prepare themselves for the office of the ministry among their countrymen; and by some acts of subsequent Assemblies, no minister was allowed to refuse a call from a parish in the north, however reluctant he might be to leave his present situation. Such was the attention shown by the General Assembly to the spiritual instruction of the Highlanders in their own language,—a degree of practical Christian wisdom which it required the lapse of centuries for the Episcopalian Establishment in Ireland even to begin to learn to imitate. It is indeed, a melancholy fact, that no Prelatic Church has ever attempted, as a church, to teach the body of the people, though individual clergymen have laboured zealously in the discharge of that all-important and imperative duty.

The necessity of an "Act for regulating transportations [translations] of ministers," arose out of some of the causes already specified. Not only was there a great deficiency of duly qualified ministers for the immediate supply of all the parishes upon the re-establishment of the Presbyterian Church, and an equal deficiency of preachers to meet the natural demands arising from the death of incumbents, but there was also a great difference in the characters of the existing ministers. Those who had conformed to Prelacy during its usurped domination, had both sustained a real and personal injury from the deadening effect on their own minds of their weak and sinful compliance, and had also sunk in the estimation of all men of sound principle and firm integrity. On the other hand, the faithful ministers, who had braved all dangers and sufferings in defence of religious liberty and truth, were regarded with great love and veneration by the people generally; and happy was that parish which could secure the ministrations of one of these honoured and revered servants of the Lord. When, therefore, any parish in which a curate, a conformed or an indulged minister, had been the incumbent, became vacant, the most strenuous endeavours were made by the parishioners to procure the translation of one of the faithful few from his own, perhaps smaller and less important sphere of labour, and his settlement among themselves. It often happened that two or more vacant parishes gave a call to the same minister, and then arose a contest who should obtain him. His own parish strove to prevent his removal,—the others were as eager to have him removed; a sharp contention not unfrequently occurred, terminated only by the decision of the superior church courts, being appealed from one to another, till it reached the General Assembly. Yet these were essentially contests of love. They were not caused by the opposition of the people to the settlement of an unacceptable minister, but by the eager anxiety of the people to obtain a good and beloved minister. The contests arising from the resistance of a religious people to the settlement among them of an irreligious and unfaithful minister, it was reserved as the disgraceful characteristic of patronage and moderatism to produce; while the contests which took place during the time when patronage did not exist, and moderatism

* Acts of Assembly.

was in its infancy, were the kindly and generous rivalries arising from a deep regard to gospel truth, and a warm affection to the zealous and devoted ambassadors of Christ. Even then, the Assembly, anxious to prevent the disagreement which might possibly arise, passed the act regulating transportations of ministers, and securing that, when such events took place, they should be guided by regard to what would most contribute to the general good of the Church.

To give a full explanation of the circumstances which caused the Assembly to pass an "Act anent Intrusion upon Kirks," might lead to too long a digression from the course of the narrative; but a few remarks are necessary. It has been already stated that a considerable number of the Prelatic clergy were expelled from their churches by the privy council in the summer of 1689. In a great majority of instances they returned, and resumed possession of both the clerical office and the temporal benefice. And in the northern counties, where they were supported by the Jacobite nobility and gentry, they did so even after Presbyterian ministers had been settled in the churches out of which they had been legally ejected. This was often done in the most violent and disorderly manner, the ejected Prelatists coming to the church accompanied by a band of Jacobite gentlemen and their serfs, rudely intruding themselves upon the assembled worshippers, expelling the Presbyterian minister, and taking forcible possession of both church and manse, in direct defiance of the law. Against this conduct the General Assembly complained, in the abovementioned act, and applied to the lords of the privy council for redress and protection. So undeniable and so flagrantly illegal were the facts adduced by the Assembly, that in the following session of parliament an act was passed on the subject, ordering the removal of those who had so intruded, and enjoining the council to take some effectual course for preventing the recurrence of similar illegal and forcible intrusions.*

[1695–96.] The Genera' Assembly met on the 17th of December 1695, and continued to sit till the 4th of January 1696, no other meeting taking place during the remainder of the latter year. None of its acts are of peculiar importance, being generally of the same tenor with those which have been already mentioned and explained. The chief subject which occupied the attentron of the Church was what ought always chiefly to occupy its attention—anxious care to promote, in the most efficient manner, the moral and religious welfare of the community. In this important task the Church was not less successful than zealous; and the happiest results began to appear throughout the kingdom. Some more direct countenance began to be given to the exertions of the Church by the king; the most valuable proof of which was the act of parliament respecting schools, realizing what had been long and earnesily sought by the Presbyterian Church of Scotland, and by no other Church in Christendom—a school in every parish throughout the whole kingdom, so far supported by the public funds as to render education accessible to even the poorest in the community.

[1697.] The year 1697 presents nothing demanding attention so far as the Church is concerned; for it is unnecessary to repeat statements respecting the steady and persevering care for the promotion of religion displayed by the Assembly in the passing of acts against profaneness and immorality—enjoining family worship—directing ministers in the discharge of their sacred duties—and urging the utmost diligence in supplying the deficiences still existing in the northern counties.

[1698.] Almost the only thing which requires mention in the year 1698, is the act of parliament commonly termed the Rabbling Act. The object of this act has been often misunderstood and misre-

* It is somewhat instructive to trace what may be termed the personal history of intrusion. To the union of Jacobitism (that is, despotism) with Prelacy, it owes its parentage. In its rash youth it showed its character in the attempt to force itself into Presbyterian churches, contrary both to the will of congregations and ministers, and to the law itself. Forming afterwards a clandestine connection with the Church, under cover of an unconstitutional enactment; and assuming a new name in its riper years, it obtained free scope for acting according to its nature, to the paralyzed astonishment of the Church whose powers it had contrived furtively to seize, and to the terror and indignation of the aggrieved community. In what appears to be its period of decrepitude, clinging to civil magistracy, and sophistically misinterpreting statute law, it still strives to perpetrate its old enormities, the moroseness of its aspect and the savage ferocity of its growl proving that its native malignity is unabated, however nearly it has reached the close of its baleful existence

presented; and reference has been made to it as a proof that riotous proceedings often took place at the settlement of ministers during the period when there was no patronage, to prevent which tumults was one of the reasons assigned for its restoration. What the real reasons for the re-imposition of patronage were, we shall have future occasion to show: meanwhile a very short statement will explain the cause of the passing of the Rabbling Act. It has been already shown that the pertinacious obstinacy of the northern Jacobites and Prelatists, both in refusing to take the oaths to government, and in retaining their churches, and intruding into those where Presbyterian ministers had been placed, rendered an act of parliament necessary to prevent such conduct. But their hostility remaining unchanged, they adopted another method of giving it scope without bringing themselves within the direct terms of the law. They privately instigated the lowest, rudest, and most immoral of the populace to assemble in a tumultuous manner at the churches to which Presbyterian ministers had been sent by the Assembly, or had been called by the more respectable and pious part of the congregation, and to offer every obstruction in their power; not unfrequently inflicting severe personal injury upon the ministers. These riotous mobs were often collected from other parishes, and in all cases they were persons who had no sense of religion themselves, so that their opposition was in no respect that of a conscientious resistance to the settlement among them of a minister whose doctrinal opinions they regarded as unsound, whose character failed to command their respect, or by whose ministrations they felt that they could not be edified. The persons, in short, who formed these riotous assemblages were not the real congregations of the parishes where they occurred, but a mere rabble of irreligious and immoral vagrants, collected together by the Jacobite politicians and the Prelatic clergy, for the purpose of creating disturbances, and preventing the peaceful settlement of Presbyterian ministers. Those who refer to such scenes, and to the act of parliament passed for preventing them, as proving that the want of patronage leads to confusion and popular tumult, must either be very ignorant of the history of the period, or must presume largely on the supposed ignorance of others.*

It has been stated that the rabbles alluded to were caused by irreligious and immoral vagrants. This expression may seem to require explanation. In a pamphlet written by the celebrated Fletcher of Salton, in the year 1698, entitled, "Second Discourse concerning the Affairs of Scotland," it is stated that the beggars and vagrants who infested the country, subsisting solely by charity, or by riot and pillage, amounted to at least two hundred thousand people. It was no difficult matter to collect together sufficient numbers to create a rabble, or riotous mob, ready to engage in mischief and depredation of any kind on the shortest notice, out of such a formidable host of lawless and degraded vagrants; and to them recourse was most unscrupulously had by those who wished to harass the Church of Scotland, and disturb the peace of the country. But the question forces itself upon the mind, "What led to the existence of such a dreadful amount of poverty and crime in Scotland at that period?" This, too, can be easily and satisfactorily explained. Twenty-eight years of tyranny and persecution had wasted the land, reducing many of its most fertile districts to the condition of a wilderness, and throwing a vast proportion of the middle and industrious classes into a state of deep poverty. The inevitable consequence was, that nearly all the lowest classes of the population were both thrown completely out of employment by the ruin of the class immediately above them, and habituated to idleness, vagrancy, and pillage, by the encouragement and example of the devastating soldiery, and the use made of them to assist in destroying the property of the respectable Presbyterians. Thus the existence of two hundred thousand vagrants, by whom the country was so grievously infested, was one of the direct results of the attempt to establish Prelacy in Scotland; and it was no wonder that such people were ready, at the instigation of those around whose paths of carnage they had so long prowled and battened, to rush anew to their wonted task of perpetrating

* See the act itself,—the tracts and pamphlets of the period,—and the Patronage Report.

insult and violence against the persons of Presbyterian ministers, and of interrupting the most sacred ordinances of religion.

It deserves also to be stated, as a point of principle, in answer to those who wish to represent the Revolution Settlement of the Church of Scotland as decidedly Erastian, and the Church itself as abandoning its own fundamental principles, and not having courage to assert its own intrinsic powers, that in 1698 the Commission of Assembly published a paper, termed, "A Seasonable Admonition," in which the following passage occurs:—"We do believe and own, that Jesus Christ is the only Head and King of his Church; and that he hath instituted in his Church officers and ordinances, order and government, and not left it to the will of man, magistrate, or church, to alter at their pleasure. And we believe that this government is neither Prelatical nor Congregational, but Presbyterian, which now, through the mercy of God, is established among us; and we believe we have a better foundation for this our church government than the inclination of the people or the laws of men."* The occasion of publishing this paper was to vindicate the conduct of the Church from the accusations brought against it by the Cameronians, and to prove that there was was no just reason for these people to continue in a state of separation from the Established Church.

[1699.] It is unnecessary to repeat that the Assembly of 1699 continued to pursue the laudable example set by its predecessors in the most strenuous exertions to promote vital religion throughout the community. But it may be observed that this Assembly expressed its approbation of the "Seasonable Admonition," and thereby gave to that faithful assertion of Presbyterian principles the sanction of the Assembled Church.

[1700.] The year 1700 presents little demanding peculiar attention. In an act appointing a national fast, one of the causes mentioned by the Assembly is, "Our continued unfaithfulness to God, notwithstanding of our solemn covenants and engagements." This may fairly be regarded as proving that the Church of Scotland had not abandoned the ground occupied by the fathers of the Second Reformation, but continued to acknowledge the binding and descending obligation of her National Covenants. In the parliament of the same year an act was passed for securing the Protestant religion and the Presbyterian church government and for preventing the growth of Popery. This was caused by the jealousy which was entertained respecting the probable effect of the alliances which the continental politics of William led him to form with Popish powers, together with the activity displayed by Popish and Jacobite emissaries in endeavouring to propagate their political and religious tenets, which were justly regarded as alike hostile to civil liberty and religious truth.

[1701.] The General Assembly held in the year 1701 was called to discharge a duty of a different kind from any that had for a considerable time occupied the attention of the Church. This was the condemnation of heresy, and the deposition of one of its ministers for holding and defending heretical opinions. Dr. George Garden, one of the ministers of Aberdeen, had espoused the wild enthusiastic notions of Antonio Bourignon, and written a book in defence of them. Refusing to retract his opinions, the Assembly first condemned the opinions themselves as heretical, and then deposed him from the office of the ministry. It would be inexpedient to state here what these heretical opinions were; but it may be mentioned in passing, that some of them are much akin to several of those with which religion has been disturbed in our own times.

[1702.] The year 1702 began its round in the midst of gloomy anticipations, which were too soon and too completely realized. When the Assembly met on the 6th of March, the commissioner, the Earl of Marchmont, communicated to them the melancholy intelligence of his majesty's dangerous illness, and warned them to expedite the despatch of all imperatively necessary business, and to prepare a Commission empowered to watch over and maintain discipline and order in the Church, whatever might take place. The Assembly manifested equal propriety and judgment in the appointment of this Commission. All the old and experienced ministers of the period antecedent to the persecution, who were still alive, were first nominated, and to

* Seasonable Admonition, p. 5.

them were added a sufficient number of such others as were most distinguished by experience and ability, ready to meet the possible exigencies of a crisis so dangerous. For it was well understood that the Jacobites anticipated an immediate change of measures upon the demise of William and the accession of Anne; and the Prelatists confidently expected a degree of direct favour more answerable to their wishes than the toleration or the comprehension schemes of the reigning monarch.

King William died on the 8th day of March, 1702, in the fifty-second year of his age, having reigned thirteen years and one month. By the Church of Scotland his memory will ever be much and justly revered, as having been, under Providence, the instrument by whom she was delivered from Prelatic tyranny and persecution. But it cannot be concealed, and ought not to be forgotten, that his systematic treatment of the Presbyterian Church was both unwise, ungrateful, and injurious. If he did not succeed in bringing her under an Erastian yoke, it was not for want of inclination to have done so. But by the gracious support of God she was enabled to be faithful to her Divine Head and King, and He did not forsake her in her hour of trial and danger. And though the Church did not in all points take the high ground to which her principles ought to have led her, and yielded compliance in matters where she ought to have maintained an attitude of uncompromising firmness, yet, remembering her wasted and weak condition, the many perilous and distracting circumstances surrounding her, and even the biassing influence of gratitude to her earthly deliverer, it seems but just to say, that instead of harsh upbraiding censure, the conduct of the Church deserves, upon the whole, the tribute of grateful approbation.

In the parliament which met in June, after the accession of Queen Anne, an act was passed, similar to those passed on former occasions, securing the Protestant religion and the Presbyterian church government. This was thought necessary, on account of the danger apprehended from the intrigues of the Jacobites, who entertained sanguine anticipations of favour from James's daughter which they could not expect from William. The proposals for a union between England and Scotland which had latterly engrossed much of William's thoughts, were again renewed and considerably forwarded, though in the midst of much hostility and opposition.

[1703.] The prospect of peace and security to the Church began again to darken in the year 1703. The language of the queen's letter appeared less favourable than previous communications of the same kind for several years past. Her majesty renewed her assurances of protection to the Presbyterian church government, "as that which she found acceptable to the inclinations of the people, and established by the laws of the kingdom." It was feared that this might be regarded as equivalent to a denial of its claim to any higher and more sacred authority. But the Assembly, in their answer, and especially in an address to her majesty, did not hesitate to assert their true position. In the latter document their language is peculiarly strong and explicit; reminding her majesty that the Reformation from Popery in Scotland was by presbyters,—that the Claim of Right had declared against Prelacy as a great and insupportable grievance,—and that by the acts of parliament founded thereon, "Presbyterian church government was settled, as agreeable to the Word of God, and most conducive to the advancement of true piety and godliness, and the establishment of peace and tranquillity, and therefore to be the only government of Christ's Church within this kingdom."* On a subsequent session, on the thirteenth day of the Assembly's meeting, the records of several synods were under consideration, in which the intrinsic power of the church courts to meet and deliberate in all spiritual matters on their own sole authority was very strongly stated; but while the Assembly was preparing to express full and entire concurrence in these sentiments, the commissioner, Lord Seafield, rose and proceeded to dissolve the meeting in her majesty's name. This was met by an immediate though brief remonstrance, and by protests from great numbers of the members; and though the Assembly did not continue to sit, there being no peculiarly urgent business before it, and hav-

* Acts of Assembly, year 1703, p. 16.

ing already continued thirteen days, the dissolution did not take place till the next day of the meeting was named, and the meeting concluded with the usual solemnities.*

Regarding their cause as rapidly rising towards the re-assumption of superiority, the Prelatic party attempted to procure from parliament an exemption from the necessity of taking the oaths to government; and anticipating success, they proceeded to renew their intrusion into parishes, and in several instances took forcible possession of the churches. But their precipitation and violence tended to defeat their object. The Duke of Argyle and the Earl of Marchmont procured the passing of an act for the protection of Presbyterian church government, expressed in the very terms of the Assembly's address to the queen, quoted above.† To narrate the further proceedings of this parliament, and in particular the passing of that remarkable act for protecting the interests and liberties of Scotland from suffering through foreign influence, is the appropriate task of the civil historian. It is merely alluded to here for the purpose of showing that the Scottish character was resuming its native bold and independent spirit, in proportion to the growing influence and energy of the Presbyterian Church, and enabling the nation to assume such an attitude as to convince English statesmen that it could not be trampled upon with impunity. Had it been otherwise, Scotland might very soon have become an English province, but an incorporating union would never have taken place.

[1704.] When the Assembly met in 1704, no time was lost in asserting the inherent rights and intrinsic powers of the Church. In the answer to the queen's letter the following significant passage occurs: "We are now again, with your majesty's countenance and favour, met in the name of our Lord Jesus Christ, in a national assembly."‡ The synod records, to avoid the ratification of which had been one great cause of the precipitate dissolving of the preceding Assembly, were deliberately produced, approved, and ratified, so that nothing was gained by the civil power, and nothing lost by the Church; or rather, the civil power was weakened by the failure of the attempted aggression, and the Church gained in character and moral strength. Some very important steps were taken by this Assembly, with regard to providing schools and other modes of religious instruction for the Highlands, which subsequently ripened into that noble institution of Christian benevolence, the Society for Propagating Religious Knowledge. Thus, in the midst of all her perils and all her contests, did the Church of Scotland persevere in discharging her duty to her Head and King, by promoting the growth and welfare of His spiritual kingdom.

[1705.] The year 1705 presents little of importance to demand attention. The records of the Church prove that great care continued to be taken to promote the interests of religion in every part of the kingdom, particularly the Highlands. But the public mind was deeply occupied with those two great political subjects,—the settlement of the order of succession to the throne, and the proposals for union between Scotland and England. The latter was the more important of the two, and caused the most intense anxiety in both kingdoms. It was felt by all parties, that unless a union upon satisfactory terms could be accomplished, a fierce devastating war was not unlikely to arise, in which Scotland would certainly receive aid from France, and both countries might sustain irreparable injury. Mutual apprehensions of danger served to counterbalance the mutual jealousies of the two kingdoms; and commissioners were appointed by the two parliaments to meet and arrange the preliminaries of a Treaty of Union. In passing this act, the Scottish parliament expressly restricted the commissioners from treating at all about the government, worship, and discipline of the Church.* The nomination of the Scottish commissioners was left to the queen, which prevented the intrigues of the parties who wished to prevent the Treaty of Union from being concluded.

[1706.] Several valuable acts were passed by the Assembly of 1706, respecting the internal purity and efficiency of the Church. One of these was of considerable importance, enjoining presbyteries to be more frequent and conscientious in visiting the several parishes within their

* Willison's Testimony, p. 31. † Acts of Parliament; Lockhart's Memoirs, vol. i. p. 65. ‡ Acts of Assembly.

* Carstares' State Papers, p. 750.

bounds, for the purpose not more of stimulating than of encouraging ministers in the discharge of their important duties. An act was also passed appointing a national fast, for the purpose of supplicating the Divine direction respecting the Treaty of Union, on the consideration of which the nation was about to enter "that all might be done to the glory of God and the good of the Church;" and the commission was directed to pay particular attention to the deliberations of parliament, and to be ready to assist with advice, or to warn by remonstrance, as might be necessary.

The Scottish parliament met on the 13th of October, to commence those deliberations which should end in the termination of its separate existence. The Duke of Queensberry was commissioner, and the Earl of Seafield chancellor. When parliament met, the whole nation was roused to the most intense and feverish anxiety and excitement as to what might be the possible result of their deliberations. The Jacobites beheld in a union the ruin of all their hopes; the Prelatists anticipated support from the Church of England if the union could be effected without the express confirmation of the Presbyterian establishment, but if that were ratified, they dreaded that their own restoration to power would be forever precluded; the Presbyterians generally were painfully apprehensive that the liberty, and even the permanent existence, of the Church would be greatly endangered by the union, from the ascendency of the Prelatic Church of England in a united parliament, and the presence of the prelates themselves in the House of Peers; and the Cameronians regarded the measure as the consummation of national guilt, being a direct violation of the great covenants by which both kingdoms were solemnly bound. The court party alone had any real wish for a union with England; yet such was the effect of so many and such conflicting grounds of hostility, that the antagonists merely neutralized each other, and rendered any well organized and vigorously combined opposition impossible. In this we cannot but see the hand of a superintending Providence, bringing order out of chaos, and overruling the elements of danger to the production of peace and safety.

Again retiring from the province of the civil historian, which the discussion of such subjects would lead us to invade, we shall but state that, after a long and highly animated debate, it was carried, that an entire incorporating union should take place, and not merely one of a federal character. Before proceeding to consider the articles of the union, the parliament then directed its attention to the security of the Presbyterian Church. The importance of this was fully understood by all parties, and gave rise not only to a new trial of strength, but to a series of intrigues by those who sought to prevent the union, and of earnest and anxious prudential management by those who favoured that measure and were friendly to the Church. The Jacobites now pretended great zeal for the Church of Scotland, and declaimed on the danger to which it would be exposed by a union—a danger which they themselves were the first to realize at a subsequent period. The Commission, which had been directed by the Assembly to meet and watch over the welfare of the Church, was greatly agitated by the dubious and gloomy aspect of affairs. But they were not allowed to fall into the pit dug for them by their enemies. The Divine Head of the Church continued to protect the interests of his spiritual kingdom, and to defeat the councils of the most cunning adversary. They joined no political party,—they yielded not to the deceitful persuasions of their foes,—they did not give way to distempered fears,—they uttered no violent and unwary declarations,—they even exerted themselves to calm the excitement which pervaded the nation, and which they might have easily roused to a fierce and universal convulsion.* At length an Act of Security was passed, in which the acts confirming the Confession of Faith and the Presbyterian form of church government were ratified and established, "to continue without any alteration to the people of this land in all succeeding generations;" and it was further declared, *that this* ACT OF SECURITY, "*with the* ESTABLISHMENT THEREIN CONTAINED, *shall be held and observed in all time coming, as a* FUNDAMENTAL AND ESSENTIAL CONDITION OF ANY TREATY OF UNION *to be concluded betwixt the two*

* Carstares' State Paper, pp. 754-758.

kingdoms, WITHOUT ANY ALTERATION THEREOF, OR DEROGATION THERETO, IN ANY SORT, FOR EVER."*

It would be very difficult, if not impossible, for language to convey more clearly and strongly the idea, that the Church of Scotland was thus intentionally placed beyond the power of the united parliament to interfere in the slightest degree with her constitutional rights and privileges; since the maintenance of her integrity unimpaired, intact, inviolable, was itself the very basis of the union, without which it would not have taken place, to interfere with which was declared to be beyond the power of the British parliament, and any infringement of which was necessarily equivalent to a virtual dissolution of that great international treaty.

The remaining Articles of Union were proposed and carried with comparative ease. And at length, after they had been accepted and ratified by the English parliament,† and returned to Scotland, they were registered by the Scottish parliament on the 25th of March, 1707, and on the 22d of April the parliament of Scotland adjourned to meet no more.

[1707.] The General Assembly met at Edinburgh on the 8th April 1707. Before their meeting the Articles of Union had been ratified by the Scottish parliament, and sent to London for the ratification of that of England. In the queen's letter to the Assembly the following sentence occurs: "We take this opportunity of renewing to you our assurance, that you shall have our protection in the free enjoyment of all the rights and privileges that by law you are possessed of;" and it is rather remarkable that her majesty makes no allusion to the topic of receiving into the Church those of the Episcopalian dissenters who should be willing to subscribe the Confession of Faith, and conform to Presbyterian government. The most important act passed by this Assembly was one respecting the Form of Process. This subject had occupied the attention of the Church for several years, and had, according to the Barrier Act, been transmitted to the presbyteries by the preceding Assembly. It was now ratified, and has ever since continued to form the chief rule of the Church of Scotland for the direction of the various ecclesiastical judicatories in the matters which come before them. It is not undeserving of notice, that this important act, completing the judicial arrangements of the Church of Scotland, took place at the very juncture of the Union, and was accordingly placed, of necessity, within the protection of the Act of Security, before the Scottish parliament, by which it was ratified, had ceased to exist. Thus the Confession of Faith,—the form of church government by Sessions, Presbyteries, Synods, and General Assemblies,—the mode of worship,—the rules of discipline,—and the process of judicial proceedings,—were all rendered as secure as the most solemn and conclusive national enactments,—the Revolution Settlement, the Act of Security, and the Articles of Union,—could make them. If they had since been thwarted, violated, or impeded, the blame must rest upon those who presumed to tamper with national faith, or who, in their endeavours to put a forced construction upon the letter of subordinate laws and statutes, grievously misconceived or utterly forgot the principles and the spirit of the constitution.

One very pernicious act was passed at this time, which has ever since continued to operate most injuriously to the best interests of the Church and people of Scotland. The lords of the Court of Session were appointed to be commissioners of teinds, and power was given to them to determine "the transporting of kirks," that is, the removal of a church from one part of the parish to another, according to the fluctuation of the population which may have rendered such a measure expedient,—and, by implication, the building of an additional church for the accom modation of an increased population. The consent of three-fourths of the heritors, in point of valuation, is declared by the act to be necessary to warrant this removal.* The effect has been, that the narrow and selfish policy of the heritors has generally been strong enough to prevent the concurrence of a sufficient number to procure the removal, however glar-

* Act of Security, Appendix.

† Carstares' State Papers, p. 760, "The Archbishop of Canterbury said, that he believed the Church of Scotland to be as true a Protestant Church as that of England, though he could not say it was so perfect."

* Dunlop's Parochial Law, p. 32.

ingly necessary for the accommodation of the people; crystallizing, as it were, the Church of Scotland into a state of rigid immobility, and rendering her unable to adapt her arrangements to the changing necessities of the country. How strangely ignorant, to say the least, statesmen and legislators have always been of what is most conducive to the true welfare of a nation, and especially, how ready to employ every practical mode of hampering the movements and obstructing the exercise of the native energies of the Christian Church, and, in particular, of the Church of Scotland. But this, and all such hostile or jealous measures, may be fairly viewed as the instinctive testimony given by worldly men to the spirituality of her character, with which they cannot sympathize, and which they regard with the natural enmity of the fallen mind.

By the Treaty of Union the Church of Scotland was placed in a new position, fitted to try severely the vitality and the power of her constitutional principles. The Act of Security had indeed precluded the British parliament from interfering with her doctrine, government, and discipline, as they existed before the passing of that act; but the removal of the seat of civil government from Edinburgh to London was certain to have an injurious effect upon the Scottish nobility and gentry, in alienating them from the Church of their native land, and accustoming them to the forms, ceremonies, want of discipline, and Erastian subserviency, of the Church of England. It was, therefore, to be expected, that early and persevering attempts would be made, both by the British Legislature and by our own Anglicized countrymen, if not to alter the government of the Church of Scotland, at least to reduce it to that condition of political thraldom in which the Church of England was held. That this should be desired by mere politicians, need excite no wonder; for it is not political sagacity, but spiritual enlightenment, which enables men to perceive and understand what are the true and essential principles of the Christian Church. They are naturally incapable of understanding on what terms alone a true Church can enter into an alliance with the State; and they therefore always regard the Church as a subordinate court, erected by the State, receiving directions from it, and necessarily subservient to it in the discharge of all its functions. And the fatal facility which the Prelatic form of church government has always shown of adapting itself to the capricious designs of statesmen, and submitting to their baneful control, has necessarily given it a recommendation in their eyes, which the Presbyterian form cannot possibly obtain, without first becoming unfaithful to its own principles.

The danger to which the Church of Scotland was exposed by the Union was very greatly increased by the admission of so many of the Prelatic curates, in weak compliance with the pernicious policy of William. It would have required the united energy and determined front of the entire Presbyterian Church to have promptly met, and triumphantly resisted, every attempted encroachment of the British parliament upon her secured rights and privileges. But this, with such a numerous band of cold friends and treacherous mercenaries within her own camp, was impossible. From this time forward, accordingly, the Church of Scotland presents the melancholy aspect of a declining and unfaithful Church, assailed by enemies without, and corrupted and betrayed by worse and more deadly foes within her own communion. To trace faithfully the sad steps of her defection must be now our painful and unwelcome task; with the perfect certainty of being compelled to record deeds and give expression to sentiments which will rouse the fierce rage of many, but with the deliberate determination to state the truth, be offended who may, and whatever amount of hostility may be thereby provoked. Let the intelligent and thoughtful man mark well the course of the Church of Scotland's procedure, as well as that of the British parliament, from the period of the Union till now, with as much fairness and candour as he can; and especially let him trace accurately, and with unprejudiced mind, the conduct of the faithful minority, testing it as rigidly as he will by reference to the fundamental principles and avowed standards of the Presbyterian Church; and he will have little difficulty in deciding who have been the defenders, and who the betrayers and the foes of civil and religious liberty, —by whom the cause of vital religion and national welfare has been promoted, and by whom retarded,—by whose ill-requited exertions the interests of the Redeemer's spiritual kingdom within our land have been maintained, and by whom they have been betrayed and violated, through the influence of secular motives, and in the spirit of a base subserviency to narrow-minded and worldly politicians.

CHAPTER IX.

FROM THE UNION TO THE RISE OF THE SECOND SECESSION IN 1752.

Position of the Church of Scotland at the Union—Memorials respecting the Poor, and beneficial Management of the Church—Political Movements in England, and Jacobite Intrigues in Scotland—Rise of erroneous Opinions in the Church of Scotland—Jacobite Intrigues; Case of Greenshields—Hostility of the British Parliament under the Administration of Harley and Bolingbroke—Act of Toleration—Oath of Abjuration—Act reimposing Patronage—Ineffectual Attempt of the Church to prevent its Enactment—Examination of the Spirit, Tendency, and Intention of that Act—Argument to prove it essentially invalid—Assertions in its Preamble refuted—Conduct of the General Assembly—Remarks—Causes of the Weakness of the Church—The Cameronians—Effects of the Abjuration Oath—Case of Burntisland—Commencement of the Process against Professor Simson for Heresy—Second Rabbling Act—Death of Queen Anne—Memorial against Patronage—The Rebellion—Professor Simson—The Auchterarder Case—First "Riding Committee"—Progress of unsound Opinions, how caused—Act restricting Patronage—Origin of the Marrow Controversy—Conduct of the Assembly—The Representers—First Case of Intrusion—Professor Simson—Boston and others—First direct Acceptance of a Presentation—Origin of the First Secession—Partial Change in the Conduct of the Assembly—Act against Intrusion—The Secession completed—Revivals at Cambuslang and Kilsyth—Violent Settlements—Opinions of the Court of Session—New Policy of the Moderate Party—Case of Inverkeithing—Deposition of Mr Gillespie—Origin of the Second Secession, the Relief, in 1752—Moderate Manifesto.

By the Act of Security, which was the basis of the Union, the Church of Scotland obtained the clearest recognition of her own principles, and the strongest ratification of her rights and privileges, which could be conveyed by legislative enactments and secured by the solemn pledge of national faith. Yet were those principles as much disliked by statesmen as they had ever been; and at the very time when the ratification was given, a powerful party was secretly plotting the violation of those rights and privileges for the security of which the faith of the sovereign and the united kingdom was pledged. The Jacobites, who wished the restoration of the exiled Stuart race, knew well that the establishment of the Presbyterian Church was the main obstacle to their resumption of power in Scotland; and the not unnatural sympathy which the English Episcopalians felt for their Scottish brethren of that persuasion, induced them to take every measure in their power for the discouragement and depression of the rival Church. Of this character was the jealous and intolerant policy of the English High-Church party, requiring the sacramental test, according to the forms of Episcopacy, before any man could be eligible to a place of public trust in civil affairs, while no such limitation was applied to them in Scotland. This was manifestly contrary to the spirit of the Union, and a grievance to every true Presbyterian. But it had still more pernicious tendencies. It was calculated to cause disregard to that sacred ordinance, by degrading it to the character of a civil qualification; and it tended to allure the Scottish nobility and gentry to conform to Prelacy, to which they were already sufficiently prone. This effect was, in all probability, what Prelatists expected and desired; but it was evident that it could not be otherwise than offensive to Presbyterians, especially when contrasted with the repeated and pressing applications made to the Church of Scotland to receive into its bosom the Prelatic curates, and to give them an equal share in the government of the Church which they had so long persecuted, and were still seeking to subvert. In the circumstances and arrangements of the Union itself, and notwithstanding the Act of Security, there was reason for the Church of Scotland to be jealous of her rights and privileges, so far as it was in the power of the Church of England to impair and obstruct them. The bitter hostility of the Scottish Jacobites and Prelatists was even increased by the Union, which opposed a mighty obstacle to their hopes, and which, they well knew, could not have been accomplished if the Church of Scotland had offered a strong and determined resistance.

Placed thus in a position surrounded with danger, the Presbyterian Church had a very difficult part to act. To act that part aright demanded the union of high-principled religious integrity, and consummate prudence. From the ruling powers of the empire she had little favour to expect, beyond what they might deem it for their own interest to give. If she could succeed in retaining and wielding the compact energies of the Scottish community, politicians would not dare to tamper with her rights and privileges; but if in that she failed, to be scorned and trampled upon by insulting adversaries was her certain doom. And unfortunately her prospect of obtaining that element of security was greatly diminished by recent events. The great mass of the Scottish people were hostile to the Union, for various causes; and the conduct of the Church in not opposing that great Treaty had alienated to a very considerable degree the minds of a large proportion of the most conscientious Presbyterians. Nothing but the most determined adherence to strict Presbyterian principles, and their exhibition in all her proceedings, could have regained the affection and the confidence of the people; and such a line of conduct it was now scarcely possible for her to follow. The baneful policy of William, which had caused the reception of so many of the Prelatic curates, had vitiated the ministerial body to such a degree, that instead of a faithful assertion and bold defence of Presbyterian principles, in government, doctrine, and discipline, the utmost that could be obtained from the General Assembly was a faint remonstrance, or a half apologetic statement of rights and privileges, or a feeble and tame petition for redress, even when much aggrieved. This increasing unsoundness of doctrine, tame and compromising spirit, and *moderate* policy, however much lauded by wily politicians, was not calculated to reinstate the Church in the affections of a people distinguished for national pride, intellectual strength, and inflexible adherence to religious principle. On the contrary, it was sure to alienate them more and more, and at the same time to encourage the foes of Presbytery to fresh aggressions. Such was the character and condition of the Church of Scotland, and such the nature of the hostile influences by which it was surrounded, and to a considerable extent interpenetrated, at the momentous period of the Union. To what extent these hostile influences prevailed, whether by external force or by internal corruption, and to what degree Presbyterian principles were repressed or allowed to fall into abeyance, remains now to be briefly but faithfully traced.

[1708.] The period immediately succeeding the Union had been employed by the Jacobites in making the most strenuous exertions to produce a counter-revolution, by means of an attempted insurrection at home, supported by an invasion from France. In this time of public danger the loyalty and zeal of the Scottish Presbyterians had been signally displayed, both ministers and people exerting themselves to the utmost in preparing to defend the constitution and government of the country. When the Assembly met in April 1708, her majesty, both by letter and through the commissioner, expressed her entire satisfaction with the conduct of the Scottish Church, and her renewed assurance of her unalterable resolution to maintain to it unimpaired all its rights and privileges. The answer of the Assembly expressed the most unswerving loyalty, and at the same time not obscurely indicated to her majesty in what manner that loyalty could be best recompensed, and the peace and welfare of the country maintained. They plainly declared, that a "pious, learned, and faithful ministry" was the greatest support, under God, of true religion and national welfare; trusting that her majesty would discourage the opposition made to the planting of such a ministry in several places, "by some that are not more disaffected to our church constitution than to your majesty's royal person and government."* Had her majesty and her government appreciated and acted upon the spirit of this suggestion, the Church and the nation must soon have entered upon a career of public tranquillity and religious purity very different from that which the historian has to record.

Two acts of this Assembly deserve attention. One was for the suppression of schism and disorders in the Church: the other, recommending ministerial visitation of families.† The first arose from the cause already specified,—the disagreement which could not but exist between the true Presbyterian ministers and the

* Acts of Assembly, year 1708. † Ibid.

admitted Prelatic curates, and also between the Established Church and the inflexible Cameronians. The second was expressly designed to promote the progress of vital and personal religion throughout the community, by giving to ministers well digested and authorative directions respecting the discharge of that very important part of their duty, so that it might not be in the power of any to neglect it, without being immediately called to account, and censured according to their demerits. Such a process was more certain to secure the stability of the Church, by resting it on the affecion and respect of the poeple, than could be done by mere acts of the legislature. But unhappily it was an act which the Prelatic conformists could not possibly discharge in a suitable manner. Too many of them had been known to their parishioners as spies and informers during the persecution, for their visits to be received with a ready and affectionate welcome; so that, when the Assembly enjoined the discharge of a duty which the previous misconduct of a large section rendered it impracticable for them to attempt, this injunction, however excellent in itself, and fitted to produce the best results when adequately performed, tended to increase the disagreement between the faithful ministers and their less zealous brethren, who disliked directions which they could not cordially and successfully obey.

[1709.] Several important transactions took place in the Assembly which met in 1709; one of which was the maturing of the Society for Propagating Christian Knowledge, which obtained the approbation of the queen in council, and has ever since continued in the discharge of its important duties, on which a large measure of the Divine favour has manifestly rested. An act was passed also for erecting public libraries, one in each presbytery throughout the kingdom; a measure well adapted to promote the knowledge and the usefulness of the ministers, by placing within their reach the means of prosecuting their own studies, which their remote situations and scanty maintenance must have greatly impeded.

Among the unprinted acts of this Assembly is one of great national importance. It is entitled, ' A memorial to be presented by the queen's commissioner to her majesty, concerning the interfering of justices of the peace with the offices of church deacons." The full purport of this memorial, and the object accomplished by it, require to be explained, and merit attention. At the period of the Reformation, it will be remembered, the Church of Scotland proposed to take upon itself the care of the poor, and to support them out of its own patrimony. The avaricious nobility frustrated this benevolent design to the utmost of their power, by seizing forcibly upon the patrimony of the Church, regardless alike of justice and humanity. But the Church, nevertheless, following the example of the Apostolic Church, appointed collections to be made for the support of the poor, and instituted the order of deacons for the proper management of the funds so raised. This method of supporting the poor was almost immediately crowned with the most remarkable success. Poverty and its dire attendants, degradation and immorality, almost disappeared, and peace, intelligence, comfort, and purity, spread their blessings over the land. But when Charles II., in 1661, abolished the Presbyterian Church, and established Prelacy on its ruins,—as attention to the religious and intellectual instruction of the poor, and the alleviation of their personal wants, formed no part of the institutions, nor had ever been regarded in the practice of the Prelatic Church,—the whole matter was intrusted to the charge of the justices of the peace, who were empowed to appoint overseers in every parish for the management of matters connected with the maintenance of the poor. The utter inefficiency of this system, attempted as it was in a time of persecution which destroyed a large proportion of the middle class, which has always been the most charitable, was demonstrated with dreadful precision, when at the Revolution it appeared that about the fifth part of the population were in a state of utter beggary and homelessness, and so fearfully degraded and demoralized as to startle and appal the most indifferent. But the Presbyterian Church was again established, and immediately resumed its hallowed labours and its charitable cares. Again was its unrivalled excellence, as a national institu tion for promoting the moral and religious welfare of the community, most signally displayed. The faithful and earnest preaching of the gospel arrested the attention of the people; schools were provided for the instruction of the young: the charitable donations of the congregations relieved the truly necessitous, and the sacred and moral atmosphere of Christianity diffused itself over the kingdom, checking and repressing vice, rebuking open crime, and imparting a more pure, healthful, and lofty tone to the feelings and desires of the renovated community. So manifestly was this the case, that the commissioner, the Earl of Glasgow, readily undertook to present the memorial, and enforced it with such statements respecting the efficiency of the Scottish system, on his own knowledge, that the justices of the peace were instructed to abstain from interfering with the management of the poor, leaving that matter to the care of the kirk-sessions, by whose judicious superintendence the country had been rescued from poverty and crime. Had it not been for this prompt and decisive conduct on the part of the Church, Scotland would have been speedily subjected to the pressure of an intolerable burden of poor-laws, similar to that under which England, notwithstanding its superior national wealth, and in spite of, not to say in consequence of, its hierarchical church, has so long groaned.

This incident would of itself convince any unprejudiced and intelligent person how much Scotland owes to its National Church, proving, at the same time, how much superior that Church is to any other in Christendom, in the efficient accomplishment of one great object for which a National Church is established —the promotion of the moral and religious welfare of the community. And yet, at the very time when the Church was thus generously taking upon herself the care of the poor, she had been recently deprived of the remains of her patrimony, the third part of the teinds, which had been given back to the patrons as a compensation for the loss of those patronages which they had obtained by conduct of the most flagrantly illegal, unjust, and wrongful character. Surely, to do good and to suffer injury,—to promote peace and to sustain persecution,—to advance the welfare of all, and to be generally calumniated,—has been more the fate of the Church of Scotland than of any Christian Church since the days of the apostles. But this is no equivocal proof that she is indeed a true Church of Christ, reviled and persecuted by the world, because she is not of the world. The success with which the exertions of the Church of Scotland had been blessed in repressing vice and irreligion, and promoting pure and personal Christianity, may be stated in the language of an acute and impartial observer, a native of England, who came to Scotland to aid in promoting the Union:—"You may pass through twenty towns in Scotland without seeing any broil, or hearing an oath sworn in the streets: whereas, if a blind man was to come from thence into England, he shall know the first town he sets his foot in within the English border, by hearing the name of God blasphemed and profanely used, even by the very little children in the streets."*

[1710.] Before the General Assembly met in 1710, a movement had taken place in England which fell little short of a revolution. This was occasioned by the notorious Sacheveral, who, by the plentiful use of a strange mixture of blind bigotry, fierce invective, and the hardy assertions of intolerant ignorance, roused the prejudices of the High-Church party and the rude populace to such a degree as to overthrow the Whig government of the Revolution and the Union, and to place a Tory administration in office, nominally headed by Harley, soon afterwards Earl of Oxford, and really by the philosophic, yet unprincipled infidel Bolingbroke. Strange as it might at first sight appear, this triumph of High-Church Episcopacy and Tory state politics tended directly to the restoration of Popery, and of the exiled claimant of the crown, the Popish Pretender. Yet every thinking person will easily perceive the natural connection which subsists between the principles of High-Church bigotry, strenuously inculcating passive obedience and non-resistance to "the right divine of kings to govern wrong," and those on which Popery itself is founded. Nor were the Scottish Jacobites inattentive

* De Foe's Memoirs, p. 428.

spectators of these changes in England, or unskilful to avail themselves of events which promised to advance the objects for which they longed. They saw well that the ascendency of High-Church politics in England presented a favourable opportunity of crushing the Presbyterian Church of Scotland, which was the most formidable obstacle they had to encounter in seeking to secure the return of the Popish Pretender. Instantly a course of deep intriguing policy was begun, conducted principally by Lockhart of Carnwath, the ablest of the Scottish Jacobites. This designing man did not expect to prevail upon the Presbyterians to strive for the recall of the Pretender; the wrongs which they had suffered were too recent for them to be induced to take such a step. But he thought that, by prevailing upon the High-Church party in the British parliament to infringe the Union, so far as to endanger the stability of the Church of Scotland, the Presbyterians might be brought to demand a repeal of the Union itself; which, if granted, would leave Scotland open to Jacobite intrigues, and, if refused, might lead to some forcible attempt to overthrow Presbytery and re-establish Prelacy, or at least throw the country into such a state of confusion as would give a greater probability of success to a French invasion and a civil war. To the artful prosecution of these deep schemes we shall have further occasion to advert.

When the Assembly met, these measures necessarily engaged their attention, though they did not deem it expedient to mention them in explicit terms. Yet there could be no doubt what was meant by such language as the following:— "We crave leave upon this occasion to assure your majesty, that we abhor all the principles that stain the glory of the reformed religion, and all the opinions that have a tendency to shake the excellent and solid foundations upon which your majesty's just title to the supreme government of your dominions, and the security of your throne in a Protestant succession against all Popish Pretenders, are happily established." It is not likely that her majesty received this address with much satisfaction, the allusion it contained to the Claim of Right and the Revolution Settlement being much less flattering to a monarch, than the glowing reference to hereditary and indefeasible right poured forth by the High-Church sycophants. A slight jar arose between the Church and the departing administration, on account of the Assembly having appointed a fast, to which the sanction of her majesty had to be procured. This was promptly granted; but the Earl of Sunderland, in a letter to Carstares, warned him against the danger which the Church might incur, if she were to repeat such a procedure on her own authority.* This was sufficiently indicative, both that the administration watched the conduct of the Church of Scotland with a jealous and unfriendly eye, and that English statesmen were alike ignorant of the character and hostile to the proceedings of the Presbyterian Church.

An act was passed by this Assembly, apparently of a very harmless, or rather of a laudable character, yet pregnant with meaning of ominous import. This was an "Act for Preserving the Purity of Doctrine," in which all persons are prohibited from uttering any opinions, or using any expressions, in relation to the articles of faith, "not agreeable to the form of sound words expressed in the Word of God and the Confession of Faith;" and further enacting, "that no minister or member of this Church presume to print, or disperse in writing, any catechism, without the allowance of the presbytery of the bounds, and of the Commission." The direct cause of framing this act was the offence taken by Principal Stirling of Glasgow, and Principal Haddow of St. Andrews, with the language of a catechism on the covenants of works and grace, written by Mr. Hamilton, minister of Airth, which these two influential men contrived to get the Assembly thus to stigmatize, without due examination, and on the strength of their representation respecting the tenor of the production. But the more remote cause, which was indeed the real moving principle of that and many subsequent events in the history of that period, is to be found in a strong leaven of unsound doctrines which was spreading rapidly in the Church, especially in that large divi-

* Carstares' State Papers, p. 786.

sion of it which was formed by the conjunction of the indulged ministers, the admitted Prelatic curates, and a considerble number of young men, who had imbibed the lax notions of a modified Arminianism, at that time becoming very prevalent both in England and on the Continent. The most sound and able divines of the Church of Scotland marked the progress of these opinions with deep regret, and set themselves to oppose them by every means in their power. It was with this view that Mr. Hamilton had written the above mentioned catechism; and it was to prevent the diffusion of it and similar productions that the leading men of the Assembly procured the passing of the act for preserving the purity of doctrine.* It may seem strange that an act so designated should in reality have been an act to prevent the defence of truth, and to permit the unchecked diffusion of error. Yet so it was; and nothing could more clearly prove the pernicious tendency of that *moderate* management so highly recommended by William, so perseveringly followed by Carstares, and so destructively successful in introducing into the Church of Scotland such a body of men, not more than half Presbyterian in their principles, doctrines, and practice, by whom she was early and deeply vitiated, ere long grievously enthralled, and from the baneful influence of whose long and dreary domination she is yet but striving painfully to recover.

[1711.] The machinations of the Jacobites for the destruction of the Church of Scotland were not only prosecuted with unremitting ardour, but began about this time to assume the aspect of near success. One event which hastened the struggle rather prematurely for the enemies of Presbstery, arose out of the attempt of one Greenshields, an Episcopalian minister, to open a meeting-house and use the English Liturgy in Edinburgh. The Prelatic party of the persecution had never used a Liturgy, with the sole exception of Burnet, afterwards bishop of Salisbury, while he was curate of Salton; being deterred probably by the remembrance of the tumult which the attempt to introduce the Liturgy in the year 1637 had caused. But now, when the Scottish Prelatists began to hope for support from their brethren in England, they thought it expedient to conform to the whole ritual of that Church. When Greenshields first made the attempt, towards the end of the year 1709, he was called before the Presbytery of Edinburgh, but declining their jurisdiction, he was interdicted by the magistrates of the city, and his meeting-house closed by their authority. The affair was brought before the Court of Session, and decided against Greenshields, his conduct being regarded as a direct infraction of the articles of the Treaty of Union. But the Jacobites and Prelatists, buoyed up by the High-Church frenzy in England, carried the matter by appeal to the House of Lords, auguring but too surely that the Church of Scotland would meet no favour and but little justice there. When the case first came to London, the whole country was in a ferment about Sacheverel's trial, so that the affair of Greenshields was laid aside till a more convenient opportunity. But after the formation of a new cabinet, and the complete ascendency of High-Church and Tory principles in the legislature, it was again brought forward, and given in favour of Greenshields, the sentence of the Court of Session being reversed, and the magistrates of Edinburgh subjected to heavy damages for wrongful imprisonment. Great was the exultation of the Prelatists and Jacobites when the decision was made; and great also was the indignation of the Presbyterians. There was a mixture of right and wrong in the decision, viewed abstractly, with regard to its essence, and to the state of the law at the time. It was right that no man should be liable to imprisonment for worshipping God according to the light of his own conscience; but according to the unrepealed laws of the country, Greenshields was guilty of a high misdemeanour, especially when it is remembered that he and all his party had refused to swear allegiance to the reigning sovereign, and were known to be engaged in plotting for the restoration of the Popish Pretender. In that view he merited punishment as guilty of rebellious conduct,—not on account of his religious

For a full account of this matter, and of the controversy respecting the Marrow of Modern Divinity, see a series of papers by Dr M'Crie, in the Christian Instructor, in the years 1831, 1832.

opinions; and his acquittal, and the fine exacted from the magistrates of Edinburgh, was a direct violation of the principles of the Revolution, and tended to shake the throne of Queen Anne, and to produce a counter-revolution. It is indeed evident that this was the very effect which the Jacobites and Bolingbroke intended and anticipated, when they pressed this decision contrary to the inclinations of the Earl of Oxford.* But, as usual, they contrived to misrepresent the whole affair, and to declaim about it as a mere act of protection to an injured Episcopalian against Presbyterian intolerance.

When the Assembly met, there was a general feeling pervading the house that a dangerous crisis was at hand. The pernicious effects of English prelatic influence were beginning to be but too apparent, not only in such a case as that of Greenshields, but in a growing tendency in various quarters to imitate the English disregard of the sanctity of the Sabbath, which had always been peculiarly maintained by the Church of Scotland. They were well aware also, that the main object of the Jacobites was to alter the succession to the throne; and they knew that Scottish Prelacy would very readily endure a Popish monarch, though the Church of England might not be equally willing to violate all Protestant principles. The attachment of the Church of Scotland was therefore very distinctly stated to the succession of the Protestant House of Hanover, both in the Assembly's letter to the Queen, and in an act passed recommending prayers to be offered up for her majesty, and for the Protestant line of succession. Several acts were also passed for the better regulation of internal matters in the worship government, and discipline of the Church — recommending family worship,—for the better observance of the Sabbath,—concerning the administration of the sacraments of baptism and the Lord's supper,—respecting students of divinity,—and appointing the questions to be put to probationers before being licenced to preach, and to ministers at their ordination. It is remarkable, that almost immediately before the occurrence of any peculiarly important or dangerous juncture in the history of the Church, there has been some arrangement made in her internal regulations, calculated to prepare her for the struggle, and to confirm her vitality when about to be severely tried. These questions to be put to probationers and ministers were calculated to deter the ungodly and worldly-minded from entering the Church, at the very time when the door of admission to such persons was about to be thrown open; and though unprincipled men can, and do break through every sacred and moral barrier, yet it cannot be doubted that the existence of such barriers has a strong tendency to preserve the sanctity of the ground which they inclose from the tread of the unhallowed intruder.

Aware of the coming dangers to be apprehended from the unprincipled statesmen who swayed the councils of the nation, the General Assembly gave specific directions to the Commission to do what might be necessary for the preservation of the rights and privileges of the Church, and empowered them to send a commission to London, if they should see cause, to watch over the progress of events, and to seek the redress of grievances.

[1712. The year 1712 must ever be regarded as a black year in the annals of the Church of Scotland. The triumph which the prelatic Jacobites had gained in the case of Greenshields, instead of satisfying, had merely encouraged them to further aggressions upon the Presbyterian Church, against which they cherished the most deadly hatred. When the British parliament met, in December 1711, their first attention was occupied in securing the ascendency of despotic principles in both houses. This was accomplished in the House of Lords by the creation of twelve new peers at once, whose votes enabled the cabinet to command a majority for the time. Early in 1712, the Jacobites, deeming their preparations complete, unmasked those batteries with which they hoped to lay prostrate the Church of Scotland. A bill was introduced into the House of Commons, purporting to be for the granting of a legal toleration to those of the Episcopalian dissenters in Scotland who wished to use the Liturgy of the Church of England; repealing, at the same time,

* Lockhart Papers, vol. i. pp. 346 347; Stuart Papers, 1711.

those acts of the Scottish parliament by which they were subjected to the jurisdiction and discipline of the Presbyterian church courts, and forbidding the civil sanction to be added to ecclesiastical sentences for their enforcement. This bill was introduced on the 21st of January; and so secretly had the Jacobites concerted their scheme, that the intention of proposing such a bill was not known till the motion was made in the House of Commons respecting it. The Commission of the General Assembly immediately sent the Rev. Messrs. Carstares, Blackwell, and Baillie, to London, with instructions to use every exertion in their power for preventing the passing of such a bill, and to watch over the threatened rights and privileges of the Church. Their earnest remonstrances were in vain. The House of Commons passed the bill, and transmitted it to the House of Lords. The Scottish Commission renewed their remonstrances, and prevailed so far as to procure the addition of the oath of abjuration to the Bill of Toleration, for the purpose of preventing Papists and Jacobites from obtaining any advantage from this bill. But the wily Jacobites contrived to have a clause inserted in the bill, requiring the ministers of the Established Presbyterian Church to come under the same obligation. There was one clause in the abjuration oath which rendered it impossible for a Presbyterian to take it without explanation. In the act of succession, settling the crown on the Hanoverian Protestant line, one of the conditions specified was, that the successor should be of the communion of the Church of England; and in he oath of abjuration, the person was required to swear allegiance to the successor *as* limited by that act. This the Presbyterians regarded as requiring them to swear that the sovereign ought to be an Episcopalian, thereby declaring a Presbyterian incapable of wearing the crown. To this they could not submit without stamping reprobation upon their own religion. But they procured from the House of Lords an alteration in that clause, changing the word *as* to *which*, thereby making the clause merely a narrative of the general limitation to a Protestant line, without any direct reference to specia conditions. The Scottish Jacobites were acute enough to perceive the import of this alteration, and had sufficient influence to procure in the House of Commons the restoration of the word *as*, well knowing the offence which it would give to the Presbyterians. They knew that the Prelatic Jacobites would not take the abjuration oath, because they regarded the Popish Pretender, whom that oath abjured, as the rightful heir to the British crown, and their great aim was to render it equally impossible for Presbyterians to take it; that both parties being placed in equal peril, so much of a mutual compromise might ensue as to leave the Prelatists undisturbed in the prosecution of their rebellious designs for the subversion of the Revolution Settlement and the restoration of a Popish king.* Too well their crafty policy succeeded. No more than one of the Prelatic clergy ever took the oath of abjuration, while every one availed himself of the toleration, and immediately began to celebrate public worship with all the pomp and ceremony in which the Church of England delights, to a degree not previously seen in Scotland since the Reformation. At the same time, so great was the dissatisfaction felt by the ministers and people of the Presbyterian Church on account of this oath, that it nearly caused a schism in the Church, the refusal to take it being regarded by many as a criterion of ministerial faithfulness, and almost a term of communion; while the people equally hated and despised those ministers who consented to take the ensnaring and dangerous bond.†

Some have endeavoured to represent this Act of Toleration as a wise and laudable scheme for securing religious liberty to all denominations of Protestant Christians. How much soever it may have ultimately contributed to that result such was not the intention, in even the slightest degree, of those by whom it was framed. They wished for toleration, that they might obtain ascendency. They were anxious to open Episcopalian chapels, only that they might soon have it in their power to shut Presbyterian churches. And they were eager to over-

* Lockhart Papers, vol. i. pp. 379-384; Burnet's Own Times, vol. ii. p. 549.

† Boston's Memoirs, p. 221, *et seq.*; Hog of Carnock's Memoirs; Wodrow, Analecta and Letters.

throw the Presbyterian Church, because they knew that the principles of religious and civil liberty had there obtained a safe retreat, till they issued forth triumphantly in the Revolution, which the Jacobites wished to d[illegible] driving from the throne the Popish tyrant, whose lawless despotism they were conspiring to restore.

The next measure brought forward by the Scottish Jacobites was of a still more pernicious character, and involved a still more direct violation of the national faith, so solemnly pledged in the Act of Security and the Treaty of Union. On the 13th of March Mr. Murray, second son of Lord Stormont, one of the Scottish members, rose and obtained leave to bring in a bill for restoring church patronage in Scotland. By this time the Scottish commissioners from the Church had returned to their own country, not anticipating any further infringement of their legal rights and privileges at that period. Availing themselves of the absence of her defenders, the enemies of the Church passed the bill with unusual rapidity through all its successive stages. On the 7th of April it passed the House of Commons, one hundred and seventy-three members voting for it, and seventy-six against it. The very next day it was carried up to the House of Lords for their consideration. By this time tidings had reached Scotland of the deadly blow aimed against the Church; and Carstares, Blackwell, and Baillie, were again sent to London, with instructions to offer the most strenuous opposition to the fatal measure. Before they arrived the bill had reached the House of Lords; and although their Lordships consented to hear them by counsel on the subject, yet this was little more than empty courtesy, for the fate of the bill had been pre-determined. So manifestly was this the case, that their lordships did not even allow time for decent deliberation on a subject of such vast international and religious importance. They heard the council for the Scottish commissioners, read the bill a second time, committed it, reported it, and read it a third time, all in one day, the fatal 12th of April. On the 14th, it was returned to the House of Commons with some slight amendments, which were agreed to without opposition; and on the 22d of April that unconstitutional and most disastrous bill received the royal assent. Whether the hand of the misguided sovereign shook when affixing the sign manual has not been recorded; but certainly at that moment she put her hand to a deed by which her right to reign was virtually rescinded, the Revolution Settlement overturned, and the Treaty of Union repealed; unless, indeed, the bill itself were to be regarded as an absolute nullity,—an idle arrangement of mere words, "full of sound and fury, signifying nothing." For it will not be disputed by any person possessing competent knowledge, that the British sovereign reigns over the united empire, solely in virtue of the Act of Security, which is the basis of Union. Any infringement of that great, and, as it may almost be termed, creative act, must therefore be either, with regard to the British parliament, a suicidal deed, and with regard to the sovereign a virtual abdication; or must be altogether and for ever null and void, incapable of acquiring any possible degree of validity, or of imposing upon any British subject the slightest shadow of obligation. It may be safely affirmed, that no jurist will ever prove that the British parliament ever did or can, pass an act greater than, and subversive of, that to which it owes its own existence. It might have dethroned the sovereign,—it might have repealed the Union; but it did not, it could not, and it never can, impair the Act of Security, unless the thing created can annihilate its creator! But the law of patronage is contrary to the Act of Security, which it was, and is avowedly beyond the power of the British legislature to violate; therefore that unconstitutional attempt to reimpose patronage was, is, and must for ever be, absolutely null and void, according to every dictate of justice, sound reason, and constitutional law.

Both the contending parties, the Church of Scotland and her enemies, regard the patronage act as a violation of the Act of Security, as appears from their respective statements. Lockhart of Carnwath says concerning it, "I pressed the Toleration and Patronage Acts more earnestly, that I thought the Presbyterian clergy would be from thence convinced that the establishment of their Kirk would in time be overturned, as it was obvious that the security thereof was not so thoroughly established by the Union as they imagined."* The commissioners of the Church had, in their address and representation to the queen, when they were in London for the purpose of opposing the passing of the Patronage Act, declared it to be "contrary to our Church constitution, so well secured by the Treaty of Union." This address the General Assembly approved and embodied in an act, thereby giving it the ratification of the whole Church. And in a meeting of the Commission of Assembly, as Wodrow states, "it was owned by all, that patronages were a very great grievance, and *sinful* in the imposers, and a breach of the security of the Presbyterian constitution by the Union."†

* Lockhart Papers, vol. i. p. 418.

† Wodrow MS. In addition to the direct statements in the text from two such opposite yet concurrent authorities as Lockhart and Wodrow, with regard to the views entertained by both parties respecting the effects intended by, or to be expected from, the Patronage Act, as calculated to impair the Scottish Church, shake the Union, and prepare for the return of the exiled Popish Pretender, the following extracts deserve attention :—"After that, an act was brought in for the restoring of patronages: these had been taken away by an act in King William's reign. It was set up by the Presbyterians from their first beginning, as a principle, that parishes had, from warrants in Scripture, a right to choose their ministers; so that they had always looked on the right of patronage as an invasion made on that. It was therefore urged, that since, by the Act of Union, Presbytery with all its rights and privileges, was unalterably secured, and since their kirk-session was a branch of their constitution, the taking from them the right of choosing their ministers was contrary to that act. Yet the bill passed through both houses, a small opposition being only made in either. By these steps the Presbyterians were alarmed when they saw the success of every motion that was made on design to weaken and undermine their establishment." (Burnet's Own Times, vol. ii. p. 595.)

"Although Mr Carstares did not succeed in his application to parliament against the bill for restoring patronages, yet his presence to London was of considerable advantage to the Church of Scotland, by giving him an opportunity of thwarting some other projects, which he considered as more dangerous in their tendency, because they affected her constitution in a more sensible manner. Some of her enemies, who were then in administration, had proposed that her annual Assemblies should be discontinued, as the source of all the opposition to the measures then pursued by the court; others were of opinion that they ought to be permitted to meet, but should be prorogued by her majesty's authority, so soon as they were constituted. And, to take away the only pretext for holding Assemblies for the future, or their sitting for any time, a bill was proposed, obliging presbyteries, under certain penalties, to settle, upon a presentation, every man to whom the Church had given license to preach, without any further trial or form." (Life of Carstares, pp. 82, 83.)

"There is no doubt that the restoration of the right of lay patrons in Queen Anne's time was designed to separate the ministers of the Kirk from the people, who could not be supposed to be equally attached to, or influenced by, a minister who held his living by the gift of a great man, as by one who was chosen by their own free voice,—and to render them more dependent on the nobility and amongst gentry, whom, much more than the common people, the sentiments of Jacobitism predominated." (Sir Walter Scott's Tales of a Grandfather, vol. ii. p. 242.)

Such was the state of affairs when the General Assembly met on the 1st of May 1712. Notwithstanding the recent violations of the Act of Security, the Duke of Athol, the commissioner, was instructed to use the language of approbation, mingled with deceitfully soothing assurances of her majesty's "firm purpose to maintain the Church of Scotland as established by law." In answer to this, the Assembly referred her majesty to the representations and petitions laid before her by the Commission, as containing the views and feelings of the Church respecting the recent proceedings of Parliament. The Assembly further embodied the representations, petitions, and addresses of the Commission in specific acts, giving them thereby the fullest sanction of the whole Church; and gave also particular instructions to the Commission to use all dutiful and proper means for obtaining redress of these grievances,—instructions which were repeated to every succeeding Commission till the year 1784. An attempt was also made by the Assembly to frame such an explanation of the abjuration oath as would enable ministers to take it without doing direct violence to their conscientious scruples; and an address was prepared to be laid before the queen, testifying their inviolate loyalty to her person and government, and their firm adherence to the principles of religious and civil liberty, and to the Protestant succession, and supplicating her majesty to employ her utmost care to protect the Church of Scotland, and to interpose her royal authority for a just redress of these recent grievances.*

The enemies of the Church of Scotland were considerably disappointed by the conduct of the General Assembly. They had expected that the passing of these iniquitous and unconstitutional laws would at once excite such an uncontrollable storm of indignation as would dissolve the Union, and throw all Scotland into the hands of the Jacobites, who would so direct the torrent of popular fury as to procure the restoration of the Pretender first to the Scottish throne, and then, by the aid of the vantage-ground so gained, and through the intrigues of Bolingbroke, to that of England. That they thoroughly misunderstood the prin-

* Acts of Assembly, year 1712.

ciples and character of Presbyterians is manifest, since they presumed to think, that in a weak and sinful revenge of wrongs sustained, true Presbyterians would perpetrate the greater wrong of aiding in replacing an avowed Papist on the throne. Presbyterians could not indeed but regard the law of patronage as sinful, since it was so far an attempt to interfere with the great Presbyterian principle of the sole Sovereignty and Headship of the Lord Jesus over his Church; but they could not fail to see, that to place a Popish monarch on the throne of the kingdom would involve an immeasurably more flagrant violation of that sacred principle. And because they thus felt and thought, the outrage which they had sustained not only brought them not one hair's-breadth nearer to a junction with the Jacobites, but as they knew by whom the nefarious deed had been instigated, they were the more confirmed in their detestation of that treacherous and tyrannical faction. This may be regarded as another proof how utterly impossible it is for mere worldly-minded men to comprehend the principles and anticipate the conduct of Christians. The Jacobites knew what they would have done, had they been so treated; but they failed miserably in their conjectures of what the Church of Scotland would do. So has it always been, so will it ever be, when the man of the world presumes to foretell the conduct of the religious man, by the consciousness of what, in similar circumstances, would be his own.

But the friends of the Church of Scotland had reason also to be disappointed by the conduct of the General Assembly. Had her councils been at that time guided by a Knox, a Melville, or a Henderson, instead of a Carstares, there can be little doubt that the Assembly would not only have declared the Act of Patronage an infraction of the Treaty of Union, as indeed was done, but also they would have declared it to be, for that very reason, necessarily and essentially invalid; and would have passed an act, strictly prohibiting all probationers, ministers, and church courts, from yielding to it the slightest degree of obedience, leaving to the civil powers to attempt enforcing it by persecution or otherwise, if they could and dared. This they might have done, and at the same time have declared with the most perfect truth, that this was not only no infringement of their own allegiance, or of the Treaty of Union, but that it was in reality the fulfilment and defence of both. Nor were the Jacobites so powerful, and the new ministry so firmly seated, as to have enabled them to attempt the violent enforcement of a law so glaringly unconstitutional, and involving such a manifest and infamous breach of national faith. But that ground may yet be taken, for the Act of Security still remains; and the time may come, at no distant date, when the Church and people of Scotland will call upon the British legislature, with a voice too distinct to be misunderstood, and too mighty to be disregarded, to rescind its own unlawful deed and to leave the Presbyterian Church in the full possession of its rights and privileges, founded in the Redeemer's Divine Sovereignty, won by the blood of her heroic martyrs, and secured by acts declared to be inviolable. He would be a strange defender of the British constitution who should insist, that to maintain it in its integrity it was necessary to perpetuate a vitiating act of national perfidy; and not less strangely would any defend the Church of England, who should assert, that her safety depended upon the permanent continuation of an act of grievous injustice committed against the Presbyterian Church of Scotland.

Not only was the Patronage Act so directly unconstitutional as to be essentially invalid, and absolutely incapable of ever acquiring validity,—not only was it forced through both houses of the legislature with such unseemly haste as to resemble the swift and stealthy motion of one who is pillaging his neighbour's property,—the very grounds of this illegal and baneful act, as stated in the preamble, were guileful misrepresentations and direct falsehoods. It begins by asserting, in general terms, that "by the ancient laws and constitution of Scotland, the presenting of ministers to vacant churches did of right belong to the patrons, till, by the act of 1690, the presentation was taken from the patrons, and given to the heritors and elders of the respective parishes." At the time of the Reformation there were nine hundred and forty parishes in Scotland, and of these, only about two hundred were subject to the presentation of lay patrons, "by the ancient laws and constitution of Scotland." Was it to regulate *these* that the act of Queen Anne was passed? It could not with truth and justice apply to more. It is not true that the presentation was given to the heritors and elders, for there was no presentation at all under the Revolution Settlement; the very word to *present*, was rigidly excluded from the act, lest some such idea might be entertained. Under the act 1690, ministers were settled, not upon the foundation of their being *proposed* by heritors and elders, but upon that of the acceptance and call of the people. This mendacious preamble further states, that "that way of calling ministers has proved inconvenient, and has not only occasioned great heats and inconveniences among those who by the foresaid act were entitled and authorised to call ministers, but likewise has been a great hardship upon the patrons, whose predecessors had founded and endowed those churches, and who had not received payment or satisfaction for their right of patronage." Instead of the "way of calling ministers" under the act 1690 having "proved inconvenient," by occasioning "great heats and inconveniencies," the very opposite is the truth. When "heats and inconveniences" did prevail, they were caused, not by the opposition to the settlement of pious and faithful ministers by turbulent Presbyterian congregations,—not even by religious congregations opposing the settlement of ungoldly ministers,—but by Jacobites, Prelatists, and mobs of vagrants who could not be termed Christians at all, hired and set on by the guileful enemies of the Church of Scotland, to obstruct her reforming progress, to prevent the consolidation of national peace and welfare, and to keep the country in such a state of confusion as might lead to the return of a Popish tyrant. The framers of that preamble were the very perpetrators of the scenes of tumult of which they complained; and the proper remedy would have been a more stringent act against those enemies of their country, the Jacobites and Prelatists of Scotland. During the whole period from 1690 to 1712, not one single instance occurred in which the great body of the people deserted a parish church, on account of the settlement of a minister under the authority of the General Assembly.*

That there were scenes of confusion is readily admitted; but these were invariably caused by a Prelatic party unlawfully obstructing the settlement of a Presbyterian minister.† And every one must see that the Prelatists in any parish could have no more right to interfere in the settlement of a Presbyterian minister, to cause confusion, and then to complain of it, than Presbyterians in England would have in the present day to impede the settlement of an Episcopalian clergyman in any parish in that country, and then to assert that the strife so caused was a proof of the evils of absolute patronage in England. The only other kind of "heats and inconveniences" which arose at times were those produced by competing calls, when two or more different parishes strove each to obtain the same individual to be their minister. The principle by which the Assembly was guided in determining cases of competing calls and transportations, was not at that time regard to the emoluments, but to the relative importance of the different parishes, invariably deciding in behalf of that parish which appeared to offer the largest sphere of public usefulness, which occasionally, from the difficulty of arriving at a certain conclusion, caused considerable delay. Yet these generous and kindly contests, as they may be termed, were far from being so numerous as has been generally asserted. Some of them were determined by the presbyteries and synods, in which case the vacancy in the parish would not extend beyond a few months. Others were carried by appeal to the Assembly; and in a very few instances the same case appeared at successive Assemblies before a final settlement took place. But the whole number of such cases mentioned in the only authoritative records, those of the General Assembly, amounted to no more than twelve or fourteen,‡ during a period of twenty-two years, in which there must have been at least six or seven hundred settlements of ministers. So utterly

* Sir Henry Moncrieff's Life of Erskine, Appendix, p. 433.

† Carstares' State Papers, p. 146.

‡ Acts of Assembly.

false is the assertion of the preamble to the Patronage Act, and so undeniably true is the statement of Sir Henry Moncrieff, that "there is no period in the history of the Church, in which the settlement of ministers was conducted with so little bustle or heat, or with as much regularity, as during the interval from 1690 to 1712."* According to Wodrow there were only five or six cases of disputed settlements which excited any degree of attention during all that period, arising out of disagreements among the parties who had the right to propose, and these were caused by improper conduct on the part of the heritors. In one of these cases, that of the parish of Cramond, in 1709-10, the two leading heritors contended, each wishing to procure the appointment of a favourite candidate; and in order to obtain a majority, "each side created new heritors to increase their party." "We are like," continues Wodrow, "to be in very sad circumstances, from the power of heritors in calling; and the same way of choosing of ministers is like to come in which was used in choosing members of parliament."† So naturally and inevitably does the secular element prove itself to be of a disruptive and disorganizing tendency, when allowed at all to intermingle among the elemental powers of spiritual matters.

It is scarcely necessary to notice the falsehood in the preamble respecting "the hardship upon the patrons, whose predecessors had founded and endowed these churches," caused by the act abolishing patronage; for every one knows that this frontless assertion is not only destitute of truth, but that in reality many of these patrons, instead of founding and endowing the Church, had been themselves founded and endowed out of its spoliation. Their predecessors had been either those rapacious and unprincipled men who robbed, defrauded, and attempted to tyrannize over the Church at the time of the Reformation, thwarting all its benevolent schemes, and impairing its national usefulness, or those mean and sycophantic minions of James VI., on whom that heartless despot bestowed with lavish hands the wealth and honours which by force or treachery he had succeeded in pillaging from the Church. If ever truth, justice, and religious principle be consulted in framing a legislative enactment respecting the patrimony of the Church of Scotland, not merely will patrons be deprived of their unhallowed power to interfere with the rights and privileges of Christ's spiritual kingdom in the appointment of his office-bearers, but they will be called to account for that stewardship into which they have unlawfully intruded, and to refund the ill-got gains which they had so long perverted and abused. Nor ought it to be overlooked, that although the act 1690 gave to patrons a right to the teinds, as compensation for the loss of their patronages (a compensation to which it would be difficult for church-spoliators to show any plausible claim), yet when their patronages were restored, they were not required to restore the teinds, as common justice would have dictated, but retained "both the purchase and the price."

Scarcely, in short, can the annals of history furnish a parallel to the infamous act reimposing patronage on the Church of Scotland. Every statement in its preamble, on the strength of which it proceeded, was either cunningly deceptive or directly false; it was manifestly contrary to the Act of Security, and therefore was either essentially and necessarily invalid, then and for ever, or to whatsoever extent its validity might be supposed to reach, to that extent it was a repeal of the Union, and a deadly stab to the British constitution; and its consequences, as subsequent times have too amply testified, have been and are fatally pernicious to the spiritual integrity and the national usefulness of the Church of Scotland. That it must be swept away sooner or later, is absolutely certain; for the reign of fraud and falsehood cannot be eternal, their very nature being self-destructive. And if the time has not yet come, it soon must, when the generous heart of England, roused by the remonstrances of the Scottish Church and people, and enlightened and directed by Him who is "Head over all things to the Church," will call upon the British legislature to remove from its records so foul a stain, so black a violation of sacred national faith, perpetrated by the unworthy hands of

* Life of Erskine, Appendix, p. 432.

† Wodrow, Analecta, quoted by Dr M'Crie in the Patronage Report, p. 363.

"the most corrupt ministry that ever sat at the helm of government."

Before passing forward from this subject, there is one remark of an explanatory nature pertaining to the history of the period, which must be made. The representations and petitions of the Commission, and the embodying of these in the Acts of Assembly, sufficiently prove the light in which the Patronage Act was regarded by the Church of Scotland, as a direct infringement upon her rights and privileges, and an unconstitutional violation of the Union. But it may be asked, why, entertaining such views, did not the Church adopt a bolder line of procedure, imitate the example of the high-souled men of other days, refuse submission, and prepare to endure persecution for conscience's sake, if come it must? Because the Church had lost the martyr spirit. And this loss was caused by the deep infusion of Prelacy, or semi-Prelacy, arising out of William's disastrous policy and the Church's sinful compliance, in the admission of the prelatic incumbents. By such men patronage could not be regarded as to any great extent a grievance, although they could not deny that it was utterly repugnant to the principles and constitution of Presbyterian church government; and therefore, while they could not oppose the representations and petitions of the Assembly, founded on principles which they themselves had subscribed, they would not have joined their better and sincerer brethren in any such decided opposition to that act as might have involved themselves in danger. Gravely to remonstrate, and then smilingly to yield, was all that these proto-moderates could do; and the faithful defenders of true Presbyterian principles,—the evangelical party of the day,—were in a manner constrained to choose between stopping when they had reached the extreme point to which their temporizing brethren would go, and incurring the hazard of an extensive and probably fatal schism, should they attempt to proceed beyond that point. Even this peril a Luther or a Knox would at once have braved, and, by braving, would have triumphed over it; for as all history, especially church history, testifies, the path of principle and the path of duty are the same; and, following their direction, the boldest course of conduct is always both the safest and the best. When the Act of Glasgow expelled nearly four hundred ministers at once, it still left a majority behind; and, though the sword of persecution was deeply bathed in blood, and the fires of persecution raged fiercely over the land for twenty-eight terrific years, the cause of the homeless and persecuted minority triumphed, because it was the cause of truth and godliness. And had a similar course been taken by the right-minded Presbyterians, though a minority, it is impossible to doubt that a similar result would have followed in a much shorter period of time. But, misled by Carstares, who was better acquainted with the wiles of state diplomacy than with the unbending firmness of Christian principle, and vitiated by the admission of the prelatic incumbents and their progeny and coadjutors, the growing Moderate party, the Church began to prefer expediency to principle, and was left to experience the bitter consequences of her want of faith, in a century of death-like spiritual lethargy, in the loss of the nation's respect and love, and in the dangers by which she is surrounded, and the agonies which she endures, in her present state of returning faithfulness and re-awakening life.

The Cameronian Covenanters, who had never joined the Church of Scotland as established at the Revolution, and who had remained for a number of years without a minister, obtained at length a minister, the Rev. John Macmillan, who was deposed in the year 1706, on account of having adopted and defended the opinions of that rigid but high-principled body. The records of the proceedings which led to his deposition reflect little credit on the Church of Scotland, either with regard to principle or prudence. For it would not be easy to prove that the Cameronians held doctrines so far different from those inculcated in the Standards of the Church, and acted upon in its purest times, as to have exposed them justly to any high degree of church censure; and while the Church was admitting prelatic curates "on the easiest terms" it was neither prudent nor seemly to deal harshly with men who might be narrow and limited in their views, but who were at least zealous and faithful Presbyterians.

When Mr. Macmillan joined these men, they gradually assumed a more regular aspect; and though they felt themselves deeply aggrieved by the cold treatment which they received, and were not slack in expressing their resentment, yet they continued to watch the course of public affairs with intense anxiety, and to stand prepared for any great and dangerous emergency. The Acts of *Toleration* and *Patronage* roused their indignation; and as the Church of Scotland had not met these public infringements of the Union and of principle with such prompt condemnation as she ought, the Cameronians resolved to declare their views in the most solemn and public manner in their power. Accordingly, on the 23d of July, the societies met in a body at Auchinsaugh, near Douglas, and after a general acknowledgment of sins, national and personal, they solemnly renewed the Covenants, making, at the same time, such specific statements in their engagement to duties as were necessary to accommodate the general obligations of the Covenants to their own case and circumstances.* There could be no impropriety in this act, viewed in itself; indeed it was one in which it would have been well if the whole body of Scottish Presbyterians had joined; but it was not followed by any consequences of such practical good as might have been expected. Unpropitious strifes and jarrings prevailed among them, fomented by a few men of greater zeal than knowledge or judgment, and prevented them from assuming, for many years, that united and harmonious aspect which could alone give them strength and importance in the community, and which in later times they acquired and continue to display.

[1713.] The subject of greatest importance which occupied the attention of the Assembly which met in 1713, was that which arose out of the oath of abjuration. A very considerable number of the best ministers refused to take that oath; and a schism was like to take place between those who felt at liberty to swear and those who did not, or the jurants and the non-jurants. And it deserves to be remarked, that the jurants were more severe against their non-jurant brethren, than the non-jurants were against them,—accusing them bitterly of being willing to disturb the peace and endanger the safety of the Church, rather than sacrifice their own scruples of conscience. Yet it was clear that the non-jurants were exposed to the pains and penalties of the law, because they refused the oath, and were willing to meet the hazard rather than violate their own conscience; whereas the jurants were exposed to no such dangers, and ought therefore rather to have striven to protect their brethren, than to have aggravated their grievances by harsh and intolerant treatment. It is creditable to Carstares, that he exerted himself strenuously to prevent the threatened schism; and procured an act of Assembly, inculcating forbearance with regard to taking or not taking the oath, representing it as comparatively a matter of indifference. Had it not been for his influence, which was very great in the Assembly, the contest would in all likelihood have proved a schism, which might have proved destructive to the Church in that period of danger.† The non-jurants, indeed, acted with extreme forbearance, notwithstanding the perils to which they were exposed. Almost the entire body of the people detested the abjuration oath; and in many instances, no sooner did a minister take it, than the congregation deserted his ministry, and flocked to the church of one who had refused. It would have been easy for the non-jurants to have raised a storm of civil commotion in the land, if they had been so disposed, but they generally did their utmost to discountenance these desertions, and continued to hold ministerial intercourse with their jurant brethren, even at the hazard of so far losing the affection of their own congregations. Even Boston had to encounter the strong displeasure of his parishioners, because, though he would not take the oath, yet he would neither speak against those who did, nor refrain from holding intercourse with them.

The Commission of the Assembly, at its meeting in August, drew up an address, which was read from all the pulpits, warning the nation against the designs of the Papists and Jacobites, pointing out the deceptive nature of their intrigues, and the evils in which their success would involve the country.‡ This address had

* Struthers' History of Scotland, p. 164, *et seq.*

† Boston's Memoirs, pp. 223-225.

‡ Willison's Testimony, pp. 42, 43.

a very beneficial influence in guarding the people against the machinations of the rebellious Jacobites, and frustrating their hopes of rousing Scotland to arm in behalf of the Popish Pretender; and contributed greatly to break the force of the insurrection when it did actually burst out two years afterwards. It proved, at the same time, how completely the most wily politicians had misunderstood the principles of the Church of Scotland, in imagining that the wrongs which she had sustained would irritate her to the commission of treason against her own Divine Head and King, by aiding in the restoration of a Popish claimant to the throne.

In the index of the unprinted acts of Assembly 1713, there are several references to the case of a Mr. William Dugud, probationer. This person had received a presentation from the crown, as patron of the parish of Burntisland, under the act 1712, and had the temerity to accept it and lay it before the presbytery of Kirkaldy. It was repelled by the presbytery, and came by appeal before the Assembly. The Assembly entered warmly into the case, deprived Mr. Dugud of his license, and caused a memorial to be drawn up, to be presented to her majesty by the commissioner, the Duke of Athol, who readily undertook the charge.* This prompt and decisive conduct on the part of the Assembly, together with the protests and resolutions of several presbyteries and synods against receiving presentations and proceeding upon them without a call from the congregation, which was then, as it previously was and still is, regarded as the primary and ruling element in forming the pastoral connection, had the effect of deterring both irreligious patrons and ambitious and wordly-minded probationers from venturing to attempt the enforcement of the perfidious and unconstitutional act reimposing patronages, till that generation was passing away.

[1714.] There is a melancholy interest attached to the year 1714, with regard to the Church of Scotland, as the first in which the General Assembly manifested a disinclination to proceed with due strictness against ministers who were accused of holding and teaching doctrines contrary to Scripture and to the Standards of the Church. There had for some time been current reports that Mr. John Simpson, professor of divinity at Glasgow, taught Arminian and Pelagian tenets; but the members of his own presbytery appear to have been unwilling to institute a process against him. The report was, however, taken up by the Rev. James Webster, one of the ministers of Edinburgh, as a matter of too serious importance to be permitted to continue without being investigated. When the case came before the Assembly, instead of remitting it to the presbytery of Glasgow, with instructions to make due inquiry, the task of conducting the prosecution was cast upon Mr. Webster, as if it had been a private affair, and not one which deeply concerned the whole Church.* The leaven of Moderatism was now beginning to put forth its corrupting power, producing laxity of principle, and that pernicious tendency to screen delinquents and to discourage men of fidelity and zeal, by which it has always been characterised.

An act was passed in this Assembly, appointing an address to be presented to her majesty, complaining of "the grievances which this Church lies under, from the growth of Popery, the insolence of Papists, and the illegal encroachments and intrusions of the Episcopal ministers and their adherents." The necessity for this act and address arose out of the riotous and outrageous proceedings of the Prelatic Jacobites of Aberdeen, who had violently taken possession of the Old Church in that city, expelling the professor of divinity, Mr. David Anderson, and his congregation, whose regular place of worship it was.† So extravagantly lawless were the proceedings of the Scottish Prelatists at this time, trusting in the favour of the infidel Bolingbroke, who, as is well known, was employing every artifice to procure the succession of the Popish Pretender, that it was found necessary to pass in parliament another Rabbling Act, to prevent them from absolutely pulling down those Presbyterian churches into which they found it difficult to intrude so as to secure possession. Yet these lawless men were at the very same time continuing to utter loud complaints of the persecution which they had to sus-

* Unprinted Acts of Assembly; Patronage Report, pp. 365, 366.

* Unprinted Acts of Assembly. † Act xii. of Assembly 1714.

tain from Presbyterians! And Scottish Prelatists can yet be found rash enough to repeat the mendacious tale! They would more consult the credit of their ancestors, and their own reputation for knowledge and veracity, did they allow the records of those times to sink into oblivion, lest it become necessary for the Church of Scotland, in her own defence, to drag anew their deeds of darkness to the light.

But while the Jacobite party were thus employing every violent and treacherous method in their power for the overthrow of the Church of Scotland, as a preliminary step to the subversion of the Revolution and the recall of the exiled Pretender to the crown, their hopes were suddenly blasted by the death of Queen Anne, on the 1st of August 1714, and the instantaneous dissolution of that corrupt administration, by whose evil deeds so dark a stain had been brought upon the latter years of her reign. The unopposed succession of the Elector of Hanover, George I., drove that fierce and unprincipled faction into a frantic and premature attempt to place by force of arms the Popish exile on the throne. The detail of the events of the unsuccessful rebellion must be left to the civil historian; but it must here be stated, that the injuries done to the Church of Scotland by Jacobite intrigues had great influence in preventing many Presbyterians, who disapproved of the Union, from joining the rebels, and thus the consequences of their evil deeds recoiled with fatal effect upon their own guilty heads.

[1715.] When the Assembly met in May 1715, its attention was chiefly occupied by two topics which have always manifested a peculiar affinity for each other by their simultaneous appearance,—unsoundness of doctrine and the grievance of patronage. An act was passed appointing a committee for preserving the purity of doctrine, and for considering the process of Mr. Webster against Professor Simson. The instructions to the committee, contained in this act, exhibit but too plainly a predetermination to throw every possible obstruction in the way of Mr. Webster, so as to render the proof of the accusation almost impossible; while every facility was given to Professor Simson to frame such evasive explanations as might eventually secure his acquittal.*

The next act of importance is "concerning the grievances of the Church from toleration, patronages," &c. This act embodies a memorial to his majesty, which the Duke of Montrose was requested to present and support. In the first part of this memorial, the Assembly pointed out the unequal character of the toleration, inasmuch as, while it gave the utmost possible freedom to Episcopalian dissenters in Scotland, notwithstanding their avowed Jacobitism, and their refusal to take the oaths of allegiance and abjuration, it did not give the same liberty to Presbyterian dissenters in England. In truth, the Act of Toleration, against which the Church of Scotland complained as a grievance, was totally different from what is properly meant by the term *toleration.* Its nature and intention was, to give encouragement to Prelacy and discouragement to Presbytery; and it was because of its unjust partiality, not because of its toleration, that the Church of Scotland regarded it as a grievance. Yet, because they complained of an act of a persecuting character, disguised under a plausible name, they have been, and still are accused of intolerance, and of cherishing a persecuting spirit. Surely neither State nor Church is bound to countenance and cherish error, though they may tolerate, pity, and attempt to instruct the erring; and surely it is not intolerance to abstain from elevating to places of public trust and influence men who are known to entertain principles whose native tendency is destructive to the public welfare.

That part of the memorial which refers to patronage deserves to be extracted, in order to show the opinions then entertained respecting that grievance. "By the act restoring the power of presentation to patrons, the legally established constitution of this Church was altered in a very important point; and while it appears equitable in itself, and agreeable to the liberty of Christians and a free people, to have interest in the choice of those to whom they entrust the care of their souls, it is a hardship to be imposed upon in so tender a point, and that frequently by patrons who have no property or residence in the parishes; and this, besides the

* Act of Assembly 1715.

snares of simonaical factions. and the many troubles and contests arising from the power of patronages, and the abuses thereof by disaffected patrons putting their power into other hands, who as effectually serve their purposes,—by patrons competing for the right of presentation in the same parish,—and by frequently presenting ministers, settled in eminent posts, to mean and small parishes, to elude the planting thereof,—by all which parishes are often kept long vacant, to the great hindrance of the progress of the gospel."* Such were the bitter fruits which patronage was beginning to bear within three years after its unconstitutional reimposition upon the Church of Scotland,—fruits which might gratify infidels and enemies of Christianity, such as Bolingbroke and the Jacobites, but which seems strange that any man professing to be a lover of religious purity and national welfare could contemplate, without immediately and strenuously exerting himself to procure the uprooting of that tree of death.

A severe act was passed by the same Assembly against some ministers, and two probationers, in the counties of Dumfries and Galloway, who manifested a strong inclination to countenance the Covenanters, and to join Mr. Macmillan, who was as yet their only regular minister, although these ministers, Messrs. Taylor, Hepburn, and Gilchrist, had held partial communion with them. It is painful to have to record, that the Church of Scotland had exhibited a more intolerant spirit in its treatment of its own better children, the remnant of the Covenanters, and those who were disposed to favour them, than it did towards the persecuting and rebellious Prelatists. It suggests too strongly the idea of severity against the weak, and a mean and timid compromise with the strong.

[1716.] Before the next meeting of the General Assembly, the kingdom had been shaken by the storm of civil war, raised by the rebellion of the Jacobites. In this dangerous period the Church of Scotland manifested the most unshaken loyalty, notwithstanding the injurious treatment which it had received since the Union. And although in many parts of the country the people, resenting their grevious wrongs, could not be prevailed upon to rise in support of the government, they were still less disposed to lend direct assistance to a Popish Pretender to the crown. They had been injured deeply in their dearest interests and most valued rights and privileges, by the acts of Queen Anne's latter years, and had obtained no redress from the new sovereign; therefore they stood comparatively aloof from the contest, merely acting upon the defensive against the rebels, under the influence of an unwise though not an unnatural resentment. But the very fact of this stern unmoving attitude, in such a time, ought to have taught a wise and paternal government to grant such an immediate and complete redress as would have restored the alienated affections of a brave, high-minded, intelligent, and religious people, whose allegiance to their king was based upon and regulated by their fear and love of God.

Nothing of peculiar importance was done by the Assembly. The case of Professor Simson was again referred to a committee, who were directed to proceed with all due expedition in preparing the matter for a final decision by next Assembly. One act was passed, of no great importance in itself, but throwing considerable light upon the subject of patronage and intrusion. It referred to that person who had signalized himself by being the first to accept a presentation after the passing of the Patronage Act,—namely, William Dugud. Upon being deprived by the Assembly of his license, he joined the Scottish Prelatists; and we find him busy raising a mob, and at its head endeavouring to effect a forcible intrusion into the church of Burntisland.* So strong is the congenial affinity between Prelacy, patronage, and intrusion, that the potential presence of any one of the three has always tended to the introduction of the others; and, when in full and united operation, the result has always been a fearful amount of worldly-mindedness in the clerical body, spiritual despotism in church courts, and spiritual lethargy throughout the community, disturbed by acts of tyranny on the part of the ecclesiastical rulers, and partially counteracted by dissent or secession.

[1717.] The course of defection on

* Assembly 1715, act ix.

* Acts xiv. and xv. of Assembly 1716; also Unprinted Acts.

which the Church of Scotland had entered became more and more apparent every year, and the Assembly of 1717 was guilty of several acts more glaringly evil than those of its predecessors. The case of Professor Simson was finally decided by this Assembly; and although it was clearly proved that he had taught Arminian and Pelagian tenets, the Assembly merely found, that he had vented some opinions not necessary to be taught in divinity; had used some expressions which are capable of bearing a bad sense, and are employed in that sense by adversaries; and that in answering the objections urged by the antagonists of the gospel, he had made use of hypotheses that tend to attribute too much to natural reason and the power of corrupt nature; which expressions and hypotheses they prohibited him from using for the future. This culpable lenity appears to have arisen in a great measure from the deplorable fact, that a large proportion of the Assembly were themselves tainted with opinions equally unsound, many of the members having been the pupils, or being the relations and personal friends of the heretical professor.* Great alarm was felt by the more sound and orthodox part of the Church, lest this unfaithful procedure should tend to encourage that proneness to innovations and to laxity of doctrine which were already but too prevalent, especially among the young and recently admitted ministers.

This alarm was instantaneously increased by another act passed by the Assembly on the very same day on which such tenderness was shown to heresy. Aware of the tendency to false doctrine rapidly springing up among young men, the presbytery of Auchterarder, with a view to prevent the growth of the evil in their bounds, prepared a series of searching questions, which were proposed to students, and required to be answered before they should receive license to preach. A young man, named William Craig, had appeared before the presbytery of Auchterarder; and though his trials were sustained in the general form, yet, because he did not give satisfaction in his answers to their own series of questions, they refused to grant him an extract of his license. He appealed to the Assembly, and laid before that court the particular question to which his answer had been the most unsatisfactory. The question, or rather article, was this:—"That I believe that it is not sound and orthodox to teach, that we must forsake sin in order to our coming to Christ, and instating us in covenant with God." The Assembly not only prohibited the presbytery of Auchterarder, and all other presbyteries, from requiring subscription to any formula but such as had been expressly approved of by the Assemblies of the Church; but further declared their "abhorrence of the foresaid proposition, as unsound, and most detestable as it stands and was offered to Mr. Craig." And the presbytery of Auchterarder was commanded to answer to the Commission what they could design by such a proposition.* Against this hasty sentence of the Assembly several of the best ministers of the Church remonstrated, but could not prevent its passing.

In the unprinted acts of this Assembly, there are two acts relating to the case of Mr. John Hay, who had been appointed to the parish of Peebles; but, although his call was signed by several heritors and elders, the opposition to his settlement by the people was so strong, that the presbytery refused to proceed with it. The first act required the presbytery to proceed with the settlement, and appointed a committee to confer with the presbytery and with the people of the parish, in order to remove, if practicable, the opposition. Not finding the opposition so easily removed, and the majority of the Presbytery being still reluctant to proceed contrary to the feelings of the people, another act was passed, "appointing certain brethren to correspond with the presbytery of Peebles, and to act and vote in their meetings at their next ensuing diet, and thereafter until the settlement of Mr. John Hay in the parish of Peebles be completed, and to concur with them in his ordination."† By this device both the opposition of the people and the conscientious reluctance of the presbytery were surmounted, and an unscrupulous hireling intruded upon an unwilling congregation. And it is of importance to mark, that this was the first instance on

* Acts of Assembly; Willison's Testimony, p. 45.

* Acts of Assembly; Boston's Memoirs, p. 266.

† Unprinted Acts of Assembly, year 1717.

record in which the superior church courts appointed an ambulatory commission, with powers to outvote and overrule the conscientious reluctance of a presbytery to inflict a grievous wrong upon the people; giving thereby a precedent to a course of procedure which was a few years afterwards matured into a system under the sway of Moderate policy during its first dynasty, when its decrees were regularly carried into effect by these "Riding Committees," as they were termed, from their dragoon-like array, and doughty achievements in the cause of spiritual despotism.

A few sentences may be necessary for explaining the conduct of the Assembly in its rash condemnation of what some of its members scornfully termed "The Auchterarder Creed." Those who are conversant with modern church history are aware, that Arminian tenets were adopted by a large proportion of the English clergymen, very soon after their condemnation by the Synod of Dort. When Prelacy was forced into Scotland by the treachery of James I. and the violence of his sons, Arminianism came along with it in its most glaring aspect; and even after the overthrow of Scottish Prelacy, the evil taint was found to have diffused itself beyond the direct Prelatists, and to have been imbibed by many of the indulged ministers. By them, and by the Prelatic incumbents, whom William's pernicious policy induced the Church of Scotland to admit at and after the Revolution, these erroneous notions were still more extensively spread throughout the Scottish Church, especially among the young ministers. Two other circumstances combined partially to modify, and yet aid in the diffusion of erroneous doctrines. For some time previous to the Revolution, considerable numbers of young men went from Scotland to Holland to be educated for the ministry, the distracted and oppressed state of their own country not permitting them to obtain the necessary instruction at home. But Holland itself had imbibed many of the tenets of Arminius, notwithstanding the counteracting influence of such men as Witsius; and several of the young Scottish students adopted these sentiments, and, returning to their native country, attempted to supersede the strong Calvinistic doctrines which had hitherto prevailed in Scotland, by the introduction of this refined Arminianism. A similar process was at the same time going on in England among the Dissenters. Baxter's writings had gained, as on many accounts they justly deserved, great celebrity; and many followed his views respecting the doctrine of grace, which are deeply tinged with Arminian notions. A controversy arose which turned chiefly on the question, "Whether the gospel is a *new law*, or constitution, promising salvation upon a certain condition?" some making that condition to be faith, others making it faith and repentance, to which others added sincere though imperfect obedience Those who maintained the affirmative were termed Neonomians, or new-law men; those who opposed this theory were by its adherents unjustly termed Antinomians. It will easily be seen that the theory of the Neonomians was essentially Arminian, though it did not assume an aspect so manifestly unscriptural. In this less offensive form it made great progress in Scotland, where, from the causes already mentioned, too many were predisposed to receive it, in preference to the sterner tenets of the genuine Presbyterian Church, whose standards they had subscribed, but were exceedingly desirous to modify and soften.

The older and sounder ministers strove to stem this tide of innovation, but with little success. The Neonomians were soon the most numerous, as they were readily joined by all the admitted Prelatists, and by the greater part of the indulged; and, as it may be easily supposed, they found most favour from men of the world, who are always delighted to hear the gospel characterized as a "milder dispensation," by which expression they are prone to understand, one that may be violated with comparative impunity. Nor was it strange that the party which loved to regard the gospel as a new and mitigated law, should be found the most compliant, when statesmen wished to mould into greater conformity with their own inclinations the constitution and government of the Church. And for this reason also, that party received a degree of political countenance and support, which their opponents, the more orthodox and truly Presbyterian party, could not hope to obtain. To counteract this growing spirit of innovation and defection, as far as might be in their power, the evangelical party exerted themselves to the utmost both in composing new works, calculated to exhibit and diffuse sound doctrine, and by republishing old ones of a similar character. They endeavoured also to make their examinations of young men preparing for the ministry, such as should not only test their religious opinions, but should likewise tend to convey sound instruction to those who might be willing to receive it. The catechism written by Mr. Hamilton of Airth, to which reference was formerly made, was one of the productions to which this scheme of the evangelical party gave birth. Hog of Carnock distinguished himself greatly by his labours in behalf of sound doctrine; and nearly all the popular works of Boston were written for the same purpose, and were of incalculable service to the cause of truth. The "Auchterarder Creed," as it was scoffingly called, presents one instance of the various attempts made by presbyteries to secure the orthodoxy of those to whom they gave license to preach, that they might preach not "another gospel," but the truth as it is in Jesus. The strong terms in which the Assembly condemned the proposition already quoted, will scarcely excite surprise, when the sentence is viewed as pronounced by polemical disputants. Yet the full amount of that polemical asperity which dictated a censure so severe against a proposition certainly true, though somewhat loosely expressed, could not be entirely accounted for without a closer view of the course adopted by the Neonomians. Instead of meeting in fair argument the accusations urged against their new system, they endeavoured to recriminate upon their antagonists, and accused them vehemently of Antinomianism. In this spirit they evidently regarded the Auchterarder proposition as containing one of the darkest of the Antinomian tenets; whereas a little more discrimination and candour, and a little less party prejudice, might have enabled them to perceive that it was intended merely to guard against the unsound doctrine, that a man must of himself first abandon sin, and cease to be a sinner, before he can be at liberty or entitled to come to Christ, and to enter into covenant with God. What they condemned in such strong terms was their own prejudiced construction of a really sound proposition, and not that orthodox tenet which it was intended to express. It will be found that these remarks apply to much of the contest which arose at this time, and so deeply agitated the Church for several dangerous years.

While sitting in the General Assembly during the discussions respecting Professor Simson and the Auchterarder proposition, the Rev. Thomas Boston happened to mention to Mr. Drummond of Crieff, that he had met with an old book called the Marrow of Modern Divinity, with which he had been much pleased. Mr. Drummond, with some difficulty, procured a copy of the work thus recommended. It was perused and approved of by Mr. Webster of Edinburgh, Mr. Hog of Carnock, and other eminent divines. Subsequently, Mr. Hog, by the advice of his friends, wrote a recommendatory preface to it, and it was republished in the course of the year 1718.* The importance of this apparently slight incident, in its ultimate bearing upon the Church of Scotland, cannot well be overestimated, as shall shortly appear.

The only other subject of importance which occurred this year, was the drawing up of a memorial by Wodrow the historian, which he sent to Colonel Erskine of Cardross, to guide that gentleman in his application to government for redress of those grievances under which the Church of Scotland groaned, especially that of patronage. The whole of this important document deserves attention, as a few sentences will prove. "Nothing can more nearly affect the present and the after generation, this National Church, and even his majesty's government, than a right, regular, and scriptural establishment as to the settling of ministers. The foundation of almost all the wrong reasonings upon this head, is a notion got into the heads of too many persons of rank and figure, that gospel ministers are a set of men whom custom hath beat in to talk a while once a-week to them upon serious subjects, and therefore are to have a maintenance and subsistence allowed them, as law accords; and such who are bound by law to give

* Boston's Memoirs, pp. 266, 267.

them their small stipends are to call and choose them; meanwhile they have no notion of a pastoral charge, or the merit in all duties and relations betwixt a minister and those for whom he must account, as well as that his hearers must give account of this great gift to them. Besides this gross notion of a gospel ministry and their maintenance, it is lamentably evident that statesmen and persons of rank and quality have of a long time been essaying to involve this Church and the judicatory thereof in their parties and designs, and to make tools of ministers to carry on their secular purposes. As to ministry brought into a church by the power of patrons, they must be dependent and servile, and so corrupt and despised. We have this to encourage us in this application, that the king, when Elector of Hanover, did express his dislike of the bill for bringing in patrons, as what would break his best friends in Scotland. I do not see that any smoothings in this affair will do. Restricting of patrons, if the people be forfeited of their just right, or obliging them to take the consent of presbyteries before they present a minister already fixed to a congregation, will but line the yoke, and make it sit closer to our necks, and perpetuate it upon us and posterity."* Such were the opinions of the sagacious and thoughtful Wodrow. Had he been filled with the spirit of prophecy, he could not more justly have characterised patrons and patronage, or more accurately have foretold the evil consequences about to follow; and it were well if men in the present times would ponder upon the danger of all attempts to devise such a restriction of that intolerable yoke as shall merely give it a firmer clasp, and render it a perpetual bondage.

[1718.] The only act of the Assembly of 1718 to which it is necessary to advert was one concerning the presbytery of Auchterarder; from which it appears, that the presbytery had given such an explanation of their meaning in the censured proposition as satisfied the Commission. They were therefore exonerated from further blame, and merely warned to abstain from using such questionable language for the future.

* See the document quoted by Dr. M'Crie, Patronage Report, pp. 364, 365.

[1719.] In the year 1719, an act of parliament was passed in consequence of the complaints and remonstrances of the Church, calculated to put an end to some of the abuses of patronage, and by many thought to be available for a great deal more. One of the glaring abuses of patronage consisted in patrons presenting to vacant charges ministers who were already in more important situations, or who were known to be so hostile to patronage that they would not accept presentations at all. By such means the parishes were kept vacant for several years, during which time the patrons retained possession of the stipend, thereby defrauding the Church of its patrimony, and the people of a minister. By this act it was declared, that if any patron should present to a vacant charge the minister of any other parish, or any person who should not accept or declare his willingness to accept of the presentation within the usual time—six months—such presentation should not be accounted any interruption of the course of time allowed to the patron for presenting, but the *jus devolutum* should take place as if no presentation had been offered. This was certainly calculated to put an end to that form of abuse; but at the time it was generally thought to be equivalent to a repeal of the Patronage Act; "and that no Presbyterian would ever expressly declare his accepting of a presentation to go so far to approve or comply with patronage, which Presbyterians had always declared to be a heavy yoke and burden on the Church of God."* And accordingly, says Willison, "there was no man that presumed to take, accept, or make use of a presentation for several years after this act was passed." It was, indeed, proposed by some, that the Assembly should follow up this act of parliament by another of their own, prohibiting all probationers and ministers from accepting presentations, on pain of the highest church censures, being persuaded that government intended to give to the Church this opportunity of getting quit of patronage without the formality of a legislative enactment. Others thought that all that was intended was only to put an end to the abuse of evasive presentations. But amid this diversity of opinion

* Willison's Testimony, p. 48.

respecting the real intention of the act, and lulled into security by regarding the dangers arising out of the exercise of patronage as now removed, and with a growing Moderate party already predominant in the church courts, who had little predilection for the original principles of Presbytery, the Church did not avail itself of this opportunity of throwing off the yoke, or at least of testing the sincerity of the friendly professions of government. By this restriction the yoke was lined, to use the words of Wodrow, and more firmly fixed than before.

In the meantime what has been termed the Marrow Controversy had begun. The republication of this work by Mr. James Hog of Carnock, with a recommendatory preface from his pen, had excited great displeasure among the leading men of the Church, who were nearly all Neonomians. Mr. Hog found it necessary to publish, early in 1719, "An Explanation of the Passages excepted against in the Marrow of Modern Divinity." Soon after this, Principal Haddow of St. Andrews, in a sermon preached at the meeting of the synod of Fife in April, directly assailed the doctrinal views contained in Marshall's Treatise on sanctification, and especially in the Marrow of Modern Divinity. This sermon having been published at the request of the synod, the discussion assumed the form of a regular controversy between the two parties in the Church,—the Evangelical and constitutional party who adhered firmly to the original and fundamental principles held by the Presbyterian Church in its purest times, and especially at the periods of the First and Second Reformations,—and the Neonomian and innovating Moderate party, who displayed an ominous readiness to accommodate the gospel to the inclinations of fallen man, and to modify the principles of Church government and discipline so as to meet the views of politicians and men of the world. No express mention was made of the Marrow in the assembly of 1719; but in the instructions given to the commission, they were directed to "inquire into the publishing and spreading of books and pamphlets tending to the diffusing of the condemned proposition of Auchterarder, and promoting a system of opinions relative thereto which are inconsistent with our Confessions of Faith; and that the recommenders of such books and pamphlets, or the errors therein contained, be called before them, to answer for their conduct in such recommendations."* The Commission entered upon the discharge of this duty with keen alacrity. They chose what they termed a "committee for preserving the purity of doctrine," who nominated a sub-committee to sit at St. Andrews, to "ripen the affair," by fixing on the persons to be called before them, and drawing up a list of questions for their examination. In a short time the following ministers were summoned to attend the committee at Edinburgh,—the Rev. Messrs. Warden of Gargunnock, Brisbane of Stirling, Hamilton of Airth, and Hog of Carnock. The answers of these ministers were declared by the Edinburgh committee to be satisfactory; and it was confidently anticipated that a favourable report would be returned to the Assembly, and that the threatened controversy would speedily terminate in peace. But this was by no means the intention of the St. Andrews sub-committee. Led on by Principal Haddow,† that small conclave was busily engaged in picking out every objectionable expression that could be found in the Marrow and in the writings of its defenders; separating these from the context, and so arranging them as to give them the appearance of a connected series of heterodox propositions, and framing the whole into a report calculated to impose upon the Assembly, which could not be expected to enter into such a minute examination of the book as it was to be supposed had been done by a committee appointed expressly for that purpose.

[1720.] When the general Assembly met in May 1720, instead of the favourable report of the Edinburgh committee, which had been expected, that of the St. Andrews sub-committee, drawn up by Principal Haddow, was laid before the house. This report had been framed with such art as to convey the impression to all who were not thoroughly acquainted with the Marrow of Modern Divinity

* Acts of Assembly, year 1719.

† There is reason to believe that Principal Haddow acted in this manner under the influence of personal enmity against Mr Hog, arising out of some disagreement which had occurred between them when students in Holland. (Gospel Truth, p. 483.)

itself, that it was a book of the most pernicious tendency, calculated to lead its readers into the most dangerous errors. In vain did its defenders attempt to procure a fair and thorough investigation of the work, for the purpose of showing that some injudicious and unguarded expressions were so modified by others, and by the general spirit of the book, that, taken collectively, the doctrine of the book was orthodox and scriptural. This which is the only fair and candid mode of ascertaining what are really an author's sentiments, was refused, and the attention of the Assembly was rigidly confined to the expressions selected by the accusers. It is perfectly evident, that by a careful selection of incautious phrases, employed incidentally by an author when his mind is mainly occupied by another topic, he may be made to seem the supporter of opinions which it is his very object to repudiate and condemn. By such a sophistical process Luther may be made the defender of Popery, and Calvin of universal redemption; by such a process Calvin, and Beza, and Knox, and the Standards of the Church of Scotland, have been made the defenders of patronage and intrusion; and by such a process the Bible itself has been made to give support to heresy. Thus misled by the sophistical report of its committee, the General Assembly was induced to pass an act condemning the Marrow of Modern Divinity, on account of the false doctrine which it was said to contain.

In the act condemning the Marrow, the passages said to contain false doctrine are arranged under five heads:—1st, Concerning the nature of faith, the charge being that assurance is made to be of the essence of faith; 2d, Universal atonement and pardon; 3d, Holiness not necessary to salvation; 4th, Fear of punishment and hope of reward not allowed to be motives of a believer's obedience; 5th, That the believer is not under the law as a rule of life. To these are added, "Six Antinomian paradoxes," which are said to be "sensed," or explained and "defended by applying to them that distinction of the law of works and the law of Christ." Assuming, on the authority of the sub-committee's report, that these heretical tenets were really contained in the Marrow of Modern Divinity, the General Assembly passed an act, on the 20th of May 1720, by which they "strictly prohibit and discharge all the ministers of this Church, either by preaching, writing, or printing, to recommend the said book, or in discourse to say any thing in favour of it; but, on the contrary, they are hereby enjoined and required to warn and exhort their people in whose hands the said book is, or may come, not to read or use the same."* It would be improper here to enter into religious controversy; but this much may be said, that the five heads condemned by the Assembly are *not* taught by the Marrow of Modern Divinity, though incidental expressions, taken apart from the context, may seem to have some such tendency; and that there are very few books to be found containing equally clear and satisfactory views of the gospel.

This act of Assembly, together with one respecting preaching catechetical doctrine, in which there are some very questionable expressions, excited great dissatisfaction and anxiety in the minds of all the sound and faithful ministers throughout the country; and the subject was discussed at the meetings of presbyteries and synods, in various quarters, particularly in the presbytery of Selkirk and the synod of Merse and Teviotdale. A correspondence was begun between Messrs. Boston of Etterick, Gabriel Wilson of Maxton, and Ebenezer Erskine of Portmoak, Wilson of Perth, and Hog of Carnock, and others, respecting the steps which ought to be taken for the vindication of the truth in this day of trouble and rebuke. It was at length agreed that a representation and petition should be given in to next Assembly, for the purpose of endeavouring to procure the repeal of the act condemning the Marrow. After several interviews had taken place, the matter was matured, and the representation prepared and signed, preparatory to its being laid before the Assembly.†

[1721.] Considerable anxiety was felt throughout the Church respecting the possible issue of the controversy, in the aspect which it had now assumed. Many

* Acts of Assembly, year 1720, act v.

† Boston's Memoirs, pp. 295-301.

who disapproved of the sentence of condemnation into which the Assembly had been betrayed by Principal Haddow, were yet afraid that the representation would not lead the Assembly to repeal an act once passed, and might end in the expulsion of the eminent divines by whom that document was signed. Great endeavours were accordingly made to induce them to withhold the representation; but having arrived at the conviction that it was an act of imperative duty, they could not be dissuaded. The representation was at length formally laid before the committee of bills, and a day was appointed on which the subject was to be discussed in the Assembly.* What the result might have been, had the discussion taken place while the minds of the members were in a state of irritation, it is impossible to say; but as the commissioner was labouring under serious indisposition, it was thought proper to shorten the sitting of the Assembly, intrusting to the Commission such business as it could not overtake. This was a propitious circumstance, as it gave both time and occasion to further investigation, besides preventing the hazard of a decision by the Assembly in a state of rash and intemperate warmth.

The most important matter intrusted to the Commission was that which related to the Representers, as the twelve ministers who had signed the representation were called. Several conferences took place between the Representers and the Commission immediately after the rising of the Assembly; but the subject was postponed to a subsequent meeting of Commission in August. At this meeting the Commission could not agree upon their own course of procedure, some being disposed to act with severity, others recommending a milder method. In November, the Representers were required to furnish written answers to a series of twelve queries which had been prepared. They perceived clearly the intention of this proposal, which was to bring them as delinquents before the Assembly, instead of being virtually the censurers of that court, as they were by their representation, which was equivalent to a complaint against its sentence condemning the Marrow. The Representers regarded this as so unusual and unfair a course of procedure, that they were not bound to comply with it; nevertheless, for the sake of truth, and for the vindication of their own characters, they judged it expedient to take these queries into consideration, and to prepare answers to be laid before the Commission at their meeting in March. One effect, not contemplated by the assailants of the Marrow, resulted from this course of procedure: the answers returned by the Representers were very carefully prepared, and being written by men of decided talents, learning, and piety, they formed an admirable exposition of a difficult point in theology, and contributed greatly to stem the tide of defection at that time so rapidly overflowing the country.*

[1722.] The answers to the queries of the Commission were produced at the meeting of that court in March 1722; and the committee for purity of doctrine immediately engaged in writing a comment upon these queries, and framing an overture on the subject, preparatory to the meeting of Assembly. When the Assembly met, it soon appeared that the opponents of the Marrow had lost, and its defenders gained, by the delay which had taken place. The attention of the Church had been directed to that work in the interval; and many ministers had come to the conclusion, that the Assembly's sentence was not warranted by any thing which it contained, if fairly and candidly interpreted as a whole. The severe censure which the leading men in the Church had intended to inflict upon the Representers was not likely to pass without strenuous opposition; and there appeared a strong probability that many might join the twelve brethren in wishing the repeal of that act against which the representation was directed. After a period of protracted and anxious discussion, an act was framed, confirming, but at the same time explaining, the former act; giving a cautious but not

* The representation was signed by the following twelve ministers:—the Rev. Messrs. James Hog of Carnock, Thomas Boston of Etterick, John Bonar of Torphichen, John Williamson of Inveresk, James Kid of Queensferry, Gabriel Wilson of Maxton, Ebenezer Erskine of Portmoak, Ralph Erskine of Dunfermline, James Wardlaw of Dunfermline, Henry Davidson of Galashiels, James Bathgate of Orwell, William Hunter of Lilliesleaf.

* Appendix to modern reprints of the Marrow, o Gospel Truth, pp. 176-238.

very orthodox statement of the doctrines held by the Church on the points under discussion; prohibiting the ministers of the Church from teaching the positions condemned, or any equivalent to them; and appointing the moderator to rebuke and admonish the twelve brethren who signed the representation.* They were rebuked and admonished accordingly, "receiving it with all gravity, and as an ornament in the cause of truth;" and immediately laying upon the table a protest against both the former act and the present sentence, asserting their liberty still to profess, teach, and bear testimony to the truths condemned.† This protest was allowed to lie on the table, but not read; and as the Assembly did not attempt to found any proceedings against the brethren on account of it, while on their part they viewed it as sufficient to exonerate their conscience, the whole matter was allowed to rest, and the imminent danger of a schism averted for the time. The sudden change in the conduct of the leading men in the Assembly from overbearing severity to comparative leniency, was caused partly by the perception that a much larger proportion of the Church disapproved of their proceedings than they had expected; but chiefly because, both in his majesty's public letter, and by the commissioner in a private conference, they were warned to abstain from every thing which might cause division in the Church.‡

Thus terminated so far as the discussion in church courts was concerned, the Marrow Controversy; but its consequences did not soon pass away. Irritated by their comparative failure in the General Assembly, the Neonomian party directed their attention to the subordinate judicatories, and did their utmost to prevent or impede the settlement in parishes of young men who were suspected to have imbibed the Marrow doctrines.§ They even framed new questions relating to these doctrines, to be put to probationers, in direct contravention of an act passed by themselves against the Auchterarder proposition; and did their utmost to harrass and annoy the twelve Representers. They assailed Gabriel Wilson with great bitterness on account of a sermon preached before the synod, prosecuting him from court to court, till he was rescued by the favourable decision of the Assembly itself; and they prevented Boston from being removed to a more salubrious situation, although aware that the air of Etterick, too keen for his delicate constitution, was hastening him to the grave.* By such a course of conduct was the first period of rising Moderatism distinguished; screening teachers of direct error, as in the case of Simson; conniving at evasive perversions of the truth, in the introduction of Neonomian views; submitting to violations of the constitutional rights and privileges of the National Church, as in the Patronage Act; and persecuting with relentless malignity their brethren the Representers, and other faithful and zealous defenders of the doctrines of grace.

[1723-4.] The records of the Church during the year 1723 and 1724 present little of peculiar importance. In the former of these the prosecution of Mr. Gabriel Wilson of Maxton was terminated by an act of Assembly, acquitting him of the charges urged against him by the inferior courts. In the latter nothing memorable occurred.

[1725.] In the year 1725, a case arose which deserves specific mention. A vacancy having taken place in one of the churches of Aberdeen, the magistrates and town-council, who, as heritors, had a right along with the session to *propose* a person to the congregation for their approbation and *call*, thought proper to avail themselves of the Patronage Act, and claimed the power of appointing absolutely, without regard to the wish of the congregation. The synod disapproved of this procedure, and the magistrates appealed to the Assembly. The Assembly directed a new call to be moderated, and "appointed the inclinations of the heads of families that attended ordinances to be consulted."† When the new call took place, one hundred and thirty-nine heads of families voted for the person proposed by the town-council, a

* Acts of Assembly, year 1722. † Boston's Memoirs, p. 306.
‡ Acts of Assembly; Wodrow, MS. Letters.
§ See the cases of Mr Hepburn's call to Edinbugh, and Mr Francis Craig's to Kinross, related by Dr M'Crie,—Christian Instructor for Febuary 1832.

* Boston's Memoirs. † Unprinted Acts o Assembly.

Mr. Chalmers, minister of Dyke, and three hundred and seven against him. The Commission of Assembly, to whom the new call was reported, sustained it, several members expressing their dissent.

[1726.] The conduct of the Commission in thus sustaining the call of Mr. Chalmers, notwithstanding the dissent of a majority of the people, was brought before the Assembly of 1726. The Assembly, by a vote, "disapproved of the Commission's proceedings in the settlement of Mr. Chalmers at Aberdeen, upon these grounds, that they acted disagreeably to the instructions of the last Assembly, particularly in not making due inquiry, and *not having due regard unto the inclinations of the people;*" but, by another vote, they refused to rescind the Commission's sentence settling Mr. Chalmers, considering it not desirable to tamper with the Commission's powers, by recalling their decision in matters which they had been empowered to determine.* This is the first instance on record of a minister settled against the dissent of the people, subsequent to the Revolution; and even the proceeding was condemned by a vote of the General Assembly, and permitted to remain unrescinded only in consequence of a point of form in judicial procedure. And it may be regarded as a somewhat curious coincidence, that Aberdeen should again, as in former times, be the spot whence wrong and outrage to the Church and people of Scotland should begin.

In the same year a new edition of the Marrow of Modern Divinity was published, to which Boston contributed a number of copious and highly valuable explanatory notes.

[1727--28.] A new accusation was brought against Professor Simson, in the year 1727, charging him with holding and teaching Arian opinions. The culpable lenity of the former sentence of Assembly seems to have encouraged the unhappy man to persevere in his course of error, sinking deeper and deeper as he advanced. The subject had been partially under the notice of the preceding Assembly; but it was now formally taken up, a committee appointed to make due inquiries, and to ripen the affair for decision. It was brought before the Assembly of 1728, and sentence of suspension from teaching and preaching was passed, till the investigation should be completed, and a final decision given. In the same year, 1728, the Commission of Assembly sustained a call by the heritors, elders, parishioners of the parish of Alves, to Mr. Gordon, minister at Boharm, against a presentation by the patron, the Earl of Moray, to another person;* indicating clearly the opinion of the church courts at that time, that a call by the people was of more importance than a presentation by a patron.

[1729.] The Assembly of 1729 gave final decision in the case of Professor Simson. He had made, upon the whole, a skillful defence, though one which proved that his own mind was deeply tainted with sophistical insincerity; partly attempting to explain away his erroneous tenets by the aid of metaphysical subtleties, partly by strenuous assertions that he really held the very doctrines of the Confession of Faith. Great reluctance was manifested by the Assembly to pass a sentence due to his demerits; and the utmost that could be obtained was a confirmation of the previous sentence of suspension, with an additional declaration, that it was not fit that he should be further employed in teaching divinity and instructing youth designed for the ministry. Against this sentence, as totally inadequate to mark a due condemnation of such deadly heresy as he had taught, Boston rose and declared his dissent, in his own name and that of all who should adhere to him; and no other person expressing adherence, he continued, "and for myself alone, if nobody shall adhere."† A deep and solemn awe filled the Assembly, to see this great and good man placing himself sublimely in uncompanioned opposition to the weak and guilty unfaithfulness of a declining Church, and not a voice was raised in condemnation of his majestic Christian fortitude. The heretical professor yielded to the letter of the sentence; did not even attempt to defend his errors from the press, as had been apprehended; and, so far as he was personally concerned, the matter gradually sunk into oblivion.

But the secular leaven introduced into

* Unprinted Acts of Assembly.

* Commission Record, p. 200. † Boston's Memoirs, p. 354.

the Church by patronage was now beginning to work more potently, and to show its true nature and tendency. During the course of this year Principal Chalmers of King's College, Aberdeen, received a presentation to the parish of Old Machar, from the college as patron. A partial call appears also to have been procured, subsequent to the presentation. In the meantime a call was given by the parishioners to a Mr. Howie, and the presbytery sustained the call in his favour. The synod, however, reversed their sentence, sustained the call to the principal, who had the presentation, and actually inducted him. The matter was brought by appeal to the Assembly, who rescinded and made void the settlement, declared the parish vacant, and appointed the moderation of a new call. But Aberdeen tactics prevailed; and though the sentence of the Assembly was a clear affirmation of the principle that the opposition of the people was, in the estimation of the Church, more powerful to prevent than a presentation could be to secure a settlement, yet the wily principal contrived to procure a majority on the moderation of the new call: and, obtaining easily from his college a new presentation, was settled in the charge.* The second instance of a settlement by means of a "riding committee," took place this year in the case of New Machar, and soon afterwards became prevalent, in order to avoid the hazard of direct collision with the conscientious unwillingness of presbyteries to take part in transactions of a character so unconstitutional, unscriptural, and violent.

[1730.] A case of a somewhat similar kind was determined by the Assembly of 1730. This was the case of the parish of Hutton, in the presbytery of Chirnside. The matter came first before the Assembly of 1728, and was referred to the Commission, who were empowered to "determine in the affair as they should find just." The Commission appointed the presbytery to proceed to the settlement of Mr. Waugh, although he was opposed by a majority in the proportion of twelve to one of the congregation. The revising committee of next Assembly recommended that the directions given by the Commission should not be approved; and this part of the transactions of the Commission was excepted in the Assembly's attestation of the record of that court. But in March 1730, the Commission again directed the presbytery to proceed to the settlement, several members dissenting from this resolution, because the settlement of Mr. Waugh "being contrary to the mind of the congregation, was contrary to the laws of the Church." When the subject came before the Assembly of 1730 for final decision, they "refused to reverse the foresaid sentence [that of 1728], in respect the Commission had been empowered to determine finally in that affair;" resting the decision not upon the propriety of the Commission's sentence, but upon the fact of their having been empowered to pass it, thus virtually condemning the deed even in its ratification.* But this was almost the last decision of this half-faithful kind, made by the Assembly, which, from this time forward, followed generally the example of artful tyranny set by the Commission, appointing deputations of unscrupulous members to visit and overrule the objections of conscientious presbyteries, and to execute the harsh sentences of superior courts, trampling scornfully under foot the feelings of the aggrieved and outraged people.

It was now but too evident that the worldly spirit introduced into the Church by the admission of the prelatic incumbents, and by the Patronage act, had done its deadly work. A considerable number of men of decided talents, but utterly destitute of true Presbyterian principles, and guided solely by regard to secular policy, had sprung up and been elevated to the most influential positions in the Church. And while the hostility of the people against the exercise of patronage, which had been comparatively slight as long as the church courts abstained from giving direct countenance to it, was now becoming daily more decided, these leading men were preparing schemes for giving to that unconstitutional mode of appointing ministers an absolute and uncontrollable power. An apparently insignificant act passed by this Assembly contained the germ of the policy by which the first dynasty of Moderatism was to be regulated. By

* Acts of Assembly, years 1729, 1730.

* Acts of Assembly, 1730.

this act the General Assembly appointed, "that the reasons of dissent against the determinations of church judicatures, in causes brought before them, should not be entered in the register, but be kept *in retentis*, to be laid before the superior judicatures."* This act contains evidently the essence of ecclesiastical despotism, and is contrary to the very spirit of a church court, which being essentially a court of conscience, and its power being ministerial, not lordly, it never can with propriety refuse to its members the right of exonerating their own conscience from the moral responsibility of any measure of which, regarding it as sinful, they cannot and dare not approve. And instead of tending to promote schism, this liberty of recording dissent actually and strongly tends to prevent it, by leaving the minds of such members at peace, satisfied with having expressed their disapprobation, and the reasons on which it is grounded, which may serve, in some happier time, to bring back the Church to the path of rectitude, from which, in their opinion, she appears to be swerving.

[1731.] The proceedings of the Assembly of 1731 did not tend to allay the feelings of dissatisfaction excited by the last act of its predecessor. Actuated by the same spirit, the Assembly refused to permit a remonstrance against violent settlements to be read; and prosecuting their headlong career, they passed an "act and overture concerning the method of planting vacant churches." The object of this overture was to secure a uniform method of supplying vacant charges, without those delays and that irritation which too often occurred. The method proposed in this overture bore considerable resemblance to that of the act 1690, but was still less favourable to the privileges of the people. The chief difference consisted in this, that by the act 1690, the heritors and elders were "to name and propose the person to the whole congregation, to be either approven or disapproven by them;" by the overture, the heritors and elders were "to elect and call one to be the minister" of the parish. It is evident that this suggested method amounted to a virtual annihilation of the call, so far as that had always previously been regarded as conveying the mind of the congregation; and it is as evident that this was directly opposed to the principles and practice of the Presbyterian Church, from the period of the Reformation.*

The case of Kinross came also before this Assembly, and was referred to the Commission. This was one of the cases, formerly alluded to, which arose out of the Marrow Controversy, the settlement of Mr. Francis Craig being opposed on account of his refusing to condemn the doctrines contained in that work. But now that patronage was beginning to assume a more arbitrary power, and the want of a call or the opposition of the people might be disregarded, the patron found a youth of sentiments similar to his own, a Mr. Stark, and proceeded to force him upon the parish, in spite of the continued resistance of the people and reluctance of the presbytery. The Commission, nothing loath to undertake the ungracious task, ordered the presbytery to admit Mr. Stark without delay; and when the presbytery refused, and appealed to the next Assembly, the settlement was made through the ready instrumentality of a "riding committee."†

[1732.] The crisis came on apace. The tyrannical conduct of the leading men of the Church, who directed the proceedings of both Assembly and Commission, had excited a wide-spread and strong feeling of discontent; and when the Assembly met, a representation and petition, signed by forty ministers, was laid on the table, imploring that venerable court to redress the grievances and check the innovations which were threatening the speedy ruin of the Church. This important paper was not even allowed to be read; and, as if to add insult to injury, the complaint against the settlement of Kinross was dismissed, and the Presbytery of Dunfermline were ordered to receive, and enrol Mr. Stark as one of their members, and to do every thing towards giving him countenance in the ministry. Several of the members protested against such arbitrary procedure, but were not permitted to record their dissent. The overture transmitted to the presbyteries last year was enacted

* Acts of Assembly.

* See this subject ably discussed in Willison's Testimony, pp. 70-76.

† Another case occurred this year of the simple acceptance of a presentation without a call, and the presentee was suspended. (Patronage Report, p 364.)

into a standing law of the Church, in direct violation of the Barrier Act, it not having received the sanction of a majority of the presbyteries. In reality it had been condemned; eighteen presbyteries approved of it, eighteen returned no opinion, twelve required material alterations, and thirty-one were absolutely against it.* Yet the leading men of the Assembly contrived to procure its enactment, though they could not but be aware of its unconstitutional character,—so eager were they to clutch the reins and wield the rod of power.

It was now all but impossible to prevent an immediate schism. The dominant party might yet have abated in their reckless career of tyranny and oppression, and the aggrieved ministers and people might have laid aside their resentment, and, while they defended purity, still have been ready to accept of peace. But pacific measures appear not to have been contemplated by either. Indignant at the treatment he had received, especially in being prevented from recording his dissent from the injurious conduct of the Assembly, the Rev. Ebenezer Erskine, from his own pulpit in Stirling, denounced in strong terms the oppressive and sinful procedure of the church courts. This was but adding fuel to the flame, and his next step fanned it into a blaze. At the meeting of the synod of Fife in October, he preached a sermon, in which he boldly and keenly censured the growing corruption and degeneracy of the Church. The synod were deeply offended, condemned his conduct, and ordered him to submit to a sharp rebuke. This he refused to do, protested against their sentence, and appealed to the next General Assembly.†

[1733.] There seemed to be yet time and opportunity to prevent the threatened deplorable division in the Church, had the Moderate leaders been willing to "change their hand and check their pride." But they appear to have thought that one act more of "firmness" would secure them a complete and lasting triumph. They passed an act of sufficiently ominous title, "concerning some of the ministers of the presbytery of Dunfermline, and for preserving the subordination of the judicatures of the Church, and good order therein." By this act the faithful ministers of that presbytery were sharply rebuked, and commanded to support and encourage Mr. Stark, and strictly forbidden to admit any of the parishioners of Kinross to sealing ordinances, without the consent of their intruded minister, on pain of the highest censure. In the same haughty spirit they proceeded to consider the contest between Erskine and the synod. They speedily approved the proceedings of the synod, and appointed Mr. E. Erskine to be rebuked and admonished by the moderator at the bar of the Assembly.—Against this sentence Mr. Erskine protested; and to this protest were added the names of William Wilson, minister at Perth, Alexander Moncrieff, minister at Abernethy, and James Fisher, minister at Kinclaven. This protest was recorded, and the case of the four brethren remitted to the Commission, with full power first to suspend them, and then to proceed to higher censure, unless they should submit, express their sorrow for their conduct and misbehaviour, and retract their protest.*

The dissevering deed might be regarded as already done, when intrusted to the Commission. When the Commission met in August, they received from many quarters strong remonstrances against the imperious course so keenly pursued by the leaders of the Church, and urgent entreaties to try the effect of milder measures. In vain: the course of Moderate policy has ever been immitigable, when civil power was on its side. The four brethren gave in a written representation, defending their conduct; but the sentence of suspension was pronounced, and they were summoned to appear again before the Commission in November. By this time the whole kingdom was in a state of the most intense excitement, and many members of Commission began to shrink, and hesitate, and recoil from the deed which they had been empowered to do. Not so the Moderate leaders: with them the thought seems to have been,—"one bold stroke more, and the victory is our own." The sentence of suspension had not been obeyed, and the Commission was empowered to proceed to a higher cen-

* Gib's Display, vol. i. p. 26.

† True State of the Process.

* Acts of Assembly.

sure. This course was opposed; the question was put, "delay" or "proceed;" the votes were equal; the moderator, Mr. John Gowdie, one of the ministers of Edinburgh, rose; a death-like stillness reigned; the cause of mercy and truth, and the peace of the Church and community, or the paltry triumph of a secularizing policy and its partizans, seemed wavering on the balanced point of that passing moment: he gave his casting vote, "*proceed*," and the fatal deed was done, which Scotland to this hour deplores, and by which the welfare of the National Church, and the cause of Christianity itself in the land, sustained a grievous and almost irreparable injury, now too clearly manifest in our present sufferings and impending dangers.

The sentence actually pronounced was a modified form of deposition, being merely that they should be loosed from their respective charges, and declared no longer ministers of this Church, all ministers being prohibited from employing them in any ministerial function. Against this sentence several ministers protested; and the four brethren gave in a protestation of their own, which was subsequently expanded into a full statement of the reasons of their "secession from the prevailing party in the Church."* The public sympathized in general with men whom they regarded as persecuted for the cause of truth, and in defence of the constitutional rights and privileges of the Church and people of Scotland. Even yet there might have been a healing measure, and some attempts were made by the better part of the Commission to prevent any decisive steps from being taken by which all hope should be precluded. But the sense of wrong appears to have stimulated in the minds of the four brethren a degree of jealousy and impatience, which caused them to regard with distrust every overture of a peaceful character, and to assume an attitude of more resolute antagonism. On the 6th day of December 1733, they constituted themselves into an Associated Presbytery, retaining possession of their charges, but abstaining for a time from any acts of jurisdiction on their own authority.*

It is unnecessary to trace minutely the subsequent steps of this deplorable secession. That it was caused by the corrupt and tyrannical procedure of the church courts, we do not affect to deny; that this corruption and tyranny flowed directly from the admission of the prelatic incumbents at and after the revolution, from the lax and heterodox tenets which they and others like to them introduced, and from the pernicious influence of patronage we do not hesitate most strongly to assert. and we think it would require a very peculiar combination of sophistry and hardihood in any man who should venture to attempt a historical refutation of the assertion. Let it never be forgotten, that these pious and eminent ministers seceded, not from the Church of Scotland, but from that "prevailing party," the Moderates of the day, by whom heresy was screened, sound doctrine condemned, discipline neglected, the rights of Christian congregations violated, and their feelings outraged, and the scriptural government of the Church changed into a system of cruel and oppressive secular tyranny.

[1734.] The heartless and destructive wrong perpetrated by the Commission in their treatment of Ebenezer Erskine and his friends, had roused the feeling of the religious part of the community to the highest pitch of regretful solicitude; and great exertions were made that the next Assembly might contain a sufficient number of right-minded men, to get, if still possible, the fatal breach repaired. Even the Moderates were willing partially to retrace their steps, not having anticipated that their guilty deed would call forth so strong an expression of national indignation. No sooner did the Assembly meet than the work of attempted conciliation began. The act of 1730, prohibiting protests, and the act of 1732, for planting vacant churches, which had been the immediate causes of dispute, were both rescinded; and an act was passed declaring that ministerial freedom was not to be held as in any degree impaired by the late decisions. Another act was passed, empowering the synod of Perth to take into consideration the case of the seceding brethren, with a view to

* It was in their protest against this sentence of the Commission that the four brethren used the memorable words, "We hereby appeal unto the first free, faithful, and reforming General Assembly of the Church of Scotland." See their "Testimony," page 28, first edition, 1734; Gib's Display, vol. i. p. 35; Re-Exhibition, &c., p. 29.

* Gib's Display, vol. i. p. 36.

their restoration to their charges, without reference to former proceedings; which was accordingly done by the synod in July.* There seemed now no real obstacle to the return of the seceding brethren into the communion of the Church. But they had taken their ground, and felt so far bound in honour to maintain it; they had published a testimony to the doctrine, discipline, and government of the Church of Scotland, avowing their unaltered adherence to these, and stating the reasons of their secession, not from the constitution of the Church, but from the prevailing party in her judicatories. And scrutinizing narrowly the recent conciliatory acts, they conceived that they still saw reason to continue separate, till the Church should not merely rescind the unconstitutional acts of which they complained, but make an explicit acknowledgment of her sinful conduct in having ever passed them.

As the seceding ministers had appealed to the first reforming Assembly, this Assembly took one step more for proving its right to such an honorable designation. A deputation was sent to London from the Commission, to solicit a repeal of the act reimposing patronages; but this deputation was unsuccessful. The uncomplying attitude maintained by the seceding ministers discouraged the Evangelical party, and cast an early blight over their fondly cherished hopes of a reunion with men whom they highly esteemed; and this disappointment tended considerably to paralyze their own reforming exertions.

[1635.] Still a reforming spirit seemed to prevail in the Church, the Moderates abating their high-handed rule, and the Evangelical party endeavouring to restore to the light the buried principles of earlier and better days. A deputation was again appointed to proceed to London, and renew the application of the church for the repeal of the Patronage Act.† This was so far attended to, that leave was given to bring in a bill for this purpose; the bill was actually drawn up by the celebrated Duncan Forbes of Culloden, but meeting little support, it was abandoned. Several acute and able pamphlets were written on the subject, by men of high eminence, such as Professor Hutcheson, Currie of Kinglassie, and others, besides the address of the Assembly to his majesty, which was written by Lord President Dundas.*

The Commission was prohibited from appointing "Riding Committees," for the purpose of executing such sentences as presbyteries and synods declined to execute. And as great complaints had been made against the style of preaching which had become prevalent among young ministers, who introduced into their sermons "little that might not have been found in Seneca and Plato," an overture was transmitted to presbyteries for their approbation, giving directions respecting a more full and faithful exhibition of the peculiar doctrines of the gospel.†

[1936.] The seceding brethren continued to stand aloof, watching jealously the proceedings of the Church, and apparently more disposed to censure omissions than to applaud the honest endeavours of the struggling Evangelical party. That faithful body continued to strive for further reformation, but with weakened energy and diminished prospects of success. The address for the repeal of the Patronage Act was engrossed in the records of the Assembly of 1736, at least to testify the views and wishes of the Church. The act concerning preaching was passed, having received the approbation of the presbyteries. It is equally admirable in spirit and in substance; and deserves the serious regard of all ministers in the Church still, as a clear and pregnant directory for sound and evangelical preaching. The questionable doctrines of Professor Campbell of St. Andrews were brought under discussion; but he succeeded in giving to them such an evasive explanation as to save him from direct censure, though he was cautioned to avoid expressions which might lead the hearers into error. The last act of this Assembly deserves peculiar mention. It is entitled, "An Act against Intrusion of Ministers into Vacant Congregations," and contains these words:—"The General Assembly considering that it is, and has been since the Reformation, the principle of this Church, that no minister shall be intruded into any church contrary to the will of

* Acts of Assembly, year 1734; Willison's Testimony, pp. 81-83. † Acts of Assembly.

* Pamphlets of the period; Randall's Tracts. † Acts of Assembly.

the congregation, do therefore seriously recommend to all judicatories of this Church, to have a due regard to this principle in planting vacant congregations, so as none be intruded into such parishes, as they regard the glory of God and edification of the body of Christ."* There seems no reason to doubt that the majority of the Assembly was perfectly sincere in passing this act, when it is viewed in connection with the proceedings of the two former Assemblies; but there is as little reason to suppose that it had the approbation of the Moderate party, who, even in that reforming Assembly, were sufficiently strong to neutralize and pervert the operation of principles which they could not openly oppose. Some proceedings of the Assembly, the Commission, and the subordinate judicatories, supporting intrusive settlements about this time, gave to the seceding ministers the opportunity of declaring their distrust of the sincerity of the Assembly, and their resolution still to continue in a state of separation.

[1737.] The year 1737 is not remarkable for any event of importance in church matters, the foolish irritation of the government, on account of the Porteous mob, led them to emit an order, that a proclamation against the leaders of that strange riot should be read from all the pulpits, "on pain of being declared incapable of sitting in any church judicatory." This was resisted by a large proportion of the Church; and it deserves to be mentioned to their credit, that some of the Moderate ministers took a decided part in resisting this unconstitutioual procedure of the civil power. The seceding brethren received this year the accession of four others, the Rev. Messrs. Ralph Erskine, Dunfermline; Thomas Mair, Orwell; Thomas Nairn, Abbotshall; and James Thomson, Burntisland; and, encouraged by this accession, they published their first Act and Testimony, by the appearance of which document the prospect of reunion was very considerably diminished.†

[1738.] Deeply as the evangelical ministers of the Church deplored the conduct of the seceding ministers in thus increasing the obstacles to their re-admission into their former communion, they continued to offer peace. An act was passed by the Assembly, in which, after stating what was viewed as improper in the conduct of the seceding ministers, it was added,—"Yet this Assembly choosing rather still to treat them in the spirit of meekness, brotherly love, and forbearance, did, and hereby do, enjoin all the ministers of this Church, as they shall have access, and especially the ministers of the synods and presbyteries within which these seceding brethren reside, to be at all pains, by conferences, and other gentle means of persuasion, to reclaim and reduce them to their duty and the communion of this Church."* But all was in vain; to no proposals of "conferences and gentle means" would they listen; but began to take steps for training young men for the ministry, granting license to probationers, and completing their organization as a distinct and separate Church.

[1739.] All endeavours to prevail upon the seceding ministers to abandon their antagonist position proving ineffectual, the Assembly of 1739 called them before the court, to answer to a libel which the Commission had been empowered to frame, should all lenient measures fail. They came, but came in the temper of determined combatants. Aware of what was in progress respecting them, they had prepared a declinature of the Assembly's jurisdiction; and, previous to their appearing in the Assembly, they constituted themselves into a presbytery, and entering as a court, gave in this document by their moderator. Its very title was conclusive: "Act of the Associate Presbytery, finding and declaring that the present judicatories of this Church are not lawful nor right constitute courts of Christ; and declining all authority, power, and jurisdiction that the said judicatories may claim to themselves over the said presbytery."† Nothing now remained but for the Assembly to pass the sentence of deposition; but even yet they lingered, reluctant to cut of all hopes of seeing men, who were by many of them very highly esteemed, restored to the bosom of the Church. At the urgent solicitations of Willison of Dundee, and others, the Assembly consented to delay

* Acts of Assembly, year 1736. † Gib's Display Re-Exhibition, &c.

* Acts of Assembly, year 1738.

* Act and Testimony, &c.; Willison's Testimony, pp. 97, 98.

passing the sentence of deposition for another year, if even yet the Secession might be averted.

1740. The seceding ministers made no attempt to avail themselves of this pause, expressed no regret for what had taken place, and, instead of giving the slightest indication of a wish for peaceful reunion, continued to pour forth sharp invectives against the faithlessness and corruption of the Church. The Assembly passed the sentence of deposition on the 15th day of May 1740, and the seceding brethren, now eight in number, ceased to be minis ers of the Church of Scotland.*

It is impossible to trace the progress and mark the conclusion of this melancholy event without feelings of the deepest regret. A calm and dispassionate view may now be taken of the whole proceeding, which could not be done by those who were personally engaged in them; and such a view may well lead us to deplore the errors and the follies of wise, good, and pious men. There can be no doubt that the pernicious and sinful course of procedure, so perseveringly followed by the church courts, was the direct occasion of the Secession; yet it is as plain that it might have been averted, had not the pride of the contending parties impelled them to use toward each other language of sinful and irritating asperity. And without any wish to stain the memory of the Erskines, whom we deeply revere as eminently evangelical divines, it must be said that they indulged in applying terms of bitter reproach and angry vituperation against the Church, which no treatment could have justified, much less that forbearance which they experienced, both in the actions and in the writings of their opponents. It may also now be seen, that they committed a great error in not returning into communion with the Church, when, by the strenuous exertions of their evangelical friends, the door of readmission was opened to them in 1734. Their return would have greatly strengthened and encouraged that faithful band to continue their arduous task of reformation, and might have averted the long reign of secular principles, cold legal and moral preaching, and uncensured immorality, which, shaken and dethroned for a few brief years during that anxious struggle, too soon recovered their ascendency, and maintained their dreary and fatal sway for almost a century. And it cannot be doubted, that if the fathers of the Secession could have foreseen what principles would be adopted by their successors in later times,—could have anticipated the deadly warfare that would be waged against the very existence of the Church of Scotland, which *they* revered and loved,—they would not have taken a single step on the path that has led to such a strange and disastrous issue.

* Acts of Assembly.

Both the Church and those who seceded from her communion sinned, when they permitted human pride and wrath to fill their hearts and overcloud their better judgment; and the third and fourth generations are suffering, and may yet more deeply suffer, from the baneful consequences of their guilty conduct. Surely a time will come, if it has not come already, when those who hold the principles for the assertion of which the Erskines and their friends unwisely seceded from the Church, and in defence of which Boston and Willison, and such men, earnestly contended within it, will unite in the one great cause, the reassertion of the Redeemer's sole Sovereignty and Headship of his Church, which cannot but be held inestimably precious equally by both, —by all who know the import and have felt the power of that sacred and glorious truth. Yes, that time must come, whether soon or late, and it may be sooner than many think; for the hour of trial, like the fierce heat of the furnace, may melt and blend into closest union, materials which, in the frigid temperature of selfishness, had long remained in hard and sullen separation, contiguous yet uncombining.

[1741.] The transactions of the Assembly which met in 1741 present nothing memorable. The elevation of Mr. James Ramsay of Kelso to the moderator's chair, indicated very plainly that the Moderate party had regained the power of which they had been deprived by the vigorous exertions of the Evangelical party in 1734. Another event proved but too clearly that their temporary loss of power had not taught them to use it with greater gentleness. A complaint of the parishioners of Bowden against the decision of the Commission, ordering the presbytery to proceed to the settlement of an unacceptable presentee, was disregarded, on the ground that the Commission had not exceeded their powers; the presbytery were ordered to proceed without delay, on pain of being censured as contumacious; and, in case of their refusal, the synod was empowered to take the necessary measures for having the sentence of the Commission executed.* This, it will be observed, was in reality equivalent to a resumption of the scheme of effective intrusion settlements by means of "riding committees," which had been prohibited by the Assembly of 1735; and though the language of the prohibition was allowed to remain for a little longer in the instructions given to the Commission, yet in a very short time the tyrannical practice was again in full operation.

The sudden and complete reacquisition of power by the Moderate party had arisen in a considerable degree from the comparative paralysis to active exertion in church courts, which seized upon their opponents when the seceding ministers not only refused to accede to the overtures of peace which were offered to them, but even repelled the advances of their former friends with reproaches, invectives, and expressions of distrust. In their dejection they retired from the struggle, in which to have secured complete success, would have demanded their most strenuous and united exertions for many years, especially as the moderate party enjoyed more of the countenance of politicians than can ever be expected by men who act solely on Christian principles. But though they in a great measure abandoned the contest in church courts, they did not sink into the lethargy of dejection in other matters. They saw well that the course of Moderate policy was both introducing into the Church ministers who cared little for the spiritual welfare of the people, provided they could secure the emoluments of the charge;† and at the same time expelling men who were faithful and able ministers of the gospel, but could not submit to Moderate despotism. The only remedy which presented itself in such a deplorable state of matters, was for every faithful minister to be doubly zealous in the discharge of his own pastoral duties, by which vital religion might be preserved in at least some portions of the land, during this period of general defection. This was accordingly done, and the results very soon began to appear.

[1742.] The year 1742 will be for ever memorable, not only in the annals of the Church of Scotland, but in the history of Christianity, on account of the remarkable revivals of genuine religion which took place at that time in various parts of the country, particularly at Cambuslang and Kilsyth. It was at Cambuslang that this remarkable manifestation of spiritual power first appeared. The minister of the parish, the Rev. Mr. Macculloch, had been peculiarly earnest in preaching the characteristic doctrines of the gospel, regeneration and justification by faith, during the greater part of the year 1741; and a greater degree of quickened attention than usual began to appear in the congregation in the course of that winter, and early in the year of 1742. At length, on the 18th of February, the people who attended meetings for prayer, which had been previously established, manifested such a degree of intense anxiety for their spiritual interests, and such deep convictions and supplicating earnestness to hear of the Saviour, that Mr. Macculloch was constrained to preach to them almost daily, and to request the assistance of his friends in the ministry from other quarters. This naturally excited the attention of the kingdom; and ministers of the most undoubted piety, and the highest character for theological attainments and soundness of judgment, hastened to the spot, to satisfy their minds by personal investigation, and returned not only convinced of the reality of what they had seen, but filled with gratitude to God that they had enjoyed the privilege of beholding so glorious a proof of the convincing and converting power of the Holy Spirit. Among these may be mentioned Dr. Webster of Edinburgh, Dr. Hamilton and Messrs. M'Laurin and Gillies of Glasgow, Willison of Dundee, Bonar of Torphichen, and Dr. Erskine of Edinburgh, at that time a young man pursuing

* Acts of Assembly.

† "What must they think of a man that tells a reclaiming parish by word and deed, '*I'll be your minister in spite of your teeth; I'll have the charge of your souls, whether ye will or not; and if ye refuse ordinances and means of salvation from me, ye shall have none!*'" (Willison's Testimony, p. 54.)

his theological studies. The celebrated Whitefield, hearing of this remarkable event, hastened to Cambuslang, and preached repeatedly with his usual eloquence, and more than usual impressiveness.

In the beginning of May a similar scene of religious awakening took place at Kilsyth, under the ministry of the Rev. James Robe, a man of considerable abilities, who had been for some time an active defender of the constitutional principles of the Church against the corrupt and secular innovations of the Moderate party. The anxiety manifested by the people of Kilsyth was not inferior to that of the people of Cambuslang; and several adjacent parishes experienced a portion of the sacred influence so graciously vouchsafed by the Divine Visitant. Mr. Robe appears to have acted with consummate prudence, exercising the most vigilant care over those who came to him in deep distress of mind under conviction of sin, giving to them the most judicious instruction in spiritual truth, and keeping a private record of all cases of religious awakening, that he might deal with each according to its own peculiarities, mark the progress of the feelings and the knowledge of the people, and be able to discriminate between what was mere excitement, and what by its fruits proved itself to be true conversion. The subsequent publication of his Narrative gave to the religious community the means of judging as to the nature and extent of the remarkable work of the Holy Spirit in Scotland at that period; and it may be safely said, that the strength of prejudice must be very great in any man who knows what vital religion is, who can peruse that judicious production, without being constrained to glorify God, who had so graciously visited his people.*

Yet it is not easy to estimate the force of prejudice. It was to be expected that irreligious men would calumniate and deride the proceedings at Cambuslang and Kilsyth, and that the Moderate ministers, the greater part of whom regarded Christianity as merely an improved system of morality, and whose sermons were generally little more than carefully composed and coldly plausible moral essays, would look upon the whole as the delusion of heated enthusiasts and fanatics; but it could scarcely have been expected that such truly pious men and experienced ministers as were the fathers of the Secession should not merely have viewed these religious revivals with distrust, but should have assailed them with excessive bitterness.* They even proceeded to the extreme absurdity of appointing a solemn fast to be held on account "of the awful symptoms of the Lord's anger with this Church and land, in sending them strong delusion that they should believe a lie, particularly when a *judicial testimony* for the Reformation principles of this Church was emitted, after all other means had proved ineffectual." These good but narrow-minded and prejudiced men seem to have come to the conclusion, that the Church of Scotland was so thoroughly corrupt that it would be derogatory to the character of the Holy God to suppose that he could deign to visit her in mercy, and to revive his own work in a Church so fearfully polluted. Their deplorable conduct at this time ought to be a warning to every Christian Church, and to every body of professing Christians, not to think of themselves more highly than they ought, lest they come to despise those whom God hath not despised.

Many serious Christians, in that eventful time, were led into speculations of a different character,—as to what might be the probable object to be effected by these remarkable manifestations of convincing and converting grace,†—whether they might not be preparatory for some great advancement of religion throughout the world, such as sacred prophecy so emphatically foretells. It is at all times hazardous to attempt to explain the meaning of any peculiar dispensations of providence or grace, in a prospective point of view, and not surprising that men should err when they make the attempt. Nor is it easy to connect peculiar dispensations with subsequent events, so as to perceive what has been produced by them, even at the lapse of a century. Yet one or two remarks may be offered of a

* See Robe's Narrative; and the testimonies of many eminent ministers of the period; also Sir Henry Moncrieff's Life of Erskine, pp. 112-123; Gillies' Collections; and Life of Whitefield.

* To their writings on this subject we do not choose to refer more specifically, wishing them rather to sink into oblivion.

† Dr. Erskine's Signs of the Times, &c.

historical character, not perhaps unworthy of consideration. It will be remembered, that in different periods of the Church of Scotland's history, God was pleased to send her a time of refreshing from His presence; and that these were invariably before a time of searching trial, as if to give her a principle of sacred life sufficiently strong to survive the period of suffering. Such was the general revival in 1596, immediately before her protracted struggle with Prelacy under James. Such were the revivals of Stewarton, Shotts, and other places, a short while before her second great contest with Prelacy in the time of Charles I., and the wasting persecution of the two following reigns. And though no direct persecution followed the revivals of Cambuslang and Kilsyth, yet the long and dreary domination of Moderatism which immediately followed was more calculated to destroy vital religion in the land than could have been the most relentless persecution; and it seems no very strained conjecture, that these gracious influences were vouchsafed to the Church at that period, to sustain her during her lengthened sojourn in a moral and religious wilderness. Certain it is that the deep and earnest spirit and feeling of vital and personal religion passed not away like a temporary excitement. Not only did many hundreds of the converts of that period continue to exhibit the beauty of holiness throughout the remainder of their lives, proving the reality of the great change which they had experienced, but also the very knowledge that such events had taken place continued to operate, silent and unseen, but with mighty efficacy, in the hearts of thousands, constraining them to believe that there was more in true spiritual Christianity than could be expressed in a cold moral harangue, and rendering them quick to mark and eager to receive instruction of a more evangelical and living character.

And here, also, it may be fittingly stated, that although the First Reformation began, as it necessarily must have done, by the conversion of Romish priests, who thus became reformed ministers, and then taught the people, yet, as the Scottish Reformers gave to the people schools as well as churches, and communicated to them the highest amount of instruction which circumstances would permit, it repeatedly happened in subsequent times, that the people remained sound and faithful in the possession of true religious principles, long after a large proportion of the ministers had fallen into error. This was strikingly the case during the time of the persecution, when so many of the ministers accepted the indulgence, while the people maintained their integrity, although exposed to at least equal perils from the vengeance of prelatic informers and the licentious and cruel soldiery. This was the case after the Revolution, when the tortuous expediencies of worldly policy corrupted the church courts, and a false system of theology became prevalent among the ministers, long before the people were tainted by such low secular views, or imbibed such erroneous doctrinal tenets. And it may be added that it was for this very purpose that the law of patronage was brought forward by the Jacobites, who saw clearly that its operation would prevent the church courts and the people from acting together; and out of the alienation which it so soon and so fatally caused, arose in a great measure the baneful policy of the moderate party, who regarded with dislike the warm interest taken by the people in religious matters, and the decided preference which they showed to evangelical doctrine. It was perfectly manifest, that if the popular mind were to be consulted in any other way than as a mere matter of form, few except evangelical ministers would ever obtain admission to the Church; and, as has been already proved, having little knowledge of, and no love for, evangelical doctrine, they had no other way of securing their own admission to the Church as a *profession*, than by exerting themselves to the utmost in weakening popular influence by the rigid enforcement of patronage. Could they have contrived at once to have reduced the people to such a state of comparative ignorance of sound doctrine as to have felt little interest in one kind of preaching more than in another, there would have been no necessity for such strenuous exertions for the repression of popular rights and popular feeling; but as this could not be accomplished with the intelligent and religious people of Scotland, there was no resource but to reduce the popular consent to a mere empty form, and to crush the popular resistance by the strong arm of an unconstitutional law, surreptitiously thrust into the statute-book by infidels and traitors. Taking all these things into consideration, it will not be denied, that true Christianity as existing among the orthodox ministers and people of Scotland, was indeed entering into a long and dreary period of trial, and greatly needed an extraordinary infusion of spiritual life, that it might not become utterly extinct before the dawning of a brighter and a happier day.

[1743-49.] It does not appear necessary to occupy space in detailing the proceedings of the Assemblies year by year from this time forward, occupied, as they chiefly were, with discussions arising out of disputed settlements, and terminating generally in the same manner, the opposition of the people being disregarded, and the presentee appointed with or without the assistance of a military force, according to the amount of the opposition which had to be overcome. Some of these cases, however, involved the question respecting the jurisdiction of the civil courts, with regard to the settlement of ministers. In the case of Dunse, for instance, in 1749, one of the applications made to the civil court was, that they would arrest the proceedings of the church court, by forbidding them to moderate a call at large, or settle any other man than the presentee. "This conclusion the Lords would not meddle with, because that was interfering with the power of ordination, or internal policy of the Church, with which the Lords had nothing to do."* Several decisions of a precisely similar character were made by the Court of Session, indicating clearly the opinion of that court, that while it fell within their province to determine whether a settlement should carry with it the civil emoluments attached to the ministerial office, they were not entitled to interfere with the spiritual proceedings of the Church, either in conferring or withholding the ministerial character. Nor is there a single instance on record, till those of recent occurrence, in which the civil courts presumed to interfere with the ecclesiastical jurisdiction of the Church, to the extent of offering an opinion whether ordination should be given or withheld, even when patrons attempted to induce them to overstep their legitimate boundaries. When the Church ordained a person who was found not to have a legal claim to the fruits of the benefice, according to the law of patronage, the civil court decided that he could not receive it, but refused to order the Church to annul the pastoral tie of ordination, or to ordain the person to whom the legal presentation had been given. Of this, the case of Lanark is a remarkable instance, in which Dr. Dick remained minister of the parish, discharging all the pastoral duties for upwards of four years, while the patron was found to be entitled to retain the stipend.*

[1750.] In the year 1750, a subject came before the Assembly which seems to have exercised great influence upon its spirit and the whole course of its proceedings for many years. This was an overture respecting the small livings in the Church, many of which were not sufficient to yield a respectable maintenance. It was decided that a committee should be appointed to draw up a report to be laid before next Assembly. The Assembly of 1750 directed Dr. Cuming, the moderator, to proceed to London at the head of a deputation, to lay the report before government, and to apply for an augmentation. The nobility, gentry, and landed proprietors in general, took the alarm, and made preparations for the most strenuous opposition, although they were in possession of the teinds, which were always regarded as the patrimony of the Church, and subject to such augmentations from time to time as might be required. One of the methods employed by the heritors to defeat this rightful claim of the Church, was a threat that the law of patronage should be more stringently applied than it had hitherto been, and that presbyteries should not be allowed to evade it, by showing any deference to the people, as they had occasion ally done.† The result was, that the

* Brown's supplement, vol. v. p. 768; Annals of the Assembly, vol. i. p. 147. See also a remarkable paper by Lord Kames in his Law Tracts.

* Annals of the Assembly, vol. i. pp. 169-180.

† Ibid. pp. 190-95, 197.

scheme was defeated, and the Moderates were made to feel that the heritors were well contented to make use of them in taking away the rights of the people by the violation of the Revolution Settlement and the Treaty of Union, but were not disposed to refund any portion of their illegal pillage, which they possessed in consequence of that violation. This disappointment seems to have paralyzed the energies of Dr. Cuming, who had been the chief leader of the Moderate party for many years, and to have been the cause of a new developement of Moderate policy, which soon afterwards appeared, under the management of an abler and a bolder man.

[1751.] The first appearance of this new aspect of Moderate policy was in the case of Torpichen, which was decided in the year 1751. It had arisen three years before, when, after the death of Mr. Bonar, the last of the Marrow-men, a Mr. Watson was presented to the parish by the patron, to whose settlement the parishioners could not be persuaded to consent. Twice was the case brought before the Assembly,—in the years 1749 and 1750,—and the presbytery of Linlithgow were each time enjoined to admit Mr. Watson. But as the opposition continued, they declined to obey the ungracious injunction. They were rebuked by the Assembly of 1751, and again ordered to proceed; but in case they should still delay, a "riding committee" was empowered to effect the settlement, which was done on the 30th of May 1751, by the aid of a military force.* This was the last instance of a settlement effected by means of a "riding committee." That device, it will be remembered, had been adopted in order to accomplish the settlement of an unacceptable presentee, without doing violence to the feelings and conscientious scruples of presbyteries. But in this case a very strenuous attempt was made by William Robertson, minister of Gladsmuir, better known by his subsequent designation, Principal Robertson, to compel the presbytery to proceed to the settlement, on pain of suspension or deposition. In this he failed; but a new opportunity soon occurred for renewing his attempt to establish a more pure despotism than the Church of Scotland had previously known, and this time with complete success.

[1752.] This opportunity arose out of the disputed settlement of Inverkeithing. Mr. Andrew Richardson, minister at Broughton, had been presented to the parish of Inverkeithing, but was not acceptable to the parishioners. The presbytery of Dunfermline hesitated to proceed with his settlement, but were ordered to admit him, with certification, that the Commission would proceed to very high censure in case of their disobedience. They still declined compliance; and the Commission which met in March 1752 issued a new command to them to proceed, the sentence of censure not being carried, though lost by a narrow majority. When the case came before the Assembly, it gave occasion to a full developement of the principles of the new Moderate policy, which Robertson was determined to introduce. The form which the discussion assumed turned upon the proposition, "How far the members of inferior judicatories are bound to give effect to the sentences of superior courts, in opposition to the dictates of their own private judgment and conscience." This had been evaded by the device of the "riding committees;" but the pregnant hint recently given by the heritors, that the law of patronage would be more strictly enforced, and presbyteries not permitted to evade it as formerly, seems to have led Principal Robertson to the idea, that it would be more expedient for the superior church courts to govern their own subordinate judicatories, and thereby to gratify the heritors and regain their favour, than to leave the matter to the civil courts, and lose all hope of propitiating the heritors, without the possibility of acquiring popular support. The result may be briefly stated. Robertson's policy prevailed. The presbytery were commanded to proceed to the ordination of Mr. Richardson; and, as if to make the deed more glaringly despotic, it was commanded that not less than five members should be regarded as a quorum,—the usual number being three. Six of the presbytery declined even then to comply; and one of these, the Rev. Thomas Gillespie of Carnock, was deposed from the office of the ministry for contumacy. The venerable man, when the sentence was pronounced,

* Ibid. pp. 156, 181, 198-212; Patronage Report, Appendix.

meekly answered, "I rejoice that to me it is given, in behalf of Christ, not only to believe on Him, but also to suffer for His sake."* This tyrannical deed gave rise to the Secession which is known by the name of the Relief, and marks the commencement of the new Moderate dynasty.

Before the ultimate decision of this case had been pronounced, the two contending parties had publicly emitted what may be termed the manifesto of each,† the manifesto of the Moderate party being the production of Dr. Robertson. As this able paper contained the principles of ecclesiastical polity which guided Robertson's administration, has been referred to with strong approbation by his successor in church power, Principal Hill, and has continued ever since to be regarded, as in a great degree, the standard of Moderate church policy, it deserves some attention. It begins by a clear and forcible statement of what Robertson regarded as the first principle of society, regulated subordination, in which private judgment is so far superseded by the authority of the ruling power, that no member of society can avoid executing the orders of the supreme authority in any other way than by withdrawing from it. This principle he immediately applies to what he terms "ecclesiastical society," and proceeds to reason to the same conclusion, asserting boldly that the conscience of subordinate members is so far superseded by the orders of their superiors, whom they are bound to obey, that they are either not entitled to plead it, or are bound to withdraw; declaring strenuously, that "if the decisions of the General Assembly may be disputed and disobeyed by inferior courts with impunity, the Presbyterian constitution is entirely overturned." This forms the very essence of his argument; and every intelligent person, especially every thoughtful Christian, will at once perceive, that the analogy on which his argument is founded commences with a false principle, and consequently that the argument is vicious throughout, and the conclusion false. This analogy assumes, that there is in the Christian Church no principle different from those natural principles which form and regulate society. It contains no recognition of the scriptural basis of ecclesiastical authority. It even leads inevitably to the conclusion, that superior ecclesiastical authority ought to supersede the conviction of conscience to such an extent as to warrant the commission of what an individual regarded as *positively sinful*. But every truly religious man, who makes the Bible his rule, must see that this analogy is false, the argument founded on it vicious, and the conclusion inept and wrong. Can men, without any higher aid, make a church and frame laws for it as they can make a monarchy or a republic? Such a low secular view of the nature of a true Church was never entertained by the great men of the First and Second Scottish Reformations; such conclusions are utterly and irreconcilably at variance with the principles and the spirit of the Presbyterian Church. On the contrary, one of the fundamental principles of Presbyterian polity is, "That all church power is *ministerial*, and not *magisterial* or *lordly*." Whence it follows, that the duty of the office-bearers in a Christian Church, met together in the name of their only and Divine Head and King, to deliberate and act for the edification of his body the Church, is to endeavour, by prayer and by searching the Scriptures with earnest faith and singleness of heart, to ascertain what is the mind and will of Christ in the matter, and then to act according to the judgment of conscience thus enlightened by the Word of God, in all gentleness and brotherly love. This is the first principle of Presbyterian Church government, flowing from the great doctrine of the Headship of Christ; and every person capable of understanding the Bible, and acquainted with the Presbyterian constitution, must see that the opposite view is equally unscriptural and unpresbyterian. And it may be very safely affirmed, that no church court, actuated by this principle, and proceeding in this manner, could ever have arrived at the conclusion, that their obedience to the laws of the gospel required of them to perpetrate that grievous violence to the

* Annals of the Assembly, vol i. pp. 222-230, 262-271; Patronage Report, Appendix.

† See these two Papers in Morren's Annals of the Assembly, vol. i. pp. 231-260.

conscience of the Christian people, the members of Christ's body, which is involved in forcing them to listen to the instructions of a false teacher, or of one who, instead of feeding and protecting the flock as a shepherd, acts towards them as a ravening wolf, regardless of their spiritual welfare, provided he can secure the fruits of the benefice. Yet such unpresbyterian, unscriptural, unchristian principles, were promulgated by Robertson as the manifesto of the Moderate party, formed the rule of his long and vigorous administration, were lauded and followed by Hill, and have ever been regarded, by subsequent Moderate leaders, as the very standards of their policy, till the present time, when, finding that their own principles would lead to the direct condemnation of some of their own party, they have discovered that supreme ecclesiastical authority resides in the Court of Session, and that they are bound in conscience to render implicit obedience to its dictates in matters of ordination. Even this is natural: men who hold a false principle are inevitably led from bad to worse, far, very far, beyond what they at first would have conceived possible. It may be added, as pointing out the ultimate bearing of these brief remarks, that while the Moderate party would readily depose a minister for mere contumacy, or disobedience to the commands of his superiors, however sinful these commands might be in themselves, although they very generally screened immorality and heresy; the Evangelical or truly constitutional party could not depose except for some deed in itself sinful, either as immoral or heretical. No man who can estimate aright the true nature of ecclesiastical jurisdiction, will hesitate a moment to say which of these two modes of procedure is that which ought to be followed by a true Christian Church.

It is not denied that the constitution of the Presbyterian Church requires the submission of the inferior to the superior courts; for were that not the case, the Church of Scotland must sink into the Independent system; and in some of their arguments the minority of that period were not sufficiently guarded against that extreme. But while sound Presbyterian polity requires this due subordination of courts, it leaves the conscience of individuals free both to protest against, and to abstain from, actively assisting to carry into effect what they think sinful, provided they offer no actual opposition, having always this resource, that it can appoint others to execute its orders when that is still held necessary.

CHAPTER X.

FROM THE PERIOD OF THE SECOND SECESSION TILL THE ASSEMBLY OF 1841.

Struggle against the new Moderate Policy—Defence of Hume and Kames—Assessment for the Poor—Cases of Nigg and Jedburgh—Overtures respecting the Elders—Home and the Theatre—Schools in the Highlands—Simony—The Relief Secession formed—Character of the Moderate Party in Preaching, Discipline, Secularity, &c.—The Schism Overtures—Intrusion Settlement at St Ninians—Increase of the Secession, and the Consequences viewed statiscally—Repeal of Popish Disabilities—Debate on Pluralities—Retirement of Principal Robertson from the General Assembly—Causes of his Retirement—Proposal of the Moderates to abolish Subscription to the Confession of Faith—Dr. Hill—Proposal to abandon the Moderation of a Call—Dr. Cook's Theory of the Settlement of Ministers—Dr. Hardy's views concerning Patronage—Discussion on the Subject of Patronage—Opinions of Dr. Hill and Dr. Cook—Declining State of Religion in Scotland—A settlement without Subscribing the Confession of Faith—The New-Light Controversy in Ayrshire—Robert Burns the Poet—Socinianism—Excitement at the Period of the French Revolution—Revival of a Religious Spirit generally—Christian Missions—Opposed by the Moderate Party—Chapels of Ease—Rowland Hill—Refusal of Ministerial Communion with all other Churches, which completes the Moderate System—Rapid Growth of Evangelism—Contest between Dr. Hill and the Edinburgh Doctors—Dr. Andrew Thomson—Dr. M'Crie—Debates on Pluralities—Dr Chalmers—Decline of Moderatism—Mission to India—Apocrypha Controversy—The Voluntary Controversy—Ascendancy of the Evangelical Party—Admission of Chapels of Ease—Subsequent Contentions and Struggles—Present Position—Concluding Remarks and Reflections.

The decision of the Assembly of 1752, in the case of Inverkeithing and the presbytery of Dunfermline, followed by the severe and despotic measure of Mr. Gillespie's deposition, gave rise to feelings of strong indignation and alarm throughout the kingdom. A general apprehension prevailed among the friends of religious liberty, that the reign of absolute and spiritual despotism was now indeed begun in Scotland, since the General Assembly had committed a deed distinctly subversive of the first principles of the Presbyterian constitution, which had always hitherto been the very citadel of freedom, civil and religious. The subject was discussed with great anxiety in many of the synods and presbyteries; overtures were framed for the purpose of obtaining a repeal of the Assembly's decision, and the restoration of Mr. Gillespie to his charge; and numerous pamphlets were written both against and in defence of the new developement of Moderate ecclesiastical polity. Great exertions were also made by the orthodox party to procure a return to next Assembly of a sufficient number of true Presbyterians to reverse the recent despotic and unconstitutional measure; and not less strenuous were the Moderates on their part to retain their ascendancy and confirm their new position.

[1753.] When the Assembly met in 1753, it speedily appeared that the struggle was to be of a very arduous and doubtful character. A comparative trial of strength arose on the question respecting the election of a legal agent for the Church, and in this Dr. Cuming, the recognised Moderate leader, was defeated. But this defeat seems to have had the effect of leading to a greater degree of union in that party, and a more determined effort to secure their predominance. The case of Mr. Gillespie came next under consideration; and the question proposed for the vote was, whether he should be restored to the exercise of his office as a minister of this Church or not. It was decided in the negative by a majority of *three.* Next day an attempt was made to procure the remission of the subject to the Commission, with power to that court to restore Mr. Gillespie, if he should make application; but this also was resisted, and again lost by the narrow majority of three.* A considerable number of ministers and elders dissented from these decisions of the Assembly, and gave in their reasons of dissent, which the ruling party prudently abstained from attempting to answer. By these reasons it was made clearly to appear that the sentence of deposition had been pronounced on account of an alleged offence, against which there existed no law declaring it to deserve deposition; while the whole practice of the Church, in similar cases, had not gone beyond censure, so that the sentence of itself was unconstitutional if tested by the laws of the Church, and unchristian by those of the Scriptures.† But the Moderate party had the possession of power, and they could therefore the more easily set aside right and disregard reason. Besides, since the laws of civil society demand complete subordination, therefore, according to the fundamental maxim of the new Moderate dynasty, "ecclesiastical society" must be governed in the same manner. Had the supporters of this principle followed it to its legitimate conclusions, they would have found themselves the advocates of the hideous doctrines of entire slavish obedience to tyranny in the State and Popery in the Church,—that is, to absolute despotism, civil and religious. For whatever takes away the right of private judgment, commanding implicit obedience, especially in matters of religion, to use the language of the Confession of Faith, "destroys liberty of conscience, and reason also," reducing men, as far as it is possible, to the condition of irresponsible and unreasoning slavery. "But you are not compelled to obey, if your conscience forbid you: it is in your power to withdraw." Such was the language of the manifesto, and still is the language of those who hold the same principles. To that the ready answer was given: "Who empowered you to frame laws contrary to the constitution of the Presbyterian Church, which you have sworn to obey and maintain, and contrary to the laws of the Christian Church, given by Him who alone is Lord of the conscience, and then to punish men because they adhere to the constitution of the Church of their fathers, and, when charged with disobeying your laws, answered, with the apostles, 'whether it is right to obey God or man, judge ye?'" Such were the opinions entertained, and arguments used, by the evangelical ministers of the Church of Scotland, in that time of struggle against a party who did not scruple to subject every spiritual consideration to the arbitrary rules of secular policy. It was not, perhaps, to be expected that secular politicians would perceive the fallacy which lay at the source of the Moderate system; but it might surely be hoped that they would be able to mark the pernicious results that have followed, and to arrive at the very simple and obvious conclusion, that the cause must be essentially bad which has produced such consequences.

* Annals of the Assembly vol. i. p. 278. † Ibid., vol. ii. p. 21.

It will not be difficult to trace the main lines of the historical demonstration.

Among the pamphlets which this contest between the two parties drew forth, by far the most remarkable was "Witherspoon's Ecclesiastical Characteristics." This was published in September 1753, and immediately acquired great celebrity, both in Scotland and England. The wrath of the Moderate party, whose maxims of ecclesiastical policy is so keenly satirized, was excessive; but they wisely abstained from attempting to answer it. And it may be safely said, that if any impartial person would take Dr. Robertson's Manifesto, and Witherson's Characteristics, and peruse them both candidly, looking also into the records of the Church courts under Robertson's administration, he would find himself constrained to admit that the Moderate policy had been fairly and justly characterised.

[1754–55.] The transactions of the years 1754 and 1755 present little deserving to be recorded. In the former the case of Biggar was terminated by a compromise. In the latter there arose a discussion, respecting the infidel writings of David Hume, which the Assembly condemned, without however, naming the author, which would not have been convenient, as he was living in terms of friendly intimacy with several of the Moderate leaders. A short time after the rising of the Assembly, Hume was defended by Dr. Blair, in a pamphlet published anonymously, to avoid the unseemliness of a teacher of religion being the avowed defender of one who made no secret of his infidelity. The speculations of Lord Kames were at the same time brought under consideration, and were virtually included in the same censure; although it seems to have been felt that they might be regarded as little more than the idle mental discussions of an eccentric man of genius, and not likely to be productive of serious injury to the cause of truth.* One apparently slight circumstance incidentally stated by Sir Henry Moncreiff, deserves to be mentioned as connected with this year; it is, that the resources of the kirk-sessions continued to be sufficient for the maintenance of the poor, without any regular assessment, till the year 1755, when the increase of the Secession, withdrawing numbers of people from the pale of the Established Church, and to the same extent dimtnishing the collections, rendered it necessary to resort, in some instances, to regular assessments to supply the growing deficiency.* This was one of the fruits of patronage on which its admirers had not probably calculated, when they planted that deadly upas tree in the vineyard of the Scottish Church. By enforcing patronage they first caused a Secession; and by continuing their infatuated procedure they nourished its growth, till the effects began to appear in the form of diminished resources for the maintenance of the poor, which they were compelled themselves to supply. Still, as if smitten with judicial blindness, they continued, and till this day continue, to enforce a system which, if persevered in, can end in nothing but the overthrow of the Presbyterian Church, and the imposition of a national poor-rate, vastly more expensive to the community, and, at the same time, a fertile nursery of immorality and crime.

[1727.] The assembly of 1756 signalized itself by its decision of the case of Nigg in Ross-shire. That parish had enjoyed the blessing of a faithful evangelical minister, Mr. John Balfour; and upon his death the next presentee was not only of a totally opposite character with regard to doctrine, but was also accused of drunkenness, which accusation was only *not proved* against him. Great opposition was made to the settlement by the pious parishioners, and equal reluctance was manifested by the majority of the presbytery to perpetuate the outrage commanded by the superior courts. But the fate of Gillespie was before their eyes; and under a strong feeling of sorrow and regret, four of the presbytery repaired to the church of Nigg, to discharge the painful duty. The church was empty; not a single member of the congregation was to be seen. While in a state of perplexity what to do in such a strange condition, one man appeared, who had it in charge to tell them, "*That the blood of the parish of Nigg would be required of*

* Annals of the Assembly, vol. ii. pp. 54-60. See also, Life of Kames, by Lord Woodhouselee.

* Life of Erskine, Appendix, p. 409

*them, if they should settle a man to the walls of the kirk.** Having delivered solemnly this appalling message, he departed, leaving the presbytery astonished and paralyzed. They proceeded no further at the time, but reported the case to the Assembly of 1756. They were rebuked for having failed in that implicit obedience which was now the rule of duty under the *Moderate* government of the Church; and the minister who was most opposed to the settlement was the very one appointed to carry it into effect. He yielded. Mr. Patrick Grant was "settled to the walls of kirk;" and the outraged people of Nigg built a meeting-house for themselves, leaving to the wretched intruder his benefice, on which to batten, without a flock to tend.

The case of Jedburg came before this Assembly, though its final decision did not take place till two years afterwards. The parishioners of Jedburgh had almost unanimously petitioned that the Rev. Mr. Boston of Oxnam, son of the celebrated Boston of Etterick, might be their minister. The presentation, however, was given to Bonar, grandson of Bonar of Torphichen; but when he found the inclinations of the people so decidedly fixed on Mr. Boston, he resigned the presentation. The patron might now have consulted the wishes of the people; but that would have been contrary to the principles of the mild government of Moderatism, and therefore a new presentation was given to another person, not likely to commit the fault of which Mr. Bonar had been guilty.

[1757.] The first subject which engaged the attention of the Assembly in the year 1757, arose out of objections against the commissions of the elders from six or seven different Presbyteries. The defect urged against these commissions was, that they did not bear that the elders were qualified according to the act 1722, in which specific mention is made that elders should be "strict in their observation of the Lord's day, and in regularly keeping up the worship of God in their families." The orthodox and constitutional ministers argued that these commissions ought to be rejected as invalid, on account of this serious defect, justly regarding personal religion as the first qualification for an office-bearer in the Church, and concluding that no man could be personally religious who neglected public and family worship. But it would not have suited Moderate policy to have held the possession of personal religion as an indispensable qualification of an office-bearer in the Church. The only qualifications which they regarded as absolutely indispensable were,—for a minister, that he had received a presentation from a patron,—and for an elder, that he possessed political influence, or was connected with those who did. And the practice was about that time introduced, which soon became the settled custom, of ordaining young lawyers to the eldership, that they might sit in Assemblies, exercise their oratorical powers, and swell the Moderate majorities. It was evident that they might discharge all these functions without any personal religion; and therefore the Moderate party strenuously resisted the attempt to have an attestation of their possessing that qualification declared to be indispensable. The Moderates were successful by a considerable majority; and thus another glaring violation of religious principle and the constitution of the Presbyterian Church was perpetrated. The evil consequences of this irreligious decision were clearly pointed out by Witherspoon, in a dissent which he laid on the table of the Assembly; and they have been completely realized, as the sufferings of the Church even yet too clearly prove.*

The next matter which came before the Assembly, after having occupied the attention of a number of the subordinate church courts in different parts of the country, was one which had its origin in the elegant studies and amusements of the Moderate clergymen. The Rev. John Home, minister of Athelstanefore, the eager supporter of Robertson in procuring the deposition of the pious and conscientious Gillespie, had composed the tragedy of Douglas; and when it was represented in the Edinburgh Theatre, both the author and many of his clerical friends were present at the representation. This gave great offence to a large proportion of the Church, both ministers and people, who very justly regarded such conduct as giving countenance to

* Annals of the Assembly, vol. ii. pp. 77-80; Patronage Report, Appendix.

* Annals of the Assembly, vol. ii. pp. 102-108.

the gross profanity and licentiousness of the stage itself, and the still grosser immoralities which haunt its precincts. The result was, that Home resigned his charge; and his play-going friends, the most distinguished of whom was Dr. Carlyle of Inveresk, submitted to be rebuked and admonished.*

[1758.] In the year 1758 Dr. Robertson was translated from Gladsmuir to Edinburgh; and from that time his ascendancy in church courts, which had already nearly superseded that of Dr. Cuming, became altogether paramount, and remained unshaken till he voluntarily withdrew upwards of twenty years afterwards. In the same year Boston of Oxnam, grieved with the proceedings of the church courts, both in their utter disregard of the feelings, wishes, and edification of the people, and in the culpable leniency shown to clerical delinquents, gave in to the presbytery of Jedburgh his demission of the charge of Oxnam, and ceased to be a minister of the Church of Scotland. The people of Jedburgh, finding all their endeavours to obtain him as minister of the parish ineffectual, built a church, and gave him a call to be their pastor. This call was signed by the town council, the session, and all the heads of families except five. On the day of his admission the magistrates attended in all their official dignity, and the new church was crowded by at least two thousand people.† He was ordained by a Mr. Mackenzie, who had once been minister of Lochbroom, but was then minister of a dissenting congregation in England, and afterwards was called to be their pastor by the injured people of Nigg. This loss to the Church of a faithful minister and a warm-hearted congregation, was a fitting celebration of Dr. Robertson's translation to Edinburgh, and accession to unlimited ecclesiastical power.

A representation was laid before this Assembly, by the Society for Propagating Christian Knowledge, respecting the deficiency of parish schools in the Highlands. From this document it appeared, that there were in the Highlands no less than one hundred and seventy-five parishes where there were no parochial schools, and where the heritors neglected or refused to provide them, notwithstanding the urgent entreaties and remonstrances of the society. In one point of view this was not strange. The greater part of the Highland heritors were both Papists and Jacobites, and consequently had no love for the propagation of religious knowledge, and as little for the extension of the Presbyterian system, which paralyzed their rebellious tendencies, as they themselves had formerly owned in their complaints against new churches and schools. But it might have been anticipated that under a Protestant government, the law which declared that there should be a school in every parish would have been put into execution, and that the supplementary exertions of this truly Christian society would not have been pleaded as an excuse by the heritors for their own neglect of duty. The discussion of this subject was ultimately attended with the most beneficial results, in the erection of about forty new churches in the Highlands, with an ordained minister in each, though the admission of these ministers into church courts did not take place till a very recent period, when a more constitutional spirit had begun to prevail.

[1759.] The only thing which merits attention in the year 1759 is the passing of the act against Simony, which had been rendered necessary to prevent the disgraceful pactions entered into between patrons and presentees in many instances, especially since the law of patronage had begun to be so steadily enforced. This kind of crime had been distinctly foreseen, as certain to arise out of patronage; and while this act condemns the sinful consequences, it by implication condems also the sinful cause.

[1760-65.] No new principles, either of evil or of good, obtained developement during the years between 1760 and 1765, and, therefore, they may be passed rapidly over, merely glancing at some events which illustrate the topics already stated. A deputation was sent to the Highlands, to explore the state of religion in those remote districts; and a full report having been laid before the Assembly, that venerable court strongly recommended the erection of new churches and parochial districts, the ministers of which were to be supported out of the royal bounty.

Annals of the Assembly, vol. ii. pp. 112-129.
† Ibid., vol. ii. pp. 154-159.

The violent settlement of Kilconquhar, on the decision of the Assembly in 1760,* caused the secession of a large body of the people of that parish, and gave occasion to the completed form which the second Secession assumed in the course of the following year. A new church was built by the aggrieved people, and on the 22d of October 1761, the Rev. Thomas Gillespie, formerly of Carnock, and the Rev. Thomas Boston, formerly of Oxnam, together with a Mr. Collier, met at Colinsburgh in Fife, and constituted themselves into the Presbytery of Relief, the reason of assuming that designation being, that they took this method of obtaining *relief* from the intolerable despotism of patronage. The course of defection, meanwhile, continued to proceed rapidly, deepening, expanding, and pouring on like an inundation. The doctrines of the gospel were superseded by cold and formal harangues respecting the "beauty of morality," and the "*good of the whole*," couched in as much elegance of style as these reverend essayists could achieve. The greater part of the pulpit productions of those times which have been preserved from oblivion are certainly not such as to do much honour to the talents, judgment, or even taste of that class of men by whom they were elaborated. Even Blair's Sermons, which reached the highest pitch of excellence that Moderate pulpit oratory could aspire to, have long since lost their factitious popularity, and sunk to that dead level of monotonous lethargy in which must for ever slumber all that is destitute of true spiritual life. But while the vital principles of the gospel were in general very carefully excluded from the sermons of the Moderate clergy, an infusion of a different nature was readily admitted. Heresy of various kinds sprang up, chiefly derived from the strong taint of Arminianism which the Prelatic incumbents introduced into the Church. Pelagianism naturally followed; and the downward progress continuing, many began to entertain views very closely bordering upon Socinianism. To this the writings of Taylor of Norwich very greatly contributed, which about this time had become extremely popular among a certain class of the Moderate ministers, especially in the west of Scotland in Galloway. But when charges of heresy against any minister were brought before the Assembly, they were invariably discouraged, and the charge repelled; and on one occasion, the faithful minister who had brought forward the charge was actually reproved for his conduct, and warned "not to be over ready to fish out heresies."* Several very glaring cases of violent intrusion occurred: such as that of Kilmarnock, in 1764; and that of Shotts, in 1765, where the presbytery had rejected Mr. Wells on his trials, as being, if not *wholly deficient*, yet so *low* and *mean* in the knowledge of divinity, that he did not come up to the character of a minister of the gospel. Yet the Assembly reversed this judgment, and ordered him to be ordained; and when the opposition of the people was so great that it could not be accomplished in the parish, he was ordained in the session-house at Hamilton. Many cases occured, also, of such atrocious immorality, that it is not fitting to stain these pages with their recital;† and yet all these cases were defended, and the delinquents screened, by the Moderates, till, in some of them, the strong indignation of insulted public decency compelled the sentence of deposition to be passed. Such were some of the glories of Principal Robertson's administration, so lauded in his own day, so closely followed by his immediate successors, and held in such high honour still by many who warmly applaud and eagerly emulate what they painfully feel and deeply deplore that they cannot rival.

It may seem a very pertinent question to ask, how such criminal conduct could be permitted to pass unpunished, much more, how it could be sheltered by church courts under the management of Principal Robertson, a high-minded, honorable man, whose own moral character was altogether unimpeachable. Simply because his views of church government were directly anti-scriptural, founded upon a worldly principle, and pervaded throughout by worldly considerations. In his mind the idea of an Established Church was exceedingly simple, and exceedingly

* Annals of the Assembly, vol. ii. p. 201.

* Annals of the Assembly, vol. ii. p. 182.

† See annals of Assembly—cases of Professor Brown, Dalrymple of Dallas, Carson of Anwoth, Park of Old Monkland, Lyell of Lady Parish, and Nisbet of Firth and Stenness.

false. He regarded it as merely a subordinate court, created by the State, and possessed of no authority but what was derived from human laws. Wherever, therefore, he found a human law, there he formed an imperative rule; and all arguments brought from the direct language of Scripture, the principles of the gospel, or the recoiling of a tender and enlightened conscience, were by him entirely disregarded. His administration certainly deserves the praise of consistency, but as certainly it was a terrible consistency of direct opposition to the fundamental principles of Christianity, and of the Presbyterian Church, to whose standards he had subscribed his name, with all the grave deliberateness required in him who in the sight of heaven takes a solemn oath. How he reconciled his own conscience to such awful principles and conduct cannot be known; and it is not for man to judge his fellow-man. Yet the cold and scarce-approving account he gave of the Reformation,—his more than ambiguous views of the Mosaic record,—the scornful terms in which Hume dared to write to him respecting John Knox and the Scottish reformers,—and his own published letters to Gibbon, not to mention other letters similar, but worse, which have never seen the light,—all concur in rendering it sadly dubious whether he did himself fully comprehend and believe the gospel.* Even in the judgment of charity such a doubt may find admission, rather than the unutterably more fearful surmise, that he and his party knew the gospel, and intentionally trampled on its holy and merciful laws,—felt the full meaning and power of the apostle's command, "Be not lords over God's heritage," yet chastised the Christian congregation with scorpions,—knew what the true bread of life was, yet gave to the people stones and serpents.

There would be no difficulty in giving a still more appalling exposure of the principles and the practice of that party, then and still known by the designation of the Moderate party, who, after a long struggle, had succeeded in usurping the government of the Church of Scotland, and under whose baleful domination truth was stifled, faithfulness punished, piety expelled, conscience outraged, heresy protected, immorality permitted to prevail almost uncensured, and the Christian community injured and despised.* But we turn from the ungracious task, and hasten forward, purposing to touch only the prominent points, that arrest the attention, and demand remark and explanation.

[1766.] The Assembly of 1766 was memorable on account of the overtures respecting schism which came before it, and occasioned a long and animated discussion. The rapid increase of the Secession had excited alarm in the minds of many who saw the pernicious consequences likely to ensue from the abandonment of the National Church by so large a proportion of the people. The overture states, that there were already no fewer than one hundred and twenty meeting-houses erected; and, viewing this as a just cause of anxiety, and contrary to the very nature of a national establishment, which is of necessity intended for the religious instruction of the whole community, it was proposed to inquire into the truth of this fact; and assuming "that the abuse of the right of patronage had been one chief occasion of the progress of the Secession, it was overtured that the General Assembly would be pleased to consider what methods may be employed to remedy so great an evil; and it was submitted whether it might not be expedient to appoint a committee to correspond with Presbyteries, and with gentlemen of property and influence, and and to report."† After a very long debate, the Assembly agreed to abandon the proposed inquiry into the number of meeting-houses. The remaining part of the overture was then discussed and rejected by a vote of ninety-nine to eighty-five.‡ Thus the supreme ascendancy of the Moderate party was again secured, after having encountered a more severe assault than had been made upon it since 1752. The arguments on both sides turned chiefly upon the subject of patronage, and were almost identical with those which are employed for and against it in the present day. Indeed, there can be little difference in the modes by which that violation of Christian principle and

* See the opinion of Wilberforce in his Practical View, p. 304, fifth edition.

* Should this view be disputed, it shall, however reluctantly, be amply proved.
† Annals of Assembly, vol. ii. p. 311. ‡ Ibid., p. 329.

of the constitution of the Presbyterian Church is assailed, and its defence attempted. "Is patronage the law of the gospel?" "It is at least the law of the land." "Is it consistent with the fundamental principles of the Reformed Presbyterian Church of Scotland?" "The civil magistrate has at least always attempted to introduce and enforce it, in spite of the opposition made by the Church." "Was it the law of the Revolution Settlement and the Union?" "No matter; it was made by the law since, and it is the law now." "Has it not alienated the affections of the people, driven them to a large and increasing Secession, and thereby frustrated so far the very object of an Established national Church?" "No matter how many leave it; they are perfectly at liberty to do so; and there will be the more ease and peace for those that remain." These were the main lines of argument employed by those who wished to remedy the evil, and those who refused to admit that it was an evil, and wished its permanent continuation; and though it was perfectly clear that Scripture, reason, constitutional law, and Christian feeling, all alike condemned it, yet the vote of a Moderate majority could set them all aside.

The same year witnessed the demission of another minister, the Rev. Mr. Baine of Paisley, who joined the Relief Secession, and became minister of one of their churches newly erected in Edinburgh. It may be mentioned, that the Seceders were by no means pleased with what was termed the schism overture, having no desire to be regarded as schismatics, and still retaining the principles of the fathers of the Secession, who earnestly declared that they did not withdraw from the Church of Scotland, but from a prevailing party, by whom its government was usurped, and all its principles violated.*

[1767-73.] The agitation caused by this keen contest did not soon pass away. Numerous pamphlets appeared on the subject from time to time, some written by ministers of the Church, some by Seceders, and some by laymen, who saw and lamented the injurious effects which the unmitigated exercise of patronage, under the management of the Moderate party, was producing. In the meantime the Moderates continued their reckless career. One instance may be briefly mentioned. Mr. Thomson, minister of Gargunnock, was presented to the parish of St. Ninians; but the whole parish was opposed to his settlement, some Episcopalians, who cared nothing about the matter, and a few non-resident heritors, being all that could be prevailed upon to concur in his call. The presbytery remonstrated with the patron, the presentee, and the General Assembly, but all in vain. Seven years of useless and evasive litigation in church courts passed over; and at length, in 1773, the Assembly issued a peremptory order to the presbytery to proceed to the ordination, and every member to be present. The presbytery met at St. Ninians; an immense crowd had assembled; and Mr. Findlay of Dollar began the religious duties which precede ordination and induction. He then paused, and called upon Mr. Thomson, who stood up to listen to the moderator's address. Instead of proceeding to put the usual questions, he made one of the most solemn and pointed appeals to the unhappy intruder that ever was addressed to a human being:—"We are met here this day to admit you minister of St. Ninians. There has been a formidable opposition made against you by six hundred heads of families, sixty heritors, and all the elders of the parish except one. This opposition has continued for seven years by your own obstinacy; and if you should this day be admitted, you can have no pastoral relation to the souls of this parish; you will never be regarded as the shepherd to go before the sheep; they know you not, and they will never follow you. You will draw misery and contempt upon yourself—you will be despised—you will be hated—you will be insulted and maltreated. One of the most eloquent and learned ministers of this Church told me lately that he would go twenty miles to see you deposed; and I do assure you that I and twenty thousand more friends to our Church would do the same. What happiness can you propose to yourself in this mad, this desperate attempt of yours, without the concurrence of the people, and without the least prospect of usefulness in this parish? Your admission into it can only be re-

* Letter by Adam Gib.

garded as a sinecure, and you yourself as *stipend-lifter* of St. Ninians, for you can have no further relation to this parish. Now, Sir, I conjure you by the mercies of God, give up this presentation; I conjure you, for the sake of the great number of souls of St. Ninians, who are like sheep going astray without a shepherd to lead them, and who will never hear you, will never submit to you, *give it up;* I conjure you, by that peace of mind which you would wish in a dying hour, and that awful and impartial account which in a little you must give to God, of your own soul, and of the souls of this parish, at the tribunal of the Lord Jesus Christ, GIVE IT UP!" There was silence, breathless, profound, awe-struck silence, for a space. At length the heartless man made answer, "I forgive you, Sir, for what you have now said—may God forgive you; proceed to obey your superiors." Again there was silence; then in a low melancholy tone of voice, Mr. Findlay, omitting all usual forms, slowly said,—"I, as moderator of the presbytery of Stirling, admit you, Mr. David Thomson, to be minister of the parish of St. Ninians, in the true sense and spirit of the late sentence of the General Assembly, and you are hereby admitted accordingly."* And thus once more absolute patronage triumphed over the principles and laws of Christianity, and another victory increased the glories of Principal Robertson's Moderate administration.

That this was a direct and legitimate consequence of the law of patronage, as administered by the Moderate party, headed by Principal Robertson, may be very easily demonstrated; but he would be a rash and daring casuist who should attempt to prove, that it was a direct and legitimate consequence of the laws of Christ, and reconcilable with the principle of his sole Headship and Sovereignty over the Church.

[1774–78.] In the year 1774 there appeared a republication of the celebrated Professor Hutcheson's "Considerations on Patronage, addressed to the Gentlemen of Scotland," which had been first published in 1736. To this was added a curious appendix, containing a view of the state of the Secession in Scotland in the year 1773, with a calculation founded on it, showing the expense which such an extensive Secession entailed on the kingdom, falling ultimately upon the possessors of fixed property, the landholders, and mercantile and commercial capitalists. The author of this paper first states, that there were in 1773 at least one hundred and ninety congregations of Seceders; and by a calculation which shows him to have been well acquainted with the principles of political economy, he proves, that the sum of money expended in the maintenance of this large Secession could not amount to less than *twelve hundred thousand pounds*, ultimately falling upon the possessors of fixed property, and all caused by the destructive patronage law, and the tyrannical conduct of the Moderate party in the Church.* If the correctness of that calculation be admitted, and the numbers of seceding congregations to be taken now at five hundred, which appears to be near the reality, the amount thereby drained from the capital of the country cannot be less than three times the sum already stated. And this enormous public burden is borne that patronage may be maintained, and ecclesiastical power secured to a party whose whole history is one wild tissue of heresy, error, or suppression of the truth in doctrine, violation of the Presbyterian constitution, ministerial unfaithfulness, sinful conniving at immorality, and the most wanton and cruel exercise of spiritual despotism, which seemed even to exult in the infliction of wrong and outrage upon a grave, intelligent, and religious people. Surely the nation will ere long awake, burst the yoke of patronage, and shake off the incubus of Moderatism, beneath which it has so long groaned.

The stream of corruption rolled on, widening and deepening as it swept along, for several successive years. During that time repeated instances occurred in which accusations of heresy were quashed or explained away, and charges of immorality mitigated, smoothed over, and dismissed. Some cases, however, occurred, too public and enormous to be thus passed by. To meet such painful cases the Moderate leaders resorted to a new device. They entered into a private arrangement with the delinquent, accord-

* Scots Magazine, vol. xxxv. pp. 614, 615.

* Considerations on Patronage; reprinted 1774.

ing to which he agreed to accept a pension out of the stipend, to withdraw from the parish, and to permit an assistant to be appointed to discharge those duties which public decency would no longer suffer him to desecrate. This was called "mercy to a weak and erring brother;" what was it to the feelings of the disgusted community?—what to the pillaged assistant?—what to the purity of the Church of Christ? Many such cases might be mentioned, from the earliest recorded instance during the domination of Principal Robertson, down till the loss of power by that party from whose corrupt policy they originated; but we forbear, under a strong feeling of shame and regret that such things could be done by men who were at least nominally Christian ministers.

[1779.] The year 1779 is chiefly remarkable for the formidable tumults, amounting almost to civil convulsions, which agitated the country in consequence of the passing of an act of parliament, relaxing the civil disabilities and penalties resting upon the adherents of Popery in England, the provisions of which were proposed to be extended to Scotland. The subject came before the General Assembly in the form of an overture for petitioning parliament against the bill, and was discussed with great ability, the Moderate party advocating the removal of these disabilities, and the Evangelical party opposing it. The discussion ended as was to be expected; for when the arguments of such men as Dr. Erskine and Mr. Stevenson of St. Madoes could not be answered, they could be overwhelmed by a vote. But though the overture was rejected on its first appearance in 1778, the tumultuary excitement of 1779 induced Robertson to retrace his steps, and consent to its being then passed as an act. The views of the orthodox party, by whom the overture was supported, were utterly averse from any thing like giving sanction to persecution. The main argument was, that while Roman Catholics ought not to be prohibited from worshipping God in their own way, nor subjected to severe penalties because they did; yet they ought not to be intrusted with political power, because their own corrupt and erroneous system of religion rendered them unfit conservators of public religious truth and moral purity, and because their allegiance to a foreign and necessarily hostile power at Rome, the enemy of religious and civil liberty, and the implacable foe of the British constitution, rendered it impossible for them to be safely intrusted with influence in a Protestant government, which they could not but regard it as a sacred duty to subvert.* These arguments were not answered then; they have not since; and our own times have furnished the most appalling demonstrations of their truth.

[1780.] Several events occurred to mark the year 1780 as memorable in the history of the Church of Scotland. Of these, the first that demands attention is the discussion respecting the propriety of a minister holding a plurality of offices, such as a church and a professorship. There had been many instances of a minister being professor of Theology or Church History, and at the same time preaching regularly every Sabbath; but in all these instances there was either no pastoral charge, or its duties were fulfilled by a colleague. The case out of which the discussion rose was that of Dr. Hill of St. Andrews, who, while professor of Greek in that university, had been appointed to a parochial charge in the city, and still continued to hold the professorship. A strong endeavour was made by the Evangelical party to prevent this plurality of offices from obtaining the sanction of the General Assembly, both as incompatible with the constitution of the Church, and as rendering it absolutely impossible that the important duties of a pastor could be adequately discharged in that parish. But Dr. Hill was already regarded as the second hope of the Moderate party, and they defended the appointment strenuously, and with complete success. There is, besides, reason to believe, that there was more in this than was allowed to meet the eye,—that it was the initiatory step in a scheme intended to introduce the system of pluralities and non-residence, resembling as closely as might be possible that system as it exists in its palmy state in England.† This, it will be admitted, was no unna-

* Life of Erskine, pp. 284-294.

† Narrative of the Proceedings of Assembly 1780, by the Rev. James Burn, minister at Forgan, pp. 29-31.

tural result of King William's "comprehension scheme," which, after the struggle of three generations, seemed ripening into an assimilation scheme.

But the most signal event by which that year was distinguished was the retirement of the celebrated Principal Robertson from the high functions which he had so long discharged, as leader of the dominant party in the General Assembly. The only direct account of the reasons which induced Robertson to withdraw from his position as leader of the Assembly while his constitution was still unbroken, and all his faculties unimpaired, is to be found in a communication from the Rev. Henry Moncreiff to Dugald Stewart, given in the appendix to his life of Robertson. "I do not know," says Sir Henry, "whether the reasons which led Dr. Robertson to retire from the Assembly after 1780 have ever been thoroughly understood. He had been often reproached by the more violent men of his party, for not adopting stronger measures than he thought either right or wise. But there was one subject which had become particularly uneasy to him, and on which he had been more urged and fretted than on all the other subjects of contention in the Church,—the scheme, into which many of his friends entered zealously, for abolishing subscription to the Confession of Faith and Formula. This he expressly declared his resolution to resist in every form. But he was so much teased with remonstrances on that subject, that he mentioned them as having at least *confirmed* his resolution to retire. He claimed to himself the merit of having prevented this controversy from being agitated in the Assemblies; but warned me, as a young man, that it would become the chief controversy of my time, and stated to me the reasons which had determined his opinions on the subject."* And this was the result of Principal Robertson's "wise and enlightened" policy during his despotic administration of ecclesiastical affairs,—the growth of a party directly opposed to the very existence of the Presbyterian constitution, till it became too strong for even his firm hand to control, and too importunately urgent for even his calm temper to endure! Could there be a more conclusive demonstration, that Moderatism is essentially anti-presbyterian and anti-scriptural,—contrary at once to the constitutional laws of both Church and State, and to the principles and regulations of the gospel? And the mighty magician whose potent words had raised the demon, had not the courage to confront and quell it;—the magnanimous man, whose touch of power had drawn from the infidel heart of unregenerate humanity this wild response, recoiled in terror, "scared by the sound himself had made." It is deeply instructive to trace the progress of an evil principle, though it is startling to see it when it appears in all its native hideousness.

We learn from other sources, that the men by whom the proposal of abolishing subscription to the Confession of Faith was most importunately urged, were Messrs. M'Gill and Dalrymple of Ayr, Wodrow of Stevenston, Oughterstan of West Kilbride, Fergusson of Kilwinning, Ross of Inch in Galloway, and a number of their neighbours and acquaintances, who held similar opinions, but were somewhat less open in asserting them. Several of these men not only embraced, but publicly taught Socinian doctrines with little or no disguise; and the small remains of conscience which they possessed impelled them to desire to get altogether free from the bond of subscription to a Confession of Faith which they did not believe, and of which their whole life and public teaching was a continual denial Principal Robertson, it appears, opposed this reckless proposal on a ground which very naturally suggested itself to his habits of thought. He knew well that the Church established by law in Scotland, is a Church publicly avowing the doctrines stated in the Confession of Faith; and he saw clearly that to permit subscription to this recognized standard to be abolished, would involve the hazard of severing the connection between Church and State, since to cease subscription to that standard was virtually to cease from being the Church established by law. The danger, however, was not so imminent as he apprehended; and the heady spirit of innovation in his mutinous followers was checked by the encounter of a comparatively slight obstacle. Some landed proprietors, of better spirit and

* Life of Robertson, Appendix, p. 297, 298.

sounder judgment than those unconstitutional innovators, hearing of their design, declared that the moment the signing of Confession of Faith was abandoned, they would consider the connection between Church and State at an end, and would therefore pay no more stipend. This was a consequence which these men were not prepared to meet, and their anxiety to obtain a greater liberty of conscience sunk into nothing compared with their dread of incurring the loss of worldly wealth. How readily do worldly-minded men understand, and how acutely feel a worldly argument, when dead to every thing of a higher and more sacred nature.

[1781-82.] When Dr. Robertson withdrew from the active management of ecclesiastial affairs, Dr. Hill of St. Andrews was immediately regarded as his successor in the high office of Moderate leader in the Assembly. But though a man of great abilities and eloquence, he never reached the pitch of absolute supremacy which had been possessed by Robertson. He cordially adopted the leading principles of his predecessor's reign, as is clearly proved by his statement and advocacy of them in the communications which he furnished to Dugald Stewart, and which are partly embodied in the Life of Robertson, partly added in the appendix to that work. But he never acquired that unquestionable ascendancy over the minds of the entire party which the great abilities and the high literary fame of Robertson had secured to him. His absence from Edinburgh contributed also not a little to prevent him from possessing that degree of influence which he might otherwise have obtained. The Edinburgh ministers, several of them men of high talent, and thoroughly versant in ecclesiastical polity, schemed, deliberated, and arranged, while Dr. Hill was attending upon his own duties in St. Andrews; and there often remained little more for him to do than to state and defend those measures which the Edinburgh Doctors had already prepared. Occasionally, too, it happened, that his opinion and theirs did not thoroughly coincide, and that his eloquence in defence of his own view was overborne by their superior management. Of this a memorable instance occurred in the year 1782.

From the time of the Reformation it had been the invariable principle of the Presbyterian Church, as stated in the Books of Discipline and in many of the acts of Assembly, that the call of the people, inviting a duly qualified person to be their minister, was an indispensable element in the formation of the pastoral tie. Even when Prelacy was forced upon the Church, the call continued to be used, and notwithstanding the imposition and reimposition of patronage, the call was never abandoned. This was a clear proof that the Presbyterian Church had at all times, and in all diversities of circumstances, regarded the call of the people as an absolutely indispensable element in the formation of the pastoral tie, whereas patronage never was declared to be either a prerequisite for, or an element in, that sacred relation between ministers and people. It was clear, nevertheless, that there was an inherent incompatibility between a call of the people and patronage; and that to whatever extent the influence of the one availed, to the same extent was the other impaired. For that reason all ministers truly Presbyterian in principle always contended earnestly against patronage, as essentially and necessarily a violation of the constitution of the Church. But when there arose a worldly-minded and unpresbyterian faction, formed out of the admitted curates and the surviving indulged ministers, that faction concurring with reimposed patronage, and therefore supported by patrons and politicians, gradually gained the ascendancy over the Church, and following their natural bent, depressed the call into a mere matter of form, and elevated the presentation of a patron into absolute supremacy. This was not fully accomplished till the despotic reign of Principal Robertson; for even Dr. Cuming publicly termed the law of patronage a "hard law," which it was necessary to obey only till it could be got mitigated or removed. But the first principle of Robertson's administration, as stated by Dugald Stewart, and corroborated by Dr. Hill, "was a steady and uniform support of the law of patronage."* He could, however, both understand and imitate the wary policy of an Augustus, and knew that it was more safe to destroy the spirit of

* Life of Robertson, p. 173.

liberty than to take away its form. He therefore continued to require the form of the call to be maintained, while he reduced it to an empty form, an unreal mockery. After his resignation of the reins of ecclesiastical government, the constitutional Presbyterians seem to have cherished a hope that the ancient spirit of the Church might be at least partially revived, and that some degree of life might be infused into her paralyzed and prostrate forms.

The subject was discussed extensively throughout the Church during the year 1781, and in 1782 overtures from the synods of Lothian, Glasgow, Fife, Perth, Angus, and Galloway, were laid before the Assembly, having for their object that the call might be revived, so as to be more than a mere matter of form, and to operate as a partial limitation to patronage. These overtures were, of course, resisted by the Moderate party; but Dr. Hill's motion against them was not sufficiently cautious to suit the wily policy of the Edinburgh conclave, and a different motion was proposed by Dr. Macknight, and carried. Dr. Macknight's motion was as follows:—"That the moderation of a call, in settling ministers, is agreeable to the immemorial and constitutional usage of this Church, and that it ought to be continued." Dr. Hill's motion admitted also that it was agreeable to the immemorial practice of the Church; but neither termed it "constitutional," nor said that it "ought to be continued," ending thus,—"dismiss these overtures, as at this time unnecessary." It was easily seen, that Dr. Hill's motion contained a virtual, and, had it been carried, it would soon have produced a real, abolition of the call itself; and the older and more wary Moderate leaders were not prepared to perpetrate so open an outrage upon the constitutional forms of the Church, though fully determined that nothing which tended to thwart patronage and Moderatism should ever be more than an empty form.

It deserves to be noted, that Dr. Cook, giving, in his Life of Dr. Hill, an account of this debate on calls, enters into a long defence of Dr. Hill's motion, resting that defence on the ground, that "call is incompatible with patronage, and therefore nugatory." The plan proposed by Dr. Cook, the call having, according to his hypothesis, been abolished, is the following:—"That the first introduction of a presentee to those whose spiritual state he is destined to superintend, should not take place till he was actually settled amongst them: That after all these matters had been arranged, a narration of the proceedings should be communicated to the people; and they should be invited to subscribe a paper, expressing their satisfaction with the presentee, and their resolution to contribute, by every method in their power, to his comfortable residence amongst them."* It is not necessary to waste words in proving that such a theory is equally unpresbyterian and absurd; but it does seem passing strange that it could ever have been seriously propounded by a native of Scotland, acquainted with the character of the strong-minded and warm-hearted Scottish people. When the people of Scotland have forgotten that ever a Presbyterian Church existed in their country, conferring upon them the inestimable blessings of civil liberty, educated intelligence, moral worth, and high spiritual privileges, and when they have consented to become the abject slaves of civil and religious despotism, then may such a scheme be tried, but not till then. The futile theory is here stated, however, for this important reason, that it is an irresistible demonstration of the perfect identity, in principle and nature, of Moderatism in former times with Moderatism now. It is constantly said by Moderates, in attempting to defend their system and themselves, that it is unfair to charge the Moderatism of the present day with all the enormities perpetrated by Moderatism in earlier and less civilized times. But till they disclaim the principles, as well as repudiate the practices, of their predecessors, they are justly liable to the charge. These principles they cannot disclaim: for their present leader has avowed and defended them, even in their most aggravated character,—nay, to an extent far beyond what his predecessors in successive Moderate dynasties ever presumed to attempt. And we shall have occasion to show, that in practice, equally as in principle, Moderatism remains unchanged.

* See the whole of this very curious argument and theory in Dr. Cook's Life of Hill, pp. 144-146

There is another incident connected with this year, to which we refer with great delight, both on account of its own pleasing character, and because it tends to explain some otherwise inexplicable peculiarities in the new Moderate dynasty.

It has been already shown that the insubordination of the heretical division of his forces was one of the chief motives that induced Robertson to retire from the management of ecclesiastical affairs. But there was another reason, which must also be stated. A tendency to revive and defend evangelical doctrines began to appear among individuals of the Moderate party; and this was felt to be a more dangerous matter than either heresy or immorality, and more likely to disturb the calm and steady progress of despotism, inasmuch as men who possess religious principles cannot be governed by mere worldly and selfish motives. The most conspicuous of the half-evangelical moderates was Dr. Thomas Hardy, recently appointed one of the ministers of Edinburgh, and professor of Church History. This distinguished man had evidently formed the plan of uniting the best men of the two parties in the Church into one body, able to control the extreme sections of both. It is impossible to say how far he might have succeeded in this laudable design had his life been prolonged; but what is of importance to notice is, that in 1782, during the agitation in the Church connected with the overtures on calls, he published a pamphlet, entitled "The Principles of Moderation, addressed to the Clergy of the Popular Interest in the Church of Scotland." A very few extracts will suffice to show the spirit of this production. "You subjoin that this transference of power in 1712 was wrong; that it was unfriendly in its intention, and has been hurtful in its effects; and that the liberty of British subjects entitles you to say, that it is a grievance, in the simple and grammatical sense of the word, and ought to be redressed. What reply do we make to this? None. We agree with you in the sentiments of the law itself; we allow that it is a hardship, or, if you will contend for a word, we say with you, it is a grievance, not such indeed as to justify resistance, but such as will warrant application for redress." "That a new arrangement must take place sooner or latter, I conclude from the state of the country. The desertion of great bodies of the people from the Establishment is the melancholy evidence of the necessity. Whatever secondary causes may be brought to account for it, there can be no manner of doubt *that it is chiefly to be ascribed to the law of patronage.*" Then, after stating that the Secession may be estimated at two hundred congregations, comprising at least one hundred thousand people, he continues,—"Methinks I hear some reckless youth, in delivering his maiden speech, exclaim on this point, 'So much the better,—they are the factious, the turbulent, the enthusiastic; the Church is happily quit; it is only her ill humours that are purged off.' Stay my young friend; you are very honest but you want experience; a few more years will convince you, that the Church is not enriched by her losses, nor strengthened by the desertion of her sons." Further, speaking of the necessity of a change, he adds,—"The exterior arrangement, therefore, ought in sound policy to correspond with the essential nature of the Establishment, otherwise the Church will never be at peace; and the experienced opposition of seventy years, joined to the revolt of one hundred thousand people, are the proofs that *absolute patronage is irreconcilable with the genius of Presbytery.*"*

The difference between this able pamphlet and Dr. Robertson's manifesto is very marked and very instructive. Dr. Hardy, though not decidedly evangelical in doctrine, was a man of great candour and integrity of mind, and his enlarged and liberal views, together with some theoretical knowledge of evangelical truth, enabled him to apprehend what really is "the essential nature" of the Presbyterian Church, and to perceive that "absolute patronage is irreconcilable with it." Dr. Robertson's peculiar theory and his want of that knowledge, left him to view it as a man of the world would do, and to regard it as in nothing essentially different from a mere secular institution having, indeed, some distinc-

* Those who cannot obtain this valuable pamphlet, will find extracts from it in Dr. Welsh's evidence in the Patronage Report, p. 260; and in the Dublin University Magazine, No. xcviii. pp. 255, 256.

tive forms which it was proper to preserve as decent and characteristic, but based upon secular maxims, governed by secular regulations, and pervaded throughout by a secular spirit. The early and lamented death of Dr. Hardy prevented the developement of his scheme; but the sacred element of evangelism which had begun to spread was destined to work with a disruptive might among the secular principles of Moderatism, disturbing repeatedly the cold continuity of their mortiferous operation, and betokening the approaching dissolution of the whole unconstitutional and unscriptural system. Even Dr. Hill, thoroughly as he had imbibed Principal Robertson's views of ecclesiastical polity, began ere long to exhibit symptoms of a tendency to evangelical doctrine; this increased with his increasing knowledge of sound theology, in the course of his studies as professor of divinity at St. Andrews: and before the close of his career his mind had acquired so full a perception of the truth as it is in Jesus, that though he still co-operated with the Moderate party generally, he had in a great measure lost their confidence as may be learned even from the cautious language of Dr. Cook, in his life of that distinguished man.

[1783-84.] During the years 1783 and 1784, the chief subject which engaged the attention of the General Assembly was that of patronage. Dr. Hardy's pamphlet seems to have excited afresh the hopes of all sound Presbyterians, that a redress of that great grievance might yet be obtained; and a number of overtures were laid before the Assembly on the subject. A regular discussion at length took place respecting these overtures in the Assembly of 1784. Dr. Hill moved that they be "rejected as inexpedient, ill founded, and dangerous to the peace and welfare of the Church." It is not necessary to state even an outline of the arguments used on both sides, in the debate which followed, after the remarks which have been made in the preceding pages. Suffice it to say, that Dr. Hill's motion was carried, and that following up the victory, he proposed to omit the clause in the instructions annually given to the Commission, which required them to apply for redress from the grievance of patronage, and in this too he was successful. The omission of this clause in the instructions annually given to the Commission is the nearest approach the Church of Scotland has ever made towards even a recognition of the patronage law, and it amounts to nothing more than ceasing openly to condemn what she has never avowedly approved. It will be remembered, that this clause was first inserted in the instructions given to the Commission by the Assembly of 1712, immediately after the passing of the perfidious and unconstitutional patronage act, and had been repeated annually ever since. Many years had elapsed since it had been attended to, the last decided public effort to procure redress having been that of 1735—36; but the retaining of the clause formed a standing testimony by the Church against the law of patronage, and so far served to exculpate her from participation in its guilt. Dr. Robertson, with his usual sagacious toleration of dead forms, permitted it to remain; but the greater rashness, or the higher degree of conscientious honesty of mind, in Dr. Hill, which had formerly led him to attempt abolishing the call induced him now to strike out a clause to which he and his party never meant that any attention should be paid. This was a very natural step for the Moderate party to take, but, thoroughly irrational and unconstitutional. Before rescinding a clause which required application to be made for the redress of what was termed a grievance, Dr. Hill ought to have persuaded the Church to declare that she had ceased to regard it as a grievance, and viewed it rather as a matter of which she now approved, and was desirous of its permanent continuation. This however, would have been too perilous an attempt even for Dr. Robertson in all his plentitude of power, as it would have caused the Secession of nearly half of the ministers and at least three-fourths of the population in the kingdom, a junction with the already existing Seceders, and the formation of a new Church, truly Presbyterian and national, whether established by law or not. Are men of that party prepared to brave a similar peril in the present day?—nay, a peril incalculably more formidable to the empire at large, and fraught with certain and irrecoverable ruin to themselves and their unscriptural cause, which would and must utterly perish in the hour of an injured nation's strong consuming vengeance.*

[1785--89.] The effects of this defeat were most disastrous. The true Presbyterian ministers, seeing all their hopes again blasted, and trampled under the feet of their triumphant antagonist, sunk into a state of comparatively torpid discouragement, and ceased to strive against what now seemed to bear the aspect of stern invincible necessity. On the other hand, the Moderate party assumed once more the haughty port of uncontrolled dominion, enforcing the law of patronage with steady and immitigable rigor. The oppressed and insulted people not only ceased to expect redress, they ceased even to ask it. They felt that opposition to patronage was of no avail. Be the presentee what he might, — a heretic, a grossly immoral person, miserably deficient in learning, or destitute of the necessary mental abilities and moral qualifications,—if he had obtained a presentation, all other objections were disregarded, and he was made the "stipend-lifter" in the parish. But he could not be made the pastor of the people. They looked on indignantly and mournfully, till the desecrating deed was done; then withdrew, built a meeting-house, and chose a pastor for themselves. In this manner the most religious part of the community was driven out of the Church, and those that remained sunk into a state of carelessness, till they ceased to feel and to regret their own calamitous condition. The rising generation grew up accustomed to such a state of matters, regardless, comparatively, of the sacredness of that day which God hallowed to himself, neglectful of public worship, and utterly destitute of personal religion, which too often the example, and even the language, of their half-infidel ministers taught them to despise and deride as hypocrisy and fanaticism. The Church of Scotland, wherever thorough Moderatism prevailed, seemed spiritually dead, and all living Christians withdrew from its polluting touch. Yet there were many truly pious ministers sprinkled over the land, shining in their own spheres apart, amid the prevailing moral darkness, like the few scattered stars that faintly break the gloom of a chill and misty night.*

Although the sagacious opposition of Dr. Robertson, and the intimated danger to their pecuniary interests, had deterred the extreme Moderates from openly expressing their desire to be released from the necessity of subscribing the Confession of Faith, yet the intention was by no means abandoned; only it was judged expedient to bring in the change gradually, by a series of precedents. In the year 1789, the presbytery of Arbroath presumed to ordain Mr. George Gleig to be minister in the church of that burgh, without requiring him to sign either the Confession of Faith or Formula.† This strange and daring conduct was brought before the Assembly; and although it deserved a very high censure, the Assembly deemed it expedient to exercise leniency in the first offence of the kind. Mr. Gleig was allowed to retain the church, upon signing the Confession of Faith in presence of the Assembly; and the presbytery was rebuked at the bar, and admonished to be more careful for the future, on pain of a higher censure. This decided expression of the mind of the Church, though accompanying a very lenient censure, had the effect of preventing that or any other presbytery from a repetition of the offence.

[1790.] Mention has been already made of the strong tendency to Socinianism prevalent in many districts of the country where Moderatism chiefly reigned, and particularly in the west of Scotland. During above ten years the west country was fiercely agitated with polemical controversy between these Socinians and their sounder brethren. The Socinian party were termed New Light men, and

* It may be noted, as proving the consistency of Moderatism in its unconstitutional career, that Dr. Cook goes even beyond Dr. Hill, and defends absolute and unlimited patronage. "The idea of a discretionary power to set aside a presentation, in particular cases, is decidedly rejected by the Moderate party." The "want of a sufficient call is no ground of rejection." "The law of patronage admits of no limitation but the defined qualifications of a presentee not existing in a particular individual." (Cook's Life of Hill, pp. 161, 162.)

* Such men as Dr. Erskine, Dr. Hunter, Dr. Davidson, Dr. Kemp, Dr. Balfour of Glasgow, Mr. Freebairn of Dunbarton, Dr Bryce Johnson of Holywood, his nephew of Crossmichael, Nisbet of Montrose, Mitchell of Kemnay, and many others who might be named, remaining within the pale of the Church, kept her alive, during this long and dreary period; and she perished not, for a blessing was in her.

† Acts of Assembly, year 1789; Scots Magazine

their opponents were called the defenders of the Old Light. In this controversy, as was to be expected, every person of irreligious and immoral character espoused the cause of the New Light or Socinian party; and what they wanted in argument they endeavoured to supply by the employment of ridicule, slander, and profane mockery of their antagonists. In an evil hour for his country and himself, the New Light party induced Robert Burns to join them, and to prostitute his high poetical genius in a cause so worthless as the defence of such unprincipled and depraved men,—nay, initiated him in depths of iniquity to which till then he had been a stranger,—nay, still more fearful,—destroyed what may be termed the natural devotional tendency of the poetical temperament, and impelled him to aim the shafts of his satire against the most sacred rites of the Church and the essential truths of the everlasting gospel. The future dark career and melancholy end of this unhappy son of genius is mainly to be ascribed to the fatal taint which his mind received from his intercourse with the Moderate, Socinian, New Light ministers of Ayrshire and their adherents. These guilty men have been already named; and their misled victim's poems will, when rightly understood, inflict upon them the retributive justice of branding their unhonoured memory with the impress of perpetual infamy.*

At length Dr. M'Gill of Ayr had the temerity to publish a work entitled, "A Practical Essay on the Death of Jesus Christ," in which the most glaring Socinianism was openly taught and maintained. This could not be overlooked. A prosecution was instituted against the author of a work so manifestly heretical. His friends, cherishing, many of them, the same sentiments, but not exposed to equal danger, because they had not given their opinions to the public in any palpable form, made every exertion in their power to shelter him from justice. A protracted litigation before the subordinate church judicatories followed. But at last the matter came before the synod of Glasgow and Ayr, and assumed an aspect so serious, that he and his friends considered it expedient for him to evade the danger of deposition, by offering to explain his meaning, acknowledge his error in what could not be explained away, and supplicate forgiveness. There were too many in the synod scarcely less heretical than he, for it to pursue a more faithful course. His explanation and apology, though very lame and impotent indeed, were sustained as satisfactory. The Synod published an account of their proceedings in the case; the condemned book sunk into that oblivion which was its natural destiny; and the worthless man was permitted to return to the perishing flock whom he could not lead to Christ, as he himself knew not the way.*

[1791-96.] It is not necessary, nor even proper in a work devoted to ecclesiastical matters, to do more than glance at those great political movements which agitate and mould the structure of society,—especially movements so vast as to shake the whole of Europe, and so recent that their vibrations have not yet settled into repose. For this reason we shall merely allude to that terrific event the French Revolution, which was on the eve of bursting forth in 1790, and which for several successive years startled and appalled the world, by the sudden changes of aspect, each more hideous and wild than the last, which it assumed, the fierce infidelity which it avowed, and the scenes of atrocious carnage which marked its dreadful progress. Even the most unreflecting were compelled to perceive what man is when without religion,—how fearful a thing the depraved, deceitful, and desperately wicked human heart can be, when left to follow its native tendency, without God, and without hope in the world. The moralist recoiled in horror; the tongue of the philosophical divine clave to the roof of his mouth; but the evangelical preacher of the gospel rushed forward, and took his stand betwixt the living and the dead. A mighty revival of genuine spiritual Christianity took place all over Britain, and great exertions were made by the

* It can be proved beyond the power of doubt, by living and unimpeachable testimony, that Burns himself, within the last fortnight of his life, expressed the deepest remorse for what these men had led him to write, and an anxious wish that he might live a little longer, to make some attempt to repair the injury he had done. And Gilbert Burns, in his latter years, repeatedly declared, that the New Light ministers were the chief subverters of all regard for religion in his brother's mind, and that he himself had not escaped unwounded, and long retained the aching scar.

* Proceedings of the Synod of Glasgow and Ayr, April, 1790.

friends of religious truth to communicate to all around them the knowledge of the gospel of peace and holiness. Numerous religious societies sprung almost simultaneously into being, and reviving Christianity began to put forth vital and expansive energies, which had lain dormant since the Reformation. With returning spiritual life returned that spiritual intelligence which enables a man to know for what object spiritual life is given. The Christian community was startled and alarmed at perceiving, that for centuries it had neglected to attempt the discharge of that very duty, the accomplishment of which is the chief end of the Christian Church Universal. It had neglected the risen Redeemer's imperative command, "Go ye into all the world, and preach the gospel to every creature under heaven." Immediately the idea of instituting Christian missions, for the purpose of fulfilling the Saviour's injunction, extending his kingdom, and promoting the salvation of perishing souls, became a leading impulse in the heart and soul of every truly spiritually-minded Christian, whether he belonged to a Dissenting, Seceding, or Established Christian Church. And in the warm fervour of renewed Christian life and love, many of the distinctions which had kept men asunder like brazen walls, melted like wax in the fire, and free scope was readily given to an amount of Christian intercourse which had for ages been unknown.

In Scotland the reviving power of this truly Christian spirit was early and strongly felt. A missionary society was formed in Glasgow, and another in Edinburgh, which held its first meeting in March, 1796, the venerable Dr. Erskine acting as its president. Circular letters were sent to every part of the country, explaining and advocating the object for the promotion of which this central missionary society was formed. These circulars gave rise to much discussion throughout the Church; and the synods of Fife and Moray transmitted overtures to the General Assembly, the general tenor of which was, that the General Assembly should "take into consideration by what means the Church of Scotland might most effectually contribute to the diffusion of the gospel over the world;" and that "an act might be passed recommending a general collection throughout the Church, to aid the several societies for propagating the gospel among the heathen nations." In this manner the great object of the Church general of Christ was brought before the notice of the Church of Scotland, assembled in its supreme court; and a fair and complete opportunity was given to both parties, into which that court is divided, to emit a public demonstration and testimony how much, or how little, of the true spirit of Christianity they respectively possessed.

This most important discussion began with a piece of very disingenuous policy on the part of the Moderates, who contrived to have both the overtures considered in one discussion. Dr. Hill had managed to exclude from the Fife overture the specific approbation of missionary exertions which it at first contained, leaving in it nothing more than a vague expression of the propriety that the Church of Scotland should in some way or other contribute to the diffusion of the gospel over the world, which any Moderate could complacently affirm, and remain inactive, as pledged to no specific object. On the other hand, the Moray overture recommended a general collection, against which plausible objections might be urged, on the ground of this having a tendency to diminish the resources of the session for the support of the poor. The Evangelical party wished the overtures to be considered separately, in the hope of carrying the general proposition in behalf of the missionary enterprise, even though the proposed method of promoting it might be rejected. Moderate tactics prevailed, and the discussion was made to include both overtures. The debate which ensued exhibited the character of Moderatism in a manner which cannot be misunderstood. One of the leading speakers on the Moderate side, Mr. George Hamilton, minister of Gladsmuir, began by some general admissions of the propriety of diffusing the gospel. "To diffuse," said he, "among mankind the knowledge of a religion which we profess to believe and to revere, is doubtless a good and important work; as to pray for its diffusion, and to expect it, is taught us in the sacred volume of Scripture."—"To spread abroad the knowledge of the gospel among barbarous and heathen nations, seems to be highly preposterous, in as far as it anticipates, nay it even reverses, the order of nature. Men must be polished and refined in their manners before they can be properly enlightened in religious truths. Philosophy and learning must, in the nature of things take the precedence." Then followed a glowing eulogium upon the "simple virtues" of the "untutored Indian." "But go,—engraft on his simple manners the customs, refinements, and, may I not add, some of the vices, of civilized society, and the influence of that religion which you give as a compensation for the disadvantages attending such a communication will not refine his morals nor ensure his happiness."—"When they shall be told that *man is saved not by good works, but by faith*, what will be the consequence? We have too much experience of the difficulty of guarding our own people against the most deplorable misapplication of this principle, to entertain a rational doubt, that the wild inhabitants of uncivilized regions would use it as a handle for the most flagrant violation of justice and morality."—"But even suppose such a nation [one already civilized,] could be found, I should still have weighty objections against sending missionaries thither Why should we scatter our forces and spend our strength in foreign service, when our utmost vigilance, our unbroken strength is required at home? While there remains at home a single individual without the means of religious knowledge, to propagate it abroad would be improper and absurd." And at length directing his attention to the idea of collections for the aid of missions, he exclaimed—"For such improper conduct censure is too small a mark of disapprobation; it would, I doubt not, be a legal subject of penal prosecution."—"Upon the whole, while we pray for the propagation of the gospel, and patiently await its period, let us unite in resolutely rejecting these overtures." Dr. Carlyle of Inveresk, who had been quite ready to spend time and money in theatrical amusements, rose and said—"I have, on various occasions, during a period of almost half a century, had the honor of being a member of the General Assembly, yet this is the first time I remember to have ever heard such a proposal made, and I cannot help also thinking it the worst time." He therefore seconded Mr. Hamilton's motion, "that the overtures be immediately dismissed."

Dr. Hill made a cautious, plausible speech, evading the main topic, animadverting sharply on the peculiarities of missionary societies, and concluding with a more guarded motion, admitting generally the propriety of aiding in the propagation of the gospel—disapproving of collections—recommending the promotion of Christianity at home—praying for the fulfilment of prophecy, and resolving to embrace any future opportunity of contributing to the propagation of the gospel. David Boyle, Esq., advocate, indulged in a furious philippic against missionary societies, as all of a political character, and dangerous to the peace of the community. Finally, the motions of Mr. Hamilton and Dr. Hill were combined, and carried by a majority of fourteen, the vote being fifty-eight to forty-four.* So well satisfied were the Moderates with the conduct of Mr. Hamilton, and with his brilliant oratory, that they soon afterwards honoured him with the title of doctor in divinity, and elevated him to the moderator's chair, as a reward for his anti-missionary exertions

Such was the obedience rendered by Moderatism to the risen Redeemer's direct command, "Go ye and make disciples of all nations,—preach the gospel to every creature under heaven;" and thus did it prove itself to be, as a system, essentially anti-christian. This may seem a harsh saying, and it is with pain and sorrow that it is said But attachment to genuine and vital Christianity requires its dead counterfeit to be detected and denounced; the love of country and of mankind demands, that whatever obstructs the true welfare of Britian and the world should be pointed out and removed; and true compassion for erring fellow-creatures, especially for erring Christian brethren, forbids the use of injudicious and criminal tenderness of language in the statement of their grievous errors, which might soothe an uneradicated evil, and leave a deadly hurt unprobed, unhealed, deeply and silently festering to death.

[1797.] While religious and moral desolation overspread the districts of the

* See an account of the Debate published in 1796.

country where Moderatism chiefly prevailed, and an alarming increase of vice, immorality, crime, and political discontent, exhibited the pernicious results of that dead form of worldly religion, there were other parts of the kingdom which still enjoyed the priceless blessing of an evangelical ministry, and where living Christianity bore its natural fruits, both in the earnestness with which the people attended upon the ministrations of their faithful pastors, and in the anxiety which the increasing population of such districts showed to obtain additional means of religious instruction, adequate to the wants of their increasing numbers. Overtures were sent to the General Assembly, from several presbyteries, for permission to erect what were termed chapels of ease in populous parishes, where additional accommodation was wanted beyond what he parish church could afford, and where also the need of an additional pastor was equally manifest. It may be easily supposed that no such requests came from the parishes where there had been violent and intrusive settlements; for in such cases, the people seceded from the National Church, and built churches of their own. But wherever there were faithful and evangelical ministers, the people manifested no desire to quit the Church of their fathers; but when the provided means were not sufficient, they were willing to build a new church in the necessitous locality, and remain within the pale of the national establishment, provided they could obtain the sanction of the General Assembly to such a measure. It might be thought that there could be no possible objection to this. Not so thought the sagacious Moderates. They perceived clearly, that in general these chapels of ease would be the resorts and the nurseries of evangelism; and as they wished the whole kingdom to be brought as speedily as possible into the same state of lethargic indifference as that in which they were themselves contentedly slumbering, they discountenanced all such proposals. After the Assembly had been repeatedly addressed on the subject, and it had become no longer possible to evade it, a committee was appointed in 1795 to inquire into the matter, and report to next Assembly. The report was received in 1796, approved of, and transmitted to the presbyteries, according to the Barrier Act, previous to its being made a standing law of the Church. In 1797, it came before the Assembly, when it appeared that *thirty-four* presbyteries disapproved of the overture, and only *thirty* approved; consequently, according to the constitutional laws of the Church, it was rejected.* Yet the Moderates, making a desperate effort in the Assembly, passed the actually rejected overture into an interim act, and re-transmitted it again to the presbyteries, in which, by dexterous management, they succeeded in procuring a majority to approve, so that the Moderate overture finally passed into a law in the year 1798.

The chief point in this act of Assembly, on account of which the Evangelical party opposed it, is the clause which proposes, that when a petition for a chapel of ease is laid before any presbytery, they "shall not pronounce any final judgment on the petition, till they shall have received the special directions of the Assembly thereon." The object of this was to put it in the power of the General Assembly, where the Moderates could secure a majority, to prevent the erection of a chapel in any dangerous place, where Evangelism was already strong, and in general to discourage the erection of chapels. And in order to accomplish this so desirable an object, as they viewed it, they did not hesitate to deprive presbyteries of their constitutional right to judge in the first instance of every ecclesiastical matter within their bounds, subject only to the review of the superior church courts by appeal. Against this glaringly unconstitutional procedure, as well as against the object which it was intended to effect, the Evangelical and constitutional party strove earnestly but unsuccessfully. Dr. Hunter, professor of theology in Edinburgh, Dr. Bryce Johnston of Holywood and Sir Henry Moncreiff, distinguished themselves in this controversy on the Evangelical side.† This conduct of the Moderate party furnishes another clear proof of the equally unchristian and unconstitutional character of their princi-

* Reasons of Dissent.

† Remarks on a paper entitled "Heads of an Argument," &c. by Sir Henry Moncrieff; Reasons of Dissent.

ples and their whole system. So recently as the preceding year they had declared it "improper and absurd to propagate the gospel abroad, while there remained a single individual at home without the means of religious knowledge." And now they did their utmost to prevent the people from procuring the means of religious instruction to themselves, and at their own expense, thereby, so far as they were able, inflicting a deadly paralysis upon the progress of Christianity both at home and abroad; violating, too, the constitution of the Presbyterian Church, that they might accomplish their purpose.

[1798–99.] Little was now wanting to complete the full developement of Moderatism, and that little was not long in being supplied. It had already done its utmost in driving the gospel out of its own circle, denying it equally to the heathen abroad and to the people at home: it had now nothing to do but to put an end to the Christian communion of all true believers, so far as its power could do so. The occasion of proceeding to this last act of degeneracy was furnished by the late celebrated Rowland Hill. This somewhat eccentric man, but most faithful and indefatigable servant of the Lord, came to Scotland about the end of July 1798, and immediately began to preach, in churches when permitted, and in the open air when he could not obtain admission to a place of worship. Edinburgh was too strongly garrisoned by Moderate divines for him to obtain access to the pulpits in that city; but he preached on the Calton Hill to great multitudes of attentive hearers. At Glasgow, Paisley, and other places in the west of Scotland, he was freely admitted to preach in the churches of the Establishment. In several other parts of Scotland he met with similar Christian brotherhood; and some of the Seceders allowed him to preach in their meeting-houses, while others refused. After his return to England, he published an account of his Scottish tour, in which he indulged freely in remarks and animadversions upon the state of religion in Scotland. There were several mistakes, much strong sense, great warmth and liberality of Christian feeling, and a considerable degree of pungent severity in his remarks, especially when expressing his opinion of the Moderate party and their adherents.*

The Moderate party were extremely displeased that Rowland Hill had been permitted to preach in several churches of the Establishment, and felt keenly galled by his pointed and severe animadversions upon their principles and conduct. And as it was known that he contemplated an early repetition of this visit, they determined to prevent the possibility that either he or any other evangelical minister of any other Church should be again permitted to preach within the pale of the Establishment. An act was accordingly passed by the General Assembly in 1799, declaring that all licences granted to probationers, "without the bounds of this Church," are invalid, and that presentations given to such persons must be refused. The ostensible reason for this part of the enactment was, to prevent incompetent persons from resorting to England or Ireland to obtain a license, by means of which they might be introduced to churches without due qualification. It had the effect, however, of preventing any man from being appointed to a church in Scotland if he had not been licensed by a Scottish presbytery,

* "The dispensation of mercy to fallen man entirely by Jesus Christ is not the subject preached by the majority; but with some, a mangled gospel, law and gospel wretchedly spliced together; with others, a mere hungry system of bare-weight morality; and with a third, what is worse still, a deliberate attack on all the truths they have engaged to uphold. The few, in comparison, orthodox among them are stigmatized by the nickname of *the wild*, while the fashionable divines on the other side of the question compliment themselves with the appellation of *the Moderate*. This epithet naturally reminds us of another, '*lukewarm*, neither cold nor hot.' In short, it is as with all who adopt the present half-way infidel system of the day, so, report says, it is with them; the cause of morality declines with the cause of the gospel; and I fear the Scots, by far the best educated and best behaved people in the British dominions, will soon be no better than their neighbours. Like their ministers, they will all become *Moderates*; first, they will be *Moderates* in religion; they will have *Moderate* notions of Jesus Christ and the gospel of salvation, for we cannot expect they will be better than their teachers; they will next be contented with a *Moderate* share of love to God, of prayer, and of repentance; they will be more *Moderate* in regard to the use of their Bibles, and be more *Moderate* in their zeal in teaching their children the Assembly's Catechism; and this will lead them to be *Moderates* in morality. In point of chastity, sobriety, honesty, &c., they will soon become *Moderate*, and be very anxious to grow in this famous fashionable *moderation*, till they become *immoderately* wicked; unless, through Divine mercy, they hear a little more of the 'grace of God that bringeth salvation,' the only doctrine that 'teacheth us to deny ungodliness and worldly lusts, and to live soberly, righteously, and godly, in this present world.'"—(Journal through the North of England, and parts of Scotland, with Remarks on the Present State of the Established Church of Scotland, &c. By Rowland Hill. Pp. 111, 112.)

whatever might be his qualifications; and it was certainly indicative of a narrow and illiberal spirit. But the concluding part of the act is that which most deserves attention. It prohibited ministers of the Establishment "from employing to preach, upon any occasion, or to dispense any of the ordinances of the gospel," persons not qualified to accept a presentation; and also, "from holding ministerial communion in any other manner with such persons."* By this act such men as Rowland Hill and Simeon of Cambridge were expressly aimed at, and excluded from every pulpit in the Established Church of Scotland, not because they were Episcopalians, but because their doctrine was evangelical; for this act was moved, carried, and enforced by the Moderate party, contrary to the feelings and the wishes of their Evangelical opponents. It may be mentioned also, that by the same Moderate party in the Assembly, a pastoral admonition was prepared and sent through the Church, warning against giving countenance to religious societies, missionary associations, itinerant preachers, and Sabbath schools, on the assumption that these were conducted by "ignorant persons, altogether unfit for such an important charge,"—and "persons notoriously disaffected to the civil constitution of the country, and who kept up a correspondence with other societies in the neighborhood." It need scarcely be said now that these accusations were altogether groundless; and it can hardly be supposed that those who uttered such charges did themselves believe them. But it was a convenient mode of fixing the brand of "sedition" upon preachers and teachers of Christianity, as was done in the days of the apostles, and has often since been repeated, when the enemies of the gospel wished to obtain a plausible pretext for persecuting its defenders.

The acts of this Assembly may be regarded as having completed the developement of the system of Moderatism. It had its origin, as a system, in the combination which early took place between the indulged ministers and the Prelatic incumbents, who were introduced into the Church by the pernicious "comprehension scheme" of King William. The perfidious act of 1712, reimposing patronage, gave it growth and fostered it into strength. Early in its progress it showed itself favourable to unsoundness of doctrine and laxity of discipline, and strongly opposed to the rights and privileges of the Christian people. Heresy was more than tolerated; the doctrines of grace and evangelical truth were condemned; legal preaching was encouraged; and a cold and spiritless morality was substituted instead of the warm life of the gospel. Increasing in power, it gave more open and vigorous exercise to its malignant nature, by violating the constitutional principles of the Presbyterian Church, perpetrating intrusive and violent settlements, repressing the remonstrances of faithful ministers, driving them out of the Church, protecting its own heterodox and immoral adherents, courting patrons and politicians, insulting and deeply grieving the religious part of the community, and causing them, even more in sorrow than in anger, to abandon the beloved National Church of their martyred fathers. Arrived at maturity, it boldly declared its principles to be entirely worldly, and its whole policy to be founded on the maxims of secular society, directly contrary to the distinct declarations of the Lord Jesus Christ, and His inspired apostles. With difficulty was it restrained from abandoning the subscription of the Confession of Faith, though even worldly policy could perceive the danger of a deed so glaringly unconstitutional. Advancing towards the stage of rigidity which is symptomatic of decline, it prohibited the missionary enterprise, and thereby declared to the world that it had so little of a Christian spirit as not to feel itself bound to discharge the great commission given by the risen and ascending Saviour to His disciples. Having refused to aid in propagating the gospel abroad, it next exerted itself in checking the extension of Christian instruction at home, by the obstructions and difficulties with which it opposed the erection of new churches; and by the act 1799, it declared against Christian communion with other Churches, however sound in their doctrine and faithful in their ministry. As a worldly system it was now complete. Vital religion had been driven out of its

* Acts of Assembly, year 1799; Cook's Life of Hill p. 175.

pale, or paralyzed within it. By declaring against the propagation of the gospel, it had almost avowedly thrown off its allegiance to Christ. By prohibiting all ministerial communion with other orthodox Protestant Christian Churches, it virtually denied the doctrine of a "Church Universal," rejected the "Communion of Saints," and disclaimed the all-pervading, heart-uniting, and love-breathing brotherly affection, infused into all true members of the household of faith, by the presence and energy of the Holy Spirit. Such did Moderatism prove itself to be, when it reached its full developement, as a system, worldly, despotic, unconstitutional, unpresbyterian, unchristian and spiritually dead,—the utter negation of every thing free, pure, lofty, and hallowed,—if indeed, it ought not rather to be said, that its essence was antipathy to every thing scriptural, holy and divine.*

But while Moderatism was thus swathing itself up in thick cerements, as if to indulge in a long and dignified repose, like a lifeless yet life-like embalmed Egyptian monarch in his hieroglyph-encrusted sarcophagus, there was an active life around it, and even a disturbed vitality, within the oppressed heart of its own torpid frame. It has been already stated, that several of the ordinary supporters of the Moderate policy held and taught the doctrines of the gospel. Not only was it necessary to retain these, because without them it would not have been possible to secure majorities in church courts, but it was also necessary to conciliate them, by occasionally passing measures contrary to the true nature of the Moderate system. Thus it was, that at the very time when that system had acquired its complete developement, it began to exhibit symptoms of disorganization, the sure harbingers of decay. But thus it is in all things essentially worldly; the point of full maturity is that where decline and fall begins. The decline of Moderatism was hastened also by the quickened life and energetic movements of society at large, which could no longer tolerate the sluggish inertness and rigid encrustation of a system unsuited to the spirit of the times. This became apparent early in the century which was on the point of commencing, and in which the contest between the worldly policy of Moderatism and the spirit of evangelical Christianity became warm, incessant, and intensely determined; every year increasing the strength and brightening the hopes of those true friends of constitutional, Presbyterian, and Christian principles, who were the genuine representatives of the Church of Scotland; and weakening both the power and the courage of their opponents, who soon began to display, not the calm and haughty confidence of superior might, but the restless and angry energy of danger and despair.

[1800-5.] It is at all times hazardous to write what may be termed contemporaneous history; both because the historian is himself exposed to the bias arising from personal predilections, and because the minds and feelings of the living generation are too much occupied by their own share of the transactions, to permit them to exercise an impartial judgment either on the events themselves, or on the narrative of the historian. Yet in matters of great and sacred principle it may be possible to state the truth both fairly and fearlessly, leaving it to future times to repel any charge of partiality which may be made. It will not be necessary, however, to do more than trace the outlines of the leading facts and principles of a period which lies within the memory of men but little past the prime and vigour of their life.

The first subject which occurred in the new century, of sufficient importance to demand attention, was that of a plurality of offices in the Church, held by the same individual. In the year 1800, Dr. Arnot, professor of divinity in St. Andrews, was presented to the parish of Kingsbarns, which is six or seven miles distant from the town. This union of offices was opposed in the presbytery by Mr. Bell, minister of Crail, but unsuccessfully. It was also opposed in the synod, and came before the Assembly, where it gave rise to one of the most animated debates that ever occurred in that venerable court. In that celebrated discussion, Principal Brown of Aber-

* It will be perceived that Moderatism is here viewed as a *system* without specific reference to those who embraced it, and without meaning to deny that there were among the Moderates many men, who were better than their system; in the same manner as the system of Popery is condemned, without denying the vital Christianity of many of its members.

deen opposed pluralities in a speech of surpassing eloquence and power, before the constitutional principles, high moral tone, clear strength of argument, and elevated Christian faithfulness of which, the firmest Moderate quailed and shrunk in conscious feebleness. But though manifestly defeated in argument, the "prevailing party" could still procure the sanction of a majority of votes; and Dr. Arnot was allowed to retain both the parish and the chair, contrary to the whole spirit of the Presbyterian constitution, and with the certainty that in such a combination of offices the duties of neither could be adequately discharged.* Although the Evangelical party failed in this constitutional struggle, a deep and lasting impression was made on the mind of the community, and public intelligence began to mark on which side of the Church integrity and faithfulness was chiefly to be found. The Moderate triumph was equivalent to a defeat; for all the sophistry which they employed could not allay the strong feeling of repugnance to such unions which had been excited, and the country rang with the clear and loud sentence of condemnation uttered indignantly against such self-interested conduct.

The celebrated Leslie case, as it has been termed, came next, and deepened the impression which that of Dr. Arnot had produced. Upon the death of Mr. John Robison, professor of natural philosophy in Edinburgh, and the promotion of Mr. Playfair from the mathematical chair to that which had become vacant, the Edinburgh ministers deemed it a convenient opportunity for securing another plurality, and immediately endeavoured to procure the appointment of Dr. Macknight to the chair of mathematics. This, however, soon appeared to be a matter of more difficult accomplishment. Two of the most distinguished professors in the university, Dugald Stewart and Playfair, wrote letters upon the subject to the lord provost; in which they proved that the duties of a professor gave full employment for the talents and industry of any man, and that a faithful discharge of them was incompatible with those important functions of a different kind which belong to a clergyman holding the pastoral office. The town-council, in whom the nomination to that chair is vested, were convinced by these arguments, and declared their intention of giving the appointment to him by whom the highest testimonials of qualification should be produced. This determination rendered it no longer doubtful who should be the successful candidate, as none of them could at all stand a comparison with Mr. John Leslie in point of scientific genius and acquirements. But in a Treatise on Heat, which that gentleman had published a short while before, he had thought proper to diverge into some metaphysical speculations on the idea of necessary connection between cause and effect. This was immediately laid hold of by the Edinburgh doctors, and an attempt was made to convict Leslie of advocating principles of an atheistical tendency. A controversy of a metaphysico-theological kind arose, in which the Moderates assailed Mr. Leslie's view, and the Evangelicals defended it, to the astonishment of the literary public, who saw in the party which they had been accustomed to regard as consisting of narrow-minded fanatics, the most enlightened defenders of true science. The subject came at length before the Assembly; and after a long and able debate, this attempt of Moderate intolerance was defeated by a majority of twelve.*

This discussion was of considerable general importance, especially in directing the public mind towards the tendency of the Moderate system. So long as that was confined to Church politics, comparatively little interest was felt respecting it; and although by one part of that system plurality of offices had been introduced, so long as that was restricted to the theological professorships, it did not attract much notice. But when it was perceived that the dominant party were endeavouring to acquire the possession of the chairs devoted to literature, science, and philosophy, it was felt that this encroaching spirit must be repelled, lest the interests of literature and science should suffer. The argument against pluralities was not indeed placed on the strongest ground by the literary part of

* Scots Magazine, year 1801.

* Pamphlets on the Leslie Controversy; Assembly Debate; Edinburgh Review, No. xiii.

the community. They looked to the injury likely to be sustained by science, if its teachers should be men whose attention was distracted by another class of duties; but Christian men deplored the evil which must be done to religion, if its teachers should devote themselves to secular employments, and neglect the eternal welfare of those over whose spiritual interests they had been appointed to watch. And the idea very readily suggested itself to the minds of reflecting people, "Surely these men must entertain a very low notion of the ministerial office and its unspeakably important duties, who can so eagerly grasp at another office, totally different in its nature, to which if they attend, they must inevitably neglect their pastoral charge." Such opinions becoming prevalent, tended greatly to weaken Moderatism, by leading men to inquire into its real character, and to contrast it with Evangelism, so long calumniated or despised.

[1805-10.] Nothing of peculiar public moment marked the years between 1805 and 1810. Perhaps the only thing which deserves to be noticed is the internal disorganization which began to appear among the Moderate party during that period. The most remarkable instance of it occurred in the different views taken by Dr. Hill of St. Andrews, and Drs. Grieve, Finlayson, and others of the Edinburgh ministers, in the case of the Duke of Hamilton against Mr. Scott, minister of Strathaven, respecting the claims of the latter for an augmentation. Dr. Hill disapproved of the strong measures advocated by the Edinburgh ministers, and stated his views to Lord Melville, who entirely agreed with him; but as the Edinburgh clergy had been in the habit of acting like a permanent committee for the management of ecclesiastical affairs, they were indignant that even Dr. Hill should have offered an opinion till he had consulted them.* The high-minded and honourable conduct of Dr. Hill prevented this disagreement from widening to an actual breach; but it put an end to that unanimity by which the course of Moderate policy had been hitherto characterised. It was indeed itself a consequence of causes previously in operation. Of these, the chief were, as already stated, the residence of Dr. Hill, the avowed leader of the Moderates, in St. Andrews, which prevented him from being generally present in the private consultations of the Edinburgh clergy; and the deeper and sounder theology of Dr. Hill himself, which rendered it impossible for him to be a thorough Moderate on all points, although he followed the principles of Robertson with regard to Church government.

In the year 1810, Dr. Andrew Thomson was appointed to one of the Edinburgh churches, and four years afterwards to St. George's, as minister of which, this distinguished and remarkable man became fully known to the public. He was one of those men who stamp the impress of their own character upon that of the age in which they live; and his appearance in the Scottish metropolis must be marked as the commencement of an era in the ecclesiastical history of his country. Soon after his arrival in Edinburgh, the "Christian Instructor" was commenced under his management as editor; and by its means the thoughts and reasonings of his powerful mind were communicated to the public like successive shocks of electricity, stirring the heart of the kingdom from its torpid lethargy, and spreading dismay among his discomfited antagonists. The public mind had indeed been already partially aroused; and instead of being allowed to sink back into dull and listless repose, the favourable moment was seized, and it was urged forward with a steady and persevering might, which could not long be successfully resisted. Every year it became more and more a matter of general conviction that some measure of ecclesiastical reform was become imperatively necessary; and as the true principles of the Presbyterian Church of Scotland were rescued from the oblivion into which they had been cast, this conviction assumed the form of a full belief, that nothing more was necessary than to restore those principles to their native and vital operation.

[1811.] By a remarkable coincidence, at the very time when Dr. Thomson had resolved to employ the mighty power of the press for the purpose of reawakening the slumbering energies of the Presbyterian Church, a potent auxiliary was on

* Dr. Cook's of Life Hill, pp. 189-207.

the point of appearing in the field, and engaging in the maintenance of the same great cause. In November 1811 was published "The Life of John Knox," by the Rev. Thomas M'Crie. A huge host of prejudices were at once scattered to the winds, or compelled to retreat to the dark lurking-places of ignorance, on the appearance of this magnificent biography. The enemies of the Church of Scotland found that it was no longer possible to accuse the great Scottish Reformer of morose and gloomy bigotry, or wild and stern fanaticism, without periling their own characters, and exposing themselves to the charge of ignorance too dark to be enlightened, and prejudices too dense to be dispelled; while the friends of scriptural truth found themselves at once admitted to the armoury of the invincible chiefs of old, from which they might obtain weapons wherewith to resist and quell the adversary. Nothing could more have borne the aspect of an express arrangement of Providence than did the propitious appearance of this noble work. Even the leading authorities in the literary world were prompt and loud in their applause; and the great principles which it contained and enforced wrought their way into the public mind, convincing, enlightening, and invigorating thousands, preparatory to their coming forward to discharge their duty in the sacred contest which the true Church of Scotland has ever waged in defence of civil and religious liberty.

[1813-17.] Another plurality case occurred in the year 1813. Mr. Ferrie, professor of civil history in St. Andrews, was presented to the parish of Kilconquhar, distant twelve miles from the university seat. The presbytery refused to sustain the presentation, unless Mr. Ferwould assure them that he would resign his professorship immediately on being settled in the parish. To this he would not consent, and the matter was carried by appeal to the Assembly. After a very long and animated debate, the sentence of the presbytery was reversed by a majority of *five*, in a very full house. Although the union of offices involving non-residence was thus once more sanctioned by the strenuous exertions of the Moderates, yet the smallness of the majority indicated that such abuses could not much longer be endured. Next year the subject was brought before the Assembly by an overture from the synod of Angus and Mearns; and after a long and full discussion, what is termed a *declaratory act* was passed, declaring it to be inconsistent with the constitution and the fundamental laws of the Church of Scotland for any minister to hold another office which necessarily required his absence from his parish, and subjected him to an authority that the presbytery to which he was a member could not control.* In the Assembly of 1815, an attempt was made to alter the judgment of the preceding year, on the ground that it was really a *new law*, and ought to have been subject to the regulations of the Barrier Act. This was successfully resisted; but a great outcry was raised by the moderate party, who asserted that the Assembly was violating the intrinsic rights of presbyteries, and insisted that the recent act should be rescinded, and an overture on the subject should be transmitted to presbyteries in the usual manner. An overture was accordingly framed by Dr. Hill in 1816, similar to the recent declaratory act, which, after passing the usual course, was confirmed by the Assembly of 1817, and became a permanent law on the subject of the pluralities, to the extent of putting an end to every such union of offices as was incompatible with residence in the parish. This was so far a reforming act, extorted from the Moderate party by the growing strength of evangelism, and the increasing intelligence and enlightenment of the age.

But that Moderatism itself was not improved, may be very easily shown by one or two illustrations. Several instances occurred about this time of ministers accused of drunkenness and immorality; and although these accusations were corroborated by evidence sufficient to satisfy almost every impartial man, they were explained away into "alleged breaches of decorum," and the culprits allowed to pass unpunished. In another case a minister was accused of criminal intimacy with a female servant; the ecclesiastical courts managed to find the charge not proven, but the civil court found the

* Acts of Assembly, year 1814; Scots Magazine

evidence sufficient to entitle the woman to legal support for herself and her infant, which the minister was obliged to give, and still was allowed to remain in the spiritual office, which he held but to desecrate.

The year 1815 is marked by one incident, apparently slight in itself, but fraught with consequences the importance of which cannot easily be overestimated. In that year was published the address of Dr. Chalmers to the parishioners of Kilmany, when he left that parish on being translated to the Tron Church, Glasgow. There are circumstances connected with that event, the history of which cannot yet be written. But every one who peruses heedfully that address, will mark the deep tone of fervent evangelical piety by which it is pervaded; and some of clearer vision may perceive in it traces of that solemn and profound emotion which fills the soul that has recently been called out of darkness into God's marvellous light, and is still tremulous with the fresh fervour of its new-born spiritual life. From that time forward the world was again to see, as in earlier and better days, how great and lovely a thing is genius of the loftiest order, hallowed by the love of God, and consecrated to His glory.

[1820-25.] In the year 1820, there occurred an instance of the fierce malignity, defeating its own purpose in its blind vindictiveness, which often characterizes the conduct of a falling party. An overture was introduced by Dr. Bryce, regarding the sharp and severe animadversions on the conduct of the Moderate party, which frequently appeared in the "Christian Instructor." A very animated discussion took place, the galled party rising into unusual eloquence under the stimulating influence of the castigation which they had often received. The motion was carried by a majority of *one*, but it gave rise to no ulterior proceedings.* The voice of an indignant public was heard, too loud to be disregarded by even that party whose characteristic it was to disregard the public voice. It might have been very convenient to hide in impenetrable darkness those deeds which could not bear the light; but the nation was not prepared to suffer the liberty of the press to be abridged for the accommodation of those who crouched in its free presence, and shrunk from its indignant rebuke. The Moderate triumph was a severe defeat It showed at once vindictiveness and impotence, and caused the loss of both respect and dread.

* Christian Instructor.

The great question of pluralities came again before the General Assembly in the year 1824. It was caused by the appointment of Dr. Macfarlan to be Principal of the University in Glasgow, and also minister of St. Mungo's in the same city. This was the first instance in which the propriety of a union of offices in the same city or parish was made the subject of a debate in the Assembly. It had been strenuously opposed in the presbytery by Dr. Macgill; but a large majority decided in favour of the union when the subject came before the supreme ecclesiastical court. It was, however, generally believed that a different result might be expected, if the question were tried on its general merits, apart from all personal considerations, such as arise when the interests of individuals are concerned. Eighteen overtures on the subject were laid on the table of the General Assembly in 1825, proving the deep interest with which it was regarded by the community at large. A debate ensued, remarkable for the accurate research into the constitutional history of the Church displayed by some, the grave and lofty views of the sacredness and importance of ministerial duties exhibited by others, and the powerful and thrilling eloquence of Chalmers and Thomson.* But again the power of numbers prevailed over the power of learning, reason, genius, and Christian principle; and a majority of twenty-six was found to defend the union of professorships with parochial charges in the seat of a university. It deserves to be remarked, although the observation may seem to be minute, that the Moderate party obtained their general majority by means of the elders, there being a positive majority of four ministers against pluralities. This fact was not unnoticed by the public, who did not fail to mark on which side of the Church they were to look for personal disinterestedness and a high sense of duty in the discharge of their

* Debates on the Plurality Question, years 1825 and 1826.

sacred functions. Nor will it be thought strange, that the elders should have so generally voted on the Moderate side, when it is remembered how, and for what purpose, that party had been in the habit of making Assembly elders. The spirit of the evangelical and reforming party was not, however, broken by this defeat. Sixteen overtures on the subject brought it again before the Assembly of 1826, and another able and brilliant debate took place. But a strong exertion had been made by the Moderate party, their full strength was mustered, and they obtained a majority of fifty-four. This was the last debate on the subject. A royal commission for visiting the universities of Scotland having been appointed, the two parties in the Church agreed to suspend the desperate struggle, and to await the decision of the commission. To this the Evangelical party might well consent; for public opinion had already expressed itself decisively against such a union of offices as rendered it absolutely impossible for the person who held them to discharge adequately the important duties of both. The opinion of the royal commission was at length given, and almost in the very terms of the motions which the Evangelical party had so long and strenuously advocated in the Assembly.* Thus one fundamental principle of the Church of Scotland was again revived and enforced, greatly to the discomfiture and dismay of that unconstitutional party which had so long held a usurped dominion over the Church, and with the usual policy of usurpers, had striven to misinterpret those laws which could not be concealed, and to conceal those that could not be misinterpreted. And as each successive great principle was brought anew to light by the true and fearless defenders of Scotland's ancient Church, a fresh vitality was poured into the nation's heart, a new intelligence enlightened the public mind, and like an iceberg pierced by the sunbeams and wasted by the rush of living waters, the cold fabric of Moderatism swayed heavily, and tottered to its fall.

[1826-30.] It has been already stated, that the infusion of evangelical principles into even the Moderate party tended greatly to cause the overthrow of Moderatism as a system; and Dr. Hardy and Dr. Hill have been mentioned as having been greatly instrumental in promoting this better spirit among their party. To their respected names must be added those of Dr. William Ritchie, Dr. Nicoll, and especially Dr. Inglis, all of whom taught evangelical doctrine, although they supported the general course of Moderate church policy. To Dr. Inglis is especial honour due, as the man by whom was first proposed, matured, and carried into effect, that measure on which so much of the Divine blessing has conspicuously rested, the Church of Scotland's Mission to India. And it is with peculiar delight that this brief tribute of respect and gratitude is paid to the memory of one who was distinguished by remarkable clearness and soundness of judgment, candour, sincerity, and frankness of mind, and a calm personal piety, deepening as he grew near the close of his life, and rendering his last years both the loveliest and the best.* So early as the year 1818, the attention of Dr. Inglis had been directed to the subject of missions, and his enlightened mind speedily detected the unchristian character of the opinions promulgated respecting it by the Moderate leaders of 1796. In 1824 he brought the matter publicly before the Assembly, and the weight of his character, and the position which he occupied, at once secured for it a degree of attention from both sides of the Church, which it could not otherwise have easily obtained. There is no reason to doubt, that if it had been brought forward by one of the Evangelical side, it would have met immediate and strong opposition; but the wisdom of Providence was clearly shown in preparing a leader of the Moderate party to be the first advocate of a measure of such a Christian character, and respecting which it was so exceedingly desirable that there should be no dissentions in a Christian Church. In 1825, a committee was appointed to consider and report on the subject; and in 1826, a "Pastoral Address to the People of Scotland," from the pen of Dr. Inglis, appeared, and tended pow-

* Report of the Royal Commission.

* It deserves to be stated to the honour of Dr. Inglis, that in the case of North Leith he declared, that, according to the Constitution of the Church, ordination to the pastoral office proceeded upon the Call alone, and that the presentation of a patron had no further effect than securing a legal right to the fruits of the benefice.

erfully to direct the attention of the kingdom to the sacred duty of propagating the gospel among the heathen, and especially in India. Collections were made and subscriptions obtained, till a sufficient fund was raised to enable the committee to proceed with their holy enterprise; and at length, in 1829, Dr. Duff, the first missionary ever sent forth by any national Protestant Church, in its corporate character, left his native land, commissioned by the Presbyterian Church of Scotland to convey to India the light of gospel truth, and to offer for her acceptance the simple, pure, efficient, and most truly apostolic form of Christianity, which is the glory and the strength of the Presbyterian Church.* It is but an act of justice to the memory of a great and far-seeing man to state, that to a suggestion made by Dr. M'Crie, at a public meeting held in Edinburgh in the year 1813, and taken up and prosecuted with characteristic energy by Sir Henry Moncreiff, was the Church of Scotland indebted for a share of legal countenance and support in India, without which she could not have sent forth her celebrated India Mission, in her corporate character as a National Church.†

Several events of great importance, partly in a religious and partly in a national point of view, occurred during this period, and would deserve to be fully stated, were they not so recent that they must still be fresh in the recollection of the public. Of these, the first in point of time was the Apocrypha Controversy, which arose in consequence of the British and Foreign Bible Society having been led to violate one of its fundamental conditions, the circulation of the pure Bible, without note or comment. The directors, induced by considerations of expediency, consented to permit the Apocrypha to be inserted in the Bible, prefaces to be prefixed, and other violations of the fundamental condition to be committed, in the hope that Romanists and others might accept the Bible in that vitiated state, who would have rejected it in its purity.‡ Against this sinful compromise the Edinburgh committee remonstrated, but without effect. A controversy arose on the subject, which soon became in reality a contest between expediency and principle. In this controversy Dr. Andrew Thomson stood forth the fearless and mighty champion of sacred truth, not quite alone, but first without a second, discomfiting every antagonist that dared the encounter. His exertions were perfectly marvellous for several successive years; and were a fair estimate made, they would prove to be equal, if not superior, to those made by any man in any department of mental labour within as short a time. It cannot be doubted that his excessive labours in that great cause hastened him, prematurely for his country and the Church, in the fifty-second year of his age, to the abodes of everlasting rest and peace. The public mind was during the same period powerfully directed towards the abolition of slavery in the West India Islands; and in this truly Christian object Dr. Thompson earned peculiar distinction, especially by one speech in which his eloquence rose to a pitch of grandeur and sublimity such as has been rarely equalled. Another event of this singularly energetic time, fertile in producing the elements both of evil and of good, must also be mentioned. In the year 1829, a bill passed the British legislature, and received the ratification of the sovereign, removing all the civil disabilities to which the adherents of the Church of Rome had been subjected, and rendering them eligible to any office of the State, with the exceptions only of the Lord Chancellorship and the Crown itself. Into any discussion respecting the merits or demerits of this measure it is scarcely our province, and not our present intention, to enter, both because it was the act of the State, not of the Church, and because its full effects upon the character and prospects of the nation have not yet been developed, although they have assumed an ominous aspect.

[1831.] The year 1831 may be regarded as the commencement of a great era, both in the ecclesiastical and in the civil history of the empire. To the civil history, we make no further allusion than merely to state, that the passing of the Reform Bill gave an impulse to the public mind, which sent it rushing with irresistible force into every channel of thought

* Acts of Assembly; Dr. Duff on India and India missions, pp. 476-491.
† Life of Dr. M'Crie, pp. 201-204.
‡ See pamphlets on the Apocrypha Controversy; and Christian Instructor.

and mental enterprise. From that time it was manifest, that no public institution, civil or sacred, could be long in a state of safety, which could not stand the most searching scrutiny, and which did not possess in itself a vital principle, that could give it spontaneous movement and ready adaptation to the spirit of the age. In what manner this was shown in political matters, let the civil historian record: our own province demands our undivided attention.

On the 9th of February 1831, Dr. Andrew Thompson was suddenly called to rest from his mighty toils; and the heart of Scotland was stunned with her great and unexpected loss. The universal sorrow of the nation bore testimony to his great and varied excellencies: the impress of his character and opinions stamped on society is his memorial.

The Assembly of that year had to discharge the painful duty of deposing Mr. Campbell, minister of the parish of Row, on account of his holding and teaching the heretical doctrine of universal redemption, together with several other erroneous tenets. The same Assembly deprived Mr. M'Lean of his license as a probationer, because he publicly avowed and preached doctrines respecting the human nature of the Divine Redeemer, similar to those held by the lamented Edward Irving. As these heretical opinions did not long continue to spread in the Church, and have since sunk into comparative oblivion, it does not seem either necessary or desirable to offer any further remarks concerning them, except to state, that while these men diverged unhappily into deplorable errors, in consequence of their fervent but ill-regulated zeal, their personal characters were unimpeachable, their piety was warm and earnest, and they were generally regarded with equal pity and esteem.

The attention of the public mind began about this time to be strongly directed to what has been termed the Voluntary controversy. The subject had indeed been so far silently working its way into the minds of many during a period of more than thirty years; but it had hitherto attracted little attention, and it was only now that, under the strong impulse given to every topic of real or speculative interest, its demands became too loud and urgent to be any longer unheard or disregarded. A few preliminary remarks are necessary to render this subject of controversy at once simple and intelligible.

It has not been considered necessary to advert particularly to the history of the Secession Church of Scotland subsequent to the formation of that new body which assumed the name of the Relief. A very brief statement of a few leading topics must now be given, as necessary to a clear view of the subject. In 1747, the Secession was divided into two parties, by a controversy about the oath taken by burgesses; which two parties were generally known by the names of Burghers and Antiburghers.* Both parties continued to adhere to the Act and Testimony of the first Seceders, though divided into two distinct synods; and as the dominant Moderate party in the National Church persevered in that course of defection in doctrine, government, and discipline, which had caused the Secession, this division, instead of weakening the Seceders, actually contributed to weaken the Church, in consequence of the new opportunities afforded and inducements held forth to draw men of all shades of opinion from the communion of a Church, whose leaders seemed to take a peculiar pleasure in despising and insulting the people. This conduct of the Moderate party caused both synods of the already estranged and alienated Secession to begin to question whether the tyranny and corruption of the Church might not be directly ascribed to her connection with the State, which seemed to lead to the infusion of a baneful secularizing influence, and might be thought to give undue power to the civil magistrate in religious matters. But as the constitution of the Church, to which by their Act and Testimony they still adhered, maintained not only the lawfulness of religious establishments, but also the duty of the civil magistrate to establish a national religious institution, they began, almost at the same time in each synod, to give a qualified assent to their own standards, and to subscribe them with evasive explanations, which was soon felt to be equally dan-

* Gib's Display, vol. ii.

gerous and irksome, not to say inconsistent with honest integrity of heart and mind.

This change of sentiment made its first appearance in a pamphlet, published by a member of the Burgher Synod about the year 1780; and having gradually gained ground in that body, it was brought before them publicly at their synodical meeting in May 1795, in a petition that acknowledged the change, and requested that the language of the Confession of Faith and Formula might be so far altered as to be rendered more consistent with the opinions entertained by a large proportion of the members. A strong opposition was made to this proposal by several of the most respectable ministers, among whom Mr. Willis of Greenock distinguished himself by the prominent and decided part which he took in defence of the fundamental principles which all had subscribed. The innovation, however, went on; a modified formula was proposed, and, after some delay, ratified by the Synod, in accordance with the new views of the majority. A small minority dissented, withdrew from the innovating party, formed themselves into a presbytery in 1799, and became known by the designation of the Old Light Burghers.*

A similar innovating process was about the same time going on in the Antiburgher synod, though it does not appear either to have begun or to have been opposed so early; and as it produced corresponding results, and has attracted more attention in consequence of the subsequent celebrity of one distinguished man, to whose great mental power it was the means of first directing public notice, it must be somewhat more fully stated. In order to escape from the unpleasant and scarcely honourable state of matters in which subscription of their standards, accompanied with evasive explanations, involved them, it was proposed in the Antiburgher Synod, that the Testimony should be enlarged, and so far modified as to adapt it to the altered circumstances which a series of years had produced.† The enlarging and modifying process thus begun, led to results which could scarcely have been contemplated by those who proposed it. The minds of those who were engaged in this attempt diverged further and further from their original position, as they proceeded in their task; and the result was, the production of a new work, which was designated, "The Narrative and Testimony." This was, however, the work of years, and was not finally adopted, so as to supersede the original Testimony, till the year 1804, although the outline of the work received the sanction of the Synod, in the form of an overture, in the year 1793. An act of Synod was passed in 1796, the tenor of which indicated darkly that the Secession Church was on the point of abandoning the principles of the Church of Scotland, and consequently of their own founders, who seceded expressly for the purpose of the more strenuously asserting those principles. Some of the ablest and best ministers of the Secession perceived the danger of these proceedings, and strove earnestly to stem the tide of defection which was rapidly drifting the great body of their Church into a contradiction of their own acts and standards. But all their remonstrances and protests were ineffectual. In May 1804, the Synod enacted their Narrative and Testimony into a term of communion. In August 1806, the Rev. Messrs. Bruce, Aitken, Hog, and M'Crie, formally abandoned their connection with the Synod, and constituted themselves into a presbytery, assuming the name of the Constitutional Associate Presbytery. The Synod deposed their more honest and conscientious brethren without delay, and even passed sentence of excommunication upon Dr. M'Crie, probably as being the most distinguished and forminable opponent of their defections. In 1807, that gifted and high-principled man published a "Statement of the Difference" between the original Testimony of the first Seceders and the new production of their descendants, proving beyond all doubt that they had abandoned their principles, and adopted others pregnant with danger to the civil and religious peace and welfare of the kingdom. This very valuable production made comparatively little impression on the public mind when it first appeared, as the deep importance of the subject was scarcely perceived beyond

* Little Naphtali, by the Rev. W. Willis, Greenock. See also Appendix to the Judicial Testimony, published by the Old Light Burghers, 1800.

† Life of Dr M'Crie, pp. 45, 46.

the limits of the Secession ; but no work which has since been published on the Voluntary controversy will more amply repay a studious perusal.* To close these preliminary remarks: In 1820, the two parties of Seceders, the Burghers and Antiburghers, again commenced the work of enlargement and compromise, abandoned some more of their original principles, opened their views more fully on the subject of hostility to all national establishments of religion, and combining on this basis, formed themselves into one body, under the name of the United Secession. Such was the condition of the Scottish Seceders, who had gradually abandoned their principles and become Dissenters, when the popular movements which were taking place throughout the kingdom encouraged them to bring prominently before the public those sentiments which had been long maturing in secret, and for which they now began to expect an early and complete triumph. Indications of this intention were given from time to time for several years; but it was not till 1830, or rather 1831, that the discussion respecting the lawfulness of a civil establishment of religion, in the form of a National Church, assumed the grave aspect of a public controversy; and it was not till 1832 that it became sufficiently important to draw into the contest the leading men both of the Secession and of the Church. Speedily, however, it reached such a degree of intensity as to engage the attention of the whole kingdom, and to make it evident, that upon the decision of this great question would depend the peace and stability of the British empire.

It will not be expected that any thing more than a very brief summary of the chief points discussed in this great controversy should be given here. And in attempting such a summary it shall be our endeavour to state nothing but what belongs to the very essence of the controversy. The subject matter of the controversy, when divested of every thing extraneous, was simply this, "Whether or not it be the duty of the State to give support and countenance to Christianity, by establishing and endowing a national institution for the purpose of imparting to the whole body of the community instruction in the faith and practice of the gospel?" Those who were opposed to all religious establishments, were of course bound to take the negative side of this proposition, and to attempt to prove, that it was not the duty of the State to interfere in religious matters, even in the slightest degree, either by supporting truth or repressing falsehood. Very few of them, however, were willing to occupy the position of maintaining a theory which clearly involved national infidelity and atheism, by the total exclusion of religion from the civil and legislative character of the nation. Those who did approach most closely to the central principle of the controversy, endeavoured to evade that conclusion, by giving such definitions of Church and State as might seem to show the impossibility of any connection between them which did not involve the most pernicious consequences. They were careful to maintain, that the power competent to states is "wholly temporal, respecting only the secular interests of society; and they seemed to think, that any possible connection which the civil magistrate could have with religion could only lead to its persecution or its corruption. Their opponents both denied the correctness of this definition of civil magistracy, and rejected the conclusion which was attempted to be deduced from it.

The defenders of national establishments of religion assumed far higher grounds than their opponents. They held civil magistracy to be an ordinance of God, whether viewed in the light of natural, or in that of revealed religion; rendering it the imperative duty of kings and states to maintain and promote, in their public and official character, the true and pure worship of Him to whom all power belongs, from whom they derive their station and authority, to whom they must render an account of all their conduct, public as well as private, and whom they are bound to recognise and revere as the King of kings and Lord of lords. This they held to be the first and highest duty of the civil magistrate, even antecedent to any express revelation. But God, the ruler and judge of the universe, having revealed his will to man, the next point of inquiry necessarily was,

* The whole of this subject is very clearly stated in the Life o Dr. M'Crie, by his Son.

whether in that revealed will there could be found any statements calculated to modify or set aside this primary law or civil magistracy. There it was found, that, under the Mosaic dispensation, the duty of kings and states to maintain and promote the worship of God was most strongly and explicitly declared; and when their opponents endeavoured to set aside the arguments deduced from the Old Testament dispensation, on the ground that its regulations were no longer binding under Christianity, this was answered, *first*, by the universally admitted principle, that what God had enacted no inferior authority could repeal; and that, therefore, all the enactments of the Mosaic dispensation must be still binding, unless it could be shown that they were either so manifestly typical as to have terminated by fulfilment, or had been expressly revealed in the gospel; *secondly*, by producing from the gospel dispensation itself such statements respecting the duties of the civil magistrate as it was manifestly impossible for him to discharge, without giving his direct sanction and authoritative support to Christianity.

They further argued, that it was impossible for the civil magistrate to perform his own peculiar duties without the support of true religion; that the true welfare of the nation, which it was his duty to promote, depended upon its moral purity, and the rectitude, impartiality, and humanity of its laws; and that the only effectual method of promoting moral purity was to be found in the propagation of the gospel, and the only sure guide in framing just, equal, and humane laws, was the Word of God. Hence it followed, that the first and most imperative duty of the civil magistrate, even when seeking to promote the physical, mental and moral welfare of the community, was to provide for and offer to the whole body of the nation, the means of instruction in the knowledge of the only living and true God, and of Christ Jesus, whom he hath sent to redeem, regenerate, and save mankind from sin and misery. It was not difficult to show that, in discharging this duty, the civil magistrate was not entitled to use his power in any manner that might amount to persecution, both because his duty was fulfilled by providing and offering the means of national religious instruction, and because in supporting Christianity, he supports a religion which pleads, entreats, persuades, but cannot and will not persecute,—whose power resides not in the sword, but in the gentle and gracious influence of heavenly love.

But the main arguments used by the assailants of religious establishments were of a secondary character, not reaching the essence of the controversy, fallacious in their own nature, and inconclusive, even if they could have been proved to be true so far as they reached. They declaimed loudly, that it was the duty of all Christians to give voluntary support to Christianity; and from this undisputed proposition they deduced two very strange and illogical conclusions,—that no other method of providing support for the public teachers of religion was permissible, —and that this was perfectly adequate to the necessities of the nation. They confounded the *right* of the pastor to be supported, with the *duty* of the people to support him; and they virtually maintained the manifest absurdity, that what was the duty of each Christian in the nation individually, was not the duty of the whole as a Christian nation collectively. Their other conclusion was resolvable into a mere question of facts. No one denied that it was the duty of all Christians to aid in propagating the gospel; but the defenders of national endowments asserted, that without a national fund applied for the support of ministers in poor and immoral localities, there would be a large proportion of the population left destitute of religious instruction, partly because too poor to provide it for themselves, and partly because too immoral and irreligious to have any regard for it. The correctness of this view was easily tried by the test of statistical investigation; and from the inquiries made by a royal commission appointed for that purpose, it appeared, that there were at least five hundred thousand souls in Scotland totally destitute of the means of religious instruction, notwithstanding the exertions of the Established Church, and the supplemental aid of all who held the Voluntary principle, and were at liberty to employ all the energies which they declared it to possess. Churchmen always said "We are eager to accept all the voluntary aid from private Christian liberality which we can obtain; and where that falls short, we call upon a patriotic and enlightened Christian legislature to supply the deficiency, by contributing to send the bread of life to thousands who are perishing for lack of spiritual knowledge."

As the advocates of the Voluntary principle could not deny the proved spiritual destitution, they attempted to evade the obvious inference, namely, that their favourite principle was not so powerful as they affirmed, by boldly declaring, that the very existence of religious establishments was the cause of that inefficiency in the Voluntary principle which could not be denied; hazarding the paradoxical assertion, that civil establishments of Christianity had been the direct source of all the errors which had corrupted the Church, paralyzed its exertions, and impeded its propagation throughout the world. In this respect the controversy assumed a historical character; and it was soon triumphantly proved, that almost every one of the most deadly errors that have crept into the Church had its origin in a period long before Christianity was established,—nay, that many of them sprang directly out of the felt defects of the Voluntary system itself, and might never have existed had there been an adequate establishment in an earlier age. A minor department of the same question furnished much scope for violent declamation against the abuses of all establishments. This was likely to be a popular theme, and was therefore much employed by the subordinate controversialists; for all those of a higher order of mind were aware that no argument, founded merely on the abuse of any thing, can be conclusively against its proper use.

But by the more intelligent opponents of the Church an attempt was made to bring essentially the same argument forward in another aspect, in which they asserted, "That in every Established Church, the very fact of entering into an alliance with the State involved such a sacrifice of the spiritual independence of the Church, as to render it incapable of exercising that freedom of government and purity of discipline which are absolutely essential to any Church of Christ which deserves the name." If it had been actually proved that there did not exist any Established Church which had not incurred the loss of due spiritual independence, that would not have proved that there *could not* be an Establishment without the sacrifice of spiritual independence. For it was not difficult to show, by analyzing the nature of Church and State till their simplest elements were reached, and pointing out the respective provinces and duties of each, that they might be of great mutual support and aid to each other, without either of them in the slightest degree yielding up that which was peculiar to itself, or encroaching on what belonged rightfully to the other; and even, that any encroachment of the one upon the other's province would inevitably not only inflict injury upon the aggrieved, but would also recoil upon the aggressor in some form at least equally calamitous. If the Church invade the functions of the State, that leads to Popery; if the State invade those of the Church, that is Erastianism; and in either case, both Church and State inflict and sustain mutual and heavy injury. And appealing to facts, it was shown, that the Church of Scotland occupied the medium between these two extremes, in her connection with the State, neither encroaching upon its functions, nor surrendering her own spiritual independence as a Church of Christ. This reference to the condition and character of the Church of Scotland was somewhat less conclusive than it would otherwise have been in consequence of the secular policy so long pursued by the unconstitutional Moderate party, which was undeniably Erastian; but the course of reformation which had been in progress for several years, the rapid increase of Evangelism, and the resuscitations of the true constitutional principles of the Presbyterian church government and discipline which had taken place, were more than sufficient to neutralize any objection drawn from the long domination of Moderatism; and it was felt by the public, and even by the ablest Voluntaries themselves that equally in principle, argument and fact, the Church had gained the victory.*

* It does not seem necessary to specify the numerous books and pamphlets written in the Voluntary controversy, as these are still in the hands of the public, and have as yet lost none of their interest.

Every person capable of fully understanding this important controversy will readily perceive, that it could not have been gained by any Church but one holding firmly the great Presbyterian principle of the sole Sovereignty and Headship of the Lord Jesus Christ over His spiritual kingdom, the Church. English Episcopacy could not have withstood the shock which the Church of Scotland encountered and repelled unshaken. This was clearly perceived by the greatest warrior and statesman of the age, when, with that intuitive penetration and sagacity by which he is distinguished, he remarked, that "the battle of Establishments must be fought in Scotland." But it must also be remarked, that the battle could not have been gained, had the struggle taken place during the domination of Moderatism. Indeed, the Moderate party seem to have been aware of their own inability to dare the encounter, as very few of them ventured to grapple with the subject, and of these few, none but Evangelical Moderates, and even they not with very distinguished success.

It might have been expected, that the merit of the Church of Scotland in this perilous conflict of principles, when she had proved herself to be the firmest bulwark of the British constitution, would have gained her some favour in the eyes not only of Christians, but of prudent politicians and enlightened statesmen. It was not the first time in her history in which the Presbyterian Church had triumphantly defended the cause of religious purity and truth, and thereby at the same time had protected civil liberty. To her it mattered not whether her assailant might be a cunning or an arbitrary monarch, an avaricious and domineering aristocracy, or a degenerate Secession, aided by a revolutionary populace. Her duty was to maintain her allegiance to her own divine Head and King, by whomsoever that sacred principle might be assailed. In all her former conflicts she had often realized the applicability to her history of her own singularly appropriate emblem and motto, the bush burning but not consumed, because the Lord was in it. And before the Voluntary controversy had fairly ceased, she was violently exposed to another fiery trial, by the instrumentality of those who should have hailed her as their protectress, had they possessed wisdom enough to comprehend the nature of the danger which had been warded off, or sufficient generosity to be grateful for their deliverance.

[1832.] The quickening progress of the Voluntary controversy directed the attention of both the assailants and the defenders of the Church of Scotland to every thing, either in her constitutional principles or in her practice, which could furnish material for assault or defence. This inevitably led the friends of the Church to mark with sharpened intelligence those abuses which rendered her peculiarly vulnerable in any part, and stimulated them to inquire carefully, whether there did not exist in her constitution principles which needed but to be recalled into sanative action, in order to restore to her a life which all her foes could not destroy. The wisest and ablest of the Evangelical ministers had always felt that the mode in which patronage was exercised in the Church was her most assailable point; that it had alienated the people, corrupted a large proportion of the ministers, diminished her usefulness, and weakened her moral influence over the public mind. But the law of patronage had now existed so long, that many who felt its arbitrary exercise to be a grievance, were nevertheless so far reconciled to the abstract idea of patronage, that they did not at all contemplate, nor even desire, its total abolition. The subject of the total abolition of patronage had indeed been brought before the public, and an anti-patronage society formed, in the year 1825, the most active member of which was Dr. Andrew Thomson. Although little effectual progress was made by this society, it directed the attention of the public mind to the subject, and in that manner probably accomplished all that its members ever expected. By such concurrent causes a very general feeling was produced, that some modification of patronage should take place, such as might render the method of appointing ministers to vacant charges less arbitrary and capricious than it had long been; and also that the argument against Establishments, based on such manifest abuses, might be weakened, if it could not be wholly removed. The chief direction, however, which the public mind took in the first instance was, to attempt such a definition of what a *call* really ought to be, and such an enforcement of it in a legitimate manner, as might restore it to a proper degree of efficiency, as a constitutional limitation of patronage.

When the General Assembly met in 1832, there were laid on the table overtures from three synods and eight presbyteries. The general tenor of these overtures was to this effect:—"That whereas the practice of church courts for many years had reduced the call to a mere formality; and whereas this practice has a direct tendency to alienate the affections of the people of Scotland from the Established Church; it is overtured, that such measures as may be deemed necessary be adopted, in order to restore the call to its constitutional and salutary efficiency." In the debate which followed, Professor Brown of Aberdeen moved, "that the overtures be remitted to a committee, with instructions to consider the subject, and to report to next Assembly." Principal Macfarlan of Glasgow moved, "that the Assembly judge it unnecessary and inexpedient to adopt the measures recommended in the overtures now before them." The latter motion was carried by a majority of forty-two; and thus the Moderate party refused even to have the subject considered, that a deliberate opinion might be formed whether the loud and general complaints of the kingdom were well-founded, and whether any method could be devised to remedy the evil and restore public tranquillity. A little more sagacity might have enabled them to perceive, that the matter could not be thus set aside and consigned to oblivion; and that a comparatively slight amendment might put an end to an agitation which was rapidly increasing in both intensity and extent, and which would soon not be satisfied without a much greater change than had yet been contemplated.

[1833.] A very short period of time after the rising of the Assembly was sufficient to prove, that the refusal of the Moderate party even to institute an inquiry into the important subject which had been before them, had greatly increased the excitement of the public mind, and directed it more forcibly than ever towards the conflicting topics of patronage and calls. This was sufficiently proved by the fact, that when the Assembly met in 1833, it appeared that the attention of the court was again to be directed to the subject by not less than forty-five overtures on calls. The general tenor of these overtures was closely similar to that of the eleven brought forward in the preceding year. Two different motions were laid before the Assembly,—one by Dr. Chalmers, the other by Dr. Cook; and a very long and able debate ensued, in which the main elements of the question were very amply developed and discussed. It was clearly proved by the whole history of the Church, that ever since the Reformation it had been a fixed principle in her constitution and laws, that no minister shall be intruded into any pastoral charge contrary to the will of the congregation; that this had been verbally admitted even by the Moderate party, though too generally disregarded in their procedure; that this principle had been subjected to various fluctuations in modes of form and application, but had never been abandoned or disclaimed; and that its most natural position and method of operation was to be found in the call given by the people, inviting a qualified person to be their pastor, without which the settlement of a minister could not be legally and constitutionally effected. Dr. Chalmers proposed, that efficiency should be given to the call by declaring, that the dissent of a majority of the male heads of families, resident in the parish and communicants, expressed with or without the assignment of reasons, ought to be of conclusive effect in setting aside the presentee, save and except where it is clearly established, that the said dissent is founded in corrupt and malicious combination, or not truly founded in any objection personal to the presentee in regard to his ministerial gifts and qualifications, either in general, or with reference to that particular parish. Dr. Cook's motion declared, that it is competent for the heads of families to give in to the presbytery objections, of whatever nature, against the presentee; that the presbytery shall consider these objections, and if they find them unfounded, or originating from causeless prejudices, they shall proceed to the settlement; but if they judge that they are well-founded, they shall reject the presentation, the presentee being unqualified. This latter motion was manifestly an evasion of the subject, as it gave no greater powers to a majority, or the whole of a congregation, than had always been possessed by any individual; but in the course of his speech, Dr. Cook distinctly admitted an important principle, which the Moderate party, ever since the days of Principal Robertson, had strenuously denied, namely, "That the Church regarded qualification as including much more than learning, moral character, and sound doctrine,—as extending, in fact, to the fitness of presentees in all respects for the particular situation to which they were appointed."* The peculiar point of Dr. Chalmers' motion was, that by declaring the dissent of a majority, with or without reasons, conclusive, it rendered intrusion impossible, while it still reserved sufficient power in the church courts to prevent that dissent from being founded on malice or mere caprice on the part of the people. Dr. Cook's motion was, however, carried by a majority of twelve, the numbers being one hundred and forty-nine to one hundred and thirty-seven. And it is worthy of notice, that in this instance again the Moderate majority was obtained by means of the elders, there being a positive majority of twenty ministers in behalf of Dr. Chalmers' motion.†

The discussion of this important question was both much more comprehensive and minute in this Assembly than in that of the preceding year, stripping off the thin disguise in which a specious sophistry had sought to involve it, clearing away many prejudices and erroneous notions that had long been prevalent, and bringing prominently to the light those great constitutional principles which had been so long kept in obscurity and abeyance. The public began now clearly to perceive, that the charge of innovation, so vehemently urged against the Evangelical party by their opponents, was altogether devoid of truth; that the insinuation of their being actuated by political motives rested on no better foundation; but that, in reality, the principles for which they were contending, were precisely those which had been held by the Scottish reformers, had been by them made the very essence and basis of the Church, and had been maintained by her in every period of her history; that her purity and efficiency as a Christian Church had been exactly proportionate to the sincerity with which they had been held, and the efficiency which had been given to their operation; and that, though these principles had been overborne and disregarded during the long and dreary reign of Moderatism, they had still been held by a faithful few within the Church, rendering it a moral certainty, that if ever that constitutional party should obtain the ascendancy, they would of necessity bring into immediate operation those principles which they had never ceased to hold, and would restore to the nation, in all its original purity and excellence, the true Evangelical and Presbyterian Church of Scotland.

But though still successful on this question, the Moderates sustained in this Assembly their first defeat as a party, and that, too, with reference to a very important measure. The ministers of chapels of ease had petitioned to be admitted to their constitutional rights, as members of church courts, and to have sessions allowed them, that they might exercise discipline in their congregations. They craved to be heard by counsel in support of their petitions. This was opposed by Dr. Cook; but, on a division, it was carried by a majority of a hundred and twenty-one to a hundred and one. The petitions were remitted to a committee, who were to report to next Assembly. A further result of this favourable deliverance, was the passing of an act by the Moderates themselves, a few days afterwards, similar to that which had been sought for by the chapel ministers, in favour of the ministers of the parliamentary churches. This act deserves unqualified approbation. By it, the parliamentary churches, as they were termed, which had been built and partially endowed in the most necessitous parts of the country chiefly in the Highlands had districts

* This view must have been since abandoned by the Moderate party; otherwise they too must have opposed the recent encroachments of the Court of Session.

† See the published debate of that year; and the Presbyterian Reviews, vol. iv.

assigned to them, which were erected into separate parishes *quoad sacra;* and the ministers of these new parishes were authorised to exercise all the functions competent to any ministers, both in their own parishes, and as members of church courts. This act was founded on a report laid before the Assembly by a committee, of which Dr. Cook was convener; and however difficult it may be to reconcile it with the ordinary policy of the Moderate party, it was in itself a just, prudent, and constitutional measure.*

[1834.] The Assembly of 1834 must ever be held as one of the most memorable whose proceedings have been recorded in the annals of the Church of Scotland. When the Erskines and other fathers of the Secession appealed to the "first free and reforming Assembly," they little thought that exactly an hundred years would elapse before that despotic party which had expelled them would lose its ascendency, and a free and reforming Assembly would actually be held. Such, however, was the case, as the shortest possible record of its proceedings will sufficiently prove. A great number of overtures on calls again brought that subject under discussion; and, from the crowded state of the house, it was manifest that the full strength of both parties was to be put forth, and that all Scotland was watching the issue with the most intense anxiety. A motion was made by Lord Moncreiff to the same purport as that made by Dr. Chalmers in the preceding Assembly, declaring that the disapproval of a majority of male heads of families, being communicants, should be deemed sufficient ground for the presbytery rejecting the person so disapproved of; and declaring further, that no person should be entitled to express his disapproval, who should refuse, if required, solemnly to declare, in presence of the presbytery, that he is actuated by no factious or malicious motive, but solely by a conscientious regard to the spiritual interests of himself or the congregation. After a long and able debate, this motion was carried by a majority of forty-six, the numbers being one hundred and eighty-four to one hundred and thirty-eight. This most important decision took place on Tuesday the 27th day of May 1834; and with it terminated the reign of Moderatism in the Church of Scotland.

* Acts of Assembly, year 1833.

On Thursday the 29th of May, the case of the chapels of ease was again brought before the Assembly, by several overtures on the subject, and the report of the committee appointed in the preceding Assembly. Although the admission of the chapel ministers seemed necessarily to follow from that of the parliamentary church ministers, it was strenuously resisted by the Moderate party, chiefly on the ostensible ground of a doubt respecting the power of the Church to admit the ministers of chapels of ease to a participation in church government, without previously asking and obtaining the consent of the legislature. As this supposed want of power equally affected the case of the parliamentary church ministers, with this sole difference, that the latter were not, like the chapel ministers, popularly elected, there is reason to believe that the unavowed objection was of a totally different nature. The vehement complaints subsequently poured forth by the leaders of that party against the admission of the chapel ministers, as having been the direct cause of Evangelical ascendency, although quite erroneous in point of fact, give a strong indication of the secret apprehensions of the Moderates, and may not unfairly be regarded as furnishing the true explanation of their conduct in this matter, both then and subsequently.* In the course of the discussion it appeared, that within the space of a century, nearly six hundred dissenting congregations had risen up in Scotland, while there had been only sixty-three chapels of ease erected during the same period. It was proved also, that this paucity of chapels had been caused, in a great measure, by the anomalous and unconstitutional position in which their ministers were placed, which rendered them comparatively inefficient, and discouraged the people from the exertions which they would otherwise have gladly made. This argument was mightily enforced by the consideration that, while the Church was thus remaining almost stationary, the population was increasing

* The exact dates are given above, because it has been asserted that the Act on Calls was passed by the support of the chapel ministers.

with great rapidity; so that vast numbers must either sink into practical heathenism and immorality, thereby becoming the enemies of all law and order, human and divine, or must join the Secession, which having now avowed the Voluntary principle, was the deadly foe of all ecclesiastical establishments. Unless, therefore, some measure were speedily taken for encouraging the erection of new churches, giving to their ministers all due and requisite powers, and making a great effort to meet the necessities of the "outfield population," it was evident that the Church of Scotland must perish in the course of a few generations, as no longer capable of accomplishing the purpose for which a National Church exists,—the instruction of the whole body of the people in the knowledge of what pertains to their mental, moral, and religious welfare. These arguments triumphed in this reforming Assembly; and the ministers of chapels of ease were, by a declaratory act, rescued from their curate-like position, empowered to perform all the functions, and authorised to enjoy all the privileges, of minist rs of the Church of Scotland, in discipline and government, as constituent members of church courts.

The only other topics of general importance connected with this Assembly were, the appointment of that committee for the purpose of promoting the erection of new churches, since so well known as the Church Extension Committee, inseparably connected with the name of Dr. Chalmers, its great founder; the appointment of a committee on the subject of the eldership, two of the reforms suggested by which have since been carried; and the sending of a deputation to London, to petition the legislature for endowments to the chapels of ease, and to the new churches which were already in contemplation, that the great destitution of the means of religious instruction in Scotland might be effectually remedied.*

It is impossible to pass the important acts of this Assembly without offering one or two remarks respecting them. The act on calls, since generally known by the name of the Veto Act, was certainly a measure of an ambiguous character. In its preamble, it contained a clear statement of the fundamental principle of the Church of Scotland, that no pastor shall be intruded on any congregation contrary to the will of the people; and so far, it was a highly meritorious and constitutional act. But it may well be questioned whether the best mode of giving due effect to that principle was adopted by rendering the dissent of the people conclusive against a presentee, instead of giving direct efficiency to the positive call of a majority. The latter mode would certainly have been more in harmony with the spirit of the principle, as well as more consistent with the procedure of the Church in her earlier and purer days. But it would have been a more direct and powerful check upon the law of patronage; and unfortunately the learned judge, by whom the motion was introduced, had no wish to see patronage abolished, or even very greatly shorn of its strength. The very nature of the act, therefore, was a compromise, containing two hostile elements in its heart; and many foresaw that it could not possibly accomplish all the good which its sanguine supporters anticipated. Doubts were also entertained whether it might not be held that it was beyond the powers of the Church to pass such an act; but the opinions of the legal advisers of the crown removed these doubts, assuring supporters of the Veto Act, that it was perfectly competent for the Church to pass an act so manifestly consistent with her legally recognised constitution. Lord Chancellor Brougham also gave it his decided approbation, as "in every respect more desirable than any other course that could have been taken."* The Church of Scotland may be accused of too great caution and timidity in framing a law which did not give full developement to her own principles; but to charge her with rashness, disregard of law, and innovation, is to set matter of fact, truth, and reason, at defiance.

[1835-39.] The Assembly of 1835 was not equal to its predecessor in prosecuting the work of reformation. Great exertions had been made by the Moderates to recover their lost dominion, by sending their adherents to the Assembly from

* For the whole proceedings of this Assembly, see the published debate, or the Presbyterian Review vol. v.

* See his Lordship's speech, quoted in Mr Hamilton's Remonstrance.

every quarter where they still retained supremacy. The Veto Act and the Chapel Act were, however, both ratified; though some decisions were given inconsistent with the spirit of the former. By dexterous management, they contrived to evade the discussion of the committee's report respecting the reformation of the eldership, and also the subject of patronage. But the Christian eloquence of Dr. Duff, on the subject of missions to the heathen, gave an elevation to the character of that Assembly which can never be forgotten. And the first report of the Church Extension Committee displayed to an astonished and admiring public the mighty energies of the Church of Scotland, when set free from the leaden enthralment of Moderate domination. In one short year, from the passing of the Chapel Act in 1834, till the Assembly of 1835, no less than sixty-four new churches had either been built or were in the process of erection,—exactly one more than had been erected during the whole preceding century. Another cheering event took place during this Assembly. The Original Burgher Synod, which had not adopted the Voluntary principle, requested the appointment of a committee to confer with them, with a view to the arrangement of preliminaries for effecting a union between that body and the Established Church of Scotland. This most desirable event took place, after due deliberation, conducted in a generous and Christian spirit on both sides, in the month of August 1839.

One decision of the Assembly of 1835 must be stated, not on account of its intrinsic claims to attention, but because of the melancholy celebrity which subsequent events have given to it. On the 14th of October 1834, a presentation by the Earl of Kinnoull was laid before the presbytery of Auchterarder, in favour of Mr. Robert Young, preacher of the gospel, appointing him to the vacant church and parish of Auchterarder. The roll of communicants had not been made up by the late minister, owing to his failing health, but was prepared under the authority of the presbytery previous to the time for moderating in the call. When that day came the call was signed by his lordship's factor, not a resident in the parish, and by two heads of families. On the other hand, two hundred and eighty-seven heads of families, communicants, subscribed a dissent or disapproval of the presentee; and as there were only three hundred and thirty on the roll, this amounted to an overwhelming majority of dissentients. The presbytery refused to sustain the call; the presentee appealed to the synod, which affirmed the sentence of the presbytery; the presentee again appealed to the Assembly, and in this manner the subject came before the supreme ecclesiastical court. The arguments in behalf of the presentee were based entirely on the alleged informality of the proceedings: the legality of the Veto Act itself was never called in question. The Assembly, on the motion of Lord Moncreiff, affirmed the sentence of the presbytery by a large majority. Such were the first stage of the proceedings in this ill-omened case.

As various important cases arose about the same time, involving a long course of litigation, during which they simultaneously occupied the attention of the civil and ecclesiastical courts, it seems expedient to trace each separately, so far as it has actually proceeded, in order to avoid the confusion which might be produced by interwisting them with each other, as they evolved in the succession of years. We shall therefore continue to follow the case of Auchterarder, so far as it has ye. proceeded, before directing our attention to the other cases.

On the 7th of July 1835, the presbytery of Auchterarder again met, and resumed consideration of the case of Mr. Young, as presentee to the parish of Auchterarder; and, in conformity with the sentence of the General Assembly, rejected him, and intimated this decision to the patron, the presentee, and the elders of the parish. Against this sentence the presentee's agent appealed to the synod of Perth and Stirling. This appeal, however, was subsequently abandoned, and an action raised in the Court of Session against the presbytery, at the instance of Lord Kinnoull, the patron, and Mr. Young, the presentee. When the case was first brought into court, the summons concluded alternatively to have it found that the presentee, or, failing him, the patron, had right to the stipend on the ground of the presentation alone, notwithstanding the refusal of the church courts to induct him. The defence of the presbytery was simple and effectual, pleading, that as *they* pretended no right to the stipend, they had been improperly called as parties in such a cause. The validity of this defence was felt by the pursuers, who sought and obtained leave to amend their summons, by the insertion of a new and totally different conclusion. The tenor of this new conclusion was, that the rejection of the presentee solely in respect of a veto of the parishioners, was illegal, and injurious to the patrimonial rights of the pursuer, and contrary to the provisions of the statutes and laws regarding the collation or settlement of ministers; and that in consequence of the presentation, the presbytery were still bound to make trial of the qualifications of the presentee, and, if found duly qualified, to receive and admit him. The conclusions respecting the stipend were intentionally left out of view, till the question respecting the legality of the veto should be determined.

The question now acquired a character of the deepest importance. The conclusion of the summons apparently assumed, that the presentee's right to be taken on trials without reference to the proceedings of the congregation at the moderating in the call, and if found qualified, to be admitted, was of the nature of a civil right;* and that the obligation on the part of the presbytery to take him on trial, and, if found qualified, to admit, and of necessity to *ordain* him, was a civil obligation. It also apparently assumed, that, if the presbytery should be held to have acted illegally, the Court of Session was the competent tribunal to review their proceedings, to direct them authoritatively in their duty with regard to admission to the pastoral office, and even, if necessary, to enforce the discharge of what should have been thus declared to be their duty. Such a conclusion was beyond all question directly subversive of both the constitution and the spiritual independence of the Church of Scotland, and consequently of the British constitution itself, on which the well-ascertained rights and privileges of the Church of Scotland form not only an integral part, but its very basis, as an essential and fundamental condition of the Treaty of Union. The Church, when entering into this action, was careful to guard against being thought to have yielded up her own spiritual jurisdiction, by strenuously maintaining, that the Court of Session had no jurisdiction whatever in regard to the matter of conferring the pastoral office, in which, and in every other manifestly ecclesiastical matter, the church courts were supreme and independent of control by any civil tribunal. The only point in which the Church admitted the power of the Court of Session, or any other civil court, to adjudicate, was with regard to the disposal of the fruits of the benefice, in case the Church should be found to have acted illegally; but even then it was denied that the Court of Session had any jurisdiction in a matter so clearly spiritual as the qualifications of a preseentee for the pastoral office, or was entitled to declare substantively against the presbytery, that their proceedings in such a matter were illegal. The Court of Session might determine whether a presentation were valid or not, and consequently whether the presentee possessed any legal claim to the fruits of the benefice in consequence of such a presentation; but when the presentation was sustained, every other step in the process of admission was exclusively within the sole jurisdiction of the ecclesiastical courts, and not subject to the review of any civil court. Be the decision what it might, the Church expressly guarded against being supposed to have consented to any abridgment of her independent spiritual jurisdiction, distinctly declaring, that she would not obey the mandate of any civil court, nor could it enforce obedience, in such matters.*

After a discussion of unprecedented length, seventeen days in all, the Court of Session, on the 8th of March 1838, by a majority of three, the numbers being eight and five, gave judgment in the case, but *not* to the full extent of the conclusion of the summons. From that the court seems to have shrunk, notwithstanding the very new and strange opinion uttered by some of the judges; and instead of finding that the presbytery were stil

* It may be remarked, that it had always formerly been held as a Presbyterian principle, that a presentee, or one who had received a call, had still no *right* whatever entitling him to *act*, but that he must remain purely *passive* till after his induction.

* See the Procurator's Speech in the Auchterarde Report, vol. i. p. 101.

bound to take the presentee on trial, and, if found qualified, to admit him, which duty they might be compelled to perform, they first repelled the objection to the jurisdiction of the court, found that the presbytery, in rejecting the presentee on the sole ground of the dissent by the people, had acted to the hurt and prejudice of the pursuers, illegally, and in violation of their duty, and contrary to certain statutes, and, in particular, contrary to the act of Queen Anne (the unconstitutional Patronage Act); and in so far repelled the defences of the presbytery, and decerned and declared accordingly. However erroneous in point of constitutional law this decision may have been, it was essentially powerless, except in so far as regarded the temporalities of the benefice; and by its evasion of the main point in the conclusion of the summons, it afforded a sufficiently intelligible inference, that the Court of Session, whatever might be its inclination, entertained grave doubts respecting its own right to interfere with the spiritual jurisdiction of the Church of Scotland.

At the next meeting of the presbytery of Auchterarder after the decision of the Court of Session, they received a memorial from the pursuers, requiring them to comply with a decision which actually enjoined nothing. They resolved to refer the matter to the synod, on which a notarial protest was taken by Mr. Young's agent, holding the members of the presbytery jointly and severally liable to damages for refusing to take him on trials. In this state the case came again before the Assembly of 1838. The decision of the Court of Session had in the meantime produced intense excitement throughout the Church. A great number of overtures were laid on the table, calling upon the Assembly to pass a declaratory act, asserting the independence of the Church upon any civil power in regard to her spiritual jurisdiction, and her determination to maintain and enforce it. A motion was made by Dr. Buchanan of Glasgow, and carried by a majority of forty-one, to this effect:—"That the General Assembly, while they unqualifiedly acknowledge the exclusive jurisdiction of the civil courts in regard to the civil rights and emoluments secured by law to the Church, and will ever give and inculcate implicit obedience to their decision in such matters, do resolve, that, as is declared in the Confession of Faith of this National Established Church,—'The Lord Jesus Christ, as King and Head of the Church, hath therein appointed a government in the hand of church officers, distinct from the civil magistrate,' and that, in all matters touching the doctrine, government, and discipline of the Church, her judicatories possess an exclusive jurisdiction, founded on the Word of God, 'which power ecclesiastical flows immediately from God and the Mediator, and is spiritual, not having a temporal head on the earth, but only Christ, the only spiritual King and Governor of his Church:' And they do farther resolve, that this spiritual jurisdiction, and the sole Headship of the Lord Jesus Christ, on which it depends, they will assert, and at all hazards defend, by the help and blessing of that great God, who, in the days of old, enabled their fathers, amidst manifold persecutions, to maintain a testimony even to the death, for Christ's kingdom and crown: And finally, that they will firmly enforce obedience to the same upon the office-bearers and members of the Church, by the execution of her laws in the exercise of the ecclesiastical authority wherewith they are invested."

By this noble and truly Presbyterian motion, it was made evident that the Church of Scotland had once more taken her position upon the ground so invincibly held by the reformers and martyrs of other days, and that the contest was for no trivial matter, but in maintenance of her allegiance to the Lord Jesus Christ, and in defence of his sole right to reign over his spiritual kingdom. The attempt to fix upon the Church the charge of a Popish usurpation of civil power was refuted by the first clause of the motion; and by the remainder it was rendered clear to every intelligent and unprejudiced person, that her appeal to the House of Lords could not imply any admission of the right of even that high court to interfere with her well-guarded spiritual jurisdiction, but merely her wish to obtain, from that supreme judicatory, protection against the illegal and unconstitutional encroachments of the Court of Session, which also necessarily affected the temporalities of the benefice, severing them during Mr. Young's life from the cure of souls.

The General Assembly authorised the presbytery of Auchterarder to appeal to the House of Lords against the decision of the Court of Session; and sanguine hopes were for a time entertained, that the sentence of that supreme tribunal would be a reversal of the decision of the inferior court. After long and able pleading, judgment was given on the 3d day of May 1839, in the following terms:—"It is ordered and adjudged by the lords spiritual and temporal in parliament assembled, that the said petition and appeal be, and is hereby, dismissed this House; and that the said interlocutor therein complained of be, and the same is hereby, affirmed." Such was the judgment of the House of Lords, guided by the opinions of ex-chancellor Brougham, and the lord chancellor Cottenham. From the published speeches of these noble and learned lords it appears, that their judgment was founded on a principle repudiated even by the Moderate party in the Church, as shown by Dr. Cook's motion in 1833, viz., that the *only* grounds on which church courts could reject a presentee (even though not an ordained person,) was disqualification in one or other of the three particulars of life, literature, or doctrine; and that, as the dissent of the people was something different from the rejection of a presentee on these grounds, it was illegal. It was even stated by Lord Brougham, that a call was "not much more than a mere ceremony"—"immaterial as a part of a valid settlement;" and his lordship declared that, if requested, he "would at once make an order upon the presbytery to admit, if duly qualified, and to disregard the dissent of the congregation."* These views were not, indeed, contained in the judgment pronounced by the House of Lords; but they served to show to the Church of Scotland that nothing less than the utter overthrow of her spiritual independence and the entire subversion of her constitution would be the inevitable result, if she swerved but a hair's-breadth from the position which she had taken, or failed but a moment in maintaining the sacred principles which she had avowed. On the cause coming back to the Court of Session, no further appearance was made for the presbytery, all matters of civil right involved being substantially settled by the decision now affirmed in the House of Lords. The pursuers accordingly obtained from the Lord Ordinary, in absence of the defenders, a decree in terms of the remaining conclusions of the summons, which previously they could not obtain from the court.

Fully aware of the nature of the crisis which had arrived, the General Assembly of 1839 prepared to deliberate on the steps now to be taken, in reference to the decision of the House of Lords in the Auchterarder case. An able and eloquent debate ensued on the conflicting motions of Dr. Chalmers and Dr. Cook, which ended in the former being carried by a majority of forty-nine, the numbers being two hundred and four to one hundred and fifty-five. The motion thus carried was to the following effect:—"Having heard the report of the procurator respecting the decision of the House of Lords, and being desirous to give and inculcate obedience to the civil courts in all civil matters, instruct the presbytery of Auchterarder to offer no further resistance to the claims of Mr. Young, or the patron, to the emoluments of the benefice: And whereas the principle of Non-Intrusion is one coeval to the Reformed Church of Scotland, and forms an integral part of its constitution, embodied in its standards, and declared in various acts of Assembly, resolve that this principle cannot be abandoned, and that no presentee shall be forced upon any parish contrary to the will of the congregation: And whereas, by the decision referred to, it appears, that when this principle is carried into effect, the legal sustentation of the ministry may be thereby suspended, and being deeply impressed with the unhappy consequences which must arise from any collision between the civil and ecclesiastical authorities, and holding it to be their duty to use every means in their power, not involving any dereliction of the principles and fundamental laws of their constitution, to prevent such unfortunate results, do therefore appoint a committee, for the purpose of considering in what way the privileges of the National Establishment, and the harmony between

* Report of Speeches, &c.

Church and State, may remain unimpaired, with instructions to confer with the Government of the country, if they shall see cause."

The purport and amount of this motion is manifest. It was the duty of the Church to obey the civil court in civil matters, when the decision of the highest tribunal had been given; and this was done by abandoning all claim to the temporalities of Auchterarder. It was equally the duty of the Church to maintain inviolate her own great principle, that no pastor be intruded upon an unwilling congregation, because it is founded on the Word of God, and embodied in her own standards, and because no sentence of a civil court, and no combination of external circumstances, could ever release her from the necessity of maintaining inviolate her allegiance to Christ, and her own constitutional principles. It was also the duty of the Church to adopt the best means in her power for obtaining the adjustment of the differences that had taken place, that harmony might be restored between the civil and the ecclesiastical authorities; and for securing this important object, a committee was appointed to make due application to the legislature. To term the conduct of the Assembly rebellion, as has been done, betrays either the marvellous strength of prejudices, or a not less marvellous obliquity of judgment, if, indeed, in many cases it may not rather arise from the vindictive wrath of defeated foes and baffled antagonists. It should ever be remembered, that the State gave its sanction to the Church, with the full knowledge that she held the very principles which she is now maintaining; and that, by embodying the Confession of Faith in the Revolution Settlement, the State actually became bound to protect the Church of Scotland in asserting the sole Headship of Christ, and her own spiritual independence, which flows from that divine source; so that, in defending these principles, instead of rebelling against the law of the land, she is defending it against lawless aggression.

Thus terminated for a time the Auchterarder case in its more public aspect; but not thus terminated the collision between the Church and the subordinate civil courts. The case of the parish of LETHENDY was the next in which these co-ordinate judicatories came into hostile contact, and in which the conduct of the Court of Session was still more glaringly unconstitutional than it had been in the case of Auchterarder, though evidently arising out of the erroneous decision therein given. The minister of Lethendy had become aged and infirm, and a petition was presented in 1835 to the patron, the Crown, that Mr. Clark might be appointed assistant and successor. No presentation was issued, as in the case of a vacancy, but a consent to the induction of Mr. Clark by the presbytery was given by a sign manual. The presbytery of Dunkeld took the ordinary steps towards the ordination; but a majority of the male heads of families, communicants, expressed their disapproval of Mr. Clark, and he was accordingly rejected. The case came before the Assembly of 1836, and the sentence of the presbytery was affirmed. In March, 1837, abou two months after the death of the aged minister, Mr. Clark raised a civil action against the presbytery, but did not bring it into Court till November of that year. When the actual vacancy occurred, the crown, admitting the validity of the previous veto, issued a presentation in favour of Mr. Kessen; the presbytery followed the usual course, and a call being signed by the people, both presentation and call were regularly sustained, and nothing remained but the ordination and induction according to the laws of the Church. By this time the Court of Session had given its decision in the Auchterarder case; and Mr. Clark, availing himself of the manifest encroachment thereby made on the jurisdiction of the Church, applied to the court for an interdict prohibiting the presbytery from proceeding to ordain Mr. Kessen. This was readily granted; and the presbytery referred the matter to the Assembly of 1838. The case was referred by the Assembly to the Commission with full powers, and the Commission, on the 30th of May, pronounced this deliverance:—"Find that admission to the pastoral charge is entirely an ecclesiastical act, subject to the exclusive jurisdiction of the ecclesiastical courts; and ordain the presbytery to proceed without delay to the induction of Mr. Kessen, upon the call in his favour, according to the rules of the Church." After the Commission rose, Mr. Clark applied for a new interdict, in a more ample form, forbidding the presbytery of Dunkeld to settle Mr. Kessen in respect of the call, or on any ground whatever, and this also was immediately granted. The subject was again referred to the Commission, which met in August the same year; and the Commission promptly and almost unanimously renewed their directions to the presbytery to disregard the interdict as illegal, being in a matter purely spiritual, and to proceed to settle Mr. Kessen, naming the day of ordination. On the 13th of September, accordingly, Mr. Kessen was ordained, upon the call of the people, to the pastoral charge of the parish of Lethendy, without reference to the civil emoluments of the benefice, and leaving these at the disposal of the civil courts. Mr. Clark immediately presented a petition and complaint to the Court of Session, calling on them to punish the members of presbytery for acting in obedience to the command of the church judicatories, whom by their ordination vows they were bound to obey, but in disregard of the mandate of a civil court, to which they were not subordinate. The court decided in favour of the applicant, found the presbytery guilty of the breach of an interdict which their lordships had no power to grant, and ordered those ministers whom they chose to regard as delinquents, to be summoned to their tribunal.

The members of presbytery obeyed the summons. On the 14th of June, 1839, a transaction took place such as had not been beheld in Scotland for nearly two centuries. A civil court, in the exercise of merely secular power, called to its bar a court of Christ, because of its having exercised a purely spiritual power, the right to do which no civil court could either give or take away. A few of the most distinguished ministers of the Church accompanied their brethren to the bar of the civil court, not to brave the civil authority, but to give the comfort of their presence to those who were called to endure the persecution of censure and reproach in the cause of the Redeemer's Headship. The Lord President, as the organ of the Court, "in the most earnest and emphatic terms," pronounced upon the servants of the Lord Jesus "the solemn censure of the Court," assuring them that it was with considerable difficulty that so lenient a measure had been adopted; that should any similar case again occur, the punishment of imprisonment would be inflicted, and its duration would depend entirely upon the "heinousness of the offence committed." This was unquestionably persecution begun in the "lenient" form of censure, rebuke, and threatening, increased by the heavy expenses, tantamount to the infliction of fines, which the presbytery were compelled to pay, and aggravated by the prospect of heavier punishment, should the Church retain its integrity, and abide by its sacred principles, which it could not abandon without violating its allegiance to its Divine King.

There was in this conduct of the Court of Session a very marked increase of its aggressions upon the spiritual jurisdiction of the Church. The decision in the Auchterarder case merely repelled the objection urged by the Church against the jurisdiction of civil courts in spiritual matters, and found that the courch courts had acted illegally in rejecting a presentee on the ground of the disapproval of the congregation, but issued no order for the presbytery to proceed; and the affirmation of this sentence by the House of Lords gave no additional efficacy to that decision. The whole amount of this ratified civil sentence was simply this: that by giving effect to the dissent of the people, the Church had forfeited her legal claims to the fruits of the benefice of Auchterarder, and in every similar case might incur a similar loss. But in the case of Lethendy the civil court not only sustained the claim of the rejected presentee, from whom the crown had withdrawn the presentation by giving it to another, but also proceeded to interdict the spiritual court from the discharge of a purely spiritual function, ordination, in which, owing to the peculiar directions of the Commission, no civil interests were involved; and inflicted censures and threatenings upon that spiritual court, because it disregarded such inter dicts as no civil court had ever before presumed to grant, and which it was in no respect warranted to do by the judgment which the House of Lords had pronounced.

The combined cases of the parish of MARNOCH and the presbytery of STRATHBOGIE next rise to view, exhibiting the full nature and extent of the contest into which the Church of Scotland has been forced, the danger to which she is exposed, and the disastrous consequences which may ensue to the best interests, moral and religious, of the entire community.

The minister of the parish of Marnoch had become so enfeebled by the infirmities of age as to be unable to preach, and employed Mr. John Edwards, a preacher, to be his assistant. This person continued to act in that capacity for three years, during which time he rendered himself so much an object of dislike among the people, that the aged minister was obliged to remove him from being assistant, in compliance with the general feeling of the parish. When the incumbent died, a presentation was issued by the trustees of the Earl of Fife, the patron, in favour of the same Mr. John Edwards, and laid before the presbytery of Strathbogie, on the 27th of September 1837. Mr. Edwards was appointed to preach, as usual, in the parish of Marnoch, and a day was appointed for moderating in the call. On that day the call was signed by proxies for the patron and for three non-resident heritors, but by one only of the heads of families on the roll of communicants, namely, Peter Taylor, innkeeper, Aberchirder. At the same time dissents were recorded by one resident heritor, the six elders composing the kirk-session, and by two hundred and fifty-four heads of families, in all two hundred and sixty-one, out of a roll of three hundred. It must have been manifest to every person, that the settlement of Mr. Edwards in a parish where he had previously officiated for three years, and yet could get but one man, an innkeeper, to sign his call, could not possibly be for edification; that though there had been no Presbyterian principle forbidding the intrusion of a pastor upon an unwilling congregation, the dictates of reason and natural feeling would have called for his rejection; and that if he had possessed the very slightest regard for the peace and welfare of the parish, he would himself have given back the presentation. But he was thoroughly imbued with the principles of Moderatism, and that explains his conduct. The agent of the patrons protested against the dissent of the people being received, alleging the illegality of the Veto Act; and the presbytery appointed a day on which charges of canvassing and caballing might be brought forward against the people. The people, conscious of their integrity, came prepared to repel these charges. The patrons now abandoned the cause, and would willingly have recalled the presentation, but the presentee was determined to establish the civil right, of which he now held himself to be in possession, regardless alike of the feelings of both patron and people. Another attempt was made by the presbytery and the presentee to browbeat the people, and when this failed, the whole matter was referred to the synod of Moray.

The synod met on the 24th of April 1838, and almost unanimously decided, that the conduct of the presbytery of Strathbogie had "been incompetent and illegal," and directed them to meet and find the presentee disqualified, according to the laws of the Church, and to intimate this sentence to all parties concerned. The presbytery met, but refused to obey this sentence; and the parishioners appealed to the General Assembly. The case then came to the Assembly of May 1838, where the proceedings of the presbytery were reversed without a vote, and they were directed to reject the presentee, and to give intimation to the parties concerned, in terms of the regulations of the Assembly relative to the calling of ministers. The advocate of the presbytery defended them by pleading, that they merely wished to have the authority of the Assembly for rejecting Mr. Edwards, that if they should be dragged into a civil court, they might have its powerful support. Their subsequent actions fully proved the insincerity of this plea. But the majority of the presbytery of Strathbogie held the principles of Moderatism and this explains their conduct.

Another presentation was issued by the patrons in favour of Mr. David Henry, the presbytery having so far obeyed the instructions of the supreme ecclesiastical judicatory as now to reject Mr. Edwards. Upon this Mr. Edwards applied to the Court of Sessions, encouraged by the recent encroachments of that court, praying that Mr. Henry should be interdicted from presenting himself to the presbytery, and that the presbytery should be interdicted from taking any steps towards his induction, as injurious to the rights and privileges which Mr. Edwards had acquired by the previous presentation. This was granted on the 30th June 1838; and on the same day Mr. Edwards raised in the same court an action of declarator against the presbytery of Strathbogie, the heritors of the parish, &c., craving that it should be found and declared to the same effect with regard to this case as had been done by the court in the analogous case of Auchterarder. This also was granted, and these documents were laid before the presbytery of Strathbogie at their meeting in July. Mr. Henry's presentation was lodged at the same time; and the whole matter was delayed till next meeting. The presbytery met again on the 17th of July, when it was moved, "That the Court of Session having authority in matters relating to the induction of ministers, and having interdicted all proceedings on the part of the presbytery in this case; and it being the duty of the presbytery to submit to their authority regularly interposed, the presbytery do delay procedure until the matters in dispute be legally determined." This vote was opposed, but carried by a majority of six to four, the actual state of the presbytery being seven of the Moderate and four of the Evangelical party. This decision was carried by appeal to the Synod, which condemned the procedure of the presbytery, but referred the case to the next General Assembly.

The Assembly of 1839 was so much occupied in the important discussions which arose out of the recent adverse decision of the House of Lords in the Auchterarder case, that they could not enter upon the consideration of that of Marnoch, but remitted it to the Commission, "with power to determine in the present reference, and any other reference, or any appeal or complaint, in regard to future proceedings in the settlement of the parish of Marnoch; enjoining the presbytery of Strathbogie, in the event of any change of circumstance, to report the matter to the Commission, who shall have power to determine thereon." The Commission accordingly took up the case, immediately after the rising of the Assembly, and "highly disapproved of the conduct of the presbytery of Strathbogie, in resolving, contrary to the principles of the Church, and the resolution of the General Assembly 1838, 'that the Court of Session have authority in matters relating to the induction of ministers, and that it was the duty of the presbytery to submit to their authority;' and in respect to their having come to such resolution, the Commission deemed it necessary to prohibit the said presbytery from taking any steps towards the admission of Mr. Edwards before the next General Assembly, in any event, as they shall be answerable."

Elated, apparently, by the decision of the House of Lords, in the Auchterarder case, Mr. Edwards applied again to the Court of Session for another declarator, containing the very conclusion from which that court had at first shrunk in the case referred to. That conclusion was granted on the 13th of June 1839, finding, "That the presbytery of Strathbogie are still bound and astricted to make trial of the qualifications of the pursuer, Mr. Edwards, and, if found qualified, to receive and admit him as minister of the parish of Marnoch." This decision was made known to the presbytery, and its Moderate majority immediately resolved to disregard the injunctions of the superior church courts, to which they had sworn obedience, and to obey the mere opinion of the Court of Session, to which they owed no obedience, nor even deference, in spiritual matters. They requested a *pro re nata* or special meeting to be called, for the purpose of taking this decree into consideration. The meeting was called, but so close upon the meeting of the Commission, that they could not have it in their power to execute any adverse decision before that court could intercept their procedure. Enraged at this cautious conduct of their moderator, who most providentially was on the Evangelical side, they broke up the meeting, and would not look at the deliverance of the Commission, which the moderator, Mr. Dewar, had procured and laid on the table. This very disgraceful conduct of the majority was brought before the Commission at its meeting in November, when the deliverances of the Assembly and of the Commission were ordered to be transmitted to the presbytery, that they might not be able to plead ignorance of their duty; and they were ordered to take them into consideration at their ordinary meeting on the 4th of December, and to appear, personally or by a legal agent, at a meeting of the Commission to be held on the 11th of the same month.

The presbytery of Strathbogie met on the 4th of December, the above mentioned documents were laid before them, the parishioners of Marnoch appeared by their agent, and requested to be heard in a statement of their objections to the settlement of Mr. Edwards. The seven Moderate ministers of Strathbogie refused to hear the parishioners, or to record their refusal, so as to admit of an appeal being taken, refusing also to receive the appeal then offered,—overbore their better brethren in the most violent and outrageous manner,—and resolved "to act in opposition to the prohibition served upon them by order of the Commission, and in obedience to the decree of the Court of Session; and further, resolved to sustain the call [*of one*] in favour of the Rev. John Edwards, and to proceed in the settlement of the said Mr. Edwards, as presentee to the church and parish of Marnoch, and appointed his trials in common form."* This motion was proposed by Mr. Allardyce, and being carried by the majority of seven, they next resolved, as if in mockery, to report the whole matter to the Commission.

The Commission met on the 11th of December, and the startling nature of the case brought together a greater number of ministers from all parts of the country than had ever been known to meet in Commission before. A long and anxious deliberation ensued; the parties were heard by their counsel; and before proceeding to determine on the course to be pursued, the counsel for the seven Strathbogie brethren was repeatedly asked, whether his clients would abstain from further disobedience to the commands of their superior church judicatories, or whether they were determined to persist in the settlement of Mr. Edwards. He answered that he was not empowered to alter or modify the statements made in the report; whence it was evident that they were determined to proceed, and intrude Edwards into the parish of Marnoch, contrary to the direct injunctions of the Assembly and Commission,—contrary to the fundamental principles of the Church, —and contrary to the great doctrine of the sole Sovereignty and Headship of the Lord Jesus Christ. To avert the perpetration of this complicated tissue of despotism and sin, the Commission was compelled to suspend the seven delinquents from the office of the ministry till the meeting of Assembly, unless reponed on declaring that they would abstain from intruding Mr. Edwards upon the people of Marnoch, Mr. Edwards being also prohibited from making further application till next meeting of Assembly. This motion was proposed by the Rev. Dr. Candlish, in a speech of extraordinary eloquence, and carried by a majority of one hundred and seven, the numbers being one hundred and twenty-one to fourteen. In consequence of this sentence of the Commission, the seven Moderate and Intrusionist ministers of Strathbogie ceased to be capable of sitting in church courts, or performing validly any judicial or ministerial function; the four Evangelical ministers became the only legal presbytery; and directions were given to them, and to a committee, to provide a supply of stated ministerial services in the parishes of the suspended ministers. The suspended ministers immediately applied to the Court of Session for a suspension of this spiritual censure, and for an interdict, to prevent the sentence from being intimated in their respective parishes, and also to prevent any other minister from preaching in these parishes. This was asking rather more than the court was ye prepared to grant; but on the 18th of December an interdict was granted, prohibiting the sentence from being intimated in the churches, churchyards, or school houses of the respective parishes, and also prohibiting all ministers from preaching in the above specified places. To this

* This is copied from their own statement in one of their interdicts.

interdict obedience was given, so far as regarded the prohibition of using the churches, churchyards, or school-houses, these being civil matters, over which the Court of Session has control; but the sentence was intimated in the open air, or in other convenient places, and ministers preached in these parishes wherever the people could assemble to hear the gospel.

Such was the state of matters at the conclusion of the year 1839; and it was now becoming apparent to the public, that such a state of matters could not long continue, without endangering the very existence of the Church, and the peace and welfare of the nation. Great exertions had been made to blind, prejudice, and mislead the public respecting the cause and nature of the contest. The cry of "rebellion" was loudly raised against the Church, by some who ought to have known that, instead of rebelling, she was opposing a revolutionary violation of the constitution; and by many who knew nothing of the matter, but who hated the Church, and were glad of any opportunity to calumniate and assail her. The Voluntaries, who had been defeated in argument, gazed on with eager delight, seeing the Court of Session so energetically engaged in attempting to give a practical confirmation of their main assertion, "that an Established Church forfeited its spiritual independence." Political antagonists swelled the crowd of false witnesses, and re-echoed the insensate charge of rebellion; but never one of tnem specified the law which had been broken, or the act of rebellion which had been committed, and the penalty which had been incurred. In this time of peril and reproach God did not desert the Church, nor withdraw his presence from her. On the 23d of July 1839, a very remarkable manifestation of the Holy Spirit's agency took place at Kilsyth, causing a revival of vital religion such as had not been witnessed in Scotland for nearly a century. Nor was it confined to Kilsyth. At Dundee, Perth, Blairgowrie, Ancrum, Jedburgh, Kelso, throughout the presbytery of Tain in Ross-shire, in Sutherlandshire, and in various other parts of Scotland, a similar awakening took place; many sinners were converted and reclaimed from their evil ways, and cold and backsliding believers were quickened and urged forward in their Christian course, with renewed zeal and faithfulness. The Church was refreshed and re-invigorated. Many whose hearts had begun to droop, were encouraged, and constrained to declare their belief, that God had visited his people; and that though cast into the furnace, the Church of Scotland could not be destroyed, for God was with her there; and the shout of her Divine King was again heard in the heart of the Scottish Zion. The bush was burning, but unconsumed, for the Lord was in it.

[1840.] The year 1840 opened in the midst of these scenes of trouble and of encouragement. In a spirit of calm resolution, the Church went forward in her sacred course; and in a spirit of furious hostility, her enemies rushed onwards to the assault. The Court of Session pronounced a judgment professing to suspend the sentence of suspension, and consequently to restore the seven ministers to the exercise of their spiritual functions; the partial interdict which they had granted was rendered perpetual; and the prohibition was extended to entire parishes of the suspended seven, so that no minister of the Church of Scotland was permitted to molest the seven by preaching the gospel, even in the open air, in these parishes. This interdict could not be obeyed without direct disobedience to the commands of Christ, to preach the gospel to every creature under heaven; and the Church therefore acted on the Divine principle, that it was right to obey God rather than man. And it must be gratefully recorded, that the Divine Head of the Church honoured the preaching of those ministers who were sent to discharge the duties of the ministry in the parishes of the suspended ministers, with a very remarkable degree of spiritual influence. The attention of the crowded audiences who waited on their ministry in barns, or temporary erections, or the open air, was deep, solemn, and often accompanied with profound emotion, and with gushing tears. The light of the gospel broke in upon a district which had long been overshadowed with the midnight darkness of extreme Moderatism; and the people rejoiced in the holy and heavenly radiance which shone around them. Many ministers returned from Strathbogie, praising God for the manifest spiritual influence which they had both marked and felt, accompanying the preaching of the gospel in that district, and counting all the perils of the Church, and all their own perils from broken interdicts, more than compensated by what they had witnessed and enjoyed. They felt that the cause was unquestionably the cause of Christ, for they felt that His presence had been with them.

At the same time it deserves to be peculiarly remarked, that the seven suspended ministers did not venture to complain to the Court of Session of the breach of interdict which had been obtained in absence. Had they done so, its validity would have been regularly tried; when there are strong reasons for believing that it would have been found incompetent for any civil court to grant such an interdict. But it was a safer policy for them to leave the point untried, raising, meanwhile, the clamorous outcry, "Obey the law," which they dared not thus test if it were a law.

In the meantime the committee which had been appointed to confer with the legislature, were exerting themselves to the utmost in the discharge of their important duty. Negociations were opened and carried on with government and with the most influential statesmen in both of the political parties in parliament. These exertions were supported by petitions from the people of Scotland, signed by no less than two hundred and sixty thousand names of Scotland's best and most religious sons, praying for protection to the Church of their fathers, and to their own sacred rights and privileges. The government at length declined to interfere, being apprehensive, probably, that to help the Church of Scotland might offend those of their supporters who were adherents of the Voluntary principle. The subject was then taken up by the Earl of Aberdeen, who had previously held intercourse with the Assembly's committee, both in interviews and by letters. Sanguine hopes were entertained by many that a bill would be introduced by that nobleman, if not such as could be wished, at least such as would secure the spiritual independence of the Church against the invasion of the Court of Session, and protect the people from the intrusion of unacceptable ministers. His lordship terminated his diplomatic labours, during which he had succeeded in deceiving many, with the production of a bill which would have ratified every aggression made by the civil courts, set aside the principle that no pastor may be intruded into a parish contrary to the will of the congregation, and left all the proceedings of the church courts subject to the review of the Court of Session.*

The Assembly of 1840 had very important duties to discharge, and it, under the guidance of its Divine Head, discharged them well. The proceedings of the Commission in the case of the suspended seven Strathbogie ministers were affirmed by a majority of eighty-four. Those men were next declared liable to high censure for their conduct; but a committee was appointed to confer with them before proceeding to express censure, with a view to recall them to some sense of their duty, if that might yet be possible. They justified their conduct, and refused to make any submission. It was then moved, that the sentence of suspension should be continued; that they should be cited to appear before the Commission in August; and that if then they still continued to refuse submission to the superior church courts, a libel, or legal indictment, should be served upon them, and the Commission should proceed till the case was ripe for the judgment of the next Assembly. This motion was carried by a majority of sixty four,—the numbers being one hundred and sixty-six to one hundred and two. The great leniency and forbearance of this procedure will be at once manifest, when it is contrasted with the conduct of the Moderate party during the administration of Principal Robertson, when ministers were instantly deposed upon declining to intrude unworthy and unacceptable presentees upon reluctant congregations. Lord Aberdeen's bill came next under consideration, and was rejected by a majority of eighty-seven,—the numbers being two hundred and twenty-one to one hundred and thirty-four. This large majority rendered it abundantly evident that the Church of

* In April 1840, the Assembly's Committee published a statement of two different methods by which a pacific adjustment might be effected,—the one founded on the veto, the other on the direct call; and in a very short time three hundred and eighty ministers, and two thousand two hundred and thirty-three elders publicly declared their satisfaction with either.

Scotland would not consent to become again subject to Erastian domination, either through Moderate management, or in dread of civil pains and penalties, or misled by the delusions of diplomatic craft. At the same time the peril to the existence of the Establishment was increasing. The speeches of Dr. Cook and other Moderate leaders, their reasons of dissent against the decision of the Assembly, and the countenance given to the suspended seven, all tended to render apparent the strong probability that, ere long, the entire Moderate party would throw aside the mask they had so long worn, and declare themselves the avowed supporters of Court of Session sovereignty, however incompatible with the sovereignty of the Lord Jesus Christ. An attempt was made by them to encourage Lord Aberdeen to press his bill through the legislature, by procuring as many signatures as possible to a declaration of satisfaction with its principles and its provisions. Only two hundred and sixty names of ministers were obtained; and, with the exception of about a dozen, these names were not such as to shed lustre or confer strength upon any cause. His Lordship withdrew his bill. Another attempt was made by the defeated Moderates to unite their party by a bond of fraternal co-operation, in the great endeavour to recover their power to perpetrate intrusions, and to stifle the voice of Evangelism. But it, too, failed, for success was uncertain; and many Moderates who would have rejoiced in the recovered ascendency of their party, were not prepared to unite in a scheme which might involve personal and pecuniary considerations. It gave occasion, however, to an Engagement among the faithful defenders of religious liberty and evangelical truth, signed on the 11th of August 1840, by which a close approach was made to the sacred National Covenant of earlier, purer, and more devoted times, and which may yet lead to the renewal of that but half-forgotten, and, as many think, still binding Covenant between the deathless moral and religious being of the nation and the King Eternal.

When the Commission met in August, it appeared that, instead of submitting, the suspended Strathbogie ministers had continued to preach, baptize, and dispense the sacraments, in defiance of the sentence of the General Assembly; that on the 8th of June they had applied to the Court of Session for an interdict against this renewed suspension, and against the preaching of any minister sent to officiate in their parishes; and that they had caused copies of that interdict to be served on ministers on the Sabbath-day, and on elders while assisting at the communion, and bearing the vessels of the sanctuary. All these fearful acts of desecration were notorious, and nothing remained but to prepare a libel, or formal accusation, against them. The motion to that effect was carried by a majority of one hundred and twenty-five,—the numbers being one hundred and ninety-one to sixty-six. The accusation was framed with great judgment and propriety, resting the main charge, not upon contumacy and insubordination,—though in the minds of many that would have been enough,—but upon their asking and receiving from a civil court power to discharge the most sacred offices, when that power had been taken away by a spiritual court, by which alone it can be either given or taken away. This was evidently receiving from the civil magistrate the keys of doctrine and discipline, which these men had sworn that the Church alone possesses, when they subscribed the Confession of Faith; consequently it involved the solemn and awful charge of denying the great doctrine of the Redeemer's sole Sovereignty, and desecrating the ordinances of His Church by administering them on the authority of the civil magistrate alone. It was evident, that if the civil court could remove the sentence of a spiritual court, and give authority to dispense spiritual ordinances, then it must itself possess all possible spiritual power, or rather, then spiritual power had no existence, and the Christian Church was but an empty name.

At the meeting of the Commission in November, the Strathbogie case was resumed, and the relevancy of the libel against the seven suspended ministers was sustained by a vote of ninety-one to fifteen; that against Mr. Edwards by a vote of seventy-five to two. Unmoved by this almost unanimous expression of condemnation, these men held on their course. Mr. Edwards had been taken on trials by the suspended seven, on the 19th day of February, and found qualified. He then applied to them to proceed with his settlement. They hesitated and delayed, as rather reluctant to take the final step. It may be that they had misunderstood the law all along, even in that particular point on which they rested their cause. They had argued often that they were "bound and astricted to take the presentee on trials; but the clause in the act 1592 says, "bound and astricted to receive and admit whatsoever qualified minister,"—leaving the whole matter of taking on trials, and determining as to qualifications, completely within the power of the Church, and not touching the spiritual act of ordination at all, which in another part of the same enactment is expressly said to "belong to the privilege that God has given to the spiritual office-bearers in the Kirk." They had, however, pronounced Mr. Edwards qualified, and they were now by their own act bound to proceed to his settlement. On the 2d of September he again applied to his seven friends; and when they still hesitated, he caused a notorial protest to be served on them, holding them liable for damages. He then raised in the Court of Session an action against the entire presbytery of Strathbogie, both the suspended and the remaining members, concluding to have them decerned to admit him, and failing to do so, to have them found liable for damages to the amount of £10,000, and £1000 additional for expenses. When the case was heard in the court, the suspended seven declared their willingness to admit Mr. Edwards, if required;—thus consenting to that court's pronouncing the order for admission sought by Mr. Edwards. The minority, the true presbytery, gave in defences, disputing the jurisdiction of the court. But the court, while the question of their own power to grant such an order at all was still under discussion in the defences offered by the presbytery, actually gave, on the 18th of December 1840, to those men who had been suspended from their spiritual office, an order to perform a spiritual function, and that simply on the ground of the consent of the seven, which could never confer on the Court of Session a jurisdiction which did not belong to it by the constitution of the empire. And certain of their Lordships of Session did not hesitate to declare, that they held it competent for that court to issue an order compelling a minister to grant admission to the Lord's Table. In this manner did the Court of Session advance, step by step, from their false position in the Auchterarder case, when they repelled the objection urged by the ecclesiastical courts against their assumption of jurisdiction in ecclesiastical matters till now; that they asserted jurisdiction in every ecclesiastical matter, however sacred, virtually putting an end to all distinction between things civil and things sacred; annihilating, so far as they were able, all spiritual jurisdiction; assuming the "power of the keys," contrary to the express language of the Confession of Faith, and the act of parliament by which it was made the law of the land. No parallel violation of law is to be found in the history of the Scottish Church and nation, except the oath of supremacy in 1661, when Charles II. caused himself to be acknowledged supreme governor in all causes, civil and ecclesiastical.

[1841.] The seventh year of Evangelical ascendency was about to commence its round, every thing indicating that the struggle between the Church and the world was rapidly approaching to a crisis. With fierce eagerness the supporters of secular power strove to throw in fresh elements of discord and of danger, while the faithful defenders of religious liberty and truth went calmly and steadily forward in the discharge of the sacred duties which they owed to the Divine Head of the Church, regarding neither the threats nor the reproaches which they were called to encounter in His cause.

On the 4th of January 1841, the suspended ministers of Strathbogie met, received a report of the proceedings in the case of Mr. Edwards, resolved to proceed with his induction, and appointed the 21st of the same month to be the day on which that deed should be committed A heavy fall of snow on the 20th had rendered the roads almost impassable; but the intense interest felt by the whole adjacent country induced great numbers to crowd to the Church of Marnoch, to the amount of probably not less than two thousand. The suspended ministers also reached the spot, accompanied by Mr. Edwards. One of the elders of Marnoch asked them for what purpose, and by what authority, they had come. Their moderator, with hesitation, answered, that they appeared as the presbytery of Strathbogie, a part of the National Church, assembled in the name of the Lord Jesus Christ. The vast audience shuddered to hear a statement so directly contrary to truth, asserted in connection with the Redeemer's name. Mr. Duncan, the legal agent for the parishioners, produced his mandate, and being refused the right of protest in the usual form, protested in the hands of a notary public. The protest was read aloud, narrating the tyrannical treatment which the parishioners of Marnoch had endured, declaring their readiness to prove objections against the life and doctrine of Mr. Edwards before any lawful presbytery, disclaiming the jurisdiction of the suspended seven, and protesting against the right of Edwards to intrude himself upon them. This being done, the parishioners arose, took their Bibles in their hands, and left the temple of their fathers, desecrated by the presence of these traffickers in religious matters; aged men and women, vigorous manhood, and opening youth, all, all alike arose, and slowly, silently, and mournfully, many of them in tears, passed outwards into the open snowy waste, banished, certainly by no court of Christ, from His Father's house of prayer. Only one parishioner of Marnoch remained, being unable to extricate himself from the agitated crowd of people from neighbouring parishes, who had come to witness the appalling scene. Some confusion then followed, these strangers not being able to repress their indignation at the outrage which they beheld their countrymen enduring. This was soon restrained by the presence of a magistrate; the confined parishioner of Marnoch obtained release and joined his fellow-sufferers, and the dread scene went on. The usual questions were put to Edwards which are put to probationers at the time of their ordination, such as the vow of obedience to superior church courts,—which at that moment both they who imposed and he who took were violating; the declaration that he had used no undue methods, either by himself or others, in procuring that call,—he having no call but that signed by Peter Taylor, and having used methods subversive of the constitution of the National Church;—and to this most solemn question, "*Are not zeal for the honour of God, love to Jesus Christ, and desire of saving souls, your great motives and chief inducements to enter into the office of the holy ministry, and not worldly designs and interests?*—he answered audibly, Yes; while at the same moments the decreets of the Court of Session, all obtained on the sole ground of "worldly designs and interests," were lying high-piled before them! At the fearful response the vast crowd heaved one long-drawn and deep gasp of awe and horror—what crime they regarded that answer as involving, need not be named. The dreadful vows were uttered; the act of ordination was profanely imitated by the authority, *not* of the Head of the Church, but of a subordinate civil court; and the perpetrators walked away from the scene amidst the hisses of the people,—Edwards in fear, though not in danger, crouching between policemen, without one to welcome him, even as stipend-lifter,—"a minister without a parishioner, a man without a friend."

Such was the atrocious deed done at Marnoch on the 21st of January 1841,—a deed to which the annals of the Church of Scotland can furnish no parallel. For in all the violent settlements effected by the Moderates of former times there was still the authority of the Church, a competent authority and the rightful one, though in all such cases wrongfully employed, involving the abuse, but not the denial of Christ's sole sovereignty; but the Marnoch crime was committed by men suspended from their spiritual functions, and by the authority of the civil court alone, as if in scorn, certainly in violation, of every feeling of humanity, every admitted principle in the constitution of Church and State, every recorded example in the sacred Scriptures, and every idea that can be conceived respecting the nature of the sole Sovereignty and Headship of the Divine Redeemer over his spiritual kingdom.

The sensation caused throughout Scotland by this renewal of the Moderate policy of other days, cannot be described. Many even of the Church's opponents began to be convinced that Moderate and Erastian policy must be essentially wrong, when they saw the hideous results to which it so directly led. Some even of the Moderates, recoiled with alarm from the thought of lending their sanction to such a deed. But the recoil was temporary, and they soon returned to the prosecution of their destructive course. The presentees to Lethendy and Auchterarder seemed to regret that they had been so far outdone by the intruder of Marnoch. New actions were raised in the Court of Session; and on the 4th of March, that court found that the presbytery of Dunkeld were still bound to take Mr. Clark on trials, this conclusion being urged expressly with a view towards ulterior proceedings to "reduce the admission of Mr. Kessen," who had already been ordained. And on the following day, 5th March, an action of damages was granted against the presbytery of Auchterarder, at the instance of the Earl of Kinnoull and Mr. Young, for £5000 to his lordship, £10,000 to the presentee, and £1000 for expenses. The court has sustained the relevancy of this action for imposing damages on the members of a spiritual court, which, even by the *statute law of the land*, is so constituted, that every one of its members, in the very act of being admitted to his office in it, is imperatively required, as a condition of holding office, to vow to submit himself to his superior judicatories, and that for no offence but that of obedience to the injunctions of these very judicatories. This judgment of the Court of Session is under appeal.

At the meeting of the Commission in March, the indictments against the suspended seven of Strathbogie and Mr. Edwards were found proven, and the cases were referred to the General Assembly for judgment. A motion was made by Dr. Candlish, expressive of sympathy with the parishoners of Marnoch, and admiration of their behaviour in such trying circumstances. This was carried by a vote of seventy-two to one, the one being Dr. Bryce, even the person who seconded the motion not having sufficient effrontery to vote for it.

On the 6th of May, the Duke of Argyle laid before the House of Lords, "a bill entitled an Act to regulate the exercise of Church Patronage in Scotland." The peculiar point of this bill was, that it secured the great principle, "that no pastor be intruded into a parish contrary to the will of the congregation," not perhaps in the best possible way, but so that under its provisions no Marnoch atrocity could again be perpetrated. It is not necessary to do more than allude to the language of misrepresentation and virulence which certain noble lords disgrace themselves by uttering against the Church of Scotland; but it deserves to be stated, that Lord Chancellor Cottenham, on a subsequent day, declared, that the sole subject of appeal in the Auchterarder case was whether the presbytery were bound to take the presentee on trials, notwithstanding the veto of the communicants; that this was the whole extent of the decision; and declined to give an opinion as to what had since taken place, thereby certainly giving no countenance to the unprecedented proceedings of the Court of Session.

The General Assembly of 1841 will ever be regarded as one of the most memorable among those to which the reader of Church history directs his special attention. The time to record its transactions fully has not yet come; but when it comes, the historian will delight to dwell upon the fearless and faithful bearing, the calm and Christian fortitude, the lofty and commanding eloquence, and the clear majestic energy of sacred principle which characterised the gifted men who met and bore back the sacrilegious aggressions of civil power upon the spiritual kingdom of the Divine Redeemer. Nor will the names of Chalmers, and Gordon, and Cunningham, and Candlish, and Dunlop, be then held unmeet to rank with those of Knox, and Melville, and Henderson, and Gillespie, and Warriston. But let it even now be recorded, that amidst all the efforts that were made to intimidate, or rouse to unseemly warmth, the defenders of the Church,—amidst all the fierce threatenings and malignant reproaches by which they were incessantly assailed,—they remained unmoved, calm, solemn, resolved, like men who knew the might of their adversaries, but feared it not, knowing that the

Lord God Almighty reigneth, and putting their trust in Him,—contending earnestly for the faith once delivered to the saints, but wielding the weapons of no carnal warfare,—conscious of the perils they had to encounter, yet careful for nothing, but in every thing by prayer and supplication making their requests known to God,—and going forward in their Master's service, strong in the Lord and in the power of his might. "Surely," was the solemn thought of many an awe-struck spectator, "surely the presence of God is here."

The main acts of this Assembly may be very briefly stated. Mr. Wright, minister of Bothwick, was deposed for heresy, by a majority of one hundred and ten. A motion declaring patronage to be a grievance, injurious to the interests of religion, the main source of the difficulties in which the Church is involved, and that its abolition is necessary to place the appointment of ministers on a right and permanent basis, was made by Mr. Cunningham, and, after a long and able debate, was lost by the narrow majority of six. The unprecedented strength of the anti-patronage party proved clearly, that the mind of the Church was taking the right direction to obtain security against the corrupting influence of secular interference in things spiritual, and secular aggression, by aiming at the abolition of the hostile element. And though not yet successful, the hour of victory cannot now be distant, several of those who opposed the motion having declared, that if the efforts then in progress for securing the efficacy of the Non-Intrusion principle should fail, they would unite with those who sought redress by an abolition of patronage. A motion approving of the Duke of Argyle's bill was carried by a majority of one hundred and twenty-five. A motion to depose the seven suspended ministers of Strathbogie was carried by a majority of ninety-seven, and they were deposed accordingly.* The settlement of Mr. Edwards was declared null and void, and the four remanent members of the presbytery of Strathbogie were instructed to proceed to the induction of Mr. Henry as minister of Marnoch. On the motion of Mr. Dunlop, an overture restoring to the people their right of electing elders was ordered to be transmitted to presbyteries, previous to its being enacted into a standing law. This most important measure had been under discussion since 1834, as essential to the restoration of the Church to a state of purity and efficiency, and was now carried by a majority of eighty-nine, completing the reformation of the Church from the abuses of Moderatism. Directions were also given to proceed by libel against refractory probationers when applying to civil courts for suspension of the decisions of ecclesiastical courts, with express reference to the cases of Auchterarder, Lethendy, and Marnoch. It may be mentioned also, that the deposed seven applied to the Court of Session for an interdict to prohibit the Assembly from passing and intimating the sentence of deposition, obtained it, and attempted to serve it, after the sentence had been pronounced, when it could be of no possible avail, except it were for the sole purpose of offering an insult to the supreme ecclesiastical court, even while its proceedings were sanctioned by the lord high commissioner, her majesty's representative. Perhaps it was fitting, that those who had done their utmost to violate the

* It must be noted, that when the motion for deposition was carried, Dr. Cook, as the leader of his party, read a declaration and protest against this decision, in which he and those adhering to him declared that they "could not cease to regard these men as still ministers, just as if the proceedings against them had never been instituted;" adding, that "although in the present case they did not submit to the judgment of the General Assembly, they would endeavour faithfully to discharge the duties which, as office-bearers in the Established Church, they were bound to perform." A copy of this protest appeared next day in the public newspapers, containing an additional clause, declaring that the protesters meant to hold communion with the deposed seven. The document had been ordered to lie on the table till next day, before being taken into consideration, to allow time for cool reflection to moderate the heat of the defeated party. The Assembly then refused to receive such a protest and declaration, the constitutional procedure being, for members, when they could not conscientiously concur, to express a dissent from, but not a protest and declaration against, a decision of the supreme court It was noticed also, that the paper actually on the table did not contain the schismatic clause which appeared in the newspapers, Dr. Cook admitting that it did not, and saying that steps had been taken to correct the published error; adding, "that it would be a matter of deep lamentation to him if any thing should occur which would lead him to bring these sad evils upon the Church, the prospect of which filled him with dismay." From this pacific termination of a procedure which had threatened an immediate schism, hopes began to be entertained that the Moderates were at length about to consent to a cessation of hostilities, and to allow a time of quiet, till a final adjustment of the perilous contest might be obtained. These hopes were soon dispelled, and ample reason given to believe, that the pacific change made on the protest had been merely a stratagem, intended to gain time till their schemes should be matured and their full strength mustered, that they might then resume the conflict, and render it a war of extermination. (See the published Report of the Assembly's Proceedings.)

British constitution should insult at once the most venerable institution in the empire and the representative of the sovereign.

It is difficult to say whether astonishment or fury predominated among the defeated Moderates. They had all along vainly imagined that their Evangelical opponents would act as they would have done themselves, and that when brought to the closing shock of the encounter, they would waver and recoil. They could scarcely yet believe that their seven champions, or rather victims, were indeed deposed. But recovering a little from their stunning amazement, they set themselves to counteract the moral influence of the Assembly's procedure by every artifice which the vindictive feelings of defeated despotism could devise. Meetings were held to express sympathy with the deposed seven. At these "sympathy meetings" were seen collected Episcopalians, Voluntaries, and men of no religious profession at all, banded together in strange alliance against the Church of Scotland in her defence of the Redeemer's crown. In each and all of them language full of distorted perversions and exaggerated mis-statements was vehemently employed; till, in concentrated bitterness, the leading enemy of the Church had the hardihood to declare in his place in the House of Lords, that the Strathbogie delinquents had been deposed "simply and exclusively for their obedience to the law of the land." Let the direct truth be stated, and deliberately considered. In the indictment against these men there were *nine* distinct charges involving the violation of their ordination vows, their desecration of divine ordinances, and their overt acts subversive of the constitution and laws of the Church, and directly opposed to the great and sacred principle of Christ's Sovereignty and Headship,—each and all purely ecclesiastical offences, arising out of their own spontaneous movements, and not one of which the law had ordered them to commit. They of their own accord applied to the Court of Session to know whether, in the opinion of that secular court, they ought to do certain ecclesiastical deeds; they received but an *opinion*, and no *order* exposing them to penalties should they disobey; and the very essence of their guilt consisted in their voluntary application to the civil court, to which in such matters the constitution of the empire had declared that they were not subordinate, after they had received the most explicit instructions and commands of the supreme ecclesiastical court, which they had solemnly vowed to obey. This is the truth; and future times will know what term to apply to those who have dared to assert the contrary.

On the 9th of June, an interdict was granted by the Court of Session, prohibiting the presbytery of Auchterarder from proceeding to the settlement of a minister in the *pastoral* charge of that parish, on such maintenance as might be secured to him by the parishoners; as if to say that in the opinion of that secular court, the usurpation of patronage must be maintained, though at the expense of thereby suppressing the preaching of the gospel and the pastoral cure of souls.

Gathering courage from the prospect of an early political change, which they expected to be likely to strengthen their cause, the defeated Moderates began to adopt a more perilous course of procedure than any on which they had previously ventured. Some of their leading men went as a deputation to London; and, while there, published what they termed "A Statement for the Presbytery of Strathbogie, and for the Minority of the late General Assembly." The leading principle of this statement was the weak and common fallacy so often refuted, and leading to such pernicious consequences, that when the civil court pronounces any matter to be within its jurisdiction, it *is* within its jurisdiction, however sacred in its own nature it may be, and that ecclesiastical courts are immediately bound to submit to every such encroachment, and to obey every decision founded upon it,—a theory which ends in the most complete and perfect Erastianism. In the conclusion of this new Moderate manifesto, its fabricators suggested, that in order to secure their ultimate triumph, the law-officers of the crown should be instructed to conduct at the public charge all such prosecutions and actions at law as might arise out of disputed settlements, similar to that of Marnoch; complacently adding, that with such an arrangement they "would have much reason to be satisfied." Doubtless they would; so that if they could neither match their faithful brethren in argument, nor overawe them by threats, they might at last wear them out by expensive suits at law and ruinous fines, their own personal comforts and pecuniary resources remaining the while untouched. Further to hasten on the crisis, they resolved to hold ministerial intercourse with the deposed, contrary to their own declaration at the recent Assembly, when giving their reasons of dissent from its sentence of deposition. And in this they proceeded so far as to assist these *laymen*, as they unquestionably were after they had been deposed, in the desecration of the sacrament of the Lord's supper. This, they well knew, was an act which the Church of Scotland could not avoid regarding as a heinous sin, and which therefore she could not permit to pass unpunished, without participating in its guilt. They had recorded their dissent; they were at perfect liberty still to declare and to maintain their sentiments; and there rested upon them no peculiar obligation to desecrate the ordinances of religion in those seven parishes of Strathbogie, which at the Assembly they had, as a party and by the mouth of their leader, disclaimed the intention of doing; but they hoped to involve their opponents in the necessity of deposing so great a number for having committed this new crime, as to give them some plausible ground for raising the loud outcry of tyranny and oppression, with a view to induce the civil power to arm and hasten to the rescue. How strongly is this tortuous, worldly, and cruel policy contrasted with the simplicity of the gospel, and the mild and much-enduring spirit of Christianity!

Such was the new aspect of affairs when the commission met on the 11th of August. The conduct of the Moderate party had brought on the long-expected crisis; and it was now manifest, that unless they should retrace their steps, or the Church should at last prove unfaithful to her principles, a great and irreparable schism was at hand. But the Divine Head of the Church did not withdraw His presence from her in this momentous hour. A report was read, containing an authentic account of what had taken place in the district of Strathbogie, and naming the ministers who had assisted the deposed men to desecrate the sacrament. Then a motion was made, that while conference should be held with these men, with the view of reclaiming them, information should be given to the several presbyteries having jurisdiction over the ministers named in the report, that they might institute disciplinary proceedings, and proceed in the matter according to the laws of the Church. And to avert, if still possible, the danger and the sin of schism, a committee was appointed to address to the said brethren a solemn remonstrance and warning, showing the guilt of their conduct, and appealing to all their better principles and feelings, not thus to persevere in rending asunder the venerable and blood-bought Church of their fathers. This motion was carried by a majority of sixty to thirteen. But all the attempts of the Evangelical majority to avert a schism and procure a pacific arrangement were in vain. Dr. Cook and Mr. Robertson, the acknowledged leaders of their party, gave in reasons of dissent, the conclusion of which was as follows: "Because the resolution now sanctioned puts an end to all hope of devising any measure by which the members of the Church might be united, and imposes upon us, and upon all who agree with us in the opinion which we have repeatedly expressed as to our present distressing condition, to take such steps as may appear most effectual for ascertaining from competent authority, whether we who now dissent, and they who concur with us, or they who continue to set at naught the law of the land and the decisions of the supreme courts in what we esteem a civil right, are to be held by the legislature of the country as constituting the Established Church, and as entitled to the privileges and endowments conferred by statute upon the ministers of that Church."

The plain meaning of this is sufficiently obvious. Moderatism now threw off all disguise, and openly avowed its intention to apply to the legislature to have itself declared the Church of Scotland, and having the sole right to the privileges and endowments of that Church, to the exclusion of Evangelism, and of every minister who continued to hold that, in the words of the Confession of Faith, which is the law of the land, "There is no other Head of the Church but the Lord Jesus Christ,"—that, "As King and Head of His Church, He hath therein appointed a government in the hand of church-officers, distinct from the civil magistrate,"—and that "The civil magistrate may not assume to himself the administration of the Word and sacraments, or the power of the keys."

There was manifestly no further use for argument; that was at an end. The appeal was to be made to the legislature, to the country, and to God. To the legislature it was necessary to show how many congregations they would deprive of their faithful and beloved pastors, if they should comply with this Moderate request. An extraordinary meeting of Commission was accordingly held on the 25th of August, when a series of resolutions were proposed, promptly and decisively encountering the threatened danger, reasserting the sacred principles of the Church, enumerating the aggressions which had been made by the civil courts on her constitutional spiritual jurisdiction, declaring a calm and settled determination to maintain unimpaired those hallowed rights and privileges which are derived from the Divine Redeemer alone, or to perish in their defence; yet, in the forgiving spirit of Christianity, offering a conference with the erring brethren, if even now they might be reclaimed from their guilty and disastrous career. These resolutions were opposed by one member, who could not find any person to second his motion, then passed in probably the largest meeting of Commission ever known, and one dissentient voice was recorded. A meeting was held on the same evening in the West Church, expressly limited to those who approved of the conduct of the Church, and were willing to encounter every hazard in her defence. This was the greatest meeting which had been held in Scotland since the ever-memorable day on which the National Covenant was signed in the Grayfriars' church-yard. From south to north, from east to west, the best and holiest office-bearers of the Church of Scotland, elders and ministers, came forth, drawn by no urgent call from any central source, but aroused by the imminent danger of our Scottish Zion, and eager to take their position on the high places of the field, and to peril all that the heart holds dearest, and even life itself if necessary, in defence of religious liberty, and of the Redeemer's glorious crown. The area of the church was crowded by about twelve hundred ministers and elders, and the double galleries of that huge fabric were densely filled with one compact continuous mass of Scotland's dauntless God-fearing men and prayerful pious matrons. One heart but seemed to throb within, one spirit to inspire, the whole vast multitude,—the heart that, fearing God, can have no other fear,—the spirit that, worshipping God, can bow before him alone.

The Moderator of the late General Assembly, the venerable Dr. Gordon, was chosen to preside. In a solemn spirit-stirring tone did that distinguished man declare his firm adherence to the great principles for which the Church of Scotland is contending, and his settled determination to maintain them at all hazards, and whatever the consequences might be. Brilliant and powerful as had often been the eloquence of Dr. Candlish, on that great night he far outshone himself, the hearts of three thousand auditors heaving, trembling, and glowing beneath the might of his living and burning words. A deputation from the Irish Presbyterian Church was present, eager to tell that a million of Erin's warm-hearted children were ready to take their stand beside their Scottish brethren, should it again be necessary to spread abroad the dreadless and unconquered old blue banner on the free winds of heaven. And not a few of those strong-minded, enterprising men, of Scottish birth and blood, who had long been settled in England's wealthier regions, were also there, anxious to testify that their warmest love and dearest hopes were with their country still, and that they held it still their highest duty and most precious privilege to rally round the venerable and beloved Church of their fathers in her hour of peril. Yet even in the midst of the strong excitemen caused by such a scene, the prevailing spirit was deep, grave, and solemnly religious; and when at the close of the proceedings, the 122d psalm was given out to be sung, and with one spontaneous impulse arose, and from three thousand tongues at once poured forth in thunderous melody the sublime anthem of prayer and praise to God.

A series of resolutions, suited to the emergency, and instinct with the calm deliberate courage of Christian faith, having been proposed to this great meeting, received its warm and unanimous approval. They bore, "That this alarming crisis was to be regarded as a solemn call for prayerful deliberation, in an humble dependence on Almighty God for strength and wisdom to meet and endure the trial; that the great principles of 'the freedom of the Church from secular control in the exercise of the spiritual government and discipline committed to her by her Divine Head,' and 'that no pastor shall be intruded on a congregation contrary to the will of the people,' cannot be abandoned, and must, at whatever hazard, and in the midst of whatever troubles, be steadfastly maintained; that the fundamental principle avowed by those who seek to have themselves recognized as exclusively constituting the Established Church of Scotland, would be subversive of the government appointed by the Lord Jesus in His Church, would sanction such desolating settlements as that of Marnoch, and cannot be submitted to by those holding the principles set forth in the preceding resolution; that even should those who hold these principles be thrust out from the Establishment, they might still, adhering to the people, and the people to them, and all co-operating in one common cause and supported by one common fund, be the Church of the nation, so that the danger with which the Presbyterian Church is threatened may be calmly contemplated and fearlessly met, while at the same time, with firm unshrinking front, and in well-compacted union, and in reliance upon Divine aid, every effort must be made to avert so great a calamity, and to add yet another triumph in this land to the cause of Christ's crown and kingdom; and that this meeting resolve to co-operate in the formation of committees, local and general, for the purpose of securing complete harmony of knowledge and feeling, unity of exertion, and concentration of energy, in warding off impending dangers, and endeavouring to effect a happy and a peaceful issue out of all the troubles by which the Church of Scotland is now surrounded, the ministers and elders present declaring their resolution to stand by each other and by the Church in the maintenance of these principles, to which they again avow their determined adherence, praying Almighty God that He would give them strength to maintain them to the end."

The Church of Scotland thus calmly, firmly, and decisively took her ground, declared her principles, and committed herself to the protection of her only Head and King, looking to Him alone for strength to meet the conflict, fortitude under the trial, and a peaceful victory in His own all-wise and gracious time. Princes and people alike were constrained to hear her solemn declaration and her dignified appeal. And it became inevitable that the question must be asked at the legislature and the whole community, and must gravely and deliberately be answered by both, whether the National Church was to be composed of the adherents of a system which had thrust out a third of the population, protected heresy and immorality, opposed Christian missions, and prohibited the communion of believers,—a system which would still surrender every thing sacred and spiritual to the control of the secular powers, and would deliberately perpetrate atrocities like that of Marnock: or whether it should be composed of those who hold, teach, and maintain the principles committed to the Church by her only Head and King, as contained in the Scriptures, and embodied in the Standards, and enforced in the government and discipline of that true Presbyterian Church which takes for its rule the Word of God alone; which was planted in our land by the firm hand of our great reformers, and watered by the blood of our martyred fathers; which was ratified by the Revolution Settlement; whose secured integrity is the very basis of the Union, and the safeguard of the British constitution; whose noble characteristic it has ever been, to give education to the young, and to preach the gospel to the poor; and whose glorious distinction among all Christian Churches it has been, and still is, to suffer in defence of the Divine Redeemer's mediatorial crown. And though there were some preliminary stages through which the conflict had to pass, before that momentous question could be so cleared from all extraneous, or merely concomitant matter, that it might be put directly and alone, in a manner becoming its great and solemn importance; yet it was not doubtful to discerning minds, that the progress of events was rapidly reducing the controversy to its primary elements, and hastening to produce a crisis, not merely in the history of the Church of Scotland, but in the religious history of the world.

CHAPTER XI.

Introductory Remarks—Progress of the Controversy—The *Liberum Arbitrium*—The Culsalmond Case—The Middle Party—Meeting of the Assembly—Outline of its Proceedings—Remarks on the Position thus finally Assumed by the Church—The Commission of August—Second Decision in the Auchterarder Case—THE CONVOCATION—Sir James Graham's Letter—Reply of the Commission—The Stewarton Case—Deputations sent through Scotland, or Preparations begun for a Disruption—Discussions in the House of Commons—Proceedings of the Civil Courts and the Moderate Party—Continued Preparations—State of Affairs at the Meeting of the Assembly—THE DISRUPTION—THE FREE ASSEMBLY—Its Proceedings—The Proceedings of the Erastianized Assembly—Lord Aberdeen's Bill—Progress of the Free Church—Bicentenary Commemoration of the Westminster Assembly—Concluding Remarks.

THE proceedings of the Church of Scotland in the General Assembly of 1842, may be regarded as having fully developed, so far as that depended on the Church, all the leading principles of her constitution, involved in the late struggle, as exhibited in her Standards. These had all been, at different times, fairly and earnestly stated and defended by the evangelical and reforming party; but some of them had not received the due sanction of a majority, so that they remained in comparative abeyance, many being afraid to bring them prominently and authoritatively forward, lest the hostility of opponents should be increased both in extent and degree. But the course of events gradually led even the most cautious to perceive, that all temporising expedients were and must be in vain; and that the time was at length come for the Church of Scotland openly to declare all her principles, and to take the ground on which she was willing to encounter every peril, and to triumph in the strength of her Divine Head, or to perish gloriously in his sacred cause. It seems expedient, therefore, to trace briefly the outline of the most important of those events which in a manner hedged in the path of the Church, leaving her but one course of procedure—to go forward—unless she were prepared to abandon all her most sacred and cherished principles, and to become the degraded slave of civil courts.

The extraordinary meeting of Commission, held on the 25th of August 1841, in consequence of the declaration of the Moderate party, that they meant to take steps for ascertaining whether they or the majority were to be regarded as constituting the Established Church,—led, as has been related, to the adoption of a series of resolutions, in which the leading principles of the Church were plainly stated, and her determination to maintain them at all hazards solemnly declared. So far the warfare of argument seemed to be at an end; for both parties had declared their principles and determinations; and it seemed only to remain for the Legislature to decide to which of them it meant to give its sanction and support. This, however, was rather a delicate matter. The new administration had scarcely assumed their offices, and it would have been a very rash course for them suddenly to have adopted the views of the minority, at the hazard, if not with the certainty, of ejecting the majority of the Church, thereby ensuring its speedy overthrow. There was instituted also, about the same time, a series of negotiations, conducted chiefly through the medium of Sir George Sinclair, with the General Assembly's Non-Intrusion Committee. These negotiations have been since published; and they show sufficiently, that the object of Government was to induce the Church to accept Lord Aberdeen's bill, formerly rejected, and again produced, with the insertion of a clause prepared by Sir George Sinclair, the effect of which *seemed* to be, to enable the Church courts, in the exercise of their discretionary liberty of judgment, to reject a presentee if they should be of opinion that the objections and reasons against his settlement, entertained by the parishioners, were so strong, or entertained by such a proportion of them, as to preclude the prospect of his ministrations proving useful to that particular congregation. This discretionary liberty of the Church courts received the designation of a *Liberum Arbitrium*, and a long, tedious, and intricate course of diplomatic management was pursued by statesmen and lawyers, with the view, apparently, of deluding the Non-Intrusion Committee into the belief that it would indeed enable the Church to give effect to her own fundamental principle in each specific case, although not by means of a general law. But at length it appeared that the conventional term, mutually employed by both the Government and the Church, was understood by each party in a manner essentially different from that in which it was understood by the other. The Church understood it to secure to the presbyteries the power of refusing to intrude any presentee into a parish contrary to the will of the people, merely in consequence of their declared unwillingness to receive him as their pastor. The Government understood it to mean the pronouncing of a judgment upon the objections or reasons stated by the people against the presentee, with liberty to the presbytery to give effect to these objections or reasons, by adopting them as their own, and thereby giving them judicial validity, but that the absolute fact of the people's continued opposition was not to form itself the ground of the presbytery's decision. In reality, a settlement of the controversy, on a ground so ambiguous, would have been equally disgraceful to the Church and insulting to the people; it would have destroyed one of her fundamental principles, and legalised possible intrusion. No sooner was that clearly seen, in spite of the misty illusions of diplomatic craft, than the Non-Intrusion Committee declared against any such mode of settlement, expressing their views in such plain terms, that the Secretary of State for the Home Department (Sir James Graham) found it impossible to evade returning a direct answer, which he did in language of an ungracious, if not insulting character; and all further negotiations between Government and the Church on that basis terminated.

During these negotiations the country was repeatedly thrown into a state of great agitation and alarm, lest the Church should be induced to consent to an unsatisfactory measure. This alarm was industriously increased by the periodical press favourable to the Moderate party, for the purpose, apparently, of sowing distrust between the Church and the people,—confidently asserting that the Non-Intrusionists were willing to abandon all their principles, and to accept any settlement which might secure to them their emoluments, let the issue with regard to the rights of the people be what it might. Never, perhaps, was the Church of Scotland in greater peril than during the course of these diplomatic transactions; and for a time it seemed as if she was fairly ensnared by the tortuous policy of weak expediency-framing friends and wily statesmen. And when these mazy entanglements were rent asunder, and she was again placed on the free and open path of rectitude, her deliverance was regarded by wise and pious men, as nothing less than the signal interposition of Divine Providence, guided by the unerring and gracious hand of her Eternal King.

While these diplomatic proceedings were in progress, various other events took place, which must be briefly stated. Two different papers were drawn up by the Non-Intrusion Committee, and presented to Government, containing in very clear and explicit language, a statement of the leading principles of the Church of Scotland involved in the present contest, a summary of the facts which had occurred during its course, and a view of the various methods by means of which these principles might be most easily and efficiently realized. In the opinion of unprejudiced men, these two papers, the "Memorial" and the "Statement," ought to have enabled the Government fully to understand the matter, and might have convinced them that they would best discharge their own duty, and promote the peace and welfare of the empire, by passing a legislative enactment, securing to the Church the free exercise of those great constitutional principles which she had declared to be essential to her very existence. As if to counteract the effect which these documents might produce, the Moderate party also drew up a "Memorial," addressed to her Majesty's Government, prepared, it appears, by a Committee appointed by that party in August. This Memorial may be regarded as one of the most important documents produced during the whole course of the controversy. It contains a statement of the principles held by the Moderate party, in their own language, and set forth by their own authority; and the most decided opponent of Moderatism could not possibly wish for better materials on which to proceed in condemning that system as essentially Erastian and unscriptural, and also, by irresistible logical inference, unchristian, and leading, as even Sir George Sinclair perceived, to infidelity. There is no reason to suppose that those by whom the Memorial was prepared and subscribed were fully aware of its true character, and of the conclusions to which it inevitably led; but while this consideration may exonerate them from moral guilt, at the expense of their intellectual capacity, it the more strongly proves the baleful character of Moderatism itself, which both involves such consequences, and blinds and deadens its adherents.

The hostile attitude assumed by the Moderates was rendered more determined, partly by the fact, that several of their leading men had not merely preached in the pulpits still held by the deposed Strathbogie Seven, but had also assisted at the pretended dispensation of the Sacrament of the Lord's Supper, conducted by men wh› were no longer ministers of the gospel; and partly by a new act of unconstitutional violence committed by another northern presbytery. Proceedings had been instituted against the ministers who had held communion with the deposed seven, in the presbyteries to which they respectively belonged; but in consequence of protests and appeals, all these cases were referred to the next General Assembly. The new cause of collision arose out of the proceedings of the Presbytery of Garioch, in the case of a presentation to the parish of Culsalmond. The main facts of the case were as follows:—

The Rev. Ferdinand Ellis, minister of Culsalmond parish, in the Presbytery of Garioch, had, it appears, been laid aside from his official duties for several years, these duties being discharged in the interim by the Rev. William Middleton, as an ordained assistant. The patron at length issued a presentation in favour of Mr. Middleton, which was sustained by the presbytery in the usual form. On the 28th of October 1841, the presbytery met at Culsalmond to moderate in the call. It then appeared that there was a majority of male heads of families communicants dissenting from the settlement of Mr. Middleton as their pastor. The majority of the presbytery (seven to five) refused to sustain this dissent as a reason to stop procedure according to the standing directions of the General Assembly, and determined to proceed with appointing a day for the settlement, as if no dissents had been offered, defending this course by the assertion that the Veto Act was illegal. The people, by their law-agent, then offered special objections against the settlement, but the majority refused to receive these objections. The minority of the presbytery complained, and protested against this conduct, appealing to the synod; as did also the people, in due form. But the majority, setting all usual forms at defiance, refused to receive these complaints and appeals, and determined to proceed to the settlement on an appointed day, contrary to a special act of Assembly passed in 1732, prohibiting presbyteries from completing a settlement when an appeal has been taken. On the 11th of November 1841, the presbytery again met, and, contrary to all legal and ordinary procedure, and in the midst of great confusion, caused by their own arbitrary and oppressive conduct, went through the form of inducting Mr. Middleton, not in the church, but in a private room in the manse. The Commission of the General Assembly, upon a petition from the parishioners, cited the parties complained against to answer before the supreme Church courts; and in the meantime prohibited Mr. Middleton from officiating in the parish, and appointed the minority of the Presbytery of Garioch to provide for the administration of sacred ordinances in the parish of Culsalmond. Mr. Middleton, and the majority of the presbytery, applied to the Court of Session to suspend the proceedings of the Commission,—to interdict the intimation or execution of its deliverance,—and to interdict also the minority of the presbytery from obeying the directions of the Commission. This interdict was refused by the Lord Ordinary (Lord Ivory); but, being carried before the First Division of the Court of Session, was granted as craved, on the 10th of March 1842. In this case the warfare of actions certainly carried both the Moderate party and the civil courts beyond their former hostile positions. The Moderate majority of the Garioch Presbytery, contrary even to the usual and declared course of that party, refused to receive special objections against the presentee; and refused also to stay procedure, in consequence of appeals to superior Church courts, contrary to all former usage, as well as to express act of Assembly. The civil courts, on their part, reviewed and interdicted a sentence of the Church court, when no civil interest was directly involved, but when a superior ecclesiastical court was interposing to check the disorderly conduct of a subordinate court in a matter undeniably spiritual.

It has been stated that the Non-Intrusion Committee ceased to hold intercourse with Government, upon discovering the essentially different interpretations put by them and those with whom they had been corresponding, respecting the meaning of that phrase, the *Liberum Arbitrium*, or free discretionary power of presbyteries, which had been proposed as the basis of a settlement. But there was a small minority of that committee who still continued to think that a settlement might, after all, be framed upon that ambiguous phrase, if not such as the Church ought to ask, yet such as she might submit to, without absolute dereliction of principle, since, as they reasoned, it was impossible that any thing more satisfactory could be obtained. Immediately some of the most active of that small minority began a course of private negotiations, partly with the most timid and undecided of those ministers who had generally acted along with the Non-Intrusionists chiefly on the ground of expediency, and partly with the least violent of the Moderates. Rumours began to arise of the formation of a middle party, which was to unite the most cautious and temperate of the other two, thereby weakening both, and assuming a new, or at least an intermediate position made up of compromises and concessions, on which a settlement might possibly be effected. At the meeting of the Synod of Glasgow and Ayr, in April, a declaration was laid before that court by Dr. Leishman, subscribed, as was said, by forty ministers, expressing their anxiety for a settlement, and giving it as their opinion, that they could conscientiously submit to Lord Aberdeen's bill, with the insertion of Sir George Sinclair's clause, if that were passed into a law. This was the first public divulgement of the course of policy intended to be pursued by the middle party; as it was then stated that they had entered into communication with Sir. James Graham, and entertained sanguine expectations that a settlement not absolutely intolerable might yet be obtained. It further appeared, from a speech of Dr. M'Culloch of Kelso, that while he had joined the middle party, and was willing to aid them with all his influence, he entertained such opinions as would have permitted him to submit to the entire sacrifice of the Non-Intrusion principle itself. This might have pleased the Moderates, but must have galled many of the forty, who sincerely detested intrusion, but had been drawn, by their love of peace, into what thus threatened to become an abandonment of principle. Still the report was most industriously propagated, that the middle party was increasing with prodigious rapidity, and would very soon form a majority of the entire Church of Scotland. The real weakness of the party, however, even numerically, was so far discovered at the meeting of the Synod of Mid-Lothian, early in May, when Dr. Simpson, the acknowledged framer and leader of the party, could obtain, even with the aid of the Moderates in the synod, but a small minority to support his views. They continued, nevertheless, to boast loudly of their secret strength, and of the favourable manner in which their overtures were met by Government. It may be added, that Sir James Graham seems to have imagined that he had now a prospect of reïntroducing the lately abandoned measure; as he induced Mr. Campbell of Monzie to postpone a bill identical with that formerly brought forward by the Duke of Argyle, expressing his hope, arising out of recent movements in Scotland, that Government might be able to introduce a measure by which the dissensions of the Scottish Church might be satisfactorily adjusted. Yet, even in this comparatively pacificatory declaration, the Home Secretary stated the principles on which alone Government could frame a measure, and these principles were essentially those of Lord Aberdeen's bill, in which the first and fundamental proposition, governing of course all the rest, was the determination to maintain what was termed "the civil rights of patrons." This *might* have opened the eyes of the middle party, had they been either able or willing to see any thing but their own preconceived wishes and impressions.

There had been several other minor, though not unimportant, events and indications during the course of these public and prominent occurrences. Men of unblemished character had been tried as implicated in what was called the Culsalmond riot, and honorably acquitted by a jury of their countrymen. A military detachment had been marched into the district of Strathbogie, without the slightest apparent reason, but merely to support the intrusion of a probationer into the parish of Glass, by means of the men who had been deposed from the ministerial office. And several glaringly arbitrary instances of despotic patronage had been perpetrated by the Home Secretary, accompanied with language indicating an insolent contempt for the feelings and the petitions of the people.

Such is a brief outline of the chief events which preceded the meeting of the Genera. Assembly, and such the general state of affairs when it met on 19th of May 1842. It seems impossible for a thoughtful mind to contemplate these mazy and complicated movements, without perceiving that they were all guided by an invisible but an Almighty hand. How many phases had the conflict assumed within the course of one short year! Encouraged, apparently, by the prospect of a change of Government, and the formation of an administration more favourable to their views, the Moderate party had cast cff their previous reserve, and declared their intention to take such steps as must inevitably cause a schism in the Church. Thence arose the great West Kirk meeting, and the noble resolutions passed there, which stirred the heart of the kingdom. Next came the period of diplomatic craft, in the negotiations respecting the *Liberium Arbitrium*,—a mode of settlement which was very early, in the course of this struggle, forced upon the consideration of the Church; and which had never been entertained but with extreme reluctance, and with the utmost danger of the sacrifice of principle. When both the Church and the people were in this state of stunned and helpless alarm, and there seemed no way of escape from a disastrous and dishonourable compromise, on a sudden, in answer doubtless to the deep-breathed prayers of thousands, these lowering clouds parted asunder, the dangers vanished, and, resuming her sacred principles, she stood again prepared fearlessly to act or suffer in their defence. The lawless deed of Culsalmond,—the military seizure of Strathbogie,—and the haughty and contumelious despotism of the Home Secretary, all doubtless intended to terrify her into submission, produced a very different result; rousing the courage of the faithful ministers to higher daring, constraining the undecided to perceive that there was now no alternative but the utter abandonment, or the resolute assertion of principle, and even imparting a noble fortitude to many who had hitherto stood timidly aloof from the conflict. Last of all came the feeble muster of the wavering middle-men, few of whom had ever truly belonged to the reforming majority, and of these few, none had ever borne a prominent part in the arduous struggle. This middle movement came in time to call off the timid and the hesitating, together with some who could better suffer for truth and purity than contend in their defence; but too late to influence those of more penetrating minds, capacious judgments, and calmly resolute hearts. It scarcely thinned the defenders of the Church; and it left no weak and assailable points in their faithful and united band. Surely in all this the overruling power and wisdom of the Redeemer was most graciously apparent! It was not by man's prudence, but by God's foreknowledge, that all had been so wonderfully ordered; and in the full and solemn perception that this had been the case, the members of the General Assembly met to deliberate, in the name, and by the authority of the Divine Head and King of the Church, on matters of the most momentous importance to His spiritual kingdom.

Her Majesty's Government had appointed the Marquis of Bute to hold the office of Lord High Commissioner. This nobleman had previously distinguished himself in promoting the cause of Church extension; and his unblemished character secured to him the respect of the entire Church. The opening of the Assembly was conducted with more than ordinary pomp; but the minds of men were too much engrossed by the deeply important nature of the matters soon to come under deliberation, to permit them to give more than a passing glance to the gorgeous pageant as it swept along. It was felt by all, that upon the proceedings of this Assembly might, or rather must, depend the present fate of the Church of Scotland; and friends and foes were wrought up to an almost equally intense pitch of excitement, in eager anticipation of the result.

After sermon by the Rev. Dr. Gordon, Moderator of the preceding Assembly, the Assembly was regularly constituted in St. Andrew's Church; and Dr. Welsh, Professor of Church History in the University of Edinburgh, was unanimously chosen to be moderator, and assumed the chair accordingly. Dr. Cook of St. Andrews, as the recognised leader of his party, then formally renewed his and their protest against the ministers of chapels of ease, or *quoad sacra* parishes, being regarded as constitutional members of Assemb y. This was immediately met by Mr. Dunlop, who declared, on the part of the majority, their firm resolution to maintain these men in all the due powers and privileges of ministers of the Church of Scotland. This incident, slight apparently in itself, gave some indication of the probable course of procedure likely to be followed by the two contending parties, each seeming to be determined to maintain every inch of the position formerly occupied. After the reading of the Queen's letter, and the respective addresses of the lord high commissioner and the moderator, a still more important discussion arose. Conflicting commissions for different parties to sit as members of Assembly, from the Presbytery of Strathbogie, were produced, the one from the pretended presbytery, constituted by the seven deposed ministers, in favour of two ministers and an elder of their own number, the other from the real presbytery, consisting of the four ministers, not deposed, and their elders, being the only parties recognised by the Church as the true Presbytery of Strathbogie. Mr. Dunlop moved, that the commission from the four be sustained, and that from the deposed seven be not received. This gave rise to a sharp discussion, in the course of which Dr. Cook moved, that, in present circumstances, the commission in favour of the representatives of the four be not sustained. The vote was taken and Mr. Dunlop's motion was carried by 215 to 85, a very large majority, in probably the fullest Assembly ever known on the first day of its meeting. This was a very important vote. It clearly indicated the overwhelming strength of the Evangelical majority, and the weakness of their opponents. It tended, accordingly, to give a tone of calm confidence to the majority; while it equally discouraged and irritated the Moderate party, by showing the certainty of their utter discomfiture.

A considerable part of Friday, the 20th of May, was occupied, as usual, in devotional exercises; and it was remarked by many, that the prayers of the various members who were called upon, were characterised throughout by a remarkable degree of fervency, and earnestness of spirit and manner. Mr. Dunlop then read a report from the joint-committee of the Five Schemes of the Church, regarding the collections, congregational and individual, contributed during the past year to these schemes. From this general report it appeared, that in the sums collected for these schemes, there had been a decided increase, not only in the aggregate, but in each particular scheme, and in some of them to a large amount. It appeared, further, that the period during which these collections had been obtained, had been only ten months, owing to an alteration in the time of making up the accounts; and that, when the whole sums raised by collections and individual subscriptions for all the public measures of the Church were united, including those for defence of the litigations in which the Church had been involved, the sum total was about £30,000, being an increase beyond the amount of the preceding year of nearly £8000. This was a result greatly more propitious than had been anticipated, on many accounts. The year had been one of great commercial and mercantile depression, throwing many thousands into absolute destitution, and exhausting the resources of the charitable in their support. In such a state of national distress, it would not have been surprising if the funds raised for religious and missionary purposes had also suffered a temporary depression. It had also been perpetually reiterated by the Moderate party and their newspaper advocates, that the dissensions within the Church had completely paralyzed all her exertions, destroyed her general usefulness, and rendered her utterly inefficient, as a national institution, for promoting the advancement of Christianity at home and abroad. The very diffusion of such gloomy assertions and predictions tended to their own realization; and it must be confessed, that the religious contributions of several congregations, where the minister was one of the Moderate party, had sunk down to about one-fourth of their former amount. This was, perhaps, more deplorable than surprising; for Moderatism had never shown itself friendly to missionary exertions; and though carried into a temporary support of these schemes by the strength of public opinion, was willing to discover some pretence for abandoning them.* Yet it is very deplorable when men, bearing the character of ministers of the gospel, avail themselves of a pretext, arising out of a controversy with their brethren, to abandon the great interests of the Redeemer's kingdom. But, in spite of such defections, and of the predictions and assertions of unscrupulous partizans, the result has proved that pity for perishing souls, and zeal for the advancement of God's glory, in the progress of the gospel all over the world, were not diminished, or rather were largely increased in the hearts of the people of Scotland; and that the existing controversy, painful and alarming as it was, had, instead of weakening, greatly strengthened their religious feelings, and stimulated their exertions. The state of the Church, in this point of view, furnished also a startling contrast to that of the nation. The difficulty of conducting the public business of the empire, with an increasing expenditure, and a diminishing revenue, not adequate to meet the public necessities, had been the direct cause of the retirement of one administration, and the accession of another; and even the new Government, in all its fresh strength, staggered and reeled in the endeavour to frame, and carry into effect, a measure by which it hoped to rescue the nation from its oppressed and sinking condition. In this very period of legislative convulsion, financial difficulty, and wide-spread national poverty, the Church was seen presenting to the service of God the gifts of a treasury more amply filled than it had ever previously been, with the free-will offerings of the people; and, at the same time emerging out of that debt in which she had been involved by the expensive litigations carried on in defence of her spiritual independence, and her people's religious liberties. Surely this was another signal manifestation that the rich blessing of God was descending upon her exertions in His service; and a great reason for her to thank Him, and take courage, and go forward undismayed. Such, unquestionably, was the general feeling of the Assembly, as was manifest, not merely by the remarks of the speakers, but also, and particularly, in the grateful tone of the subsequent devotions.

The forenoon of Saturday, the 21st, was signalized by a very spirit-stirring incident. It has been mentioned that, on

* "The contributions of the 145 ministers, who, on that occasion, voted in the majority, amount to £4023 9 8
while those of the 62 in the minority are no more than 409 4 8
Of the 145, only 10 made no contribution for any of the schemes; and a number of these were either new churches or newly settled; whereas there were no fewer than 22 out of the 62, that is more than *one-third*, who contributed nothing at all. And this, be it observed, is not accidental. The same result has been repeatedly brought out before. Then of the *quoad sacra* and parliamentary church ministers, on the same vote,
The 36 who voted with the majority contributed £413 9 2
The 5 with the minority, only . . . 5 15 0
So that the 36 *quoad sacra* ministers contribute more to the missionary schemes of the church than the whole of the 62 clerical representatives of the Moderate party put together."—*Scottish Guardian, June* 13, 1842.

the first day of the Assembly, a paper was laid on the table by the commissioners from the real Presbytery of Strathbogie, which was understood to be an interdict granted by the civil court, prohibiting them from taking their seats as members. This paper the Assembly would not read till it should have decided, according to its own principles, respecting these conflicting commissions. On Saturday, the commissioners from Strathbogie were requested to state to the house, under what circumstances of a peculiar nature they came to take their seats. Major Ludovick Stewart, the elder for Strathbogie, a war-worn, yet stately veteran, arose, holding in one hand the Court of Session's interdict, and in the other his Bible. He stated that he did not regard lightly the interdict of a civil court, for he had long been accustomed to strict discipline; but that he held that there were circumstances in which a person might be placed, when it would be criminal to obey the interdict of any earthly court. "I hold in my hands," said the venerable officer, "an authority in this holy Book, which does not prohibit me from standing forth in support of the principles of the Church of Scotland. So long as I am able, I will serve my God as faithfully as I have served my country; but there is nothing in this Book which commands me to obey such an interdict, and I will not obey anything which implies criminality to the Church of Scotland." It is impossible to describe the thrilling effect produced by this short solemn speech,—the depth of feeling which held the Assembly in silent, unbreathing fixedness of attention,—and the looks of intense sympathy and admiration with which all eyes regarded one whose earnest words and dignified aspect realized to every imagination the bodily presence of some martyred warrior of the covenant. Dr. Candlish, in a short but very impressive speech, pointed out the unparalleled character of this unconstitutional interference on the part of the Court of Session, with the powers and privileges of the Assembly; and then moved a resolution, expressive of deep and entire sympathy with those members who had been so violently obstructed, in discharge of their public duty, by the civil courts; the determination of the Assembly to support and encourage them by every means in its power; and a solemn protest against the attempt thus made, for the first time, on the part of any civil tribunal, to interfere with the constitution of the supreme courts of this Church, declaring such interference to be wholly unconstitutional, and such as the Assembly cannot recognise, when pronounced in a matter wholly ecclesiastical, and placed under the exclusive jurisdiction of this supreme ecclesiastical judicatory. Dr. Cook moved that this resolution be not adopted. The vote was taken, and Dr. Candlish's motion was carried by a majority of 97; the vote being 173 to 76.

Several other important events took place on the same day. Dr. Candlish, as convener of the Committee for Correspondence with Foreign Churches, produced two letters, one of them from the Commission, the other from the Assembly of the Church in Canada, and a third from the General Assembly of the Presbyterian Church in the United States of America. This last letter was publicly read. It expressed, in clear and emphatic terms, their sympathy with the Church of Scotland in her present troubles,—their conviction that the Lord would not forsake her when engaged in defending his own cause,—and their earnest hope and prayer that the Church might soon be, by God's blessing, delivered from her difficulties and dangers. It was moved and agreed to, that the Committee should prepare suitable answers to these interesting letters.

Reports were then given in from the Committee on the Commission record, and from the Special Commission appointed by the preceding Assembly, to attend to the state of religious affairs in the district of Strathbogie, and in other similar matters. These reports necessarily brought under the notice of the Assembly the conduct of those ministers of the Moderate party who had assisted the deposed seven of Strathbogie in the pretended dispensation of the sacrament. It was moved that these ministers should be cited to appear at the bar of the Assembly on Thursday, to answer the charge brought against them; and no opposition being made, they were cited accordingly Warrant was also granted for citing witnesses to prove, if necessary, the facts of the case. Several other accused parties were cited to appear on specified days.

In the evening, a motion was made by Mr. Cunningham, and seconded by Mr. Hetherington, to rescind that part of the Act of Assembly 1799, which prohibited all ministers of the Church of Scotland from permitting to preach in their pulpits, or holding ministerial communion with persons not qualified to receive a presentation. That act, as is well known, was passed by the Moderate party for the very purpose of preventing Mr. Simeon of Cambridge, Rowland Hill, and other evangelical ministers of the Church of England, from being permitted to preach in any pulpit of the Established Church of Scotland. It had the effect of cutting the Church off from communion with every other Church, and thereby it virtually denied the doctrine of a "Church universal," rejected the "communion of saints," and disclaimed the brotherly affection infused into all true members of the household of faith by the presence and energy of the Holy Spirit. It was thus equally sectarian and sinful in spirit and tendency, and was one of the most disgraceful and unchristian of the many guilty deeds done by Moderatism, in the name of the Church of Scotland. So much, however, was this felt to be its character, that no person spoke in its defence, at least directly; though some appeared very apprehensive that the rescinding of it might lead to a dangerous laxity in the admission of men to ministerial communion who were not sound in the faith. Though this danger could not be regarded as very great, seeing the repeal of that act would only restore the Church of Scotland to the position in which she had been placed and left by the Covenanters themselves, yet a cautionary clause was added for the satisfaction of the scrupulous. This was one of the most truly Christian decisions of this Assembly, and one, also, of very happy omen, and in most perfect accordance with the almost universal sympathy expressed by Christian Churches with the Church of Scotland in her struggles and her sufferings; contrasting, at the same time, strongly with the bigotry and intolerance of a party in the Church of England. It gave no dubious indication, that whatever worldly politicians might imagine, the Church of Scotland occupied, at that moment, the noblest and most important position of any institution, civil or ecclesiastical, in the world,—that, while they were vainly striving to circumscribe and fetter and confine her, she was snapping asunder their feeble bands, overpassing their jealousy besieging lines, and both awakening and responding to the sympathetic feelings of all living Christendom.

On Monday, May 23, the report of the Committee for classing returns to overtures was then given in; and, as it appeared that a majority of the presbyteries had approved of the overture on the Eldership, Mr. Dunlop moved that the Assembly pass it accordingly into a standing law of the Church. This was done; and it was also ordered to be recorded in the books of the kirk-session in every parish throughout the kingdom. Thus another very important reform was completed, and the sincerity of the Church, in her advocacy of the religious rights of the people, placed beyond suspicion. It had long been the practice of the Moderate party to introduce into the eldership men who favoured their views of church policy, however unfit for that office; and when the Church began her course of self-reformation, the opposition of these elders formed one of the most difficult obstacles to her endeavours, their votes repeatedly giving the preponderance to the Moderate side, when it would otherwise have been defeated. It is now the law of the Church, that the elders are to be elected by the whole male communicants of the congregation; and by the judicious use of this religious right, the people may prevent the possibility of Moderatism ever regaining the ascendency in Church courts.

The next subject which came before the Assembly, was that of Patronage. It appeared that overtures had been transmitted from 12 synods, 24 presbyteries, and 38 parishes, besides several others from associations and kirk-sessions, all praying for the abolition of patronage. Mr. Cunningham then proposed the following motion:—"That the General Assembly having considered the overtures anent patronage, resolve and declare, that patronage is a grievance, has been attended with much injury to the cause of true religion in the Church and kingdom, is the main cause of the difficulties in which the Church is at present involved, and that it ought to be abolished." In a speech of very great clearness and argumentative power, Mr. Cunningham explained, defended, and enforced this momentous question. He showed the essential distinction between the Church of Christ and any wordly institution, proving irresistibly, that having received its origin, laws and organization, from Christ alone, no merely secular power could have any right to interfere with the appointment of its office-bearers; that in regulating that matter, recourse must be had to the Word of God alone, from which it was plainly manifest, that presbyteries and Christian congregations had each a duty divinely assigned to them, while no mention was made of any function to be exercised by any third and worldly party; that every attempt to defend patronage must be based upon some secular consideration, and must involve the grievous error of setting aside or superseding the great rule, that in every thing pertaining to Christ's House, direction must be sought and taken from Him alone. Availing himself of these primary principles, he met and refuted the leading arguments generally used by the defenders of Patronage, whether viewed as arising out of the donation given by an individual, or the endowments granted by a State; for in either or both of these suppositions, the real question to be determined was, *not* whether it were natural and reasonable for the donor to retain the power of appointing a pastor who should enjoy the fruits of the endowment, but, in what manner ought the ministers of Christian churches to be appointed, so as may be most accordant with the will of Christ, and most conducive to the spiritual welfare of the people. He prov'ᴊ clearly, that to determine the question of patronage on the ground of any endowment granted by the State or an individual, or on account of any civil qualification, was most decidedly Erastian, and must introduce a hostile and destructive element into the very heart of the Church. Towards the conclusion of his unanswerable speech, Mr. Cunningham briefly alluded to the perfidious Act of Queen Anne, and to the baneful effects produced by that act, both in former times and at present, and most earnestly called upon the Church not to hesitate, from any weak or unmanly fear of consequences, from demanding the abolition of patronage, by which procedure, while boldly and fully following out the principles of the Word of God, she would also secure her best earthly support—the confidence of the free-hearted and religious people of Scotland.

A counter motion was made by the Procurator:—"That the Assembly having considered the overtures and petitions, find it inexpedient, in present circumstances, to adopt the overtures." A long and very animated discussion followed, during the course of which several rather peculiar indications respecting the state of parties and the progress of opinion appeared. It became evident that the Procurator's motion was framed by the new middle party, and that the Moderates had refrained from proposing a motion of their own, in the hope that by supporting that of the middle party, they might have the best prospect of success in their attempt to defeat the anti-patronage movement. The vote was at length taken, and the motion for the abolition of patronage carried by a majority of 69, in the fullest house ever known, the numbers being—for abolition, 216; inexpedient in present circumstances, 147; total, 363. In the year 1841, a similar motion was lost by 6; and although the Moderates so far compromised their own views in order to effect a junction with the middle party, as to move that it was inexpedient to apply for the abolition of patronage *in present circumstances*, which implied that it might be expedient in other circumstances, yet both combined sustained a complete defeat, and the Church of Scotland resumed her ancient and constitutional opposition tᵒ the great unscriptural and unpresbyterian grievance of secular patronage. The announcement of the decision was received with loud and long applause by the anxious and crowded spectators, and with warm mutual congratulations, and silent breathings of grateful thanks to God, by the faithful majority whose votes had secured the welcome victory.

On Tuesday, May 24, the Assembly proceeded to the main business of tha important day, the consideration of an overture, signed by about 150 members of Assembly, for a "Declaration against the unconstitutional encroachments of the civil courts." This singularly clear and powerful document, prepared by Mr. Dunlop, was read at full length by the clerk of the Assembly, amid the silent and deep attention of the whole house. Dr. Chalmers then moved that it be adopted as the resolution of the Assembly, which was seconded by Dr. Gordon. Dr. Cook, instead of meeting it with a direct negative, moved a series of resolutions of a different, but not directly opposite, character. The speech of Dr. Chalmers was characterized by all the lofty and fervid eloquence of that great man. He did not, indeed, attempt to follow, explain, and enforce the various leading topics of the Declaration; but taking up the subject in that point of view most suited to command the attention of a patriotic and enlightened statesman, he first removed the seeming difficulties of arriving at a right understanding of the essential elements of the question, which have been produced by misrepresenting it as little more than the personal wranglings of individuals and parties in the Church, instead of regarding it as a great constitutional question concerning the respective jurisdictions of two separate and distinct co-ordinate courts, each supreme and independent in its own province. He then drew attention to the formidable consequences which must inevitably follow, should the Legislature permit the civil court to persevere, in its encroachments upon the constitutional jurisdiction of the Church,—issuing interdicts in spiritual matters which religion and conscience were constrained to disregard,—uttering threats of pains and penalties which it could not inflict without committing the sin of persecution,—and, by assuming that the possession of superior might was equivalent to right, actually employing the argument of physical force, an argument which had already been assumed, and might ere long, after the example of the civil court, be directed with terrific power, by men who have the strength of millions of the lawless and the ungodly on their side, against all the institutions of the empire. Such an argument, so powerfully brought forward by such a man, might well have caused statesmen to pause and ponder, if they had heart to feel, and intellect to understand it,—if they had not been under the spell of a blinding and deadly infatuation.

The resolutions and the speech of Dr. Cook were alike weak and evasive, not touching, not even approaching, the essence of the subject. He proposed the rescinding of the Veto Act, and the annulling of all the penal or judicial proceedings founded on it; asserted that the doctrines of Christ's Headship, and the distinct government of the Church, might be held with such diversities of opinion, and various modes of application, as to afford no cause of irreconcilable disagreement between parties entertaining widely different views; advised that all agitation should cease, and ministers should confine themselves chiefly to their pastoral duties; and asserted, that under the existing laws of the Church, there was already sufficient security against the settlement of unqualified and unsuitable ministers. Such were the resolutions moved by Dr. Cook; and his speech was a mere explanation of them, exhibiting in its progress, not only strange feebleness of reasoning, but deplorable want of precision in the statement of principles, which in their loose and vague indefiniteness might mean any thing or nothing, and could lead to no fixed course of thought and action. Nor did he even touch upon the encroachments of the civil court, either to condemn or to approve them, nor explain in what manner his motion could rescue the Church from future similar invasions,—unless it were to be inferred, that principles so very laxly held might be abandoned whenever they should be assailed.

The speech of Mr. Dunlop was a full and complete commentary on the whole of the Declaration, leaving nothing to be desired for its explanation and defence; but as both that able document and speech have been put in the possession of entire Christendom, it cannot be necessary to insert here even the briefest outline of them.

Mr. Robertson of Ellon, as usual, came nearer the heart of the question than any other speaker on the Moderate side; but still he rather dealt with points and specialties than attempted to grapple with great principles. One of his minute criticisms on the Act 1592, respecting the presbyteries being bound and astricted to receive and admit qualified ministers, was answered by Dr. Lee, who proved that this expression could not mean persons already ordained, because out of 46 presentations granted by the king himself within a year after the passing of that Act, 27 were in favour of persons not ordained. He made also a very important admission, by stating, that he regarded the interdict granted by the Court of Session, against the preaching of the gospel, by ministers appointed by the Church, within the seven parishes of Strathbogie, as an incompetent act on the part of the civil court. This admission—although subsequently Mr. Robertson was very anxious to limit and qualify it—was gladly welcomed by the majority, as indicating the existence of some ground on which both parties might yet accordantly meet. After some further discussion, and some able speeches by Dr. Buchanan of Glasgow, Mr. Gray of Perth, and others, the vote was taken, and the motion of Dr. Chalmers carried by a majority of 131,—the numbers being 241 to 110.

The adoption of this Claim of Rights and Declaration against the encroachments of the civil courts, as the resolution of the General Assembly, was one of the most important and momentous steps ever taken by the Church of Scotland. It put an end for ever to all the ambiguities which had hitherto surrounded her position, and obscured her great principles; it placed in the most clear and prominent point of view the rights secured to her by the laws and constitution of the empire, rendering also distinctly apparent every aggression made by the civil courts upon these rights; and while it declared her firm and unalterable determination to maintain and defend all the rights, privileges, and principles essential to a Church of Christ, and secured to her by many legislative enactments, at whatever hazard, it necessarily assumed a position which even statesmen must regard with respect, and might well hesitate directly to assail, assured that it must call forth the smpathy and the admiration of all truly religious men, and that it could not possibly be overthrown without the imminent danger, if not the absolute certainty, of plunging the kingdom into the dire horrors of a wild, far-spreading revolutionary convulsion.

It may be remarked, that the greater part of the debate upon this great subject was not peculiarly animated. This arose partly from the fact, that Dr. Cook's motion, instead of directly opposing that of Dr. Chalmers, took up what may be termed a parallel position, so that the different speakers were not necessarily brought into collision, being at liberty to advocate their own peculiar views with little reference to those of the other party, consequently the discussion moved slowly forward on parallel lines, till it came to a pause rather than a conclusion. Yet several curious manifestations of opinion appeared during the debate, some of which have been already noticed, though perhaps the most remarkable were the explanations of spiritual independence and non-intrusion given by Dr. Cook and his friends. From these it appeared that, by "the spiritual independence of the Church," the Moderate party understand, the liberty enjoyed by private individuals to withdraw from the Church and become Dissenters if dissatisfied with it; and by "non-intrusion" they understand, that when an unacceptable minister is settled in a parish, the parishioners ought not to be thrust forcibly into the church, and compelled to hear the minister against their will. Something similar had previously been hinted in controversial pamphlets; but the honour of seeing the principles of Moderatism on these points revealed to the light of open day, was reserved for the General Assembly of 1842.

On Thursday, May 26, there was brought before the Assembly the case of those ministers who were reported by the Special Commission as having held communion with the deposed seven of Strathbogie, by receiving the elements of the Lord's Supper at their hands. These were, the Rev. James Robertson, minister at Ellon; Rev. James Grant, at Leith; Rev. John Cook, at Haddington; Rev. Robert Stirling, at Galston; Rev. Charles Hope, at Lamington; Rev. John Wilson, at Walston; Rev. James Bryce, late at Calcutta; Rev. Alexander Cushny, at Rayne; Rev. Thomas Hill, at Logiepert; Rev. George Peters, at Kemnay; and Rev. William Mearns, missionary at Glenrinnes—eleven in all. When they took their station at the bar Dr. Cook read a protest in his own name and in that of those who should adhere to him, against the competency of the General Assembly to entertain a motion for regarding as a ground of ecclesiastical censure the charge preferred against the ministers at the bar; declaring themselves bound, whatever judgment the Assembly may pronounce, to act as circumstances might require, in accordance with their convictions of duty. The accused brethren were then asked if they had any statements to make to the Assembly. They produced a written document, which proved to be a protest, the general purport of which was:—a complaint of the irregular and summary nature of the proceedings against them; an admission of the truth of the matters of fact with which they were charged, but a denial that these implied any thing culpable; the assertion that the sentence of deposition passed against the seven late ministers of Strathbogie was an excess of jurisdiction, and therefore incompetent, and null and void; and a declaration that they regarded their conduct as not involving matter of judicial procedure or ecclesiastical censure. Being then asked if they had any further statements to make, they answered, that if the protest should be recorded in the journals of the Assembly, they had nothing more to say. Thus, contrary to all expectation, terminated their defence.

Dr. Candlish then, in a speech of surpassing acuteness of thought, logical precision, and solemn, unimpassioned, yet impressive eloquence, proceeded to state the real and essential character of the offence committed by the accused parties. He disentangled their conduct alike from the sophistical defences of friends, and the exaggerated accusations of adversaries, placing it, when analyzed to its very elements, in the clear dry light of severely simple truth, there to be viewed and judged by itself alone. He proved that it was not of the same nature as the offence for which the seven had been deposed, and that it could not become so, till they should violate a sentence of the Assembly, pronounced immediately and directly against themselves, and should also call in the civil authority to interfere with the discipline of the Church, and to stay the censures duly pronounced against them. He further reasoned, that although their conduct might imply a desecration of the sacrament, yet it was only by inference and construction, arguing, that as even civil courts did not now condemn a man for constructive treason, so it would not become an ecclesiastical court to pass the severest censure on what was essentially a constructive crime. Thus reduced to its simplest elemental form, the offence committed by these brethren was shown to be one against the authority of the supreme court of the Church, that is, the offence of contumacy, connected with the encouragement of schismatic and divisive courses, and as such deserving direct and summary censure. Dr. Candlish also refuted several of the ordinary arguments used in defence of the conduct of these ministers, and particularly their own assertion, that they regarded the sentence of deposition as null and void; showing that they could not rationally or conscientiously assume that as not done, which they well knew had been done, but that it was their duty, both in reason and conscience, to view it as an existent reality, and then to determine what their course of procedure ought to be. He concluded his exceedingly able and luminous speech, by moving that the Assembly find the conduct of the accused ministers censurable, that a committee be appointed to deal with them, and to report on Monday, on which day they be cited to appear at the bar. To this motion the Moderate party, sheltering themselves under the protestation given in by Dr. Cook, made no opposition, and it was agreed to without a vote.

The proceedings of the Assembly on Friday, May 27, embraced some matters of considerable importance, and were characterized by faithful adherence to principle. The case of Mr. Wilson, minister of Stranraer, was brought forward. This person was charged with fraud and swindling, and had applied for, and obtained an interdict prohibiting the Presbytery from proceeding with his trial, on various grounds, one of which was, that the presbytery was vitiated by the presence of a *quoad sacra* minister. The Assembly found Mr. Wilson liable to the highest censure of the Church for applying to the civil court to impede the course of discipline, appointed a committee to deal with him, and to report on Monday, and summoned him to appear on that day. A similar course of procedure was adopted in the case of Mr. Clark, formerly presentee to Lethendy, and residing, under the authority of the Court of Session, in the manse thereof, who was charged with the crimes of drunkenness, obscenity, and profane swearing. He too had obtained an interdict against the Presbytery of Dunkeld, as vitiated by the presence in it of *quoad sacra* ministers; and for this offence he was deprived of his license, without further probation. In the course of the discussion upon this case, it was stated, that the First Division of the Court of Session had that very day, by an apparent majority of one (the real numbers being two to two, but the Lord Ordinary, Ivory, not being entitled in the circumstances to vote), affirmed the interdict prohibiting the commissioners from the true Presbytery of Strathbogie from sitting as members of Assembly, thereby assuming the power of interfering with the constitution of the supreme ecclesiastical court of the Church of Scotland; and some very important remarks were made on this subject by Mr. A. E. Monteith. Another interdict was treated in the same manner, in the case of Mr. Livingston of Cambusnethan, who had been convicted of theft, and had sought to prevent the pronouncing of judgment, by obtaining an interdict because of *quoad sacra* ministers. The sentence of deposition was pronounced by the Assembly on the spot, disregarding and condemning the interdict. The Assembly also rescinded and declared void the pretended settlement of Mr. Duguid in the parish of Glass, by the deposed ministers of Strathbogie, pronouncing him no minister of the Gospel, and depriving him of his license for his schismatic proceedings. The Culsalmond case next occupied the attention of the Assembly. Its nature has been already stated, and need not be here repeated. Dr. Cook moved, that the settlement of Mr. Middleton be not disturbed. Mr. Dunlop moved, that the complaint against it be sustained, that the settlement be rescinded, and Mr. Middleton found to have disqualified himself by his conduct; and as to the rest, reserve consideration of the conduct of the majority of the presbytery, and of Mr. Middleton, till a subsequent day. Professor Alexander moved, to reduce the settlement, on account of the irregularities of the procedure, and to send the case back to the presbytery to take the special objections. The motions of Mr. Dunlop and Professor Alexander were put against each other, and Mr. Dunlop's carried by 214 to 8. Dr. Cook then allowed Mr. Dunlop's motion to pass without another division, and next day gave in reasons of dissent, signed by himself and about 60 other members, which served to indicate the relative proportions of middle-men and decided Moderates.

The decisions of this day gave practical proof of the Church of Scotland's determination not to permit her constitution to be violated, and her discipline prevented by the interference of the civil courts; and it was a matter of no slight moment to perceive what kind of men most readily applied for, and received the Court of Session's illegal protection,—men accused of swindling, theft, drunkenness, and other gross immoralities. The judgment of public opinion cannot fail sooner or later, to ratify the emphatic language of a member of Assembly, that "Church courts discharge their whole duty regarding such interdicts, by despising them and trampling them under their feet."

On Saturday, May 28, the report of the Non-Intrusion Committee, appointed by last Assembly, was read by Dr. Gordon. After narrating the various negotiations which have been already stated, the report explicitly condemned any settlement, upon the basis of what had been termed the *Liberum Arbitrium*, being fully convinced that it would prove to be of the most undesirable nature, and would neither contain what the Church regarded as indispensable to the maintenance of her fundamental principles, nor afford due protection to the rights of the people. Dr. Candlish moved, that the report be approved of generally, and that a special commission be appointed, with reference to the present difficulties of the Church, instructing them to have respect to the several deliverances of this Assembly on the state of the affairs of the Church, and to be guided in all their proceedings and deliberations by the spirit of these deliverances; the understanding being, that the deliverances to be thus kept in view are,

—the declaration that patronage is an evil and ought to be abolished, the assertion of the Church's spiritual independence, as stated in the Declaration and Claim of Rights, and the approval of the principles laid down in the report of the Non-Intrusion Committee, namely, that the Duke of Argyle's bill is the very least that can be accepted, and the express condemnation of any measure founded on the *Liberum Arbitrium.* In the discussion that followed the proposal of this motion, Dr. Leishman spoke respecting the movement of the middle party ; and laboured to defend their proceedings, but succeeded in proving nothing more than that he and the 40 were still enveloped in the misty delusions, and held fast in the snares from which the Non-Intrusion Committee had been providentially delivered. Dr. Laurie talked imposingly of the strength of the middle party, affirming that the 40 were now increased to 400 ; and that he regarded the rise of such a party as an answer to prayer for a peaceful settlement. Mr. Mackenzie, an elder from Inverness, reminded him, that men were not to take their own convictions and impressions for answers to prayer, the test of which was, accordance with the word of God. After some further discussion, Dr. Candlish replied in a singularly brilliant and effective speech, varying from pointed retort, and half playful irony, till it rose towards the conclusion into a strain of lofty, indignant, and commanding eloquence, when he condemned the mean and paltry conduct of statesmen in balancing words and clauses, and higgling about the very lowest terms to which conscience might be screwed into uneasy submission ; instead of dealing with the subject like a great question of principle, affecting the interests of generations yet unborn, and involving the liberties of the Church, and the constitution of the State.

Dr. Leishman prudently abstained from exhibiting the weakness of the middle party by a division ; the motion was carried without a vote ; and thus the great principle of anti-patronage and spiritual independence were made the rules by which all the future contendings of the Church must be guided.

The petition of the parishioners of Rhynie, praying for permission to erect a place of worship within the boundaries of the adjoining parish, Auchendoir, brought before the notice of the Assembly a case of remarkable persecuting oppression. It appeared that they had been literally hunted out of their own parish by the Duke of Richmond, its sole proprietor, or feudal superior, and not allowed a foot of ground on which to build a church at their own expense, the parish church being wrongfully withheld by Mr. Allardyce, notwithstanding his deposition. Pitying their persecuted condition, Mr. Leith Lumsden offered them a site for a church on his property, provided the Assembly would grant permission, which was necessary, on account of its being beyond the proper ecclesiastical bounds of the parish. The prayer of the petition was granted by a majority of 152 to 60, and the thanks of the Assembly tendered to Mr. Lumsden for his Christian benevolence.* In the course of the discussion, Mr. Robertson of Ellon so far disgraced his own manly intellect, as to employ one of the quibbling arguments generally used only by the weaker men of his party,—asking why other ministers had not been appointed to the seven parishes of Strathbogie, according to the *jus devolutum*, if the previous ministers had really been deposed ? The answer was easy and conclusive ; the interdicts of the civil courts could prevent the exercise of the civil right of patronage *jure devoluto*, though they could not prevent the formation of the pastoral tie ; and, as the whole subject was still under undecided discussion, it was not deemed expedient, unnecessarily, to embarrass final arrangements by any precipitate forgone conclusion. Mr. Robertson shrunk back from the topic with evident symptoms of regret that he had touched it. The Assembly then renewed their resolutions of last year, in favour of an inquiry into the state of the poor : and in following out the recommendation in the queen's letter in behoof

* On the morning of the 13th of June, the people of Rhynie assembled in great numbers, before day-break at the site granted for the intended church, resolved to erect it before an interdict which had been threatened by the other heritors could be procured. Timber had already been prepared, and stone hewn in the adjacent mountains. Carts, labourers, masons, and carpenters plied the work with active hands and willing minds. Under their vigorous exertions the work. " rose like an exhalation ;" and ere the evening closed, a large, well executed, and commodious structure was nearly ready for the purposes of public worship. Those who think to crush the people of Scotland, may judge of the energy and resolution they have to encounter by the fact, of A CHUCH BUILT IN A DAY

of the labouring classes in distress, resolved to invite the co-operation of all parties, and took steps for the formation of a Central Committee, to be composed of persons of all denominations, at whose disposal all the funds raised by contributions and collections throughout the Church and kingdom should be placed; and then concluded the business of the week, by hearing the report on Sabbath Observance.

One incident which very impressively indicates the state of mind both of the Assembly and of the public, must here be mentioned. Intimation had been given that on Sabbath evening a meeting of the Assembly for prayer would be held in the place of worship at that time occupied by the Assembly, with particular reference to the perilous state of the Church; and a dense mass of people crowded the house at the appointed hour, leaving merely the space usually allotted to the members. The seats on the sides commonly occupied by the Evangelical majority were soon completely filled; but for a considerable time those on the Moderate side remained empty, till the assembling people, seeing that none of that party were likely to appear, took possession of them. So far as was observed, not a single Moderate minister, with the exception, if it be one, of Dr. Lee, came to join with his brethren in supplicating God to rescue the Church from distress and danger, which might surely have been conscientiously done in general terms, without specific reference to any peculiar mode of deliverance. The devotional services were conducted successively by three venerated fathers of the Church; and nothing could exceed the solemn, earnest reverential awe by which the whole vast congregation seemed to be pervaded and impressed. "God has not forsaken his people; his presence is among us here!" was the silent but deep conviction of many a grateful and adoring heart, especially when the tremulous tones of the voice of prayer told the strong emotions of the supplicating and believing soul from which it rose to heaven. And when the sacred duties closed, men returned to their abodes refreshed, encouraged, and inwardly thanking God for what they had felt, witnessed, and enjoyed.

Monday, the 30th day of May, was the last day of the Assembly's ordinary duration; and, as there was still a large amount of business to be done, the House met at the early hour of ten. The first subject of importance which was taken up, was the report of the committee which had been appointed to confer with the ministers who had held communion with the late ministers of Strathbogie. The report was produced, and the accused parties appeared at the bar. When asked if they had any thing further to say, they produced a paper, which proved to be a protest, bearing, that in thus appearing in obedience to their citation, they were not to be held as departing from their former protestation, but on account of their respect for the venerable court, and their desire to promote the peace of the church. Dr. Makellar, then, in a very calm and temperate speech, moved, that the ministers at the bar be suspended from the exercise of their judicial functions, as members of presbyteries, and all other judicatories of the Church, until after the first Wednesday of March 1843. Mr. Monteith, advocate, disapproved of this sentence, on the ground of its not being one of greater severity, and, in his opinion, not adequate to the grave nature of the offence. Professor Alexander regarded it as too severe; but, while he disapproved of the proceedings of the majority, had no sympathy with those who talked of driving them out of the Church, being fully persuaded, that "except they remained in the ship, it could not be saved." Dr. Chandlish defended the proposed sentence, and explained the reasons of its leniency, and of its peculiar character. The motion was then agreed to without a vote; and the accused ministers having reserved their right to take instruments and crave extracts, if they should require to do so, left the bar, and soon afterwards the Assembly, in whose proceedings those who were members did not attempt to take any further share, thus directly obeying the sentence.

This sentence met with probably less general approbation than any other pronounced by the Assembly, partly on account of its extreme leniency, and partly from want of being very accurately understood. It was very lenient, but not to such a degree as to involve any compromise of firmness or of principle; and it met the direct nature of the offence, as that came before the Assembly for judgment. For it must be observed, that the direct charge against them was one of disregard to the authority of the superior Church courts, which being contumacy, required to be disposed of in a summary manner, and which according to the principles of the Evangelical majority, did not necessarily infer deposition, unless it involved also some heinous sin, in which case the course of procedure must have been by way of libel. If the direct charge had been, that they had desecrated the sacraments, they might have been liable to deposition, but they must have been regularly tried by libel; and though, perhaps, their conduct was thought by very many to have actually involved that grave charge, yet, as that did not necessarily appear in the accusation brought against them, it was not legitimately before the Assembly, and could not have been founded on, without, at the very least, an apparent irregularity of procedure. Some people found fault with the sentence on another ground; arguing that, if the Assembly could suspend ministers from the exercise of their judicial functions without interfering with the ministerial, why had not this been done at first in the case of the Strathbogie seven, who were at once suspended by the Commission from all their functions. To this there is a very easy and sufficient answer. The suspension of the Strathbogie seven was not penal, but preventive,—it was not intended as punishment for a crime already committed, but to prevent them from committing a crime which they had declared their intention to commit, and which could not be prevented otherwise than by taking away their power to do it. For it must be remembered, that the Strathbogie seven had declared their intention to ordain Mr. Edwards; and as ordination is not a judicial but a ministerial act, and may be, and often has been, performed by a competent number of ministers, though not met as a presbytery, the suspension of their judicial functions would not have prevented them from being in a capacity to perform validly the act of ordination. In short, it is fully believed, that the more the sentence is examined, calmly and impartially, the more will its judicious nature become evident; and it is no slight merit, that, while its very leniency rendered its violation wholly inexcusable, it placed the Moderate party in such a position, that they must either appear to all men the wilful disturbers of the public peace, or must thenceforth be silent respecting their boasted determination to make common cause with the Strathbogie seven.

Mr. Wilson of Stranraer was then cited, and as he adhered to the interdict, was deposed.

On the application of the parties interested, clauses were sanctioned in the constitution of new churches, for the purpose of securing the property, in the event of a schism in the Establishment, to those who should adhere to the principles of non-intrusion and spiritual independence, as maintained by the present majority.

The regulations on calls were re-transmitted, with an alteration which would admit of the call being brought into effective operation. Those parts of the regulations which related to special objections were left out; and the substance of them was embodied in a separate declaratory act; by passing which *unanimously*, the Assembly declared to be wrong, in ecclesiastical law, one of the principal points on which the Court of Session had decided the Culsalmond case.

The four home missionary objects were included under one committee, to be called the Home Mission Committee.

The revised "Claim of Rights" was formally and finally adopted by the Assembly.

A committee was appointed to conduct the correspondence with foreign churches; those namely of Holland, Switzerland, Prussia, Hungary, the Protestant Church of France, the Waldensian Church, and the Presbyterian Churches in America, Ireland, and England, the Wesleyan and Calvinistic Methodists, and other orthodox Presbyterian Dissenters.

The Assembly then passed a declaration of the Church of Scotland's determination to maintain the principles on which the ministers of *quoad sacra* parishes had been admitted to the enjoyment of all the rights and privileges possessed by the other ministers of the Church. This, considering the fierce and continued hostility shown to the admission of these ministers into Church courts, and the many interdicts granted by the Court of Session on that ground, was a peculiarly important declaration, but one which it was evident might greatly increase the intensity of the contest of jurisdiction.

A resolution was passed recommending concert in prayer.

A motion was passed enjoining presbyteries to be careful in examining students and licentiates in their knowledge of the standards, history, and constitution of the Church.

Certain alterations in the form of process were agreed to, the most important of which was, that all ministers charged with heresies or immoral offences should be suspended from the exercise of their ministerial functions, from the period of their being libelled to the termination of their case. This was strenuously opposed by the Moderates, but carried without a vote. An overture was passed, and directed to be transmitted to presbyteries, the object of which was to prohibit the conjunction of professorships with ministerial charges, even within university towns, and thereby to put an end to every kind and degree of pluralities. Lastly, a day of fasting and humiliation was appointed to be observed on Thursday the 21st of July; and instructions were given that a pastoral address should be prepared to be read from all the pulpits in the Church.

With these solemn acts the Assembly closed its deliberations.

The moderator presented to the Lord High Commissioner the Claim of Rights, with an address to the Queen, requesting him to present them to her Majesty; and also an address in favour of the abolition of patronage, requesting him to present it likewise to the Queen. His Grace replied that he would have the honour of presenting the address and Claim of Rights to her Majesty, and also of presenting the anti-patronage address; but wished it to be distinctly understood, that in doing so he expressed no approbation of it. The Marquis of Breadalbane, who had signed a petition for the repeal of Queen Anne's Act, was requested to present the anti-patronage petition to the House of Lords, and Mr. Fox Maule to the House of Commons.

The moderator then addressed the house, in a speech remarkable for its eloquence of language, and solemn elevation of thought; and having concluded, he dissolved the Assembly in the name of the divine Head and King of the Church, the Lord Jesus Christ. Then turning to the Lord High Commissioner, he preferred to him the thanks of the Assembly, and expressed their united prayers for his Grace's best welfare. His Grace having also gone through the form of dissolving the Assembly, the moderator prayed; and after a portion of Scripture had been read, and the conclusion of the 122d Psalm had been sung, the apostolic benediction was pronounced, and the important Assembly of 1842 was closed.

It is impossible to reflect upon the proceedings of the General Assembly of 1842, without coming to the conclusion, that it marked an era of vast importance in the history of the Church of Scotland. It became evident to every reflecting person, that from it would be dated either the overthrow of the Presbyterian Church in this kingdom, or her THIRD REFORMATION. There remained no longer any obscurity respecting her principles, nor any retreat from her position. Statesmen and men of the world might indeed regard her with increased hostility, but they could no longer affect to misunderstand her demands. They might still view her as weak and unable to resist their political power, but they could not continue to misrepresent the contest as merely one between two rival parties in her own communion, nor pretend that her own internal disunion, and the balance of conflicting parties within her, were the reasons why they refused to take her claims and complaints into consideration. In several respects, also, her own position was greatly improved. The first vote of the Assembly, on the day of its meeting, respecting the commissions from Strathbogie, indicated the strength and determination of the majority, dispirited the Moderate party, and gave both calmness and decision to all its subsequent procedure,—the calmness of conscious strength, the decision of sound principle held in fearless integrity. The rescinding of the sectarian act of 1799 restored the Church of Scotland to Christian communion with other orthodox Christian Churches, and harmonized completely with the deep interest felt in her present struggles by all the religious-minded people of Protestant Christendom; and with the presence in the Assembly both of the deputations from England and Ireland, and also with that of pious and intelligent ministers from Prussia and Switzerland, who witnessed the proceedings with the most intense attention and delight.

By resolving to apply for the abolition of patronage, as in itself a grievance and the main cause of her present troubles, the Church not only dispelled the illusions in which her reforming movements had been so long involved, taking once more the old and well-known ground of other days, on which she might with confidence expect the high-hearted and faithful of the land to rally in her defence; but also, although almost incidentally, broke and dispersed the threatened confederacy of a middle party, uniting at the same time, more firmly than ever, the reforming majority. By the Declaration and Claim of Rights, the great principles in defence of which the contest had been waged, were brought forward in the most definite and prominent manner, clearly proved to be not a temporary conflict of parties, but the old and great struggle between the Church and the world, and the whole subject was suitably prepared to be laid before the Legislature, and displayed to the universe. And by the firm determination shown to suppress internal insurrection, by punishing, mildly yet unhesitatingly, those who held communion with deposed men,—who applied to the civil courts for interdicts to stay the course of ecclesiastical discipline,—or who entered into censurable private engagements with patrons; and also by her declared resolution to maintain the rights of *quoad sacra* ministers at all hazards, the Church proved that she was in earnest, and must conquer or perish. By occupying, distinctly and decidedly, these three positions, the Church came directly and immediately into contact with the three great worldly powers in the kingdom—the aristocracy, on the ground of anti-patronage; the legislature, through the Claim of Rights; and the courts of civil law, in defence of the *quoad sacra* ministers. These are formidable antagonists; but the Moderate party were thoroughly discomfited; the danger of disunion threatened by the middle-men disappeared; and the position was taken which the religious people of Scotland can understand, and have always shown themselves ready to defend.

And what did all this portend? Peace? Not so, but rather the preparation for a desperate and conclusive struggle. Like an army preparing to decide the war by a pitched engagement, the Church of Scotland, in the Assembly of 1842, advanced beyond the thickets, cleared the battle-ground, called in the skirmishers, seized on the strengths of the position, and took her stand arrayed beneath the sacred banner of the divine Captain of her salvation, ready in his name, and under his command, to fight the good fight of faith, "strong in the Lord and in the power of his might."

The effect of the proceedings of the Assembly upon the mind and feelings of the entire empire was sudden and great. Before its meeting, all parties and classes of men had looked forward to it with various anticipations, but all expecting that it would inevitably bring the contest nearly to a close. For some time after it rose, its proceedings formed almost the sole topic of discussion in every circle, and in every periodical publication. By some, the whole conduct of the Church was vehemently condemned; by others, not less warmly applauded. Politicians in general, of every name and shade, were loud and violent in their censure; while, on the other hand, all persons and denominations of distinguished piety and spirituality of mind, expressed great admiration of the faithfulness, zeal, and intrepidity displayed by the Church of Scotland in such a time of anxieties and perils. The only religious bodies that indicated disapproval were those tinctured with Erastianism,—such as Episcopalians, Moderates, and Middle-men. This was to be expected, because they could not sympathize with the fundamental principles of the Church of Scotland, especially in the article of spiritual independence, if indeed they understood what that great principle really meant. In the higher regions of the political world, the feeling appeared to be that of stern and unappeaseable indignation. That a Church should dare to tell statesmen that she regarded herself as altogether independent of their control, while acting in her own province, and deciding upon spiritual matters, was, in their estimation, a degree of presumption not to be endured, and they took the earliest opportunity of displaying their determined hostility to such a lofty and unpardonable claim.

The first opportunity that presented itself was on the 15th of June, the day to which the second reading of Campbell of Monzie's bill had been postponed at the request of the Government itself. On that day, instead of permitting the discussion respecting that measure to proceed, as had been expected, the Speaker directed the attention of the house to an objection in point of form, stating, that since the bill affected crown patronages, it could not be discussed without involving a breach of the royal prerogative, unless the permission of the crown were first obtained. No such objection had been urged against the previous bills of Lord Aberdeen, or the Duke of Argyle, although these equally affected crown patronages; nor had Monzie's bill been prevented on that ground at its first reading; but the ministry probably expected that they would thus display their decided disapprobation of the Church of Scotland's claims, and awe her into submission by their haughty and contemptuous treatment. If so, they only proved how little they understood both the principles which they thus scornfully rejected, and the men with whom they had to deal. A still stronger and more grave accusation might be brought against them, as statesmen. Was it prudent, was it consistent with sound constitutional policy, thus summarily to crush a bill brought forward for the redress of grievances, and the vindication of the rights and privileges of an important body of British subjects, by the mere assertion of the royal prerogative? No person who fully understands and values the true principles of British liberty will ever attempt to vindicate such conduct; and no friend of the British monarchy will ever regard it as an example to be followed, but rather as a dangerous error to be carefully shunned.

This conduct of the ministry was followed by various effects which they could scarcely have contemplated. Many people, not peculiarly friendly to the Church, exclaimed against it as a mean evasion, by which Government contrived to avoid a discussion which they dared not openly meet. It was evident that the Church was ready to lay her claims before the public, and earnestly courted the fullest possible discussion; and the counterpart idea was scarcely less evident, that this was exactly what her opponents were anxious to prevent. Her character for conscious honesty of purpose, was elevated, while that of the ministry suffered a corresponding depression. But the Church was not to be so easily baffled, and reduced to silence. If Government had resolved to turn a deaf ear to her application, she could address the kingdom. It was accordingly arranged, that on the first week of July, simultaneous meetings should be held throughout the whole of Scotland, for the purpose of stating, explaining and advocating the principles declared and defended, and the proceedings followed by the recent General Assembly. These meetings were very numerously attended; and the clear, able, and eloquent addresses of so many eminent men contributed greatly to dispel ignorance and prejudice, called forth in almost every instance the most enthusiastic expressions of approbation, and tended greatly to prepare the public mind for the important events that were soon to follow. In a great number of places associations were formed for the defence of the Church, and for the purpose of promoting the circulation of the necessary information, that Scotland might be made aware of the position of imminent peril in which her venerated and beloved Church had been placed by treacherous factions within her own pale, and by the hostility of the civil powers.

About the same time, the General Assembly of the Presbyterian Church in Ireland met at Belfast; and on the 8th of July a deputation of the General Assembly of the Church of Scotland ad dressed the Irish Assembly, and received from that body the most encouraging reception, and the warmest assurance of aid in the struggle for the defence of great and sacred principles in which she was engaged.

A new case of great importance was brought before the Court of Session on the 28th day of June. This was the Stewarton case, the nature of which it is necessary briefly to state. In consequence of the act of Assembly 1839, admitting the Associate Synod of the Secession into connection and full communion with the Church of Scotland, a congregation of that body, who had their place of worship in the village of Stewarton, Ayrshire, applied to the presbytery of Irvine, within whose bounds the village is situated, to be so received and admitted. The presbytery complied with this request; and Mr. Clelland, the minister of that congregation, having signed the Confession of Faith, his name was added to the roll, and he took his place in the presbytery. Subsequently the presbytery were interdicted from assigning a territorial district to the pastoral superintendence of Mr. Clelland, at the instance of William Cunninghame, Esq. of Lainshaw, and other proprietors. This interdict was granted in March 1840, and rendered perpetual on the 15th June same year. The presbytery, after having received the authoritative sanction of the synod of Glasgow and Ayr, and the Commission of Assembly, proceeded to point out a territorial district *quoad spiritualia* within which the minister of the Stewarton congregation should exercise his sacred functions, expressly declaring, at the same time, that no civil right belonging to any party should be held to be affected in any degree by that arrangement. The case assumed a somewhat new form shortly afterwards. Mr. Clelland having demitted his charge, a call was given by the congregation to another person to be his successor. The heritors immediately applied for a special interdict to prevent the induction of another minister into the vacant charge, which was granted on the 17th of March 1841. By another change of circumstances the case assumed a new, and still more simple and unsecular aspect. A portion of the original congregation had opposed the union with the Establishment, and raised an action to claim the right of property in the place of worship. In this action they were successful; and about the same time the person in whose favour the call had been given died. There was now a congregation without either minister or place of worship, so that the case was completely denuded of every vestige of personal rights or civil property, and it might have been expected that the case before the civil court had of itself terminated. But when the presbytery were about to moderate in a call to a minister to the congregation alone, without place of worship or civil interests of any kind being even by possibility involved, they were again met by the interdict of the civil court, prohibiting the appointment of "any minister to the new parish proposed to be erected;" and also prohibiting the presbytery from receiving into their number "any minister or elder, in respect to their alleged election or nomination to their respective offices in the said new parish."

Such were the main facts of the Stewarton case, when it was fully brought before the Court of Session. It will be evident to every one, that by the singular process of events it had been stripped of all that could even seem to involve a civil right, in the ordinary sense of that term, since it could affect neither person nor property. The question, therefore, appeared, in the simplest possible form,—"Had civil courts the power to prevent the Church of Scotland from extending the means of spiritual instruction to the community as necessity required, by forming or receiving congregations, ordaining ministers and other office-bearers, and giving to them the full possession of all the spiritual functions which in every true Presbyterian Church ordination has always been held to convey?" This, it must be evident, was an absolutely vital question; and upon its decision alone, even had there been no other cause of collision between the civil and ecclesiastical courts, must have depended the fate of the Church of Scotland. For if it be in the power of hostile heritors and civil courts to prevent the spiritual growth of the Church, while the population is rapidly increasing, they may, within the course of a single generation, reduce it to the condition of being the Church of a minority, and may then safely abolish it altogether, if so inclined. And still more, if the civil courts have the power of laying an arrest on the progress of any Christian Church, they must also be viewed as having the power to stop the progress of the Redeemer's kingdom; or at least, the power of rendering such Church no longer truly Christian, by taking from it the liberty of obeying Christ by extending his kingdom. To this the Church of Scotland could not submit, without ceasing to be a Church of Christ; consequently it was evident, that an adverse decision of this vital question would bring before her the alternative, whether to yield up her Christian character, or to abandon, if redress could not be obtained, the civil advantages and emoluments of an Established Church,—an alternative which, by any sincere Christian, must always and at once be regarded as no alternative at all.

The pleadings before the Court of this important case began on the 21st of June, and closed on the 28th of the same month. Immediately upon the close of the pleadings by the counsel for the presbytery, the Lord President drew the attention of the Court to that part of the plea by the defenders in which they declined the jurisdiction of the civil court in spiritual matters; expressing his opinion that if it were construed as the language seemed to imply, it might be regarded as seditious, and it might be necessary to commit the parties using it to immediate imprisonment! It seemed as if the spirit of James VI. had taken possession of the presiding judges, and were about to reenact the persecution of Black, and Welsh, and Melville. But the threatening storm abated; permission was granted to explain the language of the plea; and in the course of a few days an explanation was produced and accepted, which, while expressed in more cautious and guarded terms, contained a declinature of the jurisdiction of the civil court in spiritual matters, as distinct and explicit as before. The result of this discussion was so far favourable to the Church; for the explanation being allowed to be entered on the record, the plea of independence in spiritual matters was thereby secured in that case, let the ultimate decision be what it might. It was of advantage also, as incidentally vindicating the Church from the calumnious accusation, that, by pleading at all, she admitted the jurisdiction of the civil courts, and then refused to obey it, when an adverse decision was given. Yet strange as it may appear, although the Court of Session was undeniably baffled by the respectful firmness of the counsel for the Church, the Moderate party had the effrontery loudly to proclaim, that the Church had at last abandoned the plea of spiritual independence. It certainly required no little hardihood to make such an assertion in the face of printed records, to which any person might have access; yet it was made, for habit is very powerful. The final decision of the Stewarton case was then postponed, with the view, avowedly, of securing to it time for full deliberation.

On the 19th of July the Court of Session decided another element of the Auchterarder case. It will be remembered that, when the House of Lords affirmed the decision of the Court of Session, the Church yielded to that decision to the extent specified in the act 1592, leaving to the patron "the haill fruits of the benefice." But as the act of parliament respecting the Widows' Fund assigned all vacant stipends to that fund, the point was litigated whether the stipend of Auchterarder should belong to the Widows' Fund or to the Earl of Kinnoul. The decision of the Court of Session, the whole Judges being present, was in favour of the patron against the claim of the Widows' Fund, by a majority of eight to five. The First Division gave the expenses to the pursuers. This decision, however contrary to the plain meaning of an act of Parliament, had an apparent tendency to clear the question between the conflicting jurisdictions, and to diminish the subjects of litigation. For the patron's action of damages ought in equity to be regarded as having lost its ground, since the Court had decided that the presentation secured the fruits of the benefice, so that the veto of the congregation could inflict no damage upon what are termed "the patrimonial rights of the patron," or upon the presentee, who might at any time be put in possession of them. It had also another effect. It rendered the question of jurisdiction as simple and essential as in the Stewarton case; since, if any further steps were to be taken against the Church, it could only be for the purpose of attempting, by civil coercion, to compel her to perform the spiritual act of ordination, even when separated from the usual civil consequences, these having been already disposed of according to the patron's claim.

A great number of interdicts were granted on the same day, at the instance of the deposed Strathbogie seven—some on claims which they preferred, others against members sent to the Assembly from the true Presbytery of Strathbogie to the recent Assembly,—with the concurrence of her Majesty's advocate, praying the Court "to inflict such punishment, by imprisonment, fine, or otherwise, as might be considered necessary and proper." Also at the instance of other ministers who had been deposed by the late Assembly, on account of attempting to stop the course of justice when accused of flagrant crimes, by seeking and obtaining interdicts on the ground of the presence in Church courts of *quoad sacra* ministers, although no decision had yet been given by the civil court on that question. Interdicts were also granted against the Special Commission appointed to take charge of the religious interests of Strathbogie, Culsalmond, and other places in similar circumstances. And petions and complaints were applied for and subsequently granted against those who were engaged in ordaining Mr. Henry to the new Church at Marnoch, and Mr. Arthur at Stewarton, although no civil interests were involved in either of these cases. Such proceedings served very clearly to indicate the determination of the opponents of the Church to force on a speedy crisis; and they formed a very intelligible comment on what was meant by some members of the Legislature when they spoke of "allowing the law to take its course."

One strange and almost incredible case of civil interference in spiritual matters deserves to be particularly noted. On Sabbath the 7th of August, the sacrament of the Lord's Supper was dispensed at Stranraer by the deposed minister to about twenty or thirty people; and on the same by two of the ministers of the presbytery, in the church of the Reformed Presbyterians, to upwards of four hundred communicants. No sooner was it known that the use of this church had been granted to the presbytery, than an interdict was applied for to prohibit that congregation from affording even that temporary accommodation to their fellow-worshippers. Nor did the Court of Session hesitate to grant it; thus perpetrating a gross outrage upon the rights both of conscience and of private property, and assailing a body of Christians unconnected with the Establishment.

While this small, yet most harassing warfare was going on in Scotland, an event took place in England which virtually decided the conflict. This was the decision of the second appeal to the House of Lords in the Auchterarder case. The first appeal regarded the question, whether the presbytery had acted legally in refusing to ordain Mr. Young when vetoed by the communicants. The second was, whether the presbytery were liable to an action of damages in consequence of that refusal. It has already been shown that the action for damages did not, and could not proceed upon the ground of a civil injury sustained by patron and presentee; for the Court had awarded the fruits of the benefice to the patron. The Court of Session, nevertheless, had decreed that the presbytery was liable to an action of damages; and the case had been appealed to the House of Lords. On the 9th of August the case was brought before the House; and the Lord Chancellor (Lyndhurst), and Lords Cottenham, Brougham, and Campbell, guiding, as law lords, the judgment of the House in legal questions, decided that the presbytery of Auchterarder was liable to an action of damages at the instance of the patron and his presentee, for refusing to ordain Mr. Young, although no civil interest was any longer involved in the refusal. These learned Lords never once adverted to the constitution of the Church of Scotland, by which an independent ecclesiastical jurisdiction was secured to it in many unrepealed acts of parliament; but reasoning from vague generalities, totally inapplicable, and from cases in English law, affirmed the liability unanimously, and without hesitation. The necessary effect of that judgment was, that the Church courts were held liable to actions of damages for refusing to perform a purely spiritual act; and conversely, by parity of reason, for performing a purely spiritual act,—consequently, all ecclesiastical government and discipline were at once laid prostrate by that most iniquitous and unconstitutional decision. Nay, it might be truly asserted, that by this decision ecclesiastical courts were altogether abolished, for the very essence of a court is its liberty to decide according to its own conscientious conviction; and therefore, that it is no court where not only can the sentences be reversed, but the judges themselves punished for their judgment. From the moment that this judgment was passed, it became evident to every spiritually-minded and reflecting man, that unless the legislature should very speedily set it aside by a new enactment, repressing the encroachments of the civil courts, the Church of Scotland could not continue in connection with the State, but must protest, remonstrate, and retire, leaving to the "Prince of the kings of the earth," her own Head and King, to vindicate His own cause in His own time and way. Such was the grave opinion generally entertained by the evangelical body, while their narrow-minded and short-sighted opponents regarded it merely as a mode of crushing them into subjection by civil pains and penalties,—unaware, in their ignorance, that men who know and can appreciate spiritual liberty, can suffer in its defence, but cannot yield it, be the peril what it may.

On the 10th of August the Commission of Assembly held its usual quarterly meeting, and was numerously attended. Some discussion ensued respecting the delay that had taken place in presenting to the Queen the Claim of Rights, and the Address for the Abolition of Patronage; when it appeared that the delay was accidental and unintentional. The case of Abertaff was reported to the Commission, from which it appeared that the minister, Mr. Smith, had procured interdicts, not only against the presbytery, forbidding them to proceed with his trial, but also against the list of witnesses, prohibiting them from appearing to bear evidence. The case was remitted to the Assembly, and the presbytery empowered to make provision for the dispensation of religious ordinances in the parish. A communication was received from America, proposing the commemoration of the Westminster Assembly, to be held on the 1st day of July 1843, that being the day on which it first met two hundred years before. The same idea had been suggested to the Irish Assembly at Belfast, who entered cordially into the suggestion, as did also the Presbyterian Church in England. A committee was formed for the purpose of devising the best method of co-operating with all Presbyterian Churches in that important matter, which presented so favourable an opportunity of concentrating the energies of Presbyterianism, and diffusing its principles with increased vigour throughout the world.

There was a considerably numerous meeting of the Moderate party held on the morning of the 10th, Principal Haldane of St. Andrews in the chair, at which it was determined to support the deposed Strathbogie men, and to send a deputation to assist those persons in their pretended celebration of the sacrament of the Lord's Supper. This determination was announced in the newspapers of next day, rendering it publicly manifest, that, like the civil courts, the Moderates were resolved to prosecute every means of forcing on the crisis, even before it was known that the second Auchterarder decision, given by the House of Lords the preceding day, had already done the destructive deed.

A special meeting of Commission was held on the 30th of August, for the purpose of preparing an address to the Queen, on her Majesty's visit to Scotland. When the Commission met, a sharp discussion took place on a preliminary point of great importance. It was the general opinion, that as her Majesty's visit was not on State affairs, it would not be expedient to introduce the subject of the serious dangers impending over the Church into the address itself; but the majority thought it necessary to pass a motion, for the purpose of having it entered on the Commission's records, in which should be declared the determination of the Church to maintain her sacred spiritual rights and liberties, and that even with increased energy and resolution, in consequence of the increasing danger caused by recent events, together with a statement of the reason why the Commission refrained from bringing the subject before her Majesty in present circumstances. The Moderate party vehemently opposed all reference to any such subject, venturing to stigmatize the very suggestion as savouring of a want of loyalty, and certainly tending to foment strife. A very animated debate arose upon this motion, the most remarkable feature of which was, that when reference was made to the recent decision affirming liability to damages in the Auchterarder case, and when it was said, that unless that decision should be reversed, it must ere long issue in the breaking up of the Establishment, the Moderates received the declaration with shouts of exultation and mockery. This drew from Dr. Candlish an indignant rebuke, in a speech altogether worthy of himself and of the occasion, in which he nobly vindicated the principles and the loyalty of the Church of Scotland,—referring to the period when our covenanted ancestors, although firmly opposing a monarch's despotism, were yet alone found faithful to that monarch in his adversity. The motion was carried against two others, one of an intermediate, and another of a more decided character; and addresses were prepared, and deputations appointed to present them to her Majesty and Prince Albert.

This was the first meeting of a superior Church court since the second Auchterarder decision, and it was not difficult to perceive the effect of that event upon the two contending parties. The Evangelical majority displayed the grave, yet resolute bearing, the calm, deliberate courage and energy of men who were fully aware of the dangers by which they were menaced, and as fully prepared to meet them with unshrinking fortitude, relying with unwavering faith on the strength and wisdom of God to support and guide them in the hour of need. On the Moderate side, there was manifest an air of anticipated triumph, and a heartless spirit of delight in the difficulties of their opponents, though they could not but be aware that the recent decision of the House of Lords involved the breaking up, to a greater or less extent, of the Church of Scotland as an establishment. For it required no very great degree of penetration to see, that the Evangelical majority could not yield to that judgment without such a loss of character, and consequently of moral influence, as would destroy their usefulness, and at the same time confirm the Voluntary argument,—in addition to the withering effect upon themselves of a violated conscience: or, if *they* should in a body quit connection with the State, the Establishment would, by that very act, receive a shock from which it could not recover. Yet they evidently rejoiced to see the Church of Scotland in such imminent peril, being unable, apparently, to see in it any thing else but a preliminary step to their own restoration to power. Even their own explanation of their cheers, when allusion was made to the impending disruption of the Establishment, "that it was because they did not believe the announcement," implied such a disbelief in the honest integrity of their opponents as proved themselves to be destitute of that character, according to the well known maxim, that each man suspects that of others which he knows to be true of himself. It was, in short, a melancholy proof of the heartless cruelty, and want of principle, characteristic of thorough Moderatism.

Availing themselves of the opportunity presented by the presence of so many ministers in Edinburgh, the Evangelical body held several private meetings for mutual consultation respecting the course now to be adopted, in consequence of the new position in which affairs had been placed by the recent decision. It was the opinion of some of the most determined men, that the proper course would be, for presbyteries to decline proceeding to ordination in all cases of presentation, and to refer each to the next General Assembly. Others thought that the Church should regard the decision of the House of Lords as altogether incompetent, and not binding on the conscience, and should therefore proceed as if it had never been pronounced, ordaining where the presentee was acceptable and qualified, and refusing to ordain where he was rejected. At length an intermediate course received the approbation of the greater number;

and it was generally agreed, that presbyteries might proceed as under the Veto Act, carefully guarding, in each instance, against being thought to consent to the principle of the late decision, by entering on their records a strong protest, which should embody a new and explicit assertion of the constitutional principles, rights, and privileges of the Church. This plan was very soon carried into effect in several presbyteries, the example having been set by the presbytery of Edinburgh in the case of Mr. Arnot's presentation to Ratho. There can be little doubt that, in point of what may be termed theoretical propriety, the first of these plans would have been the most correct. For it is clear, that presbyteries could not be regarded as acting freely on their own responsibility as office-bearers of the Church, when inducting presentees, under the penalty of being liable to actions of damages if they should refuse, however much opposed the people might be to the persons presented, and however thoroughly convinced the presbytery might be that the appointment of a person, in such circumstances, could not be for edification. It was felt, too, that to act conscientiously in such a condition would try severely the firmness of the most determined, and might prove a grievous snare to those of weaker and more timid character. Yet it was well that an intermediate course was adopted, since it avoided hastening on the crisis prematurely, and allowed the full developement of all the evils that rendered the last step necessary.

The Queen's visit gave occasion to the manifestation of another element in the general contest. Her Majesty landed at Granton on the morning of Thursday, September 1, and proceeded to Dalkeith, where she resided with the Duke of Buccleuch. But instead of attending divine worship in the High Church of Edinburgh, as constitutionally the Presbyterian sovereign of a Presbyterian kingdom, and as George IV. on his visit had done, the dining-room at Dalkeith was turned into a temporary chapel, a pulpit being erected at the one end of it, and Mr. Ramsay, Episcopalian minister of St. John's Chapel, Edinburgh, a decided Puseyite, was sent for to officiate. How Mr. Ramsay reconciled it to *his* conscience to preach in what he would regard as an unconsecrated place, it is not easy to imagine. Again, at Drummond Castle, the Queen attended the ministrations of an Episcopalian chaplain, neglecting the Establishment, which she had sworn to support, and giving her countenance to its avowed and implacable enemy. It was not supposed that this arose from any hostility entertained by the sovereign against the Church of Scotland, but from the well known hostility of her constitutional advisers against the reforming and evangelical majority. The Earl of Aberdeen attended her Majesty, in the function, it was understood, of Home Secretary; and no one who remembered the part he had all along acted, could doubt his determined enmity against the cause, and the men whom he had attempted to delude, and then bitterly calumniated and reviled. With remarkable infatuation, the Moderate party appeared to rejoice in the evident disrespect done to the Church. They did not seem to perceive, that if the Presbyterian Church of Scotland should be overthrown, they must either join its destroyers, or perish in its ruins. The Puseyite Episcopalians rejoiced greatly in the sunshine of royal favour which thus shone around them; and their prelates presented an address of no doubtful import to her Majesty, boasting of *their* obedience to the laws. For some time after the occurrence of this event, there appeared symptoms of an incipient controversy in nearly all the periodical organs of the various parties in the country; but it was suppressed, though with very manifest difficulty, by the reluctance universally felt to say any thing that might appear personally disrespectful to the youthful and beloved Queen. There is some reason, however, to believe, that the suppressed feeling of dissatisfaction died not away, but merely sunk into the still depths of the heart of Scotland, adding another element of strength to the antiprelatic under-current that there sweeps steadily along, waiting its time to pour forth its irresistible might when the full hour of retribution shall have come.

For a short period the contest seemed to have subsided, during the busy time of harvest. But even in this interval of comparative quiescence, there were several indications of unabated hostility against the Church, on the part of the civil courts. An interdict was granted against the presbytery of Arbroath, and laid before that court on the 5th of October, forbidding them to prevent the admission to the Lord's Table of a person who had, as it was alleged, in a state of drunkenness, disturbed the public worship of God in the parish church of Inverkeillor, and had refused to submit to the requirements of church discipline. It began also to be customary for opposing heritors to apply for and obtain interdicts forbidding meetings to be held in parish churches,—a course which was extensively followed during the succeeding winter and spring, as if for the suppression of arguments which they could not answer.

But this short breathing-time was not unimproved. It allowed leisure for deliberate reflection, respecting the state of the Church, and the course of conduct which that state had rendered necessary. About the middle of October, a circular letter, signed by 32 of the most able, pious, and venerable fathers of the Church, was sent to all those ministers throughout the kingdom, who had in general acted with, and contributed to form, the Evangelical majority. In this circular, attention was directed to the peculiar character and inevitable consequences of the second Auchterarder decision, as subversive of the essential liberties of the Church, and leading certainly to its destruction, unless speedily remedied; and a general meeting or convocation was called to be held at Edinburgh on the 17th of November, the day after the ordinary meeting of the Commission. This circular was prepared and signed almost exclusively by the aged fathers in the Church,—a point of no small importance, proving that the contest was not caused and carried on merely by young and fiery controversialists, as opponents loudly and constantly asserted. And in order that the Convocation might be as numerously attended as possible, considerable sums were subscribed to defray the travelling expenses of ministers from distant parts of the country, while some parishes undertook to bear the charges of their own ministers. Accommodation was also liberally provided, by numbers of the Edinburgh citizens, for the ministers during the time of their deliberations.

The week before the Convocation met was perhaps a time of more general and fervent prayer throughout Scotland, than had been known for centuries; both ministers and people feeling, that upon the result of its momentous deliberations, would depend, not merely the existence of the Church of Scotland in all her purity and freedom, established or not, but also the character and welfare of true evangelical and spiritual religion in the country. And it must be added that during the sitting of the Convocation, the absence of the ministers did not prevent the continuation of meetings for prayer, conducted by the pious and venerable village or rural patriarchs, who knew the principles of the Church of Christ and believed them to be those for which the Church of their fathers had often suffered, and was again called on to suffer in circumstances of imminent peril.

The Commission of Assembly met on the 16th, according to its usual arrangement, and was very fully attended by the Evangelical body. Few Moderates were present, and of these, some went away almost immediately, leaving a protest against its proceedings, as illegally constituted, on account of the exclusion of Dr. Bryce, who had been suspended by the preceding Commission. A very interesting report was read by Dr. Candlish, on the arrangements for the proposed celebration of the Westminster Bicentenary; and particularly with regard to a basis for the formation of a greater degree of unity among evangelical Christian churches, than has hitherto existed. In the evening an important discussion took place concerning the state of the Church, in which was clearly pointed out the absolute necessity of taking some decided step in defence of religious liberty. A memorial was prepared, drawing the attention of Government again to the Claim of Right, and the other documents transmitted to it by last Assembly, to which no answer had yet been returned; and pointing out the new encroachments on the spiritual jurisdiction of the Church which had taken place since that time, craving redress of those grievances. No other transactions of peculiar importance took place.

Next day, the 17th of November, the CONVOCATION met. It was formally opened by a sermon, preached by Dr. Chalmers, in St. George's Church, from the text, "Unto the upright there ariseth light in darkness." (Psalm. cxii. 4.) In this sermon there was a brief, but a clear, lofty, and forcible exposition of great principles, applicable to the disturbed and perilous condition of the Church; and tending to explain, and in its explanation furnishing a very striking example of, the manner in which light might be expected to arise in the midst of darkness. It may, with truth, be said, that by nearly the entire audience, the sermon was regarded as itself an emanation of that light which it described.

On the evening of the same day, the Convocation met for deliberation in Roxburgh Street Church. Dr. Chalmers was chosen to be moderator, or chairman, it being understood, that in his absence, the next eldest of those who had been moderators of Assembly should occupy the chair, or some other minister, distinguished by piety, and venerable by years. Mr. Pitcairn of Cockpen was appointed clerk to the Convocation, and arrangements to regulate the course of procedure were made. It was resolved that each meeting should be opened with praise, reading a portion of the Word of God, and prayer;—that the meetings should be from 11 forenoon to 4 afternoon, and from 7 to 10 evening, or later if necessary; and that once, at least, during each meeting, the business should be suspended, and the Convocation should engage in prayer, in order that the course of the discussion might, from time to time, be subjected to the stilling and hallowing influence of solemn and united devotion. After the roll of those present had been prepared, the circular calling the Convocation was read, it was stated that those who had come, must of course, be held as concurring generally in the views contained in that circular. This gave rise to some discussion, from which it appeared, that there was a small number present, prepared rather to oppose than to support the leading principles stated in that document. During the course of the discussions which took place, on the second day of the Convocation, all the diversities of opinion that existed among the ministers present were fully developed; and these, considering that there were assembled about 450 men of free and independent minds, all accustomed to think and act for themselves, were exceedingly few. There were indeed but three tolerably distinct views entertained and stated in the meeting. The great majority came fully prepared to frame and carry into effect the measures which were finally adopted as the resolutions of the Convocation. It was the unhesitating conviction of the entire body, that the decisions of the civil courts were completely subversive of the constitution of the Church, and must speedily issue in its destruction, unless some adequate remedy could be procured; but the diversities of opinion arose on the questions—What ought to be regarded as an adequate remedy? and What would be the duty of the Church should no remedy be obtained? A very small number thought that what they termed "a good non-intrusion measure" might be a sufficient remedy. A somewhat more numerous party, agreeing with the majority, that no mere non-intrusion measure could be of any avail, so long as the second Auchterarder judgment stood unrepealed, still differed with regard to the duty of the Church, in the event of no remedy being granted, or no answer returned to the applications which were to be made to Government. Their argument was to the effect, that since the British Constitution had expressly guaranteed spiritual independence to the Church of Scotland, she was entitled to regard any decision of the civil courts which violated that spiritual independence, as so unconstitutional, that it was in itself, and must ever be, null and void, incapable of laying any obligation upon conscience requiring obedience,—or rather, that the duty of defending the constitution, laid a prior and greater obligation upon conscience, actually to refuse obedience. The legitimate conclusion of this argument was, that let the State do what it might, the duty of the Church would be, to resist the decisions of the civil courts, to retain her position as an Establishment, and to suffer, till the State should of itself change its persecuting course, or be compelled to do so by the righteous indignation of the community. It will be at once evident to every reflecting mind, that had the Church adopted this course of procedure the inevitable consequence would have been, a revolutionary struggle of the most appalling character. And it deserves to be especially marked, that this formidable theory of the Church's duty was entertained and asserted chiefly by those whose general leanings had been, and still were towards the middle party, and not by those who had been regarded as the advocates of extreme opinions; that, in truth, those very leaders, such as Drs. Chalmers, Candlish, Cunningham, and others, were the men by whom this perilous theory was most strenuously and ably opposed. And it is right that the whole community should know that it is chiefly owing to the wise and temperate counsels of those much maligned but most honourable and disinterested men, guided unquestionably by wisdom from above, that the Church did not adopt a course which must speedily have plunged the kingdom into the horrors of a wild and devastating civil revolution. By reasoning clear and forcible as lightning, it was shown that such a course would confound sacred and civil duties,—would confound the rights and the duties of the Church *in sacred things*, with the rights and duties of the civil magistrate *about sacred things*,—would be undertaking the defence of the civil constitution for the integrity of which the Church is not responsible, and would be interfering with that duty for which the State is alone responsible to Him who is not only " Head of the Church," but also " Prince of the kings of the earth."

But it would be inexpedient here to give a full detail of the discussions held in the Convocation; although it is not too much to say, that from them the most sage and practised, the most enlightened and philosophical statesman might have learned wisdom. It may, however, be yet regarded as a duty to lay the most important of them before the public, especially in times when the great principles which they elucidated are becoming those by which the destinies of the world are moved and moulded.

The discussions which began on the evening of the 17th of November, continued with the interval of the Sabbath-day, till the 24th, on which day a public meeting was held in Lady Glenorchy's Church, in the evening, at which addresses were delivered, stating the leading principles which the Convocation had resolved to avow and defend. The meeting of that evening, formed, indeed, a fitting conclusion to the momentous deliberations of the Convocation. The opening prayer, by Dr. Brown of Glasgow, was one of marvellous solemnity, spirituality, faith, and earnest self-denying devotedness to the glory of God, and the welfare of the Redeemer's kingdom,—full, indeed, of the Spirit of grace and supplication. And the concluding address by Dr. Candlish, not merely held the vast multitude in breathless admiration, but placing, as it did, every event, not only of the Church, but the empire and the world, full in the light of sacred truth, constrained every one to see all things, and to think, and feel, and judge of them all, as in the light of eternity, and in the presence of God.

The "Resolutions of the Convocation," the " Memorial to Government," and the "Address to the People of Scotland," have been so extensively circulated, and are so recent, that it cannot be necessary to give here even an outline of them. This only it may be necessary to state, that in the *first* series of resolutions, the leading idea embodied, was a declaration, that in the opinion of the members of Convocation, the second Auchterarder judgment contained a principle so completely subversive of all spiritual jurisdiction, that not only could the government of the Church not be conformed to that principle, but it was essentially fatal to the very existence of Church government. The *second* series of resolutions was, in truth, a necessary consequence of the first, declaring it to be the duty of the Church to terminate its connection with the State, if no measure of redress, such as was held to be indispensable, should be granted. About 20 of the ministers required a slight modification in the expression of their assent to the second series of resolutions. It was generally held, that the refusal of the State to return any answer, ought to be regarded as equivalent to a refusal of the Church's application for redress, so as to define the time when it would be her duty to relinquish the position and advantages of the Establishment. But this small party could not view the mere silence of the State as adequately deciding the path and fixing the period of duty, so as to constitute an obligation on conscience to quit the Establishment; though they adhered so far, that the Legislature would, after a reasonable time, oblige them to adopt that course on the ground of Christian expediency. With this slight modification, the second series of resolutions was signed by upwards of 350 ministers, several having been obliged to return to their homes before the conclusion; and the small party who, at first, seemed inclined to oppose, having either joined their brethern, or altogether withdrawn.

In taking the peculiarly solemn and perilous steps already specified, the Convocation did not act rashly and unwittingly. As already stated, the meeting was called, not by hasty and impetuous youth, but by the grave and aged fathers of the Church. It was composed chiefly of those most far advanced in life, on whom the feeling of nearness to the grave and the world to come most habitually rested; of those most enlarged minds, whether from genius or acquirements; of those whose piety had been most conspicuous, and whose labours had been most successful in winning souls to Christ; of all, in short, most distinguished for venerable age, deep piety, genius, talent, learning, energy of mind and character, and every kind of professional and personal eminence in the Church. It was impossible to look around the Convocation on the truly noble and dignified band of Christian ministers there assembled, without feeling constrained to say, "Whether these men remain connected with the State, or leave it, where they are, there the Church of Scotland is." And their deliberations were throughout characterised by unwonted solemnity of feeling and disinterested earnestness of purpose. The spirit of prayer, and the spirit which true prayer produces, was most distinctly manifest. They were a band of brothers, with one heart filled by the love of God, and every hour tended to the production of one mind, by the moulding and blending energies of faith and prayer. Once, and once only, did there appear symptoms of division, on the first evening of their meeting, ere heart had fully met with heart, and mind opened itself to mind. This was almost instantly repressed by a solemn, serious, and well-timed admonition, in which was pointed out the absolute necessity of calm, patient self-denial, and brotherly love, of mutual forbearance, and above all, of dependence upon God, and the constant application to Him for that wisdom which cometh from above. The danger was seen, and met; the remedy was sought, and obtained. From that time forward, all was candour, and frankness, and harmony. If any tendency to asperity of language or feeling appeared, it was instantly checked, and a deep and solemn tone reproduced. If any apparent tendency to division created alarm, it was subdued, and a sacred singleness of aim restored. And when unanimity appeared beyond what had been hoped, it drew forth, not the exultation of triumphant policy, but the hallowed spirit of grateful thanksgiving and adoration. It was a scene in which conscience was allowed its free exercise, enlightened and guided by fervent devotion; in which selfishness perished, overwhelmed by the awful importance of the subjects under deliberation, and the results which might follow; and in which the interests of time gave place to those of eternity, the feelings of earth yielded to those of heaven, and all human duties were subordinated to the duties which man owes to his great God and Saviour.

Such is a brief outline of the leading facts of the Convocation; but it was an event of too great importance to be dismissed without some remarks on its spirit and tendency. It would be difficult to show, that a meeting of ministers of the gospel has been held in modern times, if ever, in whose deliberations were involved matters of deeper moment to the welfare of the Christian Church and to the world, than that of the Convocation which met in Edinburgh on the 17th, and concluded on the 24th of November 1842. One very manifest effect of this Convocation, as appeared when its "Memorial to the Government," and its "Address to the people of Scotland" were promulgated, was the clear light in which it displayed to the world the real nature of the conflict in which the Church of Scotland was engaged,—a conflict involving the very existence of that spiritual jurisdiction which is essential to the purity and freedom of the Church general of Christ. Long had this conflict been obscured and misrepresented, as if it were either a mere struggle for ascendency between two parties in the Church courts, or a temporary collision between the civil and ecclesiastical courts on some small question respecting the boundaries of jurisdiction between them. And in this latter view, it had been frequently and confidently asserted, that the Church courts were arrogating to themselves, under the name of spiritual independence, powers which did not belong to them, which were despotic in their nature, and Popish in their tendency, and which were incompatible with the duties of subjects in a well-constituted government, and destructive of the peace and order of society. All these, and many similar charges against the conduct and pretensions of the Church, were fully met, and conclusively answered by the productions of the Convocation. The Church distinctly and amply declared, and explained both her own duty and that of the State, to the Lord Jesus Christ. By the clear exposition given of her views respecting the right and duty of the supreme civil magistrate, to be guided by his own conscience, enlightened by the Word of God, in all that he does *circa sacra*, in matters external to, but concerning the Church, she vindicated herself, in the estimation of all intelligent and right-minded men, from the accusation of attempting to usurp a Popish supremacy over the State in temporal affairs. At the same time, with equal clearness, she asserted her own divinely given, and inherent right to determine for herself, according to her own conscientious understanding of the principles and laws of her Divine Head and King, her own duty *in sacris*, in all matters essentially sacred and spiritual, subject to no control or coercion within that purely spiritual province.

But there was no reason to expect, nor was it expected, that the dense clouds of misrepresentation and calumny which had so long thickened round her path, would be at once dispelled. On the contrary, all were convinced, that the more fully these great principles were displayed, the more intensely would the hostility of the world be roused. It is well known, that the sacred truths which men cannot confute, and will not receive, they only the more vehemently deny and oppose. And while the members of Convocation held themselves imperatively bound to declare and maintain their principles, they did not expect the result to be an early and an easy triumph, but a fierce renewal of the conflict, in a spirit of embittered hatred, and with increased determination on the part of their opponents. This was indeed inevitable, unless the civil powers had resolved to grant a full and satisfactory redress. For, by the position taken, and the principles declared by the Church, the State was constrained to view the matter in its essential character, and in all its magnitude and importance. It seems probable, that Government had imagined that their silence with regard to the Claim of Right, would, of itself, be enough to overawe the Church into corresponding silence, and to deter her from making any fresh application. But the Convocation dispelled this imagination, and constrained Government to know, that the silence of the Legislature would be a culpable neglect of its duty, at the least; and when coupled with the conduct of the civil courts, would be regarded as equivalent to a sanction of all their unconstitutional and unscriptural encroachments on the sacred rights of the Church, and would, of itself, produce a result as disastrous as could be effected by the most explicit condemnation of her claims. In this manner, it was rendered unavoidable, that the mind of the State should be revealed; since evasion would, in its certain consequences, be equal to refusal of redress. Thus would it be made to appear, whether the State were prepared to acknowledge, or to disavow, its own allegiance and duty to the King of kings; whether it were prepared to redress, or to consummate the violence done to the British Constitution, by the unjust and pernicious Patronage Act of 1712; whether it were prepared to protect, or to destroy the religious, and, by inevitable consequence, the civil liberties of the people. All this was involved in the answer which the

Legislature might give to the solemn appeal made to it by the Convocation, or even by refusing to answer.

Nor could the nation fail to be deeply affected by the proceedings of the Convocation, and constrained also to declare its mind on the momentous question so clearly stated and explained. For the Address to the People rendered it unavoidable for the whole community to consider their own duty in the matter, and to determine whether they were prepared to permit their religious liberties to be utterly subverted, and the Church of their fathers overthrown, without one constitutional and legal attempt to save them; or, whether they were prepared at length to make their voice heard by the Legislature in tones too distinct and significant to be any longer disregarded. When the appeal was made, it rested for themselves to determine, whether they had become so engrossed by the cold and selfish spirit of a secular age, that they had ceased to value spiritual rights and privileges, and were only to be taught, to their loss and shame, by the result, that they had despised their birthright, and culpably forfeited the most precious blessing that God gives to nations.

The deep solemnity of the Convocation's proceedings, and the language of its Resolutions, Memorial, and Address, were well fitted to vindicate the Church from the common charge of stubborn pertinacity in adhering to principles which the civil courts had called illegal. These principles were shown to be too sacred to be yielded up, be the hazard what it might. It was proved, that they involve the very essence of Christianity,—the spiritual union of individual believers, and of every true Church, with the Lord Jesus Christ. For as every believer must obey God rather than man, in all that He has commanded, so must every Church; and to take commands from any earthly power in matters spiritual, is to allow that spiritual union to be broken. But the civil courts had interposed in matters so purely spiritual as the ordination, suspension, and deposition of ministers, in the administration of the sacraments, and in acts of discipline regarding the admission and rejection of ordinary members. If this can be done, then there can be no such thing as a spiritual kingdom of Christ upon earth, which is expressly contrary to the whole tenor of the Word of God. To such unscriptural conduct the Church can never submit. To such unscriptural conduct, whatsoever party submits, will not easily prove its claim to be regarded as a Church of Christ. These points, therefore, could not be yielded, even though the furnace should be heated seven times more than it was wont. "We must obey God rather than man;"—this is the sole answer which the Church could give.

It is an opinion entertained by many, from the aspect of our country and the world, that some great event is fast approaching. With that great event, the Church controversy in Scotland is, beyond all question, closely connected. And the Convocation was so led, as to give the fullest possible developement of its leading principle. That principle, as held by her opponents, is the supremacy of the civil courts over the ecclesiastical, not only in civil matters, which is not denied, but in all matters, however manifestly spiritual. This is equivalent to the rejection of Christ's mediatorial sovereignty; it is saying, "We will not have this man to reign over us." In England the Puseyite party seem hastening on a struggle of a dangerous character, involving all that is arrogant in the pretensions and superstitious in the practices of Popery. On the Continent there are symptoms of a vast combination of rationalistic infidelity, nominal evangelism, and Popish superstition, under the auspices of the Prussian monarch. And when to these is added, the prevalent spirit of commercial selfishness and hard-hearted utilitarianism, so characteristic of the age, it is impossible not to be struck with the wide and mighty muster of portentous elements of strife and convulsion.

Nor does it seem visionary to entertain the idea, that the present may be the very commencement of the last great conflict between the powers of light and darkness which sacred prophecy foretells as destined to precede the glories of the latter days. Every thing seems ripening and hastening on to that great, universal, and terrific struggle. The progress of events has led to the full developement of the principles held by the world with regard to Christianity; and, consequently, has drawn prominently forth that essential element in Christianity which the world most intensely hates,—its spiritual independence. The Christian Church must nevertheless continue to hold what is essential to her union with her Head and King. Thus the conflicting and antagonist powers are forming their lines, mustering their hosts, and taking up their positions; they must come speedily into direct and destructive collision. Christianity may be at first overborne and smitten prostrate; but in its weakest and most suffering hour, its Divine Head will interpose for deliverance, when His own holy arm shall alone be seen, and not man's might or prudence.

So far as this view is entertained, it must be regarded as of incalculable importance, that the Evangelical Church of Scotland, in Convocation met, renewed her Testimony in behalf of the Redeemer's Crown. From the beginning of her existence as a national Church, *that* has been her peculiar, distinctive, and very glorious province. Repeatedly has she renewed that Testimony in perilous times,—never without suffering in its behalf, and never without final success. And it may be that she is now called upon to complete her Testimony in defence of the "many crowns" worn by her Divine Head and only King, not merely against the power of despotic sovereigns as formerly, but against a still more formidable antagonist—the stern and pitiless spirit of abstract laws. If kings and judges alike,—if the world in its mightiest powers, be resolved to reject His sovereignty, the more imperatively is the Church called upon to declare in its defence,—the greater, doubtless, will be the peril, and equally the greater will be the glory when He shall take to Him his great power and reign. It would appear that the Convocation was led to take the true position, and to begin to declare aloud that great Testimony. The men of the world may slay the witnesses,—they may trample their bodies in the dust; but that triumph will be short. The spirit of the Lord will enter into them,—they will be raised into the heavens of spiritual life and power, and the city of the persecutors will perish.

The proceedings of the Convocation, the unanimity with which so many ministers had concurred in its strong and self-denying, or rather self-sacrificing resolutions, and the quickened attention and awakened sympathy begun to be manifested by the country, seemed for a time to have astonished, and even stunned the antagonists of the Church. Recovering from their amazement, they resumed their previous artifices, and plied them with increased keenness and activity. Every conceivable misrepresentation was put forth respecting the motives by which the Convocation was actuated, the temper and feelings which it displayed, and the conclusion to which it had come. Perhaps the most general calumny directed against it was, that it was a nefarious attempt to bully and overawe the Government; and that, notwithstanding the solemn pledge which had been taken before God and the world, the Convocationists would not quit connection with the State, and thereby sacrifice their emoluments, though the Legislature should refuse redress. This, of course, still proceeded upon the deplorable fact, that those who uttered these sentiments judged others according to their own standard, and knowing well that they would not themselves sacrifice wealth, station, and influence, for the sake of conscience, they could not believe that the evangelical ministers would after all make that sacrifice. Most industriously was this calumnious theory promulgated, and not without some effect, confirming the opinions of the worldly-minded, and exciting suspicions respecting the sincerity of the Church in the minds of many who would otherwise have been her eager and devoted supporters. In spite of all these misrepresentations, the cause of the Church continued steadily to advance, and to gain the favour of all who understood and valued the principles of religious liberty.

[1843.] But at length, in the midst of this comparative calm, the storm burst forth with new power and violence. A letter from Sir James Graham, Secretary of State for the Home Department, dated 4th January 1843, was received by Dr. Welsh, the Moderator of the late General Assembly, in answer to the recent Memorial of the Commission. To what extent the appearance of this document was due to the determined conduct of the Convocation, cannot be ascertained, no notice being taken of it in the letter itself; but the spirit and temper of that singular State-paper sufficiently proved that the angry feeling of a galled partizan, rather than the grave and deliberate thought of a wise statesman, had presided in its composition. It begins by a haughty admission that the Secretary of State had been "unwilling to intercept the transmission to the throne" of the Claim of Right, and the Address for the Abolition of Patronage. It then "studiously combines" these two papers, which had been by the Assembly as studiously kept separate; and proceeds to reject both applications on the ground of the necessity for defending the civil rights of patrons. A most unfair attempt is then made to represent the Church as claiming the sole power of determining what matters are spiritual, and what civil, in all questions of disputed jurisdiction,—a claim which the Church had repeatedly and most explicitly denied; but which, in truth, formed the very essence of the civil court's encroachments. This gratuitous imputation is then censured and condemned, as if it were the claim which the Church had advanced. Various other accusations, equally unfounded, are also urged against the Church; and a sufficient amount of misrepresentation and calumny having been vended, the claims of the Church are wholly and peremptorily rejected. This letter has been, by the opponents of the Church, characterised as a most able and statesmanlike document. If it be statesmanlike to misstate facts,—to put an unjust construction upon arguments,—to pervert history,—to repeat refuted calumnies,—to employ sophistry instead of reasoning,—and to repel with haughty scorn the firm but respectful appeal of a Christian Church complaining of gross wrong and outrage,—then was it indeed a statesmanlike document, and that, too, of the highest order, and Sir James Graham must ever be renowned as a most distinguished statesman. But if to pen and promulgate such a tissue would stamp infamy upon the basest partizan in some paltry political intrigue, then let the Right Honourable Baronet weigh well the sentence which truth will dictate, and posterity will loudly pronounce upon the reputed author of that document. Nor is it beyond the province of the historian, or any abuse of his privilege, in some degree to anticipate, on historical grounds, the judgment on such a matter which future times will most assuredly award and confirm.

A meeting of the Special Commission was held on the 12th of January, to take into consideration the Home Secretary's remarkable letter, and to frame to it such an answer as might meet and repel the injurious perversions with which it so lavishly abounded. It did not indeed lie directly within the province of the Special Commission to enter into formal correspondence with Sir James Graham; but a minute was framed in such a manner as to contain a complete answer, which was extracted and transmitted to the Home Office in the first instance, and then printed and published along with the letter itself. This was rendered absolutely necessary in consequence of the extensive circulation which the opponents of the Church were eagerly giving to that document. It was also resolved that a special meeting of the Commission of Assembly should be held on the 31st of January, for the purpose of having the letter of the Secretary of State laid before them, and of taking into consideration the propriety of applying to both Houses of Parliament by petition, and thus obtaining the decision of the Legislature itself as the last resource, now that the sentiments of the Government had been declared. The minute of the Special Commission was prepared by Mr. Dunlop, and though not rivalling the sententious brevity of the Home Secretary's production, was in every other respect as far superior to it as truth is to error, sound reasoning to sophistry, and high-minded integrity of principle and purpose, to the subtle wiles of diplomatic craft.

Before the Commission of Assembly met, another event had taken place, which would of itself have been subversive of the Church, if not redressed. On the 20th of January the Stewarton case was decided, denying the power of the Church to permit ministers of *quoad sacra* parishes to be members of Church courts, and decided by the usual majority of eight of the Judges against five. This decision was not unexpected, the opinions of the Judges on all ecclesiastical matters having been previously made sufficiently apparent. But although the judgment had been anticipated,—anticipated in every point of view, not only in the expectation of both the public and the Church, but also literally, by their Lordships granting interdicts, in many cases, on the ground that there were *quoad sacra* ministers in the presbyteries before they had themselves decided the question,—yet it was left to be an additional and deadly blow inflicted on the Church by the civil court. It involved, at least, two fatal elements: It assumed that the civil court had the power of regulating the constitution of Church courts, which destroyed their independence of itself; and it seemed to determine that there were to be thenceforth two orders of ministers in the Church, which would have annihilated the principle of ministerial equality, and rendered it no longer a Presbyterian Church. It was impossible, therefore, that the Church could submit to this decision, fatal alike to its primary constitution, to its spiritual independence, and to its very existence as a National Church, by rendering it incapable of extending its means of religious instruction in proportion to the necessities of an increasing population. But it came in time to complete the melancholy sum of the grievous wrongs done to the Church of Scotland by the civil courts, and to give to the Legislature the opportunity of redressing them all at once, or of taking upon itself the fearful responsibility of the whole dark series.

On the 31st of January the extraordinary meeting of the Commission of Assembly was held, for the special purpose of receiving Sir James Graham's letter, and of preparing a petition to Parliament. But before its proper business had begun, Dr. Cook directed its attention to the Stewarton decision, and in conformity with it, moved that ministers of *quoad sacra* parishes should not be enrolled, nor permitted to take part in the deliberations of the Commission. Even this was premature, as the decision of the Court of Session might be appealed to the House of Lords, and in fact was appealed as soon as it could be regularly done. Dr. Cook's motion was opposed by Mr. Dunlop, and defeated by a majority of one hundred and fifteen to twenty-three; upon which Dr. Cook and his party read a protest, and withdrew. Thus the first divisive or schismatical step was actually taken by the Moderate party, and upon no higher ground than the unconfirmed decision of a subordinate civil court.

The subject of Sir James Graham's letter was then brought before the Commission; and Dr. Candlish, in a speech of great acuteness, eloquence, and power, investigated its leading points, detected its perversions and misstatements, exposed its fallacies, and repelled its unjust accusations. He concluded by moving a series of resolutions, in which the leading points of the Home Secretary's letter were directly met, and by which the minute of the Special Commission was adopted as the Commission of Assembly's own answer. This motion was seconded by Dr. Chalmers, who, in a short but exceedingly clear and forcible speech, explained the exact position in which the Church at that moment stood, the precise nature of her claims, the manifest view in which these were regarded by the Government, the utter futility of repealing the Veto Act, the all but absolute certainty that the Evangelical body must be speedily driven from the Establishment, and the consequent duty and necessity of taking immediate measures to prepare for that event; so that, come when it might, Scotland should not be taken by surprise, and laid helpless and hopeless beneath the feet of her enemies, but might yet be rendered "an experimental garden, covered with churches and with schools." The resolutions were carried unanimously; and a petition was prepared to be transmitted to Parliament, briefly recapitulating the grievances more fully detailed in the Claim of Right, stating those which had recently taken place, and praying that the Church might be heard by certain of their number, or by their counsel, at the bar of the House of Commons in support of their petition. This concluded the business of this Commission; and it cannot fail to be remarked, that all the elements necessary for bringing the conflict to a close were at length fully developed, either in actual and vigorous operation, or so clearly indicated that their almost immediate action could not be averted. By the Stewarton decision, the last hope that the Court of Session might possibly pause in its destructive career was destroyed; by the petition to Parliament, the Church adopted a course which rendered it impossible for the Government again to prevent her claims from being brought formally before the Legislature, so as to secure such an answer as might render the path of duty plain; and in the speech of Dr. Chalmers, an indication was given that a direct and immediate appeal was about to be made to the piety and zeal of Scotland for the means of maintaining, extending, and perpetuating evangelical truth and religious liberty in the kingdom, out of the pale of the Establishment, since it was too evident that within it these were no longer to be tolerated.

It was now universally felt, by all sincere friends of the Church, that there had been enough of mere deliberation, and that the time for strenuous and united exertion had come. Nor were they unprepared for that immediate action which was imperatively necessary. There had been a meeting of elders intimated to be held on the 1st of February, the day after the Commission. This meeting was very numerously attended; and after a long and earnest discussion respecting the measures which ought to be adopted in an emergency so great, a memorial was framed to Sir Robert Peel and the other members of Government, containing a vindication of the Church from the unjust aspersions of her adversaries, a statement of the many and great benefits which had been conferred on the community by her instrumentality, and an earnest appeal to the justice and the patriotism of her Majesty's administration, praying them to interpose and preserve an institution so sacred and precious from impending destruction. But a still more important step was taken by the meeting of elders. It was resolved that a number of the most active and influential of the members should, along with the committee of ministers appointed by the late Convocation, constitute a PROVISIONAL COMMITTEE of interim administration and management; the object of which should be to commence active and energetic exertions adequate to the nature of the crisis at hand; so that when the disruption of the Church should take place, preparation might have been already made to enable the pastors to continue their ministrations without interruption, and to provide at once the means of public worship to all who might adhere to the disestablished Church throughout every part of the kingdom. The Provisional Committee was accordingly formed, and entered immediately upon the strenuous discharge of its important duties. There were three main objects to be accomplished, which naturally led to a subdivision of the committee into three main branches. It was necessary to ascertain the numbers of those who adhered to the Claim of Right, and the principles embodied in the resolutions of the Convocation; and also, by diffusing information, to dispel error and prejudice, and increase the number of such adherents. This formed the peculiar province of the statistical sub-committee. Again, it was necessary to raise funds for the erection of places of worship, when the adhering ministers should have been constrained by conscience to abandon connection with the State; and to this the attention of the building sub-committee was directed. And further, it was necessary to provide means for the support of the ministry, when compelled to relinquish all claim upon that statutory support which they had previously enjoyed, as ministers of an endowed Church. This formed the duty of the Financial Committee, in which was speedily merged the committee of the Church Defence Associations.

This general arrangement having been made, and a convener appointed to direct the operations of each sub-committee, these divisions of the Provisional Committee entered at once upon the discharge of their important duties, with a degree of wise, zealous, and active energy, altogether astonishing, meeting everywhere encouragement and success far beyond what almost any person had ventured to anticipate. In order at once to ascertain the state of the country with regard to adherents, and to diffuse sound information, the kingdom was divided into districts, and deputations were sent throughout it to address the people in explanation of the great principles at stake, to point out the almost inevitable certainty of a speedy disruption of the Church, to ascertain the number of those who were resolved to defend religious truth and liberty, and to see what provision could be made, or would be required, in every parish, town, or county, in the kingdom. The effect of these deputations was very great, and very beneficial. Long had the adversaries of the Church striven to persuade the people, that the whole controversy was merely one on the part of the ministers for power to themselves; and, to a considerable extent had the people been misled by such misrepresentations. But when the real nature of the contest was made known, and the actual state of affairs explained, with all the eloquence of truth and sincerity, the response was equally instantaneous and enthusiastic, proving that the heart of Scotland still was sound, and the mind of Scotland still held and valued the principles for which, in other days, the Scottish martyrs had borne their dying testimony.

The feelings thus awakened were not permitted to die away; the intelligence thus communicated was not permitted to be forgotten. Associations were formed throughout the whole kingdom, and placed in connection with the Provisional Committee in Edinburgh. A series of Communications were issued weekly by the Provisional Committee, containing information of what had been done and was doing in all parts of the kingdom, suggesting the most suitable measures to be adopted, giving directions how these could be most successfully carried into effect, and thus at once completely instructing and thoroughly organizing the entire adhering community. So thoroughly was the kingdom organized, and so extensive was the demand for these Communications, that there were issued of them, not under 100,000, and more frequently 150,000 every week. The enemies of the Church of Scotland began at length to perceive that she possessed a vitality and a power, the remotest idea of which had never entered into their imagination. In vain did Moderate and irreligious periodicals ply their old work of slander and falsehood. The Church held on her course, obstructed by their darkest insinuations and their loudest outcries, no more than the moon's path in the heavens is obstructed by the murky clouds and baying dogs beneath. And both friends and foes alike began to be convinced that the Church of Scotland was indeed on the point of sustaining a shock, the occurrence of which many had hitherto continued to regard as visionary,—a shock which would either separate her as a Church from the State, or, at least, expel from her communion the vast body of her most able and zealous ministers, and most pious and right-minded people. One only gleam of hope seemed yet to glimmer in the growing darkness. Might it not be, that the Legislature, having an opportunity of deliberately considering the claims and complaints of the Church, as these had been repeatedly stated and explained by herself, and being at length convinced that both Church and nation were in earnest, would, on the presenting of the Commission's petition, grant such redress as might avert the threatened calamity? To this faint gleam the eyes of many anxiously turned; but this, too, was destined to be speedily extinguished.

When the Right Honourable Fox Maule presented the petition of the Commission, he also gave notice of a motion, that the House should go into committee, to take into consideration the claims of the Church of Scotland. On the 7th of March, 1843, this motion came under discussion before the House, and occupied its attention on that and the succeeding day. This was the first opportunity that had been obtained for bringing the whole subject formally under the deliberate consideration of the House, though speeches relating to it had been uttered on various occasions. The whole question was stated with great distinctness and force of argument by Mr. Fox Maule; its legal character was explained and vindicated with remarkable ability by Mr. Rutherford; the inconsistencies of the Church's opponents were detected, and their calumnies exposed and repelled with fervid and glowing eloquence by Mr. P. M. Stewart, and Mr. Campbell of Monzie; and Sir G. Gray, in a calm and dispassionate, but generous and truly statesman-like speech, gave his support to the motion. On the other hand, Sir James Graham opposed it, repeating in an expanded form the groundless and injurious misrepresentations that formed the substance of his sententious letter,—declaring that the claim of the Church of Scotland to co-ordinate jurisdiction independent of the civil courts in spiritual matters, was "so unjust and unreasonable, that the sooner the House extinguished it the better;" the Solicitor-General evaded, but did not even attempt to meet Mr. Rutherford's legal argument; and Sir Robert Peel gave utterance to sentiments which not only proved his entire and unchangeable opposition to the claims of the Church, but also revealed the true cause of that opposition. "If," said he, "a Church chooses to participate in the advantages appertaining to an Establishment, that Church—whether it be the Church of England, the Church of Rome, or the Church of Scotland,—that Church must conform itself to the law." This declaration, delivered with even vehement emphasis, clearly proved that, in Sir Robert Peel's opinion, a Church cannot both be established, and at the same time enjoy spiritual independence,—a principle to which the Church of Scotland never assented, which gives to Voluntaries all that their argument requires for the overthrow of Establishments, and which that statesman may yet learn to be incompatible with the permanent existence of any Established Church in the present stage and condition of society. Again he declared, "My opinion is, that such claims, were you to concede them, would be unlimited in their extent. They could not be limited to the Church of Scotland. A principle, then, is involved, and if the principle be conceded by the House of Commons, why, the House of Commons must be prepared to carry it out." It was, perhaps, creditable to the candour of the Right Honourable Baronet that he made such a statement, but not equally to his prudence. For it proved that what the Church and people of Scotland dreaded at the time of the Union, and strove to prevent by the Act of Security, had at length taken place; and that the British Parliament, in violation of national faith, had destroyed the spiritual independence of the Church of Scotland, in order to prevent that great and sacred principle from extending to England, and disturbing the torpor of her wealthy but secularized and enslaved Establishment.

It is not necessary to characterise the speeches of the various other members by whom the Church of Scotland's claims were opposed, displaying chiefly, as they did, utter ignorance of the subject, with one exception. That exception was the speech of Mr. Colquhoun of Killermont, who had previously endeavoured to distinguish himself as a zealous friend and strenuous supporter of the Church of Scotland,—who had advocated her claims both in speeches and pamphlets, and who now, in her hour of extremity, not only deserted but misrepresented her cause. Nay more, he presumed to print and circulate letters to those ministers who had signed the Convocation's resolutions, in which he endeavoured, by sophistry, and by drawing guilefully pathetic pictures of the calamities which might befall their families, to persuade them to abandon the principles which they had in the most solemn manner avowed and pledged themselves to maintain. True, the temptation did not succeed, but for that no thanks were due to the tempter. And as an act of historical and retributive justice, his name is here singled out that posterity may fix upon it the brand of reprobation which it deserves.

The result was, that the motion, and by consequence the Church of Scotland's claims, were rejected by a majority of 135, the votes being 211 against, and 76 for the motion. It deserves, however, to be stated, that of the Scottish members who voted, there was a decided majority, 25 to 12, in favour of the motion, rendering it all the more manifest that the spiritual liberties of the Church of Scotland were indeed overthrown, as had at the Union been dreaded, by English and Prelatic influence.*

From this time forward it was no longer doubtful that a disruption of the Church would take place. This was indeed rendered absolutely inevitable by the destruction of every lingering hope that the Legislature might interpose in a favourable manner, and the path of duty was, at the same time, rendered clear by the removal of that obstacle which might have continued to hamper some, had no answer been obtained. So far the event was propitious, deplorable as in every other sense it must be regarded. The

* It scarcely requires to be noted, that the influence of the bishops was understood to be strenuously exerted against the claims of the Church of Scotland.

only point on which any contest could now be waged was with regard to the approaching General Assembly. As the Evangelical body had held a decided and even a growing majority since 1834, it was desirable that it should be retained, so that the Church should, by the voice of her highest court, formally relinquish her connection with the State, since she could not conform to the conditions on which alone the Legislature had now declared that the benefits of an Establishment could be granted. This, on the other hand, it was the obvious policy of the Moderate party, of the civil courts, and of the State itself to prevent; both because they would thereby diminish the effect upon the country, and would escape from the perilous necessity of actually "creating a Church," to use their own expression. Every effort accordingly was made, and every artifice employed, in order to break down the Evangelical majority. In all presbyteries where the Moderates formed the majority they returned as members of Assembly only those of their own party, a course which was perfectly legitimate, however unusual; in others they first proposed the exclusion of the *quoad sacra* ministers, and when outvoted, they withdrew, formed themselves into a separate presbytery, and chose their own members, and in a considerable number of instances a junction took place between them and the middle party, by which a majority was obtained, and persons of their own principles chosen. In some presbyteries a still more violent course was followed. Interdicts were sought and obtained to prevent *quoad sacra* ministers from sitting in presbyteries; and in one remarkable case, first the presbytery of Perth, and then the synod, were interdicted from holding their regular meetings for despatch of business, unless all such ministers were first excluded. These lawless encroachments might have been resisted, and presbyteries might have disregarded them, and proceeded according to their own constitutional rights and privileges; but they could have done so only with the certainty of being dragged before the Court of Session, and punished by heavy fines, perhaps imprisonment, for the offence of breaking the interdicts of that Court, and setting its authority at defiance. It thus became obvious, that the Church was no longer in a condition to exercise the right of choosing representatives, and that therefore a free and lawfully constituted General Assembly could not be held. In this manner the Church was absolutely shut up to one only course of procedure, to preserve her spiritual liberties as a Church of Christ.

In the meantime the preparations to meet the now inevitable disruption were carried on with increasing activity and success. New associations were rapidly formed in every quarter, great numbers readily joining who had hitherto continued to stand aloof. Large sums were subscribed, both for the erection of churches, and for the support of the ministry. Plans were prepared by a very skilful architect, according to which, places of worship might be built sufficiently commodious and comfortable, and yet at a very reduced scale of expenditure, compared with the usual cost of such buildings. Scotland began again to display her warm heart, strong mind, and unconquerable energy of character, when thus once more aroused to assert and defend her religious liberty. Nor did these quickened efforts bear at all the aspect of being called forth by the energy of despair. There was doubtless some anxiety till the final step should be taken; but there was a cheerfulness of manner, an open and warm frankness of intercourse, a fearless and manly independence of demeanour, and through all, and above all, a solemn seriousness, which told of peace, comfort, and hope, such as the world could neither give nor take away; of light, encouragement, and strength, sought and obtained from heaven; and of that fear of God which enables the heart to triumph over all other fear.

There were a few events of inferior importance which took place between the rejection of the Church's petition by the Legislature, and the meeting of Assembly,—events which did not attract much public notice, in consequence of the engrossing attention bestowed on the preparation for what was so soon to take place, and which yet deserve to be briefly mentioned. On the 21st of March the action for damages against the Presbytery of Dunkeld, arising out of the Lethendy case, was decided. Lord Cunninghame presiding in the trial. It was proved that no damage of a civil nature had been sustained by patron or presentee. A previous judgment of the Court of Session had awarded the fruits of the benefice to the patron; the presentee had been residing for a considerable time in the manse, and in the undisturbed possession of the civil emoluments; nothing, in short, was wanting to him but ordination, and the Court of Session had empowered the Moderate minority to ordain Mr. Clark themselves, so that there was not the shadow of a ground on which an action of damages could rest, it being utterly impossible for the majority to inflict any injury of either a civil or a spiritual nature. Yet Lord Cunninghame, in his charge to the jury, asserted damages to be due; and the jury, thus instructed, awarded them, though to a considerably less amount than had been claimed. At the conclusion of Lord Cunninghame's charge, certain exceptions to it were taken by Mr. Rutherford, counsel for the presbytery, so clear, searching, and indisputable, that the learned judge, even in his pride of place and power, shrunk from all discussion regarding them. The result of this trial was a very marked demonstration of the distinction between power and right; for the civil courts had assumed and exercised the power of inflicting damages, even where no injury had been sustained; but by all unprejudiced people it was felt, that in their eagerness to crush the Church courts, they had perpetrated a grievous wrong, from which the moral sense of mankind recoiled with blended feelings of shame and indignation, to see such things done under the sanction of law, and in a free and civilized, and nominally Christian country.

Not long afterwards, a discussion arose in the House of Lords which threatened to embarrass the Government in its intended course. The Earl of Aberdeen had intimated his design of again introducing his former bill, with such explanation and modifications as might be thought necessary or desirable. The speech of his Lordship gave offence to the Law Lords, who complained that such a bill as he had described, bearing the title of a declaratory enactment, would be contrary to the principles on which they had decided the Auchterarder appeals, and by declaring that to be law which they affirmed was not law, would be equivalent to a censure upon the solemn judgment of the House. Several sharp and keen altercations followed, at different times, on the same subject, the result of which was a compromise, Lord Aberdeen rendering his bill declaratory in some, and enacting in others of its clauses. This modification, however, took place at a different stage, to which reference will, in the proper place, be made.

Such was the state of affairs when the time for the meeting of the General Assembly drew near. There was scarcely a single point of the conflict which had not been fought out,—scarcely a single disputed question which had not been resolved so as to cause its primary elements to appear. During the course of the protracted struggle, every leading principle of the Church of Scotland's constitution had been assailed and overborne by the decisions of the civil courts, so that her entire government and discipline had been subverted. Kirk-sessions and presbyteries had been prevented from exercising discipline, as in the case of the parish of Inverkeillor, and Presbytery of Arbroath. The Court of Session had assumed the power of determining who were or were not to be rulers and office-bearers, as ministers and elders in the possession of all their due functions, preventing the Church from extending religious instruction to the people, and destroying the principle of Presbyterian equality of ministers, as in the case of Stewarton, affecting all *quoad sacra* parishes. It had been decided that the minority of a presbytery might supersede the majority, though fewer than the legal number required to constitute a presbytery at all, and might, in defiance of the orders of every superior Church court, transact business, and give license, induction, and ordination, as in the case of Auchterarder. The Court of Session had assumed and exercised the power of removing the sentence of deposition, and restoring deposed persons to their ecclesiastical character, as in the case of Strathbogie. Damages had been found due to a rejected presentee, against the majority of a presbytery, because they refused to ordain him, although he was in possession of the fruits of the benefice, and the civil court had empowered the minority to confer ordination, as in the case of Lethendy. And, as if to complete the utter prostration of religious liberty, the Court of Session first interdicted the Church courts from ordaining ministers on the call of the people, where no civil interests of other parties could possibly be involved, as in the cases of Marnoch and Stewarton, and then inflicted a fine upon those who had, in a matter so purely and exclusively spiritual, dared to obey God rather than man. And both Government and the Legislature had distinctly and peremptorily refused to redress these grievous wrongs, to restrain the civil courts within their own proper jurisdiction, and to protect the Church of Scotland from being again exposed to similar violent encroachments upon those sacred rights and privileges "which God has given to His Church."

There were, in these circumstances, but two possible courses for the Church to follow:—either to sink at once into the condition of a merely secular institution, the creature and the slave of the State; or, to retain her God-given principles in all their holy and free integrity, and to resign that position and those emoluments which could no longer be retained without sin and dishonour. Few of the truly religious, either ministers or people, doubted for a moment which alternative the Evangelical body would choose. But by men of the world in general, and by the Moderate party in particular, it was still believed, that when the time for quitting the Erastianized Establishment should come, by far the greater proportion would succumb, and nothing but a very few of the leading men would redeem the pledges which had been repeatedly and most solemnly made to their own conscience, to evangelical Christianity, and to their great God and Saviour. That such a supposition should be entertained, was not less discreditable to those who entertained it, than insulting and injurious to the character of evangelical Christianity. It is discreditable to any man to suspect others of dishonesty and guile, exposing him to the charge of judging them by himself, and therefore of being himself dishonest and guileful. And it is highly insulting and injurious to the character of evangelical Christianity to suspect its ministers of being men who value worldly wealth and honour more than a good conscience and the command of God. But it seemed that Lord Aberdeen had been partly persuaded that conscience did in reality exercise some power in the minds of Presbyterian ministers,—a persuasion which only led him to make a new attempt to delude it, and to bring its influence then into operation on his side. A short time before the meeting of the Assembly, he made a public statement in the House of Lords respecting the principles of such a bill as the Government might yet bring forward. This statement was considerably plausible, and made some impression on those who equally longed for a peaceful settlement and dreaded a disruption. And soon afterwards, in answer to some questions asked by the Marquis of Breadalbane, he repeated his subtle sophisms, and concluded by saying, that if the ministers should secede without seeing his newly modelled bill, "they would not be able, at the last day, to call the God of Truth to witness that they had been driven to that course by the persecution of the Legislature." This was the most deceitful and cruel part of all the deceitful and cruel course of diplomatic craft so steadily prosecuted by the Earl of Aberdeen, as became afterwards manifest when the bill was produced, and was found to contain, in an enacting clause, an express and special condemnation of that principle, without the sanctioned existence of which the Church had declared that she could not continue in connection with the State. His Lordship's diplomatic craft was again unsuccessful. Men asked the opposite question,—If the Earl of Aberdeen has a measure which will preserve the Church in its integrity as a national institution, how will *he* answer at the last day for not producing it in time to prevent her overthrow?—and if he has not, but merely means to deceive, how will he answer for this appeal to the God of *Truth?* A feeling of high-toned moral indignation, roused by this fresh insult and outrage, swept away at once the wicked sophistry, and the Church held on her course.

On the Monday before the meeting of the General Assembly, that is, on the 15th day of May, a large proportion of the ministers who had signed the resolutions of the Convocation assembled in Edinburgh, to hold a closing consultation, preparatory to the adoption of a final measure and the taking of a final step. The subject of deliberation was, whether the refusal of Government and the Legislature to the applications of the Church amounted to such a rejection of her claims for redress, as to realize the position contemplated in the second series of resolutions, and to render an immediate separation from the State an act of necessary duty. There were a few, and but a few, whom Lord Aberdeen's sophistry and appeal to God had so far influenced, that they could almost have been persuaded to consent to a brief period of prolonged delay. But when Dr. Gordon, in a speech of astonishing mental power, loftiness of principle, and Christian dignity, had detected and exposed the hollow character of the proposed mode of settlement, and insisted on the imperative necessity of maintaining principle at all hazards; and when Mr. Campbell of Monzie had further revealed and condemned the tissue of diplomatic craft with which it had been hoped that the Church might yet be ensnared and fettered; every doubt vanished, every difficulty disappeared, and with one heart and mind the band of brothers next addressed their thoughts to deliberate by what course, and in what manner, the closing event might be most suitably accomplished. Nor was this a difficult point to determine. Not only were there double returns of commissioners to the Assembly from twelve presbyteries, in consequence chiefly of the schismatical procedure of the Moderate party, but one entire presbytery was disfranchised by an interdict; and many members were also interdicted from taking their places. It was evident, therefore, that the Assembly could not be regarded as a free and lawful Assembly, duly elected according to the laws and the constitution of the Church of Scotland. The proper course accordingly was, that so soon as the Assembly should be met, and before it was constituted, a protest against it, as unconstitutional and bereft of its due freedom, should be taken by the Evangelical body, and that they should then retire and form themselves into a separate court. The propriety of this course was at once apparent, and it obtained unanimous approbation. A protest was then framed, deliberately read, and cordially, even enthusiastically adopted by the whole ministers and elders present who had signed the resolutions of the Convocation, those who had formerly given a modified adherence withdrawing that modification, and joining unreservedly with their brethren. The protest* thus resolved upon was prepared chiefly by Mr. Dunlop, and was unquestionably the most complete and the ablest document to which the whole contest had given rise, summing up the main elements of the great controversy, exhibiting the successive encroachments of the civil courts, and stating the inevitable consequences as violating both the constitution of the Church of Scotland, and the principles and laws of every true Christian Church, as contained in the sacred Scriptures, with such distinctness, perspicuity, and force, that it was impossible either to misunderstand the meaning or evade the reasoning of this unanswerable argument. With the adoption of this admirable protest terminated the private deliberations of that Evangelical majority, who, since 1834, had striven to reform and defend the beloved and venerated Church of their fathers, and who were now prepared to preserve her principles and her honour, though all else should be lost.

The day had now come,—the day big with the fate of the Church of Scotland, and without presumption it may be added, with the spiritual welfare of Christendom. It was a bright and lovely day of May—the memorable 18th—when nearly all that Scotland could produce of aristocratic grandeur, and civic authority, and legal dignity, and clerical aspiration, and ministerial worth, and upright integrity, and fervent piety, and eager curiosity, thronged the ancient capital, and poured their countless multitudes along her streets, and to every point of peculiar importance. The reign of silence in grey Holyrood was interrupted, for the annual glitter and noisy bustle of reflected royalty was there; the sombre aspect of the old town was changed into the brightness of a gorgeous procession, as her Majesty's commissioner proceeded to the cathedral church of St. Giles; and a close-pent

* The Protest, see Appendix.

crowd had already, from an early hour, filled St. Andrews, where the Assembly was ere long to meet. Slowly the hours wore past till the levee terminated, and the sermon had been preached by Dr. Welsh, the moderator of the preceding Assembly,—a sermon distinguished alike by clearness of thought, loftiness of principle, and emphatic energy of expression. Then began the active interest of the day. The streets were filled by a dense mass of human beings; and it required the utmost exertions of a large body of police to open an avenue through the multitude, such as to permit the processional movement of the commissioner to advance. As the brilliant train swept past, it was regarded by the people with utter indifference,—their beloved Church was on her trial, and what was shadowed royalty compared to that? When the slow procession passed, the vast crowd closed behind it, as the disparted ocean-wave closes behind the gliding ship. Within the Assembly Hall, in St. Andrew's Church, the tramp of steeds, the clash of military accoutrements, and the ringing swell of martial music was heard; the langour of long hours was at once thrown off, and all prepared, with sharpened eye and mind, to notice and to treasure up in memory's most retentive tablets the even awfully important events of each next trembling moment. All were keenly alive, yet all were deeply still, in the intense eagerness of curiosity, or the solemn earnestness of prayer.

The members of Assembly came thronging in by either door. On the Moderate side, there was the appearance of uncertainty and care, and somewhat, perhaps, of gloomy fear, lest after all their victory should prove more disastrous than defeat; and on the Evangelical side, there was that grave and settled seriousness of aspect, that chastened awe of mien and bearing which men wear when engaged in some great and sacred enterprise. The commissioner, the Marquis of Bute, entered, and was received with the usual ceremonies of respect. The moderator opened the meeting with prayer. Then followed a pause of brief duration, but of dead silence, unbroken save by the quickened beatings of a thousand hearts. Again the moderator spoke, uttering slowly, and firmly the following words: —"According to the usual form of procedure, this is the time for making up the roll; but, in consequence of certain proceedings affecting our rights and privileges,—proceedings which have been sanctioned by her Majesty's Government, and by the Legislature of the country, and more especially in respect that there has been an infringement on the liberties of our constitution, so that we could not now constitute this Court without a violation of the terms of the union between Church and State in this land, as now authoritatively declared, I must protest against our proceeding further. The reasons that have led me to this conclusion are fully set forth in the document which I hold in my hand, and which, with permission of the House, I shall now proceed to read." He then read the protest, laid it on the table before the clerk, and bowing to the throne where sat the Commissioner, attended by the law officers of the crown, withdrew, closely followed by all the men of distinguished genius, and talent, and learning, and piety, and faithfulness, and energy, and zeal,—by all whose lives and labours had shed fresh grace and glory on the Church of Scotland, as honoured servants of her Head and King. A long-drawn sobbing sigh, a suppressed cheer, at once of admiration and deep sympathy, swept round the Church, as the crowded spectators gazed intently on the strangely solemn scene. As man by man rose and joined the retiring band, and seat by seat was emptied on the left side of the throne, the Moderate party, the attendants of the commissioner, and the Commissioner himself, gazed on with countenances expressive of astonishment and dismay. They were beginning to learn that religious liberty was a reality which the powers of the world might assail, but could not conquer; that faith and truth had yet a home upon the earth, and that there existed a class of men to whom stainless integrity of character, and a conscience void of offence, and spiritual independence, and the glory of the Redeemer's Crown, were more precious than all that the world could give or take away. In some instances, the excited aspect of boasting and baffled scorners was even fearful; some who but a few hours before had sent intimation to Government that not thirty ministers would leave the Establishment, and whose faces, as they marked the event, grew livid and ghastly with agitation.

At the door of the church, and in the street immediately in front of it, there had been some excitement among the crowd from their closeness to the scene, and yet the impossibility of knowing what was going on within. "*When* will they come?" They will *not* come." "They *will* come," had been the abruptly interchanged exclamations, when the door opened, and "*Here they come!*" announced to the vast multitude that the deed was done, and that the Evangelical Church of Scotland was free! Instantly the whole mass of people was in motion, hats and handkerchiefs were waved aloft, and a shout, not loud nor long, but deep and earnest,—a shout, the voice of the heart rather than of the lip, burst from the countless thousands that thronged street, and door, and window, and even housetop, wherever a foot could be perched and a view obtained. And how were the ministers to work their way through that dense crowd? No civic force was there to clear a path; the military had retired; but with one similtaneous impulse the mass divided right and left, and opened an avenue in the middle of the street so broad that four might walk abreast, and through that living lane, the venerable defenders of religious liberty moved calmly and steadily on along the line of street leading to their appointed place of meeting at Tanfield Hall, on the north side of the city, in the valley formed by the water of Leith. Never, perhaps, was there a more signal instance beheld of the power which tried and trusted moral worth and religious dignity exercises over the mind of man, than in that marvellous spectacle; and frankly did many strangers, natives of other lands, who were present, declare, that in no country but Scotland could such a moral and religious triumph have been displayed. Not one single jarring incident occurred; no haste, no confusion disturbed the great and grave solemnity of the Church of Scotland's Exodus; her friends were stilled from tumultuary applause, her enemies were restrained from wrathful violence, and the presiding care of her Divine Head and King rendered her path one of serenity and peace. Yet when the protesting ministers and elders took their places in the space reserved for them in the spacious Hall, within which already at least three thousand spectators had assembled, and when Dr. Welsh opened the meeting with a prayer remarkable for solemnity of tone, comprehensiveness of thought, and even sublime fervour of devotional spirit, many a bosom could no longer restrain its full and bursting emotions, and many a grave and manly countenance was copiously bathed in tears. It was not sorrow, still less was it regret; it was the outpouring of unutterable gratitude to God for that grace which had enabled them to maintain their integrity, and to bear an unshaken testimony to the truth of Christ's mediatorial sovereignty, and for that providential goodness which had watched over them, preserved them from all strife and confusion, and given to all their proceedings that air of calm untroubled dignity which so well beseemed the sacred nature and the vast importance of the event. Another mode of relief to the full heart was obtained when that great multitude stood up to sing the praises of the Lord, in such a strain of rejoicing and adoring melody as human ears have seldom heard, and human voices seldom raised to heaven. But enough; the whole scene was far beyond description,—a scene such as to share in and behold, might have amply repaid the toils and sorrows of a lifetime,—a scene worth living to witness, worth dying to realize.

The events which followed are too recent in their occurrence, and too deeply engraved on the mind of the country, to require to be here recorded in minute detail. A few only of those which were of chief importance may be briefly stated. Dr. Welsh, in a short emphatic speech, moved that Dr. Chalmers should be chosen Moderator of this the First General Assembly of the Free Church of Scotland. The motion was carried by acclamation, and Dr. Chalmers took the chair. The 43d Psalm was then sung, prayer was again offered up to God, and the Assembly was thus regularly constituted. Dr. Chalmers then commenced the business by an address, in which he recapitulated the principles of the recent conflict, as necessarily the same on which the new

Assembly was now constituted and prepared henceforth to act; viewed the position which must now be occupied, and the course of conduct which ought to be followed towards other parties; and concluded with a beautiful statement and application of the sacred principles and heavenly affections that knit together the hearts and minds of faithful pastors and their pious people. It was then proposed by Dr. Candlish, that the Assembly should assume into their body, as members of the House, all those ministers who had signed the Protest, or a concurrence in it, together with one elder from each adhering kirk-session. This proposal was received with unanimous approbation; and thus the Assembly was put in a position to complete, by means of a formal Deed of Demision, individually signed, the separation of the Free Protesting Church of Scotland from the State, and from the Erastianized Establishment.

The time of several successive days was occupied in receiving deputations from other Churches, who expressed their concurrence in the principles and sympathy with the sufferings of the Free Church; in hearing the reports of the sub-divisions of the Provisional Committee, and of the Committees for managing the Schemes of the Church, of which the one for the conversion of the Jews obtained the precedence;* and in receiving the declared adherence of a large body of probationers, during the course of which proceeding, many very eloquent and very impressive addresses called forth the deep emotions of the vast audience. At length, on Tuesday, the 23d of May, the Act of Separation and Deed of Demission† was read, received the approbation of the Assembly, and was prepared for receiving the signatures of all adhering ministers and elders. All other business was suspended, that this momentous act might with due deliberation and solemnity be done, in the presence of the whole Assembly. The roll of names was called in the usual arrangement of synods and presbyteries. Ten by ten the members rose, moved to the platform behind the Moderator's chair, and there, with unswerving heart and steady hand, calmly completed the sacrifice of all their worldly possessions, and their station in society, for the sake, as they firmly believed and deeply felt of Christ's Crown and Covenant.* At least five hours were occupied in the deliberate execution of this singularly impressive and self-denying deed; and yet throughout this protracted period there appeared no symptom of either excitement or langour. It was the result, not of hasty and fickle passion, but of steady and unchangeable principle; it was the deed of the soul, rather than of the heart; it had been caused, and it was accomplished by the power of spiritual and eternal truth, and therefore it displayed somewhat of the majestic serenity and immoveable steadfastness of eternity itself.

As much important business connected with the reorganization of the Church required to be done, the Assembly continued its sittings with unabated zeal, attended by crowds displaying undiminished interest in its proceedings, till the evening of Tuesday, May 30, when it was closed after an address by Dr. Chalmers, in which the rare combination of genius, wisdom, and piety, which characterizes that distinguished servant of God was pre-eminently displayed. So terminated the memorable FIRST GENERAL ASSEMBLY OF THE FREE CHURCH OF SCOTLAND, having by its noble and self-denying, or rather self-sacrificing DEED OF DEMISSION, saved both the principles and the character of the true Evangelical and Presbyterian Church, for which the Scottish reformers toiled, and the Scottish martyrs died, from the imminent peril to which they were exposed by the treacherous and the faint-hearted within the camp, and the fierce hostility and subtle guile of the civil powers without. Firmly and fully had the faithful ministers redeemed all their pledges, and borne their testimony, and suffered the loss of all things in defence of the Saviour's Crown, and the sacred rights and privileges of His Church and people; but there was not a man of that God-fearing and world-defying band whose deepest thought was not, "Not we, but the grace

* It was a curious and an encouraging coincidence, that as the Church of Scotland had been the first Church that sent missionaries to the Jews so to resume that mission was the first enterprise of the Free Church.

† Deed of Demission, see Appendix.

† The number of those who signed on that day was 386; additional signatures, subsequently given, have raised it to upwards of 470.

of God in us." And when they departed, not as usual to return to homes rendered doubly dear in all their hallowed tranquillity by a period of toilful absence, but to break up their households, and to go forth as strangers and pilgrims in reality, into a world whose hostility was but too surely known, it was not with feelings of woe and despondency, but with the deep and chastened joy of hearts conscious of temptations repelled, duty discharged, trials well and fully endured, and souls graciously strengthened by inward spiritual might, and thus prepared for all that should lie before them, in acting or suffering, till their Christian warfare should be done, and they should be called to enter into the rest that remaineth for the people of God, who have "fought the good fight and finished their course."

It is a melancholy contrast to turn to the proceedings of what has been not inaptly called, the Residuary Assembly. The state of feeling in that Assembly produced by the disruption, seemed at first to be the blank confusion of utter amazement and dismay. Never, till that moment, had they realized the idea that the Evangelical ministers were men of greater sincerity and rectitude than themselves,—hence the incredulity which they had all along entertained, and the false reports which they had transmitted to Government, respecting the probability of the threatened disruption which had now taken place. It was not till the Monday that they were sufficiently recovered from their stunning astonishment to proceed to the despatch of business. But then they went forward with the blended eagerness of tyrants and servility of slaves, increased by the blind impetuosity of men acting under the spell of infatuation. Adopting, apparently, the Letter of Her Majesty's Administration* as the supreme law by which their whole conduct was to be guided, they repealed the Act on Calls, commonly denominated the Veto Act, thereby subjecting the people entirely to the despotism of patrons and Church courts, and at the same time admitting the principle, that the Church was bound to regulate its procedure according to the dictates of the civil courts; they expelled the whole of the *quoti sacra* ministers, declaring the act which gave them admission null and void from the beginning, thereby admitting the power of the civil courts to determine who were to be the members of ecclesiastical courts, consenting to the unpresbyterian theory of two orders of ministers, and allowing hostile landholders to stop at pleasure the extension of religious instruction to those who were destitute of that blessing; they rescinded the original and recently revived laws respecting the popular election of elders, thereby depriving the people of representatives and protectors in Church courts; they restored the Strathbogie men to their status as ministers, without reponing them, as if no sentence of deposition had been passed, thereby sanctioning the fatal theory, that the sentence of Church courts may be disregarded as null and void, though not proved sinful, which, if followed out, would foster insubordination, and end in dissociation and anarchy; they rescinded all the sentences of deposition passed upon ministers convicted of criminal and immoral conduct, remitting these cases to their respective presbyteries, "to take such steps in the matter as they should see fit;" and they restored the Act of 1799, thereby cutting themselves off from religious communion with every Church in the world.

Such were the proceedings of the Moderate and Erastian Assembly; and thus, in one short week, they swept away the reformation of nine years, and did their utmost to place the Establishment in the exact position which it had occupied at the end of the preceding century; as if utterly unaware, that though Moderatism may have no power of life and motion, the mind of man and the affairs of society live and advance, and that, therefore, a system unable to adapt itself to the spirit of the age cannot be maintained. But they had pleased the Government, they had harmonized with the civil courts, they had expelled the popular element and influence from their own courts, they had been relieved from the disturbing mental, moral, and spiritual energy of their evangelical antagonists, and they might surely at length hope for a period of untroubled repose. True, there was some dread that the Free Church might yet cross their path; and there was a necessity for filling the demitted charges with all convenient speed; and there

* Queen's Letter, see Appendix.

might be some uneasy misgivings about the probabilities of the future; and there could be little ground of trust in the support of an approving Providence; but they had the security of continuing to dwell in their manses and receive their stipend, though their ministry should be deserted by the people; and they had the prospect of obtaining translations to those more lucrative or dignified positions, out of which treachery, fraud, and force, had expelled their better brethren.*

Lord Aberdeen, as was previously stated, had given intimation of a bill soon to be introduced, such as ought, in his opinion, to have prevented the disruption of the Church. On the 1st of June his lordship brought forward his bill, which proved to be his former measure, somewhat altered for the worse. It had to encounter the direct opposition of the Law Lords, who affirmed that it gave power to the Church courts to infringe the rights of patrons, and was contrary to the Auchterarder decision. Well did the earl know, that no Moderate presbytery would ever dispute the authority of patrons; but to mitigate the hostility of his learned and noble antagonists, he consented that it should be both declaratory and enacting,—declaring that to be law which had yet to be enacted, and enacting that which had already been declared, and thus reducing the whole measure to a tissue of preposterous absurdity. When the bill came before the House of Commons, it was again encountered and exposed with such skill and power by the friends of the Free Church, that it narrowly escaped rejection. And after it had become law, it was so little satisfactory to the Establishment, that at the meeting of their Commission it was strongly censured by a large and influential minority of that body. So ended the glories of Aberdeen diplomacy in ecclesiastical affairs, with the dissatisfaction of all parties concerned.

Although the history of the Church of Scotland properly ends with the disestablishment of that evangelical body which had alone held and maintained the principles of its standards, and followed the example of its founders and its martyrs; yet a few sentences may be allowed in which to trace its operations in its new condition, as the Free Protesting Church of Scotland. It was well and truly said by several of the deputations from other Churches, that whatever the remaining Establishment might be called, they had no difficulty in perceiving that the Free Church was the Church of the Scottish people—that she already possessed their hearts, and had nothing to do but to go forth and possess the land. On the Sabbath after the termination of the Assembly, the ministers of the Free Church abstained from using their former places of worship, and preached in halls, or barns, or in the open air, to audiences many times more numerous, and unspeakably more intensely attentive than had ever before attended their ministrations. There was in their own devotions and instructions a fervour, a pathos, and a spirituality to which they had rarely or never before attained; and their people gazed on them and listened to them with an earnest sympathizing and admiring love, which rendered every word precious, and its impression deep and lasting. It may be safely said, that the gospel was, that day, preached in Scotland to a greater number of eager and attentive auditors than had ever before listened to its hallowed message. And yet that was but the beginning. From Sabbath to Sabbath, and on almost every weekday evening, the people sought to hear, and the ministers of the Free Church hastened to proclaim, the glad tidings of salvation. Nor did this remarkable avidity of the people to hear, and willingness of the ministers to preach, bear almost any reference to the recent controversy and its result; but both ministers and people felt themselves at last *free*, and they used that freedom in the service of their Divine Lord and Master.

At the same time, as the hearts of the people had been opened to receive the gospel, so were their hands opened to contribute towards its support and extension throughout the kingdom. Large sums were subscribed and collected for the erection of plain and humble, but comfortable places of worship, and for the due maintenance of the faithful and self-denying ministers of the Free Church Within two months after the disruption,

* A few, and but a few, of those who had generally acted along with the Evangelical body deserted at the hour of extremity. It is mercy to leave their names as far as possible in oblivion.

upwards of £240,000 had been subscribed, and nearly 800 associations formed, partly to aid in supporting, and partly that they might themselves enjoy the inestimable blessing of a pure and free gospel. Churches in all directions began to be erected; every minister and probationer was constrained to discharge double or threefold duty; and still the demand continued to increase. Nothing could be more apparent, than that a larger proportion of the people than of the ministers had abandoned the Erastian Establishment; and that if a sufficient number of ministers could have been obtained, the Free Church might have at once possessed the land, as the Church of the Scottish people.* In many localities, indeed, there were great difficulties to be surmounted, arising chiefly out of the narrow-minded and persecuting hostility of the landlords, some denying sites for the erection of churches, and others threatening to eject their tenantry and other dependents if they ventured to adhere to the Free Church. This persecuting spirit generally overshot its purpose, rousing instead of subduing the moral courage and determination of the high-hearted Scottish peasantry, calling forth the indignation of the public mind, and suggesting the perilous questions, how far such conduct was consistent with the law of toleration and British freedom of opinion, and how far the rights of property might overbear the rights of conscience.

Before the disruption took place, it had been repeatedly suggested that deputations should be sent to lay before the frank and generous people of England an account of the wrongs inflicted on the Church of Scotland. With this it had been found impracticable to comply during the contest. But now several deputations were sent, and were hailed with ready kindness and liberal sympathy—large sums being promptly contributed to aid in meeting the urgent and increasing demands for the immediate erection of places of worship for the Free Church. Warm-hearted Irish Presbyterians lent their help, both in money and in ministers, to relieve the ministers of the Free Church from some of their overwhelming toils. Even America sent, not merely the voice of encouragement, but also liberal pecuniary assistance across the wide Atlantic, requesting that a deputation might be sent to that vast continent, to communicate information, and to receive a fuller measure of substantial sympathy in return.

In the midst of these mighty and encouraging movements an event occurred, with a short outline of which this narrative must close. This was the Bicentenary Commemoration of the first meeting of the Westminster Assembly. It has already been mentioned that steps had been taken towards making suitable arrangements for the commemoration long before the disruption. The General Assembly of the Free Church did not neglect this matter in the midst of all its great and urgent exertions. A committee was appointed to make suitable arrangements, and to correspond with other Presbyterian Churches, who, holding the same standards, were equally interested in the commemoration. The first meeting of the Westminster Assembly was held on the 1st day of July 1643; and, allowing for the difference between the old and new styles, it was appointed that the commemoration should be held on the 12th of July 1843, and in the same great hall which had been occupied by the General Assembly of the Free Church. On the previous evening, an introductory sermon was preached by the Rev. Dr. Symington of the Reformed Presbyterian Church, in which the principles of Christian love were beautifully and impressively explained and enforced. The large hall was nearly filled early in the forenoon of the 12th with ministers and people from all the Presbyterian Churches in the kingdom, without distinction, and without jealousy or envy. It was soon evident that all had come together animated by the true spirit of Christian love. Most cheeringly and affectingly beautiful was the sight of ministers of all Presbyterian denominations,*—the Free Church, the United Secession, the Relief, the Original Secession, the Reformed Presbyterian, and

* It is enough to refer to the too well-known instances of Sutherlandshire, Ross-shire, the Isle of Skye, &c. &c.

* Not one minister of the Erastian Establishment gave countenance to, or took any part in, the Commemoration; but this was consistent, for how could they commemorate the Westminster Assembly, which was so decidedly opposed to Erastianism?

the English and Irish Presbyterians, thus united in one common object, commencing in the unity of the Spirit, proceeding in the harmony of oneness in heart and mind, and concluding by drawing more closely and kindly the bonds of peace. Many eloquent and powerful addresses were delivered, explaining and vindicating the great principles of Presbyterian Church government, doctrine, and discipline, as contained in the Standards framed by the Westminster Divines. It was the remark of all, that during the two days in which the commemoration was held, greater progress had been made towards realizing the sublime idea of one grand Evangelical and Presbyterian Union, than during the two centuries that had elapsed since it was first entertained by the Westminster Assembly. The meeting could not separate, the hearts of men were too full and grateful, without determining that similar meetings should again be held, and a cordial co-operation in all religious duties be begun and carried on, in the hope and with the desire that it might lead to the ultimate incorporation and thorough union of all Evangelical and Presbyterian Churches. Nor was that unity of spirit and harmony of heart confined to Presbyterians, but a cordial expression of readiness to co-operate with evangelical Episcopalians and Congregationalists was also made, and sanctioned by the warm applause of the meeting. The very existence of such a meeting as this, the unanimity of mind and brotherly love which prevailed in it, and the expansion of aim and effort, and the commencement of evangelical intercourse and co-operation which it produced, may all be fairly attributed to the principles maintained and the position taken by the Free Church of Scotland. And with this brief account of the propitious commencement of her actions and endeavours as a Free Church, ends the history of her existence as an Establishment.

Many grave and solemn thoughts must necessarily arise in the mind which has been long and intensely occupied with the history of a Christian Church. All the interests of time, and the feelings and passions that agitate human nature, seem to sink into nothingness in comparison with the interests of spiritual truth and of eternity; or, so far as they are at all regarded, they are beheld in a very different point of view from that in which they appear to the man whose mind and heart are engrossed by the objects of the passing hour. When the events of life and time are contemplated habitually in the relation which they bear to the souls of men and to eternity, the mind becomes conscious that it has attained a loftier eminence, from which it enjoys a clear perception of what would otherwise have remained obscure and indistinct. Then, all events—national, political, and even personal—are seen as they subserve or oppose those great ends for which man was created and redeemed; and with reference to that, as by a sacred standard, are they tried.

Thus viewed and estimated, the Evangelical and Presbyterian Church of Scotland appears the most perfect and beneficial, yet most persecuted Christian institution that has ever yet been established among mankind. In assuming for her first principle that sacred truth, THAT THE LORD JESUS CHRIST IS THE ONLY HEAD AND KING OF THE CHURCH, she placed her foundation, indeed, upon the Rock of Ages; but she placed it where it was certain to be assailed by all the storms and tempests which the enemy of all sacred truth, the god of this world, could raise. That she should suffer in holding this truth, was inevitable; for it is the very truth for holding and asserting which Christ himself was accused before Pilate, condemned, and crucified. "If thou let this man go, thou art not Cæsar's friend," was the argument which wrung from the Roman governor the sentence of death against Him who is King of kings and Lord of Lords. And for faithfully maintaining the same great truth has the Church of Scotland often, almost incessantly, suffered persecution, is suffering still, and must suffer so long as she continues to maintain it, till He come whose right it is to reign universally. This great principle Romanism cannot hold, because it constitutes the pope its head; Prelacy cannot hold, because it yields practically its headship to an earthly king; Voluntaryism cannot fully hold, because by not only totally withdrawing from, but absolutely denying he lawfulness of all connection with the State, it virtually denies Christ's right to reign, not only as King of the Church, but also as King of kings. It is, therefore, and has always been, the peculiar glory of the true Church of Scotland to declare, maintain, and suffer in defence of the Divine Redeemer's Mediatorial Crown.

And let it be peculiarly marked, as every stage of her history testifies, that exactly in proportion to the faithfulness with which she maintained that truth, did her Head and King honour her with His presence and His blessing, in her supreme courts held in His name, in all her inferior judicatories, in her pastors, and in her people. When most faithful in her allegiance to Him, she was always most prosperous in that which constitutes the true prosperity of a Christian Church,—in promoting the progress and the power of vital godliness throughout the nation. To that is solely owing the high eminence which the Scottish people so early gained and so long held among mankind, notwithstanding the smallness of the kingdom and the comparative barrenness of the country and severity of the climate. And in like manner, in proportion as she violated or yielded that principle, did she sink into a fatal spiritual lethargy, while the increasing, disregarded, and alienated population rapidly degenerated into vice, poverty, and turbulence. Of this, the present state of Scotland, after the long and torpid period of Moderatism, or unspirituality, is a fearful proof. Scotland is not what it was; because for several generations the Church of Scotland was under the domination of a party, the spirit of whose system was the spirit of the world, not the spirit of evangelical Christianity. Dark must have been the cloud of infatuation which rested on the minds of the Legislature, when, by its countenance and support, Moderatism was enabled to consummate its guilt by exterminating all that constituted the life and glory of the Church,—when its ancient power to paralyze, which had been shaken off, was, by the authority of civil courts and the State, raised into a power to destroy.

Yet, truth is eternal; and when a great truth has been clearly stated, it cannot perish. Repeatedly has this been proved in the case of the Church of Scotland; for repeatedly has that great truth which is her fundamental principle been for a time obscured and overwhelmed, but has again shone forth, rising from out the ruins of whatsoever had attempted its destruction. And in every successive instance of its repeated emergence it has obtained a fuller developement, and acquired a mightier power, than it had previously done. Thus, in the Second Reformation, the sole sovereignty of Christ over His Church was more amply manifested than before, and the Church was more completely freed from the clinging fetters of the world than ever it had previously been. And though that period of spiritual freedom was but of short duration, yet it presented a brief realization of what a Christian Church ought to be in its relation to Christ, to the State, and to the community. The power of the example then displayed lives still, and is even now putting forth its vital realizing energy. And when the Third Reformation, now in progress, shall have been accomplished, it will then be clearly seen, that the successive cycles through which the Church of Scotland has run, have but been expansions of each other, the moving principle being still the same, and all the elements remaining unchanged, but becoming more fully developed.

We have termed the recent, or rather the present great movement in the Church of Scotland, the Third Reformation; and under that character some of its most remarkable aspects deserve to be seriously contemplated, so far as they are yet revealed. The first peculiarity which demands attention, is that which arises out of the nature of the contest and the character of the assailants. From the period of the Revolution, and especially from that of the Patronage Act, the Church has been divided. One party, the Evangelical, has striven to act in conformity to the spirit of her sacred first principle, though that should be offensive to the world; the other, the Moderate, has attempted to hide that principle, to keep it in abeyance, and to act in conformity to the world. From this divergency at the centre, has necessarily followed a still widening divergency in the growth and progress of these tw parties. But the one which held the original principles of the Evangelical Presbyterian Church in truth and sincerity, was alone truly *the Church of Scotland;* the other was its worldly counterfeit, and for that very reason it obtained most of the world's favour. Fearful have been the consequences to Scotland of the long domination of the worldly system; but a demonstration of inestimable value has been made, which will yet be understood and applied. It has been clearly proved, that a Church really Erastian, but nominally and in form Presbyterian, is of all Protestant Churches the worst, having neither ritual to attract, nor faith and warmth to inspire and animate the people, whom at the same time it deprives of every vestige of spiritual liberty. It seems expressly calculated to produce national infidelity, by driving vital religion out of its pale, and deadening all that remain within it. If Popery has been termed the religion of fallen man, Moderatism may, with equal propriety, be termed the religion of fallen Presbyterians; or, as the same secular spirit may prevail in any church, it may be termed the religion of fallen Protestants. And yet, notwithstanding the present apparent triumph of that system, it may be safely predicted that the reign of Moderatism has passed away, and cannot again be permanently re-established. Its doom is written in the word of truth, which condemns the "earthly" and the "lukewarm," manifested in the signs of the times; urged on by the advancing spirit of the age; and will soon be pronounced alike by politicians, who will find that it can no longer subserve their purposes; and by the indignant voice of an outraged and insulted nation. The Evangelical and Presbyterian Church of Scotland has been cast out, and may be for a time trodden under foot; all ecclesiastical establishments may be overthrown; and they that dwell on the earth may rejoice because Christ's witnesses have been slain. But that Church which is willing to perish rather than surrender the Crown Rights of the Redeemer, may be persecuted, but shall not be forsaken,—may be cast down, but cannot be destroyed; for the Lord Jesus, for whom it suffers will be with it always, even to the end of the world.

Christianity, in its practical embodiment as a system, has always suffered more or less corruption by the intermingling of things civil with things spiritual. In Popery, the distinctions between them are lost by the spiritual or ecclesiastical authority engrossing all power, civil and sacred; in an Erastian Church, by the civil power assuming a right to dictate in spiritual matters; and in churches which hold what is termed the voluntary principle, an evil at least equal arises by the civil power being compelled to become virtually atheistic. The ruling principle of the Church of Scotland is different from all these; she has been constrained to encounter each of them in succession; and she has recently been exposed to the combined hostility of them all. She disclaims all power in matters civil; she will not surrender the power which Christ has given her in matters spiritual; and she fearlessly tells both governments and communities, that it is their duty to be Christians, to act as Christians, and to make it their chief object to promote Christ's kingdom and glory. For this has she been, and still is, exposed to threefold peril,—for this has she been compelled to abandon the temple where her children worshipped God, and to erect a tabernacle in the wilderness; and for this is she still pursued by the fierce wrath of her relentless enemies. But through the triple darkness of the lowering tempest which surrounds her, there may be seen the dawning brightness of a thrice glorious and peaceful day. Her conflict has now been freed from every admixture of a worldly nature on her side; all political parties have alike deserted her cause, or are banded together against her, so that she is not even tempted to put her trust in princes or the sons of men; while the masses of an irreligious and immoral population, left in that state by Moderatism, seem ready to add the fierce and irresponsible element of physical force. But for these very reasons little of worldly contamination can now cleave to her, and intermingle in her procedure; she is followed by the sympathy and the prayers of all truly evangelical Churches; she is in the condition to be most thoroughly purified by the fiery trial through which she is passing; and bereft as she is of all human help, the more manifestly will the final victory be the Lord's.

It has already been shown how remarkably the progress of events has been so guided by the hand of Providence, as to bring to the light the very central element of the last grand controversy between the Church and this world. During the earlier stages of the controversy, its true nature was apparent to comparatively few, and not at all to the greater part of the nation. As it advanced, one cause of obscurity was removed after another, and its real character became more and more manifest to all who could discern spiritual things. And at last the very essence of the mighty subject appeared distinct and alone, in the form of this direct and intelligible question,—Shall the will of Christ, or the will of man, be the supreme law and rule of the Church in spiritual matters? To this question the Church can have but one answer, and the world has but one. Often have these conflicting answers come into partial collision; but never, at any period in the history of the Christian Church, has this question been raised with such unavoidable precision, and the antagonist deliverances given with such appalling emphasis. The two contending principles which these answers embody, are now brought front to front, in the attitude of determined hostility, and till the one or other perish there can be no peace and rest for Christendom.

The same idea might be stated and illustrated in a somewhat different manner,—Is it the duty of the State to give encouragement and support to the Church of Christ, without attempting to deprive it of that spiritual independence which is necessary for the right discharge of all its spiritual duties? From the very beginning of her existence the Church of Scotland has maintained the affirmative of this great question, and it has been her constant endeavour to demonstrate to the world, that a Christian Church may be in connection with the State, thus giving to rulers the opportunity of obeying the King Eternal, and realizing the predictions of His Word; and may, nevertheless, maintain its allegiance inviolate to its own Divine King, and enjoy that spiritual freedom wherewith Christ has made his people free. The full realization of this attempt seems to be yet premature, as it has proved to be in bygone times; but something has been gained in each successive conflict; and more will yet be gained in this, both because to human view the difficulties to be surmounted are greater than ever, and because the object of the contest stands more clearly defined.

Even the fact that the antagonist power appears in the impassive form of abstract human law, though an element of peculiar danger, is equally an element of purity and hope. It is not now with persons that the Church has to contend so much as with principles; and who may doubt the issue when a human principle presumes to encounter one that is undeniably divine? Men have yet to be taught, that law itself can have no sure basis but the Word of God; and that equally those who make, and those who interpret and administer a nation's laws, are bound to regard it as their first duty both to legislate and to administer not otherwise than according to the will of Christ. And formidable as is the might of human law, it has already so far been, and will yet more be compelled to feel, that its utmost energy sinks into absolute powerlessness, when directed against conscience enlightened and upheld by Him who alone is Lord of the conscience. Then will men learn the full meaning of those simple yet sublime words. "Whether it be right in the sight of God to hearken unto you more than unto God, judge ye."

Repeatedly has the thought been suggested, during the course of this history, that civil and religious liberty exist and fall together. Nowhere has this been more signally proved than in Scotland, and never more manifestly than at present. Before the Church of Scotland could be assailed, it was necessary to violate the British constitution, as in the case of the Patronage Act of Queen Anne. Before she could be overthrown, it was necessary to subvert it, as has been too manifestly done by the recent proceedings of the civil courts and the Legislature. And in the endeavour to crush the Free Church, even the theory of toleration is set aside, and liberty of conscience is denied. And it were well for the nation, if all who value the rights and privileges of freemen were aware, that whether such be her desire or not, the Free Church of Scotland is at this moment the chief safeguard of all liberty, civil and religious. She cannot be overborne without a fatal shock being given to the very freedom of the soul, from which all other freedom springs. And those who support her antagonists may yet mourn to know, that they have been busily engaged in forging fetters for themselves.

With strangely unobservant eye and mind must that reader have perused these pages, who has not clearly perceived that the contest in which the Church of Scotland has been engaged, is precisely the same in which for centuries she has fought, and bled, and conquered. "Take from us the liberty of Assemblies, and take from us the Gospel," said John Knox. "What is Cæsar's, or what is ours, let it be given to Cæsar, but that may not derogate from Christ's right; let the God by whom kings reign have His own place and prerogative," said Alexander Henderson. "We can die, but we cannot forswear ourselves, and be false traitors to Christ," said the Covenanters. "The spiritual independence of the Redeemer's kingdom, in all matters touching the doctrine, government, and discipline of the Church, and the sole Headship of the Lord Jesus Christ, on which it depends, as also the rights and privileges of the Christian people, we will assert, and at all hazards defend, by the help and with the blessing of Almighty God," was the solemn declaration of those true-hearted Presbyterians, and faithful servants of the Lord, who have been, and still are so strenuously endeavouring to effect the Church of Scotland's Third Great Reformation. The First Reformation, like a whirlwind, dashed to the earth, and swept away the apostate and idolatrous Church of Rome, though deeply rooted in the deceived and blinded nation. The Second Reformation, after a long and painful struggle, overthrew and banished from Scotland that perjured and blood-thirsty prelatic usurpation, which the craft of one sovereign, and the fierce despotism of his three successors, had in vain attempted to erect upon the ruins of the persecuted Presbyterian Church. And the Third Reformation has been engaged in bursting asunder the fetters, and casting off the yoke of that cold, worldly, unspiritual, unchristian system, so well designated Moderatism. In each of these Reformations the Church has experienced the most desperate opposition, has been for a time overborne, and in the First and Second she ultimately obtained the victory. By the Black Acts of 1584, she was overpowered and enslaved, but regained her liberty in 1592. By the Glasgow Act of 1662, she was disestablished, silenced, driven to the mountain solitudes, and the best blood of her sons and daughters shed like water; but the revolution of 1688 terminated for a time her sufferings, sanctioned her principles, and ratified her liberties. By the recent decisions of the Civil Courts, the rejection of her Claim of Rights by the Legislature, and the Bill of Lord Aberdeen, her constitution has been again subverted, and those who continue to hold and defend it have been once more, like their forefathers, compelled to forsake their homes and places of worship, and to bear a full and public testimony against an Erastianized Establishment, and Erastian principles in the State.

But the end is not yet. If her principles be, as we believe, sacred and divine, they must and will finally conquer. And though the warfare of argument is ended, the sterner warfare of principle is yet only beginning. Other Churches are now learning the meaning of her testimony, and are employing its high and holy terms. The very sympathy which her wrongs, her sufferings, and her undaunted bearing have called forth, have tended unspeakably more to diffuse her principles than could have done her early and complete triumph in their defence, Evangelical Christianity can now lift a more erect and ennobled head in the world, since God has enabled the Free Church of Scotland to give an undeniable proof that religion is something more than a system of dead forms and vague professions,—that there are still Christians on earth, even in this secular and selfish age, to whom grace has been given to suffer the loss of all things in their Divine Redeemer's cause. Humbly and gratefully let the Free Church adore her sole Head and King, that He has not withdrawn from her that hidden spiritual life which has enabled her to dare the furnace, and will bring her unscathed through all its purifying fires. And let other Churches seek to realize a similar union with Him, both as the first and most certain step towards union with each other, and as a preparation for their own approaching hour of trial. She has already drunk deeply of the cup out of which all other Churches will have ere long, perhaps, to drink; and unspeakably the most fearful will it be for that Church which shall have to drain the dregs. For it seems evident to almost every reflecting mind, that the last great conflict between the Church and the world, foretold in sacred prophecy, has already begun. The various events which may take place during its progress cannot be fully foreseen; but the issue is certain, and it is awful,—the destruction of all that take counsel together against Jehovah, and against his Anointed. "Be wise now, therefore, O ye kings; be instructed, ye judges of the earth. Serve the Lord with fear, and rejoice with trembling. Kiss the Son, lest he be angry, and ye perish from the way, when his wrath is kindled but a little."

It would be equally presumptuous and unwise to hazard any definite opinion respecting the exact nature and probable extent and duration of the fearful conflict of irreconcilable principles which has rent asunder the Church of Scotland, expelled her genuine children from the temples where their fathers worshipped God, is rapidly spreading into other lands and rousing other Churches, and may soon convulse Christendom and the world. Enough to know that the Lord God Almighty reigneth, and that the Judge of all the earth will do right. Earnestly is it to be wished and hoped that the warfare may continue to be spiritual, not carnal,—not waged against kings, and governments, and armed troops, as in former days; but not the less arduous may be the contest, and not the less protracted may be the struggle, against an antagonist power entrenched within legal forms, and aided by the aggressive might of that modern despotism abstract human law,—forgetful, in its pride, of those high spiritual laws which mould time, which frame and govern life, which made and guide the universe, which were promulgated from heaven to lead immortal souls to its abodes of everlasting peace, and which have their sum and centre in Him who is the King Eternal. Whether the early triumph of these high spiritual laws shall glad the hearts of those who are now, exposed to every peril, their dauntless defenders,—or whether it be reserved for that day, near or remote, when angels shall proclaim, "The kingdoms of this earth are become the kingdoms of our Lord and of his Christ, and He shall reign for ever and ever,"—it becomes not short-sighted man to conjecture; but the Free Church of Scotland may, and, as we pray and trust, she will, go forward in her holy course of reformation, completing her great testimony, bearing the cross and defending the crown of her only and Divine Head and King, strong in the Lord and in the power of his might, in the spirit of faith and prayer, and hope,—encouraging her heart with these sacred words, "THE LORD IS OUR JUDGE, THE LORD IS OUR LAWGIVER, THE LORD IS OUR KING; HE WILL SAVE US."

APPENDIX.

No. I.

Note on the Death of Cardinal Beaton, p. 33.

THE attempt which has been made by Patrick Fraser Tytler, Esq., in his History of Scotland, to prove that the great and pious Scottish Reformers were implicated in some of the most criminal transactions of that dark and stormy period in which they lived, having been briefly alluded to in the body of this work, it may seem necessary to take more specific notice of his opinions than could there appropriately be done. With regard to the charge insinuated against Wishart, however, that he was concerned in a conspiracy against the life of Cardinal Beaton, little need be said, till Mr. Tytler give a satisfactory answer to the complete "Vindication of George Wishart," which appeared in the Edinburgh Christian Monitor, vol. iii. p. 475, in the year 1823. The grounds of this accusation are, the prophetic language of Wishart at the stake, which some men think more likely to have proceeded from actual knowledge of an intended assassination, than from any preternatural enlightenment granted to the dying martyr; and the casual mention in some manuscript correspondence of the period, that "a Scottishman called Wysshert," was said to have been employed by Henry VIII. in some alleged conspiracy against the life of the cardinal. The first of these conjectural suppositions we leave to those who can entertain it; because neither reasoning, nor reference to many similar well-authenticated cases, would be likely to produce conviction in their minds. Another answer might be given, which would be more satisfactory to some; neither Fox, in his account of Wishart's martyrdom, nor Knox, make any mention of his prophetic language; those, therefore, who wish to fasten this charge upon him must first prove that he spoke such words. With regard to the other, it is enough to state, that in the "Vindication" referred to above, it is proved, by direct historical testimony, that if any such person existed as is mentioned in the manuscript, he could neither have been the martyr, nor his brother the laird of Pittarow. This of itself is enough to vindicate the memory of Wishart from any such mere conjectural aspersion; for no conjecture, founded on the mere similarity of a name, loosely mentioned in the gossiping language of epistolary correspondence, may ever be allowed to set aside direct historical testimony. It would, besides, require the most incontrovertible evidence to substantiate such a charge against all the moral improbabilities, or rather impossibilities, which it has to encounter, when brought against the mild, patient, gracious, and heavenly-minded martyr, George Wishart.

Note on the Death of Rizzio, p. 68.

In the seventh volume of his History of Scotland, Mr. Tytler has directly, and even ostentatiously, charged John Knox with being "precognizant of, and implicated in," the murder, of David Rizzio. This charge has been met, and, as most people think, completely refuted, by the Rev. Thomas M'Crie, son of the distinguished biographer of Knox. It is not my intention, certainly, to retrace the ground which has been so ably occupied by Mr. M'Crie, thinking it enough to refer the reader to his answer to Mr. Tytler, as it appeared in the appendix to his "Sketches of Scottish Church History." Still, as there may be different methods of demonstrating the same truth, I think it expedient to offer, very briefly, my reasons for regarding Mr. Tytler's accusation as utterly untenable; and this, I trust, I may do without being suspected of intending any disrespect to that gentleman.

Every historian finds himself often compelled to balance conflicting evidence, in order to arrive at the truth of any subject respecting which contradictory statements have been made. The evidence thus to be estimated is to be of two kinds, —the evidence of facts, and the evidence of moral probability. These kinds of evidence sometimes seem opposed to each other, and sometimes they coincide. When they coincide, a conclusion amounting to absolute certainty is obtained; but when they are opposed to each other, the task becomes considerably difficult to determine to which of them the greatest credit is due, and very opposite conclusions will be drawn from the same data by minds differently constituted. It requires a higher cast of mind to appreciate duly the evidence of moral probability, than it does that of facts; although, no doubt, when the facts can be, or have been, fully ascertained and substantiated, nothing more is required, and the controversy is at an end. Yet such is the power of moral probability, that every man must have felt himself constrained in peculiar instances to reject instinctively the argument of facts, and to say, "I cannot believe that a man of a character so high and noble could have done a deed so base." It will not be a small amount of the evidence of facts that will suffice to set aside such an instinctive moral conviction; and when facts are brought forward with that view, they will be met by a sifting investigation whether they really occurred, and on what authority we are asked to believe that they actually took place as they are said to have done. Nothing short of the direct testimony of a sufficient number of witnesses of undoubted veracity, and adequately acquainted with the facts which they relate, will ever substantiate a charge which is instinctively felt to be morally improbable. If, for example, any person were to attempt to propagate a report that the Duke of Wellington had been detected in an act of petty theft, every man would at once indignantly feel and declare, that it was impossible; and it would require an extraordinary amount of direct evidence to induce and constrain any man to believe a report so abhorrently incredible. Not less clear and incontrovertible ought to be the evidence brought forward by him who accuses John Knox of being implicated in an act of private murder. What, then, is the amount of evidence adduced by Mr. Tytler?

The following is a brief outline of the main facts of the event. Queen Mary had joined the League of Bayonne, which was framed for the purpose of utterly exterminating Protestantism by violence. This was well known to the Scottish Protestant nobles; and her Italian secretary, David Rizzio, was believed to be the agent through whom she held intercourse with the Romish powers. The Protestant nobles resolved to seize Rizzio, bring him to trial, and condemn him to death, as a person engaged in treasonable transactions. At the same time the weak, vain, and violent Darnley conceived a strong hatred against this Italian, on the ground of an imagined guilty intercourse between him and the queen. The nobles were not reluctant to obtain Darnley's countenance to promote their own design against Rizzio's life. There was thus a double plot; and Mr. Tytler, without the shadow of evidence to support it, nay, against direct evidence to the contrary, conjectures that the nobles must have abandoned their own intention of a public trial and execution, and adopted Darnley's scheme of a private murder. Rizzio was actually seized and murdered. Soon afterwards, the blandishments of the queen prevailed over her fickle husband, and induced him to violate his engagement to the lords; and thus the conspiracy was broken up, and the betrayed noblemen fled to various quarters, to escape from the vengeance of the queen. John Knox retired to Kyle for a season, well knowing that Mary bore to him no favour, and that if she had it in her power to bring him within the sweep of her meditated vengeance, she was not likely to let slip the opportunity.

Accounts of these transactions were sent to Cecil by the Earl of Bedford, and by Sir Thomas Randolph, from Berwick, to which town several of the Scottish nobles had fled for safety. In Randolph's letter, dated the 21st of March, the names of those who were concerned in the death of Rizzio are mentioned; and in the same letter it is stated, that the intention of the lords was to have hanged him, but that a tumult arising in the court below, and fearing a rescue, they went the next way to work with him. On the 27th another letter was sent by Randolph, giving a formal and authentic list of those who were concerned in the death of Rizzio. In neither of these does the name of Knox occur. An account of the whole matter was sent to Cecil by Morton and Ruthven; and as rumour had then begun to implicate Knox and Craig, these noblemen expressly declare, that the ministers were "neither art nor part of that deed, nor participate thereof." A similar declaration is contained in Ruthven's own narrative of the event, in which he strongly exonerates the ministers. Douglas of Lochleven, another of the conspirators, disclaims the intention of murdering Rizzio, and declares that it was their purpose to punish him by order of justice. Hume of Godscroft, in his History of the House of Douglas, says the same. Every author, in short, of any credibility, gives the same general statement,—that the lords intended to bring Rizzio to a public trial, and to condemn him to death and execute him as a plotter against the religion and the liberties of the kingdom, and that the ministers were in no respect implicated in the matter.

To overwhelm the whole of the evidence thus briefly stated, Mr. Tytler brings forward the one small fact, that he found a slip of paper pinned to Randolph's first letter, which slip contained a list of those "who were at the death of Davy, and privy thereunto, and are now in displeasure with the queen, and their houses taken and spoiled." This pinned list contains the names of John Knox and John Craig. It has no signature, but is thought to be in the handwriting of a clerk employed by the Earl of Bedford,—a likely enough person to pick up the floating rumours of the day. This pinned list contains enough to prove it unworthy of credit. It states that "all these were at the death of Davy," whereas it is certain that neither Knox nor Craig were present. It further adds, that they "are now in displeasure with the queen, and their houses taken and spoiled;" yet it is known that Craig was not in displeasure with the queen, and there is no evidence that the house of Knox was "taken and spoiled." Such glaring misstatements prove this pinned slip to be a mere transcript of some popular report, such as are busily circulated without examination when any remarkable event excites the public mind, but which no man of candour or of judgment regards. It is strange reasoning, surely, to say, that because an unauthenticated rumour is false in two points, it must be true in the third. Mr. Tytler is not at liberty to change the express words of this precious document, converting *and* into *or*, that it may the better serve his purpose. He does so at the hazard of endangering his own character for candour and integrity. It must be taken as it is, without any such constructions, and then it manifests its own falsehood.

Feeling, apparently, that this small fact of the pinned list furnished but slender evidence on the strength of which to implicate John Knox in a charge of murder, Mr. Tytler attempts to corroborate it by reasoning from the known sentiments of the Reformer; that is, he leaves the evidence of facts, and enters upon the evidence of moral probability. His first and chief argument is, that Knox held it lawful for private persons to put to death notorious murderers and tyrants, provided that all redress by the ordinary courts of justice was impossible. This will not prove that Knox would either have engaged in such a deed *himself*, or would have approved of its being done *privately*; and, besides, in the case of Rizzio, the supposed emergency did not exist, the banded lords being sufficiently powerful to bring him to a public trial, as it is proved that they intended to do, his private seizure being merely to prevent the possible occurrence of a public tumult. The attempt to fasten such a charge upon the Reformer, on the ground of his holding such an abstract theory, is manifestly absurd, unless it be first proved that the case was precisely such as his theory supposed. And even then it would be necessary to show that he could, consistently with his own character, have put his theory into execution in the same manner as that in which Rizzio was killed. Now, from the whole tenor of Knox's life it is evident that he could not have committed a deliberate, contrived, private murder. Such a man, had he not been a Christian, might have killed a tyrant in his open court and surrounded by his guards, but could not have crept into his bedchamber to murder him in secret. Mr. Tytler attempts further to prove, that the murder of Rizzio was not accidental, arising out of a sudden tumultuous frenzy enhanced by the apprehension of being frustrated in the completion of their design. Strange that he does not perceive how much more improbable this renders it that Knox could have been implicated in the crime. Indeed, reasoning from Mr. Tytler's premises, and taking into consideration the high, bold, and pious character of John Knox, I do not hesitate to say, that no man who can comprehend moral evidence will ever regard the charge against him as any thing else than a charge involving a moral impossibility. And this I regard as a proof how unfit Mr. Tytler is to deal with moral evidence.

Another argument on which he builds is this: that at a subsequent period one of the ministers, defending Knox from the aspersions of King James, said, "that the slaughter of David was *allowed by Knox*, as far as it was the work of God, and not otherwise." Mr. Tytler here evidently misunderstands both the sentiment and the word used to express it. The sentiment is a sufficiently common one, nothing being more usual than for men to say, when any great criminal perishes miserably, that it is a remarkable instance of the righteous retribution of Providence, while they do not intend to express approbation of the human instrumentality by which such retribution was effected. The word *allowed* was in former times used, not to mean *permitted* an event to take place, but generally in the loose sense of *approbation of the object intended*, and often little more than *abstaining from censure.* The meaning of the sentence is plainly this: So far as the death of Rizzio may be regarded as the righteous retribution of Providence, John Knox approved, or did not condemn it; but he expressed no approbation of it, so far as it was the deed of guilty men. Rightly understood, this goes to prove that Knox was not implicated in a deed which, so far as it was man's, he *disallows.*

Mr. Tytler attempts to remove another objection to which his accusation is exposed, from the declaration of Morton and Ruthven, that none of the ministers were "art and part, or participate," in the deed. This he does by labouring to show, that in Morton's estimation, to be precognizant of an intended crime without revealing it, and to be "art and part" in it, were not equivalent expressions. He might have understood Morton's meaning better had he attended a little more accurately to his reasoning. Morton was accused of being "art and part" in Darnley's murder. This he strenuously denied; yet he owed that he knew it was intended, and did not reveal it. When asked how he could reconcile this with his denial of being art and part in it, he answered, "To whom should I have revealed it? To the queen? She was the doer thereof. The king was such a child, that there was nothing told him but he would reveal it to her again. And therefore I durst in no ways reveal it. I foreknew, indeed, and concealed it, because I durst not reveal it to any creature for my life." Morton reasons, that the primary law of self-preservation exonerated him from the accusation of being accessary to the commission of a crime of which he was precognizant, and disapproved yet concealed, because he believed that to reveal it would cause his own death, and would not prevent its being committed. But he could not have given to John Knox the same excuse which he took to himself, when he denied that "precognizance" was in such a case equivalent to "art and part," unless he had been prepared to prove that for Knox to have revealed it would have caused his own death without preventing the crime, so that to be silent was merely an act of self-preservation, and implied no approbation of the deed. In this instance also Mr. Tytler shows himself to be singularly unable to understand and apply moral evidence and reasoning.

But it is needless to traverse the whole ground of Mr. Tytler's small facts and smaller arguments. Enough has been said, I trust, to substantiate the opinion given in the body of this work, that "certainly so grave a charge, and so improbable, was never brought forward and maintained on evidence so slender, nay, so absolutely incredible." Mr. Tytler would need to beware, otherwise his character as a historian will not long stand high, either for candour and impartiality, or for soundness of judgment. There is a law of retribution which never fails in its operation. When a man assails the character of another, and fails to prove his charge, the accusation recoils, crushing him who put it in motion. And even though no consequence so serious should take place, the public may begin to draw this conclusion, that the mind which is continually prying into minute details, is liable to lose the higher faculties of comprehensiveness and discrimination, to form an undue estimate of the value of small facts, and to regard as discoveries what a mind of higher order would at once have perceived to be merely the idle rumours or the partizan insinuations of the day, and would have deemed unworthy of any notice.

No. II.

ACTS OF PARLIAMENT.

In the year 1560, on the 17th of August, the First Confession of Faith of the Reformed Church of Scotland was "professed, ratifiet, and approveit in Parliament;" the jurisdiction of the Pope was abolished; and an act was passed against idolatry, and another abolishing the mass.

In the year 1567, on the 19th of April, Queen Mary, before the last series of criminal actions which led to her imprisonment and exile, passed an act securing to all her subjects freedom from civil injury in their adherence to the Reformed faith.

But it was not till the meeting of the first parliament, held by the Regent Murray, that a full recognition was made of the Reformed Church, amounting to its establishment as the National Church of Scotland. The most important points of these acts of parliament are here given.

Act 1567, *ch.* 6. *Anent the trew and haly Kirk, and of thame that are declarit not to be of the samin.*

Item, Forsamekle as the Ministeris of the blissit Euangell of Jesus Christ, quhome God of his mercy hes now rasit vp amangis vs, or heirefter sall rais, aggreing with thame that now liues, in doctrine and administratioun of the Sacramentis, and the pepill of this realme, that professis Christ as he now is offerit in his Euangell, and do communicat with the holy sacramentis (as in the reformit Kirkis of this Realme ar publicklie administrat), according to the Confession of the Faith, Our Souerane Lord, with auise of my Lord Regent and three Estatis of this present Parliament, hes declarit and declaris the foirsaid kirk to be the onlie trew and holy Kirk of Jesus Christ within this realme, and decernis and declareis that all and sundrie quha outher gainsayis the Word of the Euangell ressauit and appreuit as the heides of the Confessioun professit in Parliament of befoir, in the yeir of God 1560 yeirs, as alswa specifiet in the Actis of this Parliament mair particularlie dois expres, and now ratifyit and appreuit in this present Parliament, or that refusis the participation of the holy sacraments as thay ar now ministrat, to be na membris of the said Kirk within this realme now presently professit swa lang as they keipe thame selfis sa deuydit fra the societie of Christis body.

Act 1567, *ch.* 7. *Anent the Admissioun of thame that sal be presentit to Benefices hauand cure of Ministrie.*

Item, It is statute and ordained by our Soveraine Lord, with advice of his dearest Regent, and three Estatis of this present Parliament, that the examination and admission of ministers, within this Realme, be only in the power of the Kirk, now openlie and publicly professed within the samin. The presentation of laic Patronages alwais reserved to the Just and auncient Patrones. And that the Patron present ane qualified persoun, within sex Moneths (after it may cum to his knawledge, of the decease of him quha bruiked the Benefice of before) to the Superintendent of thay partis, quhar the Benefice lyis, or uthers havand commission of the Kirk to that effect; utherwaies the Kirk to have power, to dispone the samin to ane qualifyed person for that time.

Providing that in caice the Patron present ane person qualified to his understanding, and failzeing of ane, ane uther within the said six Moneths, and the said Superintendent or Commissioner of of the Kirk refusis to receive and admit the person presented be the Patron, as said is: It sall be lessum [lawful] to the Patron to appeale to the Superintendent and Ministers of that province quhar the Benefice lyis, and desire the person presented to be admitted, quhilk gif they refuse, to appeal to the General Assemblie of the haill realme, be quhom the cause be and decyded, sall take end, as they decerne and declair.

Act 1567, *ch.* 12. *Anent the iurisdictioun of the Kirk.*

Item, Anent the Artickle proponit and geuin in by the Kirk to my Lord Regent and the thre Estatis of this present Parliament, anent the iurisdictioun iustlie apperteining to the trew Kirk and immaculat spous of Jesus Christ, to be declarit and expressit as the artickle at mair lenth is consuit: The Kingis Grace, with auise of my Lord Regent and thre Estatis of this present Parliament, hes declarit and grantit iurisdictioun to the said Kirk; quhilk consistis and standis, in preiching of the trew word of Jesus Christ, correction of the maneris, and administration of haly sacramentis. And declaris, that thair is na vther face of Kirk nor vther face of Religioun, than is presentlie be the faour of God establischeit within this realme. And that thair be na vther iurisdictioun ecclesiasticall acknawledgit within this realme, vther than that quhilk is and sall be within the same Kirk, or that quhilk flowis thairfra concerning the premisses; and forther, our Souerane Lord, with auis, of my Lord Regent and thre Estatis foirsadis, hes geuein and geuis power and commission to Schir James Balfour of Pittindreich, Kyncht, Priour of Pittinweem; Mark, Commendatour of Newbottill; Johne Priour of Coldinghame, Lord Preuie Seal; Maister James Makgill of Rankillour Nether, Clerk of Register; William Maitland, younger of Lethington, Secretar to our Souerane Lord; Schir Johne Bellenden of Auchinoull, Knycht, Justice Clerk; John Erskine of Dune; Maister Johne Spottiswod, Superintendent of Lowthaine; Johne Knox; Maister Johne Craig; and Maister Dauid Lindesay, Ministeris of the worde of God, To seirche furth mair speciallie, and to considder, quhat vther speciall pointis or clausis sould appertene to the iurisdictioun, priuilege, and authoritie of the said Kirk, and to declair thair mindis thairanentis to my Lord Regent and thre Estatis of this Realme at the nixt Parliament, Swa that they may tak ordour thairintill, and authories the samin be act of Parliament, as sall be fund agreable to the worde of God.

[These acts were again ratified in the years 1578, 1579, and 1581.

In 1581, a short act was passed respecting the few lay patronages at that time existing, but which the king was strenuously endeavouring to increase.]

Act 1581, *ch.* 102. *That ministeris sall be presentit be the Kingis Majestie and the lawit Patronis, to all benefices of cuir under Prelacyis.*

Item, It is statute and ordanit be our Souerane Lord, with aduise of his thre Estatis of this present Parliament, That all benefices of cuir under prelacyis, sall be presentit be our Souerane Lord, and the lawit personis, in the fauoure of abill and qualifeit ministers, apt and willing to enter in that functioun—and to discharge the dewtie thairof. And in cace any sall happin to be gevin and disponit wtherwise hereafter, decernis and declaris the giftis and dispositiounis to be null and of none availl, force, nor effect.

[Next appear the "Black Acts" of 1584

Act 1584, *ch.* 129. *An Act confirming the Kingis Majestie's Royall Power over all Statis and Subjectis within this Realme.*

Forsameklc as syndrie personis, being laitlie callit befoir the Kingis Majestie and his secreit Counsell, to answer upon certaine pointis to have bene inquirit of thame, concerning sum treasounable, seditious, and contumelious speches, utterit by thame in Pulpit, Scholis, and vtherways, to the disdane and reprooche of his Hienes, his Progenitouris, and present Counsell, contemtuouslie declinit the judgment of his Hienes and his said Counsell in that behalf, to the evill exemple of uthers to do the like, gif tymous remeid be not providit: Thairfoir our Souerane Lord, and his thrie Estatis, assembled in this present Parliament, ratifeis and apprevis, and perpetuallie confirmis the royall power and authoritie over all statis, alsweil Spirituall as Temporall, within this Realme, in the persoun of the Kingis Majestie, our Souerane Lord, his airis and successouris: And als statutis and ordanis, that his Hienes, his said airis and successouris, be thameselffis and thair counsellis, ar, and in tyme to cum sall be, juges competent to all personis his Hienes subjectis, of quhatsumever estate, degrie, functioun, or conditioun that ever they be of, Spirituall or Temporall, in all matteris quhairin they, or ony of thame, sall be apprehendit, summound, or chargeit to answer to sik thingis as sall be inquirit of thame, be our Soverane Lord and his Counsell. And that nane of thame, quhilkis sall happin to be apprehendit, callit, or summound to the effect foirsaid, presume or tak upoun hand to decline the jugement of his Hienes, his airis or successouris, or thair Counsell, in the premisses, under the pane of treasoun.

Act 1584, *ch.* 131. *Act discharging all jurisdictionis and judgmentis, not approvit be Parliament, and all Assembleis and Conventionis, without our Souerane Lordis speciall licence and commandment.*

Our Souerane Lord and his thrie Estates, assemblit in this present Parliament, dischargeis all jugementis and jurisdictionis, Spirituall or Temporall, accustomat to be usit and execute, upoun ony of his Hienes subjectis, quhilkis are not approvit be his Hienes and his saids thrie Estatis, convenit in Parliament; and decernis the same to ceis in tyme cumming, quhil the ordour thereof be first sene and considerit in Parliament, and be allowit and ratifeit be thame. Certifeing thame that sall proceid in using and exerceing of the saids jugementis and jurisdictionis, or in obeying of the same, not being allowit and ratifeit, as said is, They sall be repute, halden, callit, presewit, and punissit as usurparis, and contemnaris of his Hienes auctoritie, in example of utheris. And als it is statute and ordainit, be our Souerane Lord, and his thrie Estatis, that none of his Hienes subjectis, of quhatsumever qualitie, estate, or functioun they be of, Spirituall or Temporall, presume to tak upoun hand, to convocat, convene, or assemble thamselffis togidder, for holding of councellis, conventionis, or assembleis, to treat, consult and determinat in ony matter of Estate, Civill or Ecclesiasticall (except in the ordinare jugementis), without his Majesties speciall commandement, expres licence had and obtenit to that effect, under the panis ordinit in the lawis and actis of Parliament, agains sic as unlawfullie convocat the Kingis lieges.

Act 1584, *ch.* 132. *The Causes and Maner of Deprivation of Ministers*

Our Souerane Lord, and his thrie Estatis, assemblit in this present Parliament, willing that the word of God sall be preachit, and Sacramentis administrat in puritie and synceritie, and that the rentis, quhairon the Ministeris aucht to be sustenit, sall not be possest be unworthie personis neglecting to do thair dewties, for whilkis they accept thair benefices, being utherwayis polluted with the fraill and enorme crymis and vices after specefeit. It is, thairfoir, statute and ordainit be his Hienes, with auice of the saides thrie Estatis, that all Personis, Ministeris, or Reiddaris, or utheris providit to benefices, sen his Hienes Coronatioun (not having vote in his Hienes Parliament), suspectit culpable of heresie, papistrie, fals and erroneous doctrine, common blasphemie, fornication, common drunkennes, non-residence, pluralitie of benefices having cure, quhairunto they are providit sen the said Coronatioun, Symonie, and dilapidatioun of the rentis of benefices, contrare the lait Act of Parliament, being lawfullie and ordourlie callit, tryit, and adjudgit culpable, in the vices and causes abouewritten, or onie of thame, be the ordinare Bishop of the diocie, or utheris the Kingis Majesties Commissionaris to be constitute in Ecclesiasticall causes, sall be deprivit alsweil fra thair functioun in the Ministerie, as fra thair benefices, quhilkis sall be thairby declarit to be vacand; to be presentit and conferrit of new, as gif the personis possessouris thairof, were naturallie dead: And that it sall be esteemit and jugeit not-residence, quhair the persoun being in the function of the ministerie, providit to ane benefice, sen the Kingis Majesties Coronatioun, makis not residence at his mans, gif he ony hes; and failzeing thereof, at sum uther dwelling-place within the parochin; but remains absent thairfra, and from his Kirk, and using of his office, be the space of four Sondayis in the haill zeir, without lawfull caus and impediment, allowit be his ordinare. And quhair ony persoun is admittit to ma benefices, havand cure, sen our Soverane Lordis Coronatioun, the acceptioun of the last sall be sufficient cause of deprevatioun from the remnant, swa that he be providit to twa or ma benefices havand cure, sen the tyme of the said Coronation. And nevertheles, this present Act sall not extend to ony persoun providit to his benefice befoir the said Coronatioun, nather sall the bruking of the said office, quhairunto he was providit of befoir, induce pluralitie of benefices in this cace; bot he sall allanerlie tyne his richt of the benefice quhairunto he was providit sen the said Coronatioun allanerlie: And unioun of kirkis to ane benefice not to be jugeit pluralitie, quhill farder ordour be establissit and providit in that behalf: Likeas alswa, the personis being in the functioun of the ministerie, that sall happin to be lawfullie and ordourlie convict befoir our Soverane Lordis Justice-Generall, or utheris thair Jugeis competent of criminal causis, sick as treasoun, slachter, mutilatioun, adulterie, incest, thift, [commoun oppressioun, usurie aganes the lawis of this Realme,] perjurie, or falset: They being lykewayis lawfullie and ordourlie deprivit fra their function in the ministerie, be thair ordinair, or the Kingie Commissionaris in Ecclesiasticall causes. The benefices possest be the saidis personis to vaik, be reasoun of the said convictioun and deprivatioun. And this to have effect and execution onlie for crimis, vicis, faultis, and offenceis, that sall happin to be committit efter the dait hierof.

[That important Act commonly designated "The Great Charter of the Church," which was passed in the year 1592, demands special attention.]

Act 1592, *ch.* 116. *Act for abolishing of the Actis contrair the trew Religion. [Ratification of the libertie of the trew Kirk: Of General and Synodall Assemblies: Of Presbyteries of Disci-Pline. All laws for Idolatrie ar abrogate: Of Presentation to Benefices.]*

Our Soverane Lord and Estaittis of this present Parliament, following the loveable and gude example of their predecessours, Hes ratifiet and apprevit, and be the tenour of this present Act ratifies and apprevis, all liberties, privileges, immunities, and freedomes, quatsumever, gevin and grantit be his Hienes, his Regentis in his name, or ony of his predecessouris, to the trew and haly Kirk, presentlie establishit within this realme; and declarit in the first Act of his Hienes Parliament, the twentie day of October, the zier of God ane thousand, five hundreth, three-scoir ninetene zieres; and all and whatsumevir Actis of Parliament, and statutes maid of befoir, be his Hienes and his Regentis, anent the libertie and freedome of the said Kirk: and specialie the first Act of the Parliament, balden at *Edinburgh*, the twentie-foure day of October, the zier of God ane thousand, five hundreth, and foir-scoir ane zieres, with the haill particulare Actis thairin mentionat, quhilk sall be als sufficient as gif the samyn wer herin exprest. And all uther Actis of Parliament maid sensyne, in favouris of the trew Kirk; and siklyke, ratifies and apprevis the Generall Assemblies appointed be the said Kirk: And declaris, that it sall be lauchfull to the Kirk and Ministrie everilk zier at the leist, and ofter *pro re nata*, as occasion and necessitie sall require, to hald and keip Generall Assemblies: Providing that the Kingis Majestie or his Commissioner with thame, to be appoyntit be his Hienes, be present at ilk Generall Assemblie, befoir the dissolving thairof nominat and appoint tyme and place quhen and quhair the nixt Generall Assemblie sall be haldin: and in caise nather his Majestie nor his said Commissioner beis present for the tyme in that toun, quhair the General Assemblie beis halden, Then, and in that caise, it sall be lessum to the said Generall Assemblie, be themselffis, to nominat and appoynt tyme and place quhair the nixt Generall Assemblie of the Kirk sall be keipit and haldin, as they haif bene in use to do thir tymes bypast. And als ratifies and apprevis the Sinodall and Provinciall Assemblies, to be halden be the said Kirk and Ministrie, twyis ilk zier, as they haif bene, and are presentlie in use to do, within every Province of this realme; And ratifeis and apprevis the Presbyteries, and particulare Sessionis appoyntit be the said Kirk, with the haill jurisdictioun and discipline of the same Kirk, aggreit upon be his Majestie, in conference had be his Hienes with certane of the Ministrie convenit to that effect: of the quhilkis Articles the tenour followis. MATERIS to be entreated in Provincial Assemblies: Thir Assemblies ar constitute for wechtie materis, necessar to be entreatit be mutuall consent, and assistance of brethrene, within the Province as neid reqvyris. This Assemblie hes power to handle, ordour, and redresse all things omittit or done amisse in the particulare Assemblies. It hes power to depose the office-beareris of that Province, for gude and just causes, deserving deprivatioun: And generallie, thir Assemblies hes the haill power of the particulare Elderschippis, quhairof they are collectit. MATERIS to be entreated in the Presbyteries. The power of the Presbyteries is to give diligent labouris in the boundis committed to their chairge: That the Kirkis be kepit in gude ordour: To inquire diligentlie of the naughtie and ungodlie personis: And to travell to bring them in the way agane be admonitioun, or threatening of Goddis jugementis, or be correctioun. It appertenis to the Elderschip, to tak heid that the Word of God be puirlie preachit within thair boundis, the Sacramentis richtlie ministrat, the Discipline enterteynit, And Ecclesiasticall guidis uncorruptlie distributit. It belangis to this kynd of Assembleis, to caus the ordinances maid be the Assembleis, Provinciallis, Nationallis, and Generallis, to be kepit and put in executioun, to mak constitutionis, quhilkis concernis το πρεπον in the Kirk, for decent ordour, in the particulare kirk quhair they governe; provyding that they alter na rewlis maid be the Provinciall or Generall Assemblies: And that they make the Provinciall Assemblies foirsaidis, privie of the rewlis that they sall mak, and to abolishe constitutionis tending to the hurte of the same. It has power to excommunicat the obstinat, formale proces being led, and dew intervall of tymes observit. ANENT particulare kirkis, Gif they be lauchfully rewlit be sufficient ministeris and sessioun, Thay haif power and jurisdictioun in their awin congregation, in materis Ecclesiasticall, And decernes and declaris the said Assembleis, Presbyteries, and Sessiounes, Jurisdictioun, and Discipline thairof foirsaid, to be in all tymes cuming maist just, gude, and godlie in theselff, Notwithstanding of quhatsumevir Statutis, Actis, Cannon, Civile, or municipall Lawes, maid in the contrair: To the quhilkis and every ane of thame, thir presentis sall mak expres derogatioun. And becaus thair ar divers Actis of Parliament, maid in favour of the Papistical Kirk, tending to the prejudice of the libertie of the trew Kirk of God, presentlie professit within this realme, jurisdictioun, and discipline thairof, Quhilk stands zit in the buikis of the Actis of Parliament, not abrogat nor annullit: Thairfoir his Hienes and Estaittis foirsaidis hes abrogat, cassit, and annullit, and be the tenor hierof, abrogatis, cassis, and annullis, all Actis of Parliament maid be ony of his Hienes predecessoris, for mantenance of superstitioun and idolatrie, with all and quhatsumevir Acts, Laws, and Statutes, maid at ony tyme, befair the day and dait hierof, aganis the libertie of the the trew Kirk, jurisdictioun, and discipline thairof, as the samyn is usit and exerceisit within this realme. And in speciall, that pairt of the sevint Act of Parliament halden at [*Streviling*, the fourt day of *November*, ane thousand four hundreth, fourty-three] zeiris, commanding obedience to be gevin to *Eugin*, the Pape for the tyme: the 109 Act made be King James the *third*, in his Parliament halden at *Edinburgh*, the twenty-fourth day of *Februar*, [the zeir of God] ane thousand, four hundreth, fourscor thrie zeirs. And all utheris actis quhairby the Papis authoritie is establishit. The fourty-seven Act of King James the *third*, in his Parliament halden at *Edinburgh*, the [twenty day of *November*, ane thousand, four hundreth, three-score nine] ziers, anent the Satterday and uther vigilis to be hally dayes from Evin sang to Evin sang. ITEM, that pairt of the thirty-one Act maid be the *Queene Regent*, in the Parliament halden at *Edinburgh*, the first day of *Februar*, ane thousand, five hundreth, fifty-ane zeirs, Geving speciall licence for haldin of *Pashe* and *Zule*. ITEM, the Kingis Majesty and Estatis foresaidis declaris, that the secund Act of the Parliament haldin at *Edinburgh*, the xxij day of Maij, the zier of God ane thousand, five hundreth, four scoir, four zeires, sall naways be prejudiciall, nor derogat any thing to the privilege that God hes givin to the spirituall office-beareris in the Kirk, concerning heads of religioun, materis of heresie, excommunicatioun, collation or deprivation of ministeris, or ony sik essential censours, speciall groundit, and havand warrand of the word of God. ITEM, Our said Soverane Lord, and Estattis of Parliament forsadis, abrogatis, cassis, and annulis the XX Act of the same Parliament, halden at *Edinburgh*, the said zeir, ane thousand, five hundreth, fourscoir, four zeires, granting commission to bischoppis and utheris juges, constitute in ecclesiasticall causes, to ressaue his Hienes presentatioun to benefices, to gif collatioun thairupon, and to put ordour in all causes ecclesiasticall: quhilk his Majesty and Estatis foresaidis declaris to be expyrit in the self, and to be null in tyme cuming, and of nane availl, force, nor effect. And thairfoir ordanis all presentationis to benefices, to be direct to the particular presbyteries, in all tyme cuming: with full power to thame to giff collationis thereupon; and to put ordour to all materis and causes ecclesiasticall, within thair boundis, according to the discipline of the Kirk: Providing the forsaidis presbyteries be bund and astrictit to ressaue and admitt quhatsumeuir qualifiet minister presentit be his Majestie, or uther laic patrounes.

Act 1592, *ch.* 117. *Unqualified persons being deprived, the Benefice vaikes, and the Patron not presentand, the right of Presentation pertaines to the Presbyterie, but prejudice of the tackes, set be the person deprived.*

Our Souerane Lord, Considering the great abuses quhilkis ar laitlie croppen in the Kirk, throw the misbehaviour of sik personis as ar providit to ecclesiasticall functionis: sic as personages and vicarages within any parrochin, and thairefter neglecting thair charge, ather levis thair cure, or ellis committis sik crymes, faultis, or enormities that they are fund worthy of the sentence of deprivatioun, ather befoir thair awin presbyterie, or ellis befoir the Sinodall and Generall Assemblies. Quhilk sentence is the less regardit be thame, Because, albeit they be deprivit of their functioun and cure within the Kirk: zit they thinke they may bruike lawfully the profites and rentes of their saidis benefices, enduring their lyfetymes, Notwithstanding the said sentence of deprivatioun: Thairfore, our Soverane Lord, with avice of the Estaitis of this present Parliament, declaris, that all and quhatsomevir sentence of deprivatioun, ather pronouncit already, or that happenis to be pronouncit hereafter, be ony Presbyterie, Synodall or General Assemblie, agains ony persone or vicare within their jurisdictioun, provydit sen his Hienes coronation: (All personis provydit to personages and vicarages, quha hes voit in Parliament, Secreit Council, and Sessioun, or providit thairto of auld, befoir the Kingis coronatioun, And Maister *George Young*, Archidene of *Sanct Androis*, being specially exceptit,) is and sal be repute in all jugementis, ane just cause to seclude the persone befoir, providit, and than deprivit from all profites, commodities, rentes, and deweties of the said personage and vicarage, or benefice of cure: And that ather be way of actioun, exception, or reply. And that the said sentence of deprivatioun sal be ane sufficient cause to mak the said benefice to vaike thereby. And the said sentence being extractit and presentit to the Patroun, the said Patroun sal be bund to present ane qualifiit persone of new to the Kirk, within the space of sex monethis thairefter. And gif he failzie to do the same, the said Patroun sal tyne the richt of presentation for that tyme allanerlie: And the richt of presentation to be devolvit in the handes of the Presbytery within the quhilk benefice lyes; to the effect that they may dispone the same, and gif collatioun thereof, to sik ane qualifiit persone as they sall think expedient. Providing allwayes, in caise the Presbytery refuises to admit ane qualifiit minister, presentit to thame be the Patroun, it sall be lauchful to the Patroun to retene the haill fruitis of the same benefice in his awin handes. And forder, his Hienes and Estatis foirsaides declaris, that the deprivatioun already pronouncit, or to be pronouncit, be ony Presbytery, Synodall or Generall Assemblies, agains ony of the personis or vicaris afoirsaid, sall nawayes hurte or be prejudiciall to ony tackes, lawchfullie set be that persone deprivit, befoir his deprivatioun, to quhatsumevir personis.

[It does not seem to be generally known, that the peculiarities of the act 1592, c. 116, are directly favourable to the Church in that very respect in which they have been thought unfavourable. No express mention is made of the Second Book of Discipline, but certain of its main topics are ratified, while others are apparently passed over. Hence it has been argued that nothing has been ratified to the Church but what is specifically mentioned in the act itself, and that every other topic in the Book of Discipline must be held to have been rejected. It has been shown by Mr. Dunlop what fatal confusion such a theory would introduce, and that, therefore, it cannot be admitted. But the true reason of this peculiarity in the act appears to be the following. It is well known that when the Second Book of Discipline was laid before the privy council, certain articles were at once ratified, and others were referred to further consideration. Now, on comparing the copy of the Book of Discipline in Spotswood, in which the marginal comments of the privy council are given, with the act 1592, it is remarkable that none of those marked "*agreed*" are contained in the act, while the chief of those marked "*referred*" are. From this the conclusion seems inevitable, that having already agreed to these in the privy council, and thereby ratified them, it was not necessary to specify any but those which had been left for future consideration, and consequently, that partly by the concurrence of the privy council, and partly by the act of 1592, thus combined, almost the whole of the Second Book of Discipline was ratified, and became the law of the land, as well as the law of the Church.

[In the year 1649, the Scottish parliament, when free from external control, and at liberty to legislate solely for the good of the country, and under the influence of a religious spirit, which taught them to respect the freedom and promote the purity of Christ's spiritual kingdom, passed the following important act:—]

Act of Parliament abolishing the Patronage of Kirks, at Edinburgh, March 9, 1649.

The Estates of Parliament being sensible of the great obligation that lies upon them by the National Covenant, and by the Solemn League and Covenant, and by many deliverances and mercies from God, and by the late Solemn Engagement unto Duties, to preserve the doctrine, and maintain and vindicate the liberties of the Kirk of Scotland, and to advance the work of reformation therein to the utmost of their power; and, considering that patronages and presentations of kirks is an evil and bondage, under which the Lord's people and ministers of this land have long groaned; and that it hath no warrant in God's Word, but is founded only on the canon law, and is a custom popish, and brought into the Kirk in time of ignorance and superstition; and that the same is contrary to the Second Book of Discipline, in which, upon solid and good ground, it is reckoned amongst abuses that are desired to be reformed, and unto several acts of General Assemblies; and that it is prejudicial to the liberty of the people and planting of kirks, and unto the free calling and entry of ministers unto their charge; and the said estates, being willing and desirous to promote and advance the Reformation foresaid, that every thing in the house of God may be ordered according to his word and commandment, do therefore, from the sense of the former obligations, and upon the former grounds and reasons, discharge for ever hereafter all patronages and presentations of kirks, whether belonging to the King, or to any laick patron, Presbyteries, or others within this kingdom, as being unlawful and unwarrantable by God's Word, and contrary to the doctrine and liberties of the Kirk; and do repeal, rescind, make void, and annul all gifts and rights granted thereanent, and all former acts made in Parliament, or in any inferior judicatory, in favours of any patron or patrons whatsoever, so far as the same doth or may relate unto the presentation of kirks; and do statute and ordain, that no person or persons whatsomever shall, at any time hereafter, take upon them, under pretext of any title, infeftment, act of Parliament, possession or warrant whatsoever, which are hereby repealed, to give, subscribe, or seal any presentation to any kirk, within this kingdom; and discharges the passing of any infeftment hereafter, bearing a right to patronages, to be granted in favours of those for whom the infeftments are presented; and that no person or persons shall, either in the behalf of themselves or others, procure, receive, or make use of any presentation to any kirk within this kingdom. And it is further declared and ordained, that if any presentation shall hereafter be given, procured, or received, that the same is null, and of none effect; and that it is lawful for Presbyteries to reject the same, and to refuse to admit any to trials thereupon; and, notwithstanding thereof, to proceed to the planting of the kirk, *upon the suit and calling, or with the consent of the congregation, on whom none is to be obtruded against their will.* And it is decerned, statuted, and ordained, that whosoever hereafter shall upon the suit and calling of the congregation, after due examination of their literature and conversation, be admitted by the Presbytery unto the exercise and functioun of the ministry, in any parish within this kingdom, that the said person or persons, without a presentation, by virtue of their admission, hath sufficient right and title to possess and enjoy the manse and glebe, and the whole rents, profits, and stipends, which the ministers of that parish had formerly possesst and enjoyed, or that hereafter shall be modified by the commission for plantation of kirks. . . . And because it is needful, that the just and proper interest of congregations and Presbyteries, in providing of Kirks and ministers be clearly determined by the General Assembly, and what is to be accounted the congregation having that interest; therefore, it is hereby seriously recommended unto the next General Assembly, clearly to determine the same, and to condescend upon a certain standing way for being a settled rule therein for all times coming.

[It is not necessary to insert the tyrannical acts passed in the reigns of Charles II. and James VII., as these are sufficiently specified in the body of the work, and necessarily perished at the period of the Revolution. The Revolution Settlement follows:—]

Act 1690, *ch.* 5. *Act Ratifying the Confession of Faith, and Settling Presbyterian Church Government.*

Our Sovereign Lord and Lady, the King and Queen's Majesties, and three Estates of Parliament, conceiving it to be their bound duty, after the great deliverance that God hath lately wrought for this Church and Kingdom,—in the first place, to settle and secure therein the true Protestant religion, according to the truth of God's Word, as it hath of a long time been professed within this land: As also the government of Christ's Church within this nation, agreeable to the Word of God, and most conducive to the advancement of true piety and godliness, and the establishing of peace and tranquility within this realme: And that, by an article of the Claim of Right, it is declared that Prelacy, and the superiority of any office in the Church above Presbyteries is, and hath been, a great and unsupportable grievance and trouble to this nation, and contrary to the inclinations of the generality of the people ever since the Reformation,—they having reformed from Popery by Presbyters,—and therefore ought to be abolished: Likeas, by an Act of the last Session of this Parliament Prelacy is abolished: Therefore their Majesties, with advice and consent of the said Three Estates, do hereby revive, ratifie, and perpetually confirm, all Laws, Statutes, and Acts of Parliament made against Popery and Papists, and for the maintenance and preservation of the true reformed Protestant religion, and for the true Church of Christ within this kingdom, in so far as they confirm the same, or are made in favours thereof. Likeas, they, by these presents, ratifie and establish the Confession of Faith, now read in their presence; and voted and approved by them, as the publick and avowed Confession of this Church, containing the sum and substance of the doctrine of the Reformed Churches, (which Confession of Faith is subjoined to this present Act.) As also they do establish, ratifie, and confirm the Presbyterian Church government and discipline; that is to say, the government of the Church by Kirk-Sessions, Presbyteries, Provincial Synods, and General Assemblies, ratified and established by the 114th Act, Ja. 6, Parl. 12, anno 1592, intituled, *Ratification of the Liberty of the true Kirk, &c.*, and thereafter received by the general consent of this nation, to be the only government of Christ's Church within this kingdom; reviving, renewing, and confirming the foresaid Act of Parliament, in the whole heads thereof, except that part of it relating to Patronages, which is hereafter to be taken into consideration: And rescinding, annulling, and making void the Acts of Parliament following, viz:—Act anent Restitution of Bishops, Ja. 6, Parl. 18, cap. 2.; Act Ratifying the Acts of Assembly 1610, Ja. 6, Parl. 21, cap. 1; Act anent the Election of Archbishops and Bishops, Ja. 6, Parl. 22, cap. 1; Act intituled, Ratification of the Five Articles of the General Assembly at Perth, Ja. 6, Parl. 23, cap. 1; Act intituled, For the Restitution and Re-establishment of the ancient Government of the Church by Archbishops and Bishops, ch. 2, Parl. 1, Sess. 2, Act 1; anent the constitution of a National Synod, ch. 2, Parl. 1. Sess. 3, Act 5; Act against such as refuse to depone against delinquents, ch. 2, Parl. 2, Sess. 2, Act 2; Act intituled, Act acknowleding and asserting the right of succession to the Imperial Crown of Scotland, ch. 2, Parl. 3, Act 2; Act intituled, Act anent Religion and the Test, ch. 2, Parl. 3, Act 6; with all other acts, laws, statutes, ordinances, and proclamations, and that in so far allenarly as the said Acts, and others generally and particularly above-mentioned, or contrary or prejudicial to, inconsistent with, or derogatory from the Protestant religion and Presbyterian government now established; and allowing and declaring that the church government be established in the hands of, and exercised by, these Presbyterian ministers who were outed since the 1st of January 1661, for non-conformity to Prelacy, or not complying with the courses of the times; and are now restored by the late Act of Parliament, and such ministers and elders only as they have admitted or received, or shall hereafter admit or receive: And also, that all the said Presbyterian ministers have, and shall have right to the maintenance, rights, and other privileges, by law provided to the ministers of Christ's Church within this kingdom, as they are, or shall be, legally admitted to particular churches. Likeas, in pursuance of the premises, their Majesties do hereby appoint the first meeting of the General Assembly of this Church, as above established, to be at Edinburgh, the third Thursday of October next to come, in this instant year, 1690. And because many conform ministers either have deserted, or were removed from preaching in their churches, preceding the thirteenth day of April 1689, and others were deprived for not giving obedience to the Act of the Estates made in the said thirteenth of April 1689, intituled, Proclamation against the owning of the late King James, and appointing publick prayers for King William and Queen Mary: Therefore their Majesties, with advice and consent foresaid, do hereby declare all the churches, either deserted, or from which the conform ministers were removed or deprived, as said is, to be vacant; and that the Presbyterian ministers exercising their ministry within any of these paroches (or where the last incumbent is dead), by the desire or consent of the paroch, shall continue their possession, and have right to the benefices and stipends, according to their entry in the year 1689, and in time coming, ay, and while the Church, as now established, take further course therewith. And to the effect the disorders that have happened in this Church may be redressed, their Majesties, with advice and consent foresaid, do hereby allow the general meeting, and representatives of the foresaid Presbyterian ministers and elders, in whose hands the exercise of the Church government is established, either by themselves, or by such ministers and elders as shall be appointed and authorised visitors by them, according to the custom and practice of Presbyterian government throughout the whole kingdom, and several parts thereof, to try and purge out all insufficient, negligent, scandalous, and erroneous ministers, by due course of ecclesiastical process and censures; and, likewise, for redressing all other Church disorders. And further, it is hereby provided, that whatsoever minister, being convened before the said general meeting and representatives of the Presbyterian ministers and elders, or the visitors to be appointed by them, shall either prove contumacious in not appearing, or be found guilty, and shall be therefore censured, whether by suspension or deposition, they shall *ipso facto* be suspended from or deprived of their stipends and benefices.

Act 1690, *ch.* 23. *Act concerning Patronages.*

Our Sovereign Lord and Lady, the King and Queen's Majesties, considering, that the power of presenting ministers to vacant churches, of late exercised by patrons, hath been greatly abused, and is inconvenient to be continued in this realm, do therefore, with the advice and consent of the Estates of Parliament, hereby discharge, cass, annul, and make void the foresaid power, heretofore exercised by any patron, of presenting ministers to any kirk now vacant, or that shall hereafter happen to vaik within this kingdom, with all exercise of the said power: And also all rights, gifts, and infeftments, acts, statutes, and customs, in so far as they may be extended, or understood, to establish the said right of presentation; but prejudice always, of such ministers as are duly entered by the foresaid presentations (while in use), their right to the manse, glebe, benefice, stipend, and other profits of their respective churches, as accords: And but prejudice to the patrons of their right to employ the vacant stipends on pious uses, within the respective paroches, except where the patron is popish, in which case is to employ the same on pious uses, by the advice and appointment of the Presbytery; and in case the patron shall fail in applying the vacant stipend for the uses foresaid, that he shall lose his right of administration of the vacant stipend for that and the next vacancy, and the same shall be disposed on by the Presbytery to the uses foresaid; excepting always the vacant stipends within the bounds of the Synod of Argyle: And to the effect, the calling and entering ministers, in all time coming, may be orderly and regularly performed, their Majesties, with consent of the Estates of Parliament, do statute and declare, That, in case of the vacancy of any particular church, and for supplying the same with a minister, the heritors of the said parish (being Protestants) and the elders are to name and propose the person to the whole congregation, to be either approven or disapproven by them; and if they disapprove, that the disapprovers give in their reasons, to the effect the affair may be cognosced upon by the Presbytery of the bounds, at whose judgment, and by whose determination, the calling and entry of a particular minister is to be ordered and concluded. And it is hereby enacted, that if application be not made by the eldership, and heritors of the paroch, to the Presbytery, for the call and choice of a minister, within the space of six months after the vacancy, that then the Presbytery may proceed to provide the said parish, and plant a minister in the church, *tanquam jure devoluto*. It is always hereby declared, that this act shall be but prejudice of the calling of ministers to royal burghs by the Magistrates, Town-Council, and Kirk-Session of the burgh, where there is no landward parish, as they have been in use before the year 1660. And where there is a considerable part of the paroch in landward, that the call shall be by Magistrates, Town-Council, Kirk-Session, and the heritors of the landward paroch. And in lieu and recompense of the said right of presentation, hereby taken away, their Majesties, with advice and consent aforesaid, statute and ordain the heritors and liferenters of each paroch, and the Town-Councils for the burgh, to pay the said patrons, betwixt and Martinmas next, the sum of six hundred merks, &c., &c.

[The circumstances connected with the act 1693, and the objects it was intended to subserve, have been already mentioned in the body of the work, see pp. 309, 310.]

Act 1693. *Act for Settling the Quiet and Peace of the Church.*

Our Sovereign Lord and Lady, the King and Queen's Majesties, with advice and consent of the Estates of Parliament, ratifie, approve, and perpetually confirm the fifth act of the second session of this current parliament, entitled, Act ratifying the Confession of Faith, and settling Presbyterian Church Government, in the whole Heads, Articles, and Clauses thereof; and do further statute and ordain, that no person be admitted, or continued for hereafter, to be a minister or preacher within this Church, unless that he having first taken and subscribed the oath of allegiance, and subscribed the assurance, in manner appointed by another act of this present session of parliament, made thereanent: Do also subscribe the Confession of Faith, ratified in the foresaid fifth act of the second session of this parliament, declaring the same to be the confession of his faith, and that he owns the doctrine therein contained to be the true doctrine which he will constantly adhere to: As, likewise, that he owns and acknowledges Presbyterian Church government, as settled by the foresaid fifth act of the second session of this parliament, to be the only government of this Church, and that he will submit thereto, and concur therewith, and never endeavour, directly or indirectly, the prejudice or subversion thereof. And their Majesties, with advice and consent foresaid, statute and ordain, that uniformity of worship, and of the administration of all public ordinances within this Church, be observed by all the saids ministers and preachers as the same are at present performed and allowed therein, or shall be hereafter declared by the authority of the same; and that no minister or preacher be admitted or continued for hereafter, unless that he subscribe to observe, and do actually observe, the foresaid uniformity: And for the more effectual settling the quiet and peace of this church, the estates of parliament do hereby make a humble address to their Majesties, that they would be pleased to call a General Assembly, for the ordering the affairs of the Church, and to the end that all the present ministers possessing churches, not yet admitted to the exercise of the foresaid Church government, conform to the said Act, and who shall qualify themselves in manner foresaid, and shall apply to the said Assembly, or the other Church judicatures competent, in an orderly way, each man for himself, be received to partake with them in the government thereof: Certifying such as shall not qualify themselves, and apply to the said Assembly, or other judicatures, within the space of thirty days after meeting of the said first Assembly, in manner foresaid, that they may be deposed by the sentence of the said Assembly and other judicatures *tam ob officio quam a beneficio* (as from the office, so also from the benefice); and withal declaring, that if any of the said ministers who have not hitherto been received into the government of the Church, shall offer to qualify themselves, and to apply in manner foresaid, they shall have their Majesties' full protection, aye and until they shall be admitted and received in manner foresaid; providing always that this Act, and the benefit thereof, shall no ways be extended to such of the said ministers as are scandalous, erroneous, negligent, or insufficient, and against whom the same shall be verified, within the space of thirty days after the said application: but these and all others in like manner guilty, are hereby declared to be liable and subject to the power and censure of the

Church, as accords: And to the effect that the representation of this Church, in its General Assemblies, may be the more equal in all time coming, recommends it to the first Assembly that shall be called, to appoint ministers to be sent as Commissioners from every Presbytery, not in equal numbers, which is manifestly unequal where Presbyteries are so; but in due proportion to the churches and parishes within every Presbytery, as they shall judge convenient; and it is hereby declared, that all school-masters, and teachers of youth in schools, are and shall be liable to the trial, judgment, and censure of the Presbyteries of the bounds, for their sufficiency, qualifications, and deportment in the said office. And lastly, their Majesties, with advice and consent foresaid, do hereby statute and ordain, that the Lords of their Majesties' privy council, and all other magistrates, judges, and officers of justice, give all due assistance for making the sentences and censures of the Church and judicatures thereof to be obeyed, or otherwise effectual, as accords.

[The circumstances preceding and accompanying the Treaty of Union have been already related in the body of the work: no more is necessary than to insert here the Act of Security :—]

Act for Securing the Protestant Religion and Presbyterian Church Government, which was the basis of the Treaty of Union, at Edinburgh, January 16, 1707.

Our Sovereign Lady, and the Estates of Parliament, considering, That by the late Act of Parliament for a treaty with England, for an union of both kingdoms, it is provided, that the commissioners for that treaty should not treat of or concerning any alteration of the worship, discipline, and government of the Church in this kingdom as now by law established: which treaty being now reported to the Parliament, and it being reasonable and necessary that, *the true Protestant religion, as presently professed within this kingdom, with the worship, discipline, and government of this Church, should be effectually and unalterably secured*, therefore, her Majesty, with advice and consent of the said Estates of Parliament, do thereby establish and confirm the said true Protestant religion, and the worship, discipline, and government of this Church, to continue without any alteration to the people of this land in all succeeding generations: and more especially, her Majesty, with advice and consent aforesaid, ratifies, approves, and for ever confirms the fifth act of the first Parliament of King William and Queen Mary, entitled, "An Act ratifying the Confession of Faith, and settling Presbyterian Church Government, with the hail other Acts of Parliament relating thereto, in prosecution of the declaration of the estates of this kingdom, containing the Claim of Right, bearing date the 11th of April 1689." And her Majesty, with advice and consent aforesaid, expressly provides and declares, that the foresaid true Protestant religion, contained in the above mentioned Confession of Faith, with the form and purity of worship presently in use within this Church, and its Presbyterian church government and discipline; that is to say, the government of the Church by Kirk-Sessions Presbyteries, Provincial Synods, and General Assembly, all established by the foresaid acts of Parliament, pursuant to the Claim of Right, *shall remain and continue unalterable; and that the said Presbyterian government shall be the only government of the Church within the kingdom of Scotland.*

And further, for the greater security of the foresaid Protestant religion, and of the worship, discipline, and government of this Church, as above established, her Majesty, with advice and consent foresaid, statutes and ordains, That the universities and colleges of St. Andrews, Glasgow, Aberdeen, and Edinburgh, as now established by law, shall continue within this kingdom for ever: and that in all time coming, no professors, principals, regents, masters, or others, bearing office in any university, college, or school, within this kingdom, be capable, or admitted, or allowed to continue in the exercise of their said functions, but such as shall own and acknowledge the civil government in manner prescribed, or to be prescribed by the acts of Parliament: as also, that before or at their admissions, they do and shall acknowledge, and profess, and shall subscribe to the foresaid Confession of Faith, as the confession of their faith; and that they will practise and conform themselves to the worship presently in use in this Church, and submit themselves to the government and discipline thereof; and never endeavour, directly or indirectly, the prejudice or subversion of the same; and that before the respective Presbyteries of their bounds, by whatsomever gift, presentation, or provision they may be thereto provided.

And further, her Majesty, with advice foresaid, expressly declares and statutes, that none of the subjects of this kingdom shall be liable to, but all and every one of them, for ever free of, any oath, test, or subscription within this kingdom, contrary to or inconsistent with the foresaid true Protestant religion, and Presbyterian church government, worship, and discipline, as above established: and that the same within the bounds of this Church and kingdom, shall never be imposed upon or required of them in any sort.

And lastly, that after the decease of her present Majesty (whom God long preserve), the sovereign succeeding to her in the royal government of the kingdom of Great Britain, shall in all time coming at his or her accession to the crown, swear and subscribe, that they shall inviolably maintain and preserve the foresaid settlement of the true Protestant religion, with the government, worship, discipline, rights and privileges of this Church, as above established by by the laws of this kingdom, in prosecution of the Claim of Right: *and it is hereby statute and ordained, that this act of Parliament, with the establishment therein contained, shall be held and observed in all time coming, as a fundamental and essential condition of any treaty or union to be concluded betwixt the two kingdoms, without any alteration thereof, or derogation thereto, in any sort for ever: as also, that this act of Parliament, and settlement therein contained, shall be insert and repeated in any act of Parliament that shall pass for agreeing and concluding the foresaid treaty or union betwixt the two kingdoms; and that the same shall be therein expressly declared to be a fundamental and essential condition of the said treaty or union in all time coming.*

Act Ratifying and Approving the Treaty of Union of the two Kingdoms of Scotland and England, January 16, 1707, *founded on the foresaid Act of Security.*

The Estates of Parliament considering that Articles of Union of the kingdoms of Scotland and England were agreed on the 22d of July 1706 years, &c. * * * and sicklike, her Majesty, with advice and consent of the Estates of Parliament, resolving to establish the Protestant religion and Presbyterian church government, has passed in this session of Parliament an "Act for securing of the Protestant Religion and Presbyterian Church Government," which, by the tenor thereof, is appointed to be insert in any act ratifying the treaty, and expressly declared to be a fundamental and essential condition of the said treaty of union in all time coming, &c.

[After embodying the Act of Security, the document proceeds as follows:—]

Which Articles of Union, and act immediately above written, her Majesty, with advice and consent aforesaid, statutes, enacts, and ordains to be and continue in all time coming the sure and perpetual foundation of a complete and entire union of the two kingdoms of Scotland and England, under the express condition and provision, That this approbation and ratification of the foresaid articles and act shall be noways binding on this kingdom, until the said articles and act be ratified, approved, and confirmed by her Majesty, with and by the authority of the Parliament of England, as they are, now agreed to, approved and confirmed by her Majesty, with and by the authority of the Parliament of Scotland. Declaring nevertheless, That the Parliament of England may provide for the security of the Church of England, as they think it expedient, to take place within the bounds of the said kingdom of England, and not derogating from the security above provided for establishing of the Church of Scotland within the bounds of this kingdom. As also, the said Parliament of England may extend the additions and other provisions contained in the Articles of Union, as above insert, in favours of the subjects of Scotland, to and in favours of the subjects of England, which shall not suspend or derogate from the force and effect of this present ratification, but shall be understood as herein included, without the necessity of any new ratification in the Parliament of Scotland. And lastly, *her Majesty enacts and declares, That all laws and statutes in this kingdom, so far as they are contrary to, or inconsistent with, the terms of these articles, as above mentioned, shall from and after the Union cease and become void.*

[The insertion of the perfidious act of Queen Anne's Jacobite ministry, immediately after the Revolution Settlement and the Act of Security, is enough to show how completely the Patronage Act is a violation of national faith, and contrary to the inviolable Act of Security.]

Act 10, *Q. Anne, ch.* 12, 1711. *An Act to restore the Patrons to their ancient Rights of presenting Ministers to the Churches vacant in that part of Great Britain called Scotland.*

I. Whereas, by the antient laws and constitutions of that part of Great Britain called Scotland, the presenting of ministers to vacant churches did of right belong to the patrons, until, by the twenty-third Act of the second session of the first Parliament of the late King William and Queen Mary, held in the year one thousand six hundred and ninety, intituled, "Act concerning Patronages," the presentation was taken from the patrons, and given to the heritors and elders of the respective parishes; and, in place of the right of presentation, the heritors and liferenters of every parish were to pay to the respective patrons a small and inconsiderable sum of money, for which the patrons were to renounce their right of presentation in all times thereafter: And whereas by the fifteenth act of the fifth session, and by the thirteenth act of the sixth session, of the first Parliament of the said King William, the one intituled "An Act for encouraging of Preachers at vacant Churches benorth Forth," and the other intituled, "Act in favour of Preachers benorth Forth;" there are several burdens imposed upon vacant stipends, to the prejudice of the patron's right of disposing thereof: And whereas that way of calling ministers has proved inconvenient, and has not only occasioned great heats and divisions among those who, by the aforesaid act, were entitled and authorised to call ministers, but likewise has been a great hardship upon the patrons, whose predecessors had founded and endowed those churches, and who had not received payment or satisfaction for their right of patronage from the aforesaid heritors or liferenters of the respective parishes, nor have granted renunciations of their said rights on that account: Be it therefore enacted, by the Queen's most excellent Majesty, by and with the advice and consent of the Lords spiritual and temporal, and Commons, in this present Parliament assembled, and by the authority of the same, that the aforesaid act, made in the year one thousand six hundred and ninety, intituled, "Act concerning Patronages," in so far as the same relates to the presentation of ministers by heritors and others therein mentioned, be, and is hereby repealed and made void; and that the aforesaid fifteenth act of the fifth session, and thirteenth act of the sixth session, of the first Parliament of King William, be, and are hereby likewise repealed and made void: and that in all time coming, the right of all and every patron or patrons to the presentation of ministers to churches and benefices, and the disposing of the vacant stipends for pious uses within the parish, be restored, settled, and confirmed to them, the aforesaid acts, or any other act, statute, or custom to the contrary in any wise notwithstanding; and that from and after the first day of May one thousand seven hundred and twelve, it shall and may be lawful for her Majesty, her heirs and successors, and for every other person or persons who have right to any patronage or patronages of any church or churches whatsoever, in that part of Great Britain called Scotland (and who have not made and subscribed a formal renunciation thereof under their hands), to present a qualified minister or ministers to any church or churches whereof they are patrons, which shall, after the first day of May, happen to be vacant; and the Presbytery of the respective bounds shall, and is hereby obliged to receive and admit, in the same manner such qualified person or persons, minister or ministers, as shall be presented by the respective patrons, as the persons or ministers presented before the making of this act ought to have been admitted.

II. Provided always, that in case any patron or patrons have accepted of and received any sum or sums of money from the heritors or liferenters of any parish, or from the Magistrates or Town Council of any borough, in satisfaction of their right of presensation, and have discharged or renounced the same under their hand, that nothing herein shall be construed to restore such patron or patrons to their right of presentation; any thing in this present act to the contrary notwithstanding.

III. Provided also, and it is hereby enacted, by the authority aforesaid, that in case the patron of any church aforesaid shall neglect or refuse to present any qualified minister to such church that shall be vacant the said first day of May, or shall happen to be vacant at any time thereafter, for the space of six months after the said first day of May, or after such vacancy shall happen, that the right of presentation shall accrue and belong for that time to the Presbytery of the bounds where such church is, who are to present a qualified person for that vacancy, *tanquam jure devoluto*.

IV. And be it further enacted and declared by the authority aforesaid, that the patronage and right of presentations of ministers to all churches which belonged to archbishops, bishops, or other dignified persons, in the year one thousand six hundred and eighty-nine, before Episcopacy was abolished, as well as those which formerly belonged to the Crown, shall and do of right belong to her Majesty, her heirs and successors, who may present qualified ministers to such church or churches, and dispose of the vacant stipends thereof for pious uses, in the same way and manner as her Majesty, her heirs and successors, may do in the case of other patronages belonging to the Crown.

V. Declaring always, that nothing in this present act contained shall extend, or be construed to extend, to repeal and make void the aforesaid twenty-third act of the second session of the first parliament of the late King William and Queen Mary, excepting so far as relates to the calling and presenting of ministers, and to the disposing of vacant stipends, in prejudice of the patrons only.

[Although no real benefit arose from the Act 1719, yet it may be inserted to show, that in a purer and more faithful state of the Church it might have been of some avail.]

Excerpt from Act 5th, Geo. I. cap. 29, 1719, entitled "An Act for making more effectual the Laws appointing the Oaths for Security of the Government, to be taken by Ministers and Preachers in Churches and Meeting-houses in Scotland."

VIII. And whereas great obstructions have been made to the planting, supplying, or filling up of vacant churches in Scotland, with ministers qualified according to law, patrons presenting persons to churches who are not qualified, by taking the oatns appointed by law, or who, being settled in other churches, cannot or will not accept of such presentations: To the end that such inconveniences may be prevented for the future, be it enacted by the authority aforesaid, that if any patron shall present any person to a vacant church, from and after the first day of June, one thousand seven hundred and nineteen, who shall not be qualified by taking and subscribing the said oath in manner aforesaid, or shall present a person to any vacancy who is then or shall be pastor or minister of any other church or parish, or any person who shall not accept, or declare his willingness to accept, of the presentation and charge to which he is presented, within the said time, such presentation shall not be accounted any interruption of the course of time allowed to the patron for presenting; but the *jus devolutum* shall take place, as if no presentation had been offered: any law or custom to the contrary notwithstanding.

IX. And be it also further declared and enacted, that nothing herein contained shall prejudice or diminish the right of the Church, as the same now stands by law established, as to the trying of the qualities of any person presented to any church or benefice.

Excerpt from Act 4 and 5 William IV. c. 41.

Be it enacted, &c., that where any church, chapel, or other place of worship, in that part of Great Britain called Scotland, built or acquired and endowed by voluntary contribution, shall be erected into a parochial church, either as an additional church within a parish already provided with a parochial church, or as the church of a separate parish to be erected out of the part or parts of any existing parish or parishes, whether the same be established and erected *quoad spiritualia*, by authority of the church courts of the Established Church of Scotland, or also *quoad temporalia*, by authority of the Commissioners of Teinds, neither the King's Majesty, nor any private person, nor any body politic or corporate, having right to the patronage of the parish or parishes within which such additional churches shall be established, or out of which such new parishes shall be erected, shall have any claim, right, or title whatsoever, to the patronage of such newly established churches, or newly erected parishes; but the right of presenting ministers thereto shall be exercised according to the manner, and subject to the conditions, which shall be provided or sanctioned by the church courts establishing the said churches, or where new parishes shall be erected, as shall be prescribed and regulated by the said church courts erecting such new parishes into separate spiritual jurisdictions, subject always to such alterations as shall be made by the said courts, according to the laws of the Church from time to time.

[The object of this act was to relieve new churches from a peculiar operation of the Patronage Act, which had proved a great obstacle to their erection. It had been found, as in the case of Whitburn, for example, that when a church had been built and endowed by voluntary contribution, and a district assigned to it as a new parish, the patron of the original parish might seize upon the patronage of the new erection, even though there had been inserted into its constitution an article expressly excluding patronage, and restoring the original principle of popular election. The people would not build churches to be immediately seized by patrons, who, following the usual policy of patronage without its usual fallacious plea, usurped a supremacy where they could not even pretend a patrimonial right. The above act put an end to all such usurpation, and tended greatly to promote the great Church Extension scheme of the reforming and reviving Church of Scotland. But Moderate policy, hating these new churches because they were popular and evangelical, and free from patronage, devised methods to crush them if possible. The legality of the admission into church courts of the ministers of such churches has been strenuously denied, and protested against; yet with strange inconsistency the Moderate party placed one of these ministers in the moderator's chair. In some instances the heritors have claimed the collections made at the doors of these new churches, as belonging to the parochial funds for the support of the poor, and the Court of Session has sanctioned the unjust claim, with the perfect certainty that the attempt to enforce it would put an end to the collections, without any benefit to the heritors. In other instances the heritors have applied to the Court of Session for an interdict to prevent the Presbytery of the bounds where a new church had been erected, from assigning to it a parochial district *quoad spiritualia*, and have obtained the interdict, on the strange plea, that every man in the original parish had a right to the religious services of the parish minister, and that, therefore, to give him the additional services of another, was *an illegal interference with his civil rights!* But the most formidable aspect which the fierce hostility of Moderatism against the new churches has assumed, is that which asserts that church courts are so completely vitiated by the admission of their ministers, that no measure in which they have taken a part is legal and valid. This, too, the Court of Session has sanctioned, notwithstanding the legislative recognition of these churches in the above act of parliament, by granting interdicts to prevent the execution of sentences of deposition pronounced by Presbyteries, Synods, and the General Assembly itself, in the case of ministers convicted of heresy and theft, expressly on the ground that these sentences are invalid because pronounced by church courts in which ministers of new churches and *quoad sacra* parishes deliberated and acted as constituent members. If this decision of the civil could be carried into full effect, it would be equivalent to a new act Rescissory, as it would nullify the whole judicial procedure of the Church of Scotland since the year 1834. In this, doubtless, Moderatism would rejoice, but for one consideration : not a few Moderate ministers would immediately lose all legal claim to their stipends, their ordination and induction being rendered void, as the illegal act of a vitiated church court. They will, therefore, probably adhere to their latest policy, and strive to procure the ejection of the whole Evangelical party, that they may themselves enjoy the civil emoluments of the Church, so long as the righteous retribution of Providence will permit, till their cup is full. *Quos Deus vult perdere, prius dementat.*]

No. III.

PRINCIPLES, ACTS, AND RESOLUTIONS OF THE CHURCH OF SCOTLAND, RESPECTING THE APPOINTMENT OF MINISTERS AND PATRONAGE.

The principles of the Church of Scotland with regard to the proper method of appointing ministers to the pastoral office have been much misrepresented, and yet it appears absolutely impossible for any candid and unprejudiced person to read her standards and acts of Assembly, and to mark her general procedure, without clearly perceiving that patronage is essentially contrary to the spirit, the fundamental principles, and the constitution, of the Presbyterian Church of Scotland. There is not the slightest doubt that kings, governments, politicians, and worldly-minded men in general, whether without the Church or within it, have always striven to enact or to enforce patronage because they expected through its influence to render the Church subservient to their purposes as a mere political engine; but the true subject of inquiry is, *not* what rulers and politicians have always striven to effect,—that would only be an inquiry into *their* opinions, about which there is no doubt,—but what the Church has always declared, maintained in theory, and striven to realize in practice, as the scriptural, and therefore the best, method of appointing ministers to the pastoral office.

Beginning with the great and sacred principle, "That the Lord Jesus Christ is the only Head and King of the Church," the Presbyterian Church holds as self-evident, that the appointment of office-bearers in his spiritual kingdom must necessarily belong exclusively to its Divine King, and be regulated solely by his precepts and commands, either as given in his own words, or as embodied in the proceedings of his inspired Apostles. Applying to the Scriptures to ascertain from them the mind and will of the King of Zion in this matter, it is found, that He distinctly declares the responsibility of his people in the exercise of their private judgment what pastor they are to hear and follow. The Apostles use similar but still more explicit language, and in the few instances of the appointment of office-bearers which are recorded in the Scriptures, this at least is evident, that they were either directly chosen by the people themselves, or with their consent and approval. Hence the principle, that there cannot be a scriptural appointment to the pastoral office without the consent and approval of the Christian people, that is, of those who compose the true flock, having been admitted to the privileges of Christian communion, and thereby made citizens of Zion and members of Christ's spiritual body, the Church, of which He is the only Head. But this principle may come into operation in either of two different ways,—either by the Christian flock directly choosing their own pastor, or by expressing their consent, approval of, and willingness to receive in that relation the person offered to them. The first of these modes the Church of Scotland has always regarded as the best, because the most scriptural, natural, and direct; but when that could not be obtained, she has been willing to act upon the second, because not unscriptural, and capable, if properly administered, of securing the important objects in view, namely, the affectionate regard and confidence of the Christian people, and the appointment of an equally acceptable and efficient ministry, whom the Lord might bless in their labours for the extension of his kingdom and the edification of his people. And because the Church has believed that either of these methods of appointing ministers might be employed, though preferring the former, she has in different periods employed the one or the other, according to the force of circumstances; from which has arisen the varying aspects which this great principle has from time to time assumed; but never has she abandoned the principle itself, and never can she abandon it without ceasing to be the Presbyterian Church of Scotland, or rather, without ceasing to be a Christian Church, and becoming a mere secular institution.

A few extracts will show the truth of the preceding statement.

FIRST BOOK OF DISCIPLINE,

Drawn up by John Knox and others immediately after the Reformation in 1560.

"It appertaineth to the people, and to every several congregation to elect their minister." (*First Book of Discipline*, Fourth Head, chap. iv. sect. 2.)

"For altogether this is to be avoided, that any man be violently intruded or thrust in upon any congregation; but this liberty with all care must be reserved to every several church, to have their votes and suffrages in election of their ministers." (*Ibid*., sect. 4.)

"The admission of ministers to their offices must consist in [the] consent of the people and church whereto they shall be appointed, and approbation of the learned ministers appointed for their examination." (*Ibid*., chap. iv. sect. 8.)

SECOND BOOK OF DISCIPLINE,

Drawn up by Andrew Melville and others, and approved of by the Church of Scotland as one of her Standards, 1581.

"This ordinary and outward calling has two parts—election and ordination. Election is the choosing out of a person or persons, most able for the office that vaikes, by the judgment of the eldership, and consent of the congregation to whom the person or persons are appointed. * * * In this ordinary election it is to be eschewed that any person be intruded into any of the offices of the kirk contrary to the will of the congregation to which they are appointed, or without the voice of the eldership." (*Second Book of Discipline*, chap. iii. sect. 4, 5.)

"The liberty of the election of persons called to the ecclesiastical functions, and observed without interruption, so long as the Kirk was not corrupted by antichrist, we desired to be restored and retained within this realm; so that none be intruded upon any congregation, either by the prince or any inferior person, without lawful election, and the assent of the people over whom the person is placed,—as the practice of the apostolic and primitive Kirk, and good order, crave.

"And because this order, which God's Word craves, cannot stand with patronages and presentations to benefices used in the Pope's Kirk, we desire all them that truly fear God, earnestly to consider, that forasmuch as the names of patronages and benefices, together with the effect thereof, have flowed from the Pope and corruption of the canon law only, in so far as thereby any person was introduced or placed over kirks having *curam animarum;* and forasmuch as that manner of proceeding hath no ground in the Word of God, but is contrary to the same, and to the said liberty of election, they ought not now to have place in this light of reformation; and, therefore, whosoever will embrace God's Word, and desire the kingdom of his Son, Christ Jesus, to be advanced, they will also embrace that policy and order which the Word of God and upright estate of this Kirk crave; otherwise it is in vain that they have professed the same." (*Ibid*., chap. xii. pars. 9, 10.)

It will be observed that the language of the Second Book of Discipline varies a little from that of the First, chiefly in the precedence which it seems to give to "the judgment of the eldership," or Presbytery, in the election of ministers. The very slightest acquaintance with the history of the period is sufficient to explain that apparent difference. The people of Scotland were at that period little better than serfs and bondmen; the Presbyterian Church had indeed struck off the fetters and broken the yoke of Popery, and given them religious liberty; but they were still groaning beneath an oppressive civil despotism. The Church of Scotland, on the other hand, had obtained the sanction of the legislature to its principles so far, that it was rather perilous for the king to assail its recognised liberties, which his own hand had ratified. Holding fast her own principle, that the Christian people have a sacred right to the choice of their pastor, the Church adopted the generous part of placing herself in the front of the conflict, throwing over the people the shield of her own admitted rights and privileges, and encountering the royal despot's hostility, that she might secure to the Redeemer's flock that liberty wherewith he had made them free. At that time every article of religious freedom which was gained by the office-bearers of the Church, was gained for the people composing, with the office-bearers, the Church; and nothing in the whole conduct of our Scotish Reformers gives even the least ground of credibility to the strange assertion of Moderatism, that the sole object for which our reforming ancestors were then contending, was the acquisition of ecclesiastical power to Church Courts, regardless of the people. This, indeed, is the system of Moderatism, but not that of the true Church of Scotland.

In the year 1582, the General Assembly passed an act complaining of the "ambition, covetousness, and indirect dealing of sundry" who went about to enter into the ministry by corrupt collusion with patrons, and being in, employed unlawful means to avoid correction and punishment for their offences,—"seeking by the civil power to exempt and withdraw themselves from the jurisdiction of the Kirk,"—"and procuring letters or charges to impair, hurt, or stay the said jurisdiction." Such conduct was forbidden under the pain of excommunication; but to avoid any unnecessary collision with the civil power, it is added, "and this act to be no ways prejudicial to the laic patrons and their presentations, *unto the time the laws be reformed according to God's Word.*" Nothing could more clearly prove, that our reformers did not consider patronage to be according to God's Word.

When, in the year 1588, King James was busily prosecuting his weak and sinful policy of bestowing Church property upon his unworthy favourites, erecting titular lordships, and annexing patronages to the lands which had been wrongfully seized and wickedly gifted to wicked men, nay, giving in some instances the naked patronage without any lands, the General Assembly passed an act, complaining of this procedure, remonstrating with his Majesty, and finally "inhibiting in the mean time all Commissioners and Presbyteries, that they on no ways give collation or admission to any persons presented by said new patrons, as is above specified, unto the next General Assembly." This is a clear proof, that these new patronages were not at the time, and never since have been, recognised by the Church of Scotland as lawful and valid, but complained against as unlawful, and condemned as invalid; and be it remembered, that four-fifths of the whole patronages in Scotland were thus illegally and tyrannically created. The Church was spoiled of her own patrimony,—that property was given to the King's unworthy minions,—and then the patronage was added in virtue of the pillage which these men had received.

The last faithful Assembly, as Calderwood terms that of 1596, being well aware that there remained many abuses still to be reformed, and being desirous to reform the Church first, appointed a Committee to point out these abuses. In stating the corruptions in the office of the ministry, the following specification is made. "Thirdly, Because, by presentations, many forcibly are thrust into the ministry, and upon congregations, that utter thereafter that they were not called by God, it would be provided, that none seek presentations to benefices without advice of the Presbytery within the bounds whereof the benefice lies, and if any do in the contrary, they are to be repelled, as *rei ambitus*,"—that is, guilty of attempting to procure the office by corrupt means.

At the era of the Second Reformation, 1638, the famous Assembly of that date passed an act "anent the presenting of either pastors, or readers, and school-masters, to particular congregations," in these words: "That there be respect had to the congregation, and that no person be intruded in any office of the Kirk contrary to the will of the congregation to which they are appointed. The Assembly alloweth this article."

Several modifications of patronage took place during the intervening period between the Glasgow Assembly and the year 1649, when the Scottish parliament passed an act abolishing patronage altogether, recommending the next General Assembly to provide and enact a standing rule for the appointment of ministers. This was done at the next meeting of Assembly, on the 4th of August 1649, and is as follows:—

Directory for the Election of Ministers.

"When any place of the ministry in a congregation is vacant, it is incumbent to the Presbytery with all diligence to send one of their number to preach to that congregation, who, in his doctrine, is to represent to them the necessity of providing the place with a qualified pastor; and to exhort them to fervent prayer and supplication to the Lord, that he would send them a pastor according to his own heart; as also he is to signify, that the Presbytery, out of their care of that flock, will send unto them preachers whom they may hear; and if they have a desire to hear any other, they will endeavour to procure them a hearing of that person, or persons, upon the suit of the elders to the Presbytery.

"Within some competent time thereafter, the Presbytery is again to send one or more of their number to the said vacant congregation, on a certain day appointed before for that effect, who are to convene and hear sermon the foresaid day; which being ended, and intimation being made by the minister, that they are to go about the election of a pastor for that congregation, the Session of the congregation shall meet and proceed to the election, the action being moderated by him that preached; and if the people shall, upon the intimation of the person agreed upon by the Session, acquiesce and consent to the said person, that the matter being reported to the Presbytery by commissioners sent from the Session, they are to proceed to the trial of the person thus elected; and finding him qualified, to admit him to the ministry in the said congregation.

"But if it happen that the major part of the congregation dissent from the person agreed upon by the Session, in that case the matter shall be brought unto the Presbytery, who shall judge of the same; and if they do not find their dissent to be grounded on causeless prejudice, they are to appoint a new election, in manner above specified.

"But if a lesser part of the Session or congregation show their dissent from the election, without exceptions relevant and verified to the Presbytery; notwithstanding thereof, the Presbytery shall go on to the trials and ordination of the person elected; yet all possible diligence and tenderness must be used to bring all parties to an harmonious agreement.

"It is to be understood that no person under the censure of the Kirk because of any scandalous offence, is to be admitted to have a hand in the election of a minister.

"Where the congregation is disaffected and malignant, in that case the Presbytery is to provide them with a minister."

When Charles II., by an act at once of perfidy and of tyranny, overthrew the Presbyterian Church of Scotland, patronage was reintroduced. When the revolution drove the perfidious and despotic family of Stuart from the throne, patronage was abolished, and the rights and privileges of the Church and people restored and confirmed by the Revolution Settlement and the Act of Security, as has been fully shown in the body of the work, and in these acts themselves in the Appendix. The opposition made by the Church of Scotland to the perfidious act of 1712, which violated the Union, if it be considered valid, and, at least, violated national faith in the attempt to reimpose patronage upon the Scottish Church, has also been sufficiently stated. A strong desire to avoid prolixity alone prevents us from transcribing the Address of the Scottish Commissioners to the House of Lords against that bill; and the same reason causes us to withhold both the Address of the General Assembly to Queen Anne, and a subsequent memorial to King George I., imploring redress from the grievance of patronage. Neither shall we insert the Address of the General Assembly to King George II. in 1735, though these documents most strongly express the earnest desire of the Church of Scotland to obtain the repeal of the Patronage Act.

But the Act of Assembly 1736 must be given, for the purpose of showing the view entertained by that reforming Assembly, during the temporary ascendancy of the Evangelical and Constitutional body in the Church, with regard to their own duty and in conformity with their own principles, even though the desired redress had not been obtained.

"*Act* 1736 *against Intrusion of Ministers into vacant Congregations, and Recommendations to Presbyteries concerning Settlements.*

"The General Assembly, considering, from Act of Assembly August 6, 1575, Second Book of Discipline, chap. iii. pars. 4, 6, and 8, registrate in the Assembly books, and appointed to be subscribed by all ministers, and ratified by Acts of Parliament, and likewise by the Act of Assembly 1638, December 17 and 18, and Assembly 1715, act 9, that it is, and has been since the Reformation, the principle of this Church, 'that no minister be intruded into any parish contrary to the will of the congregation;' do therefore seriously recommend to all the judicatories of the Church, to have a due regard to the said principle in planting vacant congregations; and that all Presbyteries be at pains to bring about harmony and unanimity in congregations, and to avoid every thing that may excite or encourage unreasonable exceptions in people against a worthy person that may be proposed to be their minister in the present situation and circumstances of the Church, so as none be intruded into such parishes, as they regard the glory of God and edification of the body of Christ."

At the same time the following instruction was given to the Commission of that Assembly, and repeated to every succeeding Commission till the year 1784:—

"And the Assembly do further empower and direct the said Commission to make due application to the King and Parliament, for redress of the grievance of Patronage, in case a favourable opportunity for so doing shall occur during the subsistence of this Commission."

Extreme Moderate policy having reduced the constitutional principles of the Church and the rights of the people to a mere form, proposed in 1782 to abolish the form itself, which still survived in the call. This attempt, however, was resisted, and the following act was passed:—

"Upon a motion that the reso ution of Assembly respecting the moderation of calls sho ıld, for the satisfaction of all concerned, be converted into a declaratory act, and printed amongst the Acts of Assembly, the General Assembly agreed thereto without a vote; and in terms of said resolution did and hereby do declare, that the moderation of a call, in the settlement of ministers, is agreeable to the immemorial and constitutional practice of this Church, and ought to be continued."

Nothing further need to be stated respecting the proceedings of the Church, till the passing of the act on calls, commonly called the Veto Act, which is as follows:—

"Edinburgh, May 29, 1835.—The General Assembly declare, That it is a fundamental law of this Church, that no pastor shall be intruded on any congregation contrary to the will of the people; and, in order that this principle may be carried into full effect, the General Assembly, with the consent of a majority of the Presbyteries of this Church, do declare, enact, and ordain, That it shall be an instruction to Presbyteries, that if, at the moderating in a call to a vacant pastoral charge, the major part of the male heads of families, members of the vacant congregation, and in full communion with the Church, shall disapprove of the person in whose favour the call is proposed to be moderated in, such disapproval shall be deemed sufficient ground for the Presbytery rejecting such person, and that he shall be rejected accordingly, and due notice thereof forthwith given to all concerned; but that, if the major part of the said heads of families shall not disapprove of such person to be their pastor, the Presbytery shall proceed with the settlement according to the rules of the Church: And further declare that no person shall be held to be entitled to disapprove as aforesaid, who shall refuse, if required, solemnly to declare, in presence of the Presbytery, that he is actuated by no factious or malicious motive, but solely by a conscientious regard to the spiritual interest of himself or the congregation."

It may be expedient to transcribe the usual form of a Call.

"We, the Heritors, Elders, Heads of Families, and Parishioners of the Parish of ———, within the bounds of the Presbytery of ———, and county of ———, taking into consideration the present destitute state of the said Parish, through the want of a Gospel ministry among us, occasioned by the death of our late pastor, the Rev. ——— ———, being satisfied with the learning, abilities, and other good qualifications of you, Mr. ——— ———, Preacher of the Gospel, and having heard you preach to our satisfaction and edification, do hereby invite and call you, the said Mr. ——— ———, to take charge and oversight of this Parish, and to come and labour among us in the work of the Gospel ministry, hereby promising to you all due respect and encouragement in the Lord. We likewise entreat the Reverend Presbytery of ——— to approve and concur with this our most cordial call, and to use all the proper means for making the same effectual, by your ordination and settlement among us, as soon as the steps necessary thereto will admit. In witness whereof, we subscribe these presents, at the Church of ———, on the —— day of ———, ——— years."

That a document of such a solemn character should be held to be sufficiently subscribed by the signatures of one or two persons; and that a church court would proceed to intrude a person who could obtain but one or two signatures, upon a whole parish and congregation, in spite of their respectful, and finally of their determined opposition, even at the hazard of compelling them all to quit forever the Church of their fathers, is so strangely unnatural, oppressive, and contrary to both reason and religion, that it would not readily be thought possible, if it did not stand recorded as having actually taken place times innumerable, and if Auchterarder, Lethendy, and Marnoch could be forgotten. Still more portentously strange will it be, if the majority of the Evangelical ministers in the Church of Sc^tland be driven out of the Church, because they will not consent to become bound to perpetrate such atrocious tyranny and profanation at the command of a civil court, although contrary to the principles of the Church, contrary to the law of the land, contrary to the British Constitution, and contrary to the precepts of the Lord Jesus Christ.

No. IV.

THE PROTEST.

We, the undersigned ministers and elders, chosen as commissioners to the General Assembly of the Church of Scotland, indicted to meet this day, but precluded from holding the said Assembly by reason of the circumstances hereinafter set forth, in consequence of which a free Assembly of the Church of Scotland, in accordance with the laws and constitution of the said Church, cannot at this time be holden,—considering that the Legislature, by their rejection of the Claim of Right adopted by the last General Assembly of the said Church, and their refusal to give redress and protection against the jurisdiction assumed, and the coercion of late repeatedly attempted to be exercised over the courts of the Church in matters spiritual by the civil courts, have recognised and fixed the conditions of the Church Establishment, as henceforward to subsist in Scotland, to be such as these have been pronounced and declared by the said civil courts in their several recent decisions, in regard to matters spiritual and ecclesiastical, whereby it has been *inter alia* declared,—

1*st*, That the courts of the Church as now established, and members thereof, are liable to be coerced by the civil courts in the exercise of their spiritual functions; and in particular, in their admission to the office of the holy ministry, and the constitution of the pastoral relation, and that they are subject to be compelled to intrude ministers on reclaiming congregations, in opposition to the fundamental principles of the Church, and their views of the Word of God, and to the liberties of Christ's people.

2*d*, That the said civil courts have power to interfere with, and interdict the preaching of the gospel and administration of ordinances as authorised and enjoined by the Church courts of the Establishment.

3*d*, That the said civil courts have power to suspend spiritual censures pronounced by the Church courts of the Establishment against ministers and probationers of the Church, and to interdict their execution, as to spiritual effects, functions, and privileges.

4*th*, That the said civil courts have power to reduce and set aside the sentences of the Church courts of the Establishment, deposing ministers from the office of the holy ministry, and depriving probationers of their license to preach the gospel, with refererence to the spiritual status, functions, and privileges of such ministers and probationers,—restoring them to the spiritual office and status of which the Church courts had deprived them.

5*th*, That the said civil courts have power to determine on the right to sit as members of the supreme and other judicatories of the Church by law established, and to issue interdicts against sitting and voting therein, irrespective of the judgment and determination of the said judicatories.

6*th*, That the said civil courts have power to supersede the majority of a Church court of the Establishment, in regard to the exercise of its spiritual functions as a Church court, and to authorise the minority to exercise the said functions, in opposition to the court itself, and to the superior judicatories of the Establishment.

7*th*, That the said civil courts have power to stay processes of discipline pending before courts of the Church by law established, and to interdict such courts from proceeding therein

8*th*, That no pastor of a congregation can be admitted into the Church courts of the Establishment, and allowed to rule, as well as to teach, agreeable to the institution of the office by the Head of the Church, nor to sit in any of the judicatories of the Church, inferior or supreme, and that no additional provision can be made for the exercise of spiritual discipline among members of the Church, though not affecting any patrimonial interests, and no alteration introduced in the state of pastoral superintendence and spiritual discipline in any parish, without the coercion of a civil court.

All which jurisdiction and power on the part of the said civil courts severally above specified, whatever proceeding may have given occasion to its exercise, is, in our opinion, in itself inconsistent with Christian liberty,—with the authority which the Head of the Church hath conferred on the Church alone.

And further, considering that a General Assembly, composed, in accordance with the laws and fundamental principles of the Church, in part of commissioners, themselves admitted without the sanction of the civil court, or chosen by presbyteries, composed in part of members not having that sanction, cannot be constituted as an Assembly of the Establishment, without disregarding the law and the legal conditions of the same, as now fixed and declared:

And further, considering that such commissioners as aforesaid would, as members of an Assembly of the Establishment, be liable to be interdicted from exercising their functions, and to be subjected to civil coercion at the instance of any individual having interest who might apply to the civil courts for that purpose.

And considering, further, that civil coercion has already been in divers instances applied for and used, whereby certain commissioners returned to the Assembly this day appointed to have been holden, have been interdicted from claiming their seats, and from sitting and voting therein; and certain presbyteries have been, by interdicts directed against the members, prevented from freely choosing commissioners to the said Assembly; whereby the freedom of such Assembly, and the liberty of election thereto has been forcibly obstructed and taken away.

And further, considering that, in these circumstances, a free Assembly of the Church of Scotland by law established cannot at this time be holden, and that any Assembly, in accordance with the fundamental principles of the Church, cannot be constituted in connection with the State, without violating the conditions which must now, since the rejection by the Legislature of the Church's Claim of Right, be held to be the conditions of the Establishment.

And considering that, while heretofore, as members of Church judicatories ratified by law, and recognised by the Constitution of the kingdom, we held ourselves entitled and bound to exercise and maintain the jurisdiction vested in these judicatories with the sanction of the Constitution, notwithstanding the decrees as to matters spiritual and ecclesiastical of the civil courts, because we could not see that the State had required submission thereto as a condition of the Establishment, but, on the contrary, were satisfied that the State, by the acts of the Parliament of Scotland, for ever and unalterably secured to this nation by the Treaty of Union, had repudiated any power in the civil courts to pronounce such decrees, we are now constrained to acknowledge it to be the mind and will of the State, as recently declared, that such submissions should and does form a condition of the Establishment, and of the possession of the benefits thereof; and that, as we cannot, without committing what we believe to be sin,—in opposition to God's law, in disregard of the honour and authority of Christ's crown, and in violation of our own solemn vows,—comply with this condition; we cannot in conscience continue connected with, and retain the benefits of, the Establishment, to which such condition is attached.

We, therefore, the ministers and elders aforesaid, on this, the first occasion since the rejection by the Legislature of the Church's Claim of Right, when the commissioners chosen from throughout the bounds of the Church to the General Assembly appointed to have been this day holden, are convened together, do protest that the conditions foresaid, while we deem them contrary to, and subversive of, the settlement of Church government effected at the Revolution, and solemnly guaranteed by the Act of Security and Treaty of Union, are also at variance with God's Word, in opposition to the doctrines and fundamental principles of the Church of Scotland, inconsistent with the freedom essential to the right constitution of a Church of Christ, and incompatible with the government which He, as the Head of His Church, hath therein appointed distinct from the civil magistrate.

And we further protest, that any Assembly constituted in submission to the conditions now declared to be law, and under the civil coercion which has been brought to bear in the election of commissioners to the Assembly this day appointed to have been holden, and on the commissioners chosen thereto, is not and shall not be deemed a free and lawful Assembly of the Church of Scotland, according to the original and fundamental principles thereof, and that the Claim, Declaration, and Protest, of the General Assembly which convened at Edinburgh in May 1842, as the act of a free and lawful Assembly of the said Church, shall be holden as setting forth the true constitution of the said Church; and that the said Claim, along with the laws of the Church now subsisting, shall in nowise be affected by whatsoever acts and proceedings of any Assembly constituted under the conditions now declared to be the law, and in submission to the coercion now imposed on the Establishment.

And, finally, while firmly asserting the right and duty of the civil magistrate, to maintain and support an establishment of religion in accordance with God's Word, and reserving to ourselves and our successors to strive by all lawful means, as opportunity shall in God's good providence be offered to secure the performance of this duty agreeably to the Scriptures, and an implement of the statutes of the kingdom of Scotland, and the obligations of the Treaty of Union, as understood by us and our ancestors, but acknowledging that we do not hold ourselves at liberty to retain the benefits of the Establishment while we cannot comply with the conditions now to be deemed thereto attached—we protest, that in the circumstances in which we are placed, it is and shall be lawful for us and such other commissioners chosen to the Assembly appointed to have been this day holden, as may concur with us, to withdraw to a separate place of meeting, for the purpose of taking steps for ourselves and all who adhere to us—maintaining with us the Confession of Faith and Standards of the Church of Scotland, as heretofore understood—for separating in an orderly way from the Establishment; and thereupon adopting such measures as may be competent to us, in humble dependence on God's grace and the aid of the Holy Spirit, for the advancement of His glory, the extension of the Gospel of our Lord and Saviour, and the administration of the affairs of Christ's house, according to His Holy Word; and we do now withdraw accordingly, humbly and solemnly acknowledging the hand of the Lord in the things which have come upon us, because of our manifold sins, and the sins of this Church and nation; but at the same time, with an assured conviction, that we are not responsible for any consequences that may follow from this our enforced separation from an Establishment which we loved and prized—through interference with conscience, the dishonour done to Christ's Crown, and the rejection of his sole and supreme authority as King in his Church.

No. V.

HER MAJESTY'S LETTER TO THE GENERAL ASSEMBLY.

VICTORIA R.

Right reverend and well-beloved! We greet you well.

Faithful to the solemn engagement, which binds us to maintain inviolate the Presbyterian Church of Scotland in all its rights and privileges, we gladly renew the assurance, that we desire to extend to you the countenance and support which the General Assembly has long received from our royal ancestors.

In other circumstances, it might have sufficed to adhere to the forms which have been generally observed in our former communications to you, and to express our anxious hope that Christian charity will, as heretofore, abound among you and restrain all animosities; but in the present state of the Church, and adverting to the discussions which of late have so unhappily disturbed its peace, we desire to address you with more than usual earnestness and anxiety.

It behoves you to remember, that unity in the Church is the bond of peace; but that schism and its pernicious effects may tend seriously to endanger that religious Establishment from which Scotland has derived inestimable benefits.

The faith of our crown is pledged to uphold you in the full enjoyment of every privilege which you can justly claim: but you will bear in mind, that the rights and property of an Established Church are conferred by law; it is by law that the Church of Scotland is united with the State, and that her endowments are secured; and the ministers of religion, claiming the sanction of law in defence of their privileges, are specially bound by their sacred calling to be examples of obedience.

The act ratifying the Confession of Faith, and settling Presbyterian Church government in Scotland was adopted at the Union, and is now the act of the British Parliament. The settlement thus fixed cannot be annulled by the will or declaration of any number of individuals: those who are dissatisfied with the terms of this settlement, may renounce it for themselves; but the union of the Church of Scotland with the State is indissoluble while the statutes remain unrepealed which recognise the Presbyterian Church as the Church established by law within the kingdom of Scotland.

We cannot doubt, that your anxious consideration will be given to various important matters connected with the welfare of your Church, which require immediate adjustment.

The Act of Assembly passed in the year 1834, on the subject of calls, has come under the review of competent tribunals; and various proceedings taken in pursuance of this act have been pronounced by solemn judgments to be illegal. It has not yet been rescinded by the Assembly; and a conflict of authority between the law of the land and an act of the Church, in a matter where civil rights and civil jurisdiction are concerned, cannot be prolonged without injurious consequences.

The Church of Scotland, occupying its true position in friendly alliance with the State, is justly entitled to expect the aid of Parliament in removing any doubts which may have arisen with respect to the right construction of the statutes relating to the admission of ministers. You may safely confide in the wisdom of Parliament; and we shall readily give our assent to any measure which the Legislature may pass for the purpose of securing to the people the full privilege of objection, and to the Church judicatories the exclusive right of judgment.

There is another matter not less important, the present position of ministers in unendowed districts. The law, as confirmed by a recent judgment, has declared that new parishes cannot be created by the authority of the Church alone, and that ministers placed in such districts are not entitled to act in Church courts.

If it shall appear that the efficiency of the Church is thereby impaired, and that the means of extending her usefulness are curtailed, the law to which such effects are ascribed, may require re-consideration and amendment; but until it be so considered by the Legislature, and while it remains unaltered, we are persuaded that it will be implicitly obeyed by the General Assembly.

You will deliberate on such of these matters as fall within your cognizance attentively and calmly; and we commend you to the guidance of Divine Providence, praying that you may be directed to the adoption of wise counsels, which shall promote the permanent interests and honour of the Church, and the religious peace and moral welfare of our people.

We have again constituted and appointed our right-trusty and entirely beloved cousin, John Marquis of Bute, K. T., to be the representative of our royal person in this Assembly. And we are certain that his prudence and approved merits, and his tried attachment to the Church of Scotland, will render him acceptable unto you in the execution of the duties of his high office.

He possesses our full authority for the exercise of our royal prerogative in all matters relating to the present Assembly, in which, in obedience to our instructions to him, he may be called upon to act for us in our behalf.

We implore the blessing of God on your deliberations, trusting that He will overrule all events for the good of his Church, and for the spiritual welfare of the people committed to your charge: and we feel assured that divine grace will not be withdrawn from the labours of the ministers of the Church established in this part of the United kingdom.

And so we bid you heartily farewell.

Given at our Court at St. James's the 15th day of May 1843, in the sixth year of our reign.

By her Majesty's command.

(Signed) JAMES GRAHAM.

No. VI.

ACT OF SEPARATION AND DEED OF DEMISSION.

The ministers and elders subscribing the Protest made on Thursday, the eighteenth of this instant May, at the Meeting of the Commissioners chosen to the General Assembly, appointed to have been that day holden, against the freedom and lawfulness of any Assembly which might then be constituted, and against the subversion recently effected in the constitution of the Church of Scotland, together with the ministers and elders adhering to the said Protest, in this their General Assembly convened, did, in prosecution of the said Protest, and of the Claim of Right adopted by the General Assembly, which met at Edinburgh in May eighteen hundred and forty-two years, and on the grounds therein set forth, and hereby do, for themselves and all who adhere to them, separate from and abandon the present subsisting Ecclesiastical Establishment in Scotland, and did, and hereby do, abdicate and renounce the status and privileges derived to them, or any of them, as parochial ministers or elders, from the said Establishment, through its connexion with the State, and all rights and emoluments pertaining to them, or any of them, by virtue hereof: Declaring, that they hereby in no degree abandon or impair the rights belonging to them as ministers of Christ's gospel, and pastors and elders of particular congregations, to perform freely and fully the functions of their offices towards their respective congregations, or such portions thereof as may adhere to them; and that they are and shall be free to exercise government and discipline in their several judicatories, separate from the Establishment, according to God's Word, and the constitution and Standards of the Chnrch of Scotland, as heretofore understood; and that henceforth they are not, and shall not, be subject in any respect to the ecclesiastical judicatories established in Scotland by law; reserving always the rights and benefits accruing to them, or any of them, under the Provision of the statutes respecting the Ministers' Widows' Fund: And further, declaring that this present act shall noways be held as a renunciation on the part of such of the ministers foresaid as are ministers of churches built by private contribution, and not provided or endowed by the State, of any rights which may be found to belong to them, or their congregations, in regard to the same, by virtue of the intentions and destination of the contributors to the erection of the said churches, or otherwise, according to law; all which are fully reserved to the ministers foresaid and their congregations. And further, the said ministers and elders in this their General Assembly convened, while they refuse to acknowledge the supreme ecclesiastical judicatory established by law in Scotland, and now holding its sittings in Edinburgh, to be a free Assembly of the Church of Scotland, or a lawful Assembly of the said Church, according to the true and original constitution thereof, and disclaim its authority as to matters spiritual; yet in respect of the recognition given to it by the State, and the powers in consequence of such recognition belonging to it, with reference to the temporalities of the Establishment, and the right derived thereto from the State, hereby appoint a duplicate of this act to be subscribed by their moderator, and also by the several ministers, members of this Assembly, now present in Edinburgh, for their individual interests, to be transmitted to the clerk of the said ecclesiastical judicatory by law established, for the purpose of certiorating them, that the benefices held by such of the said ministers, or others adhering to this Assembly, as were incumbents of benefices, are now vacant; and the said parties consent that the said benefices shall be dealt with as such. And they authorize the Rev. Thomas Pitcairn and the Rev. Patrick Clason, conjunct clerks to this their General Assembly, to subscribe the joinings of the several sheets hereof; and they consent to the registration hereof in the Books of Council and Session, or others competent, therein to remain for preservation; and for that purpose constitute

their procurators, &c. In testimony whereof, these presents, written upon stamped paper by William Petrie Couper, clerk to James Crawford, junior, writer to the Signet, are, with a duplicate thereof, subscribed by the whole parties in general meeting assembled, and the joinings of the several sheets by the saids Rev. Thomas Pitcairn and Rev. Patrick Clason, as authorised as aforesaid, all at Edinburgh, the twenty-third day of May, one thousand eight hundred and forty-three years, before these witnesses,—Mr. John Hamilton, advocate, William Fraser, writer to the Signet; John Hunter, junior, writer to the Signet; and the Rev. John Jaffray, preacher of the Gospel, and secretary to the Provisional Committee, Edinburgh.

INDEX.

THE END.

www.ingramcontent.com/pod-product-compliance
Lightning Source LLC
LaVergne TN
LVHW021320110826
845150LV00003B/626

* 9 7 8 1 4 2 5 5 5 6 4 3 3 *